HIGHLIGHTS

2003 Accounting Desk Book

by Tom M. Plank, Lois Ruffner Plank, and Bryan R. Plank

The *2003 Accounting Desk Book* is a practical working tool that provides quick, authoritative, and up-to-date answers for CPAs and Financial Services Professionals applying relevant accounting principles and standards as well as tax rules. It contains all of the important pronouncements from the FASB and IASB, financial reporting presentation requirements, required and recommended disclosures, and specialized accounting topics needed to field a client's questions, brush up on the proper treatment of a transaction, or consider an engagement in a new area of practice.

Guidelines, checklists, diagrams, and step-by-step instructions simplify complex accounting issues and give public and private accountants quick answers to accounting application questions.

Aspen Publishers is offering a two-module, non-interactive self-study CPE program that can be used in conjunction with the *2003 Accounting Desk Book* (see below for more information).

TWELFTH EDITION

The Twelfth Edition of the *Accounting Desk Book* provides new and expanded coverage in these areas:

- Chapter 2, "Revenue and Expenses"—includes discussion of the FASB's and IASB's plans for accounting for share-based payments, including employee stock options.
- Chapter 5, "International Accounting"—now contains a discussion of the importance of the European Union's voting to require the use of International Accounting Standards by EU listed public companies starting January 1, 2005.

- Chapter 6, "The International Federation of Accountants"—has been revised to include complete information on the International Public Sector Accounting Standards that NATO announced just this August that it was adopting as well as IFAC's updated Code of Ethics for Professional Accountants, seven proposed standards on education, and IT monitoring guidelines on risk.

- Chapter 7, "Foreign Currency Translations and Derivative Disclosure"— reflects the latest proposed amendment to FASB 133 affecting derivative instruments and hedging activities that would become effective as of the first day of the first fiscal period beginning November 15, 2002 (January 1, 2003 for calendar year-end companies).

- Chapter 9, "The Sarbanes-Oxley Act of 2002"—this new chapter covers the legislation intended to restore the investor's faith in the stock market and breaks down the reforms that foreshadow new regulations.

- Chapter 10, "Actions of the Financial Accounting Standards Board"— has been updated to include provisions of FASB 144, *Accounting for the Impairment or Disposal of Long-Lived Assets;* FASB 146, *Accounting for Costs Associated with Exit or Disposal Activities;* and FASB 147, *Acquisitions of Certain Financial Institutions.* Discussion of the Revenue Recognition Project and the proposed Standard on Consolidation of SPEs has also been added.

- Chapter 11, "Governmental Accounting"—has been revised to reflect GASB 39 and the exposure draft on Deposit and Investment Risk Disclosures.

- Chapter 15, "Cost Accounting"—this new chapter discusses how cost accounting concepts, usually thought of only in terms of manufacturing operations, can be used in other areas of a small business or a service enterprise.

- Chapter 16, "Keep It Honest and Profitable"—this new chapter considers ways to ensure honesty and increased productivity for a business through internal controls and fraud prevention. Nine checklists are provided.

- Chapter 17, "The CPA as Financial Planner"—a completely revised chapter provides the background information needed by the CPA to qualify for, and be successful as, an AICPA-designated Personal Financial Specialist (PFS). Eight checklists are provided.

- Chapter 19, "Consideration of Real Estate as an Asset"—this new chapter discusses investing in real property and the income and expenses involved. Tax considerations involved in rental property and sale of a home are covered.

- Chapter 22, "Auditor Independence and the Audit Committee"—has been updated to reflect the SEC's new rules governing independence of auditors.

- Chapter 30, "Demystifying Funds" —this new chapter attempts to clarify many of the questions arising in connection with this popular form of investment.
- Chapter 33, "Depreciation" —a new section has been added to address provisions of the Job Creation and Worker Assistance Act of 2002 affecting the depreciation of business property.
- Chapter 34, "Independent Contractor or Employee" —has been updated with guidelines for making that determination. Also added is information on the requirements that must be met in order to receive relief from paying employment taxes.
- Chapter 40, "Tax Matters" —this new chapter details important tax considerations resulting from the Community Renewal Tax Relief Act of 2000; the Victims of Terrorism Relief Act of 2001; particularly the Economic Growth and Tax Relief Reconciliation Act of 2001; and other measures.
- Chapter 41, "The Job Creation and Worker Assistance Act of 2002" — this new chapter offers needed information on this major tax bill and its far-reaching provisions.
- Chapter 42, "Tip Income" —has been updated to reflect the U.S. Supreme Court's 6-3 favorable ruling relating to the IRS's "aggregate method" of estimating restaurant tip income.

CPE AVAILABLE

Aspen Publishers is offering a complete, two-module, non-interactive self-study CPE program that can be used in conjunction with the *2003 Accounting Desk Book*. Our goal is to provide you with the clearest, most concise, and up-to-date accounting and auditing information to help further your professional development, as well as a convenient method to help you satisfy your continuing professional educational requirements.

The CPE course has the following characteristics:

> **Prerequisites:** Basic knowledge of Accounting
> **Recommended CPE credits:** 10 hours per module
> **Level of Knowledge:** Intermediate—Builds on a basic
> level of understanding in order to relate fundamental
> principles or skills to practical situations and extend them
> to a broader range of applications. This level is for
> participants with some exposure to the field.
> **Field of Study:** Accounting and Auditing

If you are interested in taking the CPE course and examination, please contact:

> Aspen CPE
> c/o ACCPE
> 2419 Hollywood Boulevard
> Hollywood, FL 33020
> 800-394-6275

Aspen Publishers is registered with the National Association of State Boards of Accountancy (NASBA) as a sponsor of continuing professional education on the National Registry of CPE Sponsors. State boards of accountancy have final authority on the acceptance of individual courses for CPE credit. Complaints regarding registered sponsors may be registered to the National Registry of CPE Sponsors, 150 Fourth Avenue North, Nashville, TN 37219-2417; telephone (615) 880-4200; web site www.nasba.org.

ACCOUNTING RESEARCH MANAGER

Aspen Publishers' *Accounting Research Manager*™ is one of the largest and most comprehensive online databases of expert-written analytical accounting and auditing information as well as primary source data. Updated daily, it is the most timely, complete and objective resource for your financial reporting needs. Our Weekly Summary, an e-mail newsletter highlighting the key developments of the week, gives you the assurance that you have the most current information. It provides links to all FASB, AICPA, SEC, EITF, and IASB authoritative and proposal-stage literature, plus insightful guidance from financial reporting experts. With Aspen's Accounting Research Manager, you maximize your research time, while enhancing your results. Visit us at **www.arm.aspenpublishers.com** to request your free 30-day trial.

12/02

For questions concerning this shipment, billing, or other customer service matters, call our Customer Service Department at 1-800-234-1660.

For toll-free ordering, please call 1-800-638-8437.

2003
ACCOUNTING DESK BOOK

TWELFTH EDITION

2003
ACCOUNTING
DESK BOOK

*The Accountant's
Everyday Instant
Answer Book*

TWELFTH EDITION

TOM M. PLANK
LOIS RUFFNER PLANK
BRYAN R. PLANK

PUBLISHERS

1185 Avenue of the Americas, New York, NY 10036
www.aspenpublishers.com

© 2003 Aspen Publishers, Inc.
www.aspenpublishers.com

Portions of this book were published in previous editions.

Printed in the United States of America
1 2 3 4 5 6 7 8 9 0

ISBN 0-7355-3545-0

About Aspen Publishers

Aspen Publishers is a leading publisher of authoritative treatises, practice manuals, services, and journals for attorneys, corporate and bank directors, accountants, auditors, environmental compliance professionals, financial and tax advisors, and other business professionals. Our mission is to provide practical solution-based how-to information keyed to the latest original pronouncements, as well as the latest legislative, judicial, and regulatory developments.

We offer print and online products in the areas of accounting and auditing; antitrust; banking and finance; bankruptcy; business and commercial law; construction law; corporate law; criminal law; environmental compliance; government and administrative law; health law; insurance law; intellectual property; international law; legal practice and litigation; matrimonial and family law; pensions, benefits, and labor; real estate law; securities; and taxation.

Aspen Publishers products treating accounting, auditing, and corporate finance issues include:

Accounting Irregularities and Financial Fraud
Almanac of Business and Industrial Financial Ratios
Audit Committees: A Guide for Directors, Management, and Consultants
Auditor's Risk Management Guide: Integrating Auditing and ERM
Construction Accounting Deskbook
Corporate Controller's Handbook of Financial Management
CPA's Guide to Developing Effective Business Plans
CPA's Guide to Effective Engagement Letters
CPA's Guide to e-Business
CPA's Guide to Management Letter Comments
Federal Government Contractor's Manual
GAAP Handbook of Policies and Procedures
How to Manage Your Accounting Practice
Medical Practice Management Handbook
Miller Audit Procedures
Miller Compilations and Reviews
Miller European Accounting Guide
Miller Financial Instruments: A Comprehensive Guide to Accounting and Reporting
Miller GAAP Financial Statement Disclosures Manual
Miller GAAP Guide
Miller GAAP Handbook of Policies and Procedures
Miller GAAP Practice Manual
Miller GAAS Guide
Miller GAAS Practice Manual
Miller Governmental GAAP Guide
Miller Governmental GAAP Practice Manual: A Guide to GASB 34
Miller International Accounting Standards Guide
Miller IT Auditing
Miller Local Government Audits
Miller Not-for-Profit Organization Audits
Miller Not-for-Profit Reporting
Miller Revenue Recognition Guide
Miller Single Audits
Professional's Guide to Value Pricing

Aspen Publishers' *Accounting Research Manager*™ is one of the largest and most comprehensive online databases of expert-written analytical accounting and auditing information as well as primary source data. Updated daily, it is the most timely, complete and objective resource for your financial reporting needs. Our Weekly Summary, an e-mail newsletter highlighting the key developments of the week, gives you the assurance that you have the most current information. It provides links to all FASB, AICPA, SEC, EITF, and IASB authoritative and proposal-stage literature, plus insightful guidance from financial reporting experts. With Aspen's *Accounting Research Manager,* you maximize your research time, while enhancing your results. Visit us at **www.arm.aspenpublishers.com** to request your free 30-day trial.

Aspen's Miller Comprehensive Online Libraries, available at www.tax.cchgroup.com, include:

Miller GAAP Library—Miller GAAP Guide; Miller GAAP Practice Manual; Miller GAAP Financial Statement Disclosures Manual; and Miller GAAP Update Service

Miller GAAS Library—Miller GAAS Guide; Miller GAAS Practice Manual; and Miller GAAS Update Service

Miller Engagement Library—Miller Audit Procedures; Miller Compilations & Reviews; and CPA's Guide to Effective Engagement Letters

Miller Governmental GAAP Library—Miller Governmental GAAP Guide; Miller Governmental GAAP Practice Manual: A Guide to GASB 34; Miller Not-for-Profit Reporting; and Miller Governmental GAAP Update Service

Miller Governmental and Not-for-Profit Audit Library—Miller Single Audits; Miller Not-for-Profit Organization Audits; and Miller Local Government Audits

Miller International Accounting Library—Miller European Accounting Guide and Miller International Accounting Standards Guide

Original standards and pronouncements from **FASB, GASB,** and **IASB** are also available with any Miller Online Library.

ASPEN PUBLISHERS
www.aspenpublishers.com

SUBSCRIPTION NOTICE

This Aspen Publishers product is updated on a periodic basis with supplements to reflect important changes in the subject matter. If you purchased this product directly from Aspen Publishers, we have already recorded your subscription for the update service.

If, however, you purchased this product from a bookstore and wish to receive future updates and revised or related volumes billed separately with a 30-day examination review, please contact our Customer Service Department at 1-800-234-1660, or send your name, company name (if applicable), address, and the title of the product to:

ASPEN PUBLISHERS
7201 McKinney Circle
Frederick, MD 21704

About the Authors

Tom M. Plank is a specialist in SEC Accounting Rules and Regulations, new security issues registrations and annual reports and filings required by the SEC. He holds his degrees from the Graduate School of Management, University of California at Los Angeles.

Mr. Plank has served on the accounting, finance and economics faculties of various major universities in Chicago and Los Angeles. His business experience includes that of an officer and economist for a large commercial bank, a securities analyst for an investment banking firm, an account executive for a large securities firm and a consultant for various corporations for Securities and Exchange Commission filings.

Mr. Plank has published many articles in various journals and is the author of several business books: *SEC Accounting Rules and Regulations, The Age of Automation, The Science of Leadership* and several editions and supplements to the *Accounting Desk Book.* He is also the co-editor of the *Encyclopedia of Accounting Systems.*

Lois Ruffner Plank received her B.A. degree in Public Administration and International Relations from Miami University in Oxford, Ohio, with additional work in investments at the University of California at Los Angeles and at the University of Illinois.

Mrs. Plank is the co-editor of the *Encyclopedia of Accounting Systems* and co-author of several of the supplements to the *Accounting Desk Book.* She has been involved in budgeting and financial management with a government agency in Washington, D.C., and instituted a public relations and marketing program for a suburban Chicago school district.

She is an editor of professional publications and books and is a public relations consultant. Additional experience includes newspaper reporting and chief copy consultant for a national magazine.

Bryan R. Plank is a senior financial advisor and vice president at large for an international securities firm. In addition, he holds numerous licenses, certifications and credentials in securities, insurance and real estate.

Mr. Plank has 20 years of experience in training and development in the securities industry and is a frequent guest speaker at many San Diego area colleges and universities.

Mr. Plank earned university degrees from the University of Southern California and California State Polytechnic University, Pomona, with additional postgraduate work at Claremont Graduate School.

Contents

INTRODUCTION   xiii

CHAPTER 1:   Principles of Financial Statements, Disclosure,
              Analysis and Interpretation   1.01

CHAPTER 2:   Revenue and Expenses   2.01

CHAPTER 3:   Stockholders' Equity   3.01

CHAPTER 4:   Statement of Cash Flows   4.01

CHAPTER 5:   International Accounting   5.01

CHAPTER 6:   The International Federation of Accountants   6.01

CHAPTER 7:   Foreign Currency Translations & Derivative Disclosure   7.01

CHAPTER 8:   Derivatives   8.01

CHAPTER 9:   The Sarbanes-Oxley Act of 2002   9.01

CHAPTER 10:   Actions of the Financial Accounting Standards Board   10.01

CHAPTER 11:   Governmental Accounting   11.01

CHAPTER 12:   Governmental Fund Accounting   12.01

CHAPTER 13:   Not-for-Profit Exempt Organizations   13.01

CHAPTER 14:   Budgeting for Profit Planning
              and Budgetary Control   14.01

CHAPTER 15:   Cost Accounting   15.01

x   Contents

CHAPTER 16:   Keep It Honest and Profitable   16.01

CHAPTER 17:   The CPA as Financial Planner   17.01

CHAPTER 18:   Investment Vocabulary   18.01

CHAPTER 19:   Consideration of Real Estate as an Asset   19.01

CHAPTER 20:   Business Use of the Home   20.01

CHAPTER 21:   Expert Witness   21.01

CHAPTER 22:   Auditor Independence and the Audit Committee   22.01

CHAPTER 23:   The Securities and Exchange
               Commission—Organization and the Acts   23.01

CHAPTER 24:   The Securities and Exchange Commission—Materiality   24.01

CHAPTER 25:   The Securities and Exchange Commission—Private
               Securities Litigation Reform Act of 1995   25.01

CHAPTER 26:   Segment Reporting   26.01

CHAPTER 27:   E-Commerce and E-Communication   27.01

CHAPTER 28:   Internet Accounting   28.01

CHAPTER 29:   Mutual Funds   29.01

CHAPTER 30:   Demystifying Funds   30.01

CHAPTER 31:   Mutual Fund "Profile" Disclosure Option   31.01

CHAPTER 32:   Plain English Disclosure Rule   32.01

CHAPTER 33:   Depreciation   33.01

CHAPTER 34:   Independent Contractor or Employee   34.01

CHAPTER 35:   Asset Valuation for Tax Purposes   35.01

CHAPTER 36:   Change in Accounting Methods and
               Consideration of Accounting Periods   36.01

CHAPTER 37:   Practice Before the IRS and the Power of Attorney   37.01

CHAPTER 38:   Taxpayer Rights   38.01

CHAPTER 39:   The Economic Growth and Tax
               Relief Reconciliation Act of 2001   39.01

CHAPTER 40:   Tax Matters   40.01

CHAPTER 41:   Job Creation and Worker Assistance Act of 2002   41.01

CHAPTER 42:   Tip Income   42.01

CHAPTER 43:   Insurance Accounting   43.01

APPENDIX A:	Financial Planning Tables	A.0I
APPENDIX B:	Index to Journal Entries	B.0I
APPENDIX C:	Tax Terminology	C.0I
APPENDIX D:	The Going Concern Company	D.0I
APPENDIX E:	Guidelines for Interim Reporting	E.0I
APPENDIX F:	Reporting Cash Payments of Over $10,000	F.0I
INDEX		IND.0I

Introduction

The shocking events in the business world in general, and the accounting profession in particular, have brought the accountant to the forefront of world attention. Over the past year, overwhelming changes and laws have been mandated as a result. It is imperative that all accountants and auditors keep up with the new laws, rules and regulations in an industry that was already fast-paced and continually changing. The *Accounting Desk Book* is written for this purpose: to assist the accountant in his or her effort to understand and comply with both the new and existing accounting rules and regulations.

The importance of current information cannot be overemphasized. Coverage of topics, applications, examples and definitions of terms is the goal of this volume. Care has been taken to avoid abstract theory, technical jargon, complex "legalese" and textbook-type prose, which can needlessly complicate the understanding of rules and procedures. All topics are covered in a straightforward, plain English style.

The decision of the European Union to require all EU listed companies to adopt IASs by 2005 puts an added stamp of approval upon the movement toward global uniformity in accounting standards for cross-border securities offerings. Another giant step forward in this direction occurred with the International Accounting Standards Commission's beginning operation under its new Constitution.

The International Federation of Accountants is also making its presence known globally through the development of auditing and assurance-related services, and the launching of the Forum of Firms. The North Atlantic Treaty Organization (NATO) announced in August 2002 that it is adopting the

International Public Sector Accounting Standards (IPSASs) starting January 1, 2006. There appears to be a groundswell of movement toward international accounting and auditing standards by diverse groups worldwide.

Two of the timeliest chapters include a review of the *Sarbanes-Oxley Act of 2002,* and *Internet Accounting,* which explores the 20 Internet accounting issues raised by the Securities and Exchange Commission. For those who are emphasizing the AICPA's Professional Financial Specialist aspect in their practice, the chapters *The CPA as Financial Planner* and *Demystifying Funds* will be of particular interest.

After adoption of Government Accounting Standard Board Statement 34, the Board is particularly concerned with the implementation of this comprehensive overhauling of state and local government financial reporting. Phase 3 governments (those with annual revenues of less than $10 million) are finalizing plans to apply the requirements of GASB 34 in their financial statements after June 15, 2003. Meanwhile, the GASB continues to do everything it can to make the transition to the "new" governmental accounting model as painless and error-free as possible. A description of relevant new government publications and rulings is included in this volume.

It should be emphasized that the *Accounting Desk Book* is not a textbook. It is essentially a reference manual to provide the user with immediate, general answers to a large number of practical accounting, finance, tax and general business management questions.

The discussions throughout the *Accounting Desk Book* are mostly self-contained. A review of the topics does not require reference to other sources. The Contents clearly sets forth the subject matter discussed. Users will also find the Index helpful in locating needed information rapidly.

Among other topics featured are:

* Keep It Honest and Profitable
* Consideration of Real Estate As An Asset
* Auditor Independence and the Audit Committee
* E-Communication and E-Commerce
* Asset Valuation for Tax Purposes
* Tax Matters
* Actions of the Financial Accounting Standards Board
* Cost Accounting

CPE AVAILABLE

Aspen Publishers is offering two non-interactive self-study CPE courses that can be used in conjunction with the *2003 Accounting Desk Book.* Our goal is to provide you with the clearest, most concise, and up-to-date accounting and auditing information to help further your professional development, as well as a convenient method to help you satisfy your continuing professional educational requirements.

The CPE course has the following characteristics:

Prerequisites: Basic knowledge of Accounting

Recommended CPE Credit: 10 hours per module

Level of Knowledge: Intermediate—Builds on a basic level of understanding in order to relate fundamental principles or skills to practical situations and extend them to a broader range of applications. This level is for participants with some exposure to the subject.

Field of Study: Accounting and Auditing

If you are interested in taking the CPE course and examination, please contact:

Aspen CPE
c/o ACCPE
2419 Hollywood Boulevard
Hollywood, FL 33020
800-394-6275

Aspen Publishers is registered with the National Association of State Boards of Accountancy (NASBA) as a sponsor of continuing professional education on the National Registry of CPE Sponsors. State boards of accountancy have final authority on the acceptance of individual courses for CPE credit. Complaints regarding registered sponsors may be addressed to the National Registry of CPE Sponsors, 150 Fourth Avenue North, Nashville, TN 37219-2417; telephone (615) 880-4200; web site www.nasba.org.

ACCOUNTING RESEARCH MANAGER

Aspen Publishers' *Accounting Research Manager*™ is one of the largest and most comprehensive online databases of expert-written analytical accounting and auditing information as well as primary source data. Updated daily, it is the most timely, complete and objective resource for your financial reporting needs. Our Weekly Summary, an e-mail newsletter highlighting the key developments of the week, gives you the assurance that you have the most current information. It provides links to all FASB, AICPA, SEC, EITF, and IASB authoritative and proposal-stage literature, plus insightful guidance from financial reporting experts. With Aspen's *Accounting Research Manager,* you maximize your research time, while enhancing your results. Visit us at **www.arm.aspenpublishers.com** to request your free 30-day trial.

ACKNOWLEDGMENT

We would like to acknowledge Christie Ciraulo for her invaluable editorial assistance and expertise at surfin' the Web.

Chapter 1

Principles of Financial Statements, Disclosure, Analysis, and Interpretation

CONTENTS

Fair Presentation in Conformity with GAAP	**1.02**
12 Principles of Financial Statement Presentation	**1.02**
Materiality	**1.05**
Disclosures Required in Financial Statements	**1.07**
Full Disclosure	**1.08**
Disclosure in Financial Reporting	**1.09**
Disclosures Itemized	**1.11**
Restatements	**1.16**
Timing and Permanent Differences—Income Taxes	**1.18**
Timing Differences	**1.18**
Financial Statement Analysis and Interpretation	**1.21**
Four Groups of Ratios	**1.22**
The Accountant's Responsibility	**1.22**
Balance Sheet Analysis	**1.23**
Income Statement Analysis	**1.29**
Statement of Changes in Stockholders' Equity	**1.36**
FASB 130, *Reporting Comprehensive Income*	**1.37**
APB Opinion 22, *Disclosure of Accounting Policies*	**1.41**

The general objective is to provide reliable information on resources, obligations and progress. The information should be useful for comparability, completeness and understandability. The basic features involved in financial accounting are the individual accounting entity, the use of approximation and the preparation of fundamentally related financial statements.

The financial statements—balance sheet, income statement, change in stockholders' equity and statement of cash flows, as well as segment reports and interim reports—will summarize a firm's operations and ending financial position. Analysts, investors, creditors and potential investors and creditors will analyze these documents in their decision-making processes.

FAIR PRESENTATION IN CONFORMITY WITH GAAP

Fair presentation in conformity with GAAP requires that the following four criteria be met:

1. GAAP applicable in the circumstances have been applied in accumulating and processing the accounting information.
2. Changes from period to period in GAAP have been properly disclosed.
3. The information in the *underlying* records is properly *reflected* and *described* in the financial statements in conformity with GAAP.
4. A proper balance has been achieved between the conflicting needs to:
    a. Disclose the important aspects of financial position and results of operation in conformity with conventional concepts, and
    b. Summarize the voluminous underlying data with a limited number of financial statement captions and supporting notes.

12 PRINCIPLES OF FINANCIAL STATEMENT PRESENTATION

1. *Basic Financial Statements.* At minimum, these statements must include:
    a. Balance Sheet
    b. Statement of Income
    c. Statement of Changes in Stockholders' Equity
    d. Statement of Cash Flows
    e. Disclosure of Accounting Policies
    f. Disclosure of Related Notes

    Information is usually presented for two or more periods. Other information also may be presented, and in some cases required, as supplemental information (e.g., price-level statements, information about operations in different industries, foreign operations and export sales, and major customers (segment reporting)).

2. *The Balance Sheet.* A complete balance sheet must include:
   a. All assets
   b. All liabilities
   c. All classes of stockholders' equity

3. *The Income Statement.* A complete income statement must include:
   a. All revenues
   b. All expenses

4. *The Statement of Cash Flow.* A complete statement of cash flow includes and describes all important aspects of the company's financing and investing activities.

5. *Accounting Period.* The basic time period is one year. An interim statement is for less than one year.

6. *Consolidated Financial Statements.* Such statements are presumed to be more meaningful than separate statements of the component legal entities. They are *usually* necessary when one of the group owns (directly or indirectly) *over 50 percent* of the outstanding voting stock. The information is presented as if it were a *single enterprise.*

7. *The Equity Basis.* For unconsolidated subsidiaries (where over 50 percent is owned) *and for investments in 50 percent or less* of the voting stock of companies in which the investor has significant influence over investees, 20 percent or more ownership presumes this influence, unless proved otherwise. The investor's share of the net income reported by the investee is picked up and shown as income and an adjustment of the investment account—for all earnings subsequent to the acquisition. Dividends are treated as an adjustment of the investment account.

8. *Translation of Foreign Branches.* Data are translated into U.S. Dollars by conventional translation procedures involving foreign exchange rates.

9. *Classification and Segregation.* These important components must be disclosed separately:
   a. Income Statement—Sale (or other source of revenue); Cost of Sales; Depreciation; Selling Administration Expenses; Interest Expense; Income Taxes.
   b. Balance Sheet—Cash; Receivables; Inventories; Plant and Equipment; Payables; and Categories of Stockholder's Equity:
      • Par or stated amount of capital stock; Additional paid-in capital
      • Retained earnings affected by:
        —Net income or loss,
        —Prior period adjustments,

—Dividends, or

— Transfers to other categories of equity.

- Working capital—current assets and current liabilities should be classified as such to be able to determine working capital—useful for enterprises in manufacturing, trading and some service enterprises.

- Current assets—cash and other that can reasonably be expected to be realized in cash in one year or a shorter business cycle.

- Current liabilities—liabilities expected to be satisfied by the use of those assets shown as current; by the creation of other current liabilities; or in one year.

- Assets and liabilities—should *not* be offset against each other unless a legal right to do so exists, which is a rare exception.

- Gains and losses—arise from other than products or services and may be combined and shown as one item. Examples are write-downs of inventories, receivables and capitalized research and development costs—*all sizable*—as well as gains and losses on temporary investments, non-monetary transactions and currency devaluations.

- Extraordinary items or gain or loss—should be shown separately under its own title. Items distinguished by unusual nature and infrequent occurrence should be shown net of taxes.

- Net income—should be separately disclosed and clearly identified on the income statement.

10. *Other disclosures (Accounting policies and notes).* These include:

a. Customary or routine disclosures:
- Measurement bases of important assets
- Restrictions on assets
- Restriction on owners' equity
- Contingent liabilities
- Contingent assets
- Important long-term commitments not in the body of the statements
- Information on terms of equity of owners
- Information on terms of long-term debt
- Other disclosures required by the AICPA

b. Disclosure of changes in accounting policies

c. Disclosure of important subsequent events—between balance sheet date and date of the opinion

    d. Disclosure of accounting policies ("Summary of Significant Accounting Policies")

11. *Form of Financial Statement Presentation. No* particular form is presumed better than all others for all purposes. Several are used.

12. *Earnings Per Share.* This information must be disclosed on *the face of the Income Statement* and should be disclosed for:

    a. Income before extraordinary items

    b. Net Income

    Disclosure should consider:

    a. Changes in number of shares outstanding

    b. Contingent changes

    c. Possible dilution from potential conversion of:

- Preferred stock
- Options
- Warrants

MATERIALITY

There have been attempts by authoritative rule-making bodies, scholars of accounting, users of financial statements, and others to develop quantitative criteria for determining the materiality of items in the financial statements. They postulate that if Item A is X percent of a total, Item A is material. If Item B is Y percent of a total, then Item B is material, but . . . All efforts have proved fruitless, and there are no accepted quantitative standards that can be wholly relied upon for an unquestioned determination of whether an item is material or immaterial (and thus can be omitted from the financial statements or notes thereto).

    The courts to some extent have helped. However, it should be cautioned that different jurisdictions in different geographic areas of the country have established many opinions and definitions of materiality. For example, the Tenth Circuit Court of Appeals ruled that information is material if ". . . the trading judgment of reasonable investors would not have been left untouched upon receipt of such information." (*Mitchell v. Texas Gulf Sulphur Co.*) In the "landmark" *Bar Chris* case the judge said that a material fact is one ". . . which if it had been correctly stated or disclosed would have deterred or tended to deter the average prudent investor from purchasing the securities in question" (*Escott et al. v. Bar Chris Construction Corporation et al.*).

    Principally because the U.S. Supreme Court defined materiality in the *TSC Industries Inc. v. Northway Inc.* case, the following statement of the Court is considered to be an authoritative basis upon which to render a judgment of materiality:

> "An omitted fact is material if there is a substantial likelihood that a reasonable shareholder would consider it important in deciding how to vote. This standard is fully consistent with the general description of materiality as a requirement that the defect have a significant *propensity* to affect the voting process."

> [Note: This decision dealt with omissions of material information.]

> "The Securities and Exchange Commission defines *material information: 'The term* material *when used to qualify a requirement for the furnishing of information as to any subject, limits the information required to those matters as to which an average prudent investor ought reasonably to be informed.'* "

What's Material?   The accountant must decide precisely what information requires disclosure. To do this, the accountant must exercise judgment according to the circumstances and facts concerning material matters and their conformity with Generally Accepted Accounting Principles. A few examples of material matters are:

1. The form and content of financial statements.
2. Notes to the statements.
3. The terminology used in the statements.
4. The classification of items in the statements.
5. Amount of detail furnished.
6. The bases of the amounts presented (e.g., for inventories, plants, liabilities).
7. The existence of affiliated or controlling interests.

A clear distinction between materiality and disclosure should be noted. Material information involves both quantitative (data) and qualitative information. Additionally, the information must be disclosed in a manner that enables a person of "average" comprehension and experience to understand and apply it to an investment decision. Contra speaking, information disclosed in a manner that only an "expert" can evaluate is not considered within the meaning and intent of disclosure requirements.

Materiality should be thought of as an abstract concept. Many efforts to define the term can be found in the literature (e.g., accounting and auditing books, law books, and Regulation S-X). Nevertheless, in the final analysis, judgments with respect to what is material resulting from court decisions, SEC actions, accountants' interpretations, and corporate and financial officers' judgments have ultimately evolved into the subjective judgment of individuals (accountants and management) responsible for deciding what is and is not material.

DISCLOSURES REQUIRED IN FINANCIAL STATEMENTS

Following is an overview of the most important disclosures required in financial statements with a brief comment on the substance of each requirement.

Accounting Policies. Accounting Principles Board Opinion 22 (APB 22), *Disclosure of Accounting Policies,* is the applicable GAAP. (See the discussion at the end of this chapter.) The disclosure should set forth the accounting principles underlying the statements that materially affect the determination of financial position, changes in financial position, and results of operations. Also included are the accounting principles relating to recognition of revenue, allocation of asset costs to current and future periods, the selection from existing acceptable alternatives, such as the inventory method chosen, and any accounting principles and methods unique to the industry of the reporting entity.

As a general rule, the preferred position of the review of accounting policies is footnote No. 1, but a section summarizing the policies preceding the footnotes is acceptable.

Who Decides What Information Is Material? This decision is the responsibility of management working with the company's accountant. As a generalization, the *causes* for material changes in financial statement items must be noted to the extent necessary for users to understand the business as a whole. This requirement applies to all financial statements, not just to the income statement. The following items are considered material and *must* be recognized.

1. Sales and revenues. Increases or decreases in sales and revenues that are temporary or nonrecurring and their causes.
2. Unusually increased costs.
3. Informative generalizations with respect to each important expense category.
4. Financial expenses. Changes in interest expenses (and interest income); changes in the company's cost of borrowing; changes in the borrowing mix (e.g., long-term vs. short-term).
5. Other income and expense items. These may include dividend income from investees; the equity in the income or losses of investees or of unconsolidated subsidiaries.

6. Income taxes. The effective tax rate paid by corporations should be reconciled to the statutory rates. The reconciliation provides the basis for a description of the reasons for year-to-year variations in the effective tax rate to which a business is subject. Changes caused by the adoption of new or altered policies of tax-deferred accounting are considered material.
7. Material changes in the relative profitability of lines of business.
8. Material changes in advertising, research and development, new services, or other discretionary costs.
9. The acquisition or disposition of a material asset.
10. Material and unusual charges or gains, including credits or charges associated with discontinuance of operations.
11. Material changes in assumptions underlying deferred costs and the plan for the amortization of such costs.
12. The cost of goods sold, where applicable. The gross margin of an enterprise can be affected by important changes in sales volume, price, unit costs, mix of products or services sold, and inventory profits and losses. The composition of cost among fixed, semi-variable and variable elements influences profitability. Changes in gross margins by an analysis of the interplay between selling prices, costs, and volume should be explained.
13. Cash flow information.
14. Dilution of earnings per share.
15. Segmental reporting.
16. Rental expense under leases.
17. Receivables from officers and stockholders.

FULL DISCLOSURE

Full Disclosure is an attempt to present all essential information about a company in the following reports:

1. Balance Sheet
2. Income Statement
3. Statement of Changes in Stockholders' Equity
4. Statement of Cash Flows
5. Accompanying Footnotes

The objectives of financial reporting are set forth in *FASB Concepts Statement 1*. The financial statements, notes to the financial statements, and necessary supplementary information are governed by FASB standards.

Financial reporting includes other types of information, such as *Management's Discussion and Analysis,* letters to stockholders, order backlogs, statistical data, and the like, commonly included in reports to shareholders.

The Full Disclosure Principle

Financial facts significant enough to influence the judgment of an informed person should be disclosed. The financial statements, notes to the financial statements, summary of accounting policies, should disclose the information necessary to prevent the statements from being misleading. The information in the statements should be disclosed in a manner that the intended meaning of the information is apparent to a reasonably informed user of the statements.

DISCLOSURE IN FINANCIAL REPORTING

Disclosure. The heart of the compilation and disclosure of financial information is *accounting.* Yet, the idea of "adequate disclosure" stands alone as the one concept in accounting that involves all of the good things and all of the dangers inherent in the professional practice of accounting and auditing. Probably the use of the colloquialism "disclosure" best describes the all-embracing nature of the concept. That is to say, *disclosure is the name of the financial reporting game.*

For decades the profession has been inundated with disclosure literature, rules, regulations, statements, government agencies' accounting regulations, court decisions, tax decisions, intellectualizing by academics, books and seminars, all concerning what disclosure is all about.

Yet nobody has answered precisely what continues to remain the essential question: Disclosure of *what,* by *whom,* for *whom?*

The lack of definitive qualitative and quantitative criteria for what information must or need not be disclosed forces upon the independent accountant the responsibility to decide what constitutes a matter requiring disclosure, requiring an exercise of judgment in light of the circumstances and facts available at the time. The *accountant's* responsibility is confined to the expression of an opinion based upon an examination. The representations made through the statements are *management's* responsibility.

What is a material fact, and for whom does a disclosed fact have material significance? What substantive standards of disclosure must the accountant maintain? Who is to promulgate these standards? The profession? One or all of the governmental regulatory agencies? A federal board of accounting? The courts? The Congress?

One conclusion is clear, however. There is an unmistakable trend toward increasing demands upon the accounting profession for more financial information. What better evidence can be cited than the conclusion of the AICPA Study Group on the Objectives of Financial Statements? The group's report said that "... financial statements should meet the needs of those with *LEAST* ability to obtain information."

The confusion between what is and is not *material* is caused by a widely held concept—different facts have different meanings for the individual user of financial information. Information that is important to one user may be insignificant to another.

> "All information must adapt *itself* to the perception of those towards whom the information is intended."
>
> -Anonymous

It is neither possible nor economically feasible, however, for an accountant to cover in the statements every single small detail concerning a client's business. Where should the accountant draw the line? (Not many years ago, a large accounting firm had to defend a lawsuit up to the U.S. Supreme Court at a cost of several million dollars because the accountant did not question the company's chief executive officer's policy that he, alone, open the company's mail.)

Recent trends in financial reporting reflect an increase in the amount of disclosure found in financial statements. The information is communicated in the footnotes, which are an integral part of the financial statements. Although the footnotes are usually drafted in somewhat technical language, they are the accountant's means of amplifying or explaining the items present in the main body of the statements. Footnote information can generally be classified as follows:

1. *Disclosure of Accounting Policies Applied.* This information is required in order to inform the user of the statements of the accounting methods used in preparing the information that appears in statements.

2. *Disclosure of Gain or Loss Contingencies.* Because many contingent gains or losses are not properly included in the accounts, their disclosure in the footnotes provides relevant information to financial statement users.

3. *Examination of Credit Claims.* A liability, such as a bank loan, may have numerous covenants that are not conveniently disclosed in the liability section of the balance sheet.

4. *Claims of Equity Holders.* The rights of various equity security issues along with certain unique features that may apply to certain issues are commonly disclosed in footnotes to the statements.

5. *Executory Commitments.* These refer to contract obligations undertaken by the company that have not been performed, or have been only partially performed at the statement date.

In some cases a company is faced with a sensitive issue that requires disclosure in a footnote. Some examples are:

1. Related party transactions
2. Errors
3. Irregularities
4. Illegal acts

Disclosures Itemized

Following is an alphabetical listing of items requiring disclosure including short comments if applicable:

Accelerated Depreciation Methods—when methods are adopted.

Accounting Policies—(see the discussion of APB 22 at the end of this chapter.)

Allowances (depreciation, depletion, bad debts)—deduct from asset with disclosure.

Amortization of Intangibles—disclose method and period.

Amounts Available for Distribution—note the needs for any holdback retention of earnings.

Arrangements with Reorganized Debtor—disclose if a subsequent event.

Arrears on Cumulative Preferred Stock—the rights of senior securities must be disclosed on the face of balance sheet or in the notes.

Assets (interim changes in)—only significant changes required for interims.

Business Segments.

Cash-Basis Statements—fact must be disclosed in the opinion with delineation of what would have been had accrual basis been used, its significant variance.

Change in Stockholders' Equity Accounts—in a separate schedule. This does not include the changes in retained earnings statement, which is also a basic requirement.

Change to Declining Balance Method—disclose change in method and effect of it.

Changes, Accounting.

Commitments, Long-Term—disclose unused letters of credit, assets pledged as security for loans, pension plans, plant expansion or acquisition; obligations to reduce debt, maintain working capital or restrict dividend.

Commitments to Complete Contracts—only the extraordinary ones.

Consolidation Policy—method used.

Construction Type Contracts—method used.

Contingencies—disclose when reasonable possibility of a loss, the nature of, and estimated loss. Threats of expropriation, debtor bankruptcy if actual. Those contingencies which might result in gains, but not misleading as to realization. Disclosure of uninsured risks is advised, but not required. Gain contingencies should be disclosed, but not reflected in the accounts.

Contingencies in Business Combinations—disclose escrow items for contingencies in the notes.

Control of Board of Directors—disclose any stock options existing.

Corporate Officer Importance—disclose if a major sales or income factor to the company.

Current Liabilities—disclose why, if any, omitted (in notes).

Dating (Readjusted) Earned Surplus—no more than 10 years is the term now required.

Deferred Taxes—disclose and also see Timing Differences in this text.

Depreciation and Depreciable Assets—disclose the following:

1. Depreciation expense for the period.
2. Balances of major classes of depreciable assets by nature or function.
3. Accumulated depreciation by classes, or in total.
4. A general description of the methods used in computing depreciation.

Development Stage Enterprises—are required to use the same basic financial statements as other enterprises, with certain additional disclosures required. Special type statements are not permissible.

Discontinued Operations—disclose separately below continuing-operating income, net of tax, but before extraordinary items. Show separate EPS.

Diversified Company's Foreign Operations.

Earnings per share—see discussion in this text, but the following is also required in addition to the data stated there (does not apply to non-public enterprises):

1. Restatement for a prior period adjustment.
2. Dividend preference.

3. Liquidation preference.
4. Participation rights.
5. Call prices and dates.
6. Conversion rates and dates.
7. Exercise prices and dates.
8. Sinking fund requirements.
9. Unusual voting rights.
10. Bases upon which primary and fully diluted earnings per share were calculated.
11. Issues that are common stock equivalents.
12. Issues that are potentially dilutive securities.
13. Assumptions and adjustments made for earnings per share data.
14. Shares issued upon conversion, exercise, and conditions met for contingent issuances.
15. Recapitalization occurring during the period or before the statements are issued.
16. Stock dividends, stock splits or reverse splits occurring after the close of the period before the statements are issued.
17. Claims of senior securities entering earnings per share computations.
18. Dividends declared by the constituents in a pooling.
19. Basis of presentation of dividends in a pooling on other than a historical basis.
20. Per share and aggregate amount of cumulative preferred dividends in arrears.

Equity Method—as follows:

1. Financial statements of the investor should disclose in the notes, separate statements or schedules, or parenthetically:
   a. The name of each investee and percent of ownership,
   b. The accounting policies of the investor, disclosing if, and why, any over 20 percent holdings are not under the equity method,
   c. Any difference between the carrying value and the underlying equity of the investment, and the accounting treatment thereof;
2. Disclose any investments which have quoted market prices (common stocks) showing same—do not write down;
3. Present summary balance sheet and operating information when equity investments are material;
4. Same as above for any unconsolidated subsidiaries where ownership is majority;
5. Disclose material effects of contingent issuances.

Extinguishment (Early) of Debt—gains or losses should be described, telling source of funds for payoff, income tax effect, per share amount.

Extraordinary Items—describe on face of income statement (or in notes), show effect net of tax after income from continuing operations, also after business disposals if any, show EPS separately for extraordinary item. May aggregate immaterial items.

Fiscal Period Differences (in Consolidating)—disclose intervening material.

Fiscal Year Change—disclose effect only.

Foreign Items—Assets, must disclose any significant ones included in U.S. statements; gains or losses shown in body of U.S. statement; disclose significant "subsequent event" rate changes; operations, adequate disclosure to be made of all pertinent dollar information, regardless of whether consolidating or not (for foreign subsidiaries).

Headings and Captions—may be necessary to explain.

Income Taxes (and Deferred Taxes)—(see Timing Differences in this text.)

Income Taxes of Sole Proprietor or Partnership—may be necessary to disclose personal taxes to be paid if the money will come from and put a drain on the firm's cash position.

Infrequent Events—show as separate component of income and disclose nature of them.

Interim Statements—(see discussion in Appendix E.)

Inventories—disclose pricing policies and flow of cost assumption in "Summary of Significant Accounting Policies"; disclose changes in method and effect on income. Dollar effect based upon a change should be shown separately from ordinary cost of sales items.

Investment Tax Credits—disclose method used, with amounts if material. Also, disclose substantial carryback or carryforward credits.

Leases.

Legal Restrictions on Dividend Payments—put in notes.

Liability for Tax Penalties—if significant, disclose in notes. May have to take exception in opinion.

Market Value of Investments in Marketable Securities—should be written down to market value and up again, but not to exceed cost for entire portfolio per classification.

Noncumulative Preferred Stock—should disclose that no provision has been made because it is noncumulative.

Obligations (Short-Term)—disclose in notes reason any short-term obligations not displayed as current liabilities.

Partnerships, Limited—disclose fact that it's a limited partnership.

Patent Income—disclose if income is ending.

Pension Plans—must disclose the following:

1. Describe and identify employee groups covered by plan.
2. The accounting and funding policy.
3. The provision for pension cost for the period.
4. Excess, if any, of vested benefits over fund total; any balance sheet deferrals, accruals, prepays.
5. Any significant matters affecting comparability of periods presented.

Political Contributions—must disclose if material or not deductible for taxes, or if they are beneficial to an officer.

Price-Level Restatements.

Prior Period Adjustments—must disclose with tax effects. Must disclose in interim reports.

Purchase Commitment Losses—should be separately disclosed in dollars in income statement.

Purchase Method. (See Business Combinations.)

Purchase Option Cancellation Costs—yes, disclose.

Real and Personal Property Taxes—disclose if using estimates, and if substantial. All adjustments for prior year estimates should be made through the current income statement.

Real Estate Appraisal Value—for development companies, footnote disclosure might be useful.

Receivables, Affiliated Companies, Officers and Employees—should be segregated and shown separately from trade receivables.

Redemption Call of Preferred Stock—disclose in the equity section.

Renegotiation Possibilities—use dollars if estimable or disclose inability to estimate.

Research and Development Costs—disclosure must be made in the financial statements of the total research and development costs charged to expenses in each period for which an income statement is presented. Government-regulated enterprises should disclose the accounting policy for amortization and the totals expensed and deferred, but not the confidential details of specific projects, patents, new products, processes or company research philosophy. Applies the above provision for disclosure to business combinations.

Restricted Stock Issued to Employee—disclose circumstance and the restrictions.

Retained Earnings Transferred to Capital Stock—arises usually with "splitups effected as dividends" and with stock dividends; must disclose and include schedule showing transfers from retained earnings to capital stock. Also, must disclose number of shares for EPS; must show subsequent event effects.

Sale and Leaseback.

Seasonal Business (Interim Statements)—must disclose, and advisable to include 12-month period, present and past.

Stock Dividends, Split-up—must disclose even if a subsequent event and use as if made for and during all periods presented.

Stock Options—disclose status. Has effect on EPS.

Stockholders Buy/Sell Stock Agreements—disclose.

Subleases.

Termination Claims (War and Defense Contracts)—shown as current receivable, unless extended delay indicated; usually shown separately and disclosed if material, in income statement.

Treasury Stock—Shown in body of balance sheet (equity section ordinarily); should, in notes, indicate any legal restrictions.

Unconsolidated Subsidiaries—if using cost method, should also give independent summary information about position and operations.

Undistributed Earnings of Subsidiaries.

Unearned Compensation.

Unremitted Taxes—disclose only if going concern concept is no longer valid.

RESTATEMENTS

The following alphabetical listing indicates those areas that *require* a restatement (with disclosure) for all prior periods presented in the comparative financial statements:

Appropriations of Retained Earnings—any change made for the reporting of contingencies requires retroactive adjustment.

Changes in Accounting Principle Requiring Restatement:
1. Change from LIFO to another method.
2. Change in long-term construction method.
3. Change to or from "full cost" method in the extractive industries.

4. Must show effect on both net income and EPS for all periods presented.

Change in Reporting Entity—must restate.

Contingencies—restate for the cumulative effect applying the rules for contingencies.

Earnings Per Share—the effect of all restatements must be shown on EPS, separating as to EPS from continuing operations, EPS from disposals, EPS from extraordinary items and EPS from net income.

Equity Method—restatement required when first applying the method, even though it was not required before.

Extraordinary Items—if a similar one in prior period was not classified as extraordinary but is now, reclassify now for comparison.

Foreign Currency Translations—restate to conform with adoption of standards; if indeterminable, use the cumulative method. Disclose nature of restatement and effect (or cumulative effect) on income before extraordinary items, on net income, and on related per share amounts.

Income Taxes (Equity Method)—restate to comply.

Interim Financial Statements—restate for changes in accounting principle and for prior period adjustments. If it's a cumulative type change, the first interim period should show the entire effect; if in later period, full effect should be applied to the first period and restated for other periods.

Leases.

Prior Period Adjustments—must restate the details affected for all periods presented, disclose and adjust opening retained earnings. Must also do it for interim reports.

Refinancing Short-Term Obligations—restatement is permitted, but not required.

Research and Development Costs—In conforming with standards, apply retroactively as a prior period adjustment. (*No* retroactive recapitalization of costs is permissible. Applies to *purchase* combinations also. Basic rule: expense as incurred.)

Revision based on FASB Opinions—retroactive restatement is not required *unless* the new standard *specifically* states that it is required. (Note that restatements are *not* required for a change from FIFO to LIFO, nor for a change in the method of handling investment tax credits.)

Statistical Summaries (e.g., 5 years, 10 years)—restate all prior years involved in prior period adjustments.

Stock Dividends and Splits—must restate earnings per share figures and number of shares to give effect to stock dividends and splits *including* those occurring after close of period being reported on (for all periods presented).

TIMING AND PERMANENT DIFFERENCES—INCOME TAXES

Those that will not reverse or "turn around" in other periods:

1. Specific *revenues exempt* from taxability (examples):
   Dividend exclusions interest on tax-exempt securities
   Life insurance proceeds
   Negative goodwill amortization
   Unrealized gains on marketable securities
   Unrealized gains on foreign currency translations
   Tax benefits arising from stock-option compensatory plans (when booked as income)
2. Expenses that are *not* tax deductible:
   Depreciation taken on appraisal increases or donated property
   Goodwill amortization
   Premiums on officer life insurance
   Tax penalties and fines
   Unrealized losses on securities or currency translations
3. Those expenses that are predicated upon different bases for financial and tax purposes:
   Depreciation on trade-ins
   Statutory depletion vs cost depletion
   Business combinations which treat purchase as "pooling for tax return or pooling as purchase."

TIMING DIFFERENCES

Those that *will* turn around or reverse in one or more subsequent periods. Four broad categories:

1. Income—for Accounting NOW—for Taxes LATER
2. Expenses—for Accounting NOW—for Taxes LATER
3. Income—for Accounting LATER—for Taxes NOW
4. Expenses—for Accounting LATER—for Taxes NOW

Below is an explanation of these four categories:

1. Items of *income* included for accounting financial statement purposes NOW not taken on the tax return until a LATER time (examples):
   a. Gross profit on installment method date of sale/when collected on tax return.
   b. Percentage of completion method on books/completed contract method for tax return.
   c. Leasing rentals on books under financing method/actual rent less depreciation for tax return.
   d. Subsidiary earnings reported now/as received for tax return.

2. Items of *expense* taken on financial statements NOW, not taken on tax returns until LATER (examples):
   a. Accelerated depreciation used for financials/not for tax return.
   b. Contributions on financials over 5 percent limit/carried over for taxes.
   c. Deferred compensation accruals/taken when paid on tax return.
   d. Estimated costs of various kinds/taken when cost or loss becomes actual and known, such as guarantees, product warranties, inventory losses, legal settlements, segment disposals and major repairs.
   e. Depreciation based on shorter life for books than for tax return.
   f. Organization costs taken now/amortized for tax return.

3. Items of *income* taken into financial books LATER, but reported as income NOW on tax returns:
   a. Rents and royalties deferred until earned/reported when collected for tax return.
   b. Deferred fees, dues, services contracts/reported when collected for tax returns.
   c. Intercompany consolidation gains and losses/taxed now if filing separate return.
   d. Leaseback gains, amortized gains over lease-term/date of sale for tax return.

4. Items of *expense* taken into financial books LATER, but taken NOW on tax returns:
   a. Depreciation; shorter lives used for tax purposes accelerated rates on tax return/straight-line on books; certain emergency facility amortization taken on tax returns/later on books.
   b. Bond discount, premium costs taken on return/amortized on books.
   c. Certain costs that are taken for tax purposes/but deferred for financial purposes, as:
   d. Incidental costs of property acquisitions.

   e. Preoperating costs.
   f. Certain research and development costs (deferred for financial purposes).

Other Considerations Regarding Income Taxes

Interperiod tax allocation should be followed under the deferred method. Timing differences may be considered individually or grouped by similarity. Tax carryback losses (including investment tax credit carrybacks) should be recognized in the loss period in which the carryback originated. Carryforwards should not be recognized until realized (then shown as *extraordinary* item) unless there is no doubt of realization (then shown as part of operating profit or loss).

Balance Sheet Presentation of Income Taxes

Tax accounts on the balance sheet should be classified separately as to:

1. Taxes estimated to be paid currently.
2. *Net* amount of current deferred charges and deferred credits related to timing differences.
3. *Net* amount of noncurrent deferred taxes related to timing differences.
4. Receivables for carryback losses.
5. When realization is beyond doubt, show an asset for the benefit to be derived from a carryforward of losses.
6. Deferred investment credits, when this method is employed.

Income Statement Presentation of Income Taxes

All taxes based on income, including foreign, federal, state and local, should be reflected in income tax expense in the income statement.
   The following components should be disclosed separately and put on the income statement before extraordinary items and prior period adjustments:

1. Taxes estimated to be payable.
2. Tax effects of timing differences.
3. Tax effects of operating losses.

   In addition, the following general disclosures are required:

1. Amounts of any operating loss carryforwards not recognized in the loss period, with expiration dates and effect on deferred tax accounts.

2. Significant amounts of any other unused tax deductions or credits, with expiration dates.

3. Any reasons for significant differences between taxable income and pre-tax accounting income.

4. Deferred income taxes related to an asset or liability are classified the same as the related asset or liability. A deferred tax charge or credit is related to an asset or liability if reduction of the asset or liability would cause the underlying timing difference to reverse. Deferred income taxes that are not related to an asset or liability are classified according to the expected reversal date of the timing difference.

FINANCIAL STATEMENT ANALYSIS AND INTERPRETATION

Analysis techniques applied to financial statements are of interest to the corporate financial officer of any entity for a number of reasons. For one thing, that particular company's financial statements will be subject to analysis by creditors, credit grantors, and investors. Furthermore, the financial officer will want to analyze the company's statements for internal management use as well as analyze other companies' financial statements for credit purposes and perhaps for investment purposes (where an acquisition is being considered).

The financial statements are a systematic and convenient presentation of the financial position and operating performance of a business entity. The question is: What can be learned by analyzing and interpreting the information available in the statements?

There is much valuable information to be learned, as ratio analysis answers questions concerning the financial facts of a business:

1. GAAP permits a variety of accounting procedures and practices that significantly affect the results of operation reported in the statements. Statement analysis helps to evaluate the choices of alternative accounting decisions.

2. The statements for a number of successive years can be compared by the use of ratios and unusual trends and changes can be noted.

3. A company's statements can be compared with those of other similar companies in the same industry.

4. Statement analysis is the basis for estimating, or projecting, potential operating results by the development of pro forma statements.

5. The effects of external economic developments on a company's business can be applied to results as shown in the statements.

6. The balance sheet valuations can be related to the operating results disclosed in the income statement, since the balance sheet is the link between successive income statements.

7. Since ratios are index numbers obtained by relating data to each other, they make comparisons more meaningful than using the raw numbers without relating an absolute dollar figure to another statement item.

FOUR GROUPS OF RATIOS

Ratios are usually classified into four groups:

1. *Liquidity Ratios:* Measures of the ability of the enterprise to pay its short-term obligations.
2. *Profitability Ratios:* Measures of the profits (losses) over a specified period of time.
3. *Coverage Ratios:* Measures of the protection for the interest and principal payments to long-term creditors and investors.
4. *Activity Ratios:* Measures of how efficiently the company is employing its assets.

The ratios in the following discussion are those most commonly applied to measure the operating efficiency and profitability of a company. (There are hundreds of possible relationships that can be computed and trends identified.) The discussion includes an explanation of the answers that each ratio provides; each ratio's application to a specific area of a business will be noted.

THE ACCOUNTANT'S RESPONSIBILITY

In evaluating the ratios, the accountant must be mindful that the ratios are simply a measuring tool, not the final answers nor the end in themselves. They are one of the tools for evaluating the *past* performance and providing an indication of the future performance of the company. Ratios are a *control* technique and should be thought of as furnishing management with a "red flag" when a ratio has deviated from an established norm, or average, or predetermined standard.

Accordingly, ratio analysis is meaningless without an *adequate feedback* system by which management is promptly informed of a problem demanding immediate attention and correction.

While accountants are concerned primarily with the *construction* of the financial statements, particularly their technical accuracy and validity, the accountant is also relied upon by the many different users of the statements for assistance in the interpretation of the financial information. The accountant must use experience and technical skill to evaluate information and to contribute to management decisions that will maximize the optimum allocation of an organization's economic resources.

Basic Analysis Techniques

Much of the analytical data obtained from the statements is expressed in terms of ratios and percentages. (Carrying calculations to one decimal place is sufficient for most analysis purposes.) The basic analysis technique is to use these ratios and percentages in either a *horizontal* or *vertical* analysis, or both.

Horizontal Analysis. Here, similar figures from several years' financial statements are compared. For example, it may be useful to run down two years' balance sheets and compare such items as the current assets, plant assets, current liabilities and long-term liabilities on one balance sheet with the similar items on the other and to note the amount and percentage increases or decreases for each item. Of course, the comparison can be for more than two years. A number of years may be used, each year being compared with the base year or the immediate preceding year.

Vertical Analysis. Here, component parts are compared to the totals in a single statement. For example, it can be determined what percentage each item of expense on the income statement is of the total net sales, or, what percentage of the total assets the current assets comprise.

Ratios. Customarily, the *numerator* of the equation is expressed first, then the denominator. For example, fixed assets to equity means fixed assets *divided by* equity. Also, whenever the numerator is the larger figure, there is a tendency to use the word "turnover" for the result.

As indicated above, these techniques are widely used, generally in the course of one analysis.

BALANCE SHEET ANALYSIS

The significance of the balance sheet is that it shows relationships between classes of assets and liabilities. From long experience, businesspeople have learned that certain relationships indicate the company is in actual or potential trouble or is in good financial shape. For example, these relationships may indicate that the business is short of working capital, is undercapitalized generally, or has a bad balance between short- and long-term debt.

It must be emphasized that there are no fixed rules concerning the relationships. There are wide variations between industries and even within a single industry. It is often more valuable to measure these relationships against the past history of the same company than to use them in comparison with other businesses. If sharp disparities do show, however, it is usually wise not to ignore them. Many of the so-called "excesses" that in the past have led to recessions often show up in the balance sheets of individual companies. The most important balance sheet ratios and their implications for the business are discussed below.

Ratio of Current Assets to Current Liabilities

The *current ratio* is probably the most widely used measure of liquidity (i.e., a company's ability to pay its bills). It measures the ability of the business to meet its current liabilities. The current ratio indicates the extent to which the current liabilities are covered. For example, if current assets total $400,000 and current liabilities are $100,000, the current ratio is 4 to 1.

Good current ratios will range from about 2 to almost 4 to 1. However, the ratio will vary widely in different industries. For example, companies that collect quickly on their accounts and do not have to carry very large inventories can usually operate with a lower current ratio than those companies whose collections are slower and inventories larger.

If current liabilities are subtracted from current assets, the resulting figure is the *working capital* of the company; in other words, the amount of free capital that is immediately available for use in the business. One of the most significant reasons for the failure of small businesses is the lack of working capital, which makes it difficult or impossible for the business to cope with sudden changes in worsening economic conditions. Conversely, lack of a comfortable amount of working capital may prevent a small business from taking advantage of opportunities to expand in a growing economy.

The details of working capital flow are presented in the two-year comparative Statement of Cash Flows, a mandatory part of the financial statements.

An important feature of the ratios to remember is that when both factors are decreased by the same amount, the ratio is increased:

	Old	Change	New
Current Assets	$100,000	$(25,000)	$75,000
Current Liabilities	50,000	(25,000)	25,000
Working Capital	50,000	0	50,000
Ratio	2 to 1		3 to 1

By paying off $25,000 worth of liabilities (depleting Cash), you have increased the ratio from 2 to 1 to 3 to 1. Note that the *dollar* amount of *working capital* remains the same $50,000.

Conversely, should you borrow $50,000 on short-terms (increasing Cash and Current Liabilities), you would *reduce* the ratio to *11/2 to 1* ($150,000/100,000), again with the dollar amount of working capital remaining at $50,000.

A variation of the current ratio is the *acid test*. This is the ratio of *quick assets* (cash, marketable securities, and accounts receivable) to *current liabilities*. This ratio eliminates the inventory from the calculation, since inventory may not be readily convertible to cash.

Acid-Test Ratio

The current ratio does not disclose the fact that a portion of the current assets may be tied up in slow-moving inventories, which leaves the question of how long it will take to transform the inventories into finished product and how much will be realized on the sale of the merchandise. Elimination of inventories and prepaid expenses from the current assets will give better information for short-term creditors. A *quick* or *acid-test ratio* relates total current liabilities to cash, marketable securities, and receivables. If this total is $150 divided by current liabilities of $100, the acid-test ratio is 11/2 to 1, which is low compared to an industry average of 3 to 1. This means a company would have difficulty meeting its short-term obligations and would have to obtain additional current assets from other sources.

Defensive-Interval Ratio

The defensive-interval ratio is computed by dividing defensive assets—cash, marketable securities, and receivables—by projected daily expenditures from operations. This ratio measures the time span a firm can operate with present liquid assets without resorting to revenues from next year's sources. Projected daily expenditures are computed by dividing cost of goods sold plus selling and administrative expenses and other ordinary expenses by 365 days. Assuming a company has a defensive-interval measure of 150 days and an industry average of 75 days, the 150 days provides a company with a high degree of protection, and can offset the weakness indicated by low current and acid-test ratios that a company might have.

Ratio of Current Liabilities to Stockholders' Equity

This ratio measures the relationship between the short-term creditors of the business and the owners. Excessive short-term debt is frequently a danger sign, since it means that the short-term creditors are providing much or all of the company's working capital. If anything happens to concern the short-term creditors, they will demand immediate repayment and create the risk of insolvency. Short-term creditors are most often suppliers of the business, and the company's obligation to them is listed under accounts payable. However, short-term creditors may also include short-term lenders.

A general rule occasionally cited for this ratio is that for a business with a tangible capital and earnings (net worth) of less than $250,000, current liabilities should not exceed two-thirds of this tangible net worth. For companies having a tangible net worth over $250,000, current liabilities should not exceed three-fourths of tangible net worth.

Tangible net worth is used instead of total net worth because intangible assets (such as patents and copyrights) may have no actual market value if the company is forced to offer them in distress selling.

Ratio of Total Liabilities to Stockholders' Equity

The ratio differs from the preceding one in that it includes only long-term liabilities. Since the long-term creditors of a company are normally not in a position to demand immediate payment, as are short-term creditors, this ratio may be moderately greater than the preceding one without creating any danger for the company. However, the ratio should never exceed 100 percent in an industrial company. If it did, this would mean that the company's creditors have a larger stake in the enterprise than the owners themselves. Under such circumstances, it is very likely that credit would not be renewed when the existing debts matured. Utilities and financial companies can operate safely with much higher ratios because more of their liabilities are long-term.

Ratio of Fixed Assets to Stockholders' Equity

The purpose of this ratio is to measure the relationship between fixed and current assets. The ratio is obtained by dividing the book value of the fixed assets by the tangible value of stockholders' equity. A rule sometimes used is that if tangible net worth is under $250,000, fixed assets should not exceed two-thirds of tangible net worth. If tangible net worth is over $250,000, fixed assets should not exceed three-fourths of tangible net worth.

Ratio of Fixed Assets to Long-Term Liabilities

Since long-term notes and bonds are often secured by mortgages on fixed assets, a comparison of the fixed assets with the long-term liabilities reveals what "coverage" the note or bondholders have—that is, how much protection they have for their loans by way of security. Furthermore, where the fixed assets exceed the long-term liabilities by a substantial margin, there is room for borrowing additional long-term funds on the strength of the fixed asset position.

Ratio of Cost of Goods Sold to Inventory— Inventory Turnover

One of the most frequent causes of business failure is lack of inventory control. A firm that is optimistic about future business may build up its inventory to greater than usual amounts. Then, if the expected business does not materialize, the company will be forced to stop further buying and may also have difficulty paying its creditors. In addition, if a company is not selling off its inventory regularly, that item, or part of it, is not really a *current* asset. Additionally, there may be a considerable amount of unsalable inventory included in the total. For all these reasons, a business is interested in knowing how often the inventory "turns over" during the year. In other words, how long will the current inventory be on the shelves, and how soon will it be turned into money?

To find out how often inventory turns over, the average inventory is compared to the cost of goods sold shown on the income statement. (Typically, average is computed by adding opening and closing inventories and dividing the total by two.) For example, if average inventory is $2 million and cost of goods sold adds up to $6 million, during the course of the year, the company has paid for three times the average inventory. Therefore, it can be said that the inventory turned over three times, and at year-end there remained about a four months' supply of inventory on hand.

Because information about cost of goods sold and average inventory may not be readily available in published reports, another way to measure the same results is by using the ratio of net sales to inventory. In this ratio, net sales is substituted for cost of goods sold. Since net sales will always be a larger figure (because it includes the business's profit margin), the resulting inventory turnover will be a higher figure.

How large an inventory should a company carry? That depends upon many factors within a particular business or industry. What may be large or small may vary with the type of business or the time of year. An automobile dealer with a large inventory at the beginning or middle of a model year will be in a strong position. A large inventory at the end of the season places him in a weak financial position.

Ratio of Inventory to Working Capital

This is another ratio to measure over- or under-inventory. Working capital is current assets minus current liabilities. If inventory is too high a proportion of working capital, the business is short on quick assets—cash and accounts receivable. A general rule for this ratio is that businesses of tangible net worth of less than $250,000 should not have an inventory which is more than three-fourths of net working capital. For a business with tangible net worth in excess of $250,000, inventory should not exceed net working capital. The larger-size business can tolerate a condition where there are no quick assets because its larger inventory can be borrowed against; in addition, it presumably has fixed assets which can be mortgaged if necessary.

Inventory as a percentage of current assets may indicate a significant relationship when comparison is made between companies in the same industry, but not between different types of companies because of other variables.

Receivables Turnover

An important consideration for any business is the length of time it takes to collect its accounts receivable. The longer accounts receivable are outstanding, the greater the need for the business to raise working capital from other sources. In addition, a longer collection period increases the risk of bad debts. A general rule for measuring the collection period is that it should not be more than one-third greater than the net selling terms offered by the company. For example, if goods are sold on terms of 30 days net, the average collection period should be about 40 days, though this varies from industry to industry. Special rules apply in the case of installment selling.

Another way of measuring the collection rate of accounts receivable is to divide the net sales from the income statement by the average accounts receivable. This gives the accounts receivable turnover—that is, how many times during the year the average accounts receivable were collected. A comparison with prior years reveals whether the company's collection experience is getting better or worse. The faster the turnover, the more reliable the current and acid-test ratios are for financial analytical purposes.

Asset Turnover

This ratio indicates how efficiently a company utilizes its assets. If the turnover rate is high, the indication is that a company is using its assets efficiently to generate sales. If the turnover ratio is low, a company either has to use its assets more efficiently or dispose of them. The asset turnover ratio is affected by the depreciation method used. If an accelerated method of depreciation is used, the results would be a higher turnover rate than if the straight-line method is used, all other factors being equal.

Book Value of the Securities

This figure represents the value of the outstanding securities according to the values shown on the company's books. This may have little relationship to market value—especially in the case of common stock. Profitable companies often show a low net book value but report very substantial earnings. Railroads, on the other hand, may show a high book value for their common stock but have such low or irregular earnings that the stock's market price is much less than the book value. Insurance companies, banks and investment companies are exceptions. Since most of their assets are liquid—cash, accounts receivable, marketable securities—the book value of their common stock may well present a fair approximation of the market value.

Nevertheless, book value is an important test of financial strength. It is computed by simply subtracting all liabilities from total assets. The remaining sum represents the book value of the equity interest in the business. In computing this figure, it is a good idea to include only tangible assets, such as land, machinery and inventory. A patent right or other intangible may be given a large dollar value on the balance sheet, but in the event of liquidation may not be salable at all. The theory underlying the measurement of book value is that it is a good measure of how much cash and credit the company may be able to raise if it comes upon bad times. Book value is usually expressed per share outstanding.

Book value is also an important measure for the bondholders of the company. For them, the value has the significance of telling them how many dollars per bond outstanding the company has in available assets. Since they have a call on the company's assets before either the preferred stockholders or the common stockholders, a substantial book value per bond in excess of the face amount of the bond offers relative assurance of the safety of the bond—assurance that funds will be available to pay off the bonds when they become due. To find the book value of the bonds, add together the total stockholders' equity and the amount of the bonds outstanding.

For example, stockholders' equity totals $5 million. Bonded indebtedness is $2 million. From this $7 million total we subtract $1 million of intangibles. That leaves $6 million of net tangible assets. This represents a coverage of three times the total bond indebtedness, usually a fairly substantial coverage.

INCOME STATEMENT ANALYSIS

Just as with the balance sheet, most of the figures obtained from the income statement acquire real meaning only by comparison with other figures, either with similar figures of previous years of the same company or with the corresponding figures of other companies in the same or similar business.

For example, comparisons can be made between each significant item of expense and cost and net sales to get a percentage of net sales (vertical analysis) which can then be compared with other companies. Percentages are more meaningful to compare than absolute dollar amounts, since the volume of business done by one company in the same industry may vary substantially from the volume of another company.

Comparison can also be made of each of the significant figures on the income statement with the same figures for prior years (horizontal analysis). Here, too, comparisons of percentages rather than absolute dollar amounts might be more meaningful if the volume of sales has varied substantially from year to year.

Other significant comparisons are covered in the following paragraphs.

Ratio of Long-Term Debt to Equity

This ratio measures the leverage potential of the business; that is, the varying effects which changes in operating profits will have on net profits. The rule is that the higher the debt ratio, the greater will be the effect on the common stock of changes in earnings because of increased interest expenses.

Many security analysts feel that in an industrial company equity should equal at least half the total of all equity and debt outstanding. Railroads and utilities, however, are likely to have more debt (and preferred stock) than common stock because of the heavy investments in fixed assets, much of which is financed by the use of debt and preferred stock.

A stock is considered to have high leverage if the issuing company has a high percentage of bonds and preferred stock outstanding in relation to the amount of common stock. In good years, this will mean that after bond interest and preferred stock dividends are paid, there will be an impressive earnings per share figure because of the small amount of common stock outstanding.

On the other hand, that same high leverage situation could cause real difficulty with even a moderate decline in earnings. Not only would the decline eliminate any dividends for the common stock, but also could even necessitate drawing from accumulated earnings to cover the full interest on its bonds.

Earnings per Share

Probably, the most important ratio used today is the earnings per share (EPS) figure. It is a *mandatory* disclosure on all annual financial (income) statements (for public companies) and mandatory for all interim statements (though unaudited) for public companies. Moreover, the EPS must be broken out separately for extraordinary items. The standards of calculation are quite complex where preferred stock, options and convertibility are involved.

FASB 128, *Earnings per Share*

FASB 128 established new standards for computing and presenting earning per share and applies to entities with publicly held common stock or potential common stock.

It simplifies the admittedly complicated methods used for computing earnings per share previously found in APB 15, *Earnings Per Share,* and makes the requirements comparable to new international EPS standards adopted recently. In doing this, FASB 128 replaces the presentation of primary EPS with a presentation of basic EPS. It also requires dual presentation of basic and diluted EPS on the face of the income statement for all entities with complex capital structures and requires a reconciliation of the numerator and denominator of the basic EPS computation to the numerator and denominator of the diluted EPS computation.

The oft interpreted, reinterpreted, and much maligned APB 15 had required that entities with simple capital structures present a single "earnings per common share" on the face of the income statement, whereas those with complex capital structures had to present both "primary" and "fully diluted" EPS. Primary EPS showed the amount of income attributed to each share of common stock if every common stock equivalent were converted into common stock. Fully diluted EPS considers common stock equivalents and all other securities that could be converted into common stock. The two EPS figures required under FASB 128 follow:

1. Basic Earnings Per Share is computed by dividing income available to stockholders by the weighted average number of common shares outstanding during the period. Shares issued during the period and shares reacquired during the period should be weighted for the portion of the period they were outstanding. The formula would be: (Net income minus preferred dividends) divided by common stock.

    Under the old rules, U.S. companies with complex capital structures could not present a basic earnings per share figure. (A company has a complex capital structure when it has issued securities convertible into common stock or has agreements to issue common stock at some future date.) The principal difference between basic and primary earnings per share is that the latter takes into account so-called common share equivalents. In nearly every country outside of the U.S. that requires an earnings per share disclosure, the requirement calls for a basic earnings per share presentation rather than a primary EPS figure. An entity's basic earnings per share will show higher earnings per share than primary earnings per share did, but this will mean no change as far as a company's actual equity valuation is concerned.

2. Diluted EPS reflects the potential dilution that could occur if securities or other contracts to issue common stock were exercised or converted into common stock or resulted in the issuance of common stock that would then share in the earnings of the entity. It is figured in a similar manner to basic EPS after adjusting the numerator and denominator for the possible dilution. Since it is, therefore, computed in a similar manner to fully diluted EPS under APB 15, it will produce a similar earnings per share figure.

Equity Valuation Unchanged.   The new standard did not change U.S. equity valuations because:

1. Even though basic earnings per share show a higher figure than primary earnings per share, informed investors do not use basic earnings per share anyway for companies with complex capital structures because it does not take into account the potential dilutive effect of convertibles, options, warrants, and the like.
2. Most entities' dilutive earnings per share are substantially the same as their fully diluted earnings per share had been.

Resulting Changes.   Of course, the most important change introduced by the FASB 128 is the elimination of the complicated calculations necessary to arrive at primary earnings per share and replace them with the simpler calculations necessary to obtain basic earnings per share for disclosure.

In addition, diluted EPS is somewhat different from "fully diluted earnings per share." Not only is "fully" dropped, but the calculation of the figure is changed in several ways:

1. Elimination of the provision that the diluted earnings per share need not be given if the potential dilution is less than three percent.
2. Elimination of the use of the end of period stock price in the treasury stock method calculation to determine maximum dilution.
3. Elimination of the modified treasury stock method that was used to calculate potential dilution in cases when an unusually large number of options or warrants were outstanding.
4. Use of the earnings from continuing operations as the "control figure" to determine if a security or contingent issuance is antidilutive in certain situations.

The new statement not only supersedes APB 15 and AICPA Accounting Interpretation 1-102 of APB 15, it also supersedes or amends other accounting pronouncements scattered throughout accounting literature. The provisions in this Statement are substantially the same as those in International Accounting Standard 33, *Earnings per Share,* issued by the International Accounting Standards Committee at the same time.

Sales Growth

The raw element of profit growth is an increase in sales (or revenues when the company's business is services). While merely increasing sales is no guarantee that higher profits will follow, it is usually the first vital step; therefore, in analyzing a company, the sales figures for the past four or five years are important. If they have been rising and there is no reason to believe the company's markets are near the saturation point, it is reasonable to assume that the rise will continue.

When a company's sales have jumped by the acquisition of another firm, it is important to find out if the acquisition was accomplished by the issuance of additional common stock, by the assumption of additional debt, or for cash. If the company was paid for by common stock and if the acquired firm's earnings are the same on a per-share basis as those of the acquiring firm, the profit picture remains exactly as it was before. The additional sales growth is balanced by the *dilution of the equity*—that is, the larger number of shares now sharing in the earnings.

The situation is quite different if the purchase was for cash or in exchange of bonds or preferred stock. Here, no dilution of the common stock has occurred. The entire profits of the new firm (minus the interest which must be paid on the new debt or the interest formerly earned on the cash) benefit the existing shareholders.

In any event, acquisitions of new companies often require a period of consolidation and adjustment, frequently followed by a decreased rate of sales growth.

Consideration should be given to the effect of inflation on sales. A situation can exist where the increase in sales may be caused by the increase in prices. The result may be that unit sales have dropped in relation to the previous year's, but the dollar sales have increased. Comparing unit sales may be a better method of ascertaining the sales increase under certain circumstances.

Computing Operating Profit

A company's costs of operations fall into two groups: *cost of goods sold* and *cost of operations.* The first relates to all the costs of producing the goods or services matched to the revenues produced by those costs. The second includes all other costs not directly associated with the production costs, such as selling and administrative costs (usually called period expenses).

Subtracting both of these groups of costs from sales leaves *operating profit*. Various special costs and special forms of income are then added or subtracted from operating income to get *net income before taxes*. After deducting state and federal income taxes, the final figure (which is commonly used for computing the profit per share) is *net income*. When analyzing a company, however, you will often be most interested in the operating profit figure, since this reflects the real earning capacity of the company.

The best way to look at cost figures is as a percentage of sales. Thus, a company may spend 90 cents out of every dollar in operating costs. We say its cost percentage is 90 percent or, more commonly, its *operating profit margin* is 10 percent. Profit margins vary a great deal among industries, running anywhere from 1 percent to 20 percent of sales; thus comparisons should not be made between companies in different industries. The trend of the operating profit margin for a particular company, however, will give an excellent picture of how well management is able to control costs. If sales increases are obtained only by cutting prices, this will immediately show as a decrease in the margin of profit. In introducing a new product it is sometimes necessary to incur special costs to make initial market penetration, but this should be only temporary.

The most used, examined and discussed ratio within a company is the *gross profit ratio*. More significance is probably attached to this ratio than to any other because increases usually indicate improved performance (more sales, more efficient production) and decreases indicate weaknesses (poor selling effort, waste in production, weak inventory controls).

When comparing a company with others in the same field, if the company's profit margin is low by comparison, it signals troubles ahead; if it is high, the company appears to be a worthy competitor.

The terminology in the gross profit percentages is sometimes confusing and misinterpreted, especially when the word "markup" is used. As an example:

	$	%
Sales	$100	100%
Cost of Sales	80	80%
Gross Profit	$ 20	20%

In conventional usage, there is a 20 percent gross profit or margin on the sale (20/100). However, to determine the *markup*, the cost of sales is the denominator and the gross profit is the numerator (20/80 equals a 25 percent markup).

Starting with gross profit *percentage desired*, to gross 20 percent, what should the selling price be? (The only known factor is cost.)

	%	Known	As calculated
Selling price	100%	?	$150
Cost	80%	$120	120
Gross Profit	20%	?	$ 30

Selling price is always 100 percent. If cost is $120 and is equal to 80 percent of the selling price (it must be 80 percent because a gross of 20 percent was set), divide $120 by 80 percent to get the 100 percent selling price of $150.

Ratio of Net Sales to Stockholders' Equity

A company acquires assets in order to produce sales which yield a profit. If tangible assets yield too few sales, the company is suffering from underselling (the underutilization of its assets). On the other hand, the company may suffer from overtrading (too many sales in proportion to its tangible net worth). In other words, there is too heavy a reliance on borrowed funds to generate sales.

Another way of measuring the effective utilization of assets is to determine the ratio of net sales to total assets (excluding long-term investments).

In either case, comparisons of these ratios with similar ratios of other companies in the same industry can indicate the relative efficiency in utilization of assets of the company being analyzed.

Ratio of Net Sales to Working Capital

This is similar to the preceding ratio, since it measures the relationship between sales and assets. In this case, however, the ratio measures whether the company has sufficient net current assets to support the volume of its sales or, on the other hand, if the capital invested in working capital is working hard enough to produce sales.

Profit Margin on Sales

The profit margin on sales is obtained by dividing net income by net sales for the period. A ratio of 7.5 percent compared to an industry average of 4.6 percent indicates a company is achieving an above-average rate of profits on each sales dollar received.

The profit margin on sales does not indicate how profitable a company is for a given period of time. Only by determining how many times the total assets turned over during a period of time is it possible to ascertain the amount of net income earned on total assets. The rate of return on assets is computed by using net income as the numerator and average total assets as a denominator.

An average of 6.2 percent compared to an industry average of 4.9 percent is above the average of an industry and results from a high profit margin on sales.

Rate of Return on Common Stock Equity

This ratio is defined as net income after interest, taxes, and preferred stock dividends (if any) divided by average common stock-holders' equity. When the rate of return on common stock equity is higher than the rate of return on total assets, the company is considered to be trading on the equity. Trading on the equity increases a company's financial risk, but it increases a company's earnings.

Dividend Yield

The dividend yield is the cash dividend per share divided by the market price of the stock at the time the yield is determined. This ratio gives the rate of return that an investor will receive at the time on an investment in a stock or bond.

Times Interest Earned

This ratio is computed by dividing income before interest charges and taxes by the interest charge. The ratio indicates the safety of a bondholder's investment. A company that has an interest earned ratio of 5 to 1 shows a significantly safer position for meeting its bond interest obligations than a company with a lower ratio.

STATEMENT OF CHANGES IN STOCKHOLDERS' EQUITY

This statement presents an equity analysis of changes from year to year in each shareholder's account, records any additional shares issued, foreign currency translation gains/losses, dividends per share (if paid), retained earnings. This last figure indicates how well the company itself is doing by revealing how much of the profits it can retain to finance further growth opportunities. In an era of corporate raiding and takeovers, management may be wise to be sure that retained earnings are not too high, but are put to good use in increasing total earnings per share for the benefit of current stockholders.

Return on Equity

This ratio is another method of determining earning power. Here, the opening equity (capital stock plus retained earnings, plus or minus any other equity section items) is divided into the net income for the year to give the percentage earned on that year's investment.

Return to Investors

This is a relatively new ratio used mostly by financial publications, primarily for comparison of many companies in similar industries. The opening equity is divided into the sum of the dividends paid plus the market price appreciation of the period. In addition, the ratio is sometimes extended to cover five years, ten years or more.

Dividend Payout Ratio

The *dividend* per common share is divided by the *earnings* per common share to get the *percentage* of dividend payout.

The dividends on common stock will vary with the profitability of the company, but other considerations also affect the percent of payout:

1. The relative stability of the earnings
2. The need for new capital
3. The directors' judgment concerning the outlook for earnings
4. The general views of management relating to the advisability of:
   a. Plowing back a large part of earnings into the business
   b. Raising additional funds from outside sources

Dividends on the preferred stock are not subject to a year-to-year fluctuation. If the fixed dividend on *cumulative* preferred stock for any year cannot be met, the payments would accumulate and be paid before any dividends could be declared on the common stock.

FASB 130, *REPORTING COMPREHENSIVE INCOME*

FASB 130 began in conjunction with the Exposure Draft (ED) on derivatives and hedging. However, since there is much less in it to cause prolonged cotroversy, this Standard was issued requiring reporting and display of comprehensive income effective in 1998, while the new derivatives standard became effective on June 15, 2000. Financial statements from previous periods used for comparison must be reclassified in line with the provisions of Statement 130.

At the time the EDs were issued, U.S. GAAP did not use a comprehensive income concept. The idea was to issue the two EDs simultaneously in anticipation of employing the concept in connection with the derivative and other future standards.

All of the items that are required to be recognized under accounting standards as components of comprehensive income must now be reported in a financial statement that is displayed with the same degree of prominence as other financial statements.

Comprehensive Income Defined

Comprehensive income is defined in FASB Concepts Statement 6, *Elements of Financial Statements,* as "... the change in equity (net assets) of a business enterprise during a period from transactions and other events and circumstances from non-owner sources. It includes all changes in equity during a period except those resulting from investments by owners and distributions to owners."

FASB 130 considers that comprehensive income consists of two major components—net income and "other comprehensive income." The latter refers to revenues, expenses, gains and losses that, according to GAAP, are included in comprehensive income but excluded from net income. They are direct debits or credits to owners' equity that do not involve transactions with owners, such as foreign currency translation gains and losses, unrealized gains or losses on marketable securities classified as available-for-sale, and minimum pension liability adjustments. Thus, comprehensive income is the total of net income plus the revenue, expense, gain and loss changes in equity during a period which now is not included in net income.

Equity Valuation Not Affected

This new display and related disclosures will not influence equity valuations, nor is any new or additional information disclosed. It merely repackages existing disclosed data in a new format. FASB 130 may not be of particular interest to sophisticated investors, creditors, and securities firms, but it should be of interest to accountants who have the task of implementing the new format. However, this should not be a particularly onerous job since it is largely a matter of displaying known financial data rather than calculating additional figures that would change recognition of income.

On the other hand, the FASB does appear to believe that, used in conjunction with related disclosures and other information in the financial statements, the comprehensive income information could help the knowledgeable user in assessing an entity's activities, and the timing and extent of future cash flows. Further, the Board emphasizes that while a total comprehensive income figure is useful, information about its components may give more insight into an enterprise's activities.

Format for Presentation of Comprehensive Income

One aspect for the accountant to consider is the best way to use this new display to inform, but not confuse, the less sophisticated user of financial statements. Since the Statement does not require a specific financial statement format for the display of comprehensive income and its components, the accountant may be expected to make some choices.

1. The requirement to report a new "income" figure for the quarter may be displayed as *either* a performance measurement or a change in equity. Which to choose?

2. Companies are permitted to display total comprehensive income and its components in either an income statement type format or in a statement of changes in equity format. Would it be better to preserve the current income statement as a separate display and show a company's net income figure as the bottom line? Or not? (With the equity format, a statement of changes in equity must be displayed as a primary financial statement.)

3. The Standard permits companies to report only a total for comprehensive income in condensed interim financial statements issued to shareholders. Would it be less confusing to show total comprehensive income as a part of a complete display of the calculations every time rather than as a single figure?

Application of Requirements

FASB 130 applies to all companies that present a full set of general-purpose financial statements. Investment companies, defined benefit pension plans, and other employee benefit plans that are exempt from the requirement to provide a statement of cash flows by FASB 102, *Statement of Cash Flows—Exemption of Certain Enterprises and Certification of Cash Flows from Certain Securities Acquired for Resale,* are not exempt from requirements of FASB 130 if it applies in all other respects. However, it does not apply to organizations that have no items of comprehensive income in any period presented, or to not-for-profit organizations that are covered by FASB 117, *Financial Statements of Not-for-Profit Organizations.*

As mentioned above, the Statement suggests how to report and display comprehensive income and its components but does not provide guidance on items that are to be included. For this guidance, the existing and future accounting standards mentioned earlier will need to be consulted.

Components of Comprehensive Income

At this time, eight items qualify, according to GAAP, as components of other comprehensive income that, under prior standards, bypassed the income statement and had to be reported as a balance within a separate component of equity in a statement of financial position.

1. Foreign currency translation adjustments.

2. Gains and losses on foreign currency transactions that are designated as, and are effective as, economic hedges of a net investment in a foreign entity, commencing as of the designation date.

3. Gains and losses on intercompany foreign currency transactions that are of a long-term-investment nature (i.e., settlement is not planned or anticipated in the foreseeable future), when the entities to the transaction are consolidated, combined, or accounted for by the equity method in the reporting enterprise's financial statements.

4. A change in the market value of a futures contract that qualifies as a hedge of an asset reported at fair value according to FASB 115, *Accounting for Certain Investments in Debt and Equity Securities.*

5. A net loss recognized under FASB 87, *Employers' Accounting for Pensions,* as an additional pension liability not yet recognized as net periodic pension cost.

6. Unrealized holding gains and losses on available-for-sale securities.

7. Unrealized holding gains and losses that result from a debt security being transferred into the available-for-sale category from the held-to-maturity category.

8. Subsequent decreases (if not an other-than-temporary impairment) or increases in the fair value of available for-sale securities previously written down as impaired.

(This list will be expanded now that the derivatives and hedging standard is promulgated. Some gains and/or losses from those transactions will be included as part of other comprehensive income.)

Terminology

The Statement does not require that the descriptive terms "comprehensive income," "total comprehensive income," or "other comprehensive income" be used in financial statements. It permits companies to use equivalent terms, such as "total non-owner changes in equity," "comprehensive loss" or other appropriate descriptive labels. It may be that most entities will choose to use alternative terms since "comprehensive income" still has a rather hollow ring to it.

Cash Flow and Equity Valuation Not Affected

Inasmuch as all of the items included in other comprehensive income are noncash items, the FASB decided that indirect-method cash flow statement presentation would continue to begin with net income as required by FASB 95, *Statement of Cash Flows.*

FASB 130 should clarify the extent to which revenue, expense, gain and loss items are being taken directly to owners' equity, but, as mentioned above, the display of comprehensive income and its components will not affect equity valuation. Unlike the requirements in FASB 131, *Disclosures About Segments of an Enterprise and Related Information,* which calls for greatly expanded reporting on segments, the requirements of FASB 130 call for no new data. Since informed investors have always examined owners' equity to evaluate the material now collected under the other comprehensive income items, the new display should have little impact on the public's conception of a company's financial condition.

APB OPINION 22, *DISCLOSURE OF ACCOUNTING POLICIES*

APB 22 covers *Disclosure of Accounting Policies.* A description of all significant accounting policies of the reporting entity should be included as an integral part of all financial statements. Whether these statements are issued in presenting the entity's financial position, changes in the financial position, or in showing results of operations in accordance with GAAP, a description of all significant accounting policies, methods and practices of the reporting entity should be included as an integral part of all financial statements. When it is appropriate to issue one or more basic financial statements without the others, these statements should also comprise the pertinent accounting policies. Not-for-profit entities should also present details of their accounting policies as an integral part of their financial statements.

Content and Format of Disclosures

1. Disclosure of accounting policies should identify and describe the accounting principles employed by the reporting business and the methods of applying those principles which are important in the determination of financial position, changes in financial position, or results of operations. The disclosure should include decisions concerning applicability of principles relating to recognition of revenue and allocation of asset costs to current and future periods. The disclosure statement should comprise all the reasoning behind the choice of, or an explanation of, the accounting principles and methods employed that involve any of the following:

   a. Selection of one practice over another from existing acceptable alternatives.

   b. Principles and methods peculiar to the industry of the reporting firm, even when such principles and methods are characteristically followed in that industry.

   c. Unusual or innovative applications of generally accepted accounting principles or of practices and methods peculiar to that industry.

2. Examples of disclosures commonly required in regard to accounting policies include those relating to basis of consolidation, depreciation methods, amortization of intangibles, inventory pricing, accounting for

research and development costs and the basis for amortization thereof, translation of foreign currencies, recognition of profit on long-term construction-type contracts, recognition of revenue from franchising and leasing operations, and any other items deemed pertinent to give a complete picture of a firm's financial status.

3. The format follows a plan of having a separate *Summary of Significant Accounting Policies* preceding the notes to the financial statements or, in some cases, as the initial note of the statement.

Chapter 2

Revenue and Expenses

CONTENTS

Revenue (Income)	**2.01**
Expenses	**2.03**
Other Expenses (and Revenue)	**2.05**
Imputed Interest on Notes Receivable or Payable	**2.05**
Classifying and Reporting Extraordinary Items	**2.08**
Present Value Computation and Application	**2.10**
FASB's Plans for Accounting for Employee Stock Options	**2.13**
IASB Considering Fair Value for Employee Stock Options	**2.14**
SAB 101, *Revenue Recognition in Financial Statements*	**2.15**
FASB 123, *Accounting for Stock Options Issued to Employees*	**2.22**

REVENUE (INCOME)

The principles upon which net income is determined derive from the pervasive measurement principles, such as realization, and the modifying conventions, such as conservatism.

The entire process of income determination ("matching") consists of identifying, measuring and relating revenue and expenses for an accounting period. Revenue is usually determined by applying the realization principle, with the changes in net asset value interrelated with the recognition of revenue. Revenue arises from three general activities:

1. Selling products;
2. Rendering services or letting others use owned resources, resulting in interest, rent, etc;
3. Disposing of other resources (not products), such as equipment or investments.

Revenue does not include proceeds from stockholders, lenders, asset purchases or prior period adjustments.

Revenue, in the balance sheet sense, is a gross increase in assets or a gross decrease in liabilities recognized and measured in conformity with GAAP, which results from those profit-directed activities that can change owners' equity.

Revenue is considered *realized* when:

1. The earning process is complete or virtually complete, and
2. An exchange has taken place.

The objectives of accounting determination of income are not always the same as the objectives used for tax purposes.

There are various acceptable ways of determining income:

1. *Revenue* (see three general activities above):
   a. Accrual method—this is financial accounting and GAAP.
   b. Cash method—this is *not* considered financial accounting, and not GAAP, since one of the characteristics of GAAP is the *accrual* of appropriate items.
   c. Installment sales method—generally for retail stores.
   d. Completion of production method—used for precious metals.
   e. For long-term construction contracts:
      • Completed contract method.
      • Percentage-of-completion method.
   f. For leasing activities:
      • The direct financing method.
      • The operating method.
      • The sales method.
   g. The cost recovery method (used for installment sales).
   h. Consolidation method—for majority-owned subsidiaries (over 50 percent).

   i. Equity method—for non-consolidated subsidiaries and for controlled non-subsidiaries.

2. *Other* types of income requiring special determination:

   a. Extraordinary items of income.

   b. Unrealized income arising from:

- Foreign currency holdings or transactions.
- Ownership of marketable securities shown as current assets.

A *shareholder* in a corporation does *not* have income when that corporation earns income (except for a Sub-S corporation). The shareholder has, and reports for tax purposes, income only upon *distribution* of that income in the form of dividends. Generally, distributions of stock—stock dividends and stock splits—are *not* income to the shareholder, but merely an adjustment of the number of shares he holds (for the same original cost plus token costs, if any). However, there are some situations which call for the stockholder to report stock dividends as income.

If a buyer has a right of return to the seller, revenue is recognized if *all* of the following criteria are met:

1. Buyer is obligated to pay (and not contingent upon resale of the product) or has paid the seller.

2. Buyer's obligation would not be changed by theft, damage, or destruction of the product.

3. Seller does not have any significant obligation to buyer related to resale of the product by the buyer.

4. Buyer's business must have economic substance separate from the seller's business.

If these criteria are met, sales revenue and cost of sales reported in the income statement are reduced to reflect estimated returns; expected losses are accrued.

EXPENSES

Expenses are one of the six basic elements of financial accounting, along with assets, liabilities, owners' equity, revenue and net income. Expenses are determined by applying the expense recognition principles on the basis of relationships, between acquisition costs [the term "cost" is commonly used to refer to the amount at which assets are initially recorded, regardless of how determined], and either the independently determined revenue or accounting periods. Since the point in time at which revenue and expenses are recognized is also the time at which changes in amounts of net assets are recorded, income determination is interrelated with asset valuation.

All costs are not expenses. Some costs are related to later periods, will provide benefits for later periods, and are carried forward as assets on the balance sheet. Other costs are incurred and provide no future benefit, having expired in terms of usefulness or applicability—these expired costs are called "expenses." All expenses, therefore, are part of the broader term "cost." These expired costs are not assets and are shown as deductions from revenue to determine net income.

Expenses are gross decreases in assets or gross increases in liabilities recognized and measured in conformity with GAAP that result from those types of profit-directed activities that can change an owner's equity.

Recognizing Expenses

Three pervasive principles form the basis for recognizing expenses to be deducted from revenue to arrive at net income or loss:

1. Associating cause and effect ("matching")—For example, manufacturing cost of goods sold is measured and matched to the *sale* of the product. Assumptions must be made as to how these costs attach to the product—whether on machine hours, space used, or labor expended. Assumptions must also be made as to how the costs flow out (LIFO, FIFO, average costs).

2. Systematic and rational allocation—When there is no direct way to associate cause and effect and certain costs are known (or presumed) to have provided benefits during the accounting period, these costs are allocated to that period in a systematic and rational manner and to appear so to an unbiased observer. The methods of allocation should be consistent and systematic, though methods may vary for different types of costs. Examples are depreciation of fixed assets, amortization of intangibles and interperiod allocation of rent or interest. The allocation referred to here is not the allocation of expired manufacturing costs with the "cost" area to determine unit or job costs; it is rather the broader area of allocation to the manufacturing area from the unexpired asset account: Depreciation on factory building, rather than overhead-depreciation on Product A, B, or C.

3. Immediate recognition (period expenses)—Costs expensed during an accounting period because:

    a. They cannot be associated on a cause-and-effect basis with revenue, yet no useful purpose would be achieved by delaying recognition to a future period,

b. They provide no discernible future benefits, or

c. They were recorded as assets in a prior period and now no longer provide discernible future benefits.

Examples are officer salaries, most selling expenses, legal fees and most general and administrative expenses.

OTHER EXPENSES (AND REVENUE)

Gains and Losses.   Expenses and revenue from *other* than sales of products, merchandise or services may be separated from (operating) revenue and disclosed net separately.

Unusual Items.   Unusual items of expense or income not meeting the criteria of "extraordinary" should be shown as a separate component of income from continuing operations.

Extraordinary Items.   Extraordinary items are discussed elsewhere in this book. They should be shown separately—net of applicable taxes—*after* net income from continuing operations. If there are any disposals of business segments, they should be shown immediately prior to extraordinary items—also with tax effect.

IMPUTED INTEREST ON NOTES RECEIVABLE OR PAYABLE

Accounting Considerations

The AICPA sets forth the appropriate accounting when the face amount of certain receivables or payables ("notes") does not reasonably represent the present value of the consideration given or received in certain exchanges. The objective of these rules is to prevent the form of the transaction from prevailing over its economic substance. (*Present value* is the sum of future payments, discounted to the present date at an appropriate rate of interest.)

APB Opinion 21 states that:

1. When a note is received or issued solely for cash, the note is presumed to have a present value equal to the cash received. If it is issued for cash equal to its face amount, it is presumed to earn the stated rate of interest.

2. When a note is received for cash and some other rights or privileges, the value of the rights or privileges should be given accounting recognition by establishing a note discount or premium account, with the offsetting

amount treated as appropriate. An example is a five-year noninterest-bearing loan made to a supplier in partial consideration for a purchase of products at lower than prevailing market prices. Under such circumstances, the difference between the present value of the receivable and the cash lent to the supplier is regarded as (a) an additional cost of the purchased goods, and (b) interest income, amortized over the life of the note.

3. When a note is exchanged for property, goods, or services and (a) interest is not stated, or (b) it is stated but is unreasonable, or (c) the stated face amount of the note is materially different from the current cash sale price of goods (or services), the note, the sales price, and the cost of the property (goods or services) should be recorded at their fair value, or at an amount that reasonably approximates the market value of the note, whichever is more clearly determinable.

Any resulting discount or premium should be regarded as interest expense or income and be amortized over the life of the note, in such a way as to result in a constant effective rate of interest when applied to the amount outstanding at the beginning of any given period.

Opinion 21 also provides some general guides for determining an "appropriate" interest rate and the manner of amortization for financial reporting purposes.

IMPUTED INTEREST: When a sale is made for an amount that is collectible at a future time giving rise to an account receivable, the amount is regarded as consisting of a sales price *and* a charge for interest for the period of the payment deferral. APB Opinion 21 requires that in the absence of a stated rate of interest, the present value of the receivable should be determined by reducing the face amount of the receivable by an interest rate that is approximated under the circumstances for the period that payment is deferred.

This rate is the *imputed rate*. It is determined by approximating the rate the supplier pays for financing receivables, or by determining the buyer's credit standing and applying the rate the borrower would have to pay if borrowing the sum from, say, a bank.

The process of arriving at the present value of the receivable is referred to as *discounting* the sum. If the total present value of the receivable (face amount plus the imputed interest) is less than the face amount, the difference between the face value of the receivable and its present value is recognized as a discount. If the present value exceeds the face amount of the receivable, the difference is recognized as a premium.

The sale is recorded as a debit to a receivable account, a credit to a discount on the receivable, and a credit to sales at the present value as reported for the receivable. The discount is amortized as a credit to interest income over the life of the receivable. On the balance sheet any unamortized discount at the end of the accounting period is reported as a direct subtraction from the *face amount* of the receivable.

Example: A seller ships merchandise totaling $10,000 to a customer with payment deferred for five years. Seller and customer agree to impute an interest charge of 10 percent for the $10,000. The journal entries follow.

Accounts Receivable	10,000	
Sales (Present value at 10%)		6,209
Unamortized Discount		3,791
(To record the sale of merchandise at		
the present value of the receivable)		

The *interest method* is applied to amortize the discount.

End of Year 1		
Unamortized Discount	620.90	
Interest Income		620.90
(10% of $6,209.00)		
End of Year 2		
Unamortized Discount	682.99	
Interest Income		682.99
(10% of $6,829.90)		
End of Year 3		
Unamortized Discount	751.29	
Interest Income		751.29
(10% of $7,512.89)		
End of Year 4		
Unamortized Discount	826.42	
Interest Income		826.42
(10% of $8,264.18)		
Unamortized Discount	909.06	
End of Year 5		
Unamortized Discount	909.06	
Interest Income		909.06
(10% of $9,090.60)		

At the end of five years full amortization of the discount has been recorded and the face amount of the receivable results. (*Note:* Opinion 21 does not require the imputed interest method when ". . . receivables and payables arising from transactions with customers or suppliers in the normal course of business which are due in customary trade terms not exceeding approximately one year.")

CLASSIFYING AND REPORTING EXTRAORDINARY ITEMS

Income statement presentation requires that the results of *ordinary operations* be reported first, and applicable provision for income taxes provided for.
In order, the following should then be shown:

1. Results of discontinued operations:
   a. Income or loss from the operations discontinued for the portion of the period until discontinuance—shown net of tax, with the tax shown parenthetically;
   b. Loss (or gain) on disposal of the business segments, including provision for phase-out operating losses—also shown net of tax parenthetically.
2. Extraordinary items—Should be segregated and shown as the last factor used in arriving at net income for the period. Here, the caption is shown net of applicable income taxes, which are shown parenthetically. Note that extraordinary items do *not* include disposal of business segments as such, because they are segregated and shown separately prior thereto (as above).

An example of the reporting of the above:

	2002	2001
Income from continuing operations before income taxes	$ xxx	$ xxx
Provision for income taxes	xx	xx
Income from continuing operations	$ xxx	xxx
Discountinued operations (Note):		
Income from operations of discontinued		
Division B (less applicable taxes of $xx)	$ xx	
	2002	2001
Loss on disposal of Division B, including		
provision for phase-out operating losses of		
$xx (less applicable income taxes of $xx)	xx	xx
Income before extraordinary items		xxx
Extraordinary items (less applicable		
income taxes of $xx)		
(Note)		xx
Net Income	$ xxx	$ xxx
Earnings per share:		
Income from continuing operations	$ x.00	$ x.00
Discontinued operations	x.00	x.00
Extraordinary items	x.00	x.00
Net Income	$ x.00	$ x.00

Note that earnings per share should be broken out separately for the factors of discontinued operations and extraordinary items, as well as for income from (continuing) operations.

The criteria for classifying a transaction or event as an "extraordinary item" are as follows:

Extraordinary items are events and transactions that are distinguished by their unusual nature *and* by the infrequency of their occurrence. Thus, *both* of the following criteria should be met to classify an event or transaction as an extraordinary item:

1. *Unusual nature*—the underlying event or transaction should possess a high degree of abnormality and be of a type clearly unrelated to, or only incidentally related to, the ordinary and typical activities of the entity, taking into account the environment in which the entity operates.

2. *Infrequency of occurrence*—the underlying event or transaction should be of a type that would not reasonably be expected to recur in the foreseeable future, taking into account the environment in which the entity operates.

Items that are *not* to be reported as extraordinary, because they may recur or are not unusual, are:

1. Write-downs of receivables, inventories, intangibles, or leased equipment.
2. Effects of strikes.
3. Gains or losses on foreign currency translations.
4. Adjustment of accruals on long-term contracts.
5. Gains or losses on disposal of business segments.
6. Gains or losses from abandonment or sale of property, plant or equipment used in the business.

Note that some highly unusual occurrence might cause one of the above types of gains or losses and should be considered extraordinary, such as those resulting from major casualties (earthquake), expropriations and legal restrictions. Disposals of business segments, though not extraordinary in classification, should be shown separately on the income statement, just prior to extraordinary items, but after operations from continuing business.

Miscellaneous data pertaining to extraordinary items:

1. Bargain sales of stock to stockholders are *not* extraordinary items, but they should be shown separately.
2. A gain or a loss on sale of coin collections by a bank is *not* an extraordinary item.

PRESENT VALUE COMPUTATION AND APPLICATION

The procedure of computing interest on principal *and interest on interest* under-lies the concept of *compounding*. There are a number of accounting procedures (accounting for bonds, accounts receivable, accounts payable, and leases, for example) to which the compound interest formula (and variations) can be applied.

1. The *future value* of a sum of money. If $1,000 (the principal P) is deposited in a bank today, what will be the balance (S) in the account in *n years* (or *periods*) if the bank accumulates interest at the rate of *i* percent per year?

2. The *present value* of a sum of money due at the end of a period of time. What is the value *today* of the amount owed if $1,000 has to be paid, say to a creditor, *n* years from today?

3. The *future value of an annuity,* which is a series of *equal* payments made at *equal* intervals. If $1,000 a year is deposited for *n* years, how much will have accumulated at the end of the *n*-years period if the deposits earn in-terest at the rate of *i* percent per year?

4. The *present value of an annuity,* which is a series of *equal* payments made at *equal* intervals. If we are to be paid $1,000 a year for *n* years, how much is this annuity worth today, given *i* percent rate of interest?

The formula for the future value of a sum of money is the familiar compound interest formula. In the four examples to follow let:

S = The future worth of a sum of money invested today.

P = Principal, or the sum of money that will accumulate to S amount of money.

i = The rate of interest (r may be substituted).

n = Number of periods of time.

It is important to understand that a "period of time" is not necessarily one year, even though rates of interest in the United States are always under-stood to mean the rate for a period of one year. A period can be any length of time—i.e., day, week, month, year, second, minute, hour. Time is a *continuous,* not a *discrete* function.

With compound interest the total amount accumulated (S in the formula) at the end of one period earns interest during the subsequent period, or "interest on interest." The formula is:

$$S = P(1 + i)^n$$

At this point it should be emphasized that the user no longer must do the arithmetic. Not only can the problem types be solved by the use of tables, but now inexpensive hand calculators will perform the computations and give the answers. The user has simply only to enter the numbers that represent the letters in the formula. Users with computers can, of course, program the formulas for permanent storage and simply "call out" whichever formula applies to the problem at hand. With respect to the arithmetic, however, three of the variables in the equation are always known quantities; therefore, finding the value of the fourth and *un*known variable follows.

   A Word of Caution.   Computational errors caused by entering the wrong value for *n* are not uncommon. If $i = 12\%$ and the compounding period is every six months, *n* in the formula is 6. If the compounding period is quarterly *n* is 3. If the compounding period is daily (as is the case in many financial institutions savings policies) *n* becomes $i/360$—360 days in the year are applied in this country for interest calculations instead of 365. This is because the smaller the denominator, the bit more interest the *lender* collects. However, if the formula applies to a problem involving U.S. Government bonds, a 365-day year must be assumed because it enables the government to borrow a bit cheaper, relatively.

Annuities

   The previous discussion considers the accumulation of interest on a *single* payment, however the single payment may be invested. *Annuities* apply to problems that involve a series of *equal payments* (or investments, savings, etc.,) made at *equal intervals* of time. The period of time between payments is called the *payment period.* The period of time between computation of the interest accumulation is called the *interest-conversion period.* When the payment period exactly equals the interest-conversion period, the annuity is an *ordinary annuity.* The equal payments are termed rents, which are spread over equal periods of time, the first rent payment made at the *start* of the annuity, and the last payment made at the *end* of the annuity.
   The *future worth* of the annuity is the sum of the future worths of each of the separate rents. Assuming $100 invested we have $100 at time 1. At time 2 we have the $100 invested that day, plus the $100 invested at time 1, plus the interest earned during the period between time 1 and time 2. At time 3 another $100 is deposited; we now have the $100 deposited that day, the $100 deposited at time 2 plus the interest earned for one period, and the $100 deposited at time 1 plus the interest earned during the period between time 1 and time 2.
   The formula for the future worth of an annuity of $1 is:

$$S = \frac{(1 + i)^n - 1}{i}$$

   Note that the formula for the accumulation of interest on an ordinary annuity has the same variables as the compounding formula for a single payment.

To obtain S for any amount more than \$1, multiply both sides of the equation by the amount invested, by P. In this case multiply both sides of the equation by 100. As above the amount for \$1 can be found in tables (or by the use of a hand calculator).

The *present worth* of an annuity concerns the same question as the present worth of a single payment for *n years at i rate of interest*. How much would we pay today for an annuity in order to receive a given number of equal payments at equal intervals for a given number of periods in the future?

The formula for \$1 is:

$$S = \frac{1 - (1 + i)^{-n}}{i}$$

The method for accounting for the premium or discount on bonds payable are compound interest procedures. The resultant interest charges are the product of the net balance of bonds payable and the effective interest rate at the time the bonds were issued. For bonds issued at a premium, the computed interest charges will *decrease* each year as the bonds approach maturity because the net balance of the liability decreases each year due to the amortization of the premium. Conversely, for bonds issued at a discount, the computed interest charges will *increase* each year as the bonds approach maturity because of the accumulation of the discount.

A straight-line method is used for the amortization of premiums or accumulation of discounts which involves simply dividing the original premium or discount by the number of years until maturity to determine the constant annual amount of amortization or accumulation.

The most frequent application of the above formula for accounting procedures is the present value formula. For example, when a company issues bonds, cash is debited for the proceeds of the bond issue and a liability account is credited for the amount. The entries will be the present value of the bonds. Assume a bond issue sold at a premium, or for more than the typical \$1,000 par value, the present value of which we assume to be \$1,200. The entries at the time of the sale of the bonds are:

Cash	\$1,200	
Bonds Payable		\$1,200

An alternative treatment is permissible by rule:

Cash	\$1,200	
Bonds Payable		\$1,000 (par)
Premium on Bonds		200

The Premium Account is an adjunct account (an addition) to Bonds Payable. The interest charge each year is computed by multiplying the bond liability *at the end of each year* by the effective rate of interest (see the definition). The adjunct account at the end of each period is debited for the amount of interest which reduces the liability each period. *The interest charge calculation is computed on the reduced amount of the liability that occurs each year as the adjunct account is debited.* At maturity the Premium Account has a zero balance and the liability will be reduced to the maturity, or face amount (the par value of $1,000) of the bond.

Assume the bond is sold at a $200 *discount,* i.e., $200 less than the $1,000 par value. The journal entry is:

Cash	$800	
Bond Discount	200	
Bonds Payable		$1,000

The Bond Discount account is a *contra* account to bonds payable with the liability at time of issue $800. Again, for an amount deposited for the annuity of more than $1 multiply both sides of the equation by that amount. Also, again note the same variables as in the compound interest formula.

FASB's Plans for Accounting for Employee Stock Options

The accounting for employee stock options has received renewed attention. In July, 2002, important developments related to accounting for employee stock options arose from the general concern over the recognition of revenue and expenses and/or skullduggery involved therein.

Several major U.S. companies have announced their intentions to change their method of accounting for employee stock options to an approach that *recognizes an expense* for the fair value of the options granted in arriving at reported earnings. Evidently, a number of other companies also are getting on the bandwagon. The FASB is naturally quite pleased by the fact that, at long last, somebody is actually paying attention to what it had wanted done several years ago.

Forced Compromise in FASB 123

Recognizing compensation expense relating to the fair value of employee stock options granted was what the Board was trying to accomplish in FASB 123, *Accounting for Stock-Based Compensation.* At that time, to get *anything* adopted, Board members were forced to agree to an either/or compromise.

Obviously, very few companies selected the "fair value" method; in fact, many as it turns out did not even play fair in the "or" method. As a result of the recent accounting fiascoes, the fair value method is the treatment advocated by an increasing number of investors and other users of financial statements.

When the FASB developed FASB 123 in the mid-1990s, the Board proposed requiring that treatment because it believed that this was the best way to report the *actual effect* of employee stock options in a company's financial statements. The FASB modification of that proposal was in the face of strong opposition by many in the business community and in Congress that directly threatened the very existence of the FASB as an independent standard setter.

Thus, while FASB 123 provides that expense recognition for the fair value of employee stock options granted is the *preferable* approach, it permitted the continued use of existing methods. The existing (APB 25) method was modified only to the extent of requiring disclosure in the footnotes to the financial statements. This was to show the pro forma effect on net income and earnings per share as if the preferable, expense recognition method had been applied. Until now, only a handful of companies elected to follow the preferable method.

Transition Questions Raised

In response to requests by companies considering switching to the preferable method under FASB 123, the FASB is considering whether it should undertake a limited-scope, fast-track project relating to the transition provision in FASB 123. Literally applied, the existing transition provision in FASB 123 would require companies that elect to change to the preferable method to do so prospectively for stock options granted after the date of the change.

This transition provision was appropriate when FASB 123 was issued in 1995 because, at that time, companies did not have valuation information available relating to previous grants of employee stock options. However, that is no longer the case because the disclosure requirements have now been in effect since 1995, under FASB 123.

IASB CONSIDERING FAIR VALUE FOR EMPLOYEE STOCK OPTIONS

The International Accounting Standards Board (IASB) has concluded its deliberations on the accounting for share-based payments, including employee stock options, and plans to issue a proposal for public comment in the fourth quarter of 2002. That proposal would require companies using IASB standards to recognize, starting in 2004, the fair value of employee stock options granted as an *expense* in arriving at reported earnings. Although there are some important differences between the methodologies in the IASB proposal and those contained in FASB 123, the basic approach is the same—fair value measurement of employee stock options granted with expense recognition over the vesting period of the options.

The FASB has been actively working with the IASB and other major national standard setters to bring about convergence of accounting standards across the major world capital markets.

The FASB plans to issue an Invitation to Comment summarizing the IASB's proposals and explaining the key differences between its provisions and current U.S. accounting standards. The FASB will then consider whether it should propose any changes to the U.S. standards on accounting for stock-based compensation.

In the meantime, FASB 123 is still in effect and is discussed at the end of this chapter. Interpretation 44, *Accounting for Certain Transactions Involving Stock Compensation,* an interpretation of APB Opinion 25, is discussed in Chapter 10 "Actions of the Financial Accounting Standards Board." In this same chapter is a discussion of the FASB's addition of a project on revenue recognition to its agenda. The purpose is to provide more comprehensive guidance regarding when companies should record revenues.

In the meantime, the SEC's SAB 101, below, is the course to follow.

SAB 101, Revenue Recognition in Financial Statements

This Staff Accounting Bulletin (SAB) summarizes certain of the Securities and Exchange Commission staff's views in applying Generally Accepted Accounting Principles (GAAP) to revenue recognition in financial statements. The staff is providing this guidance due, in part, to the large number of revenue recognition issues that registrants encounter. For example, a March, 1999 report entitled *Fraudulent Financial Reporting 1987–1997: An Analysis of U. S. Public Companies,* sponsored by the Committee of Sponsoring Organizations (COSO) of the Treadway Commission, indicated that over half of financial reporting frauds in the study involved overstating revenue. At this point, it would be almost impossible to "fix" a figure for the number of fraudulent cases of overstated revenue.

During the upcoming 10-K season, the SEC appears to be planning to investigate cases, particularly high profile ones, of improper accounting for premature and excessive revenue recognition.

Because the SEC believes the revenue recognition accounting rules do not cover a number of areas, it is expecting companies to voluntarily correct their improper accounting by the end of the first quarter of 2000. They will then not be subject to enforcement action as long as they have not violated existing generally accepted accounting principles. This correction in most cases will be reported by companies as a one-time accounting change item.

Corrections Required

The corrections the SEC appears to be expecting are exclusion from:

1. Those collections previously included in revenue that were made when acting as an agent for a third party.
2. Revenue recorded in reciprocal barter transactions of similar products or services that do not represent the culmination of the earnings process.
3. Sales recorded before receipt of a written sales agreement.
4. Sales recorded in consignment-like arrangements.
5. Sales where the customer has not taken title and assumed the risks and rewards of ownership.
6. Bill-and-hold sales that do not have a customer business purpose.
7. Sales in situations where returns cannot be reliably estimated, such as "channel stuffing."

Conditions for Recognition

The SEC has stated that a bill-and-hold sale transaction must meet all of the following conditions to qualify for revenue recognition:

1. The risks of ownership must have been passed to the buyer.
2. The customer must commit to purchase the goods.
3. The buyer must substantiate a business purpose for the bill-and-sale transaction.
4. A fixed delivery date must be set.
5. The seller must not have any material performance obligations.
6. The goods must be ready for shipment and not available to meet other orders.

The Effect of SAB 101

Among other responses to the SEC's SAB 101, some companies will find it necessary to:

1. Exclude from revenues and/or improve the disclosure of amounts collected by the company acting as an agent. One facet of this will involve assessing whether revenue (if recognized) should be reported gross with separate display of cost of sales to arrive at gross profit or on a net basis. In their appraisal, the SEC staff considers whether the registrant:
   a. Acts as principal in the transaction.
   b. Takes title to the products.

   c. Has risks and rewards of ownership, such as the risk of loss for collection, delivery, or returns.

   d. Acts as an agent or broker (including performing services, in substance, as an agent or broker) with compensation on a commission or fee basis.

If the company performs as an agent or broker without assuming the risks and rewards of ownership of the goods, sales should be reported on a net basis.

2. Not recognize revenue from "channel stuffing" and other transactions that make it difficult to estimate product returns.

Registrants and their auditors should carefully analyze all factors, including trends in historical data, that may affect registrants' ability to make reasonable and reliable estimates of product returns.

The staff believes that the following additional factors, among others, may affect or preclude the ability to make reasonable and reliable estimates of product returns:

   a. Significant increases in or excess levels of inventory in a distribution channel (sometimes referred to as "channel stuffing").

   b. Lack of "visibility" into or the inability to determine or observe the levels of inventory in a distribution channel and the current level of sales to end users.

   c. Expected introductions of new products that may result in the technological obsolescence of and larger than expected returns of current products.

   d. The significance of a particular distributor to the registrant's business, sales and marketing.

   e. The newness of a product.

   f. The introduction of competitors' products with superior technology or greater expected market acceptance, and other factors that affect market demand and changing trends in that demand for the registrant's products.

3. Exclude from revenue consignment-like transactions. Products delivered to a consignee pursuant to a consignment arrangement are not sales and do not qualify for revenue recognition until a sale occurs. The staff believes that revenue recognition is not appropriate because the seller retains the risks and rewards of ownership of the product and title usually does not pass to the consignee.

Other situations may exist where title to delivered products passes to a buyer, but the substance of the transaction is that of a *consignment or a financing*. Such arrangements require a careful analysis of the facts and circumstances of the transaction, as well as an understanding of the rights and obligations of the parties, and the seller's customary business practices in such arrangements.

The staff believes that the presence of one or more of the following characteristics in a transaction precludes revenue recognition even if title to the product has passed to the buyer, but the buyer has the right to return the product and:

a. The buyer does not pay the seller at the time of sale, nor is the buyer obligated to pay the seller at a specified date or dates.

b. The buyer does not pay the seller at the time of sale but rather is obligated to pay at a specified date or dates, but the buyer's obligation to pay is contractually or implicitly excused until the buyer resells the product or subsequently consumes or uses the product.

c. The buyer's obligation to the seller would be changed (e.g., the seller would forgive the obligation or grant a refund) in the event of theft or physical destruction or damage of the product.

d. The buyer acquiring the product for resale does not have economic substance apart from that provided by the seller.

e. The seller has significant obligations for future performance to directly bring about resale of the product by the buyer.

4. Only include in revenue those sales backed up by a *binding* written sales agreement. (See discussion in item above.)

5. Exclude from sales all shipments where the customer has not taken title to the goods and thereby not assumed the risks and rewards of ownership. (See 3 above.)

6. Defer revenue recognition of up-front fees until the related earnings process is completed. The staff believes that up-front fees, even if nonrefundable, are normally earned as the products and/or services are delivered and/or performed over the term of the arrangement or the expected period of performance. Therefore, they should generally be deferred and recognized systematically over the periods that the fees are earned.

7. Defer recognition of revenue from refundable membership sales until the end of the refund period, except in limited circumstances when certain rigorous and demanding criteria have been met.

Because reasonable people held, and continue to hold, different views about the application of the accounting literature in this regard, pending further action in this area by the FASB, the SEC staff will not object to the recognition of refundable membership fees, net of estimated refunds, as earned revenue over the membership term in the limited circumstances where *all* of the following criteria have been met:

a. The estimates of terminations or cancellations and refunded revenues are being made for a large pool of homogeneous items (e.g., membership or other service transactions with the same characteristics such as terms, periods, class of customers, nature of service, etc.).

b. Reliable estimates of the expected refunds can be made on a timely basis.

c. There is a sufficient company-specific historical basis upon estimate the refunds, and the company believes that such experience is predictive of future events.

d. The amount of the membership fee specified agreement at the outset of the arrangement is fixed, other customer's right to request a refund.

8. End the practice of including the fair value of free services included as part of a sale transaction as revenue.

The new materiality test is the standard the SEC will use for enforcement purposes in regard to revenue recognition.

Revenue Recognition Accounting Literature

The accounting literature on revenue recognition includes both broad conceptual discussions as well as certain industry-specific guidance. Examples of existing literature on revenue recognition in December 1999, when SAB 101 was issued, included:

- Financial Accounting Standards Board (FASB) Statements of Financial Accounting Standards: 13, Accounting for Leases; 45, *Accounting for Franchise Fee Revenue;* 48, *Revenue Recognition When Right of Return Exists;* 49, *Accounting Accounting for Product Financing Arrangements;* 50, *Financial Reporting in the Record and Music Industry;* 51, *Financial Reporting by Cable Television Companies,* and 66, *Accounting for Sales of Real Estate*

- Accounting Principles Board (APB) Opinion 10, *Omnibus Opinion* -1966.

- Accounting Research Bulletins (ARB) 43 and 45, *Long-Term Construction-Type Contracts.*

- American Institute of Certified Public Accountants (AICPA) Statements of Position (SOP) 81-1, *Accounting for Performance of Construction-Type and Certain Production-Type Contracts,* and 97-2, *Software Revenue Recognition.*

- Emerging Issues Task Force (EITF) Issue 88-18, *Sales of Future Revenues;* 91-9, *Revenue and Expense Recognition for Freight Services in Process;* 95-1, *Revenue Recognition on Sales with a Guaranteed Minimum Resale Value,* and 95-4, *Revenue Recognition on Equipment Sold and Subsequently Repurchased Subject to an Operating Lease.*

- FASB Statement of Financial Accounting Concepts (SFAC) 5, *Recognition and Measurement in Financial Statements of Business Enterprises.*

If a transaction is within the scope of specific authoritative literature that provides revenue recognition guidance, that literature should be applied. However, in the absence of authoritative literature addressing a specific arrangement or a specific industry, the staff will consider the existing authoritative accounting standards as well as the broad revenue recognition criteria specified in the FASB's conceptual framework that contain basic guidelines for revenue recognition.

Based on these guidelines, revenue should not be recognized until it is realized or realizable and earned. SFAC 5 states that "an entity's revenue-earning activities involve delivering or producing goods, rendering services, or other activities that constitute its ongoing major or central operations, and revenues are considered to have been earned when the entity has substantially accomplished what it must do to be entitled to the benefits represented by the revenues." It continues "the two conditions (being realized or realizable and being earned) are usually met by the time product or merchandise is delivered or services are rendered to customers, and revenues from manufacturing and selling activities and gains and losses from sales of other assets are commonly recognized at time of sale (usually meaning delivery)."

If services are rendered or rights to use assets extend continuously over time (for example, interest or rent), reliable measures based on contractual prices established in advance are commonly available, and revenues may be recognized as earned as time passes.

The staff believes that revenue generally is realized or realizable and earned when all of the following criteria are met:

1. Persuasive evidence of an arrangement exists.
2. Delivery has occurred or services have been rendered.
3. The seller's price to the buyer is fixed or determinable.
4. Collectibility is reasonably assured.

Disclosures for Revenue Recognition

Disclosures relating to the recognition of revenue are covered in several different areas of the accounting literature:

1. A registrant should disclose its accounting policy for the recognition of revenue in line with APB Opinion 22, *Disclosure of Accounting Policies,* which states, ". . . the disclosure should encompass important judgments

as to appropriateness of principles relating to recognition of revenue . . ."
Because revenue recognition generally involves some level of judgment,
the staff believes that a registrant should always disclose its revenue recognition policy. If a company has different policies for different types of
revenue transactions, including barter sales, the policy for each material
type of transaction should be disclosed.

2. If sales transactions have multiple elements, such as a product *and* service, the accounting policy should clearly state the accounting policy for
   each element as well as how multiple elements are determined and valued. In addition, the staff believes that changes in estimated returns recognized in accordance with FASB 48 should be disclosed, if material
   (e.g., a change in estimate from 2% of sales to 1% of sales).

3. Regulation S-X requires that revenue from the sales of products, services,
   and other products each be separately disclosed on the face of the income
   statement. The SEC staff believes that costs relating to each type of revenue similarly should be reported separately on the face of the income
   statement.

4. Management's Discussion and Analysis (MD&A) requires a discussion
   of liquidity, capital resources, results of operations and other information
   necessary to an understanding of a registrant's financial condition,
   changes in financial condition, and results of operations.

Changes in revenue should not be evaluated solely in terms of volume
and price changes, but should also include an analysis of the reasons and factors contributing to the increase or decrease. To go beyond evaluation in terms
of volume and price changes, the Commission stated in Financial Reporting
Release (FRR) 36 that MD&A should "give investors an opportunity to look
at the registrant through the eyes of management by providing a historical and
prospective analysis of the registrant's financial condition and results of operations, with a particular emphasis on the registrant's prospects for the future."
    Examples of such revenue transactions or events that the staff has asked
to be disclosed and discussed in accordance with FRR 36 are:

a. Shipments of product at the end of a reporting period that significantly
   reduce customer backlog and might be expected to result in lower
   shipments and revenue in the next period.

b. Granting of extended payment terms that will result in a longer collection
   period for accounts receivable and slower cash inflows from operations,
   and the effect on liquidity and capital resources.

c. Changing trends in shipments into, and sales from, a sales channel or separate class of customer that could be expected to have a significant effect
   on future sales or sales returns.

   d. An increasing trend toward sales to a different class of customer, such as a reseller distribution channel with a lower gross profit margin than existing sales to end users.

   e. Increasing service revenue that has a higher profit margin than product sales.

   f. Seasonal trends or variations in sales.

   g. Gain or loss from the sale of an asset(s).

FASB 123, ACCOUNTING FOR STOCK OPTIONS ISSUED TO EMPLOYEES

Passage of FASB 123 in 1995 was not so much a compromise measure as an apparent agreement to get on to something else. In the final (at that time) analysis, it offered an alternative approach to the method of using APB Opinion 25, *Accounting for Stock Issued to Employees,* to account for stock options.

    The Statement set forth a preferred method for accounting for stock-based employee compensation. Companies, however, were not required to follow the new guidelines and were permitted to continue in the same accounting practice with only slight modification. The alternative approaches were:

1. The fair value method.
2. The intrinsic value method.

Fair Value Method

    In line with the effort to bring a greater degree of uniformity and understanding to financial reporting, the FASB premised the preferred method on fair value. Using this procedure, stock-based compensation cost was to be measured at the grant date based on the value of the award and to be recognized over the employee's entire service period, which is also normally the vesting period.

    For stock options granted by a public entity, the fair value is determined using an option-pricing model that considers several factors on the grant date:

1. The exercise price and expected life of the option.
2. The current price of the underlying stock and its expected volatility.
3. Expected dividends on the stock with specified exception.
4. The risk-free interest rate for the expected term of the option.

The text suggests the Black-Scholes or a binomial model. When the fair value of the option has been determined at the grant date, it is not later adjusted for:

1. Changes in the price of the underlying stock
2. Its volatility
3. The life of the option
4. Dividends on the stock
5. The risk-free interest rate

For a nonpublic enterprise, the procedure is the same, except that expected volatility need not be considered in estimating the option's fair value. Exclusion of the volatility factor in the estimation results in what is termed *minimum value*.

The Board felt, at the time, that it should be possible to reach a reasonably accurate estimate of the fair value of most stock options and other equity instruments when they are granted. However, if complicated features make this extremely difficult—even impossible—alternatives are suggested. If all else fails in finding a satisfactory estimate for the grant date, the Statement provides that the final measure of compensation cost is to be the value based on the stock price and any other pertinent information available on the first date that it is possible to reach a reasonable estimate of the value (generally, the date when the number of shares to which an employee is entitled and the exercise price are both determinable).

For nonvested or restricted stock awarded to an employee, the fair value is measured at the market price—or estimated market price, if the stock is not publicly traded—of a share of nonrestricted stock at the grant date.

Intrinsic Value Method

Stock-based compensation standards had been based on APB 25 and continued to be so for most companies. Using the intrinsic value method, compensation cost is the excess (if there is any) of the quoted market price of the particular stock over the employee's exercise price at the grant date, or at another specified measurement date, perhaps the service date.

There actually is no intrinsic value or excess of exercise price over market price of the stock at the grant date for most fixed stock option plans. Therefore, the current accounting requirements generally do not result in an expense charge for most options, and no compensation cost is recognized. On the other hand, normally a compensation cost is recognized for other types of stock compensation plans under the intrinsic value method. They are usually plans with variable, often performance-based, features.

Exceptions

Compensation costs need not be recognized for employee stock purchase plan discounts under FASB 123 if the following three conditions exist:

1. The discount is relatively small.
2. Substantially all full-time employees participate on an equitable basis.
3. Provisions in the plan do not include any stock option features.

The compensation cost of stock awards required to be settled in cash is the amount of the change in the stock price in the periods in which the changes occur.

Additional Requirements

While FASB 123 is effective for calendar year 1996 and information about options granted in 1995 must be included in the 1996 financial statements, the decade-long consideration of the controversial issue only encourages companies to account for stock compensation awards based on their fair value at the date the awards are granted with the compensation cost shown as an expense on the income statement.

Companies continuing to use the APB 25 intrinsic value method will be required to disclose—but only in a note to the financial statements—what the net income and earnings would have been had they followed the new accounting method.

Controversy

The Board had long hoped to require full-scale fair-value-type measurement and accounting for employee stock compensation using a generally accepted options pricing model; however, those outside the Board were not ready to accept a mandate. After rather overwhelming pressure for more than a year from Congress, other politicians, other government agencies, business, and CPAs in public practice as well as those with commercial and industrial companies, a majority of the Board decided to emphasize improving disclosure rather than hold out for requiring an expense charge for all options.

Many who were on the "winning side" in that tug-of-war are now in the front line of those calling for reform of the accounting for revenue recognition and expense charges.

Chapter 3

Stockholders' Equity

CONTENTS

Capital Stock	**3.02**
Retained Earnings	**3.06**
Prior Period Adjustments	**3.07**
Contingency Reserves	**3.08**
Recapitalizations	**3.09**
Changing Par or Stated Value of Stock	**3.11**
Quasi-Reorganizations	**3.11**
Stock Reclassifications	**3.12**
Substituting Debt for Stock	**3.12**
Treasury Stock	**3.13**

"Stockholders' equity" is the most commonly used term to describe the section of the balance sheet encompassing the corporation's capital and retained earnings. Other terms used are "net worth" or "capital and surplus." Stockholders' equity consists of three broad source classifications:

1. Investments made by owners: Capital Stock (Common and/or Preferred)—at par value (legal value) or stated amount. Additional Paid-In Capital—"In Excess of Par," "Capital Surplus," etc.

2. Income (loss) generated by operations: Retained Earnings—the accumulated undistributed annual profits (losses), after taxes and dividends
3.. Appraisal Capital—resulting from the revaluation of assets over historical cost (not in conformity with GAAP)

Changes in shareholders' equity, primarily in retained earnings, are caused by:

1. Periodic net income (loss) after taxes
2. Dividends declared
3. Prior period adjustments of retained earnings
4. Contingency reserves (appropriations of retained earnings)
5. Recapitalizations:
   a. Stock dividends and split-ups
   b. Changing par or stated value
   c. Reducing capital
   d. Quasi-reorganizations
   e. Stock reclassifications
   f. Substituting debt for stock
6. Treasury stock dealings
7. Business combinations
8. Certain unrealized gains and losses

CAPITAL STOCK

Capital stock is the capital contributed by the stockholders to the corporation.

Common Stock

The common stockholders are the residual owners of the corporation; that is, they own whatever is left after all preceding claims are paid off. By definition, common stock is "a stock which is subordinate to all other stocks of the issuer."

When a corporation has a single class of stock, it is often called "capital stock" instead of "common stock." The three aspects of stock ownership are (1) dividends, (2) claims against assets on liquidation, and (3) shares in management. As to these aspects of ownership, common stockholders have the following rights: (1) The amount of any/all dividend payments depends upon the profitability of the company. (2) Common stockholders have no fixed rights but, on the other hand, are limited to no maximum payment. (3) Their claim against the assets of the corporation on liquidation is last in the order of priority, following all creditors and all other equity interests. (4) The common stockholders, by statute, must have a voice in management. Their voice is often to the exclusion of all other equity interests, but they may also share their management rights with other classes of stock.

Common stock may be classified as par and no-par stock or class stock.

Par and No-Par Stock. Par stock is stock with a stated, legal dollar value, whereas no-par stock lacks such a given value. The distinction today is largely an academic one. However, state laws regarding stock dividends and split-ups and the adjustments of par value may affect the accounting treatment of such dividends.

Classes of Common Stock. Common stock may be divided into separate classes, such as class A or class B. Usually, the class distinction deals with the right to vote for separate directors, or one class may have the right to vote and one class may not. Class stock is a typical technique used where a minority group wishes to maintain control.

Preferred Stock

The second major type of capital stock is preferred stock, that which has some preference with regard to dividend payments or distribution of assets on liquidation. In the usual situation, preferred stock will have a preference on liquidation, to the extent of the par value of the stock. In addition, its right to dividends depends on whether it is classified as participating or nonparticipating right, convertible, or cumulative or noncumulative.

Participating and Nonparticipating Right. If the preferred has a right to a fixed dividend each year but has not the right to share in any additional dividends over and above the stated amount, it is nonparticipating preferred. If it is entitled to a share of any dividends over and above those to which it has priority, it is called participating. For example, a preferred may have the right to a 5 percent annual dividend and then share equally with the common stock in dividends after a dividend (equal to the preferred per-share dividend) has been paid to the common stockholders.

Convertible Preferred Stock. Convertible preferred is stock that may, at the holder's option, be exchanged for common. The terms of the exchange and the conversion period are set forth on the preferred certificate. Thus one share of $100 par preferred may be convertible beginning one year after issue into two shares of common. The preferred stockholder who converts will own two shares of common at a cost of $50 per share (this assumes the purchase of the preferred at par). A company will issue a convertible security at a time when it needs funds but for one reason or another cannot or does not wish to issue common stock. For example, in a weak stock market, common may be poorly received while a convertible preferred can be privately placed with a large institutional investor. The conversion privilege, from the point of view of the purchaser, is a "sweetener" since it affords the opportunity to take a full equity position in the future if the company prospers. The issuer may be quite satisfied to give the conversion privilege because it means that (assuming earnings rise) the preferred stock, with a prior and fixed dividend claim, will gradually be eliminated in exchange for common shares.

Accounting for a convertible preferred issue follows the usual rules. That is, when the preferred is first issued, a separate capital account will be set up, to which will be credited the par value of the outstanding stock. When conversion takes place, an amount equal to the par of the converted stock is debited to the preferred account. The common stock account will be credited with an amount equal to the par or stated value of the shares issued in exchange for the preferred. Any excess will go to capital surplus.

Both participating (1) and convertible (2) preferred stocks above must be taken into consideration when computing earnings per share.

Cumulative and Noncumulative. A corporation that lacks earnings or surplus cannot pay dividends on its preferred stock. In that case, the question arises whether the past dividend must be paid in future years. If past dividends do accumulate and must be paid off, the stock is cumulative; otherwise, noncumulative.

The preferred may share voting rights equally with the common stock; it may lack voting rights under any circumstances; or it may have the right to vote only if either one or more dividend is passed. In the latter case, the preferred may have the exclusive right to vote for a certain number of directors to be sure that its interests as a class are protected.

For cumulative stock, the dividends must be accrued each year (even if unpaid), unless issued with an "only as earned" provision. The effect on earnings per share is the extent of the reduction of net income for this accrual.

Par Value, Stated Capital, and Capital Stock Accounts

The money a corporation receives for its stock is in a unique category. It is variously referred to as "a cushion for creditors," "a trust fund," and similar expressions. The point is that in a corporation which gives its stockholders limited liability, the only funds to which the creditors of the corporation can look for repayment of their debts in the event the corporation suffers losses is the money received for stock, which constitutes the stated capital account. Consequently, most state corporation statutes require a number of steps to be taken before a corporation can reduce its stated capital. These steps include approval by the stockholders and the filing of a certificate with the proper state officer, so that creditors may be put on notice of the reduction in capital.

Stated capital is actually divided into separate accounts, each account for a particular class of stock. Thus, a corporation may have outstanding a class A common, a class B common, a first preferred, and a second preferred. Each class would have its own account, which would show the number of shares of the class authorized by the certificate of incorporation, the number actually issued and the consideration received by the corporation.

It is at this point that the distinction between par and no-par stock becomes important. Par stock is rarely sold for less than its par value, although it may be sold for more. In many states, it is illegal to sell stock at a discount from par, and even when not illegal, there may be a residual stockholder liability for that original discount to the creditors. In any case, an amount equal to the par value of the stock must be credited to its capital account, with any excess going into a surplus account.

In the case of no-par stock, the corporation, either through its board of directors or at a stockholders' meeting, assigns part of the consideration received as stated capital for the stock and treats the rest as a credit to a capital surplus account. Treating part of the consideration received as stated capital is the equivalent of giving the stock a par value.

Capital Stock Issued for Property

Where capital stock is issued for the acquisition of property in a non-cash transfer, measurement of owners' investment is usually determined by using the fair market value of the assets (and/or the discounted present value of any liabilities transferred).

When the fair value of the assets transferred cannot be measured, the market value of the stock issued may be used instead for establishing the value of the property received.

When the acquisition is an entire business, the principle of "fair value" is extended to cover each and every asset acquired (other than goodwill). If the fair value of the *whole* business is considered to be *more* than the individual values, that excess is considered to be goodwill.

The difference between fair value put on the assets received and the *par value* (stated) of the stock issued goes to the Capital-in-Excess of Par Value account (or Additional Paid-in Capital, etc.) as either a positive or negative (discount) amount. Note that this does *not* pertain to any "negative" goodwill which might have been created; said negative goodwill, if any, should be used to reduce, immediately, the noncurrent assets (except investment securities) proportionately to zero, if necessary, with any remaining excess to be deferred and amortized as favorable goodwill is amortized.

Capital in Excess of Par or Stated Value (Capital Surplus)

The term "capital surplus" is still widely used, although the preferred terminology is "capital in excess of par" or "additional paid-in capital."

The capital in excess of par account is credited with capital received by the corporation which is not part of par value or stated capital. It is primarily the excess of consideration received over par value or the amount of consideration received for no-par stock which is not assigned as stated capital.

In addition, donations of capital to the corporation are credited to this account. If stated capital is ever reduced as permitted by law, the transfer is from the capital stock account to this capital surplus account.

This account is also credited for the excess of market value over par value for stock dividends (which are not split-ups) and for the granting of certain stock options and rights.

RETAINED EARNINGS

Terminology bulletins do not have authoritative status; however, they are issued as useful guides. Accounting Terminology Bulletin No. 1 recommended that:

1. The term "surplus" be abandoned.
2. The term "earned surplus" be replaced with such terms that indicate the source, such as:
    a. Retained Earnings,
    b. Retained Income,
    c. Accumulated Earnings, or
    d. Earnings Retained for Use in the Business.

Retained earnings are the accumulated undistributed past and current years' earnings, net of taxes and dividends paid and declared.

Portions of retained earnings may be set aside for certain contingencies, appropriated for such purposes as possible future inventory losses, sinking funds, etc. A Statement of Changes in Retained Earnings is one of the basic financial statements *required* for fair presentation of results of operation and financial condition to conform with GAAP. It shows net income, dividends, prior period adjustments. A Statement of Changes in Stockholders' Equity shows additional investments by owners, retirements of owners' interests and similar events (if these are few and simple, they may be put in the notes).

Regardless of how a company displays its undistributed earnings, or the disclosures thereof, for tax purposes, the actual earnings and profits which could have been or are still subject to distribution as "dividends" *under IRS regulations* may, under some circumstances, retain that characteristic for the purpose of ordinary income taxation to the ultimate recipient. There is no requirement for this disclosure other than normal requirement for the "periods presented," which would usually show the activity in retained earnings for only two years and not prior.

Prior Period Adjustments

Only the following rare types of items should be treated as prior period adjustments and *not* be included in the determination of current period net income:

1. Correction of an error (material) in prior financial statements; and
2. Realization of income tax pre-acquisition operating loss benefits of *purchased* subsidiaries.

Corrections of errors are *not* changes in accounting *estimates.* Error corrections are those resulting from:

1. Mathematical errors;
2. Erroneous application of accounting principles; and
3. Misuse of, or oversight of, facts existing at a prior statement period.

Changes in accounting *estimates* result from *new* information or developments, which sharpen and improve judgment.

Litigation settlements and income tax adjustments *no longer* meet the definition of prior period adjustments. However, for *interim periods only* (of the current fiscal year), material items of this nature should be treated as prior interim adjustments to the identifiable period of related business activity.

Goodwill cannot be written off as a prior period adjustment.

Retroactive adjustment should be made of all comparative periods presented, reflecting changes to particular items, net income and retained earnings balances. The tax effects should also be reflected and shown. Disclosure of the effects of the restatement should be made.

Prior period adjustments must be charged or credited to the opening balance of retained earnings. They cannot be included in the determination of net income for the current period.

Beginning Retained Earnings		$1,000
Correction Depreciation Error		
$300 × .50 (net of tax)		150
Adjustment Beginning Retained Earnings		1,150
Net Income		400
Ending—Retained Earnings		$1,550
Accumulated Depreciation	$300	
Taxes Payable		150
Retained Earnings		150

CONTINGENCY RESERVES

A "contingency" is defined as "an existing condition, situation, or set of circumstances involving uncertainty as to possible gain or loss to an enterprise that will ultimately be resolved when one or more events occur or fail to occur." Loss contingencies fall into three categories:

1. Probable
2. Reasonably possible
3. Remote

In deciding whether to accrue the estimated loss by charging income or setting aside an appropriation of retained earnings, or merely to make a disclosure of the contingency in the notes to the financial statement, the following standards have been set:

A charge is accrued to income if *both* of the following conditions are met at the date of the financial statements:

1. Information available *before* the issuance of the financial statements indicates that probably the asset will be impaired or a liability incurred; and
2. A *reasonable* estimate of the loss *can* be made.

   (When a contingent loss is probable but the reasonable estimate of the loss can only be made in terms of a range, the amount shall be accrued for the loss. When some amount within the range appears at the time to be a better estimate than any other amount within the range, that amount shall be accrued. When no amount within the range is a better estimate than any other amount, the minimum amount in the range shall be accrued.)

If discovery of the above impairment occurs *after* the date of the statements, disclosure should be made and pro-forma supplementary financial data presented giving effect to the occurrence as of the balance sheet date.

When a contingent loss is only *reasonably possible* or the probable loss cannot be estimated, an estimate of the *range* of loss should be made or a narrative description given to indicate that *no* estimate was possible. Disclosure should be made; but no accrual.

When the contingency is *remote,* disclosure should be made when it is in the nature of a guarantee. Other remote contingencies are not required to be disclosed, but they may be, if desired, for more significant reporting.

General reserves for unspecified business risks are not to be accrued and no disclosure is required.

Appropriations for loss contingencies from retained earnings must be shown with the stockholders' equity section of the balance sheet, and clearly identified as such.

Examples of loss contingencies are:

1. Collectibility of receivables.
2. Obligations related to product warranties and product defects.
3. Risk of loss or damage of enterprise property by fire, explosion, or other hazards.
4. Threat of expropriation of assets.
5. Pending or threatened litigation.
6. Actual or possible claims and assessments.
7. Risk of loss from catastrophes assumed by property and casualty insurance companies including reinsurance companies.
8. Guarantees of indebtedness of others.
9. Obligations of commercial banks under "standby letters of credit."
10. Agreements to repurchase receivables (or to repurchase the related property) that have been sold.

Handling of these loss contingencies depends upon the nature of the loss probability and the reasonableness of estimating the loss. (Gain contingencies are not booked, only footnoted.)

RECAPITALIZATIONS

Essentially, a recapitalization means changing the structure of the capital accounts. It can also mean a reshuffling between equity and debt. A recapitalization may be done voluntarily by the corporation; or it may be part of a reorganization proceeding in a court, pursuant to a bankruptcy or a reorganization petition filed by the corporation or its creditors.

In almost all cases of recapitalizations, stockholder approval is required at some point during the process. This is because a recapitalization may affect

the amount of stated capital of the corporation or change the relationships between the stockholders and the corporation or between classes of stockholders.
The different categories of recapitalizations are discussed in the following
paragraphs.

Stock Split-Ups

A split-up involves dividing the outstanding shares into a larger number,
as, for example, two for one in which each stockholder receives a certificate for
additional shares equal to the amount of shares already held. The split-up is reflected in the corporate books by reducing the par value or the stated value of
the outstanding shares. Thus if shares with a par value of $10 are split two for
one, the new par becomes $5. No entry is necessary, other than a memo entry.
The stockholder adjusts his or her basis for the unit number of shares.

Reverse split. The opposite of a split-up is a reverse split, which results in
a lesser number of outstanding shares. Stockholders turn in their old certificates and receive a new certificate for one-half, for example, of former holdings. The par value or stated value is adjusted to show the higher price per
share. A reverse split is sometimes used in order to increase the price of the
stock immediately on the open market.

Stock Dividends

As far as the stockholder is concerned, a stock dividend is the same as the
stock split; the stockholder receives additional shares, merely changing the
unit-basis of holding. But the effect is quite different from the point of view of
the corporation. A stock dividend requires a transfer from retained earnings of
the *market value* of the shares. Capital stock is credited for the par value and
capital in excess of par value is credited for the excess of market price over par.
(The stockholder who has the option of receiving cash must report the dividend as ordinary income.)

Stock Split-Up Effected in the Form of a Dividend

Usually, a stock distribution is either a dividend or a split-up. However,
there is another type of distribution, which, because of certain state legal requirements pertaining to the minimum requirements for or the changing of par
value, necessitates a different nomenclature.

In those instances where the stock dividend materially reduces the market value, it is by nature and AICPA definition a "split-up." However, because

certain states require that retained earnings must be capitalized in order to maintain par value, those types of transactions should be described by the corporation as a "split-up effected in the form of a dividend." The entry would then be a reduction of retained earnings and an increase in capital stock for the *par value* of the distribution. For income tax purposes, the corporation may be required to show this reduction of retained earnings as a Schedule M adjustment and may technically still have to consider it as available for ordinary rate ultimate distribution.

CHANGING PAR OR STATED VALUE OF STOCK

This type of recapitalization involves changing from par to no-par or vice versa. This is usually done in conjunction with a reduction of stated capital. A corporation, for example, may decide to change its stock from par stock to no-par stock in order to take advantage of lower franchise fees and transfer taxes. Or no-par shares may be changed to shares having par value to solve legal problems existing under particular state statutes. A par value stock which is selling in the market at a price lower than its par must be changed if the corporation intends to issue new stock. This is necessary because of some state laws which prohibit a corporation from selling its par value stock for less than par value. In such a case, the corporation may reduce par value or may change the par to no-par; thereby, the new stock can be given a stated value equivalent to the price it can bring in the open market.

QUASI-REORGANIZATIONS

Current or future years' charges should be made to the income accounts instead of to capital surplus. An exception to this rule (called "readjustment") occurs when a corporation elects to restate its assets, capital stock and retained earnings and thus avail itself of permission to relieve its future income account or retained earnings account of charges which would otherwise be made. In such an event, the corporation should make a clear report to its shareholders of the restatements proposed to be made, and obtain their formal consent. It should present a fair balance sheet as at the date of the readjustment, in which the readjustments of the carrying amounts are reasonably complete, in order that there may be no continuation of the circumstances which justify charges to capital surplus.

As an example of how this readjustment might occur, suppose that a company has a deficit in its retained earnings (earned surplus) of $100,000. By revaluing its assets upward, it is possible for this company to create a capital surplus account for the write-up to fair value, then write off the deficit in retained earnings to that account. From then on, a new retained earnings account should be established and the fact be disclosed for ten years.

STOCK RECLASSIFICATIONS

Another category of stock recapitalization involves reclassifying the existing stock. This means that outstanding stock of a particular class is exchanged for stock of another class. For example, several outstanding issues of preferred stock may be consolidated into a single issue. Or, common stock may be exchanged for preferred stock, or vice versa. The objective in this type of reclassification is to simplify the capital structure, which in many cases is necessary in order to make a public offering or sometimes to eliminate dividend arrearages on preferred stock by offering a new issue of stock in exchange for canceling such arrearages.

SUBSTITUTING DEBT FOR STOCK

One form of recapitalization that has become popular in some areas involves substituting bonds for stock. The advantage to the corporation is the substitution of tax-deductible interest on bonds for nondeductible dividends on preferred stock. Of course, where dealing with a closely held corporation, substituting debt for stock in a manner to give the common stockholders a pro rata portion of the debt may be interpreted for tax purposes as "thin" capitalization, and the bonds may be treated as stock, regardless.

Also, to attract new money into the corporation, it is advantageous to consider the issuance of convertible debt securities bonds—to which are attached the rights (warrants) to buy common stock of the company at a specified price. The advantages of this type of security are:

1. An interest rate that is lower than the issuer could establish for nonconvertible debt;
2. An initial conversion price greater than the market value of the common stock; and
3. A conversion price that does not decrease.

The portion of proceeds from these securities that can be applied to the warrants should be credited to paid-in capital (based on fair value of both securities) and discounts or premiums should be treated as they would be under conventional bond issuance.

TREASURY STOCK

Treasury stock is stock that has previously been issued by a corporation but is no longer outstanding. It has been reacquired by the corporation and, as its name implies, held in its treasury. Treasury stock is not canceled because cancellation reduces the authorized issue of corporation stock. In some circumstances, it is permissible to show treasury stock as an asset if adequately disclosed.

Treasury Stock Shown at Cost

When a corporation acquires its own stock to be held for future sale or possible use in connection with stock options, or with no plans or uncertainty as to future retirement of that stock, the cost of the acquired stock can be shown separately as a deduction from the total of capital stock, capital surplus and retained earnings. Gains on subsequent sales (over the acquired-cost price) should be credited to capital surplus and losses (to the extent of prior gains) should be charged to that same account, with excess losses going to retained earnings. State law should be followed if in contravention.

Treasury Stock Shown at Par or Stated Value

When treasury stock is acquired for the purpose of *retirement* (or constructive retirement), the stock should be shown at par value or stated value as a reduction in the equity section; the excess of purchase cost over par (stated) value should be charged to capital surplus to the extent of prior gains booked for the same issue, together with pro-rata portions applicable to that stock arising from prior stock dividends, splits, etc. Any remaining excess may be applied pro-rata to either common stock or to retained earnings.

Treasury Stock as an Asset

If adequately disclosed, it is permissible in some circumstances to show stock of a corporation held in its own treasury as an asset. For example, pursuant to a corporation's bonus arrangement with certain employees, treasury stock may be used to pay the bonus, and, in accordance with the concept of a current asset satisfying a current liability, that applicable treasury stock might be shown as current asset. However, dividends on such stock should not be treated as income while the corporation holds the stock.

Treasury stock has neither voting rights nor the right to receive dividends. (Note: treasury stock remains *issued* stock, but not *outstanding* stock). Treasury stock can either be retired or resold. Treasury stock is an owners' equity account and is deducted from the stockholders' equity on the balance sheet.

When a company buys its own stock:
    Treasury Stock   XXX
        Cash   XXX
If the stock is resold:
    Cash   XXX
        Treasury Stock   XXX
        (The credit is the amount paid for the
        stock when purchased by the corporation)

If there is a difference between the corporation's acquisition of the stock and the resale price, the difference is debited or credited to an account Paid-In Capital from Treasury Stock Transactions for the amount of the difference between the proceeds of the resale and the amount paid by the corporation.

Under the cost method, treasury stock is shown as the last item before arriving at stockholders' equity, while under the par value method treasury stock reduces the common stock account directly under the capital stock section of stockholders' equity.

Chapter 4
Statement of Cash Flows

CONTENTS

Importance of Cash Flow	**4.01**
FASB Statement 95, *Statement of Cash Flows*	**4.03**
Classification of Cash Receipts and Cash Payments	**4.06**
Direct Method—Discussion and Illustration	**4.07**
Indirect Method—Discussion and Illustration	**4.09**
Bankers' Use of Financial Statements	**4.11**
FASB Statements Amending the Cash Flow Statement	**4.14**

The term "cash flow" refers to a variety of concepts, but its most common meaning in financial literature is the same as "funds derived from operations." The *concept* of cash flow can be used effectively as one of the major factors in judging the ability to meet debt retirement requirements, to maintain regular dividends, to finance replacement and expansion costs.

In no sense, however, can the amount of cash flow be considered to be a substitute for, or an improvement upon, the net income as an indication of the results of operations or the change in financial position.

IMPORTANCE OF CASH FLOW

The concept of cash flow was originated by security analysts. It has been stated that in evaluating the investment value of a company, cash flow is frequently regarded as more meaningful to them than net income.

Cash flow from operations data in financial summaries shows the liquid or near-liquid resources generated from operations that may be available for the discretionary use of management. Analysts have suggested that this is a useful measure of the ability of the entity to accept new investment opportunities, to maintain its current productive capacity by replacement of fixed assets, and to make distributions to shareholders without drawing on new external sources of capital.

While information about cash flow from operating activities is useful, it should be considered carefully within the framework of the complete statement of cash flows. This statement reflects management's decisions as to the use of these cash flows and the external sources of capital used relating to investing and financing activities. The implication of considering or analyzing only the cash flows generated from the operations portion of a cash flows statement is that its use is entirely at the discretion of management. In fact, certain obligations (e.g., mortgage payments) may exist even if replacement of nondepreciating assets is considered unnecessary.

In using cash flow as an analytic tool, care is required. For example, Corporation X has been capitalized with straight common stock. Corporation Y, the same size as Corporation X and comparable in other respects, has been capitalized 25 percent with common stock and 75 percent with debt. A cash flow equivalent to, say, 20 percent of each corporation's gross sales will seem to be four times as large in relation to Corporation Y's stock when compared with the common stock of Corporation X. Cash flow as a meaningful tool, therefore, will have more significance when related to industries and companies in which long-term debt is limited.

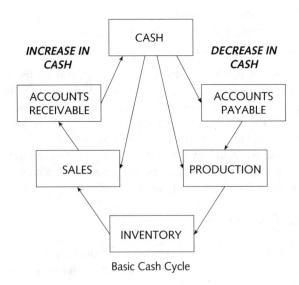

Basic Cash Cycle

One valid point in using cash flow is to put the profit margin squeeze into proper perspective. One of the most rapidly increasing costs is the depreciation charged against newly acquired plants and equipment. The use of accelerated methods of depreciation has created huge depreciation deductions which reduce profits. At the same time, accelerated depreciation creates additional cash flow and encourages further spending for facilities. In the opinion of some financial authorities, a showing of relatively high cash flow per dollar of capitalization is some compensation for a poor showing of net income per dollar of capitalization.

High cash flow is also the reason that some companies with relatively poor earnings per share are able to continue paying cash dividends per share, sometimes in excess of earnings. The SEC has noted situations where investors were misled by these cash distributions in excess of net income when not accompanied by disclosure indicating clearly that part of the distribution represented a return of capital.

In addition to profits, the extractive industries get cash flow through depletion allowances, drilling write-offs, and amortization of development costs and depreciation.

Cash flow also helps analysts judge whether debt commitments can be met without refinancing, whether the regular cash dividend can be maintained despite ailing earnings, whether the extractive industries (i.e., oils and mining) will be able to continue exploration without raising additional capital, or whether additional facilities can be acquired without increasing debt or present capital.

Relative cash flow is an important factor in deciding whether to buy or lease. But it is not necessarily true that owning property creates funds for use in expansion. The cash made available to a corporation through operations will be similar whether the business property is owned or leased. Owned property acquired by borrowed capital will require periodic payments on the debt which will have to be met before funds are available for expansion.

FASB Statement 95, *Statement of Cash Flows*

Statement 95 was issued in November, 1987. The Statement establishes the standards for reporting cash flows in the financial statements. It supersedes APB Opinion 19, *Reporting Changes in Financial Position,* and supersedes or amends prior pronouncements.

Specifically, the Statement requires disclosure of cash flows to be included in the full set of financial statements, replacing the *Statement of Changes in Financial Position.*

Business enterprises are encouraged to report cash flows from operating activities *directly* by disclosing the major sources of operating cash receipts and disbursements (the *direct* method). Enterprises can elect not to show operating cash receipts and disbursements, but will be required to disclose the same amount of net cash flow from operating activities *indirectly* by adjusting net income to reconcile the net cash flow from operating activities (the *indirect* reconciliation method) by eliminating the effects of:

1. all deferrals of past operating cash receipts and payments,
2. all accruals of expected future operating cash receipts and payments,
3. all items that are included in net income that do *not* affect operating cash receipts and payments.

It should be noted that if the direct method is applied, a reconciliation of net income and net cash flow from operating activities is required to be provided in a separate schedule.

If a reporting company has foreign business operations, the cash flows statement must disclose the currency equivalent of foreign currency cash flows, applying the current exchange rate at the time of the cash flow. The effect of changes in the exchange rates is disclosed as a separate item in the reconciliation of beginning and ending balances of cash and cash equivalents.

Information about investing and financing activities not resulting in cash receipts or payments is to be disclosed separately.

Terminology

Precise definitions to clarify the meaning of the terms related specifically to FASB 95 can be helpful to an understanding of the requirements.

Cash. Includes currency on hand, demand deposits with banks, and accounts with financial institutions that have the general characteristics of demand deposits; e.g., a depository that accepts deposits and permits withdrawals without prior notice or penalty.

Cash Equivalent. Short-term, highly liquid investments that are 1) readily convertible into known amounts of cash, and 2) near enough to maturity (see *Original Maturity*) that a change in the interest rate structure presents an insignificant risk of changes in the value of the investment.

Cash Flow. Cash receipts and cash payments resulting from investing, financing, or operating activities.

Direct Method. Shows the principal components to be operating cash receipts and payments; e.g., cash received from accounts receivable; cash paid to suppliers.

Financing Activities. Borrowing money; paying borrowings; long-term credit. In general, transactions to acquire and repay capital.

Indirect Method. Computation starts with net income that is adjusted for revenue and expense items *not* resulting from operating cash transactions (e.g., noncash transactions) to reconcile to net cash flow from operating activities. This method does not disclose operating cash receipts and payments.

Investing Activities. Making loans; collecting loans; acquiring and disposing of debt; acquiring and disposing of equity; acquiring and disposing of productive assets (e.g., plant and equipment).

Net Cash Flow. The arithmetic sum of gross cash receipts and gross cash payments which results in the net cash flow from operating activities.

Noncash and Investing Activities. Investing and financing activities that affect assets or liabilities, but do not result in cash receipts or cash payments.

Operating Activities. All transactions and other events that are not defined as investing or financing activities. Cash flows from activities which generally result from transactions and other events that enter into the determination of net income.

Original Maturity. An investment *purchased* three months from the maturity date.

NOTE: An investment *purchased more than three months from maturity is not* a cash equivalent, even though its remaining maturity on financial statement date is within the three months' rule.

Summary

The summary that follows brings together in columnar format the significant requirements of the Statement that are scattered throughout the FASB manual.

1. The objective of FASB 95 is to provide detailed information about the cash receipts and cash payments of an enterprise during a specified accounting period.

2. The statement of cash flows reports the cash effects of any enterprise's operations, investing transactions and financing transactions.

3. Related disclosures detail the effects of investing and financing transactions that affect an enterprise's financial position, but do not directly affect cash flows.

4. Net income and net cash flow from operating activities are reconciled to provide information about the *net* effects of operating transactions, other events, and financial activities.

5. The cash flows statement should explain the change during specified accounting period in cash and cash equivalents.

6. FASB 95 requires enterprises with foreign currency transactions (e.g., cash receipts and payments) to report the currency equivalent of foreign currency cash flows applying the exchange rates in effect at the time of the cash flows. (A weighted average exchange rate for the period for translation is permissible as specified in FASB 52, Para. 12.)

7. Noncash transactions have a significant effect on the cash flows of a company and should be disclosed. (Reference APB Opinion 29, *Accounting for Nonmonetary Transactions*.)

CLASSIFICATION OF CASH RECEIPTS AND CASH PAYMENTS

Resulting from Operating Activities

Cash Inflows	*Cash Outflows*
Receipts from sale of goods and services.	Payments to suppliers.
Collections on accounts.	Payments on accounts.
Collections on short- and long-term notes and other credit arrangements.	Principal payments on short- and long-term payables.
Interest and dividend receipts.	Interest payments.
Other cash receipts that do not originate from investment or financing activities.	Other cash payments that do not originate from investment or financing activities.
Generally, the cash effects of transactions that enter into the determination of net income.	Payments to employees, tax payments, etc.

Resulting from Investing Activities

Cash Inflows	*Cash Outflows*
Principal collections on loans	Loans made. Payment for debt instruments of subsidiaries.
Sale of equity securities of other enterprises.	Purchases of equity securities of other enterprises.
Sale of plant, equipment, property, and other productive assets.	Purchases of plant, equipment, property, and other productive assets.

Resulting from Financing Activities

Cash Inflows	**Cash Outflows**
Proceeds from new securities issues.	Repurchase of enterprise's equity securities.
Bonds, mortgages, notes, and other indebtedness.	Debt repayments; dividend payments.

DIRECT METHOD—DISCUSSION AND ILLUSTRATION

The direct method requires reporting the three major classes of gross cash receipts and gross cash payments, as well as their arithmetic sum to disclose the *net cash flow* from operating activities.

The Rule allows reporting entities to detail cash receipts and payments to any extent considered to be meaningful. For example, payments to suppliers might be divided between raw material purchases and other major supplies used in the business. Wage and salary payments might be divided between manufacturing, selling, and administrative expenses. Sales receipts could be divided among different sources, with an "other" operating cash receipts, if any.

The reconciliation of net income to net cash flow from operating activities must be provided in a separate schedule.

Statement of Cash Flows
Increase (Decrease) in Cash and Cash Equivalents

(Direct Method)
Year Ended December 31, 20xx

Cash flows from *operating* activities:		
Cash received from customers	$ 435,000	
Interest received	5,000	
Cash provided by operations		440,000
Cash paid to employees and suppliers	(382,000)	
Interest paid	(13,000)	
Taxes paid	(20,000)	
Cash disbursed by operations		(415,000)
Net cash flow from operations		$ 25,000

(Direct Method) *Cont'd*
Year Ended December 31, 20xx

Cash flows from *investing* activities:

Marketable securities purchases	$(32,500)	
Proceeds—marketable securities sales	20,000	
Loans made	(8,500)	
Loan collections	6,000	
Plant purchase	(80,000)	
Proceeds—sale of plant assets	37,500	
Net cash used in investing activities		$(57,500)

Cash flows from *financing* activities:

Loan proceeds	$ 22,500	
Debt repayment	(27,500)	
Proceeds—Bond issue	50,000	
Proceeds—Common Stock issue	25,000	
Dividends paid	(20,000)	
Net cash provided by financing activities		$ 50,000
Net increase (decrease) in cash		$ 17,500

The following is a more comprehensive Statement of Cash Flow from operations applying the *direct* method. This approach includes the disclosure of noncash transactions in a separate schedule formatted beneath the statement.

Statement of Cash Flows
Increase (Decrease) in Cash and Cash Equivalents

(Direct Method)
Year Ended December 31, 20xx

Cash flow from operations:

Cash from receivables	$10,000,000	
Dividend receipts	700,000	
Cash provided		10,700,000
Cash paid to suppliers	2,000,000	
Wage and salary payments	4,000,000	
Interest payments	750,000	
Taxes	1,000,000	
Cash disbursed		7,750,000
Net cash flow from operations		$2,950,000

(Direct Method) *Cont'd*
Year Ended December 31, 20xx

Cash flow from investing activities:

Property and plant purchases	(4,000,000)	
Proceeds from sale of equipment	2,500,000	
Acquisition of Corporation X	(900,000)	
Securities purchases	(4,700,000)	
Securities sales	5,000,000	
Borrowings	(7,500,000)	
Collections on notes receivable	5,800,000	
Net cash outflow from investments		$(3,800,000)

Cash flow from financing activities:

Increase in customer deposits	1,100,000	
Short-term borrowings (increase)	75,000	
Short-term debt payments	(300,000)	
Long-term debt proceeds	1,250,000	
Lease payments	(125,000)	
Common stock issue	500,000	
Dividends to shareholders	(450,000)	
Net cash provided by financing		$ 2,050,000
Foreign exchange rate change		100,000
Net increase (decrease) in cash		$ 1,300,000

Schedule—Noncash Investing and Financing Activities:

Incurred lease obligation	$ 750,000	
Acquisition of Corporation X:		
Working capital acquired (except cash)	(100,000)	
Property and plant acquired	3,000,000	
Assumed long-term debt	(2,000,000)	
Cash paid for acquisition	$ 900,000	
Common stock issued in payment		
of long-term debt	$ 250,000	

INDIRECT METHOD—DISCUSSION AND ILLUSTRATION

The indirect method (also termed the *reconciliation method*) requires *net cash flow* to be reported indirectly with an adjustment of net income to reconcile it to net cash flow from operating activities. The adjustment requires:

1. The removal from net income of the effects of all deferrals of past operating cash receipts and payments.

2. The removal from net income of the effects of all accruals of expected future operating cash receipts and payments.
3. The removal from net income of the effects of items of all investing and financing cash flows.

The reconciliation can be reported *either* within the statement of cash flows *or* in a separate schedule, with the statement of cash flows reporting only the net cash flow from operating activities. However, if the reconciliation is disclosed in the cash flow statement, the adjustments to net income must be identified as reconciling items.

Statement of Cash Flows
Increase (Decrease) in Cash and Cash Equivalents

(Indirect Method)
Year Ended December 31, 20xx

Cash flows from *operating* activities:		
Net cash flow from operating activities*		$ 25,000
Cash flows from *investing* activities:		
Marketable securities purchases	$(32,500)	
Proceeds—marketable securities sales	20,000	
Loans made	(8,500)	
Loan collections	6,000	
Plant purchase**	(80,000)	
Proceeds—sale of plant assets	37,500	
Net cash used in investing activities		$(57,500)
Cash flows from *financing* activities:		
Loan proceeds	$ 22,500	
Debt repayment	(27,500)	
Proceeds—Bond issue	50,000	
Proceeds—Common Stock issue	25,000	
Dividends paid	(20,000)	
Net cash provided by financing activities		$ 50,000
Net increase (decrease) in cash		$ 17,500

*See supplemental schedule A. (Details operating activity.)
**See supplemental schedule B. (Details investing and financing activity.)

The following is a more comprehensive Statement of Cash Flow from operations applying the *indirect* method. This approach includes the disclosure of noncash transactions in a separate schedule formatted beneath the statement.

BANKERS' USE OF FINANCIAL STATEMENTS

The accountant needs to know how financial information is used and interpreted by different kinds of statement users who have different needs for credit information. The following review concerns accountants' relationships
with banker clients and specific items in financial statements that bankers
emphasize in their analysis of financial statements that accompany loan
applications.

Of specific concern to a banker are the *trends,* both short-term and
long-term, in the prospective borrower's operating results. Sales, liquidity,
earnings, and the equity accounts give significant evidence of a company's operating performance since it has been in business and in the near-term trends
in those indicators. Banks lend money; a business has inherent risks. The more
complete and accurate the financial statements of the borrower are, the more
acceptable are the borrower's statements in a risk-evaluation examination by
a banker.

Statement of Cash Flows

(Indirect Method)
Year Ended December 31, 20xx

Net cash flow from operations		$ 2,950,000
Cash flow from investing activities:		
Property and plant purchases	(4,000,000)	
Proceeds from sale of equipment	2,500,000	
Acquisition of Corporation X	(900,000)	
Securities purchases	(4,700,000)	
Securities sales	5,000,000	
Borrowings	(7,500,000)	
Collections on notes receivable	5,800,000	
Net cash outflow from investments		$(3,800,000)
Cash flow from financing activities:		
Increase in customer deposits	1,100,000	
Short-term borrowings (increase)	75,000	
Short-term debt payments	(300,000)	
Long-term debt proceeds	1,250,000	
Lease payments	(125,000)	
Common stock issue	(500,000)	
Dividends to shareholders	(450,000)	
Net cash provided by financing		$ 2,050,000
Foreign exchange rate change		100,000
Net increase (decrease) in cash		$ 1,300,000

(Indirect Method) *Cont'd*
Year Ended December 31, 20xx

Schedule—Earnings to net cash flow
   reconciliation from operations:

Net income	$ 3,000,000	
Noncash expenses, revenues, losses, and		
gains included in income:		
Depreciation and amortization	1,500,000	
Deferred taxes	150,000	
Net increase in receivables	(350,000)	
Net increase in payables	(200,000)	
Net increase in inventory	(300,000)	
Accrued interest earned	(350,000)	
Accrued interest payable	100,000	
Gain on sale of equipment	(600,000)	
Net cash flow from operations		$2,950,000

Schedule of noncash investing and
  financing activities:

Incurred lease obligation	$ 750,000

Acquisition of Corporation X:

Working capital acquired (except cash)	$ (100,000)
Property and plant acquired	3,000,000
Assumed long-term debt	(2,000,000)
Cash paid for acquisition	$ 900,000

Common stock issued in payment of	
long-term debt	$ 250,000

The acceptability of financial statements and the verifiability of the information in the financial reports that accountants certify give the banker confidence in a borrower's accountant and in the integrity of the financial information furnished by the borrower. There should not be any deficiencies in the auditor's certificate, no violations of accounting principles (GAAP), no AICPA and SEC disclosure deficiencies, and no lack of accuracy and consistency with previous years' reports.

Evaluation of Financial Ratios

While most ratios are valuable in measuring the financial excellence of a business, certain ratios, such as the current ratio, are emphasized for particular purposes. The following discussion covers the more common purposes for which ratios are used by bankers.

Statement of Cash Flows   **1.13**

With respect to those commonly used by bankers, no one ratio can be said to be the most important, as they are all related to one another. For bank loan officers, one of the particular single items in the balance sheet is the *current ratio,* which is important because the nature of the banking business—deposits available upon demand—requires bank lending activity to be concerned predominantly with furnishing short-term loans, i.e., working capital loans. Banks as creditors attach importance to the *debt-to-net-worth ratio* and the borrower's ability to generate sufficient cash flow to service any current debt load.

Management Evaluation

Management's primary interest is efficient use of the company's assets. Management is particularly interested in the turnover ratios, such as the inventory turnover and the relationship of working capital to total sales. To the extent that assets are not being used efficiently, the company is overinvesting and realizing a smaller return than possible on its equity. On the other hand, excessive turnover is dangerous because it puts the company in a vulnerable position. Bankers are also particularly interested in trend relationships shown in the income statements for the past years. Excessive selling expenses may indicate that commissions or other payments are out of line with the market. Bank creditors will also make a comparison between a loan applicant and its competitors in all areas to indicate where improvements in operations should be expected.

Short-Term Creditors

As was stated earlier, a loan officer making short-term loans is particularly interested in the current ratio, since this is a measure of the borrower's working capital and ability to meet current debt obligations. Also discussed was the importance of the net-worth-to-debt ratio, which shows the relationship of the stockholders' investments to funds furnished by trade creditors and others, and shows a borrower's ability to stand up under pressure of debt. The sales-to-receivables ratio (net annual sales divided by outstanding trade receivables) shows the relationship of sales volume to uncollected receivables and indicates the liquidity of the receivables on the balance sheet. Another ratio important to a short-term lender is cost of sales to inventory, which shows how many times a company turns over its inventory, which shows whether inventories are fresh and salable and helps evaluate its liquidating value.

Long-Term Creditors

Since the long-term lender is looking far into the future, a banker wants to be convinced that the company's earnings will continue at least at the current level. In addition, a lending officer will study the various working capital ratios to determine if the company will have sufficient cash when needed to amortize the debt. The ratio of total liabilities to the stockholders' equity is important because the long-term lender wants to be sure that the shareholders have a sufficient stake in the business. One ratio which is used virtually solely by long-term lenders is the number of times fixed charges are earned. Fixed charges represent the interest payments on the lender's debt as well as any debt which has priority over it. When total earnings of the company are divided by total fixed charges (including preferred stock dividends, if any) the resulting figure represents the number of times fixed charges are earned.

FASB STATEMENTS AMENDING THE CASH FLOW STATEMENT

FASB 102, *Statement of Cash Flows—Exemption of Certain Enterprises and Classification of Cash Flows from Certain Securities Acquired for Resale*

This amendment of FASB 95 exempts certain entities from the requirement to provide a cash flow statement. Entities that are not required to provide a cash flow statement are as follows:

1. A pension plan classified as a defined benefit plan covered by FASB 35, *Accounting and Reporting by Defined Benefit Pension Plans,* as well as employee benefit plans (other than defined benefit pension plans).
2. Highly liquid investment companies meeting the requirements of the Investment Company Act of 1940, as well as the four conditions listed below, or an investment company that is similar to one that meets these requirements.
3. A fund maintained by an administrator, guardian, or trustee, such as a bank, for the purpose of investing and reinvesting money on a collective basis that meets the four conditions listed below. These could include a trust fund or a variable annuity fund.

An investment company, described in 2 or 3, above, must meet all of the following conditions to be exempt from providing a cash flow statement.

1. Significantly all of the investments held by the company during the accounting period are liquid.
2. Significantly all of the investments held by the company are reported at market value or the lower of cost or market value.
3. As related to average total assets, the company had little, if any debt. Average outstanding debt is used for the comparison.
4. A statement of changes in net assets is provided by the company.

FASB 104, *Statement of Cash Flows—Net Reporting of Certain Cash Receipts and Cash Payments and Classification of Cash Flows from Hedging Transactions*

This amendment of FASB 95, exempts savings institutions, credit unions, and banks from reporting gross cash flows related to customer loans, time deposits, and deposits with other financial institutions.

It also amends FASB 95 to permit cash flows resulting from futures contracts, option contracts, forward contracts, or swap contracts that are accounted for as hedges of identifiable transactions, or events to be classified in the same category as the cash flows from the items being hedged, provided that accounting policy is disclosed.

Concepts Statement 7, *Using Cash Flow Information and Present Value in Accounting Measurements*

This FASB Concepts Statement provides a framework for using future cash flows and present value as the basis for an accounting measurement. The Concepts Statement provides general principles governing the use of present value, especially when the amount of future cash flows, their timing, or both are uncertain. It also provides a common understanding of the objective of present value in accounting measurements.

The release of the Concepts Statement is the result of redeliberation and consideration of comment letters received following the issuance of EDs in 1997 and 1999. It is the first Concepts Statement relating to specific measurements and to articulate a measurement objective. The Statement applies to measurements that use cash flow information:

1. On the initial recognition of assets or liabilities.
2. In fresh-start measurements.
3. In interest methods of allocation.

It does not consider recognition questions, nor does it address when a fresh-start measurement is appropriate. The FASB expects to consider those issues on a project-by-project basis.

The Statement explains that the objective of present value in accounting measurement is to capture, to the extent possible, the economic difference between sets of estimated future cash flows. Without present value, a $1,000 cash flow due tomorrow and a $1,000 cash flow due in 10 years appear the same. Because present value distinguishes between cash flows that might otherwise appear similar, a measurement based on the present value of estimated future cash flows provides more relevant information than a measurement based on the undiscounted sum of those cash flows.

The Board concluded that to be relevant in financial reporting, present value measurements must represent some observable measurement attribute of assets and liabilities. The Board concluded that present value measurements should attempt to capture the elements that taken together would comprise fair value; that is, a market price, if one existed.

The Concepts Statement outlines techniques for:

1. Estimating cash flows and interest rates.
2. The role of risk and uncertainty.
3. The application of present value in the measurement of liabilities.

Chapter 5

International Accounting

CONTENTS

End of the European Financial Statement Tower of Babel?	**5.02**
The IASB Agenda for Improving Existing Standards	**5.03**
Steady Growth to Preeminence in Global Standard Setting	**5.04**
The IASB Announces New Work Program	**5.09**
The IASC Foundation Assessment and Certification Program	**5.12**
Preface to IFRSs	**5.13**
The IASB Proposals to Ease Transition to IAS	**5.13**
The IASB Proposes Improvements	**5.14**
The IFRIC Issues Interpretation on Web Site Costs	**5.16**
The IASB Proposes Amendment to IAS 19, *Employee Benefits*	**5.18**
The SIC Issues Six New Interpretations	**5.19**
Foundation Trustees Name Standards Advisory Council to Provide Advice to IASB	**5.21**
Revised Organization Launched	**5.21**
The IASC Standard on Agriculture (AIS 41)	**5.26**
Three Revised Standards Issued by the IASC	**5.28**
The IASC Considers Accounting by Mining and Oil and Gas Companies	**5.28**
IASC Guidance on Financial Instruments	**5.30**
Examples of Cooperative Standard Setting	**5.31**

IOSCO Is Instrumental in Launching Core Standards   **5.32**

Internationalization of the U.S. Securities Markets   **5.33**

The European Parliament's Changes to Accounting Directives   **5.36**

The OECD Is Seeking Consensus on the Tax Treatment
  of E-Commerce   **5.37**

History of the International Body   **5.41**

The Changing World Economy   **5.41**

The Importance of Global Accounting Standards   **5.42**

The Standing Interpretations Committee   **5.44**

The Role of IOSCO   **5.44**

Accounting for Developing Economies and Emerging Markets   **5.45**

The Growing Acceptance of International Standards   **5.46**

The NYSE and Securities Dealers   **5.46**

The FASB's Attitude   **5.46**

The SEC's Cautious Appraisal   **5.48**

The Adoption of IAS 40, *Investment Property*   **5.48**

Selected IASC Standards with Comparisons to U.S. GAAP   **5.49**

International Accounting Standards   **5.69**

The use of International Accounting Standards (IASs), starting January 1, 2005, by listed public companies in the European Union (EU) is considered by U.S. regulators to be an important move toward global uniformity in standards for cross-border securities offerings. A representative of the SEC, testifying before a congressional committee, viewed Europe's shift from many national accounting standards of varying quality and completeness to a single EU standard that was developed in an independent and transparent manner as an important development for both issuers and investors. It also appears to be a natural progression from the adoption of a common currency.

END OF THE EUROPEAN FINANCIAL STATEMENT TOWER OF BABEL?

Many European companies that offer securities in the United States must reconcile their own country's standards to U.S. generally accepted accounting principles (GAAP), while some use IASs. However, many prepare their financial statements in U.S. GAAP in the first place. Much of the current reporting complexities that arise from this approach would be reduced under a common EU standard.

IASs applied correctly and consistently and enforced effectively would provide a higher degree of quality and transparency in financial statements than the individual systems in the EU countries at present.

The effects of accounting standards uniformity in Europe will also be generally favorable for U.S. companies doing business abroad because it is expected that U.S. companies will continue to be able to list in the EU using U.S. GAAP.

The benefits of IAS adoption in the EU may take on even greater significance if the FASB and the International Accounting Standards Board (IASB) make substantial progress toward achieving convergence of accounting principles.

THE IASB AGENDA FOR IMPROVING EXISTING STANDARDS

The goal of a global convergence of accounting standards moved closer to reality in May 2002, when the IASB unveiled plans for a series of key improvements in the current standards that govern cross-border securities offerings.

Those changes, advanced in the form of an exposure draft, seek to foster convergence of international accounting standards by establishing uniformity in a number of murky areas of financial reporting.

In addition to eliminating accounting loopholes, such as the use of a narrow definition of "related parties" by some countries, the exposure draft also seeks to prohibit accountants from labeling items of income or expense as "extraordinary items," either in the income statement or in the notes.

The plan also eliminates certain options for accountants using IASs, including the LIFO (last-in, first-out) inventory valuation method that is used here, as well as in several other countries.

Calling the exposure draft a first step toward establishing a globally accepted set of accounting standards, IASB officials pledged to press forward to "promote convergence on high-quality solutions" in other areas where cross-border differences exist.

They are also drafting guidance for those adopting international standards for the first time and proposing to overhaul the reporting of business combinations, including reforms to accounting for goodwill, discussed below.

A Closer Look at Problems to Be Faced

While the Board is actively working on global GAAP convergence, they as well as others in the standard-setting arena are aware of problems. Politically, the issue is sensitive, as was brought out at the 2002 Accounting Standards and Financial Reporting conference of the New York Society of Security Analysts (NYSSA). There is little question that convergence is likely to take the form of moving IAS GAAP closer to U.S. GAAP. The United States has the most developed capital markets in the world, but at times the accounting standards have been unnecessarily complicated. This fact was admitted and corrected in the cooperative endeavor when the IASC and the FASB worked on developing their earnings-per-share (EPS) Standards.

The conference brought out the fact that the IASB realizes that while European companies being required to use IASs by 2005 is a giant leap forward, convergence will not be without problems. Impediments to convergence include:

1. General resistance to change.
2. The cynical, but undeniable, conviction that convergence inevitably results in a move to the lowest common denominator.
3. Recent revelations of accounting and auditing wrongdoing by some high-profile U.S. companies could slow down the process of convergence.
4. Each country or group of countries questioning whether or not their own systems would prove more effective.
5. The complexity of the U.S. accounting provisions being seen as another barrier, although some European systems, such as Germany's, have been even more convoluted. The consensus in Europe now is that simplification is essential.
6. The U.S. system provides a great deal of explicit and transparent data, but is widely seen as more open to manipulation than the European.
7. The perceived role of the U.S. auditor. European auditors are mandated to define "true and fair" value. Europe tends to see the United States as heavily dependent on the principle "buyer beware." Can the auditor be trusted?

STEADY GROWTH TO PREEMINENCE IN GLOBAL STANDARD SETTING

There is no question but that the IASB has enjoyed a steady growth in influence, and acceptance of its right to be the body to bring a reasonable degree of conformity to global financial accounting standards. Admittedly, this has not always been easy. Early gains in providing a base for an accounting system for developing nations and economies validated their efforts then. Gradually, countries like the United States, the United Kingdom and the now dissolved G4+1, at least worked together to try to bring conformity to some of the more difficult standards. Their work and other examples of cooperative standard setting are discussed later in this chapter.

The reorganization after the acceptance of the core set of accounting standards by the International Organization of Securities Commissions (IOSCO) and the inclusion of the Standards Advisory Council has given the IASB further legitimacy. But the real validation stamp has been the decision by the EU requiring that all listed companies adopt the IASs and International Financial Reporting Standards (IFRSs) by 2005.

European Union Plans to Adopt IASs and IFRSs

In June 2002, the European Union did, indeed, adopt a Regulation that will require publicly traded companies to use IASs and IFRSs in their consolidated accounts by January 1, 2005, after a formal EU endorsement process. There will be a temporary exception for companies that are currently traded in the United States and use U.S. GAAP and for companies that have issued debt instruments but not equity instruments. Those companies will be required to comply with international standards by January 1, 2007.

CSA Proposals Affecting Foreign Issuers in Canada

The Canadian Securities Administrators (CSA), the body that coordinates certain activities of the various provincial and territorial securities regulators in Canada, has issued a request for comment on proposed nationally harmonized continuous disclosure requirements for reporting issuers as well as exemptions for eligible foreign issuers. Comments were requested by September 19, 2002. Highlights, from an accounting perspective include:

1. Permission for Securities Exchange Commission (SEC) issuers to file financial statements prepared in accordance with U.S. GAAP, provided that for a two-year period after starting to use U.S. GAAP, their statements will have to be reconciled to Canadian GAAP. SEC foreign issuers may file without reconciliation to Canadian GAAP. Eligible foreign issuers (as defined) may file financial statements prepared in accordance with International Financial Reporting Standards, *without reconciliation.* Certain designated foreign issuers may file financial statements in accordance with principles in designated foreign jurisdiction. Others must reconcile.
2. Removal of any size exemption for filing of management's discussion and analysis (MD&A) of financial position and results of operations and inclusion of a requirement for Board of Directors to review MD&A.
3. The MD&A must include discussion of the outcome of previously disclosed forward-looking information, disclosures about off-balance-sheet arrangements and critical accounting policies.
4. Shortened filing deadlines for annual and interim financial statements.

The EFRAG Recommends Endorsement of IASB Standards

The European Financial Reporting Advisory Group (EFRAG), a group composed of accounting experts from the private sector in several countries, was requested by the EU Commission to review the IASB standards. They were asked to confirm that there were no remaining incompatibilities between International Financial Reporting Standards (from IAS 1 to 41 with related Standing Interpretations Committee [SIC] interpretations) and the Fourth and Seventh Directives as modified under proposals (dated November 13, 2001) still under discussion.

EFRAG reviewed IASs 1 to 41 (inclusive) and the related SIC interpretations 1 to 33 inclusive (the current standards) as of March 1, 2002. The evaluation of the current standards was based on:

1. A general review of those standards.
2. EFRAG's experience of the application of those standards in practice by various companies within Europe.
3. Their general knowledge of discussions surrounding those standards.
4. Input from standard setters and market participants.

Based on this review, EFRAG was of the opinion that the current standards met the requirements of the Regulation of the European Parliament and of the Council on the application of International Accounting Standards by EU-listed companies from 2005 onward in that:

1. They were not contrary to the true and fair principle set out in Article 2(3) of the 4th Directive and Article 16(3) of the 7th Directive.
2. They met the criteria of understandability, relevance, reliability and comparability required of the financial information needed for making economic decisions and assessing the stewardship of management.

For those reasons, they thought that it was in the European interest that the process of adoption of the current standards should be set in motion. Accordingly, they recommended endorsement of the current standards *en bloc*.

EFRAG noted that the IASB was actively reviewing a number of the current standards and changes and improvements were expected to result from this review. They will give their advice on those changes when the changes are promulgated. However, this did not in any way affect the recommendation that the current standards should be endorsed.

Expect Agreement on IASs to Help Investors and Business in the EU

The European Commission has welcomed the Council's adoption, in a single reading, of the Regulation requiring listed companies, including banks and insurance companies, to prepare their consolidated accounts in accordance with IAS from 2005 onward. The Regulation will help eliminate barriers to cross-border trading in securities by ensuring that company accounts through-out the EU are more reliable and transparent and that they can be more easily compared.

They believe that this should increase market efficiency and reduce the cost of raising capital for companies, ultimately improving competitiveness and helping boost growth. The IAS Regulation was proposed by the Commission in February 2001. It is a key measure in the Financial Services Action Plan, on which significant progress has been made recently. Unlike Directives, EU Reg-ulations have the force of law without requiring transposition into national leg-islation. Member States have the option of extending the requirements of this Regulation to unlisted companies and to the production of individual accounts.

The Commission points out that they had put forward the IAS proposal long before Enron et al., but that the Regulation is one of a series of measures that will help protect the EU from such problems. Others include the Com-mission's recent Recommendation on Auditor Independence and its proposal to amend the Accounting Directives.

European officials think that the adoption will mean that:

1. Investors and other stakeholders will be able to compare like with like.
2. It will help European firms compete on equal terms when raising capital in world markets.
3. The U.S. will be inclined to work even more actively with the EU toward full convergence of accounting standards.

New Regulatory Body Created by the EU.   To ensure appropriate po-litical oversight, the Regulation establishes a new EU mechanism to assess IAS adopted by the IASB to give them legal endorsement for use within the EU. The Accounting Regulatory Committee, chaired by the Commission and com-posed of representatives of the Member States, will decide whether to endorse IAS on the basis of Commission proposals. In its task, the Commission will be helped by EFRAG.

EFRAG provides technical expertise concerning the use of IAS within the European legal environment and participates actively in the international accounting standard-setting process.

Australian Board Considering International Standards

In July, 2002, the Financial Reporting Council (FRC) of Australia deter-mined to endorse formally the adoption of International Accounting Stan-dards and International Financial Reporting Standards (IFRSs) for Australian reporting entities by January 1, 2005. The FRC's decision is in line with

Australian government policy and legislation calling for the international convergence of accounting standards. Final approval of this proposal will require legislation.

The IASB believes that the FRC's announcement demonstrates growing support for the development and implementation of a single set of high-quality global accounting standards by 2005. Australia's adoption of international accounting standards closely followed the European Union's decision in June 2002, to adopt international standards for publicly traded companies within the EU. The addition of highly developed economies to the list of countries embracing the IASs adds validity to the international body.

Also in June, the Canadian Securities Administrators proposed for public comment that certain foreign listed companies in Canada be able to use the IASB's standards without reconciliation to Canadian generally accepted accounting principles, beginning in 2005.

The Board considers the decision of Australia's FRC as a sign of increased momentum behind the IASB's efforts. They feel that this vote of confidence will increase momentum for convergence toward high-quality international standards. The input and active participation of interested parties in Australia and the Australian Accounting Standards Board (AASB) are and will remain a vital element in ensuring the IASB's success. It is through national standard setters, such as the AASB, and the members of our various committees that the IASB feel they are able jointly to:

1. Develop high-quality solutions to accounting issues.
2. Leverage resources to research topics not yet on the international agenda so as to expedite conclusions.
3. Reach interested parties throughout the world.
4. Better understand differences in operating environments, thus fulfilling the role as a global standard setter.

UK Board Considers Amending Standards

The Accounting Standards Board (ASB) in the United Kingdom has made a start toward implementing international standards in order to ease the transition to International Financial Reporting Standards in 2005. Six proposals to amend existing UK standards were issued in mid-2002. Included are changes to the standards dealing with:

1. The effects of changes in foreign exchange rates.
2. Financial reporting in hyperinflationary economies.
3. Related-party disclosures.

4. Events after the balance sheet date.
5. Inventories and long-term contracts.
6. Property, plant and equipment.

The ASB expects to issue an exposure draft on hedge accounting soon.

THE IASB ANNOUNCES NEW WORK PROGRAM

After extensive consultation with its Standards Advisory Council, national accounting standard setters, regulators and other interested parties, the IASB
announced its new program of technical projects. These build on and carry forward the IASB's initial agenda, announced in July 2001.

The main program is made up of three elements. It is probably not too
surprising that these topics are also at the top of the FASB's list of things to do:

1. Consolidations (including special-purpose entities).
2. Revenue—definition, recognition, and related aspects of liabilities.
3. Convergence of standards on topics on which the IASB believes that a
   high-quality solution is available from existing international and national
   standards:
   a. Pension accounting.
   b. Income taxes.
   c. Segment reporting.
   d. Revaluations.

In addition, the IASB proposes to embark on active research, often in
collaboration with others, on:

1. The application of international accounting standards to small and
   medium-sized entities and in emerging economies (the small and medium
   economies project).
2. Lease accounting.
3. Accounting concepts, including a strategic review of the basic elements
   of accounting and design work on measurement, focusing initially on
   impairments.
4. Aspects of accounting for financial instruments.

The intention is that, when preparatory work on these topics is concluded, they
should be moved to the IASB's main agenda.

Longer-Range Plans

Looking further forward, the IASB will encourage the national standard setters and others to carry out initial work on projects that may in time be included in the IASB's main agenda. These projects include:

1. Management reporting in relation to financial reports (loosely termed MD&A reporting).
2. Accounting for extractive industries.
3. Accounting for public and other concessions (e.g., public to private arrangements for transport, health and other infrastructure activities).

The IASB announced that this wide-ranging program has been drawn up in consultation with representatives of the world's business community and reflects the consensus on priorities for the next stage of the IASB's work. Over the past year, the IASB has been working hard on its initial agenda (after rising from the ashes of the IASC). The chairman points to their accomplishments:

1. They have issued its Preface to International Financial Reporting Standards.
2. They have published extensive proposals for improvements to 12 standards as well as the 2 standards on financial instruments.
3. In the coming months it will publish its proposals on the first-time application of international standards.
4. They will soon publish phase 1 of the business combinations project.
5. As resources become available the IASB will phase in the new projects alongside the remaining projects from the initial agenda.

The IASB are well aware that the development of such a program must rely on the strength of their liaison relationship with national standard setters. The Board is committed to pooling resources, monitoring each others' work, sharing research findings and developing new standards together to meet the legitimate expectations of the global business community.

Moving Ahead on New Business Combination Standard

The IASB is in the process of drafting its new business combination standard (which sounds very much like the FASB's provisions in Statements 141 and 142). The major decisions thus far include:

1. Pooling-of-interests accounting (merger accounting) would be prohibited.
2. Goodwill should not be amortized. Instead, it should be carried on the balance sheet indefinitely, subject to an impairment test.

3. Intangible assets acquired in a business combination before the effective date of the new standard and recognized separately from goodwill at the effective date should be reclassified as goodwill if they are:

a. Not separable and do not arise from contractual or legal rights.

b. An assembled work force.

4. At the adoption date, the useful life of intangible assets should be re-assessed and intangible assets reclassified as having finite or indefinite lives.

5. The existing 20-year useful life rebuttable presumption for finite lived intangible assets will not be carried forward to the new standard.

The IASB is expected to issue an exposure draft of a share-based payment standard by the end of 2002. The Board tentatively decided that employee stock options result in an expense that should be recognized in income. They have also tentatively concluded that measurement of the share-based compensation should be based on the estimated fair value of the shares or options at the grant date.

The IASB Proposes Improvement of Financial Instrument Standards

The IASB published for public comment proposals to improve the two International Accounting Standards related to accounting for financial instruments—IAS 32, *Financial Instruments: Disclosures and Presentation,* and IAS 39, *Financial Instruments: Recognition and Measurement.* The proposals are in the form of an exposure draft on which comments were invited by October 14, 2002.

The IASB has focused in the near term on improving the existing standards, which are closely modeled on the approach of U.S. GAAP. While the Board has signaled its desire ultimately to develop a principles-based approach for the accounting for financial instruments, the proposed improvements are aimed at removing inconsistencies in the existing standards, providing additional guidance and easing implementation.

The IASB recognizes that to undertake a complete overhaul would require time for a comprehensive reexamination of the complex issues involved and would prolong uncertainty for the many companies required to make the transition to international standards under the new European Union regulation. Furthermore, having usable standards for financial instruments is increasingly important for investors as the use of derivatives and other financial instruments grows.

The IASB pointed out that since thousands of companies are required to implement international standards in the next few years, there is an urgent need to remove uncertainty and to make it easier to implement the standards on the reporting of financial instruments.

They consider that these exposure drafts offer a practical and timely solution to the immediate problem. In the longer term, the IASB will initiate a complete reexamination of the issue with the aim of creating a universally accepted principles based approach for financial instruments.

THE IASC FOUNDATION ASSESSMENT AND CERTIFICATION PROGRAM

With the European Union's decision to require all EU-listed companies to prepare their financial statements according to IAS and IFRSs by 2005, and with other developed economies following close behind, first-time users will need to have attained a high level of knowledge about and understanding of the application of these standards.

To satisfy the demand for high-quality learning materials and training programs and to ensure that they are available quickly, the International Accounting Standards Committee Foundation (IASC Foundation) Trustees have decided that assessment and certification programs to examine financial reporting under IAS and IFRSs should be established.

As an initial step, the Foundation has invited those experienced in providing learning materials and training programs to submit proposals for materials and programs to teach and test the understanding of financial reporting requirements under IASs and IFRSs. Once a determination of the quality of the training and materials is assessed, those approved would carry the certificate "IASC Foundation Approved Training."

The Foundation Trustees believe that, as a consequence of the EU decision as well as the increased use of IASs and IFRSs worldwide, there will be a demand to satisfy the public interest and professional requirements by demonstrating that an individual has attained a certain level of proficiency in being able to apply them. For this reason, the Trustees are considering the introduction of a two-tiered assessment program:

1. *Application Level.* Those who qualify at this level would receive a certification in IAS and IFRSs. The application level would cover basic knowledge of the Standards. The treatments and disclosures required would be examined using computer-based assessment.
2. *Advanced Level.* Those who qualify at this level would receive a diploma in IAS and IFRSs. The advanced level would cover:
    a. Application of the Standards.
    b. The concepts involved in the thinking behind the Standards.
    c. The exercise of judgment in achieving a fair presentation.

Suggestions relating to how this level could be assessed are currently being sought.

An independent board to oversee education and assessment for expertise in IAS and IFRSs will be established by the IASC Foundation Trustees.

PREFACE TO IFRSS

The IASB issued its *Preface to International Financial Reporting Standards* to set out the objectives and procedures for due process, reflecting the IASB's new structure. The Preface also explains the scope, authority and timing of application of International Financial Reporting Standards. These standards are designed to apply to the general purpose financial statements and other financial reporting of all profit-oriented entities.

The Preface provides a brief description of the purpose and function of the main structures of the new arrangements for setting global standards. As such, it is a short but essential introduction to the context within which the Board will frame its standards. It states that:

1. The IASB, based in London, began operations in 2001. It is funded by contributions from the major accounting firms, private financial institutions and industrial companies throughout the world, central and development banks, and other international and professional organizations. The 14 Board members (12 of whom are full-time) reside in 9 countries and have a variety of functional backgrounds.

   The IASB emphasizes that it is committed to developing, in the public interest, a single set of high-quality, global accounting standards that require transparent and comparable information in general-purpose financial statements. In pursuit of this objective, the IASB cooperates with national accounting standard setters to achieve convergence in accounting standards around the world.

2. Upon its inception the IASB adopted the body of IASs issued by its predecessor, the International Accounting Standards Committee.

IASB PROPOSALS TO EASE TRANSITION TO IAS

IASB published exposure draft (ED) 1, *First-time Application of International Financial Reporting Standards,* proposals on how an entity should make the transition to IFRSs from another basis of accounting. The purpose of the proposals is to ensure that all entities adopting IFRSs for the first time present comparative information in their financial statements that is as close as possible to the information provided by existing users, but within cost/benefit constraints.

The proposals, therefore, include targeted and specific exemptions, notably where retrospective application is likely to cause undue cost or effort.

The proposals would require an entity to comply with every IFRS current in the first year when it first adopts IFRSs. They would also require first-time preparers of financial statements under IFRSs to disclose how the transition to international standards affected the entity's reported financial position, financial performance and cash flows. The proposals are designed both to ensure that investors have sufficient information to analyze the entity's first financial statements using IFRSs and to minimize the cost of transition for preparers of accounts.

Replaces Requirements in SIC-8

The proposals in ED 1 would replace existing requirements in Interpretation SIC-8, *First-time Application of IASs as the Primary Basis of Accounting* by:

1. Clarifying that in most cases an entity applies only the latest version of IFRSs.
2. Proposing that an entity's estimates under IFRSs at the date of transition to IFRSs would be consistent with estimates made for the same date under an entity's previous accounting (after adjustments to reflect any difference in accounting policies), unless there is objective evidence that those estimates were in error.
3. Comparing the financial statements under IFRSs to an entity's reported financial position, financial performance and cash flows, derived from its previous accounting standards.

The Board feels that the proposals are timely, considering the growing demand for high-quality international standards and the prospect of thousands of companies turning to international accounting standards.

THE IASB PROPOSES IMPROVEMENTS

The International Accounting Standards Board in May 2002, published for public comment proposals to revise 12 of its 34 active standards. The proposals are in the form of an exposure draft, *Improvements to International Accounting Standards,* on which comments were invited by September 2002.

The ED was the first product of the IASB's Improvements project. The aim is to raise the quality and consistency of financial reporting by drawing on best practices from around the world, and removing options in international standards. (This matter of options and either/or possibilities was one of the FASB's early objections to the IASC's stance on some topics. The FASB now finds itself in the position of being criticized for having attempted to be too specific about the "hows, whys and wherefores" in many instances. As a result, too little was done too late, and there were so many loopholes that often the investor was not protected.)

Stepped-Up Efforts to Improve International Standards

The Improvements project is a first step by the new IASB to promote convergence on high-quality solutions in its objective to establish a globally accepted set of accounting standards.

The release of the exposure draft marks the IASB's initial response to the demand for the continued development and rapid improvement of international standards by market participants: regulators through IOSCO, national standard setters, the IASB's Standards Advisory Council, international corporations and others.

The project has been given added impetus by the European Union's requirement that publicly listed companies use international standards beginning on or before January 2005.

The IASB believes that investors, businesses, and policy makers worldwide are looking to the Board as the international standard setter, in partnership with national standard setters, to lead the global drive toward better financial reporting, based on convergence of standards toward high-quality solutions.

Need to Improve Existing Standards

The IASB points out that its new accounting standards will take time to develop, and in the meantime, it plans to:

1. Fix problems with existing standards now if an acceptable solution is readily available.
2. Follow up with the publication of proposals to revise the two standards on financial instruments.
3. Draft guidance for those adopting international standards for the first time.
4. Publish proposals to overhaul the reporting of business combinations, including reforms to accounting for goodwill.

Examples of the improvements to IAS proposed in the exposure draft are:

1. Those relating to *convergence* include:
   a. The definition of related parties will be extended to cover further parties (e.g., joint ventures and pension plans) and further information

(e.g., amounts of transactions and balances, terms and conditions, details of guarantees).

b. It will no longer be permissible to label items of income or expense as extraordinary items either in the income statement or in the notes.

c. Guidance on the calculation of earnings per share will be expanded and will conform to practice in a number of countries.

Among the *options* that had been permitted, the following are slated for elimination:

1. LIFO (last in, first out—an inventory valuation method sometimes used in the United States and elsewhere) will be prohibited.

2. Corrections of errors now must be accounted for retrospectively, not either through current income or retrospectively.

3. Similarly, voluntary changes in accounting policies will also have to be accounted for retrospectively and not either through current income or retrospectively.

Other planned improvements are:

1. Requirements are introduced to ensure that compliance with standards does not lead to misleading results in jurisdictions where compliance is mandatory irrespective of circumstance.

2. Disclosure is required of the critical judgments made by management in applying accounting policies.

3. Disclosure is required of the key assumptions about uncertainties made by management that could cause material adjustment of the carrying amounts of assets and liabilities in financial statements.

4. Separate disclosure is required of the amounts by which inventories have been written down.

IFRIC ISSUES INTERPRETATION ON WEB SITE COSTS

In March 2002, the IASB's Standing Interpretations Committee was renamed the International Financial Reporting Interpretations Committee (IFRIC). Under its new name, the committee issued an Interpretation to clarify the accounting for Web site costs under IAS.

The Interpretation, SIC-32, *Intangible Assets—Web Site Costs*, was submitted to the IASB for approval before the Committee's name was changed and was therefore published as an SIC Interpretation and approved by the IASB at the meeting in March.

All Interpretations issued by IFRIC are part of the binding International Accounting Standards literature. SIC-32 became effective on March 25, 2002 and is aimed at clarifying the existing requirements of IAS 38, *Intangible Assets,* as it applies to expenditure on internally developing and operating a Web site. If an enterprise applies the Interpretation and the outcome is to recognize the Web site as an intangible asset, then unless the Web site has an active market and its carrying amount is revalued regularly, the enterprise will need to amortize the expenditure over a short period.

Some of the interpretive groups sponsored by the IASB's liaison national standard setters have already issued guidance on this topic. The Committee considered those rulings when developing the Interpretation in order to ensure convergence. (The FASB, EITF and SEC have all been working for several years to figure out just how to handle accounting matters related to Web sites and Internet transactions.)

In addition, the Committee addressed the accounting treatment of expenditure on developing content that is included in a Web site. This facet was not addressed by all of those groups. Because IAS 38 applies equally to such expenditure, it was necessary to include it within the Interpretation.

Specific Provisions

The Interpretation agreed that a Web site developed by an enterprise from internal expenditure for internal or external access is an internally generated intangible asset that is subject to the requirements of IAS 38, and pointed to various paragraphs within the Standard as verification.

The Interpretation also addresses the appropriate accounting treatment for internal expenditure on the development and operation of an enterprise's own Web site for internal or external access. The Committee agreed that:

1. A Web site arising from development should be recognized as an intangible asset if, and only if, in addition to complying with the general requirements described in IAS 38 for recognition and initial measurement, an enterprise could satisfy the requirements in that IAS. In particular, an enterprise may be able to satisfy the requirement to demonstrate how its Web site will generate probable future economic benefits.
2. Any internal expenditure on the development and operation of an enterprise's own Web site should be accounted for in accordance with IAS 38:
   a. The Planning stage is similar in nature to the research phase in IAS 38. Expenditure incurred in this stage should be recognized as an expense when it is incurred.
   b. The Application and Infrastructure Development stage, the Graphical Design stage and the Content Development stage, to the extent that

content is developed for purposes other than to advertise and promote an enterprise's own products and services, are similar in nature to the development phase in IAS 38.

   c. Expenditure incurred in the Content Development stage, to the extent that content is developed to advertise and promote an enterprise's own products and services (e.g., digital photographs of products) should be recognized as an expense when incurred in accordance with a different paragraph in IAS 38.

   d. The Operating stage begins once development of a Web site is complete. Expenditure incurred in this stage should be recognized as an expense when it is incurred unless it meets the criteria in yet another section of IAS 38.

3. A Web site that is recognized as an intangible asset under this Interpretation should be measured after initial recognition by applying the requirements of IAS 38. The best estimate of a Web site's useful life should be short.

THE IASB PROPOSES AMENDMENT TO IAS 19, *EMPLOYEE BENEFITS*

The IASB published an exposure draft in February 2002 of a limited amendment to the pension accounting provisions of the standard, "Amendment to IAS 19, *Employee Benefits*: The Asset Ceiling."

Reflecting the recent fall in global equity markets, many pension plans have suffered actuarial losses. The IASB considered advice from the accounting profession that IAS 19 would have an unintended effect in some situations. The problem was produced by the interaction of two aspects of IAS 19:

1. The option to defer gains and losses in the pension fund.
2. The limit on the amount that can be recognized as an asset (the asset ceiling).

The combination of the asset ceiling and the option for an entity to defer losses can in certain circumstances require the entity to report an *increase in profit*. Equally perversely, the combination of the asset ceiling and the option for an entity to defer gains can require the entity to report a *decrease in profit*. The IASB concluded that reporting gains and losses in these circumstances is wholly inappropriate. The limited amendment would prevent their recognition.

At the same time, rather than merely fix problems as they arise, the Board decided upon a general reexamination of IAS 19 (which was adopted in 1998) with a view to the convergence of pension accounting standards worldwide.

THE SIC ISSUES SIX NEW INTERPRETATIONS

The Standing Interpretations Committee published six new Interpretations on Christmas Eve, 2001, to clarify accounting issues under the International Accounting Standards. (SIC-32 was issued in March 2002, as mentioned in the previous section, "IFRIC Issues Interpretation on Web Site Costs.") The new Interpretations follow.

SIC-27: Evaluating the Substance of Transactions in the Legal Form of a Lease. A discussion on this topic had been on the agenda for some time. It went through a number of changes, but the Committee considers the final document to be of wider application and more useful than it was at earlier stages. It highlights the significance of determining the *substance* of a transaction to determine whether that arrangement is actually a lease.

SIC-28: Business Combinations—"Date of Exchange" and Fair Value of Equity Instruments. The Interpretation dealing with the date of exchange and the fair value of equity instruments issued in a business combination clarifies the existing requirements of IAS 22.

When an acquisition is achieved in a single step, the fair value of equity instruments issued is determined at the date when the acquirer obtains control over the acquiree. The published price of a quoted equity instrument is the best evidence of its fair value; therefore, that price is used when measuring fair value. No adjustments are made for block premiums or discounts to the published price.

When approving SIC-28, the Board noted that it is considering in phase 1 of its business combinations project the date on which equity instruments issued as consideration should be measured. Any possible change to the existing requirements *as a result of that project* would be effective only after the Board has completed its due process.

SIC-29: Disclosure—Service Concession Arrangements. The disclosures required by SIC-29 should significantly improve the transparency of financial statements of enterprises that are a party to a service concession arrangement.

SIC-30: Reporting Currency—Translation from Measurement Currency to Presentation Currency. This SIC resolves the method of translating from a measurement currency determined under SIC-19 to a presentation currency. Also, during the Board's discussion of SIC-30, it noted that the Interpretation is consistent with its tentative decision in November 2001 to require translation of financial statements into a presentation currency using the method set out in IAS 21.

SIC-31: Revenue—Barter Transactions Involving Advertising Services.
The Interpretation addresses the circumstances when a Seller can reliably
measure revenue at the fair value of advertising services received or provided
in a barter transaction. The SIC agreed that revenue from a barter transaction
involving advertising cannot be measured reliably at the fair value of advertising services received. However, a Seller can reliably measure revenue at the fair
value of the advertising services it provides in a barter transaction, by reference only to non-barter transactions that:

1. Involve advertising similar to the advertising in the barter transaction.
2. Occur frequently.
3. Represent a predominant number of transactions and amount when
   compared to all transactions to provide advertising that is similar to the
   advertising in the barter transaction.
4. Involve cash and/or another form of consideration (e.g., marketable securities, non-monetary assets, and other services) that has a reliably
   measurable fair value.
5. Do not involve the same counterparty as in the barter transaction.

***SIC-33: Consolidation and Equity Method—Potential Voting Rights
and Allocation of Ownership Interests.***   This action clarifies that share call
options and other similar instruments that have the potential to give an enterprise voting power, can affect an assessment of control and significant influence.

The Interpretation addresses whether the existence and effect of potential voting rights should be considered when assessing whether an enterprise
controls or significantly influences another enterprise according to IAS 27 and
IAS 28 respectively.

It also addresses whether any other facts and circumstances related to potential voting rights should be assessed. The Committee agreed that all facts
and circumstances that affect potential voting rights should be examined, except the intention of management and the financial capability to exercise or
convert.

Effective Dates

These Interpretations were approved by the IASB at its meeting in December 2001, except SIC-32, which was adopted in March 2002. All Interpretations issued by SIC are part of the binding International Accounting Standards literature. Their effective dates are:

1. SIC-27, 29, and 31 became effective on December 31, 2001.

2. SIC-30 and 33 became effective for annual financial periods beginning on or after January 1, 2002.

3. SIC-28 became effective for acquisitions given initial accounting recognition on or after December 31, 2001.

4. SIC-32 became effective on March 25, 2002.

FOUNDATION TRUSTEES NAME STANDARDS ADVISORY COUNCIL TO PROVIDE ADVICE TO IASB

The Trustees of the International Accounting Standards Committee Foundation announced the appointment of the Standards Advisory Council (SAC) in June 2001. The members of the SAC will be asked to provide advice to the IASB on priorities in setting standards. It will also inform the Board of implications of proposed standards for both users and producers of financial accounts.

The 49-member body includes chief financial and accounting officers from some of the world's largest corporations and international organizations, leading financial analysts and academics, regulators, accounting standard setters and partners from leading accounting firms. The members of the SAC are drawn from 6 continents, 29 countries, and 5 international organizations. Additionally, the European Commission, the U.S. Securities and Exchange Commission, and the Financial Services Agency of Japan will participate as observers.

Unquestionably, this new arm of the IASC will be of the utmost importance in the quest for a globally acceptable set of accounting standards. The only question will be whether the advisors can remember that the ultimate aim is to provide the users of the finished product with the information that they need to make informed decisions.

REVISED ORGANIZATION LAUNCHED

When the Board of the International Accounting Standards Commission (IASC) unanimously approved a new Constitution in 2000, they created an organization with two main bodies. These two are the IASC Trustees, an oversight body, and the IASB, the new group of experienced accounting professionals appointed by the Trustees. This Board has the responsibility of working to develop "a single set of high-quality accounting standards that national bodies around the world can broadly support."

Additionally, the SIC was to continue as it had in the past. However, the name was subsequently changed to the International Financial Reporting

Interpretations Committee (IFRIC). A new Standards Advisory Council is expected to be the key vehicle for obtaining advice and injecting fresh thinking into the standard-making process.

Putting the New Constitution in Place

On March 8, 2001, the Trustees activated the new Constitution, effective immediately. In doing so, they established a not-for-profit Delaware corporation, the International Accounting Standards Committee Foundation, to oversee the London-based IASB. The 14-member IASB began full-time operations in April 2001, and held its first public meetings in London. In effect, the IASB is the professional standard-setting body taking up its task of attempting to create a single-set of high-quality global accounting standards.

IASC Foundation. The governance of the IASB organization is ultimately in the hands of the Trustees of the IASC Foundation. There are 19 Trustees. The IASC Foundation Constitution provides that the Trustees must:

1. Show a firm commitment to the IASC Foundation and the IASB as a high-quality global standard-setter.
2. Be financially knowledgeable.
3. Have an ability to meet the time commitment.
4. Have an understanding of, and be sensitive to, international issues relevant to the success of an international organization responsible for the development of high-quality global accounting standards for use in the world's capital markets and by other users.

The Trustees appoint the members of the IASB, the International Financial Reporting Interpretations Committee and the Standards Advisory Council. In addition they:

1. Review annually the strategy of IASB and its effectiveness.
2. Approve annually the budget of IASB and determine the basis for funding.
3. Review broad strategic issues affecting accounting standards, promote IASB and its work and promote the objective of rigorous application of International Accounting Standards (however, they are excluded from involvement in technical matters relating to accounting standards).
4. Establish and amend operating procedures for the IASB, the Standing Interpretations Committee (now the International Standards Advisory Council).

5. Approve amendments to this Constitution after following a due process, including consultation with the Standards Advisory Council and publication of an Exposure Draft for public comment.

6. Exercise all powers of the IASC Foundation except those expressly reserved to the IASB, the Standing Interpretations Committee (now IFRIC) and the Standards Advisory Council.

The Trustees are not responsible for setting International Financial Reporting Standards. That responsibility rests *solely* with the International Accounting Standards Board.

Distribution of Trustees.   The distribution of Trustees, required by paragraph 9 of the IASB Constitution, is as follows:

- *North America*—6 (5 from the United States and 1 from Canada).
- *Europe*—6 (1 each from Denmark, France, Germany, Italy, Netherlands and the United Kingdom).
- *Asia-Pacific*—4 (1 each from Australia, China-Hong Kong and Japan). There is one vacancy here.
- *Other*—3 from any area, as long as balance is maintained (1 each from Brazil, South Africa and an International Organization [the Bank for International Settlements based in Switzerland]).

The Board.   The previous Board was replaced by a new Board of fourteen individuals—twelve full-time members and two part-time members. Because the Board has sole responsibility for setting accounting standards, the foremost qualification for Board membership is technical expertise.

The Trustees reviewed more than 200 candidates for Board positions. The IASC Constitution mandated that the Board comprise individuals who represent "the best available combination of technical skills and experience of relevant business and market conditions." Further, in their selection of members, the Trustees are expected to exercise their best judgment to ensure that the Board is not dominated by any particular constituency or regional interest.

To achieve a balance of perspectives and experience, a minimum of five Board members must have a backgrounds as practicing auditors; a minimum of three, a background in the preparation of financial statements; a minimum of three must be users of financial statements; and at least one member must be from academia. The publication of a Standard, an Exposure Draft, or a final SIC Interpretation requires approval by eight of the Board's fourteen members.

In order to encourage cooperation among the new Board and national standard-setters, the Trustees appointed seven of the Board members as official liaisons to national bodies. These liaison Board members will maintain close contact with their respective national standard-setters, and will be responsible for coordinating agendas and ensuring that the new IASB and national bodies are working toward the goal of global convergence on the single set of high-quality standards.

Countries with formal liaisons are Australia and New Zealand together; Canada; France; Germany; Japan; the United States; and the United Kingdom. In addition, Board members will have frequent contacts with financial regulators and central banks, private industry, analysts, and academics throughout the world.

The International Financial Reporting Interpretations Committee. As mentioned earlier, the SIC was to continue in its form and function as previously. Its name, however, has changed as noted above. Its primary function is to review, on a timely basis within the context of existing International Accounting Standards, issues that are likely to receive divergent or unacceptable treatment where authoritative guidance is lacking. When consensus is reached on appropriate accounting treatment, the IFRIC publishes pronouncements on the application of the relevant IAS. It also recommends solutions for situations not covered by existing standards. The Committee's function is similar to that of the FASB's Emerging Issues Task Force (EITF).

The IFRIC has 12 voting members from various countries, including individuals from the accounting profession, preparer groups, and user groups. The International Organization of Securities Commissions (IOSCO) and the European Commission are nonvoting observers. To ensure adequate liaison with the Board, two Board representatives may attend IFRIC meetings as nonvoting members.

Setting up the Advisory Council. This new part of the organization was initiated in the revised Constitution to provide a formal vehicle for other groups and individuals having diverse geographic and functional backgrounds to give advice to the Board and the Trustees.

At the April meeting, the Trustees reiterated their commitment to achieving a broad and representative balance of perspectives, both professionally and geographically, through the creation of this Advisory Council. It will meet regularly with the IASB to advise the Board Members on priorities, and to inform them of ramifications of proposed standards for particular users and producers of financial accounts. Specifically, this new group must represent the diverse interests involved in the standard-setting process to ensure that the result is usable, relevant information.

The Relationship of the IASC with Other International Groups. The IASC previously had important relationships with many other international groups; for example, IOSCO, the Basel Committee, the International Federation of Accountants, and the European Commission.

The new Constitution lessens the formal ties between IASC and IFAC. They no longer have a common membership, and the IFAC Council will no longer be responsible for appointing members of the IASC Board. However, the IFAC has provided a continuing place for IASB as an observer in its governance arrangements. It is considered important for the new IASB to work hard to maintain and foster these international relationships.

And Back to Work It Was.   At its meeting in April 2001, the IASB discussed possible approaches to setting its technical agenda, identifying potential projects as :

Precedential (critical),
Convergence-related,
Leadership, and
Improvements.

Tentative allocation to each category was made and the IASB asked the staff to prepare papers for further discussion at its May meeting. *Precedential* projects are likely to include:

1. The framework.
2. Liability recognition.
3. Revenue recognition.
4. Reporting financial performance.

Convergence projects may include:

1. Business combinations.
2. Consolidation policy.
3. Revaluation of nonfinancial assets.

Leadership projects may include:

1. Banks.
2. Extractive industries.
3. Financial instruments.
4. Insurance contracts.
5. Intangible assets.
6. Leases.
7. Present value.
8. Share-based payments.

An *improvements* project may include limited revisions to most existing Standards to remove internal inconsistencies and implicit and explicit alternatives. Where appropriate, matters raised by the International Organization of Securities Commissions (IOSCO) and national standard-setters will be addressed within the project. The improvements project is expected to address topics that can be dealt with relatively quickly, and are not significant enough to be a major project on their own or to be part of a major convergence project.

In addition, and pending definitive direction from the IASB, the staff continues work on a number of projects inherited from the previous IASC Board:

1. Business Combinations
2. Business Reporting on the Internet
3. Emerging Economies
4. Extractive Industries (including Mining and Oil and Gas)
5. Financial Instruments—Comprehensive Project
6. IAS 39, *Financial Instruments—Recognition and Measurement*
7. Insurance
8. Present Value (formerly Discounting)
9. Reporting Financial Performance
10. Disclosures by Banks and Similar Financial Institutions

THE IASC STANDARD ON AGRICULTURE (AIS 41)

The Standard on Agriculture is an important one, although it deals with specialized transactions and was not part of the core set of standards. Financial support for the work on this project was originally provided by The World Bank.

The fact that the IASC had been working on this project for over six years indicates the difficulty of the issues, particularly in deciding on the relative emphases to be given to fair-value-based measurements as opposed to cost-based measurements of agricultural assets. IAS 41 prescribes the accounting treatment, financial statement presentation, and disclosures related to agricultural activity, a matter not covered in any other International Accounting Standard.

For the purpose of this Standard, agricultural activity is considered to be the management by an enterprise engaged in the biological transformation of living animals or plants (biological assets):

1. For sale.
2. Into agricultural produce.
3. Into additional biological assets.

IAS 41 requires measurement at fair value less estimated point-of-sale costs from initial recognition of biological assets up to harvest, other than when fair value cannot be measured reliably on initial recognition. A change in fair value less estimated point-of-sale costs should be included in net profit or loss for the period in which it arises.

IAS 41 *does not* deal with processing of agricultural produce after harvest. Processing grapes into wine for sale, for example, is generally accounted for under IAS 2, *Inventories.*

There is a presumption that fair value can be measured reliably for a biological asset. That presumption can be rebutted only on initial recognition for a biological asset for which market-determined prices or values are not available and for which alternative estimates of fair value are determined to be clearly unreliable. In such a case, IAS 41 requires an enterprise to measure that biological asset at its cost less any accumulated depreciation and any accumulated impairment losses.

Once the fair value of such a biological asset becomes reliably measurable, an enterprise should measure it at its fair value less estimated point-of-sale costs. In all cases, an enterprise should measure agricultural produce at its fair value less estimated point-of-sale costs.

Unique Aspects of Agriculture

The Board concluded that the Standard should require a fair value model for biological assets because of the unique nature and characteristics of agricultural activity. One of these unique characteristics is the management of biological transformation.

The financial statements of enterprises undertaking agricultural activity should reflect the effects of biological transformation, which are represented by fair value changes in biological assets. Under a transaction-based, historical cost accounting model, the effects of biological transformation are not reflected because the patterns of biological transformation often differ significantly in timing from the patterns of cost.

Fair Value Measurement Is Not Always Possible

The Board also concluded that fair value cannot be measured reliably for some biological assets. The questionable reliability of fair value measurement for some and the lack of an active market for other biological assets, in particular for those with a long growth period, poses a problem. In addition, present value of expected net cash flows is often an unreliable measure of fair value because of the necessity of using subjective assumptions. Therefore, the Board decided that there was a need to include a reliability exception for cases in which market-determined prices or values are not available and alternative estimates of fair value are determined to be clearly unreliable.

The Standard is effective for annual financial statements covering periods beginning on or after January 1, 2003. Earlier application is encouraged.

THREE REVISED STANDARDS ISSUED BY THE IASC

Standard-setting is an ongoing process, even in the most established standard-setting bodies. It is no wonder, then, that the IASC has found it necessary to publish limited revisions to three International Accounting Standards: IAS 12, *Income Taxes,* IAS 19, *Employee Benefits,* and IAS 39, *Financial Instruments: Recognition and Measurement.*

There was no specific topic that needed addressing in each, but a chain reaction set in. The revisions to IAS 39 are accompanied by consequential changes to IAS 27, *Consolidated Financial Statements and Accounting for Investments in Subsidiaries;* IAS 28, *Accounting for Investments in Associates;* IAS 31, *Financial Reporting of Interests in Joint Ventures,* and IAS 32, *Financial Instruments: Disclosure and Presentation,* and to the other two IASs named above.

Specifically, the revisions address the *income tax* consequences of dividends, *pension plan* assets, and technical application issues on *financial instruments.* The large majority of respondents supported the proposed revisions in Exposure Drafts ED66, ED67 and ED68.

The only substantive change to the proposals made in the three Exposure Drafts is that the revised definition of plan assets in IAS 19 is broadly similar to the definition proposed in ED67. However, in response to comments received on ED67, the Board extended the scope of the definition to include certain insurance policies (now described in IAS 19 as qualifying insurance policies) that satisfy the same conditions as other plan assets. These insurance policies have similar economic effects to funds whose assets qualify as plan assets under the definition proposed in ED67.

The limited revisions to the three Standards and other related Standards became operative for annual financial statements covering periods beginning on or after January 1, 2001.

THE IASC CONSIDERS ACCOUNTING BY MINING AND OIL AND GAS COMPANIES

An issues paper on financial reporting by enterprises in the extractive industries (mining and oil and gas companies) was developed with the help of a steering committee of experts on the extractive industries.

The aim of the issues paper is to identify the important accounting and disclosure issues relating to exploration and production activities in these industries, and to evaluate the merits of alternative ways of resolving the issues. To provide a focus for commentators, the issues paper sets out the tentative views that the IASC steering committee has developed on some of the most significant issues at this stage of the project.

Among the critical issues are:

1. The extent to which the costs of finding, acquiring, and developing reserves should be capitalized.
2. The methods of depreciating (amortizing) capitalized costs.
3. The degree to which quantities and values of reserves, rather than costs, should affect recognition, measurement, and disclosure.
4. The definition and measurement of reserves.

Today, there is a wide divergence in accounting standards and practices between countries and within individual countries. Even in the few countries in which financial reporting standards have been prescribed for the mining or petroleum industries, alternative treatments have been allowed and are commonly used.

Although many companies currently disclose estimated quantities of reserves in the ground, and some disclose estimated values as well, nearly all enterprises use *historical costs,* rather than *values,* as the basis of their accounting.

Two common methods illustrate the wide variety of accounting practices:

1. *The successful efforts method.* Successful efforts accounting is used by most large petroleum enterprises and many small ones, as well as by some mining enterprises. Costs that lead directly to finding reserves are capitalized, while costs that do not lead directly to reserves are charged to expense.
2. *Full-cost method.* Under full-cost accounting, all costs incurred in searching for, acquiring, and developing reserves in a large cost center such as a country or continent are capitalized as part of the cost of whatever reserves have been found. This is the practice, even though a specific cost was incurred in an effort that was clearly a failure.

Full-cost accounting is used by many small to mid-size petroleum enterprises, but rarely by mining enterprises. Many mining companies use approaches that are somewhere between the successful efforts and the full-cost methods.

There are important accounting differences, not only as to which costs are capitalized, but also as to how they are depreciated, how impairment of capitalized costs is recognized, and how provisions for future site clean-up costs are made.

The extractive industries also have unique accounting issues in such areas as revenue recognition, inventories, and arrangements that allow two or more entities to share the risks of exploring and developing reserves.

Because of widespread interest in the project, the IASC has sent the issues paper to the senior financial officials of nearly 300 extractive industries companies worldwide, with a request that they consider the issues and provide their comments.

IASC Guidance on Financial Instruments

The International Accounting Standards Committee (IASC) has issued two documents with additional guidance on implementing IAS 39, *Financial Instruments: Recognition and Measurement*. The two are:

1. *IAS 39 Implementation Guidance—Questions and Answers*. This document contains 100 questions and answers (Q&A) that have been approved for issuance in final form. These Q&A were earlier issued for public comment in three batches in May, June, and July, of 2000.
2. A fourth batch of proposed *IAS 39 Implementation Guidance— Questions and Answers*. This document contains 70 additional Q&A. IASC invited comments on these Q&A from all interested parties.

IAS 39 significantly affects corporate financial reporting by establishing for the first time a single set of rigorous and consistent principles for recognizing and measuring financial instruments under IASC standards. The IAS 39 implementation guidance issued today helps companies, auditors, and financial analysts better understand and apply the requirements in IAS 39, and helps companies implement this new approach to financial instruments consistently and effectively.

IAS 39 introduces a whole new approach to the accounting for trading, investment, and hedging activities involving financial instruments including derivatives. It is IASC's first comprehensive Standard on the subject. IAS 39 became effective for financial statements for financial years beginning on or after January 1, 2001. Therefore, it is not surprising that companies and their auditors have a lot of questions on how best and most effectively to implement IAS 39.

Issues Covered in Implementation Guides

The IAS 39 implementation guidance issued thus far includes a wide variety of difficult and diverse topics:

— The application of IAS 39 to financial reinsurance contracts, credit derivatives, financial guarantee contracts, and commodity contracts.
— Definitions of derivatives and originated loans.

— Accounting for embedded derivatives.

— Accounting for "regular way" transactions.

— Accounting for transfers of financial assets and portions of financial assets (for instance, in securitizations).

— Accounting for transaction costs.

— Fair value measurement considerations.

— Application of the effective interest method.

— Classification of financial assets as held to maturity.

— Impairment issues.

— Hedge accounting issues (such as hedge accounting considerations when interest rate risk is managed on a net basis, and hedging of risk components).

— Disclosures about financial instruments.

— Application of the transition requirements in IAS 39.

— The interaction between IAS 39 and other International Accounting Standards (such as IAS 21 on the effects of changes in foreign exchange rates).

This implementation guidance was prepared by the IASC Staff and approved for issuance by the IAS 39 Implementation Guidance Committee, which was established for this specific purpose by the IASC Board. It should come as no surprise that the members and observers on the IGC are all experts in financial instruments with backgrounds as accounting standard-setters, auditors, bankers, and banking and securities regulators.

EXAMPLES OF COOPERATIVE STANDARD SETTING

In several instances, the Financial Accounting Standards Board has worked with the IASC and with other groups to arrive at compatible standards. Among these endeavors are:

1. The FASB-IASC simultaneous effort relating to *Earnings per Share,* FASB 128 and IASC 33.

2. The FASB and the Accounting Standards Board (AcSB) of the Canadian Institute of Chartered Accountants developed almost identical Standards on Segment Reporting and Disclosure. The U.S. Standard is FASB 131. The IASC had also worked with these two groups but hesitated to require as much increased disclosure in IAS 14(rev.).

3. The United Kingdom's Accounting Standards Board (ASB)-IASC cooperation on their Standards on Impairment of Assets and also on

Provisions, Contingent Liabilities and Contingent Assets. This latter cooperative endeavor also brought them much closer to U.S. GAAP (contained in FASB 5, *Accounting for Contingencies.*)

IOSCO Is Instrumental in Launching Core Standards

In May 2000, the International Organization of Securities Commissions announced completion of its assessment of the accounting standards issued by IASC and recommended that its members allow multinational issuers to use 30 of the IASC Standards, including their related interpretations. This was with the understanding that they could be supplemented by reconciliation, disclosure, and interpretation where necessary to address outstanding substantive issues at a national or regional level. These are labeled "the IASC 2000 Standards."

IOSCO believes that use of these Standards by multinational enterprises in preparing their financial statements will facilitate cross-border offerings and listings, and will promote the further development of internationally accepted accounting standards.

IOSCO's Technical Committee published a report summarizing its assessment work, noting outstanding issues that members expect to address through supplemental treatments. IOSCO identified outstanding substantive issues relating to the IASC 2000 Standards in a report that includes an analysis of those issues and specifies supplemental treatments that may be required in a particular jurisdiction to address each of the concerns.

Those supplemental treatments are:

1. Reconciliation: Requiring reconciliation of certain items to show the effect of applying a different accounting method, in contrast with the method applied under IASC standards.

2. Disclosure: Requiring additional disclosures, either in the presentation of the financial statements or in the footnotes.

3. Interpretation: Specifying use of a particular alternative provided in an IASC Standard, or a particular interpretation in cases where the IASC Standard is unclear or silent.

In addition, as part of national or regional specific requirements, waivers may be needed relating to particular aspects of an IASC Standard, without requiring that the effect of the accounting method used be reconciled to the effect of applying the IASC method. The use of waivers should be restricted to exceptional circumstances such as issues identified by a domestic regulator when a specific IASC Standard is contrary to domestic or regional regulation.

Future Development of IASs

The practical consequences of IOSCO's decision will take some time to become fully apparent. Almost all countries of the world—the United States and Canada are the main exceptions—already accept IAS for cross-border listings, and IASC does not expect any change in the number.

They realize that a key factor will be subsequent action taken by the U.S. Securities and Exchange Commission. As is quite clear, if a foreign company submits financial statements in the United States using IAS, it must produce a reconciliation of its statements to GAAP.

The SEC published a Concept Release in February 2000 seeking comments about the possibility of greater acceptance of IAS. When the comment period ended, the SEC staff began analyzing the comments and considering their next steps. Quoting the IASC, "The United States is currently going through a period of political transition." Evidently, the international organization does not care to hazard a guess as to what that might mean.

It was pointed out that the SEC took a leading role in IOSCO's work in analyzing the core standards, and agreed with the IOSCO resolution. The wording of the resolution and the assessment of the work that has been done in IASC encourages them to expect the United States to move gradually to greater acceptance of IAS Standards. At the same time, it is realistic to expect that the SEC and FASB will continue for some time to require the disclosure of additional information by companies using international standards.

IOSCO realizes that a body of accounting standards like the IASC Standards must continue to evolve in order to address existing and emerging issues. IOSCO's recommendation assumes that it will continue to be involved in the IASC work and structure and that the IASC will continue to develop its body of standards and interpretations.

IOSCO expects to survey its membership to determine the extent to which members have taken steps to permit incoming multinational issuers to use the IASC 2000 Standards, subject to the supplemental treatments described above. At the same time, IOSCO expects to continue to work with the IASC, and will determine the extent to which IOSCO's outstanding substantive issues, including proposals for future projects, have been addressed appropriately.

INTERNATIONALIZATION OF THE U.S. SECURITIES MARKETS

Over the last few years, the number of foreign companies accessing the U.S. public markets has increased dramatically. As of December 31, 2000, there were over 1,310 foreign companies from 59 countries filing periodic reports with the Securities and Exchange Commission.

Foreign Issuers in the U.S. Market

Foreign companies raising funds from the public, or having their securities traded on a U.S. national exchange, or the NASDAQ Stock Market, are subject to the registration requirements of the Securities Act and the registration and reporting requirements of the Exchange Act. The SEC provides a separate integrated disclosure system for foreign private issuers that provides a number of accommodations to foreign practices and policies. These include:

1. Interim reporting on the basis of home country and stock exchange practice, rather than quarterly reports.

2. Exemption from the proxy rules and the insider reporting and short swing profit recovery provisions of Section 16.

3. Aggregate executive compensation disclosure rather than individual disclosure, if so permitted in an issuer's home country.

4. Acceptance of three International Accounting Standards (IASs) relating to:
   a. Cash flow statements (IAS 7).
   b. Business combinations (IAS 22).
   c. Operations in hyperinflationary economies (IAS 21).

5. Offering document financial statements updated principally on a semi-annual, rather than a quarterly basis.

6. An exemption from Exchange Act registration for foreign private issuers that have not engaged in a U.S. public offering, or whose securities are not traded on a national exchange or the NASDAQ Stock Market.

The Commission staff has also implemented procedures to review foreign issuers' disclosure documents on an expedited basis and in draft form, if requested. This helps to facilitate cross-border offerings and listings in light of potentially conflicting home-country schedules and disclosure requirements.

SEC Practice Section of AICPA Changes Rules

Reflecting the importance of audit quality in filings by foreign issuers, the SEC Practice Section of the AICPA changed sections of its membership rules to address SECPS member firms with foreign associated firms that audit SEC registrants. Under the new rules, SECPS members must seek the "adoption of policies and procedures by the international organization or individual foreign associated firms that are consistent with SECPS objectives" for audits of financial statements of SEC registrants. The SECPS member then reports to the AICPA the name and country of any foreign associated firms that demonstrates compliance with that objective. The new rules also establish minimum procedures to be performed by a knowledgeable reviewer with respect to documents to be filed with the Commission.

Interaction with the IASC

The SEC has been working with the IASC through the International Organization of Securities Commissions since 1987 to develop the set of accounting standards for cross-border offerings and listings. The Commission has always maintained that the standards should:

1. Include a core set of accounting pronouncements that constitute a comprehensive, generally accepted basis of accounting.
2. Be of high quality; in other words they must result in comparability and transparency.
3. Provide for full disclosure.
4. Be rigorously interpreted and applied.

Amendments to Disclosure Requirements

In late 1999, the Commission adopted changes to its nonfinancial statement disclosure requirements for foreign private issuers, to conform more closely to the International Disclosure Standards endorsed by IOSCO. The changes were intended to harmonize disclosure requirements on fundamental topics among the securities regulations of various jurisdictions.

For a number of years, the Securities and Exchange Commission has been working with other members of IOSCO to develop a set of International Standards for nonfinancial statement disclosures that could be used in cross-border offerings and listings. The International Disclosure Standards developed by IOSCO reflect a consensus among securities regulators in the major capital markets as to the types of disclosures that should be required for international use. The Standards cover fundamental disclosure topics such as the description of the issuer's business, results of operations and management, and the securities it plans to offer or list.

Changes to the Foreign Integrated Disclosure System

The Commission amended Form 20-F (the basic Exchange Act registration statement and annual report form used by foreign issuers) to incorporate the International Disclosure Standards. The Commission also revised the Securities Act registration forms designated for use by foreign private issuers, and related rules and forms, to reflect the changes in Form 20-F.

The amendments do not change the financial statement reconciliation (to GAAP) requirements for foreign issuers, and the SEC will continue to require disclosure on topics not covered by the International Disclosure Standards, such as disclosures relating to market risk and specialized industries such as banks. Unlike the IOSCO International Disclosure Standards, which were intended to apply only to offerings and listings of common equity securities, and only to listings and transactions for cash, the amendments to Form 20-F apply to all types of offerings and listings and to annual reports.

The Commission also revised the definition of "foreign private issuer," which determines an issuer's eligibility to use certain SEC forms and benefit from certain accommodations under Commission rules. These clarify how issuers should calculate their U.S. ownership.

THE EUROPEAN PARLIAMENT'S CHANGES TO ACCOUNTING DIRECTIVES

In amending a European Commission proposal to update two company law directives designed to introduce the principle of *fair value* accounting, members of the European Parliament voted to include banks and other financial institutions. They are among the most frequent users of derivative financial instruments.

The members believe that applying fair value to them will foster market transparency and market discipline. The Commission's proposal does not include banks and other financial institutions, because they prefer to offer similar proposals for their accounting requirements at a later stage.

The amendments, while broadly endorsing the Commission's proposals, are aimed at clarifying and improving the wording of the text. They also include a number of substantive changes in the amendments. They are intended to clarify which categories of a company, as well as which financial instruments and commodity-based contracts, fair value accounting should be applied to.

On information-related matters, Parliament is aiming for more far-reaching disclosure on derivative financial instruments. However, the intention is to allow exemptions for small companies from additional disclosure on the derivatives. In addition, the idea is that there should be no requirement to provide information if it is insignificant.

The purpose of the proposal is to bring EU legislation into line with the new International Accounting Standards (IAS) particularly IAS 39, *Financial Instruments Recognition and Measurement*. In order to take account of the widespread use of derivative financial instruments such as futures, options, forward contracts, and swaps, the IAS have moved away from the *historical cost* valuation model on which the existing directives are based. "Historical cost" is the price actually paid for an asset or liability; "fair value" is the valuation at today's market value. The proposals were unanimously approved by the EU Council of Ministers at their meeting on May 31, 2001.

THE OECD IS SEEKING CONSENSUS ON THE TAX TREATMENT OF E-COMMERCE

Representatives of the Organization for Economic Cooperation and Development (OECD) member governments are attempting to tackle the perplexing problems of how, when, and where to tax international electronic commerce.

As part of its continuing work on the taxation aspects of electronic commerce, the OECD released a set of reports and technical papers illustrating progress toward implementation of the Ottawa Taxation Framework Conditions. Taken together, these reports represent a major step toward reaching an international consensus on the accounting and taxation treatment of e-commerce.

Since the Conditions were agreed to in late 1998, the OECD, through its Committee on Fiscal Affairs, has followed a work program directed at their implementation. A key element of that work program has been an international dialogue, involving not only OECD member countries, but also the international business community and a number of nonmember economies.

In early 2001, they agreed to several important conclusions and recommendations that could provide greater certainty among businesses and consumers regarding e-commerce. The conclusions and recommendations by the Committee on Fiscal Affairs and the business/government advisory groups, cover three main areas:

1. International direct taxation.
2. Consumption taxes.
3. Tax administration.

Status of Specific Taxation Problems

On income taxes, OECD countries have now reached a broad consensus on the interpretation of existing permanent establishment rules that are fundamental for deciding where profits on the conduct of e-commerce can be taxed. They are now working on clarifying the tax treaty treatment of various types of e-commerce payments on the basis of a report just received from a business/government advisory group set up to examine this issue.

In the area of consumption taxes, OECD countries have made significant progress towards identifying pragmatic ways of achieving the desired result of effective taxation in the specific place of the consumption.

In the area of tax administration, OECD governments have reached agreement on the main administrative challenges and opportunities facing tax administrations, and on the sort of responses that governments need to consider. They are now inviting public comments on their proposals regarding consumption taxes and tax administration.

Officials of the OECD agreed there is much that various tax administrations can and should do to share their experience and expertise internationally, especially in the field of taxpayer service. They emphasize that it is important to maintain efforts to strengthen the emerging international consensus. In so doing, it will provide governments and business with the certainty that they need about how taxation rules should apply to e-commerce.

The Basis of Present Considerations

The Committee's work on e-commerce draws its impetus from the Ottawa Taxation Framework Conditions mentioned earlier. The Conditions are a set of principles about how governments should respond to the tax implications of e-commerce. These principles have since been widely recognized as representing a strong foundation for the Committee's current more detailed work. At a recent meeting in Paris, the Committee restated its commitment to a continuing dialogue with the international business community and non-OECD member economies on these issues, and approved new arrangements for continuing the dialogue.

From this basis, emerging conclusions and recommendations from the Committee on Fiscal Affairs have been made in various areas.

International Direct Tax Issues

Broad consensus was recently achieved on clarification in the Commentary on the OECD Model Tax Convention of the application of the current definition of *permanent establishment* (PE). The clarification states that for accounting and tax purposes:

1. A Web site cannot, in itself, constitute a permanent establishment.
2. A Web site hosting arrangement typically does not result in a PE for the enterprise that carries on business through that Web site.
3. An Internet service provider normally will not constitute a dependent agent of another enterprise to constitute a PE for that enterprise.
4. While a place where computer equipment, such as a server, is located *may* in certain circumstances constitute a permanent establishment, this requires that the functions performed at that place be significant as well as an essential or core part of the business activity of the enterprise.

The report of its Technical Advisory Group on Treaty Characterization of E-Commerce Payments (see detailed discussion below) is expected to help the Fiscal Affairs Committee reach an early agreement on how treaty characterization issues should be resolved and how the Commentary on the Model Tax Convention should be clarified in that respect. This clarification will address how payments for e-commerce transactions should be accounted for in relation to tax treaty purposes.

Consumption Tax Issues

The Committee endorsed tentative conclusions in a report from its Working Party on Consumption Taxes, and approved its release for public comment. The report notes that it is necessary to define the principle of taxation in the place of consumption more clearly, and to identify the collection mechanisms that can best support the practical operation of that principle.

The report proposes Guidelines to define the *place of taxation* for cross-border services and intangible property by the business establishment of the recipient business for business-to-business transactions (B2B), and to the recipient's usual place of residence for business-to-consumer transactions (B2C).

Tax Administration Issues

The Committee agreed to the tentative conclusions and future work topics identified in a report on tax administration aspects of e-commerce, and approved its publication for comment. This report addresses such issues as how tax administrations can ensure effective tax collection in an electronic environment. Attention may need to focus on strengthening this cooperation internationally. The report also identifies a range of initiatives that tax administrations across the world are already taking to improve the quality of service that they provide to taxpayers.

Further Work and Future Process

The Committee recognizes that a great deal of additional work remains to be done in several fields. The release of discussion papers is an important part of that process. Principal features of its work program for 2001–2003 include:

1. On direct taxes, work should continue in the areas of:
   a. Issues associated with the accounting for profits of a server PE.
   b. Refinement of the *place of effective management* concept in determining residence for taxation purposes.
   c. Further evaluation of the adequacy of the current treaty rules in the context of electronic commerce, taking into account possible alternatives and the possible clarification or modification of the existing rules.
2. On consumption taxes, work should continue on:
   a. The feasibility of technology-based collection mechanisms.
   b. Simplification opportunities.

    c. Means of promoting more effective international administrative co-operation.

3. On tax administration issues, the Committee should:

    a. Work to strengthen the compliance tools available to tax administrations.

    b. Share *best practice* developed worldwide.

    c. Promote further taxpayer service initiatives.

4. On process, the Committee agreed on the need to continue the dialogue with business and nonmembers, through a reinforcement of the current Technical Advisory Group (TAG) process and other initiatives to encourage cooperative international debate.

Report by TAG on Treaty Characterization

The Technical Advisory Group on Treaty Characterization, which was set up in the context of the OECD work on taxation and e-commerce, released its final report early in 2000. The report explored how various types of payments for e-commerce transactions should be accounted for in applying the tax treaties.

The report, which was unanimously approved by TAG members, deals with the determination of which provisions apply to various types of e-commerce payments, thereby, ultimately determining which country may tax these payments and under what conditions.

It includes analysis, conclusions, and recommendations concerning which treaty provisions apply in particular cases, as well as the TAG's views on how such recommendations should be applied in 28 typical categories of e-commerce transactions. Some of the TAG's principal conclusions and recommendations are:

1. Transactions that permit the customer to download digital products electronically for that customer's own use or enjoyment (for instance, when a customer orders software or music from an Internet Web site and that digital product is downloaded from the site), the payment should be accounted for as business profits rather than as a royalty payment.

2. E-commerce transactions resulting in know-how payments that constitute royalties are relatively rare. The report provides a number of criteria and examples to help distinguish the provision of *services* from the provision of *know-how.*

3. Payments for time-limited use of digital products, or for transactions such as data warehousing *cannot* be considered as payments for the use of (or the right to use) industrial, commercial, or scientific equipment. This is not, therefore, to constitute royalties under some of the conventions.

4. When payment is for various elements, but one element is predominant and the others are only ancillary and unimportant, it would be more practical to apply the accounting treatment applicable to the main part to the entire payment.

The recommendations of the report (particularly the suggestions for changes to the Commentary of the OECD Model Tax Convention that it includes) will now be examined by the Committee on Fiscal Affairs with a view to making the appropriate changes quickly to the OECD Model Tax Convention. The Tax Convention was first published in 1963 and has been regularly updated since then. It is the basic reference manual used by both OECD and non-OECD countries for the negotiation, application, and interpretation of bilateral tax treaties to coordinate their direct tax systems.

The TAG was set up in 1999 by the OECD's Committee on Fiscal Affairs with the mandate "to examine the characterization of various types of electronic commerce payments under tax conventions with a view to providing the necessary clarifications." Members of the TAG included tax officials from OECD and non-OECD countries as well as representatives from the business community.

The report follows two previous drafts released by the TAG for public comment in 2000. Those earlier drafts reflected some substantial disagreements among the members of the group. The comments received helped the TAG to resolve the disagreements at its final meeting in November, 2000; thus, the unanimous approval of the final report.

HISTORY OF THE INTERNATIONAL BODY

The International Accounting Standards Committee was established in 1973 by professional accountancy bodies (including the AICPA) from nine countries to attempt to bring some degree of order, uniformity and reliability to accounting practices and procedures in developing market countries. The IASC has delivered to the International Organization of Securities Commissions a set of core accounting standards suitable for use in cross-border listings.

With the adoption of IAS 40, *Accounting for Investments,* and 39, *Financial Instruments: Recognition and Measurement,* the IASC completed the core set of Standards identified in an agreement with the IOSCO in 1993. At that point, the IASC felt confident that it had a comprehensive set of Standards covering all of the major areas of importance to general businesses.

THE CHANGING WORLD ECONOMY

The position of accounting standard setters has changed enormously since IASC's formation. Not the least important of these positions is the attitude toward IASC. The tide has turned from a rather grudging tolerance of their activities to a realization that it's important to offer input or you may find the rest of the accounting world leaving you behind.

At the time of its inception, many countries, even some with highly developed economies, had no official accounting standards or only rudimentary ones. As the IASC pointed out, the explosion of demand for global accounting standards had been set in motion. The investing public had been made aware, by headline events in the financial newspapers, of the enormous flexibility in measuring a company's results or assets and liabilities under the existing rules. In the U.S., the Securities and Exchange Commission, in particular, had embarked upon a program to tighten up the rules relating to financial statement preparation.

These problems have not *all* been fully resolved nor are they likely to be as long as there is anyone capable of painting a corporate picture in a rosier hue than it deserves. But it's up to the standard makers—nationally and internationally—to keep trying.

The Securities and Exchange Commission publicly criticized U.S. business managers for continuing to use means available to them to disguise the pattern of income or profits over time, from what it would be with unbiased measurement, to produce the appearance of a smoother trend (and all this was before Enron).

The international organization reasoned that accounting standards can limit the opportunities for earnings management and they believe the Standards finalized by IASC do so, along with those of the many national standard setters. However, they realize that strong and independent behavior by auditors and regulators can also contribute to resolving this problem to limit the degree of judgment in applying accounting Standards and their focus is likely to shift towards enforcement activities.

Evidently, they believe the SEC concern is having a beneficial effect upon progress in standard setting and enforcement by reminding one and all that these problems continue *even in the most financially sophisticated countries of the world.*

The Importance of Global Accounting Standards

The need for global accounting standards, or at a minimum for less diversity in national standards, became painfully evident in 1998. The economic difficulties that began in Asia and spread to other regions of the world rather graphically demonstrated the interdependencies of different nations in the modern global economy.

It has been suggested that part of the blame should be placed on "accounting"—or lack of it. The IASC felt that international investors lacked confidence in the accounting of the countries where the difficulties originated.

They felt that the lack of confidence made capital more expensive than it needed to be and added to the threat of serious worldwide economic recession.

As a result, the IASC is as committed as the SEC and the FASB to the belief that "comparability" and "transparency" are key words in healthy financial markets. They acknowledge that:

1. An important emphasis in the demand for global accounting standards is *comparability* among businesses in different countries to serve the demands of international capital markets.
2. Accounting standards are needed to bring about greater *transparency* and openness in financial reporting by individual countries and their business corporations and financial institutions.

The European Union

Another important development in the demand for International Accounting Standards is taking place in Europe. A key current objective of the European Union has been the development of a single economic market. The introduction of the euro on January 1, 1999 was an important step in that direction. The single economic market would almost necessitate a single capital market with companies from the different countries competing for capital on equal terms.

Those putting up the capital must be able to assess the performance of different companies with full comparability. Said comparability is not attainable if different accounting standards are used by different companies—even if they are reporting in a common currency. IASs are the crucial to this process.

From the beginning, rather than establish a separate European Accounting Standards Board, the European Commission (EC) planned to work with the IASC to standardize accounting practices for multinational companies within the European Union. The EC's preferred option for the future development of accounting in the EU was to "oblige" listed companies to follow International Accounting Standards. Other companies would follow national codes within the framework of the European directives. Now they have decided that by 2005 all listed companies must use ISAs and IFRSs.

The European Commission concluded that there are no significant conflicts between the EC Accounting Directives and those International Accounting Standards and interpretations of the Standing Interpretations Committee that are applicable to accounting periods beginning before July 1, 1998.

Completing the Core Standards

The main focus of IASC's technical work had been the completion of the core set of Standards agreed upon with IOSCO. The work program to complete the core Standards was comprised of 40 topics classified into twelve major projects. (See later in this chapter.) In that they are now completed, the emphasis has shifted to enforcement of the Standards and reorganization of the Commission.

THE STANDING INTERPRETATIONS COMMITTEE

In 1997, faced with an ever-growing list of Standards to be revised, adopted, applied, interpreted, the IASC Board set up a Standing Interpretations Committee to consider, on a timely basis, accounting issues that were likely to receive divergent or unacceptable treatment in the absence of authoritative guidance. The SIC reviewed accounting issues within the context of existing International Accounting Standards and the IASC Framework. In developing Interpretations, the SIC worked closely with similar national committees. It also sought public input before reaching a final consensus. When consensus was reached, the SIC published authoritative pronouncements on the application of IAS and recommended solutions for situations not covered by existing standards. Its function was similar to that of the FASB's Emerging Issues Task Force. That role has now been assumed by the IFRIC.

Standard-setting requires some type of committee to provide guidance on the application of Standards. IASC considers it vital that this task be undertaken at the international level, rather than being left to national groups that could undoubtedly develop conclusions that differed from country to country, even when exemplary translations are available.

THE ROLE OF IOSCO

In May 2000, IOSCO announced completion of its assessment of the accounting standards issued by the International Accounting Standards Committee. It recommended that its members allow multinational issuers to use 30 IASC standards, as supplemented by *reconciliation, disclosure,* and *interpretation* where necessary to address outstanding substantive issues at a national or regional level. These are labeled "the IASC 2000 standards."

IOSCO believes that use of these standards by multinational enterprises in preparing their financial statements will facilitate cross-border offerings and listings, and will promote the further development of internationally accepted accounting standards.

The members of IOSCO (including the U.S. Securities and Exchange Commission) undertake their own review process before they accept financial reports prepared in accordance with International Accounting Standards for cross-border listings in their own countries. Many countries have already accepted the complete list of IASs. The other members (including the SEC) are in an advanced stage of the evaluation process.

ACCOUNTING FOR DEVELOPING ECONOMIES AND EMERGING MARKETS

Increasingly, emerging market countries and their regulatory authorities have adopted, indicated their intention to adopt, and/or based their own standards on IAS.

The IASB is continuing to work on accounting systems in developing countries and countries with emerging markets. The organization is emphasizing its commitment to help these countries with the development of accounting standards. In many of the countries, International Accounting Standards are already used as national standards. Some extra Standards, modifications and/or additional guidance may be needed to assist in applying IASs and IFRSs in countries that are only now developing market economies.

When one considers that U.S. GAAP is based upon almost 150 FASB Standards, well over 300 opinions by the FASB's Emerging Issues Task Force, APB Opinions, SEC accounting and financial reporting requirements, AICPA Position papers and Industry Accounting Guides, plus assorted other documents—fewer than 35 SICs and 50 IAS Standards might provide rather thin coverage for international accounting regulation.

However, it is apparent that U.S. and non-U.S. investors, exchanges, accountants, corporate managers, CEOs, CFOs and others in international business should become knowledgeable about the IAS and the activities of the IASB because they will increasingly play a very important part in capital formation and financial accounting worldwide.

Authorized Translations

The official language of IASB is English. It is the only language in which International Accounting Standards are approved by the Board, but they are aware that it is imperative to have reliable translations available in other languages. It is quite reasonable to assume that accounting standards will not receive effective application if they are not understood. To assure the quality of any translation, IASC has developed processes for making high-quality "authorized" translations of its Standards. A poor translation could nullify the benefits of the very carefully worded original English language Standard. German, Russian, Spanish, Latvian, Portuguese, Portuguese Brazilian, Czech, French, Chinese, Romanian, Polish, Slovenian, Bulgarian and Arabic translations have been made with other widely used languages to follow.

THE GROWING ACCEPTANCE OF INTERNATIONAL STANDARDS

Many foreign companies appear willing to adopt IAS Standards while being loath to abide by U.S. GAAP. Now that many of the international standards have been tightened and more of the U.S. requirements have been adjusted to move closer to other national standards and the IASs, the more obvious advantages to complying only with the international standards may disappear.

What originally concerned much of the regulatory hierarchy in the U.S. might be dubbed the "either/or" mentality of the IASC in its attempt to provide something for everyone. (Some have suggested that this occurred primarily because of the attempt to keep both the United States and the United Kingdom happy when their Standards were often at odds.) But subsequently the differences in these accounting systems have been reduced.

But what about the attitude of various interested groups and organizations in the United States?

THE NYSE AND SECURITIES DEALERS

The New York Stock Exchange and securities dealers have been in favor of permitting foreign corporations that have adopted the international standards to be listed on U.S. exchanges even if this means having to educate the investor on remaining discrepancies between GAAP and IAS. Many of the largest 500 corporations worldwide are not listed here principally because of what the companies have considered the too onerous U.S. GAAP requirements. Listing all of those foreign corporations would result in much greater volume; even adding two or three dozen of the largest foreign firms to the NYSE listings could certainly result in a marked increase in its market capitalization.

THE FASB'S ATTITUDE

The FASB's growing involvement with the IASC (after a very tentative, if not altogether hostile, appraisal of this outside influence) is smoothing the way toward the time when both IAS and U.S. GAAP will be regarded as being acceptable and practicable global accounting standards. Understandably, the FASB is zealously guarding its power over U.S. accounting standards. It appears that the group realizes the inevitability of compromise and cooperation inasmuch as many U.S. firms and institutions had become disenchanted with some of the gyrations necessary to meet existing or proposed requirements relating to earnings per share, derivatives, hedging.

The FASB's and the IASC's efforts toward a common goal appears to have begun in earnest with the earnings per share and segment Standards. That this cooperation became a two-way street was made easier since even the FASB admitted that the IASC's—and much of the rest of the world's—approach to figuring EPS was superior to and far less convoluted than previous U.S. requirements.

Close cooperation between the two bodies has moved IAS closer to U.S. GAAP and, at the same time, U.S. GAAP is closing the gap with international accounting standards. All along, the FASB has undoubtedly had reservations about the breadth and depth of the IASC representation actively engaged in the standard-setting process. They may have worried that what could turn out to be good enough for a foreign firm would fall short of being good enough for a U.S. firm to file in the U.S.

At least this had been the perception-that the U.S. would protect GAAP regardless. Not so. The FASB has taken steps to change or nullify several of the more divergent provisions to bring them closer to IAS requirements. And now the FASB has come out explicitly in favor of the IASC's aim of establishing a single set of Standards.

Support for the New Structure

The Board believes the restructuring when completed will create an organization that is independent, objective, and structured to operate in an open, due process environment.

These were points that the FASB has emphasized all along. They had made it evident that they could not support any structure that did not embody these principles. The FASB had taken quite seriously an attempt to show how the earlier proposed structure of the revamped IASC was too full of pitfalls. Rather than merely criticize, the Board came up with a well-thought-out list of points that needed reconsideration and/or revision.

There had been informal talks (even rumors) of the FASB becoming the *de facto* international standard setter simply by default—and by the power of the U.S. economy. The Board sincerely did not want that role, and wholeheartedly pushed for an acceptable organization coming out of the IASC. "Acceptable," to the FASB, essentially meant independent. The board did not want to see an international standard-setting committee that was subject to veto or excessive power by a board of directors, nor did it want a board of part-time individuals who might feel beholden to a corporation, accounting firm or other organization.

On their part, IASC's decision follows a global debate over what organizational structure would maximize independence while considering the needs of large and small economies as well as those of the preparers and users of financial information. The FASB, while agreeing that such an organization must be created, as mentioned above, was rather critical of the earlier proposal.

The FASB's fears were somewhat ameliorated when many of their suggestions were incorporated in the last version of the plan. While admitting that the result is a compromise, the FASB considers it at least a step forward.

THE SEC's CAUTIOUS APPRAISAL

From the very beginning, the Securities and Exchange Commission displayed cautious interest in the IASC, and as a member of IOSCO supported development of international standards. But, of course, the SEC's stated purpose is to safeguard the U.S. investor—whether naive or sophisticated, but particularly the former.

The more sophisticated investor and his adviser are aware of the fact that a foreign stock or bond is not the bargain it appears to be if insufficient data has been reported to permit an intelligent analysis of the offering. Therefore, the market drives the price of the securities down and the issuing company discovers that capital raising is more costly than necessary if management is coy about revealing the full picture of the financial status of the company. (And, of course, formal adoption of the IASs will not guarantee that an entity is actually following them.)

This truth was made abundantly clear when the SEC reported situations where a registrant prepares its financial statements in accordance with home country GAAP and in its footnotes asserts that the financial statements comply in all material respects with, or are consistent with International Accounting Standards. In some of these situations, the registrant may have applied only certain International Accounting Standards or omitted certain information without giving any explanation of why the information was excluded. The SEC routinely challenges these assertions. Where the assertion cannot be sustained, the Commission requires either changes to the financial statements to conform with International Accounting Standards, or removal of the assertion of compliance with International Accounting Standards.

THE ADOPTION OF IAS 40, *INVESTMENT PROPERTY*

With the adoption of IAS 40, *Investment Property,* to become effective on or after January 1, 2001, all of the basic core topics listed by IOSCO have now been covered.

IAS 40 concerns investment property held by all enterprises and will not be limited to enterprises whose main activities are in this area. Investment property is property (land or a building—or part of a building—or both) held (by the owner or by the lessee under a finance lease) to earn rentals or for capital appreciation or both. Investment property does not include:

1. Property held for use in the production or supply of goods or services or for administrative purposes.
2. Property being constructed for third parties.
3. Property held for sale in the ordinary course of business.
4. An interest held under an operating lease if the interest was a long-term interest acquired in exchange for a large up-front payment.

Under IAS 40, an enterprise must choose either:

1. A fair value model in which investment property should be recognized in the income statement.
2. A cost model, the same as the benchmark treatment in IAS 16, *Property, Plant, and Equipment.* Investment property should be measured at depreciated cost (less any accumulated impairment losses). An enterprise that chooses the cost model should disclose the fair value of its investment property.

The Standard requires an enterprise to apply the model chosen to all its investment property. A change from one model to the other model to the other model should be made only if the change will result in a more appropriate presentation. The standard states that this is highly unlikely to be the case for a change from the fair value model to the cost model.

In exceptional cases, an enterprise that has chosen the fair value model may conclude that it cannot determine the fair value of an investment property. In such cases the enterprise measures that investment property using the benchmark treatment in IAS 16 until the disposal of the investment property. The residual value of the investment property should be assumed to be zero. The enterprise measures all of its other investment property at fair value.

Selected IASC Standards with Comparisons to U.S. GAAP

The following are recently adopted international standards, several of which have been prepared in cooperation with the U.S. or other English speaking standard setting bodies. Each of them covers an important aspect of accounting that has been uppermost in the minds of concerned standard setters. Each of these discussions pinpoints the relationship between the international standard and the relevant GAAP accounting treatment.

IAS 33, *Earnings per Share*

The objective of the FASB and IASC earnings per share standards is to prescribe principles for the determination and presentation of earnings per share that will lead to global harmonization of earnings per share measurements and disclosures. To this end, both standard setters have concluded where appropriate two earnings per share figures should be presented, namely,

1. Basic Earnings Per Share, which is computed by dividing income available to stockholders by the weighted average number of common shares outstanding during the period. Shares issued during the period and shares reacquired during the period should be weighted for the portion of the period they were outstanding.

2. Diluted Earnings Per Share, which is computed in a similar manner to basic earnings per share after adjusting the numerator and denominator of the calculation for the effects of all potential dilutive common shares that were outstanding during the period. One difference between FASB 128, *Earnings per Share,* and IAS 33 is a matter of degree. FASB 128 requires disclosure of per-share figures for income from continuing operations on the face of the income statement and for extraordinary items, accounting changes and discontinued operations. The international standard requires only net profit per-share amounts on the face of the income statement but also encourages other disclosures.

   The IASC and FASB also differ in their view of the objective of a diluted earnings per share presentation. The IASC views the figures as an early warning to investors of possible reductions in the value of EPS while the FASB sees it as a measure of performance rather than an indicator of the future. However, except for some language differences, the basic provisions of IAS 33 are substantially the same as those of FASB 128. (These provisions are discussed more fully in connection with FASB 128 in Chapter 1.)

It is anticipated that IAS 33 will be adopted by:

1. Many countries as a national standard.
2. Stock exchanges for listing purposes.
3. Corporations with a global stock ownership.

These adoptions will be a significant contribution to facilitating global investing in common stocks.

IAS 34, *Interim Financial Reporting*

IAS 34 *Interim Financial Reporting* requires that companies that prepare interim reports apply the same accounting recognition and measurement principles used in their last annual statements. This requirement will tend to make interim earnings more volatile for non-U.S. companies that heretofore had followed U.S.-style interim reporting rules. U.S. rulings permit some interim income smoothing recognition and measurement practices. The statement also specifies that measurements in interim financial statements should be made on a financial year-to-date basis.

It does not mandate that interim reports be published in the first place, who should publish them, how often they should be prepared, or how soon they should appear after the end of an interim reporting period, if they are prepared. The IASC decided these matters were better left to the discretion of the national governments, securities regulators, stock exchanges, and accounting organizations. At present, in at least 30 countries, the securities regulators and stock exchanges do, in fact, require interim reporting. Interim reports are used by investors and creditors to check for any signs of weakness—or strength, for that matter.

IAS 34 applies to recognizing, measuring, and disclosing assets, liabilities, income, and expenses for quarterly, biannual, or any other type of interim report.

The United Kingdom's Accounting Standards Board (ASB) recently issued a nonmandatory "best practice" statement on interim reporting that is almost identical to the IASC standard. Both use the discrete method for interim reporting. Under this method, as amplified below, the interim period is treated as an accounting period distinct from the annual period. Incomplete transactions are reported, using the same principles that are used for the annual reports.

This statement will get close scrutiny from many sources including U.S. investors and creditors with worldwide interests. Interim financial reports issued by foreign companies do not conform to APB 28, *Interim Financial Reporting*. This new standard also differs in a number of significant areas from U.S. GAAP. However, U.S. accountants, investors, and financial advisors are already aware of the fact that the accounting used for interim financial reporting purposes in many countries outside of the U.S. is considerably different from U.S. GAAP. The foreign standards are similar in many respects to IAS 34.

Below is a comparison of a few of the provisions to U.S. GAAP governing interim financial reports included in Accounting Principles Board APB 28. (A discussion of other information relating to U.S. GAAP can be found in Appendix E.)

Independent Theory. IAS 34 for the most part adopts the independent theory of interim reporting. This approach regards each interim period as a discrete or "stand-alone" reporting period. That is, the events and transactions within each accounting period are to be reported in the accounting period, regardless of its length. Under the independent view, the results of operations for each interim period should be determined basically in the same manner as if the interim period were an annual accounting period. Under this approach, deferrals, accruals, and estimations at the end of each interim period are determined by following basically the same approach as in the annual reports. Thus, if an expenditure is expensed in the annual statement, it should be expensed in any interim report, regardless of the amount of the expenditure and the relationship to the annual amount or the revenues of other interim periods for that year.

Dependent Approach.   APB 28 generally follows the dependent theory of interim period reporting. This approach regards each interim period as an integral part of the annual period. According to the dependent view, interim financial data are an integral part of the annual period, and it is essential to provide investors with timely information on the progress the entity is making in realizing its annual results of operations. Therefore, the usefulness of interim data rests on the predictive relationship that it has to the annual report. Thus, each interim period should be regarded as an integral part of the annual period rather than a discrete period standing on its own.

Under this approach, deferrals, accruals, and estimations at the end of each interim period are affected by predictions about the results of operations for the remainder of the year. Thus, for example, a portion of an estimated annual expenditure that might be expensed for the entire annual period might be accrued or deferred at the end of an interim period as management allocates the estimated annual expense between interim periods on a basis that reflects time, sales volume, or production activity.

Other Differences.   If fully aware of the important differences between the two alternative interim financial reporting approaches, the user of the financial reports should be able to make an intelligent analysis of the information presented. Some of those differences are presented below:

Dependent/Independent.   Because the dependent approach gives accounting flexibility in managing interim earnings to minimize any possibility that the figures might give a misleading picture of the company's current and future performance, company management probably prefers it.

Some users believe that the dependent approach properly applied gives a better indication of a company's annual results, earnings volatility, and risks when the company is geared to such things as seasonal ups and downs of irregular sales, income and expenses. Here the independent approach may result in interim financial reports that overstate the level of risk and volatility associated with the company's actual annual earnings picture.

On the other hand, there are others who are quite sure that the independent approach produces a clearer and more timely picture of coming events in a company's financial prospects.

Mandated/Suggested.   The new Statement does not require companies complying with IAS in their annual reports to publish interim financial reports.

The IASC, however, has indicated that it intends to strongly encourage governments, security regulators, stock exchanges, international bodies, and accounting standard setters to require companies whose debt or equity securities are publicly traded to provide interim financial reports that conform to IAS 34 principles. The IASC will also encourage publicly traded companies to provide interim reports complying with the Statement's principles at least at the end of the first six months of their financial year.

U.S. GAAP does not mandate publication of interim financial reports; however, the Securities and Exchange Commission and the stock exchanges do require listed companies to publish them for the first three quarters of the fiscal year.

When interim financial reports are published, both IAS 34 and U.S. practice require that they include:

1. Condensed balance sheet.
2. Condensed income statement.
3. Condensed cash flow statement.
4. Footnote disclosures focusing on changes since the last annual report in accounting principles or estimates, unusual events, trends, and turning points.

Costs.   According to APB 28, costs and expenses that are not allocated or associated directly with product and service revenues may be expensed as incurred or allocated among interim periods based on an estimate of time expired, benefit received, or other activity associated with the period.

IAS 34 requires costs that are incurred unevenly during a company's financial year be anticipated or deferred for interim reporting only if it is appropriate to anticipate or defer those costs at the end of the financial year. An example of costs that often fall into this category are periodic major maintenance or retooling projects.

Comparability.   In the final analysis, even though the interim financial statements may look alike, the operating results for the period under the IASC proposal of a discrete approach and the U.S. GAAP integral approach will not be comparable because of the different concepts. At the same time, comparison of operating results among U.S. companies is not always possible because of discretionary accounting differences permitted for certain items under APB 28.

IAS 35, *Discontinuing Operations*

This Standard's objectives are to establish a basis for segregating information about a major operation that an enterprise is discontinuing from information about its continuing operations and to specify minimum disclosures about a discontinuing operation.

IAS 35 is a presentation and disclosure Standard that focuses on how to present a discontinuing operation in an enterprise's financial statements and what information to disclose. It does not establish any new principles for deciding when and how to recognize and measure the income, expenses, cash flows, and changes to assets and liabilities relating to a discontinuing operation. Instead, it requires that enterprises follow the recognition and measurement principles in other International Accounting Standards.

Definition of a Discontinuing Operation.   A discontinuing operation is considered in IAS 35 to be a component of an enterprise:

1. That the enterprise, pursuant to a single plan, is:
   a. disposing of substantially in its entirety,
   b. disposing of piecemeal, or
   c. terminating through abandonment.
2. That represents a separate major line of business or geographical area of operations.
3. That can be distinguished operationally and for financial reporting purposes.

Thus, a discontinuing operation is a relatively large component of an enterprise—such a business or geographical segment under IAS 14, *Segment Reporting*—that the enterprise, pursuant to a single plan, is disposing of substantially in its entirety or is terminating through abandonment or piecemeal sale.

The new Standard requires that disclosures about a discontinuing operation begin earlier, after the *earlier* of the following:

1. An enterprise has entered into an agreement to sell substantially all of the assets of the discontinuing operation.
2. The board of directors or other similar governing body has both approved and announced a detailed plan for discontinuance.

Disclosure Requirements.   Required disclosures include:

1. Description of the discontinuing operation.
2. The business or geographical segment(s) in which it is reported in accordance with IAS 14, *Segment Reporting*.
3. The date that the plan for discontinuance was announced.
4. The timing of expected completion (date or period), if known or determinable.

5. The carrying amounts of the total assets and the total liabilities to be disposed of.
6. The amounts of revenue, expenses, and pretax profit or loss from ordinary activities attributable to the discontinuing operation during that specific reporting period, and the related income tax expense.
7. The amount of any gain or loss that is recognized on the disposal of assets or settlement of liabilities attributable to the discontinuing operation, and related income tax expense.
8. The net cash flows attributable to the operating, investing, and financing activities of the discontinuing operation.
9. The net selling prices received or expected from the sale of those net assets for which the enterprise has entered into one or more binding sale agreements, and the expected timing thereof, and the carrying amounts of those net assets.

Further Considerations.   Financial statements for periods after initial disclosure must update those disclosures, including a description of any significant changes in the amount or timing of cash flows relating to the assets and liabilities to be disposed of or settled and the causes of those changes.

The disclosures would be made if a plan for disposal is approved and publicly announced after the end of an enterprise's financial reporting period but before the financial statements for that period are approved. The disclosures continue until completion of the disposal.

To improve the ability of users of financial statements to make projections, comparative information for prior periods presented in financial statements prepared after initial disclosure must be restated to segregate the continuing and discontinuing assets, liabilities, income, expenses, and cash flows.

Comparison to U.S. GAAP.   IAS 35 brings another of IASC's accounting standards closer to U.S. GAAP in that the IASC's standards now actually include a discontinuing operation standard—similar in many respects to the comparable U.S. GAAP standard, Accounting Principles Board Opinion 30 (APB 30).

However, as in most instances, this standard does vary slightly from GAAP. Two examples follow:

1. APB 30 requires the results of discontinuing operations to be reported on the face of the financial statements while IAS 35 only recommends this approach to disclosure.
2. While IASC emphasizes the timeliness of its required initial disclosure event, APB's requirement would very probably occur earlier than IAS 35's requirement. The initial disclosure event specified in IAS 35 is a

binding sales agreement or board of director's approval of a *detailed discontinuing operations plan* and a formal announcement of that plan. On the other hand, APB 30 specifies that the initial disclosure event is the date on which management having authority to approve the discontinuance commits to a formal plan to dispose of a segment of the business.

More Uniform Approach. Since many developing economies (as well as other more advanced ones) do not have specific guidance relating to discontinuing operations accounting, it is probable that the issuance of IAS 35 will inspire a number of them to adopt it outright or to develop their own national standard which will closely follow the requirements of IAS 35. Regardless, a more uniform approach to reporting discontinuing operations should result. As an additional inducement to use the principles of this Standard, appendices to IAS 35 provide illustrative disclosures and guidance on how prior period information should be restated to conform to the presentation requirements of IAS 35.

IAS 36, *Impairment of Assets*

International Accounting Standard 36, *Impairment of Assets,* prescribes the accounting and disclosure requirements specifically for impairment of:

1. Goodwill.
2. Intangible assets and property.
3. Plant and equipment.

The Standard includes requirements for identifying an impaired asset, measuring its recoverable amount, recognizing or reversing any resulting impairment loss, and disclosing information on impairment losses or reversals of impairment losses.

It prescribes how an enterprise should test its assets for impairment; that is:

1. The procedures that an enterprise should apply to ensure that its assets are not overstated in the financial statements.
2. How an enterprise should assess the amount to be recovered from an asset (the "recoverable amount").
3. When an enterprise should account for an impairment loss identified by this assessment.

The Standard does *not* cover accounting and disclosure requirements for:

1. Inventories.
2. Deferred tax assets.

3. Assets arising from construction contracts.
4. Assets arising from employee benefits.
5. Most financial assets.

Requirements of IAS 36. According to this IAS, an impairment loss should be recognized whenever the recoverable amount of an asset is less than its carrying amount (sometimes called "book value"). The Standard spells out in detail the procedures to follow when this occurs:

1. The recoverable amount of an asset is defined as the higher of:
   a. Net selling price as measured by the amount obtainable from the sale of the asset in an arm's length transaction between knowledgeable, willing parties, less the cost of disposal.
   b. Value in use as measured by the present value of the asset's estimated future cash flows including disposable cash flows, if any, expected to arise from its continuing use and eventual disposal. The discount rate should be a pretax rate that reflects current market assessments of the time value of money and the risks specific to the asset.
2. An impairment loss should be recognized as an expense in the income statement for assets carried at cost and treated as a revaluation decrease for assets carried at revalued amount.
3. An impairment loss should be reversed and income recognized when there has been a *change* in the estimates used to determine an asset's recoverable amount after the last impairment loss was recognized.
4. The recoverable amount of an asset should be estimated whenever there is an indication that the asset may be impaired. IAS 36 includes a list of indicators of impairment to be considered at each balance sheet date. In some cases, the IAS applicable to an asset may include requirements for additional reviews.
5. In determining value in use, an enterprise should use:
   a. Cash flow projections based on reasonable and supportable assumptions that reflect the asset in its current condition and represent management's best estimate of the set of economic conditions that will exist over the remaining useful life of the asset.
   b. Estimates of future cash flows should include all estimated future cash inflows and cash outflows except for cash flows from financing activities and income tax receipts and payments.
   c. A pretax discount rate that reflects current market assessments of the time value of money and the risks specific to the asset. The discount rate should not reflect risks for which the future cash flows have been adjusted.

6. If an asset does not generate cash inflows that are largely independent from the cash inflows from other assets, an enterprise should determine the recoverable amount of the cash-generating unit to which the asset belongs. IAS 36 provides explicit directions concerning these cash-generating units:

   a. "Cash-generating unit" refers to the smallest identifiable group of assets that generates cash inflows which are largely independent of the cash inflows from other assets or group of assets.

   b. The requirements for recognizing and reversing impairment losses for a cash-generating unit are the same as those for an individual asset.

   c. The concept of cash-generating units should often be used in testing assets for impairment because, in many cases, assets work together rather than in isolation.

   d. In addition, IAS 36 provides information on how to identify the cash-generating unit to which an asset belongs and further requirements on how to measure an impairment loss for a cash-generating unit and then allocate the loss between the assets of the unit.

7. Reversal of impairment losses also comes in for extensive consideration:

   a. An impairment loss recognized in prior years should be reversed if, and only if, there has been a change in the estimates used to determine recoverable amount since the last impairment loss was recognized.

   b. An impairment loss should only be reversed to the extent the reversal does not increase the carrying amount of the asset above the carrying amount that would have been determined for the asset (net of amortization or depreciation) had no impairment loss been recognized.

   c. An impairment loss for *goodwill* should be reversed only if the specific external event that caused the recognition of the impairment loss reverses.

   d. A reversal of an impairment loss should be recognized as income in the income statement for assets carried at cost and treated as a revaluation increase for assets carried at revalued amount.

8. When impairment losses are recognized or reversed, an enterprise should disclose certain information by *class of assets* and by *reportable segments*. Further disclosure is required if impairment losses recognized or reversed are *material* to the financial statements of the reporting enterprise as a whole.

Upon first adoption of IAS 36, its requirements should be applied *prospectively* only; that is, prior periods will *not* be restated.

IASC-UK Cooperation.   IAS 36 differs materially in a number of instances from U.S. Generally Accepted Accounting Principles (U.S. GAAP) and the asset impairment rules of a number of other countries. On the other hand, there are aspects of the international standard that are closer to the provisions of other established national standards.

For example, in developing IAS 36, proposals of the Accounting Standard Board (ASB) in the United Kingdom for a Financial Reporting Standard (FRS) on impairment of assets were closely monitored by the international body. The ASB and the IASC shared the same objectives for their project, and many of their views regarding requirements coincided. Therefore, the resulting standards are very similar.

Furthermore, IAS 36 provides a standard approach to the recognition, measurement, and disclosure of asset impairments by non-U.S. companies that use IAS in financial statements and also furnishes a model for the many developing economies which have not yet adopted an asset impairment standard of their own, but look often to IASC for guidance.

The IASC considers this an important step forward from the requirements and guidance for impairment losses that were previously included in their Standards. They point out that it provides more details on how to perform an impairment test and it eliminates certain alternatives, such as the option not to use discounting in measuring recoverable amount. (The "options" in many of the older IASs have been particularly worrisome to the SEC, the FASB and other standard-setting bodies.)

Differences from GAAP. As mentioned above there are a number of significant differences between IAS 36 and U.S. GAAP specified in FASB 121, *Accounting for the Impairment of Long-Lived Assets and for Long-Lived Assets to Be Disposed Of.*
Differences between the two Standards include:

1. Probably most significantly, FASB 121 *does not permit reversal* of asset impairment losses as does IAS 36—along with much of the rest of the accounting world. (It might be pointed out here that there seems to be little global consensus yet about how to account for asset impairment. Some countries have rulings similar to GAAP, others to the new IAS, others to the old IAS. Still others have standards relating to assessment of recoverability, not valuation; many have no standard at all on impairment. On the other hand, many of the emerging nations will undoubtedly adopt IAS 36.)

2. GAAP requires a *quantitative test* of asset impairment before the measurement and recognition of an asset impairment loss is necessitated. This involves figuring the expected cumulative net cash flows from continuing use of the asset, not including interest and not to be discounted less than the asset's carrying amount. IAS 36 does not include this type of test.

3. IAS 36 does not distinguish between assets to be held and used and assets to be disposed of when measuring impairment loss; FASB 121 has different impairment loss measurement approaches for the two categories.
   a. FASB 121's measurement of the impairment loss of an asset *to be used* is the difference between the asset's carrying amount and its fair value.
   b. FASB 121 measurement of the impairment loss of an asset *to be disposed of* is the asset's carrying amount less its net realizable value.
   c. IAS 36's measurement of *either* impairment loss is the asset's carrying amount less the higher of its value in use or its net realizable value (fair value minus disposal costs).
4. FASB 121 relies on *management judgment* to determine the appropriate future cash flow period and cash flows to determine the equivalent of IAS 36's value in use. Unless management can justify otherwise, IAS 36 limits the maximum future cash flow period to five years and specifies the growth rate in cash flows.

IAS 37, *Provisions, Contingent Liabilities and Contingent Assets*

IAS 37, *Provisions, Contingent Liabilities and Contingent Assets* requires that:

1. Provisions should be recognized in the balance sheet only when:
   a. An enterprise has a present obligation (either legal or constructive) as a result of a past event;
   b. More likely than not a transfer of economic benefits will be required to settle the obligation;
   c. The amount of the obligation can be measured reliably.
2. Provisions should be measured in the balance sheet at the best estimate of the expenditure required to settle the present obligation at the balance sheet date. This is the amount that an enterprise would rationally pay to settle the obligation, or to transfer it to a third party, at that date. When measuring provisions, an enterprise should take into account any risks and uncertainties. However, uncertainty does not justify the creation of excessive provisions or a deliberate overstatement of liabilities—in other words, the "big bath."

   An enterprise should discount a provision where the effect of the time value of money is material and should take future events, such as changes in the law and technological changes, into account where there is sufficient objective evidence that they will occur.
3. The amount of a provision should not be reduced by gains from the expected disposal of assets (even if the expected disposal is closely linked

to the event giving rise to the provision) or by expected reimbursements—from insurance contracts, indemnity clauses, suppliers' warranties and the like. When it is virtually certain the reimbursement will be received if the enterprise settles the obligation, the reimbursement should be recognized as a separate asset.

4. A provision should be used only for expenditures for which the provision was originally recognized and should be reversed if an outflow of resources is no longer probable.

IAS 37 sets out three specific applications of these general requirements:

1. A provision *should not be recognized* for future operating losses.
2. A provision *should be recognized* for an onerous contract in which the unavoidable costs of meeting the obligations under the contract are greater than the expected economic benefits.
3. A provision for restructuring costs *should be recognized only* when an enterprise has a detailed formal plan for the restructuring and has raised a valid expectation in those affected that it will carry out the restructuring by starting to implement that plan or announcing its main features to those affected by it; for this purpose, a management or board decision is not enough.

A restructuring provision should exclude costs—such as retraining or relocating continuing staff, marketing or investment in new systems and distribution networks—that are not necessarily entailed by the restructuring or that are not associated with the enterprise's ongoing activities.

IAS 37 replaces part of IAS 10, *Contingencies and Events Occurring After the Balance Sheet Date.* It prohibits the recognition of contingent liabilities and contingent assets. An enterprise should disclose a contingent liability, unless the possibility of an outflow of resources embodying economic benefits is remote, and disclose a contingent asset if an inflow of economic benefits is probable.

UK-IASC Cooperative Effort.   Here again, the IASC and the UK's Accounting Standards Board worked in close conjunction to develop virtually identical accounting standards. Their aim is to eliminate many of the questionable accounting practices that have been developing.

One of the most obvious is the "big bath" mentioned above and included in the "hocus pocus" practices that the SEC feels has been sullying the financial reporting process here—as well as globally. (The ploy is to report excessive liabilities currently to make future profits look even rosier at the time the liabilities are actually being incurred.)

Global Aspects. On the global front, the standards should help to lessen the diversity of provision recognition and measurement practices that have evolved along with varying accounting regulations and tax treatment of provisions. Not only do these standards cut down on the welter of provisions that were previously provided for in financial statements prepared according to UK and IAS principles, but they also move much closer to U.S. GAAP (contained in FASB 5, *Accounting for Contingencies*).

Some technical differences between GAAP and the two standards are slight enough that they should pose no problem in doing comparative valuations of U.S. and non-U.S. companies. Since provisions can significantly affect a company's balance sheet and net income, reducing the divergence in the handling of "provisions" should be considered an important step in harmonization of global accounting practices, particularly when considering the fact that many countries that have no established procedure for handling provisions and contingencies—or very haphazard ones—will now adopt IAS 37.

IAS 38, *Intangible Assets*

IAS 38 applies to all intangible assets that are not specifically handled in other IASs. Included in the lists of things it does deal with are the accounting for expenditures on advertising, training, start-up activities, research and development activities (R&D), mortgage servicing rights, customer lists, licensing agreements, motion picture patents, and copyrights. It also covers expenditures for computer software that is an integral part of a tangible asset.

The Standard does *not* apply to intangible assets covered by other IASs; financial instruments; mineral rights and expenditures for the exploration, development, and extraction of minerals, oil, natural gas—nonregenerative resources; insurance contracts.

Among those intangible assets covered by another IAS are deferred tax assets, intangible assets held for sale in the ordinary course of business, leases, employee benefits, and goodwill arising from a business transaction.

IAS 38 includes transitional provisions that clarify when the Standard should be applied retrospectively and when it should be applied prospectively.

Requirements of IAS 38. The basic features of IAS 38 include:

1. An intangible asset should be recognized initially, at cost, in the financial statement whether it has been acquired externally or generated internally, if, and only if:
   a. it is probable that the future economic benefits attributable to the asset will flow to the enterprise;
   b. cost of the asset can be measured reliably;

c. the asset falls within the classification of an *intangible* asset; that is, it is *an identifiable nonmonetary asset without physical substance held for use in the production or supply of goods or services, for rental to others, or for administrative purposes.*

2. If an intangible item does not meet both the definition and the criteria for the recognition of an intangible asset, IAS 38 requires the expenditure on this item to be recognized as an *expense* when it is incurred. An enterprise is not permitted to include this expenditure in the cost of an intangible asset at a later date.

3. Therefore, it becomes evident from the recognition criteria that all expenditures on research should be recognized as an expense. The same treatment applies to start-up costs, training costs, and advertising costs. IAS 38 also specifically prohibits the recognition as assets of internally generated goodwill, brands, mastheads, publishing titles, customer lists and such. However, as mentioned above, occasionally developmental expenditure may result in the recognition of an intangible asset—some internally developed computer software, for example.

4. In accounting for a business combination that is an acquisition, IAS 38 works in combination with IAS 22, *Business Combinations*. This reinforces the stipulation that if an intangible item does not meet both the *definition* and the *criteria* for the recognition as an intangible asset, the expenditure for this item which was included in the cost of acquisition should form part of the amount attributed to goodwill at the date of acquisition.

    Therefore, according to this Standard, purchased R&D-in-process should not be recognized as an expense immediately at the date of acquisition, but it should be recognized as part of the goodwill recognized at the date of acquisition and amortized under IAS 22 (rev.), unless it meets the criteria for separate recognition as an intangible asset.

    IAS 22 (rev.) provides that if there is sufficient evidence that the useful life of goodwill will exceed 20 years, an enterprise should amortize the goodwill over its estimated useful life and:

    a. Test goodwill for impairment at least annually in accordance with IAS 36, *Impairment of Assets.*

    b. Disclose the reasoning behind the presumption in the initial recognition that the useful life of goodwill would not exceed 20 years, and specify the factor(s) that were significant later in determining the useful life of goodwill.

        IAS 22 (rev.) does not permit an enterprise to assign an infinite useful life to goodwill.

5. Requires that after initial recognition in the financial statement, an intangible asset be measured under either the *benchmark treatment* or the allowed *alternative treatment.*

a. The benchmark treatment is historical cost less any amortization and impairment losses. It is consistent with the GAAP approach.

b. The allowed alternative treatment is the revalued amount based on fair value minus any subsequent amortization and impairment losses. However, this treatment is permitted if, and only if, fair value can be determined by reference to an active market for the intangible asset—which is fairly unlikely for *intangible* assets.

The Standard defines fair value of an asset as the amount for which that asset could be exchanged between knowledgeable, willing parties in an arm's-length transaction.

Comparison to GAAP.   IAS 38 and the comparable GAAP are similar in many respects. There are some major differences, but even here the FASB and the SEC are looking into revisions in some areas. Current differences include:

1. Here again, an international standard differs from U.S. GAAP on the revaluation issue: IAS 38 permits revaluation; GAAP does not.
2. GAAP requires that an intangible asset's amortization period not exceed forty years. IAS 38 specifies a maximum twenty-year amortization period. This is rebuttable if a longer amortization period can be justified. (The FASB has now voted to cut to twenty years the write-off time for goodwill from an acquisition.)
3. GAAP does not require an active market-based valuation for internally generated intangible assets; IAS does.
4. Except for computer software development, GAAP does not permit capitalization of development costs. On the other hand, IAS 38 requires capitalization of development costs in certain cases.

IAS 39, *Financial Instruments: Recognition and Measurement*

In March, 1999, IASC announced that it had published a comprehensive standard on accounting for financial instruments after nine years' effort and four public comment documents. This new Standard, IAS 39, *Financial Instruments: Recognition and Measurement,* will take effect for annual financial statements covering periods beginning on or after January 1, 2001. Earlier application is permitted as of the beginning of a fiscal year that ends after March 15,1999. Retrospective application is not permitted.

Financial instruments include conventional financial assets and liabilities, such as cash, trade receivables and payables, investments in debt and equity securities, and notes, bonds, and loans payable. Financial instruments also include derivatives such as futures, forwards, swaps, and option contracts.

Background. IAS 39 has been in development by IASC since 1989. Its "final" form was preceded by exposure drafts in 1991, 1994, and 1998 and by a steering committee discussion paper in 1997. In 1996, IASC adopted *Financial Instruments: Disclosure and Presentation* (IAS 32) pending completion of a standard on recognition and measurement. IAS 39 expands those disclosures and resolves the accounting questions, including the important area of accounting for hedging transactions.

IASC officials emphasized their belief that IAS 39 fills the biggest void in global accounting standards. They pointed out that of their 104 member countries only the United States has adopted a truly comprehensive standard on recognition and measurement of financial instruments and hedge accounting (FASB 133).

Need for Greater Uniformity. With the phenomenal growth of global trading (and the equally amazing growth of imaginative derivatives which are often not recognized in the financial statements), IASC suggests that investors sometimes get very unwelcome surprises when losses surface.

The IASC is aware that current accounting practices for financial instruments vary widely around the world, with the result being noncomparability and investor confusion. Even when financial assets such as investments have been recognized on the balance sheet, some companies have measured them at cost, others at lower of cost or market, and still others at fair value.

Further, in the absence of hedge accounting standards, companies often have postponed recognizing any changes in the fair values of financial instruments or, if recognized, companies have deferred the profit-or-loss effects of such changes in the balance sheet. IAS 39 addresses these and other shortcomings of current practice.

Many developing economies are adopting the International Accounting Standards outright or using them as a basis for developing their own national standards. It is probable that not only they, but also many of the developed economies, will progress to more comprehensive accounting standards for financial instruments, including derivatives. After all, both the FASB and the IASC have spent years going over the ground trying to find an effective solution to satisfy all segments of the business and financial world.

IAS 39 does not go as far in accounting for certain financial instruments as U.S. GAAP, but it does move the international standards closer. It should also reduce the global diversity of financial instrument accounting practices, particularly those dealing with debt and equity security instruments, derivatives, and hedges.

Principal Requirements. IAS 39 requires that all financial assets and all financial liabilities, including all derivatives, be recognized on the balance sheet. This means that derivatives can no longer be off-balance-sheet items.

Initially, financial assets and liabilities will be measured at cost, including transaction costs. After initial recognition, most financial assets must be remeasured at fair value; however, the following will be carried at amortized cost subject to a test for impairment:

1. Loans and receivables originated by the enterprise and not held for trading.
2. Other fixed maturity investments, such as debt securities and mandatorily redeemable preferred shares, that the enterprise intends and is able to hold to maturity.
3. Financial assets whose fair value cannot be reliably measured (limited to some equity instruments with no quoted market price and some derivatives that are linked to and must be settled by delivery of such unquoted equity instruments).

After acquisition, most liabilities will be measured at original recorded amount less principal repayments and amortization. Only derivatives and liabilities held for trading (such as short sales of securities) will be remeasured to fair value.

To record the complete amount of periodic unrealized fair value changes an enterprise will have a single, enterprise-wide option to either:

1. Recognize the entire amount in income; or
2. Recognize in income only those changes in fair value relating to financial assets and liabilities held for trading, with the value changes for nontrading instruments reported in equity until the financial asset is sold, at which time the realized gain or loss is reported in net profit or loss. For this purpose, derivatives are always deemed held for trading unless they are part of a hedging relationship that qualifies for hedge accounting.

Hedge Accounting.   The IASC considers hedging, for accounting purposes, as designating the change in value of a derivative, or in limited circumstances a nonderivative financial instrument, as an offset, in whole or in part, to the change in fair value or cash flows of a hedged item. A hedged item can be an asset, liability, firm commitment, or forecasted future transaction that is exposed to risk of change in value or changes in future cash flows. Hedge accounting recognizes the offsetting effects on net profit or loss symmetrically.

Thus, hedge accounting is permitted under IAS 39 in certain circumstances, provided that the hedging relationship is *clearly defined, measurable, and actually effective.*

IAS 39, like FASB 133, recognizes and defines three types of hedges although they are not identical.

1. Fair value hedge: a hedge of the exposure to changes in the fair value of a recognized asset or liability (such as a hedge of exposure to changes in the fair value of fixed rate debt as a result of changes in interest rates). To the extent that the hedge is effective, the gain or loss from remeasuring the hedging instrument at fair value is recognized immediately in net profit or loss.

   At the same time, the gain or loss on the hedged item adjusts the carrying amount of the hedged item and is recognized immediately in net profit or loss.

2. Cash flow hedge: a hedge of the exposure to variability in cash flows attributable to a recognized asset or liability (such as all or some future interest payments on variable rate debt) or a forecasted transaction (such as an anticipated purchase or sale). A hedge of an unrecognized firm commitment to buy or sell an asset at a fixed price in the enterprise's reporting currency is accounted for as a cash flow hedge even though it has a fair value exposure. To the extent that the gain or loss on the effective portion of the hedging instrument is recognized initially, it is recorded directly in equity. Subsequently, that amount is included in net profit or loss in the same period or periods during which the hedged item affects net profit or loss (for example, through cost of sales, depreciation, or amortization). For hedges of forecasted transactions, the gain or loss on the hedging instrument will adjust the basis (carrying amount) of the acquired asset or liability.

3. A hedge of a net investment in a foreign entity (as defined in IAS 21, *The Effects of Changes in Foreign Exchange Rates*): These are accounted for as cash flow hedges.

As we have seen above, hedge accounting is permitted when the hedging relationship is clearly defined, measurable, and actually effective. The enterprise must designate a specific hedging instrument as a hedge of a change in value or cash flow of a specific hedged item, rather than as a hedge of an overall net balance sheet position. However, the approximate income statement effect of hedge accounting for an overall net position can be achieved, in some cases, by designating part of one of the underlying items as the hedged position.

Derecognition. In addition, IAS 39 establishes conditions for determining when control over a financial asset or liability has been transferred to another party. For financial assets a transfer normally would be accounted for as a sale (derecognized) when:

1. The transferee has the right to sell or pledge the asset.
2. The transferor does not have the right to reacquire the transferred assets unless either the asset is readily obtainable in the market or the reacquisition price is fair value at the time of reacquisition.

With respect to derecognition of liabilities, the debtor must be legally released from primary responsibility for all or part of the liability either judicially or by the creditor. If part of a financial asset or liability is sold or extinguished, the carrying amount is split based on relative fair values. If fair values are not determinable, a cost recovery approach to profit recognition is taken.

Additional Disclosure Requirements. IAS 39 moves international requirements a big step in the direction of greater transparency. The principal disclosure requirements for financial instruments include:

1. Description of methods and assumptions used in estimating fair values.
2. Disclosure of whether purchases of financial assets are accounted for at trade date or settlement date.
3. Description of the enterprise's financial risk management objectives and policies.
4. For each category of hedge: a description of the hedge; which financial instruments are designated as hedging instruments; and the nature of the risks being hedged.
5. Disclosure of significant items of income and expense and gains and losses resulting from financial assets and financial liabilities, and whether they are included in net profit or loss or as a separate component of equity and, if in equity, a reconciliation of movements in and out of equity;
6. Explanation of details of securitization and repurchase agreements.
7. Description of the nature, effect, and reasons for reclassifications of financial assets from amortized cost to fair value.
8. Explanation of the nature and amount of any impairment loss or reversal of an impairment loss.

A Stop-Gap Solution. Even though IAS 39 goes a long way toward fair value accounting, the IASC considers it only a partial step. The Board decided not to require fair value measurement for the originated loans and receivables or for held-to-maturity investments at this time for a number of reasons:

1. Too drastic a change from current practice would be required in many jurisdictions.
2. The existence of portfolio linkage of those assets, in many industries, to liabilities that, under IAS 39, will continue to be measured at their amortized original amount. Banks, for example, say that they manage their depositor liabilities in tandem with their portfolios of mortgage and commercial loans.

3. Some question the relevance of fair values for financial assets intended to be held until maturity, particularly if fair value changes enter into measuring net profit or loss.

The resulting standard should probably be considered a stop-gap measure published to meet the deadline the IASC had set to submit the core set of standards to IOSCO. As noted, it also serves, at least to a certain extent, to answer the urgent need in many countries for a comprehensive financial instruments standard. While it is similar in many respects to U.S. GAAP, IAS 39 needs more work to raise it to the level of quality the IASC seeks in its standards. (As a matter of fact, there is still considerable debate about whether FASB 133 is the final word on financial instrument accounting and disclosure in this country.)

INTERNATIONAL ACCOUNTING STANDARDS

Following is a list of the International Accounting Standards currently in force or issued recently and not yet effective. Basically, they are the core group of international standards necessary for cross-border filings. Where an IAS has been superseded by a subsequent International Accounting Standard, it is not listed.

IAS 1, *Presentation of Financial Statements*
IAS 2, *Inventories*
IAS 7, *Cash Flow Statements*
IAS 8, *Net Profit or Loss for the Period, Fundamental Errors and Changes in Accounting Policies*
IAS 10, *Events After the Balance Sheet Date*
IAS 11, *Construction Contracts*
IAS 12, *Income Taxes*
IAS 14, *Segment Reporting*
IAS 15, *Information Reflecting the Effects of Changing Prices*
IAS 16, *Property, Plant and Equipment*
IAS 17, *Leases*
IAS 18, *Revenue*
IAS 19, *Employee Benefits*
IAS 20, *Accounting for Government Grants and Disclosure of Government Assistance*
IAS 21, *The Effects of Changes in Foreign Exchange Rates*
IAS 22, *Business Combinations*
IAS 23, *Borrowing Costs*
IAS 24, *Related Party Disclosures*
IAS 26, *Accounting and Reporting by Retirement Benefit Plans*

IAS 27, *Consolidated Financial Statements and Accounting for Investments in Subsidiaries*

IAS 28, *Accounting for Investments in Associates*

IAS 29, *Financial Reporting in Hyperinflationary Economies*

IAS 30, *Disclosures in the Financial Statements of Banks and Similar Financial Institutions*

IAS 31, *Financial Reporting of Interests in Joint Ventures*

IAS 32, *Financial Instruments: Disclosure and Presentation*

IAS 33, *Earnings per Share*

IAS 34, *Interim Financial Reporting*

IAS 35, *Discontinuing Operations*

IAS 36, *Impairment of Assets*

IAS 37, *Provisions, Contingent Liabilities and Contingent Assets*

IAS 38, *Intangible Assets*

IAS 39, *Financial Instruments: Recognition and Measurement*

IAS 40, *Investment Property*

IAS 41, *Agriculture*

Chapter 6

The International Federation of Accountants

CONTENTS

IPSASs Set Standards for Governments and Public Sector Bodies	**6.02**
New Accounting Standards for the Public Sector	**6.03**
The IFAC Board Takes Actions to Improve Accountability of Accountants	**6.05**
Establishment of Forum of Firms	**6.07**
Structure and Requirements of the Forum of Firms	**6.07**
IFAC Comments on the GAAP 2001 Report	**6.10**
Accounting Firms' GAAP 2000 Report	**6.11**
Implementing Projects of the IFAC	**6.12**
The IFAD and Its Vision	**6.13**
The IFAC Joins the XBRL Consortium	**6.13**
The International Auditing Practices Committee	**6.15**
Management Accountants and Their Value to Organizations	**6.21**
Code of Ethics Features New Independence Rules	**6.23**
Education Committee Releases EDs and Guideline	**6.24**
Addressing Accountant Competencies	**6.26**
IT Monitoring Guidelines on Risk	**6.27**
IFAC Issues New Paper on E-Business	**6.28**
IFAC Moves Against Money Laundering	**6.29**
Small and Medium-Sized Practices and Enterprises	**6.30**

The History of the IFAC   **6.31**
IFAC and IASC Relationship   **6.31**
Two Separate International Organizations   **6.31**
Comparison to U.S. Organizations   **6.32**
Quality Assurance   **6.32**
Financial and Management Accounting Committee   **6.33**
International Auditing Practices Committee (IAPC)   **6.33**
Information Technology Committee (ITC)   **6.37**
IFAC Forms Coalition to Advance Accountancy Development   **6.37**
Accountancy's Fight Against Corruption   **6.40**
International Public Sector Accounting Standards—
    Accrual Accounting   **6.43**

The North Atlantic Treaty Organization (NATO) announced in August 2002 that it is adopting the International Public Sector Accounting Standards (IPSASs) developed by the International Federation of Accountants' (IFAC's) Public Sector Committee for its financial statements starting January 1, 2006.

NATO also reported that most of the 14 NATO entities are adopting IPSASs even sooner than 2006. They may begin using them in January 2003 or 2004. There appears to be a groundswell of movement toward international accounting and auditing standards by diverse groups worldwide.

IPSASs SET STANDARDS FOR GOVERNMENTS AND PUBLIC SECTOR BODIES

IPSASs set out the requirements for financial reporting by governments and other public sector organizations with the ultimate objective of enhancing the accountability and financial management of governments worldwide. The Public Sector Committee receives funding from:

1. The World Bank.
2. United Nations Development Program.
3. Asian Development Bank.
4. International Monetary Fund.

Thus far, the Committee has developed 18 IPSASs as part of its *comprehensive* Standards Project to assist governments in reporting comparable, relevant, and understandable financial information.

The Organization for Economic Cooperation and Development (OECD) has adopted IFAC's International Public Sector Accounting

Standards for its own financial reporting. Its 2000 financial statements were audited against these standards. IFAC feels that the adoption of the standards will strengthen the accountability and transparency of NATO financial statements and that other entities around the world will be encouraged to adopt IPSASs.

Working Group on NATO Accounting Standards

NATO's adoption of IPSASs was based on a recommendation from a Working Group on NATO Accounting Standards that was charged with developing a comprehensive set of NATO accounting principles and standards covering all transactions and activities conducted by the Alliance. The primary objective was to harmonize accounting standards and reporting formalities across NATO. The Working Group reviewed existing accounting standards promulgated by nations and other international organizations and ultimately recommended IPSASs. The next step will be to see that the standards are actually utilized and enforced.

NEW ACCOUNTING STANDARDS FOR THE PUBLIC SECTOR

The Public Sector Committee released five new IPSASs in December 2001 and another in June 2002. The newer IPSASs are as follows:

- IPSAS 13—*Leases.* This standard prescribes for both lessees and lessors the appropriate accounting policies and disclosures to apply in relation to finance and operating leases. It includes guidance on the classification of leases, disclosures to be made in the financial statements of lessees and lessors, and accounting for sale and leaseback transactions.
- IPSAS 14—*Events After the Reporting Date.* This standard prescribes when an entity should adjust its financial statements for events that occur after the reporting date and the disclosures that it should make about other "non-adjusting" events that occur after the reporting date.
- IPSAS 15—*Financial Instruments: Disclosure and Presentation.* This standard prescribes how financial instruments are to be classified and identifies disclosures to be made in general purpose financial statements.
- IPSAS 16—*Investment Property.* This standard prescribes requirements for accounting for investment property, including the initial and subsequent measurement and disclosure of such property by governments and their agencies.
- IPSAS 17—*Property, Plant and Equipment.* This standard prescribes requirements for the initial recognition and measurement of property, plant and equipment. It also deals with subsequent measurement, depreciation, and disclosures about these assets. The standard provides a

transitional period to support the orderly implementation of its requirements and allows but does not require heritage assets to be recognized in
general-purpose financial statements.

- IPSAS 18—*Segment Reporting*. This standard establishes principles for
  reporting financial information about distinguishable activities of a gov-
  ernment or other public sector entity appropriate for:
  - —Evaluating the entity's past performance in achieving its objectives.
  - —Identifying the resources allocated to support the major activities of
    the entity.
  - —Making decisions about the future allocation of resources.

At the same time, a *Glossary of Defined Terms* was also published. The
Glossary is a useful reference because it compiles in one document the terms
defined in the 18 IPSASs released thus far by the Public Sector Committee.

These last documents, too, were issued as part of the Committee's ongoing project to develop a comprehensive body of international accounting standards for governments and their agencies around the world. A complete list of
the IPSASs is included at the end of this chapter.

The Public Sector Committee adopts a transparent due process for the
development of IPSASs that enables interested parties to monitor and provide
comment to the Committee on proposed IPSASs during the IPSAS development stage. (A brief synopsis of the 12 earlier IPSASs is at the end of this
chapter.)

Study to Assist Public Sector Entities' Transition from Cash to Accrual Basis

The Public Sector Committee has also released Study 14, *Transition to the
Accrual Basis of Accounting: Guidance for Governments and Government
Entities*. This new study identifies key issues to be addressed in the transfer
from the cash to the accrual basis of accounting and alternative approaches
that can be adopted when implementing the accrual basis in an efficient and
effective manner in the public sector.

It also identifies key requirements of IPSASs and other relevant sources
of guidance to assist in the transition from the cash basis to the accrual basis.
The Committee believes that governments and governmental entities will find
Study 14 a useful tool in dealing with complex issues necessary to implement
an accrual system. IFAC refers to the study as a "living document" that will be
updated periodically as further IPSASs are issued, and additional implementation issues and experiences are identified.

The new study contributes to the ongoing body of guidance being developed by the Public Sector Committee to enhance the accountability and

financial management of governments worldwide. As mentioned, the Committee has, thus far, developed 18 IPSASs to assist governments applying accrual accounting *to report comparable, relevant and understandable financial information.*

Some Governments Are Not Ready for Accrual Basis

The Public Sector Committee also recognizes that many governments are not yet in a position to adopt the accrual-based IPSASs. To assist these governments, the Committee has also developed an exposure draft called ED 9, *Financial Reporting under the Cash Basis of Accounting.* ED 9 sets out the requirements for the presentation of the primary financial statement under the cash basis of accounting, as well as the statement's structure and minimum content requirements. The Committee is considering field-testing this document before final release.

Standards Project—Other Guidance

Study 11, *Governmental Financial Reporting: Accounting Issues and Practices,* has been approved by the Public Sector Committee. The purpose of the Study is to make it as comfortable as possible for governments to prepare their financial reports in a usable, comparable fashion. It contains a detailed description of the common bases of accounting used by governments and provides examples of actual financial statements prepared under each basis.

The Committee is also progressing toward developing three additional accrual IPSASs to add to the 18 already in place.

IPSASs Based on the IASB's Standards

The Standards Project is a multiyear initiative with the objective of improving financial reporting in the public sector by developing a series of prescriptive standards and some associated descriptive guidance on existing government practices. Improved financial reporting will contribute to better decision making, financial management and accountability by governments.

The IPSASs are based largely on the International Accounting Standards (IASs, now International Financial Reporting Standards) developed by the International Accounting Standards Committee (now Board).

THE IFAC BOARD TAKES ACTIONS TO IMPROVE ACCOUNTABILITY OF ACCOUNTANTS

The theme of IFAC'S Board meeting in Madrid in July 2002 was "Rebuilding Public Confidence." During the meeting, the Board took actions to advance a number of public interest initiatives. In effect, this was a further demonstration of their concern expressed in the previous Board meeting in March 2002 (discussed below) about the profession's image in the face of the continuing reports of accounting irregularities. As a result:

1. The Board agreed to revise quality control standards for audit engagements and for firms performing such engagements.

2. They also approved the formal establishment of the Forum of Firms for firms that conduct or plan to conduct transnational audits. Members of the Forum must be willing to participate in international quality assurance and discipline programs as well as comply with IFAC's International Standards on Auditing and Code of Ethics.

3. Additionally, the Board also agreed to revise the requirements for IFAC member bodies regarding the establishment and maintenance of quality assurance programs for firms of practicing accountants. These programs require regular monitoring of quality control standards such as skills and competence of the firm's personnel, supervision of personnel and the acceptance and retention of clients.

4. The Board noted the adoption of the major provisions contained in IFAC's Code of Ethics for Professional Accountants by the European Union, other non-European Union countries and some accountancy institutes. They agreed to become more active in encouraging the early adoption of the Code, particularly its independence rules, and to communicate the value of the Code to members in business, especially accountants involved in the preparation of financial statements.

5. Finally, in an effort to make International Standards on Auditing more widely available to the world's accountants, thus assisting them in providing high quality work, the Board agreed that all final pronouncements issued by the International Auditing and Assurance Standards Board (IAASB) would be available free through the IFAC Web site effective January 1, 2003.

IFAC Aims to Restore Faith in Accounting Profession

At its March 2002 meeting in Tunisia, IFAC focused on advancing initiatives to strengthen the international accountancy profession. These initiatives included approval or completion of the following:

1. A project focused on restoring the credibility of financial statements in the global marketplace. The project will address worldwide problems, issues, and best practices in the areas of financial and business reporting, corporate governance and auditor performance. It will be developed by a task force comprised of members representing IFAC, audit committees, boards of directors, the investment community and financial management.

2. Inclusion of practicing accountants, academics and representatives of the business community and the public (governmental) sector in the newly formed IAASB to ensure increased transparency in the auditing standards-setting process.

3. The Board completed its discussions on the central provisions of the constitution of the Forum of Firms. Formal approval of the constitution is expected in the next few months. Membership in the Forum is open to firms that conduct transnational audits and requires a commitment to adhere to IFAC's auditing, ethics and quality control standards.

ESTABLISHMENT OF FORUM OF FIRMS

Twenty-three international accountancy firms met in London in January 2001 to develop a Global Quality Standard for firms conducting transnational audits. The intention was to ensure consistent, high-quality auditing practices worldwide as a means of protecting the interests of cross-border investors and other economic decision-makers. Their efforts were aimed at promoting global financial market stability. The IFAC sponsored the meeting, and the firms operate as a new section of IFAC known as the Forum of Firms.

The launch of the Forum of Firms is a significant step in implementing the IFAC's plan to strengthen its role as the global standard-setting, self-regulatory, and representational body for the profession's audit and assurance-related services. It is hoped that commitment to the obligations of membership in the Forum will raise the standard of the international practice of auditing and will better serve the interests of the users of the profession's services.

Globalization of business and commerce has *highlighted the inadequacy of financial reporting and auditing in accordance with purely national standards.* Decision makers need assurance that the financial information on which they base their decisions is transparent, consistent, comprehensive, and comparable across national boundaries. Through their commitment to a Global Quality Standard, audit firms that are members of the Forum of Firms should be able to provide this assurance.

STRUCTURE AND REQUIREMENTS OF THE FORUM OF FIRMS

Membership in the Forum of Firms is open to any firm that has been, or is interested in, accepting transnational audit appointments, provided the firm:

1. Agrees to conform to the Forum's Global Quality Standard.
2. Agrees to subject its assurance work to periodic external quality assurance reviews.

It would be safe to assume that the Forum's Global Quality Standard is likely to require:

1. Having audit policies and a methodology for conducting transnational audits in accordance with International Standards of Auditing.
2. Compliance with the IFAC Code of Ethics.
3. Training programs to keep partners and staff up to date on international developments in financial reporting.
4. Maintaining quality control standards and conducting regular quality assurance reviews to monitor compliance with the firm's policies and methodology.

The creation of the Forum of Firms is one prong of a four-pronged program to restructure and strengthen IFAC. The other three aspects of the program are:

1. The introduction of a program for monitoring the compliance of IFAC member bodies with IFAC standards.
2. The strengthening of the processes and broadening of the membership of the International Auditing Practices Committee, which sets International Standards on Auditing.
3. The establishment of an International Public Oversight Board to oversee the activities of IFAC and the Forum of Firms that affect the public interest.

Constitution of the Forum of Firms Approved

Forum of Firms membership consists of firms that (1) perform audits of financial statements that may be used across national borders, and (2) as mentioned, voluntarily agree to meet certain requirements. Commitment to the obligations of membership in the FOF should contribute to raising the standards of the international practice of auditing in the interest of users of the profession's services.

IFAC Board's approval of the Forum Constitution demonstrates the group's ongoing commitment to promoting consistent and high quality standards of financial reporting and auditing practices worldwide, they believe. Having approved the Constitution, the next major step is to agree on a framework and guidelines for the Forum's quality assurance process.

There are currently 23 provisional members of the Forum of Firms, including the largest accounting firms. They will be admitted to full membership upon demonstrating adherence to the Forum's Quality Standard through satisfactory completion of the quality assurance requirement.

Structure of the Forum

The Forum conducts its business primarily through the Transnational Auditors Committee, an IFAC committee whose members have been nominated by the members of the Forum. As suggested earlier, a Public Oversight Board (POB) will oversee the public interest activities and related governance and infrastructure of IFAC, particularly in the areas of audit standard setting, ethics, membership obligations and quality assurance. The Public Oversight Board will be independent of the profession.

ED on Guidelines for Performing and Reporting on Global Peer Reviews

The Transnational Auditors Committee (TAC) is an executive committee of IFAC dedicated to representing and meeting the needs of the members of the Forum. It is a key component of the international self-regulatory regime adopted by IFAC and plays a major role in encouraging member firms to meet high standards in the international practice of auditing.

Role and Responsibilities

The Transnational Auditor's Committee will:

1. Develop, maintain, and administer a global peer review program to assess the consistency of the policies and practices of members of the Forum of Firms with the Forum's Quality Standard.
2. Encourage the adoption of internationally recognized standards of accounting and auditing.
3. Regularly review issues relevant to auditors with transnational clients and provide supplementary guidance of interest to those firms.
4. Propose observers to participate on other key IFAC committees and work closely with other IFAC committees on matters of interest to Forum members.
5. Supervise the provision of additional technical material regarding the specifics of transnational work necessary to supplement the guidance already issued by IFAC.

TAC has created a Global Peer Review Subcommittee to develop the procedures and oversee the process of global peer review for members of the Forum of Firms.

IFAC COMMENTS ON THE GAAP 2001 REPORT

The *GAAP 2001* report, released by the seven largest accountancy firms, represents another critical step toward encouraging the harmonization of international standards and ultimately, the establishment of a single global financial framework, IFAC contends. In the face of all the problems confronting the accounting profession today, they believe the development of such a framework is vital to the efficient operation of global capital markets.

The report compared national accounting standards with International Financial Reporting Standards (IFRSs; formerly IASs) in 62 countries—9 more than in last year's report. It also included an analysis of changes and progress made in each country since the *GAAP 2000* report was issued. The 62 countries surveyed represent more than 95% of the world's Gross National Product and stock market capitalization. Among the significant findings are the following:

1. About one-third of the countries surveyed are showing progress in closing the gap between national and international standards.
2. About half of the countries surveyed have not implemented or proposed standards to reduce the difference.
3. Most of the major differences can be attributed to a relatively small number of standards, perhaps eight in all.
4. One of the most important differences centers on *related-party disclosure,* which is of great interest to investors and parties interested in good corporate governance.

The report also pointed out that as a result of major changes in international standards that are being considered, the *differences between national and international accounting standards will increase* unless standards setters redouble their efforts to keep pace with the changes.

Globalization of business and commerce has highlighted the inadequacy of financial reporting and auditing in accordance with purely national standards. Decision makers need assurance that the financial information on which they base their decisions is transparent, consistent, comprehensive and comparable across national boundaries. To meet this need, countries, with the support of government, standard setters and regulators, must make convergence of high-quality accounting standards a priority, IFAC emphasized.

In addition to supporting the initiatives of the International Accounting Standards Board and the firms responsible for the *GAAP 2001* report, IFAC is undertaking a number of actions to foster compliance with and convergence of international standards in four other key areas:

1. Auditing,
2. Ethics,

3. Education, and
4. Public sector accounting.

Through the newly created Forum of Firms, IFAC is also leading the development of an international self-regulatory regime for firms performing transnational audits. Such firms will be required to comply with IFAC's International Standards on Auditing and other IFAC pronouncements.

ACCOUNTING FIRMS' GAAP 2000 REPORT

The IFAC acknowledged the importance of the major accounting firms' new report, *GAAP 2000: A Survey of National Accounting Rules in 53 Countries*, issued in January 2001. The IFAC believes the report is a critical first step in understanding the current international accounting environment. The organization believes this documentation should assist the accounting profession in understanding its vital role in improving worldwide accounting practices.

The report delineates comparisons of each of the 53 sets of national accounting rules against International Accounting Standards (IASs). The study permits easy comparison against a benchmark. Diverse groups can benefit from the study. Investors need to be aware that standards differ from one country to the next. This study should underline the caution necessary in the understanding of cross-border use of financial reports. Governments, regulators, standard setters, international organizations and NGOs (nongovernmental organizations) also will find the report informative in that it provides a "snapshot" of the situation as of the end of 2000.

The *GAAP 2000* report is one part of a worldwide undertaking to address the World Bank President's challenge to the accounting profession to "Push the agenda for international harmonization of accounting standards to meet the needs of the global marketplace." This challenge was issued at the World Congress of Accountants to emphasize to preparers and users of financial statements the deleterious impact of weak reporting in an economy that is increasingly global and increasingly reliant on information.

This challenge led to the creation, by IFAC and the World Bank, of the International Forum on Accountancy Development (IFAD). It, in turn, has created the partnership necessary to encourage improvement in global accounting and auditing practices. It brings together the key international players in the field of accounting including the regulators, the major accounting firms, investors, and such organizations as the International Accounting Standards Committee (IASC), the Bank for International Settlements (BIS), the World Bank, regional development banks, the International Monetary Fund (IMF), the Organization for Economic Cooperation and Development (OECD), the United Nations Conference on Trade and Development

(UNCTAD) and others. Each has a critical role to play in improving the quality of financial reporting around the globe. The first step in achieving IFAD's program was to assess the state of accounting internationally. The major firms' report was prepared in response to this need.

IMPLEMENTING PROJECTS OF THE IFAC

The IFAC, as the representative of the international accountancy profession, has as a key component of its strategy, the creation of a global partnership that will achieve significant enhancement of the standard and consistency of global financial reporting and auditing. This partnership comprises:

1. The participants in IFAD, referred to earlier.
2. Governments and the public sector around the world.
3. The European Commission.
4. Regulators and other representatives of investor and other stake-holder interests.
5. International and national accounting and auditing standard-setters.
6. The 156 accountancy bodies in 114 countries that constitute the membership of IFAC.
7. The private sector.

With this in mind, the IFAC has enlisted its member bodies (representing more than two million accountants around the world), and the other participants listed above in implementing a strategy designed to deliver its mission. Simply stated, this mission is the worldwide development and enhancement of an accountancy profession with harmonized standards, able to provide services of consistently high quality in the public interest.

This program includes:

1. Further development of the grouping of firms engaged in transnational audit work (the Forum of Firms).
2. The executive arm, known as the Transnational Audit Committee (TAC).
3. A new IFAC Public Oversight Board that oversees the public interest activities of IFAC.
4. An IFAC Compliance Committee that will monitor compliance by member bodies with the duties of membership, and work closely with the TAC.
5. A comprehensive review of the processes of the International Auditing Practices Committee (IAPC) to ensure that it meets public expectations and delivers its work program.

IFAC believes that these initiatives that they have embarked upon, in partnership with the World Bank, regulators, other agencies, the major firms, and member bodies present a challenge to all participants. They are of critical importance in developing global capital markets in a way that will create a safe, well-ordered environment for investors and other stakeholders. At the same time, their work should increase public confidence in the accountancy profession and its services.

THE IFAD AND ITS VISION

The IFAC strengthening program, in turn, fits into the broader initiative to improve the quality of financial reporting and auditing around the world that is being implemented under the auspices of the International Forum on Accountancy Development. This organization brings together, as already mentioned, more than 30 international public and private organizations, including those representing the accounting profession, regulators, standard-setters, development banks and agencies, governments, and users and preparers of financial information.

IFAD was first presented with a "vision" for improving financial reporting and auditing on a worldwide basis in June 1999. IFAD participants endorsed the initiative at their meeting in October 1999. After 18 months of consensus-building and planning, it is now taking concrete form. IFAC considers the agreement to move ahead on the Forum of Firms to be a significant milestone. The coming year will see more, equally important implementation steps. Success will necessarily depend upon the commitment of all the interested parties represented in IFAD. (To learn more of IFAD, see the "History" section later in this chapter.)

THE IFAC JOINS THE XBRL CONSORTIUM

IFAC is a member of the consortium of organizations that are actively contributing resources and funding to ensure the success of XBRL. XBRL stands for eXtensible Business Reporting Language. More than 140 companies and professional organizations representing all sectors of global business have joined forces to develop XBRL. The purpose is the preparation and exchange of business reports and data. The initial goal of XBRL is to provide an XML-based framework that the global business information supply chain will use to create, exchange, and analyze financial reporting information including, but not limited to, general ledger information, regulatory filings such as annual and quarterly statements, audit schedules and tax schedules.

XBRL, which is freely licensed, will facilitate the automatically ex-changed and reliable extraction of financial information among various soft-ware applications anywhere in the world. The XBRL Specification and the first taxonomy for financial reporting of commercial and industrial companies un-der U.S. GAAP was released on July 31, 2000. This was a major milestone for the XBRL framework since it allows for the creation of XML-based financial statements using XBRL.

Value of XBRL

The XML-based language automatically and transparently tags each segment of computerized business information with an identification code or marker. These markers remain with the information regardless of how the information is formatted or rearranged by a browser or within software applications.

Before XBRL, no generally accepted format for reporting business data existed. The labor-intensive task of entering and reentering data into computer applications results in substantial costs and the all-too-likely risk of data entry errors. The use of XBRL streamlines this process, potentially lowering costs while helping to ensure the integrity and quality of the data.

With XBRL, once financial information is created and formatted the first time, the data can be rendered in any form; for example:

- A printed financial statement.
- An HTML document.
- A regulatory filing document.
- A raw HML file.
- Credit reports.
- Loan applications.

All of these applications can be created without manually keying information in a second time or reformatting the data.

XBRL does not change existing accounting standards, nor does it require companies to disclose additional information. Instead, it simply enhances the accessibility and usability of the financial information that companies are re-quired to report, according to IFAC.

XBRL Leads to Better Dissemination of Information

By providing easier access to accurate company financial data and more efficient analysis capabilities, XBRL will add value for anyone who creates or accesses an organization's business data. Ultimately, XBRL benefits all users in the financial information supply chain:

- Public and private companies.
- The accounting profession.
- Regulators.
- Analysts.
- The investment community.
- Capital markets.
- Lenders.
- Key third parties—software developers and data aggregators.

IFAC believes that by providing accurate and reliable information, XBRL gives industry leaders access to better information available. Ultimately, it will enable company management to more quickly access information stored in different places within the organization and to move that information both within the company and externally to their shareholders.

With less time spent on translation and data entry, financial advisors and investors, large and small, can devote more time to analysis and can perhaps screen more companies for investment opportunities. This can benefit those companies in the investment community that typically might not make it onto the investor's radar screen.

XBRL should help financial services companies to collect and update information about borrowers, automate reports to regulators and distribute or collect information related to loan portfolio sales and purchases.

Accountancy institutes worldwide consider the development of XBRL as a natural next step in the clarification and development of the fundamental language of business and a vital tool for enhancing the access and breadth of financial information available to the investing public. Additionally, XBRL will help to position accountants as valued knowledge providers and financial advisors for their clients or firms. By helping businesses leverage their use of emerging technologies such as XBRL, accountants can expand their professional opportunities and value in the marketplace, IFAC contends.

THE INTERNATIONAL AUDITING PRACTICES COMMITTEE

This committee appears to be doing its share of the work to shore up the IFAC image and standards with a multitude of projects including these publications:

1. *The Auditor's Report on Financial Statements* (Revision to ISA 700).
2. *The Auditor's Responsibility to Consider Fraud and Error in an Audit of Financial Statements.*

3. *Auditing Derivative Financial Instruments.*
4. *Assurance Engagements.*

An International Standard on Auditing

In March, 2001, IFAC proposed changes to its standard on audit reports to require the auditor to state clearly the financial reporting framework being used to prepare financial statements. IFAC's International Auditing Practices Committee has recommended these revisions to the International Standard on Auditing (ISA) 700, *The Auditor's Report on Financial Statements,* so that users may better understand the context under which the auditor's opinion is expressed.

Globalization of markets has meant that financial statements are increasingly used by foreign investors and analysts, hence clear labeling of the particular accounting and auditing frameworks is essential.

The IAPC has previously required that the auditor's report should identify which country's accounting principles have been used in audited financial statements where that is not evident. The IAPC is amending the requirement now in an effort to transform what is currently *best practice* into standard practice (*mandatory?*).

The changes to the Standard will become effective for audits of financial statements for periods ending on or after September 30, 2002.

Roles of Auditors and Bank Supervisors

Few would deny that banks play a central role in the economy:

1. They hold the savings of the public.
2. They provide a means of payment for goods and services.
3. They finance the development of business and trade.

To perform these functions securely and efficiently, individual banks must command the confidence of the public and those with whom they do business. The stability of the banking system, national and international, has, therefore, come to be recognized as a matter of general public interest. This public interest is reflected in the way banks in all countries (unlike most other commercial companies) are subject to supervision by central banks and/or specific official agencies.

In February 2001, IFAC issued for consideration, *The Relationship Between Banking Supervisors and Banks' External Auditors,* developed by the

Basel Committee on Banking Supervision and IFAC's International Auditing Practices Committee.

The tasks and responsibilities of bank supervisors and external auditors, as well as the challenges they face, have become increasingly demanding as the business of banking has become even more complex at both the national and international levels. The Basel Committee and IAPC share the view that a greater mutual understanding between banking supervisors and external auditors of each other's tasks and responsibilities improves the effectiveness of bank audits and supervision to the benefit of both disciplines, as well as the public at large.

The purpose of the proposed new International Auditing Practice Statement (IAPS) is to provide information and guidance on how the relationship between bank auditors and supervisors can be strengthened to mutual advantage, taking into account the Basel Committee's Core Principles for Effective Banking Supervision.

Specifically, this proposed Statement:

1. Describes the primary responsibilities of the board of directors and management.
2. Examines the essential features of the role of external auditor.
3. Examines the essential features of the role of supervisors.
4. Reviews the relationship between the supervisor and the auditor.
5. Describes additional ways in which auditors and the auditing profession can contribute to the supervisory process.

Both the Basel Committee and IAPC recognize that because the nature of the relationship between auditors and bank supervisors varies significantly from country to country, the guidance may not be applicable in its entirety to all countries. Nevertheless, it will provide a useful clarification of the respective roles of the two professions in the many countries where significant working relationships exist, or where the relationship is currently under study.

Both IAPC and the Basel Committee take into consideration the comments received in developing final guidance. The Statement on the relationship is expected to be published before the end of 2001.

The Basel Committee on Banking Supervision is a committee of banking supervisory authorities established by the central bank Governors of the Group of Ten countries in 1975. It consists of senior representatives of bank supervisory authorities and central banks from Belgium, Canada, France, Germany, Italy, Japan, Luxembourg, the Netherlands, Spain, Sweden, Switzerland, the United Kingdom and the United States.

Audits of Banks Are the Subject of New International Guidance

To assist auditors in addressing the unique issues associated with bank audits and to enhance the effectiveness of bank audits worldwide, at the new year, 2002, IFAC released two new International Auditing Practice Statements:

1. *Audits of the Financial Statements of Banks and the Relationship Between Banking Supervisors.*
2. *Banks' External Auditors.*

The IAPC has made it a priority to update its guidance in this area because banks play a vital role in economic life. The continued strength and stability of the banking system is a matter of general public interest. Therefore, the new practice statements highlight the tasks, responsibilities, and challenges facing external auditors and bank supervisors. They also consider special reporting relationships between auditors and bank supervisory and other regulatory authorities.

IAPS 1006, Audits of Bank Financial Statements.   This IAPS was issued after consultation with the Basel Committee on Banking Supervision (the Basel Committee), and focuses on the various stages of the audit of a bank with emphasis on those matters that are either peculiar to, or of particular importance in, such an audit. Also included are appendices that contain examples of:

1. Typical internal control procedures and substantive audit procedures for two of the major operating areas of a bank—lending and treasury operations.
2. Financial ratios commonly used in the analysis of a bank's financial condition and performance.
3. Risks and issues in securities operations, private banking and asset management.
4. Typical warning signs of fraud.

IAPS 1004, The Relationship Between Banking Supervisors and Banks' External Auditors.   This standard has been developed in conjunction with the Basel Committee. It provides information on how the relationship between bank auditors and supervisors can be strengthened to mutual advantage, taking into account the Basel Committee's *Core Principles for Effective Banking Supervision.* Specifically, this IAPS:

1. Describes the primary responsibilities of the board of directors and management.

2. Examines the essential features of the role of external auditor.
3. Examines the essential features of the role of supervisors.
4. Reviews the relationship between the supervisor and the auditor.
5. Describes additional ways in which auditors and the auditing profession can contribute to the supervisory process.

Both the Basel Committee and IAPC recognize that because the nature of the relationship between auditors and bank supervisors varies significantly from country to country, the guidance may not be applicable in its entirety to all countries. Nonetheless, it will provide a useful clarification of the respective roles of the two professions in the many countries where significant working relationships exist or where the relationship is currently under study, they believe.

Both IAPSs were exposed for comment for over a year. The IAPC and Basel Committee received valuable comments from auditors, banking supervisors, and banking organizations. As a result of this input, the practice statements include a better explanation of their approach, purpose, and scope, and a clearer delineation of the respective responsibilities and duties of the external auditor and the banking supervisor, according to the organizations.

An ISA on Auditing Fair Value Measurements Is Announced

In August 2002, to address the increasing number of complex accounting pronouncements containing measurement and disclosure provisions based on fair value, IFAC's International Auditing and Assurance Standards Board (IAASB) announced development of a new International Standard on Auditing entitled *Auditing Fair Value Measurements and Disclosures.* The ISA addresses audit considerations relating to the valuation, measurement, presentation and disclosure for material assets, liabilities and specific components of equity presented or disclosed at fair value in financial statements. Specifically, the ISA provides information on:

1. Understanding the entity's process for determining fair value measurements and disclosures and relevant control procedures.
2. Assessing the appropriateness of fair value measurements and disclosures.
3. Using the work of an expert.
4. Testing the entity's fair value measurements and disclosures.
5. Evaluating the results of audit procedures.
6. Management's process for determining fair value and management representations.
7. Communication with those charged with governance.

The appendix to the ISA discusses fair value measurements and disclosures under different financial reporting frameworks.

The organization emphasizes that it is important that auditors obtain sufficient audit evidence that fair value measurements and disclosures are in accordance with the entity's identified financial reporting framework as changes in fair value measurements that occur over time may be treated in different ways under different financial reporting frameworks.

Guidance on Fraud

In March 2001, the International Auditing Practices Committee approved two new documents: an updated International Standard on Auditing on fraud and error, and a new International Auditing Practice Statement on auditing derivatives.

The ISA, *The Auditor's Responsibility to Consider Fraud and Error in an Audit of Financial Statements,* updates and expands previous IAPC guidance. It applies to audits of financial periods ending on or after June 30, 2002. The Standard:

1. Emphasizes that when planning and performing an audit procedure, the auditor should consider the risk of material misstatements in the financial statements resulting from fraud and error.
2. Emphasizes the distinction between management fraud and employee fraud.
3. Expands the discussion of fraudulent financial reporting.
4. Includes guidance on the need to obtain management's assessment of the risk of fraud.
5. Clarifies the discussion of the inherent limitations of an audit's ability to detect fraud.

Guidance on Derivatives

The IAPS, *Auditing Derivative Financial Instruments,* provides guidance to the auditor in planning and performing auditing procedures for assertions about derivative financial instruments. The focus of the practice statement is on auditing derivatives held by end users, including banks and other financial sector entities when they are the users.

In addition to addressing auditor responsibilities with respect to assertions about derivatives, the statement also addresses:

1. Responsibility of management and those charged with governance.
2. The key financial risks.

3. Risk assessment and internal control, including the role of internal auditing.
4. Various types of substantive procedures and when they should be used.

Guidance on Assurance Services

The changing information needs of businesses and consumers are resulting in increased demands for the audit to extend beyond the traditional attest function into assurance services. The IFAC, through its International Auditing Practices Committee, is taking a leadership role in supporting the accountant as a provider of these services by developing standards and guidance in areas where the opinion of the independent auditor can add value and credibility to the information provided by directors and management. The Committee has issued the first International Standard in this area—*Assurance Engagements*—setting out guidance for professional accountants and standards for practitioners providing a broad range of assurance services.

MANAGEMENT ACCOUNTANTS AND THEIR VALUE TO ORGANIZATIONS

A major study released by IFAC's Financial and Management Accounting Committee in June 2002, presents a global, best-practice perspective on management accounting. Contemporary management accounting is an integral part of the management process focused on the effective use of resources in ongoing value creation by organizations. The study highlights the competences related to best practice in management accounting and the competences required of those taking key roles in this field of management.

Entitled *Competency Profiles for Management Accounting Practice and Practitioners,* the study builds on competency standards developed by IFAC member bodies and expands on the groundbreaking International Management Accounting Practice Statement 1, *Management Accounting Concepts.*

The study elaborates competency standards and related assessment methodologies for both management accounting practice and management accounting practitioners. The competency standards are illustrated by profiling contemporary issues related to:

1. Management practices in organizations.
2. Membership of professional associations.
3. Preparatory and continuing education associated with management practice and professional membership.

Those Toward Whom the Study Is Directed

Those who can benefit from the study and the benchmark competency standards it illustrates include:

1. Organizations seeking to move toward best practice in management accounting.
2. Professional accountants seeking to focus their work or develop their careers in the sphere of management accounting.
3. Educators, as they seek to focus and develop curricula that will contribute to the preparation of persons seeking to work in this domain of management.
4. IFAC member bodies in establishing required competences and profiling the developmental needs of their members in this sphere of management.

Study 12 provides both a benchmark and a resource for the development of practice in a range of contexts around the world. Beyond this, it is likely to open up and stimulate discussion internationally about a critical and distinctive dimension of management work.

Management Accountancy Faces a Changing Environment

A publication issued in April 2001 by the Financial and Management Accounting Committee (FMAC) presents a global perspective on the transformation of the accounting profession to a management profession. The study, entitled *A Profession Transforming: From Accounting to Management,* investigates both the causes and effects of the movement by presenting the perspectives and experiences of a dozen professional associations from around the world.

One goal of the publication is to bring to the surface the problems and solutions professional associations of accountants face in trying to understand and cope with the changes. It takes a look at the impact of the past decade of change on both the present and the future.

Such information can be useful to a wide group, including educators preparing the next generation of accountants, employers of management accountants, and professional associations that serve an increasing number of members not employed in public practice.

Currently, IFAC membership totals approximately 2.5 million accountants. More than 60% of them are employed in business. This percentage is rising steadily. The study is important for many of them who are coping with a new and still developing business environment. IFAC points out that the changed environment is one that requires new skills, increasing flexibility, and an unprecedented ability to manage change.

The study also points out that two parallel movements seem to be driving change in the accounting profession:

1. A movement to reform corporate governance as the underpinning of global capital markets, with consequent changes in financial reporting, auditing standards, and processes for institutional oversight and assurance.
2. A less visible but equally strong movement for accounting work to be absorbed into the management process of organizations. This development not only alters the competencies expected of practitioners but also makes such work accessible to those who are not accountants.

Features of the study include:

1. Twelve distinct perspectives on the changes in the profession. They were contributed by twelve professional associations in Australia, Canada, Italy, Malaysia, the UK, and U.S. chapters.
2. An introductory chapter summarizes key trends, and highlights threats and opportunities facing the management accounting profession and the associations that serve it. This overview also points out how the associations are attempting to meet the challenges.

CODE OF ETHICS FEATURES NEW INDEPENDENCE RULES

IFAC released its updated, *Code of Ethics for Professional Accountants,* featuring new rules on independence. This international Code is intended to serve as a model on which to base national ethical guidance for accountants. The Code includes principles that are applicable to all professional accountants and distinguishes between those that affect professional accountants in public practice and those that are applicable to other accountants employed in business and industry.

Although the accountancy profession throughout the world operates in an environment with different cultures and regulatory requirements, it is vital that all accountants share a commitment to a strong code of ethics. The IFAC Code states the fundamental principles that should be observed by professional accountants to meet their responsibility in protecting the public's interests.

The Ethics Committee suggests the following reasons for the need to update the independence rules:

1. Changes in the global economy.
2. Technology developments.
3. The expanding services performed by the accountancy profession.

The new rules of independence provide:

1. A conceptual framework that focuses on the factors that poses a threat to independence for all assurance engagements.
2. The safeguards that auditors should put in place to preserve their independence.
3. Examples of situations on how the conceptual approach to independence are to be applied to specific circumstances and relationships.

High-quality standards are the fundamental underpinnings of the world's financial markets, IFAC believes.

Reasons for Revisions to Guidance

IFAC's Ethics Committee issued an Exposure Draft to revise the independence statement in *Proposed Changes to the Code of Ethics for Professional Accountants*. It clarifies certain points made in the initial ED, issued in June 2000, and expands the guidance on circumstances creating threats to independence. It establishes a framework for independence requirements for assurance engagements that, if adopted, will be the international standard on which national standards should be based. Accordingly, no member body or firm would be allowed to apply less stringent standards than those stated in the revised ED.

The initial June 2000 Exposure Draft proposed a move to a conceptual framework approach that would require the identification and evaluation of threats to independence, and the application of safeguards to reduce any threats to an acceptable level. Respondents were strongly supportive of this approach and suggested that additional examples be added. The revised Statement includes such examples.

It also expands the group of people who may create threats to independence. As with the June exposure draft, immediate and close family members may create threats to independence; however, the revised Statement also discusses threats to independence that may be created by individuals who are not part of the assurance team. This includes other partners and professional staff within the firm, and the firm itself.

EDUCATION COMMITTEE RELEASES EDS AND GUIDELINE

Working to advance accounting education programs worldwide, particularly in areas where it will assist economic development, IFAC develops International Education Standards that address prequalification education and the continuing professional development of professional accountants and IFAC's Education Committee released exposure drafts of seven standards and one guideline in July 2002.

The overall goal of the proposed standards is to produce competent professional accountants. The global profession is moving toward a common base of standards in accounting, auditing, public sector accounting and ethics and is "raising the bar" in the quality and consistent application of procedures around the world. The acceptance of the need to harmonize technical and practice standards globally has never been more pronounced, the Education Committee believes. However, they add that the global profession will not properly achieve this higher application of standards without a set of robust, codified education standards. Education must be the starting point. Without robustness in education, the achievement of higher compliance with technical and practice standards will flounder.

Proposed Standards from Entry to Continuing Education

For this reason, IFAC's Education Committee has worked aggressively on the development of the following exposure drafts. They have also prepared *Introduction to International Education Standards for Professional Accountants* to provide background information about the purpose, scope, and development of the International Education Standards for Professional Accountants.

The proposed standards are:

1. *Entry Requirements*—prescribes entry requirements for candidates beginning the qualifying process for becoming professional accountants.
2. *Content of Professional Education Programs*—prescribes the professional education candidates require to qualify as professional accountants.
3. *Professional Skills and General Education*—prescribe the personal and professional skills candidates must have to qualify as professional accountants.
4. *Professional Values and Ethics*—prescribes the professional values and ethics that professional accountants need to acquire during their programs of education and practical experience. The aim of this standard is to ensure that candidates for membership of an IFAC member body are equipped with the appropriate professional values and ethics to function as professional accountants.
5. *Experience Requirements*—prescribes the practical experience and training IFAC member bodies should require their members to obtain to qualify as professional accountants. The aim of this standard is to ensure that candidates for members of an IFAC member body have acquired the

practical experience considered appropriate at the time of qualification to function as competent professional accountants.

6. *Assessment of Professional Competence*—prescribes the requirement for a process of assessment of a candidate's professional competence before admission to the profession.

7. *Continuing Professional Education and Development*—prescribes that member bodies establish a continuing professional education and development (or CPD) requirement for all accountants. This is an important aspect of serving the public interest and fosters values of continuous learning and greater professional competence among professional accountants to meet client and employer needs better.

Continuing Professional Education and Development Guidelines provides guidance to assist member bodies in establishing a requirement for an effective program of CPD for members, as prescribed in the proposed standard described above.

We strongly encourage IFAC's member organizations, accounting academics, and other interested parties to review and carefully consider the proposed standards and guideline. IFAC member bodies will be expected to comply with these standards by January 2005. Feedback on the documents is extremely important and will shape the final standards, the committee emphasized.

ADDRESSING ACCOUNTANT COMPETENCIES

A discussion paper issued in May 2001 addresses an issue fundamental to the development of the accountancy profession: How does one define and achieve professional accountancy competency? The paper, *Competence-Based Approaches to the Preparation and Work of the Professional Accountant,* explores the topic of accountant competency, providing an analysis of approaches used by various accountancy institutes around the world.

The IFAC emphasizes that the goal of accounting education and experience must be to produce competent professional accountants capable of making positive contributions over their lifetimes to the profession and society in which they work.

Accountancy bodies are coming under increasing pressure to show the public that their members are, and remain, competent. A competence-based approach to education is vital to ensuring and demonstrating that accountants possess the knowledge, skills, and professional values necessary to carry out their responsibilities.

The discussion paper seeks to:

1. Define "competence" and "capabilities."
2. Provide guidance to accountancy membership bodies on their role in developing competence and capabilities.
3. Assess various methods.

This discussion paper draws together these views within a single framework. Traditionally there have been two rather different approaches to competence:

1. Some studies have emphasized outcomes—accountants performing roles and tasks in the workplace to a defined standard.
2. Other studies have placed more emphasis on inputs contributed by the education and training process—knowledge, skills, and abilities.

The Education Committee welcomes feedback on all aspects of this discussion paper, including the definition of competence. IFAC member bodies that are using competence-based approaches can also send information about these initiatives to IFAC for future updates of the paper.

IT MONITORING GUIDELINES ON RISK

Managing Information Technology Monitoring, a guideline published by IFAC, provides information to help executives, including accountants, financial controllers, auditors, business managers, and others involved in IT decision making, better understand the principles and practices required to monitor the use of IT effectively within their organizations. It appears that IFAC is doing a very good job of helping all of the above-named executives keep pace with the fast-moving ins and outs of information technology.

IT monitoring is important because of the complexity and risks involved in those activities. The IT Governance Board, along with the Information Systems and Audit and Control Association (ISACA), were instrumental in developing this guidance. The chairman of the Board pointed out that IT monitoring is fundamental to IT governance and part of management's responsibility. It is necessary whenever IT is used within an organization. This includes planning, organization, acquisition, implementation, delivery, and support.

IT monitoring covers:

1. How IT sustains the business with operational processes and risk and control systems.
2. Whether IT complies with business strategy, standards and policy.

3. How IT improves the business with technology, process and organizational changes.

4. How IT supports enterprise growth through process knowledge and quality service.

The guideline describes the monitoring tools available to assist management in carrying out these IT monitoring responsibilities and to support effective IT governance. While recognizing that monitoring of IT is unique to an organizational environment, the guideline suggests some generic approaches that may be applied.

IT Monitoring is the sixth guideline in a series developed by IFAC's Information Technology Committee for management of small, medium-sized and large enterprises. The other guidelines in the series are:

1. Managing Security of Information. (Some detailed description of this portion of the Guidelines is included in Chapter 27, E-Commerce.)

2. Managing IT Planning for Business Impact.

3. Acquisition of Information Technology.

4. Implementation of Information Technology Solutions.

5. IT Service Delivery and Support.

IFAC ISSUES NEW PAPER ON E-BUSINESS

A paper issued by IFAC presents certain risk management aspects of e-business relevant to accounting and financial reporting from a managerial perspective. It is entitled, *E-Business and the Accountant: Risk Management for Accounting Systems in an E-Business Environment*.

Directed to the management of organizations, including accountants, *E-Business and the Accountant* points out how e-business changes the way business is conducted and that e-business consequently introduces new risks that enterprises may need to address by implementing a technology infrastructure and controls to mitigate those risks. The paper points out that e-business and its technological environment will have a significant impact on accounting systems and the evidence available to support business transactions, which in turn will lead to changes in the accounting records maintained and accounting procedures followed.

"How To" for E-Business Accounting

The document notes that accountants and auditors may be faced with new challenges and therefore may need to apply new techniques in an e-business environment, such as the development of accounting systems based on the business processes employed, to ensure that transactions:

1. Are appropriately recorded.
2. Are in compliance with local and international legislation and regulations.
3. Meet current and evolving accounting standards and guidance.

To help minimize risks in relation to these issues, the paper provides a useful framework of concepts with which accountants and others can analyze e-business from an accounting point of view. It includes:

1. Best practice guidelines on e-business accounting principles and criteria.
2. Accounting information security.
3. Accounting information processing.
4. Criteria for a functioning accounting system.

Additional information on e-business and Internet accounting is contained in Chapters 27, "E-Commerce," and 28, "Internet Accounting," on those topics.

IFAC MOVES AGAINST MONEY LAUNDERING

At the new year, 2002, IFAC urged the world's accountants to participate in efforts to combat money laundering. IFAC's Board approved the release of a white paper on anti-money laundering for dissemination to its 156 member organizations and their 2.4 million accountants and is widely disseminating the document through its Web site.

The paper explores the role of all accountants—whether they act as independent auditors, accountants in management positions, or in any other professional capacity—in ongoing public- and private-sector efforts to safeguard against money laundering. It also is designed to highlight potential indications of money laundering and to increase awareness of how professional obligations with respect to money laundering relate to and interact with corruption and transparency, privacy and consumer protection and the professional services provided by accountants. The paper draws attention to numerous risks that could lead to or reveal money-laundering situations and provides best practices to help accountants address those risks.

Accountants Asked to Play Larger Role in Detection

The IFAC emphasized the fact that, until relatively recently, the battle against money laundering and related financial crime was the exclusive domain of law enforcement. Approximately 15 years ago, forensic accountants started to join forces with law enforcement to contribute their skills in detecting possible money-laundering activity buried in the books and records of victimized financial institutions.

Specifically, since 9/11, and the U.S. Patriot's Act, even the general public in this country is well aware of money laundering per se and as a method of funneling money to terrorists in particular. However, this awareness is not limited to the American public. Governments and businesses worldwide increasingly look to the accounting profession to:

1. Aid in their monitoring and detection efforts.
2. Establish and strengthen controls and safeguards against money laundering.
3. Identify its perpetrators since they are in a good position to do so.
4. Identify the perpetrators' accomplices in organized financial crime when they become aware of them.

This white paper is part of a series of IFAC initiatives to assist the world's accountants in protecting the public interest as well as their own. In recent years, IFAC has strengthened its standard-setting role with International Standards on Auditing and Public Sector Accounting Standards. It is also in the process of establishing a global self-regulatory regime for the international profession.

SMALL AND MEDIUM-SIZED PRACTICES AND ENTERPRISES

IFAC leadership decided to undertake research into the needs of SMPs and explore member bodies' initiatives to meet these needs. Such research will then guide IFAC in determining its role with respect to SMPs.

Additionally, they supported IFAC's role in further exploring how it could best support the SME sector. IFAC has already established an SME Task Force, which specifically focuses on the needs of this constituency. Moreover, some of IFAC's committees, most notably the Information Technology and Financial and Management Accounting Committees, have issued guidance in recent months designed to be of assistance to the management of SMEs.

IFAC is not alone in its plans to aid this sector of the economic world. The Global Corporate Governance Forum (GCGF), a multidonor facility founded by the World Bank and the Organization for Economic Development (OECD) is also interested in his sector. The GCGF's purpose is to promote global, regional, and local initiatives aimed at improving the institutional framework and practices of corporate governance of middle- and low-income countries in the context of broader economic reform programs.

The History of the IFAC

Founded in 1977, the International Federation of Accountants (IFAC) with headquarters in New York, now consists of 156 national accountancy bodies from 114 countries with well over two million members in public practice, education, government service, industry, and commerce.

IFAC seems not to command the notice in the business press that the International Accounting Standards Committee receives, and decidedly not that of the SEC, FASB and GASB in this country.

IFAC and IASC Relationship

By 1982, it became obvious to the leadership of IFAC and the International Accounting Standards Committee, located in London, that their particular bailiwicks needed to be clearly established in order to avoid confusion concerning their respective roles. It was agreed that the IASC should be the sole international body to set *financial accounting and reporting standards.*

At the same time, IASC agreed to IFAC's role as the worldwide *organization for the accountancy profession.*

The Board of IFAC considered the following to be among their most important tasks:

1. Develop auditing initiatives.
2. Develop guidance and standards relating to education, ethics, management accounting, information technology and the public sector.
3. Give consideration to professional issues such as accountant's liability and the liberalization of professional services.
4. Act as primary spokesman on professional accountancy issues.

Two Separate International Organizations

IFAC emphasizes that the international accountancy profession could be considered to have two primary standard-setting bodies: IFAC and the IASC.

Associate members of IFAC are national organizations whose members work in a support role to the accountancy professions and newly formed accountancy bodies that have not yet met the full membership criteria.

Affiliate members of IFAC are international organizations that represent a particular area of interest or a group of professionals who frequently interact with accountants.

There is considerable mutual support for one another's objectives. IFAC member bodies, in addition to their responsibility to promote and use IFAC guidance, are committed to promote and implement IASC pronouncements. There is also regular contact and coordination between the two organizations at the leadership level.

This arrangement has worked for the last 15 years or so. In addition, both organizations appear to believe that it provides, on the one hand, the necessary degree of independence for the IASC Board to set accounting standards but also ensures the commitment of the accountancy profession in helping to see that these standards are actually implemented in international practice.

COMPARISON TO U.S. ORGANIZATIONS

The IFAC likens their and the IASC's roles on the international scene to those of the AICPA (with a nod to the Institute of Management Accountants and the Institute of Internal Auditors) and the FASB, respectively. The FASB is completely independent of the profession and sets accounting standards. AICPA, etc., are the professional accountancy bodies and set standards and guidelines for accountants. They also comment on FASB pronouncements and support the FASB by providing representation to the Financial Accounting Foundation (FAF) Board of Trustees, but there is no control by the profession over the FASB.

QUALITY ASSURANCE

IFAC has released an International Professional Practice Statement, *Assuring the Quality of Professional Services,* calling for the world's accountants to implement widespread quality control systems. The new statement requires firms of professional accountants to have a system of quality control that covers all of their professional work, and to provide access to continuing professional education programs focusing on quality control polices and procedures.

Additionally, it provides that each firm of professional accountants should be the subject of an external review, either by their professional body or by another firm of accountants. The review should cover the firm's quality control system and the quality of the work carried out for assurance engagements.

IFAC feels that the extension of their former guidance on quality assurance beyond the traditional audit to cover all professional services provided by practicing firms is a further demonstration of their commitment to the achievement of a profession that operates with the highest professional standards worldwide and that meets the expectations of clients, regulators, and the public at large.

FINANCIAL AND MANAGEMENT ACCOUNTING COMMITTEE

Annually, this committee publishes *Articles of Merit,* award winning articles selected from IFAC member body journals. Articles are chosen by a panel of three judges, members of the FMAC, in a "blind" selection process. Articles submitted are judged on the basis of having made, or having the potential to make "a distinct and valuable contribution to the advancement of management accounting."

In addition, the committee publishes special studies, guidance and the results of research in the area of management accounting. It also disseminates information through international forums and seminars on these issues.

Intellectual Capital. A recent study issued by this committee, *The Accountant's Role In Intellectual Capital Management,* highlights the key issues surrounding the management and measurement of *intellectual capital* and the accountant's role in this process. It refers to key research demonstrating the importance of intellectual capital in positioning a company for growth and focuses on how management accountants can contribute to an entity's overall success by identifying, valuing, reporting on, and participating in the management of the intellectual capital of the firm.

Significantly, the study recognizes that accounting for intellectual capital will ultimately require the invention of new financial and management accounting concepts and practices.

INTERNATIONAL AUDITING PRACTICES COMMITTEE (IAPC)

This committee's task is to upgrade auditing and related services standards globally by developing benchmark statements on varied auditing and attest functions to increase the credibility of financial statements. This endeavor is centered around IFAC's codification of International Standards on Auditing (ISAs) and Related Practices.

Going Concern, ISA 570. In June 1999, the IAPC approved a revision to ISA 570, *Going Concern,* dealing with the auditor's responsibility in the audit of financial statements with respect to this assumption used in the preparation of financial statements.

Since this assumption is a fundamental principle in preparation of the statements, the ISA recognizes that management has a responsibility to assess the entity's ability to continue as a going concern, even if this is not explicitly required within the financial reporting framework. The organization realizes that management's assessment may not always involve detailed analysis, particularly when the entity has a history of profitable operations and a ready access to financial resources.

Nevertheless, they believe that such an assessment should be an integral part of the auditor's consideration of the assumption, and that he or she should consider whether there are material uncertainties about the entity's ability to continue as a going concern which should be disclosed in the financial statement.

Of course, the auditor cannot predict future events or conditions that may cause an entity to cease operations. Accordingly, the absence of any reference to going concern uncertainty in an auditor's report cannot be viewed as a guarantee that the entity will continue as a going concern.

However, the new ISA recommends that, in planning the audit, the auditor should *consider* whether there are events or conditions which may cast significant doubt on the entity's ability to continue as a going concern. If so, the auditor takes them into account when making preliminary assessments of the components of audit risk and in planning audit procedures. The auditor must also remain alert throughout the audit for indications of such events and/or conditions.

As noted above, management's input is important and the auditor evaluates their assessment by considering:

1. The process management followed.
2. The assumptions made.
3. Management's plans for future action.

The auditor also considers whether management has taken into account all relevant information that has been identified as a result of his or her audit procedures.

The auditor should review the same assessment period as that used by management with the minimum period being twelve months from the balance sheet date. If management's assessment period covered a shorter period, the auditor should ask management to extend their assessment.

The auditor also needs to inquire about events or conditions beyond the period of assessment, and may ask management to determine the potential significance of any identified event or condition on their going concern assessment. If, as a result of the above procedures, an event or condition is identified that may cast significant doubt on the entity's ability to continue as a going concern, the auditor is to review management's plans for future action and request written evidence relating to questions raised by the auditor about whether or not a material uncertainty may, in fact, exist.

The auditor's report should include either a matter of emphasis paragraph, or a qualified or adverse opinion, depending upon whether or not the financial statements fully disclose the event and condition as well as the material uncertainty about the entity's ability to continue as a going concern.

If the going concern basis has been used to prepare the financial statements when it is not appropriate, the auditor should express an *adverse opinion.* At various times, the auditor may find it necessary to ask management to make or extend its assessment. If management is unwilling to do so, it is not the auditor's responsibility to rectify management's lack of analysis and the auditor must consider the need to modify the report because of insufficient appropriate evidence. Guidance is also provided on additional considerations if there has been a significant delay in signing or approving the financial statements.

The revised ISA will become effective for audits of financial statements for periods ending on or after December 31, 2000.

Assurance. Another of the committee's most important tasks involves assuring the credibility of information. As trade in goods and services spreads over the globe, the demand for reliable information spreads even faster. The changing information needs of businesses and consumers are resulting in increased demands for the audit to extend beyond the traditional attest function into assurance services. The IAPC is taking a leadership role in supporting the accountant as a provider of these services by developing standards and guidance in areas where the opinion of the independent auditor can add value and credibility to the information provided by directors and management.

Through this committee, IFAC is attempting to provide guidance on assuring the credibility of financial information with accountants assuming the role as the "primary care" providers. Building on the framework of existing auditing procedures and practices, the aim is to examine how and when these practices are effective in reporting on the reliability of information and how these practices can be improved and expanded.

As a result, IAPC released ISA 100 providing guidance in this area. The International Standard entitled *Assurance Engagements* is designed to help accountants meet the demand for services that increase the value of information for decision making.

The Standard describes the elements of an assurance engagement and the requirements for professional accountants undertaking such an engagement. In addition to providing the professional benchmark for these types of engagements, the Standard outlines the framework and general principles to be applied in developing specific standards for particular types of assurance engagements.

The proposed Standard takes into consideration comments that were received relating to an ED released in 1997, *Reporting on the Credibility of Information,* as well as another published in 1999. There was a strong view at the earlier time that although the proposal allowing for a range of assurance was conceptually sound, it appeared to pose implementation issues. The primary cause of that concern was the perceived difficulty in being able to communicate *different levels of assurance* to report users.

As a result, the later exposure draft took this into consideration. The ISA provides that:

1. Engagements should be limited to providing two levels of assurance, high and moderate.
2. Outlines the factors that would determine the appropriate level of assurance.
3. Provides guidance on reporting on the two levels of assurance.
4. Recommends that the conclusion for an assurance engagement providing a high level of assurance will generally be expressed in the form of an opinion.

Communications of Audit Matters. In June, 1999, the committee approved a new ISA, *Communications of Audit Matters with Those Charged with Governance.* It establishes standards and provides guidance on communication of audit matters arising from the audit of financial statements between the auditor and those charged with governance of an entity.

The affected personnel are those responsible for:

1. Ensuring that the entity achieves its objectives.
2. Supervising financial reporting.
3. Reporting pertinent information to interested parties.

The focus on the quality of corporate governance is sharpening as deregulated financial markets, enhanced global competition and technological progress increasingly influence corporate behavior. The auditors who should present an independent, objective view, play an important role in contributing to the achievement of the entity's objectives, particularly in relation to financial reporting.

In connection with a financial statement audit, the auditor contributes by expressing an opinion on the fairness of the financial statements in conformity with an accounting framework.

The structures of governance vary from country to country reflecting cultural and legal backgrounds. The new ISA provides guidance to the auditor who faces unfamiliar situations in attempting to determine:

1. The relevant persons charged with governance.
2. With whom audit matters should be communicated.

3. Which matters arising from the audit of the financial statements would be both important and relevant to those charged with governance in overseeing the financial reporting and disclosure process.

4. Which are audit matters of governance interest that need to be communicated and to whom.

This ISA is effective for audits of financial statements for periods ending on or after December 31, 2000.

INFORMATION TECHNOLOGY COMMITTEE (ITC)

This group is charged with keeping the worldwide accounting community abreast of the latest developments and applications relating to information technology (IT). It encourages member bodies to keep up-to-date on available hardware and software and the relationship between IT and the accounting profession.

At a recent international meeting, the committee focused on the use of IT in developing countries and approved a research program and budget. Research will involve determination of the current usage of IT in these countries and identification of the type and level of assistance which would be appropriate in developing economies.

Since being formed in 1995, the committee has begun formulating a series of guidelines to help management cope with rapidly expanding technological developments. The first guideline to be approved was *Managing Security in Information and Communications.* It emphasized the growing importance of closely managing the risks related to information technology. The other earlier guideline is *Managing Information Technology Planning for Business Impact.*

Three additional guidelines being finalized for issuance in 2000 include: *Acquiring Information Technology, Implementation of Information Technology Solutions, and IT Delivery and Support.* The expressed aim is to help executives maximize IT investments and minimize IT risks.

IFAC FORMS COALITION TO ADVANCE ACCOUNTANCY DEVELOPMENT

The organization is leading a worldwide coalition seeking to get developing and emerging national economies off to the right start in establishing accountability in the public interest through building a responsible, organized accountancy profession.

Early in 1999, IFAC, the World Bank, the International Monetary Fund, various international lending and development agencies, the regional accountancy organizations, the international financial institutions, the regulators, and the Big 5 firms agreed to create the International Forum on Accountancy Development (IFAD). The aim of the new Forum is to bring the accounting profession and International Financial Institutions (IFIs) together to develop programs to establish accountability, transparency, and general accounting know-how in those countries with the greatest needs.

With the increasing interconnectedness of countries doing business on a global scale, financial instability in one nation can very quickly bring about the same in another, as was graphically demonstrated in the recent past during the South East Asian financial crisis.

IFAC views the Forum's role as a helpmeet in formulating a comprehensive plan, establishing a common frame of reference and determining priorities and projects most likely to succeed in building the accounting capacity needed for both the public and private sectors in developing countries.

Plan of Action

Specifically, the Forum intends to:

1. Promote understanding by national governments of developing countries about the value to them of transparent financial reporting by a strong accounting profession.
2. Help harness funds and expertise to build accounting capacity in developing and transitional economies.
3. Assist in defining expectations relating to the manner in which the accounting profession should carry out its responsibilities to support the public interest in these countries.
4. Bring pressure on governments to focus more directly on the needs of developing countries.
5. Promote cooperation between governments, the profession, the international financial institutions, regulators, standard-setters, capital providers and issuers.
6. Contribute to a common strategy or framework of reference for accountancy development.

To meet these goals, the Forum will initially concentrate on developing guidance that focuses on:

1. The "cultural" issues, setting out some of the basic misunderstandings that often surround the need for transparent financial reporting and accountability.

2. Regulatory infrastructures that are likely to achieve a proper balance between the rights and responsibilities of government, shareholders, directors, and auditors.
3. Programs to enable developing economies to structure their own national standards to conform to IFAC, ISAC, and other appropriate international guidance.

IFAC knows it can't meet these goals alone. Only by working together with the other members of the Forum, who have the ability to reach their own unique constituencies, can anyone hope to overcome tremendous obstacles and achieve positive and lasting changes.

Emphasis on Developing Countries

In countries where it does not yet exist, legislative and regulatory agencies must become aware of the need to reflect the proper balance of responsibilities between government, enterprise leadership, and accountants and auditors. Transparency must be improved through better financial reporting, more accountable control environments, and management of financial risk. If all of this progresses, governments of developing nations could gain improved access to more efficient local and international financial markets for themselves and their countries' public and private sector enterprises.

The Forum will be comprised of approximately 30 organizations representing the entities most heavily involved in accountancy-capacity building projects. The initial membership of the Forum will include the following:

1. International financial institutions, providing the greater part of funding of all aid disbursed for projects within the scope of the Forum; for example, World Bank, United Nations Development Project, the European Union, the Regional Development Banks, and very large bilateral donors, notably from the Group of Seven Countries (United States, United Kingdom, Canada, Germany, France, Italy and Japan).
2. Multilateral development agencies and institutions primarily concerned with improving financial management throughout the international community, notably the International Monetary Fund, the International Organization of Supreme Audit Institutions, the United Nations Conference on Trade and Development, the Organization for Economic Development, the Basle Committee for Banking Supervision, and the International Organization of Securities Commissions.
3. The international accountancy profession, represented by IFAC, the International Accounting Standards Committee (IASC), IFAC's four "recognized" Regional Organizations, and the major firms working across the largest number of countries and undertaking projects on behalf of the development agencies and their clients.

The four regional groups are the Confederation of Asian and Pacific Accountants, Eastern Central and Southern African Federation of Accountants (ECSAFA), Fédération des Experts Comptables Européens (FEE) and the Interamerican Accounting Association (IAA). These are independent bodies which, in many cases, share IFAC's membership and have similar objectives. IFAC considers them especially effective in accomplishing their objectives because of the more intimate knowledge of the needs and resources of particular regions of the world.

Given the magnitude of the goals, it is unrealistic to expect rapid solutions. However, IFAC hopes that the Forum can help its participants bring an effective and shared focus to an essential building block of stability and growth—relevant, accurate and credible accounting information.

ACCOUNTANCY'S FIGHT AGAINST CORRUPTION

IFAC has published a discussion paper, *The Accountancy Profession and the Fight Against Corruption,* aimed at promoting debate at the national and global levels on the issue of corruption. The paper points out that while there is corruption worldwide, both public and private, it is more pervasive in some places than others.

The paper suggests that corruption has a negative impact on everyone:

1. Economic development is hampered.
2. Investors lose confidence.
3. Entrepreneurs suffer increased costs of doing business and face higher risks.
4. Country credit ratings drop.
5. Professionals, businesspersons, and government officials lose credibility.

Society at large becomes quite cynical. And the impact could be felt most deeply in developing and emerging countries where a resulting drop in aid and investment can certainly have a significant impact on economic development, and create social hardships for peoples attempting to build a better life.

Legal and Governmental Support

The IFAC may be tilting at windmills, but the organization feels that combating corruption must be carried on by all and at all levels of society. They call for a commitment by governments and the existence of a solid framework of laws, regulations, control systems and disciplinary measures that proscribe corrupt acts and prescribe strong penalties for those found guilty of them, as well as adequate protection for whistle blowers.

Just what is the accountant's role in all of this? The profession cannot carry on this battle alone but, as an integral part of society and a major player in the business world, IFAC believes it must be and is ready to play its part if there is appropriate infrastructure and public support.

The Many Faces of Corruption

Bribery, fraud, illegal payments, money laundering, smuggling and as many other forms as criminal minds may devise, IFAC finds lurking everywhere. The paper points out that often corruption takes place not only involving money, but also involving special favors or influence. Economic growth, globalization and new developments in technology provide a changing scenario in which corrupt individuals devise ever-changing forms of corruption. Thus, it concludes, it is impossible to provide an all-purpose rule book on how to contain corruption. The problem is too complex—and never-ending—but the fight must go on.

Coordinated Responsibilities

IFAC concedes that in the business world, management has a critical role in the battle against corruption. It is the management of an organization that will set the parameters by developing and enforcing systems of proper corporate governance. In the public sector, similar governance codes have been or need to be developed.

Since accountants have long been commended for high integrity, objectivity and service to the public interest, IFAC feels that their key internal positions in the public and private sectors, as well as their external responsibilities as auditors or advisors, make them essential in the efforts to reduce corruption.

In addition, the paper cites other aids to tightening the reins on corruption:

1. Most national organizations of accountants, as well as the International Federation of Accountants, have developed standards that are designed to combat corruption.
2. Ethics codes, which apply to all accountants, be they in public practice, business, industry or government, require them to follow the highest standards of objectivity and professional care.
3. Auditing standards alert practitioners to the possibility of fraud and require them to document such possibility in planning audits and to report their findings to management.
4. Codes of corporate governance and appropriate financial and other internal controls should ensure that those accountants in business or in government are aware of their responsibilities to report corruption in a similar manner.

IFAC Proposals

But where is all of this background leading? IFAC states its wish to contribute to the global and national debates which it believes should be developed to ensure that the fight against corruption moves forward. To this end:

1. It has developed the paper on corruption to raise awareness of the issues and contribute to the debate.

2. It is proposing to its 153 member bodies in 113 countries that they:

   a. Develop programs that build collaborative relationships with legislative and regulatory authorities, the legal profession, and other groups interested in strengthening the framework for good governance, transparency, and accountability, as well as the legal framework, so as to minimize corrupt practices, propose solutions based on model legislation and regulations introduced in other countries, and point out where swift action may be required.

   b. Work with government to ensure that the requisite definition of corruption is in place, the legislation proscribing corrupt acts is prepared and appropriate means of protection are developed for those who may "blow the whistle."

   c. Initiate education programs for accountants and the public to create awareness of the detrimental effects of corruption, thereby motivating public action toward its elimination, through press articles, seminars, continuing professional education courses, and speeches by leaders of the profession.

   d. Encourage the national media to make corruption a public issue by devoting attention to the types and hazards of corrupt activities, publication of studies of the harm caused by corruption, and the various steps that can be taken to prevent or expose such harm.

   e. Provide assistance including technical support, to national and international organizations fighting corruption by publicizing their activities, offering assistance in their research, and promoting their proposals.

   f. Encourage practicing firms, their clients and governments to adopt codes of conduct setting the "tone at the top" by establishing sound principles of corporate governance that expressly prohibit corrupt activity, and that provide the benefits flowing from the implementation of internal control systems that help expose corrupt activities.

   g. Encourage audit committees expressly to consider whether appropriate policies are in place to prohibit corrupt acts and to require that any such act be reported to them.

h. Promote a tax system that is efficient and equitable so as to discourage the disparity and burden that leads to corruption, and that does not allow corrupt payments to be deductible from income for tax purposes.

3. It will use its influence with organizations such as the World Bank, the IMF, the Organisation of Economic Coordination & Development (OECD) and the United Nations to encourage the development of proper legislation in all member states.

4. It will establish and maintain links with organizations such as Transparency International and the Financial Action Task Force to ensure that the profession is represented in their governing councils and periodic conferences as a means to increase its profile in the fight against corruption.

In the Final Analysis

The organization calls upon the individual accountant to carry out his or her responsibility in the anticorruption campaign. Professional skepticism is necessary when establishing business relationships, and in the review of transactions between related parties, especially when they appear to have questionable business sense. Corrupt entities and individuals must realize that accountants constitute a barrier against corruption. Above all, each individual accountant must ensure that his or her own behavior reflects an unswerving commitment to truth and honesty in financial reporting.

INTERNATIONAL PUBLIC SECTOR ACCOUNTING STANDARDS— ACCRUAL ACCOUNTING

The PSC has now issued 18 IPSASs. These authoritative international financial reporting standards for governments represent a significant step toward strengthening financial reporting by governments around the world.

The first 12 standards are briefed below. The newer 6 are discussed at the beginning of the chapter.

- IPSAS 1—*Presentation of Financial Statements.* This standard sets out the overall considerations for the presentation of financial statements, guidance for the structure of those statements and minimum requirements for their content under the accrual basis of accounting.
- IPSAS 2—*Cash Flow Statements.* This standard requires the provision of information about the changes in cash and cash equivalents during the period from operating, investing and financing activities.
- IPSAS 3—*Net Surplus or Deficit for the Period, Fundamental Errors and Changes in Accounting Policies.* This standard specifies the accounting

treatment for changes in accounting estimates, changes in accounting policies, and the correction of fundamental errors; defines extraordinary items; and requires the separate disclosure of certain items in the financial statements.

- IPSAS 4—*The Effect of Changes in Foreign Exchange Rates.* This standard deals with accounting for foreign currency transactions and foreign operations. IPSAS 4 sets out the requirements for determining which exchange rate to use for the recognition of certain transactions and balances, and how to recognize in the financial statements the financial effect of changes in exchange rates.

- IPSAS 5—*Borrowing Costs.* This standard prescribes the accounting treatment for borrowing costs and requires either the immediate expensing of borrowing costs or, as an allowed alternative treatment, the capitalization of borrowing costs that are directly attributable to the acquisition, construction, or production of a qualifying asset.

- IPSAS 6—*Consolidated Financial Statements and Accounting for Controlled Entities.* This standard requires all controlling entities to prepare consolidated financial statements that consolidate all controlled entities on a line-by-line basis. The standard also contains a detailed discussion of the concept of control, as it applies in the public sector, and guidance on determining whether control exists for financial reporting purposes.

- IPSAS 7—*Accounting for Investments in Associates.* This standard requires all investments in associates to be accounted for in the consolidated financial statements using the equity method of accounting. However, when the investment is acquired and held exclusively with a view to its disposal in the near future, the cost method is required.

- IPSAS 8—*Financial Reporting of Interests in Joint Ventures.* This standard requires proportionate consolidation to be adopted as the benchmark treatment for accounting for such joint ventures entered into by public sector entities. However, IPSAS 8 also permits, as an alternative, joint ventures to be accounted for using the equity method of accounting.

- IPSAS 9—*Revenue from Exchange Transactions.* This standard establishes the conditions for the recognition of revenue arising from exchange transactions, requires such revenue to be measured at the fair value of the consideration received or receivable, and includes disclosure requirements.

- IPSAS 10—*Financial Reporting in Hyperinflationary Economies.* This standard describes the characteristics of a hyperinflationary economy and requires financial statements of entities that operate in such economies to be restated.

- IPSAS 11—*Construction Contracts.* This standard defines construction contracts, establishes requirements for the recognition of revenues and expenses arising from such contracts, and identifies certain disclosure requirements.
- IPSAS 12—*Inventories.* This standard defines inventories, establishes measurement requirements for inventories (including those inventories held for distribution at no or nominal charge) under the historical cost system and includes disclosure requirements.

Chapter 7

Foreign Currency Translations and Derivative Disclosure

CONTENTS

FASB Statement 52, *Foreign Currency Translations*   **7.01**

FASB Statement 107, *Disclosure About Fair Value of Financial Instruments*   **7.10**

FASB Statement 133, *Accounting for Derivative Instruments and Hedging Activities*   **7.12**

FASB STATEMENT 52, FOREIGN CURRENCY TRANSLATIONS

FASB 52 covers accounting for the translation of foreign currency statements and the gain and loss on foreign currency transactions. Foreign currency transactions and financial statements of foreign entities include branches, subsidiaries, partnerships and joint ventures, which are consolidated, combined, or reported under the equity method in financial statements prepared in accordance with U.S. generally accepted financial principles.

Why is translation necessary? It is not arithmetically possible to combine, add, or subtract measurements expressed in different currencies. It is necessary, therefore, to translate assets, liabilities, revenues, expenses, gains, and losses that are measured or denominated in a foreign currency.

Definitions

An understanding of this rather complex accounting rule can be aided by becoming familiar with the terms used in the Statement. The following list of definitions will enable the accountant to apply the accounting procedures and methods outlined below.

Attribute—For accounting purposes, the quantifiable element of an item.

Conversion—Exchanging one currency for another.

Currency Exchange Rate—The rate at which one unit of a currency can be exchanged or converted into another currency. For purposes of translation of financial statements, the current exchange rate is the rate at the end of the period covered by the financial statements, or the dates of recognition in the statements for revenues, expenses, gains and losses.

Currency Swap—An exchange between enterprises of the currencies of two different countries with a binding commitment to reverse the exchange of the two currencies at the same rate of exchange on a specified future date.

Current Rate Method—All assets and liabilities are translated at the exchange rate in effect on the balance sheet date. Capital accounts are translated at *historical exchange rates.*

Discount or Premium on a Forward Contract—The foreign currency amount of a contract multiplied by the difference between the contracted forward rate and the spot rate at the date of inception of the contract.

Economic Environment—The nature of the business climate in which an entity *primarily* generates and expends cash.

Entity—In this instance, a party to a transaction which produces a monetary asset or liability denominated in a currency other than its functional currency.

Exchange Rate—The ratio between a unit of one currency and the amount of another currency for which that unit can be exchanged at a particular time. The appropriate exchange rate for the translation of income statement accounts is the rate for the date on which those elements are recognized during the period.

Foreign Currency—A currency other than the functional currency of the entity being referred to. For example, the dollar could be a foreign currency for a foreign entity. Composites of currencies, such as the Special Drawing Rights (SDRs), used to set prices or denominate amounts of loans, etc., have the characteristics of foreign currency for purposes of applying Statement 52.

Foreign Currency Transaction—A transaction in which the terms are denominated in a currency other than an entity's functional currency. Foreign currency transactions arise when an enterprise buys or sells goods or services on credit at prices which are denominated in foreign currency; when an entity borrows or lends funds and the amounts payable or receivable are denominated in foreign currency; acquires or disposes of assets, or incurs or settles liabilities denominated in a foreign currency.

Foreign Currency Translation—Amounts that are expressed in the reporting currency of an enterprise that are denominated in a foreign currency. An example is the translation of the financial statements of a U.S. company from the foreign currency to U.S. dollars.

In the translation of balance sheets, the assets and liabilities are translated at the *current exchange rate,* e.g., rate at the balance sheet date. Income statement items are translated at the *weighted-average exchange rate* for the year.

There are two steps in translating the foreign country's financial statements into U.S. reporting requirements:

1. Conform the foreign country's financial statements to GAAP.
2. Convert the foreign currency into U.S. dollars, the reporting currency.

Foreign Entity—An operation (subsidiary, division, branch, joint venture, etc.) whose financial statements are prepared in a currency other than the currency of the reporting enterprise. The financial statements are combined and accounted for on the equity basis in the financial statements of the reporting enterprise.

Foreign Exchange Contract—An agreement to exchange, at a specified future date, currencies of different countries at a specified rate, which is the *forward rate.*

Functional Currency—The currency of the primary economic environment in which an entity operates; that is, the currency of the environment in which an entity primarily generates and expends cash.

Hedging—An effort by management to minimize the effect of exchange rate fluctuations on reported income, either directly by entering into an exchange contract to buy or sell one currency for another, or indirectly by managing exposed net assets or liabilities' positions by borrowing or billing in dollars rather than the local currency. An agreement to exchange different currencies at a specified future date and at a specified rate is referred to as *the forward rate.*

Highly Inflationary Economy—Economies of countries in which the *cumulative* local inflation rate over a three-year period exceeds approximately 100 per cent, or more.

Historical Exchange Rate—A rate, other than the current or a forward rate, at which a foreign transaction took place.

Inflation—Not defined by specific reference to a commonly quoted economic index. Management can select an appropriate method for measuring inflation. An annual inflation rate of about 20% for three consecutive years would result in a cumulative rate of about 100%.

Intercompany Balance—The foreign currency transactions of the parent, the subsidiary, or both. An intercompany account denominated in the local foreign currency is a foreign currency transaction of the parent. An intercompany account denominated in dollars is a foreign currency transaction of a foreign entity whose functional currency is a currency *other than* the U.S. dollar.

Local Currency—The currency of a particular country.

Measurement—Measurement is the process of measuring transactions denominated in a unit of currency (e.g., purchases payable in British pounds).

Remeasurement—Measurement of the functional currency financial statement amounts in other than the currency in which the transactions are denominated.

Reporting Currency—The currency used by an enterprise in the preparation of its financial statements.

Reporting Enterprise—An entity or group whose financial statements are being referenced. In Statement 52, those financial statements reflect a) the financial statements of one or more foreign operations by combination, consolidation, or equity accounting; b) foreign currency transactions; c) both a) and b).

Self-Contained Operations—Operations which are integrated with the local economic environment, and other operations which are primarily a direct or integral component or extension of a parent company's operations.

Speculative Contracts—A contract that is intended to produce an investment gain (not to hedge a foreign currency exposure).

Spot Rate—An exchange for *immediate delivery* of the currencies exchanged.

Transaction Date—The date at which a transaction, such as a purchase of merchandise or services, is recorded in accounting records in conformity with GAAP. A long-term commitment may have more than one transaction date; for example, the due date of each progress payment under a construction contract is an *anticipated transaction date* credited to shareholders' equity.

Transaction Gain or Loss—Gains or losses from a change in exchange rates between the functional currency and the currency in which a foreign transaction is denominated.

Translation Adjustment—Translation adjustments translate financial statements from the entity's functional currency into the reporting currency. The amount necessary to balance the financial statements after completing the translation process. The amount is charged or credited to shareholder's equity.

Unit of Measure—The currency in which assets, liabilities, revenues, expenses, gains and losses are measured.

Weighted Average Rates—Determined on a monthly basis by an arithmetic average of daily closing rates, and on a quarterly and an annual basis by an arithmetic average of average monthly rates.

Discussion of FASB Statement 52

Statement 52 applies to the financial reports of most companies with foreign operations. The essential requirements of the Statements are:

1. Transaction adjustments arising from consolidating a foreign operation which do not affect cash flows are *not* included in net income. Adjustments

should be disclosed separately and accumulated in a separate classification of the equity section of the balance sheet.

2. Exchange rate changes on a foreign operation which directly affect the parent's cash flows must be included in net income.

3. Hedges of foreign exchange risks are accounted for as hedges without regard to their form.

4. Transaction gains and losses result from exchange rate changes on transactions denominated in currencies other than the functional currency.

5. The balance sheet translation uses the exchange rate prevailing as of the date of the balance sheet.

6. The exchange rate used for revenues, expenses, gains and losses is the rate on the date those items are recognized.

7. Upon sale (or liquidation) of an investment in a foreign entity, the amount accumulated in the equity component is removed and reported as a gain (or loss) on the disposal of the entity.

8. Intercompany transactions of a long-term investment nature are not included in net income.

9. Financial statements for fiscal years before the effective date of this Statement may be restated. If restatements are provided, they must conform to requirements of the Statement.

10. The financial statements of a foreign entity in a highly inflationary economy must be remeasured as if the functional currency were the reporting currency. A "highly inflationary economy" is defined in the Statement to be an economy that has had a cumulative inflation rate of 100%, or more, over a three-year period.

11. If material change in an exchange rate has occurred between year-end and the audit report date, the change should be reported as a subsequent event.

Background. The rapid expansion of international business activities of U.S. companies and dramatic changes in the world monetary system created the need to reconsider the accounting and reporting for foreign currency translation. In considering this topic, the FASB issued FASB Statement 52, which related to the following four areas:

1. Foreign currency transactions including buying or selling on credit goods or services whose prices are denominated in a foreign currency; i.e., currency other than the currency of the reporting entity's country.

2. Being a party to an unperformed foreign exchange contract.

3. Borrowing or lending funds denominated in a foreign currency.

4. For other reasons, acquiring assets or incurring liabilities denominated in foreign currency.

Statement 52 also applies to a foreign enterprise which reports in its currency in conformity with U.S. generally accepted accounting principles. For example, a French subsidiary of a U.S. parent should translate the foreign currency financial statements of its Italian subsidiary in accordance with Statement 52. The objective of translation is to measure and express in dollars, and in conformity with U.S. generally accepted accounting principles, the assets, liabilities, revenues, or expenses that are measured or denominated in foreign currency. In achieving this objective, translation should remeasure these amounts in dollars without changing accounting principles. For example, if an asset was originally measured in a foreign currency under the historical cost concept, translation should remeasure the carrying amount of the asset in dollars at historical cost, not replacement cost or market value.

The most common foreign currency transactions result from the import or export of goods or services, foreign borrowing or lending, and forward exchange contracts. Import or export transactions can be viewed as being composed of two elements—a sale or purchase and the settlement of the related receivable or payable. Changes in the exchange rate, which occur between the time of sale or purchase and the settlement of the receivable or payable, should not affect the measurement of revenues from exports or the cost of imported goods or services.

Foreign currency statements should be translated based on the exchange rate at the end of the reporting year. Translation gains and losses are presented in the stockholders' equity section. Also important is the accounting treatment of gains and losses resulting from transactions denominated in a foreign currency. These are shown in the current year's income statement.

Because of the proliferation of multinational companies, expanding international trade, business involvement with foreign subsidiaries, and joint ventures, FASB 52 was established, in effect, by popular demand. The stated aims of Statement 52 are to (a) provide information that is generally compatible with the expected effects of a rate change on an enterprise's cash flows and equity, and (b) reflect in consolidated statements the financial results and relationships of the individual consolidated entities as measured in their functional currencies, whether the U.S. dollar or a specified foreign currency, in conformity with U.S. generally accepted accounting principles.

The method adopted to achieve these aims is termed the *functional currency approach* which is the currency of the primary economic environment in which the entity carries on its business; in substance, where it generates and expends cash. The Statement permits a multiple measurement basis in consolidated financial statements (depending upon the country in which the subsidiary operates) because business enterprises made up of a multinational enterprise operate and generate cash flows in diverse economic environments, each with its own functional currency. When an enterprise operates in several of these environments, the results of business transactions are measured in the functional currency of the particular environment. "Measured in the functional currency" has the specific meaning that gains and losses comprising income are determined only in relation to accounts denominated in the functional currency.

Mechanically, the functional currency approach calls for eventual translation of all functional currency assets and liabilities into dollars at the current exchange rate. Under Statement 52, use of the current rate for all accounts resolves both the economically compatible results and operating margins distortions. In the past, these distortions came about with the translation of nonmonetary accounts at historical rates. The volatility of earnings distortions is alleviated by recording the translation adjustments directly into shareholders' equity.

The functional currency approach presumes the following:

1. Many business enterprises operate and generate cash flows in a number of different countries (different economic environments).

2. Each of these operations can usually be identified as operating in a single economic environment: the local environment or the parent company's environment. The currency of the principal economic environment becomes the functional currency for those operations.

3. The enterprise may be committed to a long-term position in a specific economic environment and have no plans to liquidate that position in the foreseeable future.

Because measurements are made in multiple functional currencies, decisions relating to the choice of the functional currency of a specific foreign operation will in all likelihood have a significant effect upon reported income. Even though the management of the business enterprise is entitled to a degree of latitude in its weighing of specific facts, the thinking behind adoption of this Statement is that the functional currency is to be determined based on the true nature of the enterprise and not upon some arbitrary selection which management feels might be of particular advantage to the reporting entity.

Determining the Functional Currency.   Multinational companies are involved with foreign business interests either through transactions or investments in foreign entities operating in a number of different economic environments. Each of these endeavors may be associated with one primary economic environment whose currency then becomes the functional currency for that operation. On the other hand, in a foreign country where the economic and/or political environment is so unstable that a highly inflationary economy is likely, it may be deemed wise to carry on the enterprise with the dollar as the functional currency. If the operations in situations of this nature are remeasured on a dollar basis, further erosion of nonmonetary accounts may be avoided.

When there is a reasonably stable economic situation, the national environment of each operation should be considered as the primary economic environment of the particular operation since national sovereignty is a primary consideration in relation to currency control.

Industry practice, on the other hand, may in some instances be instrumental in the determination of a primary economic environment and functional currency. If it is an industry-wide practice that pricing or other transaction attributes are calculated in a specific currency, such as prices set in dollars on a worldwide basis, that fact may be more of a determinant than local currency considerations.

The actual decisions in determining a functional currency depend to a large extent upon the operating policy adopted by the reporting company. Two broad classes of foreign operations are to be considered:

1. Those in which a foreign currency is the functional currency. This designation will have been made after receiving the facts and determining that this particular aspect of foreign business operations is largely autonomous and confined to a specific foreign economic environment. That is, ordinary operations are not dependent upon the economic environment of the parent company's functional currency, nor does the foreign operation primarily generate or expend the parent's functional currency.

2. When the workaday business of the foreign operation is deemed to be in actuality just an extension of the parent company's operation and dependent upon the economic environment of the parent company, the dollar may be designated as the functional currency. In substance, most transactions can reasonably be in dollars, thus obviating the need for foreign currency translation.

One of the objectives of Statement 52 is to provide information that is generally compatible with the expected economic effects of a rate change on an enterprise's cash flow and equity in a readily understood manner. If a foreign operation's policy is to convert available funds into dollars for current or near-term distribution to the parent, selection of a dollar functional currency may be expedient.

Therefore, reporting for investments expected to be of short-term duration, such as construction or development joint ventures, the dollar should probably be designated the functional currency. If the nature of an investment changes over a period of time, future redetermination of the appropriate functional currency may become necessary. Such redetermination is permissible only when, in actual fact, significant changes in economic facts and/or circumstances have occurred. The operative functional currency cannot be redetermined merely because management has "changed its collective mind." It becomes evident that functional currency determination should be carefully considered with the decision weighted in favor of the long-term picture rather than short-term expectations.

In the event that redetermination is necessary, three procedures should be kept in mind:

1. When the functional currency has been changed, Statement 52 provides that the prior year's financial statement need not be restated for a change in functional currency.

2. When the functional currency change is from the local currency to the dollar, historical costs and exchange rates are to be determined from translated dollar amounts immediately prior to the change.

3. When the functional currency change is from the dollar to the local currency, nonmonetary assets are to be translated at current exchange rates, charging the initial translation adjustment to equity similar to that produced when Statement 52 was adopted.

Translation.   Translation is the process of converting financial statements expressed in one unit of currency to a different unit of currency (the reporting currency). In short, translation as used in Statement 52 is the restatement into the reporting currency (the U.S. dollar) of any/all foreign currency financial statements utilized in preparing the consolidated financial statements of the U.S. parent company.

Thus, the focus for the preparation and subsequent translation of the financial statements of individual components of an organization is, as previously stated, to:

1. Provide information that is generally compatible with the expected economic effects of a rate change on the enterprise's cash flows and equity, and

2. Reflect in consolidated statements the financial results and relationships of the individual consolidated entities as measured in their functional currencies in conformity with U.S. generally accepted accounting principles.

Measurement is the process of stating the monetary value of transactions denominated in a particular unit of currency (e.g., purchases payable in British pounds). These transactions may also be figured in a unit of currency other than that in which they are denominated. This process then becomes remeasurement and is accomplished by assuming that an exchange of currencies will occur at the exchange rate in effect at the time of the remeasurement. As is evident, should the exchange rate fluctuate between the date of the original transaction and the date of the exchange, a foreign exchange gain or loss will result.

The gains or losses so recorded vary little from other trading activities and are, therefore, included in income.

It is important to note that while translations were formerly based on the premise that financial statements of a U.S. enterprise should be measured in a single unit of currency—the U.S. dollar—translation was under FASB 80, *Accounting for Futures Contracts,* a one-step process that included both remeasurement and reporting in dollars. In the newer context of the functional approach, multiple units of measure are permitted so that remeasurement is required only when (1) the accounts of an entity are maintained in a currency other than its own functional currency, or (2) an enterprise is invoiced in a transaction which produces a monetary asset or liability not denominated in its functional currency.

The subsequent translation to dollars under FASB 52 is the second step of a two-step process necessary to prepare U.S. dollar financial statements.

Foreign Currency Transactions.   Foreign currency transactions are those denominated in a currency other than the entity's functional currency. These transactions include:

1. Buying or selling goods priced in a currency other than the entity's functional currency.
2. Borrowing or lending funds (including intercompany balances) denominated in a different currency.
3. Engaging in an unperformed forward exchange contract.

As becomes evident, companies with foreign subsidiaries can readily become engaged in foreign currency transactions which must be considered when financial statements are prepared. But, in addition, companies which have no foreign branches may also in the everyday course of business become involved in foreign currency transactions.

Regardless of whether the company is entirely domestic-based or not at the transaction date, each resulting asset, liability, revenue, expense, gain, or loss not already denominated in the entity's functional currency must be so measured and recorded. At the close of each subsequent accounting period, all unsettled monetary balances are to be remeasured using the exchange rates in effect on the balance-sheet date. Gains and losses from remeasuring or settling foreign currency transactions are accounted for as current income.

FASB STATEMENT 107, DISCLOSURE ABOUT FAIR VALUE OF FINANCIAL INSTRUMENTS

Statement 107, *Disclosure About Fair Value of Financial Instruments,* defines fair value to mean the amount at which a financial instrument could be exchanged in a current transaction between willing parties, other than a forced or liquidation sale.

The rule is a broad approach to help issuers of financial statements understand what is required of them in meeting the newer, improved disclosure requirements, as well as to help minimize the costs of providing that information. Of course, the reasoning behind the stipulations in this Statement is to ensure a clearer, better defined picture of the fair value of financial instruments than has been provided in the past. This truer picture of an entity's financial activities should be of value to creditors, current and potential investors, and others in making informed decisions concerning granting credit to, investing in, or investigating more thoroughly, a particular entity.

Other impetus for enactment of this rule comes from a desire to provide another useful indicator of the solvency of a financial institution. A recent report issued by the U.S. Treasury Department has suggested that further market value information about various financial institutions could be of aid in regulatory supervision.

Since in many instances generally accepted accounting principles already necessitate disclosure, the term *fair value* use in FASB 107 in no way supersedes or modifies the set of figures obtained using *current value, mark-to-market,* or simply *market value.* It is simply an attempt to get more accurate information about financial instruments—both their assets and liabilities whether on or off the balance sheet—available for easy access.

For the purposes of this Statement, a financial instrument is cash, an ownership interest in an entity, or a contract that imposes on one entity a contractual obligation to deliver cash or another financial instrument to a second entity, or to exchange other financial instruments on potentially unfavorable terms with the second entity. The agreement gives the second entity a contractual right to receive cash or another financial instrument from the first entity, or to exchange other financial instruments on potentially favorable terms with the first entity.

If available, open-market prices are the best and easiest to obtain a measure of fair value of financial instruments. If quoted market prices or other established values are not available, estimates of fair value can be based on the quoted market price of a financial instrument with similar characteristics. Estimates can also be based on valuation techniques, such as the present value of estimated future cash flows using a discount rate commensurate with the risks involved, or using option pricing models. If it is not practicable to estimate the fair value of a particular financial instrument, reasons why it is not practicable must be thoroughly explained.

In all instances, descriptive material must be included detailing the method(s) and the basis for assumptions utilized in arriving at a stated fair value or in the failure to do so. In any event, failure to do so is not to be considered final. A continuing effort to arrive at a practicable (without incurring excessive cost) fair value should be carried out. Because the Board realizes that the cost of attempting to compute fair value in some instances would become excessive, certain types of financial instruments have been excepted from the requirements of Statement 107. These are:

1. Extinguished debt and assets held in trust in connection with a defeasance of that debt.
2. Insurance contracts, other than financial guarantees and investment contracts.
3. Lease contracts as defined in FASB Statement 13.
4. Warrant obligations and rights.
5. Unconditional purchase obligations.
6. Investments accounted for under the equity method.
7. Minority interests in consolidated subsidiaries.
8. Equity investments in consolidated subsidiaries.
9. Equity instruments issued by the entity and classified in stockholders' equity in the statement of financial position.
10. Obligations of employers and plans for pension benefits, other post-retirement benefits including health care and life insurance benefits, employee stock option, and stock purchase plans.

FASB Statement 133, Accounting for Derivative Instruments and Hedging Activities

The derivatives standard was adopted by a unanimous vote on June 1, 1998, after more than 10 years of painstaking effort by the FASB. Unquestionably, this Standard will be one of the most far-reaching accounting standards yet produced. It will also be the one that has raised the most hue and cry in every segment of the economy.

The FASB repeatedly made it clear that they would not back down on certain requirements, regardless of "special interest" objections. The Board pointed out that trillions of dollars' worth of derivative transactions are occurring in the marketplace and they believe "investors have little, if any, information about them." They believe that the new Standard will give the investor further information about an entity so that they can make more knowledgeable decisions.

The U.S. Senate, the House of Representatives, the Federal Reserve, the American Bankers Association, and assorted others entered the fray over derivatives with very little success. On the other hand, the Board had modified some of the earlier positions in response to user requests, as in the Chicago Board of Trade's concern about some of the provisions relating to hedging.

One of the most important concessions was to the projected timing of the effective date. The Standard was to have become effective June 15, 1999. This meant that for calendar-year companies it would be effective January 1, 2000. Many segments had complained that the extra time and money being expended on trying to solve Y2K problems, coping with a new derivatives Standard of such proposed magnitude by December 15, 1998, was expecting too much.

FASB Statement 137, *Accounting for Derivative Instruments and Hedging Activities—Deferral of the Effective Date of FASB Statement 133*—delayed for a year the required application of FASB 133 to June 15, 2000. However, entities that had already issued interim or annual financial statements according to the requirements of Statement 133 could not return to their previous method of accounting for derivatives or hedging activities.

FASB 137 did not change any of the requirements; it merely postponed the inevitable to give the issuers additional time to cope with Y2K considerations and digest the ramifications of the new requirements.

The FASB also appointed a special task force to aid with implementation issues on derivatives. Among the comments received from users were many related to the complicated provisions of the proposed Standard—admittedly covering very complicated financial instruments. The Board agreed with the constituents that it should be prepared to provide assistance and guidance on a timely basis: thus, the task force. The task force continues to help in identifying implementation issues and recommending conclusions to the Board.

ED Modified Somewhat, Not Substantially

FASB Standard 133 retained most of the provisions that were issued in the ED of September, 1997. All derivatives are to be reported as assets or liabilities in financial statements at their fair value. New approaches to hedge accounting are outlined. As a result, more detailed, useful disclosures of derivatives, hedging activities, and related accounting practices should furnish the investor, creditor, and user with a better picture of an entity's true financial condition. In effect, the new derivative accounting practices should then reveal the economic realities of derivative transactions to the financial statement reader.

The requirements to record all derivatives on the face of the balance sheet at fair value, and some of the new hedge accounting requirements, may very well increase the assets reported by some companies and change their return on assets. On the other hand, the result may be an increase of the liabilities reported by some companies, resulting in a change in their liabilities-to-owners'equity ratio.

Hedge Accounting

Under certain conditions, the new derivative Standard will permit management to designate a derivative as one of the following hedges—a fair value, cash flow, or foreign exchange hedge.

1. A *fair value hedge* is a hedge of the exposure to changes in the fair value of an asset or liability recognized on the balance sheet or of a firm commitment. The exposure to change must be attributable to a specific risk.

   For this type of hedge, the gain or loss is recognized in current income. This amount is offset by the gain or loss in the fair value of the hedged item. The carrying amount is adjusted to reflect the fair value gain or loss. If the hedge is working as it is intended, the adjustment to the carrying amount of the hedged item recognized in income will equal the offsetting gain or loss on the hedging derivative and there will be no net effect on earnings. If the hedge, on the other hand, is not operating as it should, earnings will be affected to the extent that the hedge is ineffective. Assessment of effectiveness is required.

2. A *cash flow hedge* is a hedge of an exposure to variability in the cash flows of an asset or liability recognized on the balance sheet, or of a forecasted transaction, that is attributable to a particular risk. Forecasted transactions include forecasted sales and purchases for which no firm commitment has been made, and interest payments on variable rate debt reported as a liability.

   The effective part of a gain or loss on a derivative designated as a cash flow hedge is initially recognized in owners' equity as part of other comprehensive income and then in earnings in the same period in which the hedged forecasted transaction affects earnings. The ineffective aspect of the gain or loss is recognized in earnings.

3. A *foreign currency exposure hedge* is a hedge of the foreign currency exposure of:

   a. A firm commitment which is a foreign currency fair value hedge.

   b. An available-for-sale debt security, a foreign currency fair value hedge.

   c. A foreign currency-denominated forecasted transaction which is a foreign currency cash flow hedge.

   d. A net investment in a foreign operation.

   The gain or loss on a derivative or nonderivative financial instrument designated as a foreign currency hedge is accounted for depending upon its designations as a fair value or cash flow hedge in the same way as outlined above for those types of hedges.

Thus, the gain or loss on a derivative financial instrument designated and qualifying as a foreign currency hedging instrument is to be accounted for as follows:

a. The gain or loss on the hedging instrument in a hedge of a firm commitment is to be recognized in current earnings along with the loss or gain on the hedged firm commitment.

b. The gain or loss on the hedging derivative in a hedge of an available-for-sale security is to be recognized in current earnings along with the loss or gain on the hedged available-for-sale security.

c. In general, the effective aspect of the gain or loss on the hedging instrument in a hedge of a foreign-currency denominated forecasted transaction is to be reported as a component of other comprehensive income, outside of earnings. It is to be recognized in earnings in the same period or periods during which the hedged forecasted transaction affects earnings. The ineffective aspect of the gain or loss on the hedging instrument and any other remaining gain or loss on the hedging instrument is to be recognized in current earnings.

d. The foreign currency transaction gain or loss on the hedging instrument in a hedge of a net investment in a foreign operation is to be reported in other comprehensive income as part of the cumulative translation adjustment. The remainder of the gain or loss on the hedging instrument is to be recognized in current earnings.

Derivatives

A derivative is a financial instrument or other contract with several distinguishing characteristics:

1. It has one or more *underlyings* and one or more *notional amounts* or payment provisions or both. Those terms determine the amount of the settlement or settlements, and in some cases, whether or not a settlement is required.

2. It requires no initial net investment or one that is smaller than would be required for other types of contracts expected to have a similar response to changes in market factors.

3. The terms require or permit net settlement; it can readily be settled net by a means outside the contract, or it provides for delivery of an asset that puts the recipient in a position not substantially different from net settlement.

An "underlying" may be one of a number of variables that is applied to the notional amount to determine the cash flows or other exchanges required by the contract—a commodity price, a per-share price, an interest rate, a foreign exchange rate, or some other variable.

"Notional amount" refers to an amount of money, a number of shares, a number of bushels, pounds, or whatever can be dreamed up to create a more exotic derivative. A contract with these characteristics is a derivative instrument according to the Statement if, by the terms at its inception or upon the occurrence of a specified event, the entire contract meets the conditions delineated above.

FASB 133 specifically states that the following transactions do not constitute derivatives for the purpose of this Statement:

1. Regular security trades.
2. Normal purchases and sales.
3. Contingent consideration from a business combination.
4. Traditional life insurance contracts.
5. Traditional property and casualty contracts.
6. Most financial guarantee contracts.

The new Statement also points out that some contracts may be accounted for as derivatives by the holder but not by the user. These would include:

1. Contracts that are both indexed to the entity's own stock and classified in stockholders' equity on their balance sheets.
2. Contracts issued in connection with stock-based compensation arrangements covered in FASB 123, *Accounting for Stock-Based Compensation.*

How FASB 133 Affects Other Accounting Literature

FASB 133 supersedes and amends several other Statements. It supersedes:

1. FASB 80, *Accounting for Futures Contracts.*
2. FASB 105, *Disclosure of Information About Financial Instruments with Off-Balance-Sheet Risk and Financial Instruments with Concentrations of Credit Risk.*
3. FASB 119, *Disclosure About Derivative Financial Instruments and Fair Value of Financial Instruments.*

It amends:

1. FASB 52, *Foreign Currency Translation,* to permit special accounting for a hedge of a foreign currency forecasted transaction with a derivative.
2. FASB 107, *Disclosures About Fair Value of Financial Instruments,* to include in Statement 107 the disclosure provisions about concentrations of credit risk from FASB 105.

FASB 133 also nullifies or modifies the consensuses reached in a number of issued addressed by the Emerging Issues Task Force.

Application to Not-for-Profit Organizations

Since the Statement applies to all entities, not-for-profit organizations should recognize the change in fair value of all derivatives as a change in net assets in the period of change. In a fair value hedge, the changes in the fair value of the hedged item attributable to the risk being hedged also are recognized.

However, because of the format of their statement of financial performance, not-for-profit organizations may *not* apply special hedge accounting for derivatives used to hedge forecasted transactions. In addition, FASB 133 does not consider how a not- for-profit organization should determine the components of an operating measure if one is presented.

Another Amendment

The Financial Accounting Standards Board issued Statement 138, *Accounting for Certain Derivative Instruments and Certain Hedging Activities—an Amendment of FASB Statement 133* in June, 2000. The Statement addresses a limited number of issues causing implementation difficulties for a large number of entities getting ready to apply Statement 133.

The Board points out that FASB 133, *Accounting for Derivative Instruments and Hedging Activities,* establishes accounting and reporting standards for derivative instruments, including certain derivative instruments embedded in other contracts, (collectively referred to as derivatives) and for hedging activities. Because of difficulties in application and interpretations, the Statement amends FASB 133 so that:

1. The normal purchases and normal sales exception is expanded.
2. The specific risks that can be identified as the hedged risk are redefined so that in a hedge of interest rate risk, the risk of changes in a benchmark interest rate would be the hedged risk.
3. Recognized foreign-currency-denominated debt instruments may be the hedged item in fair value hedges or cash flow hedges.
4. Intercompany derivatives may be designated as the hedging instruments in cash flow hedges of foreign currency risk in the consolidated financial statements even if those intercompany derivatives are offset by unrelated third-party contracts on a net basis.

Certain Board decisions based on recommendations of the Derivatives Implementation Group (DIG) to clarify Statement 133 also have been incorporated in the Statement. The Statement 138 is the result of the Board's decision, after listening to its constituents, to address a limited number of issues using the following criteria:

1. Implementation difficulties would be eased for a large number of entities.
2. There would be no conflict with or modifications to the basic model of Statement 133.
3. There would be no delay in the effective date of Statement 133.

And Yet Another Amendment!

And yet another amendment to FASB 133! Like the GASB and its efforts to make sure that everyone affected understands the workings of GASB 34 (the major overhauling of state and local accounting procedures), the FASB is trying to solve all questions raised in relation to derivatives and FASB 133.

An exposure draft, *Amendment of Statement 133 on Derivative Instruments and Hedging Activities,* has been approved to amend the definition of a derivative in paragraph 6 of FASB 133. The ED would also consider various decisions made as part of the Derivatives Implementation Group process.

The proposal resolves issues raised in connection with an implementation issue "Application of Statement 133 to Beneficial Interests in Securitized Financial Assets." Resolution would require that beneficial interests that do not qualify for the exception in paragraph 14 of Statement 133 (as amended) be evaluated. The evaluation would be to determine whether those beneficial interests in securitized financial assets (such as the interests in securitized credit card receivables) meet the amended definition of a derivative in paragraph 6 of Statement 133.

The Board concluded that other changes proposed in implementation issues are in conflict with Statement 133. In particular, an issue regarding "initial net investment," which provides proposed guidance that conflicts with the definition of a derivative. After considering alternatives for resolving this conflict, the Board decided to amend the Statement.

The Board agreed that the changes required by the ED would improve financial reporting by requiring that contracts with comparable characteristics be accounted for similarly. In particular, it should clarify under what circumstances a contract (either an option-based contract or a non-option-based contract) with an initial net investment would meet the characteristic of a derivative discussed in paragraph 6. The change would result in more consistent reporting of contracts as either derivatives or hybrid instruments.

The proposed effective date for the accounting change is the first day of the first fiscal period beginning after November 15, 2002, which, for calendar year-end companies, will be January 1, 2003.

Chapter 8
Derivatives

CONTENTS

FASB Statement 119	**8.03**
Further Disclosure Measures Needed	**8.03**
For Study and Consideration	**8.04**
Derivatives—Good and Bad	**8.04**
Three Basic Proposals	**8.05**
The SEC Takes Action	**8.06**

There is little doubt that Derivatives was the '90s buzz word in the areas of accounting, finance, banking, and investments. The SEC, the AICPA, the FASB, the GASB, the GAO, the FEI, the AIMR, the IASC, IOSCO, CBOT and myriad other worthy organizations all jumped into the fray to attempt to prevent another Orange County, California-type debacle from occurring. The losses of Procter and Gamble, other large companies, and banks had raised concern, but the fiasco of a public body so obviously misusing derivatives—and being caught—called for drastic action. How best to guard against anything like this happening again?

The Financial Accounting Standard Board's FASB 119, *Disclosures About Derivative Financial Instruments and Fair Value of Financial Instruments,* was a giant step in the right direction as far as disclosure was concerned, but it was not enough. After 10 years of wresting with the derivatives problem, the Board adopted FASB 133, *Accounting for Derivative Instruments and*

Hedging Activities. This new Standard supersedes FASBs 80, 105, and 119 and also amends FASBs 52 and 107.

Various private sector entities highlighted, pinpointed, and underlined problems associated with disclosures about these market risk sensitive instruments, as identified by users of financial reports. The Securities and Exchange Commission's study, preceding the release (in March, 1996) of their proposals for amendments to regulations governing disclosure information about derivatives and other financial instruments and the issuance in February, 1997 of amendments to SEC rules, took into consideration concerns by many organizations. For example, the Association for Investment Management and Research (AIMR), an organization of financial analysts, in a paper discussing financial reporting in the 1990s and on into the next century, noted that users are confounded by the complexity of financial instruments.

After considerable investigation into the needs of investors and creditors, the American Institute of Certified Public Accountants' (AICPA) Special Committee on Financial Reporting confirmed in a study completed in 1994 that users are confused. The users complained that business reporting is not meeting their needs in answering difficult but important questions about innovative financial instruments that companies may have entered into. They felt they needed more specific information about how companies account for those instruments, how that accounting affects the financial statements, and how risk is handled.

Other organizations have made recommendations about how to improve such disclosures on market risk sensitive instruments. These organizations include regulators, such as the Group of Ten Central Bankers, the Federal Reserve Bank of New York, the Basle Committee and the Technical Committee of the International Organization of Securities Commissions (IOSCO), and private sector bodies, such as the Group of Thirty and a task force of the Financial Executives Institute (FEI).

The SEC study found that, in general, these organizations have stressed the need to make more understandable the risks inherent in market risk sensitive instruments. In particular, they have called for additional quantitative and qualitative disclosures about market risk. For example, the Federal Reserve Bank of New York recommended a new financial statement providing quantitative information about the overall market risk of an entity. In addition, the FEI task force recommended that companies disclose some type of information that conveys overall exposure to market risk. In this regard, the FEI task force suggested two distinct approaches. One approach is to provide a high-level summary of relevant statistics about outstanding activity at period end. The second approach is to communicate the potential loss which could occur under specified conditions using either a value at risk or another comprehensive model to measure market risk.

FASB STATEMENT 119

FASB 119 prescribed, among other things, disclosures in the financial statements about the policies used to account for derivative financial instruments, and a discussion of the nature, terms, and cash requirements of derivative financial instruments. It also encouraged, but did not require, disclosure of quantitative information about an entity's overall market risk. As mentioned earlier, this was a first decisive step in the right direction, but further standards, particularly relating to *accounting* for derivatives and hedging, were considered necessary.

Standards similar to FASB 119 have been adopted by the International Accounting Standards Committee, IAS 32; the Canadian Institute of Chartered Accountants; and the Australian Accounting Standards Board. Whether all of these bodies will endeavor to expand upon the requirements in these standards remains to be seen. However, the IASC has adopted IAS 39, *Financial Instruments: Recognition and Measurement* to become effective on or after January 1, 2001. A more long-range standard relating to financial instruments including derivatives is also under consideration.

During 1994, in response, in part, to the concerns of investors, regulators, and private sector entities, the SEC staff reviewed the annual reports of approximately 500 registrants. In addition, during 1995, annual reports were reviewed by the SEC staff to assess the effect of FASB 119 on disclosures about market risk sensitive instruments. As a result of these reviews, the SEC staff observed that FASB 119 did have a positive effect on the quality of disclosures about derivative financial instruments. However, the SEC staff also concluded there was a need to improve disclosures about them, other financial instruments, and derivative commodity instruments. In particular, the SEC staff had identified the following three primary disclosure issues which should be considered when following the new rules.

FURTHER DISCLOSURE MEASURES NEEDED

1. Footnote disclosures of accounting policies for derivatives often are too general to convey adequately the diversity in accounting that exists for derivatives. As a result, it is often difficult to determine the impact of derivatives on registrants' statements of financial position, cash flows, and results of operations.

2. Disclosures frequently focus on derivatives and other financial instruments only in isolation. For this reason, it may be difficult to assess whether these instruments increase or decrease the net market risk exposure of a registrant.

3. Disclosure about financial instruments, commodity positions, firm commitments, and other anticipated transactions, *reported items,* in the footnotes to the financial statements, Management's Discussion and Analysis (MD&A), schedules, and selected financial data may not reflect adequately the effect of derivatives on such reported items. Without disclosure about the *effects* of derivatives, information about the reported items may be incomplete or perhaps misleading.

FOR STUDY AND CONSIDERATION

For one and one-half years, members of the SEC staff researched derivatives, related risk management activities, and alternative disclosure approaches to make these activities less a mystery to investors, the general public, and even many professionals who actually deal with these activities in one capacity or another, before drawing up proposals for consideration. In addition, during this period, the SEC and its staff developed a list of guiding principles to provide a foundation for proposed amendments and recommendations.

1. Disclosures should make it possible for investors to understand better how derivatives affect a registrant's statements of financial position, cash flows, and results of operations.
2. Disclosures should provide information about market risk.
3. Disclosures should clearly explain for the investor how market risk sensitive instruments are used in the registrant's business.
4. Disclosures about market risk should not focus on derivatives in isolation, but rather should point out the "opportunity" for loss inherent in all market risk sensitive instruments.
5. Disclosure requirements about market risk should be flexible enough to accommodate different types of registrants, different degrees of market risk exposure, and different ways of measuring market risk.
6. Disclosures about market risk should highlight, where appropriate, special risks relating to leverage, option, or prepayment features.
7. New disclosure requirements should build on existing disclosure requirements, where possible, to simplify the learning process for additional procedures and to minimize compliance costs to registrants.

DERIVATIVES—GOOD AND BAD

During the last several years, there has been substantial growth in the use of derivative financial instruments, other financial instruments, and derivative commodity instruments. The SEC agrees that these instruments can be effective tools for managing registrants' exposures to market risk. After all, grain futures, hedging, and the commodity market are all good heartland, conservative agricultural measures undertaken as risk prevention, not as flyers in a volatile market. However, what was an ordered, conservative approach to hedging in the 1800s began developing rapidly and spectacularly in some areas as wild speculation in the late 1900s. During 1994, some investors and registrants experienced significant, and sometimes unexpected, losses in market risk sensitive instruments due to, among other things, changes in interest rates, foreign currency exchange rates, and commodity prices. In light of these losses and the substantial growth in the use of market risk sensitive instruments, public disclosure about these instruments has emerged as an important issue in financial markets.

As mentioned, a portion of the SEC study on derivatives during 1994 and 1995 was a review of annual reports filed by approximately 500 registrants. The avowed purpose was to assess the quality of disclosures relating to market risk sensitive instruments and to determine what, if any, additional information was needed to improve disclosures about derivatives. They determined that partly because of FASB 119, disclosures reviewed in 1995 were more informative than those reviewed in 1994.

THREE BASIC PROPOSALS

It was the opinion of those reviewing the situation that the three aforementioned significant disclosure issues remain as problems. To address these specific disclosure issues, the SEC proposed guidance reminders and amendments to their basic regulations, and it is these specific proposals that have led to the new amendments to the SEC regulations:

1. Amendments to Regulation S-X requiring enhanced descriptions in the footnotes to the financial statements of accounting policies for derivative financial instruments and derivative commodity instruments. These disclosures would be required unless the registrant's derivative activities are not material. The materiality of derivatives activities would be measured by the fair values of derivative financial instruments and derivative commodity instruments at the end of each reporting period and the fair value of those instruments during each reporting period.

2. Amendments creating a new item within Regulation S-K requiring disclosure outside the financial statements of qualitative and quantitative information about derivative financial instruments, other financial instruments, and derivative commodity instruments. These disclosures would be required if the fair values of market risk sensitive instruments

outstanding at the end of the current reporting period were material or the potential loss in future earnings, fair values, or cash flows of market risk sensitive instruments from reasonably possible market movements appeared likely to be material.

3. Reminders to registrants that when they provide disclosure about financial instruments, commodity positions, firm commitments, and other anticipated transactions, such disclosure must include information about derivatives that affect directly or indirectly such reported items, to the extent the effects of such information is material and necessary to prevent the disclosure about the reported item from being misleading. For example, when information is required to be disclosed in the footnotes to the financial statements about interest rates and repricing characteristics of debt obligations, registrants should include, when material, disclosure of the effects of derivatives. Similarly, summary information and disclosures in MD&A about the cost of debt obligations should include, when material, disclosure of the effects of derivatives.

THE SEC TAKES ACTION

Disclosure of Accounting Policies for Derivative Financial Instruments and Derivative Commodity Instruments and Disclosure of Quantitative and Qualitative Information About Market Risk Inherent in Derivative Financial Instruments, Other Financial Instruments, and Derivative Commodity Instruments.

From the title of the rules released on February 3, 1997, it would almost appear that the Securities and Exchange Commission feels the ills of the "derivatives problem" can be solved if someone can just come up with the right disclosure and accounting policy formulas to make everything clear to the naive, as well as the sophisticated, investor and end user. At least they tried very hard to find that formula for the disclosure part, and appeared to have faith that the FASB would soon come up with the accounting part.

Thus, the Commission has amended rules and forms for domestic and foreign issuers to clarify and expand existing disclosure requirements for "market risk sensitive instruments." The amendments require enhanced disclosure of accounting policies for derivative financial instruments and derivative commodity instruments (derivatives) in the *footnotes* to the financial statements. In addition, the amendments expand existing disclosure requirements to include quantitative and qualitative information about market risk inherent in market risk sensitive instruments. The required quantitative and qualitative information should be disclosed *outside the financial statements and footnotes.* In addition, the quantitative and qualitative information will be provided safe harbor protection under a new Commission rule.

Disclosures about financial instruments, commodity positions, firm commitments, and anticipated transactions (reported items) must include disclosures about derivatives that *directly* or *indirectly* affect such reported items, to the extent such information is material and necessary to prevent the disclosures from being misleading. The amendments are designed to provide additional information about market risk sensitive instruments, which investors can use to better understand and evaluate the market risk exposures of a registrant.

Planned Reconsideration

The Commission recognizes the evolving nature of market risk sensitive instruments, market risk measurement systems, and market risk management strategies and, thus, intends to continue considering how best to meet the information needs of investors. In this regard, the Commission expects to monitor continuously the effectiveness of these new rules and final disclosure items, as well as the need for additional proposals.

Specifically, the Commission expects to reconsider these amendments after each of the following:

1. The FASB issues a new accounting standard for improving accounting recognition, measurement, and related discoveries for derivatives. (This should be underway with the adoption of FASB 133.)
2. Development in the marketplace of new generally accepted methods for measuring market risk.
3. A period of three years from the initial effective date of Item 305 of Regulation S-K and Item 9A of Form 20-F.

Effective Dates

The amendments became effective over a period of several months to provide registrants with time to respond to the new disclosure requirements. Some compliance dates were staggered depending upon the type of entity and its capitalization. For registrants that were likely to have experience with measuring market risk, less lead time was provided.

Provisions of Items 305 and 9A

The amendments to Regulation S-K to add Item 305, and Form 20F to add Item 9A, require disclosure of *quantitative* and *qualitative* information about market risk for derivatives and other financial instruments, and require that those disclosures be presented *outside the financial statements.* Items 305 and 9A do not pertain solely to derivatives, but also to other financial instruments. Thus, disclosures under those Items are required for registrants that have material amounts of other financial instruments, even when they have no derivatives.

These Items also *encourage* registrants to include other market risk sensitive instruments, positions, and transactions (such as commodity positions, derivative commodity instruments that are not permitted by contract or business custom to be settled in cash or with another financial instrument, and cash flows from anticipated transactions) within the scope of their quantitative and qualitative disclosures about market risk. Registrants that select the sensitivity analysis or value at risk disclosure alternatives and voluntarily include those other market risk sensitive instruments, positions, and transactions within their quantitative disclosures about market risk are permitted to present comprehensive market risk disclosures, which reflect the combined effect of both the required and voluntarily selected instruments, positions, and transactions.

Finally, if those other market risk sensitive instruments, positions, and transactions are not voluntarily included in the quantitative disclosures about market risk and, as a result, the disclosures do not fully reflect the net market risk exposures of the registrant, Items 305(a) and 9A(a) require that registrants discuss the absence of those items as a limitation of the disclosed market risk information.

Quantitative Information

Items 305(a) and 9A(a) require registrants to disclose quantitative information about market risk sensitive instruments using one or more of the following alternatives:

1. Tabular presentation of fair value information and contract terms relevant to determining future cash flows, categorized by expected maturity dates.
2. Sensitivity analysis expressing the potential loss in future earnings, fair values, or cash flows from selected hypothetical changes in market rates and prices.
3. Value at risk disclosures expressing the potential loss in future earnings, fair values, or cash flows from market movements over a selected period of time and with a selected likelihood of occurrence.

Preparation of this quantitative information also requires the registrants to categorize market risk sensitive instruments into instruments entered into for trading purposes, and instruments entered into for purposes other than trading. Within both the trading and other than trading portfolios, separate quantitative information should be presented for each market risk exposure category (i.e., interest rate risk, foreign currency exchange rate risk, commodity price risk, and other relevant market risks, such as equity price risk), to the extent material.

Registrants may use different disclosure alternatives for each of the separate disclosures.

Qualitative Information

In addition to the quantitative information, Items 305(b) and 9A(b) also require registrants to disclose qualitative information about market risk. These items require disclosure of:

1. A registrant's primary market risk exposures at the end of the current reporting period.
2. How the registrant manages those exposures (such as a description of the objectives, general strategies, and instruments, if any, used to manage those exposures).
3. Changes in either the registrant's primary market risk exposures or how those exposures are managed, when compared to the most recent reporting period and what is known or expected in future periods.

Requirements for Small Business Issuers

Small companies and registered investment companies are exempt from a portion of the new requirements. The amendments in Rule 4-08(n) of Regulation S-X and Item 310 of Regulation S-B, relating to accounting policy disclosures, apply to registered investment companies and small business issuers, along with other registrants. However, Item 305 and Item 9A do not apply to registered investment companies and small business issuers.

The Commission believes that because of the evolving nature of the disclosures and the relative costs of compliance for small business issuers, it is appropriate, at this time, to exempt them from disclosing quantitative and qualitative information about market risk. Furthermore, they will not be required to provide these market risk disclosures whether or not they file on specially designated small business forms. In addition, the Commission has extended the safe harbor for forward-looking information to Item 305 disclosures that are made voluntarily by small business issuers.

Accordingly, at this time, the Commission is not adopting amendments to Regulation S-B to incorporate an item similar to Item 305. Small business issuers, however, are required to comply with the amendment regarding accounting policies disclosures for derivatives, to comply with Rule 12b-20 under the Exchange Act and Rule 408 under the Securities Act. These rules require registrants to provide additional information about the material effects of derivatives on other information expressly required to be filed with the Commission, and to the extent market risk represents a known trend, event, or uncertainty, to discuss the impact of market risk on past and future financial condition and results of operations, pursuant to Item 303 of Regulation S-B.

Application to Foreign Private Issuers

As the interest in international securities and investment grows, it is important to keep in mind that the SEC also is charged with the responsibility of seeing that the investor has adequate information about the financial status of foreign entities.

Item 9A of Form 20-F requires disclosure by all foreign private issuers of quantitative and qualitative information about market risk. In addition, foreign private issuers that prepare financial statements in accordance with Item 18 of Form 20-F are required to provide all information required by U.S. GAAP and Regulation S-X, including descriptions in the footnotes to the financial statements of the policies used to account for derivatives.

Lack of Direction Noted

The SEC study revealed that in the absence of comprehensive requirements for accounting for derivatives, registrants had been developing accounting practices for options and complex derivatives by piecemeal application of the various APB Opinions, FASB Statements, EITF Issues, and the limited amount of such literature that did exist.

The varied applications were complicated because existing derivative literature referred to at least three distinctly different methods of accounting for derivatives: fair value accounting, deferral accounting, and accrual accounting. Further, the underlying concepts and criteria used in determining the applicability of these accounting methods were not consistent.

To illustrate: Under the fair value method, derivatives were carried on the balance sheet at fair value with changes in that value recognized in earnings or stockholders' equity. Under the deferral method, gains and losses from derivatives were deferred on the balance sheet and recognized in earnings in conjunction with earnings of designated items. Under the accrual method, each net payment or receipt due or owed under the derivative was recognized in earnings during the period to which the payment or receipt related; there was no recognition on the balance sheet for changes in the derivative's fair value.

All that is now so much history. All derivative instruments are subject to fair value accounting. And hedging rules have been clearly spelled out so that there is no longer the tug-of-war between accounting applications suggested in

FASB 52, *Foreign Currency Translation* (amended by FASB 133), and FASB 80, *Accounting for Futures Contracts* (superseded by FASB 133). Various other interpretations and opinions have also been superseded in an attempt to bring uniformity to accounting for derivatives.

As a result of lack of consistent direction during its 1994–1995 reviews of filings, the SEC staff observed that registrants, in attempting to interpret the literature, were accounting for the same type of derivative in many different ways. (We assume that it remained a moot question as to whether the interpretation was based on evidence of advantage to the registrant.) Thus, it was difficult to compare the financial statement effects of derivatives across registrants.

Building on FASB 119

In order to provide a better understanding of the accounting for derivative financial instruments, FASB 119 required disclosure of the policies used to account for such instruments, in line with the requirements of APB 22. Specifically, FASB 119 emphasized the disclosure of policies for recognizing, or not recognizing, and measuring derivative financial instruments. When recognized, the location of where those instruments and related gains and losses were reported in the statements of financial position and income must be clearly indicated.

However, FASB 119 did not provide explicit instruction concerning what must be disclosed in accounting policies footnotes to make more understandable the effects of derivatives on the statements of financial position, cash flows, and results of operations; and it does not address disclosure of accounting policies for derivative commodity instruments. Thus, to facilitate a more informed assessment of the effects of derivatives on financial statements, the amendments make explicit the items to be disclosed in the accounting policies footnotes for derivative financial instruments and derivative commodity instruments. At this time, the SEC was still very hopeful that the FASB would come up with a more effective answer to the *accounting* problem as they attempted to deal with the disclosure problem. Possibly their faith will be justified by results from FASB 133.

Disclosure Rule in Regulation S-X

The SEC's amendments to Regulation S-X require enhanced descriptions in the footnotes to the financial statements of accounting policies for derivative financial instruments and derivative commodity instruments. These disclosures are required unless the registrant's derivative activities are not material. The materiality of derivatives' activities is to be measured by the fair values of derivative financial instruments and derivative commodity instruments at the end of each reporting period, and the fair value of those instruments during each reporting period.

The amendments pertaining to accounting policies add a new paragraph to Regulation S-X to require disclosure in the footnotes to the financial statements relating:

1. Each method used to account for derivatives.
2. Types of derivatives accounted for under each method.
3. The criteria required to be met for each accounting method used (e.g., the manner in which risk reduction, correlation, designation, and/or effectiveness tests are applied).
4. The accounting method used if the specified criteria are not met.
5. The accounting for the termination of derivatives designated as hedges or used to affect directly or indirectly the terms, fair values, or cash flows of a designated item.
6. The accounting for derivatives if the designated item matures, or is sold, extinguished, terminated, or, if related to an anticipated transaction, is no longer likely to occur.
7. Where and when derivatives and their related gains and losses are reported in the statements of financial position, cash flows, and results of operations.

The amendments require registrants to distinguish between accounting policies used for derivatives entered into for trading purposes, and those that are entered into for purposes other than trading.

Disclosure of accounting policies for derivatives are required unless the registrant's derivative activities are not material. The materiality of derivatives activities is to be measured by the fair values of derivative financial instruments and derivative commodity instruments at the end of each reporting period, and the fair value of those instruments during each reporting period. In essence, the amendments clarified the application of the accounting policy disclosure requirements that had been set forth in FASB 119 for derivative financial instruments. They also extended those requirements to the disclosure of accounting policies for derivative commodity instruments.

Disclosure of Quantitative and Qualitative Information About Market Risk in Regulation S-K and Elsewhere

The amendments create a new item in Regulation S-K, requiring disclosure outside the financial statements of *quantitative* and *qualitative* information about derivative financial instruments, other financial instruments, and derivative commodity instruments. If any of the following items are material, these disclosures are required:

1. The fair values of market risk sensitive instruments outstanding at the end of the current reporting period.
2. The potential loss in future earnings, fair values, or cash flows of market risk sensitive instruments from reasonably possible market movements.

In complying with the proposed amendments requiring disclosure of quantitative information about market risk, registrants would be permitted to select any one of the three disclosure alternatives listed above as well as the necessary qualitative information. However, it must be remembered that market risk is inherent in *both derivative and nonderivative* instruments, including:

1. Other financial instruments, comprised of nonderivative financial instruments such as investments, loans, structured notes, mortgage-backed securities, indexed instruments, interest-only and principal-only obligations, deposits, and other debt obligations.
2. Derivative financial instruments—futures, forwards, swaps, options, and other financial instruments with similar characteristics.
3. Derivative commodity instruments that are reasonably possible to be settled in cash or with another financial instrument including commodity futures, commodity forwards, commodity swaps, commodity options, and other commodity instruments with similar characteristics, to the extent such instruments are not derivative financial instruments.

Generally accepted accounting principles (GAAP) and SEC rules require disclosure of certain *quantitative* information about some of these derivative financial instruments. For example, registrants are currently required to disclose notional amounts of derivative financial instruments and the nature and terms of debt obligations. However, this information is often abbreviated, is presented piecemeal in different parts of the financial statements, and does not apply to all market risk sensitive instruments. Thus, investors often are unable to determine whether, if, or how particular financial and commodity instruments actually affect a registrant's net market risk exposure. FASB 119 encouraged, but did not require, disclosure of quantitative information about the overall market risk inherent in derivative financial instruments and other instruments subject to market risk. Therefore, implementation of this portion of the amendments is spelled out in detail for both quantitative and qualitative disclosure.

General Considerations on Quantitative Disclosure

In addition to selecting and using one of the three alternative quantitative market risk disclosure methods, registrants are required to discuss material limitations that could cause that information not to reflect the overall market risk of the entity. This discussion necessarily includes descriptions of each limitation, and if applicable, the instruments' features that are not reflected fully within the selected quantitative market risk disclosure alternative.

Registrants are also required to summarize information for the preceding fiscal year, and discuss the reasons for any material changes in quantitative information about market risk when compared to the information reported in the previous period. Provision is made for companies to change their method of presentation of the quantitative information from one to another of the three alternatives. However, if they do change, they should explain why they changed, and summarize comparable information under the new method for the year preceding the year of the change.

Qualitative Information About Market Risk

A *qualitative* discussion of a registrant's market risk exposures, and how those exposures are managed, is important to an understanding of a registrant's market risk. Such qualitative disclosures help place market risk management activities in the context of the business and, therefore, are a useful complement to quantitative information about market risk. FASB 119 required that certain qualitative disclosures be provided about market risk management activities associated with derivative financial instruments held or issued for purposes other than trading. In particular, it required disclosure of the entity's objectives for holding or issuing the derivative financial instruments, the context needed to understand those objectives, and its general strategies for achieving those objectives. In addition, Statement 119 required separate disclosures about derivative financial instruments used as hedges of anticipated transactions. As indicated above, these requirements applied only to certain derivatives held or issued for purposes other than trading.

In essence, the qualitative disclosure requirements created a new requirement in Regulation S-K, which expanded certain FASB 119 disclosures to:

1. Encompass derivative commodity instruments, other financial instruments, and derivative financial instruments entered into for trading purposes.
2. Require registrants to evaluate and describe material changes in their primary risk exposures, and material changes in how those exposures are managed.

In particular, the amendments require narrative disclosure outside the financial statements of:

1. A registrant's primary market risk exposures.
2. How those exposures are managed; e.g., a description of the objectives, general strategies, and instruments, if any, used to manage those exposures.

In preparing the qualitative disclosures about market risk, the Commission expects registrants to describe their primary market risk exposures as they exist at the end of the current reporting period, and how those risks currently are being managed. Registrants also are asked to describe material changes in their primary market risk exposures and material changes in how these risks are managed as compared to what was in effect during the most recent reporting period, and what is known or expected to be in effect in future reporting periods.

These qualitative disclosure requirements apply to derivative financial instruments, other financial instruments, and derivative commodity instruments. As in the case with respect to the quantitative disclosures about market risk, the qualitative disclosures are presented separately for market risk sensitive instruments that are entered into for trading purposes, and those that are entered into for purposes other than trading. In addition, qualitative information about market risk is presented separately for those instruments used to manage risks inherent in anticipated transactions.

Finally, to help make disclosures about market risk more comprehensive, as is the case with the quantitative disclosures, the Commission also is encouraging registrants to disclose qualitative information about market risk relating to other items, such as derivative commodity instruments not reasonably possible to be settled in cash or with another financial instrument, commodity position, cash flows from anticipated transactions, and operating cash flows from nonfinancial and noncommodity instruments, e.g., cash flows generated by manufacturing activities.

Chapter 9
The Sarbanes-Oxley Act of 2002

CONTENTS

Peering into the Future	**9.02**
Types of Services Considered Unlawful	**9.02**
The Public Company Accounting Oversight Board	**9.03**
SEC Oversight of the Oversight Board	**9.06**
Accounting Standards	**9.07**
Public Company Audit Committees	**9.07**
Management Assessment of Internal Controls	**9.08**
Financial Report Requirements in the Act	**9.08**
SEC Involvement in the Act	**9.09**
Measures Relating to Corporate Officers	**9.11**
Treatment of Securities Analysts by Registered Securities Associations	**9.12**
GAO Studies	**9.12**
Amendments to the Sarbanes Senate Bill	**9.13**
All Accountants Need to Be Aware of Provisions	**9.14**

Many of the provisions of the Sarbanes-Oxley Act are direct attacks on strategies used by corporate officials—selling company stock during black-out periods, insider trading, supporting "tame" analysts to tout their stock, and shredding documents. This legislation is a concentrated effort to restore the investor's faith in the stock market.

Peering into the Future

Under pressure from accounting scandals at Enron, Congress reached an agreement with lightning speed on legislation to overhaul the rules governing the accounting profession. With the time constraint of the August congressional recess forcing their hand, House and Senate members hammered out a compromise on reform legislation in less than a week and reached an accord on July 24, 2002. The compromise called for the creation of an independent Accounting Oversight Board governed by the Securities and Exchange Commission (SEC).

Despite pressure to tone down the language and requirements of the Sarbanes-sponsored Senate bill, which placed stringent limits on the consulting services that audit firms can provide to public company audit clients, the strictures prevailed. Moreover, the act included House measures on stiffer criminal penalties for corporate crimes.

Adoption of the legislation marked a drastic shift for the accounting profession, which has, thus far, been self-regulated. The legislation makes control of the accounting profession similar to that of the brokerage industry's regulation under the National Association of Securities Dealers (NASD).

The bill places a federal government bureaucracy at the helm of accounting regulation. It is hoped that this new oversight structure will renew the faith the public had in auditors and the financial statements that they helped prepare. On the other hand, it will take a little while to see how closely the SEC and the Oversight Board itself follow the dictates of the law.

The American Institute of Certified Public Accountants (AICPA) noted that the changes demanded by the legislation would be dramatic and challenging for the accounting profession. The AICPA has pledged to work cooperatively with firms engaged in conducting public company audits in adapting to changes mandated by the new legislation. One immediate problem facing the AICPA is the appropriate role of its SEC Practice Section, within the framework of the new oversight board. At this juncture, it is a little difficult to foresee just what the role of the AICPA, Financial Accounting Standards Board (FASB), and other professional and standard-setting organizations may be.

Types of Services Considered Unlawful

The big accomplishment was to bring to fruition what the SEC and FASB had been trying to accomplish (with little success) before all the scandals came to light. Accounting firms are now barred from providing:

1. Bookkeeping or other services related to the accounting records or financial statements of public company audit clients.
2. Financial information systems design and implementation services.
3. Appraisal or valuation services, fairness opinions, or contribution-in-kind reports.
4. Actuarial services.
5. Internal audit outsourcing services.
6. Management functions or human resources.
7. Broker or dealer, investment advisor, or investment banking services.
8. Legal services and expert services unrelated to the audit.
9. Any other service that the Board determines, by regulation, is impermissible.

However, the Board does have the power to grant exceptions. Under certain conditions, some services may be performed if prior approval has been sought and granted. A similar measure in the House bill would have barred only consulting on system implementation and internal audits for audit clients. There are those who feel that Congress did not need to set hard and fast rules regarding independence and non-audit services. Some knowledgeable commenters consider those are matters better attended to by an expert regulatory body. On the other hand, if such matters are actually spelled out, obfuscation might not prevail.

The final legislation took the tougher measures proposed by the House on penalties for corporate crimes. A new securities fraud section was established to handle white-collar crime. Conviction carries a maximum penalty of a 25-year prison term, and penalties for mail and wire fraud are increased to 20 years.

THE PUBLIC COMPANY ACCOUNTING OVERSIGHT BOARD

The Oversight Board has the power to:

1. Establish auditing.
2. Set up quality control.
3. Draft ethics and independence standards for public company auditors.
4. Investigate and discipline accountants.
5. Apply oversight of foreign firms that audit the financial statements of companies under U.S. securities laws.

Because the measure was passed so quickly and powered by such emotional fervor, there may be even more need for "technical corrections" than the many which are necessary for even the most routine legislation. However, until then, qualifications for, and constraints governing, Board membership include the following:

1. The Board is made up of five financially literate members who are appointed for five-year terms.
2. Two of the members must be or have been CPAs.
3. The remaining three *must not be and cannot have been* CPAs.
4. The Chair may be held by one of the CPA members, provided that he or she has not been engaged as a practicing CPA for five years.
5. The Board's members are to serve on a full-time basis.
6. No member may, concurrent with service on the Board, share in any of the profits of, or receive payments from, a public accounting firm, other than "fixed continuing payments," such as retirement payments.
7. Members of the Board are appointed by the SEC after consultation with the Chairman of the Federal Reserve Board and the Secretary of the Treasury.
8. Members may be removed by the SEC "for good cause."

Responsibilities of the Board Related to Auditing Standards

The Oversight Board is expected to:

1. Cooperate on an ongoing basis with designated professional groups of accountants and any advisory groups convened in connection with setting auditing standards. Although the Board can, to the extent that it deems appropriate, adopt standards proposed by those groups, the *Board will have authority to amend, modify, repeal, and reject any standards suggested by the groups.* The Board is to report on these standard-setting activities to the Commission annually.
2. Require registered public accounting firms to "prepare, and maintain for a period of not less than seven years, audit work papers, and other information related to any audit report, in sufficient detail to support the conclusions reached in such report."
3. Require a second partner in public accounting firms to review and approve audit reports that registered accounting firms must adopt related to quality control standards.
4. Adopt an audit standard to implement the internal control review required by the act. This standard must require that the auditor evaluate

whether the internal control structure and procedures include records that:

a. Accurately and fairly reflect the transactions of the issuer.

b. Provide reasonable assurance that the transactions are recorded in a manner that will permit the preparation of financial statements in accordance with GAAP.

c. Include a description of any material weaknesses in the internal controls of the particular firm.

Mandatory Registration and Other Oversight Functions

The Board will be responsible for:

1. Registering public accounting firms. In order to audit a public company, a public accounting firm must register with the Board. The Board is empowered to collect a registration fee and an annual fee from each registered public accounting firm in amounts that are "sufficient" to recover the costs of processing and reviewing applications and annual reports.

   The Board is required to establish a reasonable annual accounting support fee in an amount necessary or appropriate to maintain the Board. This fee will be assessed on issuers only.

   The registration requirement also applies to foreign accounting firms that audit a U.S. company. This would include foreign firms that perform some audit work, such as in a foreign subsidiary of a U.S. company that is relied on by the primary auditor.

2. Establishing (or adopting, by rule) auditing, quality control, ethics, independence, and other *standards* relating to the preparation of audit reports for issuers.

3. Conducting inspections of accounting firms. Annual quality reviews (inspections) must be conducted for firms that audit more than 100 issues; all other inspections must be conducted every three years. The SEC or the Board may order a special inspection of any firm at any time.

4. Conducting investigations and disciplinary proceedings and imposing appropriate sanctions. All documents and information prepared or received by the Board are treated as confidential and privileged as an evidentiary matter in any proceeding in any federal or state court or administrative agency, unless they are presented in connection with a public proceeding or released in connection with a disciplinary action. However, all such documents and information can be made available to the SEC, the U.S. Attorney General, and other federal and appropriate state agencies. Disciplinary hearings will be closed unless the Board orders that they be

public, for good cause, and with the consent of the parties. Sanctions can be imposed by the Board upon a firm if it fails to supervise, within reason, any associated person with regard to auditing or quality control standards, or otherwise. No sanctions report will be made available to the public unless and until stays pending appeal have been lifted.

5. Performing such other duties or functions as necessary or appropriate.

6. Enforcing compliance with the act, the rules of the Board, professional standards, and the securities laws relating to the preparation and issuance of audit reports and the obligations and liabilities of accountants with respect to them.

7. Setting the budget and managing the operations of the Board and the staff of the Board.

SEC Oversight of the Oversight Board

The Securities and Exchange Commission:

1. Has oversight and enforcement authority over the Board.

2. Can give the Board additional responsibilities, other than those specified in the Act.

3. May require the Board to keep certain records.

4. Has the power to inspect the Board itself, in the same manner as it can with regard to self-regulatory organizations, such as the NASD.

5. Is to treat the Board as if it were a registered securities association; that is, a self-regulatory organization.

6. Requires that the Board file proposed rules and rule changes with the SEC and may approve, reject, or amend such rules.

7. Requires that the Board notify the SEC of pending investigations involving potential violations of the securities laws and coordinate its investigation with the SEC Division of Enforcement, as necessary, to protect an ongoing SEC investigation.

8. May, by order, censure or impose limitations on the activities, functions, and operations of the Board if it finds that the Board has violated the act or the securities laws. The same applies if the Board has failed to ensure the compliance of accounting firms, with applicable rules, without reasonable justification.

9. Requires that the Board must notify the SEC when it imposes any "final sanction" on any accounting firm or associated person. The Board's findings and sanctions are subject to review by the SEC. The SEC may enhance, modify, cancel, reduce, or require remission of such sanction.

ACCOUNTING STANDARDS

The SEC is authorized to recognize, as generally accepted, any accounting principles established by a standard-setting body that meets the bill's criteria, which include requirements that the body:

1. Be a private entity.
2. Be governed by a board of trustees (or equivalent body), the majority of whom are not, nor have been, associated with a public accounting firm for the past two years.
3. Be funded in a manner similar to the Board.
4. Have adopted procedures to ensure prompt consideration of changes to accounting principles by a majority vote.
5. Consider, when adopting standards, the need to keep them current and the extent to which international convergence of standards is necessary or appropriate.

PUBLIC COMPANY AUDIT COMMITTEES

The audit committee of the issuers plays an important part in overseeing many of the provisions of the Sarbanes-Oxley Act.

Qualifications and Responsibilities

Each member of the audit committee must be a member of the board of directors of the issuer and otherwise be independent. "Independent" is defined as not receiving (other than for service on the board) any consulting, advisory, or other compensatory fee from the issuer. In addition, no member may be an "affiliated" person of the issuer or of any of his or her subsidiaries. However, the SEC may make exemptions for certain individuals *on a case-by-case basis.* The SEC is expected to announce rules to require issuers to disclose whether at least one member of its audit committee is a "financial expert."

Each issuer must provide appropriate funding to the audit committee to allow the committee to carry out its responsibilities. The audit committee of an issuer, in turn, is directly responsible for the appointment, compensation, and oversight of the work of any registered public accounting firm employed by that issuer. The audit committee must also establish procedures for receiving, retaining, and handling complaints received by the issuer regarding accounting, internal controls, and auditing. In addition, the committee must engage independent counsel or other advisors that it determines necessary to carry out its duties.

Auditor Reports to Audit Committees

The accounting firm must report to the audit committee all critical accounting policies and practices to be used and any alternative disclosures and treatments of financial information within GAAP that have been discussed with management, along with the ramifications of their use and the treatment preferred by the firm. Other nonaudit services, including tax services, require preapproval by the audit committee on a case-by-case basis and must be disclosed to investors in periodic reports.

MANAGEMENT ASSESSMENT OF INTERNAL CONTROLS

The Sarbanes-Oxley Act requires that each annual report of an issuer contain an internal control report, which is to state the responsibility of management for establishing and maintaining an adequate internal control structure and procedures for financial reporting. It also must contain an assessment, as of the end of the issuer's fiscal year, of the effectiveness of the internal control structure and procedures of the issuer for financial reporting. Each issuer's auditor must attest to, and report on, the assessment made by the management of the issuer. An attestation made under this section must be in accordance with standards for attestation engagements issued or adopted by the Board. An attestation engagement may not be the subject of a separate engagement.

The legislation directs the SEC to require each issuer to disclose whether it has adopted a code of ethics for its senior financial officers and the contents of that code. It directs the SEC to revise its regulations concerning prompt disclosure on Form 8-K to require immediate disclosure "of any change in, or waiver of," an issuer's code of ethics.

FINANCIAL REPORT REQUIREMENTS IN THE ACT

Nothing is more important to a business entity, large or small, its creditors, investors, even its employees and rank-and-file officers and directors than a true and honest financial report. When ranking officers do not play by the rules (however flawed the rules) and skew that report to their own advantage, all and sundry suffer in the final analysis.

Much of the Sarbanes-Oxley Act is drafted to attempt to improve the quality and reliability of these reports.

Each financial report must be prepared in accordance with GAAP and must "reflect all material correcting adjustments . . . that have been identified by a registered accounting firm. . . ." In addition, each annual and quarterly financial report is required to disclose all material off-balance-sheet transactions and any other relationships with unconsolidated entities that may have a material current or future effect on the financial condition of the issuer.

The SEC is expected to issue rules providing that pro forma financial information must be presented in such a manner that it does not contain an untrue statement or omit a material fact that, by its omission, would make the pro forma financial information misleading.

Officer and Director Penalties.   If an issuer is required to prepare a restatement owing to *material noncompliance* with financial reporting requirements, the chief executive officer and the chief financial officer are required to reimburse the issuer for any bonus or other incentive- or equity-based compensation received during the 12 months following the issuance or filing of the non-compliant document. They must also reimburse the issuer for any profits realized from the sale of securities of the issuer during that period.

In any action brought by the SEC for violation of the securities laws, federal courts are authorized to "grant any equitable relief that may be appropriate or necessary *for the benefit of investors.*"

Improper Influence on Conduct of Audits.   It shall be unlawful for any officer or director of an issuer to take any action to fraudulently influence, coerce, manipulate, or mislead any auditor engaged in the performance of an audit for the purpose of rendering the financial statements materially misleading.

Corporate Responsibility for Financial Reports.   The CEO and CFO of each issuer are ordered to prepare a statement to accompany the audit report to certify the "appropriateness of the financial statements and disclosures contained in the periodic report, and that those financial statements and disclosures fairly present, in all material respects, the operations and financial condition of the issuer." A violation of this section must be knowing and intentional to give rise to liability.

SEC INVOLVEMENT IN THE ACT

Not only is a new Board created by the Sarbanes-Oxley Act, but the Securities and Exchange Commission is given control of it, additional oversight assignments, study problems, and added funds and laborpower to accomplish the job. Throughout this chapter, the SEC figures prominently in new and revised rules and regulations. Following are some additional areas of the Commission's role in the new legislation. Among the provisions is a section that empowers the SEC to prohibit a person from serving as an officer or director of a public company if the person has committed securities fraud. This, and many of the other measures, would seem to be iteration of provisions that have been in place, but they need to be emphasized.

Study and Report on Special-Purpose Entities.   The Commission is to study off-balance-sheet disclosures to determine (1) the extent of such transactions (including assets, liabilities, leases, losses and the use of special purpose entities) and (2) whether generally accepted accounting rules result in financial statements of issuers reflecting the economics of such off-balance-sheet transactions to investors in a transparent fashion. The Commission is to make a report containing its recommendations to Congress.

Miscellaneous Assignments.   Various sections of the legislation include the requirements placed on firms and their officers and the specifically assigned oversight tasks to the Commission. Among them are:

1. A direction that the SEC require each issuer to disclose whether it has adopted a code of ethics for its senior financial officers and the contents of that code. The SEC is also directed to revise its regulations concerning prompt disclosure on Form 8-K that requires immediate disclosure of any change in, or waiver of, an issuer's code of ethics.

2. The expectation that the SEC will issue rules providing that pro forma financial information must be presented in such a manner that it does not contain an untrue statement or omit to state a *material fact* that, by its omission, would make the pro forma financial information misleading. (Many firms that have rather straightforward financial reports have managed to produce questionable pro forma information and have defined materiality rather loosely.)

Officer and Director Penalties.   The SEC is empowered to issue an order to prohibit, conditionally or unconditionally, permanently or temporarily, any person who has violated section 10(b) of the 1934 Act from acting as an officer or director of an issuer if the SEC has found that such person's conduct demonstrates unfitness to serve as an officer or director of any such issuer:

(Section 10: It shall be unlawful for any person, directly or indirectly, by the use of any means or instrumentality of interstate commerce or of the mails, or of any facility of any national securities exchange—[b] To use or employ, in connection with the purchase or sale of any security registered on a national securities exchange or any security not so registered, or any securities-based swap agreement (as defined in section in the Gramm-Leach-Bliley Act), any manipulative or deceptive device or contrivance in contravention of such rules and regulations as the Commission may prescribe as necessary or appropriate in the public interest or for the protection of investors.)

Appearance and Practice Before the Commission.   The SEC may censure any person or temporarily bar or deny any person the right to appear or practice before the SEC if the person does not possess the requisite qualifications to represent others, lacks character or integrity, or has willfully violated federal securities laws.

Rules of Professional Responsibility for Attorneys.   The SEC is required to establish rules setting minimum standards for professional conduct for attorneys practicing before it.

Study and Report.   The SEC is ordered to conduct a study of "securities professionals" (public accountants, public accounting firms, investment bankers, investment advisors, brokers, dealers, and attorneys) who have been found to have aided and abetted a violation of federal securities laws.

Temporary Freeze Authority.   The SEC is authorized to freeze an extraordinary payment to any director, officer, partner, controlling person, agent, or employee of a company during an investigation of possible violations of securities laws.

Increased Budget for Additional Laborpower.   SEC appropriations for 2003 are increased to $776,000,000, compared to the $469,000,000 that was in the budget request. Of these funds, $98 million is to be used to hire an additional 200 employees to provide enhanced oversight of auditors and audit services required by the federal securities laws. This should also enhance the commission's general investigation and enforcement capabilities.

MEASURES RELATING TO CORPORATE OFFICERS

Because many of the problems facing corporations and the stock market at present result from actions by ranking corporate officers, a number of provisions in this legislation deal directly with corporate governance and related matters:

1. *Prohibition of Insider Trades During Pension Fund Black-Out Periods.* The Act prohibits the purchase or sale of stock by officers and directors and other insiders during black-out periods. Any profits resulting from sales in violation of this section "shall inure to and be recoverable by the issuer." If the issuer fails to bring suit or prosecute diligently, a suit to recover such profit may be instituted by "the owner of any security of the issuer."

2. *Prohibition of Personal Loans to Executives.* Generally, it will be unlawful for an issuer to extend credit to any director or executive officer.

Consumer credit companies may make home improvement and consumer credit loans and issue credit cards to its directors and executive officers, if it is done in the *ordinary course of business* on the same terms and conditions made to the general public.

3. *Timely Disclosures.* Issuers must disclose information on material changes in the financial condition or operations of the issuer on a rapid and current basis. Directors, officers, and 10 percent owners must report designated transactions by the end of the second business day following the day on which the transaction was executed.

4. *Conflicts of Interest.* The CEO, Controller, CFO, Chief Accounting Officer, or person in an equivalent position cannot have been employed by the company's audit firm during the one-year period proceeding the audit.

5. *Audit Partner Rotation.* The lead audit or coordinating partner and the reviewing partner must rotate off of the audit every 5 years.

6. *Tampering with an Official Proceeding.* The Act makes it a crime for any person to corruptly alter, destroy, mutilate, or conceal any document with the intent to impair the object's integrity or availability for use in an official proceeding or to otherwise obstruct, influence or impede any official proceeding. Perpetrators are liable for up to 20 years in prison and a fine.

7. *Sense of Congress Regarding Corporate Tax Returns.* It is the sense of Congress that the federal income tax return of a corporation should be signed by the chief executive officer of such corporation.

TREATMENT OF SECURITIES ANALYSTS BY REGISTERED SECURITIES ASSOCIATIONS

National Securities Exchanges and registered securities associations must adopt conflict-of-interest rules for research analysts who recommend equities in research reports.

GAO STUDIES

The Government Accounting Office (GAO) has also been assigned a part in the new legislations. Its task is to conduct two studies. The first is a study regarding the consolidation of public accounting firms since 1989, including the present and future impact of the consolidation and the solutions to any problems discovered. The second is a study of the potential effects of requiring the mandatory rotation of audit firms for publicly traded corporations.

Rather than relying on other laws to punish those who dispose of evidence, shred documents, and otherwise attempt to impede investigations, Congress has spelled out the crime and punishment in amendments to the Sarbanes-Oxley Act.

The Corporate and Criminal Fraud Accountability Act of 2002

It is a felony to knowingly destroy or create documents to "impede, obstruct or influence" any existing or contemplated federal investigation. Auditors are required to maintain all audit or review work papers for five years.

The statute of limitations on securities fraud claims is extended to the earlier of five years from the fraud or two years after the fraud was discovered, from three years and one year, respectively.

Employees of issuers and accounting firms are extended whistle-blower protection that would prohibit the employer from taking certain actions against employees who lawfully disclose private employer information to, among others, parties in a judicial proceeding involving a fraud claim. Whistle-blowers are also granted a remedy of special damages and attorney's fees.

A new crime for securities fraud has penalties of fines and up to 10 years of imprisonment.

White-Collar Crime Penalty Enhancement Act of 2002

The provisions include a long list of penalties that have increased the time of imprisonment and amount of fines for specified crimes as follows:

1. The maximum penalty for mail and wire fraud is increased from 5 to 10 years.
2. Tampering with a record or otherwise impeding any official proceeding is classified as a crime.
3. The SEC is given authority to seek a court freeze of extraordinary payments to directors, officers, partners, controlling persons, and agents of employees.
4. The U.S. Sentencing Commission is to review sentencing guidelines for securities and accounting fraud.
5. The SEC may prohibit anyone convicted of securities fraud from being an officer or director of any publicly traded company.
6. Financial Statements filed with the SEC must be certified by the CEO and CFO.

7. The certification must state that the financial statements and disclosures fully comply with provisions of the Securities Exchange Act and that they fairly present, in all material respects, the operations and financial condition of the issuer.

8. Maximum penalties for willful and knowing violations of this section are a fine of not more than $500,000 and/or imprisonment of up to five years.

ALL ACCOUNTANTS NEED TO BE AWARE OF PROVISIONS

Non-public companies' CPAs also need to study the implications of the act. Many of the reforms should probably be considered best practices that will result in new regulations by federal and state agencies.

Unquestionably, this act dramatically affects the entire accounting profession. It impacts not just the largest accounting firms, but also any CPA actively working as an auditor of, or for, a publicly traded company or any CPA working in the financial management area of a public company. In fact, the trickle-down or cascade effect will certainly mean that every accountant should be familiar with the new requirements in the field.

Chapter 10

Actions of the Financial Accounting Standards Board

CONTENTS

Proposed Standard on Consolidation of SPEs   **10.02**

The FAF Considers Changes to Streamline the FASB Process   **10.05**

FASB 147, *Acquisitions of Certain Financial Institutions*   **10.07**

FASB 146, *Accounting for Costs Associated with Exit or Disposal Activities*   **10.08**

FASB 144, *Accounting for the Impairment or Disposal of Long-Lived Assets*   **10.09**

FASB 145, *Rescission of FASB Statements 4, 44, and 64, Amendment of FASB Statement 13, and Technical Corrections*   **10.15**

Business Combinations: Purchase Method Procedures   **10.15**

Business Combinations: New Basis Accounting   **10.18**

New Projects to Consider Standards Overload   **10.19**

Codification and Retrievability   **10.22**

ED, on *Acquisitions of Certain Financial Institutions,* that Amends Statements 72, 144, and Interpretation 9   **10.23**

ED to Amend Definition of a Derivative and Statement 133 to Provide for More Consistent Accounting   **10.24**

FASB Issues ED to Expand Disclosure Requirements for Guarantees   **10.24**

FASB Adds Revenue Recognition Project   **10.25**

FASB 139, *Rescission of FASB Statement 53 and Amendments to FASB Statements 63, 89, and 121*   **10.26**

FASB Statement 140, *Accounting for Transfers and Servicing of*
Financial Assets and Extinguishments of Liabilities—A Replacement
of FASB Statement 125   **10.28**

Business Combinations and Intangible Assets   **10.32**

FASB 143, *Accounting for Asset Retirement Obligations*   **10.35**

FASB Joins International JWG Considering Financial Instruments   **10.39**

FIN 44, *Accounting for Certain Transactions Involving Stock*
Compensation   **10.40**

Accounting for Financial Instruments with Characteristics of Liabilities,
Equity, or Both, and *Proposed Amendment to Concepts Statement 6*   **10.43**

Improving Business Reporting: Insights into Enhancing Voluntary
Disclosures   **10.47**

Business and Financial Reporting, Challenges from the New Economy   **10.49**

FASB Report on Redundancies, GAAP-SEC Disclosure Requirements   **10.50**

All sectors of the accounting and auditing world have come under attack as a result of Enron. Rather uncharacteristically, this attack has included the Financial Accounting Standards Board (FASB) and its vaunted due process. There appear to be those who consider the FASB's work "due," but, far too often and for too long, having no "process" in place. One edge of this criticism is aimed directly at special-purpose entities (SPEs).

The Board is speeding up its timetable slightly on enacting new, stricter rules governing these vehicles. The rules are to cover *when companies are allowed to keep affiliates and their debt off their financial statements.*

PROPOSED STANDARD ON CONSOLIDATION OF SPEs

The FASB, on July 1, 2002, announced approval of the issuance of an exposure draft of a proposed Interpretation of Accounting Research Bulletin (ARB) 51 that establishes accounting guidance for consolidation of special-purpose entities. The proposed Interpretation, *Consolidation of Certain Special-Purpose Entities,* will apply to any business enterprise, public or private companies that have an ownership interest, contractual relationship or other business relationship with an SPE. The proposed guidance would not apply to not-for-profit organizations. The comment period concluded August 30, 2002.

The objective of the proposed Interpretation is to improve financial reporting by enterprises involved with SPEs. The Board emphasized that its aim is not to restrict the use of SPEs, but it is expected that when the proposal is implemented, more SPEs will be consolidated than in the past. Board members believe that most SPEs serve valid business purposes. Examples the FASB cited include:

1. Isolating assets or activities to protect the interests of creditors or other investors.
2. Allocating risks among participants.

Many SPEs that were unconsolidated before the issuance of this proposed Interpretation were reported according to the guidance and accepted practice that existed previously.

Current accounting standards require an enterprise to include in its consolidated financial statements subsidiaries in which it has a controlling financial interest. That requirement usually has been applied to subsidiaries in which an enterprise has a majority voting interest, but in many circumstances, the enterprise's consolidated financial statements do not include SPEs with which it has fundamentally similar relationships. The reason is that existing consolidation guidance focused primarily on parent-subsidiary relationships established through voting ownership interests, and the relationship between a business enterprise and an SPE is established through other means.

The FASB believes that if a business enterprise has a controlling financial interest in an SPE, the assets, liabilities and results of the activities of the SPE should be included in consolidated financial statements with those of the business enterprise, which is referred to as the primary beneficiary of the SPE.

The FASB announced that it expected to issue an Interpretation in the fourth quarter of 2002. The accounting guidance would be effective immediately upon issuance of the Interpretation for new SPEs. Companies with SPEs that existed prior to issuance of the Interpretation would be required to apply the guidance to the existing SPEs at the beginning of the first fiscal period after March 15, 2003. Calendar year-end companies would need to apply the guidance on April 1, 2003.

Earlier FASB Action Related to SPEs

A few months earlier, the FASB planned to tighten the accounting rules relating to SPEs by requiring consolidation of affiliates on a company's financial statements if those entities had *less than 10 percent in outside equity investment.* Under present rules, companies can keep SPEs off their books if independent third parties have at least a 3 percent stake. (Enron officers ignored this minute percentage.)

The board first took up the issue of consolidation 20 years ago but had backed off toughening the current standards in the face of sustained opposition from hundreds of large companies. Since the collapse of Enron Corporation, which used a variety of SPEs to hide billions of dollars of debt, the board has been spurred to revisit the issue, in the wake of widespread criticism (for not doing what they had previously been criticized for trying to do).

FASB officials had said SPEs created after August 2002 would face stricter tests of their true independence, with an emphasis on *substance over form*. Therefore, the new standards were expected to consider factors (other than a straight percentage-ownership test) to ensure that outside investors truly bear the risk of loss when they invest in unconsolidated affiliates. In some instances, independent ownership of an SPE that exceeds 10 percent by itself may not be sufficient to avoid consolidation. *FASB officials say that, apart from a specific percentage of outside interest, special-purpose entities should have to be consolidated on companies' books when it is evident that the entities are not truly independent.*

Still, the Board's tentative decision to raise the percentage threshold drew widespread speculation that many companies and their accounting firms would simply design structures to get around the new rules. However, this may not be as easy as such flaunting of the spirit of a ruling has been in the past. With most of the rest of the accounting world taking pot shots at U.S. GAAP and the U.S. "holier-than-thou" attitude about our transparent, credible and reliable system of financial accounting standards, firms that engage in skull-duggery may find borrowing a rather expensive affair.

The Board appeared to be trying to make it perfectly clear that the *substance of independence* is the message they hope to get across to companies, their managers, accountants and auditors. The 10 percent would just act as a backstop, or possibly a concession, to the way things have been viewed in the past.

Unquestionably, many existing SPEs will have to be consolidated under any new approach. Companies will find it tougher to keep debt off their financial statements and boost earnings through such off-balance-sheet instruments as synthetic leases. At the earlier timeframe, the FASB had considered that preexisting SPEs would have to meet the new 10 percent outside equity rule as well as other independence tests, starting with fiscal years beginning after December 15, 2002. Charges and gains associated with consolidation would not be included under income from continuing operations on companies' income statements, but rather as a cumulative effect of a change in accounting principles.

The FASB is well aware of the fact that new guidelines for the financing vehicles, used by Enron to hide debts, is a change that would force thousands of firms to add liabilities to their books by next year. There will undoubtedly be as much pressure exerted to thwart passage of some of these changes as there is to implement them.

Synthetic Leases

The proposed rules on special-purpose entities would cover the partnerships that Enron created, but it is believed that their greatest effect would be on synthetic leases. These are vehicles used by companies to finance property without showing indebtedness.

Special-purpose entities have long been used by many U.S. companies to finance projects in a way that allows tax benefits without *visibly* impairing balance sheets. This practice has made it possible for companies to appear not to be responsible for financial obligations that may come back to haunt them—and, certainly, to harm the investor.

In a synthetic lease arrangement, a financial institution sets up a special-purpose entity that borrows money to finance new construction or to purchase an existing building for a company. The SPE holds the title and leases the facility to the company for the term of the lease, typically three to seven years, with the possibility for renewal.

A large majority of all synthetic lease arrangements would have to be reflected on balance sheets, according to the proposed FASB plan. If the company could eventually be held accountable, then the liability should be fully disclosed on the balance sheet at the very beginning.

Stonewalled At Every Turn

There have been suggestions that unless a "new" FASB is granted greater powers and more support, the better choice would be an organization under the aegis of the SEC, which has, in effect, been forced to take actions they would previously have preferred the FASB to have taken. However, because of their bowing to pressure and inaction, the FASB has often done nothing or produced a long-delayed, watered down version of what was needed.

Previous proposals to change the rules have been opposed by accounting firms, companies and (very definitely) members of Congress, on the grounds that they would be difficult to implement and for any number of reasons. This time, the FASB has broader support, particularly from lawmakers. Twelve congressional committees have held and are holding hearings on Enron's bankruptcy. Several of the particular Congressmen who opposed the imposition of stronger controls by the FASB as well as the seeking of increased disclosure by the SEC are in the forefront of those now demanding what they had previously opposed.

Regardless of the pressure to get something done, the FASB still guarantees that there will be open due process and adequate opportunity for all of their constituents to comment.

THE FAF CONSIDERS CHANGES TO STREAMLINE THE FASB PROCESS

In light of the criticism leveled at the FASB and accountants and auditors in general, the Financial Accounting Foundation (FAF), the body that oversees, appoints members and funds the activities of the FASB, has determined to strengthen its commitment to a strong, transparent and rigorous system of financial accounting standards for America's capital markets.

FAF Trustees have admitted that in the minds of some investors the system of accounting standards along with the audited financial statements that must comply with them are being questioned. The FAF has announced it plans to do everything within its power both to review and improve the procedures and policies within its official mandate and to participate, where appropriate, in the larger debate about how to strengthen all parts of the evolving regulatory environment.

Trustees agree that there is a need for the FASB to be more flexible in responding to change and to increase the efficiency of its standard-setting process. By doing so, financial reporting standards would be enhanced.

Chairman Points to Accomplishments

In defense of the FASB, the Chairman pointed out that despite significant resistance from some of those affected, the FASB has made substantial improvements to financial reporting that have resulted in greater transparency of financial information. These include requiring:

1. That reporting entities recognize liabilities for retirement benefits when those entities promise them to employees rather than when they later pay them.

2. Significant disclosures about the separate operating segments of an entity's business so that investors can evaluate the differing risks in the diverse operations.

3. That derivative instruments and hedging transactions be reflected in financial statements. Previously they were not reflected.

4. That the acquisition of one company by another is accounted for in the same way for all entities and that the total amount paid for the acquisition is reflected in the financial statements. In the past, that was not often the case. (FASBs 141 and 142 cover this topic. To clarify purchase accounting rules, practices, and requirements, the Board is working with the International Accounting Standards Board as explained below. The Board believes such a project is necessary since current rules do not provide transparent information to users and are sometimes inconsistent with the FASB's Conceptual Framework.)

The FAF Changes FASB Voting to Increase Efficiency

In following up on its earlier proposals to increase the efficiency of the FASB's process, the Financial Accounting Foundation has decided to change the FASB's voting process from a supermajority to a simple majority vote. The decision, which received unanimous support, was made by the FAF Trustees at its quarterly meeting held in April 2002, in Washington, D.C. The change in voting of the seven-member FASB was effective immediately.

As part of its commitment to a strong, transparent and rigorous accounting standard-setting system, the FAF considered several other options. Proposed changes included a reduction in the size of the FASB from seven to five members, a simple majority versus a supermajority vote and shortened comment periods.

After full discussion of those recommendations and a review of comment letters, the Trustees determined that the change from a 5-to-2 to a 4-to-3 member voting requirement would make for a more efficient process without compromising the quality of the FASB's standard-setting process. The FAF recognized the need for the FASB to accelerate its standard-setting process and believes that this change should help to do so. At the same time, it should also reduce the lead time before an exposure draft can be published for comment or a new standard can be implemented.

FASB Reorganizes Research and Technical Activities

The FAF also discussed the FASB's reorganization of its research and technical activities to address increasing demands on staff and other resources. A study, commissioned by the FASB in the latter part of 2001, determined that the Board would be best served by reallocating its research and technical activities functions across three distinct sections rather than just one that covered all areas.

The three sections report to the Chairman of the FASB. The new directorships and their responsibilities cover the following areas:

1. Major projects and technical activities.
2. Technical application and implementation activities.
3. Planning, development and support activities.

FASB 147, *Acquisitions of Certain Financial Institutions*

The FASB issued Statement 147, *Acquisitions of Certain Financial Institutions,* on October 1, 2002. The Statement provides guidance on the accounting for the acquisition of a financial institution. It applies to all acquisitions except those between two or more mutual enterprises. (The Board has a separate project on its agenda that will provide this guidance.)

Statement 147 contains the following provisions:

1. The excess of the fair value of liabilities assumed over the fair value of tangible and identifiable intangible assets acquired in a business combination represents goodwill that should be accounted for under FASB 142, *Goodwill and Other Intangible Assets.*

2. The specialized accounting guidance in paragraph 5 of FASB 72, *Accounting for Certain Acquisitions of Banking or Thrift Institutions,* will not apply after September 30, 2002. If certain criteria in Statement 147 are met, the amount of the unidentifiable intangible asset will be reclassified to goodwill upon adoption of the new Statement.

3. Financial institutions meeting conditions outlined in FASB 147 will be required to restate previously issued financial statements. The objective of the restatement requirement is to present the balance sheet and income statement as if the amount accounted for under FASB 72 as an unidentifiable intangible asset had been reclassified to goodwill as of the date FASB 142 was initially applied. The transition provisions are effective on October 1, 2002.

4. The scope of FASB 144, *Accounting for the Impairment or Disposal of Long-Lived Assets,* is amended to include long-term customer-relationship intangible assets, such as depositor- and borrower-relationship intangible assets and credit cardholder intangible assets.

FASB 146, ACCOUNTING FOR COSTS ASSOCIATED WITH EXIT OR DISPOSAL ACTIVITIES

In July 2002, the FASB issued Statement 146, *Accounting for Costs Associated with Exit or Disposal Activities.* The Standard requires companies to recognize costs associated with exit or disposal activities *when they are incurred* rather than at the date of a commitment to an exit or disposal plan. Examples of costs covered by the standard include lease termination costs and certain employee severance costs that are associated with a restructuring, discontinued operation, plant closing, or other exit or disposal activity.

Guidance had been provided by EITF 94-3, *Liability Recognition for Certain Employee Termination Benefits and Other Costs to Exit an Activity (including Certain Costs Incurred in a Restructuring).* FASB 146 replaces it and completes work begun in FASB 144 as discussed below.

Commenting on the standard, the FASB stated that liabilities represent present obligations to others. Because a commitment to a plan, by itself, does not create a present obligation to others, the principal effect of applying Statement 146 will be on the *timing of recognition of costs* associated with exit or disposal activities. In many cases, those costs will be recognized as liabilities in periods following a commitment to a plan, not at the date of the commitment.

FASB 146 is to be applied prospectively to exit or disposal activities initiated after December 31, 2002.

FASB 144, ACCOUNTING FOR THE IMPAIRMENT OR DISPOSAL OF LONG-LIVED ASSETS

The FASB issued Standard 144, in August 2000, governing the financial accounting and reporting for the impairment or disposal of long-lived assets individually or as asset groups that include long-lived assets. An impaired long-lived asset or asset group is one whose carrying amount exceeds its fair value. This Statement:

1. Supersedes FASB 121, *Accounting for the Impairment of Long-Lived Assets and for Long-Lived Assets to Be Disposed Of.*
2. Supersedes the accounting and reporting provisions of Accounting Principles Board (APB) Opinion 30, *Reporting the Results of Operations — Reporting the Effects of Disposal of a Segment of a Business, and Extraordinary, Unusual and Infrequently Occurring Events and Transactions,* for the disposal of a segment of a business (as previously defined in that Opinion).
3. Amends ARB 51, *Consolidated Financial Statements,* to eliminate the exception to consolidation for a subsidiary for which control is likely to be temporary.

Caution from the Securities and Exchange Commission

The Securities and Exchange Commission (SEC) warned companies that it expects impaired assets to be written down to their *net realizable value.* The SEC's warning was motivated by the economic slowdown and the historical reluctance of managers to recognize asset impairment losses in a timely manner.

It was mandatory that the anticipated impact of the new standard on 2002 balance sheets and income statements be disclosed in 2001 financial reports as well as in subsequent reports.

Reasons for Issuing This Statement

Because FASB 121 did not address the accounting for a segment of a business accounted for as a discontinued operation under ARB 30, two accounting models were in use for long-lived assets to be disposed of. The Board decided to establish a single accounting model, based on the framework established in FASB 121, for long-lived assets to be disposed of by sale. The Board also decided to resolve significant implementation issues related to it.

Long-Lived Assets to Be Held and Used

FASB 144 retains the requirements of FASB 121 relating to when an impairment loss must be recognized for a long-lived asset or asset group to be held and used. Two test conditions apply. First, an impairment loss is recognized only if the carrying amount of the long-lived asset is *not recoverable* from its undiscounted cash flows. A long-lived asset or asset group's carrying amount is not recoverable if it exceeds the sum of the undiscounted cash flows expected to result from the use and eventual disposal of the long-lived asset or asset group. The estimates of future cash flows should be based on the existing service potential of the long-lived asset or asset group and include only those cash flows necessary to maintain the existing service potential. Second, an impairment loss is measured as the difference between the carrying amount and fair value of the asset when the carrying amount exceeds its fair value. A long-lived asset's cash flows should be based on the existing service potential of the long-lived asset or asset group and include only those cash flows necessary to maintain the existing service potential.

If a long-lived asset or asset group fails the first test, its fair value must be determined using the best information available. Suggested procedures include:

1. Using quoted market prices to determine fair value. The wording of FASB 144 expresses a preference for this technique but also recognizes that these may not always be available.

2. Using a present-value-based valuation technique based on assumptions marketplace participants would consider an acceptable alternative. This is the next choice the Standard suggests.

3. If market-based assumptions are unavailable, management can use its own assumptions.

To resolve implementation issues, FASB 144:

1. Removes goodwill from its scope and therefore eliminates the requirement of FASB 121 to allocate goodwill to long-lived assets to be tested for impairment.

2. Describes a probability-weighted cash flow estimation approach to deal with situations in which alternative courses of action to recover the carrying amount of a long-lived asset are under consideration or a range is estimated for the amount of possible future cash flows.

3. Establishes a primary-asset approach to determine the cash flow estimation period for a group of assets and liabilities that represents the unit of accounting for a long-lived asset to be held and used.

Long-Lived Assets to Be Disposed of by Sale

The accounting model for long-lived assets to be disposed of by sale is used for all long-lived assets, whether previously held and used or newly acquired. That accounting model retains the requirement of Statement 121 to measure a long-lived asset classified as held for sale at the lower of its carrying amount or fair value less cost to sell and to cease depreciation (amortization). *Therefore, discontinued operations are no longer measured on a net realizable value basis, and future operating losses are no longer recognized before they occur.*

If the fair value less cost to sell of an asset or asset group held for sale is lower than its carrying amount, the carrying amount is written down to its fair value less cost to sell and an operating loss is recognized for the write-down. The loss is included in the measurement of operating income, unless the long-lived asset or asset group is deemed for the purpose of the new standard to be a component of an entity.

If subsequently the fair value less cost to sell increases, the carrying amount is increased by the increase in fair value less cost to sell to the extent of previously recognized write-downs and a gain is recognized in operating income. (Any loss or gain adjustments are made only to the carrying amount of the long-lived asset whether classified as held for sale individually or as part of a group of assets.)

Long-lived assets held for sale should not be depreciated or amortized; however, interest on liabilities attributable to an asset or asset group held for sale must continue to be accrued.

Long-lived assets or asset groups held for sale should be presented separately on the balance sheet or in the notes on a gross basis. (Any gain or loss resulting from the eventual sale is recognized at the time of sale.)

In such cases, this Statement retains the basic provisions of *Opinion 30* for the presentation of discontinued operations in the income statement but broadens that presentation to include *a component of an entity* rather than *a segment of a business.*

A component of an entity comprises operations and cash flows that can be clearly distinguished, operationally and for financial reporting purposes, from the rest of the entity. A component of an entity that is classified as held for sale or that has been disposed of is presented as a discontinued operation *if* the operations and cash flows of the component will be (or have been) eliminated from the ongoing operations of the entity and the entity will not have any significant continuing involvement in the operations of the component.

Important Features of Implementation. To resolve implementation issues, FASB 144:

1. Establishes criteria beyond that previously specified in Statement 121 to determine when a long-lived asset is held for sale, including a group of as-

sets and liabilities that represents the unit of accounting for a long-lived asset classified as held for sale. Among other things, those criteria specify that:

   a. The asset must be available for immediate sale in its present condition subject only to terms that are usual and customary for sales of such assets.

   b. The sale of the asset must be probable, and its transfer expected to qualify for recognition as a completed sale, within one year, with certain exceptions.

2. Provides guidance on the accounting for a long-lived asset if the criteria for classification as held for sale is met *after* the balance sheet date but *before* issuance of the financial statements. That guidance prohibits retroactive reclassification of the asset as held for sale at the balance sheet date. Therefore, the guidance in EITF Issue 95-18, *Accounting and Reporting for a Discontinued Business Segment When the Measurement Date Occurs after the Balance Sheet Date but before the Issuance of Financial Statements,* is superseded.

3. Provides guidance on the accounting for a long-lived asset classified as held for sale if the asset is reclassified as held and used. The reclassified asset is measured at the *lower* of its:

   a. Carrying amount before being classified as held for sale, adjusted for any depreciation (amortization) expense that would have been recognized had the asset been continuously classified as held and used.

   b. Fair value at the date the asset is reclassified as held and used.

Long-Lived Assets to Be Disposed of Other Than by Sale

Long-lived assets or asset groups to be disposed of other than by sale, such as by abandonment, should be classified as *held for use* until the disposal date. When the disposal date is earlier than the asset's previously estimated useful life, future depreciation estimates are to be revised to reflect the new shorter useful life.

If long-lived assets or asset groups are to be exchanged for similar productive assets, or if distributed to owners in a spin-off are tested for recoverability before the exchange or distribution date, the cash flows used in the recoverability test should be based on the assumption that the exchange or disposal will not occur. At the exchange or disposal date, a loss should be recognized for any excess of carrying amount over the fair value of the long-lived asset or asset group exchanged or disposed of.

In summary, FASB 144 applies to a long-lived asset that is scheduled to be:

1. Abandoned.
2. Exchanged for a similar productive asset.

3. Distributed to owners in a spin-off. (In such a case, it must then be considered held and used until it is disposed of.)

The effects from other literature upon these portions of the Statement are two fold. The requirement that the depreciable life of a long-lived asset to be abandoned is revised in accordance with APB Opinion 20, *Accounting Changes.* In addition, the amendment of APB Opinion 29, *Accounting for Nonmonetary Transactions,* to require that an impairment loss be recognized at the date a long-lived asset, as mentioned above, is exchanged for a similar productive asset or distributed to owners in a spin-off when the carrying amount of the asset exceeds its fair value.

Discontinued Operations

If long-lived assets or asset groups are disposed of and are deemed for the purposes of FASB 144 to be a component of an entity, they should be reported in financial statements as discontinued operations. A component of an entity consists of those operations and cash flows that for financial reporting purposes are clearly distinguishable from the rest of the entity. In practice, a component of an entity may be:

1. A reportable or operating segment presented in the business segment disclosures included in financial statements.
2. A reporting unit to which goodwill has been assigned for goodwill testing purposes.
3. A subsidiary, or the lowest level of a group of long-lived assets and their related other assets and liabilities for which associated identifiable cash flows are largely independent of the cash flows of other groups of assets and liabilities.

The results of operations of a component of an entity either disposed of or classified as held for sale should be classified as discontinued operations if after the disposal transaction:

1. The component's cash flows and operations have been or will be eliminated from the ongoing cash flows of the company.
2. The company will not have any significant continuing involvement in the component.

Changes Should Result in Improved Financial Reporting

Prior to the issuance of FASB 144, there were a number of inconsistencies in accounting for long-lived assets or asset groups to be held for use or disposed of. These inconsistencies were confusing to investors and creditors—in fact, to all users of the financial statement information. The new standard eliminates these inconsistencies. The changes improve financial reporting by requiring that one accounting model be used for long-lived assets to be disposed of by sale, whether previously held and used or newly acquired. It also broadens the presentation of discontinued operations to include more disposal transactions. Therefore, the accounting for similar events and circumstances will be the same. Additionally, the information value of reported financial information should be improved. Finally, resolving significant implementation issues should make compliance with the requirements of the Statement easier.

Relation to FASB Conceptual Framework

In reconsidering the use of a measurement approach based on net realizable value, and the accrual of future operating losses required under that approach, the Financial Accounting Standards Board used the definition of a liability in FASB Concepts Statement 6, *Elements of Financial Statements*. The Board determined that *future operating losses* do not meet the definition of a liability.

In considering changes to FASB 121, the Board focused on the qualitative characteristics discussed in FASB Concepts Statement 2, *Qualitative Characteristics of Accounting Information*. In particular, the Board determined that:

1. Broadening the presentation of discontinued operations to include more disposal transactions provides investors, creditors, and others with decision-useful information that is relevant in assessing the effects of disposal transactions on the ongoing operations of an entity.
2. Eliminating inconsistencies resulting from two accounting models for long-lived assets to be disposed of by sale improves comparability in financial reporting among entities. Thus, it enables users to identify similarities in and differences between two sets of economic events.

FASB 144 also incorporates the guidance in FASB Concepts Statement 7, *Using Cash Flow Information and Present Value in Accounting Measurements,* for using present value techniques to measure fair value.

Later Standard Covers Other Aspects

The new standard did not address the accounting for obligations often associated with the disposal of long-lived assets or asset groups, such as employee termination benefits, restructuring charges, and lease terminations. The FASB addressed the accounting for these obligations at a later date. (See above.)

Effective Date of Statement 144

The provisions of this Statement were effective for financial statements issued for fiscal years beginning after December 15, 2001.

FASB 145, *Rescission of FASB Statements 4, 44, and 64, Amendment of FASB Statement 13, and Technical Corrections*

In April 2002, the FASB issued Statement 145, *Rescission of FASB Statements No. 4, 44, and 64, Amendment of FASB Statement No. 13, and Technical Corrections*, which updates, clarifies and simplifies existing accounting pronouncements.

The Board added this project to its agenda in August 2001 in response to constituent requests to examine the accounting for gains and losses from the extinguishment of debt.

This request was particularly important to those operating in the secondary lending market because the use of debt extinguishment is a part of their day-to-day risk management activities and Statement 4, issued in 1975, no longer addressed the needs of a changed marketplace.

FASB 145 rescinds FASB 4, which required all gains and losses from extinguishment of debt to be aggregated and, if material, classified as an extraordinary item, net of related income tax effect. As a result, the criteria in APB Opinion 30 will now be used to classify those gains and losses.

FASB 64 amended FASB 4, and is no longer necessary since FASB 4 is no more.

FASB 44 was issued to establish accounting requirements for the effects of transition to the provisions of the Motor Carrier Act of 1980. Because the transition has been completed, Statement 44 is no longer necessary.

FASB 145 amends FASB 13 to require that certain lease modifications that have economic effects similar to sale-leaseback transactions is accounted for in the same manner as sale-leaseback transactions. This amendment is consistent with the FASB's goal of requiring similar accounting treatment for transactions that have similar economic effects.

This Statement also makes technical corrections to existing pronouncements. While those corrections are not substantive in nature, in some instances, they may change accounting practice. Thus, FASB 145 appears to have taken care of a multitude of housekeeping chores.

Business Combinations: Purchase Method Procedures

The Board initially added this project to its agenda as a broad reconsideration of existing purchase accounting guidance, including that issued by the FASB, its predecessor the Accounting Principles Board and the Emerging Issues Task Force (EITF), as well as other accepted practices. Now that the purchase method of accounting for business combination is the only one permitted since the elimination of the pooling-of-interests method, it is important to get it right.

The Board believes the project is necessary, since some current purchase accounting rules and practices do not provide transparent information to users and are sometimes inconsistent with the Conceptual Framework.

The Board is joining with the International Accounting Standards Board (IASB) on the project. As a joint project, the FASB and IASB will share staff resources and research and work toward issuance of exposure drafts and final standards. Although the Boards will also coordinate the timing of deliberation on issues within the joint project, each will individually deliberate (and vote) on the issues.

The joint project broadly reconsiders aspects of the purchase method of accounting, excluding most areas deliberated by the Board in FASBs 141, *Business Combinations,* and 142, *Goodwill and Other Intangible Assets.* These areas include:

1. Measuring the value of the business combination.
2. Recognition and measurement of identifiable assets and liabilities (including such issues and contingencies and liabilities for terminating activities of an acquired entity).

Summary of Tentative Decisions

FASB members reached a tentative agreement on the following working principles for recording a business combination. The accounting for a business combination is based on the assumption that the transaction is an exchange of equal values; the total amount to be recognized should be measured based on the fair value of the consideration paid or the fair value of the net assets acquired, whichever is more clearly evident. If the consideration paid is cash or other assets (or liabilities incurred) of the acquiring entity, the fair value of the consideration paid determines the total amount to be recognized in the financial statements of the acquiring entity. If the consideration is in the form of equity instruments, the fair value of the equity instruments ordinarily is more clearly evident than the fair value of the net assets acquired and, thus, will determine the total amount to be recognized by the acquiring entity.

In a business combination, the acquiring entity obtains control over the acquired entity and is, therefore, responsible for the assets and liabilities of the acquired entity. An amount equal to the fair value, on the date control is obtained, should be assigned to the identifiable assets acquired and liabilities assumed. If the total fair value exchanged in the purchase transaction exceeds the amounts recognized for identifiable net assets, that amount is the *implied fair value* of goodwill. If the total fair value exchanged in the purchase transaction is less than the amounts recognized for identifiable net assets, that amount should be recognized as a gain in the income statement.

Other decisions reached are discussed below.

Contingent Consideration in a Business Combination

Contingent consideration issued in a business combination is an obligation of the acquirer as of the acquisition date and, therefore, should be recognized as part of the purchase price on that date. Consistent with the working principle, the initial measurement of contingent consideration should be at fair value.

Some contingent consideration arrangements obligate the acquirer to deliver its equity securities if specified future events occur. Classification of these instruments as either equity or as a liability depends on existing U.S. generally accepted accounting principles (GAAP). Presuming that the Board issues a standard on accounting for financial instruments with the characteristics of liabilities, equity, or both, prior to the issuance of guidance in this project, the guidance in that standard would apply to contingent consideration arrangements.

An exception in FASB 133, *Accounting for Derivative Instruments and Hedging Activities,* should be eliminated in order that contingent consideration arrangements that otherwise meet the definition of a derivative would be subject to the requirements of Statement 133.

Subsequent remeasurement (after the acquisition date) of contingent consideration liabilities does not result in a change to the purchase price of the business combination. These amounts, therefore, should be recorded in the income statement.

Other Measurement Issues Related to the Acquired Business

Equity securities issued, as consideration in a business combination, should be measured on the acquisition date. The description of the acquisition date in FASB 141 should be modified to clarify that the acquisition date is the date that the acquirer gains control over the target entity.

Recognition and Measurement of Identifiable Assets and Liabilities

In the acquisition of less than 100 percent of the acquired entity, the identifiable assets and liabilities of the acquired entity should be recorded at full fair value. The current practice of considering the subsidiaries' carryover basis to the extent of the noncontrolling interest should be eliminated.

If negative goodwill is present in a business combination, the acquiring entity should review the procedures used to identify and measure the net assets of the subsidiary; however, no asset acquired should be measured at an amount that is known to be less than its fair value, nor should any liability assumed or incurred be measured at an amount known to be higher than its fair value. If negative goodwill remains, the acquiring entity should recognize the amount in the income statement (recognized as an extraordinary item under FASB 141).

Preacquisition contingencies of the acquired entity that are assets or liabilities should be recognized and should be initially measured at fair value. The Board agreed to eliminate the alternative described in Statement 141 that allows for recognition under an approach consistent with FASB 5, *Accounting for Contingencies.* The issue of measuring preacquisition contingencies subsequent to the acquisition date will be addressed in the project at a later date.

The period of time permitted to recognize and measure all assets acquired and liabilities assumed (referred to as the "allocation period") ends at the earlier of one year from the acquisition date or when the acquiring entity is no longer waiting for information that it has arranged to obtain and that is known to be available or obtainable. The objective of obtaining information during the allocation period is to measure the assets acquired and liabilities assumed at their fair values as of the acquisition date. Therefore, the only information that should be considered in recording assets acquired and liabilities assumed in a business combination is information that would affect the determination of their fair values as of the acquisition date. For example, discovery during the allocation period of the need for an adjustment to the measurement of an acquired asset for an event that had not occurred as of the acquisition date would not be reflected in the purchase price allocation but would result in a *charge to earnings.*

BUSINESS COMBINATIONS: NEW BASIS ACCOUNTING

In August 1996, the Board added to its agenda a project on business combinations to reconsider APB Opinions 16, *Business Combinations,* and 17, *Intangible Assets.* In June 2001, this phase of the project was completed when FASB 141, *Business Combinations,* and FASB 142, *Goodwill and Other Intangible Assets,* were issued.

This project is a portion of the Business Combinations: Phase 2, and focuses on new basis accounting issues. The IASB has added the project to its agenda to make the new basis accounting project a joint undertaking between the IASB and the FASB.

Fresh-Start Recognition and Measurement

The project focuses on those situations in which fresh-start (a new basis at fair value) recognition and measurement of all of an entity's assets and liabilities would be appropriate. Identified conditions for application of this accounting treatment are:

1. A multiparty business combination or other new entity formation in which no single preexisting entity obtains majority ownership and control of the resulting new entity.
2. Joint venture formations.
3. Related issues, including the recognition and measurement of goodwill and other intangibles in combinations or other transactions accounted for by the fresh-start method.

In September 2000, the FASB formally approved the initial focus of Business Combinations: Phase 2 on new-basis accounting issues. The Board also approved a draft working principle for use in determining the appropriateness of recognizing a new basis of accounting. The Board decided that the scope of the project should include the issue of gain recognition in the financial statements of the entity that has transferred control over net assets to a joint venture.

During the fourth quarter in 2000, the Board discussed the recognition of a new basis of accounting in connection with the formation of a joint venture. The Board decided that a change in control over net assets from unilateral control by one entity to joint or shared control by that entity and one or more other entities should result in a new basis of accounting for those net assets in the financial statements of the jointly controlled entity. The Board also discussed gain recognition, as of the date of formation of a joint venture, in the financial statements of an investor that transfers an appreciated (or previously unrecognized) asset to the joint venture. The Board decided that an entity that exchanges appreciated (or previously unrecognized) assets for an equity interest in a joint venture should recognize a gain on the assets exchanged.

Immediate plans

During the first quarter of 2002, the FASB staff continued working with the IASB staff in developing the joint project scope and plan, which will be subject to review by both the FASB and IASB prior to further Board deliberations on fresh-start (new-basis) issues. And, as a matter of fact, as a result of more immediate pressures on both Boards, the project is temporarily on hold.

NEW PROJECTS TO CONSIDER STANDARDS OVERLOAD

The term "standards overload" is one that has been used off and on over the years by the FASB's various constituent groups to describe concerns about:

1. The volume of accounting rules.
2. The level of complexity and detail of those rules.
3. The resulting profusion of footnote disclosures.
4. The difficulty of finding all the accounting rules on a particular subject.

Those concerns surfaced in the responses to the 2001 Annual Financial Accounting Standards Advisory Council (FASAC) Survey—with respondents suggesting that the Board place a high priority (in the form of resources) on finding ways to codify and simplify the accounting literature.

In early 2002, the Board agreed to commit staff resources to a variety of projects that have a common goal of improving the usability and the effectiveness of the accounting literature. Those projects are described below.

Simplification

The Board agreed to evaluate the feasibility of issuing standards that emphasize *basic principles and objectives* rather than issue standards that include detailed rules, exceptions, and alternatives to the underlying principles. A shift to less detailed standards would place the focus on accounting for the *substance* of a transaction *rather than the form*. Such an approach would encourage those applying an accounting standard to comply not only with the letter of the law, but, more important, with the *objective* and *intent*—the spirit—of that law. Much of the rest of the accounting world including the IASB standards adhere to this principle.

The success of this project and the possible future direction of U.S. accounting standards depend upon the willingness of all those involved—preparers, practitioners and regulators to support this framework. For example, if the FASB is to issue standards that focus on underlying principles and objectives, they feel that much of the chance for improvement lies with others as well as with themselves:

1. The SEC should be willing to accept some divergence in application.
2. Preparers would need to adhere to the *spirit* of a standard and not look for the all-too-easy-to-find loopholes.
3. The auditing profession would need to enforce that spirit diligently and unquestioningly.
4. Constituents would need to accept the absence of specific guidance for many transactions. (Their reward for transparency and openness should be regaining their advantage in the capital markets.)
5. The Board must be prepared to resist requests for detailed guidance and remember that it has been impossible to codify ethical conduct.

The initial plans are to draft the framework, which will include guidelines for deciding the types of issues that should and should not be addressed in FASB standards.

The Board also plan to draft illustrations of how several existing standards might look if that framework had been applied while the standard was being developed. Once Board members have agreed in principle with the draft framework, a discussion paper explaining the framework and the illustrative standards will be distributed to, and discussed with, various constituent groups. The Board planned to begin the discussions in the summer of 2002.

Once agreed to by all parties, the framework would be applied to current and future Board agenda projects. The hope is that application of that framework would decrease the amount of time taken to issue a standard and result in standards that are easier to understand and, therefore, apply.

If future FASB standards are less detailed, the potential exists for similar transactions to be accounted for differently from entity to entity. If that different accounting produces diverse results that diminish comparability (and the relevance and reliability of financial reporting), they feel there will be a need for an authoritative body to provide implementation and interpretive guidance on those standards.

Thus, concurrent with developing a framework for more general standards, Board members plan to evaluate—in collaboration with others—how the current standard-setting structure might be modified to adapt to issuance of standards following that framework. One objective of that effort will be to make the U.S. process of issuing authoritative literature more efficient. A second objective will be to clarify the scope of each rule-making body's activities.

The initial plans are to work with a small group of representatives from the EITF, American Institute of Certified Public Accountants (AICPA), and SEC to develop a model for deciding when additional authoritative literature is necessary on a given topic and then determine the most effective segregation of duties among those bodies with respect to issuing pronouncements and providing supplemental guidance. Once that group has agreed in principle to that model, the Board plan to seek input from various constituent groups.

Cost / Benefit Analysis

Another project aimed at simplifying FASB standards will focus on improving the quality of the cost/benefit analysis performed on proposed standards by more actively engaging constituents in that analysis. The aim is to determine the costs of applying a new standard and to minimize those costs without decreasing the benefits to financial reporting. The hope is that the result will be simplified standards that are easier to understand and apply.

The FASB has always made a point of adopting a standard only when the expected benefits exceed the perceived costs. Thus, the Board currently weighs the cost/benefit relationship of each standard before issuing it. A cost/benefit section is included in the basis for conclusions of each proposed and final standard.

CODIFICATION AND RETRIEVABILITY

In response to the concerns about the ever-increasing volume of authoritative literature and the various places to research to find information on a particular topic, the Board agreed to consider a number of projects aimed at improving the retrievability and usability of the accounting literature.

The staff is in the process of developing due process procedures to be followed in current and future FASB agenda projects to ensure that future standards do not further complicate the whole process. The goal is for the Board to identify, and where possible, resolve all potential conflicts with other accounting literature—EITF, Accounting Standards Executive Committee (AcSEC), and SEC—before issuing a standard and either incorporate or refer to any existing relevant authoritative literature.

The FASB has attempted to incorporate existing ARB, APB and FASB literature in recent standards (e.g., FASBs 141 and 144); however, it is imperative to broaden the effort to encompass all authoritative literature.

Formally adopting this all-inclusive approach to setting standards should reduce the number of places necessary to search for guidance on a particular topic and reduce the volume of the literature. Since the Board will need to address inconsistencies that arise between a new standard and existing rulings (including AcSEC and SEC literature), the earlier in the process those inconsistencies are identified and addressed, the better.

The Board is planning to include references to all of the applicable U.S. accounting literature in the FASB's *Current Text* (a compilation of all FASB accounting standards categorized by subject). The next step of this project is to partner with others in developing a comprehensive *searchable online database* that will include all of the U.S. accounting requirements. It would include not only FASB and EITF literature but also AICPA and SEC literature.

Consistent with the objective of making the accounting literature easier to retrieve, the Board has agreed to consider (on an ad hoc basis) issuing documents codifying specific accounting topics. Currently, they plan to combine all of the EITF issues related to APB Opinion 25, *Accounting for Stock Issued to Employees,* in one EITF issue and then include that Issue with the rest of the APB 25 literature in a codified document. That and all future codified documents will include references to AICPA and SEC literature.

FASB and SEC Combine Efforts to Solve Disclosure Overload

In response to disclosure overload concerns, the Board has assigned an FASB staff member to work with the SEC staff on its initiative to:

1. Simplify financial disclosures.
2. Make financial statements useful for all who need to access them.
3. Produce rulings and statements that are easily understood by the ordinary investor.

The SEC staff is pursuing the idea of supplementing existing periodic disclosures with "real-time" or more current disclosures and implementing a "click-down" (hyperlinks) disclosure system. The FASB staff has agreed to act as a liaison to the SEC staff working on this initiative, provide support as appropriate and consider the implications of the SEC staff's efforts on existing and future standards.

The FASB believes that the projects described above offer the potential for improving financial reporting by facilitating retrievability and, more important, by simplifying the basic framework of financial reporting. To be successful, however, these changes will require a significant change in the mindset of preparers and constituents as well as of the Board itself.

ED, ON *ACQUISITIONS OF CERTAIN FINANCIAL INSTITUTIONS,* THAT AMENDS STATEMENTS 72, 144, AND INTERPRETATION 9

In May 2002, the FASB issued an exposure draft, *Acquisitions of Certain Financial Institutions,* that amends two existing accounting standards and an Interpretation to increase consistency of financial reporting. The proposed change would require that all financial institution acquisitions, except for those between two or more mutual enterprises, be accounted for under Statements 141, *Business Combinations,* and 142, *Goodwill and Other Intangible Assets.* The comment period concluded on June 24, 2002.

The exposure draft would amend Statement 72, *Accounting for Certain Acquisitions of Banking or Thrift Institutions,* and Interpretation 9, *Applying APB Opinions 16 and 17 When a Savings and Loan Association or a Similar Institution Is Acquired in a Business Combination.* The aim is to remove from their scope all financial institution acquisitions, except for transactions between two or more mutual enterprises. Those transactions would be accounted for under FASB Statements 141 and 142, prospectively.

In addition, the proposed Statement would amend FASB 144, *Accounting for the Impairment or Disposal of Long-Lived Assets,* to include certain long-term customer relationship intangible assets, such as depositor- and borrower-relationship assets, and credit-cardholder intangible assets.

The amendments to FASB 72 and Interpretation 9 would be effective for transactions completed after a final Statement is issued. The amendment to FASB 144 would become immediately effective upon issuance of a final Statement.

The exposure draft would require that unidentifiable intangible assets previously recognized under FASB 72 be reclassified and accounted for as goodwill if *both* of the following criteria are met:

1. The transaction in which the unidentifiable intangible assets arose was a business combination.
2. Intangible assets required to be separately recognized under Statement 141 were recognized apart from the unidentifiable intangible asset in that transaction and accounted for separately after the date of acquisition.

ED TO AMEND DEFINITION OF A DERIVATIVE AND STATEMENT 133 TO PROVIDE FOR MORE CONSISTENT ACCOUNTING

In May 2002, the FASB issued an exposure draft, *Amendment of Statement 133 on Derivative Instruments and Hedging Activities.* The draft amends FASB 133, *Accounting for Derivative Instruments and Hedging Activities,* to clarify the *definition* of a derivative.

In connection with Statement 133, Implementation Issue D1, "Application of Statement 133 to Beneficial Interests in Securitized Financial Assets," the Board addressed issues related to the accounting for beneficial interests in securitized financial assets, such as beneficial interests in securitized credit card receivables. In resolving those issues, the FASB decided that an amendment was needed to clarify the definition of a derivative, as set forth in the Statement.

The purpose of the exposure draft is to improve financial reporting by requiring that financial contracts with comparable characteristics be accounted for in the same way. The Statement would clarify under what circumstances a financial contract—either an option-based or non-option-based contract—with an initial investment would meet the characteristic of a derivative discussed in paragraph 6(b) of FASB 133. The Board believes the proposed change will produce more consistent reporting of financial contracts as either derivatives or hybrid financial instruments.

The proposed effective date for the accounting change is the first day of the first fiscal period beginning after November 15, 2002, which for calendar year-end companies will be January 1, 2003.

FASB ISSUES ED TO EXPAND DISCLOSURE REQUIREMENTS FOR GUARANTEES

In the hope of improving disclosures about loan guarantees, the FASB issued an exposure draft in May 2002 of a proposed Interpretation, *Guarantor's Ac-*

counting and Disclosure Requirements for Guarantees, Including Indirect Guarantees of Indebtedness of Others.

The proposed Interpretation would clarify and expand existing disclosure requirements for guarantees, including loan guarantees. It would also require that when a company issues a guarantee, the company must recognize a liability for the fair value, or market value, of its obligations under that guarantee. An improved disclosure and accounting treatment should provide a more faithful picture of a company's financial position and the risk it has assumed.

The Interpretation does not address the subsequent measurement of the guarantor's recognized liability over the term of the guarantee. It would also incorporate, without change, the guidance in FASB Interpretation 34, *Disclosure of Indirect Guarantees of Indebtedness of Others.*

This guidance would not apply to:

1. Guarantee contracts issued by insurance companies.
2. A lessee's residual value guarantee embedded in a capital lease.
3. Contingent rents and price rebates.

The provisions related to recognizing a liability at inception for the fair value of the guarantor's obligations would not apply to product warranties or to guarantees accounted for as derivatives.

FASB Adds Revenue Recognition Project

In a very busy May 2002, the FASB officially added a project on revenue recognition to its agenda. The purpose is to provide more comprehensive guidance regarding when companies should record revenues.

Revenue is normally the largest item in financial statements; revenue recognition issues top the list of reasons given for financial reporting restatements. It is also responsible for about 50 percent of all SEC enforcement cases that involve financial accounting and reporting cases, according to a former chief accountant at the SEC. And that was before the recent rash of restatements. The FASB's proposed project would address such matters by developing one accounting standard that would apply to a broad range of industries.

As part of its project on revenue recognition, the FASB will seek to:

1. Eliminate inconsistencies in the existing accounting literature and accepted practices.
2. Fill voids in the guidance that have recently emerged.
3. Provide further guidance for addressing issues that arise in the future.

The Board decided that while the standard is being developed, the EITF should continue to provide guidance on issues of revenue recognition based on the existing authoritative literature.

In developing the revenue recognition standard, the Board has decided to reconsider, as necessary, the guidance pertinent to revenue recognition in its Concepts Statements, particularly that in FASB Concepts Statement 5, *Recognition and Measurement in Financial Statements of Business Enterprises.*

Because of the interrelationships and interdependencies of the issues to be addressed, the Board decided that the project would be addressed in two parts being developed simultaneously. One part will take a bottom-up approach that provides an inventory of existing revenue recognition guidance and accepted practices; that inventory will help identify inconsistencies and gaps in the literature that need to be resolved. The other part will take a top-down approach that focuses on the conceptual guidance. This involves the process of developing guidance at the concepts level and standards level. The Board will test its tentative conclusions about the conceptual guidance by applying it to specific revenue recognition issues identified in the inventory. This might highlight the need for further improvements in the concepts. The simultaneous pursuit of the two parts will expedite completion of the project.

In the meantime, the SEC's Staff Accounting Bulletin (SAB) 101, *Revenue Recognition in Financial Statements,* would appear to be a good model to follow. It is discussed in Chapter 2, "Revenue and Expenses."

FASB 139, *RESCISSION OF FASB STATEMENT 53 AND AMENDMENTS TO FASB STATEMENTS 63, 89, AND 121*

The Statement rescinds FASB 53, *Financial Reporting by Producers and Distributors of Motion Picture Films.* The Statement defers to a Statement of Position developed by the American Institute of CPAs.

A business that is a producer or distributor of films and that previously applied FASB 53 is now required to follow the guidance in the AICPA's Statement of Position 00-2, *Accounting by Producers or Distributors of Films.* This Statement and the AICPA's SOP were effective for fiscal years beginning after December 15, 2000.

When Statement 53 was issued in 1981, the majority of a film's revenue resulted from distribution to movie theaters and free television. Since that time, extensive changes have occurred in the film industry. Home video, satellite and cable television, and pay-per-view television have come into existence, and international revenue has increased in significance. Because of these changes, considerable variations in the application of Statement 53 arose.

The SOP's purpose is to eradicate variations in accounting practices between producers and distributors of films and applies to all types of films and to producers or distributors who own or hold rights to them.

The SOP requires that:

1. Revenue should be recognized only when all of the following requirements are met:
   a. There is persuasive evidence that a customer sale or licensing arrangement exists.
   b. The film has been delivered or is ready for delivery and unconditional exploitation by the customer.
   c. The licensing period has begun.
   d. The revenue receivable is fixed or determinable.
   e. Collection of the revenue is reasonably assured.
2. If the above requirements are not met, revenue recognition should be deferred until they are met.
3. Licensing fee revenue recognized should be the present value of the license fee as of the time it is first recognized.
4. A flat fee covering a single film licensing arrangement should be recognized immediately when the above revenue recognition requirements are met.
5. A fee based on customer revenues should be recognized as the customer earns those revenues, and the above requirements for revenue recognition are met.
6. Film costs should be listed as a separate asset. Capitalized film costs include those costs required to bring the film to market.
7. Film cost assets should be amortized using the individual-film-forecast computation method, beginning when the film is released and revenue recognition begins. The individual-film-forecast computation method amortizes capitalized film costs in the same ratio as the current period's revenue bears to the film's estimated ultimate revenues.
8. If the fair value of a film falls below its unamortized film costs, the shortfall should be charged to income and the film's carrying amount reduced to its fair value. Any subsequent increases in fair value should not be recognized.
9. All marketing and related exploitation costs, except those direct advertising costs that qualify under existing accounting for capitalization, should be expensed as incurred.
10. Manufacturing and duplication costs should be recorded on a unit-specific basis and charged to income when the related unit's revenue is recognized.

FASB 139 also amends FASB Statement 63, *Financial Reporting by Broadcasters,* to indicate that a broadcaster is required to apply the guidance in SOP 00-2 if it owns the film (program material) that is shown on its cable, network, or local television outlets. It also amends FASB Statements 89, *Financial Reporting and Changing Prices,* and 121, *Accounting for the Impairment of Long-Lived Assets and Long-Lived Assets to Be Disposed Of.*

FASB Statement 140, Accounting for Transfers and Servicing of Financial Assets and Extinguishments of Liabilities—A Replacement of FASB Statement 125

FASB 140 replaces FASB 125, *Accounting for Transfers and Servicing of Financial Assets and Extinguishments of Liabilities,* and revises the standards for accounting for securitizations and other transfers of financial assets and collateral. It also requires certain disclosures, but it carries over most of Statement 125's provisions without reconsideration.

It provides accounting and reporting standards for transfers and servicing of financial assets and extinguishments of liabilities. Those standards are based on consistent application of a *financial-components approach* that focuses on control. Under that approach, after a transfer of financial assets, an entity:

1. Recognizes the financial and servicing assets it controls and the liabilities it has incurred.
2. Derecognizes financial assets when control has been surrendered.
3. Derecognizes liabilities when extinguished.

The Statement provides consistent standards for distinguishing transfers of financial assets that are sales from transfers that are secured borrowings.

Assets Accounted for as a Sale

A transfer of financial assets in which the transferor surrenders control over those assets is accounted for as a sale to the extent that consideration other than beneficial interests in the transferred assets is received in exchange. The transferor has surrendered control over transferred assets if and only if all of the following conditions are met:

1. The transferred assets have been isolated from the transferor—put presumptively beyond the reach of the transferor and its creditors, even in bankruptcy or other receivership.
2. Each transferee (or, if the transferee is a qualifying special-purpose entity [SPE], each holder of its beneficial interests) has the right to pledge or exchange the assets (or beneficial interests) it received. In addition, nothing prevents the transferee (or holder) from taking advantage of its

right to pledge or exchange or provide more than a trivial benefit to the transferor.

3. The transferor does not maintain effective control over the transferred assets through either:
   a. An agreement that both entitles and obligates the transferor to repurchase or redeem them before their maturity, or
   b. The ability to unilaterally cause the holder to return specific assets, other than through a cleanup call.

Measurement of Assets and Liabilities

This Statement requires that liabilities and derivatives incurred or obtained by transferors as part of a transfer of financial assets be initially measured at fair value, if practicable. It also requires that servicing assets and other retained interests in the transferred assets be measured by allocating the previous carrying amount between the assets sold, if any, and retained interests, if any, based on their relative fair values at the date of the transfer.

This Statement requires that servicing assets and liabilities be subsequently measured by:

1. Amortization in proportion to and over the period of estimated net servicing income or loss.
2. Assessment for asset impairment or increased obligation based on their fair values.

FASB 140 requires that a liability be derecognized if and only if either:

1. The debtor pays the creditor and is relieved of its obligation for the liability, or
2. The debtor is legally released from being the primary obligor under the liability either judicially or by the creditor. Therefore, a liability is not considered extinguished by an in-substance defeasance.

Implementation Guidance Provided

FASB 140 provides implementation guidance for:

- Assessing isolation of transferred assets.
- Conditions that constrain a transferee.
- Conditions for an entity to be a qualifying SPE.
- Accounting for transfers of partial interests.
- Measurement of retained interests.

- Servicing of financial assets.
- Securitizations.
- Transfers of sales-type and direct financing lease receivables.
- Securities lending transactions.
- Repurchase agreements including "dollar rolls," "wash sales," loan syndications, and participations.
- Risk participations in bankers' acceptances.
- Factoring arrangements.
- Transfers of receivables with recourse.
- Extinguishments of liabilities.

In addition to all of that, the Statement also provides guidance about whether a transferor has retained effective control over assets transferred to qualifying SPEs through removal-of-accounts provisions, liquidation provisions, or other arrangements.

It requires a debtor to:

1. Reclassify financial assets pledged as collateral and report those assets in its statement of financial position separately from other assets not so encumbered, if the secured party has the right by contract or custom to sell or repledge the collateral.
2. Disclose assets pledged as collateral that have not been reclassified and separately reported in the statement of financial position.

Additional Disclosures

FASB 140 also requires a secured party to disclose information about collateral that it has accepted and is permitted by contract or custom to sell or repledge. The required disclosure includes the fair value at the end of the period of that collateral, and of the portion of that collateral that it has sold or repledged, and information about the sources and uses of that collateral.

The Statement requires an entity that has securitized financial assets to disclose information about accounting policies, volume, cash flows, key assumptions made in determining fair values of retained interests, and sensitivity of those fair values to changes in key assumptions.

It also requires that entities that securitize assets disclose for the securitized assets and any other financial assets it manages together with them:

1. The total principal amount outstanding, the portion that has been derecognized, and the portion that continues to be recognized in each category reported in the statement of financial position, at the end of the period.

2. Delinquencies at the end of the period.
3. Credit losses during the period.

Effect upon Earlier Standards

The new Statement replaces Statement 125 and rescinds FASB Statement 127, *Deferral of the Effective Date of Certain Provisions of FASB Statement 125.* It also carries forward the actions taken by FASB 125.

Statement 125 had superseded FASB Statements 76, *Extinguishment of Debt,* and 77, *Reporting by Transferors for Transfers of Receivables with Recourse.* It amended FASB Statement 115, *Accounting for Certain Investments in Debt and Equity Securities,* to clarify that a debt security may not be classified as held-to-maturity if it can be prepaid or otherwise settled in such a way that the holder of the security would not recover substantially all of its recorded investment.

Statement 125 amended and extended to all servicing assets and liabilities the accounting standards for mortgage servicing rights now in FASB Statement 65, *Accounting for Certain Mortgage Banking Activities,* and superseded FASB Statement 122, *Accounting for Mortgage Servicing Rights.*

Statement 125 also superseded FASB Technical Bulletins 84-4, *In-Substance Defeasance of Debt,* and 85-2, *Accounting for Collateralized Mortgage Obligations (CMOs),* and amended FASB Technical Bulletin 87-3, *Accounting for Mortgage Servicing Fees and Rights.*

Special Report on FASB 140. In addition to the rather comprehensive guidance provided in the Standard, the FASB published a special report covering the most frequently asked questions about FASB 140.

The Special Report is a cumulative document, incorporating new questions and answers as well as those that have been updated and reworked from the first, second, and third editions of the FASB Special Report, *A Guide to Implementation of Statement 125 on Accounting for Transfers and Servicing of Financial Assets and Extinguishments of Liabilities.*

Most of the questions are unchanged from the previous Special Report, but many of the answers are newly updated, reflecting changes made by Statement 140. The new questions focus on the effects of various kinds of call options on sale treatment and the application of the expected cash flow technique to the measurement of the fair value of retained interests in securitizations.

Effective Dates

FASB 140 is effective for transfers and servicing of financial assets and extinguishments of liabilities occurring after March 31, 2001. It is effective for recognition and reclassification of collateral and for disclosures relating to securitization transactions and collateral for fiscal years ending after December 15, 2000. Disclosures about securitization and collateral accepted need not be reported for periods ending on or before December 15, 2000, for which financial statements are presented for comparative purposes.

BUSINESS COMBINATIONS AND INTANGIBLE ASSETS

In August, 1996, the Board added to its agenda a project on business combinations to reconsider APB Opinions 16, *Business Combinations,* and 17, *Intangible Assets.* The project is an attempt to improve the transparency of the accounting for business combinations presumably to give the user of the financial statement a clearer picture of the financial health of the new entity.

The project focuses on the accounting for goodwill and other purchased intangible assets and the fundamental issues related to the methods of accounting for business combinations, including whether there is a need for two separate and distinct methods (purchase method and pooling-of-interests method).

The project will not address how to account for in-process research and development (IPR&D) costs.

Step by Step from September 1999

Just to glance at the life cycle of the Business Combinations Exposure Draft should give one an indication that the original ideas could hardly come through the "extensive due process and deliberations" unscathed.

1. The Exposure Draft, *Business Combinations and Intangible Assets,* was issued in September, 1999. The comment period ended on December 7, 1999. The Board received more than 200 comment letters in response to the Exposure Draft.
2. In February, 2000, the Board held four days of public hearings at which 43 respondents presented their views on the 1999 Exposure Draft.
3. In April, 2000, the Board began its redeliberations of the issues addressed in the 1999 Exposure Draft.
4. The FASB Chairman testified before Congress on the business combinations project three times in 2000. He participated in oversight hearings before the Senate Committee on Banking, Housing, and Urban Affairs (March 2, 2000) and before the Subcommittee on Finance and Hazardous Materials of the Committee on Commerce in the House of Representatives (May 4, 2000). In addition, on June 14, 2000, he participated

in a roundtable discussion held by the Senate Committee on Banking, Housing, and Urban Affairs, which focused on the nature of and the accounting for goodwill.

5. At the May 31, 2000 Board meeting, a team of representatives from the investment banking community and several public accounting firms met with the Board to discuss their proposal to use a residual income valuation model to measure and account for goodwill. Under their proposal, goodwill would not be amortized but would be reviewed for impairment.

6. On September 29, 2000, the Board met with a team of representatives from the American Business Conference, Cisco Systems, Merrill Lynch & Co., Technet, and the United Parcel Service to discuss a proposed impairment test that would apply to purchased goodwill. Under that approach, goodwill would be tested for impairment when a triggering event indicates that the goodwill may have become impaired. The test for impairment would be performed by applying a discounted cash flow model to the portion of the revenue stream that can be attributed to the acquired business.

7. During October and November, 2000, Board and staff members participated in field visits with 14 companies in a variety of industries to discuss a general goodwill impairment approach developed by the FASB staff. The FASB staff then prepared a report that summarizes the information discussed at those field visits, including suggestions to change and improve the approach.

8. On October 3, 2000, Representative Christopher Cox (R-CA) introduced a bill in the House of Representatives [H.R. 5365, "Financial Accounting for Intangibles Reexamination (FAIR) Act"] that would, if enacted, postpone proposed improvements to the transparency of business combinations.

    a. On October 5, 2000, Representatives E. Clay Shaw, Jr. (R-FL), Collin C. Peterson (D-MN), Owen B. Pickett (D-VA), and Brad Sherman (D-CA), all of whom attained the professional status of licensed Certified Public Accountants, jointly issued a dear colleague letter opposing the bill.

    b. On October 10, 2000, Congressman Christopher Shays (R-CT) also issued a dear colleague letter opposing the bill.

9. On December 20, 2000 the Board decided to issue a limited revision of the 1999 Exposure Draft. The purpose of the limited revised Exposure Draft was to expose for comment the *changes to the accounting for goodwill* proposed in the 1999 Exposure Draft.

10. On January 24, 2001, the Board reconfirmed the proposal in the 1999 Exposure Draft that would require all business combinations to be accounted for using the purchase method, thus prohibiting use of the pooling-of-interests (pooling) method of accounting for business combinations.

11. On February 14, 2001, the FASB issued a revised limited Exposure Draft, *Business Combinations and Intangible Assets—Accounting for Goodwill.* During the revised Exposure Draft's 30-day comment period, it was distributed primarily through the FASB Web site. The revised limited ED contains the FASB's tentative decisions reached in December 2000, requiring use of a nonamortization approach to account for purchased goodwill.

12. Under that approach, goodwill would not be amortized to earnings, as originally proposed. Instead, it would be reviewed for impairment; that is, written down and expensed against earnings only in the periods in which the recorded value of goodwill exceeded its fair value.

13. The 30-day comment period concluded on March 16, 2001. The FASB would not issue a final Statement on business combinations and intangible assets until it had addressed issues raised in this ED and had reviewed the entire set of tentative decisions reached during redeliberations. The Board expected to issue its final Statement by the end of June, 2001.

FASBs 141 and 142 Approved

And, indeed, the FASB did conclude the voting process on its business combinations project after Board members submitted final ballots on June 29, 2001. The Board members unanimously voted in favor of the two measures: Statement 141, *Business Combinations,* and Statement 142, *Goodwill and Other Intangible Assets.*

As expected, the Statements change the accounting for business combinations and goodwill in two significant ways. Statement 141 requires that the purchase method of accounting be used for all business combinations initiated after June 30, 2001. Use of the pooling-of-interest method is prohibited.

Application of the purchase method requires identification of the acquiring enterprise. To determine which enterprise is the acquiring enterprise, all pertinent facts need to be considered, particularly the relative voting rights in the combined enterprise after the combination, the composition of the board of directors, the senior management of the combined enterprise, and which enterprise received a premium.

FASB 142 changes the accounting for goodwill from an amortization method to an impairment-only approach. Thus, amortization of goodwill, including goodwill recorded in past business combinations, ceases upon adoption of that Statement, which for companies with calendar year ends is January 1, 2002.

The Board decided that the definition of financial asset used in FASB Statement 141, *Business Combinations,* should be based on the definition of financial instrument in FASB Statement 107, *Disclosures about Fair Value of Financial Instruments.* (See the ADB.)

The Statement requires that an impairment loss recognized in the year of initial application for nonamortized intangible assets should be recognized in the same manner as goodwill; that is, as the effect of a change in accounting principle. Intangible assets that will no longer be amortized should be tested for impairment in the first interim period in which the Statement is initially applied.

Acquired intangibles other than goodwill will be amortized over their useful life which may extend beyond the current 40-year maximum amortization period. An intangible asset that is being amortized and is subsequently determined to have an indefinite useful life should stop being amortized and be accounted for in the same manner as other intangible assets deemed to have an indefinite useful life.

But this is still not the end of the business combinations project. In January 2000, the Board began discussions on a closely related project to consider purchase method procedures and new basis accounting.

The Board believes that comment letters received in the first phase of the business combinations project indicated the necessity to address the purchase method procedures. The project will reconsider purchase method guidance that was not reconsidered as part of Statements 141 and 142.

Tentatively, the project is focusing on purchase method guidance in the following areas:

1. Accounting for noncontrolling interests.
2. Determining the cost of an acquisition, and accounting for contingent consideration.
3. Recognizing assets acquired and liabilities assumed.
4. Accounting for pre-acquisition contingencies.

The Canadian Accounting Standards Board is adopting identical Standards to those adopted by the FASB with the goal of converging North American accounting standards related to business combinations.

FASB 143, Accounting for Asset Retirement Obligations

The Board concluded deliberations and unanimously voted to issue Statement 143, *Accounting for Asset Retirement Obligations.* Initiated in 1994 as a project to account for the costs of nuclear decommissioning, the Board soon expanded the scope to include similar closure or removal-type costs in other industries. These include oil and gas production facilities, landfills, mines, and environmental cleanups, etc. The existing financial reporting practices had been inconsistent and, in some cases, misleading.

The new Standard requires entities to record the fair value of a liability for an asset retirement obligation in the period in which it is incurred. When the liability is initially recorded, the entity capitalizes a cost by increasing the carrying amount of the related long-lived asset. Over time, the liability is accreted to its present value each period, and the capitalized cost is depreciated over the useful life of the related asset. Upon settlement of the liability, an entity either settles the obligation for its recorded amount or incurs a gain or loss upon settlement.

The standard is effective for fiscal years beginning after June 15, 2002, with earlier application encouraged.

Objective of the Project

The aim of the asset retirement obligations (ARO) project has been to provide accounting requirements for retirement obligations associated with these tangible long-lived assets. The obligations included within the scope of the project are those that an entity cannot avoid as a result of either the acquisition, construction, or normal operation of a long-lived asset.

The obligation must result from a long-lived asset's acquisition, construction, or normal use. The "asset" may be a functional group of assets or a component part of a group of long-lived assets for which there are separable, identifiable asset retirement obligations.

In the case of leased long-lived assets, the standard applies to a lessee's long-lived leased assets accounted for as a capital lease. It applies to the lessor if the lease is an operating lease.

Capitalization

The Board decided that an asset retirement cost should be capitalized as part of the cost of the related long-lived asset. That capitalized asset retirement cost should then be allocated to expense by using a systematic and rational method. An entity is not precluded from using an allocation method that would have the effect of capitalizing and allocating to expense the same amount of cost in the same accounting period.

Requirements

The new standard requires:

1. Recognition of a long-lived tangible asset retirement obligation liability and an offsetting increase in the amount of the related long-lived asset.
2. The obligation be measured at its fair value.
3. Allocation of the asset retirement cost in the form of additional depreciation to expense over the related asset's useful life.

4. Changes in the amount of the obligation liability subsequent to initial recognition be recognized if they arise from the passage of time and revisions to either the timing or amount of the related estimated cash flows.

5. Recognition of an interest-type charge related to the obligation.

Change in Fair Value Methodology

The Board decided that the objective for initial measurement of an ARO liability should be use of the fair value method using a valuation technique, such as expected present value, to estimate fair value.

The methodology to determine fair value under the new Standard represents a departure from past practice. The FASB now believes when the timing or amount of estimated cash flow related to an obligation is uncertain and in the absence of quoted market prices in active markets or prices for similar liabilities, fair value should be determined using an expected present value technique.

"Expected present value" refers to the sum of probability-weighted present values in a range of estimated cash flows, all discounted using the same interest rate convention. For purposes of measuring an ARO liability, an entity is required to use a discount rate that equates to a risk-free rate adjusted for the effect of its credit standing (credit-adjusted risk-free rate).

FASB's traditional present value approach used a single estimate of future cash flows, and the Board still believes the traditional approach is appropriate for measuring the fair value of assets and liabilities with contractual cash flows.

Recognition

An asset retirement obligation must be recognized when three requirements are met:

1. The obligation meets the definition of a liability.
2. A future transfer of assets associated with the obligation is probable.
3. The amount of the liability can be reasonably measured.

In order to meet the definition of a liability—the first test—the three characteristics of a liability must be satisfied:

a. The company has a present duty or responsibility to one or more other entities that entails settlement by probable future transfer or use of assets.

b. The company has little or no discretion to avoid a future transfer of use of assets.

c. An obligating event has already happened.

Obligating Events

The Standard deals with obligations arising under three circumstances:

1. Obligations incurred upon acquisition, construction, or development of an asset.
2. Obligations incurred during the operating life of an asset, either ratably or nonratably.
3. Obligations incurred any time during the life of an asset because of a newly enacted law or statute, or a change in contract provisions, or because an entity has otherwise incurred a duty or responsibility to one or more other entities.

Obligations incurred upon acquisition, construction, or development of an asset should be recognized when the cost of the long-lived asset is recognized. Those incurred during the operating life of an asset should be recognized concurrent with the events creating the obligation.

Subsequent Measurement of an ARO Liability

The Board decided that an entity should be required to use an allocation approach for subsequent measurement of an ARO liability. Under that approach, an entity is not required to remeasure an ARO liability at fair value each period. Instead, it is required to recognize changes in an ARO liability resulting from the passage of time and revisions in cash flow estimates. Those changes are then incorporated into a remeasurement of an ARO liability. The rate used to record accretion of the liability and revisions in cash flow estimates is the credit-adjusted risk-free rate applied when an ARO liability was initially measured.

Disclosures

An entity should disclose the following information in its financial statements:

1. A general description of the asset retirement obligations and of the associated long-lived assets.
2. The fair value of assets that are legally restricted for purposes of settling asset retirement liabilities.
3. If any significant change occurs in the components of an asset retirement obligation, a reconciliation of the beginning and ending aggregate carrying amount of the liability showing separately the changes attributable to:

a. The liability incurred in the current period.

b. The liability settled in the current period.

c. Accretion expense.

d. Revisions in expected cash flows.

Transition

When the Standard is first applied, the company must recognize the following on its balance sheet as if the Standard had been in effect when an asset retirement obligation was incurred:

1. A liability for any existing asset retirement obligations adjusted for cumulative interest to the date of adoption of the new standard.

2. An asset retirement cost capitalized as an increase to the carrying amount of the associated long-lived asset.

3. Accumulated depreciation on the capitalized cost.

Amounts resulting from initial application should be measured using current (as of the date of adoption) information, current assumptions, and current interest rates.

FASB JOINS INTERNATIONAL JWG CONSIDERING FINANCIAL INSTRUMENTS

Because of changes in the very nature of modern business transaction, traditional accounting concepts for the recognition and cost-based measurement of financial instruments need to be adjusted. Not only the FASB, but also the entire international business community realizes that this is necessary.

The business and investment environment changes are a result of advances in financial risk management, information technology, globalization of capital markets, and accelerated use of sophisticated derivatives and other complex financial instruments. The accounting must change also.

International Projects on Financial Instruments

Therefore, the FASB is participating in an International Joint Working Group (JWG) aimed at developing an integrated and harmonized international standard on accounting for financial instruments. Other members of the group include representatives from the International Accounting Standards Board (IASC) and from standard-setting bodies in Australia, Canada, France, Germany, Japan, New Zealand, the Nordic Federation, and the United Kingdom.

The group is working from the proposals in the IASC Discussion Paper,

"Accounting for Financial Assets and Financial Liabilities," taking into account responses received on those proposals, the views of various bodies, and work done or under way by the FASB and other national standard-setters.

Issues Similar to FASB's Projects

The International Joint Working Group is considering most of the issues that the FASB is currently considering in its own project on measuring all financial assets and liabilities at fair value, and many of the issues that the Board has already decided in FASB 140, and FASB 133, *Accounting for Derivative Instruments and Hedging Activities,* and other Statements in the financial instruments project.

The Group concluded its work by completing a Special Report, *Financial Instruments and Similar Items,* in December 2000. Comments were requested by June 30, 2001. The FASB has not yet determined what effect that international effort will have on the remaining parts of their financial instruments project. However, they have been increasingly interested in giving close consideration to international standards when feasible.

Standard-setters in other countries represented in the JWG are publishing the Special Report at approximately the same time. Comments received will be shared among all of those organizations unless respondents specify otherwise.

FIN 44, *Accounting for Certain Transactions Involving Stock Compensation*

This FASB stock option ruling in Interpretation 44, *Accounting for Certain Transactions Involving Stock Compensation,* is an interpretation of APB Opinion 25, *Accounting for Stock Issued to Employees.*

Accounting for stock options is governed by FASB 123, *Accounting for Stock-Based Compensation,* which allows companies to select one of two approaches to accounting and reporting of stock-based employee compensation plans. It was this "compromise" from requirements of a *fair value method only* standard that finally led to the adoption of FASB 123. Now, it's either intrinsic value method or fair value method.

The FASB encourages companies to adopt the fair value method, but it is not required. It is acceptable to use the intrinsic value method prescribed in APB Opinion 25, *Accounting for Stock Issued to Employees,* which is the pre-FASB 123 Standard dealing with stock-based compensation plans. If a company continues to use the Opinion 25 approach, the entity must disclose the pro forma impact on income and earnings per share of using the fair value method.

In the case of stock options, the fair value is determined using an option pricing model. Once the fair value is determined at the grant date, it is not subsequently adjusted for:

1. Changes in the price of the underlying stock.
2. The volatility of the stock.
3. The life of the option.
4. Dividends on the stock.
5. The risk free interest rate.

Delineation of Requirements

The Interpretation requires the following:

1. Compensation in the form of stock options granted to independent contractors or other providers of services and goods, who are not employees, are to be accounted for using the *fair value method.* The principal consequence of this Interpretation is that the granting company must record a stock compensation cost based on the option's fair value at the grant date over the option's life for a transaction. Previously, this may not have resulted in a stock compensation cost.
2. Non-employee board members are considered to be employees for stock option compensation accounting purposes. As a result, under the stock option plans of most companies, the practice will continue that no compensation cost will be recognized for stock options granted to non-employee directors.
3. If the exercise price of a fixed option award is reduced or repriced, the modified stock options must be accounted for as a variable option plan from the date of modification to the date the award is exercised, forfeited, or expires unexercised. The consequence for the grantor is:
   a. Very few fixed option plans will lead to a stock compensation cost.
   b. If the company's stock price exceeds the option's strike price during the stock option's life, variable option plans may result in a stock compensation cost.
4. A modification to a fixed stock option to add a reload feature requires the modified award be accounted for as a variable plan award regardless of the method used to determine the terms of the reload grant. Therefore, a reload feature provides for the automatic grant of a new option at the current market price in exchange for each previously owned share tendered by an employee in a stock-for-stock exercise.

Most reload grants awarded as modifications of a fixed plan will now result in a compensation cost if the company's stock price exceeds the reload option's strike price during the stock option's life.

5. There is no accounting consequence for changes in the exercise price or the number of shares of a stock option award as the result of an exchange of fixed stock option awards in a business combination accounted for as a pooling of interests as long as two criteria are met:

    a. The aggregate intrinsic value of the options immediately *after* the exchange is no greater than the aggregate intrinsic value of the options immediately *before* the exchange.

    b. The ratio of the exercise price per option to the market value per share is not reduced.

    (This is a very important facet of the requirements. If these two criteria are not met, a new measurement of compensation is *required.*)

6. A modification to a fixed stock option award that does *not* affect the life of the award, the exercise price, or the number of shares to be issued does not have an accounting consequence.

7. A modification that either renews a fixed award or extends the award's life requires a new measurement of compensation cost as if the award were newly granted. As a result, a compensation cost would be recognized in the case of:

    a. An employee fixed plan award over the life of the award for any significant difference between the current stock price and the stock price at the modification date.

    b. A non-employee stock grant at the fair value of the stock option at the modification date.

8. Any modification increasing the number of shares to be issued under a fixed stock option plan requires that the award be accounted for as a variable plan award from the modification date to the date the award is exercised, forfeited, or expires. The accounting consequence is that if the stock price exceeds the award's strike price during the stock option's life, after the award date a stock compensation cost will be recognized.

    A fixed option award that is canceled and replaced with a new award that results in a lower option price must be accounted for as a variable plan if the replacement award is made within six months of the cancellation date.

Possible Results of the Interpretation

Repercussions of FIN may lead to the following:

1. It potentially increases the cost of acquiring non-employee services paid for with stock options.

2. It discourages the repricing of options.

3. It encourages companies, as an alternative to repricing, to grant new stock option awards at the current market price to employees whose existing stock option award's strike prices are below the current market price.

ACCOUNTING FOR FINANCIAL INSTRUMENTS WITH CHARACTERISTICS OF LIABILITIES, EQUITY, OR BOTH, AND PROPOSED AMENDMENT TO CONCEPTS STATEMENT 6

In 1997, the FASB decided to resume deliberations on issues raised in a 1990 Discussion Memorandum, *Distinguishing Between Liability and Equity Instruments and Accounting for Instruments with Characteristics of Both.* The objective of the project is to improve the transparency of the accounting for financial instruments that contain characteristics of liabilities, equity, or both.

On October 27, 2000, the Board issued an Exposure Draft of a proposed Statement, *Accounting for Financial Instruments with Characteristics of Liabilities, Equity, or Both,* and an Exposure Draft of a proposed amendment to Concepts Statement 6 entitled *Proposed Amendment to FASB Concepts Statement 6 to Revise the Definition of Liabilities.* The deadline for comments on these EDs was April 30, 2001.

The Need for Clear Distinction

The "both" designation appears to have caused the most confusion, as might be expected. When an item is presented in one financial statement as a liability, in another as an asset, in another somewhere in limbo, confusion might be expected to result.

Financial reporting has always had difficulty dealing with financial instruments that blur the line between debt and equity, especially compound instruments like convertible debt that combine both debt and equity components.

The FASB points out that with financial innovation (creative accounting? the new economy?), both the number and complexity of such instruments are on the rise. This proposed statement would clarify the distinction between debt and equity. It would also provide better information about the rights and obligations embedded in compound instruments by requiring separate reporting of debt and equity components.

Areas of Confusion

Therefore, the FASB's motivation for a new standard might very well be a concern that some financial instruments:

1. Have the characteristics of liabilities, but are presented either between the liability and equity sections of the balance sheet or in equity.

2. Have characteristics of equity but are presented between the liabilities and equity sections of the balance sheet.

3. Have characteristics of both liabilities and equity but are classified either entirely as liabilities or entirely as equity.

The proposal would do away with these practices by requiring that the components of financial instruments be classified according to their liability or equity characteristics. The new standard would also change some aspects of the accounting for controlling and noncontrolling interests.

Classification of Components of Financial Instruments

The proposed Statement would require that an issuer of a financial instrument classify the components of that instrument as liabilities or as equity as follows:

1. A financial instrument component that represents an outstanding share of stock of the issuer that does not embody an obligation on the part of the issuer would be classified as equity.

2. A financial instrument component that embodies an obligation that requires (or permits at the issuer's discretion) settlement by issuance of equity shares would be classified as equity if it is deemed to establish an ownership relationship between the issuer and the holder. A component that embodies an obligation establishes an ownership relationship if a reporting entity can or must settle the obligation by issuing its equity shares and, to the extent that the monetary value of the obligation changes, the change is attributable to, equal to, and in the same direction as the change in fair value of the issuer's equity shares.

3. All other financial instrument components embodying obligations would be classified as liabilities.

The Board believes that separate balance sheet presentation of liability components and equity components of compound instruments more faithfully represents the rights and obligations embedded in those instruments than does presenting those components on a combined basis entirely as liabilities or entirely as equity.

With certain exceptions, the proposed statement would require that proceeds received from issuance of a compound financial instrument be allocated to its components based on the relative fair values of those components.

Requirements for Consolidated Subsidiary

The proposed statement would require the following in relation to the noncontrolling interest in a consolidated subsidiary:

1. It be displayed in the consolidated statement of financial position as a separate component of equity because it meets the definition of equity of the consolidated entity.

2. Sales of a subsidiary's shares to entities outside the consolidated group would be considered equity transactions of the reporting entity as long as that subsidiary remains consolidated. Therefore, no gain or loss would be recognized on those sales.

3. For a sale of a subsidiary's shares that results in the subsidiary's no longer being consolidated, a gain or loss would be recognized for the difference between the proceeds of that sale and the carrying amount of the interest sold in that transaction.

The proposed statement would require that an entity with one or more less-than-wholly-owned subsidiaries include amounts attributable to both the controlling interest and the noncontrolling interest in all amounts should be displayed as line items in the consolidated income statement as well as amounts displayed as components of other comprehensive income.

For companies with consolidated financial statements including one or more less-than-wholly-owned subsidiaries at any time during the initial adoption year, all financial statements of prior years would have to be restated. This restatement would need to show reversal of any gains or losses on the sale of subsidiary shares not accounted for in accordance with the new requirements.

Effects of the Proposal

If and when it is adopted, the new Standard would:

1. Change the income statement and balance sheet accounting for financial instruments with liability and equity components, such as debt convertible into common stock.

2. Change the amount reported for the total equity.

3. Change the amount reported for total liabilities.

4. Eliminate the reporting of items, such as minority interest, between the liability and equity sections of the balance sheet.

5. Eliminate in certain cases the recognition in consolidated financial statements of income from the sales of subsidiary shares.

6. Expand the earnings-per-share disclosures.

7. Change the comprehensive income display.

8. Enhance convergence of U.S. accounting standards toward similar high-quality non-U.S. accounting standards.

Liabilities Defined

As mentioned above, the proposed amendment to *Concepts Statement 6* would revise the definition of liabilities to include obligations that require or permit settlement by issuance of the issuer's equity shares but that do not establish an ownership relationship. The revision, if adopted, would facilitate and support the accounting proposals leading to the potential consequences listed above.

The amendment would reflect the Board's decision to revise the definition of liabilities to include certain obligations that a reporting entity can or must settle by issuing its equity shares.

The proposed new definition of a liability is: "Liabilities are probable future sacrifices of economic benefits arising from present obligations of a particular entity to transfer assets or provide services to other entities in the future as a result of past transactions or events. Certain obligations, primarily financial instruments or components of compound financial instruments, require or permit settlement by issuance of equity shares. If those financial instrument components establish a relationship between the issuer and the holder that is not an ownership relationship, they are liabilities."

Changes Resulting from the New Definition

Starting with this definition, the proposed standard, which deviates from current practice in many areas, would require that:

1. An issuer classify the liability components and equity components of financial instruments separately on the balance sheet. This is usually not required at present.

2. A gain or loss, if there is any, on the liability component of convertible debt must be recognized in earnings when the debt is extinguished by repayment or conversion. The manner of determining the gain or loss is new.

3. Items on the right side of the balance sheet be classified as either liabilities or equity. Currently, some items are reported between the liabilities and equity sections of the balance sheet.

4. A noncontrolling or minority interest in a consolidated subsidiary be presented in the equity section of the consolidated balance sheet. At present, this item appears between liabilities and equity.

5. A company with one or more less-than-wholly owned subsidiaries must include amounts attributable to both the controlling interest and the noncontrolling in total comprehensive income, components of other comprehensive income, and certain line items in the consolidated income statement, such as:

   a. Income from continuing operations.

   b. Discontinued operations.

   c. Extraordinary items.

   d. Cumulative effect of changes in accounting principle.

   e. Net income.

   This allocation is not required currently.

6. Sales of a subsidiary's shares to entities outside the consolidated group is an equity transaction as long as that subsidiary remains consolidated.

7. Earnings-per-share data presented on the face of the income statement include adjustments for noncontrolling interests in income to arrive at net income attributable to controlling interests. This is not required at present.

Examples of classification and measurement provisions to financial instruments with liability characteristics, equity characteristics, or both were provided in the Exposure Draft.

The new Standard would be effective for fiscal years beginning after June 15, 2002. Restatement of prior years' financial statements would be required for the effects of financial instruments within the scope of the new Standard that were outstanding at any time during the initial year of adoption.

IMPROVING BUSINESS REPORTING: INSIGHTS INTO ENHANCING VOLUNTARY DISCLOSURES

The purpose of this report is to demonstrate that companies can markedly improve their business reporting by voluntarily disclosing more available information about which the investment community and shareholders have a keen interest.

These matters include:

1. Identifying factors important to the financial success of the company.

2. Delineating management's plans and strategies for managing those factors in the past and future.

3. Specifying measurements used by management to assess its effectiveness in implementing those plans and strategies.

These were key recommendations in a broad report entitled *Improving Business Reporting: Insights into Enhancing Voluntary Disclosures.*

The recommendations resulted from a two-year project supervised by a 14-member Steering Committee of FASB constituents. The Steering Committee guided and directed the activities of a group of more than 50 professionals representing the preparer, financial statement user, auditing, and academic communities who worked on the project.

In addition to this report on voluntary disclosures, two other reports that resulted from the Business Reporting Research Project address the electronic distribution of business information and redundancies between the Securities and Exchange Commission's and the FASB's reporting requirements.

The objective of this report on voluntary disclosures is to help companies improve their business reporting by providing evidence that many leading companies are making extensive voluntary disclosures and by listing examples of those disclosures. The examples serve to provide companies with useful ideas on how to describe and explain their investment potential to investors. The basic premise underlying the Business Reporting Research Project is that improving disclosures makes the capital allocation process more efficient and reduces the average cost of capital. (And, not incidentally, avoid undue attention from the Securities and Exchange Commission.)

This project could very well be a reaction to the SEC's obviously being disillusioned by the fact that too many companies are trying to "cook the books" or resort to "creative" accounting to paint a rosier picture than the dark one that would otherwise be projected. If voluntary disclosure doesn't disclose enough, more stringent requirements will undoubtedly result.

The project studied the present practices for the voluntary disclosure of business information by six to nine companies in each of eight industries: automobiles, chemicals, computer systems, foods, oil-integrated domestic, pharmaceuticals, regional banks, and textile-apparel. The companies provided the project with copies of all materials that had been available to the public over the course of a year—materials such as annual and quarterly reports, SEC filings, press releases, fact books, and transcripts of presentations to shareholders, analysts, and potential investors. Corporate Web sites were also reviewed.

Some of the findings and recommendations noted in the report include:

1. The importance of voluntary disclosures is expected to increase in the future because of the fast pace of change in the business environment.

2. Voluntary disclosures related to matters that are important to the success of individual companies are very useful, particularly disclosures of management's view of the company's "critical success factors" and trends surrounding those factors.

3. Although some disclosures were found about unrecognized intangible assets, additional data about those assets would be beneficial because of the importance of intangibles to a company's value.

4. Voluntary disclosure should cover not only good news but also disappointments. Disclosures are most useful if they report on previously disclosed plans and goals and the results achieved in meeting those plans and goals.

5. The metrics used by companies to manage their operations and drive their business strategies often are very useful voluntary disclosures. Those metrics should be explained and consistently disclosed from period-to-period to the extent they continue to be relevant to a company's success.

BUSINESS AND FINANCIAL REPORTING, CHALLENGES FROM THE NEW ECONOMY

The FASB decided to find out if there really is a "disconnect" between the information provided in today's financial statements and the information needs of investors and creditors. In examining this issue, observers have complained about the widening gap existing between information needs of "New Economy" companies and "Old Economy" financial reporting.

Therefore, after some investigation, FASB has published a special report, *Business and Financial Reporting, Challenges from the New Economy*, that examines the relationship between the new economy and business and financial reporting.

The report reviews a range of studies and articles that compare accounting treatments for traditional assets and the challenges of new economy notions of intangible assets. The report concludes that the debate over "new" versus "old" is of very little value. The FASB appears to believe that a more important question is whether business financial reporting should change and, if so, how. (The Securities and Exchange Commission's view on the relationship between the accounting for traditional business and Internet business is discussed in Chapter 28.)

The report also concludes that the perceived shortcomings of business and financial reporting do not easily lend themselves to a simplistic and single solution.

The Board decided that there is no simple financial reporting solution to the issues raised in the report. The best set of solutions will come from national and international standard-setters working together. The issues are not limited to a specific country and probably do not lend themselves to an answer developed by one accounting standard-setter acting in isolation. Any standard-setter (foreign, domestic, or international), any SEC staff member, any preparer of financial statements, and the like, would certainly agree with all of the above.

Conclusions of Combined Effort

The report describes important contributions by groups in several nations, including the United States, the United Kingdom, Canada, Denmark, Sweden, the Netherlands, and the Organization for Economic Cooperation and Development (OECD).

The report concludes that standard-setters should focus their attention on:

1. Examination of the conceptual and practical issues surrounding recognition of internally generated intangible assets and measurement of those assets.
2. Expanded and systematic use of nonfinancial performance metrics.
3. Expanded use of forward-looking information.

An appendix to the report describes four projects that standard-setters might consider in addressing the financial reporting challenges that are a part of the new economy (in an international setting).

As the Board begins to consider whether it should add new projects to its agenda, the FASB hopes constituents will view this report as an opportunity to offer their insights on the subjects covered.

FASB Report on Redundancies, GAAP-SEC Disclosure Requirements

Redundancies that exist between generally accepted accounting principles (GAAP) and Securities and Exchange Commission financial reporting requirements create confusion and inefficiency for preparers of financial statements. To address this issue, the FASB sponsored a study as part of its Business Reporting Research Project to analyze existing reporting requirements. The report identifies and recommends measures to eliminate these redundancies in GAAP and SEC disclosure requirements.

Other objectives of the study include:

1. Review of SEC reporting requirements for one specialized industry and suggestions for improvement.
2. Recommendation of improvements to the structure and organization of disclosures within the 10-K.

The report is being sent to the SEC, FASB, and AICPA to take action in eliminating existing redundancies and to prevent their creation in the future. As directed by the Business Reporting Research Project's Steering Committee, the report focused on redundancies and was not an evaluation of the usefulness or effectiveness of disclosure requirements.

This report is the third in a series that the Business Reporting Research Project has recently completed. The first report examined the electronic distribution of business reporting information and the second focused on corporate voluntary disclosure practices, as discussed earlier.

Chapter 11
Governmental Accounting

CONTENTS

GASB 37, *Basic Financial Statements—and Management's Discussion and Analysis—for State and Local Governments: Omnibus—an Amendment of GASB Statements 21 and 34*	**11.02**
GASB 38, *Certain Financial Statement Note Disclosures*	**11.04**
Financial Reporting Guidance for Fund-Raising Foundations and Similar Organizations	**11.05**
GASB Issues ED on Deposit and Investment Risk Disclosures	**11.06**
Smoothing the Transition to GASB 34	**11.06**
A Guide for Implementing New Financial Statements	**11.07**
A Guide to Local Government Financial Statements	**11.08**
A Guide to a School District's Financial Statements	**11.09**
A Guide for Financial Analysts	**11.10**
"Cliffies" for Government Financial Statements	**11.11**
Interpretation Relating to Modified Accrual Standards	**11.12**
Review of Existing Standards	**11.13**
Business-Like Accounting Comes to State and Local Government	**11.15**
The GASB Gains Stature	**11.16**
Provisions of GASB 34	**11.16**
Background Information	**11.17**
The Time for Accountability Is Now	**11.17**
Retention of Fund Accounting	**11.18**

The All-Important Governmental Budget	**11.19**
New Information Is Readily Available	**11.19**
Required Information and Format	**11.20**
Content of MD&A	**11.22**
Government-Wide Financial Statements	**11.22**
Fund Financial Statements	**11.24**
Required Supplementary Information	**11.25**
Effective Date and Transition	**11.26**
Requirements for Prospective and Retrospective Reporting	**11.26**
Guidance on Modified Accrual Standards	**11.27**
GASB 35 for Public Colleges and Universities	**11.27**
GASB 33 on Nonexchange Transactions	**11.29**
GASB 36 on Symmetry Between Recipients and Providers in Accounting for Certain Shared Revenues	**11.30**

Phase 3 governments, those with annual revenues of less than $10 million, are finalizing plans to apply the requirements of GASB 34 in their financial statements after June 15, 2003. In the meantime, the Governmental Accounting Standards Board continues to do everything it can to make the transition of all state and local governments to the "new" governmental accounting model as painless and error-free as possible.

GASB 37, *Basic Financial Statements—and Management's Discussion and Analysis—for State and Local Governments: Omnibus—an Amendment of GASB Statements 21 and 34*

GASB 37, which was adopted in June 2001, amends GASB 21, *Accounting for Escheat Property,* and GASB 34, *Basic Financial Statements—and Management's Discussion and Analysis—for State and Local Governments.*

The amendments to Statement 21 are necessary because of the changes to the fiduciary fund structure required by Statement 34. Generally, escheat property that was previously reported in an *expendable trust fund* should now be reported in a *private-purpose trust fund* under Statement 34. Statement 37 explains the effects of that change.

The amendments to GASB 34 either:

1. Clarify certain provisions that, in retrospect, may not be sufficiently clear for consistent application, or

2. Modify other provisions that the Board believes may have unintended consequences in some circumstances.

The provisions aimed at *clarifying* previous provisions are not new but may have been unclear or confusing for the user. They include:

1. *Management's Discussion and Analysis (MD&A) requirements*— Governments should confine the topics discussed in MD&A to those listed in Statement 34 rather than consider those topics as "minimum requirements."
2. *Modified approach*—Adopting the modified approach for infrastructure assets that have previously been depreciated is considered a change in an *accounting estimate.* The effect of the change is accounted for prospectively rather than as a restatement of prior periods.
3. *Program revenue classifications*—Fines and forfeitures should be included in the broad *charges for services* category. Also, additional guidance is provided to aid in determining to which function certain program revenues pertain.
4. *Major fund criteria*—Major fund reporting requirements apply to a governmental or enterprise fund if the *same* element (for example, revenues) exceeds *both* the 10 percent *and* 5 percent criteria.

The provisions, which are modifications of the requirements of Statement 34, include:

1. Eliminating the requirement to capitalize construction-period interest for governmental activities.
2. Changing the minimum level of detail required for business-type activities in the statement of activities from *segments* to *different identifiable activities.*

The Board believed that GASB 37 would help governments implement Statement 34 and improve the usefulness of state and local governments' financial statements under the far-reaching new reporting model. Statement 38 (below) was implemented to provide users with new information and eliminate some disclosures that the Board found were no longer needed.

The provisions of Statement 37 were to be simultaneously implemented with Statement 34. For governments that had already implemented GASB 34 prior to the issuance of GASB 37, the requirements were effective for financial statements for periods beginning after June 15, 2000.

GASB 38, CERTAIN FINANCIAL STATEMENT NOTE DISCLOSURES

Statement 38 modifies, adds, and deletes various note disclosure requirements. The requirements cover such areas as:

1. Revenue recognition policies.
2. Actions taken in response to legal violations.
3. Debt service requirements.
4. Variable-rate debt.
5. Receivable and payable balances.
6. Interfund transfers and balances.
7. Short-term debt.

The new requirements are an additional attempt to address the needs of users of financial statements as determined through ongoing Board research. In discussing the benefits to users, the Board considered that with respect to interfund transfers, users of financial statements will, for the first time, be able to trace transfers from the source fund to the receiving fund and to understand why the government uses transfers.

Now users will also be able to see the purpose and extent of the use of short-term debt, which is especially important for debt issued and redeemed within the government's fiscal year.

Statement 38 is the result of the GASB's intention to ensure the continuing effectiveness of existing standards. The Board reaffirmed that most note disclosure requirements are still relevant.

The requirements of this Statement issued in June 2001 are effective in three phases based on a government's total annual revenues in the first fiscal year ending after June 15, 1999:

1. *Phase 1 governments*—The large governmental organizations with annual revenues of $100 million or more, were required to implement portions of GASB 38 for fiscal periods beginning after June 15, 2001. These governments implemented the remaining portions for fiscal periods beginning after June 15, 2002.
2. *Phase 2 governments*—Those with total annual revenues of $10 million or more but less than $100 million, applied the requirements of the Statement in financial statements for periods beginning after June 15, 2002.
3. *Phase 3 governments*—The small entities with total annual revenues of less than $10 million should apply the requirements in financial statements for periods beginning after June 15, 2003. Thus, the effective date coincides with the effective date of GASB Statement 34 for the reporting government.

FINANCIAL REPORTING GUIDANCE FOR FUND-RAISING FOUNDATIONS AND SIMILAR ORGANIZATIONS

In May 2002, the GASB issued Statement 39, *Determining Whether Certain Organizations Are Component Units, an Amendment of GASB Statement 14,* which clarifies existing accounting guidance and provides greater consistency in accounting for organizations that are closely related to a primary government. The standard provides criteria for determining whether certain organizations, such as not-for-profit foundations related to public universities and school districts, should be reported as component units based on the nature and significance of their relationship to a state or local government.

Under this ruling, state and local governments that have qualifying fund-raising foundations would be required to include, through discrete presentations, the financial activities of those foundations in their financial statements. Previously, there was no consistency in dealing with their financial matters:

1. Some entities had included the balances and transactions of their related fund-raising organizations in their financial statements.
2. Others disclosed limited information in the notes.
3. Still others provided no information at all.

GASB 39 should bring a greater level of comparability to state and local financial reporting. It amends Statement 14 to provide additional guidance to determine whether certain organizations for which the primary government is not financially accountable should be reported as component units based on the nature and significance of their relationship with a primary government.

The standard sets forth criteria on which a government is required to provide a discrete presentation that includes financial information about its own activities as well as those of the affiliated organization.

Generally, a legally separate, tax-exempt, fund-raising organization whose primary purpose is to raise or hold significant resources for the benefit of a specific governmental unit should be included as a component unit of that governmental unit's financial reporting entity.

Error Correction for Statement 39

During the final stages of production on GASB 39, an error occurred and the phrase "or its component units" was inadvertently dropped from paragraph 5 of the standard.

Paragraph 40a is added between paragraphs 40 and 41 to correct the omission.

GASB ISSUES ED ON DEPOSIT AND INVESTMENT RISK DISCLOSURES

In July 2002, GASB published an exposure draft (ED) *Deposit and Investment Risk Disclosures,* intended to provide the public with better information about the risks that could potentially impact a government's ability to provide services and pay its debts. The exposure draft would amend GASB Statement 3, *Deposits with Financial Institutions, Investments (including Repurchase Agreements), and Reverse Repurchase Agreements.* The comment period concluded in September 2002.

The Board pointed out that all investments carry some form of risk and that the public should be made aware of them in financial statements. Deposit and investment resources often represent the largest assets of governmental and fiduciary funds. Proprietary funds also report significant deposit and investment balances. These resources are critical to delivering governmental services and programs.

Financial statement disclosures would cover deposit and investment risks:

1. Credit risk disclosures would include credit quality information issued by rating agencies.
2. Interest rate disclosures would include investment maturity information, such as weighted average maturities or specification identification of the securities.
3. For investments that are highly sensitive to changes in interest rates (e.g., inverse floaters, enhanced variable-rate investments and certain asset-backed securities), disclosures would indicate the basis for their sensitivity.
4. Foreign investment disclosures would indicate the foreign investment's denomination.
5. Deposit and investment policies related to disclosed risks would be disclosed.

The effective date of the Standard would be for fiscal years beginning after June 15, 2004.

SMOOTHING THE TRANSITION TO GASB 34

After the adoption of Governmental Accounting Standard Board Statement 34, *Basic Financial Statements—and Management's Discussion and Analysis—for State and Local Governments,* in June, 1999, it is understandable that the Board appeared to be much more concerned about helping the accountants, auditors, and state and local officials "get it right" than about adopting any more new rules and regulations. Because GASB 34 is such a comprehensive overhauling of state and local government financial reporting, those involved needed time as well as helpful input to meet the requirements.

Acknowledgement of this is demonstrated by the Board's publication of:

1. An *Implementation Guide* for accountants.
2. Two *What You Should Know* guides.
3. A more sophisticated analyst's guide.
4. Three *Quick Guides.*

A GUIDE FOR IMPLEMENTING NEW FINANCIAL STATEMENTS

For those accountants faced with the daunting task of putting Statement 34 into practice, the GASB issued an *Implementation Guide* to help the preparers and auditors of state and local government financial statements understand and apply the provisions. The provisions are detailed later in this chapter.

The guide includes nearly 300 questions and answers developed by the GASB staff with the assistance of a 36-member advisory group. In addition to the question-and-answer section, the guide also includes:

1. More than 50 illustrative financial statement exhibits.
2. How-to exercises on ten of the more difficult requirements.
3. The complete standards section of Statement 34.
4. A sample financial statement for a state government.
5. A sample financial statement for a municipal government, including a complete illustrative MD&A and selected note disclosures.
6. A sample financial statement for an independent school district.

In-Depth Instructions for Compliance

The "Exercises" section furnishes step-by-step suggestions on how to comply with some of the requirements of Statement 34, including:

1. Calculating composite depreciation rates.
2. Applying group depreciation to infrastructure assets at transition and in subsequent years.
3. Calculating net asset balances for governmental activities.
4. Reporting internal service fund balances and results.
5. Determining major funds.
6. Reconciling fund financial statements to government-wide financial statements.

7. Indirectly determining direct-method cash flows.
8. Estimating historical cost using current replacement cost.
9. Calculating weighted-average age of infrastructure assets at transition.
10. Determining major general infrastructure assets.

A GUIDE TO LOCAL GOVERNMENT FINANCIAL STATEMENTS

The guide, *What You Should Know About Your Local Government's Finances: A Guide to Financial Statements,* is the GASB's first publication written specifically for citizens, taxpayers, legislators, researchers, and other people who use government financial information. The specific purpose is to highlight for financial statement users the information contained in the annual reports of local governments.

The guide is intended not only for those accustomed to using financial statements, but also as a resource for auditors and government finance officers who need to explain financial statements to elected officials, citizens, and clients.

Providing a Pathway to Information

The guide emphasizes how information in the financial statements of counties, cities, and other local governments may be used to aid in the decision-making process. This publication should be of value to a varied group of people including:

1. Entrepreneurs considering where to locate a business.
2. Investors deciding whether to buy a particular government's bonds.
3. Real estate agents developing information for a "sales pitch."
4. Developers determining a viable location for construction of a shopping mall or condominium complex.

The guide is designed to be suitable for use by a newcomer to the world of government finance as well as by the the long-time government manager or official.

It contains graphics as well as text to enhance its readability and usefulness, such as:

1. Figures and tables, including an annotated set of illustrative financial statements (complete with management's discussion and analysis) for a local government.
2. A running story that makes it easier for the reader to understand the concepts by relating them to personal financial decisions.

3. Boxes and sidebars that:
   a. Explore the issues raised in the text.
   b. Provide more detailed definitions and explanations.
   c. Offer tips on using financial statement information.
4. Easy identification of key terms that are defined in a glossary that accompanies the text.
5. An appendix containing an overview of the basics of governmental accounting and financial reporting.
6. A second appendix that explains some basic financial ratios that may be used to analyze government financial statements.

The guide covers the history-making changes in the preparation of state and local government financial statements brought about by the issuance of GASB Statement 34.

In line with the provisions of the Statement, some governments have already begun to implement these new requirements in their financial statements and others will begin complying with them over the next few years. This guide should give the preparer as well as the user of financial statements an overview of governmental accounting with particular emphasis on GASB 34's new "business" approach to accountability.

A GUIDE TO A SCHOOL DISTRICT'S FINANCIAL STATEMENTS

What You Should Know About Your School District's Finances: A Guide to Financial Statements is the second in the series of guides developed specifically for persons who use public sector financial information. It is aimed at educating readers about the information that can be found in the financial statements that public school districts will prepare under the historic changes in accounting standards that were adopted in mid-1999.

The new school district guide is designed to help anyone from public finance novices to long-time public sector managers understand school district financial statements. For the users of public school financial information (school board members, parents, taxpayers, financial analysts, and others) the guide provides insight into how the information in financial statements can be used to as a basis for decision making. The guide is also a handy reference for school district finance officers and certified public accountants seeking to understand the usefulness of the new financial statements and to explain them to citizens, elected officials, and clients.

Unlocking the Key to a School District's Fiscal Condition

Those charged with or interested in the fiscal health of public school systems should be able to use this guide to learn something about how to judge a school district's fiscal health. The GASB believes that this guide serve a double purpose: it may help the public use financial statements to hold school districts accountable; on the other hand, it may assist the districts in demonstrating their accountability to the public they serve.

The guide provides important insights into a broad range of issues, including:

1. The comparative fiscal health of a given school district in relation to previous years, as well as to similarly situated districts.
2. The reasons for a district's improved or degenerating financial condition.
3. What a school district owns and how much it owes.
4. Whether a school system will be able to pay its bills and repay its debts.
5. Looming issues that may affect a district's future finances.

Among the features contained in the school guide, which encompasses the sweeping changes the Board made to state and local government financial statements with the issuance of GASB 34, are:

1. Nearly two dozen figures and tables, including a set of annotated sample financial statements for a fictional school district.
2. Boxes and sidebars that help to explain and simplify financial statement information.
3. Clear identification of important terms and an extensive glossary.
4. Two appendices that introduce the basics of financial statement analysis and school district accounting.

A GUIDE FOR FINANCIAL ANALYSTS

The GASB has also published a guide intended to assist analysts as they incorporate the new state and local government financial statements into their work. The new publication, *An Analyst's Guide to Government Financial Statements,* introduces the financial statements that governments are beginning to prepare under GASB Statement 34.

The analyst's guide was developed specifically for regular and intensive users of public sector financial statements, including:

1. Mutual fund analysts.
2. Rating agencies.
3. Institutional investors.
4. Bond insurers.

5. Research organizations.
6. Taxpayer groups.

The Greater Depth of Information in the New Statements

This historic Standard was actually developed to provide analysts as well as other financial statement users with the more comprehensive and comprehensible data they require to assess government finances. The Board's goal in developing this guide is to help analysts more effectively assimilate the information from the new and expanded governmental financial statements into their analytical and decision-making processes.

For years the complaint about any given level of government has been, "Why can't they run it more like a business?" With the Statement, *Basic Financial Statements — and Management's Discussion and Analysis — for State and Local Governments,* establishing new requirements for state and local governments, this may happen. These requirements appear to be headed in the direction of a more businesslike approach, at least from an accountant's point of view. Governmental units must now prepare their financial reports according to GAAP. The new rules substantially change the appearance and content of government financial statements, which had previously been solely involved with fund accounts.

An Analyst's Guide to Government Financial Statements is written in an easy-to-understand style, but is more comprehensive in coverage than the two *What You Should Know* guides. It presents nearly 80 illustrations of financial statements for states, localities, school districts, public colleges and universities, and other special-purpose types of governments.

"Cliffies" for Government Financial Statements

The GASB has also published three *Quick Guides* — one each for state governments, local governments, and school districts. In an attempt to reach more of its constituents, the GASB has issued this series of "pocket" guides to assist users in understanding the financial statements that state and local governments prepare once they have fully implemented GASB Statement 34. The *Quick Guides* provide a summarized overview of the thorough introduction to government financial statements presented in the GASB's first three user guides.

They provide "need-to-know" information in brief and easy-to-read style delineating the major features of the new financial statements. They also highlight the ways in which government financial statement information may be useful to decision makers such as legislators, taxpayers, citizen groups, parents, public employees, financial analysts-even interested, involved citizens and voters.

The *Quick Guides* are directed toward school board members, legislators, and other elected officials who need a short and understandable explanation of government financial statements-and don't have the time or inclination for an in-depth indoctrination.

They are the perfect companion to the larger user guides, which are useful resources to government finance officers, accountants, and auditors who need to understand how financial statement information is used and are looking for help in explaining the new financial statements to their elected officials or clients.

INTERPRETATION RELATING TO MODIFIED ACCRUAL STANDARDS

The Board decided this Interpretation was necessary to shore up usage of modified accrual accounting used in governmental fund accounting retained by GASB 34.

Interpretation 6, *Recognition and Measurement of Certain Liabilities and Expenditures in Governmental Fund Financial Statements,* addresses concerns about the interpretation and application of existing *modified accrual standards.* The purpose of modified accrual accounting is to measure flows of current financial resources in governmental *fund financial statements.*

This Interpretation clarifies the application of existing standards for distinguishing between the portions of certain types of liabilities that should be reported as:

1. Governmental fund liabilities and expenditures.
2. General long-term liabilities of the government.

GASB 34, *Basic Financial Statements—and Management's Discussion and Analysis—for State and Local Governments,* carried forward the requirement that governmental fund financial statements be prepared using the existing financial resources measurement focus and the modified accrual basis of accounting. This traditional measurement focus and basis of accounting provides useful information related to a government's fiscal accountability, as part of the new financial reporting model. In addition, the new model provides useful information related to a government's operational accountability, including government-wide financial statements prepared on the *accrual basis* of accounting.

Concerns had been raised, however, about the interpretation and application of *existing modified accrual standards.* These concerns included:

1. Lack of comparability in the application of standards for recognition of certain fund liabilities and expenditures.
2. Perceived subjectivity of some interpretations and applications.

3. Potential circularity of the criteria for recognition of revenues and expenditures.

The objective of Interpretation 6 is to improve the comparability, consistency, and objectivity of financial reporting in governmental fund financial statements by providing a common, internally consistent interpretation of standards in areas where practice differences have occurred or could occur.

The effective date of this Interpretation was designed to coincide with the effective date of Statement 34 for the particular reporting government. Earlier application was encouraged, provided that the Interpretation and Statement 34 would be implemented simultaneously.

Review of Existing Standards

The GASB has begun a comprehensive review of existing accounting standards. One of the first results of this forward-looking activity was the redeliberation of its revised exposure draft, *The Financial Reporting Entity-Affiliated Organizations, an Amendment of GASB Statement 14.*

GASB 39, *Determining Whether Certain Organizations Are Component Units* (discussed above), resulted from this redeliberation. The Standard amends GASB 14 to provide additional guidance to determine whether certain organizations for which the primary government is not financially accountable should be reported as component units based on the nature and significance of their relationship with a primary government.

Another project in this effort was the reconsideration of the existing requirements in GASB 3, evaluating the ongoing usefulness of current requirements by taking into consideration recent federal banking reforms. This resulted in the exposure draft titled *Deposit and Investment Risk Disclosures,* also discussed above. As was indicated, the need for a new Statement is to provide the public with better information about the risks that could potentially impact a government's ability to provide services and pay its debts.

Other projects are outlined below.

Asset Impairment/Preservation Method

The objective of this project is twofold:

1. To develop criteria for when asset impairment should be recognized in the financial statements.
2. To determine whether reported changes in asset condition levels (associated with the modified approach of accounting for infrastructure assets) can be measured in monetary terms that meet the qualitative characteristics for financial reporting.

An exposure draft is planned in the near future. The preservation method portion of this project is on the Board's long-term agenda.

Conceptual Framework—Communication Methods

The objectives of this project are to:

1. Clarify the definition of general-purpose external financial reporting (GPEFR).
2. Identify and provide definitions of various methods of communicating financial and finance-related information to users.
3. Develop criteria for using each method.

During 2001, the Board continued discussions of the scope of GPEFR. They compared the tentative definitions of economic condition and its components with the objectives of GPEFR and the types of information needed to meet those objectives, according to Concepts Statement No. 1, *Objectives of Financial Reporting.*

The Board tentatively agreed that the definition of GPEFR encompasses both economic condition and service results. Further deliberations on this issue as well as the tentative definition of economic condition continued through April 2002. An exposure draft is tentatively scheduled for the first quarter of 2003.

Economic Condition

The objective of this project is to determine whether additional information on the elements of *economic condition* should be *required* in or with basic financial statements or *encouraged* to be provided in other forms of financial reporting. This project builds on the Board's tentative definitions of *economic condition* and its underlying elements of *financial position, fiscal capacity, and service capacity,* which are being developed in the Board's conceptual framework project on methods of communication in financial reporting.

This project has been tentatively divided into four phases:

1. Basic research to establish the frame of reference.
2. Board deliberations focused on the comprehensive annual financial report's (CAFR's) current statistical section, to begin in the third quarter of 2002.
3. An exposure draft is anticipated for the third quarter of 2003. The third phase of this project is on the Board's long-term agenda.
4. The fourth phase is on the Board's research agenda.

Environmental Liabilities

The objective of this project is to determine whether additional guidance is needed to account properly for, and report liabilities associated with, environmental laws and regulations (e.g., clean water, clean air, and superfund activities).

Board deliberations are scheduled in 2002, and an exposure draft is planned for the third quarter of 2003.

Other Postemployment Benefits (OPEB)

The final standards from this project will address accounting and financial reporting of postemployment benefits other than pensions by employers and plans or the entities that administer them (e.g., pension plans and public employee retirement systems that administer OPEB plans).

In the final third of 2001, the Board tentatively agreed to apply to OPEB the requirements of Statement 25, *Financial Reporting for Defined Benefit Pension Plans and Note Disclosures for Defined Contribution Plans,* with respect to:

1. Measurement focus, basis of accounting and display of financial information in the basic financial statements of fiduciary funds and similar component units.
2. Measurement and recognition criteria pertaining to specific financial statement accounts. In addition, the Board discussed several potential disclosure requirements for employers and plans. An exposure draft is planned.

BUSINESS-LIKE ACCOUNTING COMES TO STATE AND LOCAL GOVERNMENT

The Governmental Accounting Standards Board unanimously adopted the long-awaited comprehensive changes for state and local government financial reporting throughout the country in June 1999. GASB 34, *Basic Financial Statements—and Management's Discussion and Analysis—for State and Local Governments,* provides a new look and focus in reporting public finance in the U.S. The Board's action may be a response to the oft-voiced complaint, ". . . if only they'd run the government more like a business!" Now "they" must, at least from an accounting standpoint. Many big "businesses" and even more mid-size and small "businesses"—states, cities, counties, towns—adding up to a total of 87,000 in 1999, according to the GASB, are adopting the new measures.

THE GASB GAINS STATURE

This Statement can certainly be considered the most significant change in the history of governmental accounting and should signal the "coming of age" of the GASB. It represents a dramatic shift in the manner and comprehensiveness in which state and local governments present financial information to the public. When fully implemented, it will create new information and will restructure much of the fund information that governments have presented in the past.

The new requirements were developed to make annual reports more comprehensive and easier to understand and use. Now, anyone with an interest (vested or otherwise) in public finance—citizens, the media, bond raters, creditors, investors, legislators, investment bankers and others—will have readily available information about the respective governmental bodies.

Thousands of preparers, auditors, academics, and users of governmental financial statements participated during a decade and a half in the research, consideration, and deliberations that preceded the publication of GASB 34. Members of various task forces began work on this and related projects as early as 1985.

PROVISIONS OF GASB 34

Among the major innovations of Statement 34, governments will be required to:

1. Report on the *overall* state of the government's financial health, not just its individual funds as has been the case.
2. Provide the most complete information ever made available about the cost of providing services to the citizens.
3. Prepare an introductory narrative section (the Management's Discussion and Analysis—MD&A) to the basic report analyzing the government's financial performance.
4. Provide enhanced fund reporting.
5. Include information about the government's public infrastructure assets. The Statement explains these assets as long-lived assets that are normally stationary and capable of being preserved longer than most capital assets. Bridges, roads, storm sewers, tunnels, drainage systems, dams, lighting systems, and swimming pools are among those mentioned. (This is certainly the most innovative requirement introduced to governmental financial reporting.)

BACKGROUND INFORMATION

The GASB's first concepts Statement, *Objectives of Financial Reporting,* issued in 1987, identified what the Board believes are the most important objectives of financial reporting by governments. Some of those objectives reaffirm the importance of information that governmental units have historically included in their annual reports. To cover more of the original objectives, the Board felt it necessary to provide for a much broader range of information.

As a result, Statement 34 is a dual-perspective report requiring governmental bodies to retain much of the information they currently report, but also requiring them to go further in revealing their operations. The first perspective focuses on the traditional funds with some additional information required for major funds. The second perspective is government-wide to provide an entirely new look at a government's financial activities.

The Board feels that adding new material will result in reports that accomplish more of the objectives emphasized in the original concepts Statement.

THE TIME FOR ACCOUNTABILITY IS NOW

According to the GASB, state and local governments in the U.S. invest approximately $140–$150 billion annually in the construction, improvement, and rehabilitation of capital assets, including infrastructure assets like bridges, highways, and sewers. Since these expenditures represent more than 10% of the monies spent by those governments, it would appear quite natural for them to be accounted for in financial documents readily available to the public.

The majority of this infrastructure investment is financed by borrowing— selling municipal bonds and using the proceeds to pay for construction. (Enter the investor.)

The need for public accountability arises when such sums are spent and when current and future generations are committed to repay such debts. The public should know how much governments spend on infrastructure construction and how much they borrow to finance it. (Enter the taxpayer.)

The public also wants to know if government officials subsequently are caring for the infrastructure they have built with public resources. (Enter the voter.)

Although the need for information about infrastructure should be fairly obvious, the primary instruments for demonstrating fiscal accountability (the government's annual financial statements) have not previously been required to provide this information. The accounting method for preparing state and local government financial statements has focused on short-term financial resources like cash and investments. Infrastructures have been left off the balance sheet and no charge was included on the income statement for the cost of using the infrastructure assets to provide services. Because of the significant share of government spending devoted to capital assets, this has been a major omission. But with the advent of GASB 34, all of that is changing.

Opportunities for Government Consulting

Considering the number of affected governmental bodies—regardless of the considerable lead time provided—the present supply of government accountants is certainly being stretched to the limit. In addition, many have had little experience in the required more "corporate-style" accounting. Even though the smaller governments have the longest time to make the necessary changes, they face a rather daunting task as they have few, if any, accounting professionals on their staff.

Thus, the Statement opens up business opportunities for interested accountants. It should be fairly obvious that many governments need help in complying with requirements that mandate the dramatic shift in the way state and local governments present their financial information.

RETENTION OF FUND ACCOUNTING

Annual reports currently provide information about funds. Most funds are established by governing bodies (such as state legislatures, city councils, or school boards) to show restrictions on the planned use of resources or to measure, *in the short term,* the revenues and expenditures arising from certain activities. GASB 1 noted that annual reports should allow users to assess a government's accountability by assisting them in determining compliance with finance-related laws, rules, and regulations.

This new Statement requires governments to continue to present financial statements that provide fund information. The focus of these statements has been sharpened to require governments to report information about their major funds, including the general fund. In previous annual reports, fund information was reported in the aggregate by fund type. This often made it difficult for users to assess accountability of any "public servants."

Fund statements continue to measure and report the "operating results" of many funds by measuring cash on hand and other assets that can be easily converted to cash. These statements show the performance, in the short term, of individual funds using the same measures that many governments use when financing their current operations. The Board points out that if a government issues fifteen-year debt to build a school, it does not collect taxes in the first year sufficient to repay the *entire* debt; it levies and collects what is needed to make that year's required payments. On the other hand, when governments charge a fee to users for services—as is done for most water or electric utilities—fund information continues to be based on accrual accounting to ensure all costs of providing services are being measured.

THE ALL-IMPORTANT GOVERNMENTAL BUDGET

Showing budgetary compliance is an important component of government's accountability. (At the national level, with which GASB 34 has no connection, of course, THE BUDGET is undoubtedly the most widely recognized financial document.) At the state and local levels, diverse citizen groups, special interest groups, and individuals participate in the process of establishing the original annual operating budgets of the particular body.

Governments will be required to continue to provide budgetary comparison information in their annual reports. An important change that should certainly make the comparison more meaningful is the requirement to add the government's *original* budget to that comparison. Many governments revise their original budgets during the year for various reasons. Requiring governments to report that original document in addition to their *revised* budget adds a new analytical dimension and should increase the usefulness of the budgetary comparison.

Presumably, the original budget was the "best thought" of the adopting body at the time. Subsequent "revised" budgets could be the result of political pressures or personal preferences. The GASB concedes that budgetary changes are not necessarily undesirable. However, the Board decided that in the interest of accountability to those who were aware of, and may have made decisions based upon the original budget, inclusion of its contents could deter ill-considered changes. The comparison also gives the user a look at any changes that have been made. The Board suggested that this is an additional method of assessing the governmental body's ability to estimate and manage its general resources—without too many detours.

Thus, the original budget, the final appropriated budgets and the actual inflows, outflows and balances stated on the government's budgetary basis are mandated as required supplemental information (RSI) for the general fund and for each major special revenue fund that has a legally adopted annual budget. Rather than include this information in RSI, a government may elect to report these comparisons in a budgetary comparison statement as part of the basic financial statements.

NEW INFORMATION IS READILY AVAILABLE

For the first time, government financial managers are required to introduce the financial report by sharing their attitude toward and understanding of the transactions, events, and conditions reflected in the government's report and of the fiscal policies that govern its operations. The required MD&A should give the users an easily readable analysis of the government's *financial* performance for the year. Users thus have information they need to help them gauge the government's state of financial health as a result of the year's operations.

Additionally, financial managers themselves are in a better position to provide this analysis because, for the first time, the annual report also includes new government-wide financial statements prepared using accrual accounting for all of the government's activities. Most governmental utilities and private-sector companies use accrual accounting. With GASB 34, state and local governments join most of the rest of the world in using it. The reason for the change is that accrual accounting measures not just current assets and liabilities, but also long-term assets and liabilities (such as capital assets, including infrastructure, and general obligation debt). It also reports all revenues and *all* costs of providing services each year, not just those received or paid in the current year or soon after year-end. After all, government is an ongoing endeavor; officials elected or appointed come and go.

Users Benefit

These government-wide financial statements undoubtedly will help users:

1. Assess the finances of a government in its entirety, including the year's operating results.
2. Determine whether a government's overall financial position improved or deteriorated.
3. Evaluate whether a government's current-year revenues were sufficient to pay for current-year services.
4. Be aware of the cost of providing services to the citizenry.
5. Become cognizant of the way in which a government finances its programs—through user fees and other program revenues, or general tax revenues.
6. Understand the extent to which a government has invested in capital assets, including roads, bridges, and other infrastructure assets.
7. Make better comparisons between governments.

REQUIRED INFORMATION AND FORMAT

GASB 34 sets financial reporting standards for state and local governments, including states, cities, towns, villages, and special-purpose governments such as school districts and public utilities. It establishes that the basic financial statements and required supplementary information for general purpose governments should consist of:

1. *Management's Discussion and Analysis.* MD&A introduces the basic financial statements and provides an analytical overview of the

government's financial activities. Although it is required supplementary information (RSI) and one would expect to find it in the final portion of the report, governments are required to present MD&A *before* the basic financial statements. Presumably the belief is that a clearly written—plain English, perhaps—introduction provides a link between the two perspectives (fund and government-wide) to prepare the reader for a better understanding of the financial statements.

2. ***Basic Financial Statements.*** The basic financial statements must include:

   a. *Government-wide financial statements,* consisting of a statement of net assets and a statement of activities. Prepared using the economic resources measurement focus and the accrual basis of accounting, these statements should report all of the assets, liabilities, revenues, expenses, and gains and losses of the government. Each statement should distinguish between the *governmental* and *business-type activities* of the primary government and between the total primary government and the separately presented component units by reporting each in separate columns. (*Fiduciary activities,* with resources not available to finance the government's programs, are not included in the government-wide statements.)

   b. *Fund financial statements* consisting of a series of statements that focus on information about the government's major governmental and enterprise funds, including blended component units. Fund financial statements also should report information about a government's fiduciary funds and component units that are fiduciary in nature.

   c. *Governmental* fund financial statements (including financial data for the general fund and special revenue, capital projects, debt service, and permanent funds). These are to be prepared using the current financial resources measurement focus and the modified accrual basis of accounting.

   d. *Proprietary* fund financial statements (including financial data for enterprise and internal service funds) and *fiduciary* fund financial statements (including financial data for fiduciary funds and similar component units). This group is to be prepared using the economic resources measurement focus and the accrual basis of accounting.

   e. *Notes to the financial statements* are notes and explanations that provide information which is *essential* to a user's understanding of the basic financial statements.

3. ***Required Supplementary Information (RSI).*** In addition to MD&A, this Statement requires *budgetary comparison schedules* to be presented as RSI along with other types of data as required by previous GASB pronouncements. This Statement also requires RSI for governments that use the modified approach for reporting infrastructure assets.

Special-purpose governments engaged in only governmental activities (such as some library districts) or engaged in both governmental and business-type activities (such as some school districts) should normally be reported in the same manner as general purpose governments. Special-purpose governments engaged only in business-type activities (such as utilities) should present the financial statements required for enterprise funds, including MD&A and other RSI.

CONTENT OF MD&A

MD&A should provide an objective and easily readable analysis of the government's financial activities based on currently known facts, decisions, or conditions. It should be emphasized that this section is a preparation for the casual reader who is less skilled in reading financial statements as well as for the more experienced "user" to understand fully the implications of the basic report.

MD&A should include:

1. Comparisons of the current year to the prior year based on the government-wide information.
2. An analysis of the government's overall financial position and results of operations to assist users in assessing whether that financial position has improved or deteriorated as a result of the year's activities.
3. An analysis of balances and transactions of individual funds and significant budget variances.
4. A description of capital asset and long-term debt activity during the period.
5. A conclusion with a description of currently known facts, decisions, or conditions that could be expected to have a significant effect upon the financial position or results of operations.

GOVERNMENT-WIDE FINANCIAL STATEMENTS

The new annual reports contain much more comprehensive financial information. Government-wide statements now display information about the reporting government as a whole, except for its fiduciary activities. These statements include separate columns for the governmental and business-type activities of the primary government and its component parts. Government-wide statements are prepared using the economic resources measurement focus and the accrual basis of accounting. This latter requirement is a fairly dramatic step forward since heretofore governmental accounting followed only the modified-accrual basis. The statement must include a statement of net assets as well as all of the government's activities, not just those that cover costs by charging a fee for services, as currently required.

Governments should report all *capital assets,* including infrastructure assets, in the government-wide statement of net assets and generally should report depreciation expenses in the statement of activities. Infrastructure assets that are part of a network or subsystem of a network are not required to be depreciated as long as the government manages those assets using an asset management system that has certain characteristics and the government can document that the assets are being preserved approximately at (or above) a condition level established and disclosed by the government in the RSI.

To qualify for a qualified asset management system, the government must:

1. Have an up-to-date inventory of the eligible infrastructure assets.
2. Perform condition assessments of the eligible assets and summarize the results using a measurement scale.
3. Estimate each year the annual amounts necessary to maintain and preserve the assets at the established and disclosed condition level. Condition assessments are to be documented so that they can be replicated. The assessments may be performed by the government itself or by contract with an outside source.

The net assets of a government should be reported in three categories— *invested in capital assets net of related debt, restricted, and unrestricted.* Net assets are considered "restricted" when constraints are placed on their use by:

1. External sources such as creditors, grantors or contributors.
2. Laws or regulations of other governments.
3. Legal or constitutional provisions or enabling legislation.

Permanent endowments or permanent fund principal amounts included in restricted net assets should be displayed in two additional components— *expendable and nonexpendable.*

The government-wide *statement of activities* should be presented in a format that reports expenses minus program revenues, to obtain a measurement of "net (expense) revenue" for each of the government's functions. Program expenses should include all direct expenses. General revenues, such as taxes, and special and extraordinary items should be reported separately to arrive at the change in net assets for the period.

Special and extraordinary items are both significant transactions or other events, either unusual or infrequent, over which management has control. Both types should be reported separately at the bottom of the statement of activities with special items listed prior to any extraordinary items. These types of transactions or events over which a government does not have control should be disclosed in the notes to financial statements.

FUND FINANCIAL STATEMENTS

To report additional and detailed information about the primary government, separate fund financial statements should be presented for each fund category: governmental, proprietary and fiduciary.

1. *Governmental funds* report on the basic activities of the government, including general fund accounts and special revenue, capital projects, debt service, and permanent funds.
2. *Proprietary funds* cover activities that are generally financed and operated like private businesses such as enterprise (fees charged to outside users) and internal service funds.
3. *Fiduciary funds* include pension and other employee benefit and private purpose trust funds that cannot be used to support the government's own programs.

Required *governmental fund* statements are:

1. A balance sheet.
2. A statement of revenues, expenditures, and changes in fund balances.

Required *proprietary fund* statements are:

1. A statement of net assets.
2. A statement of revenues, expenses, and changes in fund net assets.
3. A statement of cash flows.

To allow users to assess the relationship between fund and government-wide financial statements, governments should present a summary reconciliation to the government-wide financial statements at the bottom of the fund financial statements or in an accompanying schedule.

Each of the fund statements should report separate columns for the *general fund* and for *other major governmental and enterprise funds*.

1. *Major funds* are funds in which revenues, expenditures/expenses, assets, or liabilities (excluding extraordinary items) are at least 10% of

corresponding totals for all governmental or enterprise funds and at least 5% of the aggregate amount for all governmental and enterprise funds. Any other fund may be reported as a major fund if the government's officials consider it to be particularly important to financial statement users.

2. *Nonmajor funds* should be reported in the aggregate in a separate column.

3. *Internal service funds* also should be reported in the aggregate in a separate column on the proprietary fund statements.

Fund balances for governmental funds should also be segregated into *reserved* and *unreserved* categories. Proprietary fund net assets should be reported in the same categories required for the government-wide financial statements. Proprietary fund statements of net assets should distinguish between current and noncurrent assets and liabilities and should display restricted assets.

Proprietary fund statements of revenues, expenses, and changes in fund net assets should distinguish between operating and nonoperating revenues and expenses. These statements should also report capital contributions, contributions to permanent and term endowments, special and extraordinary items, and transfers separately at the bottom of the statement to arrive at the all-inclusive change in fund net assets. Cash flow statements should be prepared using the direct method.

Separate fiduciary fund statements (including component units that are fiduciary in nature) also should be presented as part of the fund financial statements. Fiduciary funds should be used to report assets that are held in a trustee or agency capacity for others and that cannot be used to support the government's own programs.

Required *fiduciary fund* statements are:

1. A statement of fiduciary net assets.
2. A statement of changes in fiduciary net assets.

Interfund activity includes interfund loans, interfund services provided and used, and interfund transfers. This activity should be reported separately in the fund financial statements and generally should be eliminated in the aggregated government-wide financial statements.

REQUIRED SUPPLEMENTARY INFORMATION

To demonstrate whether resources were obtained and used in accordance with the government's legally adopted budget, RSI should include budgetary comparison schedules for the general fund and for each major special revenue fund that has a legally adopted annual budget.

The budgetary comparison schedules should include:

1. The original budget.
2. The final appropriated budgets for the reporting period.
3. Actual inflows, outflows, and balances, stated on the government's budgetary basis.

As pointed out above, the Statement also requires certain disclosures in RSI for governments that use the modified approach for reporting infrastructure assets and data currently required by earlier Statements.

EFFECTIVE DATE AND TRANSITION

The requirements of this Statement are effective in three phases based on a government's total annual revenues in the first fiscal year ending after June 15, 1999. Governments with total annual revenues (excluding extraordinary items) of $100 million or more (phase 1) should apply this Statement for fiscal years beginning after June 15, 2001. Medium-size governments with at least $10 million but less than $100 million in revenues (phase 2) should apply this Statement for fiscal years beginning after June 15, 2002. Smaller governments with less than $10 million in revenues (phase 3) should apply this Statement for periods beginning after June 15, 2003. Earlier application is encouraged.

Governments that elect early implementation of this Statement for periods beginning before June 15, 2000, should also implement GASB Statement 33, *Accounting and Financial Reporting for Nonexchange Transactions,* at the same time. (See below.)

If a primary government chooses early implementation of this Statement, all of its component units should also implement this standard early in order to provide the necessary financial information required for the government-wide financial statements.

REQUIREMENTS FOR PROSPECTIVE AND RETROSPECTIVE REPORTING

Prospective reporting of general infrastructure assets is required at the effective dates of this Statement. Retroactive reporting of all existing major general governmental infrastructure assets is encouraged at that date.

For phase 1 and phase 2 governments, retroactive reporting is *required four years after* the effective date on the basic provisions for all major general infrastructure assets that were acquired or significantly reconstructed, or that received significant improvements, in fiscal years ending after June 30, 1980. Thus, larger governments will have to report retroactively all major general infrastructure assets for all fiscal years beginning after June 15, 2005 and medium-size governments have until fiscal years beginning after June 15, 2006.

Phase 3 governments are encouraged to report infrastructure retroactively, but may elect to report general infrastructure prospectively only.

GUIDANCE ON MODIFIED ACCRUAL STANDARDS

The Governmental Accounting Standards Board issued Interpretation 6, *Recognition and Measurement of Certain Liabilities and Expenditures in Governmental Fund Financial Statements.* This Interpretation clarifies the application of standards for modified accrual recognition of fund liabilities and expenditures in governmental fund financial statements.

In GASB 34, the Board concluded that traditional governmental fund financial statements continue to provide useful information for assessing a government's fiscal accountability and should continue to be prepared with a current financial resources measurement focus and modified accrual basis of accounting. This Interpretation clarifies undefined terms and reduces differences in the ways that financial statement preparers, auditors, and others interpret and apply the standard.

The goal is to provide an interpretation that will promote more consistent and comparable reporting. The Board pointed out that the effect of the Interpretation may include both increases and decreases in accruals for governments that have applied the standards differently.

The effective date of the proposed Interpretation should coincide with the effective date of Statement 34 for the reporting government. Earlier application is encouraged, provided that this Interpretation and Statement 34 are simultaneously adopted.

GASB 35 FOR PUBLIC COLLEGES AND UNIVERSITIES

After an earlier decision by the Governmental Accounting Standards Board not to require a separate financial reporting model for public colleges and universities in order to make it easier for state and local governments to include these institutions in their financial statements, the GASB issued a proposal in July, 1999 to provide accounting and financial reporting guidance for public colleges and universities in their separately issued financial statements. That proposal became GASB 35.

This Statement amends GASB 34, *Basic Financial Statements—and Management's Discussion and Analysis—for State and Local Governments,* to include public colleges and universities within its guidance for general purpose external financial reporting.

It is anticipated that this step will make it easier to compare public institutions and their private counterparts. Such a step had been requested by GASB constituents.

Under the new guidance, public colleges and universities can report their finances as public institutions:

1. Engaged only in business-type activities.
2. Engaged only in governmental activities.
3. Engaged in both governmental and business-type activities.

A public institution is also required to include the following in separately issued financial reports, regardless of whether or not they are legally separate entities:

1. Management's discussion and analysis (MD&A).
2. Basic financial statements, as appropriate for the category of special-purpose government reporting.
3. Notes to the financial statements.
4. Required supplementary information other than MD&A.

The requirements of the Statement are effective in three phases for public institutions that are not part of another reporting entity, beginning with fiscal years beginning after June 15, 2001. All public institutions that are part of (or are component units of) a primary government are required to implement this standard at least by the same time as its primary government, regardless of the phase-in guidance contained in GASB 34.

Public colleges and universities are required to report infrastructure assets as follows:

1. Public institutions that are not part of another primary government and report as either special-purpose governments engaged only in governmental activities or engaged in both governmental and business-type activities must report infrastructure in accordance with the phase-in guidance of GASB 34 beginning with fiscal years ending after June 15, 2005.
2. Public institutions that report as special-purpose governments engaged only in business-type activities are required to report infrastructure upon implementation, without regard to the phase-in periods included in Statement 34.

GASB 33 on Nonexchange Transactions

Late in 1998, the Governmental Accounting Standards Board issued GASB Statement 33, *Accounting and Financial Reporting for Nonexchange Transactions,* which specifies the accounting and reporting for nonexchange transactions involving financial or capital resources. These transactions include most taxes, grants, and donations. The Statement is effective for periods beginning after June 15, 2000.

In a nonexchange transaction, the government gives or receives value without directly receiving or giving equal value in exchange. When there isn't an exchange, it can be difficult to decide *when* a transaction should be recognized in the financial statements. Statement 33 attempts to simplify the problem.

The timing of financial statement recognition will depend on the nature of the nonexchange transaction as well as the basis of accounting (accrual or modified accrual). The GASB has identified four classes of nonexchange transactions:

1. Derived tax revenues, such as sales and income taxes. These will be recognized when the underlying exchange on which the government imposes the tax actually occurs. An example would be when a customer buys a washing machine or refrigerator that is subject to a sales tax.
2. Imposed nonexchange revenues, such as property taxes and fines. These are to be recognized as assets when the government has an enforceable legal claim. For example, property taxes receivable generally will be recognized on the lien date, even though a lien may not be formally placed on the property at that date. Revenues will be recognized in the period in which the resources are required to be used.
3. Government-mandated nonexchange transactions, such as federal or state programs that state or local governments are required to provide. These will be recognized when all eligibility requirements are met, as specified in Statement 33. For example, when a recipient is required to incur allowable costs before reimbursement is made, the incurring of allowable costs is an eligibility requirement.
4. Voluntary nonexchange transactions, such as most grants, appropriations, donations, and endowments. These will also be recognized when the Statement 33 eligibility requirements are met. These requirements include contingencies. For example, to qualify for a grant, a recipient may be required to provide matching resources.

For revenue recognition on the modified accrual basis, resources also should be "available," as defined in existing standards. Statement 33 goes hand in hand with the Board's standards on the governmental and the college and university financial reporting models under GASB 34. The Board feels that GASB 33 will improve consistency in how governments report nonexchange transactions.

GASB 36 on Symmetry Between Recipients and Providers in Accounting for Certain Shared Revenues

GASB 36 amends GASB 33, *Accounting and Financial Reporting for Nonexchange Transactions,* which required recipients of shared derived tax or imposed nonexchange revenue to account for it differently from the provider government. This practice could have resulted in the two governments recognizing the sharing at different times.

The new Statement provides symmetrical accounting treatment for both the giver and receiver of the shared revenue. Statement 36 eliminates the timing difference by requiring recipients to account for the sharing in the same way as provider governments.

It was to be implemented simultaneously with Statement 33, which became mandatory for periods beginning after June 15, 2000.

Chapter 12

Governmental Fund Accounting

CONTENTS

Differences Between Governmental and Commercial Accounting   **12.01**
Legal Provisions   **12.02**
Is Governmental Accounting Complex? No!   **12.03**
Terminology   **12.03**
Governmental Accounting Systems   **12.08**
Objectives of Financial Reporting by Nonbusiness Organizations   **12.17**

DIFFERENCES BETWEEN GOVERNMENTAL AND COMMERCIAL ACCOUNTING

While both types of entities use double-entry bookkeeping procedures and either cash or accrual methods, and both prepare balance sheets and operating statements, there are many differences between commercial and governmental systems.

Governmental accounting is associated with: (1) an absence of a profit; (2) compliance with statutory and/or legal requirements; (3) a fundamental difference in the treatment of net worth. Commercial accounting provides accounting for preferred and common stock and retained earnings, with a paid-in capital account where appropriate. Governmental accounting treats "net worth" under account classifications *Reserve for Encumbrances or*

Unappropriated Surplus; (4) characteristically, government accounts will include a *Reserve for Contingencies* account since the projected (budgeted) reserve may not materialize as the accounting year progresses.

As will be evident in the next chapter, "New Governmental Accounting," accounting for state and local governments is in a transitional stage. Over the next several years, these entities will be adding more "business-like" requirements to their financial reporting. At the same time, the government accountant will still need to draw upon his or her knowledge of fund accounting.

The new Government Accounting Board Statement 34, *Basic Financial Statements—and Management's Discussion and Analysis—for State and Local Governments* establishes new financial reporting requirements for state and local governments. However, these entities are to continue to present financial statements that provide fund information. The focus of these fund statements has been sharpened to require governments to report information about their major funds, including the general fund. In current annual reports, fund information is reported in the aggregate by fund type. This has often made it difficult for users to assess accountability.

Fund statements will continue to measure and report the "operating results" of many funds by measuring cash on hand and other assets that can easily be converted to cash. These statements show the performance, in the short-term, of individual funds using the same measures that governments use when financing their current operations.

LEGAL PROVISIONS

In governmental accounting, legal provisions relate to budgeting and to the disposition of assets. The preparation and implementation of the projected budget and related accounting procedures are governed by certain legal provisions expressed specifically in legislation (statutory) or restrictions imposed by a nonlegislative (regulatory) authority. The accounting system must have built-in safeguards that expenditures will comply with both types of restrictions. Governmental accounting must also include revenue and expense data which facilitates the preparation of budgets for the future.

As will be seen, certain *funds* are considered less flexible in their accounting treatment. The least flexible type is the one created by a state constitution or by legislation, because the accountant must keep the books as determined by law. The most flexible is the type established by executive authority, since such authority can make changes in a fund without prior legislative approval.

In fund accounting *estimated and actual revenues* and *expenditures* are compared on an ongoing basis, e.g., reviewed by the governing bodies approving the initial budget and the appropriation for the fund. Comparisons reveal the extent to which the "actuals" are in line with the estimates (the budget) and will show significant deviations, if any, during the fiscal year of actual revenues and expenditures from the budgeted amounts.

Assets and liabilities incurred by a fund are similar to those in a commercial enterprise. Asset accounts, for example, will include cash, accounts receivable, etc., while liabilities will show accounts or vouchers payable, notes payable, bonds payable, etc.

A separate *general ledger* must be maintained for each fund related to the governmental entity's budget. Each general ledger has a self-balancing account that brings the revenue and appropriation accounts into balance at the end of the fiscal year.

As a general rule independent auditors will insist on the entity using an *accrual* system, unless the financial authorities for that specific fund can demonstrate that the financial reports would not *materially* differ if a cash accounting system is used.

Is Governmental Accounting Complex? No!

While fund accounting is perceived to be complicated, it is not any more difficult than commercial accounting. Why then is it thought to be complicated? The answer is for the same reason that we initially think any totally new and unfamiliar discipline appears difficult—the *terminology* is the culprit. It is well-settled that learning the terminology of a new discipline is 50% or more of the learning battle of anything new that one endeavors to learn. Governmental accounting terminology is indeed entirely different from commercial accounting terminology; it has a vocabulary that is totally unique to governmental accounting; no governmental accounting term can be found in any other system of accounting, whether commercial, industrial, or otherwise.

The first step, then, to acquire an understanding of fund accounting procedures is to review and become familiar with the terms. The following list of definitions will enable the user to easily apply the accounting methods for the various types of funds which are covered in the material following the definitions.

Terminology

Here is a listing of definitions applicable only to fund accounting:

Abatement. Cancellation of amounts levied or of charges made for services.

Accrued Assets. Assets arising from revenues earned but not yet due.

Accrued Expenses. Expenses resulting in liabilities which are either due or are not payable until some future time.

Accrued Revenues. Levies made or other revenue earned and not collected.

Allotment Ledger. A subsidiary ledger which contains an account for each allotment showing the amount allotted, expenditures, encumbrances, the net balance, and other related information.

Appropriation. An authorization granted by the legislative body to make expenditures and to incur obligations for specific purposes.

Appropriation Expenditure. An expenditure chargeable to an appropriation.

Appropriation Ledger. A subsidiary ledger containing an account with each appropriation.

Assessment. The process of making an official valuation of property for the purpose of taxation.

Authority Bonds. Bonds payable from the revenues of a specific public authority.

Betterment. An addition or change made in a fixed asset which prolongs its life or increases its efficiency.

Budget. A plan of financial operation embodying an estimate of proposed expenditures for a given period or purpose, and the proposed means of financing them.

Budgetary Accounts. The accounts necessary to reflect budget operations and condition, such as estimated revenues, appropriations, and encumbrances.

Capital Budget. An improvement program and the methods for the financing.

Clearing Account. An account used to accumulate total charges or credits for the purpose of distributing them among the accounts to which they are allocable, or for the purpose of transferring the net difference to the proper account.

Current Special Assessment. Assessments levied and due during the current fiscal period.

Current Taxes. Taxes levied and becoming due during the current fiscal period—from the time the amount of the tax levy is first established, to the date on which a penalty for nonpayment is attached.

Debt Limit. The maximum amount of gross or net debt legally permitted.

Debt Service Requirement. The amount of money necessary periodically to pay the interest on the outstanding debt and the principal of maturing bonded debt not payable from a sinking fund.

Deficit. The excess of the liabilities of a fund over its assets.

Delinquent Taxes. Taxes remaining unpaid on and after the date on which a penalty for nonpayment is attached.

Direct Debt. The debt which a governmental unit has incurred in its own name, or assumed through the annexation of territory.

Encumbrances. Obligations in the form of purchase orders, contracts, or salary commitments which are chargeable to an appropriation, and for which a part of the appropriation is reserved.

Endowment Fund. A fund whose principal must be maintained inviolate, but whose income may be expended.

Expendable Fund. A fund whose resources, including both principal and earnings, may be expended.

Expenditures. If the fund accounts are kept on the accrual basis, expenditures are the total charges incurred, whether paid or unpaid, including expenses, provision for retirement of debt not reported as a liability of the fund from which retired, and capital outlays.

Franchise. A special privilege granted by a government permitting the continuing use of public property.

Full Faith and Credit. A pledge of the general taxing body for the payment of obligations.

Fund Accounts. All accounts necessary to set forth the financial operations and financial condition of a fund.

Fund Group. A group of related funds.

Governmental Accounting. The preparation, reporting, and interpretation of accounts for governmental bodies.

Grant. A contribution by one governmental unit to another unit.

Gross Bonded Debt. The total amount of direct debt of a governmental unit, represented by outstanding bonds before deduction of sinking fund assets.

Indeterminate Appropriation. An appropriation which is not limited either to any definite period of time, or to any definite amount, or to both time and amount.

Inter-Fund Accounts. Accounts in which transactions between funds are reflected.

Inter-Fund Loans. Loans made by one fund to another fund.

Inter-Fund Transfers. Amounts transferred from one fund to another.

Judgment. An amount to be paid or collected by a governmental unit as the result of a court decision, including a condemnation award in payment for private property taken for public use.

Lapse. As applied to appropriations, this term denotes the automatic termination of an appropriation.

Levy. To impose taxes or special assessments.

Lump-Sum Appropriation. An appropriation made for a stated purpose, or for a named department, without specifying further the amounts that can be spent for specific activities or for particular expenditures.

Municipal. An adjective applying to any governmental unit below or subordinate to the state.

Municipal Corporation. A body or corporate politic established pursuant to state authorization, as evidenced by a charter.

Net Bonded Debt. Gross bonded debt less applicable cash or other assets.

Non-Expendable Fund. A fund the principal, and sometimes the earnings, of which may not be expended.

Non-Operating Income. Income of municipal utilities and other governmental enterprises of a business character, which is not derived from the operation of such enterprise.

Operating Expenses. As used in the accounts of municipal utilities and other governmental enterprises of a business character, the term means the costs necessary to the maintenance of the enterprise, or the rendering of services for which the enterprise is operated.

Operating Revenues. Revenues derived from the operation of municipal utilities or other governmental enterprises of a business character.

Operating Statement. A statement summarizing the financial operations of a municipality.

Ordinance. A bylaw of a municipality enacted by the governing body of the governmental entity.

Overlapping Debt. The proportionate share of the debts of local governmental units, located wholly or in part within the limits of the reporting government, which must be borne by property within such government.

Prepaid Taxes. The deposit of money with a governmental unit on condition that the amount deposited is to be applied against the tax liability of the taxpayer.

Proprietary Accounts. Accounts which show actual financial condition and operations such as actual assets, liabilities, reserves, surplus, revenues, and expenditures as distinguished from budgetary accounts.

Public Authority. A public agency created to perform a single function, which is financed from tolls or fees charged those using the facilities operated by the agency.

Public Trust Fund. A trust fund whose principal, earnings, or both, must be used for a public purpose.

Quasi-Municipal Corporation. An agency established by the state primarily for the purpose of helping the state to carry out its functions.

Refunding Bonds. Bonds issued to retire bonds already outstanding. The refunding bonds may be sold for cash and outstanding bonds redeemed in cash, or the refunding bonds may be exchanged with holders of outstanding bonds.

Related Funds. Funds of a similar character which are brought together for administrative and reporting purposes.

Reserve for Encumbrances. A reserve representing the segregation of surplus to provide for unliquidated encumbrances.

Revenue Bonds. Bonds the principal and interest on which are to be paid solely from earnings, usually the earnings of a municipally owned utility or other public service enterprise.

Revolving Fund. A fund provided to carry out a cycle of operations.

Special Assessment. A compulsory levy made by a local government against certain properties, to defray part or all of the cost of a specific improvement or service, which is presumed to be of general benefit to the public and of special benefit to the owners of such properties.

Special District Bonds. Bonds of a local taxing district, which has been organized for a special purpose—such as road, sewer, and other special districts—to render unique services to the public.

Suspense Account. An account which carries charges or credits temporarily pending the determination of the proper account or accounts to which they are to be posted.

Tax Anticipation Notes. Notes issued in anticipation of collection of taxes, usually retired only from tax collections as they come due.

Tax Levy. An ordinance or resolution by means of which taxes are levied.

Tax Liens. Claims which governmental units have upon properties until taxes levied against them have been paid.

Tax Rate. The amount of tax stated in terms of a unit of the tax base.

Trust Fund. A fund consisting of resources received and held by the governmental unit as trustee, to be expended or invested in accordance with the conditions of the trust.

Unencumbered Appropriation. An appropriation or allotment, or a part thereof, not yet expended or encumbered.

Utility Fund. A fund established to finance the construction, operation, and maintenance of municipally owned utilities.

Warrant. An order drawn by a legislative body, or an officer of a governmental unit, upon its treasurer, directing the treasurer to pay a specified amount to the person named, or to the bearer.

GOVERNMENTAL ACCOUNTING SYSTEMS

Governmental Accounting Standards Board (GASB)

The GASB was established in 1984, under the oversight of the Financial Accounting Foundation which, in turn, oversees the Financial Accounting Standards Board (FASB). Before the establishment of the GASB, the reports of governmental entities were criticized by the accounting community because they could not be interpreted in a manner consistent with the financial reports of private business organizations. The primary purpose of the GASB is to develop standards of reporting for state and local government entities; its organizational and operational structure is similar to that of the FASB, and its objective is to make the combined general purpose financial reports of governmental entities as comparable as possible to those of private business.

As a general rule the GASB will promulgate standards that parallel GAAP. However, there are instances that require a governmental entity to comply with a state law or regulatory accounting requirement that is in noncompliance with GAAP. Such reports are classified as *Special Reports or Supplemental Schedules,* which are not a part of the general purpose statements. In these cases governmental units can publish two sets of statements, one in compliance with legal requirements and one in compliance with GAAP. (An example of this problem is that it is not uncommon for some governmental entities to be required by law to apply the cash basis of accounting.)

Governmental accounting systems are developed on a *fund basis.* A fund is defined as an independent fiscal and accounting entity with a self-balancing set of accounts recording cash and other resources together with all related liabilities, obligations, reserves, and equities that are segregated for the purpose of carrying on specific activities or attaining specified objectives in accordance with applicable regulations, restrictions, and other statutory and regulatory limitations.

In addition to each fund's transactions within the fund itself, each fund in a governmental unit can have financial transactions with other funds in the same entity. The financial statements must reflect interfund transactions which result from services rendered by one fund to another.

The accrual basis of accounting is recommended for matching revenues and expenditures during a designated period of time which refers specifically to the time when revenues and expenditures are recorded as such in the accounting records.

Governmental revenues should be classified by fund and source. Expenditures should be classified by fund, function, organization unit, activity, character, and principal classes of objectives in accordance with standard recognized classifications. Common terminology and classifications should be used consistently throughout (1) the budget; (2) the accounts; and (3) the financial reports. These three elements of governmental financial administration are inseparable and can be thought of as the "cycle" of governmental financial transactions and final product of the accounting system.

Seven Types of Funds

1. The *General Fund* which accounts for all transactions not accounted for in any other fund.
2. *Special Revenue Fund* which accounts for revenues from specific sources or to finance specific projects.
3. *Debt Service Fund* which accounts for the payment of interest and principal on longterm debt.
4. *Capital Project Fund* which accounts for the receipt and disbursement of funds used for the acquisition of capital facilities.
5. *Enterprise Funds* which account for the financing of services to the public paid for by the users of the services.
6. *Fiduciary Funds: Trust and Agency Funds* which account for assets held by a governmental unit as trustee or agent for individuals, private organizations, or other governmental units.
7. *Internal Service Funds* which account for the financing of special projects and services performed by one governmental entity for an organization unit within the same governmental entity.

The accountant should:

- Maintain complete and adequate files for the initial documentation which established or restricted the fund, together with any special reporting requirements demanded.
- Keep separate detailed books of entry for each fund, separate bank account for that fund, separate identification of all property and securities.
- Under *no* circumstances should assets of separate funds be commingled. Transfers between funds should not be permitted without documentary authorization, and inter-fund receivables and payables should, in contra-effect, be equal and clearly identified, always maintaining the original integrity of each fund.
- Interest accruals, cooperative-share funding (example: government 80%—college 20% in Work Study Program), expense allowances or allocations—all should be made timely.
- Federal, state and local reporting requirements should be studied, met and reported as due to avoid stringent penalties, interest and possible loss of tax-exempt status. Options may exist regarding the handling of

payroll and unemployment taxes; they should be studied and explored for money-saving possibilities.

- Independently audited annual financial statements by fund are usually required both by organizational charter and governmental departments (especially where grant-participation is involved). Publication of the availability of these statements is sometimes mandatory (foundations).

- One area of discussion and dispute is the "compliance" feature of audits involving certain governmental agency grants. Here, the independent auditor is called upon to measure the agency's compliance with certain non-accounting rules, such as eligibility of money-recipients, internal controls and other matters not ordinarily associated with a financial audit. The integrity of the auditor's financial opinion should never be compromised by peripheral compliance requirements. In most cases, the auditor should qualify any opinion indicating the results and *extent of tests* made for compliance. The AICPA, to some extent, has spelled out guidelines for "compliance" opinions in Section 9641 of its "Statements on Auditing Standards."

- Municipal accounting techniques, procedures, format and demands are not discussed here. Their overall application involves the use of fund accounting. The main distinction is the entering of the budget—the anticipated revenues and the appropriations thereof—directly on and as part of the books of account. Progress reports then show how actual compares with anticipated. The estimates are then zeroed out at yearend. The meaning and use of "encumbrances" should also be understood. Reports for some local subdivisions, such as school boards, usually involve a strict accounting of each receipt and disbursement, including the detailing of outstanding checks.

Accounting for the General Fund (GF).   The General Fund is the type most frequently used as it accounts for revenues not allocated to specified activities by law or by contract. Every governmental entity *must* have a General Fund; none of the other types of funds are required, but are established as needed.

Entries in the GF system originally are made to Estimated Revenues and Appropriations and simultaneously a debit or credit, whichever is the case, is recorded in the Fund Balance account. For proper controls the encumbrance system is used with entries recorded when commitments are made or orders placed. This procedure has the effect of setting aside the money for the payment of future purchase orders and payment vouchers. When a purchase is actually made, the entries to an Encumbrances and Reserve for Encumbrances are reversed and those accounts cleared. (The later expenditure is not always the same as the encumbrance.) Simultaneously, the actual expenditure is recorded by a Debit to an Expenditures account and a credit to Vouchers Payable.

Taxes and service charges are budgeted in a Taxes-Receivable—Current Account. The estimated amounts should be recorded after the estimate and posting of uncollectibles, so the entries are a credit to Revenues and a credit to Estimated Uncollectible Taxes. When collections are actually received during the fiscal year, they are recorded with a debit to cash and a credit to Taxes Receivable—Current. Subsequently, it is determined that a certain amount of taxes will become delinquent as the year progresses. These amounts are recorded in a Taxes Receivable—Delinquent account (debit) and a credit to Taxes Receivable-Current. At this point an Interest and Penalties account should be opened for fees, penalties and other charges associated with the collection of delinquent taxes.

Taxes Receivable—Delinquent	xxx	
Estimated Uncollectible Current Taxes	xxx	
Taxes Receivable—Current		xxx
Estimated Uncollectible Delinquent Taxes		xxx
Interest and Penalties	xxx	
Estimated Uncollectible Interest and Penalties		xxx

At the end of the fiscal year, the accounts of the General Fund are closed out. Any differences are recorded for or against the Fund Balance.

Accounting for Special Revenue Funds (SRF).   Special Revenue Funds account for revenues obtained via specific taxes or other designated revenue sources. They are usually mandated by statute, charter, or local ordinance to fund specific functions or activities. Examples are parks, museums, highway construction, street maintenance, business licensing.

Revenue Funds resources cannot be used for any purpose other than the purpose for which the bonds were sold.

Journal entries:		
Encumbrances	xxx	
Reserve for Encumbrances		xxx
Reserve for Encumbrances	xxx	
Encumbrances		xxx
Expenditures	xxx	
Vouchers Payable		xxx
Vouchers Payable	xxx	
Cash		xxx

Taxes and service charges are budgeted in a Taxes-Receivable—Current account. The estimated amounts should be recorded after the estimate and posting of uncollectibles, so the entries are a credit to Revenues and a credit to Estimated Uncollectible Taxes; e.g.,

Taxes Receivable—Current	xxx	
Estimated Uncollectible Current Taxes		xxx
Revenues		xxx

When collections are actually received during the fiscal year they are recorded with a debit to Cash and a credit to Taxes Receivable—Current.

Accounting for Debt Service Funds (DSF).   Debt Service Fund accounts for the payment of interest and principal on long-term debt resulting from the sale of general obligation bonds. This fund does not include the accounting for special assessments and service debts of governmental enterprises.

There are three types of long-term debt:

- Term or sinking fund bonds.
- Serial bonds.
- Notes and time warrants having a maturity of *more than one year* after issuance.

The first entry in the accounting cycle for a bond fund is to record the bond authorization:

Bonds Authorized—unissued	xxx	
Appropriations		xxx
The bonds are sold:		
Cash	xxx	
Bonds Authorized—unissued		xxx

If the bonds are sold at a premium, a Premium on Bonds account is credited. If sold at a discount, a Discount on Bonds account is debited.

Accounting for the Capital Projects Fund (CPF).   Capital Projects Funds are a set of accounts for all resources used to acquire *capital* facilities (except funds financed by special assessment and enterprise funds). There must be Capital Project Funds for each authorized project to ensure that the proceeds of a bond issue, for example, are expended only as authorized. There is also a separate budget for the CPF, usually labeled the Capital Budget.

The accounting process begins with project authorization which is in memorandum form; no entry is necessary. Assuming the project is financed by the proceeds of a bond issue (as most projects are), the proceeds of the borrowing is an entry to the Cash account and a credit to Revenues for the *par value* of the bonds. If the bonds were sold at a premium, there is a credit to a Premium on Bonds account for the amount of the premium. Since GAAP requires bond premiums to be treated as an adjustment to the interest costs, the premiums are transferred *to* the Debt Service Fund established to service the debt. The entry to record the transfer is:

Premium on Bonds	xxx	
Cash		xxx

If the bonds are sold at a discount, the discount is eliminated by a transfer of the amount of the discount *from* the Debt Service Fund *to* the Capital Projects Fund.

Accounting for Enterprise Funds (EF).   Enterprise Funds finance self-supporting (not taxpayers') activities of governmental units that render services on a user charge basis to the general public. Common enterprises are water companies, electricity, natural gas, airports, transportation systems, hospitals, port authority, and a variety of recreational facilities.

In most jurisdictions, utilities and other enterprises are required to adopt and operate under budgets in the same manner as non-enterprise operations of governmental units. A budget is essential for control of each enterprise's operating results and to ensure that the resources of one enterprise are not illegally or improperly utilized by another.

The accrual basis of accounting is the required method for Enterprise Funds. As customers are billed, Accounts Receivable accounts are debited and revenue accounts *by sources* are credited.

Four financial statements are required to disclose fully the financial position and results of operations of an Enterprise Fund:

- Balance Sheet
- Revenue and Expenses
- Changes in Financial Position
- Analysis of Changes in Retained Earnings

Accounting for Trust and Agency Funds (TAF).   Trust and Agency Funds are similar; the primary difference is that a Trust Fund is usually in existence for a long period of time, even permanently. Both have fiduciary responsibilities for funds and assets that are not owned outright by the funds.

There are two types of Trust Funds, i.e., expendable and nonexpendable funds. The former allows the principal and income to be spent on designated operations, while nonexpendable funds must be preserved intact. Pension and various retirement funds are examples of expendable funds; a loan fund from which loans are made for specific purposes and must be paid back, which requires maintaining the *original amount* of the fund, is a nonexpendable fund.

Trust Funds are operated as required by statutes and governmental regulations established for their existence. Accounting for Trust Funds consists primarily of the proper recording of receipts and disbursements. Additions are credited directly to the Fund Balance account and expenditures charged directly against the Fund Balance.

An Agency Fund can be thought of as sort of a clearinghouse fund established to account for assets received for and paid to others; the main asset is cash which is held only for a brief period of time, so is seldom invested because cash is usually paid out shortly after receipt.

An Agency Fund simplifies the complexities that can result from the use of numerous fund accounting entities; e.g., instances in which a single transaction affects several different funds. All Agency Fund assets are owed to another fund, a person, or an organization. The entries for receipts and disbursements in Agency Funds are easy:

Upon receipt:		
Cash	xxx	
Fund Balance		xxx
Upon disbursement:		
Fund Balance	xxx	
Cash		xxx

Accounting for Intergovernmental Service Funds (ISF).   ISF, also referenced as Working Capital Funds and Internal Service Funds, finances and provides accountability for services and commodities provided by a designated agency of a governmental unit to other departments, agencies, etc., of the same governmental entity. Examples are motor pools, centralized garages, central purchasing, storage, facilities, and central printing services.

Funds for the establishment of ISF usually originate from three sources:

- Contributions from another operating fund—e.g., the General Fund or an Enterprise Fund.
- The sale of general obligation bonds.
- Long-term advances from other funds, which are to be repaid over a specific period of time from the earnings of a revolving fund.

As cash is expended for the benefit of other fund-users, the users are charged with the cost of the materials or services furnished by the ISF and the ISF is then reimbursed by interdepartmental cash transfers from the departments of other funds to which materials or services have been furnished.

The accounting for ISF should include all accounts necessary to compile an accurate statement of the outcome of its financial operations, and of its financial position at any given time. These accounts will usually include the fixed assets owned by the fund, accounts for buildings financed from capital Project Funds, depreciation recorded on fixed assets to obtain an accurate computation of costs and to preclude depletion of the fund's capital. The accrual basis must be used for all ISF accounting, with all charges to departments of various funds billed at the time materials or services are rendered and expenditures are recorded when incurred. Encumbrances may or may not be formally recorded in the books of account; if they are the entries would be:

Encumbrances	xxx	
Reserve for Encumbrances		xxx

If encumbrances are not recorded in the accounts, memorandum records of orders and commitments should be maintained to preclude over-obligation of cash and other fund resources.

When an ISF is established, the entry to be made will depend upon the service the fund is to provide. If the fund's capital is obtained from the General Fund, the entry would be:

Cash	xxx	
Contribution from General Fund		xxx

If a general obligation bond issue is a source of the fund's capital:

Cash	xxx	
Contribution from		
General Obligation Bonds		xxx

If fund capital is obtained from another fund of the same governmental unit the entry is:

Cash	xxx	
Advance from (name of fund)		xxx

Accounting for the General Fixed Assets Account Group (GFA).   The fixed asset accounts are maintained on the basis of original cost, or the estimated cost if the original cost is not available, as in the case of gifts. The appraised value at the time of receipt of the asset is an acceptable valuation. Otherwise, initial costs of fixed assets are obtainable from contracts, purchase vouchers, and other transaction documents generated at the time of acquisition or construction.

Depreciation on fixed assets should not be recorded in the general accounting records. Depreciation charges are computed for unit cost purposes, provided such charges are recorded in memorandum form and do not appear in the fund accounts.

Different from depreciation accounting for commercial enterprises, the depreciation of fixed assets is not recorded as an expense because there is no purpose in doing so. Property records should be kept, however, for each piece of property and equipment owned by the fund. The sum of the cost value of the properties—buildings, improvements, machinery, and equipment—should equal the corresponding balances of those accounts carried in the general ledger.

Accounting for the Long-Term Debt Group (LTD).   General Obligation Bonds and other types of long-term debt supported by general revenues are obligations of the governmental unit as a whole, not of any of the entity's constituent funds individually. Additionally, the monies from such debt can be expended on facilities that are used in the operation of several funds. Accordingly, the total of long-term indebtedness backed by the "full faith and credit" of the government should be recorded and accounted for in a separate self-balancing group of accounts titled General Long-Term Debt Group of Accounts. Included in this debt group are general obligation bonds, time warrants, and notes that have a maturity date of *more than one year* from the date of issuance.

Long-term debt is recorded in the self-balancing accounts, so do not affect the liabilities of any other fund. The reason for these accounts is to record a governmental unit's long-term debt at any point in time from the date the debt is incurred until it is finally paid. Under GAAP the proper valuation for the long-term debt liability is the sum of (1) the present discounted value of the principal payable at the stipulated maturity date in the future and (2) the present discounted value of the periodic interest payments to the maturity date.

The entries to be made at the time the bonds are sold are:

Amounts to be Provided for		
the Payment of Term Bonds	xxx	
Term Bonds Payable		xxx

The proceeds of the bond issue are entered in a Capital Projects Fund account to be expended as authorized in the Authorized Capital Outlay account.

(Note: Not-for-profit accounting for other than governmental entities uses the accrual basis of accounting—e.g., colleges and universities, voluntary hospitals, health and welfare organizations, and so on.)

OBJECTIVES OF FINANCIAL REPORTING BY NONBUSINESS ORGANIZATIONS

The main distinguishing characteristics of nonbusiness organizations include:

1. Receipts of significant amounts of resources from resource providers who do not expect to receive either repayment or economic benefits commensurate with the resources provided.
2. Operating purposes for objectives other than to provide goods or services at a profit.
3. Absence of defined ownership interests that can be sold, transferred, or redeemed, or that convey entitlement to a share of a residual distribution of resources in the event of liquidation of the organization.

These characteristics result in certain types of transactions that are largely, although not entirely, absent in business enterprises, such as contributions and grants, and in the absence of transactions with owners, such as issuing and redeeming stock and paying dividends. General purpose financial reporting by nonbusiness organizations does not attempt to meet all the information needed by those interested parties or to furnish all of the different types of information that financial reporting can provide. It is not intended to meet specialized needs of regulatory bodies, donors or grantors, or others having the authority to obtain the information they need. The most important users in the nonbusiness environment are resource providers, such as members, taxpayers, contributors, and creditors. A full set of financial statements for a period should show:

1. Financial position at the end of the period.
2. Earnings for the period.
3. Comprehensive income for the period.
4. Cash flows during the period.
5. Investments by and distributions to owners during the period.

Financial statements result from simplifying, condensing, and aggregating masses of data. As a result, they convey information that would be obscured if great detail were provided.

Chapter 13

Not-for-Profit or Exempt Organizations

CONTENTS

FASB 136, *Transfers of Assets to a Not-for-Profit Organization or Charitable Trust That Raises or Holds Contributions for Others*   **13.02**

IRS Rulings and Legislation Relating to Disclosure   **13.05**

FASB Statement 93, *Recognition of Depreciation by Not-for-Profit Organizations*   **13.08**

FASB Statement 116, *Accounting for Contributions Received and Contributions Made*   **13.09**

FASB Statement 117, *Financial Statements of Not-for-Profit Organizations*   **13.09**

FASB Statement 124, *Accounting for Certain Investments Held by Not-for-Profit Organizations*   **13.13**

FASB Project on NFPO Combinations   **13.15**

Board Deliberations   **13.16**

The Method of Accounting for a Combination of NFP Organizations   **13.17**

Accounting for nonbusiness organizations such as not-for-profit and exempt organizations has many of the same characteristics as accounting for business entities; however, there are also wide differences. Among the foremost of these are differing objectives of financial reporting by nonbusiness entities.

The main distinguishing characteristics of nonbusiness organizations include:

1. Receipts of significant amounts of resources from resource providers who do not expect to receive either repayment or economic benefits commensurate with the resources provided.
2. Operating purposes for objectives other than to provide goods or services at a profit.
3. Absence of defined ownership interests that can be sold, transferred, or redeemed, or that convey entitlement to a share of a residual distribution of resources in the event of liquidation of the organization.

These characteristics result in certain types of transactions that are largely, although not entirely, absent in business enterprises, such as contributions and grants, and in the absence of transactions with owners, such as issuing and redeeming stock and paying dividends. General purpose financial reporting by nonbusiness organizations does not attempt to meet all the information needed by those interested parties or to furnish all of the different types of information that financial reporting can provide. It is not intended to meet specialized needs of regulatory bodies, donors or grantors, or others having the authority to obtain the information they need. The most important users in the nonbusiness environment are resource providers, such as members, tax-payers, contributors, and creditors. A full set of financial statements for a period should show:

1. Financial position at the end of the period.
2. Earnings for the period.
3. Comprehensive income for the period.
4. Cash flows during the period.
5. Investments by and distributions to owners during the period.

Financial statements result from simplifying, condensing, and aggregating masses of data. As a result, they convey information that would be obscured if great detail were provided.

Following are FASB Statements, legislation, and IRS regulations relating specifically to not-for-profit organizations.

FASB 136, *Transfers of Assets to a Not-for-Profit Organization or Charitable Trust That Raises or Holds Contributions for Others*

FASB Statement 136, the most recent FASB pronouncement on not-for-profit organizations (NPOs) establishes standards for transactions in which a donor makes a contribution by transferring assets to a not-for-profit organization or charitable trust—the recipient organization.

The not-for-profit organization accepts the assets from the donor and agrees to do one of the following:

1. Use those assets on behalf of a beneficiary specified by the donor.
2. Transfer those assets to said beneficiary.
3. Transfer the return on investment of those assets to that beneficiary.
4. Transfer both the assets and the return on investments to the specified beneficiary.

It also establishes standards for transactions that take place in a similar manner but are not contributions because the transfers are any of the following:

1. Revocable.
2. Repayable.
3. Reciprocal.

It follows that the Statement requires a recipient organization that is willing to accept cash or other financial assets from a donor and to agree to abide by the stipulations spelled out above in the interest of that specified unaffiliated beneficiary. In doing so, it also agrees to recognize the fair value of those assets as a liability to the specified beneficiary concurrent with recognition of the assets received from the donor.

However, if the donor explicitly grants the recipient organization variance power, or if the recipient organization and the specified beneficiary are financially *interrelated* organizations, the recipient organization is required to recognize the fair value of any assets it receives as a contribution received.

Not-for-profit organizations are financially interrelated if:

1. One organization has the ability to influence the operating and financial decisions of the other.
2. One organization has an ongoing economic interest in the net assets of the other.

The Statement does not establish standards for a trustee's reporting of assets held on behalf of specified beneficiaries, but it does establish standards for a beneficiary's reporting of its rights to assets held in a charitable trust.

Further, it requires that a specified beneficiary recognize its rights to the assets held by a recipient organization as an asset unless the donor has explicitly granted the recipient organization variance power. Those rights are one of the following:

1. An interest in the net assets of the recipient organization.
2. A beneficial interest.
3. A receivable.

If the beneficiary and the recipient organization are financially interrelated organizations, the beneficiary is required to recognize its interest in the net assets of the recipient organization and adjust that interest for its share of the change in net assets of the recipient organization.

If the beneficiary has an unconditional right to receive all or a portion of the specified cash flows from a charitable trust or other identifiable pool of assets, the beneficiary is required to recognize that beneficial interest, measuring and subsequently remeasuring it at fair value, using a valuation technique such as the present value of the estimated expected future cash flows.

If the recipient organization is explicitly granted variance power, the specified beneficiary does not recognize its potential for future distributions from the assets held by the recipient organization. In all other cases, a beneficiary recognizes its rights as a receivable.

FASB 136 covers four conditions under which a transfer of assets to a recipient organization is accounted for as *a liability* by the recipient organization and as *an asset* by the resource provider because the transfer is revocable or reciprocal.

The four circumstances occur when:

1. The transfer is subject to the resource provider's unilateral right to redirect the use of the assets to another beneficiary.
2. The transfer is accompanied by the resource provider's conditional promise to give or is otherwise revocable or repayable.
3. The resource provider controls the recipient organization and specifies an unaffiliated beneficiary.
4. The resource provider specifies itself or its affiliate as the beneficiary and the *transfer is not an equity transaction.*
   - When the transfer is an equity transaction and the resource provider specifies itself as beneficiary, it records an interest in the net assets of the recipient organization (or an increase in a previously recognized interest).
   - When the resource provider specifies an affiliate as beneficiary, the resource provider records an equity transaction as a separate line item in its statement of activities, and the affiliate named as beneficiary records an interest in the net assets of the recipient organization. The

recipient organization records an equity transaction as a separate line item in its statement of activities.

Certain disclosures are required when a not-for-profit organization transfers assets to a recipient organization and specifies itself or its affiliate as the beneficiary or if it includes in its financial statements a ratio of fundraising expenses to amounts raised.

The Statement incorporates without reconsideration the guidance in FASB Interpretation 42, *Accounting for Transfers of Assets in Which a Not-for-Profit Organization Is Granted Variance Power,* and supersedes that Interpretation. (It states that an NPO should be considered both a *donee* and a *donor* when it receives assets from a resource provider, *and* has received explicit unilateral authority to redistribute the assets and income from the assets to a beneficiary.)

FASB 136 became effective for financial statements issued for fiscal periods beginning after December 15, 1999, except for the provisions incorporated from Interpretation 42, which continue to be effective for fiscal years ending after September 15, 1996. Earlier application was encouraged. This Statement was applicable either by restating the financial statements of all years presented or by recognizing the cumulative effect of the change in accounting principle in the year of the change.

IRS Rulings and Legislation Relating to Disclosure

At the same time that the Financial Accounting Standards Board was adopting FASB 136, the Internal Revenue Service was issuing new rulings relating to the availability to the public of financial documents revealing the details of the operations of not-for-profit (or in the parlance of the IRS, *exempt*) organizations. The new regulations increase the disclosure burden of exempt organizations — and their accountants.

These exempt organizations are entities described in Sections 501(c) and 501(d) of the Internal Revenue Code and exempt from taxation under Section 501(a). They include charitable, educational, scientific, literary, and medical organizations, trade and professional associations, sports leagues, social welfare organizations, public radio and television stations, trade and professional associations, social clubs, cemeteries, and fraternal beneficiary societies. The rules do not apply to disclosure requirements of private foundations.

Other Disclosure Requirements

Considering the huge sums of money that many of these NPOs handle, it is not surprising that in addition to other FASB Standards discussed later in this chapter, Congress has seen fit to set up some rules relating to disclosure by not-for-profits. Legislation has included the Omnibus Budget Reconciliation Act of 1987 and the Taxpayer Bill of Rights 2, passed in 1996.

The former required exempt organizations, including public foundations, to provide access for public inspection of their tax exemption applications. It also required that they (other than private foundations) allow public inspection at their principal offices of the last three years' annual reports. The Taxpayer Bill of Rights 2 provided for additional public disclosures which have been finalized in these IRS rulings.

Specific Documents for Inspection

Not only do the most recent rulings specify *what* should be disclosed, but they are very specific about *how* and *where* applicable documents are made available by the exempt organization (other than a private foundation).

The documents that must be available upon request for inspection if they apply to the particular organization include:

1. Form 990, *Return of Organization Exempt from Income Tax.*
2. Form 990BL, *Information and Initial Excise Tax Return for Black Lung Benefit Trusts and Certain Related Persons.*
3. Form 990EZ, *Short Form Return for Organization Exempt from Income Tax.*
4. Form 1023, *Application for Recognition of Exemption Under Section 501(c)(3) of the Internal Revenue Code.*
5. Form 1024, *Application for Recognition of Exemption Under Section 501(a) for Determination Under Section 120 of the Internal Revenue Code.*
6. Form 1065, *U.S. Partnership Return of Income.*

In addition to the documents themselves, other relevant information must also be made available:

For Forms 1023 or 1024, all supporting documents filed by, or on behalf of the organization in connection with that application, as well as any correspondence with the IRS should be available. If the application was filed before July 15, 1987, the organization need not supply the document unless the organization possessed a copy of the application on that date.

For Forms 990, 990-EZ, 990-BL or Form 1065, including all schedules and attachments filed with the IRS, the organization must make available its three most recent returns. However, in the interest of confidentiality, the organization should *not* including the portions of the returns that give the names and addresses of contributors.

The exempt organization must also copy documents, or portions thereof, when requested either in writing or in person.

Procedures

The ruling is quite specific about establishing the various procedures for making these documents available for public inspection.

1. It specifies the amount of fees for copying and postage the organization may charge. The organization may charge a reasonable amount for copying and mailing as long as it does not exceed the IRS fees for copies of documents (currently $1 for the first page and 15 cents for each subsequent page). They can charge for the actual cost of postage.

2. It gives instructions on *where* the documents must be available for inspection. In general, the documents must be made available at the organization's principal office, and at larger regional or district offices.

3. It sets limitations an organization may put on requests for copies of documents. Copies of documents should normally be available upon personal request the same day at the place where the documents are available for inspection. Under unusual circumstances, the organization may respond on the next business day, or on the business day following the day the unusual circumstances occurred, as long as the delay does not exceed 5 business days. Written requests must be honored within 30 days of receipt.

4. It outlines how an organization can avoid having to respond to individual requests for copies. Rather than furnish copies, an organization may put the documents on its Web page or another Internet site where there is a database of similar information. Placing the specified documents on the Internet covers the requirement to provide copies, but the organization must still allow public inspection. The regulations specify a number of criteria for posting documents on the Internet.

   a. The documents must be posted so that the public can view, download, and print them in the same format as the original document.

   b. The documents must be accessible without a fee and without having any specialized computer hardware or software.

5. It furnishes guidance to organizations that believe they are the victims of harassment campaigns. If an exempt organization has sufficient cause based on facts and circumstances to believe it is the victim of a harassment campaign, it may take certain steps:

   a. Demonstrate that a group of apparently unreasonable requests aims to disrupt the organization's operations rather than to obtain information.

   b. Refuse to respond to those requests.

c. Request the IRS district director for a determination.

d. While a determination is pending, the organization need not respond to the apparently frivolous requests.

e. Comply on a timely basis with any seemingly valid requests.

Noncompliance

The IRS has set rather stiff penalties for noncompliance:

1. An *individual* whose duty it is to make the required disclosures, but fails to comply without reasonable cause with his or her obligations on behalf of the exempt organization is subject to a penalty of $20 per return or exemption application for each day the failure continues. The maximum penalty for failure to disclose is $10,000 per return. No maximum is specified for the exemption application.

2. An exempt *organization* that willfully fails to comply with the requirement to allow public inspection or to provide copies of returns or exemption applications upon proper request is liable for a $5,000 penalty (per return or application).

3. Criminal penalties may be applied to any person or exempt organization that willfully furnishes false or fraudulent information.

FASB STATEMENT 93, RECOGNITION OF DEPRECIATION BY NOT–FOR–PROFIT ORGANIZATIONS

FASB Statement 93 provides that all not-for-profit organizations must recognize depreciation on all long-lived, tangible assets in general-purpose external financial statements. Thus, the Statement eliminates previously allowed exemptions from depreciation accounting for landmarks, monuments, cathedrals, certain historical treasures, and structures such as churches or temples used primarily as houses of worship.

However, rare works of art and historical treasures that have exceptionally long lives will continue to be exempt from depreciation accounting; but to be in line for this exemption, these assets must have recognized cultural, aesthetic, or historical value, and normally will already have had a long existence, and be expected to retain this value far into the future. Statement 93 also requires not-for-profit organizations to disclose depreciation expense periodically. The financial statement is to include:

1. Depreciation expense for the current reporting period.
2. Balance of major classes reported by nature or function.

3. Accumulated depreciation by major class or in total.
4. Description of accounting methods employed in figuring depreciation.

FASB STATEMENT 116, *ACCOUNTING FOR CONTRIBUTIONS RECEIVED AND CONTRIBUTIONS MADE*

FASB STATEMENT 117, *FINANCIAL STATEMENTS OF NOT-FOR-PROFIT ORGANIZATIONS*

In the past, differing requirements, or deficient guidelines, have led divergent forms of not-for-profit enterprises to abide by various rulings promulgated for their particular type of organization, to follow lines of least resistance, or merely to perpetuate custom. This was true whether or not the organization or the external users were gaining insightful information from the various accounting and reporting procedures. The new rules supersede any/all inconsistencies or discrepancies with previous guides, announcements, or statements.

Statement 116 specifically addresses accounting standards for contributions of cash, assets, services or unconditional promises to provide these at some future time, made or received by any organization, whether it be a not-for-profit or a for-profit business concern:

1. Contributions *received,* including unconditional promises to give, are recognized at fair market value in the period received.
2. Contributions *made,* including unconditional promises to give, are recognized as expenses at fair market value in the period when given.
3. Conditional promises to give (whether received or made) are appropriately recognized when the conditions are substantially met.

This Statement acts to tighten some of the provisions relating to measurement and recognition of volunteer services and their relevancy. It specifies that before these services can be included in revenue, they must create or enhance nonfinancial assets, be of a specialized nature, and be provided by skilled individuals contributing services that would otherwise be purchased. Therefore, the services requiring little skill or training provided by the average volunteer will not be considered as revenue or gains. On the other hand, volunteer work by trained professionals and tradesmen, such as nurses, teachers, carpenters, plumbers may be measured at fair value and recognized in the financial report with explanatory notes describing the value of service rendered to various aspects of particular programs. Recognition of these services must also be deemed to be clearly relevant and clearly measurable. If practicable, the fair value of the ordinary volunteer services contributed but not recognized as revenue should also be disclosed even though not recognized as revenue.

Both Statements 116 and 117 take into consideration three classes of contributions:

1. Permanently restricted net assets.
2. Temporarily restricted net assets.
3. Unrestricted net assets.

Statement 116 also requires accounting for the expiration of donor-imposed restrictions if/when said restrictions expire. It also establishes standards for accounting for disclosures relating to works of art, historical treasures, rare books and manuscripts—collections whether capitalized or not.

To be considered a "collection," the assets must be:

1. For the purpose of public exhibition, education or research, not an investment for financial gain.
2. Conserved, cared for, and remain unencumbered.
3. Protected by an organizational policy requiring that proceeds from the sale of any collection items be used to acquire other items for collections.

An organization is not required to recognize contributions if they are added to collections which meet the above criteria. However, when applying FASB 116, organizations are encouraged to capitalize previously acquired collections retroactively or to capitalize them on a prospective basis. One stipulation is that capitalization of selected collections or items is *not* permitted. If capitalized retroactively, these assets may be stated at their cost, at fair value at the time of acquisition, current cost or current market value.

When collections have been capitalized, additional contributed items are to be recognized as revenue or gains; if the collections have not been capitalized, these items are not recognized. There is, however, additional disclosure information required for them and for collections which have been capitalized prospectively.

1. On the face of the statement of activities, apart from revenues, expenses, gains and losses an organization that has not capitalized must report the cost of items purchased as a decrease in the appropriate class of net assets; or proceeds resulting from the sale of items; or from insurance recoveries as an increase in the appropriate class of net assets.
2. An organization that capitalizes prospectively must report proceeds from sales or insurance recoveries of items not previously capitalized separately.

3. Both those organizations that do not capitalize, or do so prospectively, must describe the collections and their significance, and the accounting conservatorship policies relating to them.

4. They must also describe and report the fair value of items lost or removed from collections for whatever reason.

5. A line in the body of the financial statement must refer directly to the note on collections.

In addition to the accounting functions which these stipulations provide, they would appear to help ensure the integrity of important collections.

The intent and purpose of FASB 117 is to begin to bring a measure of uniformity to the financial statements of NPOs, particularly for the benefit of external users. Emphasis is upon relevance and significance of the information provided, the ease with which it can be understood and interpreted, and the readiness with which financial reports can be compared with those of other not-for-profit entities.

FASB 117 stipulates that three financial statements with appropriate notes be included in all NPO financial reports:

1. Statement of financial position.
2. Statement of activities.
3. Statement of cash flows.

This latter requirement is new for not-for-profit entities and thus amends FASB 95, *Statement of Cash Flows,* in which the requirements had previously applied only to business entities. Statement 117 also *requires* Voluntary Health and Welfare Organizations (*encourages* other NPOs) to prepare an additional financial statement showing expenses in natural classifications as well as the functional classifications required of all NPOs. Organizations may continue to present other financial reports if they have found them to be beneficial in demonstrating the handling of the service aspects of the particular type of NPO.

Most organizations probably found that their accounting and reporting activities had not become more complicated and restrictive, but simplified, and at the same time, more meaningful once the initial changeover had been completed. This is particularly true if the organization carried fund accounting to the extreme and attempted to fit everything into the pattern whether or not this proved to be appropriate or useful. Statement 117 does not tamper with fund accounting *per se* but does require that the emphasis on financial reporting be placed on the entity as a whole. Thus, organizations may continue to prepare their statement of financial position showing fund groups, but the groups must be aggregated into net asset classes.

In line with the aim to give a clear picture of an NPO's liquidity, FASB 117 requires that an organization must break down its net assets into the three classes mentioned above. Further, information about the amounts and/or conditions of the two restricted categories can be made in the statement itself if this is deemed sufficient, or it may be necessary to give detailed explanations in the notes. The latter could be more frequently necessary than not, since the restrictions could range from a wealthy donor's desire to aid a "pet project" to a government grant funding a Congressional bill.

Much of the impetus for these statements was to bring about more readily usable full disclosure. Requirements will now make it more important than ever to distinguish between program and support activities and expenses. FASB 117 separates the latter into three classes:

1. Managements and general.
2. Fund-raising.
3. Membership development.

It is important for the preparer of the financial statement to be reminded that the focus should be on the *service* aspect of the NPO and how well this is being accomplished. Since it is doubtful if this information can be conveyed adequately in the body of the financial statement, the accompanying notes will be of particular relevance.

Below are some important points to keep in mind relating to the purpose of the three basic financial reports of not-for-profit entities.

Statement of Financial Position

- Present assets, liabilities and net asset figures for the organization as a whole.
- Demonstrate credit status, liquidity, ability to meet service and financial obligations, need for outside financial aid.
- Distinguish between permanently restricted assets, temporarily restricted assets, unrestricted assets.
- Disclose donor-imposed restrictions and internally imposed restrictions relating to both time and purpose.

Statement of Activities (Operating Statement for NPOs)

- Report the changes in total net assets (equities).
- Present the changes in each of the three net asset classes (not fund balances): permanently restricted, temporarily restricted, unrestricted.

- Indicate total changes in net assets.
- Disclose expenditures by functional and/or natural classification as required/recommended for a particular type of NPO.

Statement of Cash Flows

- Amends FASB 95 to require *all* NPOs to include a cash flow statement in their external financial reports.
- Present changes in cash and cash equivalents including certain donor-restricted cash used on a long-term basis.
- Present cash flow information utilizing either direct or indirect method.

FASB STATEMENT 124, ACCOUNTING FOR CERTAIN INVESTMENTS HELD BY NOT–FOR–PROFIT ORGANIZATIONS

FASB 124 is another step in the process of bringing reason, conformity, consistency, and comparability in accounting and financial reporting to the world of not-for-profit entities.

This statement is reminiscent of FASB 115, *Accounting for Certain Investments in Debt and Equity Securities,* to the extent that it covers the same securities; however, accounting treatment for NPOs is markedly different from that applied to for-profit businesses.

Fair Value Requirements

Statement 124 requires that certain equity securities and all investments in debt securities be reported at fair value. The specific equity securities are those with readily determined fair value which are not accounted for by the equity method or as investments in consolidated subsidiaries. Gains and losses are to be reported in the statement of activities. This Statement also requires specific disclosures about all investments, including the return on the investments.

Readily determinable fair value of an equity security is considered to have been met if one of the following criteria applies:

1. Sale prices or bid or asked quotations are available on an SEC registered exchange.
2. Sales prices or bid or asked prices on OTC markets if they are reported by NASDAQ or the National Quotation Bureau.
3. If the equity security is traded only on a foreign market, that market is comparable to one of those given above.

4. If a mutual fund investment, fair value per share or unit has been determined and published as the basis for ongoing transactions.

Although many NPOs have been reporting all of their investments at fair value, it has not been required; therefore, there has been a considerable degree of diversity in the various organizations' accounting and financial reporting. The FASB believes that fair value will give a truer picture of the resources available for the further growth of the program of a not-for-profit organization. In addition, not only the staff and administrators, but also the donors will have improved information to assist them in allocating their efforts and resources.

Accounting Procedures

Application of this Statement may be made in either of two ways:

1. Restating of all financial statements presented for prior years.
2. Recognizing the cumulative effect of the change in the year of adoption.

Accounting and reporting for investments by various types of not-for-profit organizations has heretofore been provided by several AICPA guides. Any guidance in those sources which is inconsistent with the provisions of FASB 124 are superseded by these new requirements in this Statement.

In addition to the accounting principles set forth in this pronouncement, any additional disclosure and accounting requirements not discussed here but included in other Statements may apply to investments held by not-for-profit entities as well as to for-profit companies. They are:

1. FASB 107, *Disclosure about Fair Value of Financial Instruments* (amended).
2. FASB 133, *Accounting for Derivative Instruments and Hedging Activities.*

Disclosure and Reporting

The Statement of Activities for each reporting period for an NPO must include the following specific items:

1. Investment income from dividends, interest, etc.
2. Net gains or losses on investments reported at other than fair value.
3. Net gains or losses on those reported at fair value.
4. Reconciliation of investment return if separated into operating and non-operating amounts.

5. Description of the policy used to decide what items should be included in determining operating costs.
6. Discussion for so doing if there is a change in that policy.

The Statement of Financial Position for each reporting period for an NPO must include the following:

1. Aggregate carrying amount of investments by major type.
2. Basis on which carrying amounts were determined for investments other than equity securities with readily determinable fair value and all debt securities.
3. Procedures used in determining fair values of investments other than financial instruments if carried at fair value. (Financial instruments are covered by the same requirement in FASB 107.)
4. Aggregate amount of any deficiencies in donor-related funds in which fair value of the assets has fallen below the level necessary to abide by donor stipulation or legal requirements.

For the most recent period, a not-for-profit organization must disclose in the Statement of Financial Position the nature of and carrying amount of any investments that represent a significant concentration of market risk.

FASB Project on NFPO Combinations

In November 1999, the FASB affirmed its earlier decision to undertake a project on combinations of not-for-profit organizations that was separate from its business combinations project. As a result of that decision, combinations of NFP organizations were excluded from the scope of Part I of the September 1999 FASB Exposure Draft, *Business Combinations and Intangible Assets.*

The objective of this project is to develop guidance on the accounting and reporting for *combinations* of NFP organizations. The following paragraphs describe the reasons for the Board deciding to undertake this separate project.

Diversity in Current Practice

Some combinations between NFP organizations have characteristics that distinguish them from business combinations. For example:

1. Some combinations do not include the exchange of cash or other assets as consideration.
2. There are differing interpretations of the application of the provisions of APB Opinion 16, *Business Combinations,* to be applied to combinations of NFP organizations.

3. This divergence occurs particularly in treating those combinations in which there is no exchange of consideration.

These differing interpretations have led to wide diversity in practice.

The Effect of Elimination of Pooling-of-Interests

Statement 141, *Business Combinations,* eliminated the pooling-of-interests method. At present, many combinations of NFP organizations are accounted for in a manner similar to the pooling method. This project is needed to provide guidance to NFP organizations in light of the Board's prohibition of the use of that method.

More Mergers

During the 1990s, the NFP health care industry underwent significant consolidation. Many expect that other segments of the NFP sector will similarly consolidate over the coming years. This project will provide timely guidance in light of the expected increase in the number of mergers and other types of combinations.

BOARD DELIBERATIONS

As of the end of the fourth quarter of 2000, the Board had substantially completed its deliberations related to the issues of:

1. The method of accounting for combinations of not-for-profit organizations.
2. The criteria to be used to identify the acquiring NFP organization.

The Board decided to suspended work temporarily in early 2001 on the NFP project while they completed work on Statements 141, *Business Combinations,* and 142, *Goodwill and Other Intangible Assets.* With the issuance of those statements, the Board returned to deliberations of the issues remaining in this project and reached decisions on:

1. Initial recognition of intangible assets acquired in a combination.
2. Accounting for collection items acquired in a combination.

The Board then decided to revisit its tentative decision that in a combination of NFP organizations, any excess of the fair value of liabilities assumed over the fair value of assets acquired should be considered goodwill. The Board planned to continue these deliberations in 2002 with the aim of issuing an ED.

The Board also agreed to delay the effective date of FASB 142, *Goodwill and Other Intangible Assets,* as it applies to combinations of not-for-profit organizations, until the Board addresses the issues related to such combinations. That means that NFP organizations will account for business combinations and acquired intangible assets following the guidance in APB Opinion 16, *Business Combinations,* and APB Opinion 17, *Intangible Assets,* until a final Statement on combinations of NFP organizations is issued and becomes effective.

Tentative Decisions Relating to Intangibles

The decisions reached by the Board to date in its project on combinations of NFP organizations are:

1. The project will be conducted following an approach that presumes that Statement 141 should apply to combinations of NFP organizations, unless a circumstance unique to such combinations is identified that calls for a different accounting treatment. This approach is being referred to as the *differences-based approach.*
2. The definition of *not-for-profit organization* in Statement 116 will be used for this project.
3. The scope of this project includes:
   a. Combinations between two or more NFP organizations.
   b. The acquisition of a for-profit business enterprise by an NFP organization. (The acquisition of an NFP organization by a business enterprise is within the scope of FASB 141.)

THE METHOD OF ACCOUNTING FOR A COMBINATION OF NFP ORGANIZATIONS

The facts and circumstances of each combination of two or more NFP organizations should be reviewed to determine the extent to which the combination is a *contribution* or a *bargained exchange.* The proposed Statement is likely to include guidance describing the types of facts and circumstances that should be considered in making that determination:

1. A combination of NFP organizations in which no consideration is exchanged should be presumed to be a nonreciprocal transfer and accounted for in a manner similar to a contribution under Statement 116.
2. A combination that includes the exchange of consideration should be presumed to be a bargained exchange and accounted for in accordance with Statement 141.

3. When the facts and circumstances provide evidence that the combination is in part an exchange and in part a contribution, the contribution inherent in that transaction should be recognized by the acquiring organization in accordance with Statement 116.

If the acquired entity is an NFP organization, the contribution recognized by the *acquiring* organization would be measured as the excess of the sum of the fair values of the identifiable assets acquired and the liabilities assumed over the fair value of the assets transferred as consideration (if any).

In the rare cases in which the sum of the fair values of the liabilities assumed exceeds the sum of the fair values of the identifiable assets acquired, the acquiring organization should initially recognize that excess as an unidentifiable intangible asset (goodwill). (The Board has decided that it will reconsider this tentative decision.)

If the acquired entity is a business enterprise, the contribution inherent in a combination should be measured as the excess of the fair value of the acquired business enterprise over the cost of that business enterprise.

Combinations That Include the Exchange of Cash or Other Assets As Consideration

The Board made the following decisions regarding the accounting for a combination of NFP organizations in which cash or other assets are exchanged as consideration. The decisions apply to both combinations between two or more NFP organizations and the acquisition of a business enterprise by a not-for-profit organization:

1. The following are examples of facts and circumstances that provide evidence that the combination is one that is in part an exchange and in part a contribution:

   a. The sum of the fair values of the assets acquired and liabilities assumed exceeds the fair value of the consideration exchanged (the excess), particularly if the amount of that excess is substantial in relation to the fair value of the net assets acquired, and no unstated rights or privileges are involved.

   b. A review of the facts and circumstances surrounding the combination, including careful study of the negotiations, provides evidence that the participants were acting as a donor and a donee and as a buyer and a seller.

2. Organizations should be provided with the following list of examples of facts and circumstances that indicate a combination is a bargained exchange:

   a. The organization or business enterprise is acquired through a competitive bidding process involving multiple potential acquirers.

    b. The amount of consideration offered by the acquiring organization was developed in consultation with acquisition advisors, was based on an estimate of the acquired entity's fair value, or both. That estimate of the acquired entity's fair value may have been developed internally by the acquiring organization or by independent valuation experts.

    c. The acquired entity's former parent or predecessor board of directors retained outside specialists to assist in negotiating the combination, used estimates of the organization's fair value to evaluate the adequacy of the offers received, or both.

    d. One or both parties to the combination retained consultants to provide an opinion on the fairness of the transaction.

    e. The provisions of NFP corporation law or involvement on the part of a state attorney general or other regulatory body influenced the terms or structure of the combination transaction.

3. In general, assets transferred (or liabilities incurred) by the acquiring organization as a requirement of a combination should be accounted for as consideration paid for the acquired entity unless the acquiring organization retains control over the future economic benefits of the transferred assets. If control over the future economic benefits of the transferred assets is retained by the acquiring organization, the asset transfer should be reported as an asset-for-asset exchange. Examples of conditions that would result in the acquiring organization retaining control over the future economic benefit or the transferred assets include:

    a. The asset transfer is repayable or refundable.

    b. The assets are transferred to a recipient that is controlled by the acquiring organization.

    c. The assets are transferred with the stipulation that they be used on behalf of, or for the benefit of, the acquired organization, the acquiring organization, or its affiliates.

4. An acquiring NFP organization should account for a regulatory required asset transfer as consideration paid for the acquired organization.

5. Communities neither own nor control NFP organizations and, therefore, a community's relationship with an NFP organization should have no effect on the method of accounting for a combination of NFP organizations.

6. Contingent consideration in a combination should be accounted for in accordance with the guidance in FASB 141.

Identifying the Acquiring Organization

There is no question but that the FASB wants to make it perfectly clear that the acquiring organization should be identified beyond a shadow of a doubt.

The Board made the following decisions regarding how the acquiring organization in a combination between NFP organizations should be identified:

1. The following general principle should be used as a guide in the process of identifying the acquirer in a combination between NFP organizations:

   In determining which organization is the acquiring organization in a combination of NFP organizations involving two or more organizations, all pertinent facts and circumstances should be considered, particularly whether one of the combining organizations has the ability to dominate the process of selecting a voting majority of the combined organization's initial governing body.

   To determine this, consideration should be given to the existence of rights to appoint members to the combined organization's governing body provided by:

   a. The combined organization's articles of incorporation.
   b. Its bylaws.
   c. Provisions in the combination agreement.
   d. Other means.

2. The FASB suggests that an appendix of implementation guidance should be provided that lists the following factors to consider in identifying the acquiring organization:

   a. Do the combined organization's articles of incorporation or bylaws state that the members of the governing body are appointed? Does one of the combining organizations have the right to appoint a voting majority of the governing body?
   b. Is the combined organization's governing body self-perpetuating?
   c. If so, has one of the combining organizations negotiated the right to select a voting majority of the combined initial governing body as part of the combination agreement?
   d. Or, does one of the combining organizations have the ability to dominate the selection of a voting majority of the governing body through means other than negotiated appointment rights, such as through disproportionate representation on the committee that selects nominees for that body?
   e. If the initial governing body is elected by the combining organizations' members, what are the relative voting rights of the combining organizations in the combined organization?
   f. Are there any other rights to appoint or designate members of the combined organization's governing body, either as of the combination date or in the near future (such as upon the expiration of the terms of some or all of the initial members)?

g. What are the powers of any sponsoring organizations and corporate members and the composition of those sponsors and members? If sponsors and corporate members have limited powers, what is the effect of those limited powers on the ability of one of the combining organizations to control the combined organization?

h. If positions on the governing body are designated positions, what is the effect of those designated positions on the ability of a combining organization to appoint a voting majority of the combined organization's governing body?

i. If the governing body delegates corporate powers to committees, what is the nature of those delegated powers? The composition of the committees?

j. What is the effect of voting requirements (such as supermajority voting requirements) on the ability of one organization to appoint or dominate the selection of a supermajority of the governing body?

k. What is the composition of senior management? What factors are considered by the combining organizations in selecting that management team?

Collection Acquired in a Combination of NFP Organizations

The Board decided that the requirements of Statement 116 would continue to be used to account for collection items that are contributed to, or purchased by, an NFP organization and added to its inexhaustible collection. They agreed that when collection items are acquired in connection with a combination of NFP organizations, the acquirer should follow the guidance in Statement 116 to account for items acquired to be added to its collection.

Identification of Intangible Assets

The criteria in FASB 141 for recognizing identifiable intangible assets should be applied in the recording of combinations of NFP organizations.

Chapter 14

Budgeting for Profit Planning and Budgetary Control

CONTENTS

Types of Budgets	**14.02**
The Sales Budget	**14.03**
The Production Budget	**14.05**
The Labor Budget	**14.07**
Materials Budget	**14.09**
Manufacturing Expense Budget	**14.11**
Capital Expenditures Budget	**14.13**
The Cash Budget	**14.15**
Zero-Base Budgeting	**14.17**
Break-Even Point Analysis	**14.20**

A budget in its simplest terms is an estimate of future events. A budget is not a purely random guess, but a forecast which is computed from historical data that has been verified and assumed with some degree of credibility. The volume of sales for the following year, for example, may be estimated by using data from past experience, present-day market conditions, buying power of the consumer and other related factors.

Merely preparing the annual budget, then leaving it unaltered for the remainder of the budget period, is not the purpose. Preparation is only the first step. The second step is for management to control the operations of the firm and to adhere to the budget. Budgetary control is the tool of management for carrying out and controlling business operations. It establishes predetermined objectives and provides bases for measuring performance against these objectives. If variations between performance and objective arise, management should alter the situation by either correcting the weakness in performance or modifying the budget. Firms that adopt budgetary control have a better control of operations and are better able to modify them to meet expectations.

In addition to a review of the rolling budgets based on previous years' expenditures and operations, two management tools related to budgeting will also be discussed: break-even analysis (BE) and zero-base budgeting (ZBB).

The objective of break-even analysis is to determine an approximation as close as possible to the changes in costs generated by changes in the volume of production. Determining the BE point is a technique that can be applied to the control of costs, in the evaluation of alternatives, in the allocations of a firm's resources, and in making decisions in virtually every phase of a company's business.

The value to budgeting in break-even analysis is that the approach can be applied to sales, profits, costs, and selling prices, to help make sound decisions for the utilization of idle plant capacity, for proposed advertising expenditures, and for proposed expansion in production levels.

ZBB is a logical process, combining many elements of management. The key components of ZBB are:

1. Identifying objectives.
2. Determining value of accomplishing each activity.
3. Evaluating alternative funding levels.
4. Establishing priorities.
5. Evaluating workload and performance measures.

What ZBB does is to recognize that the budgeting process is a management process, a decision-making process and a driving force.

TYPES OF BUDGETS

There are two principal types of annual profit budgets: the operating or earnings budget, and the financial or cash budget. The earnings budget, as its name implies, is an attempt to forecast the earnings of a company for a future period. To make such forecast, other estimates must be made. Consequently, organizations have sales budgets, production budgets (which include labor budgets, materials budgets, manufacturing expense budgets), capital expenditure budgets, administrative expense budgets, distribution expense budgets and appropriation-type budgets (e.g., advertising, research). The accuracy of each of these budgets determines the accuracy of the earnings forecast.

The cash budget, on the other hand, tries to forecast the utilization of the company's cash resources. It estimates the company's anticipated cash expenditures and resources for a period of operation. Cash budget forecasts, like the earnings forecast, depend heavily on sales forecasts. The amount of sales determines the amount of cash the company has for purposes of its operation.

THE SALES BUDGET

The foundation of the entire budget program is the sales budget. If anticipated sales of a particular product (or project) do not exceed the cost to produce and market it by an amount sufficient to reward the investors and to compensate for the risks involved, the product (project) should not be undertaken. Sales forecasting must be continuous. Conditions change rapidly; in order to direct one's efforts into the most profitable channels, there must be a continuous review and revision of the methods employed.

Forecasting Sales

A sales forecast represents the revenue side of the earnings forecast. It is a prediction as to the sales quantity and sales revenue. Sales forecasts are made for both short and long periods.

Forecasting sales with any degree of accuracy is not an easy task. For example, a firm which estimates sales with the expectation that a patent which it holds will not become obsolete may be disappointed.

In general, the business forecaster has two situations: (1) those which he or she can to some extent control, and (2) those where conditions created by others can only be observed, recorded, interpreted and applied to his or her own situation. A firm that has a monopoly due to an important patent which it owns is an example of a company which controls the situation. Forecasts made by such a company may be very accurate. In most cases, however, a company has no such control. It must attempt to interpret general conditions, the situation in its own industry, and future sales of its particular company before making forecasts.

Making the forecast is the responsibility of the sales manager, who, with the help of the district managers and the individual salespersons, determines the primary sales objectives for the year. Corrections of the forecast are made by the heads of the firm so that sales estimates will better reflect expected economic conditions. Before an estimate of sales is made, there must be a reasonable expectation that the projection is attainable. It must be based on the best evidence available. As conditions change, the forecast is revised.

If a firm desires to sell more than in the past, an analysis of past sales performances must be supplemented by other analyses. Consideration must be given to general business conditions. The effects of political and economic changes throughout the world are quickly reflected on individual business communities. Some of these factors which affect sales are wars, government regulations, and technological developments. This information should be used in appraising the probable effect of these changes on the sales of the firm for the budget period.

Market Analysis

A sales manager needs to know if the firm is getting its full share of potential customer demand as indicated by a market analysis.

The questionnaire is a popular method of reaching consumers, retailers and jobbers. Data collected give the firm valuable information, essential in arriving at a forecast of sales possibilities.

A market analysis at a given time gives a picture of the present and potential consumption of a product. This picture provides only half the significant information. The other half can be obtained by continuing the survey over a period of time to discover market trends.

Pricing Policy

The sales budget is not complete until the firm decides on a practical policy as to what price can be secured for its product(s). Generally, estimates should be made to conform with the market prices during the budget period.

The next step is to formulate the sales policies of the firm. These policies should be established relative to such considerations as territorial expansion and selection, customer selection, types and quality of products and service, prices, terms of sales, and sales organization and responsibility.

Only after a firm has thoroughly analyzed past sales experience, general business conditions, market potentials, the product to be sold, determined the prices to be charged and formulated its sales policies is it ready to develop the sales program.

Measuring Individual Performance

As a basis for measuring individual performance, a rewarding-merit sales standard could be established. A sales standard is an opinion of the best qualified judgment of performance which may reasonably be achieved under ideal conditions. By comparing this standard with the budget estimate (the figure expected) under normal conditions, management has provided the most important tool of sales control.

An example of how a comparison between the standard and budget estimate may serve as a basis for reward is the following: A saleswoman may be told to produce sales of $150,000 (standard), but the firm may expect her to produce sales of only $125,000 (budget estimate). The saleswoman does not have to be told what the firm's budget figures are. In an endeavor to reach $150,000, she is trying to better what she believes is the budget figure. Depending on how close she comes to the $150,000, the firm may devise a method of rewarding her. It should be kept in mind, however, that the standard should not be set too high, since it may have a reverse effect if the sales personnel feel it is unreachable.

THE PRODUCTION BUDGET

After the sales budget has been prepared, the next step is to prepare the production budget which specifies the quantity and timing of production requirements.

While the sales budget is prepared in anticipation of seasonal fluctuations, the production budget endeavors to smooth out the fluctuations and thus make most effective use of productive capacity. This is accomplished by manufacturing for stock over the slow periods and using the stock to cover sales during busy periods.

There are different problems for a firm that sells stock products and one that produces special-order goods. The objective for a stock-order-type firm is to coordinate sales and production to prevent excessive inventories, but at the same time to have enough stock to meet sales. A forecast of production in such a firm should enable the executive to arrange to lay out the factory so as to handle the anticipated volume most conveniently. Production in such a firm must be as evenly distributed as possible over the year. It is uneconomical to manufacture the whole period's requirements within a relatively short time at the beginning of the budget period. This involves unduly heavy capital costs of carrying the large inventory. Also, distributing the work over the entire period spreads the labor costs.

With special-order items, the production department must be prepared at all times to manufacture the goods as soon as possible after receiving the order. Production in this case has to be arranged for the best possible utilization of equipment and labor, so that idle time is reduced to a minimum.

Budgeting Production Costs

Production budgets should be rigid as long as conditions remain the same, but they should be capable of prompt adjustment when circumstances change. For example, if a company operates at 70 percent of capacity in a period and the budget was based on a production volume of 80 percent, the budget is of little use. The budget will have to be altered to show what production costs will be at the 70 percent level. It is prudent when planning production at a particular anticipated percentage level to indicate in the budget the estimates of possible production costs at different levels.

Preparing the Production Budget

The production budget period may vary in length. However, it is common practice among large corporations to use what is known as a "product year." As an example, the automobile industry will usually start with the introduction of new models. The budget year should include at least one complete cycle of operations so that money tied up in raw materials and work-in-process materials may undergo one complete liquidation. Another factor influencing the budget period is the stability of general business conditions. It is more difficult to budget operations during an unstable period, and it is advisable at these times to shorten the budget period.

The production budget should be expressed in terms of physical units. To compute the physical quantities is simple. For example, a simple computation to estimate production required is:

	Units
Estimated sales	250,000
Less opening inventory	150,000
Total requirements	100,000
Add: Closing inventory	100,000
Production required	200,000

Before computing the quantity to be produced, it is necessary to decide quantities to be in the inventory at the end of the period. This decision should be based on factors such as:

a. Adequate inventory to meet sales demands
b. Evenly distributed production to prevent shortage of material and labor
c. Danger of obsolescence
d. High costs of storing large inventories.

Available Facilities. The production program must conform with the plant facilities available and should determine the most economical use of these facilities. The capacity of the plant is measured in two ways: optimum plant capacity and normal plant capacity. All other measurements are in percentages of optimum or normal capacity. Optimum capacity of course, can never actually be attained. There are many unavoidable interruptions, such as waiting for setup of machines; time to repair machines; lack of help, tools, materials; holidays; inefficiency; etc. However, these interruptions should be looked into to determine how they can be minimized.

Management should also consider whether additional equipment is needed just to meet temporary sales demands. Later, such equipment may be idle. The replacement of old machinery with new high-speed equipment should also be considered. A careful study should help determine which step would be more profitable in the long run.

Records for each product showing the manufacturing operations necessary and a record of each machine's capability and capacity, should be maintained. Estimates must be made of material to be used, number of labor hours and quantities of service (power) required for each product. These estimates are called "standards of production performance." The establishment of these standards is an engineering rather than an accounting task. In this respect, these standards are similar to those used in standard cost accounting.

Cost of Production.   The following illustrates how cost of production is determined: Assume a concern has a normal capacity of 100 units of product. Current production budget calls for 80 units. Only one product is made; and its production requires two operations, A and B. The standard costs are: variable costs per unit of product, one unit of direct material, $2; operation A (direct labor and overhead), $3; operation B (direct labor and overhead), $5; total $10. Fixed production costs for the budget period are $500, or $5 per unit based on normal capacity. This production cost budget would then be expressed as follows:

Variable cost (80 units @ $10)	$ 800
Fixed costs (80 units @ $5)	400
Costs chargeable to production	1,200
Cost of idle capacity (500 less 400)	100
Total budgeted costs	$1,300

There is a tie-in here between estimated costs, standard costs, and production budgets.

THE LABOR BUDGET

The labor budget deals only with direct labor. Indirect labor is included in the manufacturing expense budget. (The manufacturing expense budget includes the group of expenses in addition to indirect labor, expenses such as indirect material, repairs and maintenance, depreciation and insurance.)

The purpose of the labor budget is to ascertain the number and kind of workers needed to execute the production program during the budget period. The labor budget should indicate the necessary worker-hours and the cost of labor required for the manufacture of the products in the quantities shown by the production budget.

Preparation of the Labor Budget

The preparation of a labor budget begins with an estimate of the number of labor hours required for the anticipated quantity of products. Before this can be done, it is necessary to know the quantity of items to be produced, as in the production budget. If the products are uniform and standard labor time allowances have been established, it is just a matter of multiplying the production called for by the standards to determine the labor hours required. If the products are *not* uniform but there is uniformity of operations, it is first necessary to translate production into operation requirements. Operation standards then should be established in terms of worker- or machine-hours to ascertain the quantity of labor required. The next step in preparing the labor budget is to estimate the cost of direct labor. These estimates are computed by multiplying the number of units to be produced by the labor costs per unit. The problem then is to predetermine the unit labor costs. Some of the methods of determining these costs are:

1. Day rate system.
2. Piece rate system.
3. Bonus system.

In firms where standard labor costs have been established for the products manufactured, it is necessary only to multiply the units of the product called for in the production budget by the standard labor costs.

A detailed analysis should frequently be made of the differences between actual and estimated labor costs to determine whether they are justified. An investigation may reveal inefficient workers, wasted time, defective materials, idle time, poor working conditions, high-priced workers, etc. Responsibility must be definitely placed and immediate action taken to correct those factors which are capable of being controlled.

The budgets for direct labor and manufacturing expenses are not complete until schedules of the final estimates are prepared. The form will vary, depending on the needs of the firm. The following is an example of a schedule of estimated direct labor costs where estimates are shown for each department of the firm:

X Corporation

Estimated Direct Labor Costs for the Period 1/1/xx to 12/31/xx

Dept.	Quantity to be Produced	Standard Labor Cost Per Unit	Total Estimated Labor Cost
1	127,600	$ .90	$115,000
2	127,600	1.60	204,000
3	127,600	1.12	143,000
		$3.62	$462,000

MATERIALS BUDGET

The purpose of the materials budget is to be sure that there are sufficient materials to meet the requirements of the production budget. This budget deals with the purchase of raw materials and finished parts and controls the inventory. How to estimate the material required depends on the nature of the individual company. A company manufacturing standard articles can estimate fairly accurately the amount of raw materials and the purchases required for the production program. Even where the articles are not standard, there is usually a reliable relationship between the volume of business handled and the requirements for the principal raw materials.

Tie-In to Standard Costs

In the preparation of the material budget, there is a tie-in to standard costs. Here is an example of how purchase requirements are computed:

Quantity required for production	300,000 units
Desired inventory at end of budget period	75,000 units
Total requirements	375,000 units
Less: Inventory at beginning of period	80,000 units
Purchase requirements	295,000 units

The next step is to express material requirements in terms of prices. Some firms establish standard prices based on what are considered normal prices. Differences between standard and actual purchase prices are recorded as price variance.

Factors Affecting Policy

These are:

1. The time it takes the material to be delivered after the purchase order is issued.
2. The rate of consumption of material as indicated by the production budget.
3. The amount of stock that should be on hand to cover possible delays in inventory of raw materials.

On the basis of these factors, the purchasing department working with the production department can establish figures of minimum stocks and order quantities of raw materials and parts for each product handled. Purchases in large quantities are advisable if price advantages can be obtained. Bulk purchases are advisable during periods of rising prices but not during periods of declining prices. The unavoidable time lag between order and delivery of the material is also a reason to buy in advance.

Buying in advance does not necessarily involve immediate delivery. The deliveries may be spread over the budget period in order to coordinate purchases with production and to control inventory. To control inventory, it is desirable to establish minimum and maximum quantities for each material to be carried. The lower limit is the smallest amount which can be carried without risk of production delays. If materials can be obtained quickly, the inventory can be held near the lower limit. The advantage of keeping inventory at this lower limit is that it minimizes the cost of storage and possible obsolescence. If materials cannot be obtained quickly, there is the possibility of a rise in prices, as well as an unforeseen delay in delivery which could hold up production and so it is advisable to carry more than minimum inventory.

Goods in Process

The time it takes for material to enter the factory and emerge as a finished product is frequently much longer than necessary for efficient production. Comparisons with other companies may reveal that a firm allows its goods to remain in process much longer than other firms. Investigations should be made to determine the causes of such delays and formulate remedies. These investigations are usually made in connection with the production budget.

Finished Goods

The budget of finished goods inventory is based on the sales budget. For example, if 100 units of an item are expected to be sold during the budget period, the problem is to determine how much must be kept in stock to support such a sales program. Since it is difficult to determine the exact quantity customers will demand each day, the finished goods inventory must maintain a margin of safety so that satisfactory deliveries can be made. Once this margin is established, the production and purchasing programs can be developed to replenish the stock as needed.

MANUFACTURING EXPENSE BUDGET

In preparing the manufacturing expense budget, estimates and probable expenses should be prepared by persons responsible to authorize expenditures. The general responsibility for variable expenses lies with the production manager. But the immediate responsibility for many of these expenses lies with the supervisors of the several departments. Generally, expenses are estimated by those who control them. Each person who prepares a portion of the manufacturing expense budget is furnished with data of prior periods and any plans for the budget period which may affect the amount of expenses. With these data decisions can be made about:

1. Which, if any, present expenses can be eliminated.
2. Probable effect of the sales and production forecasts on those expenses which must be incurred.

No plans for the elimination or reduction of variable expenses should be made unless it is certain that the plan can be enforced.

The responsibility for many fixed manufacturing expenses is with the general executives. Such fixed expenses include long-term leases, pension plans, patents, amortization, salaries of major production executives, etc.

In preparing the budget estimates of manufacturing expenses, a common practice is to use percentages. Each expense is taken as a percent of sales or production costs. For example, if a certain expense is estimated to be 5 percent of sales, this percentage is applied to the sales estimate to obtain the amount of this expense. The fallacy with this method is that all expenses do not vary proportionately with sales or production. A sounder method of estimating manufacturing expenses is to give individual expenses separate treatment.

In estimating the indirect labor expense, it is important to first analyze the expense for the period preceding the budget period. The requirements for additional help, or the possibility of eliminating some of the help, should be considered along with plans for increasing or decreasing any rates of compensation. Detailed schedules should be prepared, showing the nature of each job and the amount to be paid. By summarizing these schedules, an aggregate estimate can be determined.

Indirect materials expense should be estimated by first analyzing the amount consumed in prior periods. This, together with the production budget showing the proposed volume for the budget period, serves as a basis for estimating the quantities of the indirect material requirements. The probable cost of such requirements estimated by the purchasing department is the amount to be shown in the manufacturing expense budget.

Repairs and maintenance estimates are based on past experience data, supplemented by a report on the condition of the present equipment. If any additional equipment is to be installed during the budget period, recognition must be given to the prospect of additional repairs and maintenance charges. Electric power expense is in direct proportion to the production volume. The charges for depreciation of equipment can be estimated with considerable accuracy.

Insurance expense for the budget period is estimated on the basis of the insurance in force charged to production with adjustments made for contemplated changes in equipment, inventories, or coverage of hazard incident to manufacturing.

To budget manufacturing expenses effectively it is important to establish standard overhead rates.

At frequent intervals during the budget period, comparison should be made between the actual expenses in each department and the amount estimated to be spent for actual production during the period. Variations should be investigated and steps taken to correct weaknesses in the production program.

A distinction should be made between controllable and uncontrollable expenses so that the responsibility of individuals can be more closely determined. To facilitate the estimating of expenses, a further distinction is made between fixed and variable expenses. Fixed expenses are those which remain the same regardless of the variations in sales or production. Variable expenses are those which increase or decrease proportionally with changes in volume, sales or production. Maintenance is seldom treated in a separate budget. It is usually regarded as part of the manufacturing expense budget.

Following is an example of a Schedule of Estimated Manufacturing Expenses for each operation of a particular product:

Y Corporation for the Year Ended 12/31/xx

	Total	Operation 1	Operation 2	Operation 3
Variable expenses:				
Indirect materials	$ 20,000	$ 5,000	$ 10,000	$ 5,000
Indirect labor	100,000	10,000	15,000	75,000
Light and power	30,000	5,000	13,000	12,000
Telephone	5,000	3,000	− 0 −	2,000
Fixed and semi-variable:				
Factory rent	50,000	14,000	18,000	18,000
Superintendence	100,000	30,000	35,000	35,000
Depreciation	100,000	20,000	60,000	20,000
General and administrative expense	50,000	12,000	17,000	21,000
Total	$455,000	$ 99,000	$168,000	$188,000

After estimates of materials, direct labor and manufacturing expenses have been prepared, a Schedule of Estimated Cost of Production may be prepared as follows:

Z Corporation for the Year Ended 12/31/xx

	Total	Product A	Product B	Product C
Cost Element:				
Materials	$200,000	$ 80,000	$ 50,000	$ 70,000
Labor	340,000	100,000	80,000	160,000
Manufacturing expenses	70,000	30,000	30,000	10,000
Total	$610,000	$210,000	$160,000	$240,000

CAPITAL EXPENDITURES BUDGET

Since capital expenditures represent a large part of the total investment of a manufacturing concern, the capital expense budget is of great importance.

Unwise capital expenditures can seldom be corrected without serious loss to stockholders. The purpose of the capital expenditures budget is to subject such expenditures to careful examination and so avoid mistakes that cannot easily be corrected.

A carefully prepared capital expenditures budget should point out the effect of such expenditures on the cash position of the company and on future earnings. For example, too large a portion of total assets invested in fixed plant and equipment sooner or later may result in an unhealthy financial condition because of the lack of necessary working capital.

Preparation of Capital Expenditures Budget

In preparing the capital expenditures budget, the following information is recorded:

1. The amount of machinery, equipment, etc., on hand at the beginning of the budget period;
2. Additions planned for the period;
3. Withdrawals expected for the period;
4. The amount of machinery, equipment, etc., expected at the end of the budget period.

Consideration should be given to estimates of additions planned for the period. Additions will be justified if they increase the volume of production and earnings, will reduce unit costs, and the money needed can be spared. Consideration should also be given to the percentage of investment for fixed assets as compared with net worth of the firm for a number of years. Various business authorities have realized that an active business enterprise with a tangible net worth between $50,000 and $250,000 should have as a maximum not more than two-thirds of its tangible net worth in fixed assets. Where the tangible net worth is in excess of $250,000, not more than 75% of the tangible net worth should be represented by fixed assets. When these percentages are greatly exceeded, annual depreciation charges tend to be too heavy, the net working capital too moderate, and liabilities expand too rapidly for the good health of the business; alternative leasing should be considered.

The capital expenditures budget should include estimates not only for the budget period, but long-range estimates covering a period of many years. The ideal situation occurs when machinery is purchased at a time when prices are low. A long-range capital expenditures budget will indicate what machinery will be of use in the future; then, machinery may be acquired when prices are considered low. Inefficient or obsolete machines can sometimes be made into satisfactory units by rebuilding. If it is estimated that gains derived from rebuilding machinery will exceed the costs, then provision should be made in the capital expenditures budget to incur these expenses. Such expenditures are frequently called betterments and prolong the useful life of the machines. The preparation of detailed and accurate records is an essential part of the capital expenditures budget. The following information should be included in such a record:

1. Description of machines;
2. Date of requisition;
3. Cost for depreciation rate.

From the above information, it is a simple matter to complete the depreciation for the budget period.

As with other budgets, actual expenditures should be compared with the estimates, and any variation should be analyzed. In addition, a statement should be prepared showing the extent to which actual results obtained from the use of certain capital expenditures are in line with expectations. This is particularly important where substantial investments are made in labor-saving equipment, new processes or new machines.

THE CASH BUDGET

The cash budget is a composite reflection of all the operating budgets in terms of cash receipts and disbursements. Its purpose is to determine the cash resources that will be available during the entire budget program so that the company will know in advance whether it can carry out its program without borrowing or obtaining new capital or whether it will need to obtain additional capital from these sources. Thus, the company can arrange in advance for any necessary borrowing, avoiding emergencies and, more important, a cash crisis caused by a shortage.

A knowledgeable financial person goes into the market to borrow money when there is the cheapest rate. The cash budget will tell the manager when there is the need to borrow so he or she can plan accordingly. In a like manner, the manager can foresee when there will be sufficient funds to repay loans.

A cash budget is very important to a firm which does installment selling. Installment selling ties up cash resources, and a careful analysis of estimated future collections is needed to forecast the cash position of the company.

Other purposes of the cash budget are: (1) to provide for seasonal fluctuations in business which make heavy demands on funds to carry large inventories and receivables; (2) to assist the financial executive in having funds available to meet maturing obligations; (3) to aid in securing credit from commercial banks (a bank is more likely to lend funds for a definite plan that has been prepared, indicating when and how the funds will be repaid) and 4) to indicate the amount of funds available for investments, when available and for what duration.

Preparation of the Cash Budget

The main difference between a cash budget and other budgets is that in the cash budget all estimates are based on the dates when it is expected cash will be received or paid. Other budgets are prepared on the basis of the accrual of the different items (for accrual-basis companies). Therefore, in the cash budget, the budget executive cannot base the estimate of cash receipts directly on the sales budget for the obvious reason that all the cash will not be received from such sales in the same month in which they are billed. This is not true in the case of a business on a strictly cash basis.

Depreciation is another item handled differently in the cash budget. Depreciation is a cost of doing business; it increases expenses and reduces net income for financial reporting purposes. It is not, however, a cash item and is ignored in preparing the cash budget, but the amount paid for a new plant or equipment in a single year or budget period is included in full in the cash budget.

Cash receipts of a typical firm come from cash sales, collections on accounts and notes receivable, interest, dividends, rent, sale of capital assets and loans. The cash sale estimate is taken from the sales budget. The estimate of collections on accounts should be based on the sales budget and company experience in making collections. With concerns whose sales are made largely on account, the collection experience should be ascertained with considerable care. As an illustration, assume the March account sales have actually been collected as follows:

Month	%
March	6.4
April	80.1
May	8.5
June	3.6
Cash Discount Taken	1.1
Bad Debts Loss	.3
Total	100.00

If the same experience is recorded for each month of the year, it is possible to resolve the sales estimates into a collection budget. It is sometimes desirable to develop the experience separately for different classes of customers for different geographical areas. Once these figures are ascertained, they should be tested from time to time.

Cash disbursements in a typical firm are made for payroll, materials, operating expenses, taxes, interest, purchases of equipment, repayment of loans, payment of dividends, etc. With a complete operating budget on hand, there is little difficulty in estimating the amount of cash that will be required and when it will be required. Wages and salaries are usually paid in cash and on definite dates. For purchases of material (from the materials budget), the purchasing department can readily indicate the time allowed for payments. Operating expenses must be considered individually. Some items, such as insurance, are prepaid. Others, such as commissions, are accrued. So, cash payments may not coincide with charges on the operating budget.

ZERO-BASE BUDGETING

A different approach to budgeting adopted by some industrial organizations as well as not-for-profit entities and governmental units is appropriately termed *Zero-Base Budgeting*. Whether adopted wholeheartedly on a yearly basis, as a review every few years, or merely as a mind-set tool, its precepts can be of value in the budgeting process.

Expenses for industrial organizations can be divided into two categories:

1. Direct manufacturing expense, for materials, labor, and overhead.
2. Support expense, for everything else.

It is the "everything else" that causes problems at budget time, when, for example, management is beset by rising costs and must decide between decreasing the budgetary allocation for a research and development project or cutting funds for executive development. Traditionally, problems like these boil down to one question: How should the company shift its allocations around? Rather than tinker with their existing budget, many companies have implemented this budgeting method that starts at base-zero.

This approach requires that the company view all of its discretionary activities and priorities afresh, and create a different and hopefully better set of allocations for the ensuring budget year. The base-zero procedure gives management a firm grip on support allocations of all kinds, a procedure for describing all support expense minutely, classifying the alternatives to each, and sorting them all according to their importance and priority.

This technique in budgeting differentiates between the basic and necessary operations and those of a more discretionary character, thus enabling management to focus specific attention on the optional group. The basic steps for effective zero-base budgeting require justification of every dollar spent on discretionary costs, and a prescribed order of approach to the final allocation of funds:

1. Describe each optional activity in a "decision" package.
2. Evaluate and rank these decision packages by cost/benefit analysis.
3. Allocate resources based on this analysis.

Where to Use Zero-Base Budgeting

Zero-base budgeting is best applied to service and support areas of company activity rather than to the basic manufacturing operation. Since a corporation's level of manufacturing activity is determined by its sales volume, the production level, in turn, determines how much the company should spend on labor, materials, and overhead. Hence, there is not the same simple relationship between costs and benefits here as there is in the service and support areas where management can trade off a level of expenditures on a given project against the direct returns on investment. Cost benefit analysis, which is crucial to zero-base budgeting, cannot be applied directly to decisions to increase or decrease expenditures in the manufacturing areas.

The main use of zero-base budgeting occurs when management has discretion to choose between different activities having different direct costs and benefits. Such areas normally include marketing, finance, quality control, personnel, engineering and other non-production areas of company activity.

Decision Package Concept

When implementing ZBB, a company must explain the "decision package concept" to all levels of management and then present guidelines for the individual manager to use in breaking the specific activities into workable packages. Next, higher management must establish a ranking, consolidation and elimination process. The decision package is the document that identifies and describes a specific activity in such a manner that management can (1) evaluate and rank that activity against other activities competing for limited resources, (2) decide whether to approve or disapprove expenditures in that area.

The specifications in each package must provide management with the information needed to evaluate the activity. Included should be (1) a statement of the goals of the activity; (2) the program by which the goals are to be attained; (3) the benefits expected from the program and methods of determining whether they have been attained; (4) suggested alternatives to the program; (5) possible consequences of not approving the package and expenditure of funds; (6) designation of personnel required to carry out the program.

There are two basic types of decision packages:

1. Mutually exclusive packages identify alternative means of performing the same function. The best alternative is chosen and the other packages are discarded.
2. Incremental packages reflect different levels of effort that may be expended on a specific function or program. One package, the "base package," may establish a minimum level of activity, and others identify increased activity or expenditure levels.

A logical starting point for determining next year's needs is the current year's operations. Each ground level manager who has the ultimate responsibility takes the areas's forecasted expense level for the current year, identifies the activities creating this expense, and calculates the cost for each activity. At this stage, the manager identifies each activity at its current level and method of operation and does not attempt to identify alternatives or increments.

After current operations have been separated into preliminary decision packages, the manager looks at requirements for the upcoming year. To aid in specifying these requirements, upper management should issue a formal set of assumptions on the activity levels, billings, and wage and salary increases for the upcoming year. These formal assumptions provide all managers with uniform benchmarks for estimating purposes.

At the conclusion of the formulation stage, the manager will have identified all of the proposed activities as follows:

1. Business-as-usual packages.
2. Decision packages for other ongoing activities.
3. Decision packages for new activities.

The ranking process forces management to face squarely the most basic decision: How much money is available and where should it be spent to obtain the greatest good? Management arrives at the decisions by listing, and then studying all the packages identified in order of decreasing benefit to the company, and eliminating those of least value.

It is possible for one ranking of decision packages to be obtained for an entire company and judged by its top management. While this one, single ranking would identify the best allocation of resources, ranking and judging the high volume of packages created by describing all of the activities of a large company would result in an unwieldy task for top management.

This problem can be resolved by grouping decision units which may correspond to a budget unit in organizations with detailed cost-center structures, or they can be defined on a project basis.

The initial ranking should occur at the cost-center or project level so that each manager can evaluate the relative importance of the segments and rank the packages accordingly.

The manager at the next level up the ladder then reviews these rankings with the appropriate managers and uses the resulting rankings as guides to produce a single consolidated ranking for all packages presented from below.

At higher levels of a large organization, the expertise necessary to rank packages is best obtained by committee. The committee membership should consist of all managers whose packages are being ranked with their supervisor serving as chairperson.

Each committee produces its consolidated ranking by voting on the decision packages presented by its members. As at the cost-center level, the most beneficial packages are ranked highest and the least important ranked lowest.

It is best to establish the cutoff line at the highest consolidation level first, and then for the lower levels. The most effective way to establish the first cutoff is for management at the highest consolidation level to estimate the expense that will be approved at the top level and then to set the cutoff line far enough below to allow trading off between the divisions whose packages are being ranked.

The ability to achieve a list of ranked packages at any given organization level allows management to evaluate the desirability of various expenditure levels throughout the budgeting process. This ranked list also provides management with a reference point to be used during the year to identify activities to be reduced or expanded if allowable expenditure levels change.

Zero-base budgeting can be a flexible and useful tool in simplifying the budgeting process and in bringing about better resource allocation by forcing meaningful consideration of varying priorities for available funds.

BREAK-EVEN POINT ANALYSIS

The break-even point (BE) is that amount of sales necessary to yield neither income nor loss. If sales should be less than indicated by the BE point, a loss results. If the total cost of goods sold and other expenses is less than sales, and if this total varied in direct proportion to sales, operations would result in net income. BE analysis is not a budget, in itself, but is an approach in the budgeting process for dealing intelligently with the uncertainty of estimates for future operations that are based on statistical data. Breakeven analysis can be applied to sales, profit, costs, and selling price problems, and it can be used to help make sound decisions for employing idle plant capacity, planning advertising, granting credit, and expanding production. BE is a tool, and a useful one, with which to begin to approach decision problems.

BE Analysis, is an inexpensive method for analyzing the possible effects of decisions. Discounted cash flow techniques require large amounts of data expensive to develop. BE can help with the decision whether or not it is worthwhile to do more intensive, costly analysis.

BE provides a means for designing product specifications, which permits a comparison of different designs and their costs before the specifications for a specific product are accepted as the best choice cost-wise. For example, a new product with an uncertain volume is considered to be feasible if it's made with hand tools rather than with expensive capital equipment. The first method typically has higher variable costs, but lower fixed costs. This often results in a lower breakeven point for the project, and lower risks and potential profits. The fixed capital equipment approach raises the BE, but also raises the risks and profit potential for the manufacturer. BE helps to examine these trade-offs.

An important factor when using BE analysis is the nature of the user's cost structure. Some firms have a flexible labor force and standard cost analysis works well. In other businesses, however, management must treat labor costs differently. Certain skilled workers cannot be laid off when business is slow. BE analysis assumes a realistic definition of costs, both in amount and type. While fixed costs will not change with changes in revenue, variable and semi-variable costs do change with changes in sales, up or down. Product pricing can be significantly aided by using variations of breakeven analysis.

Break-Even Chart.   A break-even chart presents a visual representation of sales volume, capacity, or output when expenses and revenues are equal, i.e., a volume level at which income equals expenses. A BE chart provides a projection of the impact of output upon expenses, income, and profits which makes the chart a useful tool for profit planning and control.

The BE chart assumes that selling prices do not change, total fixed expenses remain the same at all levels of output, and variable costs increase or decrease in direct proportion to sales. The N line remains the same regardless of sales volume; the point B on the chart is the total of the fixed and variable expenses on the list on the vertical axis. The area between line M and the fixed expense line N is the amount of variable expenses at different volumes of sales. The area between line M and the horizontal axis represents the total costs at various levels of sales. Line M can be considered a total cost line, since total costs for various volumes of sales can be readily determined from it. This can be done by starting at any point on the horizontal scale and measuring upward to line M and across to the vertical scale.

The income line P starts at zero and extends through point C, which is the point at which total sales and total income are shown on both scales, about $1,200. The profit area lies to the right of break-even point D where the revenue line P crosses the total cost line M. Revenue is greater than costs above— to the right—of the break-even point D; the loss area is below—to the left—of the break-even point D.

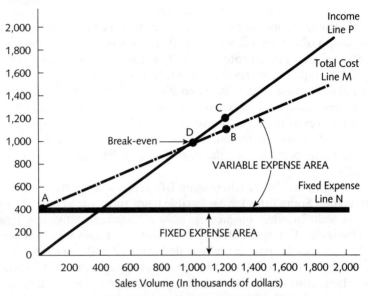

Expense and Income
(In thousands of dollars)

CONVENTIONAL BREAK-EVEN CHART

Break-Even Technique.   Break-Even is an inexpensive technique to determine whether or not it would be advisable to do more intensive and costly analysis of a proposed project. It provides a method for designing product specifications. Each design has costs which affect price and marketing feasibility by providing comparison of possible designs before the specifications are frozen by cash commitments. BE serves as a substitute for estimating an unknown factor in making project decisions. In deciding whether to go ahead with a project or to disband it, there are always variables to be considered such as costs, price, demand, and other miscellaneous factors. When most expenses associated with a proposed project can be determined, only two variables need be considered as variable items—profits (cash flow) and demand (sales). Demand is usually more difficult to estimate. By deciding that profit must at least be zero, the BE point, the demand is more easily estimated by determining what sales levels are needed to make the project a worthwhile undertaking. BE provides a way to attack uncertainty, to at least develop marketing targets for desired levels of income. One of the major problems of BE analysis is that no product exists in isolation; there are always alternative uses for an organization's funds. BE analysis helps decision makers to consider not only the value of an individual project, but how it compares to other uses of the funds and facilities.

Another problem is that BE analysis does not permit proper examination of cash flows. In considering financial commitments, the appropriate way to make investment or capital decisions is to consider the value of a proposed project's anticipated cash flows. If the discounted value of the cash flows exceeds the required investment outlay in cash, the project is acceptable. BE analysis makes restrictive assumptions about cost-revenue relationships; it is basically a negative technique defining constraints rather than looking at benefits; it is essentially a static tool for analyzing income and outflow for a single period of time.

The BE technique requires a realistic definition of costs, both in amount and type. A BE approach, therefore, should not be considered a technique to be used to make *final* investment decisions. It is a supplemental tool among the many factors a business decision maker must consider; it is an approach helpful to apply at the beginning of an analysis of a proposed solution of a business problem.

Although a complete and adequate budget may be developed without using a break-even analysis, its use adds to the understanding of estimates as shown in the following example.

Where the total cost of goods sold and other expenses is less than sales and if this total varied in direct proportion to sales, operations would always result in net income. For example, in a company in which the cost of goods sold and expenses amount to $1.80 per unit sold and the sale price is $2, on the first unit there would be net income of 20¢. On a million items, the net income would amount to $200,000.

As a practical matter, the simple example cited above is not realistic. Although some expenses may vary with volume of sales (e.g., salesperson's commissions, traveling expenses, advertising, telephone, delivery costs, postage, supplies, etc.), there are many other types of expenses which are not affected by the variations in sales. These expenses are the fixed expenses. Examples are depreciation, rent, insurance, heat, and so on.

If, going back to the above illustration, it is assumed that fixed costs and expenses amount to $40,000, at least $40,000 of costs and expenses are incurred before even one unit is sold. If a million units are sold, however, income before deducting fixed expenses is $200,000. After fixed expenses, net income is $160,000. So, the income picture goes from a loss of $40,000 (where no units are produced) to a profit of $160,000 (where one million units are produced). Somewhere between these, however, is a point represented by a certain number of units at which there will be neither income nor loss—the break-even point.

How to Compute the Break-Even Point

To determine the break-even point, let S equal the sales at the break-even point. Since sales at this point are equal to the total fixed costs and expenses

($40,000) plus variable costs and expenses ($1.80 per unit or 90 percent of sales):

$$S = \$\ 40,000 + .9S$$
$$S - .9S = \$\ 40,000$$
$$.1S = \$\ 40,000$$
$$S = \$400,000$$

Even the above illustration oversimplifies the problem. It makes the assumption that all costs and expenses can be classified as either fixed or *variable*. However, in actual operations, expenses classified as fixed expenses may become variable where sales increase beyond a certain point, and some variable expenses may not vary in direct proportion to the sales.

Rent expense, for example, may not always be a fixed expense. A substantial increase in sales may create a need for additional showroom or salesroom space or, perhaps, expenses for salesperson's offices, or salesperson's commissions may rise unexpectedly when they have gone above a certain quota.

Then, there are types of hybrid expenses which may be classified as *semifixed*. For example, executives' salaries, association dues, subscriptions to periodicals and many other expenses are not in proportion to sales. Another unreality in the above problem is that as sales increase, there is a likelihood that sale prices will decrease because of larger orders. Now let's take a look at another situation:

Net sales		$2,500,000
Costs and expenses:		
Fixed	$ 250,000	
Variable	$1,500,000	1,750,000
Net income		$ 750,000

This company currently has under consideration an investment in a new plant which will cause an increase in its fixed expenses of $200,000.

The present break-even point is as follows:

$$S = \$250,000 + .6S$$
$$S - .6S = \$250,000$$
$$.4S = \$250,000$$
$$S = \$625,000$$

If the company builds the plant, the break-even calculation will be:

$$S = \$450,000 + .6S$$
$$S - .6S = \$450,000$$

$.4S = \$450,000$
$S = \$1,125,000$

If the plant expansion is undertaken, then the sales must be increased by $500,000 for the company to maintain its net income of $750,000, as follows:

$S = \$\ 450,000 + .6S + \$750,000$
$S - .6S = \$1,200,000$
$.4S = \$1,200,000$
$S = \$3,000,000$
Increase $= \$\ 500,000\ (\$3,000,000 \text{ less } \$2,500,000)$

The situation can be analyzed using two alternatives. The maximum production with the present plant is 1,500,000 units. At an average sale price of $2 per unit, sales would be $3,000,000. With the new plant, sales are estimated to hit $5,000,000 (2,500,000 units @ $2 per unit).

	Without New Plant	With New Plant
Net Sales	$3,000,000	$5,000,000
Less: Fixed costs and expenses	250,000	450,000
	2,750,000	4,550,000
Less: Variable costs and		
expenses (60% of sales)	1,800,000	3,000,000
Net income	$ 950,000	$1,550,000

If sales do not increase, the increase in fixed costs and expenses of $200,000 would cut the net income to $550,000. The break-even point will have been boosted $500,000, and the sales will have to be increased by this amount to produce the current $750,000 of income. Alternatively, the net income can be increased by $600,000 if the sales figure is increased by $2,000,000. Although these figures are based on an assumption that all costs and expenses are fixed or variable, the break-even analysis focuses attention on the factors involved in costs and income and provides a basis for consideration of various problems.

Chapter 15

Cost Accounting

CONTENTS

What Is Cost Accounting?	**15.01**
Foundation of a Cost Accounting System	**15.04**
Items for Consideration in Developing Cost Control Systems	**15.05**
Cost Accounting Terminology for Quick Reference	**15.07**
Historical and Standard Cost Systems	**15.08**
Job Order or Process Cost Systems	**15.10**
How to Use Standard Costs	**15.12**
Direct Costing	**15.15**
Summary	**15.16**

WHAT IS COST ACCOUNTING?

The cost accounting function in an organization is a system broadly defined in terms of procedures: the gathering, sorting, classifying, resorting, reclassifying, processing (computations), summarizing, reporting and filing of information relevant to a company's costs—largely in the form of data (numbers). It measures all costs associated with doing business and providing a service.

Often, cost accounting is thought of only in terms of manufacturing operations. However, many of the concepts can be useful in other areas of a small business or a service enterprise.

15.01

What is the function of a cost accounting system? Primarily, the system accepts disorganized, meaningless raw data (input) from the environment and processes (transforms) the data into understandable form. The information then leaves the system (output) in an organized form of reports required by management to account for the production costs of a business.

Specifically, cost accounting explicitly sets forth data that relate to the costs associated with the business. This includes the assignment of costs to a particular product, process, operation or service, in the case of a service business.

The Objective of a Cost Accounting System

The primary objective of cost accounting is to provide information management can use to make the decisions necessary for the successful operation of the business. To achieve this objective, the system should be designed to provide information concerning the efficiency and effectiveness of production and service processes. The aim then, is cost reduction and increased profits.

An analysis of accurate cost data is the essence of profit planning:

1. What should be produced?
2. How much should be produced?
3. When does the law of diminishing returns kick in?
4. What price should be charged?
5. Should a particular product be discontinued?
6. Should a new product be given a "break" when dividing overhead?
7. Are costs in line with what they should be?

Management should expect cost reports to show the results of past operations in terms of costs per unit of product, costs per unit of production in each operating department, or costs per unit of service in the case of a service organization. The system should provide immediate feedback information on changes in costs from accounting period to accounting period and on *comparisons of costs with predetermined estimates or norms*. With the proper cost information, management can adjust operations quickly to changing economic and competitive conditions.

Developing a Cost System

The task of developing a cost accounting system is to determine the specific needs of management and the extent to which it is economically feasible to add detailed procedures to a basic system. The system must be easily understood by all individuals in the organization who are involved in the use of control procedures, and it must be flexible in its application. The system should be simple—that is, it must not include procedures that accumulate information that might be interesting but not particularly useful. (A common pitfall is a cost system that, itself, is more expensive than the costs to be saved.) In addition, the cost system must provide useful information in the most efficient manner. *Accurate* accounting records are particularly significant.

The cost accounting system also must be flexible, because businesspeople are often required to adapt their operations to meet changes in:

1. The needs and desires of customers.
2. Production methods caused by improved technology.
3. The economic and social environment in which the business operates.
4. Governmental regulations.

Likewise, most business ventures hope to grow and become larger. All business ventures hope to make substantial profits. New cost accounting control requirements will appear as a result of the nature of the growth process. Any system should be planned to meet changing needs with the least possible alteration of the existing system.

Fundamental cost control methods apply to most businesses and include principles applicable to an individual business. The type of production, the number of products manufactured, the size of the business, the types of costs associated with the business and the desires, capabilities and attitudes of the individuals involved in the business will all have a part in determining the structure of the cost control system.

Personnel responsible for the procedures relating to the accounting and control techniques must be constantly aware of the unique characteristics of the particular business.

Alternative Approaches

It is a rare instance that there is just one obviously right answer to any business problem. Certainly, alternative choices for the allocation of an enterprise's limited resource confront the business manager every day. Information for selecting the "right" choice is provided by a cost accounting system:

1. Is the product profitable?
2. Is the product priced to yield a predetermined profit margin?
3. What are the per-unit costs of the product?
4. Could it profitably be sold at a lower, more competitive price?

5. Should production be expanded, reduced, discontinued?
6. Are costs out of line?
7. What are the controllable costs?
8. What are the uncontrollable costs?

These are only a few items of significant information that are furnished by a well-developed cost accounting system.

FOUNDATION OF A COST ACCOUNTING SYSTEM

What input does a cost accounting system accept? An infinite amount of data within the business environment can be entered into the system. It should be emphasized that the choice of data to be entered is not random. Chance or guesswork are not acceptable determinants of data input. Rather, data selection is performed within a carefully designed framework of the information *needed* to provide the required output (reports), with the framework continually subject to modification by a feedback system. The framework is governed by a set of controls to ensure compliance with the procedures, policies and objectives the system has been designed to carry out.

The elements of the framework for a set of books to track costs are briefly described as follows:

1. The system is for a specific organization and accepts data relating only to that organization.
2. Precautions should be taken against superfluous (and expensive) input.
3. The system accepts information about transactions generated by events that have actually occurred—a purchase, for example.
4. The system accepts information that has numbers assigned to it, with dollars and cents the most common measurement.
5. The system accepts only information that has been predetermined to meet the needs of the users of the information.
6. Information entered into the system should be completely free of bias; only absolutely objective information is acceptable.
7. Information must be verifiable. Verifiability means transactions that are recorded in the same way by two or more qualified personnel acting independently of each other.
8. Information entered into the system must be consistent. Consistency prevents manipulation of data in the accounts and makes the financial information comparable from one period of time to another.

Four Group Classifications

The production activities of most businesses (of any size) can be classified into one of the following four groups:

1. **Jobbing Plants**—Jobbing plants specialize in products that are made to order and therefore not conducive to a repetitive operation. Some examples are machine shops, custom cabinet shops, builders of custom homes, printers and repair shops of all kinds—generally, custom-made products of any kind. Certain service providers, including engineers, architects and various consultants, use some job order techniques to track specific costs of a project (further explanation is given in item 4 below.)

2. **Continuous Processing Plants**—Continuous processing is used for products that are made for inventory and sale at a later date, instead of ordered in advance. The significant aspect of continuous processing is that the production process is a repetitive operation involving sequential steps in the conversion of raw materials into finished products, all the units of which are the same. Mass production techniques apply. Examples are shoe, glass, soap, paper, textile and automobile manufacturers and food processors.

3. **Assembly Plants**—Products are made up of many component parts, either manufactured by the assembler or purchased from other manufacturers. Aircraft manufacturers are one of the best examples; they subcontract various parts of the aircraft to literally hundreds of subcontractors. Automobile production is an example of both continuous processing and assembling, as many parts for automobiles are purchased from other manufacturing suppliers.

4. **Service Establishments**—Service establishments include businesses that provide various services to the public rather than manufactured products. Medical, legal, accounting, architectural, transportation, food and recreational services are examples of service businesses.

ITEMS FOR CONSIDERATION IN DEVELOPING COST CONTROL SYSTEMS

Because the cost control problems are different for each of the groups listed above, control and cost procedures must be designed for each type as well as for individual businesses within a group. Certainly not all of the items listed below will apply in every situation; however, careful consideration of this general outline should provide the basis for an effective system for any business.

Cost Accounting System—An Outline

Job Order Costs
Need for a job order cost system.
Use of journals and ledgers.
Cost control reports.
Recording job costs.

Process Costs
Need for a process cost system.
Advantages of a process cost system.
Accuracy of data provided by the
  system.
Characteristics of a process cost
  system.
Production controls.
Flow assumptions (first-in, first-out
  [FIFO] or alternatives).
Conversion cost components.
Per-unit cost information.
Spoilage problems, shrinkage,
  breakage, theft and defective
  units.
Units of production.

Accounting for Raw Materials
Determining raw materials
  requirements.
Purchasing.
Recording materials costs.
Counting and pricing materials.
Accounting for materials used.
Materials control procedures—for
  example, storing and issuing.

Accounting for Labor Costs
Labor and payroll records.
Purpose for accounting for labor
  costs.
Timekeeping.
Allocating labor costs.
By-products.
Joint products.
Distribution costs.
Transfer pricing.
Payroll preparation.
Recording payrolls.

Paying the payroll.
Individual employee earnings'
  record.
Salaried employees payroll records.
Fringe benefits.

Responsibility Accounting
Cost centers.
Profit centers.

Accounting for Overhead Costs
What is overhead? Manufacturing
  overhead? Administrative
  overhead?
Overhead costs and tight control
  systems are important.
Allocating overhead costs.
Overhead budgets (determining
  overhead rates).
Administrative (nonmanufacturing)
  overhead, such as accounting and
  other support functions.

Cost Targets
Predetermined costs.
Determining cost estimates
  (the cost standards).
Use of the standards in ledger
  accounts.
Analyzing cost deviations from the
  standards.
Standard costs for a job system.
Standard costs for a process system.

Break-Even Analysis
Cost-price-volume relationships.
Fixed costs.
Variable costs.
Production capacity levels.
Effects of changes in product price.
Effects of changes in product costs.
Unit costs.
Total costs.
Graphic method.
Incremental costs.
Single or multiproduct firms.

Cost Accounting System—An Outline (cont'd)

Budgeting and Profit Planning

Various types of budgets
(operating and capital
budgets).
Cash flow planning.
Cash budget.

Cost Allocation Techniques

Direct costing and contribution
approach.
Absorption costing.
Contribution approach.

Ratio Analysis for Control

The most commonly applied ratios,
with the emphasis on the ratios
for the expense elements of the
income statement.
How to interpret and apply the
ratios to business decisions.
Ratios as warning signals
(red flags).

Summary of Operations

Promptness.
Accuracy.
Comparative reports—with
current vs. past trends
highlighted.

Cost trends highlighted and
explained.
Cost reports for areas of specific
responsibility.
Report contents:
Direct labor hours and costs.
Indirect labor hours and costs.
Direct materials used.
Production overhead applied.
Actual overhead expense.
Variances.
Idle time costs, if any.
Overtime costs.
Spoilage costs.
Maintenance hours and costs.
Scrap costs.
Inventory status report.
New order book.
Orders shipped during the period.
New order bookings.
Interim expense and income
statements (for predetermined
periods of time—week, month;
actual versus budgeted costs
for the period. Comparisons
with prior determined periods
of time; year-to-date totals and
comparisons with prior years).

COST ACCOUNTING TERMINOLOGY FOR QUICK REFERENCE

Following are some brief definitions of various types of costs:

1. Alternative—estimated for decision areas.
2. Controllable—subject to direct control at some level of supervision.
3. Departmental—production and service, for cost distributions.
4. Differential—changes in cost that result from variation in operations.
5. Direct—obviously traceable to a unit of output or a segment of business operations.
6. Discretionary—are avoidable and not essential to an objective.
7. Estimated—are predetermined.

8. Fixed—do not change in the total as the rate of output varies.
9. Future—are expected to be incurred at a later date.
10. Historical—are measured by actual cash payments or their equivalent at the time of outlay.
11. Imputed—never involve cash outlays or appear in financial records. Imputed costs involve a foregoing on the part of the person whose costs are being calculated.
12. Incremental—are the costs that are added or eliminated if segments were expanded or discontinued.
13. Indirect—are not obviously traceable to a unit of output or to a segment of business operations.
14. Joint—exist when from any one unit source, material or process come products having different unit values.
15. Noncontrollable—are not subject to control at some level of supervision.
16. Opportunity—are those for which measurable advantage is foregone as a result of the rejection of alternative uses of resources, whether of materials, labor or facilities.
17. Out of pocket—necessitate cash expenditure.
18. Period—are associated with the income of a time period.
19. Postponable—may be shifted to future period without affecting efficiency.
20. Prime—are labor and material costs that are directly traceable to a unit of output.
21. Product—are associated with units of output.
22. Replacement—are considered for depreciation significance.
23. Standard—are scientifically predetermined.
24. Sunk—are historical and unrecoverable in a given situation.
25. Variable—do change with changes in rate of output.

HISTORICAL AND STANDARD COST SYSTEMS

Cost accounting systems vary with the type of cost used—present or future. When present costs are used, the cost system is called an historical or actual cost system. When future costs are used, the cost system is called a standard cost system. In practice, combinations of these costs are used even in actual or standard systems. Where there is an intentional use of both types of costs, it is sometimes referred to as a hybrid cost system.

Actual Cost Systems

Since an actual cost system uses costs already incurred, the system determines costs only after manufacturing operations have been performed. Under this system, the product is charged with the actual cost of materials, the actual cost of labor, and an estimated portion of overhead (overhead costs represent the future cost element in an actual cost system).

Standard Cost Systems

A standard system is based on estimated or predetermined costs. Although both estimated and standard costs are "predetermined" costs, estimated costs are based on average past experience, and standard costs are based on scientific facts that consider past experience and controlled experiments. Arriving at standard costs involves:

1. Careful selection of the exact amount of raw material and subassemblies required.
2. An engineering study of equipment and manufacturing facilities.
3. Time and motion studies.

In either system, adjustment must be made at the financial statement date to the closing inventory so that it is shown at actual cost or reasonably approximate actual cost, or at market if lower.

Also, the inventory must bear its share of the burden of overhead. The exclusion of all overheads from inventory costs does not constitute an accepted accounting procedure.

For interim statements, estimated gross profit rates may be used to determine cost of goods sold during the interim, but this fact must be disclosed.

It must be emphasized that whatever cost accounting method is chosen by a company, its purpose is primarily an internal management tool directed at:

1. Controlling costs.
2. Setting production goals.
3. Measuring efficiencies and variances.
4. Providing incentives.
5. Identifying production problems.
6. Establishing realistic relationships between unit costs, selling prices and gross margins.
7. Correcting manufacturing difficulties/errors.

Regardless of costing methods used, generally accepted accounting procedures (GAAP) must be followed for the preparation of the financial statements, wherein the valuation must be cost or market, whichever is lower.

In addition, the FIFO or last-in, first-out (LIFO) methods (or the average method) may be used under any cost system. These methods pertain to the assumption of the flow of costs, not to the actual costs themselves. Note that both methods may be used within one inventory, as long as the method is applied to that portion of the inventory consistently from period to period. Disclosures should be made of any change in method.

Elements of Cost

Production costs consist of three elements: direct materials, direct labor, and manufacturing (overhead) expenses. Direct materials are those materials that can be identified with specific units of the product. Direct labor likewise can be identified with specific units of the product. Manufacturing expenses (overhead) are costs (including indirect material or labor) that cannot be identified with specific units of the product. These costs represent expenses for the factory and other facilities that permit the labor to be applied to the materials to manufacture a product. Sometimes, overhead is further subdivided into direct overhead (manufacturing costs, other than for material and direct labor, that specifically apply to production and require no allocation from other expense areas) and indirect overhead (expenses that have been allocated into the manufacturing expense area from other more general areas). For financial statement purposes, overhead should not include selling expenses or general administrative expenses.

Integrating a Cost System

It is not essential to integrate a cost system with the rest of the accounting system, but it is highly desirable. A cost system is actually an extension of the regular system. With an integrated system, entries in the inventory account in the general ledger should represent the sums of figures taken from the cost accounting data. The general-ledger inventory accounts (e.g., finished goods, work in process and raw materials) are the control accounts and they should tie in with the amounts of physical inventories actually on hand. Discrepancies may result from errors, spoilage or thievery.

JOB ORDER OR PROCESS COST SYSTEMS

There are distinctions between cost systems other than the use of present or future costs. A job order system compiles costs for a specific quantity of a product as it moves through the production process. This means that material, labor, and overhead costs of a specific number or lot of the product (usually identifiable with a customer's order or a specific quantity being produced for stock) are recorded as the lot moves through the production cycle.

A process system compiles costs as they relate to specific processes or operations for a period of time. To find the unit cost, these figures are averaged for a specified period and spread over the number of units that go through each process. Process costing is used when large numbers of identical products are manufactured, usually in assembly-line fashion.

Keep in mind that actual or estimated costs can be used with either a job order or process cost system.

Benefits and Drawbacks

Whether the job order or process system is used depends on the type of operation. The job order system is rarely used in mass production industries. It is invariably used when products are custom made. Process costing is used when production is in a continuous state of operation, as for baking and making paper, steel, glass, rubber, sugar or chemicals.

Following are some of the relative merits and shortcomings of each method.

ADVANTAGES

Job Order System	*Process System*
Appropriate for custom-made goods	It is usually only necessary
Appropriate for increasing finished	to calculate costs each month
goods inventory in desired	A minimum of clerical work
quantities	is required
Adequate for inventory pricing	If there is only one type of
Permits estimation of future costs	product cost, computation
Satisfies cost-plus contract requisites	is relatively simple

DISADVANTAGES

Job Order System	*Process System*
Expensive to use—a good deal	Use of average costs ignores
of clerical work is required	any variance in product cost
Difficult to make sure that all	Involves calculating the stage
materials are accurately charged	of a specific job in process
to each equivalent	and the use of units
Difficult to determine cost of goods	
sold when partial shipments are made	
before completion	

How to Use Standard Costs

Smith Company manufactures only one product, glubs—a household article made out of a certain type of plastic. Glubs are made from D raw material, which goes through a single process. Glubs are turned out from D material in a fraction of a day. Smith Company has a process-type cost setup integrated with its other financial records. D material is charged to work in process through requisitions based on actual cost. Direct labor is charged to work in process based on payroll. Manufacturing expense is charged to work in process based on the number of payroll hours. Each day, a record of the number of glubs manufactured is kept. This is the responsibility of the production department.

This is the way the Smith Company process cost system operates: Every month, total figures are worked up for raw material, payroll and factory expenses. Each of these figures is then divided by the total number of glubs produced for that month to arrive at a unit cost per glub.

Following is what the unit cost accumulation for the first four months of operation shows (this example assumes no work-in-process inventory and no equivalent units):

UNIT COST PER GLUB MANUFACTURED

	First Month	Second Month	Third Month	Fourth Month	Weighted Average
Material D	$ .94	$ .91	$ .97	$1.10	$ .95
Direct Labor	1.18	1.22	2.00	.70	1.29
Manufacturing Expense	1.22	1.47	2.11	.82	1.42
	$3.34	$3.60	$5.08	$2.62	$3.66

Right now, glubs are being sold at $4.30, and the present profit appears sufficient. T. O. Smith, the president and major stockholder of the corporation, feels that if glubs were sold at $3.30 each, four times as many could be sold. He also reports that he has learned that Glubco, Inc., Smith's competitor, is going to market glubs for $3.60. Smith thinks that $3.30 is a good sales price since the cost records indicate that glubs were manufactured for as low as $2.62 in the fourth month.

Smith Company's accountant says the president is incorrect. He points out that, on the basis of the cost records for six months, the average cost is somewhere in the area of $3.55 to $3.80. Selling glubs for $3.30 would create losses. The factory foreman says that during the third and fourth months there was an error in calculating the number of glubs put into finished goods inventory. From the figures for the fourth month, it appears that the foreman is correct. The unit cost per glub is unusually low. Mr. Smith wants to know the lowest at which he can sell glubs and still make a reasonable profit. The accountant suggests setting up a cost system based on standard costs and the following information is then determined:

1. Purchasing department records indicate that material D should cost no more than 15¢ per pound. (According to the chief engineer, it takes approximately two pounds of D to produce one glub.) The 15¢ figure takes future market conditions into account.
2. A time study of half a dozen workers who produce glubs is made. The average time it takes each of these six workers to produce one glub is one-sixth of an hour. The average hourly wage of these workers is $6.00.
3. Based on reasonable levels of production for the following year, a departmental manufacturing expense or overhead is estimated to be 100 percent of direct labor.

Based on the preceding determinations, the standard cost per glub is $2.30. It is calculated as follows:

Raw Material D: two pounds at 15¢ per pound	$ .30
Direct Labor: 1/6 hour at $6.00 per hour	1.00
Manufacturing Expense: 100% of direct labor	1.00
Total	2.30

In order to produce glubs at this cost, the following points are agreed upon:

1. When more than 15¢ a pound is paid for raw material D, the excess is to be charged to a special variance account instead of the raw material account. These excesses are to be explained periodically by the purchasing department.
2. Requisitions for raw material D are to be limited to two pounds of D for each glub to be manufactured. If more than two pounds per glub is issued to meet scheduled production, the excess over two pounds is to be charged to a separate variance account. The reason for any excess will also have to be explained.
3. The daily number of direct labor hours spent making glubs is to be multiplied by six. This should equal the number of glubs produced that day. Any discrepancy here is probably due to inefficiency. The number of

inefficient hours at the standard $6 rate times the 100 percent manufacturing expense rate is to be charged to a special variance account.

4. Payroll over $6 an hour is to be charged to a variance account. Only $6 an hour is to be charged to the work-in-process account. The factory supervisor will have to explain hourly labor figures over $6 periodically.

5. Departmental variations in the 100 percent of direct labor manufacturing expense burden are to be charged or credited to separate variance accounts. This is what happened each month after this system was instituted:

Variance Accounts	Fifth Month	Sixth Month	Seventh Month	Eighth Month	Ninth Month
1. Material D Price	$ 2,100	$ 300	$ 750	$ 0	$ 0
2. Material Usage	19,500	13,000	5,000	500	400
3. Labor Efficiency	8,000	5,050	800	700	300
4. Labor Rate	400	150	(50)	400	100
5. Manufacturing Expense	0	5,000	1,000	300	(100)
	$30,000	$23,500	$ 7,500	$ 1,900	$ 700
Unit Manufactured	48,000	48,500	48,000	48,000	48,000
Variance per Unit	.63	.49	.16	.04	.01
Standard Unit Cost	2.30	2.30	2.30	2.30	2.30
Actual Cost	$ 2.93	$ 2.79	$ 2.46	$ 2.34	$ 2.31

Where there were variances, this is what was elicited from discussion with the persons responsible for the different variance accounts:

1. The purchase price for raw material D exceeded 15¢ per pound mainly because of the distance of Smith Company from where D is obtained in the South. The head of purchasing feels that D could be purchased for no more than 15¢ if there could be a small office in the South with one assistant who would remain there. It was decided to go ahead and provide the office and the additional employee.

2. The factory supervisor, together with the chief engineer, has been going over the requisitions of raw material D. More D was needed because some of the glubs had air holes in them and were not usable. It seems that the pressure used to extrude them was insufficient. The chief engineer says that he can replace the present air die channels with larger ones so that these defects do not reoccur. The supervisor knew that some glubs were scrapped in the past, but it was not until this switch to standard costs that he knew how much waste there really was.

3. The supervisor and the industrial engineer who performed the time-and-motion study discussed the labor efficiency loss. It was their opinion that:

a. There were more factory employees than needed to carry out various operations to convert D into finished glubs.
b. Some employees needed additional training.
c. Some workers were overskilled for their particular functions.
d. Other workers were not producing at reasonable levels for some as yet unknown reason.

Both the supervisor and engineer felt that a training program instructing employees in the efficient use of available tools would increase production. Further time-and-motion studies on every phase of the production process were initiated.

4. There was not much variance in labor rate, but it was hoped that the training program would release more technically skilled and higher-paid employees for use in the more complicated production steps.

At the end of the seventh month, it was obvious that the steps taken were beginning to pay off. The additional costs incurred in carrying out these steps (for example, the additional employee in purchasing and the southern office) created a manufacturing overhead variance where none had existed before; but the success in other areas outweighed this.

At the end of the ninth month, everyone agreed that the switch to standard costs had exceeded expectations. The new lower production cost would help expand the market for glubs. Smith Company was also in a good competitive position compared with Glubco since it probably could now undersell it.

This illustration shows the advantages of standard costs:

1. Control and reduction of costs.
2. Promotion and measurement of efficiencies.
3. Calculation and setting of selling prices.
4. Evaluation of inventories.
5. Simplification of cost procedures.

DIRECT COSTING

Another type of cost accounting that is used for internal purposes, but not for financial or tax reporting purposes, is direct costing. This is a method in which only those costs that are a consequence of production of the product are assigned to the product—direct material cost, direct labor cost and only variable manufacturing overhead. All fixed manufacturing costs are treated as expenses of the period.

The methods of recording costs for direct material and direct labor are similar under direct costing and conventional costing. It is in the method of reflecting manufacturing overhead that the systems differ:

1. In conventional costing, only one overhead control account is used.
2. In a direct costing system, overhead costs are classified as fixed or variable.

Two control accounts are used—a direct overhead account and an indirect overhead account. The *direct overhead account* is for variable expenses—those that vary with the volume of production. Under direct costing, direct labor, direct material and overhead costs that vary with production find their way into the inventory. The other manufacturing overhead expenses are charged off currently against income. The important reason behind direct costing is not to value inventories but to segregate expenses.

The *indirect overhead account* is for fixed expenses—those that do not vary with production. These are charged as expenses of the period rather than as costs of the finished product. Research costs, some advertising costs, and costs incurred to keep manufacturing and non-manufacturing facilities ready for use are considered expenses of the period.

The Effect of Direct Costing on Financial Statements

Direct costing, if used on the financial statements (for internal use), would produce the following results:

1. Where the inventory of manufactured goods does not fluctuate from one accounting period to the next, there should be no difference between net income using direct costing or net income using conventional costing.
2. Where the inventory does fluctuate and is increased, net income under direct costing will be lower. This is because fixed overhead costs under direct costing will have been charged to the current period instead of deferred by increasing the value of inventory. Under conventional costing, the value of the ending inventory will have been increased by these fixed overhead costs.
3. Where inventory decreases, net income under direct costing will be higher than conventional costing. The reason is that fixed overhead costs included in the value of the inventory under conventional costing will now increase the cost of goods sold, thereby reducing income.

SUMMARY

When a business enterprise becomes as operationally and financially complex as even most small and medium-sized companies are today, fairly sophisticated control and evaluation techniques must be developed to ensure an adequate level of operational efficiency and financial stability.

The historical essence of cost accounting systems has been the flow of financial resources into, through, and out of the business. It cannot be overemphasized that the ultimate objective of cost accounting is to provide relevant, valid and timely information of the cost of manufactured products or of the cost of services provided by service organizations. It is important to remember that the cost accounting process is a tool, not an end unto itself.

Also see Chapter 14, "Budgeting for Profit Planning and Budgetary Control." In many ways, budgeting is the precursor of cost accounting. Ideally, the two go hand-in-hand.

The discussion of break-even analysis in the chapter is of particular interest to the cost accountant in that it is useful for approximating as closely as possible the changes in costs generated by changes in the volume of production.

Chapter 16
Keep It Honest and Profitable

Contents

The Committee of Sponsoring Organizations (COSO)	**16.02**
The Foreign Corrupt Practices Act (FCPA)	**16.05**
Exactly What Is the Internal Control System (ICS)?	**16.12**
Fundamentals of a System of Internal Accounting Control	**16.14**
Internal Control for Inventories	**16.15**
Internal Control for Expenses	**16.23**
Internal Control for Cash	**16.27**
File Maintenance	**16.31**
Internal Controls for a Small Business Enterprise	**16.32**
Embezzlement	**16.44**
Ways to Deter Fraudulent Financial Reporting	**16.46**
Forms	
Form 16-1: General Internal Control Checklist	**16.34**
Form 16-2: Accounts Receivable and Sales Checklist	**16.36**
Form 16-3: Cash Receipts Checklist	**16.37**
Form 16-4: Inventories Checklist	**16.38**
Form 16-5: Accounts Payable, Purchases and Disbursements Checklist	**16.39**
Form 16-6: Investments Checklist	**16.41**

Form 16-7: Property, Plant and Equipment Checklist   **16.42**
Form 16-8: Insurance Checklist   **16.42**
Form 16-9: Payroll Checklist   **16.43**

Any business organization that does not have an established system of fraud control and other internal controls in place should have one; any organization that does have such a policy should review and update it periodically. If the system has developed haphazardly—reactively rather than proactively—it probably needs a thorough overhaul.

Enron is not the only cataclysmic event that has spurred change, reform, legislation and a closer look at business practices in general and accounting and auditing practices in particular. Other occurrences have also resulted in an attempt to bring honesty and increased productivity to the business world.

Action was taken in response to the series of savings and loan failures and spectacular frauds during and after the Watergate era. Increased emphasis was placed on improving the quality of financial reporting through *business ethics,* effective *internal controls,* and *corporate governance.* Concentrated effort was made to correct the existing situation and to prevent future fiascoes. In the latter attempt, the effort appears to have failed spectacularly.

THE COMMITTEE OF SPONSORING ORGANIZATIONS (COSO)

One of the reactions to that upheaval was the Committee of Sponsoring Organizations, formed in 1985 to establish and support the National Commission on Fraudulent Financial Reporting. The National Commission was organized as an independent private-sector initiative to study the causal factors that can lead to fraudulent financial reporting. It developed recommendations for public companies and their independent auditors, for the Securities and Exchange Commission (SEC) and other regulators and for educational institutions.

The National Commission (otherwise referred to as the "Treadway Commission," in honor of its first chairman, a former Commissioner of the SEC) was jointly sponsored by the five major U.S. financial professional associations:

1. The American Institute of Certified Public Accountants (AICPA).
2. The American Accounting Association (AAA).
3. The Institute of Internal Auditors (IIA).
4. The Institute of Management Accountants (IMA).
5. The Financial Executives Institute (FEI).

However, it was wholly independent of each of the sponsoring organizations and contained representatives from industry, public accounting, investment firms and the New York Stock Exchange.

The COSO Framework for Internal Control

The COSO sponsored the development and publication of *Internal Control—Integrated Framework,* which provides the COSO model. The model outlines a sound basis for establishing internal control systems and for determining their effectiveness in practice. It does not attempt to reinvent internal controls but to define them in broader terms and to provide a framework for describing and evaluating the effectiveness of internal controls within a control environment.

The COSO basis for internal controls is widely accepted:

1. It has been incorporated into generally accepted accounting principals (GAAP) with the adoption of *Statement on Auditing Standards No. 78* by the AICPA.
2. The COSO framework has also been adopted by the financial services industry in response to the Federal Deposit Insurance Improvement Act requirements for assessing internal controls.
3. The Office of Management and Budget (OMB) Circular A-123, "Management Accountability and Control," of June 21, 1995, provides the requirements for assessing controls under COSO. OMB Circular A-123 uses the term "management control" to cover all aspects of internal control over an agency's operations (operational, financial and compliance).
4. The General Accounting Office (GAO) standards provide the measure of quality against which controls in operation are assessed, and the COSO model is the model accepted by GAO.
5. Many large and small companies use the framework as the basis for their internal control procedure, as does the Small Business Administration.

Components of Internal Control

The COSO determined that a comprehensive assessment of risk and improved internal controls were necessary to manage business risk effectively. The standards and guidance developed by the committee are referred to as the COSO Internal Control Framework. According to COSO, internal control consists of five interrelated components:

1. *The control environment.* The control environment, as established by the head of the organization and senior managers, sets the tone and influences the control consciousness of employees. Control environment

factors include integrity and ethical values, employee competence, leadership philosophy and style, and assignment of authority and responsibility.

2. ***Risk assessment.*** Risk assessment is the identification and analysis of relevant risks to the achievement of the organization's objectives. It forms the basis for determining how risks should be managed.

3. ***Control activities.*** Control activities are the policies and procedures that help to ensure that management directives are carried out. They also help to ensure that necessary actions are taken to address any risks to the achievement of the organization's objectives.

4. ***Information and communication.*** Information and communication systems enable the organization's managers and employees to capture and exchange the information needed to conduct, manage and control its operations.

5. ***Monitoring.*** The entire process must be monitored to assess the quality of the internal control system's performance over time. Ongoing monitoring occurs in the course of operations:

   a. As part of regular management and supervisory activities.

   b. For employee performance of their duties.

Separate periodic evaluations assess the effectiveness of the internal control process and the ongoing monitoring procedures.

The COSO Definition of Internal Control

Internal control is a process, effected by an entity's board of directors, management and other personnel, designed to provide reasonable assurance regarding:

1. Effectiveness and efficiency of operations.
2. Reliability of financial reporting.
3. Compliance with applicable laws and regulations.

Key Concepts Considered by COSO

Following are those key concepts assumed by COSO's model and framework:

1. Internal control is a *process.* It is a means to an end, not an end in itself.
2. Internal control is effected by *people*—it is not merely policy manuals and forms, but people at every level of an organization.
3. Internal control can be expected to provide only *reasonable assurance,* not absolute assurance, to an entity's management and board.

4. Internal control is geared to the achievement of *objectives* in one or more separate but over-lapping categories.

(Note: Checklists at the end of the chapter should give a good idea of whether internal control is adequate for a particular organization.)

THE FOREIGN CORRUPT PRACTICES ACT (FCPA)

Investigations by the Securities and Exchange Commission in the mid-1970s showed that more than 400 U.S. companies admitted making questionable or outright illegal payments in excess of $300 million to foreign government officials, politicians and political parties.

When the Foreign Corrupt Practices Act (FCPA) was enacted by Congress in 1977, the act was characterized by the American Bar Association as the most extensive application of federal law to the regulation of business since the passage of the 1933 and 1934 Securities Acts. As a matter of fact, the FCPA is an amendment to the 1934 Securities Exchange Act and is generally administered by the SEC.

One reason for the significance of this statutory requirement is that it represents the first time, historically, that the U.S. Congress legislated an accounting rule. GAAP, of course, have always been developed and promulgated by private-sector authorities—the AICPA, the Financial Accounting Standards Board (FASB), the AAA and other authoritative sources. However, indications at present are that this may not hold true in the future.

Importance of the Act to the Accounting Profession

Primarily as a result of the enactment of the FCPA, internal accounting controls have become a significant point of concern for corporate management, the public accounting profession and the Securities and Exchange Commission.

Section 102 of the FCPA titled "Accounting Standards" specifies that all corporations required to file with the SEC must "Make and keep books, records, and accounts, which, in reasonable detail, accurately and fairly reflect the transactions and dispositions of the assets of the issuer."

The Accountant's Responsibility

Again, the significance of the act is the explicit statutory recognition by the federal government given to accounting controls and control systems. The accountant's responsibility is to plan a system that constantly monitors for errors, irregularities, malfeasance, embezzlement and fraudulent manipulation of the accounts. The accountant is, in fact, the monitor who must continually evaluate the effectiveness of the system and monitor compliance with the requirements of the statute. This, of course, also includes compliance with GAAP, because the statute explicitly includes GAAP in the wording of the act.

That the statutory requirement applies to publicly held corporations led, initially, to the misunderstanding that it is of no concern to public accountants who are not involved in auditing public corporations. But auditors must be mindful of the Statement on Auditing Procedure No. 1, which applies to the scope of the examination of *all companies,* whether public or private corporations, partnerships or other forms of business organizations. This Statement specifically references creditors, for example, who are a primary user of financial statements and to whom an auditor has a potential liability for materially misleading financial statements accompanying applications for credit to financial institutions, regardless of honest error or fraudulent intent.

Compliance Problems

What can an accountant do to ascertain compliance with the 1977 act? Because neither the act nor the professional literature actually specifies criteria for evaluating a system's adequacy or materiality levels, compliance can be demonstrated by an intent to comply. This makes it difficult for management, directors, independent auditors, and legal counsel to be sure of compliance with the act as far as the government is concerned.

The following suggestions may be helpful both to the accountant and to management for establishing intent to comply. There should be:

1. Records of memos and minutes of meetings held by management, the board of directors and the audit committee (if there is no audit committee, one should be instituted) concerning internal accounting control concepts. The discussions should include legal counsel, internal auditors and independent auditors.

2. Statements for the record of intention to comply.

3. A record of all company meetings with the accounting personnel and internal audit staff held to ensure that they understand the importance of compliance and are capable of monitoring compliance.

4. A written program for continuing review and evaluation of the accounting controls system.

5. Letters from the independent auditors stating that no material weaknesses in internal accounting controls were discovered during the audit or that suggested needed improvements have in fact been made. If necessary, the independent auditors' comments should also include other deficiencies discovered during the audit. Management's written plans to correct these deficiencies should be included.

6. A record of periodic review and approval of the evaluation of the system by senior management, the audit committee and the board of directors.

7. Instructional manuals for the development of methods and techniques for describing, testing and evaluating internal controls.

8. Training programs conducted for internal auditors and other company personnel responsible for internal controls.

9. Changes in internal controls to overcome identified deficiencies that are initiated and documented.

10. A formal written code of conduct appropriately communicated and monitored. (Note: the SEC regards a corporate written code of conduct as imperative. At the same time, a non-listed corporation might find that such a written code is even more important as a protection in case of litigation.)

11. Documentation that compliance testing was done by direct visual observations during the period being audited.

1988 Amendment to the FCPA

The basic act was amended in 1988 to spell out and clarify certain provisions of the act. As more and more small businesses became involved in world trade, it became essential for persons doing business overseas to understand fully the FCPA and its implications. It is an extremely important law that can result in grave consequences for those who disregard it. This law criminalizes certain conduct by or on behalf of U.S. entities doing business abroad. There are two basic parts of this law:

1. *Anti-bribery provisions,* which prohibit the payment of bribes to foreign officials to obtain business. This measure applies to *all* entities, *not* just listed companies. (See below.)

2. *Accounting provisions,* which require *public* companies to maintain accurate books and records, and an *adequate internal accounting control system.* The accounting rules apply only to companies that are required to report financial information under the Securities laws. These accounting and recordkeeping rules are broad and should be thoroughly understood.

Anti-Bribery Provisions of the FCPA

Under the FCPA, a "U.S. person" is precluded from providing certain things to a "foreign official" to get that foreign official to behave contrary to the obligations of his or her position. Specifically, the FCPA prohibits any U.S. person from corruptly proposing or giving money or other things of value to a foreign official, an official of a foreign political party, a candidate for foreign political office, or a foreign political party for the purposes of:

1. Influencing any act or decision of such foreign official in his official capacity.
2. Inducing such foreign official "to do or omit to do" any act in violation of a lawful duty of such official.
3. Inducing such official to use his or her influence with a foreign government or instrumentality thereof to affect or influence any governmental act or decision.
4. Securing any improper advantage.

Accounting Provisions: Financial Policies and Internal Control

The FCPA states that corporations filing with the SEC are required to keep an accurate accounting of all financial transactions, including payment of commissions, consulting fees, service fees, facilitating payments and gratuities. All financial transactions must be characterized accurately in company financial records. Mislabeled or hidden transactions can result in liability for the company under the accounting provisions of the FCPA.

A company's *finance policies* and *internal controls* must ensure that all such transactions are properly and fully recorded. Therefore, it is mandatory that appropriate contracts govern international relationships and that all terms and conditions regarding payment under those contracts are clearly spelled out.

The statute requires publicly held companies to develop and maintain a system of internal accounting controls sufficient to ensure:

1. That transactions are executed in accordance with management's general or specific authorization.
2. That transactions are recorded as necessary to permit preparation of financial statements in conformity with GAAP or any other criteria applicable to such statements.
3. That the system maintains accountability for assets.
4. That access to assets is permitted only in accordance with management's general or specific authorization.
5. That the recorded accountability for assets is compared with existing assets at reasonable intervals, with appropriate action taken with respect to any difference.

The Role of the Auditor.   The significance of the act, insofar as auditors are concerned, is the explicit statutory recognition given to accounting controls. The auditor's objective is to plan the examination to search for errors or irregularities that would have a material effect on the financial statements and to use skill and care in the examination of the client's internal control system. Although the independent auditor is not part of a company's internal accounting control system, the auditor must evaluate the effectiveness and monitor compliance of internal accounting control systems.

Further Discussion of the Anti-Bribery Provisions

Because the scope of the FCPA is very broad, additional discussion of the anti-bribery provisions seems appropriate. It is important to keep in mind that the act covers not only large public companies but essentially any person residing in the United States as well as businesses incorporated in the United States or those that have their principal place of business in the United States. While the original intent of the law was to cut off large bribery-type payments to foreign officials, *any business, large or small,* that exports a product outside of the United States should be aware of the law.

According to the FCPA, covered companies, their employees and agents are prohibited from making, authorizing or promising payments or gifts of money or anything of value corruptly. In other words, no person may make a payment or gift to influence the recipient in any official act, such as failing to perform an official duty. Nor can any person give a gift to induce an individual to use his or her influence with his or her government or business for the entity's business benefit. (The prohibitions apply when the recipient is a foreign official, a foreign political party, a party official, a candidate for a foreign political office or any individual who will transmit some or all of the payment or gift to an illegal recipient.) Payments for seemingly *routine* matters—for example, expediting a shipment or speed up issuance of a permit—*may* violate the FCPA.

The Department of Justice has established a Foreign Corrupt Practices Act Opinion Procedure from which any U.S. company or national may request a statement from the Department's present enforcement policy in relation to anti-bribery provisions of the FCPA regarding a proposed business arrangement or action.

Although the Department of Commerce has no enforcement role regarding the FCPA, it supplies general guidance to U.S. exporters who have questions about the FCPA and about international developments concerning the FCPA.

Relevant Definitions

A *U.S. person* is defined as:

1. Domestic concerns (i.e., U.S. citizens, residents, business entities organized under the laws of any U.S. state or territory, and business entities with their principal place of business in the United States).

2. Issuers of stock traded on a stock exchange.
3. Officers, directors, employees, agents, and stockholders of domestic concerns.

    A *foreign official* is considered to be:

1. Any officer or employee of a foreign government or instrumentality thereof or any person acting in an official capacity for or on behalf of any such government or instrumentality.
2. Officers and employees of state-owned enterprises.
3. Political parties and candidates.
4. Officers or employees of public international organizations such as the United Nations.

Sanctions for Violating the FCPA

The consequences for a violation of the FCPA are severe, both for a company and for individuals.

Fines and penalties for violations of the *anti-bribery provisions* are as follows:

1. Maximum criminal fine for a business entity is $2 million.
2. Maximum criminal fine for individuals is $100,000. Maximum imprisonment term is 5 years.
3. Civil penalty of $10,000 may also be imposed.

A fine imposed on a corporate employee or representative may not be paid directly or indirectly by the corporation.

For violations of the *accounting provisions,* there is no criminal liability, except the FCPA specifically criminalizes conduct by persons who knowingly circumvent a system of internal accounting controls or who knowingly falsify books and records. Fines and penalties are as follows:

1. Fines for individuals up to $1 million; imprisonment for up to 10 years or both.
2. Fines for corporations may be up to $2.5 million.

FCPA Red Flags

The following types of activities may involve FCPA violations:

1. Money or property passed through a consultant or representative to a public official to obtain certain government actions.

2. Use of consultants or representatives who are closely connected intermediaries with the government or a political party of the country in which the corporation is doing business.

3. Gifts or gratuities to government officials or political party officials, candidates for public office, or their families.

4. Extravagant entertaining of government officials or party leaders or their families.

5. Indirect payments to government officials or their families.

6. Use of company facilities by such government officials.

7. Negative information (flawed background) is discovered as part of due diligence.

8. A representative refuses to make FCPA-related certification.

9. A request for unusually large commissions, retainers, or other fees.

10. An unusual method of payment or payment in a third country proposed by representative.

11. Retention of a contingent fee representative when procurement decision is imminent.

1998 Amendment to the FCPA

In 1998, the International Anti-Bribery and Fair Competition Act of 1998 amended the FCPA to implement the Organization for Economic Cooperation and Development (OECD) Convention on Combating Bribery of Foreign Public Officials in International Business Transactions. The 1998 amendments:

1. Clarify that the act applies to payments to obtain any "improper advantage."

2. Assert nationality jurisdiction over U.S. companies and nationals that take any act in furtherance of a bribe, even in the absence of an interstate commerce nexus.

3. Expand the definition of foreign officials to include officials of *international public organizations*.

4. Provide for criminal liability over *foreign companies and nationals* that take any act in furtherance of a bribe *within the territory of the United States*.

5. Eliminate a *disparity in penalties* between U.S. nationals and non-U.S. nationals employed by or acting as agents of U.S. companies.

Preventing Non-Compliance

Any entity exporting products or services or preparing to export, must make sure that all employees and agents understand the requirements of the

FCPA. To emphasize the importance of abiding by the provisions of the FCPA, a business should establish written policy statements concerning proper conduct. It would be appropriate for those policy statements to address not only bribery of foreign officials but also officials in the U.S.

Individuals responsible for the actual exporting activities, especially those that may come in direct contact with foreign officials or appoint local representatives who will do so, should be especially aware of the FCPA rules. The policy should also stipulate that employees should not accept any gifts or payments that could be interpreted as intent to persuade the company to act in a certain way.

Annual Report to Congress on the OECD Convention

The third annual report to the U.S. Congress on the implementation of the Organization for Economic Cooperation and Development Anti-Bribery Convention was given by the Commerce Department on June 29, 2001.

Among other disturbing findings, the report noted that the U.S. government has received reports indicating that the bribery of foreign public officials influenced the awarding of billions of dollars in contracts around the world. For example, in the period from May 1, 2000, to April 30, 2001, the competition for 61 contracts worth $37 billion may have been affected by bribery of foreign officials. Of those contracts, U.S. firms are believed to have lost at least nine, worth approximately $4 billion. Firms from Convention signatory countries continue to account for about 70 percent of these allegations.

The government's original aim was to stop the flagrant bribery of foreign officials and to restore public confidence in the integrity of the American business system. When it became obvious that American businesses where at a disadvantage because of bribery by foreign firms, the government joined other signatories in the Convention in the hopes that this vehicle could foster fair dealings globally.

The expanded FCPA conforms with the Convention on Combating Bribery of Foreign Officials in International Business Transactions, which has been adopted by 33 countries worldwide.

EXACTLY WHAT IS THE INTERNAL CONTROL SYSTEM (ICS)?

When considering a topic of this magnitude—the importance and complexity of internal control systems—it is important to understand what they are and why they are used before getting into the nitty-gritty technical aspects. Internal control serves at least two very important functions—effective use of assets (including personnel) and prevention of fraud.

A system can be thought of as a way of thinking. That is, it involves the evaluation of both the methods and the application of those methods to an entity's controls system. Evaluation techniques require:

1. Thoughtful consideration.
2. Rigorous study and research.
3. Objective analysis.

These three attributes are ways of thinking that in turn provide an orderly approach for reviewing an organization's techniques and procedures in order to appraise the adequacy of its ICS. And, if it appears not to be working, this is the time for trying to figure out why—and to fix it.

Internal Accounting and Administrative Control

Internal control, according to the Professional Auditing Standards, is subdivided into accounting control and administrative control. Two levels of objectives are implicit in the Standard. The ultimate goals are the *safeguarding* of assets and the *reliability* of financial records.

Accounting Control.   The plan of organization and all methods, procedures and records that are concerned with, and relate directly to, safeguarding assets and the reliability of financial records are considered to be accounting controls. Consequently, they are designed to provide reasonable assurance that:

1. Transactions are executed in accordance with management's general or specific authorization.
2. Transactions are recorded as necessary:
   a. To permit preparation of financial statements in conformity with GAAP or any other criteria applicable to such statements.
   b. To maintain accountability for assets.
3. Access to assets is permitted only in accordance with management's authorization.
4. The recorded accountability for assets is compared with the existing assets at reasonable intervals and appropriate action taken with respect to any differences.

Administrative Control.   The plan of organization and all methods and procedures that are concerned mainly with operational efficiency and adherence to managerial policies, such as sales policies, employee training, and production quality control, are elements of administrative control. This is usually only indirectly related to the financial records.

Administrative control includes, but is not limited to, the plan of organization and the procedures and records that are concerned with the decision processes leading to management's authorization of transactions. Such authorization is a management function directly associated with the responsibility for achieving the objectives of the organization and is the starting point for establishing account control of transactions.

FUNDAMENTALS OF A SYSTEM OF INTERNAL ACCOUNTING CONTROL

There is, necessarily, a relationship between the size of an organization and the development of its internal control system. Although complete separation of functions and the internal auditing department may well be impossible in smaller companies, effort should be made, as much as possible, to set in place the procedures, policies, and controls that support the following guidelines:

1. *Responsibility.* There should be a plan or an organizational chart that places the responsibility for specified functions on specific individuals in the organization. The responsibility for establishing and maintaining a system of internal accounting control rests with management. The system should be continuously supervised, tested, and modified as necessary to provide reasonable (but not absolute) assurance that objectives are being accomplished, all *at costs not exceeding benefits.*

2. *Division of duties.* The idea here is to remove the handling and recording of any one transaction from beginning to end from the control of any one employee. Making different employees responsible for different functions of a transaction actually serves as a cross-check, which facilitates the detection of errors—accidental or deliberate.

3. *Use of appropriate forms and documents.* Efficient design of forms and documents aids in the administration of the internal control system. Mechanical and electronic equipment can also be used to expedite the process of checking. Both of these methods provide control over accounting data.

4. *Internal auditors.* Periodic review of all of the preceding elements of the internal control system should be carried out by an internal audit staff. The function of this staff is to check the effectiveness of the policies, procedures, and controls mentioned.

Basic Elements of a System of Internal Accounting Control

The elements of a satisfactory system of internal control include:

1. A plan of organization that provides appropriate segregation of functional responsibilities.

2. A system of authorization and record procedures adequate to provide reasonable accounting control of assets, liabilities, revenues and expenses.

3. Sound practices to follow in the performance of duties and functions of each of the organizational departments.

4. Personnel of a quality commensurate with responsibilities.

One important element in the system of internal control is the independence of the operating, custodial, accounting and internal auditing functions.

There should be a separation of duties so that *records exist outside each department to serve as controls over the activities within that department.* Responsibilities for various functions and delegation of authority should be clearly defined and spelled out in organizational charts and manuals.

Conflicting and dual responsibility must be avoided. The initiation and authorization of an activity should be separate from the accounting for it. Custody of assets should be separated from the accounting for them.

Relationship of an Internal Control System to Outside Accountants

The efficiency of an internal control system becomes important to a company's outside, independent auditors. Before determining how thorough an audit should be made, the internal control system must be reviewed. An efficient system may do away with certain audit procedures that might otherwise be necessary. Conversely, a poor internal control system may necessitate a far more costly review on the part of the auditor.

INTERNAL CONTROL FOR INVENTORIES

It is obvious that merchandising and manufacturing companies in particular need to keep a complete, secure inventory of goods held for sale. Management is responsible for determining and maintaining the proper level of goods in inventory because:

1. If inventory is too low, sales opportunities may be missed.

2. If inventory is too large, the business pays unnecessarily high costs for storing, insuring and providing security. As a result, the company's cash flow becomes one sided—cash drains out to purchase inventory, but cash does not flow in from sales.

Merchandising companies classify all goods available for sale in one inventory category. Manufacturing companies generally use three inventory categories: finished goods, work-in-process and raw materials and supplies. This chapter emphasizes inventory for manufacturing companies, but many of the principles and practices also apply to merchandising companies.

Following is a discussion of internal control procedures that can be used in conjunction with different types of inventories: goods for resale, finished goods, materials and work in process.

Inventories of Merchandise Purchased for Resale and Supplies

The departments involved in internal control in merchandise and supplies inventories are purchasing, sales, receiving, accounts receivable, and accounts payable. The following controls should be implemented:

1. The purchasing department approves the purchase orders for merchandise to be bought. In a small company, the owner or manager may be the one to approve these purchase orders, which should be sequentially numbered and traced to final destination.
2. After okays from the purchasing manager have been received, requests for price quotations are usually sent out. These requests should go to various sources, and the company quoting the lowest price will be the one from which the purchases are made, unless there is some overriding consideration.
3. In the selling department, an updated individual quantity record for each type of unit is kept on perpetual inventory stock cards. It is usually the responsibility of inventory clerks to keep these cards up to date:
   a. The number of units of merchandise ordered is entered on the inventory stock cards by one clerk.
   b. The number actually received is entered from the receiving list by a different clerk.
   c. The number sold or used is recorded by still another clerk from sales lists or salesperson's orders.

   These stock cards indicate the need for reorders. They should be checked against a purchase requisition by the manager of the selling department or other person in control of the merchandise stock. In a business too small to have a separate selling department, the owner or manager should perform these functions.

   After the number of units ordered, received and issued have been recorded on the inventory cards, the balance represents the number of units actually on hand. A well-rounded perpetual card system usually includes detailed unit costs for ready computation under the LIFO, FIFO or average method.

4. In the receiving department, the receiving clerk should not be allowed to see purchase order records or purchase requisitions. Receiving reports are checked against the perpetual inventory stock records and a notation is made on these stock record cards indicating the date, order number, and quantity received.

   Even where a business is too small to have a perpetual inventory, a receiving report should be made. It should then be checked against the purchase orders and a notation as to the day and quantity received made on those purchase orders.

5. In the accounts payable department, the receiving report is checked against the merchandise stock record, then sent to the accounts payable department, where it is verified against the seller's invoice. The purchasing agent should have approved the price on the seller's invoice before that invoice was sent to the accounts payable department.

   A clerk in the accounts payable department should verify all extension totals on the invoice. If the vendor's invoice and receiving report are in agreement, the invoice is then entered into a purchase journal or voucher register for future payment. Any discrepancy between quantity received and quantity on the seller's invoice will necessitate holding up payment until an adjustment is made by the seller.

Finished Goods Inventories

The departments involved in internal control of finished goods inventories are manufacturing, cost accounting, accounts receivable and sales. The following controls should be implemented:

1. It is necessary to ascertain the quantity of units completed from the production record and transferred to the shipping department or warehouse. The daily report of finished goods units transferred to the shipping department or warehouse indicates the number of finished units available to the sales department.

2. The unit cost of finished goods delivered to the sales department must be computed. This information is obtained from the unit cost sheet (for a process cost accounting system) or from the job-order cost card (in a job-order cost accounting system). (For more information see Chapter 15 on cost accounting.)

3. Finished goods inventory cards should be set up. For each item, the following should be recorded:

   a. The quantity received at the warehouse.

   b. The quantity shipped on orders.

   c. The balance remaining at specified unit costs.

The number of finished goods units in the warehouse or stockroom should tie in with this finished goods inventory file.

4. Periodically, a physical count of the finished goods inventory is required. It should tie in with the finished goods inventory file.

Raw Materials and Supplies Inventories

The departments involved in internal control for raw materials and supplies inventory are stores, purchasing, accounts payable, and manufacturing. The following controls should be implemented:

1. In the stores department, the storekeeper must safeguard the raw materials and supplies inventories—both physically and by accounting control. No raw materials or supplies can leave without a stores requisition. Quantity control at minimum levels is also the responsibility of the storekeeper. The storekeeper should maintain a stores record for each item, listing:

   a. The maximum and minimum quantities.

   b. Quantity ordered and number.

   c. Quantity received.

   d. Quantity issued.

   e. Balance on hand.

   When stores cards show minimum quantities, a stores ledger clerk pulls those cards from the file to make sure that materials or supplies are ordered to cover minimum needs. Quantities shown on the stores record should be verified by making an actual count of the stores items that are to be ordered. A purchase requisition is then filled out from the stores records. The quantity of each item ordered is approved by the storekeeper who knows the average monthly consumption of each item.

   The ordering of special equipment by department heads also goes through the storeroom after having the necessary executive approval. The purchase requisition is then forwarded to the purchasing agent.

   In the stores department, a receiving report is prepared in triplicate by the receiving clerk:

   a. One copy goes to the stores ledger clerk.

   b. The second is sent to the accounts payable department.

   c. The third is kept by the receiving clerk.

   The receiving clerk puts the stores items in proper places within the storeroom after preparing the receiving report. Ideally, location numbers are used to facilitate ready accessing.

The stores ledger clerk gets a copy of the receiving report and makes a record of the quantity and the order number on the stores ledger card affected by the items received.

2. In the purchasing department, the purchase agent places the order for the quantity needed on the quantity requisition. If the agent feels the quantity ordered is excessive, he or she may look into the storekeeper's purchase requisition. The next step is to request price quotations from various supply companies. The order should normally be placed with the lowest bidder. The purchase agent also verifies the prices on the seller's invoices by comparing them to the price quotations.

3. In the accounts payable department, no bill should be approved for payment until:

   a. Materials ordered have actually been received.

   b. Materials have been inspected and are in good condition.

   c. The prices of the seller's invoice match the quotations.

4. In the manufacturing department, different individuals have authority to sign stores requisitions to withdraw materials from the storeroom. Usually, a foreman prepares a stores requisition when raw materials or supplies are needed in any of the manufacturing departments.

   This requisition contains:

   a. The account name and number.

   b. The department name and number.

   c. The job order number.

   d. The quantity of material issued.

   e. The stores item name and classification symbol.

   f. The name of the person to withdraw materials from the storeroom.

   g. The unit price of the item and the total cost of items withdrawn from the storeroom.

Work-in-Process Inventory

The departments involved in internal control of work-in-process inventories are manufacturing and cost accounting. The following controls should be implemented:

1. In the manufacturing department, stores requisitions are prepared by shop foremen for materials that are to be charged to the work-in-process inventory account. Quantities of materials are obtained from engineering or administrative departments. Specifications for raw materials are

usually shown on a bill of materials (a list of different items required to complete an order). The stores requisition will specify:

a. Quantity.

b. Price.

c. Cost of each item of raw material requisitioned.

d. Job order number.

Time tickets are prepared by the workers and approved by a foreman in the department in which work is performed before it is charged to the work-in-process inventory account. Each labor operation may have a standard time for performing a certain operation, as predetermined by the engineering department. There may also be a predetermined standard wage rate, determined by the head of the manufacturing department and known by the payroll department.

The cost accounting department is responsible for the amount of manufacturing expense charged to the work-in-process inventory account.

2. In the cost department:

a. Raw material cost is computed from sales requisitions.

b. Direct labor costs are obtained from time tickets.

c. Manufacturing expense is estimated from prevailing overhead rates.

Internal control methods for the work-in-process inventory account depend on whether the firm has a process cost accounting or job-order cost accounting system.

The chief point of internal control for work-in-process inventories is computing costs. Product costs are analyzed by operations, departments and cost elements. This permits measurement of the cost of products at different stages of completion. The number of partly finished units when multiplied by a cost at a particular stage should come close to the value in the work-in-process inventory account.

Taking Count — The Physical Inventory

The two most significant factors of inventory control are knowing what should be on hand based on paper controls and then verifying what actually is on hand from a physical count.

The Perpetual System — Knowing What Should Be on Hand.   In many firms, not enough effort and emphasis are put into the timely keeping of detailed perpetual inventory stock records, the most basic control available. The nature and extent of the records to maintain vary from company to company, but at the least, there should be a constantly updated record of the units handled. The "ins" and "outs" are posted, showing the new morning's balance on hand, or rather, the balance that *should* be on hand. If expanded to the fullest, the system would also include:

1. Unit costs of acquisitions (in manufacturing, detailed material, labor and overhead costs assigned).
2. Unit sales deleted at cost (based on the company's flow-of-cost assumption of LIFO, FIFO or average costs).
3. Balance on hand extended at cost.
4. Back-order positions, write-downs, destructions and, most important, locations in the storage area (by location number or description) are shown on the individual record.
5. The total sales income for that particular unit shown on the individual record and displaying unit gross profits.

Retail stores using the gross profit method of valuing inventories usually maintain controls over entire departments, or sections of departments rather than by individual units. Extended values are at retail, showing markups and markdowns as well as bulk cost figures.

The general-ledger summary inventory asset account should (where the system provides cost-flowing movement) always tie in to the total of the subsidiary perpetual system (at least monthly). They should be matched as often as possible and all differences traced to eliminate any weaknesses in the system. The point is—know what should be on hand!

The Physical Count—Verifying What Is Actually on Hand.   At least once a year, a physical count of the entire inventory should be taken, usually as of the balance sheet date. Management, not the auditor, is responsible for taking this physical inventory. The auditor is only an observer of methods, count and valuation. Personnel may help establish the system of counting, the tags to use, the methods of ensuring a full count, the cut-off procedures and the pricing. The auditor should observe the process to be satisfied about the reasonability of the total value acceptable for attestation.

The method of tagging, counting, weighing or measuring, locating and recounting—the assignment of personnel—all the procedures should be set in advance and followed (unless properly authorized changes develop).

As to the nitty-gritty of an actual inventory count, considerations include:

1. Particular items should be counted by employees who do not have custody of the items.
2. Supervisors should be responsible for assigning each employee to a specific set of inventory tasks.

3. Employees who help take inventory are responsible for verifying the contents of any and all containers and storage places, including boxes, barrels, tubs and closets.

4. Prenumbered tally sheets are provided to all employees involved in actually taking the inventory.

5. The tally sheets provide evidence to support reported inventory levels and show exactly who is responsible for the information they include.

6. Access to inventory should be limited until the physical inventory is completed.

7. If any items are scheduled for shipping during a physical inventory, they should be segregated and not included in the count.

8. If shipments are received during a physical inventory, they also should be segregated and counted separately.

9. After the regular counting, a supervisor should verify that all items have been counted and that none has been counted twice.

The auditor should become familiar with the nature of the products handled, the terminology, the packaging, the principles of measurement and all of the precautions have been taken before the actual process is scheduled. Such education in the client's processes should not be obtained at the sacrifice of counting-time.

The auditor is concerned with the final evaluation of that physical inventory. The perpetual records, as such, and errors therein are not a necessary part of the audit process, though weaknesses should be commented upon in the management letter.

However, a history of *accurate* internal control of inventory can substantially reduce the extent of testing by the auditor. When it can be expected that variations from perpetual inventories will be small and within tolerable limits, the auditor may choose to use statistical random sampling in testing either an immediately prior physical count or in counting only those items *drawn by the auditor* (without advance notice) for random selection.

If the sample then indicates an unacceptable rate of error, the auditor may request another (or full) physical count, or may, with management's consent, adjust the overall value of the inventory to an amount indicated by the sample, with management required to investigate the error in the ensuing fiscal year. When an effective perpetual inventory control is in use, management usually cycle-counts the inventory. This may occur once or several times during the year. Unscheduled testing of bits and pieces throughout the year will keep everyone aware of attention given to the inventory; however, it must be covered entirely at least annually.

There are often *portions* of an inventory that would require more time and effort for the physical count than the relative merit of those portions warrants. Such items may be reasonably estimated (with joint approval of management and auditor), based on such elements as:

a. Last year's value.
b. Movement during the year.
c. Space occupied.
d. Weight.
e. Sales and purchases, using an estimated gross profit method.

The accuracy of a physical inventory even with the most sophisticated computerized system, may always be in doubt if there is no perpetual record for comparison. *A perpetual inventory is meaningless unless tested periodically to a physical count.* A history of accurate perpetual records can be justification for an auditor's using statistical sampling for year-end evaluation. Moreover, management itself can use statistical sampling techniques for cycle-counting. Tie-in to the general-ledger asset account should be made regularly by management. The financial statement value of the inventory must be at *cost* or *market,* whichever is lower. Standards are unacceptable, unless approximating cost.

INTERNAL CONTROL FOR EXPENSES

Each of the various types of expenses requires special internal control procedures. These procedures are covered in the following paragraphs.

Manufacturing Expenses

The departments involved in internal control of manufacturing expenses are factory production, factory service and accounts payable. The following controls should be implemented:

1. In the manufacturing service and producing department, small tools that are not constantly being used should be kept in the tool room. Each worker requiring such tools can be given metal checks, each stamped with a personal number. The tool room attendant will release a tool to a worker in exchange for a metal check bearing the worker's number. The check is retained in the tool room until the tool is returned, at which time the check is returned.

    The department supervisor has the responsibility of approving a requisition for a new tool when one wears out.

2. Charges for freight and shipping on incoming supplies should be charged to the account to which the supplies are charged. Copies of the freight or

shipping bills should be attached to supply invoices. Supplies inventory is, therefore, charged for these freight and shipping charges instead of an expense account.

3. Numerous types of shop supplies, such as brooms, oil, waste, solder, wire, are part of the raw materials and supplies inventory. They should be kept in the storeroom and issued only by a stores requisition, signed by an authorized individual. The individual who indicates the need for such supplies (usually a supervisor) should indicate the job order number or departmental expense account number to which the material is to be charged on the stores requisition.

4. Workers categorized as indirect laborers should have an identification number when they work in a specific department. A time clock card should be kept and verified by a supervisor or timekeeper.

Selling Expenses

The departments involved for internal control of selling expenses are sales and accounts payable. The following controls should be implemented:

1. Salespersons' salaries should be okayed by the sales department manager before a summary is sent to the payroll department. The basis for the summary is the salesperson's daily report. Commissions earned are verified from duplicate sales invoices mailed to the customer. These are computed in the sales department and approved by the sales department manager.

2. To prevent padding of travel expenses, many companies allow flat rates or maximum amounts for each day of the week. Unusual amounts should require an explanation from the salesperson.

3. The office manager retains control over outgoing mail and postage. A mail clerk usually affixes the postage. Control of postage expenses involves limiting the number of office workers who have access to stamps or a postage meter.

4. Telephone expenses can be controlled by maintaining a record of all outgoing calls. Long distance calls should be reported indicating the party making the call and where the call is going. From the long distance call record, telephone expenses are distributed by departments.

5. Subscriptions to publications and dues of various organizations and professional societies should be approved by the sales manager before a voucher is prepared.

6. All bills approved by the sales manager are sent to the accounting department for payment.

Administrative Expenses

The departments involved in internal control of administrative expenses are administrative and accounts payable. Internal control for administrative expenses is very similar to that for the sales department. Bills for administrative expense items should be approved by an administrative department executive before they are sent to the accounts payable department for payment.

Financial and Other Expenses

In corporations that have special departments to control financial problems in the company, a treasury department or similar department will handle expenses in the nature of interest and discount and dividends and may even supervise handling of cash. The financial department may also have the responsibility for authorizing credit extended to customers.

The departments involved in internal control for factory payrolls are timekeeping, payroll, accounts payable and the particular manufacturing division. The following controls should be implemented:

1. A credit manager in the financial department should have the responsibility for approving sales orders above a specific amount. The manager should be in constant touch with the accounts receivable department to determine whether or not a customer has been regular in payments. The treasurer has the responsibility for authorizing bad debt write-offs. The write-off itself should be made by someone in the accounts receivable department on the authority of the financial department executive — not the sales manager.

2. The financial department executive or office manager approves expenditures such as interest and bank discounts, office expenses and supplies. After approval of these items, invoices are sent to the accounts payable department.

Salaries and Wages

The departments involved in internal control for factory payrolls are timekeeping, payroll, accounts payable, and the particular manufacturing division. The following controls should be implemented:

1. In the timekeeping department, each worker is given an identifying number that will serve to identify his or her department. A badge with this number serves as identification when presence within the factory is checked each day.

2. It is the duty of a time clerk to check the presence of each worker once or twice a day, every day. This is to eliminate the possibility of one person punching the time clock for another who is absent. Absences are noted in a time book. These are then checked against the employee's time ticket, time clock card, or payroll sheet at the end of each specific pay period.

3. Care should be taken to prevent one worker punching another worker's time clock card. The time clock card indicates the number of hours the worker is present each day in the plant and can be used to verify either daily or weekly the hours shown on daily time tickets.

4. In the manufacturing department, a time ticket that lists the worker's name, number of hours worked on different jobs and labor operations, and total hours worked is prepared. It must be approved by the foreman of the department in which the work is performed.

5. In the payroll department, time tickets are verified against the time clock cards and the timekeeper's time clock book. The time ticket is then given to a clerk who inserts the hourly or piecework rate of each worker. Another clerk computes the earnings. The time tickets are then used for working up the payroll sheet. The time tickets are sent to the cost accounting department to prepare a payroll distribution sheet. The payroll sheet becomes the record by which the worker is paid. After the payroll sheet has been completely okayed, it is sent to the accounts payable department for payment. Payment to each worker, either by check or cash, should be receipted.

    In the accounts payable department, the payroll sheet serves as the basis for payment.

Office Payroll

The following controls should be implemented for the office payroll:

1. In the sales department, the sales manager approves the daily sales reports. From these reports, a record of the salesperson's days is prepared. The record is sent to the payroll department after approval by the sales manager. The manager in the sales department also approves the records of work performed by the sales office force before sending it to the payroll department.

2. In the administrative department, the office manager approves time worked by the office force and then sends it to the payroll department. Salaries of top executives are often placed on a special payroll. Their salaries are usually known by the paymaster who prepares their checks and sends them directly to the executives' offices.

3. The treasurer or financial department office manager similarly approves the work performed by the clerical personnel in his or her department.

4. Upon receiving these authorized reports from the various departments, the paymaster sets them up on a payroll sheet and after computing the applicable salary for each office worker, takes all applicable deductions and indicates a net salary for each employee.

5. In the accounts payable department, payment for these office workers' salaries is prepared from the payroll sheets.

INTERNAL CONTROL FOR CASH

Where currency is available, internal control is most necessary. Incoming checks may be used in manipulating accounts receivable and must be controlled. Accounts receivable control becomes part of cash control, and vice versa. Cash disbursements and petty cash also need special internal controls. Details follow.

Cash Receipts

The departments involved in internal control of cash receipts are selling, treasury or cashier's and accounts receivable. The following controls should be implemented:

1. In the selling department, cash sales should be recorded in a register. A numbered sales slip should be made up for each sale. These slips should be used in numerical order.

2. In the cashier's department, an employee should count the cash at the end of the day. Except for a small amount left to make change, all cash should be removed. The total daily cash receipts should be recorded on slips and placed in the same pouch as the cash itself. The pouch should then be turned over to a clerk (a different employee from the one who counted the cash in the register) who will make out a bank deposit slip. Still another clerk in the cashier's department should read the cash register totals of the day or remove the cash sales slips.

   The cash removed from the register must agree with the tape and the total of cash slips, which are numbered sequentially (all numbers must have been accounted for). The sales readings are then compared with the amount of cash removed from the registers by the cashier. Small discrepancies are charged to a cash short or over account. Larger discrepancies call for an explanation.

3. In the accounts receivable department, incoming mail should be opened by a bonded clerk. All checks, currency, and money orders are listed by this clerk on a cash-received record. The cash-received record lists date of

receipt, name of sender and amount. The record and totals are then sent to the accounts receivable department to be properly applied to the customers' accounts. The cash is sent to the cashier's office and subsequently given to the deposit clerk.

4. In the accounts receivable department, the record of cash received is used to credit customers' accounts. This record then goes to the general accounting department where it is compared with daily deposit slips of cash received from customers before it is entered on the books.

Cash Disbursements

The departments involved in the internal control of cash disbursements are accounts payable and voucher.

In the accounts payable department, purchase of any item must have prior approval from the authorized person in charge of the department in which the expenditure originates before it comes to the accounts payable department. Where a voucher system is in operation, vouchers are prepared for each expenditure. Information on the voucher matches that shown on the seller's invoice. Vouchers are entered in the voucher register after having been approved by the head of the voucher department and then placed in a pending file for future payments.

Petty Cash

The departments involved in the internal control of petty cash are selling, administrative or others in which there is a need for such petty cash funds, and accounts payable.

In any department where it is necessary to have a petty cash fund, at least two individuals should have the responsibility for handling petty cash. One individual inspects and approves the item for payment. The other has charge of the petty cash fund and pays the vouchers as they are presented. Each petty cash voucher should list the date, amount paid and name of the account to be charged. A bill or other receipt, if there is one, should be attached to the voucher. The employee who controls the petty cash fund should compare the receipts attached to the petty cash vouchers with the vouchers.

When the petty cash fund needs reimbursement, the person controlling the fund totals those petty cash vouchers which have been paid out and presents them to the accounts payable department. This department then arranges for the necessary reimbursement.

Accounts Receivable

The departments responsible for internal control of accounts receivable are accounts receivable and sales.

Copies of sales slips from the sales department are used to charge customers' accounts. Copies of any credits due customers come from the sales department. These records are sent to the accounts receivable department, where, if possible, one clerk should have the responsibility for entering only debits to customers' accounts and another for posting credits, such as for returned merchandise or receipt of a note. Still a third employee should enter the credit in the customer's account for cash received.

Sending statements at the end of each month is a good way to check the accuracy of the customer's accounts.

Notes Receivable

The departments responsible for internal control of notes receivable are treasury and accounts receivable.

In the treasury department, a record of notes held from customers is maintained. A record is then sent to the accounts receivable division where a clerk makes the proper credits. A copy is sent to the general accounting department to reflect the charge to the control account—notes receivable. The treasurer keeps the notes until maturity date or until discounted with the bank. A subsidiary note register should be kept if the company receives a large number of such notes.

Cash and Bank Reconciliations

Cash is the lifeblood of the company. It is the center upon which the whole circle of business activity pivots. Here is the reservoir through which all flows—in and out. Preferably more of the former.

It is surprising to find that tests of cash receipts and cash disbursements are usually limited by management (through intermediaries) to monthly bank reconciliations. Nothing is more effective than unannounced, non-routine, spot tests of the cash-handling procedures (for that matter, *any* business procedure) by the highest authority within the company. Think of the impact made on an employee who *knows* there may be an impromptu test by the president of the company—at any time! Imagine the psychological impact if this is done periodically, but irregularly. Such tests of the application of payments on account—receivables and payables—encourage peak, honest, performance.

Bank reconciliations by and of themselves cannot stand alone as proof of cash authenticity. They prove only the activity within that one period and serve to lend to prior reconciliations substantiation of then-listed outstanding checks. The current reconciliation is technically unproved until the outstanding checks and uncredited deposits in transit appear.

Reconciliations should be tested by someone other than the original preparer.

Block-proofs of cash should also be used occasionally to test an entire year's transactions. Here, all deposits are matched to all receipts recorded (in total); and all recorded disbursements are matched to total bank charges for cleared checks and minor items, with consideration given to opening and closing transit items.

The theory behind the mechanics of the bank reconciliation is to update the bank figures (on a worksheet) to reflect all transit items that have not yet cleared the bank, as follows:

Bank shows a balance of	$ 10,500
Add deposits in transit	2,000
	12,500
Less checks outstanding (itemized)	600
Adjusted bank balance	$ 11,900
Balance per books shows	$ 11,909
Difference	$ 9 (more on books)

Having taken the preliminary steps of determining the deposits in transit (by checking the bank credits against recorded receipts) and the outstanding checks (by checking off all returned canceled checks against the listing of those issued or carried over), a remaining difference of $9 is noted.

In the following order, the most expedient ways to find this difference are to:

1. Look at the bank statement for any bank charge not yet recorded in the general ledger.
2. Look at the books for any $9 debit (or combination) on the books and not on the statement.
3. Match the bank's opening pickup balance to the closing one on the last statement to determine whether the $9 is indicative of a transposition. Specifically,
   a. Match deposits to receipts recorded.
   b. Check general-ledger footings and subtraction.
   c. Check summary postings into the general ledger from the original source.
   d. Check footings in the books of original entry (receipts, disbursements and general journal).
4. Having exhausted the above possibilities and still not having found the difference, check the face amount of each check to the amount charged by the bank (each check is canceled with a clearance date).

5. Now match the listing of the check to the actual check. (Steps 4 and 5 are interchangeable).
6. Not yet? Prove the bank's additions.
7. If still elusive, it probably has been missed above or a transposition error has been made in listing transit checks or deposits; or, it may be an error made last month that was missed.

FILE MAINTENANCE

How costly is the time wasted in frustrating searches for misfiled data, when initial precautions and firm rules might have assured quick access to, and retrieval of, needed documents by competent, authorized personnel. One of the most important, yet least emphasized, facets of the business enterprise is the establishment and proper maintenance of an effective, accurate filing system. Following are some suggestions for doing just that:

1. Establish firm rules for filing.
2. Provide adequate accessible filing space for current files.
3. Pinpoint responsibilities for filing and accessing files.
4. Follow legal requirements for record retention.
5. Establish an annual policy of removing outdated files.
6. Utilize flow charts when appropriate.
7. Have sufficient copies of documents (e.g., purchase orders, sales shipping papers, and all papers) ultimately tied to a sales or vendor's invoice, to allow for a complete numerical file of each document.

A List of File Categories. File maintenance embraces all of the following:

1. Sales invoices to customers—both alphabetic and numeric files.
2. Vendor invoices—alphabetic, sometimes with copy of paid voucher check or numbered voucher. Some firms keep invoices segregated in an unpaid file until paid.
3. Canceled checks—kept by month in reconciled batches. Do not intermingle different batches.
4. Correspondence files—for customers, vendors, others.
5. Permanent files—organizational information, legal documents, leases, minutes and deeds. These are usually kept in fireproof areas and accessibility is limited.

6. Other:
   a. Tax files.
   b. Payroll and personnel files.
   c. Backup for journal entries.
   d. Investment files—security transactions.
   e. Petty cash voucher files.
   f. Purchasing department files—such as supplies and bids (costs).
   g. Credit department files.
   h. Prior years' books of entry.
   i. Data from subsidiary companies owned.
   j. Advertising programs, literature.

Computer Files—Considerations.   Computer files present some unique problems that should be given special consideration. At a minimum, it is important to:

1. Have security protection—access, codes, permanent tapes or disks of programs and updated balance files for accounts receivables, payables, general ledger, payrolls. Keep enough of these changing files for reruns or accumulation runs, as needed for emergencies.
2. Keep hard copy until sure replacement hard copy is accurate, or as necessary for continuous file.
3. Be prepared for manual emergency work, if the computer goes down suddenly.
4. Pinpoint responsibility for keeping logs right through storage, updating software, and general housekeeping functions.

INTERNAL CONTROLS FOR A SMALL BUSINESS ENTERPRISE

There are many definitions of a small business. The most commonly accepted one is the U.S. Department of Commerce classification of an enterprise of fewer than 500 employees as a small business concern. Using this definition, there are millions of non-agricultural small business establishments in the United States.

In a small business organization of only a few people, little reliance can be placed on internal controls involving a segregation of duties, as it is among several persons in a large organization. However, that is no excuse for ignoring the importance of some degree of internal controls. Limited personnel who perform more than one related function and are associated with the handling of a company's money should trigger an assessment of the need for the establishment of at least a modified control system.

A plan of organization that provides at least a limited segregation of functional responsibilities within the constraint of a small staff should be developed. In a small business, the segregation is not so much between employees as between the owner and employees. An alert and able owner can provide about as much control as the segregation of duties does in a large organization.

The owner of a small business usually is the key person in its management. Unlike in a large organization, in the small business, the owner represents one of the effective components of a control system—that of personal observation. Principally, the owner can personally focus attention on selective areas of the business, such as reconciling the bank statement—one of the prime areas of control for a manager with limited time and staff.

The selection of a few areas for control is an important step. A tendency to over-control must be avoided in order to prevent a negative cost benefit allocation of time and expense. There is no need to control pencils and paper clips; the effort should be directed toward areas where the risk of error and material loss are greatest. Careful evaluation can uncover areas over which no control is exercised, but that are significant enough for procedures to be established for their control.

The checklists that follow have been developed as an economic and simplified guide for the responsible person in a small business to conduct periodic internal audits for the implementation and continuous review of the activities in the various areas of the business.

Too many companies give little if any thought to fraud prevention until after the fact. Then, any plan is a reaction to a specific situation rather than well-thought-out proactive steps and procedures to prevent misappropriation in any form from taking place in the future. Here, if not earlier, the accountant can come to the rescue with a skeleton plan that can be fleshed out with input from the owner and managers. Even this plan should be reconsidered periodically.

From these checklists, which include the significant areas of any business, can be selected those areas most important to the individual user. While a small business does not need accounting controls as sophisticated and expensive as those of a large company, neither can a small business be lax and informal with respect to procedures that can prevent possible mismanagement of assets or even embezzlement or fraud. The checklists indicate procedures that can lead to a suitable system.

Internal Controls Checklists for Small Business Entities

The following checklists provided in Forms 16-1 through 16-9 should help management keep tabs on what is and is not being done to prevent fraud and to foster efficiency. (After selecting the areas that are considered to be necessary for some degree of control, the user can refer back to sections in this chapter for additional detail about each checklist deemed appropriate for the particular enterprise.)

		N/A	Yes	No	Action or Remarks
	Form 16-1 **General Internal Control Checklist**				
1.	Are accounting records kept up to date and balanced monthly?				
2.	Is a standard chart of accounts with descriptive titles in use?				
3.	Are adequate and timely reports prepared to ensure control of operations? a. Daily reports? b. Monthly financial statements? c. Ratio analysis, such as cost of goods sold or gross profit? d. Comparison of actual results with budget? e. Cash and other projections?				
4.	Do the owner/directors take an active interest in the financial affairs and reports available?				
5.	Are personal expenses kept separate from business expenses?				
6.	Are employees who are in a position of trust bonded?				
7.	Are the director and employees required to take annual vacations, and are their duties covered by another?				
8.	Are monthly bank reconciliations reviewed by the owner and director?				

	N/A	Yes	No	Action or Remarks
9. Do employees appear to be adequately trained and technically competent?				
10. Are job descriptions prepared and updated regularly to reflect current thinking?				
11. Are volunteers properly trained and supervised?				
12. Is there appropriate separation of duties?				
13. Are minutes up to date and complete?				
14. Are authorized signatories for bank accounts designated with due diligence?				
15. Are account reconciliations performed regularly by personnel independent of the bank account?				
16. Are bank statements received directly by the person doing the bank reconciliation?				
17. Are the reconciliations reviewed by a qualified appropriate independent person?				
18. Is there a built-in system of checks and balances?				
19. Are governmental reporting requirements being complied with in a timely manner?				

Form 16-2				
Accounts Receivable and Sales Checklist				
	N/A	**Yes**	**No**	**Action or Remarks**
1. Are work orders, sales orders, shipping documents and invoices prenumbered and controlled?				
2. Would the existing system disclose any shipments being made without recording a sale (such as for sales on consignment and samples)?				
3. Is a credit check approved by owner?				
4. Are sales invoices reviewed for accuracy of price, terms, extensions and footings?				
5. Is an aged trial balance prepared monthly, reconciled to the general ledger and reviewed by the owner?				

6. Are monthly statements:
  a. Reviewed by owner?
  b. Mailed to all accounts?
    Does each account have a permanently assigned "account number"?
  c. Are zero and credit balance statements mailed?				

7. Are write-offs, credit memos and special terms approved by the owner and directors?				
8. Is there sufficient separation of the receipts function and the application of payments to the accounts receivable?				
9. Are notes and other receivables under separate control?				

10. If there are any pledges receivable:
  a. Are they properly recorded?
  b. Is there collection follow-up?				

11. Is there a collections method in place either in-house or by a reputable agency?				
12. Is a schedule of late charge fees in place?				
13. Is there a schedule of charges for bounced checks?				

Form 16-3 Cash Receipts Checklist				
	N/A	Yes	No	**Action or Remarks**
1. Does the accounting system provide means to identify, classify, record and report cash transactions?				
2. Is mail opened by director or owner or someone other than the bookkeeper?				
3. Are receipts copied with payment and listed prior to turning them over to the bookkeeper?				
4. Are they subsequently traced to the cash receipts journal?				
5. Does the client have adequate documentation of cash receipts?				
6. Are checks immediately endorsed "for deposit only" and deposited promptly and intact?				
7. Are over-the-counter receipts controlled, as by cash register and prenumbered receipts?				
8. Are these reviewed by owner or director?				
9. Is there a follow-up policy established to collect on bounced checks?				
10. Are over-the-counter cash receipts compared against register tapes and a count of sales tickets?				
11. Does the bank confirm deposits directly to someone independent of the cash deposit function?				
12. Does the bank alert the cash manager to incoming wires? Are they recorded properly?				
13. Are cash receipts managed according to policy?				

	N/A	Yes	No	Action or Remarks
Form 16-4 **Inventories Checklist**				
1. Are perpetual inventories maintained?				
2. Are they verified periodically by someone not normally in charge of inventories?				
3. Where perpetual records are not in use: a. Are periodic physical counts taken by responsible employees? b. Is owner exercising control by review of gross profit margins?				
4. Are physical facilities organized to discourage pilferage by employees and others?				
5. Are policies established to ensure all employee purchases are approved by a manager? And properly logged?				
6. Are off-premises inventories controlled?				
7. Is customer's merchandise on the premises physically segregated and under accounting control?				
8. Are inventories reviewed periodically for old, obsolete, or overstocked items?				

	N/A	Yes	No	Action or Remarks
Form 16-5 **Accounts Payable, Purchases and Disbursements Checklist**				
1. Are prenumbered purchase orders used and are these approved by the owner or director?				
2. Are competitive bids required above prescribed limits?				
3. Are payments made from original invoices?				
4. Are supplier statements compared with recorded liabilities?				
5. Are all disbursements made by prenumbered checks and accounted for by someone independent of the disbursement function?				

6. Is the owner's or director's signature required on all checks?
   a. Does owner or director sign checks only when they are accompanied by original supporting documentation?
   b. Is the documentation adequately canceled to prevent reuse?
   c. Do the persons responsible for the expenditure sign "ok to pay"?
   d. Is the computer set to note the date and amount of the last payment on scheduled payments (e.g., phone and utilities bills) so that variations in billing are apparent?				

		Form 16-5 *Cont'd.* Accounts Payable, Purchases and Disbursements Checklist		
	N/A	**Yes**	**No**	**Action or Remarks**
7. Is there evidence that the following items have been checked before invoices are paid? a. Prices, trade discounts and sales tax? b. Receipt of goods or services?				
8. Are voided checks properly redeposited and stored?				
9. Is the disbursement officer independent of the accounting function?				
10. Is there a petty cash fund with one person responsible for its security and disbursement?				
11. Are vouchers used for petty cash disbursement?				
12. Are periodic reconciliations of the petty cash fund conducted by someone independent of the function?				
13. Is the size of the petty cash fund appropriate for its anticipated use?				

Form 16-6 Investments Checklist				
	N/A	**Yes**	**No**	**Action or Remarks**
1. Is access to certificates, notes and other investment documents carefully spelled out and appropriately monitored?				
2. Is the physical possession of investment securities appropriately safeguarded?				
3. Is there a formalized investment policy?				
4. Is income from investments accounted for monthly?				
5. Is there effective utilization of temporary excess funds?				
6. Are investment securities of the type specified by management policy?				
7. Do the investment maturities fit the current cash flow plan?				
8. Do the returns of the portfolio warrant the risks?				
9. Are brokers' statements reconciled to the general ledger and the investments ledger by someone independent of the function?				
10. Are brokerage confirmations sent directly to someone independent of the investment function?				
11. Are periodic inventory counts made of the securities portfolio?				
12. In case of not-for-profit organizations: a. Is dual control exercised over certificates? b. Is there a written investment policy? c. Does the board approve sales and purchases? d. Is the return on investment checked periodically by the board?				

Form 16-7 **Property, Plant and Equipment Checklist**				
	N/A	**Yes**	**No**	**Action or Remarks**
1. Are there detailed and updated records to support general-ledger totals for assets and accumulated depreciation?				
2. Are the owner or directors acquainted with assets owned?				
3. Is approval required for sale or acquisition of assets?				
4. Are there physical safeguards against theft or loss of small tools and other highly portable equipment?				
5. Is there a policy distinguishing capital and expense items?				
6. Is there a policy regarding security of building and well-being of employees?				

Form 16-8 **Insurance Checklist**				
	N/A	**Yes**	**No**	**Action or Remarks**
1. Is insurance maintained in all major cases and is this coverage reviewed periodically by a qualified individual?				
2. Is insurance coverage adapted to needs of the specific type of organization?				
3. Are insurance claims checked carefully?				
4. Fidelity bonding helps to limit the loss on fraud; however, is there an understanding of just what the insurance covers and when to file claims?				

	N/A	Yes	No	Action or Remarks

Form 16-9
Payroll Checklist

	N/A	Yes	No	Action or Remarks
1. Is owner or director acquainted with all employees and does he or she approve all new hires and changes of pay rates?				
2. Is there a folder for each employee containing full documentation, including an employment application, W4, authorizations for deductions and signed employee handbook.				
3. Are there controls to prevent the payroll from being inflated without the knowledge of owner or director by fictitious employees, padded hours or inappropriate overtime?				
4. Does the owner or director sign all payroll checks and approve all state taxes and IRS deposits?				
5. If payroll is prepared by a bank or service bureau, does the owner or director of the company periodically review each check and related journals prior to distribution to employees?				
6. Are voided checks properly redeposited and stored?				
7. Is the payroll bank reconciliation balanced by someone other than the preparer?				
8. Is the payroll paid from a separate bank account?				
9. Is someone responsible for keeping current on change in payroll tax code laws?				
10. Is someone in charge of "scheduling" eligibility for and payment of simplified employee pensions (SEPs)?				

EMBEZZLEMENT

Embezzlement is the fraudulent appropriation of property by a person whom management has trusted. *Trusted* is the key word. A company can be losing money before suspecting that an embezzlement might be taking place, because this crime is usually committed by someone in a position of trust. Losses can be small amounts taken from a cash register or large sums of money stolen through manipulating the books. A set of simple controls built into the accounting system can prevent an embezzling operation. At the least, proper controls can document incriminating evidence in the absence of which it would be difficult to estimate a loss for insurance purposes or to prove in the courts that the losses resulted from a crime.

Companies with fewer than 100 employees tend to be more vulnerable to internal thefts because the smaller company is generally more lax about internal controls than a larger establishment would be. If employees feel that they are not getting a fair deal and are not being treated with respect, they may feel justified in getting what they feel they deserve, which may be anything from products or equipment and supplies to increasingly larger sums of cash. Therefore, just as in health care for the individual, *prevention* of disease within an organization must be the watchword.

Detecting and Preventing Embezzlement

This discussion reviews procedures for the detection and prevention of dishonest practices. It can be helpful first to understand a few of the usual methods of embezzlers in diverting company funds to their own pockets. Such an understanding can be a framework for developing the record keeping and control procedures to safeguard the company's money and other property vulnerable to misappropriation by an employee. (In general, however, an embezzler's methods are limited only by his or her creativity.)

Authority in Important Areas.   As mentioned previously, by definition an embezzler is usually a trusted employee enjoying the complete confidence of his or her employer. Usually, the embezzler has authority in such important areas as managing the checkbook. The easiest opportunity is sales for cash with no recording of the transaction in the books and no relevant paperwork. Prenumbered invoices or simply cash register receipts can be used for all sales with appropriate monitoring procedures to ensure that cash sales are being recorded. In addition, when employees know written records are maintained, the temptation to embezzle is lessened.

Lapping.   A complicated method of embezzlement is termed *lapping.* Lapping involves temporarily withholding receipts, such as payments by a customer on accounts receivable, and is a continuing process that usually starts with a small amount and runs into thousands of dollars before it is detected.

Example: An employee opens mail or receives cash and checks as payment on open accounts. The employee pockets a $100 cash payment by a customer named Paul. To avoid Paul's complaining at a later time about failure for his account to be credited, $100 is next taken from a $200 subsequent payment by a customer named Peter and credited to Paul's account. The embezzler pockets the $100 difference. (Note that the amount pyramids; it has to in order for the embezzler to continue to profit.) The lapping procedure continues with the employee absconding with increasingly larger amounts of money involving a steadily increasing number of customer accounts.

Prevention requires detailed recordkeeping procedures of invoices and other supporting working papers and periodic unscheduled audits of the accounts, along with confirmation of accounts receivables. Without adequate internal control procedures, detection of lapping is difficult and can continue for years. One red flag, however, is the discovery that an employee is keeping personal records of transactions outside of the established accounting system. Another is not taking vacations For this reason, many companies and organizations such as banks and brokerage firms require employees responsible for funds management to take regular vacations; it has happened that the substitute employee discovers irregularities. Beware of brown baggers who make a habit of not leaving the premises for lunch—it may not be just an economy measure.

Check-Kiting. Check-kiting is one of the most popular operations in small and large companies alike. For a successful check-kiting operation, the employee must be in the position both to write checks and to make deposits in two or more bank accounts. One account is the embezzler's personal account and the other is the business checking account.

The check-kiter plays the float (e.g., the number of days between the deposit of a check and collection of funds). There may be several days between the date when a check drawn on Bank A is deposited in Bank B and the date the check clears Bank A for payment. An easy kite is accomplished simply by cashing a check at Bank B and then covering the amount on the morning of the day the check is expected to reach Bank A.

As the process is repeated the kited checks become increasingly large. More cash is withdrawn from Bank B and the kiting continues as long as the shortage is covered on time in Bank A. Finally, the kite breaks; this occurs when Bank A refuses to honor a check because the funds on deposit are insufficient to cover the kited check, or because the check reached Bank A a day earlier than usual.

A temporary kite can be used by a dishonest employee who has stolen cash in a separate operation. The cash shortage can be concealed at the end of an accounting period by depositing a kited check into the company account. This deposit brings the bank balance into reconciliation with the book balance on the statement date.

The best preventive measure against kiting (or to detect suspected kiting) is for the owner of the business to request cut-off statements from the bank at periodic intervals which, in turn, should be irregular intervals.

Payroll Fraud.   Payroll frauds are a frequent source of loss (and one of the more lucrative for the embezzler). The usual practice is to add the names of relatives or fictitious individuals to the company payroll, enabling the embezzler to draw several weekly paychecks instead of one. The best preventive measure is a policy that no person is added to the payroll without the personal authorization of the owner, or a responsible personnel manager in the organization. Also, frequent and regular payroll audits can reveal more paychecks being drawn than the company has employees.

Dummy Suppliers.   A typical embezzling procedure is for the dishonest employee to open an account on the books for a dummy supplier and issue checks to the nonexistent supplier for fictitious purchases. Established purchase procedures and a tight inventory controls system can discourage an employee from using false vouchers to process purchases of nonexistent merchandise.

WAYS TO DETER FRAUDULENT FINANCIAL REPORTING

In a survey conducted by the Association of Certified Fraud Examiners (ACFE) people were asked to respond to a question relating to the prevention of fraud in financial reporting. The organization noted that in the wake of Enron, there are calls for reform in the way CPAs conduct their audits. The question is, how to go about it. After compiling a list of possible solutions, the ACFE asked, "Which one of these measures do you think would likely have the greatest impact on deterring fraudulent financial reporting?" The measures and percentages of respondents who chose them follow:

- 28% Encouraging whistleblowers.
- 25% Surprise audits.
- 24% Assigning at least one certified fraud examiner to every public audit.
- 13% Requiring that auditors diligently inquire about fraud during the audit.
- 9% Requiring personal financial disclosures from insiders.

Clues for the Alert Fraudbuster

A number of clues can alert the owner or manager of a business to suspect dishonest practices:

1. An unusual increase in sales returns can conceal accounts receivable payments.
2. Unusual bad-debt write-offs can cover a fraudulent practice.
3. A decline in credit sales that is unusual can indicate possible unrecorded sales.
4. An unexpected large drop in profits or increase in expenses can be a red flag.
5. An increasing rate of slow collections of receivables can conceal an embezzlement.

In addition to an accounting system that incorporates a system of internal controls, there are precautions an owner can take to reduce the possibility of fraudulent losses:

1. A careful check of prospective employees' backgrounds.
2. Knowing the employees' personal lifestyles, insofar as possible.
3. Having company mail addressed to a post office box to which only the owner has access.
4. Having only the owner or a key person collect and open company mail.
5. Allowing only the owner to manage the funds, write checks, and make deposits.
6. Conducting periodic examination of all canceled checks, especially the endorsements on them.
7. Requiring that unusual discounts and bad-debt write-offs be approved by the owner, or manager.
8. Making sure that all employees responsible for company funds are bonded.
9. Making sure, if possible, that the preparation of the payroll and payment of employees are done by different persons, especially if cash is disbursed on payday.
10. Never signing blank checks!

Chapter 17

The CPA as Financial Planner

CONTENTS

Setting Fees for Financial Planning	**17.02**
Inflation and Financial Planning	**17.02**
Who Needs a Financial Plan?	**17.03**
Planning a Constructive Dialogue with the Client	**17.03**
Accelerating the Client Planning Process	**17.05**
Seven Key Areas of Financial Planning	**17.05**
Sample Questions for the Planning Process	**17.12**
Ramifications of Advising Clients on Investments	**17.14**
Investment Knowledge	**17.14**
Risk Tolerance	**17.15**
Market Risk	**17.19**
Asset Allocation and the Spread of Risk	**17.20**
Common Investment Mistakes	**17.30**
Good Advice	**17.31**
Accreditation Requirements for the PFS Designation	**17.32**

"Faced with a turbulent stock market, rising energy prices and other signs of an economy in flux, Americans are increasingly worried about their finances. And though individual investors admit to financial planners' expertise, few consult one." This is according to a survey commissioned by the American Institute of Certified Public Accountants' (AICPA's) personal financial specialist examination committee. The survey polled 636 Americans ages 18 to over 55 with annual income of more than $75,000.

Almost all respondents (91 percent) said they manage their finances themselves, doing their own research and obtaining advice from family, friends, the Internet, or a broker. The AICPA suggested that CPA/PFS practitioners may see potential market opportunities in this and the survey's other findings.

The CPA who is not a PFS might be interested in seeing that this is not an overcrowded niche. At present, of the 330,000 AICPA members, there are approximately 3,000 who hold the designation. For CPAs interested in obtaining the Personal Financial Specialist (PFS) designation, the requirements are given at the end of this chapter.

Setting Fees for Financial Planning

The idea of financial planning is popular. There are many plan types available, with costs from zero to thousands of dollars. Fees are usually based on a double matrix of how much money a client has and how complicated and complete the plan needs to be. Only the financial specialist can determine how much time and paperwork should be generated by a specific client's plan. Clearly, financial considerations are always a concern with a fee-related product. A survey of local fellow professionals about planner fees should help an individual entering the financial planning niche to price his or her services to scale.

Inflation and Financial Planning

A major obstacle to anyone's financial future is inflation. For example, a million dollars is not what it once was. As a matter of fact, it's about $150,000 in 1950 dollars. However, that $150,000, indexed in the Dow Jones Industrials, would be $3,000,000 now. Appropriately invested, the client's money reaps the benefits of:

1. Asset growth.
2. Income enhancement.
3. Inflation hedge.

Inflation is a major issue, but if the CPA/PFS prepares a good financial plan, with appropriately allocated investments, that plan becomes a buffer, equalizer and fighter against inflation and other risks. A millionaire today must not be cavalier with money, or he or she will not be a millionaire for very long. The planner must address these serious and ongoing client needs. Just to keep pace, the individual must have a plan that reaps at least a modest return on investment.

WHO NEEDS A FINANCIAL PLAN?

The CPA/PFS should begin with a financial plan for each client. It is a blueprint for that client's future—tailored to that individual's financial needs. In a survey of clients, friends, and professional associates, the chances are each of them supports the principles of financial planning.

Everyone needs a financial plan. As the AICPA survey confirmed, the chances are very good that few of these individuals have completed comprehensive financial plans. It is *planning* and *action* on those plans that lead to financial success.

Financial success is usually described as *the ability to meet current expenses, fund college educations and enjoy a prosperous retirement.* Weighing, evaluating, and accomplishing such goals is the responsibility of the planning specialist who can help address economic problems. The tools in the form of financial planning are available for anyone.

PLANNING A CONSTRUCTIVE DIALOGUE WITH THE CLIENT

The clients come to the office and have a meeting centered around a basic financial plan prepared for that meeting. The plan is in a format suited to the needs of the client. It concretely addresses the college saving needs, an asset allocation for the savings account, and a look at the investments in the retirement plan. The goal is to create happy and financially secure clients.

You have heard repeatedly that the clients have considered all of these financial concerns, but they have not been formalized. You as a financial planner can do much to make the session a success for the clients, with benefits that can create a lifetime pattern of planning and investments:

1. Ask the clients why they are seeking advice.
2. Determine as clearly as possible what the client perceives the family's needs to be. (It is important to establish the clients in the planning loop from the very beginning, even if they have only vague ideas of their needs.)
3. Explain in detail the planning points. The primary concern is to assess the financial security of the client.

4. Lead a frank discussion of successes and concerns with the clients.

5. Help them evaluate how closely the planning suggestions are to how they visualize their situation, and ask what they will do to implement the action points.

6. Help the clients weigh and prioritize, based on educated judgment, what is best for them. (Of course, the client ultimately has the personal responsibility for acting or not acting on advice.)

Need Based Planning

Aspects of the financial planning process include:

1. Current needs.
2. College funds.
3. Retirement.
4. Trusts and wills.
5. Insurance.
6. Mortgages.
7. Gifts and charities.
8. Asset allocation.

But clients all have different needs. The task is to determine these needs and to evaluate the level of sophistication and the amount of detail each case requires. Some clients need only a basic, boilerplate plan; others require extensive, tailored plans.

For example, a young couple several years into their working lives requires a basic plan with fundamental goals to see them along the proper path to a good financial future. On the other hand, the owner of a private company with 200 employees and a 30-year record of sales has vastly more elaborate requirements as he or she zeros in on retirement and succession planning.

The financial planner may start the client with basics, but learn that a more elaborate plan is required. CPAs are uniquely placed to gauge the extent of each client's needs because of their familiarity with every aspect of the clients' financial situation.

As the clients' assets grow and their lives become more complex, their plan will require revision and reworking. Planning is a dynamic process that involves everything from mundane number-crunching to the most trendy visualization. In other words, it is an ongoing process subject to change. The clients should understand that having a plan is a major step forward but that the plan will evolve and change in light of the unexpected events and changes that everyone experiences.

ACCELERATING THE CLIENT PLANNING PROCESS

An endless array of self-help books, computer software, and online applications can be tailored to a personalized product. The CPA is concerned primarily with getting a plan in place and implementing it; form means very little exclusive of function. A consistent review process dramatically improves the product and moves the plan toward accomplishment. The client's life changes and, as a consequence, so does the financial plan.

Fine tuning the process of financial planning is true value added from a professional standpoint in the CPA /client relationship. Together, they can determine whether the goals are being met, surpassed or not achieved. The plan should be updated and revised periodically to incorporate changes in the client's financial picture. Information useful in a plan update would be:

1. Performance on an annual basis of all securities accounts.
2. Salary changes that can affect a plan immediately.
3. Sizable gifts of financial or other assets that change the client's net worth.
4. Inheritances or bequests that have a material effect on the client's financial picture.
5. Changes in rates of saving or spending that alter the course of the plan.
6. Tax or contribution changes affecting the retirement plan.

SEVEN KEY AREAS OF FINANCIAL PLANNING

Some subjects appear in any financial plan. The client picture evolves from a format that follows this order or something similar. However, the contents are tailored for each client, either directly by the accountant or with the help of other financial service industry professionals. These subjects are:

1. *Net worth*—Establish with total clarity the client's current financial picture. Otherwise, there is no basis upon which to complete a plan. Many clients do not understand and therefore are unaware of their own financial profile. Clients are amazed to learn the simple fact that net worth is simply all assets minus all liabilities.

   Net worth is the total of the client's equity in a home, all securities in and out of retirement plans, value of business and other real estate holdings, cash value of insurance, collectibles and personal property minus all bills, taxes and loans owed. A simple net worth statement is created, but it can be broken down to more specific classifications, if needed. (See Form 17-1.)

Form 17-1
Figuring the Client's Net Worth

1. Personal Assets	Dollar Value		
Primary Residence Market Value	$		
Secondary Residence Market Value	$		
Personal Property:			
Furnishings	$		
Vehicles	$		
Jewelry	$		
2. Investment Assets			
Market Value of Securities Accounts	$		
Market Value of Retirement Accounts	$		
Market Value of Collectibles	$		
Market Value of Bank Accounts	$		
Cash Value of Life Insurance Policies	$		
Cash Value of Debts Owed to Client	$		
Cash Value of Business Owned by Client	$		
Market Value of Investment Real Estate	$		
TOTAL ASSETS	$		
3. Liabilities			
Outstanding Loan Balances:		**Dollar Cost**	
Real Estate		$	
Business		$	
Vehicles		$	
Consumer		$	
All Others		$	
Taxes Payable:			
Real Estate		$	
Income Tax		$	
TOTAL LIABILITIES		$	
4. Net Worth Calculation			**Net Worth**
Assets			$
−Liabilities			$
=Net Worth			$

For example:

a. *Liquid versus illiquid assets.* Most clients do not understand liquidity. Money market funds, most stocks and bonds and mutual funds are totally liquid. If the need is there, they can be liquidated in minutes. Many other investments are relatively illiquid—limited partnerships, private placements, most real estate and some insurance products—because they take a while to sell or liquidate.

b. *Investment versus personal assets.* Brokerage accounts are definitely investment assets. Most collectibles, such as antiques and art works, however dearly the client may prize them, are in the final analysis personal assets.

c. *Active versus passive investments.* Active investments are those over which the CPA and the client have management control. Passive investments are investments whose performance cannot be directly influenced. An IRA account, for example, is an active investment because it is self-directed. Social Security, on the other hand, is passive because the individual cannot impact what the managers do with the contributions. (This is true at the present time, but that could change.)

2. **Social security**—The client's Social Security statement should be checked to confirm and establish benefits. Are all contributions accounted for, and are projected benefits calculated correctly? This may be done for all members of the client's family.

3. **Retirement planning**—Most financial planning somehow relates to retirement planning. Clients may have little notion of how well or poorly they are prepared for retirement. Several planning steps help to clarify this picture.

a. Clients should be required to calculate, as closely as possible, their financial needs in retirement. The financial planner should remind the clients that many current needs during the earning years are unrelated to retirement needs—commuter expenses, business attire, lunch and entertainment expenses, business usage books and journals; the list is long.

b. It is important to determine whether any corporate or government retirement plans have Cost of Living Adjustments (COLAs) attached to them.

c. Clients must keep current concerning the deductibility of any of the various voluntary contribution plans they may be eligible for; they should not ignore a deductible or pre-tax contribution at the expense of a post-tax plan.

d. Both the CPA and the client should keep current with all retirement legislation. (See Form 17-2.)

Form 17-2
Retirement Planning Questionnaire

1. Where are you planning to live when you retire?
   City _____   State _____

2. Can you pay off all your debts before or at retirement?   Yes ☐   No ☐

3. Are your securities (personal wealth) and self-directed
   retirement (pension income) accounts allocated in a manner
   reflecting your future wants/needs as determined with
   the CPA?   Yes ☐   No ☐

4. Have you and your CPA addressed current and future federal
   and state income tax considerations and consequences?
   Yes ☐   No ☐

5. Have you and your CPA thoroughly and accurately mapped
   out your retirement expenses/income by projecting a current
   and future budget?   Yes ☐   No ☐

6. Will you continue to work for fulfillment and/or supplemental
   income?   Yes ☐   No ☐

---

4. *College planning*—Any client who has the responsibility for educating a
   child should address that obligation as soon as possible. The importance
   and magnitude of the event is an opportunity for the financial planner to
   make a genuinely valuable contribution to a client's life.

   College planning is not an area for procrastination. College costs have
   grossly outpaced the rate of inflation in this country. The notion of a
   child's somehow earning his or her way through college, as earlier generations did, is now completely out of the realm of possibility. Any child
   who can earn the costs of a median priced private school should probably
   be setting up his or her own business.

   Taking into consideration the age of the child/children, the accountant
   and the clients should, among other considerations, discuss when and if
   the student(s) should become part of the financial planning process, and
   whether to discuss with them the extent of the financial help they can
   expect.

   Form 17-3 is designed as a questionnaire to aid the accountant in determining what the clients' planning needs may be. The CPA may then re-
   phrase the questions to submit to clients for their input. (See Form 17-3.)

Form 17-3
College Planning Questionnaire

1. How many children will the client help through college?

2. How much will the college of choice cost?

3. What is the current age of the children?

4. How will the client get started to meet the obligations?

5. How will you, the CPA, help determine the investment choices?

6. What investment selections will you help the client use for a small child, a high school student, or a young adult?

7. What level of risk is the client prepared to assume with the college investments?

8. What investment strategies are appropriate for each student's goals?

9. Where do you, the CPA, go if you need help?

10. How do you assist the client in learning about scholarships and other financial aid?

11. How do you help the client and student reduce college costs without impairing the educational experience?

5. ***Insurance and employee benefits***—All insurance and benefit information should be identified and evaluated with two distinct goals in mind:

   a. From a practical standpoint, does the client have enough, too much or just the right amount of coverage for perceived needs? From a financial planning standpoint, needs must be addressed relative to all forms of insurance—life, fire and casualty, homeowners or renters, automobile, umbrella liability, medical, dental, long-term health care, personal property and disability.

   b. Insurance planning must also be addressed from a financial feasibility standpoint. Insurance represents a very significant financial investment. The CPA can address every opportunity to obtain the best for the least for the client.

      — The client must become aware of the fact that to have inexpensive automobile insurance with a company that is rated low for paying claims is no bargain.

      — On the other hand, to buy an umbrella liability policy (which is permitted for bundling two or three of the primary types of insurance—life, property, and automotive—with one company) is great financial planning and money management.

      —Worksheets can help in determining how much of each type of insurance the client needs and can afford.

      — For variable life and annuity products, the mutual fund selection can be determined using an asset allocation matrix that isolates the client's risk parameters. (See Form 17-4.)

6. ***Estate planning (wills, trusts, and estate documents)***—Determination should be made of needs from an estate planning standpoint, then an attorney should be selected to put together the final product. The resulting documents should be reviewed each time the financial plan is reviewed.

   Clients should always be cognizant of the fact that *estate planning is as dynamic as financial planning.* The list of life changes they go through from an estate planning standpoint are seemingly endless. For example, they may change their minds about who:

   a. Gets what.

   b. Administers their estate.

   c. Is the successor trustee.

   d. Rears the children if the parents die.

7. ***Taxes***—The CPA can do more than any other financial planner to accomplish tax-related goals for clients. He or she can help minimize taxes, invest for a tax exempt or tax deferral goal, determine exemptions, prepare forms, anticipate problems and resolve all tax issues. (See Form 17-5.)

Form 17-4
Insurance and Employee Benefits Checklist

1. Life Insurance Coverage	
Face Amount	$
Cash Value	$
Annual Premium	$
Carrier	
Type of Policy	
2. Disability Income Coverage	
Amount of Benefit	$
Annual Premium	$
Carrier	
Type of Policy	
3. Employee Benefits	
Pension Income	$
Cost of Living Adjustment Provision (If Provided)	%
Survivor Benefit	%/$
Social Security Income	$
Survivor Benefits	%/$
Other Employee Benefits	$
Other Retirement Benefits	$
4. Health Insurance Coverage	
Amount of Benefits	$
Annual Premium	$
Carrier	
Type and Scope of Coverage	
5. Dental Insurance Coverage	
Amount of Benefits	$
Annual Premium	$
Carrier	
Type and Scope of Coverage	
6. Long-Term Medical Coverage	
Amount of Benefits	$
Annual Premium	$
Carrier	
Type and Scope of Coverage	

Form 17-5
Client Tax Pointer Menu and Checklist

_____ 1. Income Planning

_____ 2. Retirement Planning

_____ 3. Investment Planning

_____ 4. Estate Planning

_____ 5. Education/Child Planning

What the Client Can Do to Facilitate the Process:

_____ 1. Keep clean expense records.

_____ 2. Save all financial statements.

_____ 3. Report any significant financial changes.

_____ 4. Address securities gain or loss before year end.

_____ 5. Schedule a mid-year planning review.

_____ 6. Practice responsible document control.

_____ 7. Collect and retain all records and organize them.

_____ 8. Leave nothing to the last minute.

SAMPLE QUESTIONS FOR THE PLANNING PROCESS

Form 17-6 provides an assortment of financial planning questions only the clients can answer because the questions are case specific. They should consider all of these questions regarding their financial status carefully because the answers are germane to their financial plan.

Answers to each of these questions may be written prior to their first financial planning meeting if the CPA has worked with them previously or after an introductory financial planning session (if they are relatively new clients).

Of course, the individual CPA/PFS will be in a position to determine whether any, all or a portion of these forms and questions are appropriate for individual clients. For that reason, they are on the CD-ROM (see Form 17-6).

Form 17-6
Financial Planning Checklist

1. Where do you work? _____

2. Your title _____ Length of service _____

3. How much is your annual income? _____

   Where does it come from? ____ _____

4. If you are responsible for paying for educational expenses, for whom?
   _____

5. When do you plan to retire? _____ _____

6. How much in post-tax dollars is required? _____

7. What pensions do you have? _____
   _____

8. What is the estimated pension income? _____

9. Is there a survivor benefit? _____

10. What self-directed plans do you have? _____

11. How much are they worth? _____

12. What are the current investments? _____

13. Do you believe these investments are appropriately allocated at present?
    _____

14. What long-term disability income coverage and life insurance do you
    carry? _____

15. Do you have a will and, if appropriate, a living trust with unified credit
    provisions? _____

16. What are your personal assets? _____

17. How much are they worth? _____

18. How much money do you save each year? _____

    Where does it go? _____

19. Do you consider your risk profile conservative, moderate, or aggressive?
    _____

20. Do you consider this allocation suitable for your risk profile? _____
    _____

RAMIFICATIONS OF ADVISING CLIENTS ON INVESTMENTS

The Investment Advisers Act of 1940 requires investment advisers to register with the Securities and Exchange Commission (SEC) and comply with certain requirements, unless exempted from registering or excepted from the definition of investment adviser.

The act defines "investment adviser" as a person who provides advice about securities for compensation, as part of a business. The definition specifically excludes the activities of an accountant that are *solely incidental* to the individual's practice of accounting. However, the SEC and the staff have traditionally interpreted the exclusion narrowly.

As more CPAs are providing comprehensive financial planning to clients (which almost necessarily requires providing advice about securities), they are increasingly registering as investment advisers. Much of the remainder of this chapter deals with information that should help the financial adviser be aware of what is entailed in becoming an investment adviser.

In 1996, changes to the act created a threshold for registering as an investment adviser with the SEC. Advisers who provide investment advice and manage more than $25 million in assets must register with the SEC. Those who manage less than $25 million are regulated by the individual states. The AICPA points out that the decision to register and the ensuing requirements involve complex legal issues. With this in mind, it is advisable to consult an attorney regarding the attendant legal issues.

As outlined at the end of the chapter, the AICPA also allows some credit toward its PFS designation for passing the examination for the following: Certified Financial Planner, Chartered Financial Consultant, Chartered Financial Analyst, National Association of Securities Dealers (NASD) Series 65, NASD Series 66 and NASD Series 7.

INVESTMENT KNOWLEDGE

The client often feels that investing has a language unto its own and that that language is as elusive as Sanskrit. In a survey to determine investment literacy and behavior, a study by the New York Stock Exchange concluded that few Americans know the basics of investing, and fewer still know how to put them to work. The CPA has a greater background familiarity with these basics because of the tax consequences of investing, but most of the experience with the investment process is passive—responding to the tax forms of clients.

The CPA can help the client along by focusing on three big concerns:

1. Determine the client's life goals.
2. Formulate an investment plan and put it into place.
3. Determine which investments will help reach those goals.

The clients should fill in their knowledge gap with a plan that teaches them how to make sound, informed financial decisions necessary to achieve their goals. This is key for retirement planning because:

1. Many employers are abandoning corporate managed pension plans.
2. Social Security faces a problematic future at best.
3. Companies are increasingly implementing retirement plans that place the burden of investment decisions on the plan participants.

Developing a sound financial plan is a value-added service for the client because it facilitates making the right investment decisions for the client's future. Because participants' feelings about this newly acquired responsibility run the gamut from exciting to horrific, the financial planner plays a key role in helping them determine the appropriate investment choices.

An endless array of investment information is readily available. Knowledgeable use of that information is the goal. There are right and wrong ways to advise the client to invest money. Investing is not as subjective as one might suppose, especially as perceived by the regulatory agencies.

Knowledgeable investing is informed investing. Informed investing is more than simply reading weekly business magazines. Planning specialists must establish a regular and systematic investigative process regarding the workings of all the investments selected for client portfolios.

Well-chosen professional investment publications, especially from SEC-regulated sources of information such as brokerage firms and mutual fund companies, are an excellent source of information for risk evaluation and other expertise. Professional financial planners provide added value for the client because they are able to sift through the myriad sources of information. They can then make an educated judgment regarding which sources to rely upon and which sources to ignore. Clients are rarely competent at performing a task like this because they do not have the resources or the background to do so.

Risk Tolerance

Determining risk tolerance is a nearly impossible task for most individuals because few are aware of the factors that should be taken into consideration. Objectivity is essential when selecting investments to fund an individual or family's future. Risk control at either extreme—conservative or high risk—demands the most objective analysis.

The value added by professional financial planning cannot be exaggerated. In the prevailing self-service approach to personal finance, millions of investors become sitting ducks for investment fraud and abuse. Much of this is a direct result of not understanding risk. An accountant offers all of his or her clients, at minimum:

1. A sounding board for each investment selection.
2. A leg up on specific areas of financial planning.
3. Knowledgeable product information.
4. Expertise about the investment industry.

Establishing the Client's Tolerance for Risk

The investor must be required to take a close look at risk. What is meant by risk? Some basic factors must be taken into consideration to establish risk in a client's financial plan, specifically, the client's:

1. Age.
2. Income and net worth.
3. Knowledge of securities.
4. "Pain tolerance."

While the first three factors are easy to measure, the fourth is a factor very difficult to determine. The client may have a conservative, moderate, speculative or high risk profile. Estimating his or her reaction to financial pressure is very important. If the client invests within a comfort level, then he or she will successfully endure the relative highs and lows of investing and the sometimes erratic behavior of the financial markets.

Crystallizing the Client Investment Profile

To acquire a clear picture of a client's investment profile, the CPA can do the following:

1. Require the client to consider the questions in Form 17-6.
2. Have the client prepare written responses to the questions in Form 17-7A.
3. Consider the factors pinpointed in Form 17-7B.
4. Meet with the client to interpret these answers.
5. Formulate an action plan.

Form 17-7A
Investment Profile

1. How secure do you consider your income and its potential for growth?

2. Do you think your present investments are right for you? Give each of them a report card grade ranging from A to F.

3. Total your fixed (financial obligations that do not change) and variable (financial obligations that do change) expenses.

4. How old are you? _____

5. How many dependents do you have? _____

6. At what age would you like to retire? (See Form 17-2.) _____

7. Estimate your required retirement income.

8. Calculate your net worth exclusive of home equity. (See Form 17-1.)

9. Do you need help to reduce the level of debt and put a savings plan into effect?

10. How do you feel about the ups and downs of the stock market?

11. How do you feel about the risk of losing money in the stock market?

12. Do you prefer low risk/low return investments to more volatile, high risk/high return ones?

13. Do you think you have the patience to see a financial plan through from beginning to end?

Form 17-7B
Investment Profile

1. Assess the security of the client's income and its potential for growth.

   _____

   _____

   _____

2. Examine the client's past investment profile and prepare a report card on these investments.

   _____

   _____

   _____

3. Determine the client's fixed and variable expenses.

   _____

   _____

   _____

4. How old is the client? _____

5. How many dependents does the client have? _____

6. At what age would the client like to retire? _____

7. Estimate the client's required retirement income and project upward for inflation. _____

   _____

   _____

8. Calculate the net worth of the client exclusive of home equity.

   _____

   _____

9. Does the client need help to reduce the level of debt and put a savings plan into effect? _____

   _____

10. What is the client's response to market volatility and how does the client perceive it as a factor in determining risk? _____

    _____

    _____

11. What is the client's response to losing money? _____

    _____

12. Does the client prefer low risk/low return investments? _____

    _____

13. Does the client exaggerate or understate his or her personal profile?

    _____

14. Does the client have the patience to see a financial plan through from beginning to end? _____

    _____

MARKET RISK

Risk in the securities industry is an attempt to assess the possibility of loss on investments. Many risks are quantifiable and not nearly as vague as many other forms of uncertainty. There are elaborate measurements of risk that the CPA and the client are not called upon to learn or understand. However, there are some forms of risk that financial planners would be advised to familiarize themselves with, because these forms of risk provide information about the investments themselves.

Taking a Closer Look at Risks

Because there are many kinds of risk, the financial planner must be aware of them as they relate to securities. Most risks in securities are measurable: they address the possible loss of the money the client has put into an investment. Common risks that affect a client investment profile are:

1. *Inflation risk*—the risk that the purchasing power of the client's funds will decrease over time. With increasing life expectancy, inflation plays a part in long-term concerns. For retired people, the concern of spiraling costs is significant, particularly if they have fixed pension income and fixed income securities.

2. *Interest rate risk*—the risk that the client will lock in a rate of return on a fixed income security that is no longer competitive with other securities. People always expect the most for each dollar. In the current environment of low interest rates on fixed income vehicles, the client needs the highest rates attainable commensurate with the level of risk. This concern is especially true with the longer duration notes and bonds because the investor is often locked in by these vehicles.

3. *Liquidity risk*—the risk that the clients will be unable to sell their investment when they need cash. The most prominent historical examples of this type of risk are private placements and limited partnerships. Many are without an orderly market, and sales are rarely accomplished quickly.

4. *Exchange risk*—the risk that an investment loses money because of currency fluctuations. Many investors realize significant cash flows in non-dollar-denominated foreign investments. Often, as these investments are exchanged for dollars, the clients net less money than they expected. Because the dollar has been such a strong currency, the foreign currency is exchanged for far fewer dollars than previously.

5. *Credit risk*—the risk that a rating sensitive investment goes down in value owing to a lowering of investment opinion. When Orange County, California, bonds went into default several years ago, many of the bonds

went from AAA (the very highest rating) to "in reorganization" (the lowest rating) in one day. The bondholders experienced immediate significant capital, cash flow and liquidity loss because of the credit collapse brought on by the county's default.

6. *Event risk*—the risk that something catastrophic will happen that affects the price of an investment. The most serious examples include:

   a. The loss of major executives in travel accidents.

   b. The nationalization of a foreign company.

   c. The discovery that a product causes terminal illness.

   d. Announcement of a major safety issue for employees and surrounding neighbors.

   Electric utilities provide classic examples of event risk that are all too familiar. Every nuclear episode in American history resulted in tremendous loss of capital and default on debt. After the event, investors could do nothing but commence endless litigation. Many of these companies have taken years to recover from such episodes.

7. *Principal risk*—the risk that the value of the investment will drop. This is most common with aggressive stock, options and futures investments. The principal value of these investments can gyrate wildly over time because they can appear to the novice investor to have "minds of their own." While physicists noted that "matter can neither be created nor destroyed," it should be obvious to the CPA that those scientists had had no experience with money management. *Principal can be created and destroyed* very quickly, indeed!

8. *Regulatory risk*—the risk that a legislative or political act will cause an investment to decline. In an environment where government regulation determines an increasingly large part of domestic corporate policy, it appears that even profit margins could be dictated by regulatory agencies.

ASSET ALLOCATION AND THE SPREAD OF RISK

In financial planning, investments and asset allocation, the key to success is diversity. This goal can be accomplished through a variety of investments in the securities industry. The determination of *how to diversify* is what asset allocation is all about. The CPA/PFS should work out with the client an appropriate blend of stocks, bonds and cash. Clients should diversify investments through asset allocation to protect the total portfolio from major downside moves without too stringently limiting upside potential. Stocks can go up, bonds can go down, balanced mutual funds can go sideways. The variations are endless, and they can all move simultaneously. By selecting a variety of investments, clients give their portfolios a better chance of remaining stable in a negative environment (for any of the asset classes) and thus of realizing maximum returns over the long term.

Asset allocation is more than a buzzword; it is a concept as old as money itself. What makes the term fresh is its usefulness for the contemporary client. The CPA/PFS can assist clients in building an investment portfolio and in achieving their financial goals using asset allocation as a tool. In today's environment, it is both profitable and smart to stick with successful applications of asset allocation because the markets are so volatile.

To summarize, the CPA/PFS takes three types of investment—stocks, bonds and cash—and stirs. Much of asset allocation is simple; but, in the real-world application, financial concepts can become complex. The specialist should be the client's interpreter for complex terms, issues and scenarios surrounding investment and asset allocation. However, there is no need to make them more difficult than they already are. Any areas that clients might find particularly interesting can be explored in depth with the CPA/PFS as mentor.

All three classes of investment—stocks, bonds and cash—perform well, poorly, neutrally, in tandem, out of sync and randomly over extended periods of time. To determine the percentage to allocate to each of these classes requires a financial plan based not on what the CPA/PFS and client think *might* happen, but on *what has happened* before and *what is currently happening* in the financial markets.

CPAs/PFSs cannot formulate a plan without a clear understanding of these securities. They must plan to consider the securities their client base will be most apt to deal with, and exclude all the techniques and vehicles that do not apply to their particular clients. Many stock and bond trading activities generate a great deal of press interest and coverage that is meaningless in the normal course of investing. CPAs/PFSs should look at stocks, bonds, and mutual funds (which are overwhelmingly made up of only stocks or bonds) for their clients, learn what they are, which kinds are available, and which are appropriate for each type of client's account.

Today, the CPAs/PFSs face a more difficult task than they did even 10 years ago. Paradoxically, while the world has shrunk because of communications and information technology, the investment universe has expanded as a consequence of communications technology. As markets fluctuate through wider and wider volatility bands, the advisor must understand and accommodate this volatility.

No CPA/PFS advises or expects a client to split savings 50/50 between the S&P 500 index and the 10-year U.S. Treasury note, then sit back and await retirement. While sometimes this might be an adequate strategy, it is no guarantee of superior returns. Personal financial needs, investment diversification, and personal risk profiles complicate such a simplistic approach. What kind of money the client needs, for what, and for how long, changes radically over a life span. A lack of diversification may expose the client to unnecessary investment risk and could result in poor long-term investment performance. The client's individual risk profile properly determined can prevent more losses than all other investment strategies combined.

Asset Allocation: How to Put It All in Place

What has been accomplished thus far is to recognize the need for a financial planning approach to investments. It then becomes necessary to:

1. Determine the client's goals (particularly as they relate to retirement and college savings).
2. Help the client implement the plan.
3. Aid the client in selecting the investments once the individual risk profile has been established.
4. Review, update, and refine the plan and strategy to confirm that the client is on course to reach those goals.
5. Check periodically to ascertain whether that course reflects the client's current thinking.

The CPA/PFS can be of great help in implementing these steps, but the plan and strategies are the clients' concern and are central to their own needs. The CPA/PFS and client should know by now the investment options in stocks, bonds and mutual funds. Now they must determine what to do to put this knowledge to work.

To allocate assets, the client is directed in the current era *toward total* return. While as time passes, this approach may change, it is currently the orientation of most securities investment. Most clients want to outpace inflation and maximize returns with a bias toward asset growth. However, they cannot ignore the attractions of cash flow from both bond interest and stock dividends.

As a secondary concern, behind the primary goal of realizing dreams, asset allocation allows the client to dream comfortably. The CPA/PFS needs to create a balance of risk to return with as little portfolio volatility as possible. Stocks and bonds often behave differently from one another. They do not move together as a single force.

Portfolio Management

While there is no need to start courses in modern portfolio theory, understanding some portfolio management basics helps in creating a diversified portfolio. For the client to achieve this, with the help of the CPA/PFS, is the most valuable aspect of investing. Asset allocation is the engine that drives the investment car. Determining this allocation is not easy, nor is portfolio management. There is much to learn before setting out to select securities for a portfolio. All the planning in the world is of no use unless it is successfully implemented by investment in a portfolio of stocks, bonds and cash. Portfolio management aims to accomplish this with:

1. Above-average returns.
2. Appropriate risk levels.
3. Diversity.
4. The long-term view.

Putting Asset Allocation to Work

The assumption of responsibility for portfolio management is the direction of asset allocation. It is the action steps of the asset allocation program. After establishing how to allocate assets from the client's financial plan, the CPA/PFS should use that plan to determine how to invest by:

1. Researching what stocks, bonds and cash to invest in. The CPA/PFS should obtain information from other financial advisors, investment publications, newspapers, books, magazines, radio, TV, investor seminars, and personal ideas.
2. Determining how to weigh a portfolio. This involves finalizing the mix of stocks, bonds and cash and evaluating choices based on suitability, risk, value, industry particulars and any other factors of interest to the CPA/PFS or client before investing.
3. Taking steps that portfolio management demands, including regular securities quote examination and regular reading about investment theory.
4. Establishing when the client should contact the CPA/PFS, such as in cases of undue volatility, especially good or poor investment performance, or when anything crops up that the client simply does not understand.
5. Instructing clients who manage their own portfolios to call for help in the event of red flags—episodes of significance to an investment that are negative in their effect.

Further Concerns

The goal is to accomplish positive things, but a similar goal is to avoid negative results. The financial specialist must watch for illogical investments—those that are unsuitable, perform all the same or are current fads:

1. *Unsuitable investments*—These are investments not suited to the clients' goals. The typical poor choices for clients are investments that exceed their risk parameters. Most familiar are investments such as hot stock funds, heavily leveraged funds, or highly specialized or concentrated

sector funds. A less obvious poor choice would be a large dividend paying stable stock in a growth portfolio.

2. ***Perform all the same***—These investments are so similar that the client cannot be said to have diversified at all. For example, selecting three different domestic small capitalization mutual funds is not investment diversity—it is investment redundancy; all are much the same and tend over time to perform the same as one another. To own six power utilities, three phone companies, and two natural gas distribution stocks sounds diversified, but, really, the client simply owns eleven utility stocks. A better allocation would be several utility stocks plus an assortment of consumer growth stocks and an insurance or bank stock.

3. ***Current fads***—The last few years have seen so many retail investment products come and go in popularity that one is hard put to select a few for examples:

   a. The limited partnership vehicle, where the client participated in partnership activities but could not lose more than his or her original investment, seems to have departed forever.

   b. The ubiquitous short-term, multimarket income funds have been rolled into other income funds, never to resurface.

   c. Current investment fads have included new issues and Internet stocks—some have tomorrows, most do not.

In summary, the CPA/PFS should assess client needs, set up an asset allocation plan that complements the financial plan and risk profile and then create a set of portfolio rules related to periodic reviews, buy/sell strategies and an overall plan that is customized to the client's needs.

What Asset Allocation Looks Like

Asset allocation relates to all this by answering the question, "What should the client invest in?" While more specific asset allocation comes in some detail later, for current uses, what the client invests in is a mixture of stocks, bonds and cash. Each asset class has volatility factors, with cash being least volatile, stocks being most volatile, and bonds somewhere in between.

Stocks.   Regarding stocks, it is important to determine whether the client should consider growth, value, domestic or foreign stocks:

1. Growth stocks increase in price and trading volume, usually from increasing earnings momentum.

2. Value stocks sell at what are perceived to be low prices relative to their liquidation and market worth.

3. Domestic stocks are in companies whose headquarters are located in the United States.
4. Foreign stocks are in companies whose headquarters are located in foreign countries.

Bonds.   With bonds, the CPA/PFS simply suggests a class of bonds suitable for the client and then creates a portfolio fit to that suitability—or invests in a strategic income mutual fund and lets a manager take care of all this for the client. Classes of bonds are:

1. Short Term: one year or less.
2. Intermediate Term: one to five years.
3. Long Term: six years or more.
4. Investment Grade: rated BBB or above.
5. Junk: rated BB or below.

As a precaution, the CPA/PFS should orient the client toward being as aggressive as the clients' risk profile and temperament allow. Investors can become so preoccupied with avoiding loss that they fail to generate suitable gains. This error results in a serious overweighing of income and neglect of growth, especially in a low interest/low inflation environment.

The Need to Diversify

To achieve their goal of financial independence in retirement and adequate savings for educational expenses, most clients fall into these broad areas of investment:

1. Capital preservation.
2. Current income.
3. Total return.
4. Long-term growth.
5. Aggressive growth.

These five sample programs should not be routinely changed. They are definitely not cursory guides to be abandoned at a whim but are commonly accepted and long-established guidelines used throughout the financial services industry. There are some compelling reasons to follow these allocations for the investors they describe. Of course, all are subject to revision and should certainly be reviewed in relation to client holdings quarterly, semiannually or at least annually. This is to make certain that the client weighting is appropriate and, if so, that the assets are still allocated as the weighting requires. If one asset class outperforms the other two by a wide margin, there could be some reallocation of assets to get the percentages back in line. Also, the exact percentages are a guideline, not hard-and-fast rules.

A description of each of these and the mix that should make up the portfolio is discussed below.

Capital Preservation.   Capital preservation, the most conservative class, is made up of 25 percent cash, 55 percent bonds, and 20 percent stock. The 25 percent cash is for client-perceived immediate or near immediate cash needs and has no volatility. The 55 percent bonds are to generate current spending income. The 20 percent equity allocation functions primarily as an inflation and asset hedge, but secondarily to generate increased net worth and capital gains over the long-term. As the most conservative strategy, the return can be only modestly rewarding because of the near absence of growth and the large percentage of money fund assets. However, the CPA assumes here the genuine need for liquidity and capital preservation at the expense of any other strategy.

With the actual potential for negative real returns (realized returns adjusted for rate of inflation), this risk parameter and asset allocation is for a very small portion of the client population. This client might be someone who is fully retired, with adequate assets for future needs. The only financial concern would be a sudden significant capital loss.

Capital preservation might be a suitable entry-level investment and asset allocation stance for a client attempting to invest for the first time. However, if that client has a very long-term outlook, the CPA/PFS could work toward a more aggressive stance over a period of time as the client became more comfortable with the process.

Current Income.   The current income class, the next asset allocation level in terms of risk tolerance, the CPA allocates 30 percent to stocks, 60 percent to bonds, and 10 percent to cash. The stocks should be total return stocks with dividends consistent with the S&P 500 dividend; the bonds should be of whatever duration the client is comfortable with; the cash is for unexpected needs. A current income allocation can be adjusted to be as conservative or moderate as the client wants to make it:

1. If conservative, the client is looking at small real returns and, it is hoped, no losses.
2. If moderate, the client can make a very good return with total return stocks, especially large capitalization ones. A more aggressive duration stance with the bonds would be in order.

The current income client is one for whom declining purchasing power, inflation, rising prices and other future dollar concerns may be a problem.

However, the problem is not a severe one because this client should have a comfortable amount of money. Similar to the prototypical capital preservation client, losses are a very significant source of unrest for the client.

Total Return.   The total return portfolio is a mixture of income and growth. It should be 40 percent stocks, 50 percent bonds, and 10 percent cash. The client can "barbell" risk (have one end speculative and the other end conservative) and have aggressive growth and moderately long-term, highest-grade bonds. Or the client can look for the middle ground with total return stocks and capital-appreciation-oriented bonds. The cash, once again, is for sudden expenses. Total return is the middle-of-the-road category that fits the middle of the bell curve for the middle client. It represents Everyman. This client is an employed individual who is trying to increase his or her net worth through securities investment and simply wants a good return without great downside risk. This client is more than happy to give up the investment grand slam home run and settle for singles, doubles, and the occasional triple or homer. Most clients are comfortable with this mix or long-term growth because these allocations approximate the financial commitment for which most clients qualify. Most clients would like to have growth and income and would be hard put to delineate a preference for either. The risk/reward tends here toward a double-digit return, without great unease in most times of market upheaval.

Long-Term Growth.   Long-term growth is set up with 70 percent stocks, 20 percent bonds, and 10 percent cash. The stock component makes investments in all areas of growth and value, capitalization and domestic and foreign. The bonds generate income to reinvest (some appreciation, ideally) and function as a hedge in down stock markets. The cash is for emergencies or special investment opportunities. Long-term growth is for the somewhat aggressive growth client who has no more than modest current income needs, but recognizes the virtues of a bond cash flow and its stabilizing influence. This client may be younger, higher income, or more aggressive than the total return client, hence the stronger predisposition toward growth. As with total return, however, the growth allocation can be very aggressive, if weighted in speculative or high-risk areas of equities. The growth component is then accentuated at the expense of the income side of the equation, but it requires significant portfolio management to accomplish significant returns. For example, for the client to realize the full benefit of such a program, considerable research would go into determining which individual equities to invest in and in what industry groups. Even if mutual funds are utilized, considerable research should go into determining which funds, from what fund family, in what types, because the goal of such a program is to hit home runs. A normal growth component with a normal rate of return would not be an adequate goal.

Aggressive Growth.   Aggressive growth, which suits people with no income needs whatsoever and few liquidity needs, is 80 percent stocks, 10 percent bonds, and 10 percent cash. The stocks are all classes, mostly pure growth with no income component; the bonds are zero coupon bonds maturing in the distant future to generate maximum capital gains potential; the cash is for special investment opportunities. Aggressive growth requires far more hands-on portfolio management than capital preservation—the opposite end of the investment spectrum—because the CPA/PFS and client need to be concerned about more aspects of the market. The aggressive growth client must spend a great deal of time trading the account and investing or, if not, he or she, must plan to hire a money manager who can handle everything. This would include discretionary trading with confirms, monthly statements, and performance reviews on a systematic basis with the CPA/PFS. The likelihood of significant losses and gains is much greater because the volatility of the account and its constituent parts is much greater. More aggressive means more risk and thus more responsibility, attention, review, activity, trading positions . . . and problems.

Warning: These are active accounts that often turn sour as short-term trading accounts using options and futures and other high-risk tools to achieve perceived maximum performance.

How to Select an Asset Allocation Option

If the client were to conclude that direct investment in stocks, bonds and cash under any of these five programs for asset allocation is beyond them, the mutual fund industry is only too happy to come to their rescue. This group of clients can create their own portfolio made up of different mutual funds. They can:

1. Select sector, index, or style funds for the equity allocation.
2. Invest in sector or strategic income funds to meet the bond allocation.
3. Have any type of money market fund that suits them for the cash.

If even this level of involvement in the selection process taxes the client's time or inclination, there are global asset allocation funds that contain domestic and foreign equities, debt and cash. Within this group is an answer to almost any investment need, because the group contains as widely variant a group of funds as any in the industry. Some are extraordinarily well diversified with hundreds of positions in numerous countries, markets and securities adding up to billions of dollars.

The best of them have betas (measure of volatility relative to the stock market) under that of the S&P 500 Index. However, some of these same funds have among the worst returns of any mutual funds in existence, either equity or debt. The class enjoys almost total flexibility because they have no real investment guidelines. This, of course, can be unnerving to many clients. But at their very best, they approach the concept of one-stop shopping investment. The task is to find a fund with an investment philosophy consistent with the risk parameters and asset allocation of the particular client—and send in the money.

Caveat emptor is still the order of the day, with required reviews and all other portfolio procedures, but most of the job is done by the fund managers.

Conclusion

A number of financial issues face client and advisor today. Among these issues are:

1. The end of "Big Brother" corporate pension plans.
2. The rocky future of Social Security.
3. The end or drastic curtailment of many government social service and entitlement programs.
4. The propensity toward increased life expectancy.
5. Skyrocketing health care costs.

The way to address these issues for the CPA/PFS and their clients is through life savings, self-directed retirement plans, college savings and other financial vehicles that in a knowledgeable and deliberate fashion solve the clients' financial problems for themselves. The CPA/PFS and client must be their own best caretakers. Financial planning, risk profile and asset allocation investment are the tools of the CPA/PFS and client relationship, they will help the CPA/PFS take better care of their clients. The sooner the individual's goals are quantified and set, the more apt the client is to achieve them.

The CPA/PFS and the client need to assess the investments using accurate performance techniques and strategies that allow the advisor to fill out an objective report card on the client's investments. After they have selected the investment, they must regularly track their performance. The CPA/PFS and client learn enough about investment appraisal and performance information sources to judge success and failure. They know to quantify everything and use quantitative analysis rather than the subjective language of adjectives such as "good" and "bad" or "safe" and "risky."

Asset allocation has characteristically appealed to, and been practiced by, large institutions and individuals with high net worth. The CPA/PFS and their clients should learn that the benefits of asset allocation apply to everyone. The primary explanation for the success of asset allocation is that diversification properly practiced actually works. The clients can index, create their own portfolio of individual securities, or select an asset allocation mutual fund. The choice is up to the CPA/PFS and his or her clients. Market timing, rampant speculation, in-and-out trading or unsuitable investments of any kind do not work for anyone. Who wins and who loses in the investment arena is easily determined: long-term, high-quality, patient investors win more often than not. There is no perfect plan or set-in-stone portfolio for everyone. Each client is different. The challenge for the CPA/PFS is to determine what is best for each and every one of them.

COMMON INVESTMENT MISTAKES

Avoiding common investment mistakes may seem to the client to be a function of logic, but in the excitement and confusion of the moment, mistakes occur. Although the risks previously addressed are beyond anyone's control, the next series of mistakes are not. The financial specialist is largely in control of the client's financial destiny. One really bad investment can ruin an entire portfolio. While it is impossible to generate record profits and performance year after year, it is relatively easy to avoid disastrous returns if the client listens to advice and avoids that "big loss."

The following disasters can be avoided by using common sense and a generous application of self-discipline. The astute CPA/PFS will not:

1. ***Put all the client's eggs in one basket.*** The securities industry calls disproportionately large securities positions "concentrated positions." The brokerage firms will not lend the normal percentages of money on concentrated positions. They consider the risks of doing so inherently excessive. They prefer that a client have a diversified portfolio—as should the planner. Enron employees who had all of their 401(k)s in company stock are an extreme example of the peril of holding a concentrated position.

2. ***Have misplaced faith in a particular stock.*** To believe in XYZ Company wholeheartedly could be likened to falling under a spell. When something goes wrong with a company, something has gone wrong, period. Stock prices per se and securities prices in general tell a story by their movements. A continually declining security often unfolds as a sad story.

3. ***Leave the client's statements and confirmations in their envelopes unopened.*** The disclosure laws exist for the investor's well-being and protection. Open all mail and act/react in a timely manner.

4. ***"Churn" the client.*** The CPA/PFS should also never let them be churned by someone else or allow them to churn themselves. Clients never traded themselves out of difficult spots by excessive trading activity. Checkmate in securities is always checkmate—and the game is over. The costs of excessive trading, which you can easily calculate, eliminate all but the most extraordinary profits. (Many former online traders learned this the hard way.)

5. ***Try to out-think the market.*** The market is smarter than any individual, even a professional analyst, and functions at speeds no human can match; it is impossible to fight against the direction of the market.

6. ***Follow a guru.*** If the CPA were to make a list of gurus going back to the gold boom of the late 1970s, how many of them would have passed the test of time?

7. ***Ignore gut reactions.*** This includes hunches, intuition and natural inclinations. The accountant's and client's first impulses, with intelligence guided by experience, are more often than not correct.

8. ***Look backward.*** The missed opportunities are in the past. Learn from experience and look ahead.

9. ***Aim too high.*** No one makes spectacular securities profits out of nowhere with no risk.

10. ***Stagnate.*** When things are not going well and have not gone well for a long time, even standing pat can be interpreted as stagnating. When this happens, it is time to decide upon a course of action.

GOOD ADVICE

Many clients are content to rely upon their life experience as their sole frame of reference for evaluating potential investments. If the clients believe the planner will achieve their goals expeditiously and cost-effectively, the CPA (from enlightened self-interest) should inject some third party into the picture. For the protection of both the adviser and the client, it is wise to enlist the aid of a qualified investment professional to increase securities knowledge. Investing has become increasingly complicated and has taken on a life of its own; no one should try to go it alone.

Whether the CPA elects to be self-reliant, seek occasional or ongoing professional advice and information, the following suggestions are sound advice. These are tried-and-true axioms that make sense and are of genuine benefit:

1. ***Cut losses.*** A client can forget a 15 percent loss in no time and it means little in the overall picture. A 50 percent loss is remembered forever.

2. ***Know what the client owns and why.*** Intermediate notes are selected for a decent cash flow and stable asset price. They cannot somehow be expected to turn into a growth stock—in any market environment.

3. ***Let profits ride.*** Sell losers, not winners. If the clients sell their winners to make up for losers, they end up with all losers.

4. ***Read quarterly and annual reports.*** Their existence is required for a reason—disclosure, disclosure, disclosure. . . .

5. ***Deal only in quality investments.*** In time, quality always wins out. It must be remembered that everyone makes mistakes. The goal is to

minimize mistakes by discarding a bad investment before the investment turns completely sour. While too much risk is a recipe for failure, without some degree of risk, there will not be adequate returns.

6. **Plan for failure.** Clients always want big returns. But it is best to have an exit strategy with any investment, should things go wrong. If XYZ Company stock is down and the clients have a red flag price to cut losses, they must abide by the initial decision regarding the investment and cut losses. To maintain control of each portfolio, the client needs a plan of action for failure as well as one for success for each investment.

Minimizing Risk

A successful strategy to minimize risk is to keep careful records of all trades and pay close attention to investment statements. With a record of investment performance, the accountant can do an adequate job of performance appraisal. No one can intelligently appraise how investments are performing without good records. Securities awareness must expand as clients become owners of more and more different investments.

ACCREDITATION REQUIREMENTS FOR THE PFS DESIGNATION

In December 2000, the AICPA announced a new set of guidelines to satisfy requirements for the Personal Financial Specialist credential. Candidates are now to be evaluated on a point system. A minimum of 100 points is required for the designation. These points are based in three specific areas: business experience, life-long learning, and examination.

To qualify for the PFS designation, an individual must:

1. Be a member in good standing of the AICPA.
2. Hold a valid and unrevoked CPA certificate issued by a legally constituted state authority.
3. Pass the PFS examination. (The requisite experience may be obtained before or after taking the PFS exam.)
4. Agree to comply with all the requirements for reaccreditation.
5. Have at least 250 hours of relevant business experience per year in personal financial planning activities for the three years immediately preceding the PFS application. This experience is drawn from six financial planning disciplines:
   a. The personal financial planning process (setting goals).
   b. Personal income-tax planning.
   c. Risk-management planning.

  d. Investment planning.
  e. Retirement planning.
  f. Estate planning.
6. Upon successful completion of the PFS exam, the applicant will be asked to submit six references to substantiate working experience in personal financial planning.

The first two requirements must be met at the time of registration in order to sit for the examination. References are required only after the applicant has been notified of successful completion of the examination. He or she then has three years in which to submit the work references. If that time has elapsed, the examination score will be invalidated. The individual will then be required to retake and pass the examination to become accredited.

Additional Information Relating to the Point System

In addition to the areas covered above in item 5, business experience also includes teaching college-level personal financial planning courses.

Life-long learning points may be earned through continuing professional education (CPE) courses, self-directed reading and research programs, conference presentations and professional writing. Advanced degrees, such as a juris doctor and master of business administration, are considered. Participants on the committees of nationally renowned personal financial planning associations also receive life-long learning credit.

As stated, all PFS candidates are required to pass an examination, the Comprehensive PFS Examination. In addition, several other certification exams are eligible for points toward accreditation: Certified Financial Planner, Chartered Financial Consultant, Chartered Financial Analyst, National Association of Securities Dealers (NASD) Series 65, NASD Series 66 and NASD Series 7. The AICPA cautions that some of these additional exams will require the applicant to obtain a greater number of points in business experience and life-long learning.

Reaccreditation Requirements

To maintain the PFS accreditation, the accountant must pay an annual reaccreditation fee and recertify his or her accreditation every three years. To do so, the requirements are:

1. Be a member in good standing of the AICPA.
2. Have a valid and unrevoked CPA certificate issued by a legally constituted state authority.

3. Have at least 750 hours of experience in personal financial planning over the preceding three years. Experience must be in each of the six financial planning disciplines listed above.

4. Take at least seventy-two hours of financial planning courses in prescribed disciplines every three years.

5. Submit a written statement of intent to continue to comply with all the requirements for reaccreditation.

6. Submit a completed internal practice review questionnaire (IPRQ), as amended from time to time. The questionnaire asks the CPA/PFS to provide information to determine whether he or she has met the reaccreditation requirements. The CPA/PFS agrees to submit supporting data, including work papers, for external review of personal financial planning activities upon request.

Every three years, all CPAs/PFSs must be reaccredited to maintain the designation. If reaccreditation requirements are not met, the accreditation ceases and all initial requirements, including examination, must be repeated to regain accreditation. A waiver may be requested and will be granted if, in the sole judgment of the AICPA, there is justification.

The Personal Financial Planning Experience Requirement

As mentioned previously, PFS candidates must have at least 250 hours of experience in personal financial planning activities in each of the three years preceding the initial accreditation application. Candidates for reaccreditation must have at least 750 hours of personal financial planning experience over the three years preceding their reaccreditation.

Although the CPA must have some experience in each of the planning areas, there is no specific or minimum amount of time required for any one area. The following summary highlights some of the services provided by CPA financial planners and provides examples of activities that may qualify as personal financial planning experience.

The Personal Financial Planning Process. In addition to all the activities involved in setting up and augmenting a basic financial plan, as described earlier, the AICPA goes even further and suggests other services that may qualify for experience. Among these are reviewing spending patterns, developing cash flow management, budgeting recommendations and performing time-value-of-money calculations.

Personal Income Tax Planning. As stated earlier, this is the area in which the CPA is already the most conversant with the clients' situation. If these are not new clients, the accountant is unquestionably already doing much of what the

AICPA considers to be qualifying experience toward the PFS designation: "Advising clients regarding the federal and state income tax consequences of their financial decisions, including matters such as timing income and deductions; making charitable contributions; utilizing net operating losses, capital losses, or passive activity losses; establishing and maintaining employee fringe benefit plans; taking retirement plan distributions; and bankruptcy. Helping clients split income among family members through the use of family partnerships, employment arrangements, gifts and trusts, installment sales, etc. Advising clients on the issues related to personal decisions such as marriage or divorce (property settlements, retirement plan asset division, alimony and child support)."

Risk Management Planning.   In this chapter, risk is considered from two very distinct aspects: that relating to the types of risk that can be ameliorated or completely covered by insurance and the types of risk encountered in investing.

The AICPA emphasizes insurance as an important aspect of managing risk. That aspect has been rather fully covered in this chapter. Certainly, it is important to analyze clients' exposure to risk and review with them methods for managing risk and to help them minimize financial risks from disability, illness, property damage, and personal and professional liability. As a part of their tax planning, the planner will automatically review with clients the income and estate tax aspects of their insurance coverage.

Investment Planning.   This is the area in which the CPA/PFS must exercise the most caution. Being a tax adviser and an investment adviser are two distinct roles. That is the reason much of this chapter is devoted to the discussion of the investment activities the AICPA includes as credit toward the PFS designation. Among their list, they include: ". . . recommending investments or helping clients build portfolios (consider registration requirements); managing client assets." A veiled caution, but a caution nonetheless.

Retirement Planning.   Added to material considered above are ". . . reviewing with clients the limits on and tax consequences of contributions to or distributions from retirement plans; planning for the post-retirement succession of a closely held business."

Estate Planning.   If the speculation about the effects of the new tax law on estate planning hold true, many CPAs may be very actively involved in this area of planning. Regardless of new legislation, the steps mentioned and the AICPA suggestions will remain: ". . . reviewing with clients the tax and probate considerations of various forms of property ownership and making recommendations on the titling of assets; recommending or reviewing various instruments (wills, powers of attorney, trusts) for use in achieving goals; planning for the post-mortem succession of a closely held business (buy-sell agreements, estate freeze techniques, valuation issues, etc.)."

Chapter 18

Investment Vocabulary

Any language has a core vocabulary of about 700 words—English, French or Russian—it doesn't matter which one. In addition, all professions have vocabularies of similar size. What we hope to accomplish here is to give basic definitions of words that crop up in most media treatments of securities and investment. While this is not an exhaustive vocabulary, nor are these complete definitions, they are most certainly working definitions of the most common words. They will help the CPA/PFS get through almost any article or conversation without feeling hopelessly confused and left out by the nomenclature of the discussion.

A

account The formal relationship between a securities entity and a client wherein the client buys and sells securities.

account executive The person responsible for executing your securities transactions.

account statement Monthly written record of a securities client's positions and transactions.

across the board Activity in the stock market where seemingly everything goes up or everything goes down in tandem.

acquisition One company buying out another.

active market Large trading volume for a period of time in either a specific security or in investment vehicles per se.

against the box Short sale of a security that the holder owns with a long position already.

American Depository Receipt (ADR) U.S. versions of foreign stocks traded domestically, mitigating against relying upon foreign exchanges to invest in their securities.

American Depository Share (ADS) Shares that make up an ADR and are the underlying security of that ADR.

American Stock Exchange (AMEX) Stock exchange in New York that is second only to the New York Stock Exchange (NYSE) in volume. It largely specializes in small and middle capitalization stocks, options, bonds and some over-the-counter (OTC) issues.

annual meeting Annual recounting of a company's activities held in a public place with management, directors, shareholders, and the press.

Annual Percentage Rate (APR) Simple annual percentage expression of the costs of a loan to consumers that must be disclosed per the Truth In Lending Act.

annual report Annual accounting in print of all the activities of a company required by the SEC.

annual return Pre-tax and expense figure resulting from total income and gain or loss being combined to create one total return figure for the year.

annualize Conversion of a return to an annual basis.

appreciation Increase in value of a security.

asset Something of measurable value.

asset allocation Determining the percentage of funds invested between cash, stock and bonds.

B

back-ended load A vanishing deferred sales charge common in mutual funds and annuities that enables investors to have their entire investment working for them at the onset of their investment.

balanced mutual fund Asset allocation fund that has a blend of stocks, bonds and cash—usually, consistent with a conservative investment pattern.

basis Cost of a security including all expenses related to the acquisition of that security.

bear market Market in which prices go down for an extended period of time.

bid and offer The prices at which people are willing to buy (bid) and sell (offer) securities to someone else.

big board Slang name for the New York Stock Exchange.

block Large number of securities.

blue chip Stock of a household-name company that has done very well over an extended number of years.

bond A debt security obligating the issuer to pay the holder interest for some period of time.

bond rating A measurement of a bond issuer's ability to pay its bondholders their interest and principal.

bottom Lowest point of something (stock, market, yield) at some measured time (day, quarter, year).

bottom-up Micro to macro look at a subject.

breakpoint Mutual fund dollar commitment that results in a lower sales fee.

breakup value Market value of the parts of a company separated from its whole.

broker Same as account executive; colloquial rather than official term.

brokered CD Certificates of deposit (CDs) sold at brokerages rather than at the bank and having the same characteristics as bank CDs.

budget Estimate of cash flow and expenses.

bull market Market in which prices go up for an extended period of time.

business cycle Recurring periods of expansion and recession in the economy.

buy Make an investment.

buy and hold Long-term investment.

buyer's market A market in which investment in securities predominates.

buying on margin Investing in securities on credit.

buyout Take over the control of a company.

C

call feature Bond issuer's ability to claim back a bond before it matures as stated in the schedule of redemption for that bond.

call option Opportunity to buy a certain amount of a security at a certain price for a certain amount of time.

callable The ability of an issuer to redeem securities before their stated maturity.

called Security is redeemed prior to maturity.

capital gain Profit realized on sale of a security.

capital gains distribution Distribution of profit, usually in December, from a mutual fund's successful trading.

capital loss Loss realized on sale of a security.

capital markets Markets where stocks and bonds are traded, both public and private.

capitalization The value of a company based on its total stock shares multiplied by the price of the stock.

cash Currency.

cash dividend Dividend paid out to shareholders in cash.

cash equivalent Securities so safe and liquid that they are just removed from being cash.

central bank A country's bank; in the U.S., the Federal Reserve System.

certificate of deposit (CD) Interest-paying debt instrument issued by banks.

certified financial planner (CFP) Financial planner who has completed the program of the Institute of Certified Financial Planners.

certified public accountant (CPA) Accountant who has completed the program required to obtain certification in the state in which he or she works as an accountant.

chairman of the board Highest ranking officer in a corporation, who presides over board meetings.

charitable remainder trust Trust that is irrevocable and that gives money to a charity, generates an income for life to the grantor, and creates tax benefits for the grantor.

chief executive officer (CEO) Actual manager of a company, as opposed to a ceremonial title, responsible for its day-to-day operation.

chief financial officer (CFO) Person who controls the purse strings of a company.

churning Excessive trading in a brokerage account.

closed-end mutual fund Mutual fund with a finite number of shares traded on a stock exchange.

common stock An equity security of a public company.

company A business.

compliance department Entity set up to see that securities activities are in accordance with the law.

confirmation Paper slip used to inform clients in writing of a securities transaction.

constant dollar plan Dollar cost averaging.

contrarian Person who does the opposite of what he or she perceives everyone else is doing.

controlling interest Enough shares to control a company.

convertible securities Securities that can be converted from one security into another; usually from a bond into stock.

cornering a market Illegally gaining control of a security.

corporate bond Bond issued by a company.

corporation Chartered legal company.

correction Downward price adjustment in a security or market.

cost basis Acquisition price of a security.

coupon Rate of return on a bond as expressed by a percentage of the face value of the bond.

crash Extraordinary drop in stock prices, usually in one day.

credit rating A measurement of an entity's ability to pay its creditors.

credit risk Chance that a debt will not be repaid.

custodial account Account created for a minor.
custodian Entity that holds securities for another entity, such as a bank holding securities for a mutual fund.
cyclical stock Stock whose price reflects the state of the economy.

D

debt instrument Written document that is issued to cover a debt.
debt security Security that is issued to cover a debt.
debt service Loan payments.
defined benefit pension plan Pension plan that pays a specific amount to a participant after a given employment tenure for the life of that participant.
defined contribution pension plan Pension plan in which there is a specific contribution allowed and the ultimate benefits are dependent upon the investment results of the plan.
delisting Removal of a security from an exchange.
denomination Face value of some financial instrument stated in currency.
derivative Security whose value is based on the value of some other security.
devaluation Lowering the value of a currency relative to the value of some other currency.
disclosure Positive and negative information required by the SEC for determination of an investment decision.
discount bond Bond selling at below its par value.
discount broker Brokerage that charges commissions below the full-service brokerage commissions.
discounting the news Price fluctuations based on anticipated news about a company.
discount rate The rate the Federal Reserve charges member banks for loans secured by various acceptable securities.
discretionary account Account in which trades may be made without first consulting with the client.
discretionary income Income left over after all obligations have been met.
disintermediation Taking funds out of a bank.
disposable income Income left over after all government tax obligations have been met.
diversification Spreading risk by investing in multiple types of investment.
dividend Earnings distribution.
dividend investment plan Reinvesting stock dividends in that company's stock to add more stock to a position on a regular basis.
dollar cost averaging Securities investment of a given amount of money at a given time interval for an indefinite period, where volatility is lessened because of the time factor.

downside risk Estimate as to how low the value of an investment can go.

downtick Trade at lower price than previous one.

down trend Security moving downward in price.

dumping Selling large amounts of stock regardless of the price offered.

E

early withdrawal penalty Fee paid to terminate a time deposit contract, usually with bank CDs.

earned income Income actively earned.

earnings momentum Accelerated earnings that tend to provoke upward price movement in stocks.

earnings per share Post-tax, post-bond and preferred stock payment amount of earnings expressed on a per-share basis.

Employee Retirement Income Security Act (ERISA) Private pension and benefit plans law enacted in 1974.

employee stock ownership plan (ESOP) Stock purchase plan set up for the employees of a company to buy their company's stock.

encumbered Owned by one party but another party has a justified claim for ownership.

endorse Transfer ownership.

entrepreneur Risk-oriented investor.

equity Ownership.

equivalent taxable yield Adjustment made to compare tax-exempt yields on an equivalent basis to taxable ones.

estate What a person owns at death.

estate planning Orderly addressing of the documentation and tax planning for the disposition of an estate.

Eurodollar Dollars in banks in Europe.

event risk Risk that something will happen to cause a lower rating of a security and a subsequent decline in price.

excess reserves Reserves of money above Federal Reserve requirement by a member bank.

exchange rate Price one currency can be bought at with another currency.

ex-dividend Time between declaration and payment of a dividend.

execution Consummate a trade.

executor/executrix Administrator of an estate.

exercise Utilize right to do something by contract, usually, with options or futures.

expense ratio A mutual fund's operating expenses expressed as a percentage of the fund's assets that are used to pay expenses plus its 12b-1 fees divided by the fund's net asset value.

F

face value Stated denomination of a security on the certificate of that security.

family of funds List of funds managed by the same company.

favorable trade balance Occurs when you export more than you import.

federal deficit Shortfall of revenue relative to expenses of the federal government.

Federal Deposit Insurance Corporation (FDIC) Federal agency that insures bank deposits.

federal funds Commercial bank deposits at the Federal Reserve Bank.

federal funds rate Bank-to-bank loan rates charged on excess deposits at the Federal Reserve.

Federal Open Market Committee (FOMC) Federal Reserve committee that sets government short-term monetary policy.

Federal Reserve Banks Group of banks making up the Federal Reserve System.

Federal Reserve Board (FRB) Board that governs the Federal Reserve.

Federal Reserve System Regulator of U.S. monetary policy and banking system.

fiduciary Entity responsible for another's assets.

fill Complete a customer's order.

Financial Accounting Standards Board (FASB) Establishes and interprets accounting terms and rules.

financial markets The total of the different markets of all types.

financial planner Person who analyzes clients' financial circumstances and prepares a plan for them to realize their goals.

financial pyramid Graphic representation of investments going from least (base) to most (peak) speculative investments.

financial statement Written financial record including balance sheet and income statement.

financial supermarket A large number of financial products sold at one company.

fiscal year A 365-day accounting period.

fixed annuity An annuity that guarantees a specific rate of return.

fixed cost Cost that remains the same regardless of outside sales effects.

fixed income investment A security whose payout rate is set.

fixed rate Loan or security whose interest rate does not change.

flat Bonds trading without interest payment accruing.

flight to quality Rush to high-grade securities in difficult times.

floating rate Loan or security whose interest rate changes.

floor broker Agent who acts for clients of a member firm on an exchange floor.

floor trader Trader who acts for him- or herself on an exchange floor.

forecasting Predicting the future.

foreclosure Seizure of property.
foreign exchange Payments between countries.
forward Buy or sell contract for a commodity.
401(K) plan Elective pre-tax contributions to a qualified tax-deferred retirement plan.
fraud Illegal detrimental behavior to obtain advantage.
front-ended load Up-front mutual fund sales charge.
full-service brokerage A financial supermarket where many financial products are available.
fully invested Asset allocation involving no cash but only stocks and bonds.
fully valued Stock prices at exactly what a company's earnings justify.
fundamental analysis Determination of the price movement of a stock based on earnings expectations as suggested by balance sheet and income statement data.
futures contract A buy or sell agreement for a specific amount of a product at a specific price for a specific time.
futures exchanges Markets where future contracts are traded.

G

general obligation (GO) bond Municipal bond backed by the full faith and credit of its issuer.
general partner Managing partner of a limited partnership with theoretically limitless liability.
going long Purchasing a security.
going private Removing a company from public ownership by buying up all its stock.
going public Making a public sale of a company.
going short Selling a security that is not owned by the seller.
gold fixing Setting of the cash (spot) price of one ounce of gold.
gold mutual fund Mutual fund made up primarily of gold and other mining shares.
gold standard Monetary system whereby currency is convertible to bullion on demand.
goldbug Someone who believes in the appreciation potential of gold.
golden handcuffs Incentives to keep a person from leaving a company.
golden parachute Corporate takeover protection for a key employee.
good faith deposit Earnest money for a securities trade.
government securities Securities issued by the U.S. government and its agencies.
grandfather clause Exemption from a new rule by virtue of prior involvement.

green shoe Provision to issue additional shares of an underwriting if demand is strong enough.

H

hard dollar fee Payment in cash for services.
high-yield bond Bonds rated BB or lower.
holding period Amount of time an owner has held an asset.
hot issue New stock issue everyone wants because these stocks tend to go up sharply in price.
hot stock Stock that is trading large relative volume and often is going up sharply in price.
hypothecation Using securities as loan collateral.

I

illiquid Cannot be immediately converted to cash.
in-the-money option Option where the underlying security is trading at a price that would be advantageous to exercise the option.
inactive security Illiquid security owing to scarcity of trading activity for any reason.
income tax Tax on income imposed by country, state or city.
indemnify Agree to pay for loss.
index Compilation of statistics (economy) or prices (securities) as a measurement standard.
index fund Fund made up of the constituents of a securities index.
index option Put or call on an index.
individual retirement account (IRA) Personally created retirement account subject to various regulations that are often altered and amended over the years.
individual retirement account rollover (IRA Rollover) Lump sum distribution deposited into an IRA account to avoid current tax consequences.
inflation Increase in prices caused by excessive demand for limited supply of goods and services.
inflation rate Rate of increase in prices of goods and services attributable to excessive demand and limited supply.
initial public offering (IPO) New stock issue that is publicly traded for the first time.
inside information Significant corporate information that has not yet been made public.

insider Person who has access to inside information about a company.

insolvent Unable to pay obligations.

institution Bank, mutual fund, pension fund, corporation, insurance company, college or union.

insurance Contract to reimburse for a loss.

insured account Accountant at a financial entity with government or private insurance coverage.

interest sensitive Reacts to upward or downward movement of rates.

intermediate term In stocks or bonds, a year or more.

intermediation Putting money on deposit at a bank.

inverted yield curve Yield curve where short-term rates are higher than long-term rates.

investment banker Firm that intermediates as broker between issue and buyers.

investment company Entity that manages mutual funds.

investment grade Bonds rated BBB or better.

investment history Pattern of investment practice through time.

investment income Income from securities.

investment strategy Asset allocation plan.

Investor Relations Department Corporate office responsible for addressing investor needs.

irrevocable trust A trust in which the beneficiary must agree to any changes in, or the termination of, that trust.

issuer Entity that issues and promotes sale of its securities.

J

joint account Account opened and owned by two or more people.

joint venture Two or more parties in contract on a project together.

jumbo certificate of deposit (jumbo CD) Usually, a certificate of $100,000 or more.

junk bond Bond rated BB or lower.

K

Keogh plan Type of tax-deferred pension plan.

kicker Usually, equity partnership in a bond deal to enhance appeal of the bond.

kiddie tax Tax filed for children's accounts as they generate taxable income or gains.

know your customer Obligation on the part of the broker to determine client suitability.

L

labor intensive Industry that requires a high number of workers.

ladder Succession of fixed income maturities set up to diversify risks associated with timing or reinvestment.

last sale Most recent sale of a security in a trading period.

last trading day Last day a futures contract can settle.

late tape Heavy trading volume that causes the tape to lag behind transactions.

lay off Usually, risk reduction.

leader Stock or group of stocks that leads an advance or decline, usually in volume activity.

leverage Borrowing.

leveraged buyout Takeover relying on borrowed funds.

liability Claim on assets.

lien Creditor's claim against an asset.

limit order Order to buy or sell at a specific price or better than the current market level.

limit price Price set in a limit order.

limited partnership Investors who have invested in a partnership, but who do not have liability beyond their investment for losses.

liquid asset Asset that can immediately be converted to cash.

liquidity Measurement of an asset's convertibility to cash.

listed security Security traded on a recognized U.S. exchange.

listing requirements Standards for inclusion on a given exchange.

load Mutual fund sales charge.

loan Borrowing of an asset by one entity from another entity.

loan value Value of collateral.

long bond The U.S. 30-Year Treasury Bond.

long position Owning a security.

long term Holding period of more than six months for a security.

long-term debt Debt issued for more than one year.

loophole Way to legally, but not always ethically, get around a rule or law.

lump sum distribution Cashing out an entire vehicle for one payment.

M

macroeconomics National economic view and study.

maintenance fee Brokerage account fee to cover costs of services and generate revenue for the brokerage.

make a market Willing to buy or sell a given security at its current price.

managed account Discretionary account where a manager allocates the asset for a fee.

management The organizational structure of a company.

management fee Comprises internal fees of a mutual fund established to cover costs of services and generate revenue for the fund.

managing underwriter Lead underwriter of an offering.

manipulation False appearance of price movement, volume or any kind of activity in a security.

margin Borrowing capability of a security.

margin account An account set up to facilitate margin trades if the customer so desires.

margin agreement Mutual agreement between brokerage and client regarding margin activity rules.

mark to the market Timely adjusted price of a security.

market Public area to buy and sell.

market analysis Study of different markets in order to project the future behavior of one particular market.

market capitalization Value of a company as determined by outstanding shares of its stock multiplied by the stock's current price.

market letter Research publication directed toward market projections.

market maker Person who will buy and sell at current prices of a security.

market order Order to buy or sell at current prices.

market price Most recent price of a security.

market research Research to evaluate a market for a product.

market risk Risk attached to a market as a whole, as reflected in any one security.

market share The part of a market that a given security or product makes up.

market timing Buying or selling of securities based on a perception of what the market as a whole may do.

market tone Psychological status of a market.

market value Security's value based on current price.

marketability Liquidity.

marketable security Liquid security.

marketing Selling.

marketplace Market.

mature economy Economy of a major nation that is in its later stages of growth.

maturity date Date on which a security comes due for payment to the holder.

medium term Intermediate-term maturity of a note.

medium-term notes (MTNs) Notes of 2-to-10-year duration that often pay monthly.

member bank A Federal Reserve Bank.

member firm Firm that has a seat on an exchange.

merchant bank Bank that facilitates investment activities.

merger The joining of two or more companies.

microeconomics Study of primary units of an economy.

missing the market Failure to execute an order in a timely fashion that is to the client's disadvantage.

momentum Rate of flow, price, or volume of a security.

monetary policy Money supply policy set by the Federal Reserve.

money center bank Bank located in one of the major financial centers of the world.

money market Trading market for short-term debt securities.

money market fund Open-ended mutual fund made up of short-term debt securities.

money supply Cash or cash deposits in the economy.

monopoly Control of something to the extent that competition is precluded.

mortgage-backed security A security issued with mortgages as its backing.

mortgage pool Collection of similar mortgage into one lot.

most active list Highest volume of traded shares on a per day basis.

moving average Trend analysis of a security price using a preset period of time as a scale.

multinational corporation Domestic company with at least one foreign branch established to operate as a foreign subsidiary.

municipal bond Bond issued without federal tax consequence by a nonfederal government entity.

municipal bond insurance Private insurance for municipal debt bought by the issuer for the benefit of the bondholder to cover interrupted payments in default or ultimately to pay off defaulted principle payments.

mutual fund Pooled money managed by an investment company for the benefit of shareholders invested in stocks, bonds, cash or other securities.

mutual fund custodian Bank where mutual fund assets are deposited for safety reasons.

N

narrow market Illiquid and low-volume market.

narrowing the spread Reducing the gap between the bid and offer on a security.

National Association of Securities Dealers (NASD) Regulators of OTC securities dealers.

National Association of Securities Dealers Automated Quotation System (NASDAQ) A price quotation system for OTC securities.

national bank Bank with a U.S. charter.

national debt Money owed by the U.S. government.

nationalization Government takeover of a company.

negative cash flow Spending in excess of income.

negotiable Transferable.

net asset value (NAV) Bid price of a mutual fund established daily after the close by adding the value of the fund's assets, subtracting its liabilities and dividing by the number of shares outstanding.

net change Change in price of a security from one day to the next.

net current assets Working capital.

net earnings Net income.

net proceeds Amount left from a transaction after all costs have been subtracted.

net sales Sales less all costs after they have been subtracted.

net transaction Securities trade with no fees attached.

net worth Amount left in assets after all liabilities have been removed by subtraction.

new account page Form filled out by broker to fulfill know-your-client regulations.

New York Stock Exchange (NYSE) Oldest and largest U.S. securities exchange.

niche Area of a company's business that distinguishes it from other companies of its type.

Nikkei Stock Exchange Tokyo stock exchange.

no-load fund Mutual fund with no front-end sales charge.

non-callable Bond or preferred stock that cannot be redeemed at the option of the issuer.

non-public information Information of a significant nature that will affect the current price of a company's securities once it becomes public.

note Usually, intermediate-term debt issues.

not rated Security unrated by any type of rating service, often simply by choice, and neither a positive nor a negative event.

O

offer Asked buy price.

offering price Price per share for an IPO or secondary offering.

offset transaction Closing trade to eliminate a position.

one-decision stock A buy-and-hold stock.

144A bonds Junk-debt private placements of low issuer cost.

open-end management company Mutual fund sales company that sells open-ended funds.

open-end mutual fund Mutual fund with an unlimited number of shares issued through a management company.

opening trade Establishes a position.

operations department Department in a brokerage firm that handles customer-related clerical functions.

option Opportunity to buy or sell a certain number of securities at a certain price for a certain amount of time.

option agreement Account document required to activate an option trading account for a client.

Options Clearing Corporation (OCC) Corporation dealing in customer-related clerical functions that manages options exchanges.

option writer Entity that sells options.

order Request for a securities transaction.

order ticket Form with request for a securities transaction written on it.

ordinary income Earned income.

organizational chart Company employment positions chart.

original cost All costs bundled together to determine price for an asset acquisition.

originator Investment banker.

OTC See **over the counter**.

other income Not normal income.

out of favor Currently unpopular with analysts and investors for performance reasons.

out-of-the-money option Options whose price does not warrant exercising the option at current levels.

overbought Unnaturally high price for a security.

overhanging supply Excessive quantity of securities available awaiting price to sell opportunity.

overheating Excessive economic expansion.

oversold Unnaturally low price for a security.

oversubscribed Banking issue with demand in excess of the available supply.

over the counter (OTC) Securities not traded on an organized exchange.

overvalued Unnaturally high price for a security from a price/earnings standpoint.

P

paper gain Unrealized gain, as no transaction has been made to take the gain.

paper loss Unrealized loss, as no transaction has been made to take the loss.

par Face value.

parent Company that owns other companies.

partnership Two or more people in business together.

passive income Income from investments deemed by the IRS to be passive investments.

passive loss Losses from investments deemed by the IRS to be passive investments.

pass-through security Security that is a packaged income product that passes through the income to the security's holders.

payment date Income payment date to security holder.

pay up To pay above the currently perceived value of a security on the belief that the security will trade still higher.

penny stocks Usually, stocks that trade at less than $10 per share are OTC and are quite speculative.

pension fund Retired workers' retirement fund.

physical commodity The underlying tangible item upon which a futures contract is based.

pink sheets Listing of thousands of OTC stocks, their current bid/offer prices and who trades them.

pledging Surrendering collateral as security for a loan or other obligation.

plow back Usually with aggressive growth stocks, to retain rather than distribute earnings.

point One percent, as it relates to debt securities; one dollar, as it relates to stocks.

poison pill Securities transaction that is activated by hostile takeover to make a company both less attractive and less susceptible to takeover.

portfolio All securities assets held.

portfolio manager Professional securities manager.

portfolio theory Risk/reward approach to evaluating securities.

position Security holding.

position building Accumulating a security holding.

power of attorney (POA) Permission to act for another in a brokerage relationship.

preferred stock Nonvoting, income producing dividend-oriented stock.

premium Payment above norm.

premium bond Bond priced above par.

premium income Option-writing income.

prepayment Debt payoff before maturity or due date has arrived.

prerefunding Replacing one bond with another before the first is due by using proceeds of the replacement bond to pay it off.

present value Future income measured in today's dollars.

price/earnings ratio (P/E) Price of a stock divided by its most recent annual earnings.

price range Usually, the 52-week high/low price of a security.

price support Usually, government support levels for commodities prices.

pricey Too high an offer price or too low a bid price.

primary dealer Entities that can deal directly with the Federal Reserve to buy government securities.

primary issue New issue of securities.

primary market New-issue market.

prime rate Rate banks charge their most creditworthy customers.

principal Total amount invested (including all costs of acquisition) in a security.

principal amount Face amount of a bond.

probate Process by which a will is administered through court system with executor.

producer price index (PPI) Wholesale price index calculated once per month.

profit Selling price minus purchase price, if to the advantage of the seller.

profit center Area of a company that on its own is expected to make money.

profit sharing Corporate plan to distribute some of its profits internally to employees.

profit taking Usually, sharp responses to broad based selling by traders who made some money, often quickly, on a security, industry group or even a market.

program trading Buying and selling by computer-driven price-monitoring schemes.

progressive tax Tax system under which the more one makes, the more taxes one pays.

projection Prediction.

pro rata Proportionate share.

prospectus SEC-required informational publication on securities offered for sale.

proxy Vote designation.

proxy fight Usually, takeover-related vote designation battle.

proxy statement SEC-required informational publication on securities vote.

Prudent Man Rule State-by-state determination of fiduciary rules.

publicly held Shares owned by the public.

public ownership Shares owned by the public.

purchasing power Margin credit line at a brokerage.

pure play Security that is without any diversification from its stated industry group.

put option Opportunity to sell a certain amount of a security at a certain price for a certain amount of time.

pyramid Leverage.

Q

qualified annuity Annuity purchased in a qualified plan.

qualified plan Tax-deferred retirement plan.

quantitative analysis Numbers-related analysis that depends on statistical interpretation of price movement.

R

raider Investor oriented toward takeover and new management.

rally Upward movement of securities prices, especially after a decline.

random walk The notion that the past is no indication of the future as securities respond only to the random-pattern current events, and these are in no way predictable.

range High/low quotes on a security over some given period of time.

rate of return Measurement of performance.

rating Credit ranking assessing default risk to debt and investment grade to equity as assigned by rating agencies.

Real Estate Investment Trust (REIT) Usually, publicly traded packaged real estate portfolio.

real rate of return Inflation-adjusted return.

rebate Purchase inducement by refund.

recession Usually, two quarters in a row of downside economic activity.

recovery Upward economic or market movement after a decline.

redemption Payoff of a debt security.

refinancing Refunding a debt issue by issuing another.

regional bank Local bank.

regional stock exchange A local exchange that for a non-New York market.

registered representative Broker.

regressive tax Tax system under which the more one makes, the fewer taxes one pays.

regulated investment company Mutual fund that conforms to IRS regulations under Regulation M.

reinsurance Insurance company risk diversification.

reinvestment Returning dividends into the original investment to grow or compound at the rate of return of the investment itself.

relative strength Price movement comparing one security to another.

reorganization Redoing a firm under bankruptcy laws.

rescind Cancel.

research and development (R&D) Creating and preparing for sale a product.

research department Security analysis area of a securities-oriented company.

retail deposit notes (RTNs) Monthly pay senior-debt notes of 5 to 20 years with 2 to 5 years of call protection that are bank issued and FDIC insured.

retail investor Person who invests.

return Profit or loss on an investment.

return on equity (ROE) Percent earnings based on price of a stock.

reversal Change of direction in a security price or market.

rich Security that is overpriced relative to past history, other stocks in its group or the market.

right of survivorship Ability to take title of something when an owner dies.

risk Downside potential.

risk adverse Avoids risk.

risk-free return Usually, short-term U.S. Treasury Bill returns.

riskless transaction Transaction in which the maker cannot lose money.

risk premium Total return potential minus a risk-free return.

rollover Investment transfer from one investment to another.

run Usually, a rapid rising price.

S

salary reduction plan Tax-deferred retirement plan so named because the contributions are pre-tax.

sale Completed transaction.

sales charge Fee paid for securities purchase.

sales literature Marketing material.

sales load Mutual fund sales charge.

savings bank Retail bank.

savings bond U.S. government bonds in $10,000 or smaller denominations; typically used for a child's savings plans.

screening Computer scanning for securities of a given parameter.

seasonal Securities that go up or down in some relationship to the time of year.

seat Euphemism for securities exchange membership.

secondary Public distribution of existing shares in a publicly traded company.

secondary market Post-original-issue markets.

secondary stock Small- or middle-capitalization stock.

sector Stock group.

sector fund Mutual fund of stock group.

secured debt Debt with collateral attached.

securities analyst Securities prognosticator.

Securities and Exchange Commission (SEC) Public protection agency that regulates the securities industry.

Securities Industry Association (SIA) Securities industry lobby.

Securities Investor Protection Corporation (SIPC) Corporations that insure customer accounts against non-market-related brokerage losses, such as default of the house.

security Investment instrument.

security ratings Investment and/or credit evaluation of companies.

sell off Dumping securities with the premise that they will go lower in price sooner than they will rise.

sell out Usually, to cover a margin debit, liquidation of a position or an account.

sell short Selling a security not owned, with the theory in mind that it will go lower in price and can be bought to close the position at a profit on a later date.

seller's market Demand exceeds supply.

selling climax Usually, market bottom induced by a drop in volume and price.

selling group Underwriters who market an issue to the public.

sentiment indicators Gauge of public investor confidence.

settle Pay.

settlement date Payment date for a securities purchase.

shakeout Elimination of secondary-level competition in an industry.

share Usually, equity unit of ownership of a security.

shareholder Owner of shares.

share repurchase plan Corporate stock buyback.

shelf registration Two-year window of opportunity to issue a public offering.

shop Retail brokerage office.

short covering Buying shares to close out a short position.

short position Shares sold short and not yet covered.

short squeeze Rising securities prices go up so far and so fast that many short-sellers, particularly those who sell on margin, are forced to cover because of the magnitude of their losses.

short term One year or less.

short-term debt Paper maturing in one year or less.

short-term gain or loss Gain or loss realized in six months or less.

simple interest Stated rate of interest divided by principal invested.

simplified employee pension (SEP) plan Plan combining aspects of an IRA and a 401(K).

single-premium deferred annuity Lump sum payment annuity that earns without tax consequences until distributions begin.

single-premium life insurance Lump sum payment whole life insurance.

Small Business Administration (SBA) Federal loan agency established to help start up businesses of risk.

small-capitalization stocks Stocks of companies with less than $500 million capitalization that are often, because of their size, more volatile than large-capitalization stocks ($1 billion or more, often quite a bit more).

small investor Usually, the stock odd-lot and modest mutual fund investor who does not have significantly large investments.

soft currency Usually, currency of an economy that has no hard assets to back up that currency and thus lacks liquidity in the currency exchange markets.

soft dollars Commission fees paid to a brokerage.

soft landing Slow but not collapsing economy.

soft market One in which supply exceeds demand.

soft spot Weak stock in a group or weak group in a market.

solvency Ability to pay debt obligations.

sovereign risk Political risk.

specialist Exchange market maker.

speculation Assumption of significant risk for unusually significant return.

spin-off Company that is removed from another company and becomes independent.

split Dividing shares without influencing capitalization with the idea that a stock will be more attractive to investors if it is at a lower price.

spread Difference between bid and offer.

squeeze Forced short-sale-position closing due to sharply rising prices.

stabilization Leveling.

staggered maturity Reinvestment risk reduction in bond portfolios by laddered maturities.

stagnation Arrested or declining economic growth.

Standard and Poor's Index (S&P 500) Widely held bundle of 500 stocks that is the generally accepted index of U.S. stock performance.

standard deviation Margin of error in a calculation.

start-up New business.

state bank State-chartered rather than federally chartered bank.

statement Client's written periodic account record.

staying power Pain tolerance in a declining market.

stock Equity ownership of shares.

stock average Standard of market measurement to gauge market performance.

stock buyback Corporation buys its own stock for an assortment of purposes.

stock certificate Piece of paper that represents equity ownership shares.

stock dividend A share rather than cash dividend.

stock exchange Organized securities trading place.

stock index Standard of market measurement to gauge market performance.

stock market Usually, Dow Jones Industrial Averages; or, an exchange where securities are traded.

stock option Opportunity to buy or sell a given amount of stock for a given amount of time at a given level of price.

stock purchase plan Internal corporate buying plan for employees.

stock symbol Series of letters to identify companies, usually, one to three letters for listed stocks and four to five letters for OTC stocks.

stockholder Entity that owns shares.

stockholder of record Owner of a share on a given day.

strategic buyout Buyout with what is perceived as an organized plan and purpose.

street Wall Street.

street name Brokerage term for collective positions of customers' securities held by their securities firm for safekeeping and convenience in the name of the firm.

strip Zero coupon treasury security.

subject Quote on a security that can be changed and is therefore not firm.

suitability rules Know-your-client requirements related especially to higher-risk securities.

support level Area in which a declining security price is expected to stabilize.

suspended trading Trading halt generated by some announcement of significance or important information.

swap One security is replaced with another.

syndicate Underwriting group.

syndicate manager Underwriting manager.

synergy The notion that the sum of the various parts of a corporate merger will somehow exceed their separate values.

synthetic Artificially created securities.

systematic investment Dollar cost averaging of mutual funds by contracted agreement with the fund family.

systematic risk Market risk.

T

take a position Long or short position in a security.

takeover Assumed control of a corporation.

taking delivery Getting a security certificate in hand and assuming possession of it.

tangible asset Real asset, such as collectibles, real estate or other physically formed property.

target Takeover candidate.

target price Stated price goal of an investor at which he or she might want to sell.

tax basis Total cost basis of an investment.

tax bracket Maximum rate of tax on a given income.

tax credit Dollar-for-dollar offset of income tax liability with a credit.

tax deferred Tax liability postponed but not avoided until effective possession has been secured.

tax-exempt security Usually, municipal bond whose interest is not taxable federally or by the state or city in which the issuer is located.

tax planning Systematic and orderly look at a tax situation with the design of reducing tax liability to a minimum.

tax selling Usually, generating losses at year-end to utilize as an offset against gains.

taxable equivalent yield Taxable yield that nets the same to a bondholder as a tax-free municipal bond would.

taxable income Total income remaining at the bottom line of the tax form after all credits and deductions.

technical analysis Price and volume indicators used as a predictor of future securities performance.

technical rally Usually, a bounce-up of prices in a downtrend perceived as being based upon technical factors.

technical sign Perceived trend by analysts.

telephone switching Usually, no-load mutual fund changes done by phone call to the fund family.

tender Surrender of a security to the transfer agent for a reason related to corporate activity.

1099 Securities tax reporting statement.

term The life of an investment with a stated maturity or duration.

test Return to support level of a security declining in price.

thin Illiquid.

tick A downward or upward movement of a stock price.

ticker tape Reporting of a trading activity on a rolling tape across a screen.

tight Active.

tight money Environment where lenders are unwilling to lend.

tip Perceived insider information considered hot.

tombstone Printed information about an underwriting in the form of an announcement.

top-down Macro-to-micro look at a subject.

topping out Pricey level that may lead to a decline.

total return Combination of cash flow and appreciation on a security.

total volume All trades for a given day in a given security.

tout Aggressive promotion to excess.

trade A purchase or sale of a security.

trade deficit Amount of imports in excess of exports.

trade surplus Amount of exports in excess of imports.

trader A person who buys and sells securities usually speculatively on a proprietary or personal basis.

trading pattern Technical phrase related to a high/low long-term trend in a security price.

trading range High/low price of a security for a specified period of time.

transaction A buy or sell order.

transaction costs Buy or sell costs.

treasuries U.S. government debt securities enjoying the full faith and credit of the U.S. government.

trend Perceived general upward or downward direction as determined by analysts.

trendline Chart used to predict trends.

triple witching hour Options, futures and options on futures expiring on the third Friday of March, June, September, and December often generating huge trading volume.

trust Document that is created to contain property for the maker under the control of a trustee, often used to avoid probate of an estate.

trust company Entity set up to assume fiduciary responsibility for trusts.

turkey Bad investment.

turnaround Favorable reversal of a downtrend.

turnover Usually, velocity of trading in a mutual fund expressed as a multiple of the fund's assets.

12b-1 fees Internal mutual fund fees assessed to the shareholder to cover assorted sales and marketing expenses.

twisting Churning.

U

undercapitalization Lack of adequate working capital.

undervalued Usually, analysts' perception that a security is trading at below its market value, liquidation value or breakup value.

underwrite Bring new securities issues to market.

underwriter Investment banker.

underwriting group Group established to broker a new securities issue to the public.

underwriting spread Difference between underwriter and public cost of a new security issue.

unearned income Income from sources other than employment compensation.

unencumbered Free and clear of debt.

Uniform Gift to Minors Act (UGMA) Child asset management act to protect minors' interests.

U.S. government securities Usually, treasuries.

unit investment trust (UIT) Packaged securities product.

unlisted security OTC security.

unloading Wholesale dumping of declining securities on the open market to avoid further losses.

unrealized gain Paper gain.

unrealized loss Paper loss.

unsecured debt Debt without collateral attached to it.

upside potential Estimate as to how high an investment can go.

uptick Trade at higher price than previous one.

up trend Security moving upward in price.

V

velocity Rate of turnover of money.

venture capital Usually, risk capital used for speculative startup companies.

vesting Acquisition of benefits by an employee by virtue of duration of tenure of employment.

Volatile Sharp and often short upward and downward movement in the price of a security.

Volume Number of units of a security traded in a fixed time period.

W

Wall Street Street in downtown Manhattan that is in the heart of the financial district and hence gives its name to the entire area.

weak market A downward market created by an absence of buyers and a proliferation of sellers.

whipsaw market Usually, trading market where some traders misgauge volatility and thus buy high and sell low.

white knight Takeover entity approved by a hostile takeover candidate in an attempt to avoid acquisition by an unwanted suitor.

wholesaler Representative of a mutual fund company to the securities industry.

windfall profit Unexpected profit due to an unpredicted positive event.

window dressing Portfolio cleaning to create a positive appearance for securities public.

window of opportunity Limited time span to consummate a particular securities transaction.

wire house Large retail brokerage firm.

withholdings Tax deductions from income and securities activity in anticipation of tax liabilities.

working capital Cash.

write-off Loss used as a tax deduction.

writer Person who sells calls or puts to generate income.

Y

yield Income return of a security.

yield curve Plot of yields at various maturity dates on a graph.

yield equivalence Tax-related comparison of the yields of various fixed income securities.

yield to call Yield rate until first call date of a bond.

yield to maturity Yield rate until maturity of a bond.

Z

zero coupon security Security stripped of its interest payments, sold at a discount, and that accretes interest to par value over the life of the security.

Chapter 19

Consideration of Real Estate as an Asset

Contents

Income-Producing Rental Property	**19.02**
Investing in Rental Real Estate	**19.15**
Importance of Real Estate to the Client	**19.16**
Selling a Home	**19.16**
It's a Real Estate Market	**19.24**

In the midst of a prolonged recession, with a moribund stock market, the residential real estate market continues to achieve record highs. In most areas, residential real estate is priced at levels not dreamed of as recently as two years ago when the recession began. Adjustable-rate loans are at historic lows; fixed-rate loans are near their lows. Builders put up homes as fast as they can—from custom-built mansions to starter condominium complexes. The appetite for residential real estate seems insatiable.

What does this mean to the tax preparer? It means that they can expect to have many more real estate transactions to address formally and even more informal client inquiries to consider.

INCOME-PRODUCING RENTAL PROPERTY

With a large segment of the population turning 18 between now and 2010, and considering leaving the nest, demand for rental housing will be on the increase. In most parts of the country, multifamily housing construction is barely keeping pace with demand, and vacancy rates are down countrywide. Fairly obviously, rental real estate income becomes an attractive consideration.

Rental income and expenses, and how to report them, is discussed in this section of the chapter. The discussion also covers casualty losses on rental property and the passive activity and at-risk rules.

Rental Income

The taxpayer must declare as income all remuneration received as rent. Rental income is *any* payment received for the use or occupation of property. If the taxpayer is a cash-basis taxpayer, all rental income should be reported for the year in which it is actually or constructively received.

In addition to amounts the taxpayer receives as normal rent payments, other amounts may be rental income:

1. *Advance rent* is any amount the taxpayer receives before the period that it covers. This, too, is included in rental income in the year the taxpayer receives it, regardless of the period covered or the method of accounting the taxpayer uses.

2. *Security deposits* are not included in income when received if the owner plans to return them to the tenants at the end of the lease. If, however, the taxpayer keeps part or all of the security deposit during any year because the tenant does not live up to the terms of the lease, then the amount the taxpayer keeps is included in income in that year. When a security deposit is to be used as a final payment of rent, it is considered *advance rent* and is include in income when received.

3. If the tenant pays to *cancel a lease,* the amount received is rent. The payment should be included in income in the year the taxpayer receives it, regardless of the method of accounting.

4. If the tenant pays for *expenses pertaining to the rental property,* the payments are rental income and the owner must include them in income. However, the taxpayer can deduct the expenses if they are deductible rental expenses.

5. When the taxpayer receives *property or services instead of money* as rent, the fair market value of the property or services must be included in rental income. If the services are provided at an agreed-on or specified

price, that price is the fair market value, unless there is evidence to the contrary.

6. If the rental agreement gives the tenant the right to buy the rental property, the payments the taxpayer receives under the agreement are generally rental income. However, if the tenant exercises the right to buy the property, the payments received for the period *after the date of sale* are considered part of the selling price.

7. If owners rent property for fewer than 15 days during the tax year that they also use as their main home, the rent received is not included in income, nor is any rental expense deductible. However, the taxpayer can deduct the interest, taxes and casualty and theft losses that are allowed for nonrental property.

8. If the taxpayer owns a part interest in rental property, he or she must report the share of the rental income from the property.

Rental Expenses

Certain expenses of renting property ordinarily can be deducted from rental income if the taxpayer rents a condominium or cooperative apartment or part of the tax property, or if the taxpayer changes his or her property to rental use. The taxpayer generally deducts these rental expenses in the year the expenses are paid:

1. If the taxpayer retains property for rental purposes, it may be possible to deduct the ordinary and necessary expenses (including depreciation) for managing, conserving or maintaining the property while it is vacant. However, the taxpayer *cannot deduct any loss of rental income* for the period the property is vacant.

2. Ordinary and necessary expenses can be deducted for managing, conserving or maintaining rental property from the time it is made available for rent.

3. Depreciation on rental property begins when it is ready and available for rent.

4. When property that had been held for rental purposes is sold, the taxpayer can deduct the ordinary and necessary expenses for managing, conserving or maintaining the property until it is sold.

5. If the taxpayer sometimes uses the rental property for personal purposes, the expenses must be divided between rental and personal use. Also, the rental expense deductions may be limited.

6. An individual who owns part interest in rental property can deduct the part of the expenses he or she paid.

Differentiating Between Repairs and Improvements

Cost of *repairs* to rental property can be deducted. Although the cost of *improvements* cannot be deducted, they can be recovered by taking depreciation. Therefore, it is important to separate the costs of repairs and improvements and to keep accurate records. These records will be needed to know the cost of improvements when the taxpayer sells or depreciates the property.

A repair keeps the property in good operating condition. It does not materially add to the value of the property or substantially prolong its life. Repainting the property inside or out, fixing gutters or floors, fixing leaks, plastering and replacing broken windows are examples of repairs.

On the other hand, when the taxpayer makes repairs as part of an *extensive remodeling or restoration* of the property, the whole job is an improvement, which is an entirely different matter. An improvement adds to the value of property, prolongs its useful life or adapts it to new uses. When the taxpayer makes an improvement to property, the cost of the improvement must be capitalized. The capitalized cost can generally be depreciated as if the improvement were separate property.

Other Deductible and Non-Deductible Rental Expenses

Other expenses the taxpayer can deduct from the rental income include advertising, cleaning and maintenance services, utilities, fire and liability insurance, taxes, interest, commissions for the collection of rent, ordinary and necessary travel and transportation and the following expenses:

1. A taxpayer can deduct the rent paid on property that he or she then turned around and used for rental purposes (i.e., sublet). If the individual buys a leasehold for rental purposes, it is permissible to deduct an equal part of the cost each year over the term of the lease.

2. The taxpayer can deduct rent paid for equipment used for rental purposes. However, in some cases, *lease contracts* are actually *purchase contracts*. If this is the case, the taxpayer cannot deduct these payments but can recover the cost of purchased equipment through depreciation.

3. If an insurance premium is paid for more than one year in advance, each year the taxpayer can deduct the part of the premium payment that will apply to that year. The total premium cannot be deducted in the year it is paid.

4. Generally, the taxpayer *cannot deduct charges for local benefits* that increase the value of the property—such as charges for putting in streets, sidewalks or water and sewer systems. These charges are nondepreciable capital expenditures. They must be added to the basis of the property. The taxpayer can deduct local benefit taxes if they are for maintaining, repairing or paying interest charges for the benefits.

5. The taxpayer can deduct mortgage interest paid on rental property.

6. Certain expenses paid to obtain a mortgage on rental property cannot be deducted as interest. These expenses, which include mortgage commissions, abstract fees and recording fees, are capital expenses. However, the taxpayer can amortize them over the life of the mortgage.

Other Expenses Involving Points

The term "points" is often used to describe some of the charges paid by a borrower when he or she takes out a loan or a mortgage. These charges are also called loan origination fees, maximum loan charges or premium charges. If any of these charges (points) are solely for the use of money, they are *interest.*

Points paid when the taxpayer takes out a loan or mortgage result in original issue discount (OID). In general, the points (OID) are deductible as interest unless they must be capitalized. How the taxpayer figures the amount of points (OID) to deduct each year depends on whether or not the total OID, including the OID resulting from the points, is insignificant or *de minimis.* If the OID is not *de minimis,* the taxpayer must use the constant yield method to figure how much he or she can deduct.

In general, the OID is *de minimis* if it is less than one-fourth of 1 percent (.0025) of the stated redemption price at maturity (generally, the principal amount of the loan) multiplied by the number of full years from the date of original issue to maturity (the term of the loan).

If the OID is *de minimis,* the taxpayer can choose one of the following ways to figure the amount allowed for deduction each year:

1. On a constant yield basis over the term of the loan.
2. On a straight-line basis over the term of the loan.
3. In proportion to stated interest payments.
4. In full at maturity of the loan.

The preparer makes this choice by deducting the OID in a manner consistent with the method chosen on the timely filed tax return for the tax year in which the loan or mortgage is issued.

The Constant Yield Method.   If the OID is *not de minimis,* the taxpayer must use the constant yield method to figure how much he or she is allowed to deduct each year.

The CPA figures the taxpayer's deduction for the first year in the following manner by:

1. Determining the issue price of the loan. For example, if the taxpayer paid points on a loan, the points the taxpayer paid from the principal amount of the loan are subtracted to get the issue price.

2. Multiplying the issue price (the result in step 1) by the yield to maturity.
3. Subtracting any qualified stated interest payments from the result in step 2. This is the amount of OID the taxpayer can deduct in the first year.

To figure the deduction in any subsequent years, it is necessary to start with the *adjusted issue price*. To obtain the adjusted issue price, the CPA adds to the issue price any OID previously deducted and then follows steps 2 and 3.

The yield to maturity is shown in the information the taxpayer receives from the lender. If the taxpayer does not receive it, the tax advisor should consult the lender to obtain this information. In general, the yield to maturity is the discount rate that, when used in computing the present value of all principal and interest payments, produces an amount equal to the principal amount of the loan.

Qualified stated interest is stated interest that is unconditionally payable in cash or property (other than debt instruments of the issuer) at least annually at a single fixed rate.

When the Loan or Mortgage Ends.   If the taxpayer's loan or mortgage ends, the accountant may be able to deduct any remaining points (OID) in the tax year in which the loan or mortgage ends. A loan or mortgage may end due to a refinancing, prepayment, foreclosure, or similar event. However, if the refinancing is with the same lender, the remaining points (OID) generally are not deductible in the year in which the refinancing occurs, but they may be deductible over the term of the new mortgage or loan.

Travel Expenses

The taxpayer can deduct the ordinary and necessary expenses of traveling away from home if the primary purpose of the trip was to collect rental income or to manage, conserve or maintain the rental property. It is important to allocate the expenses properly between rental and nonrental activities.

It is also permissible to deduct ordinary and necessary local transportation expenses if they are incurred to collect rental income or to manage, conserve or maintain the rental property.

Generally, if taxpayers use a personal car, pickup truck or light van for rental activities, they can deduct the expenses by one of two methods: actual expenses or the standard mileage rate.

Tax Return Preparation

The taxpayer can deduct, as a rental expense, the part of tax return preparation fees paid to prepare that portion of the return pertaining to rental income. It is also possible to deduct, as a rental expense, any expense paid to resolve a tax underpayment related to the rental activities.

Condominiums and Cooperatives

If the taxpayer rents out a condominium or a cooperative apartment, special rules apply. Condominiums are treated differently from cooperatives.

Condominiums. If the individual owns a condominium, the property is considered a dwelling unit in a multiunit building. This also involves owning and being responsible for a share of the common elements of the structure, such as land, lobbies, elevators, and service areas. The taxpayer and the other condominium owners usually pay dues or assessments to a special corporation that is organized to take care of the common elements.

If the owner rents the condominium to others, the CPA can deduct depreciation, repairs, upkeep, dues, interest and taxes and assessments for the care of the common parts of the structure. It is not possible to deduct special assessments paid to a condominium management corporation for improvements. Taxpayers may, however, be able to recover a share of the cost of any improvement by taking depreciation. A condominium may be the ideal way to purchase rental property, as the price is usually lower than that for a single-family home and are often in ideal locations near schools, work places and public transportation.

Since condos are governed by a set of condominium documents, a home-owners association is expected to see that the rules set down in these documents are followed. It is extremely important before purchasing a condo unit for rental or other investment purposes to review these documents closely. Some condominium documents contain rather unusual and restrictive rules about rentals, for example. Therefore, it is wise to discover any objectionable details before incurring expenses, such as for a title search and loan application fees.

Contained in the condominium documents may be a stipulation that rentals are permitted only one time per year. This is probably very desirable for those who make their main home in the particular block of condominiums. Nor would it be a problem in an area where it is preferable to find a tenant for an annual rental, but a condo located in a popular resort area may be better offered as a "seasonal rental." Rents charged in the most popular seasons are typically much higher than at other times of the year. In such a case, the owner or investor should look carefully at the rental restriction rules.

Two other important details to check are the budget and the amount set aside for reserves by the homeowners association. If any special assessments are planned for the near future, it would be foolhardy to purchase a condominium and set a rental amount only to discover that out-of-pocket money will soon be assessed for a new roof.

Condominium budgets normally chart the useful remaining life of the major systems in the building and property.

Cooperatives. If the taxpayer has a cooperative apartment that is rented to others, he or she can usually deduct as a rental expense all the maintenance fees paid to the cooperative housing corporation. However, a payment earmarked for a capital asset or improvement, or otherwise charged to the corporation's capital account cannot be deducted. For example, the taxpayer cannot deduct a payment used to pave a community parking lot, install a new roof, or pay the principal of the corporation's mortgage. The payment must instead be added to the basis of their stock in the corporation.

The amount the taxpayer was assessed for capital items is treated as a capital cost. This cannot be more than the amount by which the taxpayer's payments to the corporation exceeded his or her share of the corporation's mortgage interest and real estate taxes.

The taxpayer's share of interest and taxes is the amount the corporation elected to allocate to him or her, if it reasonably reflects those expenses for the apartment. Otherwise, the share is figured by:

1. Dividing the number of taxpayer shares of stock by the total number of shares outstanding, including any shares held by the corporation.
2. Multiplying the corporation's deductible interest by the number the taxpayer figured in step 1. This is the taxpayer's share of the interest.
3. Multiplying the corporation's deductible taxes by the number the taxpayer figured in step 1. This is the taxpayer's share of the taxes.

In addition to the maintenance fees paid to the cooperative housing corporation, the taxpayer can deduct direct payments for repairs, upkeep and other rental expenses, including interest paid on a loan used to buy the stock in the corporation.

Property Changed to Rental Use

If the taxpayer changes his or her home or other property (or a part of it) to rental use at any time other than the beginning of the tax year, he or she must divide yearly expenses, such as depreciation, taxes and insurance, between rental use and personal use.

The taxpayer can deduct as rental expenses only the part of the expense that is for the part of the year the property was used or held for rental purposes. What cannot be deducted is depreciation or insurance for the part of the year the property was held for personal use. The home mortgage interest and real estate tax expenses, however, can be included as an itemized deduction for the part of the year the property was held for personal use.

Renting Part of a Property

If the taxpayer rents part of the property, certain expenses must be divided between the part of the property used for rental purposes and the part used for personal purposes, as though they were two separate pieces of property. Expenses related to the part of the property used for rental purposes, such as home mortgage interest and real estate taxes, can be deducted as rental expenses. Expenses for the part used for personal purposes, subject to certain limitations, are deductible only if the deductions are itemized. A part of other expenses that normally are non-deductible personal expenses, such as expenses for electricity or painting the outside of the house, can also be deducted as rental expense. The taxpayer cannot deduct any part of the cost of the first phone line even if the tenants have unlimited use of it. The taxpayer does not have to divide the expenses that belong only to the rental part of the property.

If an expense is for both rental use and personal use, such as mortgage interest or heat for the entire house, the taxpayer must divide the expense between rental use and personal use. Any reasonable method for dividing the expense is permissible. It may be reasonable to divide the cost of some items (for example, water) based on the number of people using them. However, the two most common methods for dividing an expense are one based on the number of rooms in the home and one based on the square footage.

Personal Use of Dwelling Unit (Including Vacation Home)

If the taxpayer has any personal use of a dwelling unit (including vacation home) that is rented, the expenses must be divided between rental use and personal use.

If the taxpayer used the dwelling unit for personal purposes long enough during the year, it will be considered a "dwelling unit used as a home." If so, the taxpayer cannot deduct rental expenses that exceed rental income for that property. If the dwelling unit is not considered one used as a home, the taxpayer may deduct rental expenses that exceed rental income for that property subject to certain limits.

If the taxpayer uses the dwelling unit as a home and rents it fewer than 15 days during the year, no rent is included in income and no deduction is taken for rental expenses.

Definition of a Dwelling Unit

A dwelling unit can be a house, apartment, condominium, mobile home, boat, vacation home or similar property. It has basic living accommodations, such as sleeping space, a toilet and cooking facilities.

A dwelling unit *does not* include property used solely as a hotel, motel, inn or similar establishment. Property is used solely as a hotel, motel, inn or similar establishment if it is regularly available for occupancy by paying customers and is not used by an owner as a home during the year.

Dwelling Unit Used as Home

The tax treatment of rental income and expenses for a dwelling unit that the taxpayer also uses for personal purposes depends on whether the taxpayer uses it as a home. The taxpayer uses a dwelling unit as a home during the tax year if it is used for personal purposes more than the greater of:

1. 14 days or
2. 10 percent of the total days it is rented to others at a fair rental price.

If a dwelling unit is used for personal purposes on a day it is rented at a fair rental price, that day is not counted as a day of rental use in applying the 10 percent rule. Instead, it is considered a day of personal use in applying rules 1 and 2. This is moot if expenses are being divided between rental and personal use.

Fair Rental Price.   A fair rental price for property generally is an amount that a person who is not related to the taxpayer would be willing to pay. The rent charged is not a fair rental price if it is substantially less than the rents charged for other similar properties.

The following questions should be considered when comparing another property with the unit in question:

1. Is it used for the same purpose?
2. Is it approximately the same size?
3. Is it in approximately the same condition?
4. Does it have similar furnishings?
5. Is it in a similar location?

If any of the answers is no, the properties probably are not similar.

Use as Main Home Before or After Renting.   The days a taxpayer used the property as his or her main home before or after renting it or offering it for rent are not counted as days of personal use in either of the following circumstances:

1. The taxpayer rented or tried to rent the property for 12 or more consecutive months.

2. The taxpayer rented or tried to rent the property for a period of less than 12 consecutive months and the period ended because the property was sold or exchanged.

This special rule does not apply when dividing expenses between rental and personal use.

Figuring Days of Personal Use.   A day of personal use of a dwelling unit is any day it is used by any of the following persons:

1. The taxpayer or any other person who has an interest in it, unless this individual rents it to another owner as his or her main home under a shared equity financing agreement (defined later).
2. A member of the individual's family or a member of the family of any other person who has an interest in the property, unless the family member uses the dwelling unit as his or her main home and pays a fair rental price. "Family" includes only brothers and sisters, half-brothers and half-sisters, spouses, ancestors (parents, grandparents, great grandparents) and lineal descendants (children, grandchildren, great grandchildren).
3. Anyone under an arrangement that lets the taxpayer use some other dwelling unit.
4. Anyone at less than a fair rental price.

If the other person or member of the family in items 1 and 2 has more than one home, his or her main home is the one lived in most of the time.

Shared Equity Financing Agreement.   This is an agreement under which two or more persons acquire undivided interests for more than 50 years in an entire dwelling unit, including the land, and one or more of the co-owners is entitled to occupy the unit as his or her main home upon payment of rent to the other co-owner or owners.

Donation of Use of Property.   The taxpayer has used a dwelling unit for personal purposes if:

1. The taxpayer donates the use of the unit to a charitable organization.
2. The organization sells the use of the unit at a fund-raising event.
3. The "purchaser" uses the unit.

Days Used for Repairs and Maintenance.   Any day that the taxpayer spends working substantially full time repairing and maintaining a property is not counted as a day of personal use. It is not counted as a day of personal use even if family members use the property for recreational purposes on the same day.

How to Divide Expenses

If a person uses a dwelling unit for both rental and personal purposes, expenses are divided between the rental use and the personal use based on the number of days used for each purpose. When dividing the expenses, following are the correct rules:

1. Any day that the unit is rented at a fair rental price is a day of rental use even if the taxpayer used the unit for personal purposes that day. This rule does not apply when determining whether the taxpayer used the unit as a home.
2. Any day that the unit is available for rent but not actually rented is not a day of rental use.

How to Figure Rental Income and Deductions

How the taxpayer figures the rental income and deductions depends on whether the dwelling unit was used as his or her home and, if used as a home, how many days the property was rented.

If the taxpayer does not use a dwelling unit as a home, all the rental income is reported and all the rental expenses are deducted.

If the taxpayer uses a dwelling unit as a home during the year, how the rental income and deductions are handled depends on how many days the unit was rented. If the owner uses it as a home and rents it fewer than 15 days during the year, none of the rental income is included in income, nor are any expenses declared as rental expenses.

On the other hand, if the taxpayer uses a dwelling unit as a home but rents it 15 days or more during the year, all of the rental income must be declared. If the taxpayer had a net profit from the rental property for the year (that is, if the taxpayer's rental income is more than the total of the rental expenses, including depreciation), all of the rental expenses may be deducted.

However, if there was a net loss, the taxpayer's deduction for certain rental expenses is limited.

Limit on Deductions.   If rental expenses are more than the rental income, the owner cannot use the excess expenses to offset income from other sources. The excess can be carried forward to the next year and treated as rental expenses for the same property. Expenses carried forward to the next year will be subject to any limits that apply then. The taxpayer can deduct the expenses carried over to a year only up to the amount of the rental income for that year, even if the property is not used as the taxpayer's home during that particular year.

Depreciation

The taxpayer recovers the cost in income-producing property through yearly tax deductions by *depreciating* the property; that is, by deducting some of the cost on his or her tax return each year.

Three basic factors determine how much depreciation the taxpayer can deduct:

1. The taxpayer's basis in the property.
2. The recovery period for the property.
3. The depreciation method used.

The taxpayer cannot simply deduct the mortgage, principal payments or the cost of furniture, fixtures and equipment as an expense.

The taxpayer can deduct depreciation only on the part of the property used for rental purposes. Depreciation reduces the basis for figuring gain or loss on a later sale or exchange. (For further information on depreciation, see Chapter 33; for figuring the basis of property, see Chapter 35.)

Casualties and Thefts

As a result of a casualty or theft, the taxpayer may have a loss related to property and be able to deduct the loss on his or her income tax return. Damage to, destruction of or loss of property is a *casualty* if it results from an identifiable event that is sudden, unexpected or unusual. The unlawful taking and removing of money or property with the intent to deprive the taxpayer of it is a *theft*.

When the taxpayer has a casualty to, or theft of, property and receives money, including insurance, that is more than the adjusted basis in the property, he or she generally must report the gain. However, under certain circumstances, it is possible to defer paying tax by choosing to postpone reporting the gain. To do this, the taxpayer must buy replacement property within two years after the close of the first tax year in which any part of the gain is realized. The cost of the replacement property must equal or exceed the net insurance or other payment received.

Limits on Rental Losses

Rental real estate activities are considered passive activities, and the amount of loss the taxpayer can deduct is limited. Generally, taxpayers cannot deduct losses from rental real estate activities unless they have income from other passive activities. However, they may be able to deduct rental losses without regard to whether they have income from other passive activities if they "materially" or "actively" participated in the rental activity.

Losses from passive activities are first subject to the at-risk rules. At-risk rules limit the amount of deductible losses from holding most real property placed in service after 1986. However, if rental losses are less than $25,000, and the taxpayer actively participated in the rental activity, the passive activity limits probably do not apply.

If the taxpayer used the rental property as a home during the year, the passive activity rules do not apply to that home. Instead, the CPA must follow the rules explained relating to personal use above.

At-Risk Rules.   The at-risk rules place a limit on the amount the CPA can deduct as losses from activities often described as tax shelters. Losses from holding real property (other than mineral property) placed in service before 1987 are not subject to the at-risk rules.

Generally, any loss from an activity subject to the at-risk rules is allowed only to the extent of the total amount the taxpayer has at risk in the activity at the end of the tax year. The taxpayer is considered "at risk" in an activity to the extent of cash and the adjusted basis of other property contributed to the activity and certain amounts borrowed for use in the activity.

Passive Activity Limits.   In general, all rental activities (except those relating to real estate professionals) are passive activities. For this purpose, a rental activity is an activity from which the taxpayer receives income mainly for the use of tangible property, rather than for services.

Deductions for losses from passive activities are limited. The taxpayer generally cannot offset income, other than passive income, with losses from passive activities. Nor can the taxpayer offset taxes on income, other than passive income, with credits resulting from passive activities. Any excess loss or credit is carried forward to the next tax year.

Losses from Rental Real Estate Activities.   If the taxpayer or spouse actively participated in a passive real estate rental activity, he or she can deduct up to $25,000 of loss associated with the activity from the nonpassive income. This special allowance is an exception to the general rule disallowing losses in excess of income from passive activities. Similarly, the accountant can offset credits from the activity against the tax on up to $25,000 of nonpassive income after taking into account any losses allowed under this exception.

If the taxpayer is married, filing a separate return, and lived apart from a spouse for the entire tax year, the special allowance cannot be more than $12,500. If the taxpayer lived with a spouse at any time during the year and is filing a separate return, he or she cannot use the special allowance to reduce the nonpassive income or tax on nonpassive income.

The maximum amount of the special allowance is reduced if the modified adjusted gross income is more than $100,000 ($50,000 if married filing separately).

If the modified adjusted gross income is $100,000 or less ($50,000 or less if married filing separately), the CPA can deduct the taxpayer's loss up to $25,000 ($12,500 if married filing separately). If the modified adjusted gross income is more than $100,000 (more than $50,000 if married filing separately), this special allowance is limited to 50 percent of the difference between $150,000 ($75,000 if married filing separately) and the modified adjusted gross income. Generally, there is no relief from the passive activity loss limits if the modified adjusted gross income is $150,000 or more ($75,000 or more if married filing separately).

The taxpayer actively participated in a rental real estate activity if he or she (and the spouse) owned at least 10 percent of the rental property and made management decisions in a significant and bona fide sense. Management decisions include approving new tenants, deciding on rental terms and approving expenditures.

INVESTING IN RENTAL REAL ESTATE

Statistics published by the U.S. Census Bureau indicate that 75 percent of multifamily investors in rental residential real estate are over the age of 45. Of these, more than one-half own fewer than five units and earned approximately 31 percent of their income from ownership of rental properties.

Most real estate investors enter this activity in their upper-middle years because they are concerned about their retirement, have probably reached their highest potential earning power, have inherited money or real estate and have more discretionary funds available.

Four reasons are often advanced for considering real estate as an investment option:

1. *Cash flow*—It is possible in many parts of the country to have a cash flow return on real estate investment. After all of the previously listed expenses have been covered (e.g., mortgage, vacancy factor, repairs and property management) there can still be some money coming in while equity is being built up.

2. *Increase in equity*—As the mortgage is reduced and the equity increases, every mortgage payment gives the investor a greater sense of being a "man or woman of property."

3. *Appreciation*—It is within reason to expect a 4 percent appreciation level. Depending upon supply and demand and the escalation of costs, including the increased costs of construction, land and development costs, some periods will be more opportune than others. However, as long as the overall demand increases in relation to the availability of adequate housing, real estate investments will continue to appreciate.

The average single-family home sold for $23,400 in 1970; in 2000, a similar average home sold for $169,000. An approximate 8 percent annual increase with little chance of a drastic drop in value is almost always a tempting investment. But remember, location, location, location is a prime consideration.

4. *Tax savings* — The IRS permits all but actual real estate dealers to depreciate their investment properties on Schedule E when filing annual tax returns. Residential properties depreciate over 27.5 years; commercial properties, over 39 years.

Of course, the government gets a share with the sale of investment property. The investor is faced with a 20 percent capital gains tax on the increase in value of the property and the recapture of the depreciation. This cost can be deferred if the seller completes a 1031 tax-deferred exchange to trade up from property to property.

Regardless of the size of a real estate investment, it is possible to make a return, but as with *any* investment, it is important to research the market.

IMPORTANCE OF REAL ESTATE TO THE CLIENT

A client cannot expect that the tax preparer be an authority on real estate law and regulations. However, those handling tax preparation should understand that, for most of their clients, their homes are the single largest purchase and investment they will ever make. Therefore, the accountant is well-advised to credit the seriousness, consequence and priority of any questions clients ask about their residential real estate.

SELLING A HOME

This portion of the chapter explains the tax rules that apply in selling a main home. It does not cover the sale of rental property, second homes, or vacation homes.

If the taxpayer has a gain from the sale, the preparer may be able to exclude up to $250,000 of the gain from his or her income ($500,000 on a joint return in most cases). Any gain not excluded is taxable. It is not possible to deduct loss from the sale of a main home.

It is not necessary to report the sale of the main home on the tax return unless there is a gain, at least part of which is taxable.

The Main Home

The main home can be a house, houseboat, mobile home, cooperative apartment or condominium. To exclude gain under the rules, the person generally must have owned and lived in the property as the main home for at least two years during the five-year period ending on the date of sale.

If a person sells the land on which the main home is located, but not the house itself, the accountant cannot exclude any gain from the sale of the land.

If the taxpayer has more than one home, the preparer can exclude gain only from the sale of the main home. Gain from the sale of any other home must be included in income. If someone has two homes and lives in both of them, the main home is ordinarily the one lived in most of the time.

If the taxpayer uses only part of the property as the main home, the rules discussed in this chapter apply only to the gain or loss on the sale of *that part* of the property.

Rules for Sales

If the taxpayer sold the main home, as just noted, it may be possible to exclude any gain from income up to a limit of $250,000 ($500,000 on a joint return in most cases).

The main topics in this section include:

1. How to figure gain or loss.
2. Excluding gain from the sale of a home.
3. Ownership and use tests.
4. Special situations.
5. Reporting the gain.
6. Real estate and transfer taxes.

How to Figure Gain or Loss.   To figure the gain or loss on the sale of the main home, the CPA must know the selling price, the amount realized and the adjusted basis. The selling price is the total amount received for the home. It includes money, all notes, mortgages or other debts assumed by the buyer as part of the sale and the fair market value of any other property or any services received. The selling price of the home does not include amounts received for personal property sold with the home. Personal property is property that is not a permanent part of the home. Separately stated cash the taxpayer received for these items is not proceeds from the transaction.

The taxpayer may have to sell the home because of a job transfer. If the employer pays for a loss on the sale or for selling expenses, this is not include as part of the selling price.

Option to Buy.   If the taxpayer grants an option to buy his or her home and the option is exercised, then the amount received for the option is added to the selling price of the home. If the option is not exercised, the accountant must report the amount paid for the option as ordinary income in the year the option expires.

If the taxpayer can exclude the entire gain, the person responsible for closing the sale generally will not have to report it. The preparer will use sale documents and other records to figure the total amount received for the sale of the home.

Gain or Loss?   Selling expenses include commissions, advertising fees, legal fees and loan charges paid by the seller (such as loan placement fees or points). The amount realized is the selling price minus selling expenses.

While the taxpayer owned the home, he or she may have made adjustments (increases or decreases) to the basis. This adjusted basis is used to figure gain or loss on the sale of the home. (For information on how to figure the home's adjusted basis, see Chapter 35.)

To figure the gain or loss, the amount realized is compared to the adjusted basis. If the amount realized is more than the adjusted basis, the difference is a gain and, except for any part the CPA can exclude, is generally taxable. If the amount realized is less than the adjusted basis, the difference is a loss. A loss on the sale of the main home cannot be deducted.

If the taxpayer and spouse sell their jointly owned home and file a joint return, the gain or loss is figured as for one taxpayer. If the taxpayers file separate returns, each of them must figure their own gain or loss according to their ownership interest in the home. The ownership interest is determined by state law.

If the taxpayer and a joint owner other than a spouse sell their jointly owned home, each of them must figure their own gain or loss according to their ownership interest in the home. Each of them applies the rules discussed in this chapter on an individual basis.

If a person trades an old home for another home, the trade should be treated as a sale and a purchase.

Foreclosure, Repossession and Abandonment.   If the taxpayer's home was foreclosed on or repossessed, he or she has a sale. The CPA figures the gain or loss from the sale in the same way as gain or loss from any sale. But the amount of the gain or loss depends in part on whether the owner was personally liable for repaying the debt secured by the home. If the taxpayer *was not* personally liable, then the selling price includes the full amount of debt canceled by the foreclosure or repossession. If the taxpayer *was* personally liable for the amount of the debt, then the selling price includes the amount of canceled debt up to the home's fair market value. There may be ordinary income in addition to any gain or loss. If the canceled debt is more than the home's fair market value, the taxpayer has ordinary income equal to the difference. However, the income from cancellation of debt is not taxed if the cancellation is intended as a gift, or if they are insolvent or bankrupt.

Generally, the borrower will receive Form 1099-A, *Acquisition or Abandonment of Secured Property,* from his or her lender. This form will have the information the preparer needs to determine the amount of gain or loss and any ordinary income from cancellation of debt. If the debt is canceled, the borrower may receive Form 1099-C, *Cancellation of Debt.*

An owner who abandons a home may have ordinary income. If the abandoned home secures a debt for which the owner is personally liable and the debt is canceled, the taxpayer has ordinary income equal to the amount of canceled debt.

If the home is secured by a loan and the lender knows the home has been abandoned, the lender should send out Form 1099-A or Form 1099-C. If the home is later foreclosed on or repossessed, gain or loss is figured as explained in that discussion.

Effects of Transfer.   When the taxpayer transfers the home to his or her spouse, or to a former spouse in a divorce settlement, there is no gain or loss (unless the exception below applies). This is true even if the taxpayer receives cash or other consideration for the home. Therefore, the rules explained in this chapter do not apply. Nor do they apply if the individual owned the home jointly with a spouse and transfers his or her interest in the home to that spouse or a former spouse. There is no gain or loss.

Furthermore, a transfer of the home to the spouse, or former spouse incident to divorce, does not affect the basis of any new home they buy or build.

These transfer rules do not apply if the spouse or former spouse is a nonresident alien. In that case, the taxpayer will have a gain or loss.

Excluding Gain from the Sale of a Home.   An individual may qualify to exclude from income all or part of any gain from the sale of the main home. This means that, if the individual qualifies, he or she will not have to pay tax on the gain up to the limit described below. To qualify, the taxpayer must meet the ownership and use tests described later. The person can choose not to take the exclusion, but in that case must include in income the entire gain.

Maximum Amount of Exclusion.   The preparer can exclude the entire gain on the sale of the main home up to:

1. $250,000, or
2. $500,000 if all of the following are true:
   a. The owners are married and file a joint return for the year.
   b. Either the taxpayer or spouse meets the ownership test.
   c. Both the taxpayer and spouse meet the use test.
   d. During the two-year period ending on the date of the sale, neither the taxpayer nor spouse excluded gain from the sale of another home.

Reduced Maximum Exclusion.   The accountant can claim an exclusion, but the maximum amount of gain that can be excluded will be reduced if either of the following is true:

1. The seller did not meet the ownership and use tests, but sold the home because of:
   a. A change in place of employment.
   b. Health.
   c. Unforeseen circumstances, to the extent provided in regulations (as discussed below).
2. The exclusion would have been disallowed because of the rule described later, except that the seller sold the home because of:
   a. A change in place of employment.
   b. Health.
   c. Unforeseen circumstances, to the extent provided in regulations (as discussed below).

The problem is the IRS has not issued regulations defining "unforeseen circumstances." Therefore, a person cannot claim an exclusion based on unforeseen circumstances until the IRS issues final regulations — or other appropriate guidance.

More than One Home Is Sold During a Two-Year Period.   The taxpayer cannot exclude gain on the sale of a home if, during the two-year period ending on the date of the sale, he or she sold another home at a gain and excluded all or part of that gain. If the gain cannot be excluded it must be included in income. However, the CPA can still claim an exclusion if the home was sold because of the reasons discussed above.

Ownership and Use Tests.   To claim the exclusion, the taxpayer must meet the ownership and use tests. This means that during the five-year period ending on the date of the sale, the taxpayer must have:

1. Owned the home for at least two years (the ownership test).
2. Lived in the home as the main home for at least two years (the use test).

If the person owned and lived in the property as the main home for less than two years, the CPA can still claim an exclusion in some cases. The maximum amount that can be excluded will be reduced depending on the length of time spent in the home.

The required two years of ownership and use during the five-year period ending on the date of the sale do not have to be continuous. The owners meet the tests if they can show that they owned and lived in the property as their main home for either 24 full months or 730 days (365 × 2) during the five-year period ending on the date of sale.

Short temporary absences for vacations or other seasonal absences, even if the property is rented out during the absences, are counted as periods of use. The taxpayer can meet the ownership and use tests during different two-year periods. However, both tests must be met during the five-year period ending on the date of the sale.

If the owner sold stock in a cooperative housing corporation, the ownership and use tests are met if, during the five-year period ending on the date of sale, the taxpayer:

1. Owned the stock for at least two years.
2. Lived in the house or apartment that the stock entitles him or her to occupy as the main home for at least two years.

Some Exceptions.   There is an exception to the use test if, during the five-year period before the sale of the home:

1. The taxpayer becomes physically or mentally unable to care for him- or herself.
2. The taxpayer owned and lived in the home as the main home for a total of at least one year.

Under this exception, the taxpayer is considered to live in the home during any time that he or she owns the home and lives in a facility (including a nursing home) that is licensed by a state or political subdivision to care for persons in his or her condition. Anyone meeting this exception to the use test must still meet the two-out-of-five-year ownership test to claim the exclusion.

For the ownership and use tests, the preparer may be able to *add the time* owned and lived in a previous home to the time lived in the home on which the taxpayer wishes to exclude gain. This can be done if all or part of the gain on the sale of the previous home was postponed because of buying the home on which the taxpayer wishes to exclude gain.

For the ownership and use tests, the CPA adds the time the taxpayer owned and lived in a previous home that was destroyed or condemned to the time he or she owned and lived in the home on which the taxpayer wishes to exclude gain. This rule applies if any part of the basis of the home sold depended on the basis of the destroyed or condemned home. Otherwise, the taxpayer must have owned and lived in the same home for two of the five years before the sale to qualify for the exclusion.

Rules Relating to Married Persons.   If taxpayer and spouse file a joint return for the year of sale, the CPA can exclude gain if either spouse meets the ownership and use tests. If the taxpayer's spouse died before the date of sale, he or she is considered to have owned and lived in the property as the main home during any period of time when the spouse owned and lived in it as a main home.

If the home was transferred to the taxpayer by the spouse (or former spouse if the transfer was incident to divorce), he or she is considered to have owned it during any period of time when the spouse owned it.

The taxpayer is considered to have used property as the main home during any period when:

1. The taxpayer owned it, and
2. The spouse or former spouse is allowed to live in it under a divorce or separation instrument.

Business Use or Rental of a Home.   The CPA may be able to exclude the gain from the sale of a home that the taxpayer has used for business or to produce rental income if the ownership and use tests have been met.

If someone was entitled to take depreciation deductions because he or she used the home for business purposes or as rental property, the CPA cannot exclude the part of the gain equal to any depreciation allowed or allowable as a deduction for periods after May 6, 1997. If the accountant can show by adequate records or other evidence that the depreciation deduction allowed was less than the amount allowable, the amount that person cannot exclude is the smaller figure.

In the year of sale someone may have used part of a property as a home and part of it for business or to produce income. Examples are:

1. A working farm on which the house was located.
2. An apartment building in which the taxpayer lived in one unit and rented the others.
3. A store building with an upstairs apartment in which the taxpayer lived.
4. A home with a room used for business (home office) or to produce income.

If the taxpayer sells the entire property, the CPA should consider the transaction as the sale of two properties. The sale of the part of the property used for business or rental is reported differently from that used as the main home. To determine the different amounts to report, the CPA must divide the selling price, selling expenses and basis between the part of the property used for business or rental and the part used as a home. In the same way, if the owner qualifies to exclude any of the gain on the business or rental part of the home, the maximum exclusion is divided between that part of the property and the part used as a home.

The CPA generally can also exclude gain on the part of the home used for business or rental if the taxpayers owned and lived in that part of the home for at least two years during the five-year period ending on the date of the sale.

Special Situations. The following situations may affect the taxpayer's exclusion:

1. The taxpayer cannot claim the exclusion if the expatriation tax applies. The expatriation tax applies to U.S. citizens who have renounced their citizenship (and long-term residents who have ended their residency) if one of their principal purposes was to avoid U.S. taxes.
2. If the home was destroyed or condemned, any gain (for example, because of insurance proceeds received) qualifies for the exclusion.
3. Subject to the other rules in this chapter, the CPA can choose to exclude gain from the sale of a remainder interest in the taxpayer's home. If the preparer makes this choice, the owner cannot choose to exclude gain from the sale of any other interest in the home that he or she sells separately.
4. The taxpayer cannot exclude gain from the sale of a remainder interest in the home to a related person. Related persons include brothers and sisters, half-brothers and half-sisters, spouse, ancestors (parents, grandparents, great grandparents), and lineal descendants (children, grandchildren, great grandchildren). Related persons also include certain corporations, partnerships, trusts, and exempt organizations.

Reporting the Gain. It is not necessary to report the sale of the main home on the tax return unless:

1. The taxpayer has a gain and does not qualify to exclude all of it.
2. The taxpayer has a gain and chooses not to exclude it.

When the taxpayer has taxable gain on the sale of the main home that is not excluded, the entire gain realized in the transaction must be reported.

If the owner used the home for business or to produce rental income during the year of sale, the sale of the business or rental part (or the sale of the entire property if used entirely for business or rental in that year) must be reported.

Installment Sale.   Some sales are made under arrangements that provide for part or all of the selling price to be paid in a later year. These sales are called "installment sales." If the seller finances the buyer's purchase of the home, instead of having the buyer get a loan or mortgage from a bank, the sale is probably an installment sale. The CPA may be able to report the part of the gain the taxpayer cannot exclude on the installment basis.

Seller-Financed Mortgages.   If the taxpayer sells the home and holds a note, mortgage or other financial agreement, the payments receive generally consist of both interest and principal. The interest received as part of each payment must be reported separately as interest income. If the buyer of the home uses the property as a main or second home, the taxpayer must also report the name, address, and social security number (SSN) of the buyer to the Internal Revenue Service.

The buyer and seller must give each other their SSN. Failure to meet these requirements may result in a $50 penalty for each failure.

If either the seller or the buyer of the home is a non-resident or resident alien who does not have and is not eligible to get an SSN, the IRS will issue that person an ITIN. This is for tax use only. It does not entitle the holder to social security benefits or change the holder's employment or immigration status under U.S. law.

Real Estate and Transfer Taxes.   The seller and the buyer must deduct the real estate taxes on the home for the year of sale according to the number of days in the real property tax year that each owned the home.

The seller is treated as paying the taxes up to, but not including, the date of sale and can declare these taxes as an itemized deduction in the year of sale. It does not matter what part of the taxes actually were paid.

The buyer is treated as paying the taxes beginning with the date of sale. If the buyer paid the seller's share of the taxes (or any delinquent taxes owed), the payment increases the selling price of the home. The buyer adds the amount paid to his or her basis in the property.

The taxpayer cannot deduct transfer taxes, stamp taxes and other incidental taxes and charges on the sale of a home as itemized deductions. However, if the taxpayer pays these amounts as the seller of the property, they are expenses of the sale and reduce the amount realized on the sale. If the taxpayer pays these amounts as the buyer, they are included in the cost basis of the property.

It's a Real Estate Market

Those CPAs dealing with tax preparation can anticipate more and more questions from clients about the tax ramifications of their residential real estate dealings. We continue to have a positive house sales environment and will continue to have as long as we remain in a low mortgage rate environment. While it is true that most people have no tax obligation created by the sale of their primary residence, there are a number of issues related to basis, estate, second home, parents' home and business use that can crop up any day of the week.

Chapter 20

Business Use of a Home

CONTENTS

Claiming the Deduction	20.02
Principal Place of Business	20.02
Other Criteria for Determining Place of Business	20.03
Separate Structures	20.04
Figuring the Deduction	20.04
Deduction Limit	20.05
Assorted Use Tests	20.05
Exclusive Use	20.06
Part-Year Use	20.06
Day-Care Facility	20.07
Business Furniture and Equipment	20.08
Depreciation	20.11
Personal Property Converted to Business Use	20.11

Now, with email and wireless connections—and with voice mail the industry standard—not only is it hard to tell where anyone is ... but also, the public perception of someone who works from home has gone from "hardly working" to "smart businessperson." The home office means that the client is not paying for an upscale office, a receptionist, a parking valet, or even a water cooler. The client is paying for time and product.

On airplanes now, the only limit to the work time is the life of the computer battery, and even this is no longer an issue, as many airlines offer electrical outlets on seat armrests. The home office has taken to the sky!

CLAIMING THE DEDUCTION

Claiming the deduction for business use of the home may include deductions involving a house, apartment, condominium, mobile home, or boat. As pointed out later it may include an unattached garage, studio, barn, or greenhouse; however, it does not include any part of the property used exclusively as a hotel or inn. In this chapter are:

1. The requirements for qualifying to deduct expenses for the business use of the home (including special rules for storing inventory or product samples).
2. Types of expenses that can be deducted.
3. How to figure the deduction (including depreciation of the home).
4. Special rules for day-care providers.
5. Deducting expenses for furniture and equipment used in the business.
6. Records that should be kept.

The rules in this chapter apply to individuals, trusts, estates, partnerships, and S corporations. They do not apply to corporations (other than S corporations). There are no special rules for the business use of a home by a partner or S corporation shareholder.

PRINCIPAL PLACE OF BUSINESS

Rules that went into effect in 1999 make it easier to claim a deduction for the business use of a home. Under these rules, many taxpayers may qualify to claim the deduction, even though they had never qualified before. The following information explains these rules.

Under these latest rules for deducting expenses for the business use of a home, it is easier for a home office to qualify as the principal place of business. Under the old rules, a taxpayer had to consider the relative importance of the activities carried out at each business location when determining if a home was the principal place of business. The place where the taxpayer conducted the most important activities was the place where meetings were held with clients, customers, or patients, or the location where goods or services were delivered. Performing administrative or management duties in the home office was considered less important.

Before 1999, an outside salesperson's home office did not qualify as a principal place of business. The place where he or she met with customers to explain available products and take orders was considered more important than the home office where administrative duties were conducted. Beginning in 1999, however, a home office qualifies as a principal place of business for deducting expenses for the use of it:

1. If the home office is used exclusively for administration or management activities of a trade or business.
2. If the taxpayer has no other fixed location for conducting substantial administrative or management activities relating to a trade or business.

There are many activities that are administrative or managerial in nature. Some of these activities are:

1. Billing customers, clients, or patients.
2. Keeping books and records.
3. Ordering supplies.
4. Setting up appointments.
5. Forwarding orders or writing reports.

The following administrative or management activities performed at other locations will *not* disqualify a home office as a principal place of business:

1. When others conduct a taxpayer's administrative or management activities at locations other than the home.
2. The conduct of administrative or management activities at places that are not fixed locations of a business, such as in a car or a hotel room.
3. The taxpayer occasionally conducts minimal administrative or management activities at a fixed location outside of the home.
4. The taxpayer conducts substantial *non*administrative or *non*management business at a fixed location outside the home.
5. Suitable space to conduct administrative or management activities is available outside the home office, but a home office is used for those activities instead.

OTHER CRITERIA FOR DETERMINING PLACE OF BUSINESS

If the newer rules do not appear to cover the taxpayer's particular situation, the older rules may give an indication of other aspects when considering deductions for business use of the home.

It is permissible to have more than one business location, including a home, for a single trade or business. To qualify to deduct the expenses for the business use of a home, the home must be a principal place of business of that trade or business. To determine the principal place of business, all of the facts and circumstances must be considered. If, after considering the business locations, one cannot be identified as a principal place of business, then home office expenses cannot be deducted. The two primary factors to consider are:

1. The relative importance of the activities performed at each location.
2. The time spent at each location.

To determine whether a home is the principal place of business, the taxpayer must consider the relative importance of the activities carried out at each business location. The relative importance of the activities performed at each business location is determined by the basic characteristics of the business. If the business requires that meetings or conferences be held with clients or patients, or that goods or services be delivered to a customer, then the place where contacts are made must be given great weight in determining where the most important activities are performed.

If the relative importance of the activities does not clearly establish the principal place of business, such as when to deliver goods or services at both the office, in the home, and elsewhere, then the time spent at each location is important. Comparison should be made of the time spent on business at the home office with the time spent at other locations.

SEPARATE STRUCTURES

Expenses can be deducted for a separate free-standing structure, such as a studio, garage, or barn, if the structure is used exclusively and regularly for the business. The structure does not have to be the principal place of business, or a place where patients, clients or customers are met.

FIGURING THE DEDUCTION

Once it has been determined that the "home office" does qualify for a deduction, the next step is determining how much the taxpayer can deduct. Certain expenses related to the business use of a home can be deducted, but deductions are limited by the following:

1. Percentage of the home used for business, i.e., the business percentage.
2. Deduction limit.

To find the *business percentage,* the taxpayer must compare the size of the part of the home used for business to the entire house. The resulting percentage is used to separate the business part of the expenses from the expenses for operating the entire home. Any reasonable method to determine the business percentage can be used. Two commonly used methods are:

1. Dividing the square foot area of the "business space" by the total area of the home.
2. Dividing the number of rooms used for business by the total number of rooms in the home. This method can be used if the rooms in the home are all about the same size.

DEDUCTION LIMIT

If gross income from the business use of a home equals or exceeds the total business expenses (including depreciation), all of the business expenses can be deducted. If the gross income from that use is less than the total business expenses, the deduction for certain expenses for the business use is limited. The deduction of otherwise nondeductible expenses, such as insurance, utilities, and depreciation (with depreciation taken last), allocable to business is limited to the gross income from the business use of the home minus the sum of the following:

1. The business part of expenses that could be deducted even if the home was not used for business (such as mortgage interest, real estate taxes, and casualty and theft losses).
2. The business expenses that relate to the business activity in the home (for example, salaries or supplies), but not to the use of the home itself.

A self-employed individual may not include in (2) above the deduction for half of the self-employment tax.

If deductions are greater than the current year's limit, it is possible to carry over the excess to the next year. Any carryover is subject to the gross income limit from the business use of the home for the next tax year. The amount carried over will be allowable only up to the taxpayer's gross income in the next tax year from the business in which the deduction arose whether the individual lives in that particular house or home during that year or not.

ASSORTED USE TESTS

To qualify under the *regular use test,* a specific area of the home must be used for business on a continuing basis. The regular-use test is not met if the business use of the area is only occasional, even if that area is not used for any other purpose.

To qualify under the *trade or business use* test requires that part of a home be used in connection with a trade or business. If part of the home is used for some other profit-seeking activity that is not a trade or business, a deduction cannot be taken for a business use.

A taxpayer who is an employee must qualify under the *convenience-of-the-employer* test. If an employer provides suitable work space for administrative management activities, this fact must be considered in determining whether this test is met. Even if expenses qualify for a deduction for the business use of a home, the deduction may be limited. If the employee's gross income from the business use of a home is less than the employee's total business expenses, the deduction for some of the expenses—utilities, insurance, depreciation, for example—is limited.

Exclusive Use

To qualify under the *exclusive use* test, a specific area of a home must be used only for a trade or business. The area used for business can be a room or other separately identifiable space. The space does not need to be marked off by a permanent partition. If the home area in question is used both for business and personal purposes, it does not meet the requirements of the exclusive use test rule.

The exclusive use test does not have to be met if space is used for the *storage of inventory or product samples,* or for a *day-care facility.* When part of a home is used for the storage of inventory or product samples, the following 5 tests must all be met:

1. The inventory or product samples are kept for use in a trade or business.
2. The trade or business is a wholesale or retail selling of products.
3. The home is the only fixed location of a trade or business.
4. The storage space must be used on a regular basis.
5. The space is an identifiably separate space suitable for storage.

Part-Year Use

Expenses for the business use of a home *may not* be incurred during any part of the year it was not being used for business purposes. Only those expenses for the portion of the year in which it was actually used for business may be used in figuring the allowable deduction.

DAY-CARE FACILITY

If space in the home is used on a regular basis for providing day care, it may be possible to deduct the business expenses for that part of the home even though the same space is used for nonbusiness purposes. To qualify for this exception to the exclusive use rule, the following requirements must be met:

1. The space must be used in the trade or business of providing day care for children, persons 65 or older, or persons who are physically or mentally unable to care for themselves.
2. The taxpayer must have applied for, been granted or be exempt from having a license certification registration, or approval as a day-care center or as a family or group day-care home under state law. An individual does not meet this requirement if an application was rejected or license or other authorization was revoked.

If a part of the home is regularly used for day care, it is necessary to figure the percentage of that part which is used for day care, as explained above under *business percentage.* All the allocable expenses subject to the deduction limit, as explained earlier, may be deducted for that part used exclusively for day care. If the use of part of the home as a day-care facility is regular, but not exclusive, it is necessary to figure what part of available time it is actually used for business.

A room that is available for use throughout each business day and that is regularly used in the business is considered to be used for day care throughout each business day. It is not necessary to keep records to show the specific hours the area was used for business. The area may be used occasionally for personal reasons; however, a room used only occasionally for business does not qualify for the deduction.

To find that part of the available time the home is actually used for business, the total business-use time is compared to the total time that part of the home can be used for all purposes. The comparison may be based upon the hours of business use in a week with the number of hours in a week (168), or the hours of business use for the tax year with the number of hours in the tax year.

Meal Allowance

If food is provided for a day-care business, the expense is not included as a cost of using the home for business. It is a separate deduction on the taxpayer's Schedule C (Form 1040). The cost of food consumed by the taxpayer or his or her family may not be deducted. However, 100% of the cost of food consumed by the day-care recipients and generally only 50% of the cost of food consumed by employees can be deducted. However, 100% of the cost of food consumed by employees can be deducted if its value can be excluded from their wages as a de minimis fringe benefit. The value of meals provided to employees on business premises is generally de minimis if more than half of these employees are provided the meals for the taxpayer's convenience.

If cost of food for the day-care business is deducted, a separate record (with receipts) must be maintained of the family's food costs. Reimbursements received from a sponsor under the Child and Adult Food Care Program of the Department of Agriculture are taxable only to the extent they exceed expenses for food for eligible children. If reimbursements are more than expenses for food, the difference is shown as income in Part I of Schedule C. If food expenses are greater than the reimbursements, the difference is shown as an expense in Part V of Schedule C.

BUSINESS FURNITURE AND EQUIPMENT

Depreciation and Section 179 deductions may be used for furniture and equipment that an employee uses in his or her home for business or work. These deductions are available whether or not the individual qualifies to deduct expenses for the business use of a home. Following are explanations of the different rules for:

1. Listed property.
2. Property bought for business use.
3. Personal property converted to business use.

Listed Property

Special rules apply to certain types of property, called listed property, used in the home. Listed property includes any property of a type generally used for entertainment, recreation, and amusement (including photographic, phonographic, communication, and video recording equipment). But "listed property" also includes computers and related equipment.

Listed property bought and placed in service in 1998 must be used more than 50% for business (including work as an employee) to be claimed as a Section 179 deduction or an accelerated depreciation deduction. If the business use of listed property is 50% or less, a Section 179 deduction cannot be taken and the property must be depreciated using the Alternate Depreciation System (ADS) (straight-line method). Listed property meets the more-than-50%-use test for any tax year if its qualified business use is more than 50% of its total use. Allocation among its various uses must be made for the use of any item of listed property used for more than one purpose during the tax year. The *percentage of investment use may not be used* as part of the percentage of qualified business use to meet the more-than-50%-use test. However, the taxpayer should use the combined total of business and investment use to figure the depreciation deduction for the property.

If an employee uses his or her own listed property (or listed rented property) for work as an employee, the property is business-use property only if both of the following requirements are met.

1. The use is for the convenience of the employer.
2. The use is required as a condition of employment.

"As a condition of employment" means that the use of the property is *necessary* for proper performance of work. Whether the use of the property is required for this purpose depends on all the facts and circumstances. The employer does not have to tell the employee specifically to have a computer for use in the home, nor is a statement by the employer to that effect sufficient.

If, in a year after placing an item of listed property in service, the taxpayer fails to meet the more-than-50%-use test for that item of property, he or she may be required to do both of the following.

1. Figure depreciation, beginning with the year the property is no longer used more than 50% for business, using the straight-line method.
2. Figure any excess depreciation and Section 179 deduction on the property and add it to:
   a. Gross income.
   b. The adjusted basis of the property.

It is not possible to take any depreciation of the Section 179 deduction for the use of listed property unless business/investment use can be proved with adequate records or sufficient evidence to support the individual's own statements. To meet the adequate records requirement, the taxpayer must maintain an account book, diary, log, statement of expense, trip sheet, or similar record or other documentary evidence that is sufficient to establish business/investment use.

Property Bought for Business Use

The taxpayer who has bought certain property to use in his or her business can do any one of the following (subject to the limits discussed below).

1. Elect a Section 179 deduction for the full cost of the property.
2. Take part of the cost as a Section 179 deduction.
3. Depreciate the full cost of the property.

Section 179 Deduction

A Section 179 deduction can generally be claimed on depreciable tangible personal property bought for use in the active conduct of business. The taxpayer can choose how much (subject to the limit) of the cost to deduct under Section 179 and how much to depreciate. The Section 179 deduction can be spread over several items of property in any way selected as long as the total does not exceed the maximum allowable. However, the taxpayer cannot take a Section 179 deduction for the basis of the business part of the home.

Section 179 Deduction Limits

The Section 179 deduction cannot be more than the business cost of the qualifying property. In addition, the following limits apply when figuring a Section 179 deduction.

1. Maximum dollar limit.
2. Investment limit.
3. Taxable income limit.

The total cost of Section 179 property the taxpayer can elect to deduct for 2000 cannot be more than $20,000; for 2001 and 2002, it is $24,000 and after 2002, it is $25,000. This *maximum dollar limit* is reduced if the individual goes over the investment limit in any tax year.

If the cost of the qualifying Section 179 property is over the *investment limit,* the taxpayer must reduce the maximum dollar limit for each dollar over $200,000.

The total cost that can be deducted each tax year is subject to the total *taxable income limit.* This is figured on the income from the active conduct of all trade or business activities, including wages, during the tax year. The taxable income for this purpose is figured in the usual way, but without regard to all of the following.

1. The Section 179 deduction.
2. The self-employment tax deduction.
3. Any net operating loss carryback or carryforward.

DEPRECIATION

Part II of Form 4562 is used to claim a deduction for depreciation on property placed in service in 1998. It does not include any costs deducted in Part I (Section 179 deduction).

Most business property used in a home office is either 5-year or 7-year property under MACRS.

- 5-year property includes computers and peripheral equipment, typewriters, calculators, adding machines, and copiers.
- 7-year property includes office furniture and equipment such as desks, files, and safes.

Under MACRS, the half-year convention is generally used, which allows deduction of a half-year of depreciation in the first year the property is used in the business. If more than 40% of the depreciable property was placed in service during the last 3 months of the tax year, the mid-quarter convention must be used instead of the half-year convention.

PERSONAL PROPERTY CONVERTED TO BUSINESS USE

If property is used in the home office that was used previously for personal purposes, a Section 179 deduction cannot be taken for the property, but it can be depreciated. The method of depreciation depends upon when the property was first used for personal purposes.

Chapter 21

Expert Witness

CONTENTS

Engagement Letter	**21.02**
Prep Time	**21.03**
Definition of an Expert Witness	**21.04**
Function of the Expert Witness	**21.05**
Basis of Investigation	**21.05**
Exhibits	**21.06**
Understandable Testimony	**21.06**
Cross-Examination	**21.07**
Rebuttal	**21.08**
Legal Matters	**21.08**

With the plethora of high profile legal cases which have inundated the news in the last few years, we've all become trial experts. After being briefed on a variety of cases, we're aware of all the legal terms—and ramifications.

But of a less spectacular nature has been the steady increase of experts in more dignified, straightforward, less publicized cases; in fact, to the lay person, these are often downright boring. However, to the accountant who has found his niche as an "expert witness," they are not only fascinating, but can be quite remunerative. (After all, it was accounting that finally put Al Capone behind bars.) Many accountants are discovering they can increase business, gain public awareness, and enjoy using their special knowledge and experience as expert witnesses. Their financial knowledge and ability to follow a paper trail of figures gives them importance as investigators as well as witnesses in complicated court cases involving financial dealings. There can also be pitfalls along the way.

The need for the accountant as an "expert witness" has increased proportionately with the growing complexity of business affairs. For a number of years, the courts had permitted a rather liberal use of experts in trials; however, the days of relative immunity from prosecution of the expert witness seem to have ended as litigation threatened to become a national pastime. Obviously, the more lawsuits, the more losers. And the loser has to take it out on someone. (That loser may be the opposing party—or it could be the accountant's client.) Why not go after that expert who caused all the trouble? And his firm, too!

ENGAGEMENT LETTER

Therein lies the raison d'être of a well thought-out, carefully constructed engagement agreement containing buffers against both parties. This agreement needs, at the minimum, to spell out carefully:

1. What the accountant has agreed to do.
2. What information the client *must* make available to the expert witness to enable him or her to investigate the evidence and reach an opinion.
3. Lines of effective communication with both the client(s) and the attorney(s).
4. What the client can expect if the accountant is *required* to reveal on the stand any and all information on which his opinion is based.
5. That the attorney *must* keep the accountant informed in a timely fashion of any and all legal requirements such as filing times, submission of written documents, when any graphic presentations are due, and the like.

The corollary of this is, of course, that the accountant needs to guarantee to do or not do several things of concern to the client and/or attorney. If the accountant feels that he may not "fit the bill" as an expert witness in a case, he must not accept the engagement. The accountant must:

1. Possess the necessary qualifications and background.
2. Be cognizant of the accounting profession's technical and ethical standards applicable to litigation services, specifically those applying to expert witnesses.
3. Schedule adequate time and opportunity to investigate the case thoroughly.

4. Be prepared to furnish testimony in a forceful, confident manner.

5. Be prepared to defend a position "properly taken" in a polite, matter-of-fact manner in cross-examination.

6. Keep foremost in mind that the objective is to aid the client and attorney in winning the case, but *not* at the cost of the accountant's integrity.

7. Remember that the expert witness is *not* a client advocate, but an advocate of the accountant's own opinion and point of view.

8. Be positive that there can be no taint of conflict of interest that could be detrimental to the case.

9. Steer away from any engagement where there could be a possibility of divulging privileged information.

10. Withdraw as expeditiously as possible if there are any doubts about the litigation in question.

11. Adhere to the strategy of the lawyer, but here again, *not* at the expense of the accountant's integrity.

PREP TIME

Preparing for the first trial may be the most difficult part of joining the growing number of accountants entering the expert witness niche. This is the time when the accountant, if he's been lucky or hasn't served on a jury, really becomes familiar with the down-to-earth aspects of the judicial system.

There's nothing like familiarity in developing confidence and ease of presentation; therefore, preparation should include:

1. Becoming familiar with the general rules governing real-life courtroom procedure in the locale where the testimony will be given.

2. A visit to a court, preferably one where there is a trial being held involving an accountant expert witness. In metropolitan areas, this should be relatively easy.

3. When apprised of the specific court assignment of the case, the accountant should visit the particular judge's courtroom to observe his attitude and demeanor.

4. Role playing. This activity is recommended for all sorts of therapy, where it may or may not work, but it definitely works in a situation like this. (The attorneys had to play out their role for moot court in law school. Why not the accountant turning expert witness?) Partners, staff and/or family members make great critics—as well as actors in this courtroom drama. Even a full-length mirror can ask questions and talk back.

DEFINITION OF AN EXPERT WITNESS

The courts uniformly agree that the accountant possesses the qualifications of an expert witness on any subject matter falling within the scope of his experience, training, and education.

There are perhaps as many definitions of an "expert witness" as there are statutes, judges, and writers concerned with testimony. The following definition of an expert witness is designed to cover all aspect of "expert" definitions (without any whereases or wherefores): *A witness is an expert witness and is qualified to give expert testimony if the judge finds that to perceive, know, or understand the matter concerning which the witness is to testify requires special knowledge, skill, experience, training, and/or education, and that the witness has the requisite special knowledge, skill, experience, training, and/or education deemed necessary and appropriate.*

If the opposing party offers any objection to the use of an expert's testimony, the accountant's special knowledge, skill, experience, training, or education must be shown before the witness may testify as an expert. Regardless, this information should be made known to the court. A witness's special knowledge, skill, training, or education may be shown by his own testimony, but it will probably "set" better with the jury if the lawyer elicits the pertinent information from the witness relating to his or her education, experience, and specialized knowledge.

Since the basic requirement of an expert witness is that the witness possess the ability to interpret, analyze, and evaluate the significant facts on a question concerning which just a judge or a judge and jury need assistance to resolve, it is imperative that they be aware of the accountant's background. This expertise must be demonstrated in a positive but unassuming manner to be effective. No one likes a braggart.

The courts have uniformly accepted the accountant as an expert. In the majority of cases, the primary and most significant criteria in guidance of a trial court's determination of qualifications of an expert witness are based on occupational experience. Equally significant is the judicial recognition of the special knowledge acquired by an accountant relating to a particular industry, trade, occupation, or profession to qualify her as an expert on particular business and trade practices and on other factors relating to costs and gross profit margins.

In actual practice, it is rare that the trial court will refuse to permit the witness to testify as an expert because he is insufficiently qualified. Rather, any weakness or deficiency will show up in the quality and impact of the testimony rather than its admissibility.

Therefore, it is imperative that an accountant be very cautious about accepting an assignment that may be beyond his or her area of expertise.

FUNCTION OF THE EXPERT WITNESS

The function of the expert witness is to form an opinion or inference on matters when individuals in the normal course of affairs would probably not be able to do so. Therefore, an expert witness is needed in any case where by reason of his special knowledge, the expert is able to form a valid opinion on the facts while the man on the street would—or should—not.

Courts vary in their conception of when the expert is needed. Some courts maintain that expert testimony is admissible only when the subject matter is beyond the common experience of the ordinary juror who would then be unable to reach an informed opinion or draw a valid inference from the facts. In effect, they apply a "strict" test of necessity. More often, the determination is made on the basis of whether this testimony would be of "assistance" to the judge or jury.

BASIS OF INVESTIGATION

In his investigation preparatory to giving testimony, an expert may rely upon various sources. He may:

1. Rely on known facts if such facts are material to the inquiry.
2. Obtain information gained from a demonstrably reliable source.
   This could include previous audit reports, certified financial statements, books and records of the business—even though they were not kept by the expert witness—or demonstrable customs and practices within the business or industry of the client for whom the expert is testifying.
3. If the expert has firsthand knowledge of the situation, inferences or opinions may be stated directly. However, care should be taken to be absolutely sure that the practitioner states fully the facts relied upon, the reliable source, and the permissibility of the basis upon which an opinion was founded. Otherwise, the testimony will do more harm than good. If a judge and/or jury become aware of even one instance in which the accountant has slipped up, his expertise will henceforth be open to question.

In addition, the expert witness must have a thorough knowledge of the substantive issue in the case. The investigation and subsequent conclusion may be incomplete and unrelated to the issue if he either has not been informed properly of the particulars in a case, or has not done his homework thoroughly. It is also necessary that he know the issues of the case so that he can anticipate and respond promptly and forcefully to cross-examination and avoid answers that are incomplete, confusing, and irrelevant. In other words, the expert must be made privy to all relevant facts in the case as well as to the direction of the lawyer's attack or counterattack.

The "need to know" policy should not be carried so far that the accountant appears "in the dark" or at best ill-informed. Therefore, it is important for the accountant to ascertain whether the attorney is willing to work closely with the "expert witness." If the accountant finds it impossible to work in good faith with a particular attorney or law firm, he should withdraw from the case, if possible, or at least refuse to work with that individual or firm in the future. Failure to be aware of or to consider all of the facts not only diminishes the value of the expert's testimony to the case but quite often leaves the expert vulnerable to attack on cross-examination. Not only can the accountant become surprised and confused by the additional facts, but the image as an expert will be damaged in the minds of the judge and jury. The individual's credibility and reputation could be severely damaged.

Exhibits

It is almost mandatory that the expert witness prepare, or have prepared, some type of exhibit for several obvious reasons, not the least of which is the fact that very few individuals can make any sense of numbers from just *hearing* them. Oversize charts, graphs, schedules, diagrams—whatever aids the court in visualizing the accountant's findings—can be useful in focusing their attention. Visual aids not only help the expert witness explain his conclusions but they can have a greater impact on the judge and jury. *If* these graphics can be presented in an interesting, imaginative way, they might also tend to lessen the tedium of often very dry facts and figures.

This "demonstrative evidence" (in the parlance of the court) must not appear to be a way of "lecturing" to the judge and jury. At the same time, these are not people preparing for the CPA exam. The visual materials must present readily understood, clearly identifiable steps the accountant took in arriving at opinions and conclusions—not just a jumble of numbers.

It may be appropriate to provide copies of the material to the judge and the members of the jury so that they can use both eyes and ears to follow the testimony of the expert. Even then, it is probably better to have too little information on a graph or schedule than too much.

Understandable Testimony

Expert testimony is valuable only when it is understood by the judge and jury. The expert must be able to explain and defend her opinion in language reasonably understood by the layman. Everyone complains about "legalese." What about "accountantese"? It should always be kept in mind that the very reason the expert is testifying is that the subject matter is beyond the common knowledge and experience of the average juror.

A common error committed by the accounting expert is to use technical language in testimony without offering an explanation of its meaning.

Terms like *earnings per share, stockholder's equity,* and *retained earnings* may have a nice ring to them. However, if the testimony must necessarily involve technical accounting terms and concepts of this caliber, they must be defined and explained in a clear and simple manner.

CROSS-EXAMINATION

An accountant testifying as an expert may be cross-examined to the same extent as any other witness.

Therefore, the expert should assume that his opinion will be rigorously challenged on cross-examination. The fact that the subject matter is being litigated indicates conflicting theories or facts upon which an opinion may be based. In order to preserve the value and effectiveness of testimony given as an expert, the witness should anticipate what may be brought up in cross-examination. Thorough preparation, awareness of other aspects of a case, anticipation of where the "attack" may come will all aid in the individual's holding up well in this phase of a court appearance. Now is the time when the opposing counsel will attempt to discredit the expert witness concerning qualifications, knowledge of the subject matter, the validity of the source of relevant information, and the basis for arriving at the stated opinion and conclusions.

It is important for the accountant to remember that this is the lawyer's job. Since the purpose of cross-examination is to diminish or destroy the expert's conclusions, the lawyer may be argumentative, supercilious, and aggressive in an attempt to catch the witness off balance—to make the expert react too quickly and speak before thinking. Instead, this is the time when remaining courteous, unemotional, and firmly convinced of the correctness of previous statements pays off.

One of the techniques used in cross-examination is to show a contradiction or omission of facts upon which the expert founded an opinion. For this reason, it is essential that the expert make a thorough investigation, have knowledge of all relevant theories and material facts, and be prepared to support that opinion rationally on cross-examination. If the expert has adequately prepared, she can reasonably anticipate any weak or questionable aspects of the testimony and be ready to cope with them quickly and spontaneously on cross-examination.

REBUTTAL

Rebuttal testimony provides the opposing party with an opportunity to introduce evidence that refutes the prior evidence of the other side in the case. The opposing side may decide to offer in rebuttal its own expert to directly refute the testimony of the original expert. Rebuttal testimony may not go beyond the scope of the original evidence. In other words, a party may not introduce new evidence but is limited to a direct rebuttal of prior evidence. However, there is still plenty of opportunity for accounting expert witness No. 2 to question the validity of the original expert's assumptions, opinions, and conclusions concerning alternative ways of looking at a situation.

If the original expert has considered and discussed the cause for litigation from every possible angle, the impact of a rebuttal expert witness who attempts to base opinion on opposing theories and facts has basically been forestalled, because that ground has already been covered, and discarded.

LEGAL MATTERS

What are these weighty matters which the expert witness is going to investigate, form opinions concerning, testify to, be cross-examined about or offer rebuttal to? As might be expected, there may even be a "mini-niche" within this niche where the accountant could decide to specialize. Among the more likely spots are:

1. Tax cases-civil, criminal, fraud—both state and federal. It is difficult to imagine a tax case that does not involve accounting problems. Attorneys for both the government and the taxpayer can be expected to have a general knowledge of accounting principles, but they have other responsibilities in the case. Enter the practitioner investigator and witness to refute the charge of "willful attempt to evade taxes," or just an assertion of deficiency in tax payments.

2. Divorce cases. In states with community property laws, this can become extremely involved in tracing and determining which funds are community property, separate property, proceeds from separate property, commingled funds, and separate funds of various descriptions.

3. Probate proceedings. Wills, state inheritance taxes, and federal estate taxes in states with community property laws also often need testimony from investigative accountants. In fact, the distinction between separate and community property is often crucial in figuring the amount of state inheritance and federal estate taxes owed.

4. Partnership dissolution and/or valuation of partnership interest. The accountant is frequently employed as an expert to prepare a partnership

accounting of a dissolved partnership. Following is a sampling of the items that will come to the attention of the accountant in preparing her report for submission to the court:

a. Contractual agreements among the partners expressly providing for a partnership accounting for capital or profits.

b. Capital contributions reflected in the partnership agreement, additional loans, and restrictions or limitations on the right of a partner to withdraw the profits or capital.

c. Present fair market value (FMV) of property previously contributed by a partner.

d. Allocation of profits and losses for the current year in accordance with the partnership agreement.

5. Corporate suits brought by shareholders; corporate fraud cases. These involve not only large corporations, but also very small ones that have been inundated in the flood of litigation in the U.S.

The accountant must, obviously, have an understanding of the pertinent substantive law before being competent to undertake an investigation of the facts and testify as an expert witness—giving an opinion and conclusions concerning a legal as well as a financial matter.

It becomes fairly obvious that the neophyte expert witness needs to do some investigating to determine just what laws apply to the niche he has chosen to delve into. The particular state laws are undoubtedly the place to begin the investigation since each will be somewhat different—some more than others.

Chapter 22

Auditor Independence and the Audit Committee

CONTENTS

The SEC's Revised Plans for Review of Auditor Independence
Systems and Controls   **22.01**
The SEC's New Rules Governing Independence of Auditors   **22.02**
Application of Revised Rules on Auditor Independence   **22.08**
Where There's a Will, There May Be a Way   **22.11**
The Blue Ribbon Panel's Ten Commandments   **22.11**
New Rules for Audit Committees and Reviews of Interim
Financial Statements   **22.12**
The SEC Reminder to 5,000 Public Companies   **22.14**
Recent Major Accomplishments by the SEC   **22.15**

In light of recent events, the Securities and Exchange Commission has found it necessary to revise plans for review of progress in implementation of recently enacted final rules relating to auditor independence.

THE SEC'S REVISED PLANS FOR REVIEW OF AUDITOR INDEPENDENCE SYSTEMS AND CONTROLS

In March 2002, the SEC announced final plans for completing reviews of the design, implementation and operating effectiveness of each of the five largest independent auditing firms' systems for ensuring compliance with the independence rules.

Originally, these reviews were to be performed or overseen by the Public Oversight Board (POB) and its staff; however, the POB had already announced its intention to terminate its existence by March 31.

Under an agreement with the SEC and the Executive Committee of the SEC Practice Section (SECPS) of the American Institute of CPAs, the staff of the POB will continue to carry out its oversight functions. The staff will be known as the Transition Oversight Staff (TOS) and will be led by its executive director.

The TOS will assume responsibility for conducting and reporting on the review of the firms' independence systems. The staff will engage independence experts, including experts from the firms' peer reviewers, to perform operating effectiveness tests pursuant to the TOS work programs. The TOS will define and supervise the work performed by the experts.

To further assure the public of the thoroughness of the reviews and the completeness and fairness of the Oversight Staff's public report, the SEC agreed to the appointment of a former vice chairman of the POB, who is also a former chairman of the Financial Accounting Standards Board, as an independent party to oversee and issue the public report. As an independent observer/overseer, he is expected to report whether the process followed in conducting the reviews was properly defined and performed and whether the reviews are appropriately assessed and reported by the TOS.

The report is to include, among other matters:

1. A description of the scope and methodology of the work performed.
2. An evaluation of whether the firms' independence systems provide reasonable assurance that the firms comply with the independence rules.
3. Recommendations for remedying any deficiencies in those systems.
4. Recommendations to standard setters based on the best practices observed during the reviews. The assumption is that these best practices should, then, become required practices.

Preparation for the reviews began immediately and final reports are expected to be issued no later than by the first of the year 2003.

THE SEC'S NEW RULES GOVERNING INDEPENDENCE OF AUDITORS

After extensive prodding and action by the SEC, auditor independence and financial disclosure about audit committees came to the foreground in concerns relating to independence and the openness of the auditing and accounting professions.

The rather lengthy lead time, punctuated by considerable negative pressure from Congress (bipartisan and bicameral), the AICPA, three of the Big Five firms and the American Bar Association, to single out only a few, ended with the Security and Exchange Commissioners voting unanimously on November 15, 2000, to adopt new rules that modernize the requirements for auditor independence. Obviously, the measures were too little, too late to protect the investors in Enron. Until additional restrictions and guidelines are officially adopted and put in place, the measures adopted at that time are still in effect.

The three areas covered are:

1. Investments by auditors or their family members in audit clients.
2. Employment relationships between auditors or their family members and audit clients.
3. The scope of services provided by audit firms to their audit clients.

The new rules reflect the Commission's consideration of comments received on the rules it proposed in June 2000.

Principal Provisions

Significant features of the new rules include:

1. Reduction of the number of audit firm employees and their family members whose investments in, or employment with, audit clients would impair an auditor's independence.
2. Identification of certain non-audit services that, if provided to an audit client, would impair an auditor's independence. (The rules do not extend to services provided to non-audit clients.)
3. Disclosure in their annual proxy statements of certain information about non-audit services provided by the company's auditors during the last fiscal year.

Four Principles

A preliminary note to the new rules identifies four principles by which to measure an auditor's independence. An accountant is not independent when the accountant:

1. Has a mutual or conflicting interest with the audit client.
2. Audits his or her own firm's work.
3. Functions as management or an employee of the audit client.
4. Acts as an advocate for the audit client.

Financial Relationships

Compared to the previous rules, the newly adopted rules narrow significantly the number of people whose investments trigger independence concerns. Under previous rules, many partners that did not work on the audit of a client, as well as their spouses and families, were restricted from investment in a firm's audit clients. The new rules limit restrictions principally to those who work on the audit or can influence the audit.

Employment Relationships

The employment relationship rules narrow the scope of people within audit firms whose families will be affected by the employment restrictions necessary to maintain independence. The rules also identify the positions in which a person *can* influence the audit client's accounting records or financial statements. These are positions that could impair an auditor's independence if held by a close family member of that auditor.

Business Relationships

Consistent with existing rules, independence will be impaired if the accountant or any covered person has a direct or material indirect business relationship with the audit client, other than providing professional services.

A General Standard for Auditor Independence

This SEC rule is based on the widely endorsed principle that an auditor must be independent both *in fact* and *in appearance*. The new rule specifies that an auditor's independence is impaired either when the accountant is not independent *in fact* or when a "reasonable investor," after considering all relevant facts and circumstances, would conclude that the auditor would not be capable of acting without bias. The reasonable investor standard is a common construct in securities laws.

Non-Audit Services

The rules identify nine non-audit *services* that are considered inconsistent with an auditor's independence. Seven of these nine services were already restricted by the AICPA, the SEC Practice Section of the AICPA (SECPS), or the SEC. The new rules closely follow the language in the existing prohibitions.

1. Bookkeeping or Other Services Related to the Audit Client's Accounting Records or Financial Statements.   Paralleling closely the current prohibition on bookkeeping, an audit firm cannot maintain or prepare the audit client's accounting records or prepare the audit client's financial statements that are either filed with the Commission or form the basis of financial statements filed with it. Exceptions include:

a. Providing services in emergency situations, provided the accountant does not undertake any managerial actions or make any managerial decisions.

b. Bookkeeping for foreign divisions or subsidiaries of an audit client, provided certain conditions exist.

2. Financial Information Systems Design and Implementation. The auditor cannot operate or supervise the operation of the client's information technology systems (IT). However, the auditor can provide IT consulting services provided certain criteria are met. These criteria include:

a. Management acknowledges (to the auditor and the audit committee) its full responsibility for the client's system of internal controls.

b. A person within management is singled out to make all management decisions with respect to the project.

c. Management makes all the significant decisions with respect to the IT project.

d. Someone within the company evaluates the adequacy and results of the project.

e. Management does not rely on the accountant's work as the primary basis for determining the adequacy of its financial reporting system.

The issuer would also disclose the total amount of fees for IT services received from its auditor. The prohibition does not include services an accountant performs in connection with the assessment, design, and implementation of internal accounting controls and risk management controls.

3. Appraisal or Valuation Services or Fairness Opinions. The new rule bans all valuation and appraisal services. Its restrictions apply only where it is reasonably likely that the results of any valuation or appraisal would be material to the financial statements, or where the accountant would audit the results.

4. Actuarial Services. Closely following the SECPS prohibition on actuarial services, actuarial-oriented advisory services are limited in this SEC rule only when they involve the determination of insurance company policy reserves and related accounts. On the other hand, certain types of actuarial services may be performed if:

a. The audit client uses its own actuaries or third-party actuaries to provide management with the primary actuarial capabilities.

b. Management accepts responsibility for actuarial methods and assumptions.

c. The accountant does not render actuarial services to an audit client on a continuous basis.

5. Internal Audit Services.   An audit firm is permitted to perform up to 40% (measured in terms of hours) of an audit client's internal audit work. The rule does not restrict internal audit services regarding operational internal audits unrelated to accounting controls, financial systems, or financial statements. The rule provides an exception for smaller businesses by excluding companies with less than $200 million in assets. However, any internal audit services for an audit client are contingent upon management taking responsibility for and making all management decisions concerning the internal audit function.

6. Management Functions.   Consistent with previous SEC rules, an auditor's independence is impaired under the new rules when the accountant acts, temporarily or permanently, as a director, officer, or employee of an audit client, or performs any decision-making, supervisory, or ongoing monitoring function for the audit client.

7. Human Resources.   Closely paralleling the SECPS rules, an auditor is not permitted to:

a. Recruit.

b. Act as a negotiator on the audit client's behalf.

c. Develop employee testing or evaluation programs.

d. Recommend (or advise) that the audit client hire a specific candidate for a specific job.

An accounting firm can, upon request by the audit client, interview candidates and advise the audit client on the candidate's competence for financial accounting, administrative, or control positions.

8. Broker-Dealer Services.   Consistent with current AICPA rules, an auditor cannot serve as a broker-dealer, promoter, or underwriter of an audit client's securities.

9. *Legal Services.* An auditor cannot provide any service to an audit client under circumstances in which the person providing the service must be admitted to practice before the courts of a U.S. jurisdiction.

Affiliate Provisions

When it was first proposed in June 2000, the rule contained a definition of an "affiliate of an accounting firm" that many commenters felt might affect accounting firms' joint ventures with companies that are not their audit clients and the continuation of small firm alliances. These types of relationships traditionally have not been thought to impair an accountant's independence. After considering these comments, the SEC decided that it would continue to analyze these situations under existing guidance.

An "affiliate of an audit client" continues to be defined as any entity that can significantly influence, or is significantly influenced by, the audit client, provided the equity investment is material to the entity or the audit client. "Significant influence" generally is presumed when the investor owns 20% or more of the voting stock of the investee. The significant influence test is used because under GAAP it is the trigger that causes the earnings and losses of one company to be reflected in the financial statements of another company.

Contingent Fee Arrangements

The rules reiterate that an accountant cannot provide any service to an audit client that involves a contingent fee.

Quality Controls

The rules provide a limited exception from independence violations to the accounting firm if certain factors are present:

1. The individual did not know the circumstances giving rise to his or her violation.
2. The violation was corrected promptly once the violation became apparent.
3. The firm has quality controls in place that provide reasonable assurance that the firm and its employees maintain their independence.
4. For the largest public accounting firms, the basic controls must include among others:
   a. Written independence policies and procedures.
   b. Automated systems to identify financial relationships that may impair independence.

c. Training, internal inspection, and testing.

d. Disciplinary mechanism for enforcement.

Proxy Disclosure Requirement

Companies must disclose in their annual proxy statements the fees for audit, IT consulting, and all other services provided by their auditors during the last fiscal year.

Companies must also state whether the audit committee has considered whether the provision of the non-audit services is compatible with maintaining the auditor's independence.

Finally, the registrant is required to disclose the percentage hours worked on the audit engagement by persons other than the accountant's full-time employees, if that figure exceeded 50%. This requirement is in answer to recent actions taken by some accounting firms to sell their practices to financial services companies. The partners or employees often, in turn, become employees of the financial services firm. The accounting firm then leases assets, namely auditors, back from those companies to complete audit engagements. In such cases, most of the auditors who work on an audit are employed elsewhere without the public, investors, or the client being aware of the situation.

APPLICATION OF REVISED RULES ON AUDITOR INDEPENDENCE

Since the adoption of the Commission's Revised Rules on Auditor Independence, the SEC staff has received questions regarding the implementation and interpretation of the rules. They encourage these questions and related correspondence regarding auditor independence as they do to all of the rulings which may be difficult to interpret.

Frequently Asked Questions

Publications of staff responses to certain questions received are referred to as Frequently Asked Questions (FAQs). Many of the questions are rather technical, referring to a specific item on a specific schedule. Others have a more general and widespread application and give the preparer a better feel for what the SEC staff is looking for in the reports. Following is a sample of the latter variety.

Question 6
Q: Should the fees billed in prior years be disclosed so investors may compare trends in audit, information technology, and other non-audit fees?

A: The rule does not require comparative disclosures. Registrants may include such information voluntarily.

Question 7

Q: In situations where other auditors are involved in the delivery of services, to what extent should the fees from the other auditors be included in the required fee disclosures?

A: Only the fees billed by the principal accountant need to be disclosed. See Question 8 regarding the definition of "principal accountant." If the principal accountant's billings or expected billings include fees for the work performed by others (such as where the principal accountant hires someone else to perform part of the work), then such fees should be included in the fees disclosed for the principal accountant.

In some foreign jurisdictions, a registrant may be required to have a joint audit requiring both accountants to issue an audit report for the same fiscal year. In these circumstances, fees for each accountant should be separately disclosed as they are both "principal accountants."

Question 8

Q: Does the term "principal accountant" in the ruling include associated or affiliated organizations?

A: Yes. "Principal accountant" has the meaning given to it in the auditing literature. In determining what services rendered by the principal accountant must be disclosed, all entities that comprise the accountant, as defined, should be included. This term includes not only the person or entity who furnishes reports or other documents that the registrant files with the Commission, but also all of the person's or entity's departments, divisions, parents, subsidiaries, and associated entities, including those located outside of the United States.

Question 15

Q: Does the restriction on the independent accountant providing legal services to an audit client apply only to litigation services?

A: No. The Commission's rule provides that an auditor's and firm's independence would be impaired if an auditor provides to its audit client a service for which the person providing the service must be admitted to practice before the courts of a U.S. jurisdiction. This standard includes all legal services. The rule does not apply only to appearance in court or solely to litigators. The only circumstances excluded by the rule are those in which local U.S. law allows certain limited activities without admission to the bar (generally confined to advice concerning the law of foreign jurisdictions).

Additionally, as discussed in the adopting release, some firms may be providing legal services outside of the United States to registrants when those services are not precluded by local law and are routine and ministerial or relate to matters that are not material to the consolidated financial statements. Such services raise serious independence concerns under circumstances other than those meeting at least those minimum criteria.

Question 17

Q: The final rule did not define an affiliate of an accounting firm. Does the lack of a definition signal a change in the Commission's approach to this issue?

A: No. The final rule's definition of an "accounting firm" includes the accounting firm's "associated entities." As noted in the adopting release, the Commission used this phrase to reflect the staff's current practice of addressing these questions in light of all relevant facts and circumstances, and of looking to the factors identified in our previous guidance on this subject. Much of this guidance is cited in footnotes of the adopting release. The staff is available for consultations on this issue.

Question 18

Q: Did the final rule change the Commission's guidance with respect to business relationships?

A: No. The final rule is consistent with the Commission's prior guidance on business relationships. The basic standard of the Commission's prior guidance has now been codified in the rule. In addition, as the adopting release notes, much of the Commission's previous guidance has been retained and continues to apply. For example, joint ventures, limited partnerships, investments in supplier or customer companies, certain leasing interest and sales by the accountant of items other than professional services are examples of business relationships that may impair an accountant's independence.

The SEC further explained its position in a letter to an accounting firm. The Commission stated:

"The Commission has recognized that certain situations, including those in which accountants and their audit clients have joined together in a profit-sharing venture, create a unity of interest between the accountant and client. In such cases, both the revenue accruing to each party . . . and the existence of the relationship itself create a situation in which to some degree the auditor's interest is wedded to that of its client. That interdependence impairs the auditor's independence, irrespective of whether the audit was in fact performed in an objective, critical fashion. Where such a unity of interests exists, there is an appearance that the auditor has lost the objectivity and skepticism necessary to take a critical second look at management's representations in the financial statements. The consequence is a loss of confidence in the integrity of the financial statements."

Question 21

Q: The new rule permits the auditor to continue to provide certain internal audit and financial information systems design and implementation services provided certain criteria are met. Do these criteria for internal audit apply to all internal audit engagements? What are the responsibilities of management pursuant to these criteria?

A: The six criteria for internal audit services apply to all internal audit services the auditor provides to its audit client, including those services related to operational audits or for companies with less than $200 million in assets.

All of the specified criteria must be met for both internal audit and financial information systems design and implementation to ensure that management not only takes responsibility for the services and projects performed by the auditor, but also makes the required management decisions. An audit client that merely signs a letter acknowledging responsibility for the services or project, without actually meeting each of the specified conditions, is not sufficient to ensure the auditor's independence.

WHERE THERE'S A WILL, THERE MAY BE A WAY

Needless to say, all of this activity relating to auditor independence, audit committees, and related financial disclosure did not come about without some very strong impetus. When the public and average investors begin to question truthfulness as well as the usefulness of business "checks and balances," someone will take action.

THE BLUE RIBBON PANEL'S TEN COMMANDMENTS

Although described as "recommendations," the report of the Blue Ribbon Panel on Improving the Effectiveness of Corporate Audit Committees made it quite clear that not only the average investor, but also a distinguished group of those "in the know" had questions about the effectiveness of the "independent" audit process. The group comprising the Panel was formed by the New York Stock Exchange (NYSE) and the National Association of Securities Dealers (NASD or NASDAQ) in September 1998, after the SEC Chairman had publicly expressed grave concern about the "independence" of the audit process. During the deliberations of the group consisting of business, accounting, and securities professionals, testimony was provided by two dozen organizations, including the AICPA, the Financial Executives International (FEI), the Independence Standards Board (ISB), and the Institute of Management Accountants (IMA).

The panel's 71-page report listed ten recommendations for strengthening the independence of the audit committee and increasing its importance and effectiveness. These recommendations were:

1. The NYSE and NASD adopt strict definitions of independence for directors serving on audit committees of listed companies.
2. The NYSE and NASD require larger companies to have audit committees composed entirely of independent directors.

3. The NYSE and NASD require larger companies to have "financially literate" directors on their audit committees.

4. The NYSE and NASD require each company to adopt a formal audit committee charter and to review its adequacy annually.

5. The SEC requires each company to disclose in its proxy statement whether it has adopted an audit committee charter as well as other information.

6. Each NYSE and NASD listed company state in the audit committee charter that the outside auditor is ultimately accountable to the board of directors and the audit committee.

7. All NYSE and NASD listed companies ensure their charters mandate that their audit committee does communicate with the outside auditors about independence issues in accordance with Independent Standards Board regulations.

8. Generally accepted auditing rules (GAAS) require that the outside auditor discuss with the audit committee the quality and suitability, not just the acceptability, of the accounting principles used.

9. The SEC require the annual report include a letter from the audit committee clarifying that it has reviewed the audited financial statements with management as well as performed other tasks.

10. The SEC require the outside auditor to perform an interim review under SAS 71, *Interim Financial Information*, before a company files its form 10-Q.

New Rules for Audit Committees and Reviews of Interim Financial Statements

On December 15, 1999, the Securities and Exchange Commission adopted new rules aimed at improving public disclosure about the functioning of corporate audit committees and enhancing both the reliability and credibility of financial statements of public companies. These SEC rules build upon new rules adopted by the NYSE, the American Stock Exchange (AMEX), and the NASD that govern audit committees of listed companies.

The new rules also coincide with the issuance of Statement of Auditing Standard 90 by the AICPA's Auditing Standards Board. This ASB Standard requires independent auditors to discuss with the audit committee the auditor's judgment about the *quality,* and not just the *acceptability* under generally accepted accounting principles, of the company's own accounting principles as applied in its financial reporting.

Much of this activity results from the grave concern ably and loudly voiced by the SEC (particularly by the Chairman) which, in turn, led to the appointment of the Blue Ribbon Panel on Audit Effectiveness.

SEC Rules Relating to the Interim Statement

The Commission's rules require that:

1. Companies' interim financial statements must be reviewed by independent auditors before they are filed on Forms 10-Q or 10-QSB with the Commission.
2. Companies, other than small business issuers filing on small business forms, must supplement their annual financial information with disclosures of selected quarterly financial data under Item 302(a) of Regulation S-K.
3. Companies must disclose in their proxy statements whether the audit committee reviewed and discussed certain matters relating to:
   a. The ASB's Statements of Auditing Standards 61 concerning the accounting methods used in the financial statements.
   b. The Independence Standard Board's Standard 1 (concerning matters that may affect the auditor's independence) with management and the auditors.
   c. Possible recommendation to the Board that the audited financial statements be included in the Annual Report on Form 10-K or 10-KSB for filings with the Commission.
4. Companies must disclose in their proxy statements whether the audit committee has a written charter, and file a copy of their charter every three years.
5. Companies whose securities are listed on the NYSE or AMEX or are quoted on NASDAQ must disclose certain information in their proxy statements about any audit committee member who is not "independent." All companies must disclose, if they have an audit committee, whether the members are "independent." (Independence is defined in the listing standards of the NYSE, AMEX, and NASD.)

Under the new rules, timely interim auditor reviews were required beginning with the first fiscal quarter ended after March 15, 2000. Compliance with the other new requirements is required in filings after December 15, 2000.

Foreign private issuers are exempt from requirements of the new rules. The new rules include a "safe harbor" for the disclosures.

Blue Ribbon Reminders

In their final report in August, 2000, the Blue Ribbon Panel on Audit Effectiveness recommended that, among other things audit committees:

1. Obtain annual reports from management assessing the company's internal controls.

2. Specify in their charters that the outside auditor is ultimately accountable to the board of directors and audit committee.
3. Inquire about time pressures on the auditor.
4. Preapprove non-audit services provided by the auditor.

Criteria for Gauging Appropriateness

The Panel, more specifically, provided guidance that an audit committee can use to determine the appropriateness of a service. This guidance includes:

1. Whether the service is being performed principally for the audit committee.
2. The effects of the service, if any, on audit effectiveness, or on the quality and timeliness of the entity's financial reporting process. For example, what is the effect, if any, upon the technology specialists who ordinarily also provide recurring audit support?
3. Whether the service would be performed by audit personnel, and if so, whether it will enhance their knowledge of the entity's business and operations.
4. Whether the role of those performing the service would be inconsistent with the auditor's role (e.g., a role where neutrality, impartiality, and auditor skepticism are likely to be subverted).
5. Whether the audit firm personnel would be assuming a management role or creating a mutual or conflicting interest with management.
6. Whether the auditors, in effect, would be "auditing their own numbers."
7. Whether the project must be started and completed very quickly.
8. Whether the audit firm has unique expertise in the service.
9. The size of the fee(s) for the non-audit service(s).

THE SEC REMINDER TO 5,000 PUBLIC COMPANIES

The outgoing Chairman of the Securities and Exchange Commission, in one of his final actions, sent a letter in January 2001 to remind the audit chairpersons committee of the top 5,000 public companies that almost a year had passed since the SEC, the major markets, and standard-setters had adopted rules that strengthen the audit committee's independence. He reminded them that the new rules were designed to give the audit committees the *power* and the *structure* to fulfill their duty to the investing public; that they were designed to improve communications among the board, the outside auditors and the management as a result of greater disclosure.

Under the new rulings, auditors and the board are *expected* to engage in frank and meaningful discussions about the significant, but frequently gray, areas of accounting, so that both the company's and its shareholders' interests are served.

The Commission and the accounting profession have been more actively engaged in discussion relating to modernization and clarification of auditor independence as a result of increased economic pressures on the profession and greater competition and consolidation within the business world.

The discussion led to a combination of rules and disclosures that:

1. Establish clearer guidelines on the non-audit services an auditor may provide to an audit client.
2. Provide for the meaningful involvement of the audit committee in consideration of consulting services that may impair independence.
3. Require companies to state in their proxy statements whether the audit committee has considered if the provision of the non-audit services is compatible with maintaining the auditor's independence.

He also reiterated the guidance provided by the Blue Ribbon Committee.

RECENT MAJOR ACCOMPLISHMENTS BY THE SEC

In taking stock of recent accomplishments in the business world, the SEC listed improving the effectiveness of audit committees first; therefore, this appears to be a logical place to include this list.

Recent accomplishments include:

1. The Report of the Blue Ribbon Panel on *Improving the Effectiveness of Audit Committees.* This Report by a panel of representatives of investors, lawyers, accountants, stock exchanges, and businesses is causing more active corporate governance involving vigilant audit committees.
2. Improvement in the quality of earnings as a result of an initiative on inappropriate earnings management that would not have been successful without participants such as the Big Five accounting firms and the AICPA's Auditing Standards Board, who laid the groundwork for Staff Accounting Bulletin 99 on Materiality.
3. Over 200 recommendations issued by the Public Oversight Board's Panel on Audit Effectiveness (the "O'Malley Panel") to the accounting profession, audit committees, standard-setters and regulators setting forth specific steps that can be implemented to improve the quality of audits and investors' confidence in the numbers.

4. Modernized and strengthened auditor independence rules that were the result of a passionate, public dialogue among all of the capital market's participants. This dialogue served a very useful purpose and provided helpful input into crafting a final rule.

5. New disclosure rules built on the principle that each and every investor has a right to get access to information at the same time, not after a select few have profited simply because they received it in advance.

6. At a time when just under 10% of the registrants are from foreign countries, a new international accounting standard-setter was established with independent board members selected based on their technical competence, not their political or geographical ties. The leadership of the AICPA was a strong voice during this process, speaking for a competent independent standard-setter of the highest quality.

Chapter 23

The Securities and Exchange Commission— Organization and the Acts

CONTENTS

SEC Addresses: Headquarters and Regional and District Offices	**23.03**
The Securities and Exchange Commission	**23.04**
Glossary of Security and Exchange Commission Terminology	**23.05**
Securities Act of 1933	**23.16**
Registration	**23.17**
Securities Exchange Act of 1934	**23.22**
Insider Trading	**23.23**
Margin Trading	**23.23**
Division of Corporation Finance	**23.23**
Truth in Securities Laws	**23.24**
Development of Disclosure: 1933 and 1934 Acts	**23.24**
Synopsis: The Securities Act of 1933	**23.26**
Synopsis: The Securities Exchange Act of 1934	**23.31**
Public Utility Holding Company Act of 1935	**23.37**
Trust Indenture Act of 1939	**23.38**
Investment Advisers Act of 1940	**23.39**
Trust Investment Company Act of 1940	**23.39**
Corporation Reorganization	**23.40**

In a confusing and contentious regulatory environment, it is more important than ever before to understand the role, rules, and regulations of our regulatory bodies. The Securities and Exchange Commission has been in the news constantly and is a source of great curiosity to the public at large. Both tax professionals and their clients can enhance their understanding of current affairs by knowing what the SEC can—and cannot—do.

In the late 1920s there was widespread speculation in the stock market. When the market crashed in 1929, the public demanded protective action by their legislators. Congressional committees held hearings into all phases of the securities industry, investment banking, and commercial banking activities prior to the market crash. As a result of these hearings, eight Federal statutes were enacted between 1933 and 1940 (with a ninth in 1970), bringing the securities markets and the securities business under federal jurisdiction. These laws are referenced as the "truth in securities" statutes. They include the Securities Act of 1933, the Securities Exchange Act of 1934, the Public Utility Holding Company Act of 1935, the Maloney Amendment to the Securities Exchange Act of 1934, and the Federal Bankruptcy Code. Also included are the Trustee Indenture Act of 1939, the Investment Company Act of 1940, the Investment Advisers Act of 1940, the Securities Investor Protection Act (SPIC) of 1970, and the Securities Act Amendments of 1975.

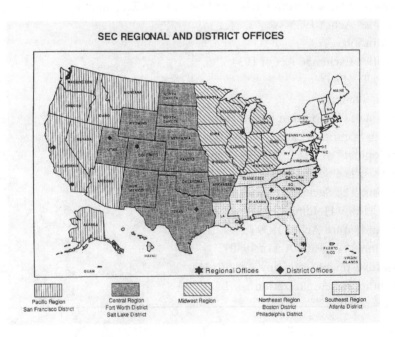

SEC REGIONAL AND DISTRICT OFFICES

★ Regional Offices   ◆ District Offices

Pacific Region	Central Region	Midwest Region	Northeast Region	Southeast Region
San Francisco District	Fort Worth District		Boston District	Atlanta District
	Salt Lake District		Philadelphia District	

SEC ADDRESSES: HEADQUARTERS AND REGIONAL AND DISTRICT OFFICES

SEC HEADQUARTERS

450 Fifth Street, NW
Washington, DC 20549
Office of Investor Education and
  Assistance
(202) 942-7040
e-mail: help@sec.gov

PACIFIC REGION

San Francisco District
Alaska, Arizona, California, Guam,
Hawaii, Idaho, Montana, Nevada,
Oregon, Washington

Pacific Regional Office
5670 Wilshire Boulevard
11th Floor
Los Angeles, CA 90036-3648
(323) 965-3998
e-mail: losangeles@sec.gov

San Francisco District Office
44 Montgomery Street
Suite 1100
San Francisco, CA 94104
(415) 705-2500
e-mail: sanfrancisco@sec.gov

CENTRAL REGION

*Fort Worth District, Salt Lake
District*
Arkansas, Colorado, Kansas,
Nebraska, New Mexico, North
Dakota, Oklahoma, South Dakota,
Texas, Utah, Wyoming

Central Regional Office
1801 California Street
Suite 4800
Denver, CO 80202-2648
(303) 844-1000
e-mail: denver@sec.gov

Fort Worth District Office
801 Cherry Street
19th Floor
Fort Worth, TX 76102
(817) 978-3821
e-mail: dfw@sec.gov

Salt Lake District Office
500 Key Bank Tower
Suite 500
50 South Main Street
Salt Lake City, UT 84144-0402
(801) 524-5796
e-mail: saltlake@sec.gov

MIDWEST REGION

Kentucky, Illinois, Indiana, Iowa,
Michigan, Minnesota, Missouri,
Ohio, Wisconsin

Midwest Regional Office
175 W. Jackson Boulevard
Suite 900
Chicago, IL 60604
(312) 353-7390
e-mail: chicago@sec.gov

NORTHEAST REGION

*Boston District, Philadelphia
District*
Connecticut, Delaware, District of
Columbia, Maine, Maryland,

Massachusetts, New Hampshire,
New Jersey, New York,
Pennsylvania, Rhode Island,
Vermont, Virginia, West Virginia

Northeast Regional Office
233 Broadway
New York, NY 10279
(646) 428-1500
e-mail: newyork@sec.gov

Boston District Office
73 Tremont Street
Suite 600
Boston, MA 02108-3912
(617) 424-5900
e-mail: boston@sec.gov

Philadelphia District Office
The Curtis Center
Suite 1120E
601 Walnut Street
Philadelphia, PA 19106-3322
(215) 597-3100
e-mail: philadelphia@sec.gov

SOUTHEAST REGION

Atlanta District
Alabama, Florida, Georgia,
Louisiana, Mississippi, North
Carolina, Puerto Rico, South
Carolina, Tennessee, Virgin
Islands

Southeast Regional Office
1401 Brickell Avenue
Suite 200
Miami, FL 33131
(305) 536-4700
e-mail: miami@sec.gov

Atlanta District Office
3475 Lenox Road, N.E.
Suite 1000
Atlanta, GA 30326-1232
(404) 842-7600
e-mail: atlanta@sec.gov

THE SECURITIES AND EXCHANGE COMMISSION

The Commission is composed of five members: a Chairman and four Commissioners. Commission members are appointed by the President, with the advice and consent of the Senate, for five-year terms. The Chairman is designated by the President. Terms are staggered; one expires on June 5th of every year. Not more than three members can be of the same political party.

Under the direction of the Chairman and Commissioners, the SEC staff ensures that publicly held entities, broker-dealers in securities, investment companies and advisers, and other participants in the securities markets comply with federal securities laws. These laws are designed to facilitate informed investment analyses and decisions by the investment public, primarily by ensuring adequate disclosure of material significant information. Conformance with federal securities laws and regulations does not imply merit of securities. If information essential to informed investment analysis is properly disclosed, the Commission cannot bar the sale of securities which analysis may show to be of questionable value. Investors, not the Commission, must make the ultimate judgment of the worth of securities offered for sale.

The Commission's staff is composed of lawyers, accountants, financial analysts and examiners, engineers, investigators, economists, and other professionals. The staff is divided into divisions and offices, including eleven regional and district offices, each directed by officials appointed by the Chairman.

GLOSSARY OF SECURITY AND EXCHANGE COMMISSION TERMINOLOGY

The Securities and Exchange Commission in Article 1, Rule 1-02, Title 17, Code of Federal Regulations (which is Accounting Regulation S-X), defines the meaning of terms used by the SEC in its Accounting Rules and Regulations. Also, many of the terms are defined as they appear in the Securities Act of 1933, the Securities Exchange Act of 1934, in Regulations S-K and D, and in the various Forms which publicly held corporations must file periodically with the SEC.

Occasionally, the Commission will use a term in a rule which in context will have a meaning somewhat different from its commonly understood meaning. Many of the definitions as they are written in the statutes and accounting regulations are lengthy and legalistic in style. The objective here is to "delegalize" the "legalese" in the interests both of clarity and brevity. The definitions are not, therefore, verbatim as developed by the Commission.

Accountant's Report. In regard to financial statements, a document in which an independent public accountant or certified public accountant indicates the scope of the audit (or examination) which has been made and sets forth an opinion regarding the financial statements taken as a whole, or an assertion to the effect that an overall opinion cannot be expressed. When an overall opinion cannot be expressed, the reasons therefore should be stated.

Accounting Principle, Change In. Results from changing one acceptable principle to another principle. A change in practice, or in the method of applying an accounting principle, or practice, is also considered a change in accounting principle.

Affiliate. One that directly or indirectly, through one or more intermediaries, controls or is controlled by, or is under common control with, the person specified (see **Person** below).

Amicus Curiae ("Friend of the Court"). An SEC advisory upon request of a court which assists a court in the interpretation of some matter concerning a securities law or accounting regulation.

Amount. When used to reference securities means:
a. The principal amount of a debt obligation if "amount" relates to evidence of indebtedness.
b. The number of shares if "amount" relates to shares.
c. The number of units if "amount" relates to any other type of securities.

Application for Listing. A detailed questionnaire filed with a national securities exchange providing information concerning the corporation's history and current status.

Assets Subject to Lien. Assets mortgaged, pledged, or otherwise subject to lien, and the approximate amounts of each.

Associate. When used to indicate a relationship with any person (see **Person** below), any corporation or organization, any trust or other estate, and any relative or spouse of such person, or any relative of such spouse.

Audit (or **examination**). When used in regard to financial statements, an examination of the statements by an accountant in accordance with generally accepted auditing standards for the purpose of expressing an opinion.

Audit Committee. A special committee of the board composed of directors who are *not* (if possible) officers of the company. The SEC wants the Audit Committee to assume the responsibility for arranging the details of the audit. In addition, an audit committee's major responsibilities include dealing with the company's financial reports, its external audit, and the company's system of internal accounting control and internal audit. The duties and responsibilities of audit committee members should be reasonably specific, but broad enough to allow the committee to pursue matters believed to have important accounting, reporting and auditing consequences.

Balance Sheet. Includes statements of assets and liabilities as well as statements of net assets unless the context clearly indicates the contrary.

Bank Holding Company. A person who is engaged, either directly or indirectly, primarily in the business of owning securities of one or more banks for the purpose, and with the effect of exercising control.

Blue Sky Laws. Terminology for State securities laws.

Broker. A person in the business of buying and selling securities, for a commission, on behalf of other parties.

Call. (See **Option** below.)

Censure. A formal reprimand by the SEC for improper profesional behavior by a party to a filing.

Certificate. A document of an independent public accountant, or independent certified public accountant, that is dated, reasonably comprehensive as to the scope of the audit made, and states clearly the opinion of the accountant in respect to the financial statements and the accounting principles and procedures followed by the registrant (see **Registrant** below).

Certification. It is the accountant's responsibility to make a reasonably unqualified certification of the financial statements. It is important for the auditor to incorporate in the certificate an adequate explanation of the scope (see **Scope** below) of the audit.

Certified. When used in regard to financial statements, examined and reported upon with an opinion expressed by an independent public or certified public accountant.

Certiorari, Writ of. An order issued by a superior court directing an inferior court to deliver its record for review.

Chapter X Bankruptcy. Voluntary or involuntary reorganization of a corporation with publicly held securities.

Chapter XI Bankruptcy. Deals with individuals, partnerships and with corporations whose securities are not publicly held. Affects only voluntary arrangements of unsecured debts.

Charter. Includes articles of incorporation, declarations of trust, articles of association or partnership, or any similar instrument, as amended, affecting the organization of an incorporated or unincorporated person.

Civil Actions. Involves the private rights and remedies of the parties to a suit; actions arising out of a contract.

Class of Securities. A group of similar securities that give shareholders similar rights.

Closed-End Investment Company. A corporation in the business of investing its funds in securities of other corporations for income and profit. Investors wishing to "cash out" of the investment company do so by selling their shares on the open market, as with any other stock.

Closing Date. Effective date (see **Effective Date** below) of a registration statement.

Comment Letters. (See **Deficiency Letter** below.)

Common Equity. Any class of common stock or an equivalent interest, including but not limited to a unit of beneficial interest in a trust or a limited partnership interest.

Compensating Balance. Restricted deposits of a borrower required by banks to be maintained against short-term loans. A portion of any demand, time, or certificate of deposit, maintained by a corporation, or by any person on behalf of the corporation, which constitutes support for existing borrowing arrangements of the corporation, or any other person, with a lending institution. Such arrangements include both outstanding borrowings and the assurance of future credit availability.

Consent Action. Issued when a person agrees to the terms of an SEC disciplinary action without admitting to the allegations in the complaint.

Consolidated Statements. Include the operating results of a corporation's subsidiary(ies) with inter-company transactions eliminated.

Control (including the terms "controlling," "controlled by," "under common control with"). The possession, direct or indirect, of the power to direct or cause the direction of the management and policies of a person, whether through the ownership of voting shares, by contract, or otherwise.

Cooling-Off Period. The period between the filing and effective date (see **Effective Date** below) of a registration statement.

Criminal Action. Suits initiated for the alleged violation of a public law.

Dealer. A person in the business of buying and selling securities for his or her own account.

Deficiency Letter. A letter from the SEC to the registrant setting forth the needed corrections and amendments to the issuing corporations' registration statement.

Delisting. Permanent removal of a listed security from a national securities exchange.

Depositary Share. A security evidenced by an American Depositary Receipt that represents a foreign security or a multiple of or fraction thereof deposited with a depositary.

Development Stage Company. A company is considered to be in the development stage if it is devoting substantially all of its efforts to establishing a new business and either of the following conditions exists.

1. Planned principal operations have not commenced.

2. Planned principal operations have commenced, but there has been no significant revenue therefrom.

Disbarment. Permanent removal of a professional's privilege to represent clients before the SEC.

Disclosure. The identification of accounting policies and principles that materially affect the determination of financial position, changes in financial position, and results of operations.

Domiciled Corporation. A corporation doing business in the state in which its corporate charter was guaranteed.

Due Diligence Meeting. A meeting of all parties in the preparation of a registration statement to assure that a high degree of care in investigation and independent verification of the company's representations has been made.

Effective Date. The twentieth (20th) day after the filing date of a registration statement or amendment unless the Commission shortens or extends that time period.

Employee. Any employee, general partner, or consultant or advisor, insurance agents who are exclusive agents of the registrant, its subsidiaries or parents. It also includes former employees as well as executors, administrators or beneficiaries of the estates of deceased employees, guardians or members of a committee for incompetent former employees, or similar persons duly authorized by law to administer the estate or assets of former employees.

Equity Security. Any stock or similar security; or any security convertible, with or without consideration, into such a security, or carrying any warrant or right to subscribe to or purchase such a security, or any such warrant or right.

Examination. (See **Audit** above.)

Exchange. An organized association providing a market place for bringing together buyers and sellers of securities through brokers.

Exempt Security. One that is not required to be registered with the SEC.

Exempt Transaction. A transaction in securities that does not require registration with the SEC.

Expert. Any specialist, accountant, attorney, engineer, appraiser, etc., who participates in the preparation of a registration statement. Broadly, any signatory to the registration statement is assumed to be an expert.

Fifty-Percent-Owned-Person. A person whose outstanding voting shares are approximately 50 percent owned by another specified person directly, or indirectly, through one or more intermediaries.

Filing. The process of completing and submitting a registration statement to the SEC.

Filing Date. The date a registration statement is received by the SEC.

Financial Statement. Includes all notes to the statements and all related schedules.

Fiscal Year. The annual accounting period or, if no closing date has been adopted, the calendar year ending on December 31.

Float. The difference on a bank's ledger and a depositor's books caused by presentation of checks and deposits in transit.

Footnote. Appended to financial statements as supplemental information for specific items in a statement.

Foreign Currency. Any currency other than the currency used by the enterprise in its financial statements.

Forms. Statements of standards with which registration statements and other filings must comply. Essentially, SEC forms are a set of instructions to guide the registrant in the preparation of the SEC reports to be filed; the forms are not required to be precisely copied.

Form S-1. A registration statement (see **Registration Statement** below) is filed on Form S-1 for companies issuing securities to the public. This form incorporates specified standards for financial statements and auditor's report.

Form 8-K. A report which is filed only when a reportable event occurs which may have a significant effect on the future of a company and on the value of its securities. Form 8-K must befiled not later than 15 days after the date on which the specified event occurs.

Form 10-K. The annual report to the SEC which covers substantially all of the information required in Form S-1. Form 10-K is due 90 days after a company's December 31 fiscal year, or by March 31 of each year.

Form 10-Q. A quarterly report containing *unaudited* financial statements. If certain types of events occur during the period, they must be reported on the Form. The 10-Q is due 45 days after the end of the first three fiscal quarters.

Going Private. The term commonly used to describe those transactions having as their objective the complete termination or substantial reduction of public ownership of an equity's securities.

Going Public. Registering a new issue of securities with the SEC. *Going public* is closely related to the process of applying for listed status on one or more of the exchanges, or registering for trading in the over-the-counter market.

Indemnification Provision. An agreement protecting one party from liability arising from the occurrence of an unforeseeable event.

Independent Accountants *(CPA)*. Accountants who certify financial statements filed with the SEC. Accountants must maintain strict independence of attitude and judgment in planning and conducting and audit and in expressing an opinion on financial statements. The SEC will not recognize any public accountant or certified public accountant that is not independent.

Information Statement. A statement on any pending corporate matters furnished by the registrant to every shareholder who is entitled to vote when a proxy is not solicited.

Initial Margin Percentage. The percentage of the purchase price (or the percentage of a short sale; see **Short Selling** below), that an investor must deposit with his/her broker in compliance with Federal Reserve Board margin requirements.

Injunction. A court order directing a person to stop alleged violations of a securities law or regulation.

Insurance Holding Company. A person who is engaged, either directly or indirectly, primarily in the business of owning securities of one or more insurance companies for the purpose, and with the effect, of exercising control.

Integrated Disclosure System (IDS). An extensive revision of the mandatory business and financial disclosure requirements applicable to publicly-held companies. It establishes a uniform and integrated disclosure system under the securities laws. The IDS adopted major changes in its disclosure systems under the Securities Act of 1933, and the Securities Exchange Act of 1934. The changes include amendments to Form 10-K and 10-Q, amendments to the proxy rules, amendments to Regulation S-K which governs the non-financial statement disclosure rules (see **Regulation S-K** below), uniform financial statement instructions, a general revision of Regulation S-X which governs the form, content, and requirements of financial statements (see **Regulation S-X** below), and a new simplified form for the registration of securities issued in business combinations.

Issuer. Any corporation that sells a security in a public offering.

Letter-of-Consent. Written permission from participating experts to include their names and signatures in a registration statement.

Line-of-Business Reporting. Registrants must report financial information regarding segments of their operations. The SEC does not define the term "line-of-business." Rather, the responsibility of determining meaningful segments that reflect the particular company's operations and organizational concepts is the responsibility of management. No more than ten classes of business are required to be reported.

Listed Status. Condition under which a security has been accepted by an exchange for full trading privileges. As long as a corporation remains listed on an exchange, it must file periodic reports to its stockholders.

Listing. A corporation applying to list its securities on an exchange must file a registration statement and a copy of the application for listing with the SEC.

Majority-Owned Subsidiary. A subsidiary more than 50 percent of whose outstanding voting shares is owned by its parent and/or the parent's other majority-owned subsidiaries.

Managing Underwriter. Underwriter(s) who, by contract or otherwise, deals with the registrant; organizes the selling effort; receives some benefit directly or indirectly in which all other underwriters similarly situated do not share in proportion to their respective interests in the underwriting; or represents any other underwriters in such matters as maintaining the records of the distribution, arranging the allotments of securities offered or arranging for appropriate stabilization activities, if any.

Margin Call. The demand by a broker that an investor deposit additional cash (or acceptable collateral) for securities purchased on credit when the price of the securities declines to a value below the minimum shareholder's equity required by the stock exchange.

Material. Information regarding any subject that limits the information required to those matters about which an average prudent investor ought reasonably to be informed.

Mutual Fund. Not legal terminology. It is a financial term commonly used in street jargon to mean an open-end investment company (see **Open-End Investment Company** below) as defined in the Investment Company Act of 1940.

National Association of Securities Dealers, Inc. (NASD). An association of brokers/dealers who are in the business of trading over-the-counter securities.

Net Sales. Income or loss from continuing operations before extraordinary items and cumulative effect of a change in accounting principle.

New York Stock Exchange (and **Regional Exchanges**). An association organized to provide physical, mechanical, and logistical facilities for the purchase and sale of securities by investors through brokers and dealers.

No-Action Letter. The SEC's written reply to a corporate issuer of securities stating its position regarding a specific filing matter.

Notification. Filing with the SEC the terms of an offering of securities that are exempt from registration.

Offering Date. The date a new security can be offered to the public.

Open-End Investment Company. A corporation in the business of investing its funds in securities of other corporations for income and profit. An open-end company continuously offers new shares for sales and redeems shares previously issued to investors who want to cash out.

Opinion. A required statement in the certification that the auditor believes the audit correctly reflects the organization's financial condition and results of operation.

Option. The contractual privilege of purchasing a security (Call) for a specified price, or delivering a security (Put) at a specified price.

Over-the-Counter Securities. Corporate and government securities that are not listed for trading on a national stock exchange.

Parent. A "parent" of a specified person(s) is an affiliate controlling such person(s) directly or indirectly through one or more intermediaries.

Pension Plan. An arrangement whereby a company undertakes to provide its retired employees with benefits that can be determined or estimated in advance.

Person. An individual, corporation, partnership, association, joint-stock company, business trust, or unincorporated organization.

Predecessor. A person from whom another person acquired the major portion of the business and assets in a single succession or in a series of related successions. In each succession the acquiring person acquired the major portion of the business and assets of the acquired person.

Prefiling Conference. A meeting of corporate officers and experts outlining the SEC requirements for the filing of a registration statement. Occasionally an SEC staff member will attend.

Previously Filed or Reported. Previously filed with, or reported in a definitive proxy statement or information statement, or a registration statement. Information contained in any such document will be assumed to have been previously filed with the exchange.

Principal Holder of Equity Securities. Used in respect of a registrant or other person named in a particular statement or report, a holder of record or a known beneficial owner of more than 10 percent of any class of securities of the registrant or other person, respectively, and of the date of the related balance sheet filed.

Promoter. Any person who, acting alone or in conjunction with one or more other persons, directly or indirectly takes initiative in founding and organizing the business or enterprise of an issuer. Any person is a promoter who, in connection with the founding and organizing of the business or enterprise of an issuer, directly or indirectly receives in consideration of services or property, or both services and property, 10 percent or more of any class of securities of the issuer or 10 percent or more of the proceeds from the sale of any class of securities. However, a person who receives such securities or proceeds either solely as underwriting commissions or solely in consideration of property shall not be deemed a promoter within the meaning of this paragraph if such person does not otherwise take part in founding and organizing the enterprise.

Prospectus. Document consisting of Part 1 of the registration statement filed with the SEC by the issuing corporation that must be delivered to all purchasers of newly issued securities.

Proxy. A power of attorney whereby a stockholder authorizes another person, or group of persons, to act (vote) for that stockholder at a shareholders' meeting.

Proxy Statement. Information furnished in conjunction with a formal solicitation in the proxy for the power to vote a stockholder's shares.

Put. (See **Option** above.)

Red-Herring Prospectus. Preliminary prospectus with a statement (in red ink) on each page indicating that the security described has not become effective, that the information is subject to correction and change without notice, and is not an offer to buy or sell that security.

Refusal. SEC action prohibiting a filing (see **Filing** above) from becoming effective.

Regional Exchanges. (See **New York Stock Exchange** above.)

Registrant. An issuer of securities for which an application, a report, or a registration statement has been filed.

Registration. Act of filing with the SEC the required information concerning the issuing corporation and the security to be issued.

Registration Statement. The document filed with the SEC containing legal, commercial, technical, and financial information concerning a new security issue.

Regulation S-K. An authoritative statement of disclosure standards under all securities acts. Regulation S-K establishes the standards of disclosure for non-financial information not included in financial statements, footnotes or schedules.

Regulation S-X. The principal document reporting for financial statements, footnotes and schedules' standards under all securities acts. No filing can be made without reference to Regulation S-X. It integrates all accounting requirements prior to February 21, 1940, into a single regulation.

Related Party. One that can exercise control or significant influence over the management and/or operating policies of another party, to the extent that one of the parties may be prevented from fully pursuing its own separate interests. Related parties consist of all affiliates of an enterprise, including its management and their immediate families, its principal owners and their immediate families, its investments accounted for by the equity method, beneficial employee trusts that are managed by the management of the enterprise, and any party that may, or does, deal with the enterprise and has ownership of, control over, or can significantly influence the management or operating policies of another party to the extent that an arms-length transaction may not be achieved. Transactions between related parties are generally accounted for on the same basis as if the parties were not related, unless the substance of the transaction is not arm's length. Substance over form is an important consideration when accounting for transactions involving related parties.

Replacement Cost. The lowest amount that would have to be paid in the normal course of business to obtain a new asset of equivalent operating or productive capability.

Restricted Security. Private offering of an issue that cannot be resold to the public without prior registration. Also called "investment letter" securities for the letter that the purchaser of such securities must submit to the SEC stating that the securities are being acquired for investment purposes, not for immediate resale.

Right. Provides current security holders the privilege of participating on a pro rata basis in a new offering of securities.

Roll-Up Transaction. Any transaction or series of transactions that, directly or indirectly through acquisition or otherwise, involves the combination or reorganization of one or more partnerships. The term includes the offer or sale of securities by a successor entity, whether newly formed or previously existing, to one or more limited partners of the partnership to be combined or reorganized, or the acquisition of the successor entity's securities by the partnerships being combined or reorganized.

Rules of Practice. Establishes standards of conduct for professionals practicing before the SEC.

Sale. Every contract of sale, disposition, or offer of a security for value (see **Security** below).

Schedule. Detailed financial information presented in a form prescribed by the SEC in Regulation S-X.

Scienter. Intent to deceive, manipulate, or defraud. Requires proof that defendant knew of material mistatements or omissions; that defendant acted willfully and knowingly.

Scope (of an Audit). A complete, detailed audit. The auditor includes in the certificate an adequate explanation of the extent of the audit.

Securities Act of 1933. Requires the disclosure of financial data for issues not exempted from registration and prohibits fraudulent acts and misrepresentations and omission of material (see **Material** above) facts in the issue of securities.

Securities Exchange Act of 1934 (The **Exchange Act**). Covers the regulation of stock market activities and the public trading of securities. The regulations covered are the disclosure of significant financial data, the regulation of securities market practices and operation, and control of credit (margin requirements) extended for the purchase and short sales of securities.

Security. Any instrument representing a debt obligation, an equity interest in a corporation, or any instrument commonly known as a security. In the Securities Act, security is defined to include by name or description many documents in which there is common trading for investment or speculation.

Some, such as notes, bonds and stocks, are standardized and the name alone carries well settled meaning. Others are of a more variable character and were necessarily designated by more descriptive terms, such as transferable share, investment contract, and in general any interest or instrument commonly known as a security.

Selling Group. Several broker/dealers who distribute a new issue of securities at retail.

Share. A share of stock in a corporation or unit of interest in an unincorporated person.

Short-Selling. Selling a security that is not owned with the expectation of buying that specific security later at a lower market price.

Significant Subsidiary. A subsidiary (including its subsidiaries) in which the registrant's (and its other subsidiaries') investments in and advances to exceed 10 percent of the total assets of the registrant and its subsidiaries consolidated as of the end of the most recently completed fiscal year. For a proposed business combination to be accounted for as a pooling of interests, this requirement is also met when the number of common shares exchanged by the registrant exceeds 10 percent of its total common shares outstanding at the date the combination is initiated, or the registrant's (and its other subsidiaries') proportionate share of the total assets, after intercompany eliminations, of the subsidiary exceeds 10 percent of the total assets of the registrant and its subsidiaries consolidated as of the end of the most recently completed fiscal year.

Small Business Issuer. An entity that (a) has revenues of less than $25,000,000; (b) is a U.S. or Canadian issuer; (c) is not an investment company; (d) if a majority-owned subsidiary, the parent corporation is also a small business issuer.

Solicitation. Any request for a proxy or other similar communication to security holders.

Sponsor. The person proposing the roll-up transaction. (See **Roll-Up Transaction** above.)

Spread. The difference between the price paid for a security by the underwriter and the selling price of that security.

Stockholders' Meeting, Regular. The annual meeting of stockholders for the election of directors and for action on other corporate matters.

Stockholders' Meeting, Special. A meeting in which only specified items can be considered.

Stop Order. An SEC order stopping the issue or listing of a security on a stock exchange.

Subsidiary. An affiliate controlled by a specified person directly, or indirectly, through one or more intermediaries.

Substantial Authoritative Support. FASB principles, standards and practices published in Statements and Interpretations, AICPA Accounting Research Bulletins, and AICPA Opinions, except to the extent altered, amended, supplemented, revoked or superseded by an FASB Statement.

Succession. The direct acquisition of the assets comprising a going business, whether by merger, consolidation, or other direct transfer. This term does not include the acquisition of control of a business unless followed by the direct acquisition of its assets.

Successor. The surviving entity after completion of the roll-up transaction, or the entity whose securities are being offered or sold to, or acquired by, limited partners of the partnerships or the limited partnerships to be combined or reorganized.

Summary Prospectus. A prospectus containing specific items of information which subsequently will be included in the registration statement.

Suspension. An SEC order temporarily prohibiting the trading of a security on the stock exchange, usually invoked by the SEC when a news release is pending which may cause a disorderly market in that security. Trading is usually resumed shortly after the information has been publicly disseminated.

Totally Held Subsidiary. A subsidiary substantially all of whose outstanding securities are owned by its parent and/or the parent's other totally held subsidiaries. The subsidiary is not indebted to any person other than its parent and/or the parent's other totally held subsidiaries in an amount which is material in relation to the particular subsidiary, excepting indebtedness incurred in the ordinary course of business which is not overdue and which matures within one year from the date of its creation, whether evidenced by securities or not.

Underwriter. (See **Managing Underwriter** above.)

Unlisted Trading Privileges. A security issue authorized by the SEC for trading on an exchange without requiring the corporation to complete a formal listing application.

Voting Securities. Securities whose holders are presently entitled to vote for the election of directors.

Warrant. A security that grants the holder the right to purchase a specific number of shares of the security to which the warrant is attached at a specified price and usually within a stated period of time.

Wholly-Owned Subsidiary. A subsidiary substantially all of whose outstanding voting securities are owned by its parent and/or the parent's other wholly-owned subsidiaries.

SECURITIES ACT OF 1933

The *truth in securities* law has two main objectives:

1. To require that investors are provided with material information concerning securities offered for sale to the public.
2. To prevent misrepresentation, deceit, and other fault in the sale of securities.

The primary means of accomplishing these objectives is by requiring full disclosure of financial information by registering offerings and sales of securities. Securities transactions subject to registration are mostly offerings of debt and equity securities issued by corporations, limited partnerships, trusts and other issuers. Federal and certain other government debt securities are not. Certain securities and transactions qualify for exemptions from registration provisions. They are included in the discussion that follows.

REGISTRATION

Registration is intended to provide adequate and accurate disclosure of material facts concerning the company and the securities it proposes to sell. This enables investors to make a thorough appraisal of the merits of the securities and exercise informed judgment in determining whether or not to purchase them.

Registration requires, but does not guarantee, the accuracy of the facts represented in the registration statement and prospectus. However, the law does prohibit false and misleading statements under penalty of fine, imprisonment, or both. Investors who purchases securities and suffer losses have important recovery rights under the law if they can prove that there was incomplete or inaccurate disclosure of material facts in the registration statement or prospectus. If such misstatements are proven, the following could be liable for investor losses sustained in the securities purchase:

1. The issuing company.
2. Its responsible directors and officers.
3. The underwriters.
4. The controlling interests.
5. The sellers of the securities.
6. Others that are affiliated with the securities of the issuer.

Registration of securities does not preclude the sale of stock in risky, poorly managed, or unprofitable companies. Nor does the Commission *approve or disapprove* securities on their merits; and it is unlawful to represent otherwise in the sale of securities. The only standard which must be met when registering securities is adequate and accurate *disclosure* of required material facts concerning the company and the securities it proposes to sell. The fairness of the terms, the issuing company's prospects for successful operation, and other factors affecting the merits of investing in the securities have no bearing on the question of whether or not securities can be qualified for registration.

The Registration Process

To facilitate registration by different types of enterprises, the Commission has special forms that vary in their disclosure requirements, but generally provide essential facts while minimizing the burden and expense of complying with the law. In general, registration forms call for disclosure of information such as:

1. Description of the registrant's properties and business.
2. Description of the significant provisions of the security to be offered for sale and its relationship to the registrant's other capital securities.
3. Information about the management of the registrant.
4. Financial statements certified by independent public accountants.

Registration statements become public immediately upon filing with the SEC. After the registration statement is filed, securities can be *offered* orally or by summaries of the information in the registration statement, but it is unlawful to *sell* the securities until the *effective date* which is on the 20th day after filing the registration statement, or on the 20th day after filing the last amendment, if any. The SEC can issue a *stop order* to refuse or suspend the effectiveness of the statement if the Commission concludes that material deficiencies in a registration statement appear to result from a deliberate attempt to conceal or mislead. A stop order is not a permanent prohibition to the effectiveness of the registration statement, or to the sale of the securities, and can be lifted and the statement declared effective when amendments are filed correcting the statement in accordance with the requirements in the stop order decision.

There are exemptions to the registration requirements:

1. Private offerings to a limited number of persons or institutions who have access to the kind of information that registration would disclose and who do not propose to redistribute the securities.
2. Offerings restricted to residents of the state in which the issuing company is organized and doing business.
3. Securities of municipal, state, federal and other governmental instrumentalities, such as charitable institutions and banks.
4. Offerings not exceeding certain specified amounts made in compliance with regulations of the Commission.
5. Offerings of small business investment companies made in accordance with the rules and regulations of the Commission.

Regardless of whether or not the securities are exempt from registration, anti-fraud provisions apply to all sales of securities involving interstate commerce or the mails.

The small business exemption from registration provides that offerings of securities under $5 million can be exempt from full registration, subject to conditions the SEC prescribes to protect investors. Certain Canadian and domestic companies are permitted to make exempt offerings.

UNITED STATES
SECURITIES AND EXCHANGE COMMISSION
Washington, D.C. 20549

FORM 10

GENERAL FORM FOR REGISTRATION OF SECURITIES
Pursuant to Section 12(b) or (g) of The Securities Exchange Act of 1934

(Exact name of registrant as specified in its charter)

(State or other jurisdiction of incorporation or organization)   (I.R.S. Employer Identification No.)

(Address of principal executive offices)   (Zip Code)

Registrant's telephone number, including area code _____

Securities to be registered pursuant to Section 12(b) of the Act:

Title of each class to be so registered	Name of each exchange on which each class is to be registered

Securities to be registered pursuant to Section 12(g) of the Act:

(Title of class)

(Title of class)

INFORMATION REQUIRED IN REGISTRATION STATEMENT

Item 1. Business.
Furnish the information required by Item 101 of Regulation S-K (§229.101 of this chapter).

Item 2. Financial Information.
Furnish the information required by Items 301 and 303 of Regulation S-K (§§229.301 and 229.303 of this chapter).

Item 3. Properties.
Furnish the information required by Item 102 of Regulation S-K (§229.102 of this chapter).

Item 4. Security Ownership of Certain Beneficial Owners and Management.
Furnish the information required by Item 403 of Regulation S-K (§229.403 of this chapter).

Item 5. Directors and Executive Officers.
Furnish the information required by Item 401 of Regulation S-K (§229.401 of this chapter).

Item 6. Executive Compensation.
Furnish the information required by Item 402 of Regulation S-K (§229.402 of this chapter).

Item 7. Certain Relationships and Related Transactions.
Furnish the information required by Item 404 of Regulation S-K (§229.404 of this chapter).

Item 8. Legal Proceedings.
Furnish the information required by Item 103 of Regulation S-K (§229.103 of this chapter).

Item 9. Market Price of and Dividends on the Registrant's Common Equity and Related Stockholder Matters.
Furnish the information required by Item 201 of Regulation S-K (§229.201 of this chapter).

Item 10. Recent Sales of Unregistered Securities.
Furnish the information required by Item 701 of Regulation S-K (§229.701 of this chapter).

Item 11. Description of Registrant's Securities to be Registered.
Furnish the information required by Item 202 of Regulation S-K (§229.202 of this chapter).

Item 12. Indemnification of Directors and Officers.
Furnish the information required by Item 702 of Regulation S-K (§229.702 of this chapter).

Item 13. Financial Statements and Supplementary Data.
Furnish all financial statements required by Regulation S-X and the supplementary financial information required by Item 302 of Regulation S-K (§229.302 of this chapter).

Item 14. Changes in and Disagreements with Accountants on Accounting and Financial Disclosure.
Furnish the information required by Item 304 of Regulation S-K (§229.304 of this chapter).

Item 15. Financial Statements and Exhibits.
(a) List separately all financial statements filed as part of the registration statement.
(b) Furnish the exhibits required by Item 601 of Regulation S-K (§229.601 of this chapter).

SIGNATURES

Pursuant to the requirements of Section 12 of the Securities Exchange Act of 1934, the registrant has duly caused this registration statement to be signed on its behalf by the undersigned, thereunto duly authorized.

_____
(Registrant)

Date _____   By _____
(Signature)*

_____
*Print name and title of the signing officer under his signature.

GENERAL INSTRUCTIONS

A. Rule as to Use of Form 10.

Form 10 shall be used for registration pursuant to Section 12(b) or (g) of the Securities Exchange Act of 1934 of classes of securities of issuers for which no other form is prescribed.

B. Application of General Rules and Regulations.

(a) The General Rules and Regulations under the Act contain certain general requirements which are applicable to registration on any form. These general requirements should be carefully read and observed in the preparation and filing of registration statements on this form.

(b) Particular attention is directed to Regulation 12B [17 CFR 240.12b-1-240.12b-36] which contains general requirements regarding matters such as the kind and size of paper to be used, the legibility of the registration statement, the information to be given whenever the title of securities is required to be stated, and the filing of the registration statement. The definitions contained in Rule 12b-2 [17 CFR 240.12b-2] should be especially noted.

C. Preparation of Registration Statement.

(a) This form is not to be used as a blank form to be filled in, but only as a guide in the preparation of the registration statement on paper meeting the requirements of Rule 12b-12 [17 CFR 240.12b-12]. The registration statement shall contain the item numbers and captions, but the text of the items may be omitted. The answers to the items shall be prepared in the manner specified in Rule 12b-13 [17 CFR 240.12b-13].

(b) Unless otherwise stated, the information required shall be given as of a date reasonably close to the date of filing the registration statement.

(c) Attention is directed to Rule 12b-20 [17 CFR 240.12b-20] which states: "In addition to the information expressly required to be included in a statement or report, there shall be added such further material information, if any, as may be necessary to make the required statements, in light of the circumstances under which they are made, not misleading."

D. Signature and Filing of Registration Statement.

Three complete copies of the registration statement, including financial statements, exhibits and all other papers and documents filed as a part thereof, and five additional copies which need not include exhibits, shall be filed with the Commission. At least one complete copy of the registration statement, including financial statements, exhibits and all other papers and documents filed as a part thereof, shall be filed with each exchange on which any class of securities is to be registered. At least one complete copy of the registration statement filed with the Commission and one such copy filed with each exchange shall be manually signed. Copies not manually signed shall bear typed or printed signatures.

E. Omission of information Regarding Foreign Subsidiaries.

Information required by any item or other requirement of this form with respect to any foreign subsidiary may be omitted to the extent that the required disclosure would be detrimental to the registrant. However, financial statements, otherwise required, shall not be omitted pursuant to this instruction. Where information is omitted pursuant to this instruction, a statement shall be made that such information has been omitted and the names of the subsidiaries involved shall be separately furnished to the Commission. The Commission may, in its discretion, call for justification that the required disclosure would be detrimental.

F. Incorporation by Reference.

Attention is directed to Rule 12b-23 [17 CFR 240.12b-23] which provides for the incorporation by reference of information contained in certain documents in answer or partial answer to any item of a registration statement.

SECURITIES EXCHANGE ACT OF 1934

The 1934 Act extends the disclosure doctrine of investor protection to securities that are listed and registered for public trading on U.S. national securities exchanges. In 1964 the SEC was authorized by Congress to include disclosure and reporting requirements to equity securities in the over-the-counter market. The object of the 1934 Act is to ensure *fair and orderly securities markets* by prohibiting certain types of activities and by setting forth rules regarding the operation of the markets and the participants.

Companies wanting to have their securities registered and listed or publicly traded on an exchange must file a registration application with the exchange and the SEC. Companies whose equity securities are traded over-the-counter must file a similar registration form. SEC rules prescribe the content of registration statements and require certified financial statements. After a company's securities have become registered, annual and other periodic reports to update information contained in the original registration statement must be filed.

The 1934 Act governs the solicitation of proxies (votes) from holders of registered securities, both listed and over-the-counter, for the election of directors and for approval of other corporate action. All material facts concerning matters on which shareholders are asked to vote must be disclosed. In 1970 Congress amended the Exchange Act to extend its reporting and disclosure provisions to situations where control of a company is sought through a tender offer to other planned stock acquisitions of over five percent of a company's equity securities by direct purchase or by a tender offer. Disclosure provisions are supplemented by other provisions to help ensure investor protection in tender offers.

INSIDER TRADING

Insider trader prohibitions are designed to curb misuse of material confidential information not available to the general public. Examples of such misuse are buying or selling securities to make profits or avoid losses based on material nonpublic information, or by telling others of the information before such information is generally available to all shareholders. The *Insider Trading Sanctions Act of 1984* allows imposing fines up to three times to profit gained or losses avoided by use of material nonpublic information. All officers and directors of a company and beneficial owners of more than ten percent of its registered equity securities must file an initial report with the SEC and with the exchange on which the stock is listed, showing their holdings of each of the company's equity securities. Thereafter, they must file reports for any month during which there was any change in those holdings, and any profits obtained by them from purchases and sales, or sales and purchases, of such equity securities within any six-month period can be recovered by the company or by any security holder on its behalf. Insiders are also prohibited from making short sales of their company's equity securities.

MARGIN TRADING

The 1934 Act authorizes the Board of Governors of the Federal Reserve System to set limits on the amount of credit which can be extended for the purpose of purchasing or carrying securities. The objective is to restrict excessive use of credit in the securities markets. While the credit restrictions are set by the Board of Governors, investigation and enforcement is the responsibility of the SEC.

DIVISION OF CORPORATION FINANCE

Corporation Finance has the overall responsibility of ensuring that disclosure requirements are met by publicly held companies registered with the SEC. Its work includes: reviewing registration statements for new securities; proxy material and annual reports the Commission requires from publicly held companies; documents concerning tender offers, and mergers and acquisitions in general.

This Division renders administrative interpretations to the public of the Securities Act and the Securities Exchange Act, and to prospective registrants, and others. It is also responsible for certain statutes and regulations pertaining to small businesses and for the Trust Indenture Act of 1939. Applications for qualification of trust indentures are examined for compliance with the applicable requirements of the law and the Commission's rules. Corporation Finance works closely with the Office of the Chief Accountant in drafting rules and regulations which prescribe requirements for financial statements.

TRUTH IN SECURITIES LAWS

The objectives of the laws are twofold. First is the protection of investors and the public against fraudulent acts and practices in the purchase and sale of securities. The second objective is to regulate trading in the national securities markets. For example:

1. "To provide full and fair disclosure of the character of securities sold in interstate and foreign commerce and through the mails, and to prevent fraud in the sale thereof, and for other purposes." (Securities Act of 1933.)
2. "To provide for the regulation of securities exchanges and the over-the-counter markets operating in interstate and foreign commerce and through the mails, to prevent inequitable and unfair practices on such exchanges and markets, and for other purposes." (Securities Exchange Act of 1934.)
3. "To provide for the registration and regulation of investment companies and investment advisers, and for other purposes." (Investment Company Act of 1940 and the Investment Advisers Act of 1940.)

DEVELOPMENT OF DISCLOSURE: 1933 AND 1934 ACTS

Two separate disclosure systems develcped under the two principal securities laws. Generally, the Securities Act of 1933 regulates the *initial* public distribution of securities. The disclosure system developed under the 1933 Act emphasizes the comprehensive information about the issuer, because it was developed primarily for companies going public for the *first time* and about which the public had very little information.

The Securities Exchange Act of 1934 regulates the trading of securities in *publicly held companies* which are traded both on the exchanges and in the over-the-counter markets. The dual disclosure system developed under the 1933 and 1934 Acts deals primarily with the form and content of financial and business data in the annual reports to the SEC and to shareholders, and concerns proxy statements as well as the dissemination of interim data. The emphasis of this disclosure system is on periodic information concerning issuers already known to security holders, and the purpose is to keep the data up-to-date.

The dual system generated a large number of registration and periodic reporting forms, each with its own set of instructions. Many publicly-held companies filed numerous registration statements and distributed related reports to the public containing the same information produced several times in slightly different forms, repeating much information that was already available within the financial community.

In addition, the audited primary financial statements prepared in conformity with GAAP that were included in the annual reports to shareholders, were not explicitly covered by the very detailed disclosure requirements in S-X. These mandated the form and content of the audited primary financial statements that were included in documents filed with the SEC and in prospectuses. However, since the financial statements had to be in conformity with GAAP there were no essential differences between the two.

Financial statements that conformed to S-X included numerous additional technical disclosures to satisfy the needs of professional financial analysts and the SEC staff. Uniform financial disclosure requirements for virtually all documents covered by either the 1933 or the 1934 Acts as well as for nonfinancial disclosures under the 1934 Act and for a major portion of those required under the 1933 Act have been formulated. To reach the objective, where identical disclosures are included both in documents filed with the Commission and distributed to security holders in prospectuses, proxy statements and annual reports, the Commission has two basic regulations. These are Regulation S-X (see Chapter 16) which covers the requirements for audited primary financial statements, and Regulation S-K which covers most of the other business, analytical, and unaudited financial disclosures.

Regulation S-K covers analytical and unaudited supplementary financial disclosures under the 1934 Act and most disclosures under the 1933 Act. One of the key requirements in Regulation S-K is the *Management's Discussion and Analysis of Financial Condition and Results of Operations*. The discussion must cover the three years presented in the audited financials and treat not only results of operations, but also financial condition and changes in financial condition. Although the requirement is for three years, the SEC suggests that when trends are being discussed, references to five years of selected financial data are appropriate.

The discussion and analysis is filed under the Securities Acts, as well as included in all annual reports and prospectuses. Accordingly, companies should document the adequacy of their systems and procedures for analyzing past results to be sure that there is an adequate and reliable information base for the management discussion and analysis, including decisions as to scope and content. Since future plans and expectations, such as capital expenditure commitments, are important in formulating management's discussion and analysis, it may be prudent to reappraise internal financial forecasting procedures periodically.

Although forward-looking information is not mandated, the specifically required information is such that financial analysts will be able to work out a forecast of future operating results. As practice develops, managements may find it preferable simply to include formal financial forecasts and comply with the safe harbor rules, rather than rely solely on the forecasts analysts will make based on data presumed to be reliable.

Form S-15. When a company acquires a business that is relatively minor when compared to the acquiring company, a process that was difficult because of the complexity and cost of registration requirements is greatly simplified by the use of Form S-15 for the registration requirements. Form S-15 enables an issuer to provide an abbreviated prospectus accompanied by the issuer's latest annual report to shareholders instead of larger documents. This procedure is limited to cases where the acquiring company's key financial indices as specified in the regulations are not affected by more than 10% by the acquired company, and where State law applicable to the merger does not require a vote by the security holders of the company being acquired. There are other restrictions, however, and it is likely this simplified procedure will be most usable for mergers where the company to be acquired is closely-held and will not become a significant part of the combined company.

Three copies of Form S-15 must be filed with the SEC. One copy must be signed manually by an officer of the registrant, or by counsel, or by any other authorized person. The name and title of the person signing Form S-15 should be typed or printed under that person's signature.

SYNOPSIS: THE SECURITIES ACT OF 1933

In 1933, the first Federal legislative act designed to regulate the securities business on an interstate basis was passed. Its expressed purpose was:

"To provide full and fair disclosure of the character of securities . . . and to prevent frauds in the sale thereof, and for other purposes." There are four things to note:

1. It related to newly-issued securities, not to those already in the hands of the public.
2. It called for full and fair disclosure of all the facts necessary for an intelligent appraisal of the value of a security.
3. It was designed to prevent fraud in the sale of securities.
4. This legislation led to the Securities Exchange Act of 1934 establishing the Securities and Exchange Commission which would administer both acts.

There are 26 sections to the Act:

Section 1. "This title may be cited as the Securities Act of 1933." Various court decisions have very liberally interpreted the meaning of "securities" as covered by the Act. One decision contains the following: ". . . that this statute was not a penal statute but was a remedial enactment . . . A remedial enactment is one that seeks to give a remedy for an ill. It is to be liberally construed so that its purpose may be realized." (SEC v Starmont, (1940) 31 F. Supp. 264.)

Section 2. Definitions. This section defines many of the terms used throughout the other sections of the Act. Importantly, it contains definitions of "security," "person," "sale," "offer to sell," and "prospectus," among many others. Several important Rules of the SEC are directly derived from this section, including Rule 134 (discussed in Section 5).

Section 3. Exempted Securities. Some securities, such as those issued or guaranteed by the United States, are exempted from the provisions of the Act.

Section 4. Exempted Transactions. Describes the transactions for which Section 5 does not apply.

Section 5. Prohibitions Relating to Intrastate Commerce and the Mails. It is unlawful to offer any security for sale "by any means or instruments of transportation or communication in interstate commerce or of the mails," unless a registration statement is in effect as to that security. It also prohibits the transportation by any means of interstate commerce or the mails of such a security for the purpose of sale or delivery after sale.

This Section further requires that any security that is registered cannot be sold without prior or concurrent delivery of an effective prospectus that meets the requirements of Section 10(a) of the Act.

There have been two important Rules promulgated by the SEC under this Section. The first, Rule 134, defines the types of advertising and of letters or other communications that can be used without prior or concurrent delivery of a prospectus. This Rule is frequently violated in letter form and also in telephone conversations. SEC Release 3844 of October 8, 1957, shows the importance of delivering a prospectus either before or at the same time that an attempt to sell is made. This Release states that a prospectus is defined to include any notice, circular, advertisement, letter, or communication, written or by radio or by television, which offers any security for sale except that any communication sent or given after the effective date of a registration statement shall not be deemed a prospectus if, prior to or at the same time with such a communication, a written prospectus meeting the requirements of Section 10 of the Act was sent or given.

Thus, any letter that gives more information than that allowed by Rule 134 becomes itself a prospectus, unless it is preceded or accompanied by the actual prospectus. A letter prospectus is in violation of Section 5 since it could not possibly comply with the requirements of Section 10.

The second, Rule 433, deals with the so-called "red-herring" prospectus which cannot be used as an offer to sell, but merely to disseminate information prior to the delivery of a regular prospectus which does offer the security for sale.

Section 6. Registration of Securities and Signing of Registration Statement. This Section details what securities may be registered and how such registration is to be done.

Section 7. Information Required on Registration Statement. This Section gives the SEC broad powers in regulating what must appear in a registration statement. In part, the section reads:

"Any such registration statement shall contain such other information, and be accompanied by such other documents, as the Commission may by rules or regulations require as being necessary or appropriate in the public interest or for the protection of investors."

Section 8. Taking Effect of Registration Statements and Amendments Thereto. Registration statements normally become effective on the twentieth day after filing, under this section. However, the SEC is empowered to determine whether or not the statement complies with the Act as to completeness and may refuse to allow the statement to become effective unless amended. If it appears to the SEC that untrue statements have been included, the Commission may issue a stop order.

Section 9. Court Review of Orders. As with any other act of Congress, provision is made so that any person who is aggrieved by an order of the administrative body (in this case the SEC) may obtain a review of the order in the Federal courts.

Section 10. Information Required in Prospectus. A prospectus must contain the same information as that contained in the registration statement. In addition, the SEC is given the authority to define the requirements for any additional material which that body considers necessary in the public interest. "Red herring" requirements and the manner of use of this type of preliminary prospectus are also detailed in this Section.

Note the application of Rule 134, discussed under Section 5, with respect to an "incomplete" prospectus.

One part of the Section, 10(3), relates to the length of time a prospectus may be used (that is, be considered an effective prospectus).

Under this Section of the Act, the SEC issued Rule 425, which requires the statement at the bottom of the first page of all prospectuses "These securities have not been approved or disapproved by the Securities and Exchange Commission nor has the commission passed upon the accuracy or adequacy of this prospectus. Any representation to the contrary is a criminal offense."

Section 11. Civil Liabilities on Account of False Registration Statement. Anyone directly connected with a company or signing the registration statement is subject to suit at law or in equity should the registration statement contain an untrue statement or fail to include a material fact necessary to make the statement not misleading.

Section 12. Civil Liabilities. If any person offers to sell or does sell a security in violation of Section 5, or uses any fraudulent means to sell a security, he or she is liable to civil suit for damages. This liability is in addition to any criminal liability arising under the Act.

Section 13. Limitation of Actions. Specified are the time limits within which civil suits may be instituted under Sections 11 and 12.

Section 14. Contrary Stipulations Void. Any provision in the sale of a security that binds the purchaser to waive the provisions of this Act or of the rules and regulations of the SEC is void. In other words, no one buying a security can relieve the seller from complying with the Act and with the rules issued under the Act.

Section 15. Liability of Controlling Persons. A dealer or broker is liable under Section 11 or 12.

Section 16. Additional Remedies. "The rights and remedies provided by this title (the Act) shall be in addition to any and all other rights and remedies that may exist at law or in equity."

Section 17. Fraudulent Interstate Transactions. As interpreted by the SEC, this section might be referred to as a "catch-all" section.

(a) "It shall be unlawful for any person in the offer or sale of any securities by the use of any means or instruments of transportation or communication in interstate commerce or by the use of the mails, directly or indirectly.

1. to employ any device, scheme or artifice to defraud, or

2. to obtain money or property by means of any untrue statement of a material fact or any omission to state a material fact necessary in order to make the statements made, in the light of the circumstances under which they were made, not misleading, or

3. to engage in any transaction, practice or course of business that operates or would operate as a fraud or deceit upon the purchaser."

Both TV and radio have been included by the SEC as "communication in interstate commerce" because it is impossible to control their area of reception.

While Section 17(a) refers only to the criminal courts in the term "unlawful," a court decision makes it clear that civil liability, in addition to criminal liability is incurred by violation of the section.

Court decisions also implement and amplify the language of the Act itself, with respect to the phrase "or by use of the mails." It would appear that Section 17 only applies to interstate mailings. However, the courts have ruled that if one used the mails *within one State* on an *intrastate* offering, and violated any provision in Section 17(a), that person is as guilty as if he or she had mailed across a state line.

Subparagraph (b) of Section 17 makes it illegal for anyone to publish descriptions of securities when the publisher is paid for such publicity, without also publishing the fact that compensation has been, or will be, received.

Section 17(c) makes the Section applicable to those securities exempted under Section 3. In other words, fraud is fraud whether in connection with exempt or other securities.

Section 18. State Control of Securities. "Nothing in this title (the Act) shall affect the jurisdiction of the Securities Commission . . . of any State. . . ."

In other words, all the provisions of the Federal act *and* all the laws of the State in which business is being conducted must be complied with.

Section 19. Special Powers of Commission. The Commission has the authority to make, amend, and rescind such rules and regulations as may be necessary to carry out the provisions of the Act. Commissioners or their representatives are also empowered to subpoena witnesses and to administer oaths.

Section 20. Injunctions and Prosecution of Offenses. The SEC is empowered to make investigations and to bring criminal actions at law against persons deemed to have violated the Act. The wording of the section is interesting in that it gives the Commission power to act "whenever it shall appear . . . that the provisions of this title (the Act) . . . have been *or are about to be* violated. . . ."

Section 21. Hearings by Commission. "All hearings shall be public and may be held before the Commission or an officer or officers of the Commission designated by it, and appropriate records shall be kept."

Section 22. Jurisdiction of Offenses and Suits. Jurisdiction of offenses and violations and certain rules in connection with them, are defined in this section. Jurisdiction is given to the District Courts of the United States, the U.S. Court of any Territory, and the U.S. District Court of the District of Columbia.

Section 23. Unlawful Representations. The fact that the registration statement for a security has been filed or is in effect does not mean that the statement is true and accurate, or that the Commission has in any way passed upon the merits of the security. It is unlawful to make any representations to the contrary.

In short, the words in the registration statement (*and* the prospectus) have been made under the penalties of fraud. The registrants are liable, even though the Commission has not certified the truth and accuracy of the statements or of the worth of the security.

Section 24. Penalties. "Any person who willfully violates any of the provisions of this title (the Act), or the rules and regulations promulgated by the Commission under authority thereof . . . shall upon conviction be fined not more than $10,000.00 or imprisoned not more than five years, or both."

Section 25. Jurisdiction of Other Government Agencies Over Securities. Nothing in the Act shall relieve any person from submitting to other U.S. Government supervisory units information required by any provision of law.

Section 26. Separability of Provisions. If any one section of the Act is invalidated, such findings will not affect other sections.

Schedule A. Sets forth the requirements for the registration of securities.

Schedule B. Sets for the registration requirements for securities issued by a foreign government or political subdivision thereof.

SYNOPSIS: THE SECURITIES EXCHANGE ACT OF 1934

The Securities Act of 1933 protects investors in the purchase of newly-issued securities. The Securities Exchange Act of 1934 concerns the regulation of trading in already issued securities.

The stated purpose of the 1934 Act is "to provide for the regulation of securities exchanges and of over-the-counter markets operating in interstate and foreign commerce and through the mails, to prevent inequitable and unfair practices on such exchanges and markets, and for other purposes."

The Act has been of importance in prohibiting abuses and manipulations through its creation of the SEC and later of the self-regulatory National Association of Securities Dealers, Inc.

The Act has 34 sections:

Section 1. Short Title. "This Act may be cited as the Securities Exchange Act of 1934."

Section 2. Necessity of Regulation. Citing that transactions in securities are affected with a national public interest, this section states that it is necessary to regulate and control such transactions and other matters in order to protect interstate commerce, the national credit, the Federal taxing power, to protect and make more effective the national banking system and Federal Reserve System, and to insure the maintenance of fair and honest markets in such transactions.

Parts of Sections 2(3) and 2(4) explain the effects of "rigged" markets and manipulative practices:

Section 2(3). Frequently, the prices of securities on such exchanges and markets are susceptible to manipulation and control, and the dissemination of such prices gives rise to excessive speculation, resulting in sudden and unreasonable fluctuations in the prices of securities which (a) cause alternately unreasonable expansion and unreasonable contraction of the volume of credit available for trade, transportation, and industry in interstate commerce . . . (c) prevent the fair valuation of collateral for bank loans and/or obstruct the effective operation of the national banking system and Federal Reserve System.

Section 2(4). "National emergencies, which produce widespread unemployment and the dislocation of trade, transportation, and industry, and which burden interstate commerce and adversely affect the general welfare, are precipitated, intensified, and prolonged by manipulation and sudden and unreasonable fluctuations of security prices and by excessive speculation on such exchanges and markets, and to meet such emergencies the Federal Government is put to such great expense as to burden the national credit."

Section 3. Definitions. In addition to defining 38 technical terms used in the Act, this Section gave the Securities Exchange Commission and the Federal Reserve System the authority to define technical, trade, and accounting terms so long as such definitions are not inconsistent with the provisions of the Act itself.

Section 4. This Section established the Securities and Exchange Commission. Prior to the Commissioners' taking office, the Securities Act of 1933 was administered by the Federal Trade Commission.

Section 5. Transactions on Unregistered Exchanges. Under this Section, it became illegal for transactions to be effected by brokers, dealers, or exchanges on an exchange unless the exchange was registered under Section 6 of the Act.

Section 6. Registration of Exchanges. Combined with Section 5, this Section sets forth the requirements for exchanges to be registered and the method of registration. Exchanges file their rules and regulations with the SEC and must agree to take disciplinary action against any member who violates the Act or violates any of the rules and regulations issued by the SEC under the Act.

Section 7. Margin Requirements. The Board of Governors of the Federal Reserve System is given the power to set margin requirements for any securities, which requirements may be changed from time to time at the discretion of the Board. Under this authority, the Board issued Regulation T and Regulation U. Regulation T governs the extension and maintenance of credit by brokers, dealers, and members of national securities exchanges. Regulation U governs loans by banks for the purpose of purchasing or carrying stocks registered on a national securities exchange.

Section 8. Restrictions on Borrowing. In four parts, this Section (a) details from whom brokers or dealers may borrow money on listed securities, (b) lays the foundation for the SEC's "net capital rule," (c) deals with pledging and co-mingling of customers' securities, and (d) states no broker or dealer may lend or arrange for the lending of any securities carried for the account of a customer without the written consent of the customer.

Section 9. Prohibition Against Manipulation. Both this Section and Section 10 deal with manipulative practices that are intended to make money for those in the Securities business at the expense of the general public.

Section 9 makes it unlawful to do certain things that constitute manipulation, such as: (a) creating a false or misleading appearance of active trading in a security, (b) giving of information to potential investors as to the likelihood of a rise or fall in price solely for the purpose of causing the market price to react to purchases or sales by such potential investors, (c) making false or misleading statements about a security, (d) "pegging" or "fixing" prices, (e) improper use of puts, calls, straddles, or other options to buy or sell. Transactions in which there is no real change in ownership are also specifically prohibited.

Section 10. Regulation of Manipulative and Deceptive Devices. Section 10 first forbids the use of short sales or stop-loss orders that violate any rules or regulations the Commission may set to protect investors. Its wording, then, becomes much more inclusive than Section 9 or the first part of Section 10, since it forbids in general "any manipulative or deceptive device or contrivance. . . ."

Section 11. Trading by Members of Exchanges, Brokers, and Dealers. Authority is given to the Commission to set rules and regulations as to floor trading by members, brokers, or dealers for their own accounts and to prevent excessive trading off the floor of the exchanges. A part of this Section deals with the roles of the odd-lot dealers and the specialist on the floor of the exchange. Further, the Section places a limitation on certain customer credit extension in connection with underwritings.

Section 11A. National Market System for Securities; Securities Information Processors. Concerns the planning, developing, operating, or regulating of a national market system.

Section 12. Registration Requirements for Securities. It is unlawful for any broker or dealer to effect transactions in a security or a national securities exchange unless a registration statement is effective for that security. Information stating how such registration is to be accomplished is given here. The SEC is given authority to allow trading on one exchange in securities that are listed on another exchange (such securities are said to have "unlisted trading privileges").

Section 13. Reports. All companies whose securities are listed on a national securities exchange must file reports at such intervals and in such form as the SEC may require. The purpose of requiring such reports was to ensure that enough information was available on any company to enable an investor to make an intelligent decision concerning the worth of its securities.

Section 14. Proxies. Paragraph (a) of this Section gives the SEC the authority to make rules and regulations as to the solicitation of proxies and makes it illegal to solicit proxies other than in accord with such rules and regulations. Several rules have been issued under this Section which detail the manner in which proxies may be solicited and the information that must be given to shareholders whose proxies are being solicited. All of these rules are designated to ensure that the recipient of a proxy solicitation will understand what it is that he or she is being asked to sign and to give enough background on the matter in question so that the shareholder can make an intelligent decision about how to vote.

Paragraph (b) relates to the giving of proxies by broker or dealers in connection with securities held for the accounts of customers. It is standard practice for broker/dealers to vote proxies for shares held in their names for customers directly in accord with the wishes of the customers themselves.

Section 15. Over-The-Counter Markets. It is mandatory that all brokers and dealers who deal in the over-the-counter market (on other than an intrastate basis) be registered with the SEC. Further, the Section states that registration will be in accord with rules and regulations issued by the Commission. "Intrastate" means that the broker or dealer deals in intrastate securities as well as doing business only within his state. Here, as elsewhere in the Act, the "use of mails," even if within one State, places the user under the Act.

Section 15 also defines the grounds for denial of registration, for suspension, or for revocation of registration. Basically, these grounds are:

1. Making false or misleading statements in the application for registration.
2. Having been convicted within the last ten years of a felony or misdemeanor involving the purchase or sale of any security or arising out of the business of a broker or dealer.
3. Being enjoined by a court from engaging in the securities business.
4. Having willfully violated any of the provisions of the 1933 Act or of the 1934 Act. (After passage of the Investment Advisers Act of 1940 and the Investment Company Act of 1940, violation of those Acts also became grounds for suspension or revocation.)

Sections 9 and 10 dealt with manipulation with respect to securities listed on a national exchange. Section 15 adds a prohibition against over-the-counter manipulation as defined by the Commission. Some of the practices that have been so defined are:

1. Excessive prices that are not fairly related to the market.
2. False representations to customers.
3. Taking of secret profits.
4. Failure to disclose control of a market.
5. Creating false impression of activity by dummy sales.
6. "Churning," or unnecessary purchases and sales in a customer's account.

Another important rule of the SEC under Section 15 seeks to protect investors by forbidding certain practices in connection with pledging or comingling of securities held for the accounts of customers. This rule specifically applies to over-the-counter broker/dealers; a similar rule, under Section 8, applies to broker/dealers who are members of or do business through members of a national exchange.

Section 15A. Registration of National Securities Associations. Aided by the Maloney Act of 1938, which amended the original Act by adding this Section, the formation of associations, such as the National Association of Securities Dealers, was authorized.

Section 15B. Concerns municipal securities dealers and transactions in municipal securities.

Section 15(c)(3) requires financial responsibility on the part of broker/dealers.

Sections 12 and 13 deal with registration and report requirements for listed securities. Section 15(d) is a corresponding list of requirements with respect to unlisted securities.

Section 16. Directors, Officers, and Principal Stockholders. Requires statements of ownership of stocks by "insiders" and other related information.

Section 17. Accounts and Records. Not only does this Section require that all brokers and dealers maintain records in accord with such rules and regulations as the SEC may set forth, but it also authorizes the SEC to make examinations of any broker's or dealer's accounts, correspondence, memoranda, papers, books, and other records whenever the Commission deems it in the public interest. Rules and regulations issued by the SEC under this Section state the types of records that must be kept. In practice, an SEC examiner may walk into a broker/dealer's office and ask that all files and books be opened for inspection. Under the law, no broker/dealer may refuse the examiner access to any and all correspondence and records. A broker/dealer can have his or her registration suspended or revoked by failure to keep copies of all correspondence or to keep books and records as required by the SEC.

Section 17A. Settlement of Securities Transactions. Concerns the clearance and settlement of securities transactions, transfer of ownership, and safeguarding of securities and funds. Congress directed the SEC to facilitate the establishment of a national system for securities clearings.

Section 18. Liability for Misleading Statements. In a rather unusual statement of law, this Section makes a person both criminally and civilly liable for any misleading statements made in connection with the requirements of Section 15 of this Act.

Section 19. Registration, Responsibilities, and Oversight of Self-Regulatory Organizations. The SEC has the power to suspend for 12 months or revoke the registration of any national securities exchange or of any security, if the Commission is of the opinion that such action is necessary or appropriate for the protection of investors. Further, authority is granted the SEC to suspend or expel from an exchange any member or officer who has violated any of the provisions of this Act.

Other provisions of this Section give the SEC broad powers in supervising the rules of national securities exchanges, which the Commission may require to be changed or amended. In other words, the SEC supervises the members of an exchange through the exchange itself as well as on an individual basis.

Section 20. Liabilities of Controlling Persons. In effect, this Section states that if A commits an illegal act under the direction of B, who controls A, then both A and B are equally liable under the law. Section 20 also makes it illegal for any "controlling person" to "hinder, delay, or obstruct" the filing of any information required by the SEC under this Act.

Section 21. Investigations; Injunctions and Prosecution. In the Securities Act of 1933, Sections 19 and 20 gave the SEC special powers in the areas of investigation, subpoenaing of witnesses, prosecutions of offenses and the like. Section 21 of this Act is similar in its provisions.

Section 22. Hearings. It is interesting to note the difference in wording with respect to hearings in the 1933 Act and in this Act. Section 21 of the 1933 Act states that "All hearings *shall* be public. . . ." Section 22 of the 1934 Act states "Hearings *may* be public. . . ."

Section 23. Rules and Regulations. Power to make rules and regulations under this Act is specifically given the SEC and the Board of Governors of the Federal Reserve System by this Section. Both bodies are required to make annual reports to Congress.

Section 24. Public Availability of Information. To protect those required to file under this Act, this Section makes it possible for certain information, such as trade secrets, to be made confidential and not a matter of public record. This Section also forbids any member or employee of the Commission to use information that is not public for personal benefit.

Section 25. Court Review of Orders and Rules. Like Section 9 of the 1933 Act, this Section reserves final judgment on any issue to the courts, rather than to the Commission itself.

Section 26. Unlawful Representations. It is unlawful to make any representation to the effect that the SEC or the Federal Reserve Board has passed on the merits of any issue. Also, the failure of either body to take action against any person cannot be construed to mean that that person is not in violation of the law.

Section 27. Jurisdiction of Offenses and Suits. Jurisdiction of violations of this Act is given to the district courts of the United States.

Section 28. Effect on Existing Law. "The rights and remedies provided by this title (the Act) shall be in addition to any and all other rights and remedies that may exist in law or at equity. . . ." The Section also leaves jurisdiction of offenses against a State law with the State.

Section 29. Validity of Contracts. No one can avoid compliance with the provisions of this Act by getting someone else to waive the requirements in any contract. Any contract that seeks to avoid the provisions of this Act are automatically void.

Section 30. Foreign Securities Exchange. It is unlawful to deal in securities whose issuers are within the jurisdiction of the United States on a foreign exchange in any manner other than that in which dealing in such securities would have to be handled in this country. In other words, the laws of the U.S. exchanges cannot be circumvented by placing business through a foreign exchange.

Section 31. Transaction Fees. Each national securities exchange is required to pay an annual fee to the Commission.

Section 32. Penalties. Individuals may be fined a maximum of $1,000,000 or sentenced to a maximum term of imprisonment of 10 years, or both, for violations of the Act.

Section 33. Separability of Provisions. An escape section that states that if any one section of the Act is found to be invalid, such findings shall have no effect on the other sections.

Section 34. Effective Date, July 1, 1934.

PUBLIC UTILITY HOLDING COMPANY ACT OF 1935

Interstate holding companies engaged through subsidiaries in the electric utility business or in the retail distribution of natural or manufactured gas are subject to regulation under the Act. These systems must register with the SEC and file initial and periodic reports. Detailed information concerning the organization, financial structure, and operations of the holding company and its subsidiaries is contained in these reports. If a holding company or its subsidiary meets certain specifications, the Commission can exempt it from part or all of the duties and obligations otherwise imposed by statute. Holding companies are subject to SEC regulations on matters such as structure of the system, acquisitions, combinations, and issues and sales of securities.

The most important provisions of the Act are the requirements for physical integration and corporation simplification of holding company systems. Integration standards restrict a holding company's operations to an *integrated utility system*. An integrated system is defined as one:

1. Capable of economical operation as a single coordinated system.
2. Confined to a single area or region in one or more states.
3. Not so large that it negates the advantages of localized management, efficient operation, and effective regulation.

The original structure and continued existence of any company in a holding company system must not necessarily complicate the corporate structure of the system or result in the distribution of voting power inequitably among security holders of the system.

The SEC can determine what action, if any, must be taken by registered holding companies and their subsidiaries to comply with Act requirements. The SEC can apply to federal courts for orders compelling compliance with Commission directives.

Acquisitions

To be authorized by the SEC, the acquisition of securities and utility assets by holding companies and their subsidiaries must meet the following standards:

1. The acquisition must not tend toward interlocking relations or concentrating control to an extent detrimental to investors or the public interest.
2. Any consideration paid for the acquisition, including fees, commissions, and remuneration, must not be unreasonable.
3. The acquisition must not complicate the capital structure of the holding company systems or have a detrimental effect on system functions.
4. The acquisition must tend toward economical and efficient development of an integrated public utility system.

Issuance and Sale of Securities

Proposed security issues by any holding company must be analyzed and evaluated by the SEC staff and approved by the Commission to ensure that the issues meet the following tests under prescribed standards of the law:

1. The security must be reasonably adapted to the security structure of the issuer, and of other companies in the same holding company system.
2. The security must be reasonably adapted to the earning power of the company.
3. The proposed issue must be necessary and appropriate to the economical and efficient operation of the company's business.
4. The fees, commissions, and other remuneration paid in connection with the issue must not be unreasonable.
5. The terms and conditions of the issue or sale of the security must not be detrimental to the public or investor interest.

Other provisions of the Act concern regulating dividend payments, intercompany loans, solicitations of proxies, consents and other authorizations, and insider trading.

TRUST INDENTURE ACT OF 1939

This Act applies to bonds, debentures, notes, and similar debt securities offered for public sale and issued under trust indentures with more than $7.5 million of securities outstanding at any one time. Even though such securities are registered under the Securities Act, they cannot be offered for sale to the public unless the trust indenture conforms to statutory standards of this Act. Designed to safeguard the rights and interests of the investors, the Act also:

1. Prohibits the indenture trustee from conflicting interests which might interfere with exercising its duties on behalf of the securities purchasers.
2. Requires the trustee to be a corporation with minimum combined capital and surplus.
3. Imposes high standards of conduct and responsibility on the trustee.
4. Precludes, in the event of default, preferential collection of certain claims owing to the trustee by the issuer.
5. Provides that the issuer supply to the trustee evidence of compliance with indenture terms and conditions.
6. Requires the trustee to provide reports and notices to security holders.

Other provisions of the Act prohibit impairing the security holders' right to sue individually for principal and interest, except under certain circumstances. It also requires maintaining a list of security holders for their use in communicating with each other regarding their rights as security holders.

In 1987 the Commission sent a legislative proposal to Congress which would modernize procedures under the Act to meet the public's need in view of novel debt instruments and modern financing techniques. This legislative proposal was adopted and enacted into law in 1990.

INVESTMENT ADVISERS ACT OF 1940

This law establishes a pattern of regulating investment advisers. In some respects, it has provisions similar to the Securities Exchange Act provisions governing the conduct of brokers and dealers. This Act requires that persons or firms compensated for advising others about securities investment must register with the SEC and conform to the statutory standards designed to protect investors.

The Commission can deny, suspend, or revoke investment adviser registrations if, after notice and hearings, it finds that grounds for a statutory disqualification exist and that the action is in the public interest. Grounds for disqualification include conviction for certain financial crimes or securities law violations, injunctions based on such activities, conviction for violating the mail fraud statute, willfully filing false reports with the SEC, and willfully violating the Advisers Act, the Securities Act, the Securities Exchange Act, the Investment Company Act, or the rules of the Municipal Securities Rulemaking Board. The SEC can recommend criminal prosecution by the Department of Justice for violations of the laws, fraudulent misconduct or willful violation of Commission rules.

The law contains antifraud provisions and empowers the Commission to adopt rules defining fraudulent, deceptive, or manipulative acts and practices. It requires that investment advisers:

1. Disclose the nature of their interest in transactions executed for their clients.
2. Maintain books and records according to SEC rules.
3. Make books and records available to the SEC for inspections.

TRUST INVESTMENT COMPANY ACT OF 1940

Activities of companies engaged primarily in investing, reinvesting, and trading in securities, and whose own securities are offered to the public, are subject to statutory prohibitions and to SEC regulations under this Act. Public offerings of investment company securities must be registered under the Securities Act of 1933. It is important that investors understand that the SEC does not supervise the investment activities of these companies and that regulation by the Commission does not imply safety of investment in them.

In addition to the registration requirement for investment companies, the law requires that they disclose their financial condition and investment policies to provide investors complete information about their activities. This Act also:

1. Prohibits investment companies from substantially changing the nature of their business or investment policies without stockholder approval.
2. Prohibits persons guilty of securities fraud from serving as officers and directors.
3. Prevents underwriters, investment bankers, or brokers from constituting more than a minority of the directors of the companies.
4. Requires that management contracts and material changes be submitted to security holders for their approval.
5. Prohibits transactions between companies and their directors, officers, or affiliated companies or persons, except when approved by the SEC.
6. Forbids investment companies to issue senior securities except under specific conditions and upon specified terms.
7. Prohibits pyramiding of such companies and cross-ownership of their securities.

Other provisions of the Act involve advisory fees, nonconformance of an adviser's fiduciary duty, sales and repurchases of securities issued by investment companies, exchange offers, and other activities of investment companies, including special provisions for periodic payment plans and face-amount certificate companies.

Investment companies must register securities under the Securities Act, and also must file periodic reports and are subject to the SEC proxy and insider trading rules.

CORPORATION REORGANIZATION

Reorganization proceedings in the U.S. Courts under Chapter 11 of the Bankruptcy Code are begun by a debtor voluntarily, or by its creditors. Federal bankruptcy law allows a debtor in reorganization to continue operating under the court's protection while the debtor attempts to rehabilitate its business and work out a plan to pay its debts. If a debtor corporation has publicly issued securities outstanding, the reorganization process may raise many issues that materially affect the rights of public investors.

Chapter 11 authorizes the SEC to appear in any reorganization case and to present its views on any issue. Although Chapter 11 applies to all types of business reorganizations, the SEC generally limits its participation to proceedings involving significant public investor interest, i.e., protecting public investors holding the debtor's securities, and participating in legal and policy issues of concern to public investors. The SEC also continues to address matters of traditional Commission expertise and interest relating to securities. When appropriate, the SEC comments on the adequacy of reorganization plan disclosure statements and participates where there is a Commission law enforcement interest.

Under Chapter 11, the debtor, official committees, and institutional creditors negotiate the terms of a reorganization plan. The court can confirm a reorganization plan if it is accepted by creditors for:

1. At least two-thirds of the amounts of allowed claims.
2. More than one-half the number of allowed claims.
3. At least two-thirds in amount of the allowed shareholder interest.

The principal safeguard for public investors is the requirement that a disclosure statement containing adequate information be transmitted by the debtor or plan proponent in connection with soliciting votes on the plan. In addition, reorganization plans involving publicly-held debt usually provide for issuing new securities to creditors and shareholders which are exempt from registration under Section 5 of the Securities Act of 1933.

Chapter 24

The Securities and Exchange Commission—Materiality

CONTENTS

SEC Staff Accounting Bulletin 99	**24.01**
Defining Materiality	**24.03**
Qualitative and Quantitative Factors Are Important	**24.03**
FASB Considerations and Opinion	**24.04**
Small Figures May Cause Big Misstatements	**24.04**
Other Considerations	**24.05**
"Managed" Earnings—Here, There, and Everywhere	**24.06**
Aggregating and Netting Misstatements	**24.07**
Intentional Immaterial Misstatements	**24.09**
The Prudent Man Concept	**24.10**
"Reasonableness" Should Not Be Unreasonable	**24.10**
The Auditor's Response to Intentional Misstatements	**24.12**
GAAP Takes Precedence Over Industry Practice	**24.13**

SEC STAFF ACCOUNTING BULLETIN 99

The Securities and Exchange Staff Accounting Bulletin (SAB) 99, *Materiality,* issued in August, 1999 delineates the staff's views concerning reliance on certain quantitative benchmarks to assess materiality in preparing financial statements and performing audits of those financial statements. The SEC has decided that the practice of adopting an arbitrary margin of error is inappropriate. SAB 99 concludes that misstatements are not immaterial simply because they fall beneath a numerical threshold.

The SEC is quick to point out that statements in the staff accounting bulletins are not rules or interpretations of the Commission, nor are they published as bearing the Commission's official approval. However, they do represent interpretations and practices followed by the Division of Corporation Finance and the Office of the Chief Accountant in *administering the disclosure requirements of the federal securities laws.* To put it bluntly, anyone ignoring this SAB, is putting himself, herself and/or their company at risk: this new materiality test is the standard the SEC will use for enforcement purposes.

It should be emphasized that SAB 99 does not constitute a new approach to the consideration of "materiality," but is an attempt to "shore up" the definition of the concept and in so doing reemphasize the Commission's foremost goal—the protection of the investor. Therefore, it provides guidance in applying materiality thresholds to the *preparation of financial statements filed with the Commission and the performance of audits of those financial statements.*

Misusing the "Rule of Thumb"

The SEC staff has been cognizant of the fact that many registrants gradually adopted as "rules of thumb" a 5% quantitative margin of error in preparing their financial statements, and that auditors also have used these thresholds in their evaluation of whether items might be considered material to users of a registrant's financial statements. One rule of thumb in particular suggests that the *misstatement* or *omission* of an item that falls under a 5% threshold is not material in the absence of particularly "egregious circumstances, such as self-dealing or misappropriation by senior management." (In this SAB, "misstatement" or "omission" refers to a financial statement assertion that would not be in conformity with GAAP.)

The staff reminds registrants and the auditors of their financial statements that exclusive reliance on this or any percentage or numerical threshold has no basis in the *accounting literature* or the *law.*

The use of a percentage as a numerical threshold, such as 5%, may provide the basis for a *preliminary* assumption that, without considering all relevant circumstances, a deviation of less than the specified percentage with respect to a particular item on the registrant's financial statements is unlikely to be material. The staff has no objection to such a "rule of thumb" as an *initial* step in assessing materiality. But the bulletin cautions that quantifying the magnitude of a misstatement in percentage terms can be only the beginning of an analysis of materiality; it cannot be used as a substitute for a *full analysis* of all relevant considerations.

DEFINING MATERIALITY

Materiality concerns the significance of an item to users of a registrant's financial statements. A matter is "material" if there is a substantial likelihood that a reasonable person would consider it important. Early in its existence, the Financial Accounting Standards Board made this clear. In its Statement of Financial Accounting Concepts 2, the FASB stated the essence of the concept of materiality as follows: *The omission or misstatement of an item in a financial report is material if, in the light of surrounding circumstances, the magnitude of the item is such that it is probable that the judgment of a reasonable person relying upon the report would have been changed or influenced by the inclusion or correction of the item.*

This Statement is almost identical to that expressed by the courts in interpreting the federal securities laws. In 1976, the Supreme Court held that a fact is material if there is "a substantial likelihood that the fact would have been viewed by the reasonable investor as having significantly altered the 'total mix' of information made available."

Thus, we see that an assessment of materiality requires that the facts be considered in the context of the "surrounding circumstances," according to accounting literature, or the "total mix" of information, in the opinion of the Supreme Court.

QUALITATIVE AND QUANTITATIVE FACTORS ARE IMPORTANT

In the context of a misstatement of a financial statement item, while the "total mix" includes the *size* in numerical or percentage terms of the misstatement, it also includes the *factual context* in which the user of financial statements appraises the financial statement item. Therefore, financial management and the auditor must consider both "quantitative" and "qualitative" factors in assessing an item's materiality. Court decisions, Commission rules and enforcement actions, and accounting and auditing literature have all considered "qualitative" factors in various contexts.

The FASB has repeatedly emphasized that materiality cannot be reduced to a numerical formula. In FASB Statement 2, the FASB noted that some commenters had urged it to promulgate quantitative materiality guides for use in various situations. The FASB decided against a blanket approach as representing only a "minority view" and went on to explain, "The predominant view is that materiality judgments can properly be made only by those who have all the facts."

According to FASB 2, an additional factor in making materiality judgments revolves around the *degree of precision* that can be attained in *estimating* the judgment item. The amount of deviation that is considered immaterial may increase as the attainable degree of precision decreases. As an example, the SAB points out that *accounts payable* usually can be estimated more accurately than can *contingent liabilities* arising from litigation or threats of it. Therefore, a deviation considered to be material in figuring accounts payable may be quite trivial when considering contingent liabilities.

FASB CONSIDERATIONS AND OPINION

The FASB's present position is that no general standards of materiality can be formulated to take into account all the considerations that enter into an experienced human judgment. The Board noted that, in certain limited circumstances, the SEC and other authoritative bodies have issued quantitative materiality guidance, citing as examples guidelines ranging from 1 to 10% with respect to a variety of disclosures. They looked at contradictory studies: one showing a lack of uniformity among auditors on materiality judgments; another suggesting widespread use of a "rule of thumb" of 5 to 10% of net income. They also considered whether an evaluation of materiality could be based solely on anticipating the market's reaction to accounting information.

In the end, the FASB rejected any simplified approach to discharging "the onerous duty of making materiality decisions" in favor of an approach that takes into account *all relevant considerations*. In so doing, it made clear that, "Magnitude by itself, without regard to the nature of the item and the circumstances in which the judgment has to be made, will not generally be a sufficient basis for a materiality judgment."

SMALL FIGURES MAY CAUSE BIG MISSTATEMENTS

Evaluation of materiality requires a registrant and its auditor to consider all the relevant circumstances, and the staff believes that there are numerous circumstances in which misstatements below 5% could well be material. As does the SEC Chairman who pointed out that given the attitude of investors in the stock market today, *everything* matters when ". . . missing an earnings projection by a penny can result in a loss of millions of dollars in market capitalization."

SAB 99 takes into consideration this concern that *qualitative factors* may cause misstatements of quantitatively extremely small amounts to be material. Thus, the bulletin, in effect, cautions the auditor that as a result of the interaction of quantitative and qualitative considerations in materiality judgments, misstatements of relatively small amounts that come to the auditor's attention *could* have a material effect upon the financial statements. Among those considerations that may well render material a quantitatively small misstatement of a financial statement item are whether the misstatement:

1. Results from an item capable of precise measurement or from an estimate and, if so, the degree of imprecision inherent in the estimate.
2. Masks a change in earnings or other trends.
3. Hides a failure to meet analysts' consensus expectations for the enterprise.
4. Actually changes a loss into income or vice versa.
5. Concerns a *segment* or other portion of the registrant's business that has been identified as playing a *significant role* in the registrant's operations or profitability.
6. Affects the registrant's compliance with regulatory requirements.
7. Affects the registrant's compliance with loan covenants or other contractual requirements.
8. Has the effect of increasing management's compensation, for example, by satisfying requirements for the award of bonuses or other forms of incentive compensation.
9. Involves concealment of an unlawful transaction.
10. Aims toward smoothing earnings artificially to give a false impression of stability.

The bulletin does not claim this to be an exhaustive list of the circumstances that may affect the materiality of a quantitatively small misstatement, but it certainly makes the decision process a little more exhausting than merely adhering to some predetermined "percentage."

OTHER CONSIDERATIONS

Other factors and situations may bring to question the materiality of a quantitatively small misstatement of a financial statement item:

1. The demonstrated volatility of the price of a registrant's securities in response to certain types of disclosures may provide guidance as to whether *investors* regard quantitatively small misstatements as material.
2. Consideration of potential market reaction to disclosure of a misstatement is by itself "too blunt an instrument to be depended on" in considering whether a fact is material. However, when management or the independent auditor expects (based, for example, on a pattern of market performance) that a known misstatement *may* result in a significant

positive or negative market reaction, that expected reaction should be taken into account when considering whether a misstatement is material.

Even if management does not expect a significant market reaction, a misstatement still may be material and should be evaluated under the criteria discussed in this SAB.

"MANAGED" EARNINGS—HERE, THERE, AND EVERYWHERE

For the reasons noted above, the staff believes that a registrant and the auditors of its financial statements should *not* assume that even small intentional misstatements in financial statements—for example those pursuant to actions to "manage" earnings—are immaterial. (Intentional management of earnings and intentional misstatements, as used in SAB 99, do not include insignificant errors and omissions that may occur in systems and recurring processes in the normal course of business.)

While the *intent* of management does not render a misstatement material, it may provide significant evidence of materiality. The evidence may be particularly revealing when management has intentionally misstated items in the financial statements to "manage" reported earnings.

In such an instance, management has presumably done so believing that the resulting amounts and trends *would be significant* to users of the registrant's financial statements. Or have the earnings been "managed" just enough to meet or marginally exceed the expectations of securities analysts who appear to be very significant players in today's volatile markets?

SAB 99 mentions that assessment of materiality should occur not only in annual financial reports, but also during the preparation of each quarterly or interim financial statement. After all, savvy investors and even less well informed ones are known to research these statements.

Consider the Investor

The staff believes that investors generally would regard as significant a management practice to overstate or understate earnings up to an amount just short of a percentage threshold in order to "manage" earnings. Investors presumably also would regard with a jaundiced eye an accounting practice that, in essence, rendered all earnings figures subject to a management-directed margin of misstatement.

The materiality of a misstatement may be judged based upon where it appears in the financial statements. For example, if a misstatement involves a segment of the registrant's operations, in assessing materiality of a misstatement to the financial statements taken as a whole, registrants and their auditors should consider:

1. The *size* of the misstatement.
2. The *significance* of that particular segment information to the financial statements as a whole.

A misstatement of the revenue and operating profit of a relatively small segment which management indicates is important to the future profitability of the entity is more likely to be material to investors than a misstatement in a segment that management has not identified as especially important. In assessing the materiality of misstatements in segment information, as with materiality generally, situations may arise in practice where the auditor will conclude that a matter relating to segment information is *qualitatively material* even though, in his or her judgment, it is *quantitatively immaterial* to the financial statements as a whole.

AGGREGATING AND NETTING MISSTATEMENTS

In determining whether multiple misstatements cause the financial statements to be materially misstated, registrants and the auditors of their financial statements should consider the effect of each misstatement separately, and in the aggregate.

Obviously, the concept of materiality takes into consideration that some information, whether viewed individually or as a part of the whole report, may be required for fair presentation of financial statements in conformity with GAAP in one context or the other. Furthermore, it is necessary to evaluate misstatements in light of quantitative and qualitative factors. It is also necessary to consider whether the following can materially misstate the financial statements taken as a whole:

1. Individual line item amounts
2. Subtotals
3. Totals

This requires consideration of:

1. The significance of an item to a particular type of business enterprise; for example, inventories to a manufacturing company. (An adjustment to inventory seen as immaterial to pretax or net income could be material to the financial statements because it could affect a working capital ratio or cause the registrant to be in default of a loan covenant.)

2. The pervasiveness of the misstatement—whether it affects the presentation of numerous financial statement items.
3. The effect of the misstatement on the financial statements taken as a whole.

Accountants and auditors should consider whether each misstatement is material, regardless of its effect when combined with other misstatements. The literature notes that the analysis should consider whether the misstatement of "individual amounts" causes a material misstatement of the financial statements taken as a whole. As with materiality generally, this analysis requires consideration of both quantitative and qualitative factors.

If the misstatement of an individual amount causes the financial statements as a whole to be materially misstated, that effect cannot be eliminated by other misstatements whose effect may be to diminish the impact of the misstatement on other financial statement items.

Quantitative materiality assessments often are made by comparing adjustments to revenues, gross profit, pretax and net income, total assets, stockholders' equity, or individual line items in the financial statements. The particular items in the financial statements to be considered as a basis for the materiality determination depend on the proposed adjustment to be made and other factors, such as those identified in this SAB. For example, an adjustment to inventory that is immaterial to pretax income or net income may be material to the financial statements because it may affect a working capital ratio or cause the registrant to be in default of loan covenants.

Aggregation May Lead to Aggravation

If a registrant's revenues are a material financial statement item and if they are materially overstated, the financial statements taken as a whole will be materially misleading even if the effect on earnings is completely offset by an equivalent overstatement of expenses. Even though *one misstatement* of an individual amount may not cause the financial statements taken as a whole to be materially misstated, it may nonetheless, when *aggregated with other misstatements,* render the financial statements taken as a whole to be materially misleading.

Registrants and the auditors of their financial statements should consider the effect of the misstatement on *subtotals* or *totals*. The auditor should aggregate all misstatements that affect each subtotal or total and consider whether the misstatements in the aggregate affect the subtotal or total in a way that causes the registrant's financial statements taken as a whole to be materially misleading.

The staff believes that, in considering the aggregate effect of multiple misstatements on a subtotal or total, accountants and auditors should exercise particular care when considering misstatement of an estimated amount with a misstatement of an item capable of precise measurement. As noted above, *assessments of materiality should never be purely mechanical;* given the imprecision inherent in estimates, there is by definition a corresponding imprecision in the aggregation of misstatements involving estimates with those that do not involve an estimate.

Registrants and auditors also should consider the effect of misstatements from prior periods on the current financial statements. For example, the auditing literature states that matters underlying adjustments proposed by the auditor but not recorded by the entity could potentially cause future financial statements to be materially misstated, even though the auditor has concluded that the adjustments are not material to the current financial statements. This may particularly be the case where immaterial misstatements recur in several years and the cumulative effect becomes material in the current year.

INTENTIONAL IMMATERIAL MISSTATEMENTS

The SEC reemphasizes their caution that a registrant may *not* make intentional immaterial misstatements in its financial statements. A registrant's management may never intentionally make adjustments to various financial statement items in a manner inconsistent with GAAP.

In any accounting period in which such actions might be taken, it could be that none of the individual adjustments would be considered material, nor would the aggregate effect on the financial statements taken as a whole be material *for the period.*

The adjustments could even be considered irrelevant; however at the same time, they could actually be unlawful. In the books and records provisions under the Exchange Act, even if misstatements are immaterial, registrants must comply with the law. Under these provisions, each registrant with securities registered pursuant to the Act, or required to file reports pursuant to it, must:

1. Make and keep books, records, and accounts, which, in *reasonable detail,* accurately, and fairly reflect the transactions and dispositions of assets of the registrant.
2. Maintain internal accounting controls that are sufficient to provide *reasonable assurances* that, among other things, transactions are recorded as necessary to permit the preparation of financial statements in conformity with GAAP.

FASB Statements of Financial Accounting Standards generally include the statement: "The provisions of this Statement need not be applied to immaterial items." This SAB does not countermand that provision of the

Statements. However, it does vanquish the 5% of net income quantitative test often applied in the past. The SEC admits that, in theory, this language in the FASBs is subject to interpretation that a registrant may intentionally record immaterial items in a manner that would unquestionably be contrary to GAAP if the misstatement were considered material. It should be carefully noted, however, that the staff believes the FASB did not intend such a conclusion. Regardless, some companies have in the past apparently interpreted the sentence in just that fashion. They evidently felt they could ignore certain immaterial transactions and misapply GAAP to so-called immaterial transactions with impunity. No more!

Both the U.S. Code and the Securities Exchange Act indicate that criminal liability may be imposed if a person knowingly circumvents or knowingly fails to implement a system of internal accounting controls or knowingly falsifies books, records, or accounts. This should make it perfectly clear that any degree of "cooking the books," setting up "cookie jar reserves," "managing," or otherwise obfuscating may result in violations of the securities laws.

THE PRUDENT MAN CONCEPT

In this context, determinations of what constitutes "reasonable assurance" and "reasonable detail" are based not on a "materiality" analysis but on the level of detail and degree of assurance that would satisfy *prudent* officials in the conduct of their own affairs. The books and records provisions of the Exchange Act, in which this is developed, originally were passed as part of the Foreign Corrupt Practices Act (FCPA). In the conference committee report regarding the 1988 amendments to the FCPA, the report stated, "The conference committee adopted the prudent man qualification in order to clarify that the current standard does not connote an unrealistic degree of exactitude or precision. The concept of reasonableness contemplates the weighing of a number of relevant factors, including the costs of compliance."

"REASONABLENESS" SHOULD NOT BE UNREASONABLE

The SEC staff is well aware of the fact that there is little authoritative guidance regarding the "reasonableness" standard in the Exchange Act. A principal statement of the Commission's policy in this area was set forth in a 1981 address by the SEC Chairman who noted that, like materiality, "reasonableness" is not an "absolute standard of exactitude for corporate records."

Unlike materiality, however, "reasonableness" is not solely a measure of the significance of a financial statement item to investors. "Reasonableness," here reflects a judgment as to whether an issuer's failure to correct a known misstatement brings into question the purposes underlying the accounting provisions of the Exchange Act. In assessing whether a misstatement results in a violation of a registrant's obligation to keep books and records that are accurate "in reasonable detail," registrants and their auditors should consider, in addition to the factors discussed above concerning an evaluation of a misstatement's potential materiality, the following factors.

1. *The significance of the misstatement.* Though the staff does not believe that registrants need to make in-depth determination of significance regarding all immaterial items, it is "reasonable" to treat misstatements whose effects are clearly inconsequential differently from possibly more significant ones.

2. *How the misstatement arose.* It is undoubtedly never "reasonable" for registrants to record misstatements or not to correct known misstatements, even immaterial ones, as part of an ongoing effort directed by or known to senior management for the purposes of "managing" earnings. On the other hand, insignificant misstatements that arise from the operation of systems or recurring processes in the normal course of business generally will not cause a registrant's books to be inaccurate "in reasonable detail."

   To carry it a step further, the SEC appears to be emphasizing the caution that criminal penalties *will be imposed* where acts of commission or omission in keeping books or records or administering accounting controls *are deliberately aimed at* falsification, or circumvention of the accounting controls set forth in the Exchange Act. (This would also include the deliberate falsification of books and records and other conduct calculated to evade the *internal accounting controls requirement* which is about to come under close scrutiny by the Commission. See below.)

3. *The cost of correcting the misstatement.* The books and records provisions of the Exchange Act do not require registrants to make major expenditures to correct small misstatements. (To put it succinctly, thousands of dollars should ordinarily not be spent conserving hundreds.) Conversely, where there is little cost or delay involved in correcting a misstatement, failure to do so is unlikely to be "reasonable."

4. *The clarity of authoritative accounting guidance with respect to the misstatement.* In instances where reasonable individuals could differ about the appropriate accounting treatment of a financial statement item, a failure to correct it may not render the registrant's financial statements inaccurate "in reasonable detail." On the other hand, when there is little basis for reasonable disagreement, the case for leaving a misstatement uncorrected is decidedly weaker.

The SEC acknowledges that there may be additional indicators of "reasonableness" that registrants, their accountants and auditors may take into consideration. Because the judgment is seldom unanimous, the staff will be inclined to continue to defer to judgments that "allow a business, acting in good faith, to comply with the Act's accounting provisions in an innovative and cost-effective way."

THE AUDITOR'S RESPONSE TO INTENTIONAL MISSTATEMENTS

The Exchange Act requires auditors to consider several courses of action when discovering an illegal act which is defined as ". . . an act or omission that violates any law, or any rule or regulation having the force of law."

The statute specifies among other things that:

1. These obligations are triggered regardless of whether or not the illegal acts are considered to have a material effect upon the financial statements of the issuer.
2. The auditor is required to inform the appropriate level of management of an illegal act unless it is clearly "inconsequential."
3. When an auditor discovers an intentional misstatement of immaterial items in a registrant's financial statements which violates the Exchange Act and thus is an illegal act, the auditor must take steps to see that the registrant's audit committee is "adequately informed" about the illegal act. (Since the provisions of the Act are triggered regardless of whether an illegal act has a material effect on the registrant's financial statements, when the illegal act is a misstatement in the registrant's financial statements, the auditor is required to report that illegal act to the audit committee irrespective of any "netting" of the misstatements with other financial statement items.)

Auditors who become aware of intentional misstatements may also be required to:

1. Reevaluate the degree of audit risk involved in the audit engagement.
2. Determine whether to revise the nature, timing, and extent of audit procedures accordingly.
3. Consider whether to resign.

Cases of intentional misstatements may serve as a signal of the existence of reportable conditions or material weaknesses in the registrant's system of internal accounting control that should have been designed to detect and deter improper accounting and financial reporting.

Management's Role

As stated by the National Commission on Fraudulent Financial Reporting (also known as the Treadway Commission) in its 1987 report, the *tone* set by top management, the corporate environment, or the culture within which financial reporting occurs is the most important factor contributing to the integrity of the financial reporting process. Even if there is an in-depth set of written rules and procedures, if this tone is lax or permissive, fraudulent financial reporting is more likely to occur.

Here again, it is up to the auditor to report to a registrant's audit committee any *reportable conditions or material weaknesses* in a registrant's system of internal accounting control that he or she uncovers in the course of the examination of the registrant's financial statements.

GAAP TAKES PRECEDENCE OVER INDUSTRY PRACTICE

It has been argued that registrants should be permitted to continue to follow an *industry* accounting practice even though that practice is—or has become—inconsistent with authoritative accounting literature. Such a situation might occur:

1. If a practice is developed when there are few transactions.
2. The accounting results are clearly inconsequential.
3. That particular industry practice never changed despite a subsequent growth in the number or materiality of such transactions.

Regardless of how or why the practice had developed, this may *not* be considered a valid argument for its continued use. Authoritative literature *always* takes precedence over industry practice that is contrary to GAAP.

Determining Appropriate Accounting Treatment

As pointed out above, SAB 99 is not intended to change current law or guidance in the accounting or auditing literature. This SAB and the authoritative accounting literature cannot specifically address all of the novel and complex business transactions and events that may occur. Accordingly, registrants may at times account for, and make disclosures about these transactions and events based on analogies to similar situations or other factors.

The SEC staff may not, however, always be convinced that a registrant's determination is the most appropriate under the circumstances. When disagreements occur after a transaction or an event has been reported, the consequences may be severe for registrants, auditors, and, most important, for the *users of financial statements* who have a right to expect consistent accounting and reporting for, and disclosure of, similar transactions and events.

The SEC, therefore, encourages registrants, their accountants and auditors to discuss on a timely basis with the staff proposed accounting treatments for, and disclosures about, transactions or events not specifically covered by the existing accounting literature. This caution should also apply in instances where there is any question in the mind of any of the entity's "team" concerning the appropriateness of a particular procedure. In more forceful terms, "Don't let creative accounting get you or your firm into trouble."

Chapter 25

The Securities and Exchange Commission—Private Securities Litigation Reform Act of 1995

CONTENTS

Provisions of the Act	**25.03**
Certification Filed with Complaint	**25.05**
Nonwaiver of Attorney Privilege	**25.05**
Appointment of Lead Plaintiff	**25.05**
Additional Notices Required Under Federal Rules	**25.05**
Consolidated Actions	**25.06**
Rebuttable Presumption	**25.06**
Discovery	**25.06**
Selection of Lead Counsel	**25.06**
Restrictions on Professional Plaintiffs	**25.06**
Recovery by Plaintiffs	**25.06**
Restrictions on Settlements Under Seal	**25.07**
Restrictions on Payment of Attorneys' Fees and Expenses	**25.07**
Disclosure of Settlement Terms to Class Members	**25.07**
Attorney Conflict of Interest	**25.08**
Security for Payment of Costs in Class Actions	**25.08**
Misleading Statements and Omissions	**25.08**
Required State of Mind	**25.09**
Sanction for Willful Violation	**25.09**

Causation of Loss **25.09**

Limitation on Damages **25.09**

Private Class Actions **25.10**

Multiple Actions **25.10**

Presumption in Favor of Attorneys' Fees and Costs for
Abusive Litigation **25.10**

Rebuttal Evidence for Sanctions Against Abusive Litigation **25.10**

Availability of Documents **25.10**

Stay Pending Decision on Motion Exemption Authority **25.10**

Exemption Authority **25.11**

Effect on Other Authority of the Commission **25.11**

Definition of Forward-Looking Statements **25.11**

Safe Harbor for Forward-Looking Statements **25.12**

Class Action Reforms **25.13**

Proportionate Liability and Contributions **25.13**

Reduction of Damage **25.13**

Right of Rescission **25.13**

Aiding and Abetting **25.13**

Stay of Discovery and Preservation of Evidence **25.14**

Protections for Senior Citizens and Qualified Investment
Retirement Plans **25.14**

Racketeer Influenced and Corrupt Organization Act (RICO) **25.14**

Proportionate Liability **25.14**

Indemnification Agreements **25.15**

Rule of Construction **25.15**

The Act's Exception Provision **25.16**

Conclusion **25.16**

To reduce the number of frivolous class action lawsuits, Congress passed the Private Securities Litigation Reform Act of 1995 (the Act). The Act revises the securities laws that professional investors and class action lawyers have used against corporations, accountants, and securities underwriters to win billions of dollars in damages. A safe harbor provision now protects companies from the legal liability for forecasts that subsequently proved to be incorrect, as well as for statements that were inaccurate when they were made. Key personnel of a large number of national CPA firms and various state CPA associations urged members of Congress to support reforms in the bill; the passage of the bill is considered to be significantly helpful to business corporations and the accounting and investment banking professions. The law encourages the dissemination of forward-looking information and forecasts, using easily understood language that lessens the possibility of frivolous lawsuits by the users of financial statements. The Act's fundamental purpose is to address concerns, raised in a number of Congressional hearings over a four-year period, that the securities litigation system was misaligned in a way that overcompensated weak cases to the detriment of strong cases, and that served investor interests poorly.

PROVISIONS OF THE ACT

The following are some of the Act's provisions:

1. The Act implements a system of proportionate liability in which peripheral defendants pay only their fair share of a judgment. Less accountable defendants will pay a proportionate share of the damages, but parties that knowingly engage in fraudulent actions are still subject to the fullest extent of joint and several liability. Proponents of the bill argued that joint and several liability in the previous law caused plaintiffs' lawyers to target rich defendants.

   The proportionate liability of proportionately liable defendants can exceed their percentage of responsibility in two respects. First, if the liability share of any codefendant is found to be uncollectible within six months of entry of the judgment, proportionately liable defendants will be liable for the uncollectible portion in proportion to their share of responsibility, up to 50% of each covered person's proportionate share. Second, plaintiffs with net worth of under $200,000 and who incur damages equal to more than 10% of their net worth could still enforce their judgment against all defendants jointly and severally.

   The Act also clarifies a number of open issues concerning the operation of rights of contribution among codefendants. A defendant who settles a private action is discharged from all claims of contribution brought by other persons, and any subsequent judgment in the action is reduced by the greater of the percentage of responsibility of the settling defendant or the amount paid to the plaintiff by the settling defendant. A defendant against whom a judgment is not collectible is subject to contribution and to continuing liability to the plaintiff. A proportionate share of responsibility has a contribution claim against other defendants, except settling defendants, or any other person responsible for the conduct. All claims for contribution are to be determined based on the percentage of responsibility of the claimant and of each person who would have been liable if joined in the original action. Contribution claims are subject to a six-month statute of limitations.

2. A significant part of the Act for the various professions is its system of proportionate liability which the professions had urged Congress to adopt as part of the legislation. For example, a defendant who is found only to have acted carelessly, and did not *knowingly* commit fraud, would be responsible for a proportionate amount of the damages instead of for the fullest amount of money possible as under the old law.

3. All defendants involved in the action remain jointly and severally liable to investors with a net worth under $200,000 who lost more than 10% of their net worth. Defendants liable for their proportionate share are also liable for up to an additional 50% of their share to help pay for insolvent codefendants.

4. The Act encourages voluntary disclosure of forward-looking information to investors by establishing a carefully designed safe harbor rule. The safe harbor protects statements made and meaningful cautionary risk disclosures that identify factors that could alter actual results.

5. Language was added to the safe harbor provision to make certain that forward-looking information has meaningful support behind it. The safe harbor does not protect those who knowingly make a false or misleading statement.

6. The 1995 Act requires that auditors immediately disclose illegal acts discovered in the course of an audit. Auditors must notify the SEC of illegal acts ignored or improperly considered by management. This puts a time limit on when illegal acts must be reported to the SEC. The board of directors has *one* business day to report to the SEC that the independent auditor has reported a material illegal act, and the auditor has determined that senior management and the board of directors have not taken appropriate actions, or are not expected to take appropriate action. If the independent auditor does not receive a copy of the board of directors' report to the SEC within the one business day period, the independent auditor must resign from the engagement or furnish the SEC with a copy of the original fraud report. This requirement ensures immediate reporting of illegal acts.

7. The Act gives the SEC the power to sue people or companies for aiding and abetting others who commit fraud. The provision is designed to ensure the SEC's enforcement authority which prevents aiding and abetting from not being considered an actionable offense in private securities fraud lawsuits.

8. The law does not require the loser of a case to pay all attorneys' fees, but it does impose sanctions against attorneys who file frivolous lawsuits. If a court finds that either the plaintiff's or the defendant's attorneys made arguments that were legally irrelevant or lacking evidentiary support, the court must impose sanctions unless it is a trifling violation. Reasonable

attorneys' costs and fees are presumed to be adequate reimbursement. The statute of limitations is not changed with respect to the three-year time limit for filing securities fraud lawsuits. Current law permits actions to be brought within one year after discovery of an alleged violation, and no more than three years after the alleged violation occurred.

CERTIFICATION FILED WITH COMPLAINT

Each plaintiff seeking to serve as a representative party on behalf of a class must provide a sworn certification, which shall be personally signed by the plaintiff and filed with the complaint, that states that the plaintiff has reviewed the complaint and authorized this filing, and states that the plaintiff did not purchase the security that is the subject of the complaint at the direction of plaintiff's counsel or in order to participate in any private action.

NONWAIVER OF ATTORNEY PRIVILEGE

The certification filed shall not be construed to be a waiver of the attorney-client privilege.

APPOINTMENT OF LEAD PLAINTIFF

No later than 20 days after the date on which the complaint is filed, the plaintiff or plaintiffs shall cause to be published, in a widely circulated national business-oriented publication or wire service, a notice advising members of the purported plaintiff class of the action, and the claims asserted therein. Not later than 60 days after the date on which the notice is published, any member of the purported class may move the court to serve as lead plaintiff of the purported class.

No later than 90 days after the date on which a notice is published, the court shall consider any motion made by a class member who is not individually named as a plaintiff in the complaint or complaints, and shall appoint as lead plaintiff the member or members of the purported plaintiff class that the court determines to be most capable of adequately representing the interests of class members who is referred to as the *most adequate plaintiff.*

ADDITIONAL NOTICES REQUIRED UNDER FEDERAL RULES

Notice required under the early notice requirement should be in addition to any other required notice.

Consolidated Actions

If more than one action on behalf of a class asserts substantially the same claim or claims for pretrial purposes or trial, the court will appoint the most adequate plaintiff as lead plaintiff for the consolidated actions.

Rebuttable Presumption

The court shall adopt a presumption that the most adequate plaintiff in any private action is the person or group of persons who has either filed the complaint, or made a motion in response to a notice in the determination of the court, and has the largest financial interest in the relief sought by the class.

Discovery

Discovery relating to whether a member or members of the purported plaintiff class is the most adequate plaintiff can be conducted by a plaintiff only if the plaintiff first demonstrates a reasonable basis for a finding that the presumptively most adequate plaintiff is incapable of adequately representing the class.

Selection of Lead Counsel

The most adequate plaintiff will, subject to the approval of the court, select and retain counsel to represent the class.

Restrictions on Professional Plaintiffs

A person may be a lead plaintiff, or an officer, director, or fiduciary of a lead plaintiff, in no more than five securities class actions brought as plaintiff class actions.

Recovery by Plaintiffs

The share of any final judgment or of any settlement that is awarded to a representative party serving on behalf of a class shall be equal, on a per share basis, to the portion of the final judgment or settlement awarded to all members of the class. However, the court may permit lead plaintiffs to recover reasonable costs and expenses, including lost wages.

RESTRICTIONS ON SETTLEMENTS UNDER SEAL

The terms and provisions of any settlement of a class action should not be filed under seal, except that on motion of any party to the settlement, the court can order filing under seal for those portions of a settlement agreement as to which good cause is shown for a filing under seal.

RESTRICTIONS ON PAYMENT OF ATTORNEYS' FEES AND EXPENSES

Total attorneys' fees and expenses awarded by the court to counsel for the plaintiff class shall not exceed a reasonable percentage of the amount of any damage and prejudgment interest actually paid to the class.

DISCLOSURE OF SETTLEMENT TERMS TO CLASS MEMBERS

Any proposed or final settlement agreement that is published or otherwise disseminated to the class will include a cover page summarizing the information contained in the following statements:

Statement of plaintiff recovery.   The amount of the settlement proposed to be distributed to the parties to the action, is determined in the aggregate and on an average per share basis.

Agreement of the amount of damages.   If the settling parties agree on the average amount of damages per share that would be recoverable if the plaintiff prevailed on each claim alleged, a statement concerning the average amount of such potential damages per share, and a statement from each settling party should be made.

Disagreement on the amount of damages.   If the parties do not agree on the average amount of damages per share that would be recoverable if the plaintiff prevailed on each claim alleged, a statement from each settling party must be made concerning the issue or issues on which the parties disagree.

Inadmissibility for certain purposes.   A statement made concerning the amount of damages shall not be admissible in any federal or state judicial action or administrative proceeding, other than an action or proceeding arising out of such statement.

Statement of attorneys' fees or costs sought.   If any of the settling parties or their counsel intend to apply to the court for an award of attorneys' fees or costs from any fund established as part of the settlement, a statement indicating which parties or counsel intend to make such an application, the amount of such fees and costs determined on an average per share basis, and a brief explanation supporting the fees and costs sought is required. Such information will be clearly summarized on the cover page of any notice to a party of any proposed or final settlement agreement.

Identification of lawyers' representatives.   The name, telephone number, and address of one or more representatives of counsel for the plaintiff class who will be reasonably available to answer questions from the class.

Reasons for settlement.   A brief statement explaining the reasons why the parties are proposing the settlement must be made.

Other information.   Information that might be required by the court.

ATTORNEY CONFLICT OF INTEREST

If a plaintiff class is represented by an attorney who directly owns or otherwise has a beneficial interest in the securities that are the subject of a litigation, the court shall make a determination of whether such ownership or other interest constitutes a conflict of interest sufficient to disqualify the attorney from representing the plaintiff class.

SECURITY FOR PAYMENT OF COSTS IN CLASS ACTIONS

In any private action that is certified as a class action, the court may require an undertaking from the attorneys for the plaintiff class, the plaintiffs' class, or both, in such proportions and at such times as the court determines are just and equitable for the payment of fees and expenses that may be awarded.

The Act does permit a court to require plaintiffs, defendants, or their attorneys to post a bond for the payment of fees and expenses that may be awarded.

MISLEADING STATEMENTS AND OMISSIONS

In actions in which the plaintiff alleges that the defendant made an untrue statement of a material fact, or omitted a material fact necessary to prevent the statements from being misleading, the complaint must specify the following:

1. Each statement alleged to have been misleading,
2. The reason or reasons why the statement is misleading, and

3. If an allegation regarding the statement or omission is made on information and belief, the complaint should state the specific facts on which that belief is based.

REQUIRED STATE OF MIND

In any private action in which the plaintiff may recover money damages only on proof that the defendant acted with a particular state of mind, the complaint shall state specifically which facts give rise to a strong inference that the defendant acted with the required state of mind.

SANCTION FOR WILLFUL VIOLATION

A party aggrieved by the willful failure of an opposing party to comply with this Act may apply to the court for an order awarding appropriate sanctions.

CAUSATION OF LOSS

In any private action, the plaintiff shall have the burden of proving that the act or omission of the defendant alleged to violate this Act caused the loss for which the plaintiff seeks to recover damages.

LIMITATION ON DAMAGES

Stock prices frequently have a tendency to recover part of their market price after the initial price adjustment to adverse news about a company. If a security recovers some or all of its market price during the 90-day period after the dissemination of information correcting the misstatement or omission that is the basis for the action, damages will be capped at the difference between the price paid for the security and the mean trading price of the security during the 90-day period.

If the plaintiff sells or repurchases the subject security prior to the expiration of the 90-day period, the plaintiff's damages shall not exceed the difference between the purchase or sale price paid or received, as appropriate, by the plaintiff for the security and the mean trading price of the security during the period beginning immediately after dissemination of information correcting the misstatement or omission and ending on the date on which the plaintiff sells or repurchases the security. For the purposes of this rule, the *mean trading price* of a security shall be an average of the daily trading price of that security, determined as of the close of the market each day during the 90-day period.

Private Class Actions

The provisions of this Act shall apply in each private action arising that is brought as a plaintiff class action.

Multiple Actions

If more than one action is filed on behalf of a class asserting substantially the same claim or claims, only the plaintiff or plaintiffs in the first filed action will be required to cause notice to be published.

Presumption in Favor of Attorneys' Fees and Costs for Abusive Litigation

The court shall adopt a presumption that the appropriate sanction for failure of any responsive pleading, or dispositive motion to comply with any requirement of the court, is an award to the opposing party of the reasonable attorneys' fees and other expenses incurred as a direct violation.

Rebuttal Evidence for Sanctions Against Abusive Litigation

The presumption may be rebutted only upon proof by the party, or attorney against whom sanctions are to be imposed, that the award of attorneys' fees and other expenses will impose an unreasonable burden on that party or attorney and would be unjust, and the failure to make such an award would not impose a greater burden on the party in whose favor sanctions are to be imposed. If the party or attorney against whom sanctions are to be imposed meets its burden, the court shall award the sanctions that the court deems appropriate.

Availability of Documents

Any document filed with the Commission or generally disseminated shall be deemed to be readily available.

Stay Pending Decision on Motion Exemption Authority

In any private action, the court shall stay discovery, other than discovery that is specifically directed to the application of an exemption, during the tendency of any motion by a defendant for summary judgment that is based on the ground that the statement or omission upon which the complaint is used is a forward-looking statement, and the exemption provided precludes a claim for relief.

EXEMPTION AUTHORITY

The Commission may provide presumptions from any provision of this Act that is consistent with the public interest and the protection of investors as determined by the Commission.

EFFECT ON OTHER AUTHORITY OF THE COMMISSION

Nothing in the Act limits, either expressly or by implication, the authority of the Commission to exercise similar authority or to adopt similar rules and regulations with respect to forward-looking statements under any other statute under which the Commission exercises rule-making authority.

DEFINITION OF FORWARD-LOOKING STATEMENTS

Forward-Looking Statement. The term means a statement containing a projection of revenues, income including income loss, earnings including earnings loss per share, capital expenditures, dividends, capital structure, or other financial items. These could include, but are not limited to, the following:

- A statement of the plans and objectives of management for future operations, including plans or objectives relating to the products or services of the issuer.
- A statement of future economic performance, including any such statement contained in a discussion and analysis of financial condition by the management or in results of operations included pursuant to the rules and regulations of the Commission.
- Any statement of the admissions underlying or relating to any other statement.
- Any report issued by an outside reviewer retained by an issuer, to the extent that the report assesses a forward-looking statement made by the issuer.
- A statement containing a projection or estimate of such other items as may be specified by rule or regulation of the Commission.

SAFE HARBOR FOR FORWARD-LOOKING STATEMENTS

Liability for forward-looking statements such as earnings or sales forecasts has had the undesirable effect of discouraging companies from sharing such information with investors, despite keen market interest in this information. This has become a particular concern for high technology and biotech companies which tend to have volatile stock prices, and therefore are frequent targets of class action lawsuits when projections are not realized. While the primary beneficiaries of the safe harbor are issuers and their officers, the Act also offers useful protection to broker-dealers in their roles as underwriters and analysts. The safe harbor is offered to:

1. An issuer who, at the time that the statement is made, is subject to the reporting requirements of the Exchange Act.
2. A person acting on behalf of such issuer.
3. An outside reviewer retained by such issuer making a statement on behalf of such issuer.
4. An underwriter, with respect to information provided by such issuer or information derived from information provided by the issuer.

In addition, the safe harbor excludes certain categories of issuers and transactions, most notably issuers who have been subject to criminal or SEC enforcement sanctions within the preceding three years, issuers that are investment companies, and statements made in connection with a tender offer or initial public offering, or that are included in an audited financial statement. The safe harbor generally applies to a forward-looking statement if it is identified as a forward-looking statement, and is accompanied by meaningful cautionary statements identifying important factors that could cause actual results to differ materially from those in the forward-looking statement; or is immaterial; or the plaintiff fails to prove the forward-looking statement was made with actual knowledge; or if made by a business entity was made by and with the approval of an executive officer of that entity, and made or approved by such officer with actual knowledge by that officer that the statement was false or misleading.

Oral statements made by an issuer, or by a person acting on behalf of such issuer, can also be covered under a corollary formulation of the safe harbor. Under the corollary, an oral statement qualifies for the safe harbor if the oral statement is accompanied by a cautionary statement pointing out that the oral statement is a forward-looking statement, that actual results may vary, and identifying an available written document setting out the meaningful cautionary statements identifying important factors that could cause actual results to differ that are required by the primary safe harbor.

The safe harbor was drafted in such a way that even if a forward-looking projection or estimate did not contain adequate cautionary language, a plaintiff would still have to prove that the speaker had actual knowledge that the statement was false or misleading. The safe harbor directs courts to stay all discovery, except for discovery directed at the applicability of the safe harbor, while a motion to dismiss based on the safe harbor is pending.

CLASS ACTION REFORMS

The Act creates a procedure for the court to appoint as lead plaintiff the plaintiff with the largest financial interest. The Act also adopts other class action reforms, such as prohibiting the payment of referral fees to securities brokers.

PROPORTIONATE LIABILITY AND CONTRIBUTIONS

The Act generally limits joint and several liability to persons who knowingly commit a violation of the securities laws. The Act requires a defendant to pay 50% more than its proportionate share of damages in certain cases where other defendants' shares are uncollectible, and preserves joint and several liability for plaintiffs with a net worth under $200,000 whose damages exceed 10% of their net worth. The Act clarifies certain issues regarding the operation of rights of contribution.

REDUCTION OF DAMAGE

The Act provides that a defendant can reduce damages by proving that all or part of the decline in the value of the securities was caused by factors other than the alleged misstatement or material omission in the prospectus.

RIGHT OF RESCISSION

The Act provides a right of rescission to the buyer of a security if the security was sold in violation of the registration or prospectus delivery requirements, or if it was offered or sold by means of a prospectus or oral communication which included an untrue statement of a material fact or omitted to state a material fact.

AIDING AND ABETTING

The Act gives the SEC (but not private plaintiffs) authority to bring civil injunctive actions and to seek civil money penalties against any person who knowingly provides substantial assistance to another person in violation of the Exchange Act to the same extent as the person to whom such assistance is provided.

STAY OF DISCOVERY AND PRESERVATION OF EVIDENCE

A stay of discovery is required while a motion to dismiss is pending, other than a particular discovery needed to preserve evidence. Any party to the action with actual notice of the allegations contained in the complaint shall treat all documents, data compilation, and tangible objects that are in the custody or control of such person and that are relevant to the allegations, as if they were the subject of a continuing request for production of documents from an opposing party. A party aggrieved by the willful failure of an opposing party to comply with this requirement may apply to the court for sanctions. The use of the term *willful failure* should give protection from liability for inadvertent violations.

PROTECTIONS FOR SENIOR CITIZENS AND QUALIFIED INVESTMENT RETIREMENT PLANS

The SEC must determine whether senior citizens or qualified retirement plans have been adversely impacted by abusive securities fraud litigation and whether they are adequately protected from such litigation by the Act. If the SEC finds any such adverse impact or lack of adequate protection, it is to submit to Congress a report containing recommendations for protection from securities fraud, or for protection from abusive litigation.

RACKETEER INFLUENCED AND CORRUPT ORGANIZATION ACT (RICO)

The Act eliminates private RICO liability, with its accompanying exposure to treble damages, for conduct that would have been actionable as fraud in the purchase or sale of securities. This does not apply to an action against any person who is criminally convicted in connection with the fraud, in which case the statute of limitations will begin to run from the date the conviction becomes final.

PROPORTIONATE LIABILITY

Major accounting firms argued that joint and several liability under the antifraud provisions of the securities laws had created an unjustifiable liability exposure in cases where their role was relatively peripheral, but their potential deep-pocket liability for the more culpable conduct of others was enormous. Accounting firms argued that this disproportionate liability exposure was forcing them to curtail audit services for companies that were regarded as high risks for potential litigation, particularly start-up firms and firms with volatile stock prices in the high technology and biotech sectors. In place of joint and several liability, accounting firms sought a limited system of proportionate liability, so that the liability of less culpable defendants would bear some relationship to their degree of responsibility for the damages incurred.

The Act provides that a defendant in an action is jointly and severally liable only if the person who tries the facts specifically finds that the defendant *knowingly committed* a violation of the securities laws. The provision provides an extensive clarification of the term, which essentially requires that the defendant engaged in conduct with actual knowledge of the facts and circumstances that make the conduct a violation of the securities laws. The Act also expressly provides that *reckless conduct* will not be construed to constitute a knowing commission of a violation of the securities laws. The Act also takes pains to avoid supporting the argument that recklessness is a sufficient standard for anti-fraud liability by providing that nothing in the Act should be construed to create, affect, or in any manner modify, the standard of liability associated with any action arising under the securities laws. For defendants who are not found to have committed a knowing violation of the securities laws, the Act offers a qualified form of proportionate liability. Such a defendant is only liable for the portion of the judgment that corresponds to its percentage of responsibility.

In determining the percentage of responsibility for each defendant, the person examining the facts must consider:

1. The nature of the conduct of each covered person found to have caused or contributed to the loss incurred by the plaintiff or plaintiffs.
2. The nature and extent of the causal relationship between the conduct of each such person and the damages incurred by the plaintiff or plaintiffs.

INDEMNIFICATION AGREEMENTS

The indemnification agreement expressly permits a defendant to recover attorneys' fees and costs incurred in connection with an action in which the defendant prevails. The Act does not change the enforceability of indemnification contracts in the event of settlement.

RULE OF CONSTRUCTION

The Act clarifies two points:

1. Nothing in the Act is to be deemed to prevent the SEC from restricting or otherwise regulating private actions under the Exchange Act.
2. Nothing in the Act is to be deemed to create or ratify any implied right of action.

The Act's Exception Provision

The Act's exception for material of little value could alleviate a concern about the Act's use of the term *substantial* in relation to complaints. The word *substantial* might be used to argue that plaintiffs' complaints are to be subjected to a less rigorous scrutiny than papers filed by other parties. The ability to rebut any finding of a violation by showing that the finding was of little value suggests that the standard probably will be the same for both plaintiffs and defendants. Although it is not clear whether there is some distinction intended between substantial and irrelevancy, *the exception provision* in the Act was not the intention of Congress to hold defendants to a more stringent standard than plaintiffs.

Conclusion

The Act reforms many of the procedures that govern private class actions. It is intended to address a number of concerns about securities class actions, such as the race to the courthouse to file cases within days or even hours of a sharp stock price decline; the ability of attorneys to select plaintiffs with nominal holdings to bring a class action case; the lack of opportunities for institutional investors to participate in litigation brought on their behalf; and the lack of effective notice to investors of the terms of class action settlements. Institutional investors are encouraged to take a more active role in securities class action lawsuits. Within 20 days of filing a class action lawsuit, the plaintiff must provide notice to members of the purported class. The notice is to identify the claims alleged in the lawsuit and indicate that potential members have 60 days from publication to file a motion to seek to serve as lead plaintiff. If more than one action is filed, only the plaintiff in the first action is required to file the notice. The notice must be filed in a widely circulated business publication.

Once designated by the court, the lead plaintiff is authorized to select and retain counsel for the class. It is unclear whether this provision would encompass other related powers, such as to replace counsel, to direct litigation strategy, or to reject or give preliminary approval to settlements. The amount of autonomy that courts actually give to lead plaintiffs to manage the case could have a significant impact on whether institutional investors will avail themselves of this new procedure.

Chapter 26
Segment Reporting

CONTENTS

FASB Statement 131, *Disclosures About Segments of an Enterprise and Related Information*	**26.01**
Security and Exchange Commission Response to FASB 131	**26.07**
Segment Information Added to Interim Reports	**26.13**
Codification Update, Revised Section 501.06	**26.14**
A Parting Thought	**26.16**

FASB STATEMENT 131, DISCLOSURES ABOUT SEGMENTS OF AN ENTERPRISE AND RELATED INFORMATION

Continuing the newfound path of developing Standards with other standard setting bodies, the FASB issued Statement 131, *Disclosures About Segments of an Enterprise and Related Information* in conjunction with the Accounting Standards Board (AcSB) of the Canadian Institute of Chartered Accountants. Simultaneously, the two bodies published almost identical statements that become effective in 1998. FASB 131 supersedes FASB 14, *Financial Reporting for Segments of a Business Enterprise*.

At the same time as the U.S. and Canadian groups were working together, the International Accounting Standards Committee (IASC) was also

26.01

working closely with them to revise International Accounting Standard (IAS)14, *Reporting Financial Information by Segment.* However, after the many discussions to minimize differences that did effectively reduce the gap, the international organization still decided to publish its own Standard. That group declined to go as far in requiring increased disclosure in IAS 14 (rev.), *Segment Reporting,* as the U.S. and Canadian pronouncements required.

Reporting Requirements

FASB 131 sets forth stricter requirements than previously for the way a business reports financial and related information about reportable operating segments in annual and interim reports. The Statement does not apply to non-public business enterprises nor to not-for-profit organizations.

The requirements went into effect for the first annual statement after December 15, 1997, but quarterly interim statements were not due until after the first annual disclosure. Thus, the interim statements did not begin until 1999. Then, comparative information for interim periods in the first year was to be reported in financial statements for the second year.

FASB 131 establishes new standards for related financial and other disclosures in relation to:

1. Products and services.
2. Geographical areas.
3. Major customers.

This information must be reported whether the business actually uses it in making operating decisions or not—unless preparing information that is not used internally would be impracticable. The enterprise must also:

1. Provide background information about the manner in which the operating segments were established.
2. Describe the particular products and/or services provided by each segment.
3. Explain any differences between the measurements used in reporting segment information and those used in their general-purpose financial statements.
4. Explain any changes in the measurement of segments from one reporting period to another.
5. Indicate shifts in a company's sources of profits, geographical risk, and investment requirements.

Objectives of the Standard

It would appear that the FASB considers this a refinement of the general principles of good general-purpose financial reporting. The Board apparently feels that providing the required segment information will better the financial statement user's ability to:

1. Understand the enterprise's performance.
2. Estimate the enterprise's prospects relating to future cash flows.
3. Arrive at better informed judgments about the enterprise as a whole.

Information from Within

Generally, this Standard requires that the information be reported on the same basis as the enterprise uses *internally* for evaluating segment performance and deciding how to allocate resources to segments. This leads to new data being disclosed by companies and should be useful to investment analysts and informed investors. They become privy to much of the operations information that goes to upper management to assist them in their decision making.

Reporting financial information under FASB 131 is based on the *management approach* in contrast to the *industry approach* that was used in FASB 14. While this Standard required reporting of information about major customers, and some data was provided on related product and service groups, it was felt that the industry approach was too subjective. So much discretion was left to the reporting company in the application of FASB 14 that unfavorable earnings figures could be hidden (by switching industry groupings around, for example).

Management Approach

The management approach is based on the way management organizes the segments within a company for making operating decisions and assessing performance. Because of this, the segments should be evident from the structure of the company's organization. Therefore, financial statement preparers should be able to provide the additional required information without a great amount of additional time and effort.

The management approach should result in consistent descriptions of a company in its annual report since it focuses on financial information that an enterprise's decision makers have been using to make their decisions regarding company operations. The components that management establishes for that purpose are referred to in FASB 131 as operating segments.

According to the FASB, if management were to change the internal structure of their organization to the extent that the operating segment lines were altered, the changed reporting may be handled in one of two ways:

1. By restating segment information for earlier periods, including interim periods.
2. By disclosing segment information for the current period under both the old and the new bases of segmentation unless it is impracticable to do so.

IASC's Revised Segment Reporting Standard

As mentioned, the release of the IASC's revised Standard on segment reporting was delayed while efforts were made to synchronize it with the new segment disclosure Standards developed by the FASB and Canadian standard setters. The original IAS 14 was revised to bring it into line with the common disaggregated disclosure requirements agreed upon by the IASC and the FASB, and embodied in FASB 131.

The IASC went along with the FASB/Canadian measures as far as to adopt the management approach in which a company's internal structure and its system of internal financial reporting to senior management is normally the basis for identifying reportable segments and, thus, for its segment disclosures. Unlike the two North American standards, IAS 14 (rev.) does allow management under some circumstances to depart from the management approach.

It also differs from them in another respect. The IASC Standard requires that segment data disclosures be prepared using the accounting policies adopted for the company's consolidated financial statements. In contrast, FASB 131 requires the same accounting as management uses internally to be used in its segment data disclosures.

Operating Segments Defined

FASB 131 defines an operating segment as a component of an enterprise:

1. That engages in business activities from which it may earn revenues and incur expenses.
2. Whose operating results are regularly reviewed by the enterprise's chief operating decision maker regarding decisions about resources to be allocated to the segment and to assess its performance.
3. For which discrete financial information is available.

(The term "chief operating decision maker" identifies a function, not a person with that title. The person's or persons' function is to allocate resources to and assess the performance of the company's segments. A chief operating decision maker is frequently a company's chief executive officer or chief operating officer, but it also could be a group of decision makers, for example, the company's president, executive vice presidents and others.)

No More Secrets

As with other recent exposure drafts and standards, there was a storm of protest raised about the requirements. Most of the complaints were leveled at the increased disclosure requirements that respondents felt would result in competitive harm. They felt that the specificity of the required reporting would place them at a disadvantage by giving competitors and suppliers sufficient information to figure out their profit margins on particular products.

Strangely enough, when the SEC requested comment on whether the proposed revisions, if adopted, would have an adverse effect on competition, or would impose a burden on competition that was neither necessary nor appropriate in furthering the purposes of the Securities Act and the Exchange Act, no commenter addressed the issue. Therefore, based upon this apparent lack of concern and further study, the Commission determined that there would be no adverse effect on competition, and that the rule changes would not impose any unnecessary burden on competition that is not appropriate in furthering the purposes of the federal securities laws.

Segment Quantitative Thresholds

A company must report separately information about an operating segment that meets any of the following quantitative thresholds:

1. Its reported revenue, including both sales to external customers and intersegment sales or transfers, is 10% or more of the combined revenue, internal and external, of all reported operating segments. (The *revenue* test.)
2. The absolute amount of its reported profit or loss is 10% or more of the greater, in absolute amount, of one of the following:
   a. The combined reported profit of all operating segments that did not report a loss.
   b. The combined reported loss of all operating segments that did report a loss. (The *profitability* test.)
3. Its assets are 10% or more of the combined assets of all operating segments. (The *asset* test.)

Information about operating segments that do not meet any of the quantitative thresholds may be disclosed separately.

FASB 131 permits combining information about operating segments that do not meet the quantitative thresholds with information about other operating segments that do not meet the quantitative thresholds to produce a reportable segment only if the operating segments have similar economic characteristics and share a majority of the following aggregation criteria:

1. The nature of the products and services.
2. The nature of the production process.
3. The type or class of customers for their products and services.
4. The methods used to distribute their products or provide their services.
5. If applicable, the nature of the regulatory environment (banking, insurance, or public utilities, for example).

If the total of external revenue reported by operating segments is less than 75% of the enterprise's total consolidated revenue, additional operating segments must be identified as reportable segments. This must be done even if the segments do not meet the quantitative threshold criteria until at least 75% of total consolidated revenue is included in reportable segments.

Finally, an "all other" category is to be set up for disclosure about other business activities and operating segments that are not reportable under the previously mentioned quantitative threshold criteria. Sources of the revenue included in this category must be revealed.

Rules for Single Segment Entities

FASB 131 includes disaggregated disclosure requirements for companies that have a single reportable segment and whose business activities are not organized on the basis of differences in related products and services or differences in geographical areas of operations. Disclosures about products and services, geographical areas, and major customers are required of these companies. As a result:

1. The expanded disclosure of operating segment income statements and asset data should enhance investors' understanding of an operating segment's performance, cash flows, and investment requirements.
2. The operating segment data presentation should be more consistent with other parts of a company's annual report.

Other Aspects

Under FASB 131, the following take effect.

1. Disclosures about different parts of a business are required, but the basic income statement and balance sheet are not changed.
2. Entities may no longer claim that their business consists of only one segment if, in fact, it does not.
3. Operating segment data will be reported quarterly.

4. Reporting geographic operating data by countries should aid in the evaluation of performance and risk resulting from the global nature of present day business and commerce. The cultural, economic, political, and social data resulting from this disclosure and reporting should better serve top management as well as creditors and investors in evaluating a company as a whole—not just particular segments.
5. The FASB has taken the first big step in its consolidations projects. Consolidations policy and procedure, and unconsolidated entities are still to come.

In the final analysis, FASB 131 attempts to provide information for the user of financial statements about the different types of business activity in which a company engages, the different environments in which it operates, and the nature of its client base.

SECURITY AND EXCHANGE COMMISSION RESPONSE TO FASB 131

As a result of the promulgation of FASB 131, the Security and Exchange Commission adopted technical amendments to Regulations S-X, S-K, and Schedule 14A in order to bring SEC reporting requirements in line with new disclosures relating to a business enterprise's operating segments. These steps also required consistent changes to Form 20-F and a section of the Codification of Financial Reporting Policies (CFRP).

Since FASB 14 had required corporations to disclose certain financial information by "industry segment" as defined in that statement and by geographic area, the SEC had adopted amendments to their rules to integrate that information to be furnished under FASB 14 with the narrative and financial disclosures required in various SEC disclosure forms.

The SEC agreed to adopt the rules in FASB 131 essentially as proposed. They believe that this is in keeping with their long-standing policy to rely upon the private sector for the promulgation of generally accepted accounting principles (GAAP). The Commission felt this step was also in line with their goal of integrating existing accounting information into the narrative disclosure in documents mandated by the federal securities laws. However, as frequently happens, the SEC retains some of their more stringent requirements while adopting the FASB rules.

Operating Segment Disclosure Rules Change

FASB 14 required (and the Commission's rules and forms have required) disclosure along industry segment lines. An "industry segment," as defined by FASB 14, is "a component of an enterprise engaged in providing a product or service or a group of related products and services primarily to unaffiliated customers ... for a profit."

Recognizing that businesses often evaluate their operations using criteria not necessarily related to the products or services offered to the public, the FASB replaced the industry segment reporting standard with one that requires businesses to report financial information on the basis of "operating segments." Under FASB 131, an operating segment is a component of a business, for which separate financial information is available, that management regularly evaluates in deciding how to allocate resources and subsequently assess performance thereof.

Although FASB 131 did not adopt any new accounting principles relating to measurement or recognition, it did change how a business should identify its segments. It also changed the types of information to be disclosed for each segment.

FASB 14 required an issuer to report its revenues, operating profit (loss), and identifiable assets if a segment's revenues, operating profit, or identifiable assets were 10% or more of all the industry segments' revenues, operating profits, or assets, respectively. The entity was to reconcile these three items to the consolidated amounts in the financial statements. In addition, FASB 14 required each segment to report depreciation, depletion, amortization, capital expenditures, equity in net income of unconsolidated subsidiary or equity-method investee, and the effect of a change in accounting principle on operating profit (loss).

By contrast, FASB 131 requires that a company provide for each reportable segment quantitative disclosure of two basic items—total assets and a measure of profit or loss. The newer standard defines neither segment profit (loss) nor assets. Instead as stated above, management is required to determine what is reportable based on how they operate their business. In addition, companies must disclose the following items for each segment, but only if management includes them in measuring segment profit or loss:

1. Revenues from external customers.
2. Revenues from other operating segments.
3. Interest income.
4. Interest expense.
5. Depreciation, depletion, and amortization.
6. Unusual items.
7. Equity in net income of equity method investees.
8. Income taxes.
9. Extraordinary items.
10. Significant noncash items other than depreciation, depletion, and amortization.

A company must also disclose for each segment the amount of investment in equity-method investees and total expenditures for additions to long-lived assets if it includes the amount in its determination of segment assets.

The company must reconcile the totals of the reportable segments' amounts for all of these listed items to consolidated amounts.

The FASB required more items to be disclosed per segment under the new Standard because analysts have long wanted more information and, as mentioned above, most of the items required were already available in management reports.

The SEC, therefore, amended their narrative and financial reporting rules to conform their segment reporting requirements to the FASB's revised accounting standards. However, the Commission retained certain requirements relating to disclosure of principal products or services and major customers that traditionally have differed from the FASB Standards.

Description of Business—Item 101

In the past, Regulation S-K had required issuers to disclose in the "business description" sections of documents that they filed with the Commission, pertinent financial information based on GAAP's old "industry segment" standard. Now, registrants report segment information in accordance with GAAP's operating segment standard.

Principal Products or Services. Historically, the SEC has required a discussion, by segment, of the principal markets for and methods of distribution of each segment's products and services. On the other hand, GAAP required, and continues to require, only disclosure of the types of products and services from which each segment derives its revenues, without reference to principle markets and distribution methods. The SEC continues to believe such information is also useful to investors; consequently, the provision is retained in their rules.

The SEC also requires registrants to disclose the amounts of revenues from each class of similar products and services based on quantitative thresholds. Specifically, the issuer must state the amount or percentage of total revenue contributed by any class of similar products or services that accounted for 10% or more of consolidated revenue in any of the last three fiscal years, or if total revenue did not exceed $50,000,000 during any of those three fiscal years, 15% or more of consolidated revenue. The Commission amended their rules to conform with FASB 131 requirements, but retained some of their own previous provisions.

FASB 131 requires disclosure of revenues from external customers for each product and service or each group of similar products and services, regardless of amount, unless it is impracticable to do so. It appears, then, to require more disclosure than SEC rules. FASB 131 provisions result in *disclosure of a range of amounts of products and services, depending upon how a company defines a class of related products or services.* In fact, the SEC decided that Statement 131 could well require disclosure of amounts below the existing 10% threshold of SEC requirements.

However, the Commission believes that a clearly stated minimum threshold for disclosure is desirable. Such a measure should eliminate any possible ambiguity resulting from attempts to apply an unwritten materiality threshold to small amounts of reportable revenues. The SEC, therefore, decided to retain the thresholds.

Retroactive Restatement of Information. The SEC has required issuers to restate retroactively previously reported financial information when there has been a material change in the way they group products or services into industry segments and that change affects the reported segment information. FASB 131 provides that if an issuer changes the structure of its internal organization in a manner that causes the composition of its reportable segments to change, the issuer must restate the corresponding information for earlier periods unless it is impracticable to do so. In their final rule, the SEC conforms the language of Item 101 with the language of FASB 131 regarding when a company must restate information.

Property—Item 102

Regulation S-K Item 102 requires descriptions of an issuer's principal plants, mines, and other "materially important" physical properties. Companies must identify the industry segment(s) that use the described properties. An updating of the item reflects FASB 131 financial statement reporting requirements.

Management's Discussion and Analysis

Regulation S-K Item 303, which requires management to include a discussion and analysis of an issuer's financial condition and results of operations, provides:

"Where in the registrant's judgment a discussion of segment information or other subdivisions of the registrant's business would be appropriate to an understanding of such business, the discussion shall focus on each relevant, reportable segment or other subdivision of the business and on the registrant as a whole."

The Commission has in the past relied on the FASB's definition for segment disclosure in Management's Discussion and Analysis (MD&A), and intends to continue to rely on the FASB's standards, thereby allowing issuers to use the management approach under FASB 131. No rule change is necessary.

Under the language in Item 303, a multi-segment registrant preparing a full fiscal year MD&A should analyze revenues, profitability (or losses) and total assets of each significant segment in formulating a judgment as to whether a discussion of segment information is necessary to an understanding of the business.

Although the SEC did not adopt changes to the language of Item 303, they did amend the CFRP which provides informal guidance about MD&A. (See later in this chapter.) The revisions in Item 303 conform the Codification's language with that of FASB 131, and add a new footnote, that reads:

> "Where consistent with the registrant's internal management reports, FASB 131 permits measures of segment profitability that differ from consolidated operating profit as defined by GAAP, or that exclude items included in the determination of the registrant's net income. Under FASB 131, a registrant also must reconcile key segment amounts to the corresponding items reported in the consolidated financial statements in a note to the financial statements. Similarly, the Commission expects that the discussion of a segment whose profitability is determined on a basis that differs from consolidated operating profit as defined by GAAP or that excludes the effects of items attributable to the segment also will address the applicable reconciling items in Management's Discussion and Analysis.

> "For example, if a material charge for restructuring or impairment included in management's measure of the segment's operating profit or loss, registrants would be expected to discuss in Management's Discussion and Analysis the applicable portion of the charge, the segment to which it relates and the circumstances of its incurrence. Likewise, the Commission expects that the effects of management's use of non-GAAP measures, either on a consolidated or segment basis, will be explained in a balanced and informative manner, and the disclosure will include a discussion of how that segment's performance has affected the registrant's GAAP financial statements."

In short, SEC wants to make it clear that they expect a narrative discussion in MD&A of items that affect the operating results of a segment but that are not included in segment operating profit defined by management.

Where consistent with the registrant's internal management reports, FASB 131 permits measures of segment profitability that differ from consolidated operating profit as defined by GAAP, or that exclude items included in the determination of the registrant's net income. Under FASB 131, a registrant also must reconcile key segment amounts to the corresponding items reported in the consolidated financial statements in a note to the financial statements.

Similarly, the Commission expects that the discussion of a segment whose profitability is determined on a basis that differs from consolidated operating profit as defined by GAAP, or that excludes the effects of items attributable to the segment, will also explain the applicable reconciling items in MD&A.

For example, if a material charge for restructuring or impairment relates to a specific segment, but is not included in management's measure of the segment's operating profit or loss, registrants would be expected to discuss in MD&A:

1. The applicable portion of the charge.
2. The segment to which it relates.
3. The circumstances relating to how and why the charge was incurred.

The Commission expects that the effects of management's use of non-GAAP measures, either on a consolidated or segment basis, will be explained in a balanced and informative manner, and the disclosure will include a discussion of how that segment's performance has affected the registrant's GAAP financial statements.

Form 20-F

Form 20-F is the registration statement and annual report for foreign private issuers promulgated under the Securities Exchange Act of 1934. Form 20-F has permitted a foreign registrant that presents financial statements according to United States GAAP to omit FASB 14 disclosures if it provides the information required by Item 1 of the form. A reference to FASB 131 replaces that to FASB 14.

Much of the material required by the FASB Standards is supplied in Item 1, which requires registrants to disclose sales and revenues by categories of activity and geographical areas, as well as to discuss each category of activities that provides a disproportionate contribution to total "operating profit" of the registrant.

Other Reporting Requirements

Geographic Areas.   Now companies must disclose revenues from external customers deriving from:

a. Their country of domicile.
b. All foreign countries in total from which the company derives revenues.
c. An individual foreign country, if material.

A company must also disclose the basis for attributing revenues from external customers to individual countries.

The Standard requires an issuer to disclose long-lived assets other than financial instruments, long-term customer relationships of a financial institution, mortgage and other servicing rights, and deferred policy acquisition costs. It is also necessary to include deferred tax assets located in its country of domicile and in all foreign countries, in total, in which the enterprise holds assets. If assets in an individual foreign country are material, an issuer must disclose those assets separately.

Even those companies whose segments were defined by geography, continue to report designated information based on geographic areas, unless the information is already provided as part of the reportable operating segment information required by the accounting standards. Consistent with FASB 131, rules no longer will require companies to disclose geographic information relating to profitability, unless their segments are defined by geographic areas, or export sales.

Major Customers. Since the adoption of FASB 14, GAAP has required disclosure of revenues from major customers. FASB 131 now requires issuers to disclose the amount of revenues from each external customer that amounts to 10% or more of an enterprise's revenue as well as the identity of the segment(s) reporting the revenues.

The accounting standards had never before required issuers to identify major customers. On the other hand, the SEC has historically required naming a major customer if sales to that customer equal 10% or more of the issuer's consolidated revenues and if the loss of the customer would have a material adverse effect on the issuer and its subsidiaries. The Commission believes that the identity of major customers is material information to investors.

This disclosure improves a reader's ability to assess risks associated with a particular customer. Additionally, material concentrations of revenues related to a particular customer may be judged more accurately. Consequently, the SEC continues to require this information.

SEGMENT INFORMATION ADDED TO INTERIM REPORTS

GAAP historically has not required segment reporting in interim financial statements. In FASB 131, the FASB changed its position. Under the new accounting standards, issuers must include in condensed financial statements for interim periods the following information about each reportable segment:

1. Revenues from external customers.
2. Intersegment revenues.
3. A measure of segment profit or loss.
4. Total assets for which there has been a material change from the amount disclosed in the last annual report.
5. A description of differences from the last annual report in the basis of segmentation or in the basis of measurement of segment profit or loss.

6. A reconciliation of the total of the reportable segments measures of profit or loss to the enterprise's consolidated income before income taxes, extraordinary items, discontinued operations, and the cumulative effect of changes in accounting principles.

Thus, issuers must now disclose in interim financial statements, including those filed with the Commission, condensed financial information about the segments identified as reportable segments for purposes of their annual reports.

CODIFICATION UPDATE, REVISED SECTION 501.06

The Codification of Financial Reporting Policies (CFRP) contains current Commission interpretive guidance relating to financial reporting and is updated whenever it is deemed necessary. In this case the new guidance information results from the technical amendments to Regulations S-X and S-K.

Segment Analysis

In formulating a judgment as to whether a discussion of segment information is necessary to an understanding of the business, a multi-segment registrant preparing a full fiscal year MD&A should analyze revenues, profitability, and the cash needs of its significant segments.

To the extent any segment contributes in a *materially disproportionate* way to those items, or where discussion on a consolidated basis would present an incomplete and misleading picture of the enterprise, *segment discussion* should be included.

Examples could include:

1. When there are legal or other restrictions upon the free flow of funds from one segment, subsidiary, or division of the registrant to others.
2. When known trends, demands, commitments, events, or uncertainties within a segment are reasonably likely to have a material effect on the business as a whole.
3. When the ability to dispose of identified assets of a segment may be relevant to the financial flexibility of the registrant.
4. Other circumstances in which the registrant concludes that segment analysis is appropriate to an understanding of its business.

The following example illustrates segment disclosure for a manufacturer with two segments. The two segments contributed to segment profit amounts that were disproportionate to their respective revenues. The registrant should discuss:

1. Sales and segment profit trends.
2. Factors explaining such trends.
3. Where applicable, known events that will impact future results of operations of the segment.

Financial Information About Segments

Each segment must report, as defined by GAAP, revenues from external customers, a measure of profit or loss and total assets. A registrant must report this information for each of the last three fiscal years or for as long as it has been in business, whichever period is shorter. If the information provided in response to *this* paragraph conforms with GAAP, a registrant may include in its financial statements a cross reference to this data instead of presenting duplicate information in the financial statements; conversely, a registrant may cross reference to the financial statements.

If a registrant changes the structure of its internal organization in a manner that causes the composition of its reportable segments to change, the registrant must restate the corresponding information for earlier periods, including interim periods, unless it is impracticable to do so.

Following a change in the composition of its reportable segments, a registrant must disclose whether it has restated the corresponding items of segment information for earlier periods. If it has not restated the items from earlier periods, the registrant is to disclose, in the year in which the change occurs, the segment information for the current period under both the old basis and the new basis of segmentation, unless it is impracticable to do so.

Financial Information About Geographic Areas

1. The registrant must state the following for the last three fiscal years, or for each fiscal year the registrant has been engaged in business, whichever period is shorter:
   a. Revenues from external customers attributed to:
   - The registrant's country of domicile.
   - All foreign countries, in total, from which the registrant derives revenues.
   - Any individual foreign country, if material. The registrant must disclose the basis for attributing revenues from external customers to individual countries.

   b. Long-lived assets, other than financial instruments, long-term customer relationships of a financial institution, mortgage and other servicing rights, deferred policy acquisition costs, and deferred tax assets, located in:

- The registrant's country of domicile.
- All foreign countries, in total, in which the registrant holds assets.
- Any individual foreign country, if material.

2. A registrant must report the amounts based on the financial information that it uses to produce the general-purpose financial statements. If providing the geographic information is impracticable, the registrant must disclose that fact. A registrant may wish to provide, in addition to the information required by this Section, subtotals of geographic information about groups of countries. If the disclosed information conforms with GAAP, the registrant may include a cross reference to this data instead of presenting duplicate data that is in its financial statements; conversely, a registrant may cross-reference to the financial statements.

3. A registrant is required to describe any risks attendant to the foreign operations and any dependence on one or more of the registrant's segments upon its foreign operations. Or the registrant might consider it more appropriate to discuss this information in connection with one or more of the segments in an individual foreign country.

A Parting Thought

The SEC has been concerned about the sometimes dubious manner in which some companies have been interpreting these segment disclosure rules. They point out that it should not be too difficult a task. After all, the disclosures are supposed to be based upon how management evaluates performance and makes decisions about allocating resources to segments.

Chapter 27

E-Commerce and E-Communication

CONTENTS

Accounting Issues	**27.02**
Topics for Consideration	**27.02**
E-Business Accounting Principles and Criteria	**27.07**
Taxing Problems	**27.10**
Cautions for E-Communication Web Site Use	**27.11**
International Guidance Helps Auditors Address E-Commerce Risks	**27.12**
The IASC Study: *Business Reporting on the Internet*	**27.14**
FASB's Business Reporting Research Project	**27.16**
The SEC on Reporting in the New Economy	**27.17**
Electronic Data Interchange (EDI)	**27.18**
The CPA WebTrust and Small Business	**27.18**
Congress Learns About SysTrust	**27.20**
The AICPA Plans to Combine WebTrust and SysTrust	**27.21**
Glossary of Terms	**27.23**
An E-Business Checklist	**27.27**

Forecasts of Internet business—variously called e-commerce, e-business, EC, e-tail, cyber-business or virtual markets—are so astronomical that they strain credibility. Internet commerce is growing in exponential leaps and bounds.

The term "e-commerce" has already been superseded by the term "e-business." E-commerce can be described as obtaining and distributing goods and services over the Internet using digital technology. Even though many use the terms interchangeably, the more encompassing term "e-business" can be defined as including all activities conducted by a business over the Internet. This definition for e-business extends beyond the definition of e-commerce by covering a digital approach to the whole enterprise, including other parts of the IT system and other non-transactional activities, such as recruiting employees through the Internet.

It is estimated that e-business will reach $1.3 trillion by 2003 in this country alone. And according to the SEC, e-trading is there already, "In today's hot-wired financial markets, modern technology allows traders to move money anywhere in the world at lightning speed, more than $1.5 trillion everyday—a sum equal to world trade for four months."

Web-based technologies and their support structures are changing on an average of every four to eight months. Along the way, e-commerce is creating new ways to sell, to advertise, and to communicate with customers, suppliers, employees and shareholders. And the accountant is faced with attempting to determine how to account for these evolving technologies.

Properly reporting the acquisition and then disposal of technology (with its rapid turnover) will be only one of the many new issues organizations will have to deal with.

The accounting issues raised by e-commerce factors will undoubtedly call for new accounting and auditing standards that haven't even been thought of yet. Some of the older ones will require very careful consideration.

In effect, the Internet is not only creating new business, it is creating new ways to do business and to be in business. And therein lies the work for the accountant.

ACCOUNTING ISSUES

A study called "Electronic Commerce Trends, Technology and the Security, Control and Audit Implications" was prepared for the Institute of Internal Auditors (IIA) with partial funding from the International Federation of Accountants (IFAC). That report emphasized the need for accountants and auditors of an organization to work closely with management in setting up and developing their e-business and e-communication systems. The study identifies many accounting issues that must be considered.

TOPICS FOR CONSIDERATION

The following is a discussion of some of these accounting problems and considerations relating to them.

Software

The considerable software infrastructure needed to implement an e-commerce strategy will be obtained from software vendors or developed internally. Existing U.S. software related accounting rules governing these transactions are expected to remain unchanged.

Vendor Software.   AICPA Statement of Position (SOP) 97-2, *Software Revenue Recognition,* requires that revenue should be recognized on software or software systems arrangements that do not require significant production, modification, or customization of software when delivery has occurred and all of the following tests are met:

1. Persuasive evidence that a sale or lease arrangement exists.
2. Delivery of the product or service has occurred.
3. The seller must not retain any specific performance obligation.
4. The vendor's fee is fixed or determinable.
5. Appropriate recognition is given to the likelihood of returns.
6. Collectibility is probable.

Revenue from software or software system arrangements that require significant production, modification, or customization of software should be accounted for using long-term construction-type contract accounting.

The vendor fee in software arrangements that consist of multiple elements, such as upgrades, must be allocated to the various elements. The portion of a fee allocated to an element should be recognized when the revenue is earned and realized.

Internally Developed Software.   *Accounting for the Cost of Computer Software Developed for Internal Uses* (SOP 98-1) requires the costs associated with the acquisition and development of software for internal use to be *capitalized* when both of the following occur:

1. Management authorizes and commits to funding a computer software project and believes that it is probable that the project will be completed and the software will be used to perform the function intended.
2. Conceptual formulation, design, and testing of possible software project alternatives have been completed.

Capitalization of costs should cease when the computer software development project is substantially completed and ready for its intended use. This point occurs when substantially all testing is complete.

Thus, companies developing their e-commerce software internally, will find it necessary to:

1. Capitalize the direct costs of the development.
2. Amortize the capitalized cost over the software's useful life.

A high level of uncertainty typically accompanies the introduction of new software applications, such as e-commerce. How reliable are the decisions to commence capitalization of e-commerce development costs and the choice of their related amortization periods?

If there is a question of application for U.S. companies, the issue is of even more concern when dealing with non-U.S. companies. Many of them rely heavily on local accounting standards which may or may not make provision for accounting for software.

Acquisitions and Mergers

Growth through mergers and acquisitions has become a popular e-commerce strategy. E-commerce companies are seeking to benefit from economies of scale by rapidly expanding their share of existing markets and entering new markets. In nearly all of these business combinations, the accounting for in-process research and development and goodwill could be major issues because of the large amount of money involved and the level of uncertainty associated with potential benefits. An acquired company could present a sizable goodwill factor involving market share, software, and people not on the balance sheet.

New accounting rules are now applicable in FASB 141 and FASB 142, which are discussed in Chapter 10.

Contingency Losses

There is a high level of uncertainties associated with e-commerce related contingency losses. Transactions often involve purchases of products and services where the purchaser does not physically inspect the product purchased or interview the service provider directly.

This is not a new phenomenon. Catalog sales companies have operated in this way for many years. The change that the expansion of e-commerce brings is that many companies without any experience in this type of transaction are now engaged in it.

The e-commerce accounting issue that this development raises for these inexperienced companies is:

How do you estimate reliably such contingency losses as returns, volume discounts, and other sales allowances when you do not have an historical record on which to base your estimates of future losses and adjustments?

This uncertainty issue is more important to companies in the U.S. and those other countries, such as the UK, that have contingency losses recognition rules that require reasonable estimates of contingency losses and strictly prohibit the establishment of general reserves.

Start-Up Activities

E-commerce is not a single technology, but rather a sophisticated combination of technologies and consumer-based services integrated to form a new way of conducting business. This new form, however, is still itself in a start-up mode. The future of e-commerce is bright and viable; the application, however, has not been fully integrated into the business mainstream. For many companies, the introduction of e-commerce sales activities could be considered a start-up activity.

Start-up activities are defined broadly as those onetime activities related to opening a new facility, introducing a new product or service, conducting business in a new territory, conducting business with a new class of customer or beneficiary, initiating a new process in an existing facility, or commencing some new operation. Start-up activities include activities related to organizing a new entity.

According to generally accepted accounting practices (GAAP), start-up activity costs must be expensed as incurred. For U.S. companies that add e-commerce sales activities to their traditional business practices, the question will be: Is this a start-up activity?

If it is not, the costs may be capitalized. Again, this raises the issue of the level of uncertainty associated with the amortization period selected. Outside of the U.S., entities and their investors are confronted with a variety of different accounting treatments of e-commerce start-up sales activities.

Since these e-commerce start-up costs can be very material, management, their shareholders and potential investors need to be aware of the costs and the accounting for them.

Nondisclosure

In many companies, e-commerce activities are not carried out by a specific organizational unit. Often these activities will spread throughout the operating activities of many organizational units.

Under U.S. operating segment disclosure rules, as well as those of many other countries, only the organizational unit's operating results need be disclosed. If a company chooses to stick by the rules, investors may not be given the company's e-commerce-related operating results. Since, as noted above, e-commerce start-up activities are often unprofitable, nondisclosure may be detrimental to the interests of investors at least in the short run.

Credit Losses

Electronic payment systems are often an integral part of e-commerce activities. From the accounting point of view, this can be good news and bad news.

From the vendor's point of view, it can be good news since often the buyer's payment is guaranteed by a third party, such as a credit card issuer, that absorbs the bad debt risk. This reduces the uncertainty associated with establishing bad debt reserves.

On the other hand, it can be bad news for the party absorbing the credit risk. With the expansion of e-commerce, many products, customers, sellers, and services outside of the prior experience of the credit grantor will be paid for electronically. Again, the lack of a historical record raises the level of uncertainty associated with making estimates about future events, which in this case is the appropriate level of the bad debt reserve.

Asset Impairments

Radical changes in the way business is conducted have always led to asset impairments. Therefore, it should be expected that the growth of e-commerce may lead to the impairment of some asset groups. In some cases, asset groups used in traditional business activities may be made obsolete by the introduction of e-commerce. In fact, the rapid evolution of e-commerce and its associated technologies will define technical obsolescence in terms of months, not years. The "new" assets may be impaired very quickly. In other circumstances, some asset groups devoted to e-commerce may become impaired as a result of the inability of the company to implement its e-commerce strategy successfully.

Historically, management has been slow to recognize asset impairment losses. This attitude will probably not change; therefore, balance sheets of companies engaging in e-commerce could very possibly include overvalued assets.

Customer Solicitation Costs

Many of the companies engaged in e-commerce will have to spend considerable sums of money to build their e-commerce customer base. Some may capitalize part of these customer solicitation costs.

U.S. accounting standards generally require these customer solicitation costs to be expensed as incurred. The only exception is the cost of direct mail advertising. It can be capitalized only if the company can base the amortization period choice on a reasonable estimate of the direct mailings' response rate. Since for many companies, e-commerce will be a new business activity, they will not have a historical record of response rates upon which to base their estimate of future response rates.

Outside of the U.S., advertising costs are generally accounted for under the local intangible assets rules, which may permit capitalization of advertising costs. Companies with limited e-commerce experience that capitalize direct mail advertising costs must be very cautious since their historical response-rate record may be inadequate.

Materiality

Under generous interpretations of what is *material,* the sales, costs, assets, and liabilities of a company's e-commerce start-up activities may be regarded as *immaterial.* This could be a problem. In recent years, some managers have adopted the point of view that since U.S. GAAP does not apply to immaterial items, they can account for immaterial items in any way they choose.

As shown in Chapter 24 *Materiality,* the SEC has changed all of this. A cavalier attitude toward materiality is unacceptable practice. The new definition of materiality in essence says, "if it's material to investors, it's material." Under this test, relatively small amounts can be material in a high price-earnings ratio-valued stock situation.

Uncertainty

E-commerce is a new form of business and, like many new business forms, there can often be a high level of uncertainty associated with the future prospects of many of those engaging in it. Since accounting involves many estimates of future events, this uncertainty can create major accounting problems involving contingency loss estimates, recognition of intangibles, asset impairment loss recognition, and amortization period choices. Consequently, the reliability of management estimates will be crucial to the welfare of the entity.

E-BUSINESS ACCOUNTING PRINCIPLES AND CRITERIA

Management is responsible for the attainment of the enterprise's objectives *in accordance with the business strategy it has defined.* If an e-business system is used for this purpose, it is important that those in management make appropriate arrangements to manage the ensuing risks. An enterprise's e-business strategy, as an integral part of the information technology (IT) strategy, ordinarily includes consideration of *all aspects of business risks, including IT risks.* Consequently:

1. Management assesses IT risks with respect to information reliability.
2. Information reliability, in turn, depends on IT system reliability.
3. IT system reliability depends on IT controls.

It is important that management implements IT controls that operate effectively to help ensure that an IT system performs reliably. Information generated by an IT system will be reliable where that system is capable of operating without material error, fault, or failure during a specified period. This also applies to accounting information. The following *principles* may be used to evaluate whether processed accounting information is reliable:

1. Principles for accounting information security.
2. Principles for appropriate accounting information processing.

The reliability of accounting information relating to the entire e-business process is increased if the accounting system satisfies both accounting information security principles and the principles for appropriate accounting information processing.

The principles for appropriate accounting information processing are fulfilled where the e-business system and the entire IT system safeguards comply with the following general criteria for the input, processing, output and storage of information and data about e-business transactions:

1. Completeness.
2. Accuracy.
3. Timeliness.
4. Assessability.
5. Order.
6. Inalterability (logging of alterations).

The *completeness* criterion refers to the extent and scope of processed e-business transactions—that is, the recipient of transactions determines that all transactions are input completely into the e-business system. Each transaction should be individually identifiable and recorded separately. The completeness of the recorded entries should be demonstrably preserved throughout processing and for the duration of the retention period.

In accordance with the *accuracy* criterion, processed information should accurately reflect e-business transactions—that is, recorded transactions should reflect the actual events and circumstances in conformity with the applicable financial reporting framework.

Under the *timeliness* criterion, e-business transactions should be recorded on a timely basis—that is, as soon as possible after the transaction has occurred. When time elapses between the occurrence of a transaction and its recording, further appropriate action may become necessary to determine completeness and accuracy of the entry recorded.

Under the criterion of *assessability,* each item and disclosure in the financial statements should be verifiable in that it can be traced back to individual entries in the books and records and to the original source documents that support that entry. Furthermore, the criterion of assessability implies that an expert third party should be able to gain an insight into the transactions and position of the enterprise within a reasonable period of time.

To meet the *order* criteria, accounting entries in an accounting system should be organized in both chronological order (a journal function) and by nature (by type of asset, liability, revenue or expense—a ledger function). Transactions and their recording should be identifiable and capable of conversion into human-readable format in a reasonable period of time.

In accordance with the criterion of *inalterability,* no entry or record may be changed after the posting date so that its original content can no longer be identified, unless the change to the original content can be identified by means of a log of such alterations. Therefore, alterations of entries or records should be made in a way that both the original content and the fact that changes have been made are evident or can be made evident. For program-generated or program-controlled entries (automated or recurring vouchers), changes to the underlying data used to generate and control accounting entries would also be recorded. This applies, in particular, to the logging of modifications of settings relevant to accounting or the parameterization of software and the recording of changes to master data.

Before accepting a transaction for processing, it would be useful to verify the following:

1. That all transaction details have been entered by the customer.
2. The authenticity of the customer.
3. The availability of the products or services to be supplied.
4. The reasonableness of the order, for example, to identify an unusually large quantity resulting from an input error, or to identify erroneous duplicate orders.
5. The pricing structure applied, including delivery costs, where appropriate.
6. The method of payment or credit worthiness of the customer.
7. The non-repudiability of the transaction in that its author cannot later deny having entered into it.

In an e-business process, it is often not possible to provide evidence of transactions by way of conventional vouchers. Despite this fact, transactions should continue to be supported by appropriate documentary evidence (i.e., the source document entry function).

TAXING PROBLEMS

What of the tax accountant? The accounting for e-commerce will require organizations to review current policies and procedures. Accounting concerns such as recording multiple tax payments, which might not be an issue in a paper-based trading environment, could quickly become a major concern. Very possibly, other tax concerns will develop with many more questions than answers:

1. How soon will the federal government decide that it really should get its share from all of these Web sites?
2. Will there be a flat electronic tax applied to every e-business transaction?
3. How will an organization account for and respond to different tax regulations governing commerce as they vary by country, by state, by county, by city?
4. Will there be some form of interstate or intercountry tax?
5. How would these taxes (if forthcoming) affect the cost of doing e-business?
6. Who will collect the appropriate taxes, and how will the taxes be submitted to the proper taxing authority?
7. Will electronic transactions be taxed in their city/state/country of origin or at some other destination (or all of the above)?
8. What new procedures will be designed to account for varying tax revenue, which will be transferred to organizations in distant countries and various states?

These and many additional questions, which affect tax accounting for Web-based commerce, will need to be addressed on an international level. In the meantime, they are being considered here on a national level.

Commission on Electronic Commerce

Even discounting the global aspects of Internet taxation, there are more than enough questions relating to domestic taxes. "The Internet Tax Freedom Act," enacted by Congress in October 1998 established a three-year moratorium on "new Internet tax" and set up the Advisory Commission on Electronic Commerce. It is made up of 19 members—13 representatives from governmental and nonprofit entities and 6 from private-sector industry.

They are assigned the task of conducting a thorough study of "Federal, state and local and international taxation and tariff treatment of transactions using the Internet and Internet access and other comparable intrastate, interstate or international sales activities."

Consensus appears to be growing to extend the ban on levying "new" taxes on the Internet for as much as three-to-five years beyond the present cutoff date of October 22, 2001. In the end, it was extended for only two years to November 1, 2003. But what of the "old" taxes? Yes, there are some and there could be more, regardless of a moratorium.

1. Consumers in some areas are supposed to pay use taxes on those purchases on the Internet for which no sales tax was paid. (In fact, some states include the appropriate tax form in their income tax package as a reminder.)

2. Sales tax must be paid if the buyer lives in a state in which the e-business has a facility such as a retail store, warehouse, or factory in that state. (Therefore, many e-retailers that actually do have a physical site of any variety have located them in the states that have no retail sales tax— Alaska, Delaware, Montana, New Hampshire, and Oregon.)

3. Then there is the distinction between "new" and "old." If the state and local governments begin losing too much tax revenue from e-commerce, they might decide that sales tax is an "old" tax and just extend it to e-commerce.

CAUTIONS FOR E-COMMUNICATION WEB SITE USE

With the Internet now playing an increasingly important role in investing and financial reporting, the Securities and Exchange Commission Private Securities Litigation Reform Act of 1995 (see Chapter 25) may be cited frequently. It is important that companies be aware of pitfalls that could lead to a new wave of litigation.

Following are several cautions that could reduce the legal risks from electronic disclosures, particularly those associated with company Web sites:

1. Meaningful, obvious, clearly worded cautionary disclaimers must accompany any and all "forward-looking" statements.

2. Some of these forward-looking statements may appear in varied guises: transcripts of speeches, press conferences, and quotes should be treated as written disclosures and must include an appropriate written disclaimer situated as closely as possible to the statement.

3. A full set of financial statements and notes should always be included. "Selected" portions, summations, "fractured"financial statements, even a complete set without the footnotes, could be an invitation for litigation.

4. A company should not commit to update disclosures and should include on its Web site disclaimers regarding the absence of any obligation to do so. However, the site should be monitored very closely for any information that is outdated or misleading.

5. Management should be wary of any "selectivity" relating to analysts. Do not frame, inline, or link to analysts' sites or include analysts' comments on the company's site. If a list of analysts covering the company is provided, the names of *all* analysts must be included, not just those with favorable comments.

6. Probably the most cogent advice relating to "chat rooms" (for the company as well as the investor) has come from the chairman of the SEC in a much publicized speech:

   "Chat rooms, which increasingly have become a source of information and misinformation for many investors, have been compared to a high-tech version of morning gossip or advice at the company water cooler. But, at least you knew your co-workers at the water cooler. For the future sake of this medium, I encourage investors to take what they see over chat rooms—not with a grain of salt—but with a rock of salt."

   Obviously, it is in the best interest of the company to establish well-defined policies for employee participation in chat room discussions about their jobs and their organization.

7. Keeping in mind the seemingly never-ending abilities of the "hackers" to access a mainframe and compromise a Web site, it is paramount that there should be continuing reevaluation of a system's security measures.

INTERNATIONAL GUIDANCE HELPS AUDITORS ADDRESS E-COMMERCE RISKS

Increasing use of the Internet for e-business related to various modes of business relationships is introducing new elements of risk that need to be considered by accountants when planning and performing the audit of financial statements. These business relationships include:

- Business to consumer.
- Business to business.
- Business to government.
- Business to employee.

To assist auditors in identifying and assessing these risks, IFAC's International Auditing Practices Committee (now the International Auditing and Assurance Standards Board, or IAASB) issued a new practice statement, *Electronic Commerce—Effect on the Audit of Financial Statements,* in May, 2002. (The IAASB is an IFAC committee that works to improve the uniformity of auditing practices and related services throughout the world by issuing pronouncements on a variety of audit and assurance functions and by promoting their acceptance worldwide.)

Such usage is introducing new elements of risk that need to be considered by accountants when planning and performing the audit of financial statements.

Impetus for the study was the realization that growth of Internet activity without close attention *by the entity* to those risks could affect the auditor's assessments of the risks. It was pointed out that an entity's e-commerce strategy could affect the security of the financial records and the completeness and reliability of the financial information produced. Even with "due diligence" by the most sophisticated IT technician, hackers appear to be able to access almost any computer. But that doesn't mean that every effort should not be made to enhance security.

Focus of Attention

To assist auditors in identifying and assessing the risks, this new International Auditing Practice Statement (IAPS) helps auditors address e-commerce issues by focusing on the following:

1. The level of skills and knowledge required to understand the effect of e-commerce on the audit.
2. The extent of knowledge the auditor should have about the entity's business environment, activities and industries.
3. Business, legal, regulatory, and other risks faced by entities engaged in e-commerce activities.
4. Internal control considerations, such as an entity's security infrastructure and transaction integrity.
5. The effect of electronic records on audit evidence.

The guidance in this statement is particularly relevant to the application of three International Standards on Auditing (ISAs): ISA 300, *Planning;* ISA 310, *Knowledge of the Business;* and ISA 400, *Risk Assessments and Internal Controls.*

The statement was written for situations in which an organization engages in commercial activity over a public network, such as the Internet. However, much of the guidance it contains can also be applied when the entity uses a private network.

While much of the guidance will be helpful to accountants engaged in auditing entities organized primarily for e-commerce activities, or "dot.coms," it is not intended to deal with all audit issues that could be addressed in the audit of such entities. Furthermore, additional accounting information related to e-commerce is provided in a paper described below.

IFAC Issues New Paper on E-Business

"E-Business and the Accountant: Risk Management for Accounting Systems in an E-Business Environment" issued by IFAC presents certain risk management aspects of e-business relevant to accounting and financial reporting from a managerial perspective.

Directed to the management of organizations, including accountants, "E-Business and the Accountant" points out how e-business changes the way business is conducted and that e-business consequently introduces new risks that enterprises may need to address by implementing a technology infrastructure and controls to mitigate those risks. The paper points out that e-business and its technological environment will have a significant impact on accounting systems and the evidence available to support business transactions, which in turn will lead to changes in the accounting records maintained and accounting procedures followed.

The document notes that accountants and auditors may be faced with new challenges and regulations and may need to:

1. Apply new techniques in an e-business environment.
2. Develop accounting systems based on the business processes employed.
3. Ensure that transactions are appropriately recorded.
4. See that transactions are in compliance with local and international legislation and regulations.
5. Abide by current and evolving accounting standards and guidance.

To help minimize risks in relation to these issues, the paper provides a useful framework of concepts with which accountants and others can analyze e-business from an accounting point of view. It includes best practice guidelines on e-business accounting principles and criteria, such as accounting information security and accounting information processing. It also outlines criteria for a functioning accounting system.

THE IASC STUDY: *BUSINESS REPORTING ON THE INTERNET*

The International Accounting Standards Committee published a study of business and financial reporting on the Internet in November, 1999, as the first step in a possible project to develop accounting standards in that area.

The study examines:

1. The current technologies available for electronic business reporting.
2. What companies around the world are actually doing (this involved a detailed analysis of the Web sites of the 30 largest companies in each of 22 countries, 660 companies in all).

3. The sort of standards for electronic business reporting that are needed now, within the constraint of today's technologies.
4. The shortcomings of financial reporting on the Internet within current technologies.
5. The technological changes that are on the horizon and how they can improve electronic reporting.

Changes in Paper Financial Reports

Technology has altered irreversibly not only the physical medium of corporate financial reporting, but also its traditional boundaries. The Committee realized that paper reports are being supplemented—and, for many users, replaced—by electronic business reporting, primarily via the Internet. They became aware that investors and lenders had moved far beyond traditional financial statements and related note disclosures.

Four experts from the academic world authored the IASC study, *Business Reporting on the Internet.* It illustrates to accounting policy makers the nature of changes occurring in business reporting and explains how those changes are affecting the dissemination of accounting and financial information.

The study also identifies the effects those changes may have on accounting standard-setting in the future. The report charts a course of IASC—and, in fact, the rest of the accounting world—to follow in helping to ensure that high-quality electronic data is available for the users of business and financial information.

A Code of Conduct for Web-Based Business Reporting

Among other recommendations, the study urges IASC to adopt a Code of Conduct for Web-based business reporting. The report is designed to enhance the quality of business reporting information provided on the Web by corporations. The authors of the suggested Code are quick to point out that it is not intended to be a permanent solution to resolving the issues related to business reporting online since technology will continue to change and develop, and user expectations and demands will change. A complete draft of a proposed Code is included in the report.

E-Business Reporting Language

The study recommends that a global electronic business reporting language (BRL) be developed to meet the needs of those who look to the Internet for financial and operating information.

Those represented in the consortium should include:

1. The IASC.
2. Global information distributors.

3. Software developers.
4. Securities regulators.
5. National accounting standard setters.
6. International accounting firms.
7. Others. (Presumably "others" will become evident as e-business and e-communication become better defined!)

FASB's Business Reporting Research Project

Many organizations are interested in this new information technology and do in-depth studies to discover the advantages as well as the pitfalls of its use. The FASB is one of the most recent to publish a very comprehensive study.

The Three-Part Study

The report, *Electronic Distribution of Business Reporting Information,* published in January 2000, is the first section of a broader study—the Business Reporting Research Project. The objective of the FASB is to determine the kind of business information corporations are reporting outside of financial statements.

The first portion describes the electronic distribution of business information and investigates the possibilities and problems of the Internet on the reporting process.

The second will deal with the redundancies between SEC and FASB reporting requirements, thus helping to eliminate overlapping and duplication.

A third portion will discuss the results of 10 selected industries' business reporting practices.

Objectives of the First Study

Growth of the Internet as a medium for delivering business reporting information has altered the way that information flows from companies to investors and creditors. The structure will continue to change as companies bring new technologies to the process and as information users find new ways to access and analyze information.

The stated objectives of the first FASB study were to:

1. Survey the state of reporting information over the Internet.
2. Identify notable practices.

Financial Information Online

More and more companies are using the Internet to disseminate information about themselves. This includes stock quotes and the latest annual report, as well as forward-looking information, detailed plans about new products and services, and other material from outside the financial statements.

The Internet offers vast amounts of fiinancial information available to the nonspecialist investor and allows delivery of that information instantaneously and at very low cost. Any investor with a computer and a modem can obtain information that was previously available, as a practical matter, only to a limited range of company officials, professional investment analysts, and the financial press.

Some of the present practices observed in the report include:

1. Transcripts of management presentations.
2. Analyst's reports on the company.
3. Traditional financial information.
4. Live and archived audio-visual versions of meetings that were previously open only to selected analysts.

The FASB report discusses legal and other issues that are of interest to companies using or thinking about using the Internet for distributing business information.

THE SEC ON REPORTING IN THE NEW ECONOMY

As the Securities and Exchange Commission makes quite evident, they are not about to let e-communication and e-trading progress too far without adequate protection for the investor. New industries, spurred by new services and new technologies, are creating new questions and challenges that must be addressed.

Rules for valuation of manufacturing inventory or assessing what a factory is worth are well established. But what of the value of R&D invested in a software program, or the value of a user base on an Internet shopping site? As intangible assets continue to grow in size and scope, more and more people are questioning whether the true value—and the drivers of that value—is being reflected in a timely manner in publicly available disclosure.

To look into these questions, a group of leaders from the business community, academia, the accounting profession, standard-setting bodies, and corporate America is being formed to examine whether the current business reporting framework can more effectively handle these changes in our economy.

As always, the SEC embraces free market principles to foster greater competition, while ensuring effective regulatory oversight to protect investor interest. To that effect, they are simultaneously taking a very close look at the many complaints about online trading.

ELECTRONIC DATA INTERCHANGE (EDI)

Electronic commerce involves individuals as well as organizations engaging in a variety of electronic business transactions (without paper documents) using computer and telecommunication networks. These networks can be either private or public, or a combination of the two. Actually the big leap in e-business has been in conducting business over the Internet (specifically the Web).

This is due to the Web's surge in popularity and the acceptance of the Internet as a viable transport mechanism for business information. The use of a public network-based infrastructure like the Internet can reduce costs and make it feasible for small as well as large companies to extend their services and products to a broad customer base.

Electronic commerce has been defined as a means of conducting business electronically via online transactions *between merchants and consumers;* traditionally, the definition of electronic commerce had focused on EDI as the primary means of conducting business electronically *between entities having a preestablished contractual relationship.*

EDI involves computer application-to-computer application transmission of business documents in a predetermined, standard format. While e-commerce is targeted for global trading and is suited to anyone interested in online commerce, EDI is best suited for a selected group of trading partners.

EDI improves business operations dealing with high volumes of transactions by providing electronic information exchange between those trading partners. Such an established electronic connection reduces data entry errors by eliminating repetitive tasks and lowers administrative overhead costs associated with paper-based processing methods.

E-commerce and EDI, whatever its nature, will require accounting professionals of those organizations using the new technology to reexamine the nature of the entity's business practices and the manner in which transactions are recorded. This might be especially true for organizations which, up until their entrance into e-commerce, had only domestic trading partners and never sold directly to the consumer. E-commerce is changing the conduct of business, as most organizations have known it.

THE CPA WEBTRUST AND SMALL BUSINESS

WebTrust is a comprehensive seal of assurance for e-commerce sites developed jointly by the American Institute of Certified Public Accountants (AICPA) and the Canadian Institute of Chartered Accountants (CICA). The designers believe that WebTrust can help small businesses build consumer confidence necessary for electronic commerce to reach its full potential.

Testimony Before the House

In testimony before the House Committee on Small Business, one AICPA official suggested that small Web-based businesses rely upon the accounting profession to provide assurance services like CPA WebTrust which are designed to make cyberspace a safer place to shop. Another of the AICPA officials identified their goal, as trusted CPAs, to raise awareness of WebTrust to the point where consumers around the world seek out small business Web sites with WebTrust seals as the safest, most secure place to shop on the Internet.

Advantages of Assurance Services

The AICPA considers WebTrust a way to level the playing field for small, online businesses. Although they do not benefit from nationally recognized brand names, they still may assure their customers that the Web site has met the most comprehensive e-commerce standards to protect consumers online.

These standards, known as the *WebTrust Principles and Criteria,* ensure that the site:

1. Discloses its business practices for e-commerce transactions to Web site visitors.
2. Follows these business practices.
3. Has appropriate controls so that transactions executed at the site are completed as ordered.
4. Protects the privacy of customer information and financial data.

The program licenses CPAs to certify the sites to ensure that electronic transactions meet high standards. Those that do will display the CPA WebTrust "seal," assuring consumers that these sites are trustworthy and reliable, and that consumer information will remain confidential.

Handling Consumer Complaints

WebTrust provides a consumer complaint mechanism that allows consumers to resolve problems about product quality and customer service. This mechanism enhances the assurance service with binding third-party arbitration. Consumers or businesses that have problems with a WebTrust certified company can file a claim online with the independent third party, the National Arbitration Forum, through a link provided on the CPA WebTrust site.

The designers anticipate that giving credibility to small business Web sites through WebTrust can help an entity to:

1. Build a worldwide customer base.
2. Develop global electronic commerce.
3. Deliver on their sales promises.
4. Build a loyal, online customer base.
5. Build consumer confidence.
6. Help reduce risk of online fraud.

AICPA officials testified that they believe WebTrust, CPAs and their international counterparts to be uniquely qualified to examine online businesses to determine:

1. If the business is legitimate.
2. Its transactions are secure.
3. The information it collects from consumers is kept private.

CONGRESS LEARNS ABOUT SYSTRUST

The Enron matter has focused significant attention on the audit and financial statements. Some of the discussion concerns the increasing need for more timely information and the *reliance* on information systems. Recently, a representative of the AICPA addressed Congress regarding the profession's perspective and its related service offering, SysTrust.

What Are SysTrust Services?

More organizations have become dependent on information technology to run their businesses, produce products and services and communicate with customers and business partners. The AICPA representative pointed out that it is critical that their systems be secure, available when needed, and consistently able to produce accurate information. An unreliable system can trigger a chain of business events that negatively affect a company, its customers, suppliers, and business partners. In response to this business need, the AICPA and the Canadian Institute of Chartered Accountants (CICA) introduced a new professional service called SysTrust, which enables a CPA to provide assurance that a system is reliable.

SysTrust uses the following four principles to evaluate whether a system is reliable:

1. *Availability*—Does the system operate and provide information in accordance with its stated availability and is it accessible when routine processing and maintenance must be performed?

2. *Security*—Is the system protected against unauthorized physical and logical access? Logical access is the ability to read or manipulate data through remote access. Restricting system access helps prevent:

   a. Potential abuse of system components,

   b. Theft of system resources,

   c. Misuse of system software, and

   d. Improper access to and use of information.

3. *Integrity*—Is system processing complete, accurate, timely and authorized?

4. *Maintainability*—Can the system be updated to provide continued availability, security and integrity?

Criteria were established for each of these principles to enable a CPA to evaluate the reliability of a system. These criteria are included in the document, *AICPA/CICA SysTrust Principles and Criteria for Systems Reliability, Version 2.0*.

THE AICPA PLANS TO COMBINE WEBTRUST AND SYSTRUST

The AICPA/CICA is releasing for comment an exposure draft of the *Trust Services Principle and Criteria*. The principles and criteria contained in this program supersede Version 3.0 of the WebTrust principles and criteria and Version 2.0 of the SysTrust principles and criteria and were effective for examination periods beginning after August 31, 2002.

The exposure draft information included transition information, the revised principles and criteria, reporting examples and illustrative disclosures for e-commerce. The *Trust Services Principles and Criteria* are intended to address user and preparer needs regarding issues of security, availability, processing integrity, online privacy and confidentiality within e-commerce and non-e-commerce systems.

Services Have Not Reached a Broad Market

Evidently, this step is being taken because neither attestation service— WebTrust nor SysTrust—has been the successful product the AICPA had hoped each would be. Lack of acceptance of the products can be demonstrated by the fact that, after several years, WebTrust's Web site lists only 26 Web sites that display the WebTrust seal. A representative of the AICPA claimed that "hundreds" of the much less expensive SysTrust engagements have been completed. Hence, the overhaul and at a time when businesses might be more interested in attestation services.

The AICPA will combine the separate principles for each service into one set of principles for a broader program that would apply to future WebTrust and SysTrust engagements. The merged services could also be applied to other attest and consulting work.

It is planned that the program will have one licensing standard for practitioners, rather than the separate standards now required by WebTrust and SysTrust. Another change could be that electronic reports or seals, similar to those awarded to WebTrust, would be added to SysTrust, which now uses paper-based certification.

The two trust services, jointly developed by the AICPA and the CICA in the late 1990s, provide guidance that enables auditors to issue opinions on the key technologies employed by most businesses today. SysTrust attests to the reliability of client companies' internal technology systems, and WebTrust attests to the reliability of Web sites and associated electronic commerce systems and business practices.

The reason the AICPA gives for the move toward one set of principles is an effort to alleviate confusion about the programs and to increase CPAs' potential to derive consulting engagements from them.

The new approach, in essence, revises the three criteria (availability, security and integrity) shared by both services so that they can be applied to both services. Principles that apply only to WebTrust—those related to protecting the privacy of Web site visitors—will remain applicable only to that service.

Having one set of principles for both services would alleviate that market confusion and could also make it easier for CPAs to provide either or both of the services, according to the AICPA. The organization has said that the reported number of completed engagements is misleading because practitioners have handled numerous SysTrust and WebTrust engagements in which they performed only the portion of the attest service that was requested by the client. Although the clients are not added to a completed engagement count for either service, in each case, CPAs have provided a value-added and billable service, the AICPA explained.

Both WebTrust and SysTrust are available in modules, meaning that client companies can request attestation of only the particular part of the service that applies to their businesses. Consultants agree that the planned merger would help eliminate any confusion. Combining WebTrust and SysTrust could make a strong, less confusing statement, to a public that will discover it needs these services.

GLOSSARY OF TERMS

This glossary provides common definitions of some of the terms in contacts with clients or e-business vendors. Some of the definitions have been simplified for conciseness and ease of understanding. We are all familiar with many of the terms, although we would be hard-pressed actually to define them, thus:

Affiliate Programs. Cooperative arrangements that involve providing a link to another Web site in exchange for a commission on purchases made by users following that link to the other Web site.

Access Provider. An intermediary remote computer system through which a user may then connect to the Internet.

Acrobat Reader. A software application from Adobe that provides the formatted display of documents in portable document format (see PDF).

Applet. A JAVA program designed to perform a specific task within a larger program. Applets may be embedded and run from within another application such as a Web page.

Applications Programming Interface. A program or data mapping mechanism that allows separate applications to work together by mapping data in one application to the format required in another application.

Application Service Provider (ASP). An organization that provides software applications over the Internet. A common example is an Internet Service provider (ISP).

ADSL. See Asymmetric Digital Subscriber Line.

ASP. See Application Service Provider

Asymmetric Digital Subscriber (ADSL). A dedicated connection to the Internet that is suitable for individual and small business use. It is quicker for downloads than for uploads.

Authentication (authorization). The process a computer used to "verify" a user attempting to access the computer. Authentication may include user names, passwords, encryption, digital security certificates and signatures and other forms of security checking prior to allowing access to a computer, Web site, systems, files or data.

Auto-Responder. A feature of some e-mail programs that can be set to provide an automatic response to incoming messages. It is frequently used by business to acknowledge the receipt of a customer's messages and to provide a timeframe for the response. It is also used by individual employees to send a response to messages when they are out of the office.

Backbone. A top-level, high-speed connection to the Internet that serves as a major access point for ISPs and major users of the Internet (e.g., large business).

Bandwidth. The amount of information that can be carried through a communication system in a set time.

Banner. A graphical display, usually an ad, that is displayed on a Web page.

Bit. A single binary value, either 0 or 1, used to store data or provide instructions to a computer. Bits are collected in multiples, called bytes, to form the instructions to run the computer.

Bookmarks/Favorites. A list of Web pages visited and to which one will likely return that are created by Internet browsers, such as Netscape and Internet Explorer. These bookmarks are direct links to the Web page.

Browser. A user interface program that allows access to the Internet. The most well-known browsers are Internet Explorer and Netscape Navigator.

Business Intelligence (BI). Organizing, searching, analyzing and reporting trends or business specific information from data contained in Web sites, business applications and/or databases.

Business Process Reengineering (BPR). Analysis and reengineering of specific business processes and management systems to eliminate redundancy and non-value-added steps and to improve efficiency and performance.

Certificates. A security mechanism used in Internet communications to ensure that the Web site and data or communications conducted with it are trusted and secure.

C-Commerce (Collaborative Commerce). Technology-enabled business interactions among anyone involved in a business process, including internal employees, suppliers, business partners and customers.

Contact Center. A component of customer relationship management (CRM), that is a centralized support center for all customer contact channels, including phone, e-mail, Internet, fax, mail or other forms of communication between customers and their providers of goods or services.

Cookie. A small text file that is put on users' hard drives when they visit a Web page so that other Web pages can remember certain information about the user.

Customer Relationship Management (CRM). An organizational strategy to maximize revenue, profitability and brand loyalty by focusing business processes and information analysis around customer intelligence. Key investment in technologies that connect internal business systems with external customer-facing systems to improve response to customer demands and related product, revenue and profitability mixes.

Database Management System (DBMS). Software that enables systematic data storage and retrieval in a repeatable mechanism to create, update and report on large amounts of data.

Data Mining. Sorting and analyzing trends or meaningful patterns across large amounts of data.

Digital Signature. A code that can be attached to a transmission (e.g., e-mail message, order request) that authenticates the sender.

Domain Name. A name designated to represent a location on the Internet, such as the address for a Web site.

Domain Name Server (DNS). A server that associates a number (an Internet Protocol, or IP address) with a text-based domain name.

DNS. See Domain Name System.

E-Business. All activities conducted by a business over the Internet.

E-Commerce. The procurement and distribution of goods and services over the Internet using digital technology.

E-Marketplace. An online marketplace where buyers and sellers can exchange goods and services. Normally relates to business-to-business transactions.

Encryption. The encoding of a message or electronic transmission to prevent unauthorized access.

Enterprise Resource Planning (ERP). Large-scale business software applications that support key management functions of the enterprise, such as financial, manufacturing, human resources, procurement, customer relationship management and other key business processes.

Favorites. See Bookmarks.

FAQ. See Frequently Asked Questions.

Firewall. Hardware and software used to prevent unauthorized access to a computer or network.

Frequently Asked Questions (FAQs). A list of answers to commonly asked questions, especially on a Web site.

GIF. See Graphics Interchange Format.

Graphical User Interface (GUI). A graphical tool that allows users to access the features and functionalities of a software application. On the Web, it refers to the parts of the Web site the users actually see, and would not include the back end software such as the database and programs that power the site.

Graphics Interchange Format (GIF). One of the two common formats for graphics on the Web (the other being JPEG).

Hyperlink. A highlighted link or graphic within a hypertext document or Web page that will take the user to another place within the same Web page or to another Web site or page.

Intranet. A secure network within a company accessible only by internal users of the company network. Intranets are protected by firewalls and other security mechanisms that prevent unsecure parties from accessing internal data.

Java. A programming language developed by SUN Microsystems that has been widely adopted for developing Internet applications.

JPEG. A compression format used for Internet graphics or images.

Knowledge Management (KM). An organizational strategy to use technology to capture, organize, access and manage the "knowledge" assets of a business. The deployment of "content management" systems to provide storage, search, retrieval and use of information assets across collaborative groups of people within an organization.

Middleware. Software applications that support integration of different data, programs, databases, and Web sites across or between multiple computer systems.

PDF (Portable Document Format). A file format created by Adobe that delivers and displays an entire document with text and complex graphics in a single readable file.

PDA (Personal Digital Assistant). Any small, mobile, handheld device that creates, stores and retrieves data. Many PDAs may also connect to the Internet through wireless technology for sending and retrieving data such as e-mail.

Permission Marketing. Involves persuading customers to physically request that marketing information be sent to them (sometimes called opt-in marketing).

Personalization. Individual user's ability to configure their own preferences for information selection and display on their access pages to a Web site or application.

POP (Post Office Protocol or Point Of Presence). Refers to the way that e-mail software gets mail from a mail server. Point of presence usually refers to the locations where a dial-up connection to a mail server is available.

Portal. A Web site used as a primary starting point to get to other Web sites. It often refers to search directories such as Yahoo and Search engines such as Google.

Search Directory. A human-compiled directory of information on the Web sorted under meaningful categories (e.g., Yahoo, About, open directory).

Search Engine. A computer program that automatically seeks out Web sites, creates an index of these sites and then allows you to search the index (e.g., Altavista, Alltheweb, Hotbot).

Secure Sockets Layer (SSL). A communication protocol developed to securely transmit data on the Internet. Data is encrypted prior to being transferred over SSL to its destination. Many Web sites support SSL to confidentially process user information, such as credit card payments.

Service-Level Agreement (SLA). An agreement between an ASP and a user that describes the level of service expected throughout the duration of the contract.

SLA. See Service-Level Agreement.

SPAM. A term used to describe unsolicited and unwanted messages sent to an e-mail address or to an online discussion group.

Splash Page. An initial web page that is used to capture the user's attention and is usually a lead-in to the home page.

Structure Query Language (SQL). A standard programming language use for updating and retrieving data from a database.

SSL. See Secure Sockets Layer.

Stickiness. A term used to describe the ability of a Web site to keep users on the site. Usually measured by the average length of time visitors spend on a Web site.

Supply Chain Management (SCM). Technology-based applications that support and optimize the process of planning, producing, ordering, stocking, delivering and supporting goods, services and information from a supplier to a customer.

T1 (also T3). High-speed, high-bandwidth, dedicated connections to the internet. T1 offers 20 times the bandwidth of a 56K modem. A T3 connection is made up of 28 T1 lines.

24/7. Refers to services offered 24 hours a day, 7 days a week.

Traffic. Refers to the amount of visitors that a Web site receives.

Telephony. A general term applied to any type of voice communication as opposed to data communication.

URL. See Uniform Resource Locator.

Uniform Resource Locator (URL). Another way of describing a Web page address. When a URL is entered into a Web browser, it will be bring the user to that site.

Viral Marketing. Involves using the customer as a sales person to encourage others to use a product/service.

Web Site. Generally a set of Web pages all located within the same URL.

World Wide Web (or WWW or the Web). A series of hypertext markup language (HTML) documents all connected using the Internet.

www. See World Wide Web.

Workflow Management. Supports the ability to define specific business rules or data events that are automatically routed to users and managers for review or action.

AN E-BUSINESS CHECKLIST

Keys to the success of any project include executive support and constant communication. Usually a steering committee of executives is established to report regularly on a project. This allows project decisions to be made quickly. Any business policy or business process change requires this. "Quickly" is often important because usually any decision that delays a project adds costs to the project.

Using this checklist could assist in developing successful project policies.

1. Is there an executive who can serve as a project liaison with senior management?

    ☐ yes   ☐ no

2. Is there a cross-departmental team of both business and Information Technology users assigned to the implementation of the project?
□ yes □ no

3. Are the business objectives of both the organization and the project clearly identified and agreed upon?
□ yes □ no

4 Are business and information managers fully aware of the plans and strategies of the organization?
□ yes □ no

5. What benefits and improvements can be expected from this project, and how will they be measured?

_____

_____

_____

6. Which business processes will be improved, and how will customers benefit?

_____

_____

_____

7. Are the people involved in the project development and implementation capable and reliable?
□ yes □ no

8. Are there sufficient resources to implement the new project while adequately supporting the old system?
□ yes □ no

9. Has the total cost of the project been identified and estimated, including staffing, training, and any external consulting that may be required?
□ yes □ no

10. Has a detailed business case, supported by resource and technical plans, been prepared along with a proper project proposal?
□ yes □ no

11. Can the implementation of the project be "phased" in stages to deliver incremental early successes as opposed to the "big bang" approach in which success is not identified until the entire project is complete?
□ yes □ no

12. Is there an experienced project leader dedicated full time to the management of the teams, tasks, and external consultants on a daily basis?
□ yes □ no

13. Have effective means of communicating developments and progress to all staff members been put in place?

    ☐ yes   ☐ no

14. Have the role, responsibilities and time commitment of the people involved been clearly set out and accepted by them?

    ☐ yes   ☐ no

15. Are information and communication strategies and systems reviewed frequently?

    ☐ yes   ☐ no

16. Is it possible to benchmark the business and information systems against those of the company's peers and competitors?

    ☐ yes   ☐ no

17. Does the project help achieve the strategic objectives of the business?

    ☐ yes   ☐ no

Chapter 28

Internet Accounting

CONTENTS

Issues Related to Internet Accounting	**28.02**
Targeted Areas in Accounting for Internet Activities	**28.02**
Quality Accounting Needed	**28.03**
EITF 01-9, Accounting for Considerations from Vendor to Retailer	**28.04**
Gross versus Net	**28.07**
Definition of Software	**28.16**
Revenue Recognition	**28.19**
Updated Status of EITF 00-22 Relating to Various Incentives	**28.30**
Prepaid/Intangible Assets versus Period Costs	**28.31**
Miscellaneous Issues	**28.33**
Catch-All Issue for Problems Not Yet Considered	**28.36**
If All Else Fails	**28.37**
Top 10 Technologies and Tech Issues	**28.38**

With anything new, many and varied practices spring up. Some variations are a result of different people attempting to explain a similar situation in as logical a manner as possible. Other variations have arisen as a result of less fair-minded individuals attempting to show a situation to the best advantage for themselves. Or it may be that the variations stem from mere ineptitude to downright chicanery.

This phenomenon is as true of Internet business accounting practices as it is of any other innovation. Who better to try to bring order to a rather chaotic state of development than the Chief Accountant's Office of the Security and Exchange Commission?

The SEC's stated purpose is to protect the investor. How companies recognize revenue for the goods and services they offer and, in turn, how this appears on their financial report have become increasingly important issues. Some investors have been known to value Internet-based companies on a multiple of revenues, rather than a multiple of gross profit or earnings. Such a valuation may be satisfactory for a while, but may lead to dismay down the road.

The last year has borne out this concern. Many Internet company stocks that were once $100, $200, or even $300-level stocks are now trading at penny stock levels. Their previous lofty price levels were based upon earnings expectations that never would have existed had shareholders' investment practices conformed to conventional beliefs related to balance sheets, financial statements, and other commonly accepted accounting standards.

Furthermore, a recently completed study by a major brokerage analyst indicates that, with a historic snapshot of stocks that fell to penny stock levels over the past decade, the likelihood of these stocks recovering anything approaching their previous levels is virtually nil.

Issues Related to Internet Accounting

Late in 1999, the Chief Accountant of the SEC sent a letter to the Director of Research and Technical Activities of the Financial Accounting Standards Board. He suggested that the Emerging Issues Task Force (or another standard-setting body) should deal with a list of issues that had arisen in Internet businesses.

Attached to the letter was a list of 20 accounting issues developed by the SEC staff. The list included those issues they believed warranted consideration by a standard-setting body with suggested priority levels for addressing each of the issues (priority levels 1–3). However, they expected that all of the issues should eventually be addressed.

The staff agreed that several issues could best be addressed by staff announcements.

Targeted Areas in Accounting for Internet Activities

The list comprises accounting on issues the SEC staff had dealt with in registrant filings, as well as issues identified through input from accounting firms. One or more of the following applies to all of these issues:

1. There appears to be a diversity in practice.

2. The situation does not appear to be addressed in existing accounting literature.

3. The SEC staff is concerned that the developing practice may be inappropriate under generally accepted accounting principles (GAAP).

Some of the issues arise because of the new business models used in Internet operations, while others are issues that also exist in businesses with no Internet operations. It was pointed out that advertising partnerships, coupon and rebate programs, and complex equity instruments, while perhaps more common in Internet businesses, were in use long before the Internet. As a general rule, the SEC staff believes that Internet companies engaging in transactions that are similar to transactions entered into by traditional companies should follow the already established accounting models for those transactions.

The SEC believes that all of the issues discussed deserved further consideration by the accounting and financial reporting community. Each issue represents an area in which investors benefit from improved financial information and consistency as a result of providing additional guidance on the issue. In order to maximize the benefits of providing such guidance, the Commission believes it is important that guidance address not only recognition and measurement questions, but also classification and disclosures.

For each issue, the SEC staff added comments regarding the issue, and an assessment of the priority for addressing the issue.

QUALITY ACCOUNTING NEEDED

After careful consideration of the "call to accountability" letter from the SEC's chief accountant, it would appear that the Task Force (and the SEC, for that matter) really believe that the new economy is not so much in need of "new accounting," as of *quality* accounting. Basically, the Emerging Issues Task Force (EITF) has resolved many of the issues by reference to interpretations and guidance found in existing accounting pronouncements. Regardless of the rather complex list of perceived abuses and inconsistencies referred to, the solutions do not appear to require radical changes to traditional accounting models.

In addition to the EITF's discussion and consensus in the attempt to correct the various questionable accounting practices of Internet companies, the Financial Accounting Standards Board (FASB) is planning a Standard on revenue recognition. The SEC Accounting Bulletin (SAB) 101 is reliable guidance relating to revenue recognition, but it is *required* for publicly traded companies only. On the other hand, until the FASB does adopt a Standard in two or three years, all accountants and companies would be wise to know it well.

EITF 01-9, ACCOUNTING FOR CONSIDERATIONS FROM VENDOR TO RETAILER

In attempting to bring a little more organization to various aspects of accounting for vendor/customer/reseller transactions, EITF Issue 01-9 *Accounting for Consideration Given by a Vendor to a Customer or a Reseller of the Vendor's Products,* brings together three EITF Issues on the topic. This might almost be called a "vendor's omnibus issue."

Issues 00-14, *Accounting for Certain Sales Incentives;* 00-22, *Accounting for "Points" and Certain Other Time-Based or Volume-Based Sales Incentive Offers, and Offers for Free Products or Services to be Delivered in the Future;* and 00-25, *Vendor Income Statement Characterization of Consideration from a Vendor to a Retailer,* have addressed various aspects of the accounting for consideration given by a vendor to a customer or a reseller of the vendor's products. Issue 01-9 is an effort to codify and reconcile the Task Force consensuses on those varied but related Issues. It also identifies other related interpretive issues that resulted from this codification.

Issues 1 and 2 are basically concerned with income statement treatment of cash consideration, including sales incentives. The Task Force reached a consensus requiring a *reduction in revenue* for cash consideration (including sales incentives) given by vendors unless *both* of the following conditions are true:

1. The vendor has received, or will receive, a benefit that is sufficiently separable from the customer's purchase of products and services from the vendor.
2. A reasonable estimate of the fair value of this benefit is available.

When these conditions are met, the consideration is to be treated as a cost. The excess of consideration paid over the fair value of the benefit received must be reported as a *reduction in revenue.*

Vendors must also treat as cost any "free" products or services given to customers. Although the EITF did not reach a consensus on the income statement display of such costs, the SEC staff considers such costs to be *components of cost of sales.* Slotting fees and other similar product development or placement fees are to be reported as *reductions in revenue.* Because this EITF applies to both intermediate and final resellers, their cooperative advertising and marketing programs are subject to this consensus.

Issue 1.   Issue 1 considers how a vendor should account for an offer to a customer (in connection with a current revenue transaction) for free or discounted products or services from the vendor that is redeemable by the customer at a future date without a further exchange transaction with the vendor.

The Task Force reached a consensus that transactions that involve offers by a vendor to a customer for free or discounted products or services are multiple deliverable transactions. This issue refers back to Issue 00-21 for further evaluation.

Issue 2.   Issue 2 covers how to clarify the scope and application of paragraph 16 of EITF 00-25, which addresses vendor consideration at the inception of the relationship with a customer or reseller. The Task Force reached a consensus that paragraph 16 of Issue 00-25:

1. Applies to variable consideration, including equity instruments accounted for in accordance with Issue 96-18, for which a measurement date has not yet occurred.
2. Precludes a vendor from recharacterizing as an expense consideration that otherwise meets the conditions in paragraph 16 that permits expense characterization, if a portion of that consideration is not immediately recognized in the income statement. This also applies if, by the time that consideration is recognized in the income statement, there is cumulative revenue from the reseller.
3. Does not preclude a vendor from characterizing as an expense that portion of consideration that a vendor remits, or is obligated to remit, at the beginning of the overall relationship with a reseller that exceeds the amount of probable future revenue to be received from the reseller.

The Task Force also agreed that a purchase commitment or exclusive arrangement is not necessary to conclude that future revenues are probable. Financial statements for annual or interim periods beginning after December 15, 2001, must reflect these consensuses.

Issue 3.   Issue 3 considers whether the consensus on Issue 2 of Issue 00-14 (regarding when to recognize and how to measure a sales incentive when there is a loss on the sale) should apply to arrangements within the scope of Issue 00-25. This applies to arrangements for which the sum of the consideration from the vendor and the vendor's estimated cost of sales are expected to exceed the estimated revenues from the reseller.

The Task Force reached a consensus that Issue 2 of Issue 00-14 should not apply to arrangements within the scope of Issue 00-25.

Issue 4.   Issues 4, 5, and 6 are particularly concerned with:

1. The timing—when to recognize the transaction.
2. How to measure the cost of the incentive.

In Issue 4, relating to sales incentive offered without charge to the customer and voluntarily by the vendor, the Task Force reached a consensus requiring the recognition of the cost of such incentives at the later of the following:

1. The date at which the related revenue is recognized by the vendor.
2. The date at which the sales incentive is offered.

This consensus was to be applied no later than in financial statements for annual or interim periods beginning after December 15, 2001. Additionally, Issue 4 is concerned with how the impact of changes in estimates (or other factors based on the guidance in paragraphs 14-17 of Issue 00-25 that result in fluctuations in negative revenue during multiple financial reporting periods) should be presented in the income statement.

The Task Force reached a consensus that for the purposes of applying the guidance in paragraphs 14 through 17 of Issue 00-25, each financial reporting period must stand on its own. If an amount is classified as an expense in one period, amounts presented in the income statement for that period must not be reclassified later, even if that approach results in a credit to expense in a later period.

Issue 5.   Issue 5 deals with whether the Issue 00-25 income statement characterization applies to the amortization of an exclusive arrangement that is valued in a purchase business combination.

The Task Force reached a consensus that the Issue 00-25 income statement characterization model does not apply to the amortization of an exclusive arrangement acquired and recognized as an intangible asset in a business combination. The Task Force also noted that this issue is more closely related to Issue 01-3 than to Issue 01-9. Accordingly, this issue will be moved to Issue 01-3.

Issue 6.   Issue 6 asks whether the consensus on Issue 2 of Issue 00-25 applies to consideration that consists of other than cash or equity instruments, or whether consideration that consists of other than cash or equity instruments should always be characterized as an expense when recognized in the income statement.

The Task Force reached a consensus that consideration that is not in the form of cash, equity instruments, or "credits" (that the reseller can apply against trade amounts owed to the vendor) should always be characterized as an expense in the income statement. There were those Task Force members who observed that ultimately the form of the consideration should unquestionably dictate the accounting based on this consensus.

Not the Last Word.   Elsewhere in this chapter, Problem 3 is related to EITF 00-14 and 00-25 and Problems 5 and 14 are related to EITF 00-14.

Post Script: This "inactive issue," 02-E, might be properly included as a postscript to Issue 01-9 in that it is concerned with what that issue *does not* cover.

Issue 02-E, *Accounting for Consideration Received from a Vendor by a Customer (Including a Reseller of the Vendor's Products)* in EITF 01-9, *Accounting for Consideration Given by a Vendor to a Customer (Including a Reseller of the Vendor's Products)*, as seen above, requires consideration given by a *vendor to a customer* to be characterized as a *reduction of revenue* unless certain conditions are met. However, the *customer's accounting* for consideration received from a vendor *is not addressed* by Issue 01-9 or other authoritative literature. The issue is how the customer should account for consideration received from a vendor.

GROSS VERSUS NET

Some of the more significant issues facing Internet businesses surround whether to present grossed-up revenues and cost of sales, or merely report the net profit as revenues, similar to a commission. The significance is greater because of the importance often placed on the revenue line in the valuation of Internet stocks.

Problem 1

The question of gross versus net revenue and cost display has arisen several times in connection with an Internet company that distributes or resells third-party products or services. Because the Internet is a new distribution channel and can be used in the distribution of tangible assets, intangible assets, and services, the existing practices used for making this determination are not always sufficient. (Priority level 1.)

Status of Problem 1

The FASB's Emerging Issues Task Force reached a consensus on this first issue in EITF 99-19, "Reporting Revenue Gross as a Principal versus Net as an Agent" at the July, 2000 meeting. The issue addressed was *when* a vendor should report revenue as the gross amount billed to a customer rather than the net amount earned by the vendor in the transaction. At the July meeting, the EITF affirmed as a consensus the tentative conclusion reached at the May 2000 meeting, with minor modifications to the indicators.

Consensus is that none of the indicators should be considered presumptive or determinative. However, the relative strength of each indicator should be considered. The members of the Task Force believe that the primary obligor, general inventory risk, and pricing latitude are the strongest indicators that would point to recording revenue gross. They also amended the consensus to allow transition to mirror the required implementation in SAB 101, *Revenue Recognition in Financial Statements.* (See Chapter 2.)

This attempt to reach consensus on when it is appropriate for a company to record revenue on a gross basis when acting as a principal versus on a net basis when acting as an agent has not been easy. For example, during EITF's May meeting, the EITF observed that an Internet retailer who had only credit and inventory risk during the time period goods were in transit would not qualify for gross revenue recognition.

Materials prepared by the FASB staff for the EITF's May 2000 meeting discussion of gross versus net revenue recognition indicate the variety of issues considered. The staff made the following suggestions to the EITF's members:

a. The answer to the question of when it is appropriate to recognize and report gross revenues turns on the risks assumed by the vendor in an exchange of goods and services with a customer.

b. Indicators taken alone or in combination that gross revenue recognition may be appropriate include that the vendor, from the customer's perspective, is the primary obligor; the vendor is primarily responsible for the fulfillment of the ordered product or service; the vendor has a credit loss risk; the vendor has an inventory loss risk; the vendor adds significant value to the products or services ordered by a customer; and the vendor has complete latitude to set prices of products or services ordered.

c. Some gross revenue recognition indicators are more persuasive than others. For example, taking title to inventory before a customer orders is more to the point than taking title to inventory after the customer orders.

d. No one indicator necessarily dictates gross revenue recognition. For example, while a vendor's failure to take title for the goods sold to a customer may be a strong indicator of net revenue recognition, taking title alone may not be enough to justify gross revenue recognition.

e. Some sale transactions and industry revenue recognition practices may be beyond the scope of the EITF consensus because of existing accounting standards. These include sale of financial assets, lending transactions, insurance and reinsurance transactions, and revenue recognition practices in airline, casino, construction contractor, and investment companies.

Problem 2

The staff pointed out that a number of press articles had commented on the following issue: Many Internet companies enter into advertising barter transactions with each other in which they exchange rights to place advertisements on each others' Web sites. There has been diversity in practice in accounting for these transactions. The staff believes a prerequisite to reflecting these transactions in the accounting records is that the value of the transaction must be reliably measurable. In addition, the staff believes registrants should be making transparent disclosure that will clearly convey to investors the accounting being used. (Priority level 1.)

Status of Problem 2

The Emerging Issues Task Force reached consensus in EITF 99-17 that the fair value of bartered advertising transactions can be included in revenue (with an offsetting amount charged to revenue) so long as the recording entity has a history of receiving cash in a similar advertising deal transacted during the last six months. If not, the company cannot book the cash.

A "cash" transaction can serve as support for revenue recognition of advertising barter transactions only up to the dollar amount of the cash transaction. Once that dollar amount has been reached, the "cash" transaction cannot serve as evidence of fair value for any other barter transaction. In other words, a cash transaction cannot support more than its original value or quantity in barter transactions. The following disclosures are required for advertising barter transactions, for each income statement period that is presented:

a. Disclosure of the amount of revenue and expense recorded from advertising barter transactions.

b. If the fair value of the advertising barter transactions is not determinable, information must be provided that clearly explains the volume and type of advertising surrendered and received, such as the number of pages or minutes or the overall percentage of advertising volume.

c. The EITF intends the barrier to recording barter transaction revenue at its fair value to be high. The evidence must be persuasive to overcome the presumption that the barter transaction should be recorded at zero or its historical cost. Reciprocal cash transactions between counterparties are considered to be barter transactions (i.e., each company places advertising with the other for a cash payment). The fair value of barter transactions must be disclosed in a footnote.

This EITF ruling was effective for transactions occurring after January 20, 2000.

Problem 3

Internet service providers (ISPs) and personal computer (PC) retailers at times offer a rather substantial rebate to purchasers of new PCs who contract for a given period of Internet service. It appears that:

a. Most of the rebate cost is borne by the ISP while a portion is borne by the PC retailer.
b. The retailer provides advertising and marketing for the arrangement.
c. The rebate, or a portion thereof, must be returned by the consumer to the ISP if the consumer breaks the contract with the ISP.

Some ISPs and retailers believe their portion of the cost of the rebate should be a marketing expense, as opposed to a reduction of revenues. The SEC staff generally believes that such rebates should be considered a reduction of revenues.

Status of Problem 3

The SEC staff felt that a staff announcement indicating that discounts like these should be accounted for as reductions of revenue was appropriate and adequate. The Task Force thought otherwise. Two of the EITFs, 00-14 and 00-25, deal with this to some extent, and to related issues. (For provisions included in Issue 00-14, *Accounting for Certain Sales Incentives,* please see Problem 5, which seems to have been solved by this consensus.) A discussion of EITF 00-25, *Accounting for Consideration from a Vendor to a Retailer in Connection with the Purchase or Promotion of the Vendor's Products,* follows:

Since the EITF reached a consensus on EITF 00-14, questions have been raised about the income statement characterization of consideration (other than that directly addressed in Issue 00-14) from a vendor to an entity that resells the vendor's products.

The term "vendor" is used to represent a product seller, such as a manufacturer or distributor, who sells to an entity that resells the vendor's products. The term "retailer" is used to represent that reseller entity, whether that entity is another distributor, a conventional retailer, or another type of reseller.

Examples of arrangements within the scope of this Issue include, but are not limited to, arrangements labeled as follows:

a. "Slotting fees." A vendor pays or agrees to pay a fee to a retailer to obtain space for the vendor's products on the retailer's store shelves.
b. Cooperative advertising arrangements. A vendor agrees to reimburse a retailer for a portion of the costs incurred by the retailer to advertise the vendor's products.

c. "Buydowns." A vendor agrees to reimburse a retailer up to a specified amount for shortfalls in the sales price received by the retailer for the vendor's products over a specified period of time.

Although many of the arrangements within the scope of this Issue (in particular, slotting fees) result in cash payments by a vendor to the retailer, the form of the consideration may be "credits" that the retailer can apply against trade amounts owed to the vendor, or against equity instruments of the vendor. Measurement of consideration in the form of vendor equity instruments is outside the scope of this Issue.

Guidance currently exists in:

a. EITF 96-18, *Accounting for Equity Instruments That Are Issued to Other Than Employees for Acquiring, or in Conjunction with Selling, Goods or Services,* which requires that equity instruments issued be recognized in the same period and in the same manner as if cash were paid.

b. Issue 00-14, which requires that a reduction in or refund of the selling price of the product or service resulting in a sales incentive be classified in the issuer's financial statements as a reduction of revenue.

EITF 00-25 Progress.   However, the issues requiring attention from the Working Group considering EITF 00-25 are:

a. ***Issue 1:*** For nonrefundable consideration from a vendor to a retailer to obtain shelf space for the vendor's products, the period(s) and manner in which the vendor should recognize the consideration.

b. ***Issue 2:*** Whether consideration from a vendor to a retailer is: (i) Adjustment of the selling prices of the vendor's products to the retailer and, therefore, should be deducted from revenue when recognized in the vendor's income statement; or (ii) A cost incurred by the vendor for assets or services provided by the retailer to the vendor and, therefore, should be included as a cost or expense when recognized in the vendor's income statement.

c. ***Issue 3(a):*** The period(s) and manner (that is, capitalize versus expense) in which the entity should recognize the measured cost of nonrefundable up-front consideration paid to a counterparty if future specific performance (by providing or purchasing goods or services) is not required by the counterparty in order to earn the consideration.

d. ***Issue 3(b):*** Whether a cost that is evaluated to be an asset under Issue 1, above, should be recognized in a different manner (classified as contra-equity) if the consideration paid is equity instruments of the entity.

e. *Issue 4:* If consideration from a vendor to a retailer results in negative revenue, whether the negative revenue amount should be included within revenues or expenses in the statement of operations.

In January 2001, the Task Force reached a tentative conclusion on Issue 2 that consideration from a vendor to any downstream purchaser of the vendor's products, even when that purchaser is not a direct customer of the vendor, is presumed to be a reduction to the selling prices of the vendor's products and, therefore, should be characterized as a reduction of revenue when recognized in the vendor's income statement.

That presumption is overcome and the consideration should be characterized as a cost incurred if, and to the extent that, a benefit is received from the retailer that meets both of the following:

a. The vendor receives, or will receive, an identifiable benefit (goods or services) from the retailer in return for the consideration. In order to meet this condition, the identified benefit must be sufficiently separable from the vendor's arrangement to sell its goods or services such that the vendor would have entered into an exchange transaction with parties other than a retailer customer in order to receive that benefit.

b. The vendor has sufficient, objective, and reliable evidence to estimate the fair value of the benefit. For example, if the benefit received from the retailer is advertising and the benefit's fair value estimate is based on the cost of "similar" advertising, that advertising must have characteristics reasonably similar to the advertising received from the retailer with respect to:

   (i) Circulation, exposure, or saturation within an intended market.

   (ii) Timing (time of day, day of week, daily, weekly, 24 hours a day/7 days a week, and season of the year).

   (iii) Prominence (page on Web site, section of periodical, location on page, and size of advertisement that relates to vendor's brands or products).

   (iv) Demographics of readers, viewers, or customers.

   (v) Duration (length of time advertising will be displayed).

If the amount of consideration exceeds the estimated fair value of the benefit received, that excess amount should be characterized as a reduction of revenue when recognized in the vendor's income statement.

The Task Force did not discuss Issues 1, 3, or 4; therefore, further discussion is expected at a future meeting. (See discussion of issue 01-9 earlier.)

Problem 4

Shipping and handling costs are a major expense for Internet product sellers. Most sellers charge customers for shipping and handling in amounts that are not a direct pass-through of costs. Some display the charges to customers as revenues and the costs as selling expenses, while others net the costs and revenues. The staff believes that practice for non-Internet mail-order companies is to net the revenues and expenses, although diversity may exist.

In either situation, the staff noted that Internet companies generally do not provide any separate disclosure of shipping revenues and costs (e.g., by reporting shipping revenue and costs as separate line items, or by providing footnote disclosure of the gross shipping revenues and costs).

The staff noted that there was diversity in practice that should be eliminated, but that the issue related to a smaller portion of revenues and costs than some of the other items. (Priority level 2 .)

Status of Problem 4

There are two questions here: (1) how a seller of goods should classify in the income statement amounts billed to a customer for shipping and handling, and (2) how the seller should classify in the income statement costs incurred for shipping and handling. The Task Force reached a consensus in EITF 00-10 in the first instance that all amounts billed to a customer in a sale transaction related to shipping and handling, if any, represent revenues earned for the goods provided and should be classified as revenue.

In the second, they decided that the classification of shipping and handling costs is an accounting policy decision that should be disclosed pursuant to Opinion 22, *Disclosure of Accounting Policies.* A company may adopt a policy of including shipping and handling costs in cost of sales. If shipping costs or handling costs are significant, and are not included in cost of sales (that is, if those costs are accounted for together or separately on other income statement line items), a company should disclose both the amount(s) of such costs and the line item(s) on the income statement that include them.

Problem 5

Some Internet companies have concluded that a free or heavily discounted product or service, as is provided in introductory offers (e.g. a free month of service, six CDs for a penny) should be accounted for as a sale at full price, with the recognition of marketing expense for the discount. The staff notes that an AICPA Technical Practice Aid Section relating to "One-Cent Sales"addresses this issue, concluding that, "The practice of crediting sales and charging advertising expense for the difference between the normal sales price and the 'bargain day' sales price of merchandise is not acceptable for financial reporting."

The SEC staff believes that a staff announcement indicating that discounts like these should be accounted for as reductions of revenue is appropriate.

Here, again, the EITF thought otherwise. (Much of their thinking is contained in Issue 00-14.)

Status of Problem 5

Issue 1.   A sales incentive is offered voluntarily by a vendor and without charge to customers. This incentive can be used by a customer as a result of a single exchange transaction; it will not result in a loss on the sale of a product or service. The issue is when to recognize and how to measure the cost of the sales incentive. (Here the term "vendor" includes a manufacturer that sells its products to retailers or other distributors.)

Consensus: The Task Force reached consensus on Issue 1 that for a sales incentive that will not result in a loss on the sale of a product or service, a vendor should recognize the "cost" of the sales incentive at the latter of the following:

a. The date at which the related revenue is recorded by the vendor.
b. The date at which the sales incentive is offered (which would be the case when the sales incentive offer is made after the vendor has recognized revenue; for example, when a manufacturer issues coupons offering discounts on a product that it already has sold to retailers).

Certain sales incentives entitle a customer to receive a reduction in the price of a product or service by submitting a form or claim for a refund or rebate of a specified amount of a prior purchase price charged to the customer at the point of sale (for example, mail-in rebates and certain manufacturer coupons). The Task Force reached consensus that a vendor should recognize a liability (or "deferred revenue") for those sales incentives at the latter of (a) or (b), above, based on the estimated amount of refunds or rebates that will be claimed by customers. However, if the amount of future rebates or refunds cannot be reasonably and reliably estimated, a liability (or "deferred revenue") should be recognized for the maximum potential amount of the refund or rebate (that is, no reduction for "breakage" should be made). The ability to make a reasonable and reliable estimate of the amount of future rebates or refunds depends on many factors and circumstances that will vary from case to case. However, the Task Force reached consensus that the following factors may impair a vendor's ability to make a reasonable and reliable estimate:

a. Relatively long time periods in which a particular rebate or refund may be claimed.
b. The absence of historical experience with similar types of sales incentive programs with similar products, or the inability to apply such experience because of changing circumstances.
c. The absence of a large volume of relatively homogeneous transactions.

Issue 2.   A sales incentive is offered voluntarily by a vendor and without charge to customers. This incentive can be used by a customer as a result of a single exchange transaction; it will result in a loss on the sale of a product or service. The issue is when to recognize and how to measure the cost of the sales incentive.

Consensus: For sales incentives within the scope of this Issue that will result in a loss on the sale of a product or service (Issue 2), the Task Force reached consensus that a vendor should not recognize a liability for the sales incentive prior to the date at which the related revenue is recognized by the vendor. However, the Task Force observed that the offer of a sales incentive that will result in a loss on the sale of a product may indicate an impairment of existing inventory under ARB 43.

Issue 3.   A sales incentive is offered voluntarily by a vendor and without charge to customers. This incentive can be used by a customer as a result of a single exchange transaction. The issue is how the cost of the sales incentive should be classified in the income statement.

Consensus: For Issue 3, the Task Force reached consensus that when recognized, the reduction in or refund of the selling price of the product or service resulting from any cash sales incentive should be classified as a reduction of revenue. However, if the sales incentive is a free product or service delivered at the time of sale (for example, a gift certificate or free airline ticket that will be honored by another, unrelated entity), the cost of the free product or service should be classified as an expense (as opposed to a reduction of revenues). That is, the free item is an element in the exchange transaction and not a refund or rebate of a portion of the amount charged to the customer.

While the Task Force did not reach consensus on the classification of the expense associated with free products, the SEC Observer indicated that the SEC staff believes that the expense associated with a free product or service delivered at the time of sale of another product or service should be classified as cost of sales. The Task Force observed that sales incentives in the form of options or warrants to purchase stock or the issuance of shares of stock of the vendor are multiple-element transactions that are outside the scope of this Issue.

Companies should have applied the consensuses no later than in (a) annual financial statements for the fiscal year beginning after December 15, 1999, or (b) financial statements for the fiscal quarter beginning after March 15, 2001, whichever is later. Earlier adoption was encouraged.

Problem 6

Several Internet-based businesses have experienced service outages. Related costs may include:

a. Refunds to customers/members.

b. Costs to correct the problem that caused the outage.

c. Damage claims.

The facts and circumstances surrounding these situations are likely to be very diverse, making the development of general guidance difficult. They add that issues could include:

a. When to accrue the refunds and costs.

b. Whether refunds that are not required but are given as a gesture of good-will are reductions of revenues, or a marketing expense, or "other."

c. The "other" could be imaginative; therefore, the SEC staff decided upon a Priority level 3 for this item.

Status of Problem 6

The staff indicated that the diversity of facts, circumstances, and causes surrounding the outages and handling could make general guidance difficult. Thus far, the issue is not being discussed. Although some indication may be drawn from 00-14.

DEFINITION OF SOFTWARE

The SEC noted several issues that relate to whether Web sites themselves and files or information available on Web sites should be considered software, and therefore be subject to the provisions of SOPs 97-2, *Software Revenue Recognition,* and 98-1, *Accounting for the Costs of Computer Software Developed or Obtained for Internal Use,* and/or FASB 86, *Accounting for the Costs of Computer Software to Be Sold, Leased, or Otherwise Marketed.*

Problem 7

In EITF Issue 96-6, the SEC staff expressed its view that the costs of software products that include film elements should be accounted for under the provisions of FASB 86. As such, revenue from the sale of such products should be accounted for under the provisions of SOP 97-2. By analogy, the staff believes that guidance should be applied to software with other embedded elements, such as music. However, EITF 96-6 did not discuss accounting for the costs of computer files that are essentially films (e.g., MPEG, RealVideo), music (e.g., MP3), or other content. A number of questions may arise relating to these files, including whether a company purchasing the rights to distribute music in the MP3 format should account for those costs under FASB 50,

Financial Reporting in the Record and Music Industry, or FASB 86. Similarly, it is not clear whether the revenue from the sales of MP3 files falls under SOP 97-2.

The staff indicated that as the areas of software, film, music, and so on continue to converge, it is important to be able to identify which accounting models apply to various transactions. In addition, resolving this Issue may be necessary in order to resolve Issue 8. (Priority level 2.)

Status of Problem 7

This item is on the agenda of the Task Force, but has not yet been discussed, as noted in Issue 00-X1 at the end of this chapter.

Although these two issues do not deal directly with the problem as posed by the SEC, they do concern both directly and indirectly issues relating to software and might be of interest in dealing with the accounting questions.

Issue 02-G, *Recognition of Revenue from Licensing Arrangements on Intellectual Property.* Licensing arrangements can take many forms, such as arrangements with a specific term or those with an unlimited term. The accounting for licensing arrangements varies in practice. Some may view the licensing of intellectual property as indistinguishable from a lease of a physical asset in which the total arrangement fee should be recognized over the contract term, while others may view such licensing arrangements as indistinguishable from the licensing of software or motion picture rights in which revenue is recognized once the license has been conveyed and the seller has no further obligations. The latter group believes their approach is fully consistent with the guidance in AICPA SOP 97-2, *Software Revenue Recognition,* and SOP 00-2, *Accounting by Producers or Distributors of Films.* The issue is when to recognize revenue from licensing arrangements on intellectual property.

Status: To be discussed at a future meeting.

Related to the Issue above is Issue 00-20, which has been considered a possible answer to some of the questions raised relating to the accounting for the costs of computer files that are essentially films, music, or other content.

Issue 00-20, *Accounting for Costs Incurred to Acquire or Originate Information for Database Content and Other Collections of Information.* Some companies derive revenues from making databases and other collections of information available to users. Those collections of information may be made available electronically or otherwise. The Issue is how the costs of developing or acquiring those collections of information should be accounted for (that is, capitalized and amortized or charged to expense as incurred).

Status: This Issue will be discussed at a future meeting, pending further progress by the FASB on its project Disclosures about Intangibles.

Last discussed: September 2000.

Problem 8

Costs of developing a Web site, including the costs of developing services that are offered to visitors (chat rooms, search engines, e-mail, calendars, etc.) are significant costs for many Internet businesses. In fact, the staff concluded that it is the largest cost for many of them. The SEC staff believes that a large portion of such costs should be accounted for as software developed for internal use in accordance with SOP 98-1, *Accounting for the Costs of Computer Software Developed or Obtained for Internal Use.* The staff notes that SOP 98-1 states, "If software is used by the vendor in providing the service but the customer does not acquire the software or the future right to use it, the software is covered by this SOP."

A letter to the FASB noted the staff view that a large portion of Web site development costs should be accounted for in accordance with this SOP, as software developed for internal use. However, at that time some companies were not following the requirements of SOP 98-1 for such costs.

The letter pointed out that even during the development of 98-1, some participants had questioned the wisdom of capitalizing software development costs. However, an answer was reached after significant comment and debate that requires capitalization when certain conditions have been met. (Priority level 1.)

Status of Problem 8

The Task Force reached consensus in EITF 00-2, on Web site development costs, effective for quarters beginning after June 30, 2000.

Organizations thinking about or in the process of developing a Web site must be aware of accounting guidance covering various stages of development and use: the planning stage, the development stage, and the operating stage.

a. Costs incurred during the planning stage are to be expensed as incurred. This includes developing a project plan, determining functions and technology, identifying needed hardware, Web applications, and graphics, choosing vendors and software packages—any and all necessary planning aspects.

b. Costs related to acquiring or developing software that operates a Web site should be accounted for under SOP 98-1 and should generally be capitalized if the entity does not intend to market the software externally. This includes developing software and graphics, obtaining and registering a domain name, developing HTML Web pages or templates, installing applications on servers, creating initial hypertext links, and testing Web applications.

If at the time the software is being developed, the organization that owns the site has, or is developing, a plan to market the software externally, the organization should account for the software under FASB 86. Accounting for related computer hardware and Web site content (the information on the Web site) is not addressed in EITF 00-2. This will be discussed as a separate EITF issue.

Fees incurred for Web site hosting should be expensed over the period of benefit. Data input costs should be expensed as incurred. Software acquired or developed to integrate a database with a Web site should usually be capitalized.

c. Costs incurred at the operating stage are generally expensed as incurred. Such costs include training employees, administration, maintenance, registering the Web site with Internet search engines, updating graphics, creating new links, and performing security reviews.

However, costs that add additional functions or features to the Web site (including graphics) should be accounted for as new software following the guidance in SOP 98-1 for upgrades and enhancements if the new software will not be marketed externally.

REVENUE RECOGNITION

As with any new business model, issues exist regarding the recognition of revenue for various types of Internet activities.

Problem 9

Auction sites usually charge both up-front (listing) fees and back-end (transaction-based) fees. The staff understands that the listing fees are being recognized as revenue when the item is originally listed, despite the requirement for the auction site to maintain the listing for the duration of the auction.

In addition, some auction sites recognize the back-end fees as revenue at the end of the auction, despite the fact that the seller is entitled to a refund of the fee if the transaction between the buyer and seller doesn't close. (Note: The auction house is merely a facilitator and takes no part in assisting in closing the transaction.) Given that many popular sites have recently started up auction services, this issue may become more prevalent.

The SEC staff comments relating to the front-end stated that a staff announcement indicating that fees like this should be recognized over the listing period (the period of performance) is appropriate.

The comments relating to the back-end indicated that the staff believes the facts and circumstances of the agreements among the auction site, the buyers, and the sellers may vary significantly, making it difficult to provide applicable guidance. (Priority level 3.)

Status of Problem 9

The issue relating to auction sites is on the agenda of the EITF but has not been discussed. (See Issue 00-X2 at the end of this chapter.)

Problem 10

Some purchasers of software do not actually receive the software. Rather, the software application resides on the vendor's or a third party's server, and the customer accesses the software on an as-needed basis over the Internet. The customer is paying for two elements—the right to use the software, and the storage of the software on someone else's hardware. The latter service is often referred to as "hosting." When the vendor also provides the hosting, several revenue recognition issues may arise:

a. There may be transactions structured in the form of a service agreement providing Internet access to the specified site, without a corresponding software license. In such instances, it may not be clear how to apply SOP 97-2.

b. When the transaction is viewed as a software license with a service element, it is not clear how to evaluate the delivery requirement of SOP 97-2.

The staff commented that this type of arrangement seems to be growing in popularity, although it is not all that common at this point. (Priority level 2.)

Status of Problem 10

In March, 2000, the EITF reached a consensus on EITF 00-3, *Application of AICPA Statement of Position 97-2, "Software Revenue Recognition," to Arrangements That Include the Right to Use Software Stored on Another Entity's Hardware.* EITF 00-3 addresses the accounting issues related to software hosting arrangements. In general, it states that if the customer does not have the option to physically take possession of the software, the transaction is not within the scope of SOP 97-2, and revenue should be recognized ratably over the hosting period as a service arrangement.

However, if the customer has the option to take physical delivery of the software and specific pricing information is available for both the software and hosting components of the arrangement, then the software revenue may be recognized when the customer first has access to the software and revenue from the hosting component should be recognized ratably over the hosting period.

Implementation of EITF 00-3 was required for the year ending December 31, 2000.

Problem 11

An Internet business may provide customers with services that include access to a Web site, maintenance of a Web site, or publication of certain information on a Web site for a period of time. Certain companies have argued that, because the incremental costs of maintaining the Web site and/or providing access to it are minimal (or even zero), this ongoing requirement should not preclude up-front revenue recognition. The staff has historically objected to up-front revenue recognition in these cases, even with an accrual of the related costs.

The SEC staff believes that a staff announcement indicating that fees like this should be recognized over the performance period, which would be the period over which the company has agreed to maintain the Web site or listing, is appropriate. No priority was assigned.

Status of Problem 11

This problem has not been discussed by the EITF as noted under Issue 00-X3 at the end of this chapter. However, number 10 of the frequently asked questions (FAQ) relating to revenue recognition in SAB 101 appears to answer the questions:

Question   In each of the following situations, when should the company receiving the fee recognize the related revenue?

Example 1: A company charges users a fee for nonexclusive access to its Web site that contains proprietary databases. The fee allows access to the Web site for a one-year period. After the customer is provided with an identification number and trained in the use of the database, there are no incremental costs that will be incurred in serving this customer.

Example 2: An Internet company charges a fee to users for advertising a product for sale or auction on certain pages of its Web site. The company agrees to maintain the listing for a period of time. The cost of maintaining the advertisement on the Web site for the stated period is minimal.

Example 3: A company charges a fee for hosting another company's Web site for one year. The arrangement does not involve exclusive use of any of the hosting company's servers or other equipment. Almost all of the projected costs to be incurred will be incurred in the initial loading of information on the host company's Internet server and setting up appropriate links and network connections.

Answer   Some propose that revenue should be recognized when the initial setup is completed in these cases because the ongoing obligation involves minimal or no cost or effort and should be considered perfunctory or inconsequential. However, the staff believes that the substance of each of these transactions indicates that the purchaser is paying for a service that is delivered over time. Therefore, revenue recognition should occur over time, reflecting the provision of service. In certain cases, the arrangement with the customer may be a multiple-element arrangement, with separate revenue recognition for those initial services.

Question 4 of this document (FAQ) discusses multiple-element arrangements:

Question   Although SAB 101 does not establish a framework for accounting for multiple-element arrangements, what factors would the staff consider in assessing whether an arrangement is accounted for as a multiple-element arrangement?

Answer   SAB 101 does not modify existing practice in accounting for multiple-element arrangements. Recognizing the diversity in practice in the accounting for multiple-element arrangements, and the complexity of these arrangements, the staff asked the Emerging Issues Task Force (EITF) and the Auditing Standards Board (ASB) to provide additional accounting and auditing guidance on those transactions. The EITF has added Issue 00-21, *Accounting for Multiple-Element Revenue Arrangements,* to its agenda to address the accounting issues. Pending additional guidance, registrants should use a reasoned method of accounting for multiple-element arrangements that is applied consistently and disclosed appropriately. In response to questions, the SEC staff has stated that it will not object to a method that includes the following conditions:

1. To be considered a separate element, the product or service in question represents a separate earnings process. The staff notes that determining whether an obligation represents a separate element requires significant judgment. The staff also notes that the best indicator that a separate element exists is that a vendor sells or could readily sell that element unaccompanied by other elements.

2. Revenue is allocated among the elements based on the fair value of the elements. The fair values used for the allocations should be reliable, verifiable, and objectively determinable. The staff does not believe that allocating revenue among the elements based solely on cost plus a profit

margin that is not specific to the particular product or service is acceptable because, in the absence of other evidence of fair value, there is no objective means to verify what a profit margin should be for the particular element(s).

Additional guidance on allocating among elements may be found in SOP 81-1, paragraphs 35 through 42; SOP 97-2, paragraphs 9 through 14; and SOP 98-9, *Modification of SOP 97-2, Software Revenue Recognition, with Respect to Certain Transactions.* All of the methods of allocating revenue in those SOPs, including the residual method discussed in SOP 98-9, are acceptable. If sufficient evidence of the fair values of the individual elements does not exist, revenue would not be allocated among them until that evidence exists. Instead, the revenue would be recognized as earned, using revenue recognition principles applicable to the entire arrangement as if it were a single-element arrangement. Prices listed in a multiple-element arrangement with a customer may not be representative of fair value of those elements because the prices of the different components of the arrangement can be altered in negotiations and still result in the same aggregate consideration.

Updated Status of Problem II

That this issue is not cut, dried, and put on the shelf is obvious from the fact that the Task Force discussed it over a two-day period in late June 2002. At that time, it was scheduled for further discussion. In addition, the *SEC Observer* expressed the view that Issue 00-21 and perhaps Issue 00-22 should be reinstated by the Task Force. The Task Force agreed and the FASB followed up by agreeing to consider adding to the Board's agenda a narrow project that would address Issues 00-21 and 00-22. Consistent with previous requests by the Task Force, the Board is taking into consideration whether the due process afforded a Board project would represent a better forum in which to deal, in greater depth, with the issues and views of constituents on certain matters.

To review: Issue 00-21, *Accounting for Revenue Arrangements with Multiple Deliverables.* Many companies offer complete solutions to their customers' needs. Those solutions may involve:

1. The delivery or performance of multiple products.
2. Services to be performed.
3. Rights to use assets.
4. Performance may occur at different points in time or over different periods of time.

The arrangements are often accompanied by initial installation, initiation, or activation services, and generally involve either a fixed fee or a fixed fee coupled with a continuing payment stream. The continuing payment stream generally corresponds to the continuing performance and may be:

1. A fixed payment.
2. Variable payment based on future performance.
3. Composed of a combination of fixed and variable payments.

The issue is how to account for those arrangements.

On the other hand, many software transactions do *not* involve "complete solutions." Therefore, identification of separate components and elements of software transactions and their fair value are necessary to take into consideration for determining the timing of revenue recognition. So, how should "separate components/elements" and "separate deliverables" be defined? The task force considered that tentative conclusions of EITF 00-21 provided some insight into a potential resolution. It states that a deliverable should be segmented and accounted for separately if:

1. There is objective and reliable evidence of fair value to allocate the consideration to the separate deliverables.
2. The deliverable meets at least one of the following criteria at the inception of the arrangement:
   a. It does not affect the quality of use or value to the customer of other deliverables in the arrangement.
   b. It can be purchased from an unrelated vendor without affecting the quality of use or value to the customer of the remaining deliverables in the arrangement.

Software companies may consistently include or exclude all deliverables in an arrangement from revenue (and recognize a liability) for the arrangement if all of the following conditions are met:

1. The deliverable does not affect the quality of use or value of other deliverables or could be purchased from another vendor without loss of the quality of use or value of other deliverables.
2. Any vendor obligation relating to nonperformance would not result in a refund, revenue reversal, or concession.
3. The deliverable is inconsequential or perfunctory.

No allocation is permitted in the absence of verifiable fair value. Third-party evidence may not be a reliable indicator of vendor specific objective evidence (VSOE) if the product or service is unique to the vendor. When objective and verifiable evidence of fair value is available for the undelivered item(s) but not for one or more delivered items in the arrangement, the residual method (SOP 98-9) can be used to allocate revenue when:

1. The undelivered item meets all other applicable criteria for separate accounting.
2. The fair value of all the undelivered items is less than the total arrangement fee.

It is important to keep in mind that the residual method cannot be used to *establish* the fair value of an undelivered item.

Below is the treatment of the discount:

1. The residual method, established in SOP 98-9, allocates the entire discount to the delivered elements.
2. The relative fair value allocation method established in SOP 97-2 allocates a proportionate amount of the entire discount to each unit of accounting in the arrangement based on the fair value of each unit without regard to the discount.

Revenue Recognition for Multiple Element Arrangements

For more than a year, the Emerging Issues Task Force, its working group and the staff of the FASB had worked on providing this tentative guidance on accounting for multiple element arrangements in relation to revenue recognition.

In July 2001, the chief account of the SEC stepped into the picture. The SEC commended the EITF, its working group and the FASB staff for their hard work. However, the Commission felt that the process that led to the tentative conclusion and comments about the model had made it clear that significant effort must be made to reach an *operational solution* that is consistent with the *fundamentals* of existing GAAP and that provides adequate transparency and protection for investors. In addition, the SEC felt that the tentative conclusions in EITF 00-21 made it clear that developing guidance for revenue recognition related to *multiple element arrangements* is a broad project with many implications that has "outgrown" the size and nature of a project contemplated by the mission of the EITF.

This view had been reflected in comments by some of those task force members, who had stated that the issue requires more *due process and public comments* than can be provided by the EITF's process. The SEC pointed out that several FASB constituents had expressed similar views at the Financial Accounting Standards Advisory Council and in letters to the SEC staff. The SEC concurs with that viewpoint.

The SEC Requests the IASB to Consider the Revenue Recognition Project

At that time, the SEC asked the International Accounting Standards Board (IASB) to undertake a project in partnership with national standard setters, including the FASB, to develop a comprehensive accounting standard for revenue recognition. (This action may well have been the impetus behind the FASB's putting the project on revenue recognition on their agenda.)

The SEC staff would have objected to an EITF consensus on the issue pending completion of a comprehensive revenue recognition standard subject to full due process. Until further standards are developed, they felt that registrants should disclose their accounting policy for revenue recognition. In addition, the staff would not object to a registrant's accounting provided it complied with the broad principles in SAB 101 and the related Frequently Asked Questions document on SAB 101.

The EITF 00-21 working group has met numerous times to address the issue of revenue recognition for multiple element arrangements, including gathering information from various affected industries. Largely because of those working group efforts, it has become clear that this is, indeed, a broad project. Some of the specific observations the SEC staff has noted include:

1. Many of the issues are fundamental revenue recognition questions with ramifications well beyond accounting for multiple element arrangements. As examples, the issues include providing answers to the following questions:
   a. What is a revenue element?
   b. What is a separate earnings process?
   c. What constitutes delivery?
   d. How is fair value of the separable elements in the arrangement determined?

2. As pointed out above, the SEC emphasized that other models for multiple element accounting already exist in GAAP, including SOP 81-1, *Accounting for Performance of Construction-Type and Certain Production-Type Contracts,* and SOP 97-2, *Software Revenue Recognition.* The tentative conclusion would be another model added to the mix, not a comprehensive solution.

3. The question of vendor performance (or lack thereof) is an issue involved in many types of revenue transactions including multiple elements. This issue should be discussed in a broader context.

4. The staff is concerned that, as broad as this issue is, and the resulting implications for all companies that commonly enter into such transactions today, greater due process is necessary to ensure all significant issues have

been identified, and there has been adequate input received to afford a transparent standard for investors.

5. Additional time for due process would allow standard setters to study actual practice given the enhanced disclosures now being made as a result of SAB 101.

6. Revenue is often the single largest item in the financial statements, while *revenue recognition is the single largest issue involved in restatements of financial statements causing the greatest losses for investors.* The development of a high-quality standard for revenue recognition needs to be based on research of these issues and provide adequate investor protection.

The SEC recommended that the IASB work in close partnership with national standard setters on this project. They believe the FASB should play an active leading role on this project. They are of the opinion that such a project provides a significant opportunity for convergence of international accounting standards (including U.S. Standards) toward a single high-quality standard, which would level the playing field for companies worldwide. Convergence should result in "best of breed" accounting standards by drawing on the knowledge of both international and national standards setters.

No final decision had been reached when Issue 00-21 was discussed in June 2002, although there had been numerous meetings and discussions, and several models had been prepared.

Problem 12

Many Internet companies enter into various types of advertising arrangements (sometimes with other Internet companies) to provide advertising services over a period of time. These arrangements often include guarantees on "hits," "viewings," or "click-throughs."

It is not clear how the provider of the advertising takes progress toward these minimums into account in assessing revenue recognition. This issue could show up in various other industries as well (sales reps who guarantee they will reach a certain level of sales, advertising in other kinds of media, etc.).

The SEC staff mentioned that the terms of these arrangements vary somewhat from contract to contract. The issues that arise in some, but not all, of these contracts may be addressed in SAB 101, *Revenue Recognition in Financial Statements.* (Priority level 3.)

Status of Problem 12

It would be a good idea for the accountant to pay close attention to the disclosure requirements of SAB 101 until or if the Task Force considers taking a look at this problem. (See Issue 00-X4 at the end of this chapter.)

Problem 13

There are a growing number of "point" and other loyalty programs being developed in Internet businesses (similar to the airline and hotel industry programs). There are several well-known companies whose business model involves building a membership list through this kind of program. In some cases, the program operator may sell points to its business partners, who then issue them to their customers based on purchases or other actions. In other cases, the program operator awards the points in order to encourage its members to take actions that will generate payments from business partners to the program operator.

Several issues related to these programs have arisen:

a. The program operators believe that their customers are the companies for whom they provide advertising and marketing services. They view the redemption of the points or other reward as the "cost of sales," not as a revenue-generating activity. Therefore, they do not believe the fact that delivery under the reward occurs later should require revenue deferral. The SEC staff has accepted this argument only when the contracts with the business partners do not require the issuance or offer of any award, and speak merely to performing the advertising, marketing, or customer acquisition activities.

   In other cases, the staff has required that some amount of revenue be deferred until the points are redeemed, to reflect that the substance of the arrangement involves multiple elements, one of which has not yet occurred. The same issue could also exist in customer acquisition programs. For example, offers exist whereby an ISP offers six months of free service to people who open accounts at certain online brokerages.

b. When revenue is recognized up front with an accrual of the redemption costs, a question arises as to whether companies should estimate "breakage" (the amount of rewards that will expire unused). Many Web-based businesses have loyalty programs that would also face this issue. For example, many sites issue rewards that can be used towards future purchases at the site. In recording the liability for those rewards, some argue that the gross amount of the rewards issued should be recorded, while others believe that the recorded amount should be reduced for an estimate of the rewards that will not be used, if this "breakage" can be reliably estimated. (Priority level 2.)

Status of Problem 13

There has been a great deal of discussion on this problem. The issues and discussion are in EITF 00-22, *Accounting for Points and Certain Other*

Time-Based or Volume-Based Sales Incentive Offers, and Offers for Free Products or Services to Be Delivered in the Future. The Task Force has reached no final decisions and there is no additional guidance, but they have identified the issues and reached some tentative conclusions.

The issues are:

Issue 1.   How a vendor should account for an offer to a customer, in connection with a current revenue transaction, for free or discounted products or services delivered by the vendor that is redeemable only if the customer completes a specified cumulative level of revenue transactions or remains a customer for a specified time period.

Issue 2.   How a vendor should account for an offer to a customer, in connection with a current revenue transaction, for free or discounted products or services from the vendor that is redeemable by the customer at a future date without a further exchange transaction with the vendor.

Issue 3.   How a vendor should account for an offer to a customer to rebate or refund a specified amount of cash that is redeemable only if the customer completes a specified cumulative level of revenue transactions or remains a customer for a specified time period.

Issue 4.   How a vendor should account for an offer to a customer, in connection with a current revenue transaction, for free or discounted products or services delivered by an unrelated entity (program operator) under an arrangement between the program operator and the vendor that is redeemable only if the customer completes a specified cumulative level of revenue transactions or remains a customer for a specified time period.

Issue 5.   How a program operator should account for award credits sold (directly or indirectly) to other vendors and consumers.

At the January 2001 meeting, the Task Force reached consensus on Issue 3—that a vendor should recognize a rebate or refund obligation as a reduction of revenue.

Measurement of the obligation should be based on the estimated number of customers that will ultimately qualify for a "prize." However, if the amount of future rebates or refunds cannot be reasonably estimated, a liability (or "deferred revenue") should be recognized for the maximum potential amount of the refund or rebate (that is, no reduction for "breakage" should be made). The Task Force reached a consensus that the following factors may impair a vendor's ability to make a reasonable estimate of the amount of future rebates or refunds:

a. Relatively long periods in which a particular rebate or refund may be claimed.

b. The absence of historical experience with similar types of sales incentive programs with similar products, or the inability to apply such experience because of changing circumstances.

c. The absence of a large volume of relatively homogeneous transactions.

The Task Force also reached consensus that changes in the estimated amount of rebates or refunds, and retroactive changes by a vendor (that is, an increase or a decrease in the rebate amount that is applied retroactively) to a previous offer, should be recognized using a cumulative catch-up adjustment. The vendor should adjust the balance of its rebate obligation to the revised estimate immediately. The vendor should then reduce revenue on future sales based on the revised refund obligation rate as computed.

Entities should have applied the consensus on Issue 3 for the fiscal quarter ending after February 15, 2001. Amounts in prior years presented should be reclassified as a reduction of revenue.

UPDATED STATUS OF EITF 00-22 RELATING TO VARIOUS INCENTIVES

After reaching consensus on Issue 3, the Task Force requested that the FASB staff, together with the Working Group established to address EITF 00-21, on multiple deliverables, make additional progress on the Issue 00-21 model before further developing a revenue recognition approach for EITF 00-22. The Board may add to its agenda a narrow project that would address Issues 00-21 and 00-22. Consistent with previous requests by the Task Force, the Board is considering whether the due process afforded a Board project would represent a better forum in which to comprehensively consider the issues and the views of constituents. (Also see EITF 01-9, above.)

EITF 00-22 basically covers all industries that use point or other loyalty programs to draw and retain customers, including the airline and hospitality industries. Thus, this falls into the category of both old and new economy accounting situations.

The EITF has not yet reached a consensus on the Issue as a whole. In the final analysis, specific industries would be excluded from the scope of the study and discussions inasmuch as many industries are already addressed by higher-level GAAP and rulings; however, there are definite holes in existing guidance. One source points out that the AICPA Industry Audit Guide *Audits of Airlines* does not even mention accounting for frequent-flyer programs (and these are certainly not new or "new economy" means or methods of building a customer base).

PREPAID/INTANGIBLE ASSETS VERSUS PERIOD COSTS

Internet businesses often make payments to obtain members or customers or to obtain advertising space, distribution rights, supply agreements, and so on. In some cases, the questions of whether to capitalize or expense such costs and of assessing impairment of the rights obtained are not straightforward. Although similar payments are made by companies that do not have Internet operations, the frequency with which this issue arises is higher in Internet companies.

Problem 14

Businesses often make payments for long-term contractual rights (e.g., Internet distribution rights) that are intended to be exploited only through Internet operations. The contractual rights meet the definition of an asset, but the measurement of the probable economic benefits is difficult. Some companies have asserted that these rights are immediately impaired, as their best estimate of the expected cash flows would indicate the asset is not recoverable.

The SEC staff has objected in these situations, and believes impairment should not be recorded unless it can be shown that conditions have changed since the execution of the contract. The evaluation of impairment of these kinds of assets is complicated because, as discussed earlier, the contractual rights purchased may be covered by different accounting standards, depending on the subject of the rights.

The staff pointed out EITF Issue 99-14 discusses *whether* impairment of such contracts should be assessed, but not *how.* They believe that guidance on how to assess impairment is *critical,* and should be provided either as implementation guidance to Issue 99-14 or in a separate issue. Therefore, the staff assigned it priority level 1.

Status of Problem 14

As mentioned above, the staff considers it of primary importance either to "finish" EITF 99-14 or to consider the "how" as a separate item. However, at this point the issue is not being discussed.

Problem 15

Many Internet companies enter into various types of advertising arrangements (sometimes with other Internet companies) in which one entity pays the other an up-front fee (or guarantees certain minimum payments over the course of the contract) in exchange for certain advertising services over a period of time. The payers in these arrangements have at times recognized an immediate loss on signing the contract, arguing that the expected benefits are less than the up-front or guaranteed payments.

The staff has indicated that it views these payments as being similar to payments made for physical advertising space, and that any up-front payment should be treated as prepaid advertising costs.

Status of Problem 15

No priority level was assigned to this problem, but the staff suggested that guidance on these arrangements can be provided along with guidance on Problem 14. Inasmuch as Problem 14 was assigned a level 1 priority, it would follow that this problem also needs expeditious attention. However, at present it is not being discussed.

Problem 16

Internet businesses often make large investments in building a customer or membership base. Several examples of this are:

a. Sites that give users rewards (points, products, discounts, services) in exchange for setting up an account with the site.
b. Sites that make payments to business partners for referring new customers or members.
c. Businesses that give users PCs and Internet service for free if they are willing to spend a certain minimum amount of time on the Internet each month and are willing to have advertisements reside permanently on their computers.

In each of these cases, a question may arise as to whether the costs represent customer acquisition costs or costs of building a membership listing that qualify for capitalization, for example, by analogy to FASB 91, *Accounting for Nonrefundable Fees and Costs Associated with Originating or Acquiring Loans and Initial Direct Costs of Leases.* (Priority Level 3.)

Status of Problem 16

As evidenced by the priority level 3 assigned by the staff, this is not a pressing problem. They point out that most companies appear to be expensing such costs as incurred; therefore, there is little diversity in practice to make it urgent that this issue be addressed. If and when the issue is addressed, the model should apply broadly to costs of building customer and membership lists.

At present, the Accounting Standards Committee (AcSec) of the AICPA is considering the matter.

Miscellaneous Issues

Problem 17

Issued equity instruments often have conversion or exercisability terms that are variable based upon future events, such as the attainment of certain sales levels or a successful initial public offering (IPO). The issuer's accounting does not appear to raise new issues as it is covered in EITF Issues 96-18, *Accounting for Equity Instruments That Are Issued to Other Than Employees for Acquiring, or in Conjunction with Selling, Goods or Services,* and 98-5, *Accounting for Convertible Securities with Beneficial Conversion Features or Contingently Adjustable Conversion Ratios.*

For the holders, the instruments may be within the scope of FASB 133, *Accounting for Derivative Instruments and Hedging Activities.* However, because one or more of the underlyings are often based on the holder's or issuer's performance, FASB 133 will not always apply. In addition, it is not clear that the change in fair value of the instrument should be entirely recognized as a derivative holding gain or loss, versus an increase or decrease in revenues or operating expenses.

The SEC staff believes this issue seems to fit well with other issues being considered by the Derivatives Implementation Group (DIG). (Priority level 2.)

Status of Problem 17

In March 2000, the EITF reached consensus on EITF 00-8, *Accounting by a Grantee for an Equity Instrument to Be Received in Conjunction with Providing Goods or Services.* This Issue addresses 1) the date a grantee should use to measure the fair value of the equity instruments received, and 2) how the grantee should account for an increase in fair value as a result of reaching designated performance milestones. On the first issue, the Task Force reached consensus that the grantee should measure the fair value of the equity instruments using the stock price and other measurement assumptions as of the earlier of either of the following dates:

a. The date the parties come to a mutual understanding of the terms of the equity-based compensation arrangement and a commitment is made for performance by the grantee to earn the equity instruments (a "performance commitment" in the context of the definition in Issue 96-18).

   b. The Task Force reached consensus on the second issue that:

      — If on the measurement date the quantity or any of the terms of the equity instrument are dependent on the achievement of a market condition, then the grantee should measure revenue based on the fair value of the equity instruments inclusive of the adjustment provisions.

      — That fair value would be calculated as the fair value of the equity instruments without regard to the market condition plus the fair value of the commitment to change the quantity or terms of the equity instruments if the market condition is met.

      — If on the measurement date the quantity or any of the terms of the equity instruments are dependent on the achievement of grantee performance conditions, changes in fair value of the equity instrument that result from an adjustment to the instrument upon the achievement of a performance condition should be measured as additional revenue from the transaction.

      — Changes in fair value of the equity instruments after the measurement date unrelated to the achievement of performance conditions should be accounted for in accordance with any relevant literature on the accounting and reporting for investments in equity instruments, such as Opinion 18, FASB 115, and FASB 133.

Problem 18

FASB 131, *Disclosures about Segments of an Enterprise and Related Information,* defines segments based on the information reviewed by top management in making decisions. Therefore, if top management reviews information about the Internet portion of a company's business separately from other operations, the Internet operations should be considered a separate operating segment.

Status of Problem 18

Because this is what they do, ensuring that FASB 131 is properly applied in this area and others will undoubtedly be a focus of the SEC staff. No priority level was assigned, nor was any further action by an outside group requested. The FASB staff implementation guide, "Segment Information: Guidance on applying Statement 131," is also pertinent.

Problem 19

The staff has noted that classification of expenses between various categories (costs of sales, marketing, sales, R&D) sometimes varies significantly among Internet companies for costs that appear similar. Examples include Web site development costs and expenses related to the various contractual rights discussed above.

The staff agreed that it is difficult to identify common elements between the classification issues that have arisen, making the preparation of general guidance difficult. (Priority level 3.)

Status of Problem 19

Since this is not really a new issue, the staff is keeping a close watch, but no discussion is being carried on at present.

Problem 20

When a company prints a coupon in the newspaper, it is common practice to record a liability and marketing expense for the estimated number of coupons that will be redeemed. The Internet provides several new methods of distributing coupons that may raise questions within the existing accounting models. For example:

a. Product or service providers post coupons online, often for long periods of time.
b. Internet retailers or service providers send e-mails inviting the receiver to get a discount on a purchase.

The staff commented that the area of accounting for coupons, rebates, and discounts is growing more significant, but it is not limited to Internet businesses. Developing a robust model to account for these arrangements would be helpful. (Priority level 2.)

Status of Problem 20

In accordance with the Emerging Issues Task Force Issue 00-14, *Accounting for Certain Sales Incentives* (EITF 00-14), expenses related to coupon redemptions, formerly classified as marketing and sales expense, are now recorded as a reduction of sales. EITF 00-14 required the implementation of this change effective within all reporting periods beginning in the first fiscal quarter beginning after May 18, 2000, and also requires all prior periods to be reclassified to reflect this modification. The accounting guidance for such programs provided by the EITF consensus No. 00-14 indicates that the Task Force reached a consensus on the issue relating to a sales incentive. This will not result in a loss on the sale of a product or service; therefore, a vendor should recognize the "cost" of the sales incentive at the latter of the following:

a. The date at which the related revenue is recorded by the vendor.
b. The date at which the sales incentive is offered (which would be the case when the sales incentive offer is made after the vendor has recognized revenue; for example, when a manufacturer issues coupons offering discounts on a product that it already has sold to retailers).

EITF 00-25, *Vendor Income Statement Characterization of Consideration from a Vendor to a Retailer,* picks up where EITF 00-14 left off.

However, when all is said and done, what results is that for coupons, rebates, and discounts offered voluntarily by vendors to customers:

a. Cash sales incentives used at the time of sale should be recognized as a revenue reduction at the time of sale.
b. Cash incentives that give the customer the right to receive a refund or rebate should be recognized as a reduction of revenue at the sale date based upon an estimate of the amount of incentives claimed by the ultimate customer.
c. A free product or service incentives delivered at the time of sale should be recorded at cost as an expense at the time of sale.

The consensus was applicable to the first fiscal quarter starting after May 18, 2000.

(Additional discussions of EITF 00-14 and 00-25 are found at the beginning of this chapter and in Status of Problems 5 and 3, respectively.)

CATCH-ALL ISSUE FOR PROBLEMS NOT YET CONSIDERED

That the Emerging Issues Task Force of the FASB took the SEC letter from the SEC chief accountant seriously, and at least worked at considering and discussing all of the concerns raised by the SEC, is supported by the following.

Issue 99-V, "Remaining Issues from the SEC's October 18, 1999 Letter to the EITF." At the November 17-18, 1999 EITF meeting, Task Force members agreed that the issues identified in the SEC's October 18, 1999 letter to the Task Force should be addressed by the Task Force. This Issue is a placeholder for those issues that have not specifically been given an EITF Issue number.

Status: Issues identified under this Issue, either have been added to the EITF agenda as EITF Issues (both separately and in combination) (see Issues below) or have been removed from EITF consideration.

Issue 00-X1, "Accounting for the Costs of Computer Files that Are Essentially Films, Music, or Other Content." A description for this Issue is not available at this time.

Status: This Issue is currently inactive pending further progress on active EITF Issues, receipt of additional information, or further developments in practice.

Issue 00-X2, "Accounting for Front-End and Back-End Fees." A description for this Issue is not available at this time.

Status: This Issue is currently inactive pending further progress on active EITF Issues, receipt of additional information, or further developments in practice.

Issue 00-X3, "Accounting for Access, Maintenance, and Publication Fees." A description for this Issue is not available at this time.

Status: This Issue is currently inactive pending further progress on active EITF Issues, receipt of additional information, or further developments in practice.

Issue 00-X4, "Accounting for Advertising or Other Arrangements Where the Service Provider Guarantees a Specified Amount of Activity." A description for this Issue is not available at this time.

Status: This Issue is currently inactive pending further progress on active EITF Issues, receipt of additional information, or further developments in practice.

IF ALL ELSE FAILS

The Office of Internet Enforcement (OIE), formed in July, 1998, administers the Enforcement Division's Internet program. The Internet has brought significant benefits to investors; most notably, enhanced access to information (both in speed and quantity) and lower costs to execute trades. At the same time, unfortunately, the Internet has opened new avenues for fraud artists to attempt to swindle the investing public. To combat this online fraud, the OIE:

1. Identifies areas of surveillance.
2. Formulates investigative procedures.
3. Provides strategic and legal guidance to Enforcement staff nationwide.
4. Conducts Internet investigations and prosecutions (a task it shares with the entire Enforcement staff).
5. Performs training for Commission staff and outside agencies.
6. Serves as a resource on Internet matters for the entire Commission.

In addition, the OIE coordinates the activities of the "CyberForce"— a group of over 200 Commission attorneys, accountants, and investigators nationwide—whose purpose is Internet surveillance. OIE, along with the SEC's Office of Investor Education and Assistance, manages the SEC Complaint Center, which receives hundreds of complaints per day.

The OIE coordinates Internet-related "Enforcement Sweeps," in which similar types of Internet misconduct are targeted for investigation and, where appropriate, prosecution. This allows for the coordinated filing of Enforcement actions and allows the Commission to deliver its message more forcefully and effectively. The OIE also serves as a liaison on Internet matters with other regulatory agencies and both national and international law enforcement agencies.

According to Commission officials, the SEC's online Enforcement Complaint Center receives more than 120 complaints every day concerning Internet-related potential securities violations. Since 1995, the Enforcement Division has brought more than 30 cases of Internet-related securities fraud involving such scams as phony offerings, market manipulations, affinity frauds (targeting a particular ethnic group), and pyramid and Ponzi schemes.

Top 10 Technologies and Tech Issues

The specters of the Enron collapse and the 9/11 terrorist attacks evidently influenced the 2002 Top 10 Technologies list from the AICPA. They are:

1. Business and financial reporting applications.
2. Training and technology competency.
3. Information security and controls.
4. Quality of service.
5. Disaster recovery.
6. Communication technologies/bandwidth.
7. Remote connectivity tools.
8. Web-based and Web-enabled applications.
9. Finding IT personnel.
10. Messaging applications, such as e-mail, fax, voicemail, and instant messaging.

Business and financial reporting applications rose to the top of the list, probably as a result of concerns raised in the wake of Enron. In what came as a surprise to the AICPA, privacy concerns did not make the top 10 but placed only 11th according to the chair of the Top Technologies Task Force. The issues were drawn from an online AICPA survey.

Chapter 29
Mutual Funds

CONTENTS

Kinds of Distributions   **29.01**

Foreign Tax Deduction or Credit   **29.03**

Basis   **29.03**

Sales, Exchanges and Redemptions   **29.04**

Investment Expenses   **29.07**

Background of SEC Final Rules and Amendments on Independent
    Fund Advisors   **29.08**

The SEC Adopts Final Rules and Amendments on Fund Governance   **29.10**

The Role of Independent Directors of Investment Companies   **29.11**

Amendments to Exemptive Rules to Enhance Director Independence
    and Effectiveness   **29.14**

Additional Rule Changes   **29.15**

Disclosure Requirements   **29.16**

KINDS OF DISTRIBUTIONS

There are several kinds of distributions that a shareholder can receive from a mutual fund. They include:

1. Ordinary dividends.

2. Capital gain distributions.
3. Exempt-interest dividends.
4. Return of capital (nontaxable) distribution.

Tax-Exempt Mutual Fund

Distributions from a tax-exempt mutual fund—one that invests primarily in tax-exempt securities—can consist of ordinary dividends, capital gains distributions, undistributed capital gains, or return of capital like any other mutual fund. These contributions follow the same rules as a regular mutual fund. Distributions designated as exempt-interest dividends are not taxable.

A mutual fund may pay exempt-interest dividends to its shareholders if it meets certain requirements. These dividends are paid from tax-exempt interest earned by the fund. Since the exempt-interest dividends keep their tax-exempt character, the taxpayer does not have to include them in income, but may need to report them on his or her return. The mutual fund will send the taxpayer a statement within 60 days after the close of its tax year showing the amount of exempt-interest dividends. Although exempt-interest dividends are not taxable, they must be reported on the tax return if one is required to be filed. This is an information reporting requirement and does not convert tax-exempt interest to taxable interest.

Return of Capital

A distribution that is not out of earnings and profits is a return of the investment, or capital, in the mutual fund. The return of capital distributions are not taxed as ordinary dividends and are sometimes called tax-free dividends or nontaxable distributions that may be fully or partly taxable as capital gains.

A return of capital distribution reduces the basis in the shares. The basis cannot be reduced below zero. If the basis is reduced to zero, the taxpayer must report the return of capital distribution on the tax return as a capital gain. The distribution is taxable if, when added to all returns of capital distribution received in past years, it is more than the basis in the shares. Whether it is a long-term or short-term capital gain depends on how long the shares had been held.

Reinvestment of Distributions

Most mutual funds permit shareholders to automatically reinvest distributions, including dividends and capital gains, in more shares in the fund. Instead of receiving cash, distributions are used to purchase additional shares.

The reinvested amounts must be reported to the IRS in the same way as if the reinvestment were received in cash. Reinvested ordinary dividends and capital gains distributions must be reported as income; reinvested exempt-interest dividends are not reported as income.

FOREIGN TAX DEDUCTION OR CREDIT

Some mutual funds invest in foreign securities or other instruments. A mutual fund may choose to allow an investor to claim a deduction or credit for the taxes the fund paid to a foreign country or U.S. possession. The notice to the fund's investors will include their share of the foreign taxes paid to each foreign country or possession, and the part of the dividend derived from sources in each country or possession.

BASIS

The basis in shares of a regulated investment company (mutual fund) is generally figured in the same way as the basis of other stock. The cost basis of purchased mutual fund shares often includes a sales fee, also known as a *load charge*. In certain cases, the entire amount of a load charge incurred after October 3, 1989, cannot be added to the cost basis, if the load charge gives the purchaser a reinvestment right.

Commissions and Load Charges

The fees and charges paid to acquire or redeem shares of a mutual fund are not tax deductible. They are usually added to the cost of the shares and increase the basis. A fee paid to redeem the shares is usually a reduction in the redemption price (sales price) in the case of mutual funds.

Keeping Track of the Basis

The investor in mutual funds should keep careful track of his or her basis because the basis is needed to figure any gain or loss on the shares when they are sold, exchanged, or redeemed. When mutual fund shares are bought or sold, the confirmation statements should be kept to show the price paid for the shares, and the price received for the shares when sold. If the shares are acquired by gift or inheritance, the investor needs information that is different from that in a confirmation statement for figuring the basis of those shares. The basis of shares of a mutual fund is important to know in figuring a gain or loss, with the basis dependent upon how the shares are acquired.

Shares Acquired by Inheritance

If mutual funds shares are inherited shares, the basis is the fair market value (FMV) at the date of the decedent's death, or at the alternate valuation date, if chosen for estate tax purposes. In community property states, each spouse is considered to own half the estate. If one spouse dies and at least half of the community interest is includable in the decedent's gross estate, the FMV of the community property at the date of death becomes the basis of both halves of the property.

Adjusted Basis

After mutual fund shares are acquired, adjustments may need to be made to the basis. The adjusted basis of stock is the original basis, increased or reduced. The basis is increased in a fund by 65 percent of any undistributed capital gain that is included in the taxpayer's income. This has the effect of increasing the basis by the difference between the amount of gain included in income and the credit claimed for the tax considered paid on that income. The mutual fund reports the amount of undistributed capital gain.

Reduction of the Basis

The basis must be reduced in the fund by any return of capital distributions received from the fund. The basis is not reduced for distributions that are exempt-interest dividends.

SALES, EXCHANGES AND REDEMPTIONS

When mutual fund shares are sold, exchanged, or redeemed, the investor will usually have a taxable gain or deductible loss. This includes shares in a tax-exempt mutual fund. The amount of the gain or loss is the difference between the adjusted basis in the shares and the amount realized from the sale, exchange, or redemption.

Gains and losses are figured on the disposition of shares by comparing the amount realized with the adjusted basis of the owner's shares. If the amount realized is more than the adjusted basis of the shares, a gain results; if the amount realized is less than the adjusted basis of the shares, a loss results. The amount received from a disposition of mutual fund shares is the money and value of any property received for the shares disposed of, minus expenses of sale such as redemption fees, sales commissions, sales charges, or exit fees.

The exchange of one fund for another fund is a taxable exchange, regardless of whether shares in one fund are exchanged for shares in another fund that has the same distributor or underwriter without paying a sales charge. Any gain or loss on the investment in the original shares as a capital gain or loss must be reported in the year in which the exchange occurs. Service charges or fees paid in connection with an exchange can be added to the cost of the shares acquired. Mutual funds and brokers must report to the IRS the proceeds from sales, exchanges, or redemptions. The broker must give each customer a written statement with the information by January 31 of the year following the calendar year the transaction occurred. The broker must be given a correct taxpayer identification number (TIN); a social security number is acceptable as a TIN.

Identifying the Shares Sold

When mutual fund shares are disposed of, the investor must determine which shares were sold and the basis of those shares. If the shares were acquired all on the same day and for the same price, figuring their basis is not difficult; however, for shares that are acquired at various times, in various quantities, and at various prices, determining the cost basis can be a difficult process. Two methods can be used to figure the basis, the cost basis, or the average basis.

Under the cost basis one of the following methods can be chosen:

1. Specific share identification.
2. First-in first-out (FIFO).

If the shares sold can be definitely identified, the adjusted basis of those particular shares can be used to figure a gain or loss. The shares can be adequately identified, even if bought in different lots at various prices and times, if:

1. The buyer specifies to the broker or other agent the particular shares to be sold or transferred at the time of the sale or transfer.
2. The buyer receives confirmation of the specification from his or her broker in writing within a reasonable time.

The confirmation by the mutual fund must state that the seller instructed the broker to sell particular shares. The owner of the shares has to be able to prove the basis of the specified shares at the time of sale or transfer.

If the shares were acquired at different times or at different prices, and the seller cannot identify which shares were sold, the basis of the shares acquired initially (first-in, first-out) is used as the basis of the shares sold. Therefore, the oldest shares still available are considered sold first. An adequate record should be kept of each purchase and any dispositions of the shares, until all shares purchased at the same time have been disposed of completely.

Average Basis

The average basis can be used to figure a gain or loss when all or part of the number of shares in a regulated investment company are sold. This choice can be made only if acquired at various times and prices, and the shares were left on deposit in an account handled by a custodian or agent who acquires or redeems those shares. The investor may be able to find the average basis of the shares from information provided by the fund. Once the average basis is used, it must continue to be used for all accounts in the same fund. However, a different method can be used for the shares in other funds.

To figure average basis, one of the following methods can be used:

1. Single-category method.
2. Double-category method.

Single-Category Method.   In the single-category method, the average cost is found of all shares owned at the time of each disposition, regardless of how long the shares were owned. Shares acquired with reinvested dividends or capital gains distributions must be included. Even if only one category is used to compute the basis, it is possible to have short-term or long-term gains or losses. To determine the holding period, the shares disposed of are considered to be those acquired first. The following steps are used to compute the basis of shares sold:

1. The cost of all shares owned is added.
2. The result of Step 1 is divided by the number of shares owned. This gives the *average basis* per share.
3. The result of Step 2 is multiplied by the number of shares sold. This gives the basis of the shares sold.

The basis of the shares determined under average basis is the basis of all the shares in the account at the time of each sale. If no shares were acquired or sold since the last sale, the basis of the remaining shares at the time of the next sale is the same as the basis of the shares sold in the last sale.

Double-Category Method.   In the double-category method, all shares in an account at the time of each disposition are divided into two categories: short-term and long-term. The adjusted basis of each share in a category is the total adjusted basis of all shares in that category at the time of disposition, divided by the total shares in the category.

The investor can specify to the custodian or agent handling the account from which category the shares are to be sold or transferred. The custodian or agent must confirm in writing the seller's specification. If the investor does not specify or receive confirmation, the shares sold must first be charged against the long-term category and then any remaining shares sold against the short-term category.

When a share has been held for more than one year, it must be transferred from the short-term category to the long-term category. When the change is made, the basis of a transferred share is its actual cost or adjusted basis; if some of the shares in the short-term category have been disposed of, its basis falls under the average basis method. The average basis of the undisposed shares would be figured at the time of the most recent disposition from this category.

Holding Period

When mutual fund shares are disposed of, the holding period must be determined. The period starts by using the trade date—the *trade date* is the date on which the holder of the shares bought or sold the mutual fund shares. Most mutual funds will show the trade date on confirmation statements of the purchases and sales.

INVESTMENT EXPENSES

The expenses of producing taxable investment income on a *nonpublicly* offered mutual fund during the year are generally deductible expenses; these include counseling and advice, legal and accounting fees, and investment newsletters. These are deductible as miscellaneous itemized deductions to the extent that they exceed 2 percent of adjusted gross income. Interest paid on money to buy or carry investment property is also deductible.

A nonpublicly offered mutual fund is one that:

1. Is not continuously offered pursuant to a public offering.
2. Is not regularly traded on an established securities market.
3. Is not held by at least 500 persons at all times during the tax year.

Generally, mutual funds are *publicly* offered funds. Expenses of publicly offered mutual funds are not treated as miscellaneous itemized deductions because these mutual funds report only the net amount of investment income after the investor's share of the investment expenses has been deducted. Expenses on the shares of nonpublicly offered mutual funds can be claimed as a miscellaneous itemized deduction subject to the 2 percent limit.

Expenses cannot be deducted for the collection or production of exempt-interest dividends. Expenses must be allocated if they were for both taxable and tax-exempt income. One accepted method for allocating expenses is to divide them in the same proportion that the tax-exempt income from the mutual fund is to the total income from the fund.

The amount that can be deducted as investment interest expense must be limited in two different ways. First, the interest cannot be deducted for the expenses borrowed to buy or carry shares in a mutual fund that distributes only tax-exempt dividends. Second, investment interest is limited by the amount of investment income. Deductions for interest expense are limited to the amount of net investment income. Net investment is figured by subtracting investment expenses other than interest from investment income. Investment income includes gross income derived from property held for investment, such as interest, dividends, annuities, and royalties. It does not include net capital gains derived from disposing of investment property, or capital gains distributions from mutual fund shares. Investment interest that cannot be deducted because of the 2% limit can be carried forward to the next tax year, provided that net investment income exceeds investment interest in the later year.

BACKGROUND OF SEC FINAL RULES AND AMENDMENTS ON INDEPENDENT FUND ADVISORS

Mutual funds are organized as corporations, trusts or limited partnerships under state laws and thus are owned by their shareholders, beneficiaries or partners.

Like other types of corporations, trusts or partnerships, a mutual fund must be operated for the benefit of its owners. However, unlike most business organizations, mutual funds are typically organized and operated by an investment adviser who is responsible for the day-to-day operations of the fund. In most cases, the investment adviser is separate and distinct from the fund it advises, with primary responsibility and loyalty to its own shareholders.

Therefore, the "external management" of mutual funds presents inherent conflicts of interest and potential for abuses that the Investment Company Act and the Securities and Exchange Commission (SEC) have addressed in different ways.

One of the ways that the Act addresses conflicts between advisers and funds is by giving mutual fund boards of directors, and in particular the disinterested directors, an important role in fund governance. In relying upon fund boards to represent fund investors and protect their interests, Congress avoided the more detailed regulatory provisions that characterize other regulatory schemes for collective investments.

The SEC has similarly relied extensively on independent directors in rules that exempt funds from provisions of the Investment Company Act.

SEC Study of Role of Independent Directors

The SEC pointed out that millions of Americans had been investing in mutual funds, which experienced a tremendous growth in popularity over the previous 20 years. In 1999 and 2000, because of that growth and the growing reliance on independent directors to protect fund investors, the SEC felt compelled to study:

1. The governance of investment companies.
2. The role of independent directors.
3. SEC rules that rely on oversight by independent directors.
4. The information that funds are required to provide to shareholders about their independent directors.

They held a roundtable discussion at which independent directors, investor advocates, executives of fund advisers, academics and experienced legal counsel offered a variety of perspectives and suggestions. After evaluating the ideas and suggestions offered by roundtable participants, the SEC proposed a package of rule and form amendments that were designed to:

1. Reaffirm the important role that independent directors play in protecting fund investors.
2. Strengthen their hand in dealing with fund management.
3. Reinforce their independence.
4. Provide investors with better information to assess the independence of directors.

In addition to input from the roundtable, in response to their usual policy of requesting comments to proposed rule changes, amendments and additions, the SEC received 142 comment letters on the proposals, including 86 letters from independent directors.

Commenters generally supported the efforts to enhance the independence and effectiveness of fund directors, although many offered recommendations for improving portions of the proposals. Many of these letters were taken into consideration in formulating the final rules and amendments.

Early Results of Study

The SEC believes that the efforts to improve the governance of mutual funds on behalf of mutual fund investors began to have effect even before the final adoption. The roundtable discussions and proposed rules provoked a great deal of discussion among directors, advisers, counsel, and investors about governance practices and policies. After the roundtable, an advisory group organized by the Investment Company Institute (ICI) made recommendations regarding fund governance in a "best practices" report.

Many boards adopted the recommendations set forth in the ICI Advisory Group Report. Some groups of independent directors hired independent counsel for the first time. Director nomination and selection procedures have been revised.

During the next year, Commissioners and members of the staff began meeting with independent directors and sharing ideas and concerns regarding the governance of mutual funds. A former SEC chairman established the Mutual Fund Directors Education Council, a broad-based group of persons interested in fund governance and operations. Their main purpose is to foster the development of educational activities designed to promote the efficiency, independence, and accountability of independent fund directors.

The American Bar Association formed a task force to examine the role of counsel to independent directors, and the task force released a report offering guidance to counsel and fund directors regarding standards of independence for counsel, and guidelines for reducing potential conflicts of interest (ABA Task Force Report).

All of these initiatives have focused attention on the important role of independent directors, and their importance in promoting and protecting the interests of fund shareholders.

THE SEC ADOPTS FINAL RULES AND AMENDMENTS ON FUND GOVERNANCE

In January 2001, the SEC adopted amendments to certain exemptive rules under the Investment Company Act of 1940 relating to investment company governance based upon changes that were proposed in October 1999. Many of the proposed rule and form amendments were basically those initially proposed. However, the final amendments, summarized below, contain several modifications made as a result of suggestions made during the comment period. In line with the original proposals, the rule and form changes cover three areas:

1. Rule amendments relating to directors.
2. Conditions for reliance on certain exemptive rules.
3. Changes in disclosure requirements.

These amendments are designed to enhance the independence and effectiveness of boards of directors of investment companies and to better enable investors to assess the independence of those directors.

THE ROLE OF INDEPENDENT DIRECTORS OF INVESTMENT COMPANIES

The SEC's first order of business was adopting amendments to require (for funds relying on these "certain exemptive rules") that:

1. Independent directors constitute a majority of the fund's board of directors.
2. Independent directors select and nominate other independent directors.
3. Any legal counsel for the fund's independent directors is an independent legal counsel—that is, he or she does not also represent the fund's management or close affiliates.

The three new conditions are generally the same as had been proposed, though some clarifications and modifications were made. Specifics of these items are discussed in some detail below.

Independent Directors Constitute Majority of Fund's Board

Rather than the 40 percent previously required by the Investment Company Act of 1940, the Commission adopted a simple majority independence requirement. They had originally proposed a two-thirds supermajority requirement, but adopted the simple majority in response to public comments.

According to the adopting release, a majority independence requirement will permit, under state law, the independent directors to have a strong influence on fund management. It should enable them to represent shareholders better by being in a stronger position to elect officers, call meetings and solicit proxies.

To allow funds time to implement this provision, compliance is required after July 1, 2002.

In connection with this new requirement, the Commission also adopted a new rule that suspends the board composition requirement *temporarily* in the event of the death, disqualification or bona fide resignation of a director. The final rule provides that if the remaining directors can fill the vacant board position, the suspension is for 90 days; if a shareholder vote is required, the suspension is for 150 days. This time period begins to run when the fund no longer meets the board composition requirement, even if the fund is not yet aware of its non-compliance. The effective date for this specific rule was February 15, 2001.

Independent Directors Select, Nominate Other Independent Directors

This rule amendment was adopted substantially as proposed. The adopting release clarifies that a fund's adviser may be involved in the nomination process. The independent directors must maintain control of the nomination process; however, the adviser may suggest candidates at the independent directors' invitation and provide administrative assistance in the selection and nomination process.

The self-nomination requirement is not intended to supplant or limit the ability of shareholders under state law to nominate directors. At the same time, the involvement of shareholders or the adviser does not excuse the independent directors from their responsibility to canvass, recruit, interview and solicit candidates.

The self-nomination requirement is prospective only. Current independent directors who were selected through a different process may continue to serve as independent directors but—beginning after July 1, 2002—all *new* independent directors must be researched, recruited, considered and formally named by the existing independent directors.

Legal Counsel for Independent Directors Must Be an "Independent Legal Counsel"

This rule's conditions were modified in response to the large number of comments the SEC received relative to it. The proposal defined "independent legal counsel" in narrow terms. Many commenters felt that this explicit definition of "independent" could have unintended negative results:

1. Discouraging the independent directors from even consider selecting their own counsel.
2. Limiting the pool of eligible counsel unnecessarily.
3. In some instances, possibly forcing independent directors to terminate longstanding relationships with counsel.

In line with the final rule, as well as with the proposal, independent directors are not required to have counsel. However, if they do, that counsel must be an "independent legal counsel," as determined by the independent directors. A "person"—the lawyer, his or her firm and partners and employees—is considered an independent legal counsel if the independent directors:

1. Determine that any representation of the fund's investment adviser, principal underwriter, administrator or their control persons during the past two fiscal years is or was "sufficiently limited" that it is unlikely to adversely affect the professional judgment of the person in providing legal representation.

2. Have obtained sufficient background information from the counsel for them to determine at that time that any relationship is, indeed, "sufficiently limited." The legal counsel must update the independent directors promptly on any relevant information if the counsel begins or materially increases his or her representation of a management organization or control person.

Directors may rely on information provided by counsel for these decisions.

The final rule requires that the independent directors determine whether a person is an independent legal counsel at least annually. The basis for the determination must be recorded in the board's meeting minutes. If the board receives information from counsel concerning his or her representation of a management organization or a control person, the fund can continue to rely on the relevant exemptive rules for up to three months. This period should provide sufficient time for the independent directors to make a new determination about the counsel's independence under the circumstances or, on the other hand, to hire a new independent legal counsel.

The SEC states that in making the determination of whether counsel is an independent legal counsel, the judgment of the independent directors must be *reasonable* and should take into consideration all relevant factors in evaluating whether the conflicting representations are sufficiently limited. For example, the independent directors should consider such factors as:

1. Is the representation current and ongoing?
2. Does it involve a minor or substantial matter?
3. Does it involve the fund, the adviser, or an affiliate, and if an affiliate, what is the nature and extent of the affiliation?
4. The duration of the conflicting representation.
5. The importance of the representation to counsel and his firm, including the extent to which counsel relies on that representation economically.
6. Does it involve work related to mutual funds?
7. Whether or not the individual who will serve as legal counsel was or is involved in the representation. (In the opinion of the SEC, this would exclude a lawyer from simultaneously representing the fund's adviser and independent directors in connection with such matters as the negotiation of the advisory contract or distribution plan or other *key areas* of conflict between the fund and its adviser.)

Compliance with the independent legal counsel provision also became effective July 1, 2002.

AMENDMENTS TO EXEMPTIVE RULES TO ENHANCE DIRECTOR INDEPENDENCE AND EFFECTIVENESS

In amending the 10 rules to exempt funds and their affiliates from certain prohibitions of the Act, the SEC added conditions to the Exemptive Rules to require that, for funds relying upon those rules, the independence and effectiveness of independent directors must be guaranteed. The efforts in that direction have been discussed above.

The SEC pointed out that some commenters questioned the need to amend the rules, because each rule already requires independent directors to approve separately some of the fund's activities under the rule. In truth, these rules were selected because they require the independent judgment and scrutiny by the independent directors in overseeing activities that are beneficial to funds and investors *but involve inherent conflicts of interest between the funds and their managers.* The amendments are designed to increase the ability of independent directors to perform their important responsibilities under each of these rules.

Amendments to Exemptive Rules

The 10 rules exempting funds and their affiliates from certain stipulations of the Investment Company Act make the following actions possible:

1. Permission for funds to purchase securities in a primary offering when an affiliated broker-dealer is a member of the underwriting syndicate.
2. Permission to use fund assets to pay distribution expenses.
3. Permission for fund boards to approve interim advisory contracts without shareholder approval.
4. Permission for securities transactions to take place between a fund and another client of the fund's adviser.
5. Permission for mergers between certain affiliated funds.
6. Permission for funds and their affiliates to purchase joint liability insurance policies.
7. Specific conditions under which funds may pay commissions to affiliated brokers in connection with the sale of securities on an exchange.
8. Permission for funds to maintain joint insured bonds.
9. Permission for funds to issue multiple classes of voting stock.
10. Permission for the operation of interval funds by enabling closed-end funds to repurchase their shares from investors.

ADDITIONAL RULE CHANGES

Other rule changes affecting independent directors and their qualification duties and responsibilities have been adopted, including:

Joint Insurance Policies

A rule of the Investment Company Act has been amended so that funds may now purchase joint "errors and omissions" insurance policies for their officers and directors, but *only* if the policy does not exclude:

1. Bona fide claims brought against any independent director by a co-insured.
2. Claims brought by a co-insured in which the fund is a co-defendant with an independent director.

This provision became effective July 1, 2002.

Independent Audit Committees

The SEC also adopted a new rule exempting funds from the Act's requirement that shareholders vote on the selection of the fund's independent public accountant if the fund has an audit committee composed *wholly* of independent directors.

The rule will permit continuing oversight of the fund's accounting and auditing processes by an independent audit committee instead of the shareholder vote. Commenters agreed that the shareholder ratification had become largely perfunctory and that an independent audit committee could exercise more meaningful oversight.

Consistent with the proposed rule, the final rule provides that a fund is exempt from having to seek shareholder approval if:

1. The fund establishes an audit committee composed solely of independent directors to oversee the fund's accounting and auditing processes.
2. The fund's board of directors adopts an audit committee charter setting forth the committee's structure, duties, powers, and methods of operation or sets out similar provisions in the fund's charter or bylaws.
3. The fund maintains a copy of such an audit committee charter. Some commenters questioned whether the proposed rule would require the audit committee to supervise a fund's day-to-day management and operations. The rule does not require, nor was it intended, that an audit committee perform daily management or supervision of a fund's operations.

The effective date for this particular rule was February 15, 2001.

Qualification as an Independent Director

A new rule conditionally exempts individuals from being disqualified from serving as independent directors because they invest in index funds that hold shares of the fund's adviser or underwriter or their controlling persons. The rule as *proposed* would have applied only if the value of securities issued by the adviser or controlling person did not exceed 5 percent of the value of any index tracked by the index fund. The SEC has *modified the final rule* to provide relief if a fund's investment objective is to replicate the performance of one or more "broad-based" indices. The effective date for this rule was February 15, 2001.

In addition, the SEC has rescinded a rule that provides relief from a section of the Investment Company Act defining when a fund director is considered to be independent. The SEC had proposed amending the rule to permit a somewhat higher percentage of a fund's independent directors be affiliated with registered broker-dealers, under certain circumstances. The enactment of the Gramm-Leach-Bliley Act amended the Act to establish new standards for determining independence under the same circumstances, thus making the proposed amendments redundant. The rescission became effective on May 12, 2001.

Recordkeeping Requirements

The rule was amended to require funds to preserve for at least six years any record of:

1. The initial determination that a director qualifies as an independent director.
2. Each subsequent determination of whether the director continues to qualify as an independent director.
3. The determination that any person who is acting as legal counsel to the independent directors is an independent legal counsel.

These requirements are designed to permit the SEC's staff to monitor a fund's assessment of director independence. Compliance with this requirement was required after July 1, 2002.

DISCLOSURE REQUIREMENTS

As is to be expected the SEC has adopted rule and form changes that will require funds to *disclose additional director information* beyond that currently available in a fund's statement of additional information (SAI) and proxy statements. The amendments were adopted with several modifications to tailor them more closely to the goal of providing shareholders with better information without overburdening directors.

All of these new registration statements and post-effective amendments that are annual updates to effective registration statements, proxy statements for the election of directors, and reports to shareholders filed on or after January 31, 2002 must comply with the new disclosure requirements. The new requirements are discussed below.

Basic Information About Fund Directors

The Commission has adopted, as they had proposed, requirements that basic information about the identity and experience of directors should be outlined in tabular form and included in the fund's annual report to shareholders, the SAI and any proxy statement for the election of directors. Specifically, the table must disclose detailed information about each and every director:

1. Name, address, and age.
2. Current positions held with the fund.
3. Term of office and length of time served.
4. Principal occupations during the past five years.
5. Number of portfolios overseen within the fund complex (as opposed to the current requirement to disclose the number of registered investment companies overseen).
6. Other directorships held outside the fund complex.
7. The relationship, events, or transactions that make each "interested" director an "interested person" of the fund.

The annual report is required also to include a statement that the SAI has additional information about the directors that is available without charge upon request.

Ownership of Equity Securities in Fund Complex

The proposed requirement to disclose the amount of equity securities of funds in a fund complex owned by each fund director was adopted with certain modifications, as described below.

Disclosure of Amount Owned.   The SEC responded to comments that fund disclosure of the dollar amount of directors' fund holdings was not necessary to demonstrate alignment of directors' interests with those of shareholders and would impinge on directors' privacy. The provision adopted requires disclosure of a director's holdings of fund securities using specified dollar ranges rather than an exact dollar amount. Commenters considered the exact amount impinged too greatly upon the director's privacy. The rule incorporates the following dollar ranges: none; 0–$10,000; $10,001–$50,000; $50,001–$100,000; over $100,000.

Beneficial Ownership.   The SEC received a number of comments requesting clarification about the types of director holdings that would be disclosed under the proposal. Based on these comments, the Commission reevaluated the proposal to require disclosure of securities owned beneficially and of record by each director.

Under the original proposal, beneficial ownership would have been determined in accordance with a rule of the Exchange Act, which focuses on a person's voting and investment power. In view of the objective of providing information about the alignment of directors' and shareholders' interests, they believe that disclosure of record holdings should not be required and that the focus of beneficial ownership should be on whether a director's economic interests are tied to the securities rather than on his or her ability to exert voting power or to dispose of the securities.

As a result, disclosure of director holdings will be required only in those instances where the director's economic interests are tied to the securities and will not be triggered solely by his or her ability to exert voting power or to dispose of the securities.

Disclosure of Ownership of Funds Within the Same Family of Investment Companies.   The proposal that directors disclose their aggregate holdings in a fund complex was modified to require disclosure of:

1. Each director's ownership in every fund that he oversees.
2. Each director's aggregate ownership of all funds that he oversees within a fund family.

The ownership in specific funds demonstrates a director's alignment of interests with shareholders. The SEC realized that a director may have legitimate reasons for not having shares of a specific fund in his or her portfolio; however, the adopting release states that the requirement to disclose aggregate ownership should help to negate any inference that otherwise could be made about why a director has chosen not to own shares of a particular fund.

To determine a director's holdings in a fund complex, the SEC agreed with public comments that the proposed definition of fund complex was too broad. Instead, the Commission adopted a more specific definition of "family of investment companies," to include only funds that have the same investment adviser or principal underwriter and actually publicize themselves to investors as related companies for purposes of investment and investor services.

The equity ownership information must be included in the SAI and any proxy statement relating to the election of directors. For the proxy statement, the equity ownership information must be provided as of the most recent practicable date, as proposed, in order to ensure that shareholders receive up-to-date information when they are asked to vote to elect directors.

For the SAI, the SEC modified the proposal to require that the equity ownership information be provided as of the end of the last completed calendar year. They believe that this modified time period requirement facilitates our goal that investors receive equity ownership information to evaluate whether directors' interests are aligned with their own and imposes less of a burden on directors, especially those who serve multiple funds with staggered fiscal years.

Conflicts of Interest. Consistent with the proposal, fund SAIs and proxy statements will be required to disclose three types of circumstances that, according to the adopting release, could affect the allegiance of fund directors to shareholders. These are the positions, interests and transactions and relationships of directors and their immediate family members with the fund and persons related to the fund. The proposal was modified in several significant respects in response to comments that it was too broad.

Persons Covered. The final rule excludes "interested" directors from the conflict of interest disclosure requirements in both the SAI and proxy statement.

In addition, the SEC narrowed the scope of "immediate family members" covered by the disclosure requirements to a director's spouse, children *residing in the director's household,* including step and adoptive children and dependents of the director. The SEC concluded that these are family members from whom directors can reasonably be expected to obtain the required information. Thus, in contrast to the proposal, the final disclosure requirements do not apply to the director's parents, siblings, children not residing with the director or in-laws.

On the other hand, the SEC did not go to the extent of adopting a suggestion made by some commenters to limit disclosure about positions, interests and transactions and relationships of a director's family members to those about which the director has actual knowledge.

The SEC excluded administrators from the persons related to the fund that are covered by the requirements. This exclusion is limited to administrators that are not affiliated with the fund's adviser or principal underwriter. Entities (including administrators) that control, are controlled by or are under common control with the adviser or principal underwriter will be covered by the disclosure requirements.

Despite these modifications narrowing the disclosure requirements, the adopting release strongly suggests examining any circumstances that could *potentially impair* the independence of independent directors, regardless of whether or not such circumstances are actually spelled out in the SEC's disclosure requirements.

Threshold Amounts. The SEC adopted a $60,000 threshold for disclosure of interests, transactions and relationships. For this provision, it is necessary for a director's interest to be aggregated with those of his immediate family members.

The adopting release warns funds that the $60,000 threshold should not be equated with materiality. The statement is made that "a transaction between a director and a fund's adviser may constitute a material conflict of interest with the fund or its shareholders that is required to be disclosed, regardless of the amount involved, if the terms and conditions of the transaction are not comparable to those that would have been negotiated at 'arm's length' in similar circumstances."

Time Periods. The SEC also modified some of the proposed time periods for disclosure of conflicts of interest in the proxy statement and SAI. In the proxy statement, disclosure of positions and interests of directors and their immediate family members is required, as proposed, for a five-year period. Disclosure of material transactions and relationships must be provided from the beginning of the last two completed fiscal years. In the SAI, disclosure of positions and interests of directors and their immediate family members, as well as disclosure of material transactions and relationships is required for the two most recently completed calendar years, rather than fiscal years.

Routine, Retail Transactions and Relationships. The adopting release clarifies that the exception from the disclosure requirements for routine, retail transactions and relationships, such as credit card or bank or brokerage accounts (unless the director is accorded special treatment), extends to residential mortgages and insurance policies as well as other routine transactions not specifically enumerated.

The Board's Role in Fund Governance. The SEC has adopted, as proposed, disclosure requirements in the proxy rules and SAI relating to board committees. Funds must identify each standing committee of the board in both the SAI and any proxy statement for the election of directors. Funds also are required to provide:

1. A concise statement of the functions of each committee.
2. Names of the members of the committee.
3. Information regarding the number of committee meetings held during the last fiscal year.

4. An indication of whether the nominating committee would consider nominees recommended by fund shareholders; if so, procedures for submitting recommendations should be provided.

Approval of the Advisory Contract.   Funds must also disclose in the SAI the board's basis for approving an existing advisory contract. In response to comments that this disclosure would become "boilerplate," the adopting release specifies that boilerplate language is not adequate; funds are required to provide appropriate detail regarding the board's basis for approving an existing advisory contract, including the particular factors forming the basis for this determination.

Separate Disclosure.   Funds must present all disclosure for *independent directors* separately from disclosure for *interested directors* in the SAI, proxy statements for the election of directors and annual reports to shareholders. The SEC felt this would aid shareholders in understanding information about directors and in evaluating the effectiveness of independent directors to oversee fund operations.

Compliance Date for Disclosure Amendments.   All new registration statements and post-effective amendments that are annual updates to effective registration statements, proxy statements for the election of directors and reports to shareholders filed on or after January 31, 2002, must comply with the disclosure amendments. Based on the comments, the SEC felt that this would provide funds with sufficient time to make the necessary changes to disclosure documents.

Chapter 30

Demystifying Funds

CONTENTS

The Mutual Fund Industry	**30.02**
What You Buy Is What You Get	**30.03**
What Are Mutual Funds?	**30.03**
Open-Ended and Closed-Ended Mutual Funds	**30.05**
Mutual Fund Sales Costs	**30.06**
Stock Mutual Funds	**30.10**
Bond Funds	**30.12**
Selecting a Mutual Fund—Professional Rating Services	**30.16**
Periodicals: Benefits to the CPA and Client	**30.17**
Computer Software: Benefits to the CPA and Client	**30.17**
Internet Services: Benefits to the CPA and Client	**30.18**
Advice on Mutual Funds Advice	**30.18**
General Guidelines on Selecting a Mutual Fund	**30.19**
Steps to Avoid	**30.19**
Conclusion	**30.20**

Everybody loves mutual funds. The average mutual fund investor is a Baby Boomer 44 years old, married, employed, with investments in three different funds in two different mutual fund families. The household income is $60,000 per year, and the family has $50,000 in assets. In addition, the average fund owner knows absolutely nothing about what he or she owns.

The basic cause of confusion regarding mutual funds is the rapid growth and expansion of this nation's, and the entire investment world's, reliance upon this vehicle. The mutual fund vehicle is asked to be both the savior and the scapegoat for the investing public.

Approximately 90,000,000 people, representing over 50,000,000 U.S. households, own funds. The primary source of this meteoric rise in numbers is retirement plan assets. The shift from corporate-managed pension plans to self-directed retirement vehicles opened an ever-widening gate for the novice investor. Today, it is rarely the company's responsibility for planning successful employee pensions; usually, it is financially naive employees responsible for selecting successful investments for themselves. This has given new meaning to the term "dartboard investing."

Currently, almost 50 percent of all mutual fund assets are invested in stocks, with about 25 percent in bonds, and the remainder in money market funds. This is a compromised breakdown because there is a wide variety of fund types, many of which defy conventional asset labels and commingle asset types. Not every formula is the same.

THE MUTUAL FUND INDUSTRY

Wall Street is as fond of mutual funds as are investors. From a traditional investment banking standpoint, issuer products have been largely stocks or bonds. Furthermore, most of the attention was concentrated on the institutional investors, who would buy most of the stocks or bonds in a banking issue for their own use—investment, pension plans, cash flow needs, or whatever. In recent years, however, mutual funds (overwhelmingly directed toward the retail investor) have assumed a larger and larger slice of the investment banker pie. Not surprisingly, Wall Street pays attention.

Both open-ended and closed-ended mutual funds have generated enormous banking fees and enjoyed enthusiastic acceptance with investors. "Enthusiastic acceptance" describes a huge asset shift—and assets mean a lot to Wall Street. Of late, the most institutionally driven of investment banking firms have signed mutual fund distribution contracts with the large retail wire houses and discount brokerage firms. This is a revenue expanding and gathering activity for both.

Today, the retail investor directly owns half of all U.S. financial assets and will acquire more as savings and retirement investment expands and grows. Much of this money resides in mutual fund investments. The scramble is still unfolding regarding how this class will grow and best be harnessed by both institutions and investors.

Another measure of the fund industry's success is its seemingly daily consolidation. Mutual fund families are on a merger course that rivals the consolidation mania of the rest of the financial services industry itself. As the families consolidate, so do the funds. Happily, all this appears beneficial for the investor, too, because the investor has more funds to choose from within the expanded family groups.

To summarize, mutual fund management is a primary source of income to the financial services industry. That income is largely impervious to market fluctuations because funds need management in bad years as well as good years. Long-term investing is simply that: there will be both up and down cycles. It is the overall, long-term, extended holding period (5–10-year) return that is important to the investor because the long time frame is where the benefits lie—not short term. The investor, once again, pays fees no matter what goes on with the markets.

WHAT YOU BUY IS WHAT YOU GET

On the other hand, investors can get quite a bit for what they pay. The average mutual fund investor owns $25,000 worth of funds. Almost 80 percent of those funds are selected with the help of an investment professional. There are three basic types of funds: stock, bonds and money market funds. Three-quarters of all fund owners own stock funds, half own bond funds, and half own money market funds. Almost all owners own two or three of the three types of funds. Half are comfortable with risk, a quarter are somewhat speculatively inclined, and almost 10 percent are either totally risk adverse or totally high risk oriented, putting them at either extreme of the investor bell curve. Each investor's fee facilitates finding each investor the correct fit.

How do the mutual fund investors get what they pay for? Probably only a small percentage of fund investors understand diversification and asset allocation. Consequently, most investors in mutual funds don't know what they own. Only a fraction of investors could ever hope to duplicate their fund performance on their own. Quite simply this is what they pay for—high returns from investments they may know nothing about and have no input in selecting. This represents an enormous opportunity for the CPA/PFS to add value.

WHAT ARE MUTUAL FUNDS?

What are these behemoths we call mutual funds? They're everyone who wants to commingle their money to work more aggressively to increase their wealth. They prefer to do it with a collectively huge sum of money rather than individually with a small amount of money. The benefit to the investor is that a small amount of money makes an investor part-owner in fabulous wealth that is invested for them according to a prospectus plan.

For the most part, they are pooled assets historically created for two types of investors. These investors were people with little time or with moderate amounts of money—as little as $100. Like most antiquated investment rules, these investor profiles have expanded with time, but the rules still apply to the most representative types of mutual fund shareholders, those with little time and moderate amounts of money. These pooled assets make investing easier because, once the investor designates a fund type, the mutual fund management company assumes responsibility for everything else. The selection, diversification, buying and selling—all are the direct responsibility of the manager.

If the manager has selected correctly, funds can perform extremely efficiently. Consequently, people with a lot of money invest in funds for the extraordinary level of performance they can enjoy. Many of the investment banking firm mutual funds were created for this group. A mutual fund can own hundreds or even thousands of individual issues. This makes the whole process cost-effective. Purchases in bigger blocks generate fewer fees. In addition, some investors who enjoy spending time studying investments spend it examining and rating different funds. They do this because mutual fund investment can be a cost-efficient way to diversify assets. Most funds have diversification above and beyond almost any investor's dreams.

There is a major disadvantage to all of this. By delegating responsibility to a manager, the investor loses control over the investment and, thus, his or her money. The investor's choice is confined to buying and selling the fund. Many investors view security selection as a sport. It is important for the CPA to rein in this activity.

Direct stock and bond investment costs end as soon as the client buys the security; mutual fund fees are ongoing. Fund fees only rarely are tied to returns. In other words, fees are rarely dictated by performance. Usually, they are fixed, regardless of how the market or how the funds behave. With high turnover (of assets in the fund) and increasingly modest disclosure requirements (of activity generated within the mutual fund), interested investors often have no idea (other than asset class) what they own or what they have earned.

To top it off, the primary fund support document, the prospectus, may be difficult to understand. However, recent prospectus requirements were cut and edited to modest-sized disclosure documents by the Securities and Exchange Commission's Rule on the "Profile" disclosure option. Another SEC Rule mandates the use of "Plain English" for disclosure documents. (Both SEC Rules are explained in other chapters.)

Not all funds have these various disadvantages. Furthermore, many have them to a lesser extent than their more confusing or complicated mutual fund rivals. It is true that some mutual funds' portfolio guidelines are almost impossible to understand. Incredibly enough, however, mutual fund companies are regularly rated, based on the reporting documents to shareholders and their shareholder relations departments. But their portfolio guidelines never win awards for clarity.

OPEN-ENDED AND CLOSED-ENDED MUTUAL FUNDS

There are two types of mutual funds: open ended and closed ended. By far the most common, popular and largest are open ended, so-called because they can continue to take in new money every trading day, thus creating new shares that represent a pro rata portion (the investor's share of the pot) of the fund's assets. Open-ended funds are listed in the mutual fund section of the business section of the newspaper, fund family by fund family. They are priced by their net asset value (total net value of the fund divided by the number of shares in the fund) at the close of the trading day. There are no fluctuating quotes during the course of the market day.

Closed-ended funds, on the other hand, trade throughout the day on an exchange the same way stocks do—their prices fluctuate during the course of the day and are listed and quoted daily under their proper exchange listing. Closed-ended funds are always listed under the exchange quotes (in alphabetical order) of the exchange on which they are listed (usually the New York Stock Exchange and American Stock Exchange). They are not priced by their net asset value the way open-ended funds are. The two can vary widely—market (price) value and underlying asset value. Most closed-ended funds sell at either a premium (above) or a discount (below) to their underlying net asset value. Net asset value is total fund assets remaining after total fund liabilities, such as trading fees and margin interest, have been subtracted. XYZ Fund owns $125,000,000 of stock (after all liabilities are subtracted from fund assets) and there are 10,000,000 shares outstanding. Therefore, the net asset value is $12.50 ($125,000,000 divided by 10,000,000 shares = $12.50).

Closed-ended funds tend to be a bit more esoteric as investment items than open-ended funds because little about them is as cut-and-dried as open-ended funds. Discounts to (prices below) their net asset value are much more common than premiums (prices above), so people tend to assume there is something wrong with closed-ended funds per se. Many of the funds are made up of foreign, illiquid, or small capitalization securities; therefore, many investors are wary of investing in something they are unfamiliar with and do not understand. Closed-ended funds often employ leveraging (borrowing) to enhance cash flow, gains or total return—many clients want nothing to do with leveraged securities purchases in any form and should avoid closed-end funds altogether.

MUTUAL FUND SALES COSTS

Far more popular than worrying about closed-ended funds and their investment practices is the issue of mutual fund costs. A large library could be filled with the book, magazine, newspaper, TV and radio coverage of mutual fund costs. They all so thoroughly contradict one another and come to such contrary conclusions that, other than as a cure for insomnia, they may be collectively without value. As an introduction to mutual fund costs, the CPA/PFS must remember there are no free lunches in the mutual fund industry. Mutual fund companies are not philanthropic entities. They are in the business of making money for themselves and their clients. If they don't, they don't survive.

Definitions of Sales Fees of Mutual Funds

The issue of cost arises because there is a multiplicity of pricing matrixes for the same or very similar products. The sales fees of mutual funds are called "loads." There are front-ended loads, no-loads, back-ended (trailing) loads, and level-load funds. In addition, there are internal charges, called 12(b)-1 fees and management fees, which serve to further muddy the waters. Enumerated, stated and defined are all the loads:

1. *Load*—the different types of sales charges associated with open-ended mutual fund purchases.
2. *Front-ended load*—up-front pay for the purchase.
3. *No-load*—no direct purchase or sell costs are associated with investment. However, there are internal fees (to make up for no direct sales charges), which can be considerable.
4. *Back-ended (trailing) load*—a fee is attached if the fund is liquidated within a stated time period that declines at stated intervals, usually yearly, as ownership continues.
5. *Level-load*—a combination of front-ended and back-ended (trailing) load in which a reduced front-ended charge is paid upon purchase and a reduced back-ended (trailing) load is paid if the investment is liquidated early in holding period.
6. *Internal charges*—fees paid within the fund itself for the ongoing expenses of the fund.
7. *12(b)-1 fees*—fees charged to fund assets for mutual fund advertising and sales.
8. *Management fees*—administrative and trading costs charged to the fund assets.

The Significance of Fund Costs

To an investor, these charges are at best inconsequential and at worst blinding. At one end of the spectrum, there are investors who ignore the costs of a product and simply invest passively, regardless of the price. At the other end, are investors who ignore every characteristic of a fund except its costs. The realistic approach lies somewhere between the two extremes. The consequence of mutual fund costs is significant because of the nature of mutual fund investing itself. A single year of sales and related fees may not seem like much, but mutual fund investment is perceived as a long-term commitment. With time (as these fees never go away), the costs of a fund are clearly significant, because they affect fund performance. The more sophisticated a fund's investment mission, the more sizable are their fees. There are no superexpensive plain-vanilla index funds; there are no bargain-basement leveraged, international, multi-sector commodities pools. Often, then, but not always, the investors pay for what they get. However, it is a mistake to assume that the highest fees necessarily guarantee the investor the best manager or performance. The highest fees simply provide the investor with the most costly securities—much of the time.

High costs generate virulent controversy because investors do not like to pay them and, as already stated, the costs do not go away. It is incorrect to assume that someone who attacks mutual fund fees is simply a crank unwilling to pay fair value for services rendered. Studies suggest that, when mutual funds perform above the average of income funds, their success is directly related to modest costs. Conversely, these studies suggest that, when funds perform below the average, they lose too much return to the cost of the fees. Internal fees rarely scale down as funds grow in size; some studies suggest that fees tend to go up as funds do better! So, one is at a loss to determine exactly what is fair. "Fair" pricing structure in mutual funds may be impossible to define, but everyone is well advised to pay attention to all of these costs.

How Mutual Fund Costs Affect Performance

Less subjectively, it can be said that a lot of effort has been expended trying to answer questions about mutual fund costs and almost all of that effort focuses on performance. How do costs affect performance? Respected research offers conflicting data. One company that researches, evaluates, and comments on mutual funds, has concluded that, over the long run (10 years), fund returns are not influenced by the type of sales charges a fund family uses. This company perceives the real issue to be whether investors receive fair value for whatever expense they generate determining their mutual fund selections.

The company addresses investor need by looking at:

1. What the investor can expect from a fund.
2. Products offered by the different fund families—by segregating all the various types of funds and defining them in plain English.
3. Value added by the fund family—by determining the role played in various fund classes and types by managers, trading costs and management fees.

Of mutual fund sales, 25 to 30 percent are no-load. Much of the no-load sales are in defined contribution retirement plans, an area that load-fund families are aggressively targeting. More and more investors feel the need to consult professional advice and are unwilling to go the investment route solo with direct-marketed (not broker-sold) mutual funds. Supporting the point, more and more direct-marketed fund families have sprouted broker-marketed fund subsidiaries, often with different names. Broker-sold funds, through the CPA/ personal financial specialist (PSF) may be less risky than direct-marketed funds for the novice investor. The financial advisor can help select the clients' fund choices and provide them with research and documentation. Most investors cannot confidently or wisely select mutual funds on their own.

Even more confusing, a financial journal has concluded that no-load mutual fund investors made more money than load investors, but that their superior results came from more aggressive investment. The problem with this conclusion is that it does not:

1. Address the suitability of the specific mutual fund for the investor.
2. Take into consideration the goals set by the individual investor.
3. Consider how asset allocation was able to offset market upsets to the good or detriment of the fund.

It is difficult to congratulate an investor group on performance achieved as a happy by-product of ignorance of their own investment profile. On the other hand, if professional advisors tend to defer to a conservative investment posture to police clients "for their own good," the clients must wonder what is going on. Until the mid-1990s, pension plan investment tended to be biased toward capital preservation and low volatility.

Hindsight demonstrates in this instance that professional advice that is too conservative is fully as undesirable as the opposite stance. It can be very difficult for the CPA to ascertain a clear picture of how a mutual fund is doing in relation to individual client's needs.

Conclusions About Mutual Fund Costs

It should be clear that cost problems in the mutual fund industry are not going away. Perhaps most inequitable is the fact that all of the costs in all of the sale configurations are borne by the investors. The investor pays for everything. Almost no fund fees are tied to the performance of the mutual fund. Consequently, the investor reads all about the gains of mutual funds but has no familiarity with the costs incurred by the fund itself. Many assumptions are made about mutual funds because the investor believes that they all behave the same as the other funds of their class and variety. They do not.

For a moment, the CPA should look at the conventional buying and selling of securities. One of the most incorrect statements made about the financial services entities that sell securities is that the industry does not care whether the market goes up or down. The conventional belief is that, buying or selling, the client has to pay a commission, so the broker makes out no matter what. Well, that's just plain silly. What is true is that the money managers who manage mutual funds often do not share the responsibility for good or bad results with mutual fund shareholders the way they do with other financial commitments. To say managers are neither rewarded for good performance nor penalized for bad is incorrect and an exaggeration. They receive better bonuses if all goes well; they are fired if things do not. However, the fund companies themselves receive the same fees regardless of the results. While it is true clients exit poor performing funds, their money tends to remain with the same mutual fund family—they simply switch to a better-performing fund within that family. The fund company still gets their fees.

Direct-sales clients can come and go as they please because they pay no direct sales fees to inhibit their departure; however, broker-sold fund families have better retention because sales regulatory principles that govern broker practices discourage switching between fund families. One would be hard put to determine which is the better practice.

So . . . What's the Answer?

The SEC requires mutual fund families to share in gains and assume responsibilities in losses if a performance-based fee program is implemented. Over an extended holding period, the fees might be the same with or without a performance-based fee program. To determine that would require still another industry study. One would suspect that the gigantic fund families (as they continue to consolidate) would not really care much. However, smaller companies with specialized funds would experience significant revenue volatility. Particularly acute would be problems that a prolonged downturn in their markets would create because these companies would lose assets. For example, any specialty fund loses money under management when its area of specialization falls out of favor.

The Answer Is . . . .

Like so many seemingly simple investment questions, there are sadly no simple answers. The global investment public continues to rely on the mutual fund industry to manage assets; therefore, the way that industry is compensated will be scrutinized. Who knows what will come of it?

Costs are more relevant an issue to the investor than ever before with their shift toward allocating capital to equity funds. The reason for this is that the cost of equity funds so grossly exceeds that of debt funds. All debt funds charge about the same amount of money to do the same thing, which is why they all tend to have about the same yield. This is anything but the case with equity funds. In a bull market, the return on successful equity funds is so high that most clients cannot see the costs that they are paying to own the funds. This is not a good situation, because it creates opportunities for shareholder abuse. However, in a bear market, every client is aware of where every penny (that they do not receive) goes. Hence, fund fees and sales charge abuses are less apt to be a problem. The issue of costs with income funds (which generate a cash flow to the client as opposed to growth, as with an equity fund) is largely self-policed in a low interest rate environment. Excessive costs eliminate yield, which is the reason most investors buy debt funds. Thus, costs tend to remain low or investors do not invest in the fund. If costs are high, they eat up the yield and investors select a different fund for their income.

Stock Mutual Funds

Again, in an equity bull market, performance can conceal a multitude of sins, let alone bury internal costs. Until 1994, a terrible year for both equity and debt securities, stock and bond fund cash flows were about equal. By 2000, the net inflow to bond funds became essentially zero. Equities account for nearly 40 percent of all household financial assets, much of them contained in mutual funds concentrating in equities. The retail investor has, for several years, been a net seller of directly owned equities.

Interestingly, from a performance standpoint, most equity mutual funds, if compared to the Standard & Poor's 500 Index, do not do well. The S&P 500 is the accepted measurement and usual index for equity performance measurement. Large equity funds have a difficult time beating their index (once again, usually, but by no means always, the S&P 500). Some of the index funds have a hard time duplicating the performance of their index.

What's an Investor to Do?

A head-banging exercise in equity fund investment futility is to try to pick funds with the aid of mass media periodical rankings. None of these publications agrees on much of anything and their choices are often atrocious performers, even if their selection is not entirely capricious. They do seem to try, and yet routinely fail. So, the CPA/PFS and client can go ahead and read periodical rankings, but they must keep in mind the lack of reliability.

Special and Sector Equity Funds

While nobody can begin to sort out magazine fund rankings, what is true is that if such specialized sectors as real asset funds, emerging economy funds, socially responsible funds, or other esoteric types suit the client's fancy, the CPA should learn a lot about how to evaluate funds. Nothing out there can help very much. Many of these funds are completely uncharacteristic and capricious in their investment styles. They often have abominable performance by any standard of measurement and are despised by the rating services. The financial planner is going to have to take down and tear apart each fund one by one to glean any uniqueness or value for the client. They are often bad investments.

Equity Funds: Costs and Conclusions

To conclude remarks on equity funds, the CPA and client cannot afford to ignore investment costs. The most common measurement of costs is expense ratios. They are a statement of costs expressed as a percentage of assets. For example, if the net asset value of a fund is $25.00 and the expenses total 50 cents, then 2 percent of the assets go to expenses. The expense ratios vary from less than 1 percent to as much as 10 percent in growth-oriented mutual funds. Once again, there is no correlation, good or bad, between expenses and performance over time. However, a "study of studies" suggests that:

1. Large capitalization fund performance is affected negatively by large fees.
2. Small capitalization stock fund performance is related positively to high expense ratios.
3. There is no correlation between costs and global fund performance. Therefore, it cannot be that the more esoteric the investment, the more money needs to be spent on the funds.

With equity mutual funds, there is really only one way to find a correlation between costs and performance. The solution is to take a long list of stock funds, break down what their expenses are allotted to, and determine whether any particular expense correlates with either positive or negative performance. Nobody wants to be the one to try to do it, though. Can anyone imagine calling a variety of privately owned investment companies to ask them for a list of their expenses, broken down item by item, for each fund? "Go fish!"

BOND FUNDS

A bond fund is a mutual fund made up almost entirely, but by no means exclusively, of bonds. There are numerous income-generating securities that can end up in a bond fund—from simple money market instruments to the sophisticated synthetics or derivatives. Their primary purpose is to generate a cash flow the investor can use for immediate spending.

Bond fund costs, happily, are clearer and easier to understand than equity fund costs. Since bond funds tend to be specialized and simple to categorize, they are easier than stock funds to evaluate. Bond funds, in brief, usually under perform their indexes, especially on a risk-adjusted, post-expense basis. In a low-interest-rate environment, the only way a manager can perform at or above his or her index is to increase his risk significantly (on a relative basis to that index and to funds like it).

In addition, the manager can try to enhance the return with strategies that few individual investors would ever consider, let alone try to do or be able to understand, on their own. At the most elementary level, very few individuals use margin to buy bonds on credit, either for income or gain. At its most sophisticated, money managers have sizable commitments to synthetically created securities, derivatives of conventional bonds, uncommon option and futures strategies . . . the list is endless.

While the aggressive management of bond funds is not categorically bad (investors do, after all, pay a fund manager to do better than they think they can do on their own), the investment public has seen some mind-boggling bond fund disasters over the last 20 years. Many of these misfortunes arose because a fund manager failed to realize exceptional returns for his or her shareholders. Although it is ludicrous to say fund managers' errors were made in an effort to offset large expenses, this strategy did play a role in these fiascoes. For example, common sense dictates that if a manager of anything—mutual fund or fast food restaurant—has large expenses, the manager tries to do the best he or she can to cover expenses.

Bond and Other Income Fund Costs

One service has claimed that risks and high expense ratios in income funds go hand in hand, especially large 12(b)-1 fees. Bond fund promotion costs through 12(b)-1 fees are so large that the effects on yield are perceptible. Evidently, aside from assuming more credit risk, expensive funds have longer duration (more volatility), use margin (leveraged purchases) and employ options and futures strategies (high risk) more often. Another of the largest managers of income funds was accused for years of buying premium bonds in its income funds only to beef up yields to cover enormous advertising costs. Of course, premiums disappear as bonds approach par value at maturity, so a lot of money just disappears from net asset value—but cash flow stays higher in the meantime.

How much of all this quibbling becomes "chicken and egg" controversy is arguable. The 12(b)-1 fees are so controversial and confusing that one can safely predict an eventual legislated end to their existence. The consumer is confused by the blend of internal sales, management and distribution fees, and logic suggests that these fees in their current form cannot last much longer. Full disclosure of costs would mitigate most of the problems attached to mutual fund fees.

Junk Bond Funds

Before addressing fund selection, there are a few special types of bond funds the financial planner should understand. Even in an equity-obsessed universe, these income funds generate a large amount of press coverage and should be understood by the financial advisor. The most notorious of all bond vehicles, in or out of a mutual fund, are junk bonds. Junk bonds are lower-rated debt that is not investment or "bank quality" debt—which must be rated BBB or better. Despite the general antipathy generated by the sector, the fact remains that junk (or high-yield bonds, to be less pejorative) generates large cash flow and excellent total return. It took a while, after Michael Milken, but lower-rated debt has returned to the generally high level of performance conventionally associated with this investment before the junk market collapse.

Junk bonds historically have returned about 50 percent more than Treasury bonds. In a time when few companies default, where there is little inflation and the economy usually chugs along quite nicely, the risks of lower-rated debt (particularly diversified in a large mutual fund investment pool) seems well worth the risk to many investors. Of particular note is that, as more companies continue to turn their performance around for the better, credit upgrades resulting from these turnarounds can only enhance the value of junk bond portfolios. An example would be all the debt issued to fund the growth and development of the major high-tech companies. When the companies were created in the 1960s and 1970s, those that were able to issue debt were rated very low. However, as some of these companies became large capitalization companies of immense value, their debt was upgraded accordingly and traded in line with the higher-quality debt to which they became comparable.

Global Bond Funds

Global bond funds enjoy reputations similar to junk bond funds. Most countries have debt that is rated below investment grade. Many countries enjoy decent ratings simply because their debt is guaranteed or backed by the U.S. government. Thanks to the collapse of short-term multimarket income funds several years ago (when much foreign debt either defaulted or dropped like a stone as the dollar strengthened), many clients respond to the mention of global bond funds with genuine loathing. The reason for this antipathy is that the short-term multimarket income funds fell apart never to recover, and they generated legal proceedings that continue to this day.

Global bond funds are sophisticated investments with multiple risks that are rather difficult to understand. Without an elaborate discussion of bond fund risks, suffice it to say that if global debt is a client's interest rate vehicle of choice, the CPA/PFS must do some homework preparatory to selecting a fund and investing the client's hard-earned money in it.

The CPA must learn about those countries that a "chosen" fund invests in. It would be unwise under any circumstances to invest in countries the client does not like. On the other hand, it would be interesting for the client to invest in countries that he or she does like. The CPA must always remember—debt securities are loans; hence, loans should be made to countries clients want to lend their money to, because that is exactly what they are doing. Then, it is important to examine the nature of the fund's currency exposure—do they own mostly dollar-denominated securities? Or are they all tied up with a lot of soft currency paper? As has been discussed, the CPA should determine whether the fund's expense ratio is consistent with the costs of implementing the investment strategy stated in its prospectus. For example, a plain vanilla fund without leverage or advanced trading strategies should have significantly lower expenses than one with sophisticated futures, options, currency and derivative plays.

Emerging Markets Bond Funds

Closely aligned to global bond fund investing are emerging markets bond fund investing. While global funds can invest in domestic and foreign debt from highest to lowest quality, emerging market bond funds invest only the debt of developing nations. The debt of emerging nations by definition is often of highest credit risk, illiquid and tied to currencies that are not traded on global markets. The fact that these currencies are often pegged to the dollar helps stabilize them, but the risks attached to these countries can quickly eliminate this advantage. It is safe to say that most emerging nation debt funds trade like high-risk equity funds with an income kicker (in the form of cash flow) attached to them. The emerging debt fund group is a vehicle designed to generate a huge cash flow, but certainly things go wrong. Every kind of risk can apply to a greater or lesser extent to emerging market debt.

Insured Municipal Bond Funds

The last bond fund the CPA should learn about is the insured municipal bond fund. Many investors become very concerned with municipal bond fund problems—problems they think owning an insured fund will cure. What they want is so many layers of protection that they ignore the fact that they may give up more income than their concern justifies. For example, if a person wants insured debt, he or she should invest in direct ownership of individual issues. Then, the investor will have fixed cash flow and fixed maturity, which do not exist in funds.

Now, to be totally contradictory, if there are high-yield (lower-rated) mutual funds of a state, the CPA should examine these offerings. The default risk of municipal debt is slight. Funds managers have mind-numbing diversity to consider in any single state's municipal funds; there are hundreds of issuers and thousands of issues. A good municipal fund manager might generate very high yields for the client unconstrained by conventional rating.

Bond Funds and Risk

Bond funds have significant risk. The types of risk associated with income-oriented investment that directly apply to income mutual funds follow:

Interest Rate Risk.   There's not a thing anyone can do about interest rates, unless they are on the Federal Reserve Board. If the CPA and the client are afraid of rates rising and eroding the value of a fund position, they should switch into the fund family's money market fund or intermediate term bond fund. Rate issues generate much less significant principal risk in intermediate-term maturities than in long-term ones. Of course, for all practical purposes, principal is not at risk in a money market fund, regardless of rate fluctuations.

Credit Risk.   If the CPA and client do not like lower-rated debt because of a fear of default, the client should not own any lower-rated debt, period. The incremental return is not worth the fact that the client will never stop worrying about his or her position.

Sector Risk.   Sector risks are very real. Most single state municipal funds are very responsive to their state's financial well-being. However, the municipal markets are comparatively stable, state to state, because they operate in fairly benign isolation and suffer from a chronic supply shortage of bonds. On the other hand, with most high-risk global, junk or emerging market funds, an investor must exercise great restraint, from an asset allocation standpoint. High yield seduces many investors with visions of chunks of cash flow dancing in their heads into overcommitting assets. Concentrated positions in low-rated and high-risk securities makes no sense in income-oriented investments—to place 25 percent of your principal at risk to generate 4 percent more income per year is hardly sound money management. Junk funds are good for income enhancement, but the client cannot overcommit to them. Murphy's Law is fully operative with greedy income investors. They are always punished.

Style Risk.   The CPA/PFS must be well-versed in leverage, options and futures strategies, derivatives and foreign exchange risk before employing these strategies to invest the clients' money in funds. Also, the financial advisor must read the prospectuses and quarterly reports of all these funds to determine which employ risk or risk management strategies and to attempt to learn exactly how they affect the performance of the funds.

SELECTING A MUTUAL FUND—PROFESSIONAL RATING SERVICES

How do the CPA and client select mutual funds? There is not a single investor out there who does not have an opinion on mutual fund selection. Most professionals rely upon one or more of the professional rating services. They are providers of services that the CPA and client can purchase direct, buy from professional advisors or find at local libraries that have a strong investment information presence.

With the American urge to quantify and rank anything, the CPA and client can even attempt to rate the rating services, but there is no reason to recommend it. They all have more to offer investors than anyone can ever use. It is best to screen funds with as many services as are available. However, all they address is the past; they cannot be held accountable for the future.

Most use some sort of a grading system similar to the way movies are rated. As with movies, they often conceal as much as they reveal. The ratings are no substitute for personal involvement. For example, stars are used to screen types of funds. If a style of fund is made up of 15 to 20 funds and almost all of them are 1- to 2-star funds (on a scale of 1 to 5, 5 being high), the CPA and client must have the courage of their convictions before allocating to that sector. More narrowly, if the CPA and client pick a universe made up of 30 to 40 funds and 3 of them are 5 stars and the remainder are 2, 3, and a few 4 stars, then the CPA and client should certainly look at the three 5-star funds first.

Grading Mutual Fund Professional Rating Service Analysts

The CPA/PFS must learn to analyze the analysts. For example, few bond funds are 5-star funds, compared with balanced (equity and debt geared toward total return of both growth and income) or equity funds. There is a perception, however misguided, that bond fund managers do little to earn their money and they do little to enhance bond fund performance legitimately. Does that mean the investor should not buy a bond fund? Absolutely not—they are simply unpopular or uninteresting to mutual fund analysts. To summarize, the CPA and client must use ratings and rating services responsibly—as a tool of logic and research. They are of benefit because they perform a task nobody can perform on their own, but the CPA must learn how to read them and what they mean. Do be careful to read between the lines.

How to Access Professional Rating Service Information on Mutual Funds

The retail public dissemination of mutual fund information has been carried on by the rating services for 20 years now. This information was formerly the province of institutions alone. These services went from statistical disseminators to consumer advocates and industry reformers. As a reader of the editorials in their various guides (whichever the CPA elects to use), the financial advisor or client will learn that they are aggressive people. It is not a stretch to say that every mutual fund investor owes these services a debt of gratitude for all they have done for the investor over the past decade. Their database has been used to destroy myth after myth after myth about mutual funds.

The companies most likely to apply to the CPA and their clients are the purely retail services. For the most part, all do the same thing—provide hard copy and software subscriptions. Investors can benefit from them all; they should inspect everything that is available.

All of the services receive ample criticism. Much of the criticism centers on the services' inability to predict the future (which they do not try to do), the lack of dependability of their star systems (which they readily acknowledge), and their inapplicability for fund-trading strategies (which is a pastime that does not work and they discourage). If the CPA or client wants to be a student of mutual fund investment, these are the textbooks.

PERIODICALS: BENEFITS TO THE CPA AND CLIENT

In addition to rating service publications, financial magazines often produce excellent comparative spreadsheets in their mutual fund lists. As with any analytical service in any field, the rankings are to be viewed very carefully—the writer's and editorial staff's likes and the financial planner's and clients' interests might not be the same. The primary benefit to the CPA and client is that the periodicals deal with a huge number of funds and can be used as a starting point to narrow down the focus to the more detailed commentaries available elsewhere.

COMPUTER SOFTWARE: BENEFITS TO THE CPA AND CLIENT

Various services provide software loaded with charts and information. The CPA can customize his or her fund searches with databases used by professional fund managers. The personal computer has proven to be a valuable tool, tremendously beneficial for the retail investor willing to make the financial, time and learning commitment necessary to negotiate the minefields of computer securities services.

INTERNET SERVICES: BENEFITS TO THE CPA AND CLIENT

Information sifting on the computer may ultimately prove to be the only way to keep timely track of mutual funds. The CPA can find a biography on almost any manager, find the most recent portfolios of many funds and certainly find past performance on any public fund.

ADVICE ON MUTUAL FUNDS ADVICE

While the preceding information, well used, can help the CPA and client both to police current holdings and to search for new possibilities, the fact remains that no method of research will ever guarantee success. However, these are some ideas to consider that are perceived as generally helpful:

1. "Past performance is no indication of future returns" is a sentence printed in bold type on every piece of mutual fund literature legitimately distributed in the U.S. Beware of astronomical performance claims, particularly unaudited ones. There are ways to compute past performance that, while observing the rules, really gild the lily regarding true returns. Buyers beware!

2. Assess risk to determine whether a fund actually fits the client risk parameter. Many services attempt to assess risk and the CPA and client should be aware that what seems and what is, on the risk front, are often two entirely different matters. For example, most people who buy mutual funds in banks think FDIC insurance covers their fund investments. Not so.

3. Once again, there are absolutely no free lunches. The CPA and client can determine for themselves how to elect to pay for mutual fund investments. Costs in funds are a given. No one can avoid expenses of significance attached to mutual funds. The financial advisor and client should simply accept this fact if they are going to invest a significant amount of assets in these vehicles.

4. Shop around. Which funds in the proper style post a history that is compatible with that notion of reality for that type of investment? Then, the CPA should do the same cost studies done with any other major family purchase.

General Guidelines on Selecting a Mutual Fund

To select funds, the CPA should consider this advice:

1. Know why a client should invest in a certain fund and what the client wants from it.
2. Scan research tools for as large a universe of choices as the fund type includes.
3. Narrow the field by negative feedback—anything that doesn't jibe, get rid of immediately.
4. Find all research and marketing material available on the funds that remain in the group and cull this herd.
5. If there are several choices left, go with an instinctive choice and invest the money.

Steps to Avoid

There are many ways to subvert best efforts and lose potential return. Some thoughts to keep in mind:

1. Most investors evidently do not realize (earn) the return their funds post because they tend to buy high and sell low. They switch around too often, usually chasing last period's best performers. By its very nature, fund investment is supposed to be long term.
2. If the client takes out income and distributions for any reason other than need, he or she is making a big mistake. Posted results of funds always assume reinvestment of all distributions. At any given time, as much as 75 percent of the return of the S&P 500 has been as a consequence of the reinvestment of dividends and those dividends' subsequent appreciation.
3. If clients ignore the tape because they cannot acknowledge mistakes but move so fast it is obvious they do not know what they are doing, fund-switch services and hotlines are perfect for them. Then they can lose money much more quickly and get it over with sooner. The CPA has no time for such clients as "investors."
4. New funds should not be ignored categorically, especially those with a high turnover rate. New funds often outperform their more established rivals, and high-turnover funds in aggressive growth are often found at the top of their class.
5. The CPA can do much to see that the client's long-term goals are being met. Once they have selected the client's funds and invested the money,

they are not done. The responsibilities of an educated financial advisor and investor never end.

6. Keeping careful track of the client's funds and their price fluctuations is mandatory. The CPA should read the semiannual portfolio summaries to determine the contents of the funds. Could the advisor happily have the client own these items through direct investment? The CPA should assume the responsibility of determining that fund portfolios remain consistent with the client's goals and objectives. This is particularly true from a risk/reward standpoint.

7. With funds in taxable accounts, the CPA must help determine post-tax rate of return. The rating services data sheets can help, as they calculate post-tax returns at the maximum marginal tax rate. With a post-tax rate of return, the CPA can determine whether (on a risk-adjusted basis), the client is at the bottom of the ladder (least risk for potential return) or appropriately invested. The CPA can be of immeasurable value in this exercise. He or she can see to it that the client gets the numbers right and can use reason (rather than emotion) to evaluate the investments.

CONCLUSION

There is a lot to think about here. Mutual funds have gone from one of the least popular investment vehicles on the U.S. investment scene to the most widely disseminated in fewer than 20 years. Funds can become only more and more predominant. In an era of rapidly expanding financial self-determination, it benefits CPAs/PFSs to become as expert as they are capable of becoming as quickly as possible. Mutual fund selection is alternately the most intimidating and most exciting of investment processes. Unfortunately, most people assume it is the simplest and safest. The CPA won't make this mistake.

Chapter 31

Mutual Fund "Profile" Disclosure Option

CONTENTS

Need for Simplified Disclosure Information **31.02**

Profile Requirements Under Rule 498 **31.03**

Profiles for Tax-Deferred Arrangements **31.03**

Pilot Profile Program **31.03**

Other Investment Companies Excluded from Profile Option **31.04**

Multiple Funds Described in a Profile **31.04**

Cover Page **31.04**

Risk/Return Summary **31.05**

Other Disclosure Requirements **31.08**

Application to Purchase Shares **31.10**

Filing Requirements **31.10**

Modified Profiles for Certain Funds **31.10**

The Securities and Exchange Commission has adopted a new Rule that permits an open-end management investment company (mutual fund) to offer investors a user-friendly disclosure document called a "profile." This document summarizes key information about the fund, including the fund's investment strategies, risks, performance, and fees, in a concise, standardized format.

A fund that offers a profile will be able to give investors a choice of the amount of information that they wish to consider before making a decision about investing in the fund; investors will have the option of purchasing the fund's shares after reviewing the information in the profile or after requesting and reviewing the fund's prospectus (and other information). An investor deciding to purchase fund shares based on the information in a profile will receive the fund's prospectus with the confirmation of purchase.

The SEC also adopted amendments to Rule 497 under the Securities Act to require a fund to file a profile with the Commission at least 30 days prior to the profile's first use. At the same time, they adopted revisions to the prospectus disclosure requirements in Form N-1A, the registration statement used by funds. The revisions should *minimize* prospectus disclosure about technical, legal, and operational matters that generally are common to all funds and thus *focus prospectus disclosure on essential information* about a particular fund. The reasoning is that the simplified general information should enable the average investor to make better informed decisions about investing in that fund.

NEED FOR SIMPLIFIED DISCLOSURE INFORMATION

As more investors turn to funds for professional management of current and retirement savings, funds have introduced new investment options and shareholder services to appeal to investors. While benefiting from these developments, investors also faced an increasingly difficult task in choosing from the many different fund investments. The SEC, fund investors, and others realized it was in everyone's best interest to improve fund disclosure documents to help investors evaluate and compare them.

In the Commission's view, the growth of the fund industry and the diversity of fund investors warranted a new approach to fund disclosure to offer more choices in the format and the amount of information available about these investments. (Particularly, it would seem, since so many relatively "uninitiated" investors were testing the mutual fund market.)

The Profile summarizes key information about a fund, including its investment objectives, strategies, risks, performance, fees, investment adviser and portfolio manager, purchase and redemption procedures, distributions, tax information and the services available to the fund's investors.

It was designed to provide summary information about a fund that could assist an investor in deciding whether to invest in that particular fund immediately, or to request additional information about it before deciding whether or not to buy shares in it.

Rule 498 requires a fund to mail the prospectus and other information to the requesting investor within 3 business days of a request. An investor deciding to purchase fund shares based on the Profile receives the fund's prospectus with the purchase confirmation.

PROFILE REQUIREMENTS UNDER RULE 498

1. ***Standardized Fund Summaries.*** The profile includes concise disclosure of 9 items of key information about a fund in a specific sequence.

2. ***Improved Risk Disclosure.*** A risk/return summary (also required at the beginning of a fund's *prospectus*) provides information about a fund's investment objectives, principal strategies, risks, performance, and fees.

3. ***Graphic Disclosure of Variability of Returns.*** The risk/return summary provides a bar chart of a fund's annual returns over a 10-year period that illustrates the variability of those returns and gives investors some idea of the risks of an investment in the fund. To help investors evaluate a fund's risks and returns relative to "the market," a table accompanying the bar chart compares the fund's average annual returns for 1-, 5-, and 10-year periods to that of a broad-based securities market index.

4. ***Other Fund Information.*** The profile includes information on the fund's investment adviser and portfolio manager, purchase and redemption procedures, tax considerations, and shareholder services.

5. ***Plain English Disclosure.*** The Commission's plain English disclosure requirements, which are designed to give investors understandable disclosure documents, apply to the profile. The plain English rule requires the use of plain English writing principles, including short sentences, everyday language, active voice, tabular presentation of complex material, no legal or business jargon, and no multiple negatives. (For a discussion of this rule, see Chapter 21.)

PROFILES FOR TAX-DEFERRED ARRANGEMENTS

Rule 498 also permits a fund that serves as an investment option for a participant-directed defined contribution plan (or for certain other tax-deferred arrangements) to provide investors with a profile that includes disclosure that is tailored for the plan (or other arrangement).

Profiles tailored for such use can exclude information relating to the purchase and sale of fund shares, fund distributions, tax consequences, and fund services otherwise required in a profile.

PILOT PROFILE PROGRAM

The Commission tested various options for improving fund disclosure documents in a pilot program conducted with participation by the Investment Company Institute (ICI) and several large fund groups, in which the funds used profile-like summaries with their prospectuses. The Pilot Profile summarized important information about specific funds to determine whether investors found these profiles helpful in making investment decisions. Focus groups conducted on the Commission's behalf responded positively to the profile concept, indicating that a disclosure document of this type would assist them in making investment decisions. Fund investors participating in a survey sponsored by the ICI also strongly supported the profile idea.

OTHER INVESTMENT COMPANIES EXCLUDED FROM PROFILE OPTION

The Commission has decided that other types of investment companies, such as closed-end investment companies, unit investment trusts, and separate accounts that offer variable annuities do not come within the scope of Rule 498. It is available only to mutual funds.

Although the Agency recognizes that a short, summary disclosure document such as the profile could potentially benefit investors in other types of investment companies, it has concluded that it would be prudent to assess the use of profiles by mutual funds over a period of time before considering a rule to allow other types of investment companies to use similar summary documents. As the Commission gains experience with funds' use of the profile and analyzes the results of other pilot profile programs that are underway, it will undoubtedly consider expanding use of the concept to other types of investment companies if things work out as well as they anticipate.

MULTIPLE FUNDS DESCRIBED IN A PROFILE

The SEC decided that a profile that describes more than one fund can be consistent with the goal of a summary disclosure document that assists investors in evaluating and comparing funds. In fact they believe that describing more than one fund or class of a fund in a profile can be a useful means of providing investors with information about related investment alternatives offered by a fund group (e.g., a range of tax-exempt funds or different types of money market funds) or about the classes of a multiple class fund. However, profiles describing multiple funds must be organized in a clear, concise, summary manner in a format designed to communicate the information effectively. Thus, a profile that offers the securities of more than one fund or class does not need to repeat information that is the same for each one described in the document.

COVER PAGE

Rule 498 requires the cover page of a fund's profile to include certain basic information about the fund and to disclose that the profile is a *summary disclosure document.* The cover page identifies it as a "profile" without using the term "prospectus." It includes a legend explaining the profile's purpose, and displays the fund's name. A fund also could describe its investment objectives or its type or category (e.g., that the fund is a growth fund or invests its assets in a particular country). The cover page must state the approximate date of the profile's first use.

Required Legend

The new rule requires the following legend on the cover page, or at the beginning, of a profile:

"This profile summarizes key information about a Fund that is included in the Fund's prospectus. The Fund's prospectus includes additional information about the Fund, including a more detailed description of the risks associated with investing in the Fund that you may want to consider before you invest. You may obtain the prospectus and other information about the Fund at no cost by calling _____."

A toll-free (or collect) telephone number that investors can use to obtain the prospectus and other information must be provided. The fund may also indicate, as applicable, that the prospectus and other information is available on the fund's Internet site or by e-mail request.

When additional information is requested, a 3-business day mailing requirement applies. Since many funds use intermediaries in distributing or servicing their shares, revised Rule 498 also permits the legend to state that additional information in such a case may be obtained from financial intermediaries. The 3-business day rule applies here also.

RISK/RETURN SUMMARY

The first 4 items of the profile must contain information that would be substantially identical to the proposed risk/return summary at the beginning of every prospectus. The following discussion summarizes the main features of the risk/return summary required by Form N-1A and discusses specific disclosure required in the profile.

Fund Investment Objectives/Goals

To assist investors in identifying funds that meet their general investment needs, the risk/return summary requires a fund to disclose its investment objectives or goals.

Principal Investment Strategy

The risk/return summary requires a fund to summarize, based on the information provided in its prospectus, how the fund intends to achieve its investment objectives. The purpose of this disclosure is to provide a summary of the fund's principal investment strategies, including the specific types of securities in which the fund invests or will invest principally, and any policy of the fund to concentrate its investments in an industry or group of industries.

In addition, a fund (other than one that has not yet been required to deliver a semi-annual or annual report) must provide the following disclosure:

"Additional information about the Fund's investments is available in the Fund's annual and semi-annual reports to shareholders. In the Fund's annual report you will find a discussion of the market conditions and investment strategies that significantly affected the Fund's performance during the last fiscal year. You may obtain either or both of these reports at no cost by calling _____."

Principal Risks of Investing in the Fund

Summary Risk Disclosure.   The risk summary gives a fund the option to include disclosure in its profile about the types of investors for whom the fund is intended and the types of investment goals that may be consistent with an investment in the fund.

Special Risk Disclosure Requirements.   A mutual fund profile is required to provide a special disclosure in the risk summary for money market funds to the effect that, "An investment in the Fund is not insured or guaranteed by the Federal Deposit Insurance Corporation or any other government agency. Although the Fund seeks to preserve the value of your investment at $1.00 per share, it is possible to lose money by investing in the Fund."

A fund advised by or sold through a bank would disclose in the risk summary of its profile: "An investment in the Fund is not a deposit of the bank and is not insured or guaranteed by the Federal Deposit Insurance Corporation or any other government agency."

Risk/Return Bar Chart and Table.   The risk/return summary requires a fund's profile to include a bar chart showing the fund's annual returns for each of the last 10 calendar years and a table comparing the fund's average annual returns for the last 1, 5, and 10 fiscal years to those of a broad-based securities market index.

Obviously, this provision requires a fund to have at least one calendar year of returns before including the bar chart. It requires a fund whose profile does not include a bar chart, because the fund does not have annual returns for a full calendar year, to modify the narrative explanation to refer only to information presented in the table. The provision also requires the bar chart of a fund in operation for fewer than 10 years to include annual returns for the life of the fund.

To show a fund's highest and lowest returns (or "range" of returns) for annual or other periods as an alternative, or in addition, to the bar chart, the Profile ruling requires that a fund disclose (in addition to the bar chart) its best and worst returns for a quarter during the 10-year (or other) period reflected in the bar chart. This information is aimed at disclosing the variability of a fund's returns and the risks by pointing out that a fund's shares may very well be subject to short-term price fluctuations.

Presentation of Return Information.   To help investors use the information in the bar chart and table, the profile risk/return summary requires a fund to provide a brief narrative explanation of just how the information illustrates the variability of the fund's returns.

Bar Chart Return Information.   The risk/return summary requires calendar-year periods for both the bar chart and table. Under Rule 498, the average annual return information in the table in a fund's profile risk/return summary must be as of the most recent calendar quarter and updated quarterly.

Bar Chart Presentation.   The bar chart may include return information for more than one fund. However, the presentation of the bar chart is subject to the general requirement that disclosure should be presented in a format designed to communicate information *clearly and effectively.*

The risk/return summary requires a fund offering more than one class of shares in a profile to include annual return information in its bar chart for only one class. The ruling permits a fund to choose the class to be reflected in the bar chart, subject to certain limitations: the chart must reflect the performance of a class that has returns for at least 10 years (e.g., a fund could not present a class in the bar chart with 2 years of returns when another class has returns for at least 10 years). In addition, if two or more classes offered in the profile have returns for less than 10 years, the bar chart must reflect returns for the class that has returns for the longest period.

Fees and Expenses of the Fund

The risk/return summary requires a bar chart showing the fund's fees and expenses, including any sales loads charged in connection with an investment in the fund. The fee table must be included in both the profile and the prospectus. This emphasis underlines the SEC's belief that fees and expenses of a fund figure high in a typical investor's decision to invest in a fund. The fee table is designed to help them understand the costs of investing in a particular fund and to compare those costs with the costs of other funds.

OTHER DISCLOSURE REQUIREMENTS

The profile of a fund must include not only the risk/return summary, but also disclosure about other key aspects of investing in the fund—the other items to be disclosed in sequence: Investment Adviser, Sub-Adviser(s) and Portfolio Manager(s) of the Fund.

The profile requirements are very precise in this respect. This section requires:

1. Identification of the fund's investment adviser.
2. Identification of the fund's sub-adviser(s) (if any):
   a. A fund need not identify a sub-adviser(s) whose sole responsibility for the fund is limited to day-to-day management of the fund's holdings of cash and cash equivalent instruments, unless the fund is a money market fund or other fund with a principal investment strategy of regularly holding cash and cash equivalent instruments.
   b. A fund having three or more sub-advisers, each of which manages a portion of the fund's portfolio, need not identify each such sub-adviser, except that the fund must identify any sub-adviser that is (or is reasonably expected to be) responsible for the management of a significant portion of the fund's net assets. For purposes of this paragraph, a significant portion of a fund's net assets generally will be deemed to be 30% or more of the fund's net assets.
   c. State the name and length of service of the person or persons employed by or associated with the fund's investment adviser (or the fund) who are primarily responsible for the day-to-day management of the fund's portfolio and summarize each person's *business experience* for the last five years.

      A fund with three or more such persons, each of whom is (or is reasonably expected to be) responsible for the management of a portion of the Fund's portfolio, need not identify each person, except that a fund must identify and summarize the business experience for the last five years of each person who is (or is reasonably expected to be) responsible for the management of a significant portion of the fund's net assets. For purposes of this paragraph, a significant portion of a fund's net assets generally will be deemed to be 30% or more of the fund's net assets.

Purchase of Fund Shares

Under Rule 498, a fund must disclose the minimum initial or subsequent investment requirements, the initial sales load (or other loads), and, if applicable, the initial sales load breakpoints or waivers.

Sale of Fund Shares

Rule 498 also requires a fund to state that its shares are redeemable; to identify the procedures for redeeming shares (e.g., on any business day by written request, telephone, or wire transfer); to identify any charges or sales loads that may be assessed upon redemption (including, if applicable, the existence of waivers of these charges).

Fund Distributions and Tax Information

Rule 498 requires a mutual fund's profile to describe how frequently the fund intends to make distributions and what reinvestment options for distributions (if any) are available to its investors.

It also requires a fund to disclose whether its distributions to shareholders may be taxed as ordinary income or capital gains and that the rates shareholders pay on capital gains may be taxed at different rates depending upon the length of time that the fund holds its assets.

If a fund expects that its distributions, as a result of its investment objectives or strategies, primarily will consist of ordinary income or capital gains, it must provide disclosure to that effect. Funds subject to this requirement would include, for example, those often described as "tax-managed," "tax-sensitive," or "tax-advantaged," which have investment strategies to maximize long-term capital gains and minimize ordinary income.

If a fund has a *principal* investment objective or strategy to achieve tax-managed results of this type, the fund would be required to provide disclosure to that effect in the discussion of its investment objectives.

For a fund that describes itself as investing in securities generating tax-exempt income, it must provide, as applicable, a general statement to the effect that a portion of the fund's distributions may be subject to federal income tax.

Other Services Provided by the Fund

A fund profile should provide a brief summary of services available to the fund's shareholders (e.g., any exchange privileges or automated information services), unless this information has already been provided in earlier sections of the profile. A fund should disclose only those services that generally are available to typical investors in the fund.

APPLICATION TO PURCHASE SHARES

The profile may include an application that a prospective investor can use to purchase the fund's shares as long as the application explains with equal prominence that an investor has the option of purchasing shares of the fund after reviewing the information in the profile or after requesting and reviewing the fund's prospectus (and other information) before making a decision about investing in the fund.

FILING REQUIREMENTS

A profile is to be filed with the Commission at least 30 days before the date that it is first sent or given to a prospective investor. The first profile filing must be accompanied by the submission of a profile in the format in which it will be distributed to investors. Subsequent filings will not require the additional formatted profile. An amended form of any profile must be filed with the Commission within 5 business days after it is used.

MODIFIED PROFILES FOR CERTAIN FUNDS

Funds can tailor disclosure for profiles to be used for investments in defined contribution plans qualified under the Internal Revenue Code, and for funds offered through variable insurance contracts. The Commission believes that this revision will help to ensure that profiles contain information that investors will find meaningful and useful.

Rule 498 permits a profile for a fund offered as an investment option for a plan to include, or be accompanied by, an enrollment form for the plan. An application or enrollment form for a variable insurance contract may accompany the profile for the funds that serve as investment options; however, this is only if the form also is accompanied by a full prospectus for the contract.

The Rule also permits funds to modify the legend and other disclosure in profiles intended for use in connection with defined contribution plans, other tax-deferred arrangements described in the Rule, and variable insurance contracts.

Chapter 32

Plain English Disclosure Rule

CONTENTS

Investor Protection   32.02
Prospectus Simplification   32.02
Plain English Pilot Program   32.03
Rule 421(d), *The Plain English Rule*   32.03
Rule 421(b), *Clear, Concise, Understandable Prospectuses*   32.04
Revisions to Regulations S-K and S-B   32.06
Comments on the Plain English Requirements   32.10
Updated Staff Legal Bulletin 7   32.11

The Securities and Exchange Commission has adopted a Plain English Disclosure rule incorporating changes made as a result of comments received and the lessons learned from participants in the plain English pilot program. The rule requires issuers to write the *cover page, summary,* and *risk factors section* of prospectuses in plain English. The previous requirements for those sections have been changed to the extent they conflicted with the plain English rule. In conjunction with this rule, the SEC also provides issuers more specific guidance on how to make the entire prospectus clear, concise, and understandable.

The Commission believes that using plain English in prospectuses will lead to a better informed securities market in which investors can more easily understand the disclosure required by the federal securities laws. The rule became effective on October 1, 1998, with the compliance date being the same.

INVESTOR PROTECTION

Obviously, the intended purpose of financial reporting should be full and fair disclosure. In fact this is one of the cornerstones of investor protection under federal securities laws. The SEC points out that if a prospectus fails to communicate information clearly, investors do not receive the basic protection intended.

Yet prospectuses have often employed complex, legalistic language, confounding all but the most erudite lawyers, accountants or financial experts. The Commission emphasizes that the proliferation of complex transactions and securities (including all manner of derivatives) has only magnified this problem. A major challenge facing the securities industry and its regulators is the assurance that financial and business information reaches investors in a form they can read *and understand.*

The SEC anticipates, and many public comment letters concur, that implementation of the plain English rule will:

1. Allow investors to make better-informed assessments of the risks and rewards of investment opportunities.
2. Reduce the likelihood that investors make investment mistakes because of incomprehensible disclosure documents.
3. Reduce investors' costs of investing by lowering the time required to read and understand information.
4. Increase consumers' interest in investing by giving them greater confidence in their understanding of investments.
5. Reduce the number of costly legal disputes because investors are more likely to understand disclosure documents better.
6. Lower offering costs because investors will ask issuers fewer questions about the offering.

All well and good, but how is all of this expected to happen?

PROSPECTUS SIMPLIFICATION

The Commission stated that the new rules will change the face of every prospectus used in registered public offerings of securities. They expect these prospectuses will be simpler, clearer, more useful, and hopefully, more widely read and understood when clarity prevails:

1. The new rules require issuers to write and design the cover page, summary, and risk factors section of their prospectuses in plain English. Issuers will also have to design these sections to make them inviting to the reader. The new rules will *not* require issuers to limit the length of the summary, limit the number of risk factors, or prioritize risk factors.

2. The SEC is also providing guidance to issuers on how to comply with the current rule that requires the entire prospectus to be clear, concise, and understandable. The goal is to dispense with legalese and repetitions that tend to blur the pertinent information (and facts) that investors actually need in making informed decisions.

With that in mind, the Office of Investor Education and Assistance produced a handbook with practical tips on document presentation. A *Plain English Handbook: How to Create Clear SEC Disclosure Documents,* outlining methods and techniques on how to apply plain English principles to the disclosure documents, is the resulting publication.

PLAIN ENGLISH PILOT PROGRAM

To test plain English in disclosure documents, the Division of Corporation Finance experimented with a pilot program in 1996 for public companies willing to file plain English documents under either the Securities Act of 1933 or the Securities Exchange Act of 1934. More than 75 companies volunteered to participate in the pilot program. Many participants got into the spirit of the project to the extent that they even prepared disclosure documents that are not subject to the plain English rule: proxy statements, footnotes to financial statements, management's discussion and analysis of financial condition and results of operations.

Assessment of the results of the pilot program affirmed the SEC's belief that preparing documents in plain English increases investors' understanding and helps them make informed investment decisions. Thus, the package of rules adopted, as well as the handbook, should enable issuers to improve dramatically the clarity of their disclosure documents.

RULE 421(D), *THE PLAIN ENGLISH RULE*

Basic rules outline how prospectuses must be prepared. This new ruling requires preparation of the front portion of the prospectus in plain English.

The plain English principles apply to the organization, language, and design of the front and back cover pages, the summary, and the risk factors section. Also, when drafting the language in these front parts of the prospectus, the preparer must comply substantially with six basic principles:

1. Short sentences.
2. Definite, concrete, everyday language.
3. Active voice.
4. Tabular presentation or bulleted lists for complex material, whenever possible.
5. No legal jargon or highly technical business terms.
6. No multiple negatives.

Does this all sound very reminiscent of your high school English teacher preparing you to write term papers? It should. And it does seem strange that it takes a Final Rule of the Securities and Exchange Commission to remind prospectus preparers of these basic rules for written communication. (Unless obfuscation is their objective.)

A number of comment letters noted that the rule *dictates* how to write the front of the prospectus. The SEC observed marked improvement in the clarity of disclosure when pilot participants used these recognized, basic principles of clear writing. They decided that the benefits to investors supported *mandating* the use of the principles for the front of the prospectus.

In addition, the cover page, summary, and risk factors section must be easy to read. The text and design of the document must highlight important information for investors. The rule permits the issuer to use pictures, charts, graphics, and other design features to make the prospectus easier to understand.

RULE 421(B), *CLEAR, CONCISE, UNDERSTANDABLE PROSPECTUSES*

This ruling currently requires that the entire prospectus be clear, concise, and understandable. These stipulations are in addition to the plain English rule, which applies only to the front of the prospectus.

Amendments to Rule 421(b) also provide guidance on how to prepare a prospectus that is actually clear, concise, and understandable. The amendments set out four general writing techniques and list four conventions to *avoid* when drafting the prospectus. In effect, these amendments codify earlier interpretive advice.

Amended Rule 421(b) requires use of the the following techniques when writing the entire prospectus:

1. Presentation of information in clear, concise sections, paragraphs, and sentences. Whenever possible, the use of short explanatory sentences and bullet lists.
2. Use of descriptive headings and subheadings.
3. Avoidance of frequent reliance on glossaries or defined terms as the primary means of explaining information in the prospectus. Definition of terms in a glossary or other section of the document only if the meaning is unclear from the context. Use of a glossary only if it facilitates understanding of the disclosure.
4. Avoidance of legal and highly technical business terminology.

How to Comply

The new note to Rule 421(b) provides further guidance on how to comply with the rule's general requirements. Because they make the document harder to read, the note lists the following tactics to *avoid:*

1. Legalistic or overly complex presentations that make the substance of the disclosure difficult to understand.
2. Vague boilerplate explanations that are readily subject to differing interpretations.
3. Complex information copied directly from legal documents without any clear and concise explanation or interpretation of the provision(s).
4. Repetitive disclosure that increases the bulk of the document, but fails to further clarify the information.

Technical Terminology

Several comment letters stated that the SEC should permit public companies to use legal and technical business terminology. The argument was that high tech companies must use technical terms to distinguish their products or services from others in the industry. The Commission agreed that certain business terms may be necessary to describe operations properly, but cautioned against using excessive technical jargon that only competitors or industry specialists could understand.

The focus of the Plain English Rule is that the disclosure in the prospectus is for the benefit of the *investors*. When too many highly technical terms are employed, the investor soon becomes bogged down in a welter of verbiage and little if anything is "disclosed." If technical terms are unavoidable, the preparer must attempt to make their meaning perfectly clear at the onset.

Legal Documents

Several comment letters noted that some investors, particularly institutional investors, want to read the specific terms of contracts or of the securities offered. For example, the SEC concedes an investor may want to read the specific language of a loan agreement's financial covenants or an indenture's default provisions.

The current rule permits summarizing an exhibit's key provisions in the prospectus. The issuer is also required to file material contracts and any instruments that define the rights of security holders. The SEC believes this approach generally serves the needs of all investors in the market.

If the language from an exhibit in the prospectus cannot be summarized adequately, then the explicit language may be included, but it must be presented clearly and its meaning to the investor explained precisely.

REVISIONS TO REGULATIONS S-K AND S-B

The following revisions to Regulation S-K and S-B, covering requirements applicable to nonfinancial portions of the registration statements, annual and interim reports to stockholders, proxy, and other information statements, are addresses to specific sections of the narrative portions of the disclosure documents. Evidently the SEC hopes that prospective customers and stockholders will be given a better opportunity to understand the written portions of a prospectus and other relevant documents whether they really grasp the financial import of the documents or not. (Regulation S-B applies specifically to "small" businesses.)

Item 501—Forepart of Registration Statement and Outside Front Cover Page of Prospectus

The formal design requirements for the prospectus cover page have been eliminated but the issuer is required to limit the front cover of the prospectus to one page. It is expected that the revisions will result in a cover page written and designed to focus investors on *key information* about the offering and encourage them to read the important information in the prospectus. The SEC also expects the amendments to give the flexibility needed to design a cover page tailored to the specific company and the offering.

Under the revised disclosure item, the issuer is free to use pictures, graphs, charts, and other designs that accurately depict the company, business products, and financial condition; however, design features and font types that make the disclosure difficult to read or understand are taboo.

The formalized requirements on how to present the mandatory legends on the cover page have been amended. The only restrictions on presentation of these legends are:

1. The legends must be prominent.
2. The print type must be easy to read.

The Commission has amended Item 501 to provide two plain English examples of the legend that state the Commission has not approved the offering. The item also provides a plain English example of the legend that states the prospectus is not yet complete. It is commonly printed in red ink and referred to as the "red herring" legend.

The Commission has amended the requirements detailing information that must always be included on the prospectus cover page. The goal is to have the cover page focus only on *key information* about the offering. The issuing company is cautioned to avoid moving unnecessary information to this page.

Original plans were to eliminate the requirement to refer to the risk factors on the cover page; however, comment letters suggested the mandate be retained. Therefore, the cover page must now not only reference the risk factors section but must also cite the page number on which the risk factors begin.

Cover Page Format

Retained on the cover page from previous requirements are:

1. Company name.
2. Title, amount, and description of securities offered.
3. Selling securities holder's offering.
4. Bona fide estimate of range of maximum offering price, and numbers of securities.
5. If price not set, indication of how price will be determined.
6. State-required legends.
7. Date of prospectus.

Adopted changes to Regulation S-K—Item 501 to the prospectus cover page include:

1. Cross reference to risk factors *must include page number.*
2. Bullet list or other design that highlights the information showing *price, underwriting commission, and proceeds of the offering* replaces formatted distribution table.

3. Bullet list or other design that highlights the *best efforts disclosure* replaces the formatted distribution table.

4. Commission legend retained in plain English. Reference to *state securities commissions* to be included.

5. Information concerning *underwriters' over-allotment option and the number of shares* retained on the cover page. Expenses of the offering, the number of shares, commissions paid by others, and other non-cash consideration and finder's fees *moved* to the plan of distribution section.

6. Identification of market for securities, trading symbol, underwriters, and type of underwriting arrangements.

7. Prospectus "Subject to Completion" legend retained in plain English.

8. Cover limited to one page.

Limited Partnership Offerings Risk

Several comment letters suggested that the plain English rule and the revised disclosure requirements should replace earlier interpretive advice on cover page disclosure for *limited partnership* offerings.

The SEC acknowledges that under existing advice, the cover page must list the offering's key risks, resulting in repetitious disclosure of those risks. However, they feel that the unique nature of limited partnership offerings and the risks they present to investors warrant requiring the issuer to highlight these risks on the cover page. Of course, the cover page, summary, and risk factors section must otherwise comply with the plain English rule and the revised disclosure requirements being adopted.

Item 502—Inside Front and Outside Back Cover Pages

Item 502's amended requirements for the inside front cover page and outside back cover page of the prospectus now significantly limit the information required on these pages. The hope is that this will give further freedom to the issuer to arrange the information in the prospectus from the *investor's viewpoint.*

The Commission prefers that the required table of contents immediately follow the cover page, but the ruling permits the preparer to have the flexibility to include it on either the inside front or outside back cover page of the prospectus. However, if a prospectus is delivered to investors electronically, the table of contents must come immediately after the cover page so that investors need not scroll to the end of the prospectus to see how it is organized.

Although some comment letters recommended elimination of the requirement to disclose the dealer's prospectus delivery obligations, the SEC decided to retain this disclosure on the outside back cover page. They suggest this disclosure is helpful to dealers in reminding them of their legal obligation to deliver the prospectus

Following are disclosures *previously required* on the inside front or outside back cover pages and their *new location* adopted under Regulation S-K—Item 502:

1. Availability of Exchange Act reports generally—moved to description of business section or, for short-form registration statements, to the incorporation by reference disclosure.
2. Identification of market for securities—moved to cover page.
3. Availability of annual reports to shareholders with financial statements for foreign issuers and others not subject to proxy rules—moved to description of business section.
4. Availability of Exchange Act reports incorporated by reference in short-form registration statements—moved to incorporation by reference disclosure.
5. Stabilization legend—moved to plan of distribution section.
6. Passive market-making activities legend—deleted. Disclosure retained in plan of distribution section.
7. Dealer prospectus delivery page—retained on outside back cover as noted above.
8. Enforceability of civil liability provisions of federal securities laws against foreign persons—moved to description of business section.
9. As mentioned above, the table of contents may still be located on either the inside front cover or the outside back cover unless it is sent electronically. Then it must be on the inside front cover.

In line with other changes, Forms S-2, S-3, S-4, F-2, F-3, and F-4 are also being amended.

Along with the list of reports incorporated by reference, the issuer must include information on:

1. How investors may obtain a copy of these reports.
2. How investors may obtain copies of the other reports filed with the SEC.

Item 503—Summary Information, Risk Factors, and Ratio of Earnings to Fixed Charges

Summary Information. If a summary is included, it must be brief and in plain English. Further, if a summary description of the company's business operations or financial condition is included, the information must be written in plain English even if not identified as a "summary."

Length of the summary is not mandated, but the SEC emphasizes that this section should *highlight the most important features* of the offering. It *should not* include a lengthy description of the company's business and business strategy. They suggest this detailed information is better included in the disclosure in the body of the prospectus.

Although there is no list of items that must be in a summary (if there is one), since the financial statements are an important part of the disclosures made by public companies, the SEC believes the issuer should continue to *highlight financial information* in the summary in a manner readily understood by the user.

Risk Factors.   When a risk factors section is included in the prospectus, the risk factors must be detailed in plain English avoiding trite "boilerplate" risk factors. Any risk factors must be explained in context so investors can understand the specific risk applicable to that particular company and its operations.

Ratio of Earnings to Fixed Charges.   Where a summary or similar section is included in the prospectus, amended Item 503 requires showing the ratio of earnings to fixed charges as part of the summarized financial data.

Issuers offering debt securities must show a *ratio of earnings to fixed charges.* Those registering preference equity securities must show the *ratio of combined fixed charges and preference dividends to earnings.* The issuer must present the ratio for each of the last five fiscal years and the latest interim period for which financial statements are presented in the document.

If the proceeds from the sale of debt or preference securities are used to repay any outstanding debt or to retire other securities, and the change in the ratio would be ten percent or greater, a ratio showing the application of the proceeds, the *pro forma ratio,* must be used. If a ratio indicates less than one-to-one coverage, the dollar amount of the deficiency is to be disclosed. The pro forma ratio may be shown only for the most recent fiscal year and the latest interim period. The net change in interest or dividends from the refinancing should be used to calculate the pro forma ratio.

COMMENTS ON THE PLAIN ENGLISH REQUIREMENTS

Forty-five comment letters on the plain English proposals generally favored requiring plain English for the front of prospectuses—the cover page, summary, and risk factors section—to ensure that investors receive clear information. They believe that requiring plain English will focus all parties involved in the offering process—issuers, underwriters, trustees, and counsel—on clear and readable disclosure.

Other comment letters raised the following general concerns about the rule:

1. Will the plain English rule increase a registrant's liability?
2. How will the staff review and comment on plain English filings?
3. Will the Commission deny acceleration of a filing if it does not comply with the plain English rule?

After studying these questions, the SEC has concluded that issuers really have little, if any cause, for concern: *following the new rulings* should not alter established procedures and practices for handling relevant matters.

COST FACTORS

While project participants who responded to benefit-cost questions had incurred some additional document preparation costs, the majority estimated them to be low and predicted that they would fall over time. The participants anticipated little added, and perhaps even lower, overall cost. Some even predicted they might save money on printing and distribution costs and on the amount of time spent on answering investors' questions. Based on the experiences of pilot program participants, the SEC believes that the substantial benefits to investors of plain English—and the probable ongoing cost savings to issuers—justify the short-term cost to public companies of learning to prepare documents in plain English.

UPDATED STAFF LEGAL BULLETIN 7

In June, 1999, The SEC updated Staff Legal Bulletin 7 relating to the Plain English requirements for registration statements filed on or after October 1, 1998, with the Division of Corporation Finance. This bulletin is not a rule, regulation, or statement of the Securities and Exchange Commission, nor have its contents been approved or disapproved by the agency.

Risk Factor Guidance

According to the staff members responsible for reviewing the filings, the most vexing problem for most issuers involved risk factor disclosures. Amended Item 503(c) of Regulation S-K specifies that issuers should not present risks that could apply to any issuer or any offering. Further, the subheadings must adequately describe the risk that follows.

Item 503(c) seems to be the least understood of the plain English requirements. For this reason, the SEC has provided additional information as well as sample risk factor disclosures and subheadings to help preparers comply with Rule 421(d) of Regulation C and Item 503(c) of Regulation S-K.

Types of Risk

Risk factors loosely fall into three broad categories:

1. *Industry Risk*—risks companies face by virtue of the industry they're in. For example, many REITs run the risk that, despite due diligence, they will acquire properties with significant environmental issues.
2. *Company Risk*—risks that are specific to the company. For example, a REIT owns four properties with significant environmental issues and cleaning up these properties will be a serious financial drain.
3. *Investment Risk*—risks that are specifically tied to a security. For example, in a debt offering, the debt being offered is the most junior subordinated debt of the company.

When drafting risk factors, the issuer should specifically link each risk to the specific industry, company, or investment, as applicable.

Cautions and Suggestions Relating to Risk Disclosure

After the staff had gained several months' experience issuing plain English comments under the new rule and amendments, they thought it would be helpful to list some of the comments that had been recorded most frequently. By alerting filers to these comments before they file subsequent registration statements, the SEC hopes filers will be able to avoid making these types of mistakes in the future.

Of course, the following selected, abridged comments do not encompass all of the varied plain English comments that were issued. Each prospectus is different and many of the comments issued are unique to the organization of and disclosure in individual prospectuses.

Following are several of the types of cautions made relative to risk disclosure:

1. More than one risk factor should not be "bundled" under one subheading. In order to give the proper prominence and weight to each risk presented, it should be given its own descriptive subheading.
2. Risks should be presented in concrete terms. For example, a reference to "risks due to the 'costs' associated with the benefit plans" is too vague. A better understanding of the risks would be gained by a statement that the "costs" are not expenses of running the plans, but result from the

added compensation expense that stems from the shares purchased by or granted to employees and executives under those plans.

3. In each risk factor, the risk should be clearly and succinctly stated as quickly as possible without undue introductory background material and extensive detailed discussion.

4. The issuer should provide the information investors need to assess the magnitude of the risk. For example, a statement that "increases in short-term interest rates could have a material adverse effect" on XYZ Bank's profitability raises more questions than it provides information.

   Why? Are a substantial percentage of XYZ's interest-earning assets in long-term investments that pay fixed rates while the interest paid to depositors fluctuates? If so, what percentage of interest-earning assets are in long-term investments? Explain.

5. Item 503(c) of Regulation S-K states that issuers should not "present risk factors that could apply to any issuer or to any offering."

   For example, a risk disclosed under "Dependence on Key Personnel" could apply to nearly any issuer in an industry or in almost any industry. If general risk factors are retained in a prospectus, they must be clearly explained. How do they apply to a particular industry, company, or offering? Why is there a concern about losing key personnel? Are they about to retire? Are they not bound by employment contracts?

6. If the subheadings in the risk factors section are too vague and generic they will not adequately describe the risk that follows as is required in Item 503(c) of Regulation S-K.

   For example, the subheading "Competition" is certainly not descriptive because all companies operating in a free market economy are subject to competition.

7. To the extent possible, generic conclusions about the risk should be avoided. Statements like ". . . would have a material adverse effect on . . ." operations, financial condition, or business are too imprecise. Instead, there should be specific disclosure of *how* operations, financial condition or business would be affected *by what* specific risk.

8. In an introductory paragraph to the risk factors section, the issuer should not "hedge" against noncompliance by stating that there might be risks not considered material at the time that could become material. Or by making a blanket statement that there might be unidentified risks. The issuer must disclose all risks considered material at the time.

Glossaries and Defined Terms

Rule 421(b) specifies that the issuer "must avoid frequent reliance on glossaries or defined terms as the primary means of explaining information in the prospectus. Define terms in a glossary or other section of the prospectus only if the meaning is unclear from the context. Use a glossary only if it facilitates understanding of the disclosure."

Obviously, then, there are times when a glossary should be used. The bulletin suggests the following:

1. Terms used in a prospectus which are understood only by industry experts should be included in a glossary.
2. If the meanings of terms cannot be made clear from the context or explained concisely where they are first used, then the glossary is appropriate.
3. It is not necessary to use a glossary to define commonly understood abbreviations, like SEC, or acronyms, like NASDAQ.
4. A glossary should not be used to define terms that have been created solely for the purpose of the registration statement. In fact, with the exception of brand or trade names used to identify the type of security being offered, new terms should not be created.

Creating terms that exist only for use in a prospectus forces investors to learn a new vocabulary before they can begin to understand the disclosure. The issuer should eliminate over-reliance on defined terms as a primary means of explaining information in the prospectus, and instead, disclose material information in a clear, concise, and understandable manner.

Documents Incorporated by Reference

Some, but not all of the documents incorporated by reference into registration statements are subject to the plain English rule and amendments.

1. The information incorporated by reference in response to a general requirement need not comply with the plain English rule. For example, Item 12 on Form S-3 requires incorporation by reference of the issuer's recent Exchange Act reports in their entirety. The reports need not be rewritten.
2. However, any information incorporated by reference to satisfy a specific disclosure requirement must comply with the applicable plain English rule and amendments. For example, on Form S-3, if the filer incorporates by reference risk factors from a Form 10-K to satisfy Item 3, the risk factors must comply with Rule 421(d).

Post-Effective Amendments to Registration Statements

A post-effective amendment to a Form S-3 that, when first filed, was not subject to plain English will trigger the plain English requirements in two instances. A post-effective amendment must be rewritten to comply if:

1. It incorporates by reference audited financials that are more recent than those incorporated in any earlier post-effective amendment or the original registration statement.
2. Enough time has elapsed since the last post-effective amendment or the original registration statement that the issuer is required to post-effectively amend the prospectus under Section 10(a)(3) of the Securities Act of 1933.

Use of Legal Documents in Prospectus

Under Rule 421(b) of Regulation C, the issuer must avoid copying complex information directly from legal documents without any clear and concise explanation of the information. Language in the body of the prospectus should not be taken directly from the underlying indenture, shareholder agreements, rights plan, merger agreement, statute on dissenters rights, employment agreement, or similar document. The disclosure relating to such documents should be revised so that it is clear, concise, and understandable.

In the event that the issuer feels the language as it appears in the underlying legal documents is indispensable to a prospectus, it is necessary to:

1. Present it clearly, using bullet lists and concise sections and paragraphs.
2. Explain how that particular document affects investors.

Highly Technical Business Description in Plain English

Under the plain English rule, an issuer with a highly technical business should provide a brief, general description of the business with, if necessary, concrete examples to illustrate the description.

By comparing the following two descriptions of Computational Systems, Inc., it is obvious that it is possible to describe a tech-business effectively in plain English. The first example is from CSI's 1996 10-K, prior to the adoption of the plain English rules. The second is from the summary of a merger proxy that CSI filed during the company's participation in the Division's plain English pilot program:

1. ***Computational Systems, Inc. 10-K***

   "The Company primarily designs, produces and markets an integrated family of advanced predictive maintenance products and services for use in large scale, continuous run manufacturing facilities. The Company's Reliability-Based Maintenance products and services help customers detect potentially disruptive conditions in the operation of their machinery before damage or complete mechanical failure occurs, thereby allowing maintenance to be scheduled at the most appropriate time."

2. ***Computational Systems, Inc./Emerson Electric Company's merger proxy***

"CSI's primary business is the design manufacture, and sale of a family of high-tech instruments that help companies determine when their industrial machines are in need of repair or adjustment. CSI also offers services to help its customers better manage the maintenance of their equipment. CSI's products and services help its customers keep their production lines running and maintain the quality of their products which may be adversely affected by an improperly functioning production line machine. CSI's customers are primarily large manufacturing, processing or power generating companies."

If the issuer must include technical terms that are understood only by industry experts, every effort must be made to explain these terms where they are first used. Where this is simply not possible, a glossary is acceptable.

In addition, technical terms and industry jargon are not appropriate for concise explanations.

Clarity, Not Brevity, Is the Goal

The goal of plain English is clarity, not brevity. Writing disclosure in plain English can sometimes actually increase the length of particular sections of a prospectus. The aim should be to reduce the length of a prospectus by writing concisely and eliminating redundancies—not by eliminating substance.

Electronic Filers Selected for Review

The Division of Corporation Finance has announced that, because issuers are required to file their registration statements electronically on EDGAR, the staff did not want them to send paper copies of their filings. However, in the plain English adopting release, if a registration statement that is subject to the new plain English rule is selected for review, the staff will need paper copies.

When issuers file their registration statements electronically on the EDGAR system, the document's layout is lost. Because the plain English rule is intended to enhance the readability of the prospectus through language *and design,* the staff needs to see the layout of the plain English sections as they are delivered to investors.

At present, the staff member assigned to a filing will call to request paper copies of the prospectus. The SEC is working to upgrade the EDGAR system to give issuers the option of filing an exact duplicate of the paper copy sent to investors, but this may not occur for some time.

Plain English and Acceleration Requests

The staff may ask the Commission to deny acceleration of a registration statement where the issuer has not made a good faith effort to comply with the plain English rule and amendments. The issuer must make a bona fide effort to make the prospectus reasonably concise, readable, and in compliance with the plain English requirements.

Cover Page Reminders

1. If the cover page exceeds the one page limit imposed by the rule, much of the information included is probably too detailed. The information that is not required by Item 501 of Regulation S-K and other information that is not key to an investment decision should be moved off the cover page. More in-depth information should be in the summary.

   Superfluous information such as the par value of common stock, highly technical explanations of industry operations, and minute details about the mechanics of a possible merger obscure the information that is key to potential investors' decisions.

2. Using all capital letters, cascading margins, narrow margins and dense text all impede readability of the text on the cover page. Since requirements limit this page to information that is key to an investment decision, it is very important that it be readable and visually inviting. The layout must highlight the information required by Item 501 and encourage investors to read the prospectus.

3. Item 501(a)(5) of Regulation S-K requires the issuer to highlight the cross reference to the risk factors section by using prominent type or in another manner. In other words, the cross reference should be visually distinctive from the other text on the cover page. Highlighting this cross reference using bold-faced and italicized type is suggested. Placing the cross reference in all capital letters is not recommended.

Comments Relating to the Summary

1. *Like information* should be grouped together. For example, if in a summary the items that discuss how a transaction directly affects shareholders are mixed with information on other topics, a naive investor could very easily become confused. If the exchange ratio, the tax consequences

for payments on fractional shares, discussions of regulatory matters, termination fees, conditions to the merger, and such are not organized in a logical order, even a sophisticated investor would be at a loss.

2. In the summary, the issuer should carefully consider and identify those aspects of an offering that are the *most significant* and determine how best to highlight them in clear, plain language. It is not necessary to explain at length technical steps a company must take, such as creating a merger subsidiary, directors' reasons for the merger, or the conflicts of interest that may result. This type of information would not be helpful for a shareholder making an investment decision.

3. The summary should not contain a lengthy description of the company's business and business strategy. Disclosure of this nature appears later in the prospectus. Detailed information is better suited for the body of the prospectus. If the issuer feels it important to highlight key aspects of the entity's business strategy, listing these in a bullet-point format, with one sentence per bullet point, is acceptable.

Sample Cautions for the Entire Prospectus

1. Long sentences make it difficult to understand on the first reading, particularly if there are embedded lists of information in paragraph form. Rather than including lists in paragraph form, they should be broken out, and each item marked with a bullet point, a number, or a letter.

2. Sentences containing parenthetical phrases disrupt the flow of information and make the sentences very long. As a result, investors may have to read them several times to understand the disclosure. Possible ways to eliminate parenthetical phrases are:

   a. If the information in the parenthetical phrase is part of the sentence, it may be set off by commas.

   b. If the parenthetical phrase does not fit as part of the sentence, it should be a separate sentence.

3. The use of footnotes should be avoided where possible. Some suggestions are:

   a. If the text in a footnote applies to an entire financial table, the footnoted material could be included in the narrative discussion that precedes the table.

   b. If a number of footnotes repeat the same text of a table, the information could be moved to the introductory paragraph.

   c. The footnoted material could be included in a column in the table.

4. A prospectus should be organized from the shareholders' perspectives. Information about the mechanics of a merger, for instance, is not

important to investors. How the proposed transactions will affect their investments is important to them.

5. Redundancy should be consciously avoided. The only type of repetition that is appropriate in the prospectus would be:

   a. Introduction of topics on the cover page.

   b. Expansion of those topics in a summary fashion while summarizing other key aspects of the transaction in the summary.

   c. Discussion of those and the remaining topics in greater detail in the body of the prospectus.

6. Informative subheadings provide readers with helpful navigational cues. They should be descriptive and specific to a particular prospectus. If subheadings would work equally well in any other company's disclosure document, they are probably too vague to be helpful.

7. A prospectus should never be written from the perspective of someone who is already quite familiar with the transaction and the entities involved. For example, references to "certain circumstances," "certain matters," "certain amendments," "certain persons," and "certain extraordinary matters" would make sense to someone who is already familiar with these transactions. But, would the shareholders be? Probably not. The term "certain" should be replaced with a brief description of what makes the information qualify as "certain."

8. Legalese and industry jargon should not be used in a prospectus. Instead, concepts should be explained in concrete, everyday language. As always, any industry terms should be used in context so those potential investors who do not work in the industry can understand the disclosure.

Chapter 33
Depreciation

CONTENTS

Types of Property	**33.02**
What Cannot Be Depreciated	**33.02**
When Depreciation Begins and Ends	**33.03**
Using the Section 179 Deduction	**33.04**
The Modified Accelerated Cost Recovery System (MACRS)	**33.07**
Dispositions	**33.11**
General Asset Accounts	**33.12**
Provisions in 2002 Tax Law	**33.14**
Special Depreciation Allowance	**33.14**
New York Liberty Zone Benefits	**33.19**

Depreciation is a decrease in the value of property over the time the property is being used. Events that can cause property to depreciate include wear and tear, age, deterioration, and obsolescence. It is possible to get back the cost of certain property by taking deductions for depreciation. For example, depreciation deduction may be taken for equipment used in business or for the production of income. Special depreciation provisions in the Job Creation and Worker Assistance Act of 2002 are detailed at the end of this chapter.

TYPES OF PROPERTY

To determine if property is a depreciation deduction, the property must be defined as either tangible or intangible.

Tangible property is property that can be seen or touched. There are two main types of tangible property, real property, such as land, buildings, and generally anything built or constructed on land, growing on land, or attached to the land; and personal property including cars, trucks, machinery, furniture, equipment and anything that is not real property.

Intangible property is generally any property that has value but cannot be seen or touched. It includes items such as computer software, copyrights, franchises, patents, trademarks, and trade names. Generally, if intangible property is depreciable the straight line method is used. It allows for the same amount of depreciation each year.

In general, only the owner using the property for business or for producing income may claim depreciation.

Only the property meeting all the following requirements may be depreciated.

1. It must be used in business or held to produce income.
2. It must be expected to last more than one year. In other words, it must have a useful life that extends substantially beyond the year it is placed in service.
3. It must be something that wears out, decays, gets used up, becomes obsolete, or loses its value from natural causes.

WHAT CANNOT BE DEPRECIATED

Property placed in service and disposed of in the same year may not be depreciated.

Tangible Property

The following are types of tangible property that cannot be depreciated, even though they are used in business or held to produce income.

1. The cost of land may not be depreciated because land does not wear out, become obsolete, or get used up. The cost of land generally includes the cost of clearing, grading, planting, and landscaping, because these expenses are all part of the cost of the land itself.
2. Inventory is any property held primarily for sale to customers in the ordinary course of business and may not be depreciated.
3. Generally, containers are part of inventory and cannot be depreciated.

4. Equipment held to build capital improvements may not be depreciated.

5. Leased property may be depreciated only if the incidents of ownership for the property are retained. Leased property to use in business or for the production of income cannot be depreciated because the incidents of ownership are not retained. A lessor generally can depreciate its cost even if the lessee has agreed to preserve, replace, renew, and maintain the property. However, if the lease provides that the lessee is to maintain the property and return to the lessor the same property or its equivalent in value at the expiration of the lease in as good condition and value as when leased, the cost of the property may not be depreciated.

   "Incidents of ownership" include the legal title, the legal obligation to pay for it, the responsibility to pay its maintenance and operating expenses, the duty to pay any taxes and the risk of loss if the property is destroyed, condemned, or diminishes in value through obsolescence or exhaustion.

6. Generally, a deduction for depreciation may not be taken on a term interest in property created or acquired after July 27, 1989, for any period during which the remainder interest is held, directly or indirectly, by a person related to the owner.

Intangible Property

There are two types of intangible property that can never be depreciated.

1. Goodwill may never be depreciated because its useful life cannot be determined. However, if a business was acquired after August 10, 1993 (after July 25, 1991, if elected), and part of the price included goodwill, it may be possible to amortize the cost of the goodwill over 15 years.

2. In general, trademark and trade name expenses must be capitalized. Neither trademarks nor trade names may be depreciated or amortized if acquired before August 11, 1993 (before July 26, 1991, if elected). It may be possible to amortize over 15 years the costs of trademarks and trade names acquired after August 10, 1993 (after July 25, 1991, if elected).

WHEN DEPRECIATION BEGINS AND ENDS

Property may be depreciated when it is placed in service for use in a trade or business or for the production of income. It is no longer depreciable when the cost has been fully recovered or other basis or when it is retired from service, whichever happens first.

For depreciation purposes, property is placed in service when it is ready and available for a specific use, whether in a trade or business, for the production of income, a tax-exempt activity, or a personal activity. Even if the property is not being used, it is in service when it is ready and available for its specific use.

Property permanently withdrawn from use in trade or business or from use in the production of income is considered retired from service and is no longer depreciable. Property can be retired either when sold or exchanged, when it is abandoned or when it is destroyed.

USING THE SECTION 179 DEDUCTION

The Section 179 deduction is a means of recovering the cost of property through a current deduction rather than through depreciation. Section 179 of the Internal Revenue Code allows for the deduction of all or part of the cost of certain qualifying property in the year it is placed in service. This would be done instead of recovering the cost by taking depreciation deductions over a specified recovery period. However, there are limits on the amount that can be deducted in a year.

What Costs Can and Cannot Be Deducted

The Section 179 deduction may be used for the cost of qualifying property acquired for use in trade or business, but not for the cost of property held only for the production of income.

Only the cost of property acquired by purchase for use in business qualifies for the Section 179 deduction. The cost of property acquired from a related person or group may not qualify.

If an asset is purchased with cash and a trade-in, a Section 179 deduction can be claimed based only on the amount of cash paid. The Section 179 deduction does not include the adjusted basis of the trade-in used in the purchase.

Qualifying Property

Property qualifying for the Section 179 deduction is depreciable property and includes the following.

1. Tangible personal property.
2. Other tangible property (except buildings and their structural components) used as:
   a. An integral part of manufacturing, production, or extraction or of furnishing transportation, communications, electricity, gas, water, or sewage disposal services,

b. A research facility used in connection with any of the activities in above, or

c. A facility used in connection with any of the activities for the bulk storage of fungible commodities.

3. Single purpose agricultural (livestock) or horticultural structures.
4. Storage facilities (except buildings and their structural components) used in connection with distributing petroleum or any primary product of petroleum.

Generally, a Section 179 deduction may not be claimed based on the cost of leased property. However, a Section 179 deduction may be claimed based on the cost of the following:

1. Property manufactured or produced and leased to others.
2. Property purchased and leased to others if both of the following apply.
   a. The term of the lease (including options to renew) is less than half of the property's class life.
   b. For the first 12 months after the property is transferred to the lessee, the total business deductions allowed on the property (other than rent and reimbursed amounts) is more than 15% of the rental income from the property.

Partial Business Use

When property is used for both business and nonbusiness purposes, the Section 179 deduction may be used if the property is used more than 50% for business in the year it was placed in service. The part of the cost of the property that is for business use is the cost of the property multiplied by the percentage of business use. The result is the business cost.

Nonqualifying Property

Generally, the Section 179 deduction cannot be claimed on the cost of any of the following.

1. Property held only for the production of income.
2. Real property, including buildings and their structural components.
3. Property acquired from certain groups or persons.
4. Air conditioning or heating units.
5. Certain property used predominantly outside the U.S.

6. Property used predominantly to furnish lodging or in connection with the furnishing of lodging.
7. Property used by certain tax-exempt organizations.
8. Property used by governmental units.
9. Property used by foreign persons or entities.
10. Certain property leased to others by a noncorporate lessor.

Electing the Deduction

The Section 179 deduction is not automatic. An individual must elect to take a Section 179 deduction. For purposes of the Section 179 deduction, property is considered placed in service in the year it is first made ready and available for a specific use. This use can be in a trade or business, the production of income, a tax-exempt activity, or a personal activity. If property is placed in service in a use that does not qualify it for the Section 179 deduction, it cannot later qualify in another year even if it is changed to business use. Records must be kept that show the specific identification of each piece of qualifying Section 179 property. These records must show how the property was acquired, the person it was acquired from and when it was placed in service.

How to Figure the Deduction

The total business cost an individual can elect to deduct under Section 179 in 2000 is $20,000; in 2001 and 2002, it is $24,000; after 2002, it is $25,000. This maximum dollar limit applies to each taxpayer, not to each business. The full amount does not have to be claimed. A percentage of the business cost of qualifying property may be deducted under Section 179. Then it may be possible to depreciate any difference in the cost not deducted under Section 179. If more than one item of qualifying property is acquired and placed in service during the same year, it is possible to divide the deduction among the items in any way, as long as the total deduction is not more than the limits.

If there is only one item of qualifying property and it does not cost more than the dollar limit, the deduction is limited to the lesser of the following.

1. An individual's taxable income from trade or business.
2. The cost of the item.

The Section 179 deduction must be figured before figuring the depreciation deduction. The amount deducted under Section 179 must be subtracted from the business/investment cost of the qualifying property. The result is called the unadjusted basis and is the amount used to figure any depreciation deduction.

Deduction Limits

The Section 179 deduction cannot be more than the business cost of the qualifying property. In addition, the following limits must be applied to the Section 179 deduction.

1. Maximum dollar limit. The total cost of Section 179 property that can be elected for deduction cannot be more than the amounts listed above.
2. Investment limit. If the cost of the qualifying Section 179 property placed in service in a year at present is over $200,000, the maximum dollar limit for each dollar over $200,000 must be reduced (but not below zero). If the business cost of Section 179 property placed in service is $200,000 plus the maximum dollar limit, or more, a Section 179 deduction cannot be taken for more than the total, and cannot be carried over.
3. Taxable income limit. The total cost that can be deducted each year is limited to the taxable income from the active conduct of any trade or business during the year. Generally, an individual is considered to be actively conducting a trade or business if he or she meaningfully participates in the management or operations of the trade or business.

THE MODIFIED ACCELERATED COST RECOVERY SYSTEM (MACRS)

The Modified Accelerated Cost Recovery System (MACRS) consists of two systems that determine how to depreciate property. The main system is called the General Depreciation System (GDS) and the second system is called the Alternative Depreciation System (ADS).

The main difference between the two systems is that ADS generally provides for a longer recovery period and uses only the straight line method of depreciation to figure a deduction. Unless specifically required by law to use ADS, GDS is generally used to figure a depreciation deduction.

Both systems simplify the way to figure the deduction by providing three preset conventions. These conventions determine the number of months for which depreciation may be claimed both in the year the property is placed in service, and in the year in which the property is disposed of. The conventions are as follows:

1. Mid-month convention. Used for all nonresidential real property and residential rental property. The property is treated for tax purposes as if use began or ended in the middle of the month.
2. Mid-quarter convention. Used if the basis of property placed in service during the last three months of the tax year is more than 40% of the

total bases of all property placed in service for the entire year (excluding nonresidential real property, residential rental property, and property placed in service and disposed of in the same year). The property is treated for tax purposes as if use began or ended in the middle of the quarter.

3. Half-year convention. Used for all other property. The property is treated for tax purposes as if use began or ended in the middle of the year.

MACRS provides four methods of figuring depreciation on property:

1. The 200% declining balance method over a GDS recovery period.
2. The 150% declining balance method over a GDS recovery period.
3. The straight line method over a GDS recovery period.
4. The straight line method over an ADS recovery period.

What to Depreciate Under MACRS

MACRS applies to most tangible depreciable property placed in service after 1986. MACRS must be used to depreciate all real property acquired before 1987 that has been changed from personal use to a business or income-producing use after 1986.

Knowing Which System to Use

Most tangible depreciable property falls within the *general* rule of MACRS, which is also called the General Depreciation System (GDS). Because GDS permits use of the declining balance method over a shorter recovery period, the deduction is greater in the earlier years.

However, there are specifications for the use of each system.

Both GDS and ADS have pre-established class lives for most property. Under GDS, most property is assigned to eight property classes based on these class lives. These property classes provide the number of years over which the cost of an item in a class may be recovered.

Some examples of this:

3-year property. Any race horse over 2 years old when placed in service. Any other horse over 12 years old when placed in service.

5-year property. Automobiles, taxis, buses, and trucks; computers and peripheral equipment; some office machinery; breeding cattle and dairy cattle.

However, ADS must be used for the following property:

1. Any tangible property used predominantly outside the U.S. during the year.
2. Any tax-exempt use property.
3. Any tax-exempt bond-financed property.
4. Any property used predominantly in a farming business and placed in service during any tax year in which the individual makes an election not to apply the uniform capitalization rules to certain farming costs.
5. Any imported property covered by an executive order of the President of the United States.

What Cannot Be Depreciated Under MACRS

MACRS cannot be used to depreciate the following property.

1. Intangible property.
2. Any motion picture film or video tape.
3. Any sound recording.
4. Certain real and personal property placed in service before 1987.

Any property that can be properly depreciated under a method of depreciation not based on a term of years may be excluded from MACRS.

Property Placed in Service Before 1987.   There are special rules that prevent the use of MACRS for property placed in service by anyone (for any purpose) before 1987 (before August 1, 1986, if MACRS was elected). These rules apply to both personal and real property. However, the rules for personal property are more restrictive. And although there are some exceptions to these rules, they do offer a basic guideline from which to work.

Personal Property.   MACRS may not be used for most personal property acquired after 1986 (after July 31, 1986, if MACRS was elected) if any of the following apply.

1. The individual or a relative owned or used the property in 1986.
2. The property was acquired from a person who owned it in 1986 and as part of the transaction the user of the property did not change.
3. The property was leased to a person (or someone related to this person) who owned or used the property in 1986.

4. The property was acquired in a transaction in which:
   a. The user of the property did not change, and
   b. The property was not MACRS property in the hands of the person from whom the individual acquired it because of (2) or (3).

Real Property.   MACRS may not be used for certain real property. This includes real property acquired after 1986 (after July 31, 1986, if MACRS was elected) if any of the following apply.

1. The individual or a relative owned the property in 1986.
2. The property was leased back to the person (or someone related to this person) who owned the property in 1986.
3. The property was acquired in a transaction in which some of the individual's gain or loss was not recognized. MACRS applies only to that part of the basis in the acquired property that represents cash paid or unlike property given up. It does not apply to the substituted portion of the basis.

Certain Nontaxable Transfers of Property.   MACRS does not apply to property involved in certain nontaxable transfers. This applies to property used before 1987 and transferred after 1986 to a corporation or partnership if its basis is determined by reference to the basis in the hands of the transferor or distributor. If MACRS was elected, it also applies to property used before August 1, 1986, and transferred after July 31, 1986, to a corporation or partnership if its basis is determined by reference to the basis in the hands of the transferor or distributor.

The nontaxable transfers covered by this rule include the following:

1. A distribution in complete liquidation of a subsidiary.
2. A transfer to a corporation controlled by the transferor.
3. An exchange of property solely for corporate stock or securities in a reorganization.
4. A contribution of property to a partnership in exchange for a partnership interest.
5. A partnership distribution of property to a partner.

Election to Exclude Property from MACRS

If property is depreciated under a method not based on a term of years, such as the unit-of-production method, that property may be excluded from MACRS.

Use of Standard Mileage Rate

If the standard mileage rate is used to figure a tax deduction for a business automobile, it is treated as having made an election to exclude the automobile from MACRS.

How to Figure the Deduction

Once it is determined that the property may be depreciated under MACRS and whether it falls under GDS or ADS, the following information must be known about the property.

1. Its basis. Generally, this refers to the cost plus amounts paid for items such as sales tax, freight, installation, and testing.
2. Its property class and recovery period. This refers to the member of years over which the cost "basis" of the property is recovered.
3. The date it was placed in service. This refers to the date the item was actually first used—not when it was purchased.
4. Which convention to use—mid-month, mid-quarter, or half-year.
5. Which depreciation method to use:
   a. GDS or ADS
   b. Which class the property is in.
   c. What type of property it is.

DISPOSITIONS

A disposition is the permanent withdrawal of property from use in a trade or business or in the production of income. A withdrawal can be made by sale, exchange, retirement, abandonment, involuntary conversion, or destruction. Generally gain or loss on the disposition of property is recognized by a sale. However, nonrecognition rules may allow for postponement of some gain.

If property is disposed of before the end of its recovery period, it is called an early disposition. If that property is depreciated under MACRS, a depreciation deduction for the year of disposition is allowed. The depreciation deduction is determined for the year of disposition.

With the exception of gain on the disposition of residential rental and nonresidential real property, all gain on the disposition of property depreciated under MACRS is included in income as ordinary income, up to the amount of previously allowed depreciation deducted for the property. There is no recapture for residential rental and nonresidential real property.

GENERAL ASSET ACCOUNTS

It is possible to group separate properties into one or more general asset accounts. They then can be depreciated as a single item of property. Each account can include only property with similar characteristics, such as asset class and recovery period. Some property cannot be included in a general asset account. There are additional rules for passenger automobiles, disposing of property, converting property to personal use, and property that generates foreign source income.

Once a general asset account is established, the amount of depreciation for each account is achieved by using the depreciation method, recovery period, and convention that applies to the property in the account. For each general asset account, the depreciation allowance is recorded in a separate depreciation reserve account.

Property used in both a trade or business (or for the production of income) and in a personal activity in the year in which it was first placed in service may not be in a general asset account.

How to Group Property in General Asset Accounts

Each general asset account must include only property placed in service in the same year and that has the following in common:

1. Asset class.
2. Recovery period.
3. Depreciation method.
4. Convention.

The following rules also apply when establishing a general asset account.

1. No asset class. Property without an asset class, but with the same depreciation method, recovery period, and convention, placed in service in the same year, can be grouped into the same general asset account.
2. Mid-quarter convention. Property subject to the mid-quarter convention can only be grouped into a general asset account with property that is placed in service in the same quarter.
3. Mid-month convention. Property subject to the mid-month convention can only be grouped into a general asset account with property that is placed in service in the same month.
4. Passenger automobiles. Passenger automobiles subject to the limits on passenger automobile depreciation must be grouped into a separate general asset account.

Dispositions and Conversions

Property in a general asset account is considered disposed of when any of the following occurs:

1. It is permanently withdrawn from use in trade or business or from the production of income.
2. It is transferred to a supplies, scrap, or similar account.
3. It is sold, exchanged, retired, physically abandoned, or destroyed.

Note the following:

1. The retirement of a structural component of real property is not a disposal.
2. The unadjusted depreciable basis and the depreciation reserve of the general asset account are not affected by the disposition of property from the general asset account.
3. Any property changed to personal use must be removed from the general asset account.

Unadjusted Depreciable Basis.   The unadjusted depreciable basis of an item of property in a general asset account is the same amount used to figure gain on the sale of the property, but it is figured without taking into account any depreciation taken in earlier years. The unadjusted depreciable basis of a general asset account is the total of the unadjusted depreciable bases of all of the property in the account.

Adjusted Depreciable Basis.   The adjusted depreciable basis of a general asset account is the unadjusted depreciable basis of the account minus any allowed or allowable depreciation based on the account.

Disposition of Remaining Property.   If all or the last item of property is disposed of in a general asset account, the adjusted depreciable basis of the general asset account can be recovered. Under this rule, the general asset account ends and the amount of gain or loss for the general asset account is figured by comparing the adjusted depreciable basis of the general asset account with the amount realized. If the amount realized is more than the adjusted depreciable basis, the difference is a gain. If it is less, the difference is a loss. If there is a gain, the amount that is subject to recapture as ordinary income is limited.

Change to Personal Use.   An item of property in a general asset account becomes ineligible for general asset account treatment if it is used in a personal activity. Once the property has been converted to personal use, it is removed from the general asset account as of the first day of the year in which the change in use occurs and make the appropriate adjustments are made.

PROVISIONS IN 2002 TAX LAW

For those who depreciate business property acquired and placed in service after September 10, 2001, the *Job Creation and Worker Assistance Act of 2002* contains provisions that may affect depreciation deduction for that property.

The new law made several changes in the tax rules. Some of the changes apply to property placed in service during 2001. Those changes and what the taxpayer should do if affected by them are outlined below. The new law contains the following provisions:

1. Depreciation deductions of 30 percent (a special depreciation allowance and special New York Liberty Zone depreciation allowance) for the year qualified property are placed in service after September 10, 2001.
2. An increased dollar limit on the section 179 deduction for qualified Liberty Zone property purchased after September 10, 2001.
3. A shorter recovery period for qualified Liberty Zone leasehold improvement property placed in service after September 10, 2001.
4. An increase in the maximum depreciation deduction for 2001 for a qualified passenger automobile placed in service after September 10, 2001.

Those who may qualify for an increased deduction under any of these new rules should file the revised 2001 Form 4562 (dated March 2002) for 2001 calendar or fiscal years and 2000 fiscal years ending after September 10, 2001. Since many individuals and corporate entities had already filed their tax returns, instructions are provided below for those who wish to amend their filing.

SPECIAL DEPRECIATION ALLOWANCE

A special depreciation allowance for qualified property placed in service after September 10, 2001, has been approved. The allowance is an additional deduction of 30 percent of the property's depreciable basis. To figure the depreciable basis, the taxpayer must first multiply the property's cost or other basis by the percentage of business/investment use and then reduce it by the amount of any Section 179 deduction and certain other deductions and credits for the property.

The allowance is deductible for both regular tax and alternative minimum tax (AMT) purposes. There is no AMT adjustment required for any depreciation figured on the remaining basis of the property. In the year the allowance is claimed—generally the year the property is placed in service—the depreciable basis of the property must be reduced by the allowance before figuring the regular depreciation reduction.

Qualified Property

To qualify for the special depreciation allowance, the property must meet the following requirements;

1. It is new property of one of the following types:
   a. Property depreciated under the MACRS with a recovery period of 20 years or less.
   b. Water utility property.
   c. Computer software that is not a Section 197 intangible. (The cost of some computer software is treated as part of the cost of hardware and is depreciated under MACRS.)
   d. Qualified leasehold improvement property.
2. It meets the following tests:
   a. Acquisition date test.
   b. Placed-in-service-date test.
   c. Original use test.
3. It is not excepted property.

Qualified Leasehold Improvement Property. Qualified leasehold improvement property is generally any improvement to an interior part of a building that is nonresidential real property, provided all of the following requirements are met:

1. The improvement is made under or pursuant to a lease by the lessee (or any sublessee) or the lessor of that part of the building;
2. That part of the building is to be occupied exclusively by the lessee (or any sublessee) of that part; and
3. The improvement is placed in service more than three years after the date the building was first placed in service.

However, a qualified leasehold improvement does *not* include any improvement for which the expenditure is attributable to any of the following:

1. The enlargement of the building,
2. Any elevator or escalator,

3. Any structural component benefiting a common area, or
4. The internal structural framework of the building.

Generally, a binding commitment to enter into a lease is treated as a lease, and the parties to the commitment are treated as the lessor and lessee. However, a binding commitment between related persons is not treated as a lease.

Related Persons.   For this purpose, the following are related persons:

1. Members of an affiliated group.
2. The persons listed in items 1 through 9 under Related Persons on page 8 of Publication 946 (except that "80% or more" should be substituted "for more than 10%").
3. An executor and a beneficiary of the same estate.

Tests to Be Met.   To qualify for the special depreciation allowance, the property must meet all of the following tests:

1. *Acquisition date test*—Generally, the property must have been acquired either:
   a. After September 10, 2001, and before September 11, 2004, but only if no written binding contract for the acquisition was in effect before September 11, 2001, or
   b. Pursuant to a written binding contract entered into after September 10, 2001, and before September 11, 2004.
      Property manufactured, constructed, or produced by owners for their own use meets this test if the manufacture, construction, or production of the property was begun after September 10, 2001, and before September 11, 2004.
2. *Placed-in-service-date test*—Generally, the property must be placed in service for use in the taxpayer's trade or business or for the production of income after September 10, 2001, and before January 1, 2005.
      However, certain property placed in service before January 1, 2006, may meet this test. Transportation property and property with a recovery period of 10 years or longer meet the test if one of the following applies:
   a. The property has an estimated production period of more than two years, or
   b. The property has an estimated production period of more than one year and it costs more than $1 million.
      Transportation property is any tangible personal property used in the trade or business of transporting persons or property. For property that

qualifies for the special depreciation allowance solely because of the one-year extension of the placed in service date, only the part of the basis attributable to manufacture, construction, or production before September 11, 2004, is eligible for the special depreciation allowance.

If taxpayers sold property they placed in service after September 10, 2001, and leased it back within three months after the property was originally placed in service, the property is treated as placed in service no earlier than the date it is used under the leaseback.

3. *Original use test*—The original use of the property must have begun with the taxpayer after September 10, 2001. "Original use" means the first use to which the property is put, whether or not by the present owner. Additional capital expenditures incurred after September 10, 2001, to recondition or rebuild the property meet the original use test.

Excepted Property. The following property does not qualify for the special depreciation allowance:

1. Property used by any person before September 11, 2001.
2. Property required to be depreciated using ADS. This includes listed property used 50 percent or less in a qualified business use.
3. Qualified New York Liberty Zone leasehold improvement property.

Qualified New York Liberty Zone leasehold improvement property is any qualified leasehold improvement property (as defined earlier) if all of the following requirements are met:

1. The improvement is to a building located in the New York Liberty Zone,
2. The improvement is placed in service after September 10, 2001, and before January 1, 2007; and
3. No written binding contract for the improvement was in effect before September 11, 2001.

Election Not to Claim the Allowance

A taxpayer can elect not to claim the special depreciation allowance for qualified property. If this election is made for any property, it applies to all property in the same property class placed in service during the year. To make this election, a statement should be attached to the individual's return indicating he or she elects not to claim the allowance and the class of property for which the election is being made. Points to take into consideration:

1. *When to make election*—Generally, the election must be made on a timely filed tax return (including extensions) for the year in which the

property is placed in service. However, if the timely filed return was filed for the year without making the election, the election can be made by filing an amended return within six months of the due date of the original return (not including extensions). The election statement should be attached to the amended return. At the top of the election statement, this statement should be printed: "Filed pursuant to Section 301.9100-2."

2. *Revoking an election*—Once an election has been made not to deduct the special depreciation allowance for a class of property, it cannot be revoked without IRS consent. A request to revoke the election is subject to a user fee.

Rules for Returns Filed Before June 1, 2002

The following rules apply if qualified property was placed in service after September 10, 2001, and the return filed before June 1, 2002. The rules apply to returns for 2000 fiscal years that end after September 10, 2001 as well as 2001 calendar and fiscal years:

1. *Claiming the allowance*—If the allowance was not claimed on the individual's return and he or she did not make the election *not to claim* the allowance, it is possible to do either of the following to claim the allowance:

   a. File an amended return by the due date (not including extensions) of the return for the year following the year the property was placed in service. A notation, "Filed Pursuant to Rev. Proc. 2002-33," should be printed at the top of the amended return.

   b. File Form 3115, *Application for Change in Accounting Method,* with the return for the year following the year the property was placed in service. The return must be filed by the due date (including extensions). The notation, "Automatic Change Filed Under Rev. Proc. 2002-33," should be written on the appropriate line of Form 3115. A copy of the completed Form 3115 (with signature) must also be filed with the IRS National Office no later than when the original is filed with the return.

2. *Electing not to claim the allowance*—Generally, the taxpayer elected not to claim the special depreciation allowance for a class of property if:

   a. The taxpayer filed the return in a timely manner (including extensions) for the year the qualified property was placed in service and a statement with the return indicated that the allowance was not being claimed, or

   b. The taxpayer filed the return in a timely manner, filed an amended return within six months of the due date of the original return (not including extensions) and indicated on a statement with the amended return that the allowance was not being claimed.

The statement must indicate that the taxpayer is not deducting the special depreciation allowance and the class of property to which the election applies. The statement can be either attached to or written on the return. You can, for example, write "not deducting 30%" on Form 4562.

3. *Deemed election* - Taxpayers not following either of the procedures described above to elect *not to claim* the allowance may still be treated as making the election if they:

   a. Filed the return for the year the property was placed in service and claimed depreciation, but not the special allowance, for any class of property, and

   b. Did not file an amended return or a Form 3115 within the time prescribed for claiming the special allowance (see above).

Passenger Automobiles

The limit is increased on the depreciation deduction (including any Section 179 deduction) for any passenger automobile that is qualified property (defined earlier) placed in service after September 10, 2001, and for which the individual claims the special depreciation allowance. Generally, the limit is increased from $3,060 to $7,660. However, if the automobile is a qualified electric car, the limit is increased from $9,280 to $23,080 ($22,980 if placed in service in 2002).

The increased maximum depreciation deduction does not apply if the individual elected not to claim the special depreciation allowance as explained earlier under Election Not to Claim the Allowance and Rules for Returns Filed Before June 1, 2002.

NEW YORK LIBERTY ZONE BENEFITS

Several benefits are available for property placed in service in the New York Liberty Zone (Liberty Zone). They include a special depreciation allowance for the year the property was placed in service, an increased Section 179 deduction, and the classification of certain leasehold improvement property as five-year property.

The New York Liberty Zone is the area located on or south of Canal Street, on or south of East Broadway and east of its intersection with Canal, and on or south of Grand Street and east of its intersection with East Broadway in the Borough of Manhattan in the City of New York, New York.

Special Liberty Zone Depreciation Allowance

A special depreciation allowance is permitted for qualified Liberty Zone property placed in service after September 10, 2001. The allowance is an additional deduction of 30 percent of the property's depreciable basis. To figure the depreciable basis, it is necessary first to multiply the property's cost or other basis by the percentage of business/investment use and then reduce that amount by any Section 179 deduction and certain other deductions and credits for the property.

The allowance is deductible for both regular tax and alternative minimum tax (AMT) purposes. There is no AMT adjustment required for any depreciation figured on the remaining basis of the property. In the year the allowance is claimed (generally the year the property is placed in service), the depreciable basis of the property must be reduced by the allowance before figuring regular depreciation deduction.

It is not permissible to claim the special Liberty Zone depreciation allowance for property eligible for the special depreciation allowance explained earlier. It is important to remember that qualified property is eligible for *only one* special depreciation allowance.

Qualified Liberty Zone Property

For a 2001 calendar or fiscal year and a 2000 fiscal year that ends after September 10, 2001, property qualifies for the special Liberty Zone depreciation allowance if it meets the following requirements.

1. It is one of the following types of property:
   a. Used property depreciated under MACRS with a recovery period of 20 years or less.
   b. Used water utility property.
   c. Used computer software that is not a section 197 intangible.
   d. Certain nonresidential real property and residential rental property (defined later).
2. It meets the following tests:
   a. Acquisition date test.
   b. Placed-in-service-date test.
   c. Substantial use test.
   d. Original use test.
3. It is not excepted property.

Nonresidential real property and residential rental property is qualifying property only to the extent it rehabilitates real property damaged, or replaces real property destroyed or condemned, as a result of the terrorist attack of September 11, 2001. Property is treated as replacing destroyed or condemned property if, as part of an integrated plan, such property replaces real property included in a continuous area that includes real property destroyed or condemned.

For these purposes, real property is considered destroyed (or condemned) only if an entire building or structure was destroyed (or condemned) as a result of the terrorist attack. Otherwise, the property is considered damaged real property. If certain structural components of a building (such as walls, floors, or plumbing fixtures) are damaged or destroyed as a result of the terrorist attack, but the building is not destroyed (or condemned), then only costs related to replacing the damaged or destroyed structural components qualify for the special Liberty Zone depreciation allowance.

Qualifying Tests.   To qualify for the special Liberty Zone depreciation allowance, the property must meet all of the following tests:

1. *Acquisition date test*—The property must have been acquired by purchase after September 10, 2001, and there must not have been a binding written contract for the acquisition in effect before September 11, 2001.

   Property manufactured, constructed, or produced for the owner's own use meets this test if the manufacture, construction, or production of the property was begun after September 10, 2001.
2. *Placed-in-service-date test*—Generally, the property must be placed in service for use in trade or business or for the production of income before January 1, 2007 (January 1, 2010, in the case of qualifying nonresidential real property and residential rental property).

   If the property placed in service after September 10, 2001, was sold and leased back within 3 months after the property was originally placed in service, the property is treated as placed in service no earlier than the date it is used under the leaseback.
3. *Substantial use test*—Substantially all use of the property must be in the Liberty Zone and in the active conduct of a trade or business in the Liberty Zone.
4. *Original use test*—The original use of the property in the Liberty Zone must have begun after September 10, 2001.

Used property can be qualified Liberty Zone property if it has not previously been used within the Liberty Zone. Also, additional capital expenditures incurred after September 10, 2001, to recondition or rebuild the property meet the original use test if the original use of the property in the Liberty Zone began with the new owner.

Excepted Property. The following property does not qualify for the special Liberty Zone depreciation allowance:

1. Property eligible for the special depreciation allowance explained earlier in Qualified Property under Special Depreciation Allowance.
2. Property required to be depreciated using ADS. This includes listed property used 50 percent or less in a qualified business use.
3. Qualified New York Liberty Zone leasehold improvement property (defined earlier in Excepted Property under Special Depreciation Allowance).

If office furniture is new property, it qualifies for the special depreciation allowance but not for the special Liberty Zone depreciation allowance. If, for example, a computer is used property that had not previously been used in the Liberty Zone, it qualifies for the special Liberty Zone depreciation allowance, but not the special depreciation allowance.

Election Not to Claim the Liberty Zone Allowance

It is permissible not to claim the special Liberty Zone depreciation allowance for qualified property. If this election is made for any property, it applies to all property in the same property class placed in service during the year. To make this election, a statement must be attached to the tax return indicating the election not to claim the allowance and the class of property for which the election is being made.

Generally, the election must be made on a timely filed tax return (including extensions) for the year in which the property was placed in service.

However, if the timely filed return for the year was made without making the election, it would still be possible to make the election by filing an amended return within six months of the due date of the original return (not including extensions). The election statement should be attached to the amended return. At the top of the election statement, "Filed pursuant to Section 301.9100-2" should be noted.

Once the election not to deduct the special Liberty Zone depreciation allowance for a class of property is made, it cannot be revoked without IRS consent. A request to revoke the election is subject to a user fee.

The rules that apply to the special depreciation allowance discussed earlier in Rules for Returns Filed Before June 1, 2002 under Special Depreciation Allowance also apply to the special Liberty Zone depreciation allowance.

Increased Section 179 Deduction

Under Section 179 of the Internal Revenue Code, it is possible to choose to recover all or part of the cost of certain qualifying property, up to a limit, by deducting it in the year placed in service. For tax years beginning in 2000, that limit was $20,000. For tax years beginning in 2001 and 2002, that limit is generally $24,000. If the cost of qualifying Section 179 property placed in service in a year is over $200,000, the dollar limit must be reduced (but not below zero) by the amount of the cost over $200,000.

The dollar limit on the Section 179 deduction is increased for certain property placed in service in the Liberty Zone. The increase is the smaller of the following amounts:

1. $35,000.
2. The cost of Section 179 property that is qualified Liberty Zone property placed in service during the year.

Chapter 34

Independent Contractor or Employee?

CONTENTS

Determining Who Is an Employee and Who Is an Independent Contractor	**34.02**
Worker Classification	**34.05**
Accountant's Concern?	**34.05**
Section 530 Relief Requirements	**34.06**
The Decision: Employee or Independent Contractor?	**34.07**
Primary Categories	**34.07**
Checklist	**34.14**
Emphasis on Categories	**34.16**
New Procedures for Processing Employment Tax Cases	**34.16**

Whether a person is an employee or independent contractor has been an area of uncertainty for many years. In August 1996, during the 104th Congress, changing and strengthening the "safe harbor" provisions were enacted as part of the *Small Business Jobs Protection Act*. The changes allow small businesses to rely on previous IRS actions and determinations to avoid reclassification of independent contractors as employees. The legislation does, however, still leave open the key question of what exactly is an independent contractor.

To make the definition of an independent contractor as clear as possible under current law, the IRS issued a training manual for IRS personnel on the independent contractor issue; introduced procedures for facilitating rapid determinations and appeals; and reduced penalties where a business acts in good faith to classify its independent contractors.

DETERMINING WHO IS AN EMPLOYEE AND WHO IS AN INDEPENDENT CONTRACTOR

Before it is possible to treat payments made for services, it is necessary to know the business relationship that exists between the employer and the person performing the services. The person performing the services may be:

1. An independent contractor.
2. A common-law employee.
3. A statutory employee.
4. A statutory nonemployee.

These four categories are discussed below. A later section points out the differences between an independent contractor and an employee. If an individual who is not an employee under the common-law rules is employed by a business, generally it is not necessary to withhold Federal income tax from that individual's pay. However, in some cases the employer may be required to withhold under backup withholding requirements on these payments.

Independent Contractors

People such as lawyers, contractors, subcontractors, public stenographers, and auctioneers who follow an independent trade, business, or profession in which they offer their services to the public, are generally not employees. However, whether such people are employees or independent contractors depends on the facts in each case. The general rule is that an individual is an independent contractor if the person for whom the services are performed, has the right to control or direct *only the result* of the work and *not the means and methods* of accomplishing the result.

Common-Law Employees

Under common-law rules, anyone who performs services for an entity is an employee if the employer can control what will be done and how it will be done. This is so even when the employee is given freedom of action. What matters is that the employer has the right to control the details of the services performed.

If there is an employer-employee relationship, it makes no difference how it is labeled. The substance of the relationship, not the label, governs the worker's status. Nor does it matter whether the individual is employed full or part time.

For employment tax purposes, no distinction is made between classes of employees. Superintendents, managers, and other supervisory personnel are all employees. An officer of a corporation is generally an employee; however, an officer who performs no services or only minor services, and neither receives nor is entitled to receive any pay, is not considered an employee. A director of a corporation is not an employee with respect to services performed as a director.

It is generally necessary to withhold and pay income, Social Security, and Medicare taxes on wages paid to common-law employees. However, the wages of certain employees may be exempt from one or more of these taxes.

Leased Employees. Under certain circumstances, a corporation furnishing workers to various professional people and firms is the employer of those workers for employment tax purposes. For example, a professional service corporation may provide the services of secretaries, nurses, and other similarly trained workers to its subscribers.

The service corporation enters into contracts with the subscribers under which the subscribers specify the services to be provided and the fee to be paid to the service corporation for each individual furnished. The service corporation has the right to control and direct the worker's services for the subscriber, including the right to discharge or reassign the worker. The service corporation hires the workers, controls the payment of their wages, provides them with unemployment insurance and other benefits, and is the employer for employment tax purposes.

Statutory Employees

If workers are independent contractors under the common law rules, such workers may nevertheless be treated as employees by statute ("statutory employees") for certain employment tax purposes if they fall within any one of the following four categories and meet the three conditions described under Social Security and Medicare taxes, below. The four categories are:

1. A driver who distributes beverages (other than milk) or meat, vegetable, fruit, or bakery products, or one who picks up and delivers laundry or dry cleaning, if the driver is the entity's agent or is paid on commission.
2. A full-time life insurance sales agent whose principal business activity is selling life insurance, annuity contracts, or both, primarily for one life insurance company.

3. An individual who works at home on materials or goods that are supplied and that must be returned to a business establishment, if the business also furnishes specifications for the work to be done.

4. A full-time traveling or city salesperson who works on the entity's behalf and turns in orders to the business from wholesalers, retailers, contractors, or operators of hotels, restaurants, or other similar establishments. The goods sold must be merchandise for resale or supplies for use in the buyer's business operation. The work performed must be the salesperson's principal business activity.

Social Security and Medicare Taxes.   Social Security and Medicare taxes must be withheld from the wages of statutory employees if all three of the following conditions apply:

1. The service contract states or implies that substantially all the services are to be performed personally by them,

2. They do not have a substantial investment in the equipment and property used to perform the services (other than an investment in transportation facilities), and

3. The services are performed on a continuing basis for the same payer.

The Federal Unemployment Tax Act (FUTA) and Income Tax.   For FUTA tax, the term employee means the same as it does for Social Security and Medicare taxes, except that it does not include statutory employees in categories 2 and 3 above. Thus, any individual who is an employee under category 1 or 4 is also an employee for FUTA tax purposes and subject to FUTA tax.

Income taxes are not to be withheld from the wages of statutory employees.

Statutory Nonemployees

There are two categories of statutory nonemployees: direct sellers and licensed real estate agents. They are treated as self-employed for all federal tax purposes, including income and employment taxes, if:

1. Substantially all payments for their services as direct sellers or real estate agents are directly related to sales or other output rather than to the number of hours worked.

2. Their services are performed under a written contract providing that they will not be treated as employees for federal tax purposes.

Direct Sellers.   Direct sellers include persons falling within any of these three groups:

1. Persons engaged in selling (or soliciting the sale of) consumer products in the home or place of business other than in a permanent retail establishment.

2. Persons engaged in selling (or soliciting the sale of) consumer products to any buyer on a buy-sell basis, a deposit-commission basis, or any similar basis prescribed by regulations, for resale in the home or at a place of business other than in a permanent retail establishment.

3. Persons engaged in the trade or business of delivering or distributing newspapers or shopping news (including any services directly related to such delivery or distribution).

Direct selling includes activities of individuals who attempt to increase direct sales activities of their direct sellers and who earn income based on the productivity of their direct sellers. Such activities include providing motivation and encouragement; imparting skills, knowledge or experience; and recruiting.

WORKER CLASSIFICATION

With the exception of statutory employees, work classification is based upon a common law standard for determining whether the worker is an independent contractor or employee. That standard essentially asks whether the business has the right to *direct and control the worker.* The courts have traditionally looked to a variety of evidentiary facts in applying this standard, and the IRS has adopted those facts to assist in classifying workers.

ACCOUNTANT'S CONCERN?

When conducting an audit, the auditor needs to assist taxpayers in identifying all of the evidence relative to their business relationships with workers. Many taxpayers may not be aware of what information is needed to make a correct determination of worker classification. This is especially true of small business owners who may not be aware of the relief available under Section 530 of the Revenue Act of 1978, resulting from worker reclassification. An auditor's examination should actively consider Section 530 during an examination, including furnishing taxpayers with a summary of Section 530 at the beginning of an examination.

Essentially, an accountant's responsibility is similar to an IRS tax examiner's responsibility as set forth by the Treasury Department which states:

"The examiner has a responsibility to the taxpayer and to the government to determine the correct tax liability and to maintain a fair and impartial attitude in all matters relating to the examination. The fair and impartial attitude of an examiner aids in increasing voluntary compliance. An examiner must approach each examination with an objective point of view."

Section 530 Relief Requirements

A business has been selected for an employment tax examination to determine whether certain workers were correctly treated as independent contractors. However, the employer will not owe employment taxes for those workers if the employer meets the relief requirements described below. If the employer does not meet these relief requirements, the IRS will need to determine whether the workers are, in fact, independent contractors or employees and whether employment taxes are actually owed for those workers.

To receive relief from paying employment taxes, three requirements must be met: reasonable basis, substantive consistency and reporting consistency.

Reasonable Basis.   To establish a reasonable basis for not treating the workers as employees, an employer must show that:

1. It reasonably relied on a court case about federal taxes or a ruling issued by the IRS.
2. The business was audited by the IRS at a time when similar workers were treated as independent contractors and the IRS did not reclassify those workers as employees.
3. Workers were treated as independent contractors because that was how a significant segment of that particular industry treated similar workers.
4. The employer relied on some other reasonable basis—for example, on the advice of a business lawyer or accountant who knew the facts about the particular business and that industry.

The employer does not have a *reasonable basis* for treating the workers as independent contractors and therefore will not meet the relief requirements if his or her decision was not made on the basis of one of these criteria.

Substantive Consistency.   In addition, the employer (and any predecessor business) must have treated the workers, and any similar workers, as independent contractors. If similar workers were treated as employees, this relief provision is not available.

Reporting Consistency.   Form 1099-MISC must have been filed for each worker, unless the worker earned less than $600. Relief is not available for any year in which the required Forms 1099-MISC were not filed. If they were filed for some workers but not others, relief is not available for the workers for whom they were not filed.

The Decision: Employee or Independent Contractor?

An employer must generally withhold income taxes, withhold and pay Social Security and Medicare taxes, and pay unemployment tax on wages paid to an *employee.* An employer does not generally have to withhold or pay any taxes on payments to *independent contractors.* This is the important distinction.

To determine whether an individual is an employee or an independent contractor under the common law, the relationship of the worker and the business must be examined. All evidence of control and independence must be considered. In any employee–independent contractor determination, all information that provides evidence of the degree of control and the degree of independence must be considered.

Primary Categories

Officially termed the *worker classification issue,* the focus is centered on three main areas that the IRS has concluded are primary categories of evidence to draw a distinction between an employee and an independent contractor. The essence of the distinction is whether or not the employer has the right to direct and control the worker. The three areas are:

1. Behavioral control.
2. Financial control.
3. Relationship of the parties.

Those three areas provide evidence that substantiates the right to direct or control the details and means by which the worker performs the required services. Training is important in this context. Significant are such workplace developments as evaluation systems and concern for customer security in conjunction with business identification. All relevant information must be considered and weighed to determine whether a worker is an independent contractor or an employee.

Virtually every business will impose on workers, whether contractors or employees, some form of instruction. How else would a worker know what he or she is supposed to do, what duties to perform? This fact alone, however, is not sufficient evidence to determine a worker's status. As with every relevant fact, the problem is to determine whether the employer has retained the right to control the *details* of a worker's performance, or instead has given up the business's right to control those details. Accordingly, the weight of evidence in any case depends on the *degree* to which instructions apply with respect to *how the job gets done rather than to the end result.*

Behavioral Control

Behavioral control concerns whether there is a right to direct or control how the worker performs the specific task for which he or she is engaged. Instructions and training are the main factors in considering the degree of behavioral control.

An employee is generally subject to the business's instructions about when, where, and how to work. Following are types of instructions about how to do work:

1. When and where to do the work.
2. What tools or equipment to use.
3. What workers to hire or to assist with the work.
4. Where to purchase supplies and services.
5. What work must be performed by a specified individual.
6. What order or sequence to follow.

The degree of instruction depends on the scope of instructions, the extent to which the business retains the right to control the worker's compliance with the instructions, and the effect on the worker in the event of noncompliance. All these provide useful clues for identifying whether the business keeps control over the manner and means of work performance, or only over a particular product or service. The more detailed the instructions are that the worker is required to follow, the more control the business exerts over the worker, and the more likely the business retains the right to control the methods by which the worker performs the work. Absence of detail in instructions reflects less control.

Although the presence and extent of instructions is important in reaching a conclusion as to whether a business retains the right to direct and control the methods by which a worker performs a job, it is also important to consider the weight to be given those instructions if they are imposed by the business only in compliance with governmental or governing body regulations. If a business requires its workers to comply with established, municipal building codes related to construction, for example, the fact that such rules are imposed by the business should be given little weight in determining the worker's status. However, if the business develops more stringent guidelines for a worker in addition to those imposed by a third party, more weight should be given to these instructions in determining whether the business has retained the right to control the worker.

The nature of a worker's occupation also affects the degree of direction and control necessary to determine worker status. Highly trained professionals such as doctors, accountants, lawyers, engineers, or computer specialists may require very little, if any, training and instruction on how to perform their services for a particular business. In fact, it may be impossible for the business to instruct the worker on how to perform the services because it may lack the essential knowledge and skills to do so. Generally, professional workers who are engaged in the pursuit of an independent trade, business, or profession in which they offer their services to the public are independent contractors, not employees. In analyzing the status of professional workers, evidence of control or autonomy with respect to the financial details of how the task is performed tends to be especially important, as does evidence concerning the relationship of the parties.

An employment relationship can also exist when the work can be done with a minimal amount of direction and control, such as work done by a store clerk, or gas station attendant. The absence of a *need* to control should not be confused with the absence of the *right* to control. The right to control as an incident of employment requires only such supervision as the nature of the work requires. The key fact to consider is whether the business retains the *right* to direct and control the worker, regardless of whether the business actually exercises that right.

Evaluation systems are used by virtually all businesses to monitor the quality of work performed by workers, whether independent contractors or employees. In analyzing whether a business's evaluation system provides evidence of the right to control work performance, or the absence of such a right, an auditor should look for evidence of how the evaluation system may influence the worker's behavior in performing the details of the job.

If an evaluation system measures compliance with performance standards concerning the details of how the work is to be performed, the system and its enforcement are evidence of control over the worker's behavior. However, not all businesses have developed formal performance standards or evaluation systems. This is especially true of smaller businesses.

Training is the established means of explaining detailed methods and procedures to be used in performing a task. Periodic or ongoing training provided by a business about procedures to be followed and methods to be used indicates that the business wants the services performed in a particular manner. This type of training is strong evidence of an employer-employee relationship.

Financial Control

Financial control concerns the facts which illustrate whether there is a *right* to direct or control how the worker's activities are conducted.

Factors to be considered are the business aspects of the worker's activities; significant investment, if any; unreimbursed expenses; services available to the relevant market; method of payment; and opportunity for profit or loss. These factors can be thought of as bearing on the issue of whether the recipient has the right to direct and control the means and details of the business aspects of how the worker performs services.

A significant investment is evidence that an independent contractor relationship may exist. It should be stressed that a significant investment is not necessary for an independent contractor. Some types of work simply do not require large expenditures. Even if large expenditures, such as costly equipment, are required, an independent contractor may rent the equipment needed at fair rental value. There are no precise dollar limits that must be met in order to have a significant investment. The size of the worker's investment and the risk borne by the worker are not diminished merely because the seller or lessor receives the benefit of the worker's services.

The extent to which a worker chooses to incur expenses and costs impacts his or her opportunity for profit or loss. This constitutes evidence that the worker has the right to direct and control the financial aspects of the business operations. Although not every independent contractor needs to make a significant investment, almost every independent contractor will incur an array of business expenses either in the form of direct expenditures or in the form of fees for pro rata portions of one or several expenses. Businesses often pay business or travel expenses for their employees. Independent contractors' expenses may also be reimbursed. An independent contractor can contract for direct reimbursement of certain expenses, or can seek to establish contract prices that will reimburse the contractor for these expenses. Attention should center on *unreimbursed* expenses, which better distinguish independent contractors and employees, inasmuch as independent contractors are more likely to have unreimbursed expenses. If expenses are unreimbursed, then the opportunity for profit or loss exists. Fixed ongoing costs that are incurred regardless of whether work is currently being performed are especially important. However, employees may also incur unreimbursed expenses in connection with the services they perform for their businesses. Relatively minor expenses incurred by a worker, or more significant expenses that are customarily borne by an employee in a particular line of business, would generally not indicate an independent contractor relationship.

An independent contractor is generally free to seek out business opportunities, as independent contractors' income depends on doing so successfully. As a result, independent contractors often advertise, maintain a visible business location, and are available to work for the relevant market. An independent contractor with special skills may be contacted by word of mouth and referrals without the need for advertising. An independent contractor who has negotiated a long-term contract may find advertising equally unnecessary, and may be unavailable to work for others for the duration of a contract. Other independent contractors may find that a visible business location does not generate sufficient business to justify the expense. Therefore, the absence of these activities is a neutral fact.

The method of payment can be helpful in determining whether the worker has the opportunity for profit or loss. A worker who is compensated on an hourly, daily, weekly, or similar basis is guaranteed a return for labor. This is generally evidence of an employer-employee relationship, even when the wage or salary is accompanied by a commission. In some lines of business, such as law, it is typical to pay independent contractors on an hourly basis. Performance of a task for a flat fee is generally evidence of an independent contractor relationship, especially if the worker incurs the expenses of performing the services. A commission-based worker can be either an independent contractor or employee. The worker's status will depend on the worker's ability to realize a profit or incur a loss as a result of services rendered.

The ability to realize a profit or incur a loss is probably the strongest evidence that a worker controls the business aspects of services rendered.

Also to be considered is whether the worker is free to make business decisions that affect his profit or loss. If the worker is making decisions that affect the bottom line, the worker likely has the ability to realize profit or loss. It is sometimes thought that because a worker can receive more money working longer hours or receive less money by working less, he has the ability to incur a profit or loss. This type of income variation, however, is also consistent with employer status and does not distinguish employees from independent contractors.

Not all financial control facts need be present for the worker to have the ability to realize profit or loss. For example, a worker who is paid on a straight commission basis, makes business decisions, and has unreimbursed business expenses, likely would have the ability to realize a profit or loss, even if the worker does not have a significant investment and does not market her services.

Relationship of the Parties

There are other facts that recent court decisions consider relevant in determining worker status. Most of these facts reflect how the worker and the business perceive the relationship to each other. It is much more difficult to link the facts in this category directly to the right to direct and control *how* work is to be performed than the categories discussed above. The relationship of the parties is important because it reflects the parties' *intent* concerning control. Courts often look at the intent of the parties because the intent is most often stated in their contractual relationship. A written agreement describing the worker as an independent contractor is viewed as evidence of the parties' intent that a worker is an independent contractor. However, a contractual designation, in and of itself, is not sufficient evidence for determining worker status. The facts and circumstances under which a worker performs services determine a worker's status. The *substance* of a relationship, not a label, governs the worker's status. The contract may be relevant in ascertaining methods of compensation, expenses that will be incurred, and rights and obligations of each party with respect to *how* work is to be performed. In addition, if it is difficult, if not impossible, to decide whether a worker is an independent contractor, the intent of the parties, as reflected in the contractual designation, is an effective way to resolve the issue.

Questions sometimes arise concerning whether a worker who creates a corporation through which to perform services can be an employee of a business that engages the corporation. If the corporate formalities are properly followed, and at least one nontax business purpose exists, the corporate form is generally recognized for both state law and federal law, including federal tax purposes. Disregarding the corporate entity is generally an extraordinary remedy, applied by most courts only in cases of clear abuse, so the worker will usually not be treated as an employee of the business, but as an employee of the corporation. (It should be noted that the fact that a worker receives payment for services from a business through the worker's corporation does not automatically require a finding of independent contractor status with respect to those services.)

Employee Benefits.   Providing a worker with employee benefits has traditionally been linked with employee status and, therefore, can be an important factor in deciding an independent contractor-employee relationship. If a worker receives employee benefits, such as paid vacation days, paid sick days, health insurance, life or disability insurance, or a pension, this constitutes some evidence of employee status. The evidence is strongest if the worker is provided with employee benefits under a tax-qualified retirement plan, 403(b) annuity, or cafeteria plan, because by statute, these benefits can be provided to employees only. If an individual is excluded from a benefit plan because the worker is not considered an employee by the business, this is relevant though not conclusive in determining the worker's status as an independent contractor. If the worker is excluded on some other grounds, the exclusion is irrelevant in determining whether the worker is an independent contractor or an employee. This is because none of these employee benefits is required to be provided to employees. Many workers whose status as bona fide employees is unquestioned receive no employee benefits, as there is no requirement that all workers be covered.

Termination Rights.   The circumstances under which a business or a worker can terminate their relationship have traditionally been considered useful evidence bearing on the status the parties intended the worker to have.

However, in order to determine whether the facts are relevant to the worker's status, the impact of modern business practices and legal standards governing worker termination must be considered. A business's ability to terminate the work relationship at will, without penalty, provides a highly effective method to control the details of how work is performed, and indicates employee status. On the other hand, in the traditional independent contractor relationship, the business could terminate the relationship only if the worker failed to provide the intended service, which indicates the parties' intent that the business does not have the right to control how the work was performed. In practice, businesses rarely have complete flexibility in discharging an employee. The business may be liable for pay in lieu of notice, severance pay, "golden parachutes," or other forms of compensation when it discharges an employee. In addition, the reasons for which a business can terminate an employee may be limited, whether by law, by contract, or by its own practices.

A worker's ability to terminate work at will was traditionally considered to illustrate that the worker merely provided labor and tended to indicate an employer-employee relationship. In contrast, if the worker terminated work, and the business could refuse payment or sue for nonperformance, this indicated the business's interest in receiving the contracted product or service, which tended to indicate an independent contractor relationship. In practice, however, independent contractors can enter into short-term contracts for which nonperformance remedies are inappropriate; or they may negotiate limits on their liability for nonperformance. Typical examples are professionals, such as doctors and attorneys, who can terminate their contractual relationship without penalty.

Businesses can successfully sue employees for substantial damages resulting from their failure to perform the services for which they were engaged. As a result, the presence or absence of limits on workers' ability to terminate the relationship, by themselves, no longer constitutes useful evidence in determining worker status. A business's ability to refuse payment for unsatisfactory work continues to be characteristic of an independent contractor relationship.

Permanent/Indefinite Relationship. The existence of a permanent relationship between the worker and the business is relevant evidence in determining whether there is an employer-employee relationship. If a business engages a worker with the expectation that the relationship will continue indefinitely, rather than for a specific project or period, it is a factor that is generally considered evidence of an intent to create an employment relationship.

A relationship that is created with the expectation that it will be indefinite should not be confused with a long-term relationship. A long-term relationship may exist between a business and either an independent contractor or an employee. The relationship between the business and an independent contractor can be long-term for several reasons:

1. The contract may be a long-term contract.
2. Contacts can be renewed regularly due to superior service, competitive costs, or lack of alternative service providers.

A business can also have a relationship with an employee that is long-term, but not indefinite. This could occur if temporary employment contracts are renewed, or if a long-term, but not indefinite, employment contract is entered into. As a result, a relationship that is long-term, but not indefinite, is a neutral fact that should be disregarded.

A temporary relationship is a neutral fact that should be disregarded. An independent contractor will typically have a temporary relationship with a business, but so too will employees engaged on a seasonal project, or on an "as needed" basis. The services performed by the worker, and the extent to which those services are a key aspect of the regular business of the company, are germane. In considering this, it should be remembered that the fact that a service is desirable, necessary, or even essential to a business does not mean that the service provider is an employee. The work of an attorney or paralegal is part of the regular business of a law firm. If a law firm hires an attorney or paralegal, it is likely that the law firm will present the work as its own. As a result, there is an increased probability that the law firm will direct or control the activities. However, further facts should be examined to see whether there is evidence of the *right* to direct or control before a conclusion is reached that these workers are employees. It is possible that the work performed is part of the principal business of the law firm, yet it has hired workers who are outside specialists and may be independent contractors.

CHECKLIST

The 20 factors indicating whether an individual is an employee or an independent contractor follow:

1. *Instructions.* An employee must comply with instructions about when, where, and how to work. Even if no instructions are given, the control factor is present if the employer has the right to control how the work results are achieved.
2. *Training.* An employee may be trained to perform services in a particular manner. Independent contractors ordinarily use their own methods and receive no training from the purchasers of their services.

3. *Integration.* An employee's services are usually integrated into the business operations because the services are important to the success or continuation of the business. This shows that the employee is subject to direction and control.

4. *Services Are Rendered Personally.* An employee renders services personally. This shows that the employer is interested in the methods as well as the results.

5. *Hiring Assistants.* An employee works for an employer who hires, supervises, and pays workers. An independent contractor can hire, supervise, and pay assistants under a contract that requires their contractor to provide materials and labor and to be responsible only for the result.

6. *Continuing Relationship.* An employee generally has a continuing relationship that may exist even if work is performed at recurring although irregular intervals.

7. *Set Hours of Work.* An employee usually has set hours of work established by an employer. Independent contractors generally can set their own work hours.

8. *Full-Time Required.* An employee may be required to work or be available full-time. This indicates control by the employer. An independent contractor can work when and for whom he or she chooses.

9. *Work Done on Premises.* An employee usually works on the premises of an employer, or works on a route or at a location designated by an employer.

10. *Order or Sequence Set.* An employee may be required to perform services in the order or sequence set by an employer. This shows that the employee is subject to direction and control.

11. *Reports.* An employee may be required to submit reports to an employer, which shows that the employer maintains a degree of control.

12. *Payments.* An employee generally is paid by the hour, week, or month. An independent contractor is usually paid by the job or on a straight commission.

13. *Expenses.* An employee's business and travel expenses are generally paid by an employer. This shows that the employee is subject to regulation and control.

14. *Tools and Materials.* An employee is normally furnished significant tools, materials, and other equipment by an employer.

15. *Investment.* An independent contractor has a significant investment in the facilities used in performing services for someone else.

16. *Profit or Loss.* An independent contractor can make a profit or suffer a loss.

17. *Works for More than One Person or Firm.* An independent contractor is generally free to provide services to two or more unrelated persons or firms at the same time.

18. *Offers Services to General Public.* An independent contractor makes services available to the general public.

19. *Right to Fire.* An employee can be fired by an employer. An independent contractor cannot be fired as long as results are produced that meet the specifications of the contract.

20. *Right to Quit.* An employee can quit a job at any time without incurring liability. An independent contractor usually agrees to complete a specific job and is responsible for its satisfactory completion, or legally is obligated to make good for failure to complete it.

EMPHASIS ON CATEGORIES

Since the publication of the training manual for IRS personnel on worker classification, there has been less reliance upon the common law standard or the list of 20 factors. The three categories (behavioral control, financial control, and relationship of the parties) are relied upon more heavily for the determination. However, it is wise to consider all aspects of the arrangement. In fact, the IRS cautions, "In each case, it is very important to consider all the facts—no single fact provides the answer."

And it is not only the employer who considers the independent contractor/employee situation a morass. At one point in the ongoing attempts to decipher the complex tax code tax lawyers, CPAs and corporate tax officers came up with a list of high priority suggestions for simplifing the tax situation: drop the minimum tax; standardize the rules on classifying workers as employees or independent contractors; clarify the eight tax incentives for education.

The following addition to the Internal Revenue Code may not help in the worker classification process, but it does provide Tax Court review rights.

NEW PROCEDURES FOR PROCESSING EMPLOYMENT TAX CASES

The Taxpayer Relief Act of 1997 (TRA'97) created Section 7436 of the Internal Revenue Code, which provides Tax Court review rights concerning certain employment tax determinations.

Code Notice 98-43 provides information about how taxpayers can petition for Tax Court review of employment tax determinations under the provision that became effective August 5, 1997. Attached to this notice as Exhibit 1 is a "Notice of Determination Concerning Worker Classification Under Section 7436."

With respect to taxpayers whose workers are the subject of an employment tax determination as to whether they are independent contractors, or, in fact, employees, the attached Notice of Determination addressed to a taxpayer will constitute the "determination" that is a prerequisite to invoking the Tax Court's jurisdiction.

The new Section of the Code contains the following provisions:

1. The Tax Court has the jurisdiction to review determinations by the IRS that workers are employees for purposes of Subtitle C of the Code.
2. And that the organization for which services are performed is not entitled to relief from employment taxes under Section 530 of the Revenue Act of 1978.
3. The determination must involve an actual controversy relating to independent contractor/employee status.
4. The determination is made as part of an examination of worker classification.

Section 7436 can be conducted pursuant to the Tax Court's simplified procedures for small tax cases set forth in the new Section of the Code and Rule 295 of the Tax Court's Rules of Practice and Procedure. Currently, taxpayers can elect, with the concurrence of the Tax Court, to use these simplified procedures if the amount of employment taxes placed in dispute resulting from workers being designated as independent contractors is $50,000 or less for each calendar quarter involved.

Issues to Which Section 7436 Applies

Section 7436(a) provides the Tax Court with jurisdiction to review the IRS's determinations that one or more individuals performing services for the taxpayer are employees of the taxpayer, not independent contractors, for purposes of Subtitle C of the Code, or that the taxpayer is not entitled to relief under Section 530 with respect to such individuals.

Thus, 7436(a) does not:

1. Provide the Tax Court with jurisdiction to determine any amount of employment tax or penalties.
2. Provide the Tax Court with jurisdiction to review other employment tax issues.
3. Apply to employment-related issues not arising under Subtitle C, such as the classification of individuals with respect to pension plan coverage or the proper treatment of individual income tax deductions.

Additionally, insofar as 7436(a) only confers jurisdiction upon the Tax Court to review determinations that are made by the IRS as part of an employment tax examination, other IRS determinations that are not made as part of an examination, including those that are made in the context of private letter rulings or Form SS-8, "Determination of Employee Work Status for Purposes of Federal Employment Taxes and Income Tax Withholding," are not subject to review by the Tax Court under this provision.

The IRS will issue a Notice of Determination only after the IRS has determined both that:

1. One or more individuals performing services for the taxpayer are employees for purposes of Subtitle C.
2. The taxpayer is not entitled to relief under Section 530. This will provide taxpayers with the opportunity to resolve both issues in one judicial determination.

Taxpayers Eligible to Seek Review

Section 7436(b) provides that a pleading seeking Tax Court review of the IRS's determination can be filed only by "the person for whom the services are performed." Thus, workers may not seek review of the IRS's determinations under these provisions. In addition, because there must be an actual controversy, review may not be sought by a third party who has not been determined by the IRS to be the employer.

Notice of Determination

The IRS will inform taxpayers of a determination by sending the taxpayer a Notice of Determination by certified or registered mail. The Notice of Determination will advise taxpayers of the opportunity to seek Tax Court review, and it provides information on how to do so. Attached to the notice will be a schedule showing each kind of tax with its proposed employment tax adjustment for the specific taxpayer by calendar quarter.

This schedule will be provided to enable the taxpayer to determine eligibility to elect use of the small tax case procedures under Section 7436(c). Currently, the small tax case procedures may be available if the amount of employment taxes in dispute is $50,000 or less for each calendar quarter involved.

In most cases, a taxpayer who receives a Notice of Determination will have previously received a "thirty-day letter," which the IRS sends to taxpayers in unagreed examination cases. The thirty-day letter lists the proposed employment tax adjustments to be made and describes the taxpayer's right either to agree to the proposed employment tax adjustments or, alternatively, to protest the proposed adjustments to the Appeals Division within thirty days of the date of the letter.

If the taxpayer does not respond to the thirty-day letter by agreeing to the proposed adjustments or, alternatively, by filing a protest with the Appeals Division, the taxpayer will receive, by certified or registered mail, a Notice of Determination. Under normal procedures, if the taxpayer does not respond to the thirty-day letter, the taxpayer should generally expect to receive the notice within sixty days after expiration of the thirty-day period beginning with the date on the thirty-day letter. If no notice is received during this period, the taxpayer may wish to contact the local Internal Revenue Service office to check on the status of the case.

If the taxpayer responds to the thirty-day letter by filing a protest with the Appeals Division (or if the case proceeds to Appeals by way of the employment tax early referral procedures), and the worker classification and Section 530 issues are not settled on an agreed basis in the Appeals Division, the taxpayer will then receive a Notice of Determination.

Taxpayers are encouraged to resolve cases in nondocketed status by requesting use of the early referral procedures in appropriate cases.

Prerequisite for Seeking Review

Because a Notice of Determination constitutes the IRS's determination of worker classification, it is a jurisdictional prerequisite for seeking Tax Court review of the IRS's determinations regarding classification of the worker as an independent contractor or an employee, and Section 530 issues (see above). Tax Court proceedings seeking review of these determinations can not begin prior to issuance of the notice.

Time of Filing

Section 7436(b)(2) provides that a taxpayer's petition for review must be filed with the Tax Court before the 91st day after the IRS mails its Notice of Determination to the taxpayer by certified or registered mail. If the taxpayer discusses the case with the IRS during the period before the 91st day following the mailing of the notice, the discussion will not extend the period in which the taxpayer may file a petition with the Tax Court.

A taxpayer who does not file a Tax Court petition within the allotted time retains the right to seek judicial review of the employment tax determinations by paying the tax and filing a claim for refund, as required by the Code. If the claim for refund is denied, the taxpayer may file a refund suit in district court or the Court of Federal Claims.

Appeals Jurisdiction

Cases docketed in the U.S. Tax Court will be referred by District Counsel to the Appeals Division of the IRS for consideration of settlement unless the Notice of Determination was issued by Appeals. Cases in which Appeals issued such a Notice of Determination may be referred to them unless District Counsel determines that there is little likelihood that a settlement of all or a part of the case can be achieved in a reasonable period of time. Appeals will have sole settlement authority over docketed cases referred to them until the case is returned to District Counsel.

Suspension of the Statute of Limitations

The ruling provides that the suspension of the limitations period for assessment in Section 6503(a) of the Code applies in the same manner as though a notice of deficiency had been issued. Thus, the mailing of the Notice of Determination by certified or registered mail will suspend the statute of limitations for assessment of taxes attributable to the worker classification and Section 530 issues. Generally, the statute of limitations for assessment of taxes attributable to these issues is suspended for the 90-day period during which the taxpayer can begin a suit in Tax Court, plus an additional 60 days thereafter.

Moreover, if the taxpayer does file a timely petition in the Tax Court, the statute of limitations for assessment of taxes attributable to the issues will be suspended during the Tax Court proceedings, and for 60 days after the decision becomes final.

Restrictions on Assessment

This same ruling provides that the restrictions on assessment in Section 6213 of the Code apply in the same manner as if a notice had been issued. Thus, the IRS is precluded from assessing the taxes prior to expiration of the 90-day period during which the taxpayer can file a timely Tax Court petition.

If he or she does file, this generally precludes the IRS from assessing the taxes until the decision of the Tax Court has become final. If the taxpayer does not file a timely Tax Court petition before the 91st day after the Notice of Determination was mailed, the employment taxes attributable to the workers described in the Notice of Determination can then be assessed.

Agreed Settlements

If the taxpayer wishes to settle the employment issues on an agreed basis before issuance of a Notice of Determination, the taxpayer must formally waive the restrictions on assessment. This will generally be accomplished by execution of an agreed settlement that contains the following language: "I understand that, by signing this agreement, I am waiving the restrictions on assessment provided in Sections 7436(d) and 6213(a) of the Internal Revenue Code of 1986."

The IRS will not assess employment taxes attributable to those issues unless either a Notice of Determination has been issued to the taxpayer and the 90-day period for filing a Tax Court petition has expired or, alternatively, the taxpayer has waived the restrictions on assessment.

If the IRS erroneously makes an assessment of taxes attributable to those issues without first either issuing a Notice of Determination or obtaining a waiver of restrictions on assessment, the taxpayer is entitled to an automatic abatement of the assessment. However, once any such procedural defects are corrected, the IRS can reassess the employment taxes to the same extent as if the abated assessment had not occurred.

Section 1454 of the Tax Relief Act (TRA) of 1997 was effective as of August 5, 1997. Thus, assessments that were made prior to the August 5, 1997 effective date of the Act are not subject to this legislation or the procedures discussed above. All employment tax examinations involving worker classification and/or Section 530 issues that were pending as of August 5, 1997 became subject to the legislation.

Chapter 35

Asset Valuation for Tax Purposes

CONTENTS

Cost Basis of Assets	**35.02**
Adjusted Basis of Property	**35.08**
Basis Other Than Cost	**35.11**

Basis is the amount of an investment (equity) in property for tax purposes. The basis of property is used to figure depreciation, amortization, depletion, and casualty losses. It is also used to figure gain or loss on the sale or other disposition of property. It is important to keep accurate records of all items that affect the basis of property so that these computations can be made quickly and accurately.

This discussion is divided into three sections:

1. Cost Basis.
2. Adjusted Basis.
3. Basis Other Than Cost.

The basis of property bought is usually its cost. It may also be necessary to capitalize (add to basis) certain other costs related to buying or producing the property.

The original basis in property is adjusted (increased or decreased) by certain events. If improvements are made to the property, the basis is increased. If deductions are taken for depreciation or casualty losses, the basis is reduced.

Basis in some assets cannot be determined by cost. This includes property received as a gift or inheritance. It also applies to property received in an involuntary conversion and in certain other circumstances.

Cost Basis of Assets

The basis of property bought is usually its cost. The cost is the amount paid in cash, debt obligations, other property, or services. Cost also includes amounts paid for the following items:

1. Sales tax.
2. Freight.
3. Installation and testing.
4. Excise taxes.
5. Legal and accounting fees (when they must be capitalized).
6. Revenue stamps.
7. Recording fees.
8. Real estate taxes (if assumed for the seller).

Certain other costs related to buying or producing property may have to be capitalized.

For property bought on any time-payment plan that charges little or no interest, the basis of that property is the stated purchase price, minus the amount considered to be unstated interest. There generally is unstated interest if the interest rate is less than the applicable federal rate. When a trade or business is purchased, this generally includes all assets used in the business operations, such as land, buildings, and machinery. The price is spread among the various assets, including any Section 197 intangibles such as goodwill.

Stocks and Bonds

The basis of stocks or bonds bought is generally the purchase price plus any costs of purchase, such as commissions and recording or transfer fees. If a person gets stocks or bonds other than by purchase, the basis is usually determined by the fair market value (FMV) or the previous owner's adjusted basis. Adjustments to the basis of stocks for certain events that occur after purchase will be necessary.

When it is possible to identify the shares of stock or the bonds sold, their basis is the cost or other basis of the particular shares of those stocks or the particular bonds. If someone buys and sells securities at various times in varying quantities, and no one can identify the shares sold, the basis of the securities is the basis of the securities acquired first.

For mutual fund shares acquired at different times and prices, it is appropriate to use an average basis.

Real Property

In a purchase of real property, certain fees and other expenses become part of the cost basis in the property.

If the purchaser pays the real estate taxes the seller owed on real property bought, and the seller did not reimburse the buyer, those taxes are part of the basis. The buyer cannot deduct them as taxes.

If a buyer reimburses the seller for taxes the seller paid, the buyer can usually deduct that amount as an expense in the year of purchase. That amount is not included in the basis of the property.

If the buyer did not reimburse the seller, the buyer must reduce the basis by the amount of those taxes.

Settlement Costs.   A buyer can include in the basis of property the settlement fees and closing costs that are for buying the property. A buyer cannot include fees and costs for getting a loan on the property. (A fee for buying property is a cost that must be paid even if the buyer bought the property for cash.)

The following items are some of the settlement fees or closing costs buyers *can* include in the basis of the property:

1. Abstract fees (abstract of title fees).
2. Charges for installing utility services.
3. Legal fees (including title search and preparation of the sales contract and deed).
4. Recording fees.
5. Surveys.
6. Transfer taxes.
7. Owner's title insurance.
8. Any amounts the seller owes that the buyer agrees to pay, such as back taxes or interest, recording or mortgage fees, charges for improvements or repairs, and sales commissions.

Settlement costs do not include amounts placed in escrow for the future payment of items such as taxes and insurance.

The following items are some settlement fees and closing costs a buyer *cannot* include in the basis of the property:

1. Fire insurance premiums.
2. Rent for occupancy of the property before closing.

3. Charges for utilities or other services related to occupancy of the property before closing.
4. Charges connected with getting a loan. The following are examples of these charges:
   a. Points (discount points, loan origination fees).
   b. Mortgage insurance premiums.
   c. Loan assumption fees.
   d. Cost of a credit report.
   e. Fees for an appraisal required by a lender.
5. Fees for refinancing a mortgage.

If these costs relate to business property, items (1) through (3) are deductible as business expenses. Items (4) and (5) must be capitalized as costs of getting a loan and can be deducted over the period of the loan.

Points and Mortgages. If a buyer pays points to obtain a loan (including a mortgage, second mortgage, line of credit, or a home equity loan), the points are not added to the basis of the related property. Generally, a buyer can deduct the points over the term of the loan.

Special rules may apply to points the buyer and the seller pay when obtaining a mortgage on the purchase of a main home. If certain requirements are met, the buyer can deduct the points in full for the year in which they are paid. The basis of the home is reduced by any seller-paid points.

If a person buys property and assumes (or buys subject to) an existing mortgage on the property, the basis includes the amount the buyer pays for the property plus the amount to be paid on the mortgage.

If an individual builds property or has assets built, the expenses for this construction are part of the basis. Some of these expenses include the following items:

a. The cost of land.
b. The cost of labor and materials.
c. Architect's fees.
d. Building permit charges.
e. Payments to contractors.
f. Payments for rental equipment.
g. Inspection fees.

In addition, if the owner of a business uses employees, material, and equipment to build an asset, the basis would also include the following costs:

1. Employee wages paid for the construction work.
2. Depreciation on equipment owned while it is used in the construction.

3. Operating and maintenance costs for equipment used in the construction.
4. The cost of business supplies and materials used in the construction.

These expenses may not be deducted. They must be capitalized; therefore, they are included in the asset's basis. On the other hand, it is necessary to reduce the basis by any work opportunity credit, welfare-to-work credit, Indian employment credit, or empowerment zone employment credit allowable on the wages paid in (1). The value of the owner's own labor, or any other labor not paid for, is not to be included in the basis of any property constructed.

Business Assets

If property is purchased to use in a business, the basis is usually its actual cost. If the owner constructs, creates, or otherwise produces property, the costs must be capitalized as the basis. In certain circumstances, the project may be subject to the uniform capitalization rules.

Uniform Capitalization Rules. The uniform capitalization rules specify the costs added to basis in certain circumstances. Uniform capitalization rules must be used when any of the following applies to a trade, business, or any activity carried on for profit:

1. Production of real or tangible personal property for use in the business or activity.
2. Production of real or tangible personal property for sale to customers.
3. Acquisition of property for resale.

Property is produced when it is constructed, built, installed, manufactured, developed, improved, created, raised, or grown. Property produced for someone under a contract is treated as produced by that person up to the amount paid or costs incurred for the property.

Tangible personal property includes films, sound recordings, video tapes, books, or similar property.

Under the uniform capitalization rules, a person must capitalize all direct costs and an allocable part of most indirect costs incurred due to production or resale activities.

The following are not subject to the uniform capitalization rules:

1. Property someone produces that he or she does not use in trade, business, or activity conducted for profit.
2. Qualified creative expenses paid or incurred as a freelance (self-employed) writer, photographer, or artist that are otherwise deductible on the freelancer's tax return.

3. Property someone produced under a long-term contract, except for certain home construction contracts.

4. Research and experimental expenses allowable as a deduction under Section 174 of the Internal Revenue Code.

5. Costs for personal property acquired for resale if the current (or predecessor's) average annual gross receipts for the three previous tax years do not exceed $10 million.

Intangible Assets.   Intangible assets include goodwill, patents, copyrights, trademarks, trade names, and franchises. The basis of an intangible asset is usually the cost to buy or create it.

The basis of a *patent* is the cost of development, such as research and experimental expenditures, drawings, working models, and attorneys' and governmental fees. If research and experimental expenditures are deducted as current business expenses, they cannot be included in the basis of the patent. The value of the inventor's time spent on an invention is not part of the basis.

For an author, the basis of a *copyright* will usually be the cost of getting the copyright plus copyright fees, attorneys' fees, clerical assistance, and the cost of plates that remain in the author's possession.

The value of the author's time, or any other person's time that was not paid for, is not included.

The purchase price of a *franchise, trademark,* or *trade name* is the basis unless the payments can be deducted as a business expense.

Allocating the Basis

When multiple assets are purchased for a lump sum, the amount paid is allocated among the assets received. This allocation is used to figure the basis for depreciation and gain or loss on a later disposition of any of these assets.

The buyer and the seller may agree to a specific allocation of the purchase price among the multiple assets in the sales contract of a lump-sum sale. If this allocation is based on the value of each asset, and the buyer and the seller have adverse tax interests, the allocation generally will be accepted.

Acquisition of a Trade or Business.   In the acquisition of a trade or business, the purchase price is allocated to the various assets acquired. It is this Section that has been changed by the IRS.

For asset acquisitions occurring *after* January 5, 2000, the allocation must be made among the following assets in proportion to (but not more than) their fair market value (FMV) on the purchase date, in the following order:

1. Certificates of deposit, U.S. Government securities, foreign currency, and actively traded personal property, including stock and securities.

2. Accounts receivable, mortgages, and credit card receivables that arose in the ordinary course of business.

3. Property of a kind that would properly be included in inventory if on hand at the end of the tax year, and property held by the tax-payer primarily for sale to customers in the ordinary course of business.

4. All other assets except Section 197 intangibles, goodwill, and going concern value.

5. Section 197 intangibles, except goodwill, and going concern value.

6. Goodwill and going concern value (whether or not they qualify as Section 197 intangibles).

For asset acquisitions occurring *before* January 6, 2000, the allocation must be made among the following assets in proportion to (but not more than) their fair market value on the purchase date, in the following order:

1. Certificates of deposit, U.S. Government securities, foreign currency, and actively traded personal property, including stock and securities.

2. Accounts receivable, mortgages, and credit card receivables that arose in the ordinary course of business.

3. Property of a kind that would properly be included in inventory if on hand at the end of the tax year, and property held by the tax-payer primarily for sale to customers in the ordinary course of business.

4. All other assets except Section 197 intangibles, goodwill, and going concern value.

5. Section 197 intangibles, except goodwill and going concern value.

6. Section 197 intangibles in the nature of goodwill and going concern value.

The buyer and seller may enter into a written agreement as to the allocation of any consideration or the FMV of any of the assets. This agreement is binding on both parties unless the IRS determines the amounts are not appropriate.

Both the buyer and seller involved in the sale of business assets must report to the IRS the allocation of the sales price among Section 197 intangibles and the other business assets.

Land and Buildings.   When a purchaser obtains buildings and the land on which they stand for a lump sum, the basis of the property is allocated among the land and the buildings to figure the depreciation allowable on the buildings.

The basis of each asset is obtained by multiplying the lump sum by a fraction. The numerator is the FMV of that asset, and the denominator is the FMV of the whole property at the time of purchase. If there is uncertainty about the FMV of the land and buildings, the basis can be allocated based on their assessed values for real estate tax purposes.

Demolition costs, and other losses incurred for the demolition of any building, are added to the basis of the land on which the demolished building was located. The costs may not be claimed as a current deduction.

A modification of a building will not be treated as a demolition if the following conditions are satisfied:

1. 75% or more of the existing external walls of the building are retained in place as internal or external walls.
2. 75% or more of the existing internal structural framework of the building is retained in place.

If the building is a certified historic structure, the modification must also be part of a certified rehabilitation.

If these conditions are met, the costs of the modifications are added to the basis of the building.

Subdivided Lots. If a tract of land is purchased and subdivided, the basis for *each* lot must be determined. This is necessary because the gain or loss must be figured on the sale of each individual lot. As a result, the entire cost in the tract is not recovered until all of the lots have been sold.

To determine the basis of an individual lot, multiply the total cost of the tract by a fraction. The numerator is the FMV of the lot, and the denominator is the FMV of the entire tract.

If a developer sells subdivided lots before the development work is completed, it is possible (with IRS consent) to include, in the basis of the properties sold, an allocation of the estimated future cost for common improvements.

ADJUSTED BASIS OF PROPERTY

Before figuring gain or loss on a sale, exchange, or other disposition of property, or figuring allowable depreciation, depletion, or amortization, it is usually necessary to make certain adjustments to the basis of the property. The result of these adjustments to the basis is the adjusted basis.

Increases to Basis

The basis of any property is increased by all items properly added to a capital account. These include the cost of any improvements having a useful life of more than one year.

Rehabilitation expenses also increase basis. However, any rehabilitation credit allowed for these expenses must be subtracted before adding them to the basis. If any of the credit must be recaptured, the basis is increased by the recapture amount.

Separate accounts must be kept for additions or improvements to business property. Also, the basis of each modification is depreciated according to the depreciation rules that would apply to the underlying property, had they been placed in service at the same time as the addition or improvement.

The following items increase the basis of property:

1. The cost of extending utility service lines to the property.
2. Legal fees, such as the cost of defending and perfecting title.
3. Legal fees for obtaining a decrease in an assessment levied against property to pay for local improvements.
4. Zoning costs.
5. The capitalized value of a redeemable ground rent.

Assessments for Local Improvements.   The basis of property is increased by assessments for items such as paving roads and building ditches that increase the value of the property. They may not be deducted as taxes. However, charges for maintenance, repairs, or interest charges related to the improvements can be deducted as taxes.

Deducting versus Capitalizing Costs.   Costs that can be deducted as current expenses are not added to the basis. Amounts paid for incidental repairs or maintenance that are deductible as business expenses cannot be added to the basis. However, certain other costs can be either deducted or capitalized. If they are capitalized, they are included in the basis. If they are deducted, they are not included.

The costs that can be either deducted or capitalized include the following:

— Carrying charges, such as interest and taxes, that someone pays to own property, except those carrying charges that must be capitalized under the uniform capitalization rules (discussed earlier).
— Research and experimentation costs.
— Intangible drilling and development costs for oil, gas, and geothermal wells.
— Exploration costs for new mineral deposits.
— Mining development costs for a new mineral deposit.
— Costs of establishing, maintaining, or increasing the circulation of a newspaper or other periodical.

— Cost of removing architectural and transportation barriers for people with disabilities and the elderly. If someone claims the disabled access credit, they must reduce the amount deducted or capitalize by the amount of the credit.

Decreases to Basis

The following items reduce the basis of property:

— Section 179 deductions.
— Deduction for clean-fuel vehicles and refueling property.
— Nontaxable corporate distributions.
— Deductions previously allowed (or allowable) for amortization, depreciation, and depletion.
— Exclusion of subsidies for energy conservation measures.
— Credit for qualified electric vehicles.
— Postponed gain from sale of home.
— Investment credit (part or all) taken.
— Casualty and theft losses and insurance reimbursements.
— Certain canceled debt excluded from income.
— Rebates received from a manufacturer or seller.
— Easements.
— Gas-guzzler tax.
— Tax credit or refund for buying a diesel-powered highway vehicle.
— Adoption tax benefits.

A few of the more timely of these items are discussed below.

Environmental Considerations.   The basis is decreased in a car by the *gas-guzzler (fuel economy) tax* if the owner begins using the car within one year of the date of its first sale for ultimate use. This rule also applies to a subsequent owner who buys the car and begins using it not more than one year after the original sale. If the car is imported, the one-year period begins on the date of entry or withdrawal from the warehouse if that is later than the date of the first sale for ultimate use. If an income tax credit or refund has been received for a *diesel-powered highway vehicle* purchased before August 21, 1996, the basis is reduced by the credit or refund allowable.

If a deduction is taken for *clean-fuel vehicles or clean-fuel vehicle refueling property,* the basis is decreased by the amount of the deduction. Any subsidy received from a public utility company for the purchase or installation of an *energy conservation measure* for a dwelling unit can be excluded from gross income. The basis of the property for which the subsidy was received is reduced by the excluded amount.

Depreciation. The basis of property is decreased by the depreciation that was deducted, or could have been deducted, on tax returns under the method of depreciation chosen. If less depreciation was taken than could have been taken, the basis should be decreased by that amount. If no depreciation deduction was made, the basis is reduced by the full amount permitted. If more was deducted than should have been, the basis is decreased by the amount equal to the depreciation that should have been deducted, plus the part of the excess depreciation deducted that actually reduced the tax liability for the year. In decreasing the basis for depreciation, the amount deducted on the tax returns as depreciation, and any depreciation capitalized under the uniform capitalization rules, must be included.

BASIS OTHER THAN COST

There are many instances in which cost *cannot be used* as basis. In these cases, FMV or the adjusted basis of property may be used. Adjusted basis is discussed above; FMV is discussed in this section.

Fair market value (FMV) is the price at which property would change hands between a buyer and a seller, neither having to buy or sell, and both having reasonable knowledge of all necessary facts. Sales of similar property on or about the same date may be helpful in figuring the property's FMV.

Property Received for Services

If someone receives property for services, the property's FMV should be included in income. The amount included in income becomes the basis. If the services were performed for a price agreed upon beforehand, it will be accepted as the FMV of the property if there is no evidence to the contrary.

Bargain Purchases. A bargain purchase is a purchase of an item for less than its FMV. If, as compensation for services, someone purchases goods or other property at less than FMV, the difference between the purchase price and the property's FMV is included in income. The basis in the property is its FMV (the purchase price plus the amount included in income).

If the difference between the purchase price and the FMV represents a qualified employee discount, the difference should not be included in income. However, the basis in the property is still its FMV.

Taxable Exchanges

A taxable exchange is one in which the gain is taxable or the loss is deductible. A taxable gain or deductible loss is also known as a recognized gain or loss. If someone receives property in exchange for other property in a taxable exchange, the basis of the property received is usually its FMV at the time of the exchange. A taxable exchange occurs when a taxpayer receives cash or gets property not similar or related in use to the property exchanged.

Involuntary Conversions

If property is received as a result of an involuntary conversion, such as a casualty, theft, or condemnation, the basis of the replacement property is figured using the basis of the converted property.

If replacement property is similar or related in service or use to the converted property, the replacement property's basis is the old property's basis on the date of the conversion. However, the following adjustments should be made:

1. Decrease the basis by the following:
   a. Any loss recognized on the conversion.
   b. Any money received that is not spent on similar property.
2. Increase the basis by the following:
   a. Any gain recognized on the conversion.
   b. Any cost of acquiring the replacement property.

Money or property not similar or related in service or use to the converted property may be received. If the recipient buys replacement property similar or related in service or use to the converted property, the basis of the new property is its cost decreased by the gain not recognized on the conversion.

If more than one piece of replacement property is purchased, the basis is allocated among the properties based on their respective costs.

Nontaxable Exchanges

A nontaxable exchange is an exchange in which the recipient is not taxed on any gain and cannot deduct any loss. When property is received in a nontaxable exchange, its basis is usually the same as the basis of the property transferred. A nontaxable gain or loss is also known as an unrecognized gain or loss.

Like-Kind Exchanges

The exchange of property for the same kind of property is the most common type of nontaxable exchange. To qualify as a like-kind exchange, both the property transferred and the property received must be held by the transferor for business or investment purposes. There must also be an exchange of like-kind property.

The basis of the property received is the same as the basis of the property given up. Exchange expenses are generally closing costs. They may include such items as brokerage commissions, attorney fees, and deed preparation fees. They should be added to the basis of the like-kind property received.

Related Persons.   If a like-kind exchange takes place directly or indirectly between related persons and either party disposes of the property within two years after the exchange, the exchange no longer qualifies for like-kind exchange treatment. Each person must report any gain or loss not recognized on the original exchange. Each person reports it on the tax return filed for the year in which the later disposition occurs. If this rule applies, the basis of the property received in the original exchange will be its fair market value.

These rules generally do not apply to the following kinds of property dispositions:

1. Dispositions due to the death of either related person.
2. Involuntary conversions.
3. Dispositions in which neither the original exchange nor the subsequent disposition had as a main purpose the avoidance of federal income tax.

Generally, related persons are ancestors, lineal descendants, brothers and sisters (whole or half), and spouses. Other "related" persons may, for example, include two corporations, an individual and a corporation, a grantor and a fiduciary, or other business arrangements.

Partially Nontaxable Exchange.   A partially nontaxable exchange is an exchange in which someone receives unlike property or money in addition to like property. The basis of the property received is the same as the basis of the property given up, with the following adjustments:

1. Decrease the basis by the following amounts:
   a. Any money received.
   b. Any loss recognized on the exchange.
2. Increase the basis by the following amounts:
   a. Any additional costs incurred.
   b. Any gain recognized on the exchange.

If the other party to the exchange assumes the liabilities, the debt assumption is treated as money received in the exchange.

Partial Business Use of Property.   If someone has property used partly for business and partly for personal use, and exchanges it in a nontaxable exchange for property to be used wholly or partly in their business, the basis of the property received is figured as if two properties had been exchanged . The first is an exchange of like-kind property. The second is personal-use property on which gain is recognized and loss is not recognized.

The adjusted basis in the property should first be figured as if someone transferred two separate properties. The adjusted basis of each part of the property is figured by taking into account any adjustments to basis. The depreciation taken or that could have taken is deducted from the adjusted basis of the business part. The amount realized for the property should then be figured and allocated to the business and nonbusiness parts of the property.

The business part of the property may be exchanged tax-free. However, any gain must be recognized from the exchange of the nonbusiness part. The taxpayer is deemed to have received, in exchange for the nonbusiness part, an amount equal to its FMV on the date of the exchange. The basis of the property acquired is the total basis of the property transferred (adjusted to the date of the exchange), increased by any gain recognized on the nonbusiness part.

If the nonbusiness part of the property transferred is the main home, it may be possible to exclude from income all or a portion of the gain on that part.

Property Transferred from a Spouse

The basis of property transferred to a spouse or transferred in trust for one's benefit by a spouse (or former spouse if the transfer is incident to divorce) is the same as the spouse's adjusted basis. However, the basis must be adjusted for any gain recognized by the spouse or former spouse on property transferred in trust. This rule applies only to a transfer of property in trust in which the liabilities assumed, plus the liabilities to which the property is subject, are more than the adjusted basis of the property transferred.

If the property transferred is a series E, series EE, or series I U.S. Savings Bond, the transferor must include in income the interest accrued to the date of transfer. The basis in the bond immediately after the transfer is equal to the transferor's basis increased by the interest income includable in the transferor's income. The transferor must, at the time of the transfer, turn over the records necessary to determine the adjusted basis and holding period of the property as of the date of transfer.

Inherited Property

The basis in property inherited from a decedent is generally one of the following:

1. The FMV of the property at the date of the individual's death.

2. The FMV on the alternate valuation date, if the personal representative for the estate chooses to use alternate valuation.
3. The value under the special-use valuation method for real property used in farming or other closely held business, if chosen for estate tax purposes.
4. The decedent's adjusted basis in land to the extent of the value that is excluded from the decedent's taxable estate as a qualified conservation easement.

If a federal estate tax return does not have to be filed, the basis in the inherited property is its appraised value at the date of death for state inheritance or transmission taxes.

Appreciated Property. The above rule does not apply to appreciated property received from a decedent if a taxpayer or spouse originally gave the property to the decedent within one year before the decedent's death. The basis in this property is the same as the decedent's adjusted basis in the property immediately before his or her death, rather than its FMV.

Appreciated property is any property whose FMV on the day it was given to the decedent is more than its adjusted basis.

Community Property

In community property states (Arizona, California, Idaho, Louisiana, Nevada, New Mexico, Texas, Washington, and Wisconsin), husband and wife are each considered to own half the community property. When either spouse dies, the total value of the community property, even the part belonging to the surviving spouse, generally becomes the basis of the entire property.

For this rule to apply, at least half the value of the community property interest must be includable in the decedent's gross estate, whether or not the estate must file a return.

Farm or Closely Held Business

Under certain conditions, when a person dies, the executor or personal representative of that person's estate may choose to value the qualified real property on other than its FMV. In that-case, the executor or personal representative values the qualified real property based on its use as a farm or its use in a closely held business. If the executor or personal representative chooses this method of valuation for estate tax purposes, that value is the basis of the property for the heirs. The qualified heirs should be able to get the necessary value from the executor or personal representative of the estate.

If a qualified heir received special-use valuation property, the basis in the property is the estate's or trust's basis in that property immediately before the distribution. The basis is increased by any gain recognized by the estate or trust because of post-death appreciation. Post-death appreciation is the property's FMV on the date of distribution minus the property's FMV either on the date of the individual's death or the alternate valuation date. All FMVs should be figured without regard to the special-use valuation.

It is possible to elect to increase the basis in special-use valuation property if it becomes subject to the additional estate tax. This tax is assessed if, within ten years after the death of the decedent, the property is transferred to a person who is not a member of the family, or the property stops being used as a farm or in a closely held business.

Property Changed to Business or Rental Use

When property held for personal use is changed to business use or to produce rent, its basis for depreciation must be figured. An example of changing property held for personal use to business use would be renting out a former main home.

The basis for depreciation is the lesser of the following amounts:

1. The FMV of the property on the date of the change.
2. The adjusted basis on the date of the change.

If the property is later sold or disposed of, the basis of the property used will depend upon whether gain or loss occurred. The basis for figuring a gain is the adjusted basis when the property is sold. Figuring the basis for a loss starts with the smaller of the adjusted basis or the FMV of the property at the time of the change to business or rental use. This amount is then adjusted for the period after the change in the property's use to arrive at a basis for loss.

Chapter 36

Change in Accounting Methods and Consideration of Accounting Periods

CONTENTS

New Automatic Approval Procedures for Accounting Period Changes	**36.02**
Significant Changes	**36.05**
Change in Method of Accounting Defined	**36.05**
Filing Form 3115	**36.06**
Method Change with Adjustment	**36.07**
Method Change Using a Cutoff Method	**36.07**
Initial Method	**36.07**
IRS Approval	**36.08**
Reflections of Income	**36.08**
Need for Adjustment	**36.08**
90-Day and 120-Day Window Periods	**36.09**
Under Examination	**36.10**
Application Procedures	**36.10**
Consolidated Groups	**36.11**
Separate Trades or Businesses	**36.12**
Resolving Timing Issues: Appeals and Counsel Discretion	**36.12**
Resolving Timing Issues: Discretion of Examining Agent	**36.14**
Method Changes Initiated by the IRS	**36.14**

Accounting Periods   **36.16**

Changes During the Tax Year   **36.26**

Several pronouncements were issued in May 2002 by the Internal Revenue Service in connection with changes in accounting periods that should make life easier for the tax practitioner and small business owners, in particular. The automatic approval procedures and safe harbors for requesting changes should provide greater certainty to taxpayers and free the IRS to devote much needed laborpower and resources to more pressing matters.

The guidance was not based on a sudden decision; in fact, these procedures are actually based on guidance that was rather fully developed in 2001. This is part of an ongoing effort by the IRS to identify areas in which requests to adopt, change or retain accounting periods can be expedited or permitted automatically. Therefore, the guidance should be very helpful to taxpayers and tax practitioners who want to switch accounting periods to a more logical or tax efficient timeframe.

NEW AUTOMATIC APPROVAL PROCEDURES FOR ACCOUNTING PERIOD CHANGES

Notices 2001-34 and 2001-35 had indicated the IRS thinking in regard to changes in accounting periods. Revenue Procedure 2002-35 finalized the guidance in Notice 2001-35 regarding automatic approval procedures for accounting periods for partnerships, S corporations, electing S corporations and professional service corporations.

Rev. Proc. 2002-39 is the result of guidance outlined in Notice 2001-34 relating to requests for changes in accounting periods. Rev. Proc. 2002-37, issued at the same time, provides automatic approval procedures for corporations.

Revenue Procedure 2002-37

Rev. Proc. 2002-37 outlines the procedures that certain corporations are required to follow to be regarded as having automatic approval for a change in their annual accounting period. A corporation complying with the new procedures will be deemed to have established a sufficient business purpose and to have obtained IRS approval for the change.

The revenue procedure states that it is the exclusive procedure to be used by corporations within its scope and then specifies the types of corporations covered or excluded. The final guidance:

1. Provides more flexibility for changing to or from a 52–53-week tax year and for changes to, or retention of, a natural business year by a corporation that satisfies the 25 percent gross receipts test.
2. Shortens from 6 years to 48 months, the required time between a requested change and a prior accounting period change. It also adds to the list of changes that will not be considered prior changes for purposes of the new 48-month rule.
3. Adds to the list of corporations outside of the scope of the procedure in the areas of interests in a pass-through entity, controlled foreign corporations, foreign personal holding companies and corporations with a required tax year.
4. Provides additional guidance for exceptions to the record-keeping/book-keeping conformity rule and the prevention of the carryback of capital losses generated in the short period resulting from the accounting period change.

Revenue Procedure 2002-38

Rev. Proc. 2002-38 provides the exclusive procedures for certain partnerships, S corporations, electing S corporations and personal service corporations, to obtain automatic approval to adopt, change or retain an annual accounting period.

Consistent with the changes for corporations promulgated in Rev. Proc. 2002-37, this procedure also provides more flexibility in changing to or from a 52–53-week tax year, changes to a required or natural business year satisfying the 25 percent gross receipts test, the new 48-month period between the requested change and the prior accounting period change and the restrictions on the carryback of capital losses from the short period. In addition, it provides:

1. Guidance relating to changes to a year corresponding to the ownership.
2. Guidance specifying that, under certain circumstances, a partnership can retain its current tax year for one year, even though a minor percentage change in ownership would have otherwise required a change in the tax year.
3. That a professional service corporation may automatically change its tax year even if it makes an S corporation election for the tax year immediately following the short period.

4. Restrictions that prevent using the guidance to change an annual accounting period while under examination.

5. Guidance that permits S corporations and electing S corporations to disregard the ownership interests of certain tax exempt entities when determining their tax year.

Except in specified circumstances, the entities that are subject to Rev. Proc. 2002-38 will be required to compute their income and keep their books and records (including financial statements) on the basis of the requested tax year. The guidance also extends the due date for filing a Form 1128 to the due date of the taxpayer's federal income tax return (including extensions) for the first effective year, and provides audit protection for accounting period changes made within the scope of the procedure.

Revenue Procedure 2002-39

In contrast to the automatic procedures for corporations and pass-through entities that are covered in Rev. Procs. 2002-37 and 2002-38, Rev. Proc. 2002-39 provides guidance to all taxpayers when obtaining IRS approval to adopt, change or retain an annual accounting period and for establishing a business purpose for the change.

The business purpose requirement is a facts-and-circumstances test, although a business purpose is deemed satisfied for an accounting period that corresponds to the taxpayer's required tax year, ownership tax year or natural business year. The natural business year again is based on the 25 percent gross receipts test.

Safe harbors are provided in connection with annual business cycles and seasonal businesses. The revenue procedure states that the safe harbors are designed to require reliance on a facts-and-circumstances test only in rare situations. Excepted from the scope of this general guidance are, on the one hand, requests for automatic approval and, on the other, requests in which the taxpayer is under examination or where the accounting period is already an issue in a proceeding.

In the earlier exception, the IRS advised taxpayers to check the rules for automatic approval before filing a request with the IRS for a change.

Effective Date

The effective date for all three Revenue Procedures—2002-37, -38 and -39—is generally for applications filed on or after May 10, 2002. All three provide for similar elections of retroactive application.

Previously, to simplify the procedures to obtain IRS consent for taxpayers to change methods of accounting for federal income tax purposes, the IRS had modified and/or eliminated a number of the complicated rules governing changes in these accounting methods. The purpose of the new procedures is to provide incentives to encourage prompt, voluntary compliance with proper tax accounting principles. Under this approach, a taxpayer usually receives more favorable terms and conditions by filing a request for a change in method before the IRS contacts the taxpayer for an examination. A taxpayer who is contacted for an examination and required by the IRS to change his or her method of accounting generally receives less favorable terms and conditions and may also be subject to penalties.

SIGNIFICANT CHANGES

Probably the single most important change for the taxpayer was that Form 3115 requesting a change in method may now be filed any time during the year. Other new rules reduce or eliminate many of the complex provisions of the previous procedure including:

1. The Category A and Category B, and Designated A and Designated B have been eliminated.
2. The 90-day window at the *beginning* of an examination has been eliminated.
3. The 30-day window for taxpayers under *continuous examination* has been increased to 90 days.
4. The number of consecutive months the taxpayer is required to be under examination has been reduced from 18 to 12.
5. The definition of "under examination" has been clarified.
6. The consent requirement for taxpayers before an appeals officer or a federal court has been replaced with a notification procedure.
7. The various adjustment periods have been replaced with a single 4-year adjustment period for both positive and negative adjustments.
8. Several of the terms and conditions relating to the adjustment have been eliminated.

CHANGE IN METHOD OF ACCOUNTING DEFINED

A change in method of accounting includes a change in the overall plan of accounting for gross income or deductions, or a change in the treatment of any material item. A *material item* is any item that involves the proper time for the inclusion of the item in income or the taking of the item as a deduction.

In determining whether a taxpayer's accounting practice for an item involves timing, the relevant question is whether the practice permanently changes the amount of the taxpayer's lifetime income. If the practice does not permanently affect the taxpayer's lifetime income, but does or could change the taxable year in which income is reported, it involves timing and is, therefore, a method of accounting.

Consistency: Although a method of accounting may exist under this definition without a pattern of consistent treatment of an item, a method of accounting is not adopted in most instances without consistent treatment. The treatment of a material item in the same way in determining the gross income or deductions in two or more consecutively filed tax returns, without regard to any change in status of the method as permissible or not permissible, represents consistent treatment of that item. If a taxpayer treats an item properly in the first return that reflects the item, however, it is not necessary for the taxpayer to treat the item consistently in two or more consecutive tax returns to have adopted a method of accounting. If a taxpayer has adopted a method of accounting under the rules, the taxpayer cannot change the method by amending prior income tax returns.

Classification: A change in the classification of an item can constitute a change in the method of accounting if the change has the effect of shifting income from one period to another. A change in method of accounting does not include correction of mathematical or posting errors, or errors in the computation of a tax liability.

Filing Form 3115

Except as otherwise provided, a taxpayer must secure the consent of the Commissioner before changing a method of accounting for federal income tax purposes. In order to obtain the Commissioner's consent for a method change, a taxpayer must file a Form 3115, *Application for Change in Accounting Method* during the taxable year in which the taxpayer wants to make the proposed change.

The Commissioner can prescribe administrative procedures setting forth the limitations, terms, and conditions deemed necessary to permit a taxpayer to obtain consent to change a method of accounting. The terms and conditions the Commissioner can prescribe include the year of change, whether the change is to be made with an adjustment or on a cutoff basis, and the adjustment period.

Unless specifically authorized by the Commissioner, a taxpayer cannot request, or otherwise make, a retroactive change in method, regardless of whether the change is from a permissible or an impermissible method.

METHOD CHANGE WITH ADJUSTMENT

Adjustments necessary to prevent amounts from being duplicated or omitted must be taken into account when the taxpayer's taxable income is computed under a method of accounting different from the method used to compute taxable income of the preceding tax year. When a change in method is applied, income for the taxable year preceding the year of change must be determined under the method of accounting that was then employed. Income for the year of change and the following taxable years must be determined under the new method as if the new method had always been used.

Required adjustments can be taken into account in determining taxable income in the manner and subject to the conditions agreed to by the Commissioner and the taxpayer. In the absence of an agreement, the adjustment is taken into account completely in the year of change, which limits the amount of tax where the adjustment is substantial. However, under the Commissioner's authority to prescribe terms and conditions for changes in method, specific adjustment periods are permitted that are intended to achieve an appropriate balance between mitigating distortions of income that result from accounting method changes and providing appropriate incentives for voluntary compliance.

METHOD CHANGE USING A CUTOFF METHOD

Certain changes can be made in a method and without an adjustment, using a cutoff method. Under a cutoff method, only the items arising on or after the beginning of the year of change are accounted for under the new method. Certain changes, such as changes in the last-in first-out (LIFO) inventory method, *must* be made using the cutoff method. Any items arising before the year of change or other operative date continue to be accounted for under the taxpayer's former method of accounting. Because no items are duplicated or omitted from income when a cutoff method is used to make a change, no adjustment is necessary.

INITIAL METHOD

A taxpayer can generally choose any permitted accounting method when filing the first tax return. IRS approval is not needed for the choice of the method. The method chosen must be used consistently from year to year and clearly show the taxpayer's income. A change in an accounting method includes a change not only in an overall system of accounting, but also in the treatment of any material item. Although an accounting method can exist without treating an item the same all the time, an accounting method is not established for an item, in most cases, unless the item is treated the same every time.

IRS APPROVAL

After a taxpayer's first return has been filed, the taxpayer must get IRS approval to change the accounting method. If the current method clearly shows the income, the IRS will consider the need for consistency when evaluating the reason for changing the method used. The following changes require IRS approval:

1. A change from the cash method to an accrual method or vice versa unless this is an automatic change to an accrual method.
2. A change in the method or basis used to value inventory.
3. A change in the method of figuring depreciation, except certain permitted changes to the straight-line method for property placed in service before 1981.

   Approval is not required in the following instances:

1. Correction of a math or posting error.
2. Correction of an error in computing tax liability.
3. An adjustment of any item of income or deduction that does not involve the proper time for including it in income or deducting it.
4. An adjustment in the useful life of a depreciable asset.

REFLECTIONS OF INCOME

The important point to remember is that methods of accounting should clearly reflect income on a continuing basis, and that the IRS exercises its discretion and in a manner that generally minimizes distortion of income across taxable years on an annual basis. Therefore, if a taxpayer asks to change from a method of accounting that clearly reflects income, the IRS, in determining whether to consent to the taxpayer's request, will weigh the need for consistency against the taxpayer's reason for desiring to change the method of accounting.

NEED FOR ADJUSTMENT

The adjustment period is the applicable period for taking into account an adjustment, whether positive (an increase in income) or negative (a decrease in income), required for the change in method of accounting. Adjustments necessary to prevent amounts from being duplicated or omitted are taken into account when the taxpayer's taxable income is computed under a method of accounting different from the method used to compute taxable income for the preceding taxable year. When there is a change in method of accounting, income for the year preceding the year of change must be determined under the method of accounting that was then employed, and income for the year of change and the following years must be determined under the new method of accounting.

90-DAY AND 120-DAY WINDOW PERIODS

A taxpayer under examination cannot file a Form 3115 to request a change in accounting methods except as provided in the 90-day window and 120-day window periods, and the consent of the district director. A taxpayer filing a Form 3115 beyond the time periods provided by the 90-day and 120-day windows will not be granted an extension of time to file except in unusual and compelling circumstances.

A taxpayer can file a Form 3115 during the first 90 days of any taxable year if the taxpayer has been under examination for at least 12 consecutive months as of the first day of the taxable year. The 90-day window is not available if the method of accounting the taxpayer is requesting to change is an issue under consideration at the time the Form 3115 is filed, or is an issue the examining agent has placed in suspense at the time.

A taxpayer requesting a change under the 90-day window must provide a copy of the Form 3115 to the examining agent at the same time the original form is filed with the IRS. The form must contain the name and telephone number of the examining agent, and the taxpayer must attach to the form a separate statement signed by the taxpayer certifying that, to the best of his or her knowledge, the same method of accounting is not an issue under consideration or an issue placed in suspense by the examining agent.

A taxpayer can file a Form 3115 to request a change in accounting method during the 120-day period following the date an examination ends regardless of whether a subsequent examination has commenced. The 120-day window is not available if the method of accounting the taxpayer is requesting to change is an issue under consideration at the time the form is filed or is an issue the examining agent has placed in suspense at the time of the filing.

A taxpayer requesting a change under the 120-day window rule must provide a copy of the Form 3115 to the examining agent for any examination that is in process at the same time the original form is filed with the IRS. The form must contain the name and telephone number of the examining agent, and must have a separate signed statement attached certifying that, to the best of the taxpayer's knowledge, the same method of accounting is not an issue under consideration or an issue placed in suspense by the examining agent.

Under Examination

A taxpayer is "under examination" if the taxpayer has been contacted in any manner by a representative of the IRS for the purpose of scheduling any type of examination of any of its federal income tax returns. If a consolidated return is being examined, each member of the consolidated group will be considered under examination for purposes of the accounting method change requirements.

However, according to the 1997 ruling, on the date a new subsidiary becomes affiliated with a consolidated group, a 90-day window period can be provided within which the parent of the group may request a method change on behalf of the new member, unless the subsidiary itself is already under examination. Previously, if a consolidated group was being examined, each member of the consolidated group was considered under examination regardless of the tax year under examination.

An examination of a taxpayer, or consolidated group of which the taxpayer is a member, is considered to end at the earliest of the date:

1. The taxpayer or consolidated group of which the taxpayer is a member receives a "no-change" letter.
2. The taxpayer or consolidated group of which the taxpayer is a member pays the deficiency — or proposed deficiency.
3. The taxpayer or consolidated group requests consideration by an appeals officer.
4. The taxpayer requests consideration by a federal court.
5. The date on which a deficiency, jeopardy, termination, bankruptcy, or receivership assessment is made.

A taxpayer under examination cannot ask to change an impermissible method of accounting if under examination for the year in which the taxpayer adopted the method, and it was an impermissible method of accounting in the year of adoption. A taxpayer under examination cannot ask to change a method to which it changed without permission if under examination for the year in which the unauthorized change was made. Under any other circumstance, a taxpayer under examination can change an accounting method only if the taxpayer requests the change under the applicable procedures, terms, and conditions set forth in the regulation.

Application Procedures

The IRS can decline to process any Form 3115 filed in situations in which it would not be in the best interest of sound tax administration to permit the requested change. In this regard, the IRS will consider whether the change in method of accounting would clearly and directly interfere with compliance efforts of the IRS to administer the income tax laws.

A change in the method of accounting filed must be made pursuant to the terms and conditions provided in the regulations. The rule notwithstanding, the IRS can determine, based on the unique facts of a particular case, terms and conditions more appropriate for a change different from the changes provided in the regulations.

In processing an application for a change in an accounting method, the IRS will consider all the facts and circumstances, including whether:

1. The method of accounting requested is consistent with the Tax Code regulations, revenue rulings, revenue procedures, and decisions of the United States Supreme Court.
2. The use of the method requested will clearly reflect income.
3. The present method of accounting clearly reflects income.
4. The request meets the need for consistency in the accounting area.
5. The taxpayer's reasons for the change are valid.
6. The tax effect of the adjustment is appropriate.
7. The taxpayer's books and records and financial statements will conform to the proposed method of accounting.
8. The taxpayer previously requested a change in the method of accounting for the same item but did not make the change.

If the taxpayer has changed the method of accounting for the same item within the four taxable years preceding the year of requesting a change for that item, an explanation must be furnished stating why the taxpayer is again requesting a change in the method for the same item. The IRS will consider the explanation in determining whether the subsequent request for change in method will be granted.

CONSOLIDATED GROUPS

Separate methods of accounting can be used by each member of a consolidated group. In considering whether to grant accounting method changes to group members, the IRS will consider the effects of the changes on the income of the group. A parent requesting a change in method on behalf of the consolidated group must submit any information necessary to permit the IRS to evaluate the effect of the requested change on the income of the consolidated group. A Form 3115 must be submitted for each member of the group for which a change in accounting method is requested. A parent can request an identical accounting method change on a single Form 3115 for more than one member of a consolidated group.

SEPARATE TRADES OR BUSINESSES

When a taxpayer has two or more separate and distinct trades or businesses, a different method of accounting may be used for each trade or business, provided the method of accounting used for each trade or business clearly reflects the overall income of the taxpayer as well as that of each particular trade or business. No trade or business is separate and distinct unless a complete and separate set of books and records is kept for that trade or business. If the reason for maintaining different methods of accounting creates or shifts profits or losses between the trades or businesses of the taxpayer so that income is not clearly reflected, the trades or businesses of the taxpayer are not separate and distinct.

RESOLVING TIMING ISSUES: APPEALS AND COUNSEL DISCRETION

An appeals officer or counsel for the government may resolve a timing issue when it is in the interest of the government to do so. To reflect the hazards of litigation, they are authorized to resolve a timing issue by changing the taxpayer's method of accounting using compromise terms and conditions or they may use a nonaccounting method change basis using either an alternative-timing or a time-value-of-money resolution.

Requirement to Apply the Law to the Facts

An appeals officer or counsel for the government resolving a timing issue must treat the issue as a change in method of accounting. The law must be applied without taking into account the hazards of litigation when determining the new method of accounting. An appeals officer or government official can change a taxpayer's method of accounting by agreeing to terms and conditions that differ from those applicable to an "examination-initiated" accounting method change.

The appeals officer may compromise on several points:

1. The year of change (by agreeing to a later year of change).
2. The amount of the adjustment (a reduced adjustment).
3. The adjustment period (a longer adjustment period).

If an appeals officer agrees to compromise the *amount* of an adjustment, the agreement must be in writing.

A change in a taxpayer's method of accounting ordinarily will *not defer the year of change* to later than the most recent taxable year under examination on the date of the agreement finalizing the change, and in no event will the year of change be deferred to later than the taxable year that includes the date of the agreement finalizing the change.

Alternative Timing

An appeals officer can resolve a timing issue by not changing the taxpayer's method of accounting, and by the IRS and the taxpayer agreeing to alternative timing for all or some of the items arising during/prior to and during, the taxable years before appeals or a federal court. The resolution of a timing issue on an alternative-timing basis for certain items will not affect the taxpayer's method of accounting for any items not covered by the resolution.

Time-Value-of-Money

An appeals officer or government counsel may resolve a timing issue by not changing the taxpayer's method of accounting, and by the IRS and the taxpayer agreeing that the taxpayer will pay the government a specified amount that approximates the time-value-of-money benefit the taxpayer derived from using its method of accounting for the taxable years before appeals or a federal court. This approach is instead of the method of accounting determined by the appeals officer to be the proper method of accounting. The "specified amount" is reduced by an appropriate factor to reflect the expense of litigation. The specified amount is not interest and cannot be deducted or capitalized under any provision of the law. An appeals officer may use any reasonable manner to compute the specified amount.

Taxpayer's Advantage

As outlined above, these IRS requirements, which are part of the "new" IRS image, cover timing problems that have been resolved by the IRS on a nonaccounting-method change basis. They provide terms and conditions for IRS-initiated changes that are intended to encourage taxpayers to *voluntarily request a change from an impermissible method of accounting* rather than being contacted by an agent for examination. Under this approach, a taxpayer who is contacted for *examination* and required to change methods of accounting by the IRS generally receives less favorable terms and conditions than if the taxpayer had filed a request to change before being contacted for examination.

The new regulations may be consistent with the policy of encouraging prompt voluntary compliance with proper tax accounting principles, but they appear to have some limitations. It is now easier for the taxpayer to change an accounting method, but the IRS ordinarily will not initiate an accounting method change if the change will place the taxpayer in a more favorable position than if the taxpayer had been contacted for examination. An examining agent will not initiate a change from an impermissible method that results in a negative adjustment. If the IRS declines to initiate such an accounting method change, the district director will consent to the taxpayer requesting a voluntary change.

RESOLVING TIMING ISSUES: DISCRETION OF EXAMINING AGENT

An examining agent proposing an adjustment on a timing issue will treat the issue as a change in method of accounting. In changing the taxpayer's method of accounting, the agent will properly apply the law to the facts without taking into account the hazards of litigation when determining the new method of accounting. An examining agent changing a taxpayer's method of accounting will impose an adjustment.

The change can be made using a cutoff method only in rare and unusual circumstances when the examining agent determines that the taxpayer's books and records do not contain sufficient information to compute the adjustment and the adjustment is not susceptible to reasonable estimation. An examining agent changing a taxpayer's method of accounting will effect the change in the earliest taxable year under examination (or, if later, the first taxable year the method is considered impermissible) with a one-year adjustment period.

METHOD CHANGES INITIATED BY THE IRS

If a taxpayer does not regularly employ a method of accounting that clearly reflects his or her income, the computation of taxable income must be made in a manner that, in the opinion of the Commissioner, does clearly reflect income. The Commissioner has broad discretion in determining whether a taxpayer's method of accounting clearly reflects income, and the Commissioner's determination must be upheld unless it is clearly unlawful.

The Commissioner has broad discretion in selecting a method of accounting that properly reflects the income of a taxpayer once it has been determined that the taxpayer's method of accounting does not clearly reflect income. The selection can be challenged only upon showing an abuse of discretion by the Commissioner.

The Commissioner has the discretion to change a method of accounting even though the IRS had previously changed the taxpayer to that method if it is determined that the method of accounting does not clearly reflect the taxpayer's income. The discretionary power does not extend to requiring a taxpayer to change from a method of accounting that clearly reflects income to a method that, in the Commissioner's view, more clearly reflects income.

The accounting method of a taxpayer that is under examination, before an appeals office, or before a federal court, can be changed except as otherwise provided in published guidance. The service is generally precluded from changing a taxpayer's method of accounting for an item for prior taxable years if the taxpayer timely files a request to change the method of accounting for the item.

Retroactive Method Change

Although the Commissioner is authorized to consent to a retroactive accounting method change, the taxpayer does not have a right to a retroactive change, regardless of whether the change is from a permissible or impermissible method.

Except under unusual circumstances, if a taxpayer who changes the method of accounting is subsequently required to change or modify that method of accounting, the required change or modification will not be applied retroactively provided that:

1. The taxpayer complied with all the applicable provisions of the consent agreement.
2. There has been no misstatement nor omission of material facts.
3. There has been no change in the material facts on which the consent was based.
4. There has been no change in the applicable law.
5. The taxpayer to whom consent was granted acted in good faith in relying on the consent, and applying the change or modification retroactively would be to the taxpayer's detriment.

New Method Established

An IRS-initiated change that is final establishes a new method of accounting. As a result, a taxpayer is required to use the new method of accounting for the year of change and for all subsequent taxable years unless the taxpayer obtains the consent of the commissioner to change from the new method or the IRS changes the taxpayer from the new method on subsequent examination. As indicated above, the IRS is not precluded from changing a taxpayer from the new method of accounting if the IRS determined that the new method does not clearly reflect the taxpayer's income. A taxpayer who executes a closing agreement finalizing an IRS initiated accounting method change will not be required to change or modify the new method for any taxable year for which a federal income tax return has been filed as of the date of the closing agreement, provided that:

1. The taxpayer has complied with all the applicable provisions of the closing agreement.
2. There has been no taxpayer fraud, malfeasance, or misrepresentation of a material fact.
3. There has been no change in the material facts on which the closing agreement was based.
4. There has been no change in the applicable law on which the closing agreement was based.

Required Change or Modification of New Method

The IRS may require a taxpayer to change or modify the new method in the earliest open taxable year if the taxpayer fails to comply with the applicable provisions of the closing agreement, or upon a showing of taxpayer's fraud, malfeasance, or misrepresentation of a material fact. The taxpayer can be required to change or modify the new method in the earliest open taxable year in which the material facts have changed, and can also be required to change or modify the new method in the earliest open taxable year in which the applicable law has changed. For this purpose, a change in the applicable law includes:

1. A decision of the U.S. Supreme Court.
2. The enactment of legislation.
3. The issuance of temporary or final regulations.
4. The issuance of a revenue ruling, revenue procedure, notice, or other guidance published in the Internal Revenue Bulletin.

Except in rare and unusual circumstances, a retroactive change in applicable law is deemed to occur when one of the events described in the preceding sentence occurs and not when the change in law is effective.

ACCOUNTING PERIODS

Taxable income must be figured on the basis of a tax year. A *tax year* is an annual accounting period for keeping records and reporting income and expenses. The tax years usable are:

1. A calendar year.
2. A fiscal year.

The tax year is adopted in the first year that an income tax return is filed. The tax year must be adopted by the due date, not including extensions, for filing a return for that year. The due date for individual and partnership returns is the 15th day of the 4th month after the end of the tax year. "Individuals" include sole proprietorships, partners, and S corporation shareholders. The due date for filing returns for corporations and S corporations is the 15th day of the 3rd month after the end of the tax year. If the 15th day of the month falls on a Saturday, Sunday, or legal holiday, the due date is the next business day.

Calendar Year

If a calendar year is chosen, the taxpayer must maintain books and records and report income and expenses from January 1 through December 31 of each year. If the first tax return uses the calendar year and the taxpayer later begins business as a sole proprietor, becomes a partner in a partnership, or becomes a shareholder in an S corporation, the calendar year must continue to be used unless the IRS approves a change. Anyone can adopt the calendar year. However, if any of the following apply, the calendar year must be used:

1. The taxpayer does not keep adequate records.
2. The taxpayer has no annual accounting period.
3. The taxpayer's tax year does not qualify as a fiscal year.

Fiscal Year

A fiscal year is 12 consecutive months ending on the last day of any month except December. A 52–53-week tax year is a fiscal year that varies from 52 to 53 weeks. If a fiscal year is adopted, books and records must be maintained, and income and expenses reported using the same tax year.

A 52–53-week tax year may be elected if books and records are kept, and income and expenses are reported on that basis. If this election is chosen, the tax year will be 52 or 53 weeks long, and will always end on the same day of the week. The tax year can end only on the same day of the week that:

1. Last occurs in a particular month.
2. Occurs nearest to the last day of a particular calendar month.

To make the choice, a statement with the following information is attached to the tax return for the 52–53-week tax year:

1. The month in which the new 52–53-week tax year ends.
2. The day of the week on which the tax year always ends.

3. The date the tax year ends. It can be either of the following dates on which the chosen day:

    a. Last occurs in the month in (1).

    b. Occurs nearest to the last day of the month in (1).

When depreciation or amortization is figured, a 52–53-week tax year is considered a year of 12 calendar months unless another practice is consistently used. To determine an effective date, or apply provisions of any law, expressed in terms of tax years beginning, including, or ending on the first or last day of a specified calendar month, a 52–53-week tax year is considered to:

1. Begin on the first day of the calendar month beginning nearest to the first day of the 52–53-week tax year.
2. End on the last day of the calendar month ending nearest to the last day of the 52–53-week tax year.

If the month in which a 52–53-week tax year ends is changed, a return must be filed for the short tax year if it covers more than 6 but less than 359 days. If the short period created by the change is 359 days or more, it should be treated as a full tax year. If the short period created is 6 days or less, it is not a separate tax year. It is to be treated as part of the following year.

A corporation figures tax for a short year under the general rules described for individuals. There is no adjustment for personal exemptions.

Improper Tax Year

A calendar year is a tax year of 12 months that ends on December 31, and a fiscal year is a tax year of 12 months that ends on the last day of any month except December, including a 52–53-week tax year. If business operations start on a day other than the last day of a calendar month and adopt a tax year of exactly 12 months from the date operations began, the taxpayer has adopted an *improper* tax year. The requirements for a calendar or fiscal tax year, including a 52–53-week tax year, have not been met. To change to a proper tax year, one of the following requirements must be met:

1. An amended tax return should be based on a calendar year.
2. IRS approval should be sought to change to a tax year, other than a calendar year.

Business Purpose Tax Year

A business purpose tax year is an accounting period that has a substantial business purpose for its existence.

In considering whether there is a business purpose for a tax year, significant weight is given to tax factors. A prime consideration is whether the change would create a substantial distortion of income. The following are examples of distortions of income:

1. Deferring substantial income or shifting substantial deductions from one year to another to reduce tax liability.
2. Causing a similar deferral or shifting for any other person, such as a partner or shareholder.
3. Creating a short period in which there is a substantial net operating loss.

The following nontax factors, based on convenience for the taxpayer, are generally not sufficient to establish a business purpose for a particular year:

1. Using a particular year for regulatory or financial accounting purposes.
2. Using a particular pattern, such as typically hiring staff during certain times of the year.
3. Using a particular year for administration purposes, such as:
   a. Admission or retirement of partners or shareholders.
   b. Promotion of staff.
   c. Compensation or retirement arrangements with staff, partners, or shareholders.
4. Using a price list, model year, or other item that changes on an annual basis.
5. Deferring income to partners or shareholders.

Natural Business Year

One nontax factor that may be sufficient to establish a business purpose for a tax year is an annual cycle of business, called a "natural business year." A natural business year exists when business has a peak and a nonpeak period. The natural business year is considered to end at or soon after the end of the peak period. A business whose income is steady from month-to-month all year would not have a natural business year as such. A natural business year is considered a substantial business purpose for an entity changing its accounting period. The IRS will ordinarily approve this change unless it results in a substantial deferral of income or another tax advantage.

The IRS provides a procedure for a partnership, an S corporation, or a personal service corporation to retain or automatically change to a natural business year as determined by the 25% test. It also allows an S corporation to adopt, retain, or change to a fiscal year that satisfies the "ownership tax year test." The 25% test uses the method of accounting used for the tax returns for each year involved. To figure the 25% test:

1. The gross sales and services receipts for the most recent 12-month period that includes the last month of the requested fiscal year are totaled for the 12-month period that ends before the filing of the request. Gross sales and services receipts for the last 2 months of that 12-month period are then totaled.
2. The percentage of the receipts for the 2-month period is then determined by dividing the total of the 2-month period by the total for the 12-month period. The percentage should be carried to two decimal places.
3. The percentage following steps 1 and 2 should then be figured for the two 12-month periods just preceding the 12-month period used in 1.

If the percentage determined for each of the three years equals or exceeds 25%, the requested fiscal year is the *natural business year.* If the partnership, S corporation, or personal service corporation qualifies for more than one natural business year, the fiscal year producing the higher average of the three percentages is the natural business year. If the partnership, S corporation, or personal service corporation does not have at least 47 months of gross receipts—which may include a predecessor organization's gross receipts—it cannot use this automatic procedure to obtain permission to use a fiscal year.

If the requested tax year is a 52–53-week tax year, the calendar month ending nearest the last day of the 52–53-week tax year is treated as the last month of the requested tax year for purposes of computing the 25% test.

An S corporation or corporation electing to be an S corporation qualifies for automatic approval if it meets the ownership tax year test. The test is met if the corporation is adopting, retaining, or changing to a tax year and shareholders holding more than 50% of the issued and outstanding shares of stock on the first day of the requested tax year have, or are all changing to, the same tax year.

Change in Tax Year

A tax year change must be approved by the IRS. A current Form 1128 must be filed by the 15th day of the end calendar month after the close of the short tax year to get IRS approval. The *short tax year* begins on the first day after the end of the present tax year and ends on the day before the first day of the new tax year. If the short tax year required to effect a change in tax years is a year in which the taxpayer has a net operating loss (NOL), the NOL must be deducted ratably over a 6-year period from the first tax year after the short period.

A husband and wife who have different tax years cannot file a joint return. There is an exception to this rule if their tax years began on the same date and ended on different dates because of the death of either or both. If a husband and wife want to use the same tax year so they can file a joint return, the method of changing a tax year depends on whether they are newly married. A newly married husband and wife with different tax years who wish to file a joint return can change the tax year of one spouse without first getting IRS approval.

The correct user fee must be included, if any. The IRS charges a user fee for certain requests to change an accounting period or method, certain tax rulings, and determination letters. The fee is reduced in certain situations and for certain requests, such as a request for substantially identical rulings for related entities.

Year of Change

While this heading and the one above are similar, the connotation is somewhat different. The year of change is the taxable year for which a change in the method of accounting is effective, that is, the first taxable year the new method is used even if no affected items are taken into account for that year. The year of change is also the first taxable year for taking an adjustment and complying with all the terms and conditions accompanying the change.

Partnership

A partnership must conform its tax year to its partners' tax years unless the partnership can establish a business purpose for a different period. The rules for the required tax year for partnerships are:

1. If one or more partners having the same tax year own a majority interest—more than 5%—in partnership profits and capital, the partnership must use the tax year of those partners.
2. If there is no majority interest tax year, the partnership must use the tax year of its principal partners. A principal partner is one who has a 5% or more interest in the profits or capital of the partnership.
3. If there is no majority interest tax year and the principal partners do not have the same tax year, the partnership generally must use a tax year that results in the least aggregate deferral of income to the partners.

If a partnership changes to a required tax year because of these rules, the change is considered to be initiated by the partnership with IRS approval. No formal application for change in the tax year is needed. Any partnership that changes to a required tax year must notify the IRS by writing at the top of the first page of its tax return for its first required tax year: *Filed Under Section 806 of the Tax Reform Act of 1986.*

The tax year that results in the least aggregate deferral of income is determined by:

1. Figuring the number of months of deferral for each partner using one partner's tax year. The months of deferral are found by counting the months from the end of that tax year forward to the end of each other partner's tax year.
2. Each partner's months of deferral figured in step (1) are multiplied by that partner's share of interest in the partnership profits for the year used in step (1).
3. The amounts in step (2) are added to get the aggregate (total) deferral for the tax year used in step (1).
4. Steps (1) through (3) are repeated for each partner's tax year that is different from the other partners' years.

The partners' tax year that results in the lowest aggregate—total—number is the tax year that must be used by the partnership. If more than one year qualifies as the tax year that has the least aggregate deferral of income, the partnership can choose any year that qualifies. If one of the tax years that qualifies is the partnership's existing tax year, the partnership must retain that tax year.

S Corporations

If a business meets the requirements of a small business corporation, it can elect to be an S corporation. All S corporations, regardless of when they became an S corporation, must use a *permitted tax year.* A permitted tax year is the calendar year or any other tax year for which the corporation establishes a business purpose.

Personal Service Corporations

A personal service corporation must use a calendar year unless it can establish a business purpose for a different period or it makes a Section 444 election (discussed below). For this purpose, a corporation is a personal service corporation if all of the following conditions are met:

1. The corporation is a C corporation.
2. The corporation's principal activity during the testing period is the performance of personal services.
3. Employee-owners of the corporation perform a substantial part of the services during the testing period.
4. Employee-owners own more than 10% of the corporation's stock on the last day of the testing period.

The principal activity of a corporation is considered to be the performance of personal services if, during the testing period, the corporation's compensation costs for personal service activities is more than 50% of its total compensation costs.

Generally, the *testing period for a tax year is the prior tax year.* The testing period for the first tax year of a new corporation starts with the first day of the tax year and ends on the earlier of the following dates:

1. The last day of its tax year.
2. The last day of the calendar year in which the tax year begins.

The *performance of personal services* involves any activity in the fields of health, veterinary services, law, engineering, architecture, accounting, actuarial science, performing arts, or certain consulting services.

An employee-owner of a corporation is a person who:

1. Is an employee of the corporation on any day of the testing period.
2. Owns any outstanding stock of the corporation on any day of the testing period.

A further clarification of the definition of an independent contractor by the 1997 Act states, "A person who owns any outstanding stock of the corporation and who performs personal services for or on behalf of the corporation is treated as an *employee* of the corporation. This rule applies even if the legal form of the person's relationship to the corporation is such that the person would be considered an independent contractor for other purposes."

Section 444 Election

A partnership, S corporation, or personal service corporation can elect under Section 444 of the Internal Revenue Code to use a tax year different from its required tax year. Certain restrictions apply to the election. In addition, a partnership or S corporation may have to make a payment for the deferral period. The Section 444 election does not apply to any partnership, S corporation, or personal service corporation that establishes a business purpose for a different period.

A partnership, S corporation, or personal service corporation can make a Section 444 election if it meets all the following requirements:

1. It is not a member of a tiered structure.
2. It has not previously had a Section 444 election in effect.
3. It elects a year that meets the deferral period requirement.

The determination of the *deferral period* depends on whether the partnership, corporation, or personal service corporation is retaining its current tax year or adopting or changing its tax year with a Section 444 election.

A partnership, S corporation, or personal service corporation can make a Section 444 election to *retain* its tax year only if the deferral period of the new tax year is three months or less. The deferral period is the number of months between the beginning of the retained year and the close of the first required tax year.

If the partnership, S corporation, or personal service corporation is *changing* to a tax year other than its required year, the deferral period is the number of months from the end of the new tax year to the end of the required tax year. The IRS will allow a Section 444 election only if the deferral period of the new tax year is less than the shorter of:

1. Three months.
2. The deferral period of the tax year being changed. This is the tax year for which the partnership, S corporation, or personal service corporation wishes to make the Section 444 election.

If the tax year is the same as the required tax year, the deferral period is zero.

A Section 444 election is made by filing a form with the IRS by the earlier of:

1. The due date of the income tax return resulting from the 444 election.
2. The 15th day of the 6th month of the tax year for which the election will be effective. For this purpose, the month in which the tax year begins is counted, even if it begins after the first day of that month. The Section 444 election stays in effect until it is terminated. If the election is terminated, another Section 444 election cannot be made for any tax year. The election ends when any of the three corporations does any of the following:

1. Changes its tax year to a required tax year.
2. Liquidates.
3. Willfully fails to comply with the required payments or distributions.
4. Becomes a member of a tiered structure.

The election also ends if:

1. An S corporation's election is terminated. However, if the S corporation immediately becomes a personal service corporation, it can continue the Section 444 election of the S corporation.

2. A personal service corporation ceases to be a personal service corporation. If the personal service corporation elects to be an S corporation, it can continue the election of the personal service corporation.

Corporations

A new corporation establishes its tax year when it files its first return. A newly reactivated corporation that has been inactive for a number of years is treated as a new taxpayer for the purpose of adopting a tax year. A corporation other than an S corporation, a personal service corporation, or a domestic international sales corporation (C-DISC) can change its tax year without getting IRS approval if all the following conditions are met:

1. It must not have changed its tax year within the 10 calendar years ending with the calendar year in which the short tax year resulting from the change begins.

2. Its short tax year must not be a tax year in which it has a net operating loss.

3. Its taxable income for the whole tax year, if figured on an annual basis, is 80% or more of its taxable income for the tax year before the short tax year.

4. If a corporation is one of the following for either the short tax year or the tax year before the short tax year, it must have the same status for both the short tax year and the prior tax year.

   a. Personal holding company.

   b. Foreign personal holding company.

   c. Exempt organization.

   d. Foreign corporation not engaged in a trade or business within the United States.

5. It must not apply to become an S corporation for the tax year that would immediately follow the short tax year required to effect the change.

The corporation must file a statement with the IRS office where it files its tax return. The statement must be filed by the due date for the short tax year required by the change. It must indicate the corporation is changing its annual accounting period, and show that all the preceding conditions have been met. If the corporation does not meet all the conditions because of later adjustments in establishing tax liability, the statement will be considered a timely application to change the corporation's annual accounting period to the tax year indicated in the statement.

The IRS will waive conditions (1) and (5) above, as well as conditions (2) and (3)(c) outlining automatic approval criteria for a corporation that:

1. Meets all the other conditions.
2. Elected to be an S corporation for the tax year beginning January 1, 1997.
3. It must:
   a. Write "Filed" at the top of the forms required.
   b. Write "Attention, Entity Control" on the envelope.
   c. Mail the forms to the IRS where the corporation files its return.

Corporations can automatically change their tax year if it cannot meet the five conditions and has not changed its annual accounting period within 6 calendar years or in any of the calendar years of existence, and if the corporation is *not any of the following:*

1. A member of a partnership.
2. A beneficiary of a trust or an estate.
3. An S corporation.
4. An interest-charging DISC or a foreign sales corporation (FSC).
5. A personal service corporation.
6. A controlled foreign corporation.
7. A cooperative association.
8. Certain tax-exempt organizations.

CHANGES DURING THE TAX YEAR

A corporation, other than an S corporation, a personal service corporation, or a domestic international sales corporation (IC-DISC) can change its tax year without getting IRS approval if all the following conditions are met:

1. It must not have changed its tax year within the 10 calendar years in which the short tax year resulting from the change begins.
2. Its short tax year must not be a tax year in which it has a net operating loss (NOL).
3. Its taxable income for the short tax year, when figured on an annual basis, annualized, is 80% or more of its taxable income for the tax year before the short tax year.
4. If a corporation is one of the following for either the short tax year or the tax year before the short tax year, it must have the same status for both the short tax and the prior tax year.

5. It must not apply to become an S corporation for the tax year that would immediately follow the short tax year required to effect the change.

The corporation must file a statement with the IRS office where it files its tax return. The statement must be filed by the due date, including extensions, for the short tax year required by the change. It must indicate the corporation is changing its annual accounting period, and that all the preceding conditions have been met.

Certain corporations can *automatically* change their tax year by meeting all the following criteria:

1. It cannot meet the conditions listed earlier.
2. It has not changed its annual accounting period within 6 calendar years of existence, or in any of the calendar years of existence, if less than 6 years.

Chapter 37

Practice Before the IRS and the Power of Attorney

CONTENTS

Expanding the Confidentiality Privilege	**37.01**
Practicing Before the IRS	**37.02**
Becoming a Recognized Representative	**37.02**
Methods of Enrollment	**37.05**
Rules of Practice	**37.05**
The Power of Attorney	**37.07**

EXPANDING THE CONFIDENTIALITY PRIVILEGE

The confidentiality protection for communications between a taxpayer and attorney has been expanded to communications involving tax advice between a taxpayer and any *federally authorized tax practitioners*. These tax practitioners include attorneys, certified public accountants, enrolled agents, enrolled actuaries, and certain other individuals allowed to practice before the Internal Revenue Service. This provision became effective for communications occurring after July 21, 1998.

This protection applies only to the advice given to the taxpayer by any of these individuals. Tax advice is considered to be advice in regard to a matter that is within the scope of the practitioner's authority to practice. The confidentiality protection is applied to communications that would be privileged if between the taxpayer and an attorney, and that relate to noncriminal tax matters or to tax proceedings brought in federal court by or against the United States.

This protection of tax advice communications does not apply to certain written communications between a federally authorized tax practitioner and a director, shareholder, officer, employee, agent, or representative of a corporation. It does not apply if the communication involves the promotion of the direct or indirect participation of the corporation in any tax shelter.

PRACTICING BEFORE THE IRS

A person is practicing before the IRS if he or she:

1. Communicates with the IRS for a taxpayer regarding taxpayer's rights, privileges, or liabilities under laws and regulations administered by the IRS.
2. Represents a taxpayer at conferences, hearings, or meetings with the IRS.
3. Prepares and files necessary documents with the IRS for a taxpayer.

Just preparing a tax return, furnishing information at the request of the IRS, or appearing as a witness for a taxpayer, does not constitute practicing before the IRS.

BECOMING A RECOGNIZED REPRESENTATIVE

Any of the following individuals can practice before the IRS. However, any individual who is recognized to practice—a recognized representative—must file a written declaration with the IRS that he or she is qualified and authorized to represent a taxpayer.

Those individuals include:

1. Any attorney who is not currently under suspension or disbarment from practice before the IRS and who is a member in good standing of the bar at the highest court of any state, possession, territory, commonwealth, or in the District of Columbia.
2. Any Certified Public Accountant who is not currently under suspension or disbarment from practice before the IRS and who is qualified to practice as a CPA in any state, possession, territory, commonwealth, or in the District of Columbia.
3. Any enrolled agent.

4. Any individual who is enrolled as an actuary by the Joint Board for the Enrollment of Actuaries. The practice of enrolled actuaries is limited to certain Internal Revenue Code sections that relate to their area of expertise, principally those sections governing employee retirement plans.

5. Any individual other than an attorney, CPA, enrolled agent, or enrolled actuary who prepares a return and signs it as the return preparer is an unenrolled return preparer. Also, any individual who prepares a return and is not required to sign it as the preparer is considered to be an unenrolled preparer.

    These individuals are limited in their practice. They can represent a taxpayer concerning the tax liability only for the year or period covered by the return that he or she prepared. Also, an unenrolled return preparer is permitted to represent taxpayers only before the Examination Division of the IRS and is not permitted to represent taxpayers before the Appeals, Collection, or any other division of the IRS.

    Unenrolled return preparers cannot perform the following activities for another taxpayer:

    a. Sign claims for a refund.

    b. Receive refund checks.

    c. Sign consents to extend the statutory period for assessment for or collection of tax.

    d. Sign closing agreements regarding a tax liability.

    e. Sign waivers of restriction on assessment or collection of a tax deficiency.

6. Because of their special relationship with a taxpayer, the following unenrolled individuals can represent the specified taxpayers before the IRS, provided they present satisfactory identification and proof of authority to represent.

    a. An individual can represent himself or herself before the IRS and does not have to file a written declaration of qualification and authority.

    b. An individual family member can represent members of his or her immediate family. Family members include a spouse, child, parent, brother, or sister of the individual.

    c. A *bona fide* officer of a corporation (including parents subsidiaries, or affiliated corporation), association, organized group, or, in the course of his or her other official duties, an officer of a governmental unit, agency, or authority can represent the organization of which he or she is an officer.

    d. A trustee, receiver, guardian, personal representative, or executor can represent a trust or estate.

e. A regular full-time employee can represent his or her employer. An employer can be, but is not limited to, an individual, partnership, corporation (including parents, subsidiaries, or affiliated corporations), association, trust, receivership, guardianship, estate, organized group, governmental unit, agency, or authority.

An unenrolled individual can represent any individual or entity before IRS personnel who are outside the United States.

Denial of Right to Limited Practice

The IRS Director of Practice, after giving notice and an opportunity for a conference, can deny eligibility for limited practice before the IRS to any unenrolled preparer or other unenrolled individual who has engaged in disreputable conduct. This conduct includes, but is not limited to, the list of items under Disreputable Conduct.

Authorization for Special Appearance

An individual can be authorized to practice before the IRS or represent another person in a particular matter. The prospective representative must request this authorization in writing from the Director of Practice. It is granted only when extremely compelling circumstances exist. If granted, the IRS will issue a letter that details the conditions related to the appearance and the particular tax matter for which the authorization is granted.

The authorization letter should not be confused with a letter from an IRS service center advising an individual that he or she has been assigned a *Centralized Authorization File* number which identifies an assigned representative. The issuance of a number does not indicate that a person is either recognized or authorized to practice before the IRS. It merely confirms that a centralized file for authorizations has been established for the representative under that number.

Who Cannot Practice

Individuals cannot practice before the IRS either because they are not eligible to practice, or because they have lost the privilege as a result of certain actions. The following individuals generally cannot practice before the IRS:

1. Individuals convicted of any criminal offense under the revenue laws of the U.S.
2. Individuals convicted of any offense involving dishonesty or breach of trust.

3. Individuals under disbarment or suspension from practicing as attorneys, CPAs, public accountants, or actuaries in any state, possession, territory, commonwealth, or in the District of Columbia, or before any federal court, or any body or board of any federal agency.

4. Individuals who are disbarred or suspended from practice before the IRS because they refuse or have refused to comply with the regulations governing practice before the IRS.

METHODS OF ENROLLMENT

The Director of Practice can grant an enrollment to practice before the IRS to an applicant who has demonstrated special competence in tax matters by passing a written examination administered by the IRS. Enrollment also can be granted to an applicant who qualifies because of past service and technical experience in the IRS. In either case certain application forms must be filed. An applicant must never have engaged in any conduct that would justify suspension or disbarment by the IRS.

An *enrollment card* will be issued to each individual whose application is approved. The individual is enrolled until the expiration date shown on the enrollment card. To continue practicing beyond the expiration date, the individual must request renewal of the enrollment.

RULES OF PRACTICE

An attorney, CPA, enrolled agent, or enrolled actuary authorized to practice before the IRS who is referred to as a practitioner has the duty to perform certain acts and is restricted from performing other acts. Any practitioner who does not comply with the rules of practice or engages in disreputable conduct is subject to disciplinary action. Also, unenrolled preparers must comply with most of these rules of practice and conduct to exercise the privilege of limited practice before the IRS.

Practitioners must promptly submit records or information requested by officers or employees of the IRS. When the IRS requests information concerning possible violations of the regulations by other parties, the practitioner must provide it and be prepared to testify in disbarment or suspension proceedings. A practitioner can be exempt from these rules if he or she believes in good faith and on reasonable grounds that the information requested is privileged or that the request is of doubtful legality.

A practitioner who knows that his or her client has not complied with the revenue laws, or has made an error in or omission from any return, document, affidavit, or other required paper has the responsibility to advise the client promptly of the noncompliance error or omission.

Required Due Diligence

A practitioner must exercise due diligence when performing the following duties:

1. Preparing or assisting in the preparation, approving, and filing of returns, documents, affidavits, and other papers relating to IRS matters.
2. Determining the correctness of oral or written representations made by him or her to the Department of the Treasury.
3. Determining the correctness of oral or written presentations made by him or her to clients with reference to any matter administered by the IRS.

Restrictions

Practitioners are restricted from engaging in certain practices:

1. A practitioner must not unreasonably delay the prompt disposition of any matter before the IRS.
2. A practitioner must not knowingly, directly or indirectly, employ or accept assistance from any person who is under disbarment or suspension from practice before the IRS.
3. He or she must not accept employment as an associate, correspondent, or subagent from, or share fees with, any person under disbarment or suspension by the IRS.
4. He or she must not accept assistance from any former government employee where provisions of these regulations or any federal law would be violated.
5. If a practitioner is a notary public and is employed as counsel, attorney, or agent in a matter before the IRS, or has a material interest in the matter, he or she must not engage in any notary activities relative to that matter.
6. A partner of an officer or employee of the executive branch of the U.S. Government, or of an independent agency of the U.S. or of the District of Columbia, cannot represent anyone in a matter before the IRS in which the officer or employee has or had a personal or substantial interest as a government employee. There are similar and additional restrictions on former government employees.

Disreputable Conduct

Disreputable conduct by a practitioner includes such things as:

1. Committing any criminal offense under the revenue laws, or committing any offense involving dishonesty or breach of trust.
2. Knowingly giving or participating in the giving of false or misleading information in connection with federal tax matters.
3. Willful failure to file a tax return, evading or attempting to evade any federal tax or payment, or participating in such actions.
4. Misappropriating, or failing properly and promptly remit funds received from clients for payment of taxes.
5. Directly or indirectly attempting to influence the official action of IRS employees by the use of threats, false accusations, duress, or coercion, or by offering gifts, favors, or any special inducements.
6. Being disbarred or suspended by the District of Columbia or by any state, possession, territory, commonwealth, or any federal court, or any body or board of any federal agency.
7. Knowingly aiding and abetting another person to practice before the IRS during a period of suspension, disbarment, or ineligibility, or maintaining a partnership so that a suspended or disbarred person can continue to practice before the IRS.
8. Contemptuous conduct in connection with practice before the IRS, including the use of abusive language, making false accusations and statements, or circulating or publishing malicious or libelous matter.
9. Giving a false opinion knowingly, or recklessly, or through gross incompetence, or following a pattern of providing incompetent opinions in questions arising under the federal tax laws.
10. Soliciting employment by prohibited means.

THE POWER OF ATTORNEY

A power of attorney is a taxpayer's written authorization for an individual to act for him or her in tax matters. If the authorization is not limited, the individual can generally perform all acts that a taxpayer can perform. The authority granted to an unenrolled preparer cannot exceed that shown under the special rules of limited practice.

Any representative, other than an unenrolled preparer, can usually perform the following acts:

1. Represent the taxpayer before any office of the IRS.
2. Record the interview.

3. Sign an offer or a waiver of restriction on assessment or collection of a tax deficiency, or a waiver of notice of disallowance of claim for credit or refunds.
4. Sign a consent to extend the statutory time period for assessment or collection of a tax.
5. Sign a closing agreement.
6. Receive, but not endorse or cash, a refund check drawn on the U.S. Treasury. The taxpayer must specifically sign a form showing the name of the individual designated to receive the refund check.

The representative named under a power of attorney is not permitted to sign the taxpayer's income tax return unless the signature is permitted under the Internal Revenue Code and the related regulations of the Tax Regulations. The taxpayer can authorize this in the taxpayer's power of attorney.

The regulation permits a representative to sign a client's income tax return if the client is unable to make the return for any of the following reasons:

1. Disease or injury.
2. Continuous absence from the United States for a period of at least 60 days prior to the date required by law for filing the return.
3. Other good cause if specific permission is requested of and granted by the IRS.

If a taxpayer wants a representative to receive a refund check, the taxpayer must specifically so authorize it in the power of attorney. However, if the representative is an income tax return preparer, the representative cannot be authorized to endorse or otherwise cash the client's check related to income taxes.

The appointed representative can substitute a representative or delegate authority to a new representative only if this is specifically authorized under the power of attorney. A power of attorney is generally terminated if the client becomes incapacitated or incompetent. The power of attorney can continue, however, in the case of the taxpayer's incapacity or incompetency if the taxpayer had previously authorized that it be continued.

When a Power of Attorney Is Required

A taxpayer should submit a power of attorney when he or she wants to authorize an individual to represent him or her before the IRS, whether or not the representative performs any of the other acts discussed earlier. A power of attorney is most often required when a taxpayer wants to authorize another individual to perform at least one of the following acts on his or her behalf:

1. Represent the taxpayer at a conference with the IRS.
2. Prepare and file a written response to the IRS.

A taxpayer can appoint an unenrolled return preparer as his or her representative. The preparer can represent the taxpayer only before revenue agents and examining officers. Also, the preparer can represent a taxpayer concerning his or her tax liability only for the period covered by a return prepared by the preparer.

The IRS will accept a non-IRS power of attorney, but a transmittal form must be attached in order for the power of attorney to be entered into the *Centralized Authorization File.* If a power of attorney document other than the required transmittal form is used, it must contain the following information:

1. The taxpayer's name and mailing address, Social Security number, and/or employer identification number.
2. An employee plan number, if applicable.
3. The name and mailing address of the taxpayer's representative.
4. The types of tax involved.
5. The federal tax form number.
6. The specific years or periods involved.
7. For estate tax matters, the decedent's date of death.
8. A clear expression of the taxpayer's intention concerning the scope of authority granted to his or her representative.
9. The taxpayer's signature and date.

The taxpayer must also attach to the non-IRS power of attorney a signed and dated statement made by the taxpayer's representative. This statement, which is referred to as the *Declaration of Representative* is included with the transmittal form filed.

Filing a Power of Attorney

The power of attorney is filed with each IRS office with which the taxpayer deals. If the power of attorney is filed for a matter currently pending before an office of the IRS, it should be filed with that office. Otherwise, the power should be filed with the service center where the related return was, or will be, filed.

When a Power of Attorney Is Not Required

The following situations do not require a power of attorney:

1. A power of attorney is not required when a person is merely furnishing information at the request of the IRS.
2. A power of attorney is not required to authorize the IRS to disclose information concerning a tax account to an individual (whether or not the individual is authorized to practice before the IRS) or other party, such as a corporation, a partnership, or an association.

The Tax Matters Partner or Person (TMP)

A TMP is authorized by law to perform various acts on behalf of a partnership or Subchapter S corporation. This includes the power to delegate authority to represent the TMP and to sign documents in that capacity, but certain acts performed by the TMP cannot be delegated.

The Fiduciary

A fiduciary, trustee, executor, administrator, receiver, or guardian, stands in the position of the taxpayer and acts as the taxpayer. Therefore, a fiduciary does not act as a representative and should not file a power of attorney. A fiduciary should file Form 56, *Notice Concerning Fiduciary Relationship,* to notify the IRS of the fiduciary relationship.

Completed Documents

A power of attorney will be recognized after the Form 56 is received, reviewed, and determined by the IRS to contain the required information. However, until a power of attorney is entered into the Centralized Authorized File (CAF), IRS personnel, other than the individual to whom the form is submitted, may be unaware of the authority of the taxpayer's representative and request an additional copy.

When the IRS receives a complete and valid power of attorney, the IRS will take action to recognize the representative. This involves processing the document into the CAF system. The power of attorney is not considered valid until all required information is entered on the document. The individual named as representative will not be recognized to practice before the IRS until the document is complete and accepted by the IRS.

In most instances, the recognition involves processing the document by recording the information on the CAF which enables the IRS to automatically direct copies of mailings to an authorized representative and to instantly recognize the scope of authority granted.

After the power of attorney is filed, the IRS will recognize the taxpayer's representative. However, if it appears the representative is responsible for unreasonably delaying or hindering the prompt disposition of an IRS matter by failing to furnish, after repeated requests, nonprivileged information, the IRS can bypass the representative and contact the taxpayer directly.

Revoking a Power of Attorney

If a taxpayers wants to revoke an existing power of attorney and does not want to name a new representative, there are two ways to do it:

1. By sending a *revocation copy* of a previous appointment form to each office of the IRS where forms were originally filed.
2. By sending a *revocation statement* to the service center where a return was filed that was covered by the power of attorney.

Unless a taxpayer wants to revoke a power of attorney for which no form was filed, a letter can be written requesting the revocation with a copy of the power of attorney to be revoked. The letter should be signed and dated and sent to each office of the IRS where the taxpayer originally filed the non-IRS power of attorney.

Unless a taxpayer specifies otherwise, a newly filed power of attorney concerning the same matter will revoke a previously filed power of attorney, but not a previously filed tax authorization. A newly filed tax information authorization will revoke a previously filed tax authorization concerning the same matter, but will not revoke a power of attorney concerning that matter.

Chapter 38

Taxpayer Rights

CONTENTS

New image for the IRS	**38.01**
Declaration of Taxpayer Rights	**38.02**
Examinations, Appeals, Collections, and Refunds	**38.04**
The IRS Collection Process	**38.06**
Employment Taxes for Employers	**38.11**
Award of Administrative Costs	**38.12**
Explanation of Claim for Refund Disallowance	**38.13**
Tax Court Proceedings	**38.14**
Additional Provisions for Taxpayer Rights	**38.15**

NEW IMAGE FOR THE IRS

Along with their tax bills, taxpayers receive publications delineating their rights and obligations in handling various and sundry tax problems. Some of the points made are reminiscent of those previously publicized in the Taxpayer Bill of Rights 1, 2, and 3. (The last may be better known as the *IRS Restructuring and Reform Act of 1998,* but more on that below.) These two publications emphasize some of the measures adopted in the Congressional Bills, but are also based on IRS regulations and other legislation. They are not a Taxpayer

38.01

Bill of Rights 4. Regardless, it does appear that the Service is attempting to serve the public and make tax paying as painless as possible.

At some point, between the time that Congress passed the 1998 bill and the IRS started sending out information publications for the 1998 tax season, it had picked up a subtitle and become known as the *Taxpayer Bill of Rights 3*.

In fact, the IRS states, "The *IRS Restructuring Reform Act of 1998* contains the Taxpayer Bill of Rights 3. It preserves the balance between safeguarding the rights of the individual taxpayers and enabling the Internal Revenue Service to administer the tax laws efficiently, fairly, and with the least amount of burden to the taxpayer."

Under this bill, taxpayer rights have been expanded in several areas:

1. The burden of proof will shift to the IRS in certain court proceedings.
2. In certain cases, taxpayers may be awarded damages and fees, and get liens released.
3. Penalties will be eased when the IRS exceeds specified time limits between when a return is filed and when the taxpayer is notified of a tax liability.
4. Interest will be eliminated in certain cases involving federally-declared disaster areas.
5. There are new rules for collection actions by levy.
6. Innocent spouse relief provisions have been strengthened.
7. In certain situations, taxpayer-requested installment agreements must be accepted. Taxpayers will get annual status reports of their installment agreements.

Included are requirements that IRS employees are now required to be more polite and responsive. For example, any IRS correspondence not computer generated must include the name and telephone number of an employee whom a taxpayer can contact. The new law also establishes a nine-member board to oversee the general administration of the agency. And to assure that key decision making will not remain in the self-protecting hands of IRS career employees, six of the board's members will be "outsiders." Many of these provisions are contained in the material that follows.

Declaration of Taxpayer Rights

The first part of this discussion explains some of a taxpayer's most important rights. The second part explains the examination, appeal, collection, and refund procedures.

I. *Protection of a Taxpayer's Rights.* IRS employees will explain and protect a taxpayer's rights throughout his or her contact with the IRS.

II. *Privacy and Confidentiality.* The IRS will not disclose to anyone the information given to the IRS, except as authorized by law.

III. *Professional and Courteous Service.* If a taxpayer believes an IRS employee has not treated him or her in a professional, fair, and courteous manner, the employee's supervisor should be told. If the supervisor's response is not satisfactory, the taxpayer should write to the IRS District Director or Service Center Director.

IV. *Representation.* A taxpayer can either represent himself or herself or, with proper written authorization, have someone else as a representative. The taxpayer's representative must be a person allowed to practice before the IRS, such as an attorney, certified public accountant, or enrolled agent.

If a taxpayer is in an interview and asks to consult such a person, then the IRS must stop and reschedule the interview in most cases. Someone may accompany the taxpayer to an interview, and make recordings of any meetings with the IRS examining agent, appeal or collection personnel, provided the taxpayer tells the IRS in writing 10 days before the meeting.

V. *Payment of Only the Correct Amount of Tax.* Taxpayers are responsible for paying the correct amount of tax due under the law—no more, no less. If a responsible taxpayer cannot pay all of his or her tax when it is due, it may be possible to make monthly installment payments. Arrangements for payments are made with the IRS.

VI. *Help with Unresolved Tax Problems.* The National Taxpayer Advocate's Problem Resolution Program can help a taxpayer who has tried unsuccessfully to resolve a problem with the IRS. A local Taxpayer Advocate can offer special help for a significant hardship as a result of a tax problem. The taxpayer may call toll-free or write to the Taxpayer Advocate at the IRS office that last contacted him or her.

VII. *Appeals and Judicial Review.* If a taxpayer disagrees with the IRS about the amount of a tax liability or certain collection actions, it is the taxpayer's right to ask the Appeals Office to review the case. The taxpayer also has the right to ask a court to review the case.

VIII. *Relief from Certain Penalties and Interest.* The IRS will waive penalties when allowed by law if a taxpayer can show he or she has acted reasonably and in good faith or relied on the incorrect advice of an IRS employee. The IRS will waive interest that is the result of certain errors or delays caused by an IRS employee.

Examinations, Appeals, Collections, and Refunds

Examinations (Audits).   The IRS accepts most taxpayers' returns as filed. If the IRS inquires about a return or selects it for examination, it does not suggest the taxpayer is dishonest. The inquiry or examination may or may not result in more tax. A case can be closed without change, or the taxpayer may receive a refund.

The process of selecting a return for examination usually begins in one of two ways:

1. Computer programs are used to identify returns that may have incorrect amounts. These programs may be based on:
   a. Information returns, such as Forms 1099 and W-2.
   b. Studies of past examinations.
   c. Certain issues identified by compliance projects.
2. Information is used from outside sources that indicate that a return has incorrect amounts. These sources include:
   a. Newspapers.
   b. Public records.
   c. Individuals.

If it is determined that the information is accurate and reliable, this information may be used to select a particular tax return for examination.

Examinations by Mail.   The IRS processes many examinations and inquiries by mail. They will send a letter to a taxpayer with either a request for more information or a reason the IRS believes a change in a return may be needed. The taxpayer can respond by mail or can request a personal interview with an examiner. If the taxpayer mails the requested information or provides an explanation, the IRS may or may not agree with the taxpayer's explanation, and will explain the reasons for any changes. The IRS urges taxpayers not to hesitate to write about anything they do not understand.

By Interview.   If the IRS notifies a taxpayer that they will conduct an examination through a personal interview, or the taxpayer requests such an interview, the taxpayer has the right to ask that the examination take place at a reasonable time and place that is convenient for both the taxpayer and the IRS. If an examiner proposes any changes to a return, the examination will make clear the reasons for the changes. If the taxpayer does not agree with these changes, he or she can meet with the examiner's supervisor.

Repeat Examinations.   If the IRS examined a return for the same items in either of the two previous years and proposed no change to the taxpayer's tax liability, he or she should contact the IRS as soon as possible so that the IRS can determine if the current examination should be discontinued.

Appeals.   If a taxpayer does not agree with an examiner's proposed changes, he or she can appeal them to the Appeals Office of the IRS. Most differences can be settled without expensive and time-consuming court trials. If the taxpayer does not want to use the Appeals Office or disagrees with its finding, the case can be taken to the U.S. Tax Court, U.S. Court of Federal Claims, or the U.S. District Court where the taxpayer lives. If a case is taken to court, the IRS will have the burden of proving certain facts. These would include whether the taxpayer:

1. Kept audit records to show the tax liability.
2. Cooperated fully with the IRS.
3. Met certain other conditions.

If the court agrees with the taxpayer on most issues in a case, and finds that the IRS position was largely unjustified, the taxpayer may be able to recover some of the administrative and litigation costs. However, the taxpayer cannot recover these costs unless he or she tried to resolve a case administratively, including going through the appeals system, and giving the IRS the information necessary to resolve the case.

Innocent Spouse Relief.   Generally, both spouses are responsible, jointly and individually, for paying the full amount of any tax, interest, or penalties due on their joint return. However, one spouse may not have to pay the tax, interest, and penalties related to the other spouse or former spouse.

New tax law changes make it easier to qualify for innocent spouse relief and add two other ways to get relief through "separation of liability" and "equitable relief." Thus, there are now three types of relief available:

1. Innocent spouse relief which applies to all joint filers.
2. Separation of liability, which applies to joint filers who are divorced, widowed, legally separated, or have not lived together for the past 12 months.
3. Equitable relief, which applies to all joint filers and married couples filing separate returns in community property states.

Innocent spouse relief and separation of liability apply only to items incorrectly reported on the return. If a spouse does not qualify for innocent spouse relief or separation of liability, the IRS may grant equitable relief.

Refunds.   A taxpayer can file a claim for a refund if he or she thinks too much tax was levied. The claim must generally be filed within 3 years from the date the original return was filed, or 2 years from the date the tax was paid, whichever is later. The law generally provides for interest on a refund if it is not paid within 45 days of the date the return was filed or the refund was claimed.

THE IRS COLLECTION PROCESS

There are steps the IRS can take to collect overdue taxes. The information in this discussion applies to all taxpayers—for individuals who owe income taxes and employers who owe employment tax. Special rules that apply only to employers are given at the end of this discussion.

By law, taxpayers have the right to be treated professionally, fairly, promptly, and courteously by IRS employees. Some of those rights are to:

1. Disagree with claims on the tax bill.
2. Meet with an IRS manager if the taxpayer disagrees with the IRS employee who handles the tax case.
3. Appeal most IRS collection actions.
4. Transfer a case to a different IRS office.
5. Be represented by someone when dealing with IRS matters.
6. Receive a receipt for any payment he or she makes.

Disagreement with an IRS Decision.   If a taxpayer disagrees with a decision of an IRS employee at any time during the collection process, the taxpayer can ask the employee's manager to review the case. The employee will then refer the taxpayer to a manager who will either speak with the taxpayer then or return a call by the next work day.

If the taxpayer disagrees with a manager's decision, the taxpayer has the right to file an appeal which enables him or her to appeal most collection actions taken by the IRS, including filing a lien, placing a levy on the taxpayer's wages or bank account, or seizing a taxpayer's property.

Someone to Represent a Taxpayer.   When dealing with the IRS, a taxpayer can choose to represent himself or herself, or can have an attorney, a certified public accountant, an enrolled agent, or any person enrolled to practice before the IRS as a representative.

Problem Resolution Program.   This program ensures that taxpayers' problems are handled promptly and properly. If repeated attempts have been made to sort out a tax problem with the IRS, but have been unsuccessful, then the taxpayer can first ask any IRS employee or manager for help. If the problem continues, the taxpayer may ask for an appointment with the Taxpayer

Advocate in the local IRS office. The Taxpayer Advocate determines whether the taxpayer qualifies for the Problem Resolution Program.

IRS Sharing Information.   By law the IRS can share a taxpayer's information with city and state tax agencies and, in some cases, with the Department of Justice, other federal agencies, and with people the taxpayer authorizes to receive that information. Such information can also be shared with certain foreign governments under tax treaty provisions.

The IRS can contact other sources, such as neighbors, banks, employers or employees, to investigate a case. However, after January 18, 1999, the new law provides that before contacting other persons, the IRS must notify the individual that, in examining or collecting tax liability, they may contact third parties. In addition, the new law requires the Service to provide a list of persons who were questioned. This information is to be provided periodically and upon request.

The notification provision does not apply in the following circumstances:

1. Pending criminal investigations.
2. When providing notice would jeopardize collection of any tax liability.
3. Where providing notice may result in reprisal against any person.
4. When the taxpayer authorized the contact.

If a taxpayer is involved in a bankruptcy proceeding, the proceeding may not eliminate the tax debt, but it may temporarily stop IRS enforcement action from collecting a debt related to the bankruptcy.

If a Taxpayer Owes Child Support.   If a taxpayer is entitled to a federal or state tax refund while still owing unpaid taxes or child support, the IRS can apply the refund toward the debt and send the taxpayer the remaining balance, if there is any.

When a Taxpayer Can't Pay.   When a tax return is filed, the IRS checks to see if the mathematics is accurate and if the taxpayer has paid the correct amount. If the taxpayer has not paid all that is owed, the IRS will send a bill called a *Notice of Tax Due and Demand for Payment.* The bill will include the taxes, plus penalties and interest, and the IRS encourages a taxpayer to pay the tax bill by check or money order as quickly as possible.

If the taxpayer has received a bill for unpaid taxes, the entire amount should be paid, or the IRS should be notified why the taxpayer cannot pay. If the taxpayer does not pay the taxes owed and makes no effort to pay them, the IRS can ask the taxpayer to take action to pay by selling or mortgaging any assets, or getting a loan. If the taxpayer still makes no effort to pay the taxes owed or to work out a payment plan, the IRS can also take more serious action, such as seizing the taxpayer's bank, levying his or her wages, or taking other income or assets.

If a Taxpayer Believes the Bill Is Wrong.   If a taxpayer believes a bill is wrong, the IRS should be contacted as soon as possible by:

1. Calling the number on the bill.
2. Writing to the IRS office that sent the bill.
3. Visiting the local IRS office.

To help IRS consideration of the problem, the taxpayer should send a copy of the bill along with copies (not originals) of any records, tax returns, and canceled checks that will help the IRS understand why the taxpayer believes the bill to be wrong. When writing to the IRS, the taxpayer should state clearly why he or she believes the bill is wrong. If the IRS finds the taxpayer is correct, the account will be adjusted, and, if necessary, the taxpayer will be sent a corrected bill.

If the total amount owed cannot be paid immediately, as much as possible should be paid. By paying that portion, the amount of interest and penalty will be reduced. The taxpayer should call, write, or visit the nearest IRS office to explain the situation. The IRS will ask for a completed form, *Collection Information Statement,* to help them consider the amount the taxpayer can pay based upon the taxpayer's monthly income and expenses. The IRS will then help to figure out a payment plan that fits the situation. The IRS will work with the taxpayer to consider several different ways to pay what is owed:

1. The taxpayer may be able to make monthly payments through an installment agreement.
2. The taxpayer may be able to apply for an offer in compromise.
3. The taxpayer may qualify for a temporary delay, or the case may be considered a significant hardship.

An Installment Agreement.   Installment agreements allow the full payment of taxes in smaller, equal monthly payments. The amount of each installment payment is based on the amount of tax owed and the taxpayer's ability to pay that amount within the time available to the IRS to collect the tax debt.

Previously, the IRS did not have to agree to accept the payment of taxes in installments. However, as of July 22, 1998, they must enter into an installment agreement for the payment of income tax if the taxpayer meets all of the following conditions on the date he or she offers to enter into the agreement:

1. The total income tax owed is not more than $10,000.
2. In the last 5 years, the taxpayer (and spouse if the liability relates to a joint return) has:
   a. Filed all required income tax returns.

b. Paid all taxes shown on the returns filed.

c. Not entered into an installment agreement to pay any income tax.

3. The taxpayer shows (and the IRS agrees) that the individual cannot pay the income tax in full when due.

4. The taxpayer agrees to pay the tax in full in 3 years or less.

5. The taxpayer agrees to comply with the tax laws while the agreement is in effect.

An installment agreement is a reasonable payment option for some taxpayers, but they should be aware that an installment agreement is more costly than paying all the tax owed and may be more costly than borrowing funds to pay the full amount. Why? Because the IRS charges interest and *penalties* on the tax owed and also charges interest on the unpaid penalties and interest that have been charged to the taxpayer's account. This means that while the taxpayer is making payments on his or her tax debt through an installment agreement, the IRS continues to charge interest and penalties on the unpaid portion of that debt.

The interest rate on a bank loan or on a cash advance on a credit card may be lower than the combination of penalties and interest the IRS charges. There is also another cost associated with an installment agreement. To set up the payment program, the IRS charges a $43 user fee. If a taxpayer owes $10,000 or less in tax, the taxpayer can call the number on the tax bill to set up a plan. The IRS will inform the taxpayer what has to be done to begin immediately.

If more than $10,000 is owed, the IRS may still be able to set up an installment agreement with the taxpayer based on the completed form, *Collection Information Statement.* Even though a taxpayer agrees to an installment plan, the IRS can still file a *Notice of Federal Tax Lien* to secure the government's interest until the taxpayer makes the final payment.

However, the IRS cannot levy against the taxpayer's property:

1. While a request for an installment agreement is being considered.

2. While an agreement is in effect.

3. For 30 days after the request for an agreement has been rejected.

4. For any period while an appeal of the rejection is being evaluated by the IRS.

If an installment agreement is arranged, the taxpayer can pay with personal or business checks, money orders, certified funds, or payroll deductions the employer takes from the taxpayer's salary and regularly sends to the IRS, or by electronic transfers from the employee's bank account or other means.

An installment agreement is based on the taxpayer's financial situation. If a change in the financial situation makes it necessary to change the terms of the installment agreement, the IRS will inform the taxpayer by letter 30 days before changing the established plan. The payments on an installment agreement must be paid on time; if a payment cannot be made, the IRS should be informed immediately. The IRS can end an agreement if the taxpayer does not furnish updated financial information when the IRS requests it, or if the taxpayer fails to meet the terms of the agreement.

An agreement could end if the taxpayer misses a payment, or does not file or pay all required tax returns. In that case, the IRS can take enforced collection action. In some cases, the IRS will accept an offer in compromise. On the other hand, if taxes are not paid when they are due, the taxpayer may be subject to a failure- to-pay penalty of 5% of the unpaid taxes for each month they are not paid. But if a return was filed on time, the penalty will be reduced to 2.5% for any month beginning after 1999 in which the taxpayer has an installment agreement in effect.

Offer in Compromise.   In some cases, the IRS may accept an Offer in Compromise to settle an unpaid tax account, including any interest and penalties. With such an arrangement, they can accept less than the amount owed when it is doubtful that they would be able to collect all of the taxpayer's debt any time in the near future.

Temporary Delay.   If the IRS determines that the taxpayer cannot pay *any* of a tax debt, they may temporarily delay collection until the taxpayer's financial condition improves. If the IRS does delay collection, the debt will increase because penalties and interest are charged until the full amount is paid. During a temporary delay, the IRS will review the individual's ability to pay, and may file a *Notice of Federal Tax Lien* to protect the government's interest in the taxpayer's assets.

A Significant Hardship.   The IRS can consider whether a significant hardship exists for a taxpayer to pay a tax liability. It would be judged a significant hardship if the taxpayer cannot afford to maintain even the necessities to live day to day (adequate food, clothing, shelter, transportation, and medical treatment). Other cases that can be considered as significant hardship by law:

1. An immediate threat of adverse action.
2. Delay of more than 30 days in resolving taxpayer account problems.
3. Incurring significant costs (including fees for professional representation) if relief is not granted.
4. Irreparable injury to, or long-term adverse impact on, the taxpayer if relief is not granted.

A taxpayer may apply for emergency relief if facing a significant hardship. He or she should call the toll-free IRS Taxpayer Assistant number or visit the district's Taxpayer Advocate. A qualifying taxpayer will be assisted in filling out the form, *Application for Taxpayer Assistance Order.*

EMPLOYMENT TAXES FOR EMPLOYERS

To encourage prompt payment of withheld income and employment taxes, including Social Security taxes, railroad retirement taxes, or collected excise taxes, Congress passed a law that provides for the trust fund recovery penalty. (These taxes are called *trust fund taxes* because the employer actually holds the employee's money in trust until making a federal tax deposit in that amount.)

If the IRS plans to assess an employer for the trust fund recovery penalty, they will send a letter stating that the employer is the *responsible* person. An employer has 60 days after receiving the letter to appeal the IRS proposal. If the employer does not respond to the letter, the IRS will assess the penalty and send a *Notice and Demand for Payment*. The IRS can apply this penalty even if the employer has gone out of business.

Responsible Person. A responsible person is a person or group of people having the duty to perform and the power to direct the collecting, accounting, and paying of trust fund taxes. This person may be:

1. An officer or an employee of a corporation.
2. A member or employee of a partnership.
3. A corporate director or shareholder.
4. A member of a board of trustees of a nonprofit organization.
5. Another person with authority and control over funds to direct their disbursement.

Assessing the Trust Fund Recovery Penalty. The IRS may assess the penalty against anyone who:

1. Is responsible for collecting or paying withheld income and employment taxes, or for paying collected excise taxes.
2. Willfully fails to collect or pay them.

For *willfulness* to exist, the responsible person must:

1. Have known about the unpaid taxes.
2. Have used the funds to keep the business going or allowed available funds to be paid to other creditors.

Employment Taxes. Employment taxes include the amount the employer should *withhold* from employees for both income and Social Security tax, plus the amount of Social Security tax paid on behalf of each employee.

If the employer fails to pay employment taxes on time, or if required to but did not include payment with the return, the IRS will charge interest and penalties on any unpaid balance. They may charge penalties of up to 15% of the amount not deposited, depending on how many days late the payment is.

If withheld trust fund taxes are not paid, the IRS may take additional collection action. They may require the employer to:

1. File and pay the employee's taxes monthly rather than quarterly, or
2. Open a special bank account for the withheld amounts, under penalty of prosecution.

AWARD OF ADMINISTRATIVE COSTS

Rules for awarding reasonable administrative costs and certain fees incurred after January 18, 1999 include:

Qualified Offer Rule. The taxpayer can receive reasonable costs and fees as a prevailing party in a civil action or proceeding when all of the following occur:

1. The taxpayer makes a qualified offer to the IRS to settle the case.
2. The IRS rejects that offer.
3. The tax liability (not including interest) later determined by the Court is not more than the qualified offer.

The Court can consider the IRS not to be the prevailing party in a civil action or proceeding based on the fact that the IRS has lost in other courts of appeal on substantially similar issues.

Qualified Offer. This is a written offer made by the taxpayer during the qualified offer period. It must specify both of the following:

1. The amount of the taxpayer's liability (not including interest).
2. That it is a qualified offer when made.

It must remain open until the earliest of the following dates:

1. The date the offer is rejected.
2. The date the trial begins.
3. 90 days from the date of the offer.

The qualified offer period is the period beginning with the date that the 30-day letter is mailed by the IRS to the taxpayer and ending on the date that is 30 days before the date the case is first set for trial.

Administrative costs can be awarded for costs incurred after the earliest of the following dates:

1. The date of the notice of deficiency.
2. The date the first letter of proposed deficiency is sent that allows an opportunity to request administrative review in the IRS Office of Appeals.
3. The date the taxpayer receives the IRS Office of Appeals' decision.

Attorney Fees.   The basic rate of an award for attorney fees has been raised from $110 to $125 per hour and it can be higher in certain circumstances. Those circumstances now include the difficulty level of the issues in the case and the availability of tax expertise locally. The basic rate is subject to adjustment each year.

Attorney fees now include the fees paid for the services of anyone who is authorized to practice before the Tax Court or before the IRS. In addition, attorney fees can be awarded in civil actions taken for unauthorized inspection or disclosure of the taxpayer's tax return or return information.

Fees can be awarded in excess of the actual amount charged if all of the following apply:

1. The fees are charged at less than the $125 basic rate.
2. The taxpayer is represented for no fee, or for a nominal fee, as a pro bono service.
3. The award is paid to the taxpayer's representative or to the representative's employer.

EXPLANATION OF CLAIM FOR REFUND DISALLOWANCE

The IRS has the obligation to explain the specific reasons that a claim for refund is disallowed or partially disallowed. Claims for refund can be disallowed based on a preliminary review or on examination by a revenue agent. This means that the taxpayer must receive one of the following:

1. A form explaining that the claim is disallowed for one of the following reasons:
   a. The claim was filed late.
   b. It was based solely on the unconstitutionality of the revenue acts.
   c. It was waived as part of a settlement.

    d. It covered a tax year or issues that were part of a closing agreement or an offer in compromise.

    e. It was related to a return closed by a final court order.

2. A revenue agent's report explaining the reasons that the claim is disallowed.

Tax Court Proceedings

Burden of Proof.   Generally, for court proceedings resulting from examinations started after July 22, 1998, the IRS has the burden of proving any factual issue if the taxpayer has introduced credible evidence relating to the issue. However, the taxpayer must also have done all of the following:

1. Complied with all substantiation requirements of the Internal Revenue Code.
2. Maintained all records required by the Internal Revenue Code.
3. Cooperated with all reasonable requests by the IRS for information regarding the preparation and related tax treatment of any item reported on a tax return.
4. Had a net worth of $7 million or less at the time the tax liability is contested in any court proceeding if the tax return is for a corporation, partnership, or trust.

Use of Statistical Information.   The IRS has the burden of proof in court proceedings that are based on any reconstruction of an individual's income solely through the use of statistical information on unrelated taxpayers.

Penalties.   The IRS has the burden of proof in court proceedings with respect to the liability of any individual taxpayer for any penalty, addition to tax, or additional amount imposed by the tax laws.

Refund or Credit of Overpayments Before Final Decision.   Beginning July 22, 1998, any court with proper jurisdiction, including the Tax Court, has the authority to order the IRS to refund any part of a tax deficiency that the IRS collects from the taxpayer during a period when the IRS is not permitted to assess, levy, or engage in any court proceeding to collect that tax deficiency. In addition, the court can order a refund of any part of a tax deficiency that is not at issue in a taxpayer's appeal to the court. The court can order these refunds before its decision on the case is final. Generally, the IRS is not permitted to take action on a tax deficiency during the following periods.

1. The 90-day (or 150-day if outside of the United States) period that the taxpayer has to petition a notice of deficiency to the Tax Court.
2. The period that the case is under appeal.

Under prior law, no authority existed for ordering the IRS to refund any amount collected during an Impermissible period, or to refund any amount that was not at issue in an appeal, before the final decision of the Tax Court.

Small Case Procedures.   For proceedings beginning after July 22, 1998, small tax case procedures are available for disputes that involve $50,000 or less. Under prior law, small tax case procedures were limited to disputes involving $10,000 or less. Small tax case procedures can be used, at the taxpayer's request and with the Tax Court's concurrence, for income, estate, gift, certain employment, and certain excise taxes. The proceedings are conducted as informally as possible. Neither briefs nor oral arguments are required. Most taxpayers represent themselves, although they may be represented by anyone admitted to practice before the Tax Court.

ADDITIONAL PROVISIONS FOR TAXPAYER RIGHTS

The rules were expanded for awarding reasonable administrative costs and certain fees incurred after January 18, 1999. Reasonable costs and fees can be received as a prevailing party in a civil action or proceeding when all the following occur:

1. A qualified offer is made to the IRS to settle the case.
2. The IRS rejects the offer.
3. The tax liability (not including interest) later determined by the Court is not more than the amount of the qualified offer.

A *qualified offer* is a written offer made by a taxpayer during the qualified offer period. It must specify both of the following.

1. The amount of the liability (not including interest).
2. That it is a qualified offer when made. It must also remain open until the earliest of the following dates.
   a. The date the offer is rejected.
   b. The date the trial begins.
   c. 90 days from the date of the offer.

A *qualified offer* period is the period beginning with the date that the 30-day letter is mailed by the IRS to the taxpayer and ending on the date that is 30 days before the date the case is first set for trial.

Administrative costs can be awarded for costs incurred after the earliest of the following dates.

1. The date of the notice of deficiency.
2. The date the first letter of proposed deficiency is sent that allows the taxpayer an opportunity to request administrative review in the Appeals Office of IRS.
3. The date the taxpayer receives the Appeals Office of IRS decision.

Attorney Fees

The basic rate of an award for attorney fees has increased from $110 to $125 ($140 for 2000) per hour and it can be higher in certain circumstances. Those circumstances now include the difficulty level of the issues in the case and the availability of tax expertise locally. The basic rate is subject to adjustment each year.

Notice of IRS Contact of Third Parties

The IRS must notify a taxpayer *before* IRS can contact third parties when examining or collecting a tax liability. Third parties may include neighbors, banks, employees, or employers. The IRS must periodically, and upon request, provide notice of specific contacts. This is effective for contacts made after January 18, 1999.

This provision does not apply in the following circumstances:

1. When there is a pending criminal investigation.
2. When providing notice would jeopardize collection of any Tax liability.
3. Where providing notice may result in reprisal against any person.
4. When the taxpayer authorized the contact.

Last Date for Filing Tax Court Petition

Beginning in 1999, each notice that the IRS mails out must specify the last date on which a timely petition can be filed with the Tax Court. This date is the 90th day after the date that the notice of deficiency is mailed by the IRS.

Explanation of Claim for Refund Disallowance

Beginning January 19, 1999, the IRS must explain to the taxpayer the specific reasons why a claim for refund is disallowed or partially disallowed. This puts into law an existing practice of the IRS. Claims for refund can be disallowed based on a preliminary review or an examination by a revenue agent. This means the taxpayer must receive a form explaining that the claim is disallowed for one of the following reasons.

1. It was filed late.
2. It was based solely on the unconstitutionality of the revenue acts.
3. It was waived as part of a settlement.
4. It covered a tax year or issues that were part of a closing agreement or an offer in compromise.
5. It was related to a return closed by a final court order.
6. A revenue agent's report explaining the reasons that is disallowed.

Chapter 39

The Economic Growth and Tax Relief Reconciliation Act of 2001

CONTENTS

A Timeline for Key Provisions in the 10-Year Cut Plan   **39.02**
CPA/PFSs May Benefit Most from the Tax Relief Act   **39.03**
Income Tax Rate Cuts   **39.03**
Alternative Minimum Tax Relief   **39.05**
Estate Tax Relief   **39.05**
Gift Tax   **39.06**
Marriage Penalty Relief   **39.06**
Child-Related Tax Relief   **39.07**
Dependent Care Tax Credit   **39.08**
Education Tax Cuts   **39.09**
Retirement Savings and Pension Provisions   **39.11**
Benefits for Business Taxpayers   **39.13**

Many taxpayers were confused by the whys and wherefores of what they considered a windfall check as a result of the Economic Growth and Tax Relief Reconciliation Act (EGTRRA) of 2001. It was all because of the creation of a new 10% rate bracket that resulted in "advance refund" checks being issued to most taxpayers by October 1, 2001. The new 10% rate technically started January 1, 2002.

A credit was available to taxpayers in 2001 which, in effect, accelerated to a 10% income tax rate bracket benefit for 2001. This meant $300 for most taxpayers, $600 for joint filers and $500 for heads of household in 2001 in the form of advance refund checks. The checks were sent to all eligible taxpayers (dead or alive) based on their 2000 returns. Trusts and estates, nonresident aliens, and taxpayers claimed as dependents were not eligible for the refund.

Other facets of the $1.35 trillion tax cut covering 10 years with 85 major provisions, 441 Internal Revenue Code changes, and reams and reams of official documents may have a more lasting effect, but not a greater initial impact.

A Timeline for Key Provisions in the 10-Year Cut Plan

2001
- A 10% tax bracket was created (applies to first $6,000 of annual taxable income for individuals, $12,000 for married couples).
- As of July 1, other income tax rates dropped from 39.6% to 38.6%; 36% to 35%; 31% to 30%; 28% to 27%.
- The child credit was increased from $500 to $600.
- The Treasury Department began mailing refunds in late summer.

2002
- Tuition deduction began, with a $3,000 deduction allowed for individual taxpayers with less than $65,000 annual income ($130,000 for married couples).
- An increase in annual contribution limits to IRAs began.
- An increase in annual contribution limits to 401(k)s began.
- The estate tax phaseout began. The individual exemption on estates increased to $1 million from $675,000.

2004
- Income tax rates drop another 1 percentage point.
- College tuition deduction rises to a limit of $4,000.

2005
- The child credit increases to $700.
- Marriage penalty relief begins: Changes in the standard deduction for married couples and adjustment of their 15% rate begin to take effect.

2006
- All rate reductions are fully phased in: Income tax rates drop from 37.6% to 35%; 34% to 33%; 29% to 28%; 26% to 25%.

- The increase in the 401(k) contribution limit is completed; it reaches $15,000 from the present $10,500.

2008
- The increase in the IRA contribution limit is completed; it reaches $5,000.

2009
- The marriage penalty relief is fully phased in.
- The child credit increases to $800.
- The individual estate tax exemption rises to $3.5 million.

2010
- The child credit increases to $1,000.
- The estate tax is repealed.

2011
- If not picked up by a future Congress, these provisions will cease to be in effect.

CPA/PFSs May Benefit Most from the Tax Relief Act

The relief measure portion of the law forms the largest tax cut in over 20 years. Enter the tax CPA/PFS who is required to reconsider many tax and other financial planning decisions. The new law presents a complicated array of back-loaded benefits, with varying effective dates covering 10 years. Some provisions are retroactive; some started in 2002 but required immediate planning to max-imize benefits; others won't start for 5, 10, or more years, but could affect deci-sions made earlier.

The conscientious CPA began immediately "crunching the numbers" for clients because of the need to consider the time-based phase-in projections and recommendations in the Act. The law raises many new opportunities, pit-falls, and complications. Taxpayers and their accountants cannot afford to over-look them. The various provisions underscore the need not only for tax plan-ning but also for much broader personal financial planning during the next 10 years. This is necessary even without the complication of more tax legislation that followed.

Income Tax Rate Cuts

The centerpiece of the EGTRRA is a $958 billion consolidation and reduction of the marginal tax rates for individuals. Most taxpayers came out ahead under these rate cuts, which started with the creation of the new 10% rate bracket mentioned earlier. All other individual income tax rates, except the 15% rate, were also cut for 2001, effectively by 0.5 percent across the board for the 2001 tax year. Those cuts, however, were not subject to advance refunds.

The retroactive rate cuts for 2001—from the across-the-board benefit of the new 10% rate to the reduced 27.5, 30.5, 35.5 and 39.1% effective rates for 2001 taxpayers, may have at first seemed small. And, in fact, they were when compared to benefits gained from rate cuts made over the next five years, when the new tax rates really kick in.

There are now six rate brackets for individuals. The new 10% rate is taken from the current 15% bracket. For 2002–2007, the new 10% bracket applies to the first $12,000 of income for couples, $6,000 for singles, and $10,000 for heads of household. This changes to $14,000, $7,000, and $10,000, respectively, after 2008. Thereafter, it is adjusted for inflation.

As mentioned, the savings becomes more dramatic along the line. For example, tax savings from the rate tax cut for married couples filing jointly, projected for 2006 and thereafter show that:

- With $60,000 taxable income, the annual tax savings will be $701.
- With $100,000 taxable income, the annual tax savings will be $2,740.
- With $200,000 taxable income, the annual tax savings will be $7,901.
- With $300,000 taxable income, the annual tax savings will be $10,676.

Ways and Means

Figuring out winners and losers by running through the numbers based on the new tax rate schedules is the easy part. More complicated is assessing the relative importance that lower rates will have in future tax planning strategies. Below is a short list of some of the areas the PFS and client should consider:

1. Use of the lower tax brackets is one method of family income shifting. As long as the family member is not subject to the "kiddie tax"(under 14 years of age), shifting up to $6,000 in income (for example, dividend or interest income) to a child or other family member can save 25% in taxes even when the new rates are fully phased in. In other words, the saving is the difference between the 10% and 35% brackets.

2. The planning opportunities after a phased-in rate cut will be based on postponing the recognition of income until a lower-rate year, i.e., to a year during the phase-in of the new rates or to a post-2006 year. On the other hand, lower rates on ordinary income will take some of the value off converting wages to incentive stock options and other equity-based remuneration.

3. Personal service corporations were taxed at a flat 35% rate in 2001 and regular corporations were taxed at graduated rates from 15 to 38%. With personal income tax rates moving substantially lower than the average corporate rate, the probability is that many businesses may consider switching to sole proprietorships, partnerships, and S corporations rather than continuing as C corporations.

4. A rate cut makes tax-exempt investments less competitive unless they are able to match the change with higher yields. Similarly, the benefits of operating as a tax-exempt organization are devalued as the general tax rate decreases.

ALTERNATIVE MINIMUM TAX RELIEF

Those who are subject to the AMT will receive no rate reduction. Rates are still 26% for the first $175,000 of AMT income after applying a $45,000 exemption (unadjusted for inflation since 1986), and 28% for the balance. According to projections, the number of taxpayers subject to the AMT under its current form will increase sixfold by the time all benefits under this new tax law are phased in.

The new law, however, does begin to address a part of the AMT problem. It makes permanent the use of the child credit to offset AMT and repeals the AMT offsets of refundable credits. It also increases the AMT exemption for joint filers by $4,000 and for single taxpayers by $2,000, but only for the 2001–2004 period. All indications are that this is not the end of Congressional interest in the AMT. Its increasingly threatening impact upon the middle-class taxpayer will almost force Congress to "fix" or eliminate the tax. But at what cost? (For a further discussion of the "AMT problem," see Chapter 41, "Job Creation and Worker Assistance Act of 2002.")

ESTATE TAX RELIEF

Personal Financial Specialists, take note. A financial columnist in a top U.S. newspaper began a column as follows: "The estate tax may be headed for the graveyard but estate planning isn't." The columnist, as well as many lawyers, accountants, and affluent clients, is well aware of some of the convoluted provisions. Estate planning may very well become more, rather than less, complicated as planners ponder the estate tax "repeal" and the way certain property is taxed. Some may contemplate the wisdom of attempting to break into trusts set up under the old rules.

Congress and the President may claim to have repealed the "death tax." However, it is dead for only one year—2010. Because of budgetary restrictions, the new law allows the current estate tax rules, rates, and exemptions to come back in force in 2011, if Congress doesn't reverse course and completely repeal the estate tax or "revise" it.

Regardless, at this point, the estate tax continues with increasing exemption from $1 million to $3.5 million through 2009 until 2010, when it is repealed only for that year. In order to come within budget limitations and still accomplish the repeal, the estate tax relief that has been scheduled for the interim years (2001–2009) has also been significantly scaled back.

Estate tax repeal has become estate tax complexity leading to a great deal of uncertainty. Many in finance and government believe that the prospect of the automatic reinstatement of 2001 estate tax rules in 2011 will force Congress to face the entire issue again, possibly in a very altered political climate. Then the PFS and clients will have still another legislative maze to confront.

Slowly, Slowly It Phases Out

Year	Top Estate Tax Rate	Exemption Amount
2002	50%	$1 million
2003	49%	$1 million
2004	48%	$1.5 million
2005	47%	$1.5 million
2006	46%	$2 million
2007	45%	$2 million
2008	45%	$2 million
2009	45%	$3.51 million
2010	repealed	N/A
2011	55%	$1 million

GIFT TAX

The new law is designed to prevent significant use of gifts to transfer income-laden property from higher- to lower-rate taxpayers. Therefore, a modified gift tax is still in place. Starting in 2010, gifts in excess of a lifetime $1 million exemption would be subject to a gift tax equal to the top individual income tax rate at that time.

MARRIAGE PENALTY RELIEF

Dual-income married couples, who now often pay more tax than two singles with the same combined income, will get modest tax relief eventually. This relief, which starts in 2005, has two phases—an expanded 15% tax bracket and a larger standard deduction.

One of the inequities in the current tax code relating to both-employed married couples is that the standard deduction is less than twice the size of a single person's standard deduction. Moreover, the income thresholds where higher tax brackets kick in for marrieds also aren't at twice the level for singles. Consequently, if a dual-income couple were to live together rather than marry, they'd get bigger deductions and pay less tax.

To solve this, the standard deduction for a married couple filing jointly, which currently amounts to 160% of the standard deduction for singles, will rise to 174% in 2005, then to 200% of the standard deduction for singles in 2009.

The 15% tax bracket for married couples will also eventually rise until it's twice the 15% bracket for singles. These changes would save a relatively low-income couple up to $225 a year. High-income couples could save as much as $594 if they don't itemize deductions.

Statistically, most taxpayers above the new 25% tax bracket will not be taking the standard deduction and, therefore, will continue to be subject to the current marriage penalty. On the other hand, expansion of the 15% rate will not impact those who currently are in the 15% bracket; that is, single taxpayers with taxable incomes of under $27,050 and married taxpayers with taxable incomes below the $45,200 level.

CHILD-RELATED TAX RELIEF

One of the more generous and more immediate tax breaks in the tax package is the doubling of the current child tax credit to $1,000, phased in over 10 years. The increase was effective for tax years beginning after December 31, 2000.

The credit for parents of dependent children aged 16 or younger increases gradually and will not be fully implemented until 2011. Retroactive application increased the credit to $600 for 2001. The phase-in schedule for the child credit is:

- $600—2001 to 2004
- $700—2005 to 2008
- $800—2009
- $1,000—2010 and after

A middle-income family with three young children saw its child tax credit rise in 2001 from $1,500 to $1,800. However, only parents of a child younger than 8 years of age at that time will realize the $1,000 for that child when the credit is fully phased in. Assuming a 3.25% annual inflation rate, the $1,000 credit will be worth only $747 in current dollars by 2010.

However, in addition, the 2001 law allows the credit to be claimed against the alternative minimum tax permanently, and repeals the AMT offset of refundable credits. The credit is made refundable to the extent of 10% of the taxpayer's earned income in excess of $10,000 for 2001–2004, increasing to 15% after 2004.

And it does mean more when parents realize that a "tax credit" reduces their tax bill dollar for dollar, rather than a "reduction" which merely reduces the amount of income subject to taxation.

The downside: Those who earn more than the set amounts can lose all or part of this credit. The credit is reduced by $50 for each $1,000 when the income exceeds $110,000 if married or $75,000 if single.

The upside: For working low-income parents, the credit is partially refundable even if they pay no income tax. The formula for figuring how much of the credit could be refunded is complex. Therefore, if the family does not get help, they could conceivably lose the credit.

Adoption Credits

Tax credits that help defray the cost of adoption are boosted and made permanent. The maximum credit, currently $5,000, rose to $10,000 in 2002. Those who adopt special needs children (credit currently $6,000) will be able to claim a $10,000 tax credit in the year the adoption is completed, regardless of whether they had qualified adoption expenses.

Employer-paid adoption assistance of up to $10,000 per child will also is tax-free. But both breaks begin to phase out once a family's income exceeds $150,000 annually, although the new law does double the present income phase-out starting point of $75,000. The new limits are effective starting in 2002.

Employer-Provided Child Care Facilities

After 2001, employers are allowed a credit of 25% of qualified expenses for employee child care and 10% of qualified expenses for child care resource and referral services, up to $150,000 per year credit.

DEPENDENT CARE TAX CREDIT

The law increases the dependent care credit rate from 30 to 35%, and increases the amount of eligible employment-related expenses from $2,400 to $3,000, and from $4,800 to $6,000 for more than one qualifying individual. It also increased the beginning point of phase-out income to $15,000 of adjusted gross income, starting in 2002.

EDUCATION TAX CUTS

Educational incentive provisions was expanded. Eventually, incentives may become so attractive that even the least inclined will decide they can't afford not to take advantage of educational opportunities.

Among those who should pay close attention to all of the new and existing education provisions is the family CPA, whether he or she specializes in financial planning or not. With so many stipulations with a growing number of provisos, it is necessary to compare and choose judiciously those provisions that provide the greatest benefit for the specific case and individual. Much depends upon the economic status of the family or individual and the age of the intended student.

Among education-related tax breaks, provisions, and changes included in the Act were:

1. Expansion of definitions relating to, and increase in flexibility of, qualified State programs.
2. Expansion of qualified State tuition plans to include approved private college and university prepaid tuition plans.
3. More generous deductions for student loan interest.
4. A temporary above-the-line college tuition deduction.
5. Permanent extension of the employee exclusion for employer-provided educational assistance. Graduate-level work is now included.
6. Expanded contribution limits to education IRAs.
7. Penalty-free contributions to education IRAs and qualified state tuition programs may be made in the same year.
8. HOPE and Lifetime Learning tax credits may be claimed in the same year as education IRA distributions, as long as the IRA distribution is not used to pay for the same costs used to claim the education credit.

College Tuition Deduction

This law introduced an above-the-line deduction for qualified higher education expenses:

For 2002–2003, a single taxpayer with adjusted gross income below $65,000 ($130,000 if married) is entitled to an above-the-line tuition deduction of $3,000 each year.

In 2004 and 2005, the deduction increases to $4,000 for those with that same AGI. Single taxpayers with incomes up to $80,000 and joint filers with incomes up to $160,000 are permitted a maximum deduction of $2,000 in 2004 and 2005.

After 2005, this deduction is scheduled to sunset to fit the bill's budget restrictions. The deduction cannot be claimed in the same year as a HOPE or Lifetime Learning credit for the same student.

Education Savings Accounts

Distributions from education Individual Retirement Accounts or "education savings accounts" were declared free from federal taxation if they are used to pay for qualified education expenses. The legislation expanded the importance of education IRAs to future family savings plans. (PFSs take note!)

The new law raised the limit dramatically, from $500 to $2,000. It also exempts special-needs beneficiaries from the prohibition against contributions being made after a beneficiary turns 18. Starting in 2002, contributions are allowable not only from individuals, but also from corporations, tax-exempt organizations, and other entities. Contributions counted toward any tax year will be permissible until April 15 of the following year, rather than being cut off on December 31.

The AGI ceiling of those who may contribute to an education savings account has also been raised. The current contribution phase-out range for joint filers of $150,000–$160,000 jumps to $190,000–$220,000—twice the range for single filers.

In one of the more controversial provisions in the new law, proceeds in education savings accounts are now available to pay for elementary and secondary school tuition—public and private—as well as the costs of higher education. Covered expenses include tutoring, computer equipment, room and board, uniforms, and extended day program costs.

Enhanced Student Loan Deductions

The 2001 law permits more student loan interest to be deducted. Prior rules permitted taxpayers to deduct up to $2,500 in student loan interest above-the-line. The deduction also had been severely limited by the rule that a taxpayer's adjusted gross income had to fall under a certain threshold and the interest had to be attributable to payments made during the first 60 months in which interest payments were required. The law removed these restrictions. It raised the income phase-out thresholds to $55,000–$65,000, from $40,000–$50,000, for singles, and to $100,000–$130,000, from $60,000–$75,000, for joint filers. These amounts are adjusted annually for inflation after 2002.

It repealed both the annual dollar limit on the amount of the deduction and the 60-month limit. Voluntary payments, such as interest-only payments made while a loan is in forbearance, are also eligible for above-the-line deductibility under EGTRRA.

Qualified Tuition Plans

The law expands the scope of qualified tuition programs and alters the tax treatment of distributions. Prior to this law, taxpayers could prepay higher education tuition costs only under State-sponsored qualified tuition programs. Now, approved private colleges and universities are able to sponsor qualified tuition programs as well. Additionally, distributions from State-sponsored qualified tuition programs were excludable from gross income if made after December 31, 2001. Distributions from the non-State programs would be excludable if made after December 31, 2003.

Employer-Provided Assistance

As mentioned earlier, EGTRRA makes permanent the employer-provided educational assistance exclusion (up to $5,000 annually), and extends coverage for both undergraduate and graduate courses.

RETIREMENT SAVINGS AND PENSION PROVISIONS

The Act provides several improvements to retirement savings programs, including increases in income and contribution limits for Individual Retirement Accounts (IRAs). These were generally effective beginning in 2002.

Although reduced tax rates leave taxpayers with more money to put in IRAs or 401(k) plans, they also make saving for retirement on a tax-deferred basis less of a priority. One clear exception is that lower tax rates should make Roth IRAs more attractive, especially for those who believe tax rates will go up in the future, when they will be withdrawing IRA assets.

Other modifications include increases in deferrals, overall contributions, and deductions; increases in the compensation base for qualified retirement plans and government-sponsored programs; plus provisions for catch-up contributions to both IRAs and other retirement programs for taxpayers age 50 and older.

Pension reform comprises over a third of the new law in terms of the bill's text. Retirement savings incentives, including expansion of IRAs and 401(k)plans, are projected to cost $40 billion. Retirement savings and pension reform in total is pegged at approximately $50 billion.

Other provisions:

1. Simplify or ease nondiscrimination testing requirements.
2. Permit rollovers among IRAs and other retirement plans.
3. Liberalize some distributions rules.

4. Simplify some administrative and reporting requirements.
5. Correct technical issues for S Corporation Employee Stock.
6. Shorten vesting schedules.
7. Permit workers to become vested and eligible for employer matching contributions in three rather than five years.
8. Increase portability of pension assets.

As mentioned above, the 2001 law permits greater contributions to tax-advantaged savings plans, such as qualified plans including 401(k)s and IRAs. To be more specific, following are some of the changes to qualified plan and contribution limits.

IRA Contribution Limits

The contribution limits for both traditional and Roth IRAs will gradually increase to an annual cap of $5,000. The progression is $3,000 for 2002–2004; $4,000 for 2005–2007; and $5,000 for 2008 and after, with annual adjustments for inflation after 2008.

Catch-Up Contributions

Taxpayers age 50 and over will be permitted to contribute catch-ups to their IRAs: an additional $500 in 2002–2005; $1,000 in 2006 and all years thereafter. These catch-up payments can be deductible or made to a Roth IRA, if the base-line AGI limits are met for regular contributions for the year.

Defined Contribution and Defined Benefits Plan Limits

Beginning in 2002, the limit on annual additions to a defined contribution plan increased to $40,000. The annual limit on benefits under a defined benefits plan increased from $140,000 to $160,000.

401(k) Contribution Limits

The limit on salary reduction contributions to IRC § 401(k)-type plans (including 403(b) annuities and salary reduction SEPs) will increase from $10,500 to $15,000 by 2006. The progression was a rise to $11,000 in 2002, and an increase of an additional $1,000 each year until 2006.

Contribution Tax Credit

Lower-income workers are entitled to a tax credit, rather than just a tax deduction, for contributions to retirement savings. Joint filers earning less than $30,000 are entitled to the maximum 50% credit.

Additional Qualified Plan Provisions

The limit on maximum annual elective deferrals to a SIMPLE plan will increase to $10,000 by 2005. It began with $7,000 in 2002 and increase $1,000 each year until the $10,000 limit is reached in 2005. The limit on compensation taken into account under a qualified plan rises to $200,000. It will be increased for inflation in $5,000 increments.

BENEFITS FOR BUSINESS TAXPAYERS

Business taxpayers were included in this section of the law with provisions that:

1. Raise the limit on an employer's deduction for contributions to certain types of defined contribution plans to 25% of compensation.
2. Modernize and streamline pension laws to encourage small businesses to offer pension plans.
3. Provide tax credits for small business start-up costs and matching contributions.
4. Modify some of the "top-heavy" rules.

Chapter 40
Tax Matters

CONTENTS

Need to Adjust Withholding or Estimated Tax Payments for 2002   **40.02**

2001 Changes Affecting Later Years   **40.02**

Tax Benefits for Education   **40.06**

Changes in Earned Income Credit   **40.12**

Child-Oriented Tax Benefits and Considerations   **40.13**

Additional Changes for Later Years   **40.16**

Retirement and Benefit Plans   **40.16**

Community Renewal and Environmental Credits and Deductions   **40.27**

Estate and Gift Taxes   **40.29**

Excise Taxes   **40.30**

Miscellaneous Tax Items   **40.31**

Many of the changes discussed in this chapter result from the Economic Growth and Tax Relief Reconciliation Act of 2001 (EGTRRA), including a *sunset provision* adopted to comply with the Congressional Budget Act of 1974. This provision states that the changes from the act will not apply in tax years beginning after 2010 unless extended by future legislation. (See Chapter 39 for an explanation of the EGTRRA basic provisions.)

Some of the changes covered in this chapter are:

- Tax rate reductions.
- Changes to various credits, among them, the earned income credit, adoption credit, and child tax credit.
- Changes to the student loan interest deduction.
- Increase in the allowable amount of individual retirement arrangement (IRA) contributions.
- Higher contribution and benefit limits for retirement plans.
- Additional contributions to retirement plans allowed for those age 50 and over.

NEED TO ADJUST WITHHOLDING OR ESTIMATED TAX PAYMENTS FOR 2002

If a taxpayer's tax for 2002 will be more or less than his or her 2001 tax, it may be necessary to adjust the withholding or estimated tax payments accordingly. If the tax will decrease, the taxpayer can get the benefit of lower taxes throughout the year. If more will be owed, a penalty can be avoided when filing the 2002 tax return by adjusting the amount withheld.

2001 CHANGES AFFECTING LATER YEARS

Several broad items that took effect in 2001 but have not been widely publicized or are the result of tax legislation enacted after EGTRRA affect future tax filings are discussed in the paragraphs immediately following.

Tax Benefits for Parents of Kidnapped Children

A child who has been kidnapped may still qualify the taxpayer for the following tax benefits:

1. The exemption deduction for a dependent.
2. A filing status of head of household or qualifying widow(er) with dependent child.
3. The child tax credit.
4. The earned income credit.

Both of the following statements must be true:

1. The child must be presumed by law enforcement authorities to have been kidnapped by someone who is *not* a member of the taxpayer's family or the child's family.

2. The child must have qualified as the taxpayer's dependent for the part of the year before the kidnapping (or, in the case of the earned income credit and filing status determinations, the child must have lived with the taxpayer for more than half of the part of the year before the kidnapping).

If both statements are true, the child is treated as the taxpayer's dependent for the year. The child is also treated as continuing to live with the taxpayer after the kidnapping. This may enable the taxpayer to qualify for the tax benefits listed.

This special treatment for a kidnapped child applies until the child is returned. However, the last year this treatment can apply is the earlier of:

1. The year the child is determined to be dead.
2. The year the child would have reached age 18.

Restitution Made to Holocaust Victims

Payments received by Holocaust victims (or their heirs) as restitution for Nazi persecution are not taxable. The taxpayer also does not include them in any computations in which the taxpayer would ordinarily add excludable income to the adjusted gross income, such as the computation to determine the taxable part of Social Security benefits.

Postponed Tax Deadlines in Disaster Areas

The IRS may postpone for up to one year certain tax deadlines of people who are affected by a Presidentially declared disaster. The tax deadlines the IRS may postpone include those for filing income and employment tax returns, paying income and employment taxes and making contributions to a traditional IRA or Roth IRA. If any tax deadline is postponed, the IRS will publicize the postponement in the area and publish a news release, revenue ruling, revenue procedure, notice, announcement or other guidance in the Internal Revenue Bulletin.

Tax Relief for Victims of Terrorist Attacks

The Victims of Terrorism Tax Relief Act of 2001 provides tax relief for those injured or killed as a result of terrorist attacks, certain survivors of those killed as a result of terrorist attacks, and others who were affected by terrorist attacks. The act does the following:

1. Forgives federal income tax liabilities of individuals who die as a result of:
   a. The April 19, 1995, attack on the Alfred P. Murrah Federal Building (Oklahoma City).

b. The September 11, 2001, terrorist attacks against the United States.

c. The terrorist attacks involving anthrax occurring after September 10, 2001, and before January 1, 2002.

2. Provides for the tax-free treatment of the following types of income:

a. Qualified disaster relief payments made after September 10, 2001, to cover personal, family, living or funeral expenses incurred because of a terrorist attack.

b. Certain disability payments received in tax years ending after September 10, 2001, for injuries sustained in a terrorist attack.

c. Certain death benefits paid by an employer to the survivor of an employee because the employee died as a result of a terrorist attack.

d. Debt cancellations made after September 10, 2001, and before January 1, 2002, if the debts were canceled because an individual died as a result of a terrorist attack.

e. Payments from the September 11th Victim Compensation Fund of 2001.

3. Allows the IRS to postpone for up to one year certain tax deadlines of people who are affected by a terrorist attack.

4. Reduces the estate tax of individuals who die as a result of the Oklahoma City terrorist attack, the September 11 terrorist attack, and the anthrax attacks.

Redesignation of Estimated Tax Payments

As a result of the economic disruptions caused by the September 11, 2001, terrorist attacks, some people believe their tax liability for the current year will be lower than the total of the estimated tax payments they have already made.

The IRS will allow them to redesignate their estimated tax payments as deposits of employment taxes and income taxes withheld. If, as a result of the redesignation, the amount of the estimated tax payments is reduced below the amount required to pay the estimated tax obligation, they may be liable for an underpayment penalty.

Afghanistan Designated a Combat Zone

By Executive Order, Afghanistan was designated a combat zone beginning September 19, 2001. Certain benefits are available to members of the Armed Forces serving in combat zones.

Survivor Benefits for Public Safety Officers

For tax years beginning after 2001, a survivor annuity received by the spouse, former spouse or child of a public safety officer killed in the line of duty will generally be excluded from the recipient's income, regardless of the date of the officer's death. Survivor benefits received before 2002 are excludable only if the officer died after 1996.

Election Out of the Installment Method

For sales occurring after December 16, 1999, accrual-basis persons were required to report installment sales under the accrual method of accounting. The Installment Tax Correction Act of December 28, 2000, repealed that requirement.

If someone entered into an installment sale after December 16, 1999, and filed an income tax return by April 16, 2001, reporting the sale on an accrual method, he or she has IRS approval to revoke the effective election out of the installment method.

To revoke the election, the CPA must file an amended return for the year of the installment sale (and any other year affected by the sale), reporting the gain on the installment method. The taxpayer generally has three years from the due date of the original return to file an amended return.

The Cash Method of Accounting

For tax years ending on or after December 31, 2001, a qualifying small-business taxpayer can choose to use the cash method of accounting and not account for inventories. A qualifying small-business taxpayer is anyone with average annual gross receipts of more than $1,000,000 but less than or equal to $10,000,000 who is not prohibited from using the cash method of accounting under Section 448 of the Internal Revenue Code. Certain other requirements must be met. These rules do not apply to persons with average annual gross receipts of $1,000,000 or less.

Securities Futures Contracts

A securities futures contract is a new financial product that is a contract of sale for future delivery of a single security or of a narrow-based security index. Gain or loss from the sale or exchange of the contract will generally have the same character as gain or loss from transactions in the property to which the contract relates. Any capital gain or loss on a sale or exchange of the contract will be considered short term, regardless of how long the contract is held.

Lower Tax Rates for Capital Gain

Beginning in 2001, the 10 percent capital gain rate is lowered to 8 percent for qualified five-year gain. Qualified five-year gain is long-term capital gain from the sale of property that was held for more than five years and that would otherwise be subject to the 10 percent or 20 percent capital gain rate.

Medical Savings Accounts Program Extended and Renamed

A medical savings account (MSA) is a tax-exempt trust or custodial account with a financial institution (e.g., a bank or an insurance company) in which the taxpayer can save money for future medical expenses. To qualify for an MSA, taxpayers must be employees of a small employer or self-employed. They must also have a health plan with a high deductible and have no other health insurance coverage except permitted coverage. The pilot project for MSAs was scheduled to end December 31, 2000, but has been extended until December 31, 2002. MSAs have also been renamed Archer MSAs.

TAX BENEFITS FOR EDUCATION

The following items explain the changes to tax benefits for education.

Employer-Provided Educational Assistance

The tax-free status of up to $5,250 of employer-provided educational assistance benefits each year for undergraduate-level courses was scheduled to end for courses beginning after 2001. This benefit has been extended indefinitely, and, beginning in 2002, it also applies to graduate-level courses.

Qualified Tuition Programs

Beginning in 2002, changes apply to what were formerly known as qualified state tuition programs. They have also been renamed qualified tuition programs (QTPs).

Distributions from State-Maintained QTPs.   A distribution from a QTP established and maintained by a state (or an agency or instrumentality of the state) can be excluded from income if the amount distributed is used for higher education. Previously, the beneficiary was required to pay tax on any earnings from a QTP unless the earnings were tax free under some other provision of the law.

QTPs Maintained by Educational Institutions.   Someone can make contributions to a QTP established and maintained by one or more eligible educational institutions. Any earnings distributed before January 1, 2004, will be taxable. Previously, contributions could be made only to a QTP established and maintained by a state (or an agency or instrumentality of the state).

Rollovers of QTPs to Family Members.   For purposes of rollovers, and changes of designated beneficiaries, the definition of family members is expanded to include first cousins of the beneficiary.

Rollovers of QTPs Without Changing Beneficiary.   Amounts in a QTP can be rolled over, tax free, to another QTP set up for the same beneficiary. However, the rollover of credits or other amounts from one QTP to another QTP for the benefit of the same beneficiary cannot apply to more than one transfer within any 12-month period.

Qualified Expenses.   Calculation of the amount that is considered reasonable for room-and-board expenses has been changed. Taxpayers must contact the educational institution for their qualified room-and-board costs.

Special Needs Beneficiaries.   The definition of "qualified higher-education expenses" has been expanded to include expenses of a special needs beneficiary that are necessary for that person's enrollment or attendance at an eligible institution.

Coordination with Coverdell ESAs.   Taxpayers can make contributions to QTPs and Coverdell education savings accounts (ESAs) (the new name for education IRAs) in the same year for the same beneficiary. Previously, they could only make contributions to one program or the other.

Coverdell ESAs (Formerly Education IRAs)

Beginning in 2002, the following changes apply to Coverdell education savings accounts.

Maximum Contribution.   The most someone can contribute each year to a Coverdell ESA is increased from $500 to $2,000, a rather sizable jump.

Income Limits.   If the taxpayer files a joint return, the amount he or she can contribute to a Coverdell ESA will be phased out (gradually reduced) if his or her modified adjusted gross income (MAGI) is more than $190,000 but less than $220,000. The taxpayer will not be able to contribute to a Coverdell ESA if the MAGI is $220,000 or more. This is an increase in the phaseout range for married people filing joint returns (which was between $150,000 and $160,000 in 2001).

Contribution Due Dates. The final date on which someone can make contributions to a Coverdell ESA for any year has been extended to the due date of the return for that year (not including extensions). Calendar-year taxpayers will have until April 15, 2003, to make their contribution for the 2002 tax year. In previous years, contributions were required to be made by December 31.

Correcting Excess Contributions. The 6 percent excise tax on excess contributions will not apply to any excess contributions withdrawn by June 1 of the following year if the *earnings* on the excess are also withdrawn. Previously, these amounts had to be withdrawn by the due date for the beneficiary's return or, if no return was required, by April 15, of the following year.

Qualified Expenses. The definition of qualified education expenses has been expanded to include elementary and secondary education expenses. Qualified elementary and secondary education expenses include expenses for:

1. Tuition, fees, academic tutoring, special needs services in the case of a special needs beneficiary, books, supplies and other equipment incurred in connection with enrollment or attendance as an elementary or secondary school student at a public, private or religious school.
2. Room and board, uniforms, transportation and supplementary items and services (including extended day programs) that are *required* or *provided* by a public, private, or religious school in connection with such enrollment or attendance.
3. The purchase of computer technology or equipment or Internet access and related services, if such technology, equipment or services are to be used by the beneficiary and the beneficiary's family during any of the years the beneficiary is in school (not including expenses for computer software designed for sports, games, or hobbies unless the software is predominantly educational in nature).

Special Needs Beneficiaries. The taxpayer can continue to make contributions to a Coverdell ESA for a special needs beneficiary after his or her 18th birthday. A person can also leave assets in a Coverdell ESA set up for a special needs beneficiary after the beneficiary reaches age 30.

Coordination with HOPE and Lifetime Learning Credits. Taxpayers can claim the HOPE or lifetime learning credit in the same year they take a tax free distribution from a Coverdell ESA, provided the distribution from the

Coverdell ESA is not used for the same expenses for which the credit is claimed. Previously, individuals could not claim the HOPE or lifetime learning credit if they received a tax-free withdrawal from a Coverdell ESA and did not waive the tax-free treatment of the withdrawal.

Coordination with Qualified Tuition Programs. Taxpayers can make contributions to Coverdell ESAs and qualified tuition programs in the same year for the same beneficiary. Previously, they could make contributions to only one program or the other.

New Deduction for Higher-Education Expense

Beginning in 2002, taxpayers may be able to deduct qualified tuition and related expenses paid during the year for themselves, their spouse or a dependent, *even if they do not itemize deductions.*

Qualified Tuition and Related Expenses. Qualified tuition and related expenses are tuition and fees required for enrollment or attendance at an *eligible educational institution.* They may be paid for the expenses of:

1. The taxpayer.
2. His or her spouse.
3. A dependent for whom they claim an exemption.

Student activity fees and fees for course-related books, supplies and equipment are included in qualified tuition and related expenses *only* if the fees must be paid *to the institution as a condition of enrollment or attendance.*

An eligible educational institution is any college, university, vocational school or other post-secondary educational institution eligible to participate in a student aid program administered by the Department of Education. This encompasses virtually all accredited, public, non-profit, and proprietary (privately owned profit-making) post-secondary institutions. (The particular educational institution should be able to tell the taxpayer if an educational institution is eligible.)

A person must reduce qualified expenses by the amount of any tax-free educational assistance received. Tax-free educational assistance includes:

1. Scholarship.
2. Pell grants.
3. Employer-provided educational assistance.
4. Veterans' educational assistance.
5. Any other nontaxable payments (other than gifts, bequests or inheritances) received for education expenses.

Expenses that are not considered "qualified tuition and related expenses" include the cost of:

1. Medical expenses (including student health fees).
2. Insurance.
3. Room and board.
4. Transportation.
5. Similar personal, living, or family expenses.

This is true even if the fee must be paid to the institution as a condition of enrollment or attendance. Qualified tuition and related expenses generally do not include expenses that relate to any course of instruction or other education that involves sports, games or hobbies or any noncredit course. However, if the course of instruction or other education is part of the student's degree program, these expenses can qualify.

Maximum Deduction.   For tax years beginning in 2002 and 2003, the taxpayer may be able to deduct up to $3,000 paid for qualified tuition and related expenses as an adjustment to income. For 2004 and 2005, the taxpayer may be able to deduct up to $4,000.

Income Limits.   For tax years beginning in 2002 and 2003, the CPA can deduct up to $3,000 of qualified tuition and related expenses if the MAGI is not more than $65,000 ($130,000 on a joint return). If the MAGI is more than $65,000 ($130,000 on a joint return), the CPA cannot take the deduction.

For tax years beginning in 2004 and 2005, the taxpayer can deduct up to $4,000 of qualified tuition and related expenses if the MAGI is not more than $65,000 ($130,000 on a joint return). If the MAGI is more than $65,000 ($130,000 on a joint return) but not more than $80,000 ($160,000 on a joint return), the accountant can deduct up to $2,000 of qualified tuition and related expenses. If the MAGI is more than $80,000 ($160,000 on a joint return), the deduction cannot be taken.

For purposes of this deduction, the MAGI is the adjusted gross income shown on the taxpayer's income tax return plus any foreign earned income exclusion, foreign housing exclusion or deduction, exclusion of income for bona fide residents of American Samoa and exclusion of income from Puerto Rico.

Coordination with Credits and Other Deductions.   The taxpayer cannot deduct any amount for qualified tuition and related expenses for a year if:

1. A HOPE credit or lifetime learning credit is claimed with respect to expenses of the individual for whom the tuition and related expenses were paid.
2. The expense can be deducted under any other provision of the law.

Coordination with Exclusions.   The CPA must reduce the qualified tuition and related expenses by:

1. Expenses used to figure the amount of interest on qualified U.S. savings bonds that the taxpayer excluded from income because it was used to pay qualified higher-education expenses.
2. Expenses used to figure the amount of any tax-free withdrawals from a Coverdell ESA.
3. Expenses used to figure the portion of any distribution of earnings from a QTP a person excludes from income because the earnings were used to pay the beneficiary's qualified higher-education expenses.

Limits on Eligibility.   The student cannot claim the deduction for qualified tuition and related expenses if any of the following applies:

1. Another taxpayer is entitled to claim an exemption for that individual as a dependent on his or her return. This is true even if the other taxpayer does not actually claim the exemption.
2. The filing status is married filing separate return.
3. The student is a non-resident alien and has not elected to be treated as a resident alien for the tax year.

Year of Deduction.   Generally the taxpayer can deduct only those expenses for a year that are in connection with enrollment at an institution of higher education during the same year. However, it is possible to deduct expenses paid in a year if they are for an academic period beginning within the year or during the first three months of the next year.

Student Name and ID Number.   To take the deduction, the taxpayer must show on the income tax return the name and taxpayer identification number (usually the Social Security number) of the person for whom the expenses were paid.

Termination.   This new deduction is not available for tax years beginning after 2005.

Student Loan Interest Deduction

If the taxpayer pays interest on a student loan, the CPA may be able to deduct the interest as an adjustment to income.

Elimination of 60-Month Limit.   Beginning in 2002, the requirement that the taxpayer can deduct only interest on student loans paid during the first 60 months that interest payments are required is eliminated.

Limit on Deduction Based on MAGI.   Beginning in 2002, the amount of the taxpayer's student loan interest deduction will be phased out (gradually reduced) if the modified adjusted gross income is between $50,000 and $65,000 ($100,000 and $130,000 if a joint return is filed). Someone will not be able to take a deduction for student loan interest if the MAGI is $65,000 or more ($130,000 or more if a joint return is filed). For 2001, the deduction was phased out if the MAGI was between $40,000 and $55,000 ($60,000 and $75,000 if a joint return was filed). The CPA could not take a deduction for student loan interest if the MAGI was $55,000 or more ($75,000 or more if a joint return was filed).

Prior to 2002, the MAGI, for purposes of deducting the student loan interest, was the *adjusted gross income as shown on the return modified by adding back* any:

1. Exclusion of foreign earned income.
2. Exclusion of or deduction for foreign housing.
3. Exclusion of income for bona fide residents of American Samoa.
4. Exclusion of income from Puerto Rico.

Beginning in 2002, the taxpayer must *also add back any deduction of qualified tuition and related expenses.*

Tax-Exempt Bond Financing for Qualified Public Educational Facilities

Beginning in 2002, the private activities for which state and local tax-exempt bonds may be issued will be expanded to include providing qualified public educational facilities. A qualified public educational facility is any school facility that is:

1. Part of a public elementary school or a public secondary school, and
2. Owned by a private, for-profit corporation under a public-private partnership agreement with a state or local educational agency.

The issuer of the bond should be able to tell the taxpayer whether the bond is tax exempt or not.

CHANGES IN EARNED INCOME CREDIT

The following items explain the changes to earned income credit:

1. The amount of earned income credit someone can claim is based, in part, on his or her *earned income.* For tax years after 2001, earned income will

no longer include non-taxable employee compensation. Non-taxable employee compensation includes such amounts as salary deferrals and reductions, excludable dependent care benefits and excluded combat pay.

2. For tax years after 2001, the taxpayer will no longer need to figure *modified* adjusted gross income. The earned income credit will be figured using AGI, *not* MAGI.

3. For tax years after 2001, if two or more persons may be able to claim the same qualifying child, the qualifying child can be claimed only by:

   a. The parents, if they file a joint return.

   b. The parent, if only one of the persons is the child's parent.

   c. The parent with whom the child lived the longest during the year, if two of the persons are the child's parent.

   d. The parent with the highest AGI if the child lives with each parent for the same amount of time during the year.

   e. The person with the highest AGI, if none of the persons is the child's parent.

4. For tax years beginning in 2002, the definition of an eligible foster child is changed. The child will have to live with the taxpayer only for more than half of the tax year. Previously, the child must have lived with the taxpayer the entire year.

5. For tax years beginning in 2002, the earned income credit will no longer be reduced by the amount of alternative minimum tax shown on the tax return.

6. For tax years after 2003, the IRS will disallow earned income credit if the Federal Case Registry of Child Support Orders shows that the taxpayer is the noncustodial parent of a child claimed as a qualifying child for earned income credit.

CHILD-ORIENTED TAX BENEFITS AND CONSIDERATIONS

Following are several tax measures that are oriented in the direction of child care and benefits.

Child Tax Credit Increased and Expanded

The maximum child tax credit for each qualifying child was increased from $500 to $600 beginning in 2001.

The additional child tax credit has also been expanded to include taxpayers with fewer than three qualifying children. If they have taxable earned income of more than $10,000, the taxpayers may be able to claim the credit.

Previously, they had to have three or more qualifying children to claim the additional child tax credit. The additional child tax credit may give a refund even if the taxpayer does not owe any tax.

Effect of Child Tax Credit on Welfare Benefits

Any refund received as a result of taking the additional child tax credit will not be considered income when determining whether the taxpayer is eligible for the following programs, or how much they can receive from them. However, if the amounts they receive are not spent within a certain period of time, they may count as an asset (or resource) and affect eligibility. The programs affected are:

1. Temporary Assistance for Needy Families (TANF).
2. Medicaid and supplemental security income (SSI).
3. Food stamps and low income housing.

Tax Benefits for Adoption Extended and Expanded

Under current law, taxpayers can take a tax credit for expenses paid to adopt a child. In addition, they can exclude from income certain amounts paid or reimbursed by their employer for qualifying adoption expenses under an adoption assistance program. Beginning in 2002, there are significant changes to the credit and exclusion:

1. The credit, which was scheduled to end after 2001 (except for children with special needs), has been permanently extended. The exclusion, which was scheduled to end after 2001, has also been made permanent.
2. Beginning in 2002, the maximum credit and exclusion will increase to $10,000. Beginning in 2003, a $10,000 credit or exclusion will be allowed for the adoption of a child with special needs, regardless of whether the taxpayer has qualifying expenses.
3. The income limit based on *modified adjusted gross income* will also increase. For persons with MAGI of $150,000 or less, the credit or exclusion will not be affected. Incomes between $150,000 and $189,999 will reduce credit or exclusion. Incomes of $190,000 or more will eliminate the credit or exclusion.

Child and Dependent Care Credit Increase

Beginning in 2003, the following changes will be made to the child and dependent care credit:

1. The credit amount can be as much as 35 percent (previously 30 percent) of qualified expenses.

2. The maximum adjusted-gross-income amount that qualifies for the 35 percent rate will be increased from $10,000 to $15,000.

3. The limit on the amount of qualifying expenses will be increased from $2,400 to $3,000 for one qualifying individual and from $4,800 to $6,000 for two or more qualifying individuals.

Credit for Employer-Provided Child Care

An employer can receive a tax credit of 25 percent of the qualified expenses paid for employee child care and 10 percent of qualified expenses paid for child care resource and referral services. This credit cannot exceed $150,000 each year:

Expenses that qualify for this credit include the following:

1. Expenses to acquire, construct, rehabilitate or expand depreciable property for use as a qualified child care facility. This property cannot be part of the taxpayer's or the employee's main home.

2. Expenses to operate a qualified child care facility, including the costs related to training employees, scholarship programs and any increased compensation to employees with higher levels of child care training.

3. Expenses paid to a qualified child care facility under contract to provide child care services to employees.

Qualified child care expenses do not include expenses in excess of the fair market value of the care.

A qualified child care facility is a facility that:

1. Is used mainly to provide child care assistance.

2. Has enrollment open to employees.

3. Has as its enrollees at least 30 percent of the employees' dependents, if the facility is the main trade or business.

4. Does not discriminate in favor of highly compensated employees.

5. Meets the requirements of all applicable laws and regulations, including the licensing of the facility as a child care facility.

Qualified child care resource and referral expenses are amounts paid or incurred under contract to provide child care resource and referral services to employees. The business cannot claim the credit on these expenses if the services offered discriminate in favor of highly compensated employees.

If the business takes a credit for expenses to acquire, construct, rehabilitate or expand a facility, the basis in the facility must be decreased by the amount of that credit.

ADDITIONAL CHANGES FOR LATER YEARS

The following are a few reminders of some of the major changes that will take place in the future:

1. Beginning in 2005, the standard deduction for a single individual and a married individual filing a separate return will be the same. The standard deduction for a married couple filing a joint return will gradually increase until, in 2009, it is twice the amount of the standard deduction for a single individual.
2. Beginning in 2005, the 15 percent income-tax-rate bracket for a married couple filing a joint return will be gradually expanded until, in 2008, it is twice the size of the 15 percent bracket for a single filer.
3. Beginning in 2006, the overall limit on certain itemized deductions will gradually be eliminated.
4. Beginning in 2006, the phaseout of exemptions for taxpayers whose adjusted gross income is above certain threshold amounts will gradually be eliminated.

RETIREMENT AND BENEFIT PLANS

Because Social Security, old-fashioned pension plans and modest saving accounts have long since provided insufficient funds for even the most circumspect retirement, additional ways and means to save are constantly being improved and expanded as explained below.

Social Security and Medicare Taxes

For 2002, the employer and employee will continue to pay:

1. 6.2 percent each for Social Security tax (old age, survivors, and disability insurance), and
2. 1.45% each for Medicare tax (hospital insurance).

For Social Security tax, the maximum amount of 2002 wages subject to the tax has increased to $84,900. For Medicare tax, all covered 2002 wages are subject to the tax.

Credit for Pension Plan Start-Up Costs

Eligible employers who begin a new pension plan for their employees may be able to receive a tax credit of 50 percent of the first $1,000 of qualified start-up costs of the plan. The credit is available for each of the first three years of the plan. In order to qualify, an employer:

1. Must have had 100 or fewer employees who received at least $5,000 of compensation during the preceding year.
2. Must have qualified start-up costs. These are any ordinary and necessary expenses paid to:
   a. Begin or administer an eligible employer plan.
   b. Educate employees about the plan.
3. Must have an eligible employer plan that meets the requirements of a defined benefit or defined contribution plan (including a 401[k] plan), savings incentive match plan for employees (SIMPLE) or simplified employee pension (SEP).

New Credit for Contributions to Retirement Plans and IRAs (Saver's Credit)

Beginning in 2002, employees who make eligible contributions to an employer-sponsored retirement plan or to an individual retirement arrangement (IRA) may be able to take a tax credit. The amount of the saver's credit is based on the contributions made and the credit rate. The credit rate can be as low as 10 percent or as high as 50 percent, depending on the adjusted gross income. The lower the income, the higher the tax credit. The credit rate also depends on filing status.

This credit is scheduled to expire for tax years beginning after 2006.

A testing period has been instituted that consists of the year for which the taxpayer claims the credit, the period after the end of that year and before the due date (including extensions) for filing the return for that year, and the two tax years before that year.

Eligible Contributions and Reductions. Eligible contributions and reductions are enumerated and explained as follows:

1. Traditional or Roth IRA and salary reduction contributions to a 401(k) plan (including a SIMPLE 401[k] plan).
2. A Section 403(b) annuity, an eligible deferred compensation plan of a state or local government (a governmental 457 plan), a SIMPLE IRA plan or a salary reduction SEP (SARSEP).
3. Voluntary after-tax employee contributions to a tax-qualified retirement plan or Section 403(b) annuity. (For purposes of the credit, an employee contribution will be voluntary as long as it is not required as a condition of employment.)

4. Eligible contributions are *reduced* by the sum of:

   a. Any taxable distribution from a qualified retirement plan or from an eligible deferred compensation plan received during the testing period (defined below).

   b. Any distribution from a Roth IRA or a Roth account received during the testing period that is not a qualified rollover contribution to a Roth IRA or is not a rollover to a Roth account. A distribution from a Roth IRA that is not rolled over reduces eligible contributions, even if the distribution is not taxable.

5. A distribution that is a return of a contribution to an IRA (including a Roth IRA) made during the year for which someone claims the credit *does not reduce eligible contributions if:*

   a. The distribution is made before the due date (including extensions) of the tax return for that year.

   b. A person does not take a deduction for the contribution.

   c. The distribution includes any income attributable to the contribution.

6. Any distributions the spouse receives are treated as received by the taxpayer if they file a joint return for the year of the distribution and for the year for which they claim the credit.

7. After the contributions are reduced, the maximum annual contribution on which individuals can base the credit is $2,000 per person.

8. The amount of the credit in any year cannot be more than the amount of tax that the taxpayer would otherwise pay (not taking into account any re- fundable credits or the adoption credit) in any year. If the tax liability is reduced to zero because of other non-refundable credits, such as the HOPE credit, the taxpayer will not be entitled to this credit.

Persons Ineligible to Receive Saver's Credit. A person cannot claim the credit if:

1. He or she is under the age of 18.

2. He or she is a full-time student (explained below).

3. Someone else, such as a parent, claims an exemption on his or her tax return.

4. His or her adjusted gross income (see below) is more than:

   a. $50,000 if the filing status is married filing jointly.

   b. $37,500 if the filing status is head of household.

   c. $25,000 if the filing status is either single, married filing separately, or qualifying widow(er).

An ineligible student is one who during some part of each of five calendar months (not necessarily consecutive) during the calendar year is:

1. A full-time student at a school that has a regular teaching staff, course of study and regularly enrolled body of students in attendance.
2. A student taking a full-time, on-farm training course given by a school that has a regular teaching staff, course of study and regularly enrolled body of students in attendance or a state, county or local government.

A person is a full-time student if they are enrolled for the number of hours or courses the school considers to be full time. (Tax breaks for students are described elsewhere in this chapter.)

In addition to the individual's usual adjusted gross income, he or she must add any exclusion or deduction claimed for the year for:

a. Foreign earned income.
b. Foreign housing costs.
c. Income for residents of American Samoa.
d. Income from Puerto Rico.

Individual Retirement Arrangements

The most that can be contributed to the *traditional IRA* for 2002 is the lesser of:

1. $3,000 (up from $2,000), or
2. The compensation that must be included in income.

If the worker is 50 or older in 2002, the most that can be contributed to the traditional IRA for 2002 is the lesser of:

1. $3,500 (up from $2,000), or
2. The compensation that must be included in income.

Besides being able to contribute a larger amount in 2002, a person may be able to deduct a larger amount.

Increased Roth IRA Contribution Limit. If contributions on someone's behalf is made only to Roth IRAs, the contribution limit for 2002 generally is the lesser of:

1. $3,000 (up from $2,000), or
2. The compensation that must be included in income.

If the taxpayer is 50 or older in 2002 and contributions on his or her behalf are made only to Roth IRAs, the contribution limit for 2002 generally is the lesser of:

1. $3,500 (up from $2,000), or
2. The compensation that must be included in income.

However, if the MAGI is above a certain amount, the contribution limit may be reduced.

Increased Contributions to Both Traditional and Roth IRAs.   If contributions are made to both a Roth IRA and a traditional IRA, the contribution limit for 2002 is the *lesser of:*

1. $3,000 ($3,500 if the worker is 50 or older in 2002) minus all *contributions* (other than employer contributions under a SEP or SIMPLE IRA plan) for the year to all IRAs other than Roth IRAs.
2. *Compensation* that must be included in income minus all contributions (other than employer contributions under a SEP or SIMPLE IRA plan) for the year to all IRAs other than Roth IRAs.

However, if the MAGI is above a certain amount, the contribution limit may be reduced.

Rollovers from Traditional IRAs into Qualified Plans.   A person can roll over tax free a distribution from the traditional IRA made after 2001 into a qualified plan. The part of the distribution that can be rolled over is the part that would otherwise be taxable (includable in income). Qualified plans may, but are not required to, accept such rollovers. Rules applicable to other rollovers, such as the 60-day time limit, apply.

Tax Treatment of Rollovers from an IRA into an Eligible Retirement Plan Other Than an IRA.   For distributions made after 2001, if the taxpayer rolls over a distribution from an IRA into an eligible retirement plan other than an IRA, the part of the distribution rolled over is considered to come first from amounts other than after-tax contributions in any traditional IRA.

This means a distribution from an IRA with after-tax contributions can be rolled over into a qualified plan if there is enough taxable income in other IRAs to cover the after-tax part. The effect of this is to maximize the amount in the traditional IRAs that can be rolled over to a qualified plan.

Generally, a rollover is tax free only if a person makes the rollover contribution by the 60th day after the day he or she receives the distribution.

Beginning with distributions after 2001, the IRS may waive the 60-day requirement where it would be against equity or good conscience not to do so.

For distributions made after 2001, no hardship distribution can be rolled over into an IRA.

Qualified Plans

Plan administrators are now required by the Internal Revenue Code to provide to employees written notice of plan amendments that significantly reduce the rate of future benefit accrual. For plan amendments taking effect after June 6, 2001, the employer or the plan will have to pay an excise tax if *both* of the following occur:

1. A defined benefit plan or money purchase pension plan is amended to provide for a significant reduction in the rate of future benefit accrual.
2. The plan administrator fails to notify the affected individuals and the employee organizations representing them of the reduction.

Retirement Planning Services.   Beginning in 2002, if the employer has a qualified retirement plan, qualified retirement planning services provided to taxpayers (or spouses) by the employer will not be included in their income. Qualified retirement planning services include retirement planning *advice* and *information.* However, the value of any tax preparation, accounting, legal or brokerage *services* provided by the employer will still be included in income.

Deductions Limits Changed.   For years beginning after 2001, the following deduction limits apply:

1. The maximum deduction for contributions to a *profit-sharing plan* increases from 15 percent to 25 percent of the compensation paid or accrued during the year to eligible employees participating in the plan. Compensation for figuring the deduction for contributions includes elective deferrals.
2. For *defined benefit plans,* in years beginning after 2001, the maximum deduction for contributions can be as much as the plan's unfunded current liability.
3. *Elective deferrals* will not be subject to the deduction limits that apply to qualified plans. Also, elective deferrals are not taken into account when figuring the amount the taxpayer can deduct for employer contributions that are not elective deferrals.

Elective Deferrals (401[k] Plans).   The limit on elective deferrals for participants in 401(k) plans (excluding SIMPLE plans) increases for tax years beginning after 2001. The limit for 2002 is $11,000 with $1,000 increases for each year up to and including 2006. The $15,000 limit is subject to adjustment after 2006 for cost-of-living increases.

For tax years beginning after 2001, a plan can permit participants who are age 50 or over at the end of the plan year to make *catch-up contributions.* The catch-up limit for 2002 is $1,000 with $1,000 increases for each year up to and including 2006. The $5,000 limit is subject to adjustment after 2006 for cost-of-living increases.

The catch-up contribution a participant can make for a year cannot exceed the lesser of the following amounts:

1. The catch-up contribution limit, or
2. The excess of the participant's compensation over the elective deferrals that are not catch-up contributions.

Limits on Contributions and Benefits.   For years beginning in 2002, the maximum annual benefit for a participant under a *defined benefit plan* increases to the lesser of the following amounts:

1. 100 percent of the participant's average compensation for his or her highest three consecutive calendar years.
2. $160,000 (subject to cost-of-living increases after 2002).

For years beginning in 2002, a *defined contribution plan's* maximum annual contributions and other additions (excluding earnings) to the account of a participant increases to the lesser of the following amounts:

1. 100 percent of the compensation actually paid to the participant (up to a maximum of $200,000 for 2002 subject to cost of living increases after 2002).
2. $40,000 (subject to cost-of-living increases after 2002).

Involuntary Payment of Benefits.   A qualified plan may provide for the immediate distribution of a participant's benefit under the plan if:

1. The participant's employment is terminated.
2. The present value of the benefit is not greater than $5,000.

For distributions made beginning in 2002, benefits attributable to rollover contributions and earnings on the contributions can be ignored in determining the present value of these benefits.

For distributions made after the Department of Labor adopts final regulations implementing rules on fiduciary responsibilities relating to this provision, a plan must provide for the automatic rollover of any distribution of more than $1,000 to an IRA under this provision. However, the participant may choose otherwise. The plan administrator must notify the participant in writing that the distribution can be transferred to another IRA.

Plan Amendments Conform to EGTRRA.   Master and prototype plans are amended by sponsoring organizations. However, the taxpayer or accountant may need to request a determination letter regarding a master or prototype plan believed to be a nonstandardized plan if changes are made to adopt some provisions enacted by the Economic Growth and Tax Relief and Reconciliation Act (EGTRRA) of 2001.

The user fee for requesting a determination letter does not apply to certain requests made after 2001 by an eligible employer. An eligible employer is one who has 100 or fewer employees with at least one employee who is not highly compensated participating in a qualified plan.

Simplified Employee Pensions (SEPs)

For plan years beginning after 2001, the maximum deduction for contributions to an SEP increases from 15 percent to 25 percent of the compensation paid or accrued during the year to the eligible employees participating in the plan.

Elective Deferrals (SARSEPs) Increased.   For tax years beginning in 2002, the limit on elective deferrals for participants in SARSEPs increases. The limit for 2002 is $11,000 with $1,000 increases for each year up to and including 2006. The $15,000 limit is subject to adjustment after 2006 for cost-of-living increases.

For tax years beginning in 2002, a plan can permit participants who are age 50 or over at the end of the plan year to make *catch-up contributions.* The catch-up limit for 2002 is $1,000 with $1,000 increases for each year up to and including 2006. The $5,000 limit is subject to adjustment after 2006 for cost-of-living increases.

The catch-up contribution that a participant can make for a year cannot exceed the lesser of the following amounts:

1. The catch-up contribution limit.
2. The excess of the participant's compensation over the elective deferrals that are not catch-up contributions.

SIMPLE Plans

The limit on salary reduction contributions to a SIMPLE plan increases in 2002. The limit for 2002 is $7,000 with an increase of $1,000 to $10,000 in 2005 and later years. The $10,000 limit is subject to adjustment after 2005 for cost-of-living increases.

For tax years beginning after 2001, a SIMPLE plan can permit participants who are age 50 or over at the end of the plan year to make catch-up contributions. The catch-up limit for 2002 is $500 with $500 increases for each year, up to and including 2006 and beyond. The $2,500 limit is subject to adjustment after 2006 for cost-of-living increases.

The catch-up contribution a participant can make for a year cannot exceed the lesser of the following amounts:

1. The catch-up contribution limit.
2. The excess of the participant's compensation over the elective deferrals that are not catch up contributions.

403(b) Plans

Recent legislation has made several changes to the way the CPA determines the maximum amount that can be contributed to the 403(b) account:

1. In years prior to 2002, the maximum amount contributable (MAC) to a 403(b) plan was the least of:
   a. The maximum exclusion allowance (MEA).
   b. The limit on annual additions.
   c. The limit on elective deferrals.
   The MEA has been repealed. Therefore, MAC for years beginning in 2002 is the lesser of the limit on annual additions or the limit on elective deferrals.
2. For years prior to 2002, MAC for church employees would be figured as indicated above. However, certain church employees could use a minimum exclusion allowance instead of MEA to figure MAC. For years after 2001, the minimum exclusion allowance has been repealed. Therefore, MAC for church employees for years beginning in 2002 is the lesser of the limit on annual additions or the limit on elective deferrals.
3. For years beginning in 2002, the alternative limits on annual additions have been repealed. Therefore, none of the following can be used to figure the limit on annual additions:
   a. The year of separation from service limit,

b. The "any year limit", or

c. The overall limit.

4. For 2002, the limit on annual additions has increased to the lesser of $40,000 or the includable compensation for the most recent year of service. For 2001, the limit on annual additions was the lesser of $35,000 or 25 percent of compensation.

5. Beginning in 2002, the includable compensation for the most recent year of service will not include money received five years after termination of service with the employer.

6. Beginning in 2002, the includable compensation for the most recent year of service does not include contributions made by the church during the year to the 403(b) account of foreign missionaries.

7. For 2002, the limit on elective deferrals has been increased from $10,500 to $11,000. The limit on elective deferrals will increase by $1,000 each year through 2006.

8. Beginning in 2002, people age 50 or older may be able to make additional catch-up contributions of up to $1,000 to the 403(b) account. The limit on catch-up contributions will increase each year by $1,000 through 2006.

9. Beginning in 2002, taxpayers contributing to both a 403(b) plan and a 457 plan in the same year are not required to reduce the maximum deferral limit of the 457 plan by the amount of contributions made to the 403(b) account. If they contribute to a 457 plan in 2002, they should see the plan administrator for contribution limits.

10. If someone makes a direct trustee-to-trustee transfer beginning in 2002 from the governmental 403(b) account to a defined benefit governmental plan, the transferred amount is not includable in gross income if it is used to purchase permissive service credits or repay contributions and earnings that were previously refunded under a forfeiture-of-service credit under another plan maintained by a state or local government employer within the same state.

11. Effective for distributions after 2001, an individual can roll over, tax free, money and other property that would otherwise be taxable from an eligible retirement plan to a 403(b) plan. In addition, an individual can roll over, tax free, money and other property that would otherwise be taxable from a 403(b) plan to an eligible retirement plan.

Section 457 Deferred Compensation Plans

Beginning in 2002, the special limit on elective deferrals for Section 457 plans no longer applies. Deferrals under these plans are subject to the general limit for elective deferrals ($11,000 for 2002). The special catch-up limit in the last three years before retirement is twice the general limit amount. Also beginning in 2002, deferrals under Section 457 plans are no longer coordinated with other plans in applying the deferral limit.

Beginning in 2002, if a taxpayer receives a distribution or payment under a qualified domestic relations order (QDRO) from an eligible state or local government Section 457 plan in which the spouse or former spouse is a participant, the taxpayer must pay the tax on it. For distributions or payments before 2002, the plan participant would have had to pay the tax. Under the new law, the plan participant still must pay the tax if the distribution or payment is made to a child or other dependent.

Beginning in 2002, amounts in eligible state or local government Section 457 plans are generally deferred from tax until paid to the taxpayer. Before 2002, these amounts generally became subject to tax when either paid or otherwise *made available.*

For distributions made beginning in 2002, eligible state or local government Section 457 plans are qualified retirement plans for rollover purposes. A person may be able to roll over certain distributions to and from these plans.

The tax on early distributions may apply to a distribution made after 2001 from an eligible state or local government Section 457 plan to the extent it is attributable to amounts rolled into the plan from another type of qualified retirement plan.

Beginning in 2002, if a person contributes to both a 403(b) plan and a Section 457 plan in the same year, it is not necessary to reduce the maximum deferral limit of the 457 plan by the amount of contributions made to the 403(b) account. If there is a contribution to a Section 457 plan in 2002, it is advisable to see the plan administrator for contribution limits.

Excise Tax for Non-deductible (Excess) Contribution

For years beginning in 2002, when figuring the 10 percent excise tax, it is permissible to choose not to take into account as non-deductible contributions for "any year contributions" to a defined benefit plan that are not more than the full funding limit figured without considering the current liability limit.

It is necessary to apply the overall limits on deductible contributions:

1. First to contributions to defined contribution plans, and
2. Then to contributions to defined benefit plans.

Taxpayers using this new exception cannot also use the exception under Section 4972(c)(6) of the Internal Revenue Code.

Rollovers

A person may be able to roll over the nontaxable part of a retirement plan distribution (such as the taxpayer's after-tax contributions) made beginning in 2002 to another qualified retirement plan or traditional individual retirement account. The transfer must be made either through a direct rollover to a qualified plan that separately accounts for the taxable and nontaxable parts of the rollover or through a rollover to an individual retirement account.

Other Changes to Rollovers.   A hardship distribution made after 2001 from any retirement plan is not an eligible rollover distribution.

It is necessary to complete the rollover of an eligible rollover distribution by the 60th day following the day on which the individual received the distribution from the employer's plan. However, the 60-day period may be extended for distributions made after 2001 in certain cases of casualty, disaster or other events beyond reasonable control.

For distributions beginning in 2002, an employee's surviving spouse who receives an eligible rollover distribution may roll it over into an eligible retirement plan, including an IRA, a qualified plan, a Section 403(b) annuity, or a Section 457 plan. A surviving spouse who received an eligible rollover distribution *before* 2002, could only roll it over into an IRA.

Before making an eligible rollover distribution, the administrator of a qualified retirement plan must provide a written explanation of various qualified retirement plan rollover rules. For most distributions made after 2001, the explanation must also tell how the distribution rules of the plan they roll the distribution over to may differ in their restrictions and tax consequences from the rules that applied to the plan making the distribution.

Deemed IRAs

For plan years beginning after 2002, a qualified retirement plan can maintain a separate account or annuity under the plan (a deemed IRA) to receive voluntary employee contributions. If the separate account or annuity otherwise meets the requirements of an IRA, it will be subject only to IRA rules. An employee's account can be treated as a traditional IRA or a Roth IRA.

COMMUNITY RENEWAL AND ENVIRONMENTAL CREDITS AND DEDUCTIONS

Various tax advantages are available for individuals, and particularly businesses, that operate in disadvantaged areas or consider environmental clean-air provisions.

Tax Incentives for Empowerment Zones and Renewal Communities

The Community Renewal Tax Relief Act of 2000 generally extends empowerment zone status for existing zones through 2009, provides new or enhanced tax benefits to businesses in empowerment zones and authorizes up to nine new zones.

The act also authorizes as many as 40 renewal communities in which businesses will be eligible for tax incentives, such as a 15 percent credit on the first $10,000 of the wages of certain employees, special cost recovery for commercial revitalization expenses, an increased Section 179 deduction and paying no tax on any capital gain from the sale of certain qualifying assets. In addition, the act creates a new-markets tax credit for equity investments in qualified community development entities.

Rollover of Gain from Sale of Empowerment Zone Assets

Taxpayers can choose to roll over certain gains from the sale of qualified empowerment zone assets purchased after December 21, 2000, if all the following tests are met:

1. They hold a qualified empowerment zone asset for more than one year and sell it at a gain.
2. The gain from the sale is a capital gain.
3. During the 60-day period beginning on the date of the sale, the taxpayer buys a replacement qualified-empowerment-zone asset in the same zone as the asset sold.

Increased Section 179 Deduction for Enterprise Zone Businesses

The dollar limit on the Section 179 deduction is increased for 2002 and later years if the taxpayer's business qualifies as an enterprise zone business. The increase is the smaller of the following amounts:

1. $35,000.
2. The cost of Section 179 property that is also qualified zone property.

Environmental Clean-Up Cost Deduction

The deduction for qualified environmental clean-up costs was scheduled to expire for costs paid or incurred after 2001. It has been extended to include costs the taxpayer pays or incurs before 2004.

Electric and Clean Fuel Vehicles

The maximum deduction for clean fuel vehicles and credit for qualified electric vehicles are 25 percent lower for 2002 than they were for 2001. Both the credit and the deduction will be phased out completely by 2005.

ESTATE AND GIFT TAXES

Increased Exclusion for Gifts

The annual exclusion for gifts of present interests made to a donee during the calendar year has been increased to $11,000.

Beginning with gifts made in 2002, the applicable exclusion amount for lifetime gifts has been fixed at $1 million.

The applicable exclusion amount is the amount on which the unified credit (applicable credit amount) is based. An estate tax return for a U.S. citizen or resident needs to be filed only if the gross estate exceeds this amount.

The annual exclusion for gifts made to spouses who are not U.S. citizens is increased to $110,000.

Reduction of Maximum Estate and Gift Tax Rate

For estates of decedents dying, and gifts made, beginning in 2002, the maximum rate for the estate tax and the gift tax will be reduced. For 2002, the maximum tax rate is 50 percent with a 1 percent reduction each year until it is 45 percent for 2007 through 2009.

For estates of decedents dying, and gifts made, the benefit of the graduated rates will no longer be phased out for estates and gifts in excess of $10 million.

Reduction of Credit for State Death Taxes

For estates of decedents dying in 2002, the credit allowed for state death taxes will be limited to 75 percent of the amount that would otherwise have been allowed. For estates of decedents dying in 2003 and 2004, the credit will be limited to 50 percent and 25 percent, respectively.

For estates of decedents dying after 2004, the state death tax credit will be replaced with a deduction for state death taxes.

Changes to Installment Payment Provisions

For estates of decedents dying after 2001, several rules applicable to qualifying for installment payments of estate tax have been changed:

1. The allowable number of partners and shareholders in a closely held business is increased from 15 to 45.
2. Stock in qualifying lending and finance businesses is treated as stock in an active trade or business company.
3. The rules regarding non-readily-tradable stock and holding company stock are clarified.

Increase in Generation-Skipping Transfer (GST) Exemption

The generation-skipping transfer (GST) lifetime exemption in 2002 is increased by $40,000 to $1,100,000. The annual increase can be allocated only to transfers made during or after the year of the increase.

The lifetime exemption amount for generation-skipping transfers is later increased to $1,500,000 for 2004 and 2005; $2,000,000 for 2006–2008; $3,500,000 for 2009.

The estate and generation-skipping transfer taxes have been repealed for the estates of decedents dying and generation-skipping transfers made in 2010. New rules will go into effect at that time regarding the basis of assets transferred at death. The gift tax continues, but at reduced rates.

Repeal of QFOBI Deduction

The deduction for qualified family-owned business interest (QFOBI) has been repealed beginning with the estates of decedents dying in 2004.

EXCISE TAXES

The following changes were effective for calendar quarters beginning after September 30, 2001:

1. Taxpayers or CPAs must file Form 720, *Quarterly Federal Excise Tax Return,* by the last day of the month following the calendar quarter for which the return is made. The rule that allowed them to file by the last day of the second month following the calendar quarter for certain taxes has been eliminated. Now it is not necessary to deposit excise taxes for a calendar quarter if the net tax liability for the quarter is not more than $2,500.

2. One deposit rule applies for all taxes that have to be deposited other than those deposited under the alternative method. They must be deposited under the regular method by the 14th day following the semimonthly period. If the 14th day falls on a Saturday, Sunday or legal holiday, the taxes must be deposited by the immediately *preceding* day that is not a Saturday, Sunday or legal holiday. The deposit date for taxes deposited under the alternative method was not changed. The previous-deposit rules (the 9-day rule, 14-day rule and 30-day rule) have been eliminated.

Amount to Deposit and Safe Harbor Rules

Deposit of taxes for a semimonthly period generally must be at least 95 percent of the net tax liability incurred during that period, unless the safe harbor rule applies. Previously, the deposit had to equal the amount of the net tax liability. The current liability safe harbor rule has been eliminated. However, for people depositing taxes that were in effect during the look-back quarter, the look-back quarter safe-harbor rule still applies.

Air Transportation Taxes

For transportation beginning in 2002, the tax on transportation of persons by air is increased to $3.00 for each domestic segment. The percentage tax remains at 7.5 percent. The tax on the use of international air travel facilities will be $13.20 per person for flights that begin or end in the United States, or $6.60 per person for domestic segments that begin or end in Alaska or Hawaii (applies only to departures).

Luxury Tax

For 2002, the luxury tax on a passenger vehicle is reduced to 3 percent of the amount of the sales price that exceeds the base amount. The base amount for 2002 is $40,000.

MISCELLANEOUS TAX ITEMS

Following is an assortment of tax items that will be of concern to the taxpayer and accountant in the next several years.

Estimated Tax for Higher-Income Taxpayers

For installment payments for tax years beginning in 2002, the estimated tax safe harbor for higher-income individuals (other than farmers and fishermen) has been modified. If the 2001 adjusted gross income was more than $150,000 ($75,000 if married filing a separate return), the taxpayer will have to pay the smaller of 90 percent of the expected tax for 2002 or 112 percent of the tax shown on the 2001 return to avoid an estimated tax penalty.

Certain Withholding Rates Decreased

For 2002, the withholding rates on the following items have been decreased:

1. Gambling winnings—The rate has been decreased to 27 percent.
2. Unemployment compensation—The rate has been decreased to 10 percent.
3. Federal payments—Withholding on certain federal payments is voluntary. The elective rates have been decreased to 7 percent, 10 percent, 15 percent, and 27 percent.
4. Backup withholding—The rate has been decreased to 30 percent.
5. Supplemental wages—The rate has been decreased to 27 percent.

Depreciation and Section 179 Deduction

The total cost of Section 179 property that it is possible to elect to deduct is increased from $20,000 to $24,000 for 2002. Beginning in 2003, the total amount will increase to $25,000.

If the business filed the 2001 return on a calendar-year basis, or on a fiscal-year basis or for a short tax year and the third or fourth quarter of the 2001 tax year includes September 11, 2001, it is possible to elect to apply the half-year convention to all property placed in service during the year. It would otherwise be subject to the midquarter convention under the Modified Accelerated Cost Recovery System.

Work Opportunity Credit and Welfare-to-Work Credit

The work opportunity credit and the welfare-to-work credit are scheduled to expire for wages paid to individuals who began working for the taxpayer after 2001.

Meal Expenses When Subject to "Hours of Service" Limits

Generally, taxpayers can deduct only 50 percent of their business-related meal expenses while traveling away from the home for business purposes. They can deduct a higher percentage if the meals take place during, or incident to, any period subject to the Department of Transportation's "hours of service" limits. These limits apply to workers who are under certain federal regulations, and the amount that can be deducted is 65 percent for 2002 and 2003.

Standard Mileage Rate

For 2002, the standard mileage rate for the cost of operating a car, van, pickup or panel truck is increased to 36-1/2 cents a mile for all business miles.

Self-Employed Health Insurance Deduction

For 2002, this deduction increases to 70 percent of the amount paid for medical and qualified long-term care insurance for the taxpayer and his or her family. After 2002, the deduction will increase to 100 percent.

Self-Employment Tax

The self-employment tax rate on net earnings does not change for 2002. This rate, 15.3 percent, is a total of 12.4 percent for Social Security (old age, survivors, and disability insurance) and 2.9 percent for Medicare (hospital insurance).

The maximum amount subject to the Social Security part for tax years beginning in 2002 has increased to $84,900. All net earnings of at least $400 are subject to the Medicare part.

Foreign Earned Income Exclusion Increased

Beginning in 2002, the maximum foreign earned income exclusion increases from $78,000 to $80,000.

Chapter 41

The Job Creation and Worker Assistance Act of 2002

CONTENTS

Highlights of New Bill	**41.02**
New Five-Year Carryback for Net Operating Loss	**41.02**
Business Incentives	**41.04**
IRAs and Other Retirement Plans	**41.06**
Contributions to Defined Benefit Plans	**41.08**
Discharge of S Corporation Indebtedness	**41.08**
Electronic Filing of 1099s	**41.09**
The New York City Liberty Zone	**41.09**
Individual Incentives	**41.10**
Technical Corrections	**41.13**
Issues Yet to Be Resolved	**41.15**

The Job Creation and Worker Assistance Act of 2002 (HR 3090) is a somewhat scaled-back version of measures the Administration and Republicans proposed immediately after September 11th. The final bill is a major tax bill with a number of far-reaching provisions. The new package contains $38.7 billion in tax incentives spread over 10 years and goes a long way toward trying to help New York City recover from the tragedy.

It includes one of the business community's most sought after tax incentives, a 30 percent depreciation bonus. The new law also made several tax breaks retroactive to the 2001 tax year, affecting 2001 tax returns that had already been filed.

HIGHLIGHTS OF NEW BILL

The Job Creation and Worker Assistance Act of 2002 is an economic stimulus package that includes provisions to boost business, extend unemployment assistance, provide relief to New York City businesses and provide for retirement in addition to miscellaneous and technical measures. Highlights of the act follow:

1. A five-year carryback period for net operating losses.
2. A temporary 30 percent depreciation bonus.
3. Special tax breaks for post 9/11 New York City reconstruction.
4. Limit on the use of the non-accrual experience method of accounting for service providers.
5. Pension changes, such as the new tax credit for certain pension plan start-up costs, an increased contribution limit for simplified employee pensions, figuring 403(b) catch-up.
6. Electronic filing of Forms 1099.
7. Reversal of the Supreme Court's S corporation decision in *Gitlitz* v. *Commr.*
8. New deductions available for educator expenses.
9. Extension of many expiring tax credits and deductions, including the welfare-to-work and work opportunity credits.

NEW FIVE-YEAR CARRYBACK FOR NET OPERATING LOSS

Taxpayers generally can carry back net operating losses (NOLs) two years. The new law temporarily extends the general carryback period from two to five years. In addition, three-year NOLs, like casualty losses, can be carried back five years.

The losses must arise in tax years ending in 2001 and 2002. Taxpayers would be given one opportunity to elect out of this treatment and their election is final. It is also possible to choose not to carry back an NOL and only carry it forward. The new law also allows a taxpayer's NOL deduction to reduce its alternative minimum taxable income (AMTI) up to 100 percent.

Individuals, estates and trusts can file Form 1045, *Application for Tentative Refund.* Corporations can file Form 1139, *Corporation Application for Tentative Refund.* The instructions for these forms have been revised to reflect the new law.

Under the new law, those having an NOL for a tax year ending during 2001 or 2002 must generally carry back the entire amount of the NOL to the five tax years before the NOL year (the carryback period). However, they can still choose to carry back an NOL to the two (or three, if applicable) years before the NOL year. Any remaining NOL can be carried forward for up to 20 years.

Those who have already filed a return for a tax year ending during 2001 or 2002 and who did not apply the new five-year carryback for an NOL have a limited opportunity to do so.

Elected to Forgo Carryback Period

If a taxpayer elected to forgo the carryback period but now wants to apply the five-year carryback period, he or she can do so by filing either Form 1045, *Application for Tentative Refund,* or Form 1040X to amend the tax return. Estates and trusts must file Form 1045 or an amended Form 1041, *U.S. Income Tax Return for Estates and Trusts.* They should type or print across the top of the form "Revocation of NOL carryback waiver pursuant to Rev. Proc. 2002-40."

Those who elected to forgo the carryback period and still want to forgo a carryback should do nothing. The previous election applies to forgoing the five-year carryback period.

A Change of Mind

Individuals and entities that applied a two- or three-year carryback period but now want to apply the five-year carryback period can do so by filing either Form 1045 or Form 1040X. Estates and trusts should file Form 1045 or amended Form 1041. They should type or print across the top of the form "Amended refund claim pursuant to Rev. Proc. 2002-40."

For those who applied a two- or three-year carryback period and still want to use that period should do nothing. They will be considered to have made an election to forgo the five-year carryback period in favor of the two- or three-year carryback period.

Those who neither elected to forgo the carryback period nor applied the two- or three-year carryback period but now want to forgo the five-year period and apply a two- or three-year period can do so by filing either Form 1045 or Form 1040X. Estates and trusts should file Form 1045 or amended Form 1041. If they do not choose the two- or three-year period, the five-year period will apply.

The appropriate form should have been filed by October 31, 2002. (Since much of this legislation was passed after the main IRS publications and deadlines were adopted, it is not far-fetched to expect that the deadlines will be extended.)

BUSINESS INCENTIVES

Most of the tax breaks under the new law go to businesses rather than to the individual taxpayer. Two of the measures, the five-year carryback period for net operating losses (explained previously), and the temporary 30 percent depreciation bonus (discussed in Chapter 33, "Depreciation") apply retroactively to affect 2001 tax returns. Businesses affected by the 9/11 tragedy in New York City have a set of special tax breaks to help them in the rebuilding and recuperating process.

Tax Incentives for New York Liberty Zone

New tax benefits are provided for the parts of New York City damaged in the terrorist attacks on September 11, 2001. These benefits apply to the newly created New York Liberty Zone, which is the area located on or south of Canal Street, East Broadway (east of its intersection with Canal Street), or Grand Street (east of its intersection with East Broadway), in the Borough of Manhattan.

Tax benefits for the New York Liberty Zone include the following:

1. A special depreciation allowance equal to 30 percent of the adjusted basis of qualified Liberty Zone property. It is allowed for the year the property is placed in service.
2. No alternative minimum tax depreciation adjustment for qualified Liberty Zone property.
3. Classification of Liberty Zone leasehold improvement property as five-year property.
4. Authorization of the issuance of tax-exempt New York Liberty bonds to finance the acquisition, construction, reconstruction and renovation of nonresidential real property, residential rental property and public utility property in the Liberty Zone.
5. An increased Section 179 deduction for certain Liberty Zone property.
6. Extension of the replacement period from two years to five years for certain property involuntarily converted as a result of the terrorist attacks on September 11, 2001, but only if substantially all of the use of the replacement property is in New York City.

Work Opportunity Credit Expanded in Liberty Zone. The work opportunity credit is expanded to include a new targeted group consisting generally of employees who perform substantially all their services either in the New York Liberty Zone (defined above) or elsewhere in New York City for a business that relocated from the Liberty Zone because of the destruction or damage of its place of business by the September 11, 2001, terrorist attack. The credit is available to employers for wages paid to new employees and existing employees for work performed during 2002 or 2003. Certain limits apply.

Credit for Pension Plan Start-Up Costs

The credit for pension plan start-up costs is now allowed for plans that *become effective after* December 31, 2001. Previously, the credit was allowed only for plans *established after* December 31, 2001.

Non-Accrual Experience Method of Accounting

Under current law, taxpayers using the accrual method of accounting may exclude from income amounts from the performance of services that they anticipate will not be collected. Beginning in 2002, under the new law, the non-accrual experience method of accounting is available only for amounts to be received for the performance of qualified services and for services provided by certain small businesses in the fields of health, law, engineering, architecture, accounting, actuarial science, performing arts and consulting, or if the average annual gross receipts for the three prior tax years does not exceed $5 million. As under current law, the non-accrual experience method will not apply to amounts on which interest or a late payment penalty is charged.

Extension of Empowerment Zone Tax Incentives

The Empowerment Zone tax incentives have been extended as follows:

1. State and local governments had been granted authority to issue *qualified zone academy bonds* to raise funds for the use of qualified zone academies. The amount of bonds that could be issued was limited to $400 million each year for 1998, 1999, 2000 and 2001. This provision has been extended to provide for an additional $400 million of bonds to be issued each year for 2002 and 2003. These bonds are among the tax incentives for empowerment zones and other distressed communities.

2. Another of these incentives is the *Indian employment credit* that was scheduled to expire for tax years beginning after 2003. It has been extended to include a tax year beginning in 2004.

3. The *welfare-to-work credit* that was scheduled to expire for wages paid to individuals who began working for an employer after 2001 has been extended to include wages paid to qualified individuals who begin work in 2002 or 2003.

4. The *work opportunity credit* that was scheduled to expire for wages paid to individuals who began working for an employer after 2001 has been

extended to include wages paid to qualified individuals who begin work in 2002 or 2003. In addition, for 2002 and 2003, the work opportunity credit is expanded by creating a new targeted group, consisting generally of employees who work in the Liberty Zone or, in certain cases, in New York City outside the Liberty Zone.

Extensions of Expiring Business Tax Credits

Many temporary tax credits and deductions expired December 31, 2001, or soon thereafter. In addition to the tax incentives just mentioned immediately above, the new law extends for two years, until December 31, 2003, or slightly beyond, the:

1. Cover over payments to Puerto Rico and the Virgin Islands.
2. Tax on failure to comply with mental health parity requirements.
3. Suspension of reduction of deductions for mutual life insurance companies.
4. Credit for producing electricity from wind, biomass and poultry litter.
5. Renewable electricity production credit, to include electricity produced by facilities placed in service after 2001 and before 2004.
6. Taxable income limit on percentage depreciation from marginal production of oil and natural gas that was scheduled to expire for tax years beginning after 2001, to tax years beginning before 2004.
7. Maximum clean-fuel vehicle deduction and qualified electric vehicle credit. These were scheduled to be 25 percent lower for 2002, and both were scheduled to be phased out completely by 2005. The full deduction and credit are now allowed for qualified property placed in service in 2002 and 2003. The phase-out of the deduction and the credit will begin in 2004, and no deduction or credit will be allowed for property placed in service after 2006.
8. Other energy incentives.

IRAS AND OTHER RETIREMENT PLANS

Changes and modifications to several retirement plans figured in provisions in the 2002 tax bill. Among them are the following.

Simplified Employee Pensions (SEPs)

Contribution limits were increased for plan years beginning after December 31, 2001. The annual limit on the amount of employer contributions to an SEP increases to the lesser of the following amounts:

1. 25 percent of an eligible employee's compensation.
2. $40,000 (subject to cost-of-living adjustments after 2002).

For years beginning after 2001, the following changes apply to the SEP deduction limit:

1. Elective deferrals under a salary reduction (SARSEP) are not subject to the deduction limit that applies to employer contributions. Also, elective deferrals are not taken into account when figuring the amount that can be deducted for employer contributions that are not elective deferrals.
2. Compensation for figuring the deduction for employer contributions includes elective deferrals under a SARSEP.

403(b) Plans

The 403(b) plans, also referred to as tax-sheltered annuity (TSA) plans, are retirement plans for certain employees of public schools, employees of certain tax-exempt organizations and certain ministers.

When figuring allowable catch-up contributions, all contributions made by the employer on the individual's behalf to the following plans are combined:

1. Qualified retirement plans.
2. 403(b) plans.
3. Simplified employee pensions (SEP).
4. Savings Incentive Match Plan for Employees (SIMPLE) plans.

The total amount of the catch-up contributions to all plans maintained by the employer cannot exceed the annual limit. For 2002, the limit was $1,000.

If a distribution includes both pre-tax contributions and after-tax contributions, the portion of the distribution that is rolled over is treated as consisting first of pre-tax amounts (contributions and earnings that would be included in income if no rollover occurred). This means that if the rollover amount is at least as much as the pre-tax portion of the distribution, it is not necessary to include any of the distribution in income.

For a minister or church employee, all of the individual's years of service as an employee of a church or a convention or association of churches are treated as years of service with one employer. Prior law required church employees and ministers to figure years of service separately for each employer.

As a minister or church employee, all contributions made to 403(b) plans on behalf of an individual, as an employee of a church or a convention or association of churches, are considered made by one employer.

For a foreign missionary, contributions to a 403(b) account will not be treated as exceeding the limit on annual additions if the contributions are not more than the greater of:

1. $3,000.
2. The individual's includible compensation.

Deemed IRAs

For plan years beginning after 2002, a qualified employer plan can provide for voluntary employee contributions to a separate account or annuity that is deemed to be an IRA.

For this purpose, a qualified employer plan includes a deferred compensation plan (Section 457(b) plan) maintained by a state, a political subdivision of a state or an agency or instrumentality of a state or political subdivision of a state.

The term "qualified employer plan" also includes:

1. A qualified pension, profit-sharing, or stock bonus plan (Section 401(a) plan).
2. A qualified employee annuity plan (Section 403(a) plan).
3. A tax-sheltered annuity plan (Section 403(b) plan).

CONTRIBUTIONS TO DEFINED BENEFIT PLANS

Last year, the Treasury discontinued the sale of 30-year bonds. Part of the fallout was a negative effect on interest rates used to determine additional required contributions for defined benefit plans. An artificially low rate makes a plan look like it is underfunded, since its funding liability is calculated with the use of an interest rate that has to fall within a permissible range. Currently it is between 90 percent and 105 percent. The new law expands the permissible range up to 120 percent for 2002 and 2003.

DISCHARGE OF S CORPORATION INDEBTEDNESS

In *Gitlitz v. Commr.*, 531 US 206 (2001), the U.S. Supreme Court surprised many observers by relying on the "plain language" of the Code to find that while IRC paragraph 108(a) provides that discharge of indebtedness income (DOI) ceases to be included in gross income when the S corporation is insolvent, it does not provide that the DOI ceases to be an item of income for purposes of allowing the shareholder an increase in basis that, in turn, can allow the pass through of otherwise suspended corporate losses.

The new law reverses the Supreme Court's decision. The discharged amount excluded from an S corporation's income is expressly not treated as an item of income by a shareholder. Consequently, the shareholder's basis is not increased. Generally, HR 3090 applies to discharges of indebtedness income after October 11, 2001.

The Court's decision temporarily put S corporation shareholders at a decided advantage over other business entities, particularly partnerships, when hard times hit. Now, that changes.

ELECTRONIC FILING OF 1099s

Copies of some information returns must be presented to the named individual either in person or in a statement sent by first-class mail in a specified format. The new law now allows information returns to be sent electronically, as long as the recipient agrees.

Subpart F

Generally, under Subpart F, some foreign personal holding company income, such as income from a financial services company, is taxable to domestic shareholders even if it is not distributed to them. Five years ago, Congress temporarily exempted income derived from the active conduct of banking, financing and insurance from foreign personal holding company income. U.S. tax is deferred until the income is repatriated. Under the new law, taxpayers will be eligible to defer U.S. tax until the income is repatriated through December 31, 2006.

THE NEW YORK CITY LIBERTY ZONE

New York City residents were promised special tax breaks to help rebuild after September 11, 2001. HR 3090 gives taxpayers enhanced depreciation and expensing as well as other breaks. However, only taxpayers in a special "Liberty Zone"—southern Manhattan—will be able to take advantage of the special new look incentives.

These tax breaks are in addition to those already in the Victims of Terrorism Tax Relief Act of 2001, signed on January 23, 2002. Highlights include:

1. Expensing—The maximum Section 179 deduction amount for qualifying property used in the Liberty Zone is increased, by the lesser of $35,000 or the cost of the qualifying property put in service during the taxable year.

2. Depreciation—Added to normal first-year depreciation deduction is an amount equivalent to 30 percent of the qualified property's adjusted basis, applicable for both regular and alternative minimum tax purposes.

3. Work Opportunity Tax Credit (WOTC)—A new targeted group is added for Liberty Zone taxpayers:

   a. Individuals substantially performing all their services in the recovery zone for a business in the Liberty Zone.

   b. Individuals substantially performing all of their services in New York City for a business relocated from the Liberty Zone to someplace else within New York City as a result of the terrorist attacks.

4. Converted property—Instead of the usual two-year period, a five-year replacement period applies to involuntarily converted property as a result of the terrorist attacks, if replaced with property to be substantially used in New York City.

5. Qualified leasehold improvements—For Section 168 depreciation purposes, five-year property includes qualified leasehold improvement property put in service after September 10, 2001 and before January 1, 2007.

INDIVIDUAL INCENTIVES

With additional tax rebates and accelerated rate cuts jettisoned from the final stimulus compromise, HR 3090 does not have as broad an impact on individuals as was expected based on earlier versions of the economic stimulus legislation. Nevertheless, a significant number of individuals are affected by the introduction of two new tax breaks and the extension of two others.

Personal Credits Still Allowed Against AMT

The provision that allowed certain non-refundable personal credits to reduce both an individual's regular tax and any alternative minimum tax has been extended and will be in effect for 2002 and 2003. This provision as it applies to the AMT, was originally scheduled to expire after 2001. Without the extension, these credits could not have been used to reduce any AMT in 2002 or 2003.

In 1998, Congress enacted some limited AMT relief when it allowed individual taxpayers to temporarily use the personal credits, such as the adoption, disability, child, and education credits, against regular tax liability and AMT. The Economic Growth and Tax Relief Act of 2001 (EGTRRA) made permanent the use of the child tax and adoption credits. However, EGTRRA did not extend the other personal credits beyond their cut-off date of December 31, 2001. This bill does. After that date, only the child tax and adoption credits will be permitted to be used to their fullest extent. On the other hand, the AMT is not a forgotten issue as discussed below.

Whither the Alternative Minimum Tax?

Even though they seldom agree on anything, particularly anything to do with taxes—raising, lowering, simplifying, whatever . . . , Republicans, Democrats, the Internal Revenue Service, the American Institute of CPAs (AICPA), and those who have recently been or are about to be hit by it are all agreed that something needs to be done about the Alternative Minimum Tax. However, total agreement ends there. The something takes many forms.

This section of the tax code was written 30 years ago to plug loopholes that were permitting a few wealthy taxpayers to figure out ways to use tax preferences and deductions to wiggle out of any federal tax liability.

Figures show that only 19,000 U.S. taxpayers were affected by the AMT in 1970, but that number rose to 1.5 million in 2001. Left uncorrected, the AMT will make the federal income tax considerably more complex and expensive for 17 million American families by 2010, according to the Joint Economic Committee.

Few of those likely to be hit with the AMT restrictions are even aware of this tax. Many tax practitioners have warned that a widespread taxpayer revolt could be the result if millions of middle-income Americans begin losing their deductions and exemptions.

Varied Approaches to Modifying the Thrust of the AMT. As was pointed out, Congress has been skirting the edges of the problem with minor tax code changes allowing individuals to use personal credits to offset AMT tax liability during the 2000 and 2001 tax years—a provision now extended through 2003. But the lack of any clear consensus on how far to go in whittling back the AMT has effectively stalled more substantive reform efforts.

More than two dozen bills were pending on Capitol Hill in the spring and summer of 2002 to cut back on the spread of the AMT. These measures included stock option gains exclusions, farm subsidies, state and local income tax refunds, foreign tax credits and other preference items from the Alternative Minimum Tax. Other bills would phase out the individual alternative tax altogether by 2006.

The AICPA, which has repeatedly criticized the AMT as a major contributor to unnecessary tax code complexity, has recommended a somewhat less drastic cure involving the elimination of itemized deductions and personal exemptions as adjustments to regular taxable income in calculating taxable income for AMT purposes.

National Taxpayer Advocate Approach. The IRS National Taxpayer Advocate has called for relief from the tax, a provision that penalizes "unintended targets . . . because they have large families, live in high-tax cities or states, or earn their income in a variety of ways other than direct compensation, such as stock options."

In presenting the annual report to Congress earlier this spring, the Taxpayer Advocate released an analysis that concluded that calculating the AMT is one of the 20 most serious problems encountered by American taxpayers.

Although the report included several possible ways for excluding middle-income taxpayers from the alternative tax bite, the presenter told Congress that the simplest solution might be to establish a new threshold for the AMT.

She personally favors the alternative proposal of establishing a gross income threshold, below which a taxpayer will not be subject to the AMT. This proposal has the advantage of providing relief to those taxpayers who must spend hours to determine whether they are subject to the tax at all, the report explained.

If this proposal were adopted, the taxpayer could look at a line on his or her return and check it against the threshold for his or her filing status. The face of the return would tell them whether they were subject to the AMT or not.

Deduction for Educator Expenses

The new law includes an education tax incentive in an above-the-line deduction for classroom expenses. Eligible educators can deduct, as an adjustment to income, up to $250 in qualified expenses. They can deduct these expenses even if they do not itemize deductions on Schedule A (Form 1040). This adjustment to income is for expenses paid or incurred in tax years beginning during 2002 or 2003. Previously, these expenses were deductible only as a miscellaneous itemized deduction subject to the 2 percent of adjusted gross income limit.

An eligible educator is one who, for the tax year, meets the following requirements:

1. Is a teacher, instructor, counselor, principal or aide for kindergarten through grade 12.
2. Works at least 900 hours during a school year in a school that provides elementary or secondary education, as determined under state law.

Qualified Expenses. These are unreimbursed expenses paid or incurred for books, supplies, computer equipment (including related software and services), other equipment and supplementary materials used in the classroom. For courses in health and physical education, expenses for supplies are qualified expenses only if they are related to athletics.

To be deductible as an adjustment to income, the qualified expenses must be more than the following amounts for the tax year:

1. The interest on qualified U.S. savings bonds the individual excluded from income because the taxpayer paid qualified higher education expenses.
2. Any distribution from a qualified tuition program that was excluded from income.
3. Any tax-free withdrawals from the taxpayer's Coverdell education savings account.

Change in Child and Dependent Care Expenses

For the purpose of figuring the child and dependent care credit, the spouse is treated as having at least a minimum of earned income for any month that he or she is a full-time student or not able to care for himself or herself. Beginning in 2003, this amount is increased to $250 a month if there is one qualifying person and to $500 a month if there are two or more qualifying persons. The same rule applies for the exclusion of employer-provided dependent care benefits.

Archer Medical Savings Accounts

Although Archer Medical Savings Accounts (MSAs) have failed to meet initial expectations of popularity, continuing them past their initial cut-off date had significant bipartisan support. HR 3090 extends MSAs through December 31, 2003.

Foster Care

Payments to a qualified foster care provider by state or local governments or a tax-exempt placement agency generally are excluded from income. HR 3090 expands the definition of payments and the definition of who may be considered a foster care individual.

TECHNICAL CORRECTIONS

This tax law makes numerous technical corrections to 2001's big tax cut vehicle, EGTRRA, and to some earlier tax laws. Many of the technical corrections create substantive changes. Several of these measures are based on what Congress *intended to indicate* in original provisions that were poorly drafted. Many Congressional bills come in for "technical corrections." It just seems that this bill may have had more because of its size and because of the rush to get the stimulus to work. It also has a much higher profile than more run-of-the-mill measures.

EGTRRA Corrections

Several of the corrections to the EGTRRA follow:

1. *Adoption credit*—The transition rule for the credit, the dollar amount for special-needs children, and employer-provided assistance for special-needs adoptions are clarified.

2. *Child tax credit*—The refundable portion of the child tax credit will continue to be determined as it was pre-EGTRRA.

3. *HOPE credit*—Taxpayers may claim the education IRA exclusion and the HOPE credit in the same year.

4. *Benefit and contribution limits*—HR 3090 corrects the dollar amounts used for indexing future cost of living adjustments.

5. *Credit for new retirement plans*—The EGTRRA also gave eligible small businesses a credit for new retirement plan expenses. Under HR 3090, to take advantage of the credit, the plan must be first effective after December 31, 2001.

6. *Catch-up contributions*—One of EGTRRA's most significant reforms was the allowance of catch-up contributions for qualifying taxpayers over age 49. HR 3090 clarifies that a person who reaches age 50 by the end of the tax year is eligible to make catch-up contributions as of the beginning of the year.

7. *Retirement plan rollovers*—When a spouse consents to a cash-out of the plan benefits, this measure clarifies when rollover amounts may be disregarded.

8. *Notice of pension reductions*—EGTRRA requires plan participants to receive notice of significant future reductions in benefits. This tax bill clarifies that the notice requirement applies only to qualified defined benefit plans and, depending on the type of the reduction, only if the benefit is significant.

9. *Deduction limits*—EGTRRA increased the cap on annual deductible contributions to an SEP to 25 percent of compensation. Thus, the deduction limit is brought into conformity with the 25 percent defined contribution plan limit.

Corrections of Earlier Laws

Among the more important clarifications to pre-EGTRRA laws are:

1. Taxpayer Relief Act of 1997. Treatment of disposition of interest in passive activity.

2. Technical and Miscellaneous Revenue Act of 1988. The wash sale rules that generally apply to losses from the sale of stock or securities do not apply to any loss arising from a Section 1256 contract. A Section 1256 contract is any:

   a. Regulated futures contract.

   b. Foreign currency contract.

   c. Nonequity option.

   d. Dealer equity option.

   e. Dealer securities futures contract.

Issues Yet to Be Resolved

Even before this bill was passed with a strong bipartisan vote, there was talk of another bill to come later in the year, but most in Congress evidently agreed that getting one law signed and in effect was better than delaying too long to try to come to agreement on other points.

In addition to the individual AMT discussed previously, several other provisions have been given consideration by Congress, including:

1. Repeal of the corporate AMT.
2. Prescription drug benefits for senior citizens.
3. Acceleration of the 100 percent health benefits for the self-employed.
4. The research and development (R&D) tax credit. As it stands, the R&D credit is scheduled to expire June 30, 2004.
5. Reduced payroll taxes for small businesses.
6. A $300 rebate for certain low-income individuals.
7. An immediate reduction in the individual 27 percent income tax rate to 25 percent.

Chapter 42
Tip Income

CONTENTS

Tip Rate Determination/Education Program	**42.01**
Basic Rules Relating to Tip Income Reporting	**42.04**
Tip Rates	**42.08**
Annual Review	**42.09**
Allocated Tips	**42.10**
Supreme Court Ruling on "Aggregate Method"	**42.12**

What's the big deal? An estimated $9 billion a year in unreported, untaxed tip income, that's what. Reporting all tip income has always been required by law. When the significant extent to which taxpayers were ignoring the law became evident, the IRS stepped up the emphasis on the requirements for both employee and employer to report tip income.

TIP RATE DETERMINATION/EDUCATION PROGRAM

The Tip Rate Determination/Education Program (TRD/EP) was first promoted in the gaming industry (casino industry) in Las Vegas, Nevada, and has spread to the food and beverage industry. Other industries whose employees receive tips include beauty parlors, barber shops, taxi companies, and pizza delivery establishments.

The Tip Rate Determination/Education Program created in 1993 is a national program used in all states. The employer has the option to enter into one of two arrangements under this program: the Tip Rate Determination Agreement (TRDA) or the Tip Reporting Alternative Commitment (TRAC) created in June 1995.

With the introduction of the new programs, four options became available for tip reporting:

1. Tip Rate Determination Agreement (TRDA).
2. Tip Reporting Alternative Commitment (TRAC).
3. The status quo—the old basic method following the requirements listed below without any "formal" agreement.
4. Examination of Tip Income Reporting.

Under the Tip Rate Determination/Education Program (TRD/EP), the employer may enter into either the TRDA or TRAC arrangement. The IRS will assist applicants in understanding and meeting the requirements for participation. Many similarities exist between the two new alternatives, but there are some differences. Following is a descriptive list of the requirements for each, particularly in reference to the food and beverage industry:

TRDA

1. Requires the IRS to work with the establishment to arrive at a tip rate for the various restaurant occupations.
2. Requires the employee to enter into a Tipped Employee Participation Agreement (TEPA) with the employer.
3. Requires the employer to get 75% of the employees to sign TEPAs and report at or above the determined rate.
4. Provides that if employees fail to report at or above the determined rate, the employer will provide the names of those employees, their social security numbers, job classification, sales, hours worked, and amount of tips reported.
5. Has no specific education requirement relating to legal responsibility to report tips under the agreement.
6. Participation assures the employer that prior periods will not be examined during the period that the TRDA is in effect.
7. Results in the mailing of a notice and demand to employer for the employer's portion of FICA taxes on unreported tips determined for the six month period used to set the tip rate(s).
8. Prevents employer (only) assessments during the period that the agreement is in effect.

TRAC

1. Does not require that a tip rate be established, but it does require the employer to:
   a. Establish a procedure where a directly tipped employee is provided (no less than monthly) a written statement of charged tips attributed to the employee.
   b. Implement a procedure for the employee to verify or correct any statement of attributed tips.
   c. Adopt a method where an indirectly tipped employee reports his or her tips (no less than monthly). This could include a statement prepared by the employer and verified or corrected by the employee.
   d. Establish a procedure where a written statement is prepared and processed (no less than monthly) reflecting all cash tips attributable to sales of the directly tipped employee.
2. Does not require an agreement between the employee and the employer.
3. Affects all (100%) of the employees.
4. Includes a commitment by the employer to educate and reeducate quarterly all directly and indirectly tipped employees and new hires of their statutory requirement to report all tips to their employer.
5. Participation assures the employer that prior periods will not be examined during the period that the agreement is in effect.
6. Prevents employer (only) assessments during the period that the agreement is in effect.
7. Assures that employers comply with all tax reporting, filing, and payment obligations.
8. Requires employers to maintain and make available records to the IRS.
9. Emphasizes that employees earning $20 or more a month in tips must report them to the employer.

In return, the IRS generally will not perform a tip examination on employers complying with the TRAC guidelines. In contrast, an establishment whose employees underreport their tips could be liable for back FICA taxes.

The approach has helped lead to increased tip reporting, but the IRS believes there is still ample room for improvement. In the food and beverage sector alone, tip reporting jumped from $3.9 billion in 1993 to $5.2 billion in 1995 to more than $7 billion in 1998. However, estimates placed the amount of annual tips going to those same workers at $18 billion annually.

TRAC Agreement Revised

The IRS has been working cooperatively with the restaurant industry in response to industry concerns regarding some aspects of the TRAC program.

In late 1999, the IRS took steps to reduce the administrative burdens of restaurant operators by making several changes in the regulations:

1. The IRS will no longer revoke TRAC agreements in cases where employers make a good-faith effort at following the guidelines but employees still fail to report tips. Instead of pursuing the employers in such situations, the IRS will focus on the employees who are not in compliance with tip reporting.

2. Another change involves restaurants with locations in different IRS Districts. Under the new plan, the restaurant's headquarter operations will work directly with their local IRS office on TRAC issues. This streamlined approach will be simpler and more straightforward than the old system, where different locations of a company had to deal with different people in different IRS Districts.

3. The third change involves the expiration date of the TRAC program. Instead of ending in May, 2000, the program will now run through May, 2005, with the possibility of its being extended even longer.

About 10,000 companies, representing more than 30,000 locations, have already entered the agreements, and the IRS hopes more will follow in the months ahead as a result of this shifting of more responsibility to the employee.

Instituting the Program

To enter into one of the arrangements, an employer should submit an application letter to the area IRS Chief, Examination/Compliance Division, Attn: Tip Coordinator. The Tip Coordinator can provide a letter format as well as extensive information on the two separate arrangements.

All employers with establishments where tipping is customary should review their operations. Then, if it is determined that there is or has been an underreporting of tips, the employer should apply for one of the two arrangements under the TRD/EP. Employers currently with the TRDA in effect may revoke the arrangement and simultaneously enter into a TRAC.

The particular advantage to the employer who adopts one of these programs is that no subsequent tip examination is imposed as long as terms of the arrangement have been met and all tips have been reported.

BASIC RULES RELATING TO TIP INCOME REPORTING

The following discussion concerns how tip income is taxed and how it should be reported to the IRS on the federal income tax return. The employees of food and beverage companies are the main subjects of this review; the record keeping rules and other information also apply to other workers who receive tips.

As pointed out earlier, all tips that are received by employees are taxable income and are subject to federal income taxes. Employees must include in gross income all tips received directly from customers, and tips from charge customers paid to the employer, who must pay them to the employee. In addition, cash tips of $20 or more that an employee receives in a month while working for any one employer are subject to withholding of income tax, social security retirement tax, and Medicare tax. The employee should report tips to the employer in order to determine the correct amount of these taxes.

Tips and other pay are used to determine the amount of social security benefits that an employee receives when he or she retires, becomes disabled, or dies. Noncash tips are not counted as wages for social security purposes. Future Social Security Administration (SSA) benefits can be figured correctly only if the SSA has the correct information. To make sure that an employee has received credit for all his or her earnings, the employee should request a statement of earnings from the SSA at least every other year. The SSA will send the person a statement that should be carefully checked to be sure it includes all of the employee's earnings.

Every large food and beverage business must report to the IRS any tips allocated to the employees. Generally, tips must be allocated to be paid by employees when the total tips reported to an employer by employees are less than 8% of the establishment's food and beverage sales of that employee. This necessitates the employer and employees keeping accurate records of the employee's tip income.

Daily Tip Record

The employee must keep a daily tip record so he or she can:

1. Report tips accurately to the employer.
2. Report tips accurately on a tax return.
3. Prove tip income if the taxpayer's return is ever questioned.

There are two ways to keep a daily tip record:

1. The employee can keep a daily "tip diary."
2. The employee should keep copies of documents that show the tips, such as restaurant bills and credit card charge slips.

The employee can start record keeping by writing his or her name, the employer's name, and the name of the business if it is different from the employer's name. Each workday, the employee should write and date the following information in a tip diary.

1. Cash tips received directly from customers or other employees.
2. Tips from credit card charge customers that the employer pays the employee.
3. The value of any noncash tips received, such as tickets, passes, or other items of value.
4. The amount of tips the employee paid out to other employees through tip pools, tip splitting, or other arrangements, and the names of the employees to whom tips were paid.

Reporting Tips to the Employer

The employee must report tips to the employer so that:

1. The employer can withhold federal income tax, social security taxes, and Medicare taxes.
2. The employer can report the correct amount of the employee's earnings to the Social Security Administration. This will affect the employee's benefits when the employee retires or becomes disabled, or the family's benefits upon the employee's death.

What Tips to Report

Only cash, check, or credit card tips should be reported to the employer. If the total tips for any one month from any one job are less than $20, they should not be reported to the employer. The value of any noncash tips, such as tickets or passes, is not reported to the employer because the employee does not have to pay social security and Medicare taxes on these tips. The employee will, however, report them on his or her individual tax return. The following information should be written on the report to be given to the employer:

1. Name, address, and social security number.
2. The employer's name, address, and business name if it is different from the employer's name.
3. The month, or the dates of any shorter period, in which the tips are received.
4. The total amount of tips the employee received.

The employee must sign and date the report and give it to the employer. The employee should keep a copy of the report for his or her personal records. The report is to be completed each month and given to the employer by the tenth of the next month.

Employer Records for Tip Allocation

Large food and beverage establishments are required to report certain additional information about tips to the IRS. To make sure that employees are reporting tips correctly, employers must keep records to verify amounts reported by employees. Certain employers must allocate tips if the percentage of tips reported by employees falls below a required minimum percentage of gross sales. To allocate tips means to assign an additional amount as tips to each employee whose reported tips are below the required percentage. The rules apply to premises in which:

1. Food and beverages are provided for consumption on the premises.
2. Tipping is customary.
3. The employer normally employed more than ten people on a typical business day during the preceding calendar year.

Tip allocation rules do not apply to food and beverage establishments where tipping is not customary such as:

1. A cafeteria or fast food restaurant.
2. A restaurant that adds a service charge of 10% or more to 95% or more of its food and beverage sales.
3. Food and beverage establishments located outside the United States.

The rules apply only if the total amount of tips reported by all tipped employees to the employer is less than 8%, or some lower acceptable percentage of the establishment's total food or beverage sales, with some adjustments. If reported tips total less than 8% of total sales, the employer must allocate the difference between 8% of total sales, or some lower acceptable percentage approved by the IRS, and the amount of tips reported by all tipped employees. The employer will exclude carryout sales, state and local taxes, and sales with a service charge of 10% or more when figuring total sales.

Usually, the employer will allocate to all affected employees their share of tips every payroll period. However, the employer should not withhold any taxes from the allocated amount. No allocation will be made to the employee if the employee reports tips at least equal to the employee's share of 8% of the establishment's total food and beverage sales.

Penalty for Not Reporting Tips

If the employee does not report tips to his or her employer as required, the employee can be subject to a penalty equal to 50% of the social security and Medicare taxes owed. The penalty amount is in addition to the taxes owed.

The penalty can be avoided if the employee can show reasonable cause for not reporting the tips to the employer. A statement should be attached to the tax return explaining why the tips were not reported to the employer. If an employee's regular pay is not enough for the employer to withhold all the taxes owed on the regular pay plus reported tips, the employee can give the employer money to pay the rest of the taxes, up to the close of the calendar year.

If the employee does not give the employer enough money, the employer will apply the regular pay and any money given by the employee in the following order:

1. All taxes on the employee's regular pay.
2. Social security and Medicare taxes on the reported tips.
3. Federal, state, and local income taxes on the reported tips.

Any taxes that remain unpaid can be collected by the employer from the employee's next paycheck. If withholding taxes remain uncollected at the end of the year, the employee must make an estimated tax payment. To report these taxes, a return must be filed even if the employee would not otherwise have to file. If the employer could not collect all the social security and Medicare taxes owed on the tips reported to the employer, the uncollected taxes must be shown by the employer on a Form W-2. The employee must then also report these uncollected taxes on his or her return.

TIP RATES

Depending on the Occupational Category and the employer's business practices, tips can be *measured* in different ways.

1. *Actual tips* generally apply to Employees in Occupational Categories (O.C.) where pooling of tips is common. The tips are pooled during a shift and the total is split among the employees of the O.C. who worked the shift.
2. *Tip rates* generally apply to employees in O.C. where pooling of tips is not common. The rate may be a percentage of sales, a dollar amount, or other accurate basis of measurement per hour or shift, a dollar amount per drink served, a dollar amount per working hour, or other accurate measurement.

Methods for Determining Tip Rates

The employer will determine tip rates for the O.C. based on information available to the employer, historical information provided by the district director, and generally accepted accounting principles (GAAP). The rates will specify whether the tips are received as a percentage of sales, a dollar amount per hour or shift, a dollar amount per drink served, a dollar amount per dealing hour in a casino, or on another basis.

Initial Tip Rate

The initial tip rate for each O.C. is shown where pool and split tips methods are used by the employees.

ANNUAL REVIEW

The employer will review annually, on a calender year basis, changes in the tip rates assigned to its O.C. In connection with the review, the employer can review its O.C. The initial rates for each O.C. will apply to the first full calendar year of the review.

Employer Submission

If the employer believes that a revision of one or more rates or O.C. is appropriate, the employer will submit proposed revisions to the District Director by September 30. If the employer fails to submit a proposed rate revision by September 30 of the taxable year, the employee will be treated as having submitted the rate in effect for the current year.

District Director Review

The District Director will review the proposed rates and notify the employer in writing of the approval or disapproval by November 30. If the District Director does not approve one or more proposed rates, the existing rate or rates will be continued until no later than the last day of the following February.

The effective date of revised rates and O.C. will become effective on the later of January 1 of the calendar year, or on the first day of the month following the date the employer and the district director agree upon a revised rate. The district director can examine a participating employee's tip income for any period if an employee reports tips at a rate less than the tip rate for the employee's occupational category.

These amounts must be an additional tax on the employee's tax return. The employee may have uncollected taxes if his or her regular pay was not enough for the employer to withhold all the taxes the taxpayer owed, but did not give the employer enough money to pay the rest of the taxes. The employee must report these uncollected taxes on a return.

ALLOCATED TIPS

Allocated tips are tips that the employer assigned to an employee in addition to the tips the employee reported to the employer for the year. The employer will have done this only if the employee worked in a restaurant, cocktail lounge, or similar business that must allocate tips to employees, and the reported tips were less than the employee's share of 8% of food and drink sales. If allocated tips are shown on a return, and if social security and Medicare taxes were not withheld from the allocated tips, these taxes must be reported as additional tax on a return.

Allocation Formula

The allocation can be done either under a formula agreed to by both the employer and the employees or, if they cannot reach an agreement, under a formula prescribed by IRS regulations. The allocation formula in the regulations provides that tip allocations are made only to directly tipped employees. If tips are received directly from customers, the employees are directly tipped employees, even if the tips are turned over to a tip pool. Waiters, waitresses, and bartenders are usually considered directly tipped employees. If tips are not normally received directly from customers, the employee is an indirectly tipped employee. Examples are busboys, service bartenders, and cooks. If an employee receives tips both directly and indirectly through tip splitting or tip pooling, the employee is treated as a directly tipped employee.

If customers of the establishment tip less than 8% on average, either the employee or a majority of the directly tipped employees can petition to have the allocation percentage reduced from 8%. This petition is made to the district director for the IRS district in which the establishment is located. The percentage cannot be reduced below 2%.

A fee is required to have the IRS consider a petition to lower the tip allocation percentage. The fee must be paid by check or money order made out to the Internal Revenue Service. (The user fee amount for 1998 is $275; the district director in the taxpayer's area will know if this amount has changed.)

The employees' petition to lower the allocation percentage must be in writing, and must contain enough information to allow the district director to estimate with reasonable accuracy the establishment's actual tip rate. This information might include the changed tip rate, type of establishment, menu prices, location, hours of operation, amount of self-service required, and whether the customer receives the check from the server or pays the server for the meal. If the employer possesses any relevant information, the employer must provide it to the district upon request of the employees or the district director.

The employees' petition must be consented to by more than one-half of the directly tipped employees working for the establishment at the time the petition is filed. If the petition covers more than one establishment, it must be consented to by more than one-half of the total number of directly tipped employees of the covered establishments. The petition must state the total number of directly tipped employees of the establishment(s) and the number of directly tipped employees consenting to the petition.

The petition may cover two or more establishments if the employees have made a good faith determination that the tip wages are essentially the same and if the establishments are:

1. Owned by the same employer.
2. Essentially the same type of business.
3. In the same Internal Revenue Service region.

A petition that covers two or more establishments must include the names and locations of the establishments and must be sent to the district director for the district in which the greatest number of covered establishments are located. If there is an equal number of covered establishments in two or more districts, the employees can choose which district to petition. Employees who file a petition must promptly notify their employer of the petition. The employer must then promptly furnish the district director with an annual information return form showing the tip income and allocated tips filed for the establishment for the three immediately preceding calendar years.

The employer will report the amount of tips allocated to employees on the employees' Form W-2 separately from wages and reported tips. The employer bases withholding only on wages and reported tips. The employer should not withhold income, social security, and Medicare taxes from the allocated amount. Any incorrectly withheld taxes should be refunded to the employee by the employer.

If an employee leaves a job before the end of the calendar year and requests an early Form W-2, the employer does not have to include a tip allocation on the Form W-2. However, the employer can show the actual allocated amount if it is known, or show an estimated allocation. In January of the following year, the employer most provide Form W-2 if the early Form W-2 showed no allocation and the employer later determined that an allocation was required, or if the estimated allocation shown was wrong by more than 5% of the actual allocation.

If an employee does not have adequate records for his or her actual tips, the employee must include the allocated tips shown on the Form W-2 as additional tip income on the tax return. If the employee has records, allocated tips should not be shown on the employee's return. Additional tip income is included only if those records show more tips received than the amount reported to the employer.

SUPREME COURT RULING ON "AGGREGATE METHOD"

In 2002, a 6-3 ruling by the Supreme Court upheld a move by federal tax collectors to force employers to pay the 7.65% Social Security tax on all income received by their workers, including tips. The dispute originally arose over the method used to calculate the total tip income, specifically in restaurants.

At some previous time, restaurant owners had been told that they could rely on reports from their servers and bartenders. However, tips were being notoriously underreported as was pointed out in the first paragraph of this chapter.

In the early 1990s, the IRS decided to survey credit card slips to calculate how much waiters and waitresses were actually receiving in tips. From this information, the Service would use the average tip to estimate the total of tips. For example, if customers on average added a 15% tip on their credit cards, the IRS would assume that customers tipped 15% on all of the restaurant's income, including cash payments. The owner could be assessed back taxes based on this amount.

The restaurant industry objected strenuously, claiming that customers who pay in cash often leave lower tips and that some leave no tip whatsoever. However, the Supreme Court Justices discounted such complaints and upheld the estimates based on credit card receipts as a reasonable way to assess the taxes owed by a restaurant.

In the specific instance, the IRS estimated the tips for 1992 as $368,374, not the $220,845 that the servers had reported. The IRS sent the owner an $11,286 bill for back taxes for 1992 to cover his share of the employee Social Security taxes, known officially as the Federal Insurance Contribution Act (FICA) taxes.

Steps Toward a Decision

A Circuit Court of Appeals judge had then ruled the IRS was not empowered to "slap an employer" with back tax assessments based on "rough and somewhat inflated estimates." However, the U.S. Solicitor General appealed the issue to the Supreme Court. It was pointed out that the amount of reported tips to the IRS rose from $8.5 billion in 1994 to $14.3 billion in 1999 after the tax agency pressed for better compliance. This demonstrated rather graphically that tip income had been greatly underreported.

There is no question but that the restaurant owners can challenge the accuracy of their tax assessments. However, the majority opinion of the Supreme Court stated that their objections do not "show the aggregate estimate method is an unreasonable way of ascertaining unpaid FICA taxes for which the employer is indisputably liable."

Reaction to the Decision

Leaders of the National Restaurant Association, which represents 200,000 eating establishments, denounced the decision and said they would take their fight to Congress. They feel that the ruling may affect all employers, like hotels, casinos and taxi companies whose employees receive tips.

An IRS lawyer stressed that the "aggregate estimate" method (the term given to this system of determining tax owed) has not been widely used so far. Moreover, it was emphasized that it is brought into the picture only when it appears restaurants are underpaying their taxes.

Understandably, the Commissioner for the IRS favored the Supreme Court decision and feels that it upholds the IRS's ability to make sure all Americans pay a fair share of taxes. The IRS plans to continue working cooperatively with the restaurant industry and other industries where tips are common.

With the 6-3 decision in the books, the IRS does not anticipate any particular change in the manner of determining and collecting the taxes on tip income.

Reaction to the Decision

Chapter 43

Insurance Accounting

CONTENTS

The IASC Paper on Insurance Accounting   **43.01**

Financial Accounting Standards Board Statements That
    Cover Accounting and Reporting by Insurance Enterprises   **43.06**

THE IASC PAPER ON INSURANCE ACCOUNTING

As one of the final steps to fill out their core of basic standards for financial reporting, the International Accounting Standards Committee (IASC) published an Issues Paper on Insurance in December, 1999. The Issues Paper developed by IASC's Steering Committee on Insurance is the first step in this project.

It includes the following topics:

1. The different forms of insurance contract and specific characteristics that are relevant in determining the appropriate accounting treatment.
2. Accounting and disclosure issues and arguments for and against possible solutions to those issues.
3. The tentative views of the Steering Committee at this early stage of the project.

It was published together with an accompanying booklet that contains the following:

1. Illustrative examples; 82 are shown.
2. Summaries of relevant national standards and requirements in 17 countries.
3. Summaries of the main features of the principal contracts found in 8 countries.
4. A glossary of terms used in the paper.
5. Summaries of the tentative views expressed in the paper.

It seems obvious from the scope of the booklet that there is a need to bring about at least partial convergence of accounting treatment for insurance.

The chairman of IASC's steering committee on insurance pointed out that the industry is becoming increasingly important as an international industry.

This takes on particular significance when considering the diversity in accounting practices for insurers. Not only are insurance industry accounting practices significantly different in a number of countries, but even within the same country, accounting practices for insurance varies.

It follows that this makes it difficult for users to compare financial statements issued by insurers in different countries, and even by insurers within the same country.

With the worldwide emphasis on the need for transparency and comparability in financial reporting, it becomes apparent that accounting for insurance needs serious attention. Insurers need to provide more relevant and reliable information that the users of their financial statements can rely upon as a basis for economic decisions.

The information disclosed by insurers should enable users to compare the financial position and financial performance of insurers in different countries. That information should also be comparable with information disclosed about similar transactions by enterprises that are not insurers.

Insurance Contracts

The project addresses accounting for insurance contracts (or groups of contracts), rather than all aspects of accounting by insurance enterprises.

An insurance contract is a contract under which one party (the insurer) accepts an insurance risk by agreeing with another party (the policyholder) to make payment if a specified uncertain future event occurs.

Exceptions are an event that is only a change in a specified variable:

1. Interest rate.
2. Security price.
3. Commodity price.

4. Foreign exchange rate.
5. Index of prices or rates.
6. Credit rating or credit index.
7. Similar variable.

The following are examples of contracts that meet the definition of an insurance contract:

1. Insurance against damage to property.
2. Insurance against product liability, professional liability, civil liability or legal expenses.
3. Life insurance (although death is certain, it is uncertain when death will occur or, for some types of life insurance, whether death will occur at all within the period covered by the insurance).
4. Annuities and pensions (for annuities, the uncertain future event is the survival of the annuitant).
5. Disability and medical coverage.
6. Performance bonds and bid bonds (under which an enterprise under-takes to make a payment if another party fails to perform a contractual obligation, for example, an obligation to construct a building).
7. Product warranties issued either directly by a manufacturer or dealer or indirectly by an insurer.
8. Financial guarantees; for example, of a loan.
9. Title insurance (insurance against the discovery of defects in title to land that were not apparent when the insurance contract was written. In this case, the uncertain future event is the discovery of a defect in the title, not the defect itself).
10. Travel assistance (compensation in cash or in kind to policyholders for losses suffered while they are traveling).
11. Catastrophe bonds (bonds that provide for reduced payments of princi-pal and/or interest if a specified event occurs).
12. Contracts that require a payment based on climatic, geological, or other physical variables (referred to as weather derivatives).
13. Reinsurance (insurance contracts between a direct insurer and a rein-surer, or between two reinsurers, in order to limit the risk exposure of the first insurer).

Types of Insurance Risk

The Steering Committee believes that the feature that distinguishes insurance contracts from other financial instruments is the risk that the insurer will need to make payment to another party if a specified uncertain future event occurs. They also believe that a contract that transfers only price risk (i.e. a derivative) should not be included in the definition of an insurance contract and should fall within the scope of the financial instruments project. Therefore, the Committee proposes that the definition of insurance contract should exclude contracts where the only uncertain future event that triggers payment is *a change in one of the seven variables* listed above.

This is consistent with IAS 39, *Financial Instruments: Recognition and Measurement.* Thus it is appropriate to describe the risk that is present in an insurance contract as *insurance risk* and the risk that is present in a derivative financial instrument as *price risk.*

Insurance risk covers a number of different types of risk, including:

1. Occurrence risk: the possibility that the number of insured events will differ from those expected.
2. Severity risk: the possibility that the cost of events will differ from expected cost.
3. Development risk: a residual category. It refers generally to changes in the amount of an insurer's obligation after the end of a contract period. Such changes may result from the late identification of insured events that occurred during the contract period; the possibility that claims will settle more quickly or in amounts greater than expected; that courts may interpret the insurer's liability differently than expected; other factors that may change the insurer's initial estimate of costs to settle incurred claims.

Recognition and Measurement

The objective should be to measure the assets and liabilities that arise from insurance contracts (an asset-and-liability measurement approach), rather than to defer income and expense so that they can be matched with each other (a deferral-and-matching approach).

Insurance liabilities (both general insurance and life insurance) should be discounted.

The measurement of insurance liabilities should be based on current estimates of future cash flows from the current contract. Estimated future cash flows from renewals are:

1. Included if the current contract commits the insurer to pricing for those renewals.
2. Excluded if the insurer retains full discretion to change pricing.

In the view of a majority of the Steering Committee, catastrophe and equalization reserves are not liabilities under IASC's framework. There may be a need for specific disclosures about low-frequency, high-severity risks, perhaps by segregating a separate component of equity.

The measurement of insurance liabilities should reflect risk to the extent that risk would be reflected in the price of an arm's length transaction between knowledgeable, willing parties. It follows that the sale of a long-term insurance contract may lead in some cases to the immediate recognition of income. The Steering Committee recognizes that some may have reservations about changing current practice in this way.

1. Overstatement of insurance liabilities should not be used to impose implicit solvency or capital adequacy requirements.
2. Acquisition costs should not be deferred as an asset.
3. All changes in the carrying amount of insurance liabilities should be recognized as they arise. In deciding what components of these changes should be presented or disclosed separately, the Steering Committee will monitor progress by the Joint Working Group on Financial Instruments.

Anticipated Requirement of Full Fair Value Accounting

The Steering Committee is working on the assumption that IAS 39, *Financial Instruments: Recognition and Measurement* will be replaced before the end of the Insurance project by a new IAS that will require full fair value accounting for the substantial majority of financial assets and liabilities.

The Committee believes that:

1. If such a standard exists, portfolios of insurance contracts should also be measured at fair value. IASC defines fair value as "the amount for which an asset could be exchanged or a liability settled between knowledgeable, willing parties in an arm's length transaction."
2. In a fair value accounting model, the liability under a life insurance contract that has an explicit or implicit account balance may be less than the account balance.
3. Determining the fair value of insurance liabilities on a reliable, objective and verifiable basis poses difficult conceptual and practical issues, because there is generally no liquid and active secondary market in liabilities and assets arising from insurance contracts.

General Discussion of Measurement Issues

To avoid excessive detail, the Issues Paper discusses measurement issues in fairly general terms. The Steering Committee will develop more specific guidance on measurement issues at a later stage in the project.

Pending further discussion, the Steering Committee is evenly divided on the effect of future investment margins. Some members believe that future investment margins should be reflected in determining the fair value of insurance liabilities. Other members believe that they should not.

For participating and with-profits policies:

1. Where the insurer does not control allocation of the surplus, unallocated surplus should be classified as a liability.

2. Where the insurer controls allocation of the surplus, unallocated surplus should be classified as equity (except to the extent that the insurer has a legal or constructive obligation to allocate part of the surplus to policyholders).

Liability classification is the default to be used unless there is clear evidence that the insurer controls allocation of the surplus.

For investment-linked insurance contracts, premiums received may need to be split into a risk component (revenue) and an investment component (deposit).

The accounting for reinsurance by a reinsurer should be the same as the accounting for direct insurance by a direct insurer.

Presentation and Disclosure

These proposals include the following:

1. Amounts due from reinsurers should not be offset against related insurance liabilities.

2. Most of the disclosures required by IAS 32, *Financial Instruments: Disclosure and Presentation,* and IAS 37, *Provisions, Contingent Liabilities and Contingent Assets,* are likely to be relevant for insurance contracts. Some of the disclosures required by IAS 39 may not be needed in a fair value context.

3. Other items that may require disclosure are regulatory solvency margins, key performance indicators (such as sum insured in life, retention/lapse rates, level of new business) information about risk adjustments and information about value-at-risk and sensitivity.

FINANCIAL ACCOUNTING STANDARDS BOARD STATEMENTS THAT COVER ACCOUNTING AND REPORTING BY INSURANCE ENTERPRISES

Four statements apply to insurance entities. The basic document is FASB 60, *Accounting and Reporting by Insurance Enterprises.* It has been amended and amplified by the three other statements in the following discussions.

FASB 97, *Accounting and Reporting by Insurance Enterprises for Certain Long–Duration Contracts and for Realized Gains and Losses from the Sale of Investments*

FASB Statement 97 amends Statement 60 by concluding that the accounting methods required by Statement 60 are not appropriate for insurance contracts in which the insurer can vary amounts charged or credited to the policyholder's account or the policyholder can vary the amount of premium paid.

The Statement outlines the accounting methods for three different classifications of long-duration life and annuity products. These classifications are:

1. Universal life-type policies.
2. Limited payment policies.
3. Policies not covering significant mortality or morbidity risks.

Universal Life-Type Policies.   Universal life-type policies must utilize a retrospective deposit method. The liability for this type of policy will be equal to the gross account balances before deduction of surrender charges. Revenues reported will be made up of charges assessed against the policy for mortality, expenses, and surrenders. These charges are presumed to be earned in the period during which they were assessed; however, charges, such as front-end fees, for example, assessed a limited number of times are deferred as unearned revenue.

For universal life-type policies, acquisition costs will be deferred and amortized in relation to present value of estimated future gross profits. Interest accrues to the unamortized balance of the deferred acquisition costs. The estimated gross profits are computed from estimated future mortality charges minus the estimated benefit claims exceeding:

1. The related account balances.
2. Expense charges minus the policy's estimated administration costs.
3. Estimated surrender charges.
4. Estimated future earnings based on investment yields of the policyholder's account balances, minus the estimated interest to be credited to account balances.

When the estimates of future gross profits are reevaluated, the amortization of deferred acquisition costs accrued to date must be adjusted and recognized in current operations. Any deferred revenues, including deferred front-end fees, are recognized as income on the same basis as the amortization of deferred acquisition costs.

Limited-Payment Policies.   Limited-payment policies consist of life insurance and annuity policies with fixed and guaranteed terms having premiums that are payable over a period shorter than the period during which benefits are paid. The premiums for this type of policy are reported as revenues (reserves are computed in accordance with rulings set forth in Statement 60). However, the accumulated profit, formerly shown as a percentage of premiums, is deferred. The amount of coverage must be related to life insurance in force or expected future annuity benefit payments.

Policies Not Covering Significant Mortality or Morbidity Risk. Policies not covering significant mortality or morbidity risks, such as *guaranteed investment contracts* (GICs) and some types of annuities, are shown as interest-bearing or other financial instruments, rather than as insurance contracts. Therefore, the accounting for these policies would show the account balance as a liability, and premiums as deposits rather than as revenues. Deferred acquisition costs would primarily be amortized in relation to future interest margins.

Policies including accident and health insurance not falling under one of these three classifications remain within the requirements of Statement 60.

Statement 97 also requires that property/casualty and stock life insurance companies must provide one-step income statements for realized investment gains or losses instead of the currently required two-step statement. The latter shows operating income after taxes but before net realized investment gains or losses. The one-step income statement presents realized investment gains or losses on a pretax basis with revenues, investment income, and expenses to show income before taxes.

FASB 113, *Accounting and Reporting for Reinsurance of Short-Duration and Long-Duration Contracts*

Definitions.   The following definitions of terms relate to this Statement. They will be helpful in understanding their exact meaning in this Statement.

Amortization—The act or process of extinguishing a debt, usually by equal payments over a specific period of time. The liquidation of a financial obligation on an installment basis.

Assuming Enterprise—The receiving company in a reinsurance contract. The assuming enterprise (or reinsurer) receives a reinsurance premium and, in turn, accepts an obligation to reimburse a ceding enterprise under specified terms; reinsures on a risk or exposure.

Ceding Enterprise—The company seeking a reinsurance contract. The ceding enterprise exchanges a reinsurance premium for the right to reimbursement from the assuming enterprise under specified terms. The insurer that cedes all or part of the insurance or reinsurance it has written to another insurer. Also known as the *direct writer.*

Contract Period—The length of time over which the specified terms are covered by the reinsured contracts.

Covered Period—Same as contract period (above).

Fronting Arrangements—Reinsurance provisions in which the ceding enterprise issues a policy to the assuming enterprise to reinsure all or substantially all of the insurance risk.

Incurred but Not Reported (IBNR)—Refers to losses that have occurred but have not been reported to the insurer or reinsurer.

Indemnification—Action of compensating for the actual loss or damage sustained; the fact of being compensated; the payment made for loss or damage.

Insurance Risk—The risk caused by the uncertain nature of the underwriting risk relating to the amount of net cash flows from premiums, commissions, claims, and claim settlement expenses paid as a result of contract specifications and the equally uncertain nature of the timing risk, which involves the timing of the receipt and payment of those cash flows. Actual or imputed investment returns are not an element of insurance risk. An insurance risk encompasses the possibility of adverse events occurring outside the control of the insured.

Long-Duration Contract—A contract expected to cover a prolonged period of time; in contrast to a short-duration contract (*see* Short-Duration Contract). While the time element is obvious from the long/short descriptive terms applied, the nature of the services rendered and the degree of control by the insurance company also differ. Along with insurance coverage, the long-duration carrier provides additional services and functions for the policyholder, including loans secured by the insurance policy, various options for payment of benefits, etc. The contract is usually not unilaterally controlled as is the short-duration type. It is customarily noncancellable, guaranteed renewable, and has fixed contract terms.

Most life and title insurance policies are considered long-duration contracts, while accident and health insurance policies depend on the expected term of coverage for the determination of long- or short-duration.

Offsetting—Showing a recognized asset and a recognized liability as a net amount on a financial statement. As a result of offsetting the assets and liabilities in reinsurance contracts, pertinent information could be lost and financial statement relationships altered.

Prospective Reinsurance—Reinsurance in which an assuming enterprise agrees to reimburse a ceding enterprise for losses that may be incurred as a result of future insurable events covered under contracts subject to the reinsurance. A reinsurance contract may include both prospective and retroactive reinsurance provisions.

Reinsurance—A device whereby an insurance company lessens the catastrophic hazard in the operation of the insurance mechanism; insurance for the insurer.

Reinsurance Receivables—All amounts recoverable from reinsurers for past and unpaid claims and claim settlement expenses, including estimated amounts receivable for unsettled claims, claims incurred but not reported, or policy benefits.

Reinsurer—See Assuming Enterprise.

Retroactive Reinsurance—Reinsurance in which an assuming enterprise agrees to reimburse a ceding enterprise for liabilities incurred as a result of past insurable events covered under contracts subject to reinsurance. A reinsurance contract may include both prospective and retroactive reinsurance provisions.

Retrocession—The process by which the reinsurer, or assuming enterprise, in turn, becomes a party in a reinsurance contract with still other reinsurers.

Settlement Period—The estimated period over which a ceding enterprise expects to recover substantially all amounts due from the reinsurer under the specified terms of the reinsurance contract.

Short-Duration Contract—An insurance policy not expected to cover an extended period of time. A carrier primarily provides insurance for a short, fixed period. The insurance carrier has more one-way control than in the long-duration contract (*see* Long-Duration Contract). The various specified terms of the contract, including amount of premiums and coverage, may be altered or canceled at the end of any contract period by the insurance company. Short-duration contracts include most property and liability policies and, to a lesser extent, some short-term life policies.

Statutory Accounting—The accounting system followed by insurance companies as required by the statutes of the various states. These procedures are geared to the National Association of Insurance Commissioners' (NAIC's) standardized reporting format. Differs in some instances from GAAP, but because the principal emphasis is on reflecting the ability of the insurer to meet its contract commitments, tends to be conservative.

General Provisions of the Statement.   FASB Statement 113, *Accounting and Reporting for Reinsurance of Short-Duration and Long-Duration Contracts* amends FASB Statement 60, *Accounting and Reporting by Insurance Companies,* and was effective for fiscal years starting after December 15, 1992. This rule eliminated the former practice of reporting assets and liabilities related to insurance contracts net of the effects of reinsurance. Statement 60, which is the basic document dealing with specialized insurance accounting and reporting practices, had continued the statutory accounting practice of offsetting reinsurance assets and liabilities. However, this procedure is now considered inconsistent with the generally accepted criteria for offsetting. Under this rule, the practice is eliminated for general-purpose financial statements.

Beginning in 1993, reinsurance receivables and prepaid reinsurance premiums are reported as assets. Reinsurance receivables include amounts related to (a) claims incurred but not reported and (b) liabilities for future policy benefits. Estimated reinsurance receivables are recognized in a manner consistent with the related liabilities.

Statement 113 set up a method of determining whether a specific contract qualified for reinsurance accounting. The accounting standard revolves around determination of whether the reinsurance is long-duration or short-duration, and, if short-duration, whether it is prospective or retroactive insurance. A contract must result in a reasonable possibility that the reinsurer may realize a significant loss from assuming insurance risk, or the contract does not qualify for reinsurance accounting, but must be accounted for as a deposit. All reinsurance contracts prohibit the reinsurance from recognizing immediately a gain if there remains a chance of liability to the policyholder by the ceding enterprise.

To further clarify the financial picture, the reinsurer is required to provide footnote disclosures explaining all facets of the terms, nature, purpose, and effect of ceded reinsurance transactions. In addition, disclosures of concentrations of credit risk associated with reinsurance receivables and prepaid premiums are also required under the provisions of FASB 105, *Disclosures of Information About Financial Instruments with Off-Balance-Sheet Risk and Financial Instruments with Concentrations of Credit Risk.*

Cause for Concern.   A portion of the impetus for consideration, or reconsideration, of the accounting and reporting for reinsurance has evolved from the general concern about the highly visible failure of some insurance companies. Risk relating to reinsurance has been considered germane to some of the failed enterprises.

Among the concerns voiced in regard to reinsurance have been:

1. The effect of reinsurance accounting relating to contracts that did not provide indemnification for the ceding party against loss or liability.
2. The fact that FASB Statement 60 did not provide sufficient guidance relating to reinsurance accounting. Among other weaknesses, this led to acceleration of the recognition of income relating to reinsurance contracts.
3. The absence of requirements for disclosure of reinsurance transactions. The policyholder was seldom aware of any reinsurance arrangement.
4. The inconsistency between the widespread use of *net* accounting for reinsurance-related assets and liabilities in spite of not meeting the established criteria for offsetting.

Therefore, the thrust of the Statement is: (a) as already noted, to address these perceived problems; (b) to provide guidance in the determination of whether specific reinsurance contracts actually make provision for indemnification of the ceding enterprise to qualify for reinsurance accounting; and (c) to establish the necessary accounting methods.

Statement 113 did *not* change practice in accounting for reinsurance *assumed* other than to require certain disclosures relating to reinsurance by all insurance companies.

For short-duration contracts to qualify for reinsurance accounting, there should be a positive answer to the following questions:

1. Does the reinsurer assume significant insurance risk under the reinsurance provisions of the underlying insurance contracts?
2. Is there a reasonable possibility that the assuming enterprise may be faced with a significant loss as a result of this contract?
3. Is there a possibility of a significant variation in the amount or timing of payments by the reinsurer?

A ceding company's evaluation of whether it is reasonably possible for a reinsurer to realize a significant loss should be based on a present value analysis of cash flows between the ceding and assuming enterprises under reasonably possible outcomes. When the ceding company reaches the conclusion that the reinsurer is not exposed to the possibility of significant loss, the ceding company can decide that it is indemnified against loss or liability related to insurance risk only if *substantially all* of the insurance risk relating to the reinsured portion of the specific underlying insurance policy has been assumed by the reinsurer. Thus, any insurance risk remaining with the ceding company must be of little or no importance or of a trivial nature if the ceding company decides to consider itself indemnified against loss or liability.

For a long-duration contract to qualify for reinsurance accounting, there must be a reasonable probability that the reinsurer may realize significant loss from assuming the insurance risk. FASB Statement 97, *Accounting and Reporting by Insurance Enterprises for Certain Long-Duration Contracts and for Realized Gains and Losses from the Sale of Investments,* defines long-duration contracts that do not subject the insurer to mortality or morbidity risks as investment contracts. Consistent with that definition, if a contract does not subject the reinsurer to the reasonable possibility of significant loss from the events insured by the underlying insurance contracts, it does not indemnify the ceding enterprise against insurance risk.

FASB 113 mandates that reinsurance contracts can lead to recognition of immediate gains only if the reinsurance contract is a legal replacement of one insurer by another and the ceding company's liability to the policyholder is extinguished.

Amounts paid for prospective reinsurance of short-duration insurance contracts must be accounted for as prepaid reinsurance premiums. They are to be amortized over the remaining contract period in proportion to the amount of insurance protection provided.

Amounts paid for retroactive reinsurance of short-duration insurance contracts must be reported as insurance receivables to the extent those amounts do not exceed the recorded liabilities relating to the reinsured contracts. If the recorded liabilities exceed the amount paid, reinsurance receivables should be increased to reflect the difference and the resulting gain should be deferred. The deferred gain is to be amortized over the estimated remaining settlement period. If the amount paid for retroactive reinsurance exceeds the recorded related liabilities, the ceding company must increase the related liabilities or reduce the reinsurance receivable, or both, at the time the reinsurance contract is entered into. The excess is charged to earnings.

If, when both prospective and retroactive provisions are included in a single short-duration reinsurance transaction and it is deemed impracticable to account for every provision separately, retroactive short-duration reinsurance contract accounting must be used. Amortization of the estimated costs of insuring long-duration insurance contracts depends on whether the reinsurance contract is long- or short-duration. These costs should be amortized over the remaining life of the underlying insured contracts if the contract is long-duration, or over the reinsurance contract period if the reinsurance contract is short-duration. Determining whether a contract that reinsures a long-duration insurance contract is long- or short-duration is a matter of judgment.

Disclosure Requirments.   The financial statements of all insurance companies must now disclose the following information:

1. The nature, purpose, and effect of ceding and reinsurance transactions on the insurance company's operations.
2. The ceding company must disclose the amount of earned premiums ceded and recoveries recognized under reinsurance contracts in footnotes to the financial statement, unless these are reported separately in the statement of earnings.
3. Premiums from direct business, reinsurance assumed, and reinsurance ceded, on both a written and earned basis, must be disclosed for short-duration contracts.
4. For long-duration contracts, premiums and amounts assessed against policyholders from direct business, reinsurance assumed and ceded, and premiums and amounts earned must be disclosed.
5. Companies must detail the methods used for income recognition on their reinsurance contracts.

FASB 120, *Accounting and Reporting by Mutual Life Insurance Enterprises and by Insurance Enterprises for Certain Long–Duration Participating Contracts*

FASB 120 is the result of considerable cooperation between the Financial Accounting Standards Board and the American Institute of CPAs to provide guidance in accounting, reporting, and disclosure procedures to mutual life insurance companies. Prior to the enactment of this standard and those rulings cited below, these companies reported financial information to their creditors and policyholders primarily following the statutory provisions of various state insurance regulatory bodies. The companies are now to report insurance and reinsurance activities according to GAAP.

The thrust of this Statement is to apply the provisions of FASB 60, *Accounting and Reporting by Insurance Enterprises;* FASB 97, *Accounting and Reporting by Insurance Enterprises for Certain Long-Duration Contracts and for Realized Gains and Losses from the Sale of Investments,* and FASB 113, *Accounting and Reporting for Reinsurance of Short-Duration and Long-Duration Contracts,* to mutual life insurance enterprises, assessment enterprises and to fraternal benefit societies. Certain participating life insurance contracts of those same enterprises have also been addressed in the AICPA's Statement of Position 95-1, *Accounting for Certain Activities of Mutual Life Insurance Enterprises.* Both become effective for financial statements for fiscal years beginning after December 15, 1995.

The three earlier FASB Statements had specifically exempted mutual life insurance enterprises from their requirements. FASB Interpretation 40, *Applicability of Generally Accepted Accounting Principles to Mutual Life Insurance and Other Enterprises,* did not address or change the exemption of mutual life insurance companies from these Statements. Interpretation 40 had been scheduled to become effective earlier but the date was changed to permit simultaneous application with FASB 120 and SOP 95-1.

It was because there seemed to be little authoritative accounting guidance relative to the insurance and reinsurance activities of mutual life insurance enterprises that the FASB, along with the AICPA, decided to extend the requirements of the above mentioned standards to them. The AICPA's Statement of Position 95-1 sets guidelines for participating insurance contracts of mutual life insurance companies when:

1. They are long-duration participating contracts that are expected to pay dividends to policyholders based on the actual experience of the insurer.
2. The annual policyholder dividends are paid in a way that identifies divisible surplus, then distributes that surplus in approximately the same proportion that the contracts are estimated to have contributed to that surplus. Otherwise, accounting and reporting for these contracts are covered by the four basic FASB insurance enterprise standards listed above.

The effect of initially applying FASB 120 was reported retroactively through restatement of all previously issued annual financial statements presented for comparative purposes for fiscal years beginning after December 15, 1992.

Appendix A
Financial Planning Tables

The following tables, involving the effects of interest factors, are useful in various forms of future business planning.

SIMPLE INTEREST TABLE

Example of use of this table:
  Find amount of $500 in 8 years at 6% simple interest.
  From table at 8 yrs. and 6% for $1   1.48
  Value in 8 yrs. for $500 (500 × 1.48) $740

Number of Years	3%	4%	5%	6%	7%	8%	9%	10%
1	1.03	1.04	1.05	1.06	1.07	1.08	1.09	1.10
2	1.06	1.08	1.10	1.12	1.14	1.16	1.18	1.20
3	1.09	1.12	1.15	1.18	1.21	1.24	1.27	1.30
4	1.12	1.16	1.20	1.24	1.28	1.32	1.36	1.40
5	1.15	1.20	1.25	1.30	1.35	1.40	1.45	1.50
6	1.18	1.24	1.30	1.36	1.42	1.48	1.54	1.60
7	1.21	1.28	1.35	1.42	1.49	1.56	1.63	1.70
8	1.24	1.32	1.40	1.48	1.56	1.64	1.72	1.80
9	1.27	1.36	1.45	1.54	1.63	1.72	1.81	1.90
10	1.30	1.40	1.50	1.60	1.70	1.80	1.90	2.00
11	1.33	1.44	1.55	1.66	1.77	1.88	1.99	2.10
12	1.36	1.48	1.60	1.72	1.84	1.96	2.08	2.20
13	1.39	1.52	1.65	1.78	1.91	2.04	2.17	2.30
14	1.42	1.56	1.70	1.84	1.98	2.12	2.26	2.40
15	1.45	1.60	1.75	1.90	2.05	2.20	2.35	2.50
16	1.48	1.64	1.80	1.96	2.12	2.28	2.44	2.60
17	1.51	1.68	1.85	2.02	2.19	2.36	2.53	2.70
18	1.54	1.72	1.90	2.08	2.26	2.44	2.62	2.80
19	1.57	1.76	1.95	2.14	2.33	2.52	2.71	2.90
20	1.60	1.80	2.00	2.20	2.40	2.60	2.80	3.00
21	1.63	1.84	2.05	2.26	2.47	2.68	2.89	3.10
22	1.66	1.88	2.10	2.32	2.54	2.76	2.98	3.20
23	1.69	1.92	2.15	2.38	2.61	2.84	3.07	3.30
24	1.72	1.96	2.20	2.44	2.68	2.92	3.16	3.40
25	1.75	2.00	2.25	2.50	2.75	3.00	3.25	3.50
26	1.78	2.04	2.30	2.56	2.82	3.08	3.34	3.60
27	1.81	2.08	2.35	2.62	2.89	3.16	3.43	3.70
28	1.84	2.12	2.40	2.68	2.96	3.24	3.52	3.80
29	1.87	2.16	2.45	2.74	3.03	3.32	3.61	3.90
30	1.90	2.20	2.50	2.80	3.10	3.40	3.70	4.00
31	1.93	2.24	2.55	2.86	3.17	3.48	3.79	4.10
32	1.96	2.28	2.60	2.92	3.24	3.56	3.88	4.20
33	1.99	2.32	2.65	2.98	3.31	3.64	3.97	4.30
34	2.02	2.36	2.70	3.04	3.38	3.72	4.06	4.40
35	2.05	2.40	2.75	3.10	3.45	3.80	4.15	4.50
36	2.08	2.44	2.80	3.16	3.52	3.88	4.24	4.60
37	2.11	2.48	2.85	3.22	3.59	3.96	4.33	4.70
38	2.14	2.52	2.90	3.28	3.66	4.04	4.42	4.80
39	2.17	2.56	2.95	3.34	3.73	4.12	4.51	4.90
40	2.20	2.60	3.00	3.40	3.80	4.20	4.60	5.00

COMPOUND INTEREST TABLE

Example of use of this table:
Find how much $1,000 now in bank will grow to in 14 years at 6% interest.
From table 14 years at 6%   2.2609
Value in 14 years of $1,000 $2,260.9

Number of Years	6%	6 1/2%	7%	7 1/2%	Interest Rate 8%	8 1/2%	9%	9 1/2%
1	1.0600	1.0650	1.0700	1.0750	1.0800	1.0850	1.0900	1.0950
2	1.1236	1.1342	1.1449	1.1556	1.1664	1.1772	1.1881	1.1990
3	1.1910	1.2079	1.2250	1.2422	1.2597	1.2772	1.2950	1.3129
4	1.2624	1.2864	1.3107	1.3354	1.3604	1.3858	1.4115	1.4376
5	1.3332	1.3700	1.4025	1.4356	1.4693	1.5036	1.5386	1.5742
6	1.4135	1.4591	1.5007	1.5433	1.5868	1.6314	1.6771	1.7237
7	1.5030	1.5539	1.6057	1.6590	1.7138	1.7701	1.8230	1.8875
8	1.5938	1.6549	1.7181	1.7834	1.8509	1.9206	1.9925	2.0668
9	1.6894	1.7625	1.8384	1.9172	1.9990	2.0838	2.1718	2.2632
10	1.7908	1.8771	1.9671	2.0610	2.1589	2.2609	2.3673	2.4782
11	1.8982	1.9991	2.1048	2.2156	2.3316	2.4531	2.5804	2.7136
12	2.0121	2.1290	2.2521	2.3817	2.5181	2.6616	2.8126	2.9714
13	2.1329	2.2674	2.4098	2.5604	2.7196	2.8879	3.0658	3.2537
14	2.2609	2.4148	2.5785	2.7524	2.9371	3.1334	3.3417	3.5628
15	2.3965	2.5718	2.7590	2.9588	3.1721	3.3997	3.6424	3.9013
16	2.5403	2.7390	2.9521	3.1807	3.4259	3.6887	3.9703	4.2719
17	2.6927	2.9170	3.1588	3.4193	3.7000	4.0022	4.3276	4.6777
18	2.8543	3.1066	3.3799	3.6758	3.9960	4.3424	4.7171	5.1221
19	3.0255	3.3085	3.6165	3.9514	4.3157	4.7115	5.1416	5.6087
20	3.2075	3.5236	3.8696	4.2478	4.6609	5.1120	5.6044	6.1416
21	3.3995	3.7526	4.1405	4.5664	5.0338	5.5465	6.1088	6.7250
22	3.6035	3.9966	4.4304	4.9089	5.4365	6.0180	6.6586	7.3639
23	3.8197	4.2563	4.7405	5.2770	5.8714	6.5295	7.2578	8.0635
24	4.0489	4.5330	5.0723	5.6728	6.3411	7.0845	7.9110	8.8295
25	4.2918	4.8276	5.4274	6.0983	6.8484	7.6867	8.6230	9.6683
26	4.5493	5.1414	5.8073	6.5557	7.3963	8.3401	9.3991	10.5868
27	4.8223	5.4756	6.2138	7.0473	7.9880	9.0490	10.2450	11.5926
28	5.1116	5.8316	6.6488	7.5759	8.6271	9.8182	11.1671	12.6939
29	5.4183	6.2106	7.1142	8.1441	9.3172	10.6527	12.1721	13.8998
30	5.7434	6.6143	7.6122	8.7549	10.5582	11.5582	13.2676	15.2203
31	6.0881	7.0442	8.1451	9.4115	10.8676	12.5407	14.4617	16.6662
32	6.4533	7.5021	8.7152	10.1174	11.7370	13.6066	15.7633	18.2495
33	6.8408	7.9898	9.3253	10.8762	12.6760	14.7632	17.1820	19.9832
34	7.2510	8.5091	9.9781	11.6919	13.6901	16.0181	18.7284	21.8816
35	7.6860	9.0622	10.6765	12.5688	14.7853	17.3796	20.4139	23.9604
36	8.1479	9.6513	11.4239	13.5115	15.9681	18.8569	22.2512	26.2366
37	8.6360	10.2786	12.2236	14.5249	17.2456	20.4597	24.2538	28.7291
38	9.1542	10.9467	13.0792	15.6142	18.6252	22.1988	26.4366	31.4583
39	9.7035	11.6582	13.9948	16.7853	20.1152	24.0857	28.8159	34.4469
40	10.2857	12.4160	14.9744	18.0442	21.7245	26.1330	31.4094	37.7193

Compound Interest Table (*Cont'd*)

Number of Years	10%	11%	12%	13%	14%	15%	16%	17%
1	1.1000	1.1100	1.1200	1.1300	1.1400	1.1500	1.1600	1.1700
2	1.2100	1.2321	1.2544	1.2769	1.2996	1.3225	1.3456	1.3689
3	1.3310	1.3576	1.4049	1.4428	1.4815	1.5208	1.5608	1.6016
4	1.4647	1.5180	1.5735	1.6304	1.6389	1.7490	1.8106	1.8738
5	1.6105	1.6350	1.7623	1.8424	1.9254	2.0113	2.1003	2.1924
6	1.7715	1.8704	1.9738	2.0819	2.1949	2.3130	2.4363	2.5651
7	1.9487	2.0761	2.2106	2.3526	2.5022	2.6600	2.8262	3.0012
8	2.1435	2.3045	2.4759	2.6584	2.8525	3.0590	3.2784	3.5114
9	2.3579	2.5580	2.7730	3.0040	3.2519	3.5178	3.8029	4.1084
10	2.5937	2.8394	3.1058	3.3945	3.7072	4.0455	4.4114	4.8068
11	2.8531	3.1517	3.4785	3.8358	4.2262	4.6523	5.1172	5.6239
12	3.1384	3.4984	3.8959	4.3345	4.8179	5.3502	5.9360	6.5800
13	3.4522	3.8832	4.3634	4.8980	5.4924	6.1527	6.8857	7.6986
14	3.7974	4.3104	4.8871	5.5347	6.2613	7.0757	7.9875	9.0074
15	4.1772	4.7845	5.4735	6.2542	7.1379	8.1370	9.2655	10.5387
16	4.5949	5.3108	6.1303	7.0673	8.1372	9.3576	10.7480	12.3303
17	5.0544	5.8950	6.8660	7.9860	9.2764	10.7612	12.4676	14.4264
18	5.5599	6.5435	7.6899	9.0242	10.5751	12.3754	14.4625	16.8789
19	6.1159	7.2633	8.6127	10.1974	12.0556	14.2317	16.7765	19.7483
20	6.7274	8.0623	9.6462	11.5230	13.7434	16.3665	19.4607	23.1055
21	7.4002	8.9491	10.8038	13.0210	15.6675	18.8215	22.5744	27.0335
22	8.1402	9.9335	12.1003	14.7138	17.8610	21.6447	26.1883	31.6292
23	8.9543	11.0262	13.5523	16.6266	20.3615	24.8914	30.3762	37.0062
24	9.8497	12.2391	15.1786	18.7880	23.2122	28.6251	35.2364	43.2972
25	10.8347	13.5854	17.0000	21.2305	26.4619	32.9189	40.8742	50.6578
26	11.9181	15.0793	19.0400	23.9905	30.1665	37.8567	47.4141	59.2696
27	13.1099	16.7386	21.3248	27.1092	34.3899	43.5353	55.0003	69.3454
28	14.4209	18.5799	23.8838	30.6334	39.2044	50.0656	63.8004	81.1342
29	15.8630	20.6236	26.7499	34.6158	44.6931	57.5754	74.0085	94.9270
30	17.4494	22.8922	29.9599	39.1158	50.9501	66.2117	85.8498	111.0646
31	19.1943	25.4104	33.5551	44.2009	58.0831	76.1435	99.5858	129.9456
32	21.1137	28.2055	37.5817	49.9470	66.2148	87.5650	115.5195	152.0363
33	23.2251	31.3082	42.0915	56.4402	75.4849	100.6998	134.0027	177.8825
34	25.5476	34.7521	47.1425	63.7774	86.0527	115.8048	155.4431	208.1226
35	28.1024	38.5748	52.7996	72.0685	98.1001	133.1755	180.3140	243.5034
36	30.9128	42.8180	59.1355	81.4374	111.8342	153.1518	209.1643	284.8990
37	34.0039	47.5280	66.2318	92.0242	127.4909	176.1246	242.6306	333.3319
38	37.4048	52.7561	74.1796	103.9874	145.3397	202.5433	281.4515	389.9983
39	41.1447	58.5593	83.0812	117.5057	165.6872	232.9248	326.4837	456.2980
40	45.2592	65.0008	93.0509	132.7815	188.8835	267.8635	378.7211	533.8687

Compound Interest Table (*Cont'd*)

Number of Years	18%	19%	20%	21%	22%	23%	24%	25%
1	1.1800	1.1900	1.2000	1.2100	1.2200	1.2300	1.2400	1.2500
2	1.3924	1.4161	1.4400	1.4641	1.4884	1.5129	1.5376	1.5625
3	1.6430	1.6851	1.7280	1.7715	1.8158	1.8608	1.9066	1.9531
4	1.9387	2.0053	2.0736	2.1435	2.2153	2.2888	2.3642	2.4414
5	2.2877	2.3863	2.4883	2.5937	2.7027	2.8153	2.9316	3.0517
6	2.6995	2.8397	2.9859	3.1384	3.2973	3.4628	3.6352	3.8146
7	3.1854	3.3793	3.5831	3.7974	4.0227	4.2592	4.5076	4.7683
8	3.7588	4.0213	4.2998	4.5949	4.9077	5.2389	5.5895	5.9604
9	4.4354	4.7854	5.1597	5.5599	5.9874	6.4438	6.9309	7.4505
10	5.2338	5.6946	6.1917	6.7274	7.3046	7.9259	8.5944	9.3132
11	6.1759	6.7766	7.4300	8.1402	8.9116	9.7489	10.6570	11.6415
12	7.2875	8.0642	8.9161	9.8497	10.8722	11.9911	13.2147	14.5519
13	8.5993	9.5964	10.6993	11.9181	13.2641	14.7491	16.3863	18.1898
14	10.1472	11.4197	12.8391	14.4209	16.1822	18.1414	20.3190	22.7373
15	11.9737	13.5895	15.4070	17.4494	19.7422	22.3139	25.1956	28.4217
16	14.1290	16.1715	18.4884	21.1137	24.0855	27.4461	31.2425	35.5271
17	16.6722	19.2441	22.1861	25.5476	29.3844	33.7587	38.7408	44.4089
18	19.6732	22.9005	26.6233	30.9126	35.8489	41.5233	48.0385	55.5111
19	23.2144	27.2516	31.9479	37.4043	43.7357	51.0736	59.5678	69.3889
20	27.3930	32.4294	38.3375	45.2592	53.3576	62.8206	73.8641	86.7361
21	32.3237	38.5910	46.0051	54.7636	65.0963	77.2693	91.5915	108.4202
22	38.1420	45.9233	56.2061	66.2640	79.4175	95.0413	113.5735	135.5252
23	45.0076	54.6487	66.2473	80.1795	96.8893	116.9008	140.8311	169.4065
24	53.1090	65.0319	79.4968	97.0172	118.2050	143.7880	174.6306	211.7582
25	62.6686	77.3880	95.3962	117.3908	144.2101	176.8592	216.5419	264.6977
26	73.9488	92.0918	114.4754	142.0429	175.9363	217.5368	268.5120	330.8722
27	87.2597	109.5892	137.3705	171.8719	214.6423	267.5703	332.9549	413.5903
28	102.9665	130.4112	164.8446	207.9650	261.8636	329.1115	412.8641	516.9878
29	121.5005	155.1893	197.8135	251.6377	319.4736	404.8072	511.9515	646.2348
30	143.3708	184.6753	237.3763	304.4816	389.7578	497.9128	634.8199	807.7935
31	169.1773	219.7636	284.8515	368.4227	475.5046	612.4328	787.1767	1009.7419
32	199.6292	261.5187	341.8218	445.7915	580.1156	753.2923	976.0991	1262.1774
33	235.5625	311.2072	410.1862	539.4077	707.7410	926.5496	1210.3629	1577.7218
34	277.9638	370.3366	492.2235	652.6834	863.4441	1139.6560	1500.8500	1972.1522
35	327.9972	440.7006	590.6682	789.7469	1053.4018	1401.7769	1861.0540	2465.1903
36	387.0368	524.4337	708.8018	955.5938	1285.1502	1724.1855	2307.7069	3081.4879
37	456.7034	624.0761	850.5622	1156.2685	1567.8833	2120.7482	2861.5586	3851.8598
38	538.9100	742.6505	1020.6746	1399.0849	1912.8176	2608.5203	3548.3302	4814.8248
39	635.9138	883.7542	1224.8096	1692.8927	2333.6375	3208.4800	4399.9295	6018.5310
40	750.3783	1051.6675	1469.7715	2048.4002	2847.0377	3946.4304	5455.9126	7523.1638

PERIODIC DEPOSIT TABLE

Example of use of this table:
How much is $1,000 a year invested at 6% worth in 20 years?
At 6% for 20 years, the figure is   38.993
For $1,000 a year, the amount is $38,993

Number of Years	6%	7%	8%	9%	10%	11%	12%	13%
1	1.060	1.070	1.080	1.090	1.100	1.110	1.120	1.130
2	2.183	2.215	2.246	2.278	2.310	2.342	2.374	2.407
3	3.375	3.440	3.506	3.573	3.641	3.710	3.779	3.850
4	4.637	4.751	4.867	4.985	5.105	5.228	5.353	5.480
5	5.975	6.153	6.336	6.523	6.716	6.913	7.115	7.323
6	7.394	7.654	7.923	8.200	8.487	8.783	9.089	9.405
7	8.897	9.260	9.637	10.028	10.436	10.859	11.300	11.757
8	10.491	10.978	11.488	12.021	12.579	13.164	13.776	14.416
9	12.181	12.816	13.487	14.193	14.937	15.722	16.549	17.420
10	13.972	14.784	15.645	16.560	17.531	18.561	19.655	20.814
11	15.870	16.888	17.977	19.141	20.384	21.713	23.133	24.650
12	17.882	19.141	20.495	21.953	23.523	25.212	27.029	28.985
13	20.015	21.550	23.215	25.019	26.975	29.095	31.393	33.883
14	22.276	24.129	26.152	28.361	30.772	33.405	36.280	39.417
15	24.673	26.888	29.324	32.003	34.950	38.190	41.753	45.672
16	27.213	29.840	32.750	35.974	39.545	43.501	47.884	52.739
17	29.906	32.999	36.450	40.301	44.599	49.396	54.750	60.725
18	32.760	36.379	40.446	45.018	50.159	55.939	62.440	69.749
19	3$.786	39.995	44.762	50.160	56.275	63.203	71.052	79.947
20	38.993	43.865	49.423	55.765	63.002	71.265	80.699	91.470
21	42.392	48.006	54.457	61.873	70.403	80.214	91.503	104.491
22	45.996	52.436	59.893	68.532	78.543	90.148	103.603	119.205
23	49.816	57.177	65.765	75.790	87.497	101.174	117.155	135.831
24	53.865	62.249	72.106	83.701	97.347	113.413	132.334	154.620
25	58.156	67.676	78.954	92.324	108.182	126.999	149.334	175.850
26	62.706	73.484	86.351	101.723	120.100	142.079	168.374	199.841
27	67.528	79.698	94.339	111.968	133.210	158.817	189.699	226.950
28	72.640	86.347	102.966	123.135	147.631	177.397	213.583	257.583
29	78.058	93.461	112.283	135.308	163.494	198.021	240.333	292.199
30	83.802	101.073	122.346	148.575	180.943	220.913	270.293	331.315
31	89.890	109.218	133.214	163.037	200.138	246.324	303.848	375.516
32	96.343	117.933	144.951	178.800	221.252	274.529	341.429	425.463
33	103.184	127.259	157.627	195.982	244.477	305.837	383.521	481.903
34	110.435	137.237	171.317	214.711	270.024	340.590	430.663	545.681
35	118.121	147.913	186.102	235.125	298.127	379.164	483.463	617.749
36	126.268	159.337	202.070	257.376	329.039	421.982	542.599	699.187
37	134.904	171.561	219.316	281.630	363.043	469.511	608.831	791.211
38	144.058	184.640	237.941	308.066	400.448	522.267	683.010	895.198
39	153.762	198.635	258.057	336.882	441.593	580.826	766.091	1012.704
40	164.048	213.610	279.781	368.292	486.852	645.827	859.142	1145.486

COMPOUND DISCOUNT TABLE

This table shows the present or discounted value of $1 due at a given future time. For example, assume property which will revert to a lessor in 10 years will then be worth $1,000. The present value of this reversion, computed at an assumed rate of 4% on the investment, is found by finding the factor on the 10-year line in the 4% column. The factor .6756 is multiplied by 1000 to obtain the answer of $675.60.

Years	4%	4-1/2%	5%	5-1/2%	6%	6-1/2%	7%	7-1/2%	8%	9%	10%	11%
1	0.9615	0.9569	0.9524	0.9479	0.9434	0.9390	0.9346	0.9302	0.9259	0.9174	0.9091	0.9009
2	.9246	.9157	.9070	.8985	.8900	.8817	.8734	.8653	.8573	.8417	.8264	.8116
3	.8890	.8763	.8638	.8516	.8396	.8278	.8163	.8050	.7938	.7722	.7513	.7312
4	.8548	.8386	.8277	.8072	.7921	.7773	.7629	.7488	.7350	.7084	.6830	.6587
5	.8219	.8025	.7835	.7651	.7473	.7299	.7130	.6966	.6806	.6499	.6209	.5935
6	.7903	.7679	.7462	.7252	.7050	.6853	.6663	.6480	.6302	.5963	.5645	.5346
7	.7599	.7343	.7107	.6874	.6651	.6435	.6227	.6027	.5835	.5470	.5132	.4816
8	.7307	.7032	.6768	.6516	.6274	.6042	.5820	.5607	.5403	.5019	.4665	.4339
9	.7026	.6729	.6446	.6176	.5919	.5673	.5439	.5216	.5002	.4604	.4241	.3909
10	.6756	.6439	.6139	.5854	.5584	.5327	.5083	.4852	.4632	.4224	.3855	.3522
11	.6496	.6162	.5847	.5549	.5268	.5002	.4751	.4514	.4289	.3875	.3505	.3173
12	.6246	.5897	.5568	.5260	.4970	.4697	.4440	.4199	.3971	.3555	.3186	.2858
13	.6006	.5643	.5303	.4986	.4688	.4410	.4150	.3906	.3677	.3262	.2897	.2575
14	.5775	.5400	.5051	.4726	.4423	.4141	.3878	.3633	.3405	.2992	.2633	.2320
15	.5553	.5167	.4810	.4479	.4173	.3888	.3624	.3380	.3152	.2745	.2394	.2090
16	.5339	.4945	.4581	.4246	.3936	.3651	.3387	.3144	.2919	.2519	.2176	.1883
17	.5134	.4732	.4363	.4024	.3714	.3428	.3166	.2924	.2703	.2311	.1978	.1696
18	.4936	.4528	.4155	.3815	.3503	.3219	.2959	.2720	.2502	.2120	.1799	.1528
19	.4746	.4333	.3957	.3616	.3305	.3022	.2765	.2531	.2317	.1945	.1635	.1377
20	.4564	.4146	.3769	.3427	.3118	.2838	.2584	.2354	.2145	.1784	.1486	.1240
21	.4388	.3968	.3589	.3249	.2942	.2665	.2415	.2190	.1987	.1637	.1351	.1117
22	.4220	.3797	.3418	.3079	.2775	.2502	.2257	.2037	.1839	.1502	.1228	.1007
23	.4057	.3633	.3256	.2919	.2618	.2349	.2109	.1895	.1703	.1378	.1117	.0907
24	.3901	.3477	.3101	.2766	.2470	.2206	.1971	.1763	.1577	.1264	.1015	.0817
25	.3751	.3327	.2953	.2622	.2330	.2071	.1842	.1640	.1460	.1160	.0923	.0736
26	.3607	.3184	.2812	.2486	.2198	.1945	.1722	.1525	.1352	.1064	.0829	.0663
27	.3468	.3047	.2678	.2356	.2074	.1826	.1609	.1419	.1252	.0976	.0763	.0597
28	.3335	.2916	.2551	.2233	.1956	.1715	.1504	.1320	.1159	.0895	.0693	.0538

Compound Discount Table (Cont'd)

Years	4%	4-1/2%	5%	5-1/2%	6%	6-1/2%	7%	7-1/2%	8%	9%	10%	11%
29	0.3207	0.2790	0.2429	0.2117	0.1846	0.1610	0.1406	0.1228	0.1073	0.0822	0.0630	0.0485
30	.3083	.2670	.2314	.2006	.1741	.1512	.1314	.1142	.0994	.0754	.0573	.0437
31	.2965	.2555	.2204	.1902	.1643	.1420	.1228	.1063	.0920	.0691	.0521	.0394
32	.2851	.2445	.2099	.1803	.1550	.1333	.1147	.0988	.0852	.0634	.0474	.0354
33	.2741	.2340	.1999	.1709	.1462	.1251	.1072	.0919	.0789	.0582	.0431	.0319
34	.2636	.2239	.1904	.1620	.1379	.1175	.1002	.0855	.0730	.0534	.0391	.0288
35	.2534	.2142	.1813	.1535	.1301	.1103	.0937	.0796	.0676	.0490	.0356	.0259
36	.2437	.2050	.1727	.1455	.1227	.1036	.0875	.0740	.0626	.0449	.0323	.0234
37	.2343	.1962	.1644	.1379	.1158	.0973	.0818	.0688	.0580	.0412	.0294	.0210
38	.2253	.1878	.1566	.1307	.1092	.0914	.0765	.0640	.0537	.0378	.0267	.0189
39	.2166	.1797	.1491	.1239	.1031	.0858	.0715	.0596	.0497	.0347	.0243	.0171
40	.2083	.1719	.1420	.1175	.0972	.0805	.0668	.0554	.0460	.0318	.0221	.0154
41	.2003	.1645	.1353	.1113	.0917	.0756	.0624	.0515	.0426	.0292	.0201	.0139
42	.1926	.1574	.1288	.1055	.0865	.0710	.0583	.0480	.0395	.0268	.0183	.0125
43	.1852	.1507	.1227	.1000	.0816	.0667	.0545	.0446	.0365	.0246	.0166	.0112
44	.1780	.1442	.1169	.0948	.0770	.0626	.0509	.0415	.0338	.0225	.0151	.0101
45	.1712	.1380	.1113	.0899	.0726	.0588	.0476	.0386	.0313	.0207	.0137	.0091
46	.1646	.1320	.1060	.0852	.0685	.0552	.0445	.0359	.0290	.0190	.0125	.0082
47	.1583	.1263	.1009	.0807	.0647	.0518	.0416	.0334	.0269	.0174	.0113	.0074
48	.1522	.1209	.0961	.0765	.0610	.0487	.0389	.0311	.0249	.0160	.0103	.0067
49	.1463	.1157	.0916	.0725	.0575	.0457	.0363	.0289	.0230	.0147	.0094	.0060
50	.1407	.1107	.0872	.0688	.0543	.0429	.0339	.0269	.0213	.0134	.0085	.0054
51	.1353	.1059	.0831	.0652	.0512	.0403	.0317	.0250	.0197	.0123	.0077	.00488
52	.1301	.1014	.0791	.0618	.0483	.0378	.0297	.0233	.0183	.0113	.0070	.00440
53	.1251	.0970	.0753	.0586	.0456	.0355	.0277	.0216	.0169	.0104	.0064	.00396
54	.1203	.0928	.0717	.0555	.0430	.0333	.0259	.0201	.0157	.0095	.0058	.00357
55	.1157	.0888	.0683	.0526	.0406	.0313	.0242	.0187	.0145	.0087	.0053	.00322
56	.1112	.0850	.0651	.0499	.0383	.0294	.0226	.0174	.0134	.0080	.0048	.00290
57	.1069	.0814	.0620	.0473	.0361	.0276	.0211	.0162	.0124	.0073	.0044	.00261
58	.1028	.0778	.0590	.0448	.0341	.0259	.0198	.0151	.0115	.0067	.0040	.00235
59	.0989	.0745	.0562	.0425	.0321	.0243	.0185	.0140	.0107	.0062	.0036	.00212
60	.0951	.0713	.0535	.0403	.0303	.0229	.0173	.0130	.0099	.0057	.0033	.00191

PRESENT WORTH TABLE—SINGLE FUTURE PAYMENT

Example of use of this table:
 Find how much $10,000 payable in 12 years is worth now at an interest rate of 6%.
 From table for 12 years 6%   .4970
 Present value of $10,000 in 12 years (10,000 × .4970) $4,970

Number of Years	6%	7%	8%	9%	10%	11%	12%	13%
1	0.9434	0.9346	0.9259	0.9174	0.9091	0.9009	0.8929	0.8850
2	0.8900	0.8734	0.8573	0.8417	0.8264	0.8116	0.7972	0.7831
3	0.8396	0.8163	0.7938	0.7722	0.7513	0.7312	0.7118	0.6931
4	0.7921	0.7629	0.7350	0.7084	0.6830	0.6587	0.6355	0.6133
5	0.7473	0.7130	0.6806	0.6499	0.6209	0.5935	0.5674	0.5428
6	0.7050	0.6663	0.6302	0.5963	0.5645	0.5346	0.5066	0.4803
7	0.6651	0.6227	0.5835	0.5470	0.5132	0.4816	0.4523	0.4251
8	0.6274	0.5820	0.5403	0.5019	0.4665	0.4339	0.4039	0.3762
9	0.5919	0.5439	0.5002	0.4604	0.4241	0.3909	0.3606	0.3329
10	0.5584	0.5083	0.4632	0.4224	0.3855	0.3522	0.3220	0.2946
11	0.5268	0.4751	0.4289	0.3875	0.3505	0.3173	0.2875	0.2607
12	0.4970	0.4440	0.3971	0.3555	0.3186	0.2858	0.2567	0.2307
13	0.4688	0.4150	0.3677	0.3262	0.2897	0.2575	0.2292	0.2042
14	0.4423	0.3878	0.3405	0.2992	0.2633	0.2320	0.2046	0.1807
15	0.4173	0.3624	0.3152	0.2745	0.2394	0.2090	0.1827	0.1599
16	0.3936	0.3387	0.2919	0.2519	0.2176	0.1883	0.1631	0.1415
17	0.3714	0.3166	0.2703	0.2311	0.1978	0.1696	0.1456	0.1252
18	0.3503	0.2959	0.2502	0.2120	0.1799	0.1528	0.1300	0.1108
19	0.3305	0.2765	0.2317	0.1945	0.1635	0.1377	0.1161	0.0981
20	0.3118	0.2584	0.2145	0.1784	0.1486	0.1240	0.1037	0.0868
21	0.2942	0.2415	0.1987	0.1637	0.1351	0.1117	0.0926	0.0768
22	0.2775	0.2257	0.1839	0.1502	0.1228	0.1007	0.0826	0.0680
23	0.2618	0.2109	0.1703	0.1378	0.1117	0.0907	0.0738	0.0601
24	0.2470	0.1971	0.1577	0.1264	0.1015	0.0817	0.0660	0.0532
25	0.2330	0.1842	0.1460	0.1160	0.0923	0.0736	0.0588	0.0471
26	0.2198	0.1722	0.1352	0.1064	0.0829	0.0663	0.0525	0.0417
27	0.2074	0.1609	0.1252	0.0976	0.0763	0.0597	0.0470	0.0369
28	0.1956	0.1504	0.1159	0.0895	0.0693	0.0538	0.0420	0.0326
29	0.1846	0.1406	0.1073	0.0822	0.0630	0.0485	0.0374	0.0289
30	0.1741	0.1314	0.0994	0.0754	0.0573	0.0437	0.0334	0.0256
31	0.1643	0.1228	0.0920	0.0691	0.0521	0.0394	0.0298	0.0226
32	0.1550	0.1147	0.0852	0.0634	0.0474	0.0354	0.0266	0.0200
33	0.1462	0.1072	0.0789	0.0582	0.0431	0.0319	0.0238	0.0177
34	0.1379	0.1002	0.0730	0.0534	0.0391	0.0288	0.0212	0.0157
35	0.1301	0.0937	0.0676	0.0490	0.0356	0.0259	0.0189	0.0139
36	0.1227	0.0875	0.0626	0.0449	0.0323	0.0234	0.0169	0.0123
37	0.1158	0.0818	0.0580	0.0412	0.0294	0.0210	0.0151	0.0109
38	0.1092	0.0765	0.0536	0.0378	0.0267	0.0189	0.0135	0.0096
39	0.1031	0.0715	0.0497	0.0347	0.0243	0.0171	0.0120	0.0085
40	0.0972	0.0668	0.0460	0.0318	0.0221	0.0154	0.0107	0.0075

PRESENT WORTH TABLE—PERIODIC FUTURE PAYMENT

Example of use of this table:
   To find the cost now of $1,000 of income per year for 20 years at 7%.
   From table for 20 years at 7%   10.5940
   Cost of $1,000 per year ($1,000 × 10.5940) $10,594

Number of Years	Interest Rate							
	6%	7%	8%	9%	10%	11%	12%	13%
1	0.9434	0.9346	0.9259	0.9174	0.9091	0.9009	0.8929	0.8850
2	1.8334	1.8080	1.7833	1.7591	1.7355	1.7125	1.6901	1.6681
3	2.6730	2.6243	2.5771	2.5313	2.4869	2.4437	2.4018	2.3612
4	3.4651	3.3872	3.3121	3.2397	3.1699	3.1024	3.0373	2.9745
5	4.2124	4.1002	3.9927	3.8897	3.7908	3.6959	3.6048	3.5172
6	4.9173	4.7665	4.6229	4.4859	4.3553	4.2305	4.1114	3.9975
7	5.5824	5.3893	5.2064	5.0330	4.8684	4.7122	4.5638	4.4226
8	6.2098	5.9713	5.7466	5.5348	5.3349	5.1461	4.9676	4.7988
9	6.8017	6.5152	6.2469	5.9952	5.7590	5.5370	5.3282	5.1317
10	7.3601	7.0236	6.7101	6.4177	6.1446	5.8892	5.6502	5.4262
11	7.8869	7.4987	7.1390	6.8052	6.4951	6.2065	5.9377	5.6869
12	8.3838	7.9427	7.$361	7.1607	6.8137	6.4924	6.1944	5.9176
13	8.8527	8.3577	7.9038	7.4869	7.1034	6.7499	6.4235	6.1218
14	9.2950	8.7455	8.2442	7.7862	7.3667	6.9819	6.6282	6.3025
15	9.7122	9.1079	8.5595	8.0607	7.6061	7.1909	6.8109	6.4624
16	10.1059	9.4466	8.8514	8.3126	7.8237	7.3792	6.9740	6.6039
17	10.4773	9.7632	9.1216	8.5436	8.0216	7.5488	7.1196	6.7291
18	10.8276	10.0591	9.3719	8.7556	8.2014	7.7016	7.2497	6.8399
19	11.1581	10.3356	9.6036	8.9501	8.3649	7.8393	7.3658	6.9380
20	11.4699	10.5940	9.8181	9.1285	8.5136	7.9633	7.4694	7.0248
21	11.7641	10.8355	10.0168	9.2922	8.6487	8.0751	7.5620	7.1016
22	12.0416	11.0612	10.2007	9.4424	8.7715	8.1757	7.6446	7.1695
23	12.3034	11.2722	10.3711	9.5802	8.8832	8.2664	7.7184	7.2297
24	12.5504	11.4693	10.5288	9.7066	8.9847	8.3481	7.7843	7.2829
25	12.7834	11.6536	10.6748	9.8226	9.0770	8.4217	7.8431	7.3299
26	13.0032	11.8258	10.8100	9.9290	9.1609	8.4881	7.8957	7.3717
27	13.2105	11.9867	10.9352	10.0266	9.2372	8.5478	7.9426	7.4086
28	13.4062	12.1371	11.0511	10.1161	9.3066	8.6016	7.9844	7.4412
29	13.5907	12.2777	11.1584	10.1983	9.3696	8.6501	8.0218	7.4701
30	13.7648	12.4090	11.2578	10.2737	9.4269	8.6938	8.0552	7.4957
31	13.9291	12.5318	11.3498	10.3428	9.4790	8.7331	8.0850	7.5183
32	14.0840	12.6466	11.4350	10.4062	9.5264	8.7686	8.1116	7.5383
33	14.2302	12.7538	11.5139	10.4644	9.5694	8.8005	8.1354	7.5560
34	14.3681	12.8540	11.5869	10.5178	9.6086	8.8293	8.1566	7.5717
35	14.4982	12.9477	11.6546	10.5668	9.6442	8.8552	8.1755	7.5856
36	14.6210	13.0352	11.7172	10.6118	9.6765	8.8786	8.1924	7.5979
37	14.7368	13.1170	11.7752	10.6530	9.7059	8.8996	8.2075	7.6087
38	14.8460	13.1935	11.8289	10.6908	9.7327	8.9186	8.2210	7.6183
39	14.9491	13.2649	11.8786	10.7255	9.7569	8.9357	8.2330	7.6268
40	15.0463	13.3317	11.9246	10.7574	9.7791	8.9511	8.2438	7.6344

Appendix B

Index to Journal Entries

INDEX TO JOURNAL ENTRIES EXAMPLES
References Are to Journal Entry Numbers

Appraisals:
    Write-up—85
    Depreciation on—86
Appropriation of retained earnings—39
Bond premium:
    Initial entry—51
    Amortizing—52
    Interest payment—53
Business combinations:
    Purchase method—102, 103
    Pooling—104
Common stock:
    Dividend declared—37
    Payment of—38
Consolidation:
    Adjust opening investment—99
    Adjust to opening fair value—100
    Intercompany eliminations—101
Corporation—opening investment with goodwill—6
Customer check bounces—20
    Redeposited—21

Depreciation:
    First-year special allowance—24
    Then straight-line followup—25
Equity method:
    Original investment—93
    Adjust underlying equity at purchase—94
    Receipt of cash dividend—95
    Pick up share of investee income (including extraordinary item)—96
    Set up deferred taxes—97
    Set up actual tax liability—98
Federal income tax—netting extraordinary item—54
Foreign currency translation:
    Year 1—adjust payable—87
    set up deferred tax—88
    Year 2—payment on account—89
    adjust payables, year-end—90
    set up actual tax expense—91
    adjust deferred tax—92
Fund accounting:
    See Municipal accounting
    Membership-type organization:
        initial dues received—105
        purchase of building with mortgage—106
        first mortgage payment—107
        to close year's income—108
        transfer building and mortgage to plant fund—109
        in plant fund—set up building and mortgage—110
Goodwill:
    In consolidation—99 & 100
    In purchase method—102
    In equity method—94
Imputed interest on notes receivable:
    Original receipt of note—48
    Set up imputed interest—49
    Year 2—amortize interest income—50
Installment sales method:
    Original sale—30
    Payment on account—31
    Profit entry—32
Interest cost capitalized—120
Inventory—year-end entries:
    See Sampling—67 & 68

Adjusting standard figures:
    to physical count—69
    to actual cost—70
    Year 2—to new actual—71
Investment tax credit—deferral method:
    Initial deferral—34
    Year 2—amortization of—35
Lease—for lessee:
    Capitalizing present value, with contra liability—55
    First rental payment—56
    Interest entry, first payment—57
    Amortizing asset (depreciation)—58
Marketable securities:
    As current asset:
        Adjust to year 1 market—77
        Year 2—selling part of stock—78
        —adjust to market—79
    As non-current asset:
        Adjust to year 1 market—80
        Year 2—selling part of stock—81
        —adjust to market—82
Municipal accounting:
    Booking the budget—111
    Actual year's transactions:
        Issue purchase orders—112
        Invoices received—113
        Tax levy—114
        Actual revenues received—115 & 116
        To zero budget accounts and adjust fund balance—117
Notes receivable discounted—22
    Note paid by customer—23
Officer life insurance:
    Paying premium on—59
    Set up cash surrender value—60
    Loan taken on policy—61
Partnership dissolution:
    First sale of assets—72
    Cancel one partner's overdrawn account—73
    Paying liabilities—74
    Sale of remaining assets at loss and apportioning loss to remaining
    partners—75
    Distributing remaining cash to zero capital accounts—76

Partnership incorporates—5
Partnership—opening investment—2
Partnership—opening investment, with goodwill—3
Partnership—opening investment, skill only—4
Partnership—splitting net profit—46
Partnership—withdrawals—45
    Closing withdrawals to capital—47
Pooling—104
Preferred stock—accumulating dividend—36
    Payment of dividend—38
Prior period adjustment (litigation)—40
Purchase method of business combination (includes goodwill)—102
    Amortizing goodwill and discount income—103
Recurrent and correcting monthly entries:
    Correction:
        set up gain on sale of machinery—13
    Recurrent:
        depreciation—14
        accrue real estate taxes—15
        accrue payroll—16
        accrue payroll taxes—17
        allocate overhead—18
        adjust inventory to closing—19
Sampling:
    Adjust inventory per sample valuation—67
    Year 2—readjust to physical count—68
Sole proprietor—opening investment—1
Standard cost variances:
    Raw material price variance—62
    Direct labor rate and time variance—63
    Overhead variance—64
    Adjust closing inventory—65
    Adjust inventory for variances—66
Stock acquisitions:
    Equity method—93 to 98
    Consolidation—99 to 101
Stock dividend:
    3% taxable dividend (to recipient)—41
    Nontaxable dividend (to recipient)—42
Stock options—employee compensation entries
Stock split-up—44
    effected in the form of a stock dividend—43
Subchapter S corporation:
    First year's net income—27

Retitling prior retained earnings—28
New distribution—29
Summary monthly entries:
Purchase journal—7
Cash disbursements—regular account—8
Cash disbursements—payroll account—9
Sales book—10
Cash receipts book—11
Petty cash box—12
Tax loss carryback—26
Treasury stock:
Purchase of—83
Sale of—84
Voiding own check—33

SAMPLE JOURNAL ENTRIES

OPENING INVESTMENT—Sole Proprietorship:
[1]

Cash	5,000	
Building (fair value)	45,000	
A. Able, Net Worth		50,000

OPENING INVESTMENT—Partnership:
[2]

Cash	30,000	
Inventory	30,000	
B. Baker (50%), Capital		30,000
C. Charles (50%), Capital		30,000

PARTNERSHIP INVESTMENT—with Goodwill:
[3]

Building (fair value)	45,000	
Goodwill	15,000	
A. Able (50%), Capital		60,000

Able contributes building for ½ share
of partnership.

PARTNERSHIP INVESTMENT—Skill, no funds:
[4]

A. Able, Capital	3,000	
B. Baker, Capital	3,000	
C. Charles, Capital	6,000	
D. Dog, Capital		12,000

Dog gets 10% of partnership
for the skill he'll contribute.
Ratios will now be:

Able	(25% less 10%)	22.5%
Baker	(same)	22.5%
Charles	(50% less 10%)	45.0%
Dog	(as granted)	10.0%
		100.0%

PARTNERSHIP INCORPORATES:
[5]

Cash	30,000	
Inventory—Raw Material	30,000	
Building (fair value)	45,000	
Capital Stock (par $10; 10,000		
shares issued; 100,000 auth.)		100,000
Additional Paid-in Capital		5,000

Shares issued: A. 2250; B. 2250;
C. 4500; D. 1,000. Note that partnership
goodwill is not carried over to corporation.

CORPORATE INVESTMENT—with Goodwill:
[6]

Machinery & Equipment (fair value)	9,000	
Goodwill	1,000	
Capital Stock (1,000 shares)		10,000

Issuing 1,000 shares to E. Easy
@ $10 par for machinery contributed.

CORPORATION MONTHLY ENTRIES—The
corporation records all entries into the general
ledger *through* summary entries made in the general
journal from the books and sources of original entry:
[7] *Summary of Purchase Journal,* where all vendor
    invoices are entered:

Purchases—Raw Material	10,000	
Shop Supplies	2,000	
Office Supplies	1,000	
Office Equipment	3,000	
Utilities	1,000	
Freight Out	2,000	
Advertising	1,000	
Accounts Payable		20,000

[8] *Summary of Cash Disbursement, Regular Cash A/C:*

Cash—Payroll A/C	13,000	
Petty Cash	200	
Accounts Payable	14,500	

Federal Tax Deposits Made	5,100	
Bank Charges	2	
Cash—Regular A/C		32,602
Cash Discounts Taken		200

[9] *Summary of Cash Disbursement, Payroll A/C:*

Direct Labor—Shop	12,500	
Indirect Labor—Shop	1,500	
Salaries—Sales Dept.	2,000	
Salaries—G & A	4,000	
Cash—Payroll A/C (net pay)		13,000
W/H Tax Pay—Federal		4,400
FICA Tax Withheld		1,200
SUI & Disability W/H		300
State Income Taxes W/H		600
Savings Bonds W/H		500

[10] *Summary of Sales Book:*

Accounts Receivable	35,000	
Sales Returns & Allowances	500	
Sales—Product L		18,000
Sales—Product M		16,600
Sales Taxes Payable		900

[11] *Summary of Cash Receipts Book:*

Cash—Regular A/C	30,500	
Cash Discounts Allowed	500	
Accounts Receivable		30,000
Machinery and Equipment		1,000

[12] *Summary of Petty Cash Box:*

Postage	40	
Entertainment	60	
Travel Expense	30	
Misc. Expense	20	
Petty Cash		150

[13] *General Journal Entries during month:*

Depreciation—M & E	10	
Machinery and Equipment	400	
Gain on Sale of Machinery		410

To correct entry from cash receipts:

Basis	$ 600	
Deprec.	10	(1/60th)
	590	
S.P.	1000	
Gain	$ 410	

[14]

Depr.—Bldg (1/40 × 45,000 × 1/12)	94	
Depr.—M&E (1/5 × 8,400 × 1/12)	140	
Depr.—OE (1/5 × 3,000 × 1/12)	50	
Amortization (1/40 × 1,000 × 1/12)	2	
Accum Depr.—Bldg		94
Accum Depr.—M&E		140
Accum Depr.—OE		50
Goodwill		2

[15]

Real Estate Taxes	300	
Accrued Taxes—RE		300
1/12th of estimated $3,600 for yr		

[16]

Direct Labor (3125)	2,500	
Indirect Labor (375)	300	
Salaries—Selling (500)	400	
Salaries—G & A (1000)	800	
Accrued Salaries (5000)		4,000
To accrue 4/5 of last payroll in month.		

[17]

W/H Tax Payable—Federal	3,300	
FICA Tax Withheld	900	
FICA Tax Expense—employer	900	
Federal Tax Deposits Made		5,100
FICA Tax Expense—employer	300	
SUI & DISAB Expense	600	
FUI Expense	100	
Accrued Taxes—Payroll		1,000
To zero deposit account against withholding accounts and to book employer FICA expense and estimated unemployment tax for month.		

[18]

Overhead	6,106	
Depr.—Bldg (60% of 94)		56
Depr.—M&E (all)		140
Indirect Labor (all)		1,800
Payroll Tax Exp (70% of 1900)		1,330
Shop supplies (all considered used)		2,000

Utilities (60% of 1000)		600
Taxes—RE (60% of 300)		180

To allocate expenses to overhead.
Taxes based on payroll proportion.
Other allocations based on space occupied.

[19]

Inventory—Raw Materials	(15,000)	
Inventory—Work in Process	none	
Inventory—Finished Goods	15,369	
Cost of Production—Inventory Change		369

To increase or (decrease) inventory
accounts to reflect new month-end inventory
as follows:

Raw Material:

Opening Inventory	$ 30,000
Purchases	10,000
Less used in production	(25,000)
Closing inventory	15,000
To adjust opening	$ (15,000)

Finished Goods:

Materials used (above)	$ 25,000
Direct labor costs	15,000
Overhead costs	6,106
3 units produced	46,106
1 unit unsold (1/3)	$ 15,369

(none at hand at beginning)
No work in process this month.

(The entries through here are all related with respect to the dollars shown. From here on, they are independent with respect to each CAPITAL HEADING, but related within the headed area.)

CUSTOMER'S CHECK BOUNCES
[20]

Accounts Receivable (Mr. A.)	100	
Cash (Disbursements)		100

To record bank charge for
Mr. A's check return—insufficient funds.

[21]

Cash (Receipts)	100	
Accounts Receivable (Mr. A.)		100

For re-deposit of above, per customer's instructions.

NOTES RECEIVABLE DISCOUNTED
[22]

Cash	9,900	
Interest Expense	250	
Notes receivable Discounted		10,000
Interest Income		150

For proceeds from customer note discounted,
due 90 days @ 6%, discount rate 10%.

[23]

Notes Receivable Discounted	10,000	
Notes Receivable		10,000

To offset. Customer note paid, per bank notice.

FIRST-YEAR DEPRECIATION
[24]

Depreciation Expense—M & E	2,000	
Accumulated Depr—M & E		2,000

For maximum first-year depreciation
taken on 6/30 purchase of extruder.
See next entry for regular deprec.

[25]

Depreciation—M & E	400	
Accumulated Depr—M & E		400

To take straight-line on above:

Cost	$ 10,000
Less 1st yr. Depr	(2,000)
S/L basis	8,000
Over 10 yrs—per yr	$ 800
Six months this yr (no salvage value).	$ 400

TAX LOSS CARRYBACK
[26]

FIT Refund and Interest Receivable	106,000	
Income Tax (Current Yr. Income Statement)		100,000
Interest Income		6,000

To set up receivable for carryback tax
refund due, plus interest.

SUBCHAPTER S EQUITY ENTRIES

End of Year 1:

[27]

Net income for Current Year	30,000	
Undistributed Earnings—Post-Election		30,000

To close year's net income into new Sub-S
undistributed earnings Equity account.

[28]

Retained Earnings	55,000	
Retained Earnings—Pre-Election		55,000

To retitle opening retained earnings
account and keep it separate from
earnings after Sub-S election.

[29]

Post-Election Dividends	10,000	
Cash		10,000

For cash distributions made of current
earnings. (NOTE: State law may require
a *formal* declaration of a dividend for
corporations. If this is true, and there
is no such declaration, this must be
treated as a *loan receivable* from
stockholders.)

INSTALLMENT SALES METHOD
[30]

Accounts Receivable	1,000	
Cost of Installment Sale		700
Deferred Gross Profit on Installment Sales		300

For original sale. (GP% is 30%)

[31]

Cash	300	
Accounts Receivable		300

For payment on account.

[32]

Deferred Gross Profit on Installment Sales	90	
Realized Gross Profit		90

To amortize 30% of above collection to
realized income.

VOIDING YOUR OWN CHECK (Issued in a prior period)
[33]

Cash (Ck # 1601)	1,500	
Rent Expense		1,500

To void check # 1601 (last month).
Check reported lost. Payment stopped.
Replaced with this month's
check # 1752. (See CD book)

INVESTMENT TAX CREDIT—THE DEFERRAL METHOD
[34]

Taxes Payable	7,000	
Deferred Investment Tax Credits		7,000

To set up investment tax credit under
the deferred method. *Note:* The tax expense
for this year on the income statement does
not reflect the use of this credit.

Year 2:

[35]

Deferred Investment Tax Credits	700	
Income Tax Expense		700

To amortize 1/10th, based on 10-year
life of asset to which applicable.

ACCUMULATED PREFERRED STOCK DIVIDENDS
[36]

Dividends (Income Statement)	30,000	
Dividends Payable (Liability)		30,000

To accrue this year's commitment, 6%
of $500,000. *Note:* There was no "only
as earned" provision attached to this issue.

DIVIDEND DECLARATION—COMMON STOCK
[37]

Retained Earnings	100,000	
Common Stock Extra Dividend Declared—(show in Equity Section)		100,000

To segregate common stock extra
dividend from accumulated earnings (until
paid), 10¢ per share, 1,000,000 shares.

PAYMENT OF ABOVE TWO DIVIDENDS
[38]

Dividends Payable	30,000	
Common Stock Extra Dividend Declared	100,000	
Cash		130,000

For payment of dividends.

APPROPRIATION OF RETAINED EARNINGS
[39]

Retained Earnings	50,000	
Reserve Appropriation for Inventory Declines (Equity Section)		50,000

To set aside retained earnings for possible
inventory losses—per Board resolution.

[40]

Retained Earnings—(1/1 opening)	150,000	
Accounts Payable (XYZ Co.)		150,000

To record prior year billing error made by
supplier, XYZ Co., on invoice #___,
dated 12/10. Error not discovered by
XYZ until after closing of our books and
issuance of statements. Error is considered
material enough to treat as prior period
adjustment. Item was not in inventory at 12/31.

STOCK DIVIDEND

Usually:

[41]

Retained Earnings (at market)	45,000	
Common Stock (par $10, 3,000 shares)		30,000
Additional Paid-in Capital		15,000

For 3% stock dividend distributed on
100,000 shares—3,000 shares issued.
Market value $15 at dividend date.

Sometimes:

[42]

Additional Paid-in Capital	30,000	
Common Stock (par $10, 3,000 shares)		30,000

For non-taxable distribution out of
Paid-in Capital.

SPLIT-UP EFFECTED IN THE FORM OF A STOCK DIVIDEND
[43]

Retained Earnings (at par)	1,000,000	
Common Stock (par $10, 100,000 shs)		1,000,000

For split in the form of a stock dividend
(to conform with state law). One share
issued for each share outstanding.
100,000 shares at par of $10.

STOCK SPLIT-UP
[44]

Common Stock (100,000 shares @ $10.)	memo	
Common Stock (200,000 shares @ $5.)		memo

Memo entry only. To record stock split-up
by showing change in par value and in
number of shares outstanding. One share
issued for each outstanding. Par changed
from $10 to $5.

STOCK OPTIONS FOR EMPLOYEES AS COMPENSATION

PARTNERSHIP WITHDRAWALS
[45]

S. Stone, Withdrawals	15,000	
T. Times, Withdrawals	5,000	
Cash		20,000
For cash withdrawals.		

PARTNERSHIP PROFIT ENTRY
[46]

Net Income—P & L a/c	100,000	
S. Stone, Capital (50%)		50,000
T. Times, Capital (50%)		50,000
To split profit as follows:		
Per P & L closing account	$ 80,000	
Add back above included in P & L account	20,000	
Profit to distribute	$ 100,000	

[47]

S. Stone, Capital	15,000	
T. Times, Capital	5,000	
S. Stone, Withdrawals		15,000
T. Times, Withdrawals		5,000
To close withdrawal accounts to capital accounts.		

IMPUTED INTEREST (ON NOTES RECEIVABLE)
[48]

Notes Receivable (Supplier A—6 yrs)	1,000,000	
Cash		1,000,000
For loan made to supplier. Received non-interest bearing note, due 6 yrs.		

[49]

Cost of Merchandise (from supplier A)	370,000	
Unamortized Discount on Notes Receiv.		370,000
To charge imputed interest of 8% on above note, due in 6 years, to cost of merchandise bought from A.		

Year 2:

[50]

Unamortized Discount on Notes Receiv.	50,000	
Interest Income		50,000

To amortize this year's applicable imputed
    interest on note.

BOND DISCOUNT, PREMIUM AND ISSUE COSTS
[51]

Cash	2,025,000	
Unamortized Bond Issue Costs	15,000	
Bonds Payable (8%, 10 yrs)		2,000,000
Unamortized Premium on Bonds		40,000

To set up face value of bonds, issue costs
and net cash proceeds received.

Year 2:

[52]

Unamortized Premium on Bonds	4,000*	
Unamortized Bond Issue Cost		1,500*
Interest Expense (difference)		2,500

To set up approximate amortization.
(*Should actually be based on present values.)

[53]

Interest Expense	160,000	
Cash		160,000

To record actual payment of bond interest.
8% of $2,000,000.

FEDERAL INCOME TAX—INTERIMS—
AND EXTRAORDINARY ITEM
[54]

Income Tax (on continuing operations)	350,000	
Extraordinary Loss (tax effect)		50,000
Taxes Payable		300,000

To set up FIT at end of First Quarter
based on full year's 50% rate and to
segregate tax applicable to extraordinary item.

Statement should show:

Net from continuing operations	$ 700,000
Less FIT	(350,000)
	350,000
Extraordinary loss	
(net of $50,000 tax effect)	50,000
Net Income	$ 300,000

CAPITALIZING A LEASE (LESSEE)

At contracting:

[55]

Capitalized Leases	1,920,000	
Long-Term Lease Liability		3,600,000
Unamortized Discount on Lease		(1,680,000)

To capitalize lease of $25,000 per month
for 12 years @ 12% imputed interest
rate. Estimated life of asset is 15 years.
Present value used, since fair value is
higher at $2,000,000.

(*Note:* The two credit items shown are
netted and shown as *one net liability* on
the balance sheet. The liability (at present value)
should always equal the asset value, also at
present value. Future lease payments are broken
out, effectively, into principal and interest.)

Month-end 1:

[56]

Long-Term Lease Liability	25,000	
Cash		25,000

First payment on lease.

[57]

Interest Expense	18,950	
Unamortized Discount on Lease		18,950

For one month's interest.
1% of $3,600,000 less $1,680,000, less
initial payment on signing of contract
of $25,000 (*entry not shown*) or $1,895,000.

[58]

Depreciation Expense	10,667	
Accumulated Depr of Capitalized Lease		10,667

One month:
$1,920,000 \times 1/5 \times 1/12$

CASH SURRENDER VALUE—OFFICER LIFE INSURANCE

[59]

Officer Life Insurance—expense	1,500	
Cash		1,500

For payment of premium. *Note:* Expense is
not deductible for tax purpose and is a
permanent difference.

[60]

Cash Surrender Value-Officer Life Ins.	1,045	
Officer Life Ins. expense		1,045
To reflect increase in C.S.V. for year		

[61]

Cash	5,000	
Loans Against Officer Life Insurance		5,000
(Displayed against the asset "C.S.V.")		
To record loan against life policy. No intent		
to repay within the next year.		

STANDARD COST VARIANCES

[62]

Purchases—Raw Mat (at stand)	200	
Accounts Payable—actual		188
Variance—material price		12

[63]

Direct Labor—at standard	50	
Variance—Direct Labor rate	10	
Payroll—actual direct labor		58
Variance—Labor Time		2

[64]

Overhead—at Standard	75	
Variance—overhead	15	
Overhead itemized actual accounts		90

Adjusting Inventories:

[65]

Inventory—Raw Materials at standard	100	
Finished Goods—at standard	75	
Cost of Production—at standard		175
To adjust inventory accounts to reflect		
end-of-month on-hand figures at standards.		

[66]

Variance—material price	xx	
Variance—labor time	xx	
Variance—direct labor rate		xx
Variance—overhead		xx
Contra Inventory Asset a/c (variances		
to offset standard and reflect cost)		xx

To pull out of variance accounts that portion which
is applicable to inventory, in order to keep an isolated
contra account, which in offset to the "standard" asset
account, reflects approximate cost. The portion is
based on an overall ratio of variances to production
and inventory figures (at standard). (If normal, apply
to cost of sales for interims.)

ADJUSTING INVENTORY FOR SAMPLING RESULTS
[67]

Cost of Sales		50,000	
Inventory			50,000

To reduce inventory by $50,000 based
on sampling results:

Inventory per computer run	$1,000,000
Estimated calculated inventory	
per sample	950,000
Reduction this year	$ 50,000

Year 2:

[68]

Inventory		10,000	
Cost of Sales			10,000

To adjust inventory to actual based on actual
physical count of entire inventory. Last year-end
sample error proved to be 4%, not 5%.

ADJUSTING CLOSING INVENTORY FROM CLIENTS STANDARD COST TO AUDITOR'S DETERMINED (AND CLIENT AGREED) ACTUAL COST, AND TO REFLECT PHYSICAL INVENTORY VS. BOOK INVENTORY DIFFERENCES
[69]

Inventory—Finished Goods (Standard)	25,000	
Cost of Sales		25,000

To adjust general ledger inventory (at
standard) to actual physical inventory
count, priced out at standard. Actual is
$25,000 more.

[70]

Cost of Sales	80,000	
Inventory—Finished Goods (Asset		
Contra Cost account)		80,000

To set up a contra account reducing asset
account, which is at standard costs, effectively to
audited actual cost or market, whichever lower.

Year 2: (End of Year)

[71]

Inventory—Finished Goods (Asset		
Contra Cost account)	50,000	
Cost of Sales		50,000

To reduce the contra account to the new
year-end difference between the "standard"
asset account and the actual cost determined
for this new year-end inventory.

PARTNERSHIP DISSOLUTION:

Balance Sheet

Cash	$ 20,000
Assets other	35,000
Liabilities	(25,000)
A Capital (50%)	(20,000)
B Capital (30%)	(14,000)
C Capital (20%)	4,000
	-0-

[72]

Cash	15,000	
Assets other		15,000

For sale of some assets at book value.

[73]

A Capital (⅝)	2,500	
B Capital (⅜)	1,500	
C Capital		4,000

C cannot put in his overdraw—to apportion
his deficit.

[74]

Liabilities	25,000	
Cash		25,000

To pay liabilities

[75]

Cash	10,000	
Loss on Sale of Assets other	10,000	
Assets other		20,000
A Capital (⅝)	6,250	
B Capital (⅜)	3,750	
Loss on Sale of Assets other		10,000

Selling remaining assets and apportioning loss

[76]

A Capital (remaining balance)	11,250	
B Capital (remaining balance)	8,750	
Cash		20,000

To distribute remaining cash and zero
capital accounts.

NOTE THE SHARING OF C'S DEFICIT AND
OF THE LOSS ON ASSET SALE *BEFORE*
DISTRIBUTING REMAINING CASH.

MARKETABLE SECURITIES

Shown as Current Assets:

[77]

Unrealized Loss—to P & L	1,500	
Valuation Allowance—Current		1,500

To write down 100 U.S. Steel:

Cost 1/1	$10,000
Market 12/31	8,500
Unrealized Loss	$ 1,500

Year 2:

[78]

Cash	4,500	
Realized Loss—P & L	500	
Marketable Securities—Current		5,000

Sold 50 @ 90	$ 4,500
Cost 50 @ 90	5,000
Realized Loss	$ 500

[79]

Valuation Allowance—Current	1,250	
Valuation Adjustment—Current (P&L Gain)		1,250*

To adjust valuation allowance a/c
(current) for remaining securities
left in portfolio:

50 US Steel—cost 100	$ 5,000
Market, this year end—95	4,750
Bal. should be	250 Cr.
Balance in valuation a/c	1,500 Cr.
Debit valuation a/c	$ 1,250 Dr.

*Note: Unrealized *gains* are called
"valuation adjustments." Unrealized
losses are called "unrealized losses."

Shown as Noncurrent Asset:

[80]

| Unrealized Noncurrent Loss (Equity section) | 1,000 | |
| Valuation Allowance—Noncurrent | | 1,000 |

To write down 100 shares GM from cost of
60 to market value at 12/31 of 50.

Year 2:

[81]

Cash	2,900	
Realized Loss—P & L	100	
Marketable Securities—Noncurrent		3,000

Sold 50 GM @ 58	$ 2,900
Cost 50 GM @ 60	3,000
Realized loss	$ 100

[82]

| Valuation Allowance—Noncurrent | 1,000 | |
| Unrealized Noncurrent Loss (Equity Section) | | 1,000 |

To adjust valuation allowance a/c
(Noncurrent) as follows:

Cost 50 GM @ 60	$ 3,000
Market now @ 65	N/A
(Higher than cost)	
Valuation a/c should be	-0-
(Because market is higher than cost)	
Balance in valuation a/c	1,000 Cr.
Debit to correct	$ 1,000 Dr.

TREASURY STOCK

Purchase of:

[83]

| Treasury Stock—at Cost | 125,000 | |
| Cash | | 125,000 |

Purchase of 1,000 shares @ 125
market. Par value $50.
No intent to cancel the stock.

Sale of:

[84]

Cash	140,000	
Treasury Stock—at Cost		125,000
Additional Paid—in Capital		15,000

For sale of treasury stock @ 140.

APPRAISAL WRITE-UPS
[85]

Building	350,000	
Appraisal Capital (Equity Section)		350,000

To raise building from cost of $400,000 to
appraised value of $750,000 per requirement
of the lending institution.

Year 2:
[86]

Depreciation—Building	21,667	
Accumulated Depreciation—Building		21,667

To depreciate based on appraised value:
(400,000 for 40 years; 350,000 for 30 yrs)
Building was 10 years old at appraisal.

FOREIGN CURRENCY EXCHANGE
[87]

Unrealized Loss (balance sheet)	10,000	
Accts Payable—Foreign		10,000

To adjust liabilities payable in Swiss Francs
to US Dollars at 12/31:

Exchange rate at 12/31 .40	$40,000
Booked at (100,000 frs) .30	30,000
More dollars owed	$10,000

[88]

Deferred Taxes	5,000*	
Unrealized Loss		5,000*

To show deferred tax effect (50% rate
times $10,000 above)
*Less Foreign or Domestic Dividend
Credits, if Applicable

Year 2:
[89]

Accounts Payable—Foreign	20,000	
Cash		19,000
Realized gain (Books, not Tax)		1,000

For payment of 50,000 Swiss Francs at
exchange rate of .38

[90]

Accounts Payable—Foreign	500	
Balance Sheet		500

To restate liability at year-end:

50,000 Frs @ .39	$ 19,500	
Booked to last yr.	20,000	
(Gain)	$ (500)	

[91]

Taxes Payable	2,000	
Income Tax Expense	500	
Deferred Taxes		2,500

To transfer to actual taxes payable
(from deferred) that portion applying
to the payment of $19,000. Original debt
in dollars was $15,000. 50% tax rate on
$4,000 or $2,000, plus $500—to offset
2,500 booked to last 12/31.

[92]

Income Tax Expenses	250	
Deferred Taxes		250

To adjust deferred taxes to equal 1/2 of 4,500
(19,500 liability now, less original liability of
15,000) for $2,250 tax deferral.

THE EQUITY METHOD

[93]

Investment—Oleo Co.	275,000	
Cash		275,000

Purchase of 25% of Oleo's stock, at cost
(25,000 shares @ $11).

[94]

Investment—Oleo Co.	40,000	
Deferred Good Will in Oleo		40,000

To set up additional underlying equity in
Oleo Co. at date of acquisition—to
write-off over 40 years.

[95]

Cash	5,000	
Investment—Oleo Co.		5,000

For receipt of 20¢ per share cash
dividend from Oleo.

[96]

Investment—Oleo Co.	27,500	
Income from Equity Share of Undistributed Earnings of Oleo continuing operations		25,000
Income from Equity Share of Undistributed Extraordinary Item of Oleo		2,500

To pick up 25% of the following reported
Oleo annual figures:

Net income after taxes, but before Extraordinary item	$100,000
Extraordinary Income (net)	10,000
Total net income reported	$110,000

[97]

Income Tax Expense—Regular	12,500*	
Income Tax Expense—Extra Item	1,250*	
Deferred Taxes		13,750*

To set up 50% of above income as accrued
taxes. Expectation is that Oleo will
continue paying dividends.

*Dividend Tax Credit, if any, should reduce
these Amounts

[98]

Deferred Taxes	2,500*	
Income Taxes Payable		2,500*

To set up actual liability for tax on
cash dividends received.

*Dividend Tax Credit, if any, should reduce
these Amounts

CONSOLIDATION

Trial Balances
Now-at
12/31-End of Year

	A Co.	B Co.	Fair Value Excess at Acquisition
Cash	10,000	6,000	
A/R	20,000	10,000	
Inventory	30,000	5,000	
Equip	50,000	30,000	5,000
Investment Cost	40,000		
Liabilities	(30,000)	(5,000)	(1,000)
Common Stock	(20,000)	(10,000)*	
Retained Earnings	(50,000)	(20,000)*	
Sales	(80,000)	(40,000)	
Costs of Sale	20,000	14,000	
Expenses	10,000	10,000	
	-0-	-0-	
	(Parent)	(Sub)	

*Unchanged from opening balances.

At year-end there were $5,000 intercompany receivables/
payables. The parent had sold $5,000 worth of product

to the subsidiary. The inventory of the subsidiary was $1,000 over the parent's cost.

Consolidating Entries:

[99]

Excess Paid over Book Value	10,000	
Investment Cost		10,000

To reduce investment cost to that of the subsidiary's equity at time of purchase (unchanged at 12/31).

[100]

Equipment	5,000	
Liabilities		1,000
Excess Paid over Book Value		4,000

To reflect fair value corrections at time of consolidation for the combination of current year-end trial balances.

[101]

B Co. Equity	30,000	
Investment Cost		30,000
Sales	5,000	
Costs of Sale		5,000
Costs of Sale	1,000	
Inventory		1,000
Liabilities	5,000	
Accounts Receivable		5,000
Excess paid over book value (expense)	150	
Goodwill		150

To eliminate intercompany dealings, debt, investment, and to amortize goodwill.

Consolidated figures will then be:

Cash	16,000
A/R	25,000
Inventories	34,000
Equipment	85,000
Investment cost	—
Goodwill	5,850
Liabilities	(31,000)
Common Stock	(20,000) (Opening)
Ret. Earnings	(50,000) (Opening)
Sales	(115,000)
Cost of sales	30,000
Expenses	20,150
	-0-

The year's consolidated net income (before provision for income taxes) is $64,850.

PURCHASE METHOD OF BUSINESS COMBINATION
[102]

Accounts Receivable (present value)	50,000	
Inventory (current cost or market, lowest)	40,000	
Building (fair value)	110,000	
Equipment (fair value)	30,000	
Investments, non-current securities-market	5,000	
Goodwill	16,200	
Accounts Payable—(present value)		25,000
Long-term Debt—(face value)		30,000
Unamortized discount on long-term debt		
(to reflect present value)		(3,800)
Common Stock (Par $10; 10,000 shares)		100,000
Additional Paid-in Capital		100,000

To reflect, by the purchase method, the purchase of Diablo Company assets and liabilities for 10,000 shares of common stock; total purchase price of contract $200,000 based on market price of stock at date of consummation of $20 per share (1/1).

[103]

Amortization of Goodwill (1/40)	405	
Goodwill		405
Unamortized discount o n long-term debt	760	
Discount Income (approx 1/5th)		760*

To amortize pertinent Diablo items, first yearend. Goodwill on straight-line basis—40 years.
*Should be calculated present value computation.

POOLING METHOD OF BUSINESS COMBINATION
[104]

Inventory	43,000	
Cash	5,000	
Accounts Receivable	60,000	
Reserve for Doubtful Accounts		7,000
Building	75,000	
Accumulated Depreciation—Building		15,000
Equipment	100,000	
Accumulated Depreciation—Building		60,000
Investments—non-current securities	4,000	
Accounts Payable		25,500
Long-Term Debt		30,000
Common Stock (10,000 shs @ par $10)		100,000
Additional Paid-in Capital		49,500

To reflect the pooling of Diablo items, per *their book value* on date of consummation.

FUND ACCOUNTING

Initial transactions:

[105]

| Cash | 100,000 | |
| Dues Income | | 100,000 |

For initial membership dues received.

[106]

Building	50,000	
Mortgage Payable		40,000
Cash		10,000

Purchase of building for cash and mortgage.

[107]

Interest Expense	2,400	
Mortgage Payable	2,000	
Cash		4,400

For first payment on mortgage.

[108]

| Net income (100,000 less 2,400) | 97,600 | |
| Current Fund Balance | | 97,600 |

To close year's income

[109]

Mortgage Payable	38,000	
Current Fund Balance	12,000	
Building		50,000

To transfer building and mortgage to plant fund.

Plant Fund Entry:

[110]

Building	50,000	
Mortgage Payable		38,000
Plant Fund Balance		12,000

To set up building in plant fund.

Note that interest expense is to be borne by the current fund every year as a current operating expense used in the calculation of required dues from members. Also, the principal sum-payments against mortgage are to come out of current fund assets, with no interfund debt to be set up, until such time as a special drive is held for plant fund donations for improvements and expansion.

MUNICIPAL ACCOUNTING—CURRENT OPERATING FUND

To book the budget:

[111]

Estimated Revenues	600,000	
Appropriations		590,000
Fund Balance		10,000

Actual year's transactions:

[112]

Encumbrances	575,000	
Reserve for Encumbrances		575,000

To enter contracts and purchase orders issued.

[113]

Expenditures—itemized (not here)	515,000	
Vouchers Payable		515,000
Reserve for Encumbrances	503,000	
Encumbrances		503,000

To enter actual invoices for deliveries received and service contracts performed and to reverse applicable encumbrances.

[114]

Taxes Receivable—Current	570,000	
Revenues		541,500
Estimated Current Uncollectible Taxes		28,500

To enter actual tax levy and to estimate uncollectibles at 5%.

[115]

Cash	55,000	
Revenues		55,000

For cash received from licenses, fees, fines and other sources.

[116]

Cash	549,500	
Estimated Current Uncollectible Taxes	8,000	
Taxes Receivable		549,500
Revenues		8,000

For actual taxes collected for this year.

To close out budget accounts:

[117]

Revenues	604,500	
Appropriations	590,000	
Estimated Revenue		600,000
Expenditures		515,000
Encumbrances		72,000
Fund Balance		7,500

To zero budget accounts and adjust fund balance.

DISCS—DEEMED DISTRIBUTIONS (Parent's Books)

1975—under old law

[118]

DISC Dividends Receivable (previously taxed)	110,000	
Deemed Distribution from DISC (income)		110,000

To pick up 1/2 of DISC's net of $220,000.

1976—under the new law

[119]

DISC Dividends Receivable (previously taxed)	189,375	
Deemed Distribution from DISC (income)		189,375

As follows:

Facts:

Gross export receipts average for 1972–1975	$1,100,000
Gross exportreceipts — 1976	$1,300,000
Net DISC income — 1976 only	$ 250,000

Since the 1976 net income is over $150,000, the graduated relief in the 1976 law does not apply, and the calculation is:

67% of 1,100,000 = 670,000

670,000 ÷ 1,300,000 = 51.5%

51.5% × 250,000 =	$128,750
250,000 − 128,750 = 121,250	
121,250 × 50% =	60,625
Total Deemed Distributions	$189,375

[120]

Capitalization of Interest Costs		
Qualifying Asset	10,000	
Accrued Interest		10,000

[121]

Employee Compensation	50,000	
Accrued Vacation		50,000

Appendix C
Tax Terminology

Accountant's Report. When used regarding financial statements, a document in which an independent public or certified public accountant indicates the scope of the audit (or examination) which has been made and sets forth an opinion regarding the financial statements taken as a whole, or an assertion to the effect that an overall opinion cannot be expressed. When an overall opinion cannot be expressed, the reasons must be stated.

Accounting Method. A set of rules used to determine when and how income and expenses are reported.

Adjusted Issue Price. The issue price increased by any amount of discount deducted before repurchase, or, in the case of convertible obligations, decreased by any amount of premium included in gross income before repurchase.

Adjusted Sales Price. The amount realized, reduced by the aggregate for work performed on the old residence to assist in its sale. The reduction only applies to work performed during the 90-day period ending on the day on which the contract to sell the old residence is entered into.

Adverse Party. Any person having a substantial beneficial interest in the trust which would be adversely affected by the exercise or nonexercise of the authority which he/she possesses regarding the trust.

Affiliate. An affiliate of, or a person affiliated with, a specific person is one who directly or indirectly, through one or more intermediaries, controls, or is controlled by, or is under common control with, the person specified. (See **Person** below)

Affiliated Group. One or more chains of includable corporations connected through stock ownership with a common parent corporation which is an includable corporation. (See **Includable Corporation** below). The ownership of stock of any corporation means the common parent possesses at least 80 percent of the total voting power of the stock of such corporation and has a value equal to at least 80 percent of the total value of the stock of that corporation.

Alien. A foreigner is an alien who has filed his/her declaration of intention to become a citizen, but who has not yet been admitted to citizenship by a final order of a naturalization court.

American Aircraft. An aircraft registered under the laws of the United States.

American Vessel. Any vessel documented or numbered under the laws of the United States, and includes any vessel which is neither documented nor numbered under the laws of the United States nor documented under the laws of any foreign country, if its crew is employed solely by one or more citizens or residents of the United States or corporations organized under the laws of the United States or of any State.

Amount. When used regarding securities, the principal amount if relating to evidences of indebtedness the number of shares if relating to shares, and the number of units if relating to any other kind of security.

Amount Loaned. The amount received by the borrower.

Annual Accounting Period. The annual period, calendar year or fiscal year, on the basis of which the taxpayer regularly computes his/her income in keeping the books.

Annual Compensation. Includes an employee's average regular annual compensation, or such average compensation over the last five years, or such employee's last annual compensation if reasonably similar to his or her average regular annual compensation for the five preceding years.

Annuity Contract. A contract which may be payable in installments during the life of the annuitant only.

Applicable Installment Obligation. Any obligation which arises from the disposition of personal property under the installment method by a person who regularly sells or otherwise disposes of personal property of the same type on the installment plan. The disposition of real property under the installment method which is held by the taxpayer for sale to customers in the ordinary course of the taxpayer's trade or business, or the disposition of real property under the installment method which is property used in the taxpayer's trade or business, or property held for the production of rental income, but only if the sale price of such property exceeds $150,000.

Associate. Indicates a relationship with any person, and means 1) any corporation or organization of which such person is an officer or partner or is directly or indirectly the beneficial owner of 10 percent or more of any class of equity securities, 2) any trust or other estate in which such person has a substantial beneficial interest or for which such person serves as trustee or in a similar fiduciary capacity, and 3) any relative or spouse of such person, or any relative of such spouse, who has the same home as such person or who is a director or officer of the registrant or any of its parents or subsidiaries.

Audit (Examination). When used regarding financial statements, an examination of the statements by an accountant in accordance with generally accepted auditing standards for the purpose of expressing an opinion.

Balance. With respect to a reserve account or a guaranteed employment account, the amount standing to the credit of the account as of the computation date.

Bank. A bank or trust company or domestic building and loan association incorporated and doing business under the laws of the United States, including laws relating to the District of Columbia, or of any State, a substantial part of the business of which consists of receiving deposits and making loans and discounts, or of exercising fiduciary powers similar to those permitted to national banks under authority of the Comptroller of the Currency, and which is subject by law to supervision and examination by State or Federal authority having supervision over banking institutions.

Bank Holding Company. A person who is engaged, either directly or indirectly, primarily in the business of owning securities of one or more banks for the purpose, and with the effect, of exercising control. (See **Person** below)

Basis of Obligation. The basis of an installment obligation is the excess of the face value of the obligation over an amount equal to the income which would be returnable were the obligation satisfied in full.

Below-Market Loan. Any demand loan for which the interest is payable on the loan at a rate less than the applicable Federal rate, or in the case of a term loan (see **Term Loan** below) the amount loaned exceeds the present value of all payments due under the loan.

Bond. Any bond, debenture, note, or certificate or other evidence of indebtedness, but does not include any obligation which constitutes stock in trade of the taxpayer or any such obligation of a kind which would properly be included in the inventory of the taxpayer if on hand at the close of the taxable year, or any obligation held by the taxpayer primarily for sale to customers in the ordinary course of trade or business.

C Corporation. With respect to any taxable year, a corporation which is not an S corporation for such year.

Calendar Year. A period of 12 months ending on December 31. A taxpayer who has not established a fiscal year must make his/her tax return on the basis of a calendar year.

Capital Asset. Property held by a taxpayer, whether or not connected with a trade or business. The term does not include stock in trade of the taxpayer or other property of a kind which would properly be included in the inventory of the taxpayer if on hand at the close of the taxable year, or property held for sale to customers in the ordinary course of a trade or business.

Capital Expenditure. Any cost of a type that is properly chargeable to a capital account under general Federal income tax principles. Whether an expenditure is a capital expenditure is determined at the time the expenditure is paid with respect to the property. Future changes in law do not affect whether an expenditure is a capital expenditure. Capital expenditures do not include expenditures for items of current operating expense that are not properly chargeable to a capital account—so called *working capital* items.

Capital Gain. The excess of the gains from sales or exchanges of capital assets over the losses from sales or exchanges.

Carrier. An express carrier, sleeping car carrier, or rail carrier providing transportation.

Certified. When used regarding financial statements, examined and reported upon with an opinion expressed by an independent public or certified public accountant.

Charitable Contribution. A contribution or gift to or for the use of a corporation, trust, community chest, fund, or foundation operated exclusively for religious, charitable, scientific, literary, or educational purposes, or to foster national or international amateur sports competition if no part of its activities involves the provision of athletic facilities or equipment. A contribution or gift is deductible only if it is used within the United States or any of its possessions.

Charter. Articles of incorporation, declarations of trust, articles of association or partnership, or any similar instrument affecting, either with or without filing with any governmental agency, the organization or creation of an incorporated or unincorporated person (see **Person** below).

Child. Son, stepson, daughter, stepdaughter, adopted son, adopted daughter, or for taxable years after December 31, 1958, a child who is a member of an individual's household if the child was placed with the individual by an authorized placement agency for legal adoption pursuant to a formal application filed by the individual with the agency.

Child Care Facility. Any tangible property which qualifies as a child care center primarily for children of employees of the employer, except that the term does not include any property not of a character subject to depreciation, or located outside the United States.

Citizen. Every person born or naturalized in the United States and subject to its jurisdiction.

Collapsible Corporation. A corporation formed or availed of principally by the manufacture, construction, or production of property, for the purchase of property which is in the hands of the corporation, or for the holding of stock in a corporation so formed or availed of with a view to the sale or exchange of stock by its shareholders. The term includes distribution to its shareholders, before the realization by the corporation manufacturing, constructing, producing, or purchasing the property of ⅔ of the taxable income to be derived from such property, and by the realization by such shareholders of gain attributable to such property.

Common Equity. Any class of common stock or an equivalent interest including, but not limited to a unit of beneficial interest in a trust or a limited partnership interest.

Common Trust Fund. A fund maintained by a bank exclusively for the collective investment and reinvestment of moneys contributed thereto by the bank in its capacity as a trustee, executor, administrator, or guardian, or as a custodian of accounts which the Secretary determines are established pursuant to a State law, and which bank has established that it has duties and responsibilities similar to the duties and responsibilities of a trustee or guardian.

Company. Corporations, associations, and joint-stock companies.

Complete Liquidation. (See **Distribution** below)

Computation Date. The date, occurring at least once each calendar year and within 27 weeks prior to the effective date of new rates of contributions, as of which such dates are computed.

Constructive Sale Price. An article sold at retail, sold on consignment, or sold otherwise than through an arm's length transaction at less than the fair market price.

Contributions. Payments required by a State law to be made into an unemployment fund by any person on account of having individuals in his/her employ, to the extent that such payments are made without being deducted or deductible from the remuneration of the employed individuals.

Control. The ownership of stock possessing at least 80% of the total combined voting power of all classes of stock entitled to vote and at least 80% of the total number of shares of all other classes of stock of the corporation.

Controlled Foreign Corporation. Any foreign corporation if more than 50% of the total combined voting power of all classes of stock of such corporation entitled to vote, or the total value of the stock of such corporation, is owned, directly or indirectly, by and for a foreign corporation, foreign partnership, foreign trust, or foreign estate shall be considered as being owned proportionately by its shareholders, partners, or beneficiaries.

Controlled Group of Corporations. One or more chains of corporations connected through stock ownership with a common parent corporation if stock possessing at least 80% of the total combined voting power of all classes of stock entitled to vote or at least 80% of the total value of shares of all classes of stock of each of the corporations, and the common parent corporation is owned by one or more of the other corporations.

Convertible Obligation. An obligation which is convertible into the stock of the issuing corporation, or a corporation which, at the time the obligation is issued or repurchased, is in control of (see **Control** above) or controlled by the issuing corporation.

Cooperative Bank. An institution without capital stock organized and operated for mutual purposes and without profit, which is subject by law to supervision and examination by State or Federal authority having supervision over such institutions.

Cooperative Housing Corporation. A corporation having one and only one class of stock outstanding, each of the stockholders of which is entitled, solely by reason of ownership of stock in the corporation, to occupy for dwelling purposes a house, or an apartment in a building, owned or leased by the cooperative housing corporation. No stockholder of the housing corporation is entitled to receive any distribution that is not out of earnings and profits of the corporation except on a complete or partial liquidation of the corporation.

Corporate Acquisition Indebtedness. Any obligation evidenced by a bond, debenture, note, or certificate or other evidence of indebtedness issued by a corporation to provide consideration for the acquisition of stock in another corporation; or the acquisition of the assets of another corporation in accordance with a plan under which at least two-thirds in value of all the assets (excluding money) is used in trades and businesses carried on by the corporation.

Corporation. Includes associations, joint-stock companies, and insurance companies.

Currency Swap Contract. A contract involving different currencies between two or more parties to exchange periodic interim payments on or prior to maturity of the contract. The swap *principal amount* is an amount of two different currencies which, under the terms of the currency swap contract, is used to determine the periodic interim payments in each currency and which is exchanged upon maturity of the contract.

Date of Original Issue. The date on which the issue was first issued to the public, or the date on which the debt instrument was sold by the issuer. In the case of any debt instrument which is publicly offered, it is the date on which the debt instrument was issued in a sale or exchange.

Debt Instrument. A bond, debenture, note, or certificate or other evidence of indebtedness.

Deficiency. The amount by which the tax imposed exceeds the sum of the amount shown as the tax by the taxpayer upon his/her return, if a return was made by the taxpayer and an amount indicated as the tax. *Deficiency* includes the amounts previously assessed or collected without assessment as a deficiency over the amount of rebates.

Deficiency Dividends. The amount of dividends paid by the corporation on or after the date of the determination (see **Determination** below), before filing claims which would have been includable in the computation of the deduction for dividends paid for the taxable year with respect to which the liability for personal holding company tax exists, if distributed during such taxable year. No dividends are considered as *deficiency dividends* unless distributed within 90 days after the determination.

Deficiency Dividend Deduction. No deduction is allowed unless the claim therefore is filed within 120 days after the determination.

Demand Loan. Any loan which is payable in full at any time on the demand of the lender.

Dependent. Any of the following individuals *over half* of whose support for the calendar year in which the taxable year of the taxpayer begins was received from the taxpayer or treated as received from the taxpayer:

1. A son or daughter of the taxpayer, or a descendant of either.
2. A stepson or stepdaughter of the taxpayer.
3. A brother, sister, stepbrother, or stepsister of the taxpayer.
4. The father or mother of the taxpayer, or an ancestor of either.
5. A stepfather or stepmother of the taxpayer.
6. A son or daughter of a brother or sister of the taxpayer.
7. A brother or sister of the father or mother of the taxpayer.
8. A son-in-law, daughter-in-law, father-in-law, mother-in-law, brother-in-law, sister-in-law, of the taxpayer.
9. An individual, other than an individual who at any time during the taxable year was the spouse, who, for the taxable year of the taxpayer, has as his/her principal place of abode the home of the taxpayer and is a member of the taxpayer's household.

Depositary Share. A security, evidenced by an *American Depositary Receipt,* that represents a foreign security or a multiple of or fraction thereof deposited with a depositary.

Determination. A decision by the Tax Court or a judgment, decree, or other order by any court of competent jurisdiction, which has become final.

Development Stage Company. A company which is devoting substantially all its efforts to establishing a new business and either of the following conditions exists:

1. Planned principal operations have not commenced.
2. Planned principal operations have commenced, but there has been no significant revenue therefrom.

Distiller. Any person who produces distilled spirits from any source or substance.

Distribution. A *distribution* is treated as in complete liquidation of a corporation, if the distribution is one of a series of distributions in redemption of all of the stock of the corporation pursuant to a plan.

Dividend. Any distribution of property made by a corporation to its shareholders out of earnings and profits of the taxable year, or from the most recently accumulated earnings and profits, computed at the close of the taxable year, without regard to the amount of earnings and profits at the time the distribution was made.

Domestic. When applied to a corporation or partnership, created or organized in the United States or under the laws of the United States or of any State.

Domestic Building and Loan Association. A domestic building and loan association, a domestic savings and loan association, or a federal savings and loan association.

Earned Income. Wages, salaries, or professional fees, and other amounts received as compensation for personal services rendered by an individual to a corporation which represent a distribution of earnings or profits rather than a reasonable allowance as compensation for the personal services actually rendered. *Earned income* includes net earnings from self-employment to the extent such net earnings constitute compensation for personal services actually rendered.

Educational Organization. An organization which normally maintains a regular faculty and curriculum and normally has regularly organized body of students in attendance at the place where its educational activities are carried on.

Employee. Any officer of a corporation; any individual who, under the usual common law rules applicable to determining the employer-employee relationship, has the status of an employee; any individual who performs services for remuneration for any person as an agent-driver engaged in distributing products; a full-time life insurance salesperson; a home worker performing work; a traveling or city salesperson.

Employee Stock Purchase Plan. A plan which provides that options are to be granted only to employees of the employer corporation, or of its parent or subsidiary corporation, to purchase stock in any such corporation; and such plan is approved by the stockholders of the granting corporation within 12 months before or after the plan is adopted.

Under the terms of the plan, no employee can be granted an option if the employee, immediately after the option is granted, owns stock amounting to 5% or more of the total combined voting power or value of all classes of stock of the employee corporation or of its parent or subsidiary corporation. Under the plan, options are to be granted to all employees of any corporation whose employees are granted any of such options by reason of their employment by such corporation, except employees who have been employed less than 2 years, or employees whose customary employment is 20 hours or less per week, or employees whose customary employment is for not more than 5 months in any calendar year.

Employer. With respect to any calendar year, any person who during any calendar quarter in the calendar year or the preceding calendar year, paid wages of $1500 or more, or on each of some 20 days during the calendar year or during the preceding calendar year (each day being in a different calendar week) employed at least one individual in employment for some portions of the day.

Employment. Any service of whatever nature performed by an employee for the person employing him or her, irrespective of the citizenship or residence of either within the United States; or any service in connection with an American vessel or American aircraft under a contract of service which is entered into within the United States or during the performance of which and while the employee is employed on and in connection with such vessel or aircraft when outside the United States. The term also includes any service of whatever nature performed outside the United States by a citizen or resident of the United States as an employee of an American employer, or if it is service, regardless of where or by whom performed, which is designated as employment or recognized as equivalent to employment under an agreement entered into under the Social Security Act.

Endowment Contract. A contract with an insurance company which depends in part on the life expectancy of the insured, which may be payable in full during the insured's life.

Energy Property. Property that is described in at least one of 6 categories:

1. Alternative energy property.
2. Solar or wind energy property.
3. Specifically defined energy property.
4. Recycling equipment.
5. Shale oil Equipment.
6. Equipment for producing natural gas from geopressured grime.

Property is not *energy property* unless depreciation or amortization is allowable and the property has an estimated useful life of 3 years or more from the time when the property is placed in service.

Enrolled Actuary. A person who is enrolled by the Joint Board for the Enrollment of Actuaries.

Equity Security. Any stock or similar security, or any security convertible, with or without consideration, into such a security, or carrying any warrant or right to subscribe to or purchase such security, or any such warrant or right.

Exchanged Basis Property. Property having a basis determined in whole or in part by reference to other property held at any time by the person for whom the basis is determined.

Executor. The administrator of the decedent, or, if there is none appointed, qualified, and acting within the United States, then any person in actual or constructive possession of any property of the decedent.

Farm. Includes stock, dairy, poultry, fruit and truck farms; also plantations, ranches, and all land used for farming operations.

Farmer. All individuals, partnerships, or corporations that cultivate, operate, or manage farms for gain or profit, either as owners or tenants.

Fiduciary. A guardian, trustee, executor, administrator, receiver, conservator, or any person acting in any fiduciary capacity for any person.

Fifty-Percent-Owned Person. A person approximately 50% of whose outstanding voting shares is owned by the specified person either directly or indirectly through one or more intermediaries (see **Person**).

Financial Statements. Include all notes to the statements and all related schedules.

Fiscal Year. An accounting period of 12 months ending on the last day of any month other than December; the 52–53 week annual accounting period, if such period has been elected by the taxpayer. A fiscal year is recognized only if it is established as the annual accounting period of the taxpayer and only if the books of the taxpayer are kept in accordance with such fiscal year.

Foreign. A corporation or partnership which is *not* domestic.

Foreign Currency Contract. A contract which requires delivery of, or settlement of, and depends on the value of, a foreign currency which is a currency in which positions are also traded through regulated futures contracts. The contract is traded in the interbank market, and is entered into at arm's length at a price determined by reference to the price in the interbank market.

Foreign Earned Income. The amount received by any individual from sources within a foreign country or countries which constitutes earned income attributable to services performed by such individual. Amounts received are considered to be received in the taxable year in which the services to which the amounts are attributable are performed.

Foreign Estate (Foreign Trust). An estate or trust, as the case may be, the income of which comes from sources without the United States which are not materially connected with the conduct of a trade or business within the United States.

Foreign Insurer or Reinsurer. One who is a non-resident alien individual, or a foreign partnership, or a foreign corporation. The term includes a nonresident alien individual, foreign partnership, or foreign corporation which will become bound by an obligation of the nature of an indemnity bond. The term *does not include* a foreign government, or municipal or other corporation exercising the taxing power.

Foreign Investment Company. Any foreign corporation which is registered under the Investment Company Act of 1940, as amended, either as a management company or as a unit investment trust, or is engaged primarily in the business of investing, reinvesting, or trading in securities, commodities, or any interest in property, including a futures or forward contract or option.

FSC (Foreign Sales Corporation). Any corporation which was created or organized under the laws of any foreign country, or under the laws applicable to any possession of the United States, has no more than 25 shareholders at any time during the taxable year, does not have any preferred stock outstanding at any time during the taxable year, and during the taxable year maintains an office located outside the United States in a foreign country, or in any possession of the United States. The term *FSC* does not include any corporation which was created or organized under the laws of any foreign country unless there is in effect between such country and the United States a bilateral or multilateral agreement, or an income tax treaty which contains an exchange of information program to which the *FSC* is subject.

Foreign Trading Gross Receipts. The gross receipts of any FSC which are from the sale, exchange, or other disposition of export property, from the lease or rental of export property for use by the lessee outside the United States, or for services which are related and subsidiary to any sale, exchange, lease, or rental of export property by such corporation.

Foundation Manager. With respect to any private foundation, an officer, director, or trustee of a foundation responsible for any act, or failure to act, and for the employees of the foundation having authority or responsibility, and for their failure to act.

General Partner (see **Partner**). The person or persons responsible under state law for directing the management of the business and affairs of a partnership that are subject of a roll-up transaction (see **Roll-Up Transaction**) including, but not limited to, a general partner(s), board of directors, board of trustees, or other person(s) having a fiduciary duty to such partnership.

General Power of Appointment. The power which is exercisable in favor of the decedent, his/her estate, his/her creditors, or the creditors of the estate.

Generation-Skipping Transfer. A taxable distribution, a taxable termination, and a direct skip. The term does not include any transfer to the extent the property transferred was subject to a prior tax imposed; and such transfers do not have the effect of avoiding tax.

Gift Loan. Any below-market loan where the forgoing of interest is in the nature of a gift (see **Below-Market Loan**).

Gross Income. All income derived from whatever source; income realized in any form, whether in money, property, or services; income realized in the form of services, meals, accommodations, stock, or other property, as well as in cash. Gross income, however, is not limited to the items enumerated.

Head of Household. An individual is considered a head of a household if, and only if, such individual is *not* married at the close of his/her taxable year, is not a surviving spouse, (see **Surviving Spouse**) maintains as his/her home a household which constitutes more than one-half of such taxable year the principal place of abode as a member of such household.

Holder. Any individual whose efforts created property held; any other individual who has acquired an interest in such property in exchange for consideration in money or money's worth paid to such creator of the invention covered by the patent, if such individual is neither the employer of the creator, nor related to the creator.

Housing Expenses. The reasonable expenses paid or incurred during the taxable year by or on behalf of an individual for housing in a foreign country for the individual, spouse and dependants.

Includable Corporation. Any corporation except those exempt from taxation, foreign corporations, insurance companies subject to taxation, regulated investment companies, and real estate investment trusts subject to tax.

Income Recognition. Dividends are included in income on the ex-dividend date; interest is accrued on a daily basis. Dividends declared on short positions existing on the record date are recorded on the ex-dividend date and included as an expense of the period.

Income Tax Return Preparer. Any person who prepares for compensation, or who employs one or more persons to prepare for compensation, any return of tax or any claim for refund of tax. The preparation of a substantial portion of a return or claim for refund is treated as if it were the preparation of such return or claim for refund.

A person is *not* an *income tax return preparer* merely because such person furnishes typing, reproducing, or other mechanical assistance, or prepares a return or claim for refund of the employer, or of an officer or employee of the employer, by whom the person is regularly and continuously employed.

Indian Tribal Government. A governing body of a tribe, band, pueblo, community, village, or a group of native American Indians, or Alaska Native.

Individual Retirement Account. A trust created or organized in the United States for the exclusive benefit of an individual or his/her beneficiaries, but only if the written governing instrument creating the trust meets the following requirements:

1. The trustee is a bank, or such other person who demonstrates that the manner in which such other person will administer the trust will be consistent with the requirements of this section.
2. No part of the trust funds will be invested in life insurance contracts.
3. The interest of the individual in the balance of the account is non-forefeitable.
4. The assets of the trust will not be commingled with other property except in a common trust fund or common investment fund.

Individual Retirement Annuity. An annuity contract, or an endowment contract issued by an insurance company which meets the following requirements:

1. The contract is not transferable by the owner.
2. Under the contract, the premiums are not fixed.
3. Any refund of premiums will be applied before the close of the calendar year following the year of the refund toward the payment of future premiums or the purchase of additional benefits.
4. The entire interest of the owner is nonforfeitable.

Influencing Legislation. Any attempt to have an effect on legislation by trying to impact the opinions of the general public or any segment thereof through communication with any member or employee of a legislative body, or with any government official or employee who may participate in the formulation of the legislation. It does not include any communication with a government official or employee *other than* one whose *principal purpose* is to affect legislation.

Insurance Company. A company whose primary and predominant business activity during the taxable year is the issuing of insurance or annuity contracts, or the reinsuring of risks underwritten by insurance companies. It is the character of the business actually done in the taxable year which determines whether a company is taxable as an insurance company. Insurance companies include both stock and mutual companies, as well as mutual benefit insurance companies. A voluntary unincorporated association of employees, including an association formed for the purpose of relieving sick and aged members, and the dependants of deceased members, is an insurance company.

Interest. Return on any obligation issued in registered form, or of a type issued to the public, but does not include any obligation with a maturity (at issue) of not more than 1 year which is held by a corporation.

International organization. A public international organization entitled to the privileges, exemptions, and immunities as an international organization under the *International Organizations Immunities Act.*

Investment in the Contract. As of the annuity starting date, the aggregate amount of premiums or other consideration paid for the contract, minus the aggregate amount received under the contract before such date, to the extent that such amount was excludable from gross income under prior income tax laws.

Itemized Deductions. Those allowable other than the deductions allowable in arriving at adjusted gross income and the deduction for personal exemptions.

Joint Return. A single return made jointly by a husband and wife.

Life Insurance Contract. An *endowment contract* which is not ordinarily payable in full during the life of the insured.

Lobbying Expenditures. Amounts spent for the purpose of influencing legislation (see **Influencing Legislation**).

Local Telephone Service. Any telephone service not taxable as long distance telephone service; leased wire, teletypewriter or talking circuit special service, or wire and equipment service. Amounts paid for the installation of instruments, wire, poles, switchboards, apparatus, and equipment, are not considered amounts paid for service.

Long Distance Telephone Service. A telephone or radio telephone message or conversation for which the toll charge is more than 24 cents and for which the charge is paid within the United States.

Long-Term Capital Gain. A gain from the sale or exchange of a capital asset held for more than 1 year, if and to the extent such gain is taken into account in computing gross income.

Long-Term Capital Loss. A loss from the sale or exchange of a capital asset held for more than 1 year, if and to the extent that such loss is taken into account in computing taxable income.

Long-Term Contract. A building, installation, construction or manufacturing contract (see **Manufacturing Contract**) which is not completed within the taxable year in which it is initiated.

Lottery. A numbers game, policy, and similar types of wagering (see **Wager**).

Lowest Price. Determined without requiring that any given percentage of sales be made at that price, and without including any fixed amount to which the purchaser has a right as a result of contractual arrangements existing at the time of the sale.

Majority-Owned Subsidiary Company. A corporation, stock of which represents in the aggregate more than 50% of the total combined voting power of all classes of stock of such corporation entitled to vote, is owned wholly by a registered holding company, or partly by such registered holding company and partly by one or more majority-owned subsidiary companies, or by one or more majority-owned subsidiary companies of the registered holding company.

Managing Underwriter. An underwriter(s) who, by contract or otherwise, deals with the registrant, organizes the selling effort, receives some benefit, directly or indirectly, in which all other underwriters similarly situated do not share in proportion to their respective interests in the underwriting, or represents any other underwriters in such matters as maintaining the records of the distribution, arranging the allotments of securities offered, or arranging for appropriate stabilization activities, if any.

Manufacturing Contract. A long-term contract which involves the manufacture of unique items of a type which is not normally carried in the finished goods inventory of the taxpayer, or of items which normally require more than 12 calendar months to complete regardless of the duration of the actual contract.

Material. Information required for those matters about which an average prudent investor ought reasonably to be informed.

Mathematical or Clerical Error:

1. An error in addition, subtraction, multiplication, or division shown on any return.
2. An incorrect use of any table provided by the IRS with respect to any return, if such incorrect use is apparent from the existence of other information on the return.
3. An entry on a return of an item which is inconsistent with another entry of the same or another item on the return.
4. An omission of information which is required to be supplied to substantiate an entry on the return.
5. An entry on a return of a deduction or credit in amount which exceeds a statutory limit, if such limit is expressed as a specified monetary amount, or as a percentage, ratio, or fraction, and if the items entering into the application of such limit appear on the return.

Municipal Bond. Any obligation issued by a government or political subdivision thereof, if the interest on such obligation is excludable from gross income. It does not include such an obligation if it is sold or otherwise disposed of by the taxpayer within 30 days after the date of its acquisition.

Net Capital Gain. The excess of the net long-term capital gain for the taxable year over the net short-term capital loss for that year.

Net Capital Loss. For corporations, the excess of the losses from sales or exchanges of capital assets only to the extent of gains from such sales or exchanges. For taxpayers other than a corporation, losses from sales or exchanges of capital assets are allowable only to the extent of the gains from such sales or exchanges, plus the lower of $3,000 ($1,500 in the case of a married individual filing a separate return), or the excess of such losses over such gains.

Net Earnings from Self-Employment. The gross income derived by an individual from any trade or business carried on by such individual, less the deductions allowed which are attributable to such trade or business.

Net Long-Term Capital Gain. The excess of long-term capital gains for the taxable year over the long-term capital losses for such year.

Net Long-Term Capital Loss. The excess of long-term capital losses for the taxable year over the long-term capital gains for such year.

Net Operating Loss. The excess of the deductions allowed over the gross income. In the case of a taxpayer other than a corporation, the amount deductible on account of losses from sales or exchanges of capital assets cannot exceed the amount includable on account of gains from sales or exchanges of capital assets.

Net Short-Term Capital Gain. The excess of short-term capital gains for the taxable year over the short-term capital losses for such year.

Net Short-Term Capital Loss. The excess of short-term capital losses for the taxable year over the short-term capital gains for such year.

Nonadverse Party. Any person who is not an adverse party (see **Adverse Party,** above).

Nonrecognition Transaction. Any disposition of property in a transaction in which gain or loss is *not* recognized in whole or in part.

Notional Principal Contract. A contract that provides for the payment of amounts by one party to another at specified intervals calculated by reference to a specified index upon a *notional principal amount* in exchange for a specified consideration or a promise to pay similar amounts.

Obligation. Any bond, debenture, note, certificate, or other evidence of indebtedness.

Operating Foundation. Any private foundation which makes distributions directly for the conduct of the activities constituting the purpose or function for which the foundation is organized and operated, equal to substantially all of the lesser of its adjusted net income, or its minimum investment return.

Option. The right or privilege of an individual to purchase stock from a corporation by virtue of an offer of the corporation continuing for a stated period of time, whether or not irrevocable, to sell such stock at a price determined under an option price, or price paid under the option. *Option Price* means the consideration in money or property which, pursuant to the terms of the option, is the price at which the stock subject to the option is purchased.

The individual owning the option is under no obligation to purchase, and the right or privilege must be evidenced in writing. While no particular form of words is necessary, the written option should express, among other things, an offer to sell at the option price and the period of time during which the offer will remain open. The individual who has the right or privilege is the *optionee* and the corporation offering to sell stock under such an arrangement is referred to as the *optionor.*

Organizational Expenditures. Any expenditure which is incident to the creation of a corporation, chargeable to capital accounts, and is of a character which, if expended incident to the creation of a corporation having a limited life, would be amortizable over such life.

Overpayment. Any payment of an Internal Revenue tax which is assessed or collected after the expiration of the period of limitation properly applicable thereto.

Owner-Employee. An owner of a proprietorship, or, in the case of a partnership, a partner who owns either more than 10% of the capital interest, or more than 10% of the profits interest, of the partnership.

Paid or Incurred (Paid or Accrued). Defined according to the method of accounting upon the basis of which the taxable income is computed.

Parent. Of a specified person, (see **Person**) is an affiliate controlling such person directly, or indirectly, through one or more intermediaries.

Parent Corporation. Any corporation, other than the employer corporation, in an unbroken chain of corporations ending with the employer corporation if each of the corporations other than the employer corporation owns stock possessing 50% or more of the total combined voting power of all classes of stock in one of the other corporations in the chain.

Partially Pooled Account. A part of an unemployment fund in which all contributions thereto are mingled and undivided. Compensation from this part is payable only to individuals to whom compensation would be payable from a reserve account or from a guaranteed employment account but for the exhaustion or termination of such reserve account or of a guaranteed employment account. (See **Pooled Fund.**)

Partner. A member of a partnership.

Partner's Interest, Liquidation Thereof. The termination of a partner's entire interest in a partnership by means of a distribution, or a series of distributions, to the partner by the partnership. A series of distributions means distributions whether they are made in one year or in more than one year. Where a partner's interest is to be liquidated by a series of distributions, the interest will not be considered as liquidated until the final distribution has been made. One which is not in liquidation of a partner's entire interest is a *current distribution.* Current distributions, therefore, include those in partial liquidation of a partner's interest, and those of the partner's distributive share.

Partnership. A syndicate, pool, group, joint venture or other unincorporated organization through or by means of which any business, financial operation, or venture is carried on, and is not a corporation, trust, or estate.

Partnership Agreement. Includes the original agreement and any modifications thereof agreed to by all the partners or adopted in any other manner provided by the partnership agreement. The agreements or modifications can be oral or written.

Payroll Period. A time frame for which a payment of wages is ordinarily made to the employee by the employer. The term *miscellaneous payroll period* means one other than a daily, weekly, biweekly, semimonthly, monthly, quarterly, semiannual, or annual period.

Pension Plan Contracts. Any contract entered into with trusts which at the time the contracts were entered into were deemed to be trusts and exempt from tax. Includes contracts entered into with trusts which were individual retirement accounts, or under contracts entered into with individual retirement annuities.

Person. Includes an individual, a trust, estate, partnership, association, company, or corporation, an officer or employee of a corporation or a member or employee of a partnership, who is under a duty to surrender the property or rights to property to discharge the obligation. The term also includes an officer or employee of the United States, of the District of Columbia, or of any agency or instrumentality who is under a duty to discharge the obligation.

Personal Holding Company. Any corporation if at least 60% of its adjusted ordinary gross income for the taxable year is personal holding company income, and at any time during the last half of the taxable year more than 50% in value of its outstanding stock is owned, directly or indirectly, by or for not more than 5 individuals. To meet the gross income requirement, it is necessary that at least 80% of the total gross income of the corporation for the taxable year be personal holding company income (see **Personal Holding Company Income**).

Personal Holding Company Income. The portion of the adjusted ordinary gross income which consists of dividends, interest, royalties (other than mineral, oil, or gas royalties or copyright royalties), and annuities.

Political Organization. A party, committee, association, fund, or other organization, whether or not incorporated, organized and operated primarily for the purpose of directly or indirectly accepting contributions or making expenditures for an exempt function activity. A political organization can be a committee or other group which accepts contributions or makes expenditures for the purpose of promoting the nomination of an individual for an elective public office in a primary election, or in a meeting or caucus of a political party:

1. **Exempt Function Activity.** Includes all activities that are directly related to and support the process of influencing or attempting to influence the selection, nomination, election, or appointment of any individual to public office, or office in a political organization.

2. **Segregated Fund.** A fund which is established and maintained by a political organization or an individual separate from the assets of the organization or the personal assets of the individual. The amounts in the fund must be for use only for an exempt function, or for an activity necessary to fulfill an exempt function. A segregated fund established and maintained by an individual may qualify as a political organization.

Pooled Fund. An unemployment fund or any part thereof other than a reserve account (see **Reserve Account**) or a guaranteed employment account, into which the total contributions of persons contributing thereto are payable, in which all contributions are mingled and undivided, and from which compensation is payable to all eligible individuals.

Predecessor. A person from whom another person acquired the major portion of the business and assets in a single succession, or in a series of related successions. In each of these successions the acquiring person received the major portion of the business and assets of the acquired.

Previously Filed or Reported. Previously filed with, or reported in, a definitive proxy statement or information statement, or in a registration statement under the Securities Act of 1933.

Principal Holder of Equity Securities. Used regarding a registrant or other person named in a particular statement or report, a holder of record or a known beneficial owner of more than 10 percent of any class of equity securities of the registrant or other person, respectively, as of the date of the related balance sheet filed.

Principal Underwriter. An underwriter in privity of contract with the issuer of the securities as to which he or she is underwriter.

Promoter. Any person who, acting alone or in conjunction with others, directly or indirectly, takes initiative in founding and organizing the business or enterprise of an issuer. Any person who in so doing received in consideration of services or property, or both services and property, 10 percent or more of any class of securities of the issuer or 10 percent or more of the proceeds from the sale of any class of securities. However, a person who receives such securities or proceeds with or solely as underwriting commissions or solely in consideration of property will not be deemed a promoter within the meaning of this paragraph if such person does not otherwise take part in founding and organizing the enterprise.

Property Used in the Trade or Business. That property used in a trade or business of a character which is subject to an allowance for depreciation, held for more than 1 year, and *real* property used in a trade or business, held for more than 1 year, and which is not a copyright, a literary work, musical, artistic composition, or similar property. Also *not* included in the definition is property of a kind which would properly be includable in the inventory of the taxpayer if on hand at the close of the taxable year, nor property held by the taxpayer primarily for sale to customers in the ordinary course of the trade or business.

Qualified Assets. The nature of any investments and other assets maintained, or required to be maintained, by applicable legal instruments in respect of outstanding face-amount certificates. If the nature of the qualifying assets and amount thereof is not subject to the provisions of the Investment Company Act of 1940, a statement to that effect should be made.

Qualified Individual. An individual whose tax home is in a foreign country and who is a citizen of the United States and establishes that he/she has been a bona fide resident of a foreign country (or countries) for an uninterrupted period which includes an entire taxable year, or a citizen or resident of the United States and who, during any period of 12 consecutive months, is present in a foreign country (or countries) during at least 330 full days in such period.

Qualified Pension, Profit-Sharing, Stock Bonus Plans and Annuity Plans. Compensation is paid under a deferred payment plan, and bond purchase plan. The plan is a definite written program and arrangement which is communicated to the employees and which is established and maintained by an employer.

In the case of a *pension plan,* to provide for the livelihood of the employees or their beneficiaries after the retirement of such employees through the benefits determined without regard to profits.

In the case of a *profit-sharing plan,* to enable employees or their beneficiaries to participate in the profits of the employer's trade or business, or in the profits of an affiliated employer who is entitled to deduct any contributions to the plan pursuant to a definite formula for allocating the contributions and for distributing the funds accumulated under the plan.

In the case of a *stock bonus plan,* to provide employees or their beneficiaries benefits similar to those of profit-sharing plans, except that such benefits are distributable in stock of the employer, and that the contributions by the employer are not necessarily dependent upon profits.

Real Estate Investment Trust (REIT). A corporation, trust, or association which meets the following conditions:

1. Is managed by one or more trustees or directors. A trustee means a person who holds legal title to the property of the *real estate investment trust,* and has such rights and powers as will meet the requirement of centralization of management. The trustee must have continuing exclusive authority over the management of the trust, the conduct of its affairs, and the disposition of the trust property.
2. Has beneficial ownership which is evidenced by transferable shares or by transferable certificates of beneficial interest and must be held by more than 100 persons determined without reference to any rules of attribution.
3. In case of a taxable year beginning before October 5, 1976, does not hold any property, other than foreclosure property, primarily for sale to customers in the ordinary course of its trade or business.
4. Is neither a financial institution, nor an insurance company.
5. Beneficial ownership of the REIT is held by 100 or more persons.
6. The REIT would not be a personal holding company if all of its gross income constituted personal holding company income.

Recomputed Basis. With respect to any property, its adjusted basis recomputed by adding to it all adjustments reflected on account of deductions allowed or allowable to the taxpayer or to any other person for depreciation or amortization.

Recovery. Regarding the recovery of tax benefit items, gross income does not include income attributable to the recovery during the taxable year of any amount deducted in any prior taxable year to the extent such amount did not reduce the amount of tax imposed.

Recovery Exclusion. Regarding a bad debt, prior tax, or delinquency amount, it is the amount determined in accordance with regulations of the deductions or credits allowed, on account of such bad debt, prior tax, or delinquency amount, which did not result in a reduction of the taxpayer's tax under corresponding provisions of prior income tax laws.

Registrant. The issuers of the securities for which an application, a registration statement, or a report is filed.

Related Parties. All affiliates of an enterprise, including its management and their immediate families, its principal owners and their immediate families, its investments accounted for by the equity method, beneficial employee trusts that are managed by the management of the enterprise, and any party that may, or does, deal with the enterprise and has ownership of, control over, or can significantly influence the management or operating policies of another party, to the extent that an arm's-length transaction may not be achieved.

Reorganization, A Party To. Includes a corporation resulting from a *reorganization,* and both corporations in a transaction qualifying as a reorganization where one corporation acquires stock or properties of another corporation. A corporation remains a *party to* the reorganization although it transfers all or part of the assets acquired as a controlled subsidiary. A corporation controlling an acquiring corporation is a party to the reorganization when the stock of the controlling corporation is used in the acquisition of properties.

Repurchase Premium. the excess of the repurchase price paid or incurred to repurchase the obligation over its adjusted issue price (see **Adjusted Issue Price**).

Reserve Account. A separate account in an unemployment fund, maintained with respect to a person, or group of persons, having individuals in his, her, or their employ, from which account (unless such account is exhausted) is paid all and only compensation payable on the basis of services performed for such person, or for one or more of the persons comprising the group.

Restricted Securities. Investment securities which cannot be offered for public sale without first being registered under the Securities Act of 1933.

Return. Any return, statement, schedule, or list, and any supplement thereto, filed with respect to any tax imposed by the law.

Roll-Up Transaction. Any transaction or series of transactions that, directly or indirectly, through acquisition or otherwise, involve the combination or reorganization of one or more partnerships and the offer or sale of securities by a successor entity, whether newly formed or previously existing, to one or more limited partners of the partnerships to be combined or reorganized.

Rules and Regulations. All needful *rules and regulations* approved by the Commissioner for the enforcement of the Code. Includes all rules and regulations necessary by reason of the alterations of the law in relation to Internal Revenue.

S Corporation. Regarding any taxable year, a small business corporation for which an election is in effect for such year (see **Small Business Corporation**).

Section 1245 Property. Any property, other than livestock, which is or has been property of a character subject to an allowance for depreciation or subject to an allowance for amortization and is personal property, or other property if such property is tangible, but not including a building or its structural components.

Section 1250 Property. Any *real* property, other than Section 1245 property, which is or has been property of a character subject to an allowance for depreciation.

Self-Employment Income. The net earnings from self-employment derived by an individual during any taxable year, except if such net earnings for the taxable year are less than $400.

Share. A *unit* of stock in a corporation, or unit of interest in an unincorporated person.

Short-Term Capital Gain. A gain from the sale or exchange of a capital asset held for not more than 1 year, if and to the extent such gain is taken into account in computing gross income.

Short-Term Capital Loss. A loss from the sale or exchange of a capital asset held for not more than 1 year, if and to the extent that such loss is taken into account in computing gross income.

Significant Subsidiary. A *subsidiary,* including its subsidiaries, which meets any of the following conditions:

1. The registrant's and its other subsidiaries' investments in and advances to the subsidiary exceed 10 percent of the total assets of the registrant and its subsidiaries consolidated as of the end of the most recently completed fiscal year for a proposed business combination to be accounted for as a pooling-of-interests. This condition is also met when the number of common shares exchanged by the registrant exceeds 10 percent of its total common shares outstanding at the date the combination is initiated.

2. The registrant's and its other subsidiaries' proportionate share of the total assets, after intercompany, eliminations, of the subsidiary exceeds 10 percent of the total assets of the registrant and its subsidiaries consolidated as of the end of the most recently completed fiscal year.

3. The registrant's and its other subsidiaries' equity in the income from continuing operations before income taxes, extraordinary items and cumulative effect of a change in accounting principle of the subsidiary exceeds 10 percent of such income of the registrant and its subsidiaries consolidated for the most recently completed fiscal year.

Small Business Corporation. A domestic corporation which is not an ineligible corporation, e.g., a member of an affiliated group, and which does not have more than 35 shareholders, does not have as a shareholder a person, other than an estate or trust, who is not an individual, and does not have a nonresident alien as a shareholder.

Standard Deduction. The sum of the basic standard deduction and the additional standard deduction.

Straight Debt. Any written unconditional promise to pay on demand or on a specified date a sum certain in money if the interest rate and interest payment dates are not contingent on profits or the borrower's discretion, not convertible into stock, and the creditor is an individual, an estate, or a trust.

Subsidiary Corporation. (See **Parent Corporation.**)

Substituted Basis Property. Property which is transferred basis property, or exchanged basis property.

Summarized Financial Information. The presentation of summarized information as to the assets, liabilities and results of operations of the entity for which the information is required.

Support. Includes food, shelter, clothing, medical and dental care, education, etc. The amount of an item of *support* will be the amount of expense incurred by the one furnishing such item. If the item of *support* furnished an individual is in the form of property or lodging, it is necessary to measure the amount of such item of support in terms of its fair market value.

Surviving Spouse. A taxpayer whose spouse died during either of his/her two taxable years immediately preceding the taxable year, and who maintains as his/her home a household which constitutes for the taxable year the principal place of abode as a member of such household.

Tax Court. The United States Tax Court.

Tax-Exempt Obligation. Any obligation if the interest on such obligation is not includable in gross income.

Taxable Gifts. The total amount of gifts made during the calendar year, less the deductions provided.

Taxable Income. Gross income minus the deductions allowed, other than the standard deduction (see **Standard Deduction**). For individuals who do not itemize deductions for the taxable year, it is adjusted gross income, minus the standard deduction, and the deductions for personal exemptions.

Taxable Transportation. Transportation by air which begins and ends in the United States or in the 225-mile zone. The term *225-mile zone* means that portion of Canada and Mexico which is not more than 225 miles from the nearest point in the continental United States. The term *Continental United States* means the District of Columbia and the States other than Alaska and Hawaii.

Taxable Year. The taxpayer's annual accounting period if it is a calendar year or a fiscal year, or the calendar year if the taxpayer keeps no books or has no accounting period. (See **Annual Accounting Period** and **Calendar Year.**)

Term Loan. Any loan which is not a demand loan (see **Demand Loan**).

Tips. Wages received while performing services which constitute employment, and included in a written statement furnished to the employer.

Toll Telephone Service. A telephonic quality communication for which there is a toll charge which varies in amount with the distance and elapsed transmission time of each individual communication.

Totally Held Subsidiary. A subsidiary substantially all of whose outstanding equity securities are owned by its parent and/or the parent's other totally held subsidiaries, and which is not indebted, in an amount which is material in relation to the particular subsidiary, excepting indebtedness incurred in the ordinary course of business which is not overdue and which matures within 1 year from the date of its creation whether evidenced by securities or not. Indebtedness of a subsidiary which is secured by its parent by guarantee, pledge, assignment, or otherwise, is excluded.

Tract of Real Property. A single piece of real property, except that two or more pieces of real property should be considered a tract if at any time they were contiguous in the hands of the taxpayer, or if they would be contiguous except for the imposition of a road, street, railroad, stream, or similar property.

Trade or Business. Includes the performance of personal services within the United States at any time within the taxable year. Includes the performance of the functions of a public office.

Transferred Basis Property. Property having a basis determined in whole or in part by reference to the basis in the hands of the donor, grantor, or other transferor.

Trust. As used in the Internal Revenue Code, an arrangement created either by a will or by an *inter vivos* declaration whereby trustees take title to property for the purpose of protecting or conserving it for the beneficiaries under the ordinary rules applied in chancery or probate courts. Usually the beneficiaries of such a trust do no more than accept the benefits thereof and are not the voluntary planners or creators of the trust arrangement.

Undistributed Foreign Personal Holding Company Income. The taxable income of a *foreign personal holding company.*

Undistributed Personal Holding Company Income. The amount which is subject to the personal holding company tax.

United States Property. Any property which is a tangible property located in the United States, stock of a domestic corporation, an obligation of a United States resident, or any right to the use in the United States of a patent or copyright, an invention, model, or design (whether or not patented).

Unrealized Receivables. Any rights, contractual or otherwise, to payments for goods delivered, or to be delivered, to the extent that such payment would be treated as received for property other than a capital asset. Includes services rendered, or to be rendered, to the extent that income arising from such right to payment was not previously includable in income under the method of accounting employed. The basis for unrealized receivables includes all costs or expenses attributable thereto paid or accrued, but not previously taken into account under the method of accounting employed.

Unrecognized Gain. Any position held by the taxpayer as of the close of the taxable year, the amount of gain which would be taken into account with respect to such position if such position were sold on the last business day of such taxable year at its fair market value.

Valuation of Assets. The balance sheets of registered investment companies, other than issuers of face-amount certificates, which reflect all investments at value, with the aggregate cost of each category of investment and of the total investments reported shown parenthetically.

Voting Shares. The sum of all rights, other than as affected by events of default, to vote for election of directors; the sum of all interests in an unincorporated person (see **Person**).

Wager. Any *bet* with respect to any sporting event or a contest placed with a person engaged in the business of accepting such bets. Includes any bet placed in a wagering pool with respect to a sports event or a contest, if such pool is conducted for profit, and any bet placed in a lottery (see **Lottery**) conducted for profit.

Wages. All remuneration for services performed by an employee for an employer, including the cash value of all remuneration, including benefits.

Welfare Benefits Fund. Any fund which is part of a plan of an employer, and through which the employer provides welfare benefits to employees or their beneficiaries.

Wholly Owned Subsidiary. A subsidiary substantially all of whose outstanding voting shares (see **Voting Shares**) are owned by its parent and/or the parent's other wholly owned subsidiaries.

Year. Any 12 *consecutive* months.

Appendix D
The Going Concern Concept

The concept that financial statements are prepared on the basis of a "going concern" is one of the basics relating to financial accounting. There is an underlying presumption in the standards set for financial accounting that a business, once started, will continue functioning and operating. For example, the use of historical costs for building and property, which are currently more valuable, presupposes that the *use* of that property will generate more advantages than would present disposition. Deferrals to future periods through systematic allocations also indicate a presumption of longevity.

This presumption of continuance as a going concern is never stated by the independent auditor—never worded in his or her own opinion. On the *contrary,* it is when there appears to be danger of the firm's *not* being able to continue as a going concern that the auditor makes the assertion that "the statements have been prepared on the basis of a going concern," and that he or she is *unable* to express an opinion because of major uncertainties, then described. Therefore, the actual use of the terminology, "going concern," in the auditor's opinion indicates trouble.

Two types of problems may dictate against an entity's continuation as a going concern:

1. Operational uncertainties which may present two different types of situations giving cause for concern:
   a. Progressive deterioration of a firm's financial stability resulting from changing markets, outmoded or inefficient plant and facilities, inept management. This, in turn, leads to declining earnings or actual losses,

reduced cash balances and eventually an inability to meet current liabilities. Such uncertainties may result in gradual deterioration or, less frequently, in a very sudden turnaround of a previously profitable firm.

b. A start-up business that may never get off the ground. This is the enterprise that begins with high hopes but has not yet met with success nor achieved a solid financial footing. In the event of even a minor setback at this juncture, the firm's continuation may be open to question particularly in relation to the liquidity of its assets. What assets it has are probably tied up in inventories, specialized plant and equipment and deferred charges.

2. External difficulties beyond the control of an entity. These may be as a result of governmental controls, natural disasters such as earthquakes or floods, mandatory product recalls or devastating lawsuits. Any of these or other potential catastrophes could drain an entity beyond its financial capacity to recover.

Following is a random listing of factors which could be indicative of *possible* failure to continue as a going concern:

1. Inability to satisfy obligations on due dates.
2. Inability to perform contractual obligations.
3. Inability to meet substantial loan covenants.
4. A substantial deficit.
5. A series of continued losses.
6. The presence of major contingencies which could lead to heavy losses.
7. Catastrophes which have rendered the business inoperable.
8. Negative cash flows from operations.
9. Adverse key financial ratios.
10. Denial of usual trade credit from suppliers.
11. Necessity of finding new sources of financing.
12. Loss of key personnel.
13. Loss of a principal customer.
14. Work stoppage and labor disputes.

Appendix E
Guidelines for Interim Reporting

Guidelines for interim reporting by publicly traded companies have been established by the AICPA (and the SEC). For those private companies which do not bear the same responsibility for full and adequate disclosure to public shareholders, the guideline for public disclosure should be studied and followed, where feasible and relevant, for possible selfprotection against insurgent parties, since adherence to standards would probably be more defensible than nonadherence.

Following are the standards for determining applicable information and the appropriate guidelines for minimum disclosure:

1. Results should be based on the same principles and practices used for the latest annual statements (subject to the modifications below).
2. Revenue should be recognized as earned for the interim on the same basis as for the full year. Losses should be recognized as incurred or when becoming evident.
3. Costs may be classified as:
   a. Those associated with revenue (cost of goods sold);
   b. All other costs expenses based on:
      1. Those actually incurred, or
      2. Those allocated, based on: time expired, or benefits received, or other period activity.

4. Costs or losses (including extraordinary times) should not be deferred or apportioned unless they would be at year end. Advertised costs may be apportioned in relation to sales for interims.

5. With respect to inventory and cost of sales:

    a. LIFO basis should not be liquidated if expected to be replaced later, but should be based on expected replacement factor;

    b. Inventory losses should not be deferred because of cost or market rule; and conversely, later periods should then reflect gains on market price recoveries. Inventory losses should be reflected if resulting from permanent declines in market value in the interim period in which they occur; recoveries of such losses would be gains in a later interim period. If a change in inventory value is temporary, no recognition is given.

    c. With standard costs, variances which are expected to be absorbed by year end should be deferred for the interim, not expensed. Unplanned purchase price or volume variance, not expected to turn around, is to be absorbed during the period;

    d. The estimated gross profit method may be used, but must be disclosed.

6. The seasonal nature of activities should be disclosed, preferably including additional 12-month-to-date information with prior comparative figures.

7. Income taxes:

    a. Effective yearly tax rate (including year-end applicable tax-planned advantages) should be applied to interim taxable income;

    b. Extraordinary items applicable to the interim period should be shown separately net of applicable tax and the effect of the tax not applied to the tax on ordinary net income.

8. Extraordinary and unusual items including the effects of segment disposals should be disclosed separately, net of tax, for the interim period in which they occur, and they should not be apportioned over the year.

9. Contingencies should be disclosed the same as for the annual report.

10. Changes in accounting practices or principles from those allowed in prior periods should be disclosed and, where possible, those changes should be made in the first period of the year.

11. Retroactive restatement and/or prior period adjustments are required under the same rules applying to annual statements.

12. The effect of a change in an accounting estimate, including a change in the estimated effective annual tax rate, should be accounted for in the period in which the change in estimate is made. No restatement of previously reported interim information should be made for changes in estimates, but the effect on earnings of a change in estimate made in a current interim period should be reported in the current and subsequent interim periods, if material in relation to any period presented, and

should continue to be reported in interim financial information of the subsequent year, for as many periods as necessary to avoid misleading comparisons.

MINIMUM DATA TO BE REPORTED ON INTERIM STATEMENTS:

1. Sales or gross revenues, provisions for income taxes, extraordinary items (including related tax), cumulative effect of changes in accounting principles or practices, and net income;
2. Primary and fully diluted earnings per share data for each period presented;
3. Seasonal revenue, costs and expenses;
4. Disposal of business segments and extraordinary items, as well as unusual or infrequent items;
5. Contingencies;
6. Changes in estimates, changes in accounting principles or practices;
7. Significant changes in balance sheet items;
8. Significant changes in tax provisions;
9. Current year-to-date, or the last 12 months, with comparative data for prior periods;
10. In the absence of a separate fourth-quarter report, special fourth-quarter adjustments and extraordinary, infrequent or unusual items which occurred during that fourth quarter should be disclosed in a note to the annual financial statement;
11. Though not required, condensed balance sheet data and funds flow data are suggested to provide better understanding of the interim report.
12. If a fourth quarter is not presented, any material adjustment to that quarter must be commented upon in the annual report.

Interim reports are usually prepared by management and issued with that clear stipulation.

Accounting firms which issue reports for interim periods are to be guided by auditing standards set for "Reports on a Limited Review of Interim Financial Information" in Section 722 of Statements on Auditing Standards, April, 1981.

ACCOUNTING CHANGES IN INTERIM STATEMENTS

FASB 3, *Reporting Accounting Changes in Interim Financial Statements* amended APB Opinion No. 28, *Interim Financial Reporting* with respect to reporting an accounting change in interim financial reports that have a *cumulative effect.*

The following disclosures of accounting changes that have cumulative effects on income from continuing operations, net income, and related per share amounts for the interim period in which the change is made must be included in interim reports:

1. In the interim period in which the new accounting principle is adopted, disclosure should explain the nature and justification for the change.
2. Disclosure should be made of the effect of the change in the interim period in which the change is made.
3. The effect of the change for each pre-change interim period of that fiscal year should be disclosed.
4. The cumulative effect of the change should be shown on retained earnings at the beginning of that fiscal year, if the change is made in other than the first interim period of the company's fiscal year.
5. In the interim period in which a change is made, disclosure must include amounts computed on a *pro forma* basis for the interim period in which the change is made and for any interim periods of prior fiscal years for which financial information is being presented.
6. In financial reports for a subsequent interim period of the fiscal year in which a new principle is adopted, disclosure must include the effect of the change on income from continuing operations, net income, and related per share amounts for the post-change interim period.

Appendix F

Reporting Cash Payments of Over $10,000

Often smugglers and drug dealers use large cash payments to "launder" money from illegal activities. Laundering means converting "dirty" money or illegally gained money to "clean" money. Congress passed the Tax Reform Act of 1984 and the Anti-Drug Abuse Act of 1988 requiring the payment of certain cash payments of over $10,000 to be reported to the Internal Revenue Service. Any person in a trade or business who receives more than $10,000 in a single transaction or in related transactions must report the transaction to the IRS. The government can often trace the laundered money through payments that are reported. Compliance with the law provides valuable information that can stop those who evade taxes and those who profit from the drug trade and other criminal activities.

A "person" includes an individual, a company, a corporation, a partnership, an association, a trust, or an estate. A report does not have to be filed if the entire transaction, including the receipt of cash, takes place outside of:

1. The 50 states.
2. The District of Columbia.
3. Puerto Rico.
4. A possession or territory of the United States.

However, a report must be filed if the transaction, including the receipt of cash, occurs in Puerto Rico or a possession or territory of the United States and the person is subject to the Internal Revenue Code.

A transaction occurs when:

1. Goods, services, or property are sold.
2. Property is rented.
3. Cash is exchanged for other cash.
4. A contribution is made to a trust or escrow account.
5. A loan is made or repaid.
6. Cash is converted to a negotiable instrument such as a check or bond.

Payments to be reported include:

1. A sum over $10,000.
2. Installment payments that cause the total cash received within one year of the initial payment to total more than $10,000.
3. Other previously unreportable payments that cause the total cash received within a 12-month period to total more than $10,000.
4. Those received in the course of a trade or business.
5. Those received from the same buyer or agent.
6. Those received in a single transaction or in related transactions.

A DESIGNATED REPORTING TRANSACTION

A designated reporting transaction is the retail sale of any of the following:

1. A consumer durable, such as an automobile or boat. A consumer durable is property other than land or buildings that is suitable for personal use and can reasonably be expected to last at least one year under ordinary usage.
2. Has a sales price of more than $10,000.
3. Tangible property.
4. A "collectible," including works of art, rugs, antiques, gems, stamps, coins.
5. Travel or entertainment, if the total sales price of all items sold for the same trip or entertainment event in one transaction, or related transactions, is more than $10,000. The sales price of items such as air fare, hotel rooms, and admission tickets are all included.

RETAIL SALES

The term "retail sales" means any sale made in the course of a trade or business that consists mainly of making sales to ultimate consumers. Thus, if a business consists mainly of making sales to ultimate consumers, all sales made in the course of that business are retail sales. This includes sales of items that will also be resold.

DEFINITION OF CASH

In this context, cash is considered to be:

1. The coins and currency of the U.S. and any other recognized country.
2. Cashier's checks, bank drafts, traveler's checks, and money orders received if they have a face value of $10,000 or less and were received in:
   a. A designated reporting transaction.
   b. Any transaction in which the receiver knows the payer is trying to avoid the reporting of the transaction.

A check drawn on an individual's personal account is not considered cash; however, a cashier's check, even when labeled a "treasurer's check" or "bank check," is considered cash.

EXCEPTIONS TO DEFINITION OF CASH

A cashier's check, bank draft, traveler's check, or money order received in a designated transaction is not treated as cash if:

1. It is the proceeds from a bank loan. As proof that it is proceeds from a bank loan, a copy of the loan document, a written statement or lien instructions from the bank, or similar proof are acceptable as evidence,
2. If received in payment on a promissory note or an installment sales contract, including a lease that is considered a sale for federal tax purposes. This exception applies if:
   a. The receiver uses similar notes or contracts in other sales to ultimate consumers in the ordinary course of trade or business.
   b. Total payments for the sale are received on or before the 60th day after the sale, and are 50% or less of the purchase price.
3. For certain down payment plans in payment for a consumer durable or collectible, or for travel and entertainment, and *all three* of the following statements are true:
   a. It was received under a payment plan requiring one or more down payments, and payment of the remainder before receipt of goods or service.

  b. It was received more than 60 days before final payment was due.
  c. Similar payment plans are used in the normal course of the trade or business.

TAXPAYER IDENTIFICATION NUMBER (TIN)

The receiver must furnish the correct TIN of the person or persons from whom the cash is received. If the transaction is conducted on behalf of another person or persons, the receiver must furnish the TIN of that person or persons. There are three types of TINs:

1. The TIN for an individual, including a sole proprietor, is the individual's social security number (SSN).
2. The TIN for a nonresident alien individual who needs a TIN, but is not eligible to get an SSN, is an IRS individual taxpayer identification number (ITIN). An ITIN has nine digits, similar to an SSN.
3. The TIN for other persons, including corporations, partnerships, and estates, is the employer identification number.

A nonresident alien individual or a foreign organization does not have to have a TIN, and so a TIN does not have to be furnished for them, if *all* the following are true:

1. The individual or organization does not have income effectively connected with the conduct of a trade or business in the United States, or an office or place of business or a fiscal or paying agent in the United States, at any time during the year.
2. The individual or organization does not file a federal tax return.
3. In the case of a nonresident alien individual, the individual has not chosen to file a joint federal income tax return with a spouse who is a U.S. citizen or resident.

RELATED TRANSACTIONS

Any transaction between a buyer, or an agent of the buyer, and a seller that occurs within a 24-hour period are related transactions. If a person receives over $10,000 in cash during two or more transactions with one buyer in a 24-hour period, he or she must treat the transactions as one transaction and report the payments. For example, if two products are sold for $6,000 each to the same customer in one day, and the customer pays the seller in cash, they are related transactions. Because they total $12,000, they must be reported.

Transactions can be related if they are more than 24 hours apart if the person knows, or has reason to know, that each is one of a series of connected transactions. For example, a travel agent receives $8,000 from a client in cash for a trip. Two days later, the same client pays the agent $3,000 more in cash to include another person on the trip. These are related transactions and must be reported.

When a person receives $10,000 or less in cash, the person may voluntarily report the payment if the transaction appears to be suspicious. A transaction is suspicious if it appears that a person is trying to cause the receiver not to report, or is trying to cause a false or incomplete report, or if there is a sign of possible illegal activity.

The amount received and when it was received determines when it must be reported to the IRS. Generally, a report must be filed within 15 days after receiving payment. If the first payment is not more than $10,000, the seller must add the first payment and any later payments made within one year of the first payment. When the total cash payments are more than $10,000, the buyer must file within 15 days. After a report is filed, a new count of cash payments received from that buyer within a 12-month period must be reported to the IRS within 15 days of the payment that causes the additional payments to total more than $10,000. The report can be filed in the seller's local IRS office.

A written statement must be given to each person named on the report to the IRS. The statement must show the name and address of the person who receives the payment, the name and telephone number of a contact person, and the total amount of reportable cash received from the person during the year. It must state that the information is being reported to the IRS. The statement must be sent to the buyer by January 31 of the year after the year in which the seller receives the cash that caused the information to be filed with the IRS. The individual making the report must keep a copy of every report filed for five years.

PENALTIES

There are civil penalties for failure to:

1. File a correct report by the date it is due.
2. Provide the required statement to those named in the report.
3. If the person receiving the cash payment intentionally disregards the requirement to file a correct form by the date it is due, the penalty is the larger of:
   a. $25,000.
   b. The amount of cash the person received and was required to report, up to $100,000.

There are criminal penalties for:

1. Willful failure to file a report.
2. Willfully filing a false or fraudulent report.
3. Stopping or trying to stop a report from being filed.
4. Setting up, helping to set up, or trying to set up a transaction in a way that would make it seem unnecessary to file a report.

Interference with or prevention of the filing of a report as well as actual willful failure to file sa report may result in a substantial fine, imprisonment, or both. The fine can be up to $250,000 ($500,000 for corporations). An individual may also be sentenced to up to five years in prison. Both a fine and a prison sentence may be imposed.

The penalties for failure to file can also apply to any person, including a payer, who attempts to interfere with or prevent the seller, or business, from filing a correct report. This includes any attempt to *structure* the transaction in a way that would make it seem unnecessary to file a report by breaking up a large cash transaction into small cash transactions.

Index

A

AASB. *See* Australian Accounting Standards Board (AASB)
Abandonment, real estate, 19.18–19.19
Accountability, governmental, 11.17–11.18
The Accountancy Profession and the Fight against Corruption, 6.40
Accountant as expert witness. *See* Expert witness
Accounting literature on revenue recognition, 2.19–2.20
Accounting methods, change in, 36.01–36.27. *See also* Change
Accounting Standards Board (ASB), United Kingdom, 5.31, 5.58–5.59, 5.61
  New Work Program, 5.09
Accounts payable
  internal control system, checklist, 16.39–16.40
Accounts receivable
  internal control system, 16.28–16.29
    checklist, 16.36
Accrual accounting
  IFAC, Public Sector Committee (PSC), 6.43–645
  income determination, 2.02
ACFE. *See* Association of Certified Fraud Examiners (ACFE)
Acid test ratio, 1.25
Acquisitions. *See also* Business combinations
  acquisition date test, depreciation, 33.16, 33.21
  e-commerce, 27.04
  trade or business, basis of, 35.06–35.07

Actions of Certain Financial Institutions (Exposure Draft), 10.21–10.22
Activity ratios, 1.22
Actuarial services, 22.05–22.06
Adjusted basis of property, 35.08–35.11. *See also* Asset valuation
Administrative expenses
  internal control system, 16.25
Adoption credits, 39.08
ADS. *See* Alternative depreciation system (ADS)
Advertising
  international accounting, 5.19–5.20
  Internet accounting, 28.08–28.09
Afghanistan, designation as combat zone, 40.04
Aggressive growth
  diversification, 17.28
Agriculture, Standard on
  international accounting. *See* International Accounting
AICPA (American Institute of Certified Public Accountants), 2.05–2.07
  Enron scandal, effect of, 9.02
  SEC practice section, 5.34–5.35
  Special Committee on Financial Reporting, 8.02
  Statement of Auditing Standards 90, 22.12
  Study Group on the Objectives of Financial Statements, 1.10
  SysTrust, 27.20–27.22
  WebTrust, 27.18–27.20. *See also* E-commerce and E-communication
Air transportation taxes, 40.31

AJCPA
  XBRL Consortium, 6.13–6.15. *See also* International Federation of Accountants
Alfred P. Murrah Federal Building (Oklahoma City), bombing
  tax relief for victims of, 40.03–40.04
Alternative depreciation system (ADS), 33.07, 33.08–33.09
Alternative minimum tax (AMT)
  personal credits against AMT, 41.10–41.12
  relief, 33.14–33.15, 39.05
Annual Financial Accounting Standards Advisory Council (FASAC) Survey, 10.19
Annuities, 2.11–2.13. *See also* Revenue and expenses
Anthrax attacks, tax relief for victims of, 40.03
Anti-bribery provisions, FCPA. *See* Foreign Corrupt Practices Act (FCPA)
APB (Accounting Principles Board)
  Opinion 10, 2.19
  Opinion 16, *Accounting for Business Combinations,* 10.32–10.35, 13.15. *See also* Business combinations
  Opinion 17, *Intangible Assets,* 10.32–10.35
  Opinion 21, 2.05–2.07
  Opinion 22, *Disclosure of Accounting Policies,* 1.07, 1.41–1.42, 2.20–2.21
  Opinion 25, *Accounting for Stock Issued to Employees,* 10.40
  Opinion 29, *Accounting for Nonmonetary Transactions,* 4.06
  Opinion 30, 5.55
Appraisal services, 22.05
Appreciation, real estate, 19.15–19.16
ARB (Accounting Research Bulletin)
  51, *Consolidated Financial Statements,* 10.02
Archer MSAs, 40.06, 41.13
ASB. *See* Accounting Standards Board (ASB), United Kingdom
Assembly plants, cost accounting, 15.05
Assessments for local improvements as increase in property basis, 35.09
Asset, real estate as. *See* Real estate as asset
Asset allocation
  investments, advising clients on, 17.20–17.29
    bonds, 17.25
    concerns, 17.23–17.24
    current fads, 17.24
    description of asset allocation, 17.24–17.25
    diversification, overview, 17.25–17.28. *See also* Diversification
    how to allocate assets, 17.22
    portfolio management, 17.22–17.23
    selection of option, 17.28–17.29
    similar performance of investments, 17.24
    steps, 17.23
    stocks, 17.24–17.25
    unsuitable investments, concerns, 17.23–17.24

Asset impairment/preservation method
  governmental accounting, 11.13–11.14
Asset impairments related to e-commerce, 27.06
Asset turnover, 1.28
Asset valuation for tax purposes, 35.01–35.16
  adjusted basis of property, 35.08–35.11
    assessments for local improvements, 35.09
    decreases, 35.10
    deducting versus capitalizing costs, 35.09–35.10
    environmental considerations, 35.10–35.11
    increases, 35.08–35.11
  basis other than cost, 35.11–35.16. *See also* Basis in property other than cost
    closely held business, 35.15–35.16
    community, 35.15
    farm, 35.15–35.16
    inherited property, 35.14–35.15
    involuntary conversions, 35.12
    like-kind exchanges, 35.12–35.14. *See also* Like-kind exchanges, basis of
    nontaxable exchanges, 35.12
    property changed to business or rental use, 35.16
    services, property received for, 35.11
    spouse, property transferred from, 35.14
    taxable exchanges, 35.12
  cost basis of assets, 35.02–35.08
    allocating, 35.06–35.08. *See also* Basis in property
    business, 35.05–35.06. *See also* Business assets
    mutual fund shares, 35.03
    real property, 35.03–35.05. *See also* Real property, cost basis of
    stocks and bonds, 35.02–35.03
    time-payment plan, 35.02
Association of Certified Fraud Examiners (ACFE), 16.46
Assurance Engagements, 6.35
Assurance of financial credibility, 6.35–6.36
Assuring the Quality of Professional Services, 6.32
At-risk rules, rental property, 19.14
Attorney fees, raise in rates of, 38.13, 38.16
Audit Committee. *See* Auditor independence and Audit Committee
Auditing Fair Value Measurements and Disclosures, 6.19–6.20
Auditor independence and Audit Committee, 22.01–22.16
  actuarial services, 22.05–22.06
  appraisal services, 22.05
  Blue Ribbon Panel on Improving the Effectiveness of Corporate Audit Committees, 2.11–2.12
  bookkeeping services, 22.04–22.05
  broker-dealer services, 22.06
  fairness opinions, 22.05
  financial information systems design and implementation, 22.05

human resources, 22.06

internal audit services, 22.06

legal services, 22.07

management functions, 22.06

non-audit services, 22.04–22.07

SEC's new rules for Audit Committees and Review of interim financial statements, 22.12–22.13

appropriateness, gauging, 22.14

Blue Ribbon Panel, 22.13–22.14

public companies, SEC reminder to, 22.14–22.15

SEC's new rules governing independence of auditor, 22.02–22.11

affiliate provisions, 22.07

application of rules, 22.08–22.11

business relationships, 22.04

contingent fee arrangements, 22.07

employment relationships, 22.04

financial relationships, 22.04

four principles to measure independence, 22.03–22.04

frequently asked questions, 22.08–22.11

general standard, 22.04

non-audit services, 22.04–22.07

overview, 22.01–22.02

principal provisions, 22.03

proxy disclosure requirement, 22.08

quality controls, 22.07–22.08

valuation services, 22.05

Audits by IRS, 38.04

appeals, 38.05

equitable relief, 38.05

innocent spouse relief, 38.05

by interview, 38.04

by mail, 38.04

refunds, 38.05–38.06

repeat, 38.04–38.05

separation of liability, 38.05

Audits of Airlines, 28.30

Australia

Financial Reporting Council (FRC) of Australia, 5.07–5.08

international standards considered by, 5.07–5.08

Australian Accounting Standards Board (AASB), 5.07–5.08

Average basis for selling mutual fund shares, 29.06–29.07

B

Back-ended (trailing) load

mutual funds, 30.06

Balance sheet, 1.03–1.04

analysis, 1.23–1.24

income taxes, presentation of, 1.20

Bankruptcy

Chapter 11, 23.40–23.41

IRS procedure in case of, 38.07

Banks and banking

bankers' use of financial statements, 4.11–4.14. *See also* Cash flows

bank supervisors, function of, 6.16–6.17

internal control system, bank reconciliations and cash, 16.29–16.31

International Auditing Practices Committee, 6.16–6.19

Bar Chris case, 1.05

Bargain purchases, 35.11

Basel Committee, IASC's relationship with, 5.24

on Banking Supervision, 6.17–6.19

Basis in property

allocating, 35.06–35.08

land and buildings, 35.07–35.08

trade or business, acquisition of, 35.06–35.07

subdivided lots, 35.08

Basis in property other than cost, 35.11–35.16

closely held business, 35.15–35.16

community property, 35.15

farm, 35.15–35.16

inherited property, 35.14–35.15

involuntary conversions, 35.12

like-kind exchanges, 35.12–35.14. *See also* Like-kind exchanges, basis of

property changed to business or rental use, 35.16

services, property received for, 35.11

bargain purchases, 35.11

spouse, property transferred from, 35.14

taxable exchanges, 35.12

Behavioral control

independent contractor or employee, 34.08–34.09

Block-proofs of cash, 16.30

Blue Ribbon Panel on Improving the Effectiveness of Corporate Audit Committees, 2.11–2.12

interim financial statements, 22.13–22.14

Boilerplate, avoiding in prospectus, 32.10. *See also* Plain English Disclosure Rule

Bond Discount account, 2.13

Bond mutual funds, 30.11–30.16

costs, 30.11–30.12

emerging markets bond funds, 30.13–30.14

global bond funds, 30.12–30.13

insured municipal bond funds, 30.14–30.15

junk bond funds, 30.12

municipal bond funds, 30.14–30.15

risk, 30.15–30.16

credit risk, 30.15

interest rate risk, 30.15

sector risk, 30.15–30.16

Bonds

asset allocation, 17.25

cost basis of, 35.02–35.03

qualified public educational facilities, tax-exempt bond funding, 40.12

qualified zone academy bonds, 41.05

Book value, 5.57
  of securities, 1.28–1.29
Break-even analysis (BE), 14.02. *See also* Budgeting
      for profit planning and budgetary control
Broker-dealer services, 22.06
Budget, governmental, 11.19
Budgeting for profit planning and budgetary control,
      14.01–14.25
  break-even analysis (BE), 14.02
    chart, 14.21–14.23
    computing break-even point, 14.23–14.25
    defined, 14.20–14.21
    objective, 14.02
    value of, 14.02
  capital expenditures budget, 14.13–14.15
    preparation, 14.14–14.15
    purpose, 14.13–14.14
  cash budget, 14.15–14.17
    depreciation, 14.16
    differences from other budgets, 14.16
    preparation, 14.16–14.17
    purposes, 14.15–14.16
  definition, 14.01
  labor budget, 14.07–14.09
    actual vs. estimated costs, analysis of, 14.08
    cost estimates, 14.08
    direct labor only, 14.07
    operation requirements, 14.08
    preparation, 14.08–14.09
    purpose, 14.08
    schedule of estimated direct labor costs, 14.09
    unit costs, determining, 14.08
  manufacturing expense budget, 14.07–14.08,
      14.11–14.13
    controllable and uncontrollable expenses, dis-
        tinction, 14.12
    electric power expense, 14.12
    fixed expenses, responsibility for, 14.11
    fixed vs. variable expenses, 14.12
    goods in process, 14.10–14.11
    indirect labor expense, 14.07–14.08, 14.12
    indirect materials expense, 14.12
    insurance expense, 14.12
    percentages, use of, 14.11–14.12
    preparation, 14.14–14.15
    repairs and maintenance expense, 14.12
    schedule of estimated manufacturing expenses,
        sample, 14.13
  materials budget, 14.09–14.11
    factors affecting policy, 10, 14
    finished goods, 14.11
    inventory, controlling, 14.10
    purpose, 14.09
    standard costs, tie-in to, 14.09–14.10
    time lag between order and delivery, 10–14, 11, 14
  production budget, 14.05–14.07
    available facilities, confirmation with, 14.06–
        14.07

    budgeting costs, 14.05–14.06
    cost of production, 14.07
    preparing, 14.06–14.07
    standards of production performance, 14.07
    for stock products vs. special-order goods, 14.05
  sales budget
    forecasting sales, 14.03–14.04
    generally, 14.02–14.03
    individual performance, measuring, 14.04–14.05
    market analysis, 14.04
    pricing policy, 14.04
    questionnaire, use of, 14.04
    sales policies, formulating, 14.04
  types of budgets, 14.02–14.03
  zero-base budgeting (ZBB), 14.02, 14.17–14.20
    categories, two, 14.17
    decision package concept, 14.18–14.20
    where to use, 14.18
Buildings, allocating cost basis of, 35.07–35.08
Business, cost basis of, 35.02
  allocating, 35.06–35.08
*Business and Financial Reporting, Challenges from
      the New Economy,* 10.49
Business assets, cost basis of, 35.05–35.06
  intangible assets, 35.06
  tangible personal property, 35.06
  uniform capitalization rules, 35.05–35.06
Business combinations
  international accounting, 5.10–5.11, 5.19
  new basis accounting, 10.18–10.19
  not-for-profit organizations, accounting methods,
      13.17–13.21
    acquiring organization, identifying, 13.19–13.21
    collection acquired, 13.21
    exchange of cash or other assets as considera-
        tion, 13.18–13.19
    intangible assets, identification of, 13.21
  purchase method procedures, 10.15–10.17
    assets and liabilities, recognition and measure-
        ment, 10.17–10.18
    contingent consideration, 10.17
    measurement issues, acquired businesses, 10.17
    tentative decisions, 10.16–10.17
Business Combinations and Intangible Assets, 10.31–
      10.35. *See also* Financial Accounting Stan-
      dards Board
Business Combinations Exposure Draft, 10.32–10.34
Business incentives
  Job Creation and Worker Assistance Act of 2002
    empowerment zone tax incentives, 41.05–41.06
    expiring business tax credits, 41.06
    non-accrual experience method of accounting,
        41.05
    pension plan start-up costs, credit for, 41.05
    tax incentives for New York City Liberty Zone,
        41.04–41.05
Business purpose tax year, 36.18–36.19
  natural, 36.19–36.20

Business Reporting on the Internet, 27.14–27.16. *See also* E-commerce and E-communication
Business taxpayers, benefits for, 39.13
Business use of home, 20.01–20.11
  assorted use tests, 20.05–20.06
  business furniture and equipment, 20.08–20.10
    listed property, 20.08–20.09
    property bought for business use, 20.09–20.10
  convenience-of-the employer test, 20.06
  day-care facility, 20.07–20.08
    meal allowance, 20.07–20.08
  deductions
    business percentage, 20.05
    claiming, 20.02
    figuring, 20.04–20.05
    limit, 20.05
    Section 179, 20.10
  depreciation, 20.11
  exclusive use test, 20.06
  part-year use, 20.06–20.07
  personal property converted to business use, 20.11
  principal place of business, 20.02–20.03
    criteria for determining, 20.03–20.04
  property bought for business use, 20.09–20.10
  Section 179 deduction, 20.10
  separate structures, 20.04
  trade or business use test, 20.06

C

Calendar year for taxpayer, 36.17
Canada, foreign issuers, 5.05
Canadian GAAP, 5.05
Canadian Institute of Chartered Accountants, 5.31, 26.01
  SysTrust, 27.20–27.22
Canadian Securities Administration, 5.05
Capital expenditures budget, 13–14.15, 14. *See also* Budgeting for profit planning and budgetary control
Capital gain, lower tax rates, 40.06
Capital in excess of par, 3.06
Capitalization, 10.36
Capital Project Fund, 12.09, 12.12–12.13
Capital stock, 3.02–3.06. *See also* Stockholders' equity
Capital surplus, 3.06
Cash
  disbursements, internal control system, 16.28
  internal control for. *See* Internal control system
Cash budget, 14.02–14.03, 14.15–14.17. *See also* Budgeting for profit planning and budgetary control
Cash flow, real estate, 19.15
Cash flow hedge, 7.14
Cash flows, statement of, 4.01–4.16
  bankers' use of financial statements, 4.11–4.14

current ratio, 4.13
debt-to-net-worth ratio, 4.13
financial ratios, evaluation of, 4.12–4.13
long-term creditors, 4.13–4.14
management evaluation, 4.13
short-term creditors, 4.13
cash cycle, basic, 4.02
classification of cash receipts and cash payments, 4.06–4.07
  from financing activities, 4.07
  from investing activities, 4.06
  from operating activities, 4.06
concept, 4.01
definition, 4.01
direct method, 4.03–4.04, 4.07–4.09
FASB 95, *Statement of Cash Flows,* 4.03–4.06
  direct method, 4.03–4.04, 4.15
  indirect reconciliation method, 4.04
  summary, 4.05–4.06
  terminology, 4.04–4.05
FASB 102, *Statement of Cash Flows—Exemption of Certain Enterprises and Classification of Cash Flows from Certain Securities Acquired for Resale,* 4.14
FASB 104, *Statement of Cash Flows—Net Reporting of Certain Cash Receipts and Cash Payments and Classification of Cash Flows from Hedging Transactions,* 4.15
importance, 4.01–4.03
indirect method, 4.09–4.10
indirect reconciliation method, 4.04
reconciliation method, 4.04, 4.09–4.10
Cash method of accounting, 40.05
  income determination, 2.02
Cash receipts
  internal control system, 16.27–16.28
  checklist, 16.38
Casualties, rental property, 19.13
Centralized Authorized File (CAF) of IRS, 37.09, 37.10
Change in accounting methods and consideration of accounting periods, 36.01–36.27
  accounting periods, 36.16–36.26
    business purpose tax year, 36.18–36.19
    calendar year, 36.17
    change in tax year, 36.20–36.21
    corporations, 36.17, 36.20, 36.25–36.26
    fiscal year, 36.17–36.18
    improper tax year, 36.18
    "individuals," 36.17
    natural business year, 36.19–36.20
    partnerships, 36.17
    personal service corporations, 36.22–36.23
    S corporation shareholders, 36.17, 36.20, 36.22
    Section 444 election, 36.22, 36.23–36.25
    short tax year, 36.20
    sole proprietorships, 36.17
    tax year, 36.16–36.21

Change in accounting methods and consideration of
    accounting periods (*cont.*)
  adjustment, 36.07
    need for, 36.08–36.09
  appeals officer, 36.12–36.13
  application procedures, 36.10–36.11
  automatic approval procedures, new, 36.02–36.05
  business purpose tax year, 36.18–36.19
    natural, 36.19–36.20
  calendar year, 36.17
  consolidated groups, 36.11–36.12
  corporations, 36.17, 36.20, 36.25–36.26
    automatic change, 36.27
    changes during tax year, 36.26–36.27
  counsel for government, role of, 36.12–36.13
  cutoff method, 36.07
  definition of change, 36.05–36.06
    classification, 36.06
    consistency, 36.06
    material item defined, 36.05
  domestic international sales corporation
    (IC-DISC), 36.25
  effective date, 36.04–36.05
  under examination by IRS, 36.10
  examining agent, role of, 36.14
  fiscal year, 36.17–36.18
  Form 3115, *Application for Change in Accounting
    Method,* 33.18, 36.01–36.27
    filing, 33.06
  improper tax year, 36.18
  income, reflections of, 36.08
  "individuals," 36.17
  initial method, 36.07
  IRS approval, 36.08
  IRS-initiated method changes, 36.14–36.15
    with LIFO inventory method, 36.07
    method changes initiated by IRS, 36.14–36.15
    method change using cutoff method, 36.07
    method change with adjustment, 36.07
    new, 36.15–36.16
    required change or modification of new
      method, 36.16
    retroactive, 36.15
  natural business year, 36.19–36.20
  ownership tax year test, 36.19–36.20
  partnerships, 36.17, 36.21–36.22
  permitted tax year, 36.22
  personal service corporations, 36.22–36.23
  retroactive method change, 36.15
  Revenue Procedure 2002-37, 36.02–36.03
  Revenue Procedure 2002-38, 36.03–36.04
  S corporations, 36.17, 36.20, 36.22
  Section 444 election, 36.22, 36.23–36.25
    deferral period, 36.24
  separate trades or businesses, 36.12
  significant changes, 36.05
  sole proprietorships, 36.17
  tax year, 36.16–36.21
    change in, 36.20–36.21

    year of change, 36.21
  timing issues, 36.12–36.14
    alternative, 36.13
    application of law to facts, 36.12–36.13
    examining agent, discretion of, 36.14
    taxpayer's advantage, 36.13–36.14
    time-value-of-money, 36.13
  user fee, 36.31
  window periods, 36.09
  year of change, 36.21
"Channel stuffing," 2.16, 2.17
Chapter 11 bankruptcy, 23.40–23.41
Chat rooms, 27.12
Check-kiting, 16.45–16.46
Child and Adult Food Care Program, 20.08
Child and dependent care credit, 40.14–40.15, 41.13
Child care facilities, employer-provided, 39.08
Child credit increases, 39.07–39.08
Children
  child-oriented tax benefits and considerations,
    40.13–40.15
    child and dependent care credit, 40.14–40.15,
      41.13
    child tax credit, effect on welfare benefits, 40.14
    employer-provided child care, 40.15
  earned income credit, 40.12–40.13
  education. *See* Education, tax benefits for
  foster care, 41.13
  kidnapped children, tax benefits for parents of,
    40.02–40.03
  special needs, Coverdell ESAs, 40.08
Child support owed by taxpayer, IRS procedure in
    case of, 38.07
Child tax credit, effect on welfare benefits, 40.14
Circular A-123, "Management Accountability and
    Control," 16.03
Clean fuel vehicles, 40.29
Closely held business, basis of, 35.15–35.16
Code of Ethics for Professional Accountants, 6.23–6.24
Codification of Financial Reporting Policies (CFRP),
    26.14–26.16
  financial information about geographic areas,
    26.15–26.16
  financial information about segments, 26.15
  segment analysis, 26.14–26.16
COLAs. *See* Cost of living adjustments (COLAs)
Collections, standards for accounting disclosures of,
    13.10
College planning, 17.08–17.09
College tuition deduction, 39.09–39.10
Combat zones
  Afghanistan, designation as, 40.04
Commercial and governmental accounting, differ-
    ences between, 12.01–12.02
Commission on Electronic Commerce, 27.10–27.11
Committee of Sponsoring Organizations (COSO),
    2.15, 16.02–16.05
  described, 16.02–16.03
  internal control, framework for, 16.03–16.05

components of internal control, 16.03–16.04
control activities, 16.04
control environment, 16.03–16.04
definition, 16.04
information and communication, 16.04
key concepts, 16.04–16.05
monitoring, 16.04
risk assessment, 16.04
Common law employees
independent contractor or employee, 34.02 34.03
Common stock, 3.02–3.03
classes, 3.03
classification of, 3.03
definition, 3.02–3.03
par/no-par, 3.03
rights of owners, 3.02 3.03
Community property, basis of, 35.15
Community renewal and environmental credits and
deductions, 40.27–40.29
Community Renewal Tax Relief Act of 2000, 40.28
*Competency: Profiles for Management Accounting
Practice and Practitioners,* 6.21
Completion of production method to determine income, 2.02
Compounding, 2.10–2.11
Comprehensive income, 1.37–1.41
cash flow not affected, 1.40–1.41
components, 1.39–1.40
definition, 1.38
equity valuation not affected, 1.38, 1.40–1.41
terminology, 1.40
Condominiums
rental property, 19.07–19.08
Confidentiality
between taxpayer and federally authorized tax
practitioner, 37.01–37.02
Conflicts of interest
attorneys, Private Securities Litigation Reform
Act of 1995, 25.08
independent fund advisors, disclosure, 29.19–29.21
Sarbanes-Oxley Act of 2002, 9.12
Consolidated groups, accounting changes for, 36.11–
36.12
Consolidation method
to determine income, 2.02
international accounting, 5.20
Constant yield method, "points," 19.05–19.06
Consulting opportunity in governmental accounting,
11.18
Contingency losses related to e-commerce, 27.04–
27.05
Contingency reserves, 3.08–3.09. *See also* Stockhold-
ers' equity
Contingent fee arrangements, 22.07
Continuous processing plants, cost accounting, 15.05
Contributions. *See specific topics*
Convenience-of-the employer test
business use of home, 20.06
Convertible preferred stock, 3.03–3.04

Cooperatives
rental property, 19.08
Corporate and Criminal Fraud Accountability Act of
2002, 9.13
Corporations, tax filing date for, 36.17, 36.25–36.26
automatic change, 36.27
changes during tax year, 36.26–36.27
domestic international sales corporation
(IC-DISC), 36.26
Corruption, IFAC's fight against, 6.40. *See also* International Federation of Accountants
COSO. *See* Committee of Sponsoring Organizations
(COSO)
Cost accounting, 15.01–15.16
actual cost systems, 15.08–15.09
alternative approaches, 15.03–15.04
assembly plants, 15.05
benefits of, 15.11
continuous processing plants, 15.05
control systems, items for consideration, 15.05–
15.07
defined, 15.01–15.02
developing cost system, 15.02–15.03
direct costing, 15.15–15.16
drawbacks, 15.11
elements of cost, 15.10
elements of production costs, 15.10
foundation of system, 15.04–15.05
general-ledger inventory accounts, 15.10
group classifications, 15.05
historical and standard cost systems, 15.08–15.11
integrating cost system, 15.10
jobbing plants, 15.05
job order systems, 15.10–15.11
objectives of system, 15.02
outline of cost accounting system, 15.06–15.07
process costs systems, 15.10–15.11
service establishments, 15.05
standard cost systems, 15.09–15.10
how to use, 15.12–15.15
unit cost accumulation, 15.12
terminology, 15.07–15.08
Cost basis
assets, 35.02–35.08. *See also* Asset valuation for
tax purposes
selling mutual fund shares, 29.05
Cost of goods sold
ratios of cost of goods sold to inventory, 1.27
sales growth, 1.33
Cost of living adjustments (COLAs), 17.07
Cost recovery method to determine income, 2.02
Coverage ratios, 1.22
Coverdell ESAs, 40.07–40.09
contribution due dates, 40.08
excess contributions, correcting, 40.08
HOPE credit, coordination with, 40.08–40.09
income limits, 40.07–40.08
lifetime learning credits, coordination with, 40.08–
40.09

Coverdell ESAs (*cont.*)
  maximum contributions, 40.07
  qualified expenses, 40.08
  qualified tuition programs, coordinating with, 40.09
  special needs beneficiaries, 40.08
CPA as financial planner. *See* Financial planner
CPA WebTrust, 27.18–27.20. *See also* E-commerce
    and E-communication
Credit claims, disclosure, 1.10
Credit losses related to e-commerce, 27.06
Credit manager
  internal control system, 16.25
Credit risk, 17.19–17.20
  bond mutual funds, 30.15
Cumulative preferred stock, 3.04
Currency
  international accounting, 5.19
Current ratio, 4.13
Customer solicitation costs related to e-commerce,
    27.06–27.07

D

Day-care facility
  business use of home, 20.07–20.08
    meal allowance, 20.07–20.08
Death taxes, 39.05–39.06, 40.29
Debt Services Fund, 12.09, 12.12
Debt-to-net-worth ratio, 4.13
Decision package concept of zero-base budgeting,
    14.18–14.20
Declaration of Representative, 37.09
Deductions. *See specific topic*
Deemed IRAs, 40.27
  Job Creation and Worker Assistance Act of 2002,
    41.08
Defensive-interval ratio, 1.25
Defined benefit plans
  contributions, Job Creation and Worker Assis-
    tance Act of 2002, 41.08
  limits, increase in, 39.12
Defined contribution plans
  limits, 39.12, 40.22
Demystifying mutual funds. *See* Mutual funds
Dependent care tax credit, 39.08–39.09
Deposit and investment risk disclosures (Exposure
    Draft), 11.06–11.07
Deposit of taxes
  excise taxes, 40.31
Depreciation, 33.01–33.23
  acquisition date test, 33.16, 33.21
  alternative minimum tax (AMT) relief, 33.14–33.15
  automobiles, general asset accounts, 33.12
  beginning and ending, 33.03–33.04
  business use of home, 20.11
  in cash budget, 14.16
  definition, 32.01

dispositions, 33.11
general asset accounts, 33.11–33.12
  adjustable depreciable basis, 33.13
  automobiles, 33.12
  dispositions and conversions, 33.13–33.14
  personal use, change to, 33.13–33.14
  remaining property, disposition of, 33.13
  unadjusted depreciable basis, 33.13
ineligibility for
  goodwill, 33.03
  intangible property, 33.03
  tangible property, 33.02–33.03
  trademarks and trade names, 33.03
modified accelerated cost recovery system
    (MACRS), 33.07–33.11
  alternative depreciation system (ADS), 33.07,
    33.08–33.09
  conventions to figure deduction, 33.07–33.08
  deduction, figuring, 33.11
  election to exclude property from, 33.10
  General Depreciation System (GDS), 33.07,
    33.08
  mileage rate, standard, use of, 33.11
  nontaxable transfers of property, certain, 33.10
  150% declining balance method, 33.08
  personal property, 33.09–33.10
  property, methods to figure deduction for, 33.08
  property placed in service before 1987, 33.09–
    33.10
  real property, 33.10
  straight line method, 33.08
  200% declining balance method, 33.08
  what cannot be depreciated under MACRS, 33.09
  what to depreciate, 33.08
  which system to use, 33.08–33.09
New York City Liberty Zone Depreciation, 33.14,
    33.17, 33.19–33.23
  election not to claim, 33.22
  qualified liberty zone property, 33.20–33.22
  qualifying tests, 33.21
  Section 179 deduction, increased, 33.22–33.23
  special Liberty Zone Depreciation Allowance,
    33.20
original use test, 33.17, 33.21
placed in service date test, 33.16–33.17, 33.21
property, types of
  intangible, 32.02
  tangible, 32.02
real estate as asset
  rental property, 19.13
related persons, 33.16
Section 179 deduction of Internal Revenue Code,
    using, 33.04–33.07, 40.32
  costs that can/cannot be deducted, 33.04
  electing deduction, 33.06
  figuring deduction, 33.06–33.07
  limits on deduction, 33.07
  nonqualifying property, 33.05–33.06

partial business use, 33.05
  qualifying property, 33.04–33.05
  what it provides, 33.04
special depreciation allowance, 33.14–33.19
  acquisition date test, 33.16, 33.21
  alternative minimum tax (AMT) relief, 33.14–33.15
  automobiles, 33.19
  claiming allowance, 33.18
  deemed election, 33.19
  election not to claim, 33.17–33.18
  excepted property, 33.17
  original use test, 33.17
  passenger automobiles, 33.19
  placed in service date test, 33.16–33.17, 33.21
  qualified leasehold improvement property, 33.15–33.16
  qualified property, 33.15–33.18
  related persons, 33.16
  returns filed before June 1, 2002, 33.18–33.19
  substantial-use test, 33.21
  2002 tax law, provisions, 33.14
  types of property, 33.02
Derivatives, 8.01–8.15
  definition, amendment, 10.23–10.24
  direction, lack of, 8.10–8.11
  disclosure measures, need for, 8.03–8.04
  effective dates, 8.07
  fair value accounting for derivative instruments, 8.10
  FASB 119, *Disclosures About Derivative Financial Instruments and Fair Value of Financial Instruments,* 8.01–8.15
  Financial Executives Institute (FEI) task force, 8.02
  proposals, three basic, 8.05–8.06
  qualitative disclosure, 8.12–8.14
    market risk, about, 8.14–8.15
  qualitative information, 8.09
  quantitative disclosure, 8.12–8.14
  reconsideration, 8.07
  Regulation S-B, 8.09
  Regulation S-K, 8.05–8.09
  Regulation S-X, 8.11–8.12
  Securities and Exchange Commission
    action by, 8.06–8.07
    foreign private issuers, application to, 8.10
    Items 305 and 9A, amendments, 8.08–8.09
    small business issuers, requirements for, 8.09–8.10
    speculation and, 8.04–8.05
    study, 8.02, 8.04
Developing economies, accounting for, 5.45
  coalition to advance accountancy development, 6.39–6.40
Diesel-powered highway vehicle, decrease in property basis for, 35.10–35.11
Dilution of equity, 1.33
Direct costing, 15.15–15.16
  financial statements, effect on, 15.16

Direct mail advertising costs related to e-commerce, 27.06
Direct method, 4.03–4.04, 4.07–4.09
Direct overhead account, 15.15
  indirect overhead account, 15.15–15.16
Direct sellers
  independent contractor or employee, 34.04–34.05
Disaster areas, postponed tax deadlines, 40.03
Disclosure
  content and format of, 1.41–1.42
  credit claims, 1.10
  equity holders, claims of, 1.10
  financial reporting, 1.09–1.16
  financial statements, 1.07–1.09
    full disclosure principle, 1.09
    required in, 1.07 1.08
  footnotes, 1.11
  full disclosure principle, 1.09
  independent fund advisors, SEC final rules and amendments, 29.17
  itemized, 1.11–1.16
  materiality, distinction between, 1.06
  voluntary, report on, 10.47–10.48
Disclosure of Accounting Policies, 1.07
Discontinued operations
  long-lived assets, FASB statement 144, 10.12–10.13
  reporting, 2.08
Discounts, 2.06
  Internet accounting, 28.13–28.15
Dispositions, 33.11
Diversification
  aggressive growth, 17.28
  capital preservation, 17.26
  current income, 17.26–17.27
  importance of, 17.20, 17.25–17.28. *See also* Asset allocation
  long-term growth, 17.27
  total return, 17.27
Domestic international sales corporation (IC-DISC), 36.25, 36.26
Dummy supplies, 16.46
Dwelling unit, defined, 19.09–19.10

E

Earned income credit, 40.12–40.13
Earnings budget, 14.02–14.03. *See also* Budgeting for profit planning and budgetary control
Earnings per share (EPS)
  generally, 1.05
  ratio, 1.30–1.33
E-business. *See also* E-commerce and E-communications
  IFAC paper issued on, 6.28–6.29
E-Business and the Accountant: Risk Management for Accounting Systems in an E-Business Environment, 6.28–6.29, 27.14

E-commerce and E-communication, 27.01–27.29
  accounting issues, 27.02–27.07
    acquisitions and mergers, 27.04
    asset impairments, 27.06
    contingency losses, 27.04–27.05
    credit losses, 27.06
    customer solicitation costs, 27.06–27.07
    direct mail advertising, 27.06
    materiality, 27.07
    nondisclosure, 27.05
    software, 27.03–27.04
    start-up activities, 27.05
    uncertainty, 27.07
  Business Reporting Research Project, 27.16–27.17
  CPA WebTrust and small business, 27.18–27.20
  e-business
    accounting principles and criteria, 27.07–27.09
    accuracy criterion, 27.08
    assessability criterion, 27.09
    checklist, 27.27–27.29
    completeness criterion, 27.08
    glossary of terms, 27.23–27.27
    inalterability criteria, 27.09
    order criteria, 27.09
    superseding of term by, 27.02
    timeliness criterion, 27.08
  e-communication Web site use, cautions for,
      27.11–27.12
    chat rooms, 27.12
    Private Securities Litigation Reform Act, 27.11
  Electronic Data Interchange (EDI), 27.18
  FASB Business Reporting Research Project,
      27.16–27.17
    *Electronic Distribution of Business Reporting
      Information,* 27.16–27.17
  glossary of terms, 27.23–27.27
  IASC Study, Business Reporting on the Internet,
      27.14–27.16
    code of conduct for Web-based business report-
      ing, 27.15
    e-business reporting language, 27.15–27.16
    paper financial reports, changes in, 27.15
  international guidance on risk, 27.12–27.14
  risk, international guidance on, 27.12–27.14
  SEC on reporting, 27.17–27.18
  SysTrust, 27.20–27.22
    Congress and, 27.20
    defined, 27.20–27.21
    WebTrust, plans to combine, 27.21–27.22
  tax considerations, 27.10–27.11
    Commission on Electronic Commerce, 27.10–
      27.11
    The Internet Tax Freedom Act of 1998, 27.10
    OECD, 5.37–5.41
  WebTrust, 27.18–27.20
    assurance services, advantages of, 27.19
    customer complaints, handling, 27.19–27.20
    House testimony, 27.19
    National Arbitration Forum, 27.20

    SysTrust, plans to combine, 27.21–27.22
    Web Trust Principles and Criteria, 27.19
Economic Growth and Tax Relief Reconciliation Act
      of 2001 (EGTRRA), 39.01–39.13
  adoption credits, 39.08
  "advance" refund checks, 39.01
  alternative minimum tax, personal credits against,
      41.10
  business taxpayers, benefits for, 39.13
    alternative minimum tax relief, 39.05
  catch-up contributions to IRAs, 39.12
  child care facilities, employer-provided, 39.08
  child credit, increase in, 39.07–39.08
  college tuition deduction, 39.09–39.10
  contribution tax credit, 39.12
  defined contribution/benefits plan limits, 39.12
  dependent care tax credit, 39.08–39.09
  education savings accounts, 39.10
  education tax cuts, 39.09
  employer-provided assistance, 39.11
  estate tax, 39.05–39.06
  401(k) contribution limits, 39.12
  gift tax, 39.06
  income tax rate cuts, 39.03–39.04
  IRA contribution limits, 39.12
  marriage penalty relief, 39.06–39.07
  pension provisions, 39.11–39.13
  personal service corporations, taxation of, 39.05
  qualified plans, conformity to, 40.23
  qualified tuition plans, 39.11
  retirement savings programs, 39.11–39.13
  Roth IRAs, 39.11
  SIMPLE plan, increase in deferrals to, 39.13
  student loan deductions, enhanced, 39.10–39.11
  technical corrections, 41.14
  timeline, 39.02–39.03
EDGAR, 32.16
EDI (Electronic Data Interchange), 27.18
Education, tax benefits for. *See also* Higher education
      expense, new deduction for
  Coverdell ESAs, 40.07–40.09
  employer-provided educational assistance, 40.06
  HOPE and Lifetime Learning credits, 39.09
    Coverdell ESAs, coordination with, 40.08–40.09
  qualified public educational facilities, tax-exempt
      bond funding, 40.12
  qualified tuition programs (QTPs), 40.06–40.07
  student loan interest deduction, 40.11–40.12
  tax cuts, 39.09
Education Committee, IFAC, 6.24–6.26
  accountant competencies, 6.27
Education IRAs. *See* Coverdell ESAs
Education savings accounts, 39.10
Education tax cuts, 39.09
  HOPE and Lifetime Learning credits, 39.09
    Coverdell ESAs, coordination with, 40.08–40.09
Educator expenses, deduction for, 41.12–41.13
EFRAG. *See* European Financial Reporting Advi-
      sory Group (EFRAG)

EGTRRA. *See* Economic Growth and Tax Relief Reconciliation Act of 2001 (EGTRRA)
Elective deferrals
  401(k) plans, 40.22
  SARSEPs, 40.23
Electric and clean fuel vehicles, 40.29
Electric power expense, 14.12
Electronic Data Interchange (EDI), 27.18
Electronic filing
  1099s, 41.09
  Plain English Disclosure rule, 32.16–32.17
Embezzlement, 16.44–16.46
  check-kiting, 16.45–16.46
  detecting and preventing, 16.44–16.45
  dummy supplies, 16.46
  lapping, 16.44–16.45
  payroll fraud, 16.46
Emerging Issues Task Forces of FASB, and Internet accounting, 28.03–28.07
  EITF 00-8, *Accounting by a Grantee for an Equity Instrument to Be Received in Conjunction with Providing Goods or Services,* 28.33–28.34
  EITF 00-22, 28.30
  EITF 00-25, *Vendor Income Statement Characterization of Consideration from a Vendor to a Retailer,* 28.36
  EITF 01-9, *Accounting for Consideration Given by a Vendor to a Customer or a Reseller of the Vendor's Products,* 28.04–28.07
  EITF 099-19, *Reporting Revenue Gross as a Principal versus Net as an Agent,* 28.07
Emerging markets
  accounting for, 5.45
  bond funds, 30.13–30.14
Employee benefits
  financial planning, 17.10–17.11
  independent contractor or employee, 34.12
  international accounting, 5.18
Employee or independent contractor, 34.01–34.21. *See also* Independent contractor or employee *for detailed treatment*
Employee stock options
  revenue and expenses, 2.13–2.15
    additional requirements, 2.24
    controversy, 2.24
    exceptions, 2.24
    fair value, 2.14–2.15, 2.22–2.23
    forced compromise, 2.13–2.14
    intrinsic value method, 2.23
    transition questions, 2.14
Employer-provided assistance, 39.11
Employer-provided child care facilities, 39.08–39.09
Employer-provided educational assistance, 40.06
Employment tax
  employers, 38.11–38.12
  independent contractor or employee, 34.16–34.21
    appeals jurisdiction, 34.20
    assessment, restrictions, 34.20
    eligibility to seek review, 34.18
    notice of determination, 34.18–34.19
    prerequisite for seeking review, 34.19
    Section 7436, 34.17–34.18
    settlements, agreed, 34.20–34.21
    statute of limitations, suspension of, 34.20
    timing of filing, 34.19
Empowerment zones, 40.28, 41.05–41.06
Engagement letter
  expert witness, 21.02 21.03
Enron scandal, effect of, 16.02
  e-commerce and e-communication, 27.20
  Sarbanes-Oxley Act of 2002, 9.02
  special-purpose entities, consolidation of, 10.03
Enterprise funds, 12.09, 12.13
Environmental clean-up cost deduction, 40.28–40.29
Environmental considerations as cause for decrease in property basis, 35.10–35.11
Environmental liabilities
  governmental accounting, 11.15
Equity
  dilution, 1.33
  real estate, 19.15
Equity holders, claims of
  disclosure, 1.10
Equity method
  to determine income, 2.03
Estate planning, 17.10
Estate tax
  changes in, 39.05–39.06
  installment payment provisions, 40.30
  maximum tax rate, reduction, 40.29
  state death taxes, reduction of credit for, 40.29
Estimated tax
  higher-income taxpayers, 40.31–40.32
  payments for 2002, need to adjust, 40.02, 40.04
Ethics
  Code of Ethics for Professional Accountants, 6.23–6.24
Euro, 5.43
European Commission
  IASC's relationship with, 5.24
European Financial Reporting Advisory Group (EFRAG), 5.05–5.06
European Parliament's changes to accounting directives, 5.36
European Union (EU), 5.43
  agreement on IASs to help investors and businesses, 5.06–5.07
  new regulatory body created by, 5.07
Event risk, 17.20
Excess contributions
  excise tax, 40.26–40.27
Exchange risk, 17.19
Exchanges of mutual funds, 29.04–29.07. *See also* Mutual funds
Excise taxes, 40.30–40.31
  deposit of taxes, 40.31
  non-deductible (excess) contributions, 40.26–40.27

Excise taxes (*cont.*)
  safe harbor, 40.31
Exclusive use test
  business use of home, 20.06
Exempt organizations, 3.01–3.21. *See also* Not for-
  profit organizations
Expatriate tax
  sale of home, 19.23
Expenses
  internal control for. *See* Internal control system
  real estate
    "points," 19.05–19.06
    rental property, 19.04–19.05
    travel expenses, 19.06
  revenue and, 2.01–2.24. *See also* Revenue and
    expenses
Expert witness, 21.01–21.09
  basis of investigation, 21.05–21.06
  cross-examination, 21.07
  defined, 21.04
  demonstrative evidence, 21.06
  engagement letter, 21.02–21.03
  exhibits, 21.06
  function of, 21.05
  legal matters, 21.08–21.09
  prep time, 21.03
  rebuttal, 21.08
  understandable testimony, 21.06–21.07
Expiring business tax credits, 41.06
Extraordinary items, reporting, 2.08–2.09. *See also*
  Revenue and expenses

F

FAF. *See* Financial Accounting Foundation (FAF)
Fairness opinions, 22.05
Fair value accounting
  agriculture, 5.27–5.28
  for derivative instruments, 8.10
  employee stock options, 2.14–2.15
  full, for insurance contracts, 43.05
Fair value hedge, 7.14
Fair value measurements
  auditing, 6.19–6.20
Fair value requirements
  NPOs, 13.13–13.14
Farm property, basis of, 35.15–35.16
FASAC. *See* Annual Financial Accounting
  Standards Advisory Council (FASAC)
  Survey
FASB
  5, *Accounting for Contingencies,* 5.62
  14, *Financial Reporting for Segments of a Business
    Enterprise,* 26.01
  40, *Applicability of Generally Accepted Account-
    ing Principles to Mutual Life Insurance and
    Other Enterprises,* 43.14

  42, *Accounting for Transfers of Assets in Which a
    Not-for-Profit Organization Is Granted Vari-
    ance Power,* 13.05
  52, *Foreign Currency Translation,* 7.01–7.10, 8.11
  60, *Accounting and Reporting by Insurance Enter-
    prises,* 43.10, 43.14
  80, *Accounting for Futures Contracts,* 7.10, 8.11
  87, *Employers' Accounting for Pension Plans,* 1.40
  95, *Statement of Cash Flows,* 1.40, 4.03–4.06, 13.11
  97, *Accounting and Reporting by Insurance Enter-
    prises for Certain Long-Duration Contracts
    and for Realized Gains and Losses from Sale
    of Investments,* 43.12, 43.14
  102, *Statement of Cash Flows—Exemption of Cer-
    tain Enterprises and Certification of Cash
    Flows from Certain Securities Acquired for
    Resale,* 1.39
  105, *Disclosures of Information about Financial
    Instruments with Off-Balance-Sheet Risk and
    Financial Instruments with Concentrations of
    Credit Risk,* 43.11
  107, *Disclosure about Fair Value of Financial In-
    struments,* 7.10–7.12, 10.34
  113, *Accounting and Reporting for Reinsurance of
    Short-Duration and Long-Duration Con-
    tracts,* 43.08–43.14
  115, *Accounting for Certain Investments in Debt
    and Equity Securities,* 1.40, 13.13
  116, *Accounting for Contributions Received and
    Contributions Made,* 13.09
  117, *Financial Statements of Not-for-Profit Organi-
    zations,* 1.39, 13.09–13.13. *See also* Not-for-
    profit organizations
  119, *Disclosures about Derivative Financial Instru-
    ments and Fair Value of Financial Instru-
    ments,* 8.01–8.15. *See also* Derivatives
  120, *Accounting and Reporting by Mutual Life In-
    surance Enterprises and by Insurance Enter-
    prises for Certain Long-Duration Participat-
    ing Contracts,* 43.13–43.14
  121, *Accounting for Impairment of Long-Lived
    Assets and for Long-Lived Assets to Be Dis-
    posed Of,* 5.59–5.60
  123, *Accounting for Stock Options Issued to Em-
    ployees,* 2.13–2.14, 2.22–2.24
  124, *Accounting for Certain Investments Held by
    Not-for-Profit Organizations,* 13.13–13.15
  128, *Earnings per Share,* 1.31–1.33
  130, *Reporting Comprehensive Income,* 1.37–1.41,
    1.40
  131, *Disclosures about Segments of an Enterprise
    and Related Information,* 1.40, 26.01–26.16.
    See also Segment reporting
  Securities and Exchange Commission's re-
    sponse to, 26.07–26.13
  133, *Accounting for Derivative Instruments and
    Hedging Activities,* 7.12–7.18, 10.17, 28.33
    amendment of, 10.22–10.23

136, *Transfers of Assets to a Not-for-Profit Organization or Charitable Trust That Raises or Holds Contributions for Others,* 13.02–13.05

137, *Accounting for Derivative Instruments and Hedging Activities—Deferral of Effective Date of FASB Statement,* 7.13

139, *Rescission of FASB Statement 53 and Amendments to FASB Statements 63, 89, and 121,* 10.26–10.27

140, *Accounting for Transfers and Servicing of Financial Assets And Extinguishments of Liabilities,* 10.28

143, *Accounting for Asset Retirement Obligations,* 10.35

144, *Accounting for the Impairment or Disposal of Long-Lived Assets,* 10.09–10.14

145, *Rescission of FASB Statements 4, 44, and 64, Amendment of FASB Statement 13, and Technical Corrections,* 10.15

146, *Accounting for Costs Associated with Exit of Disposal Activities,* 10.08

147, *Acquisitions of Certain Financial Institutions,* 10.07–10.08

FASB Project on NPO combinations, 13.15–13.17
board deliberations, 13.16–13.17
intangibles, decisions relating to, 13.17
mergers, 13.16
pooling-of-interests, effect of elimination, 13.16

FCPA. *See* Foreign Corrupt Practices Act (FCPA)

Federal Reserve Bank of New York
derivatives, 8.02

Federal Unemployment Tax Act (FUTA)
independent contractor or employee, 34.04

Fees. *See specific topic*

Fiduciary, 37.10

Fiduciary Funds, 12.09

Financial Accounting Foundation (FAF)
FASB process, changes considered in order to streamline, 10.05–10.07

Financial Accounting Standards Board (FASB). *See also* FASB
long-lived assets, 10.08–10.14

Financial Accounting Standards Board (FASB), actions of, 10.01–10.50
Actions of Certain Financial Institutions (Exposure Draft), 10.21–10.22
Annual Financial Accounting Standards Advisory Council (FASAC) Survey, 10.20
business combinations
new basis accounting, 10.18–10.19
purchase method procedures, 10.15–10.17
Business Combinations and Intangible Assets, 10.32–10.35
Business and Financial Reporting, Challenges from the New Economy, 10.49–10.50
Business Combinations Exposure Draft, 10.32–10.33
Business Reporting Research Project, 10.47–10.49

codification, 10.22

Concepts Statement 6, proposed amendment to, 10.43–10.47

consolidation of SPEs, proposed standard on, 10.02–10.03

derivative, amendment of definition, 10.24

disclosure overload, combined efforts of SEC and FASB, 10.22–1023

disposal activities, 10.08–10.09

FIN 44, *Accounting for Certain Transactions Involving Stock Compensation,* 10.40–10.43
fair value method, 10.40
reload feature, 10.41
requirements, delineation of, 10.40–10.41
results, possible, 10.42

Financial Accounting Foundation (FAF), 10.05 10.07

financial instruments with characteristics of liabilities, equity, or both, accounting for, 10.43–10.47
changes resulting from new definition of liabilities, 10.46–10.47
components, classification of, 10.44
confusion areas, 10.43–10.44
consolidated subsidiary, requirements for, 10.45–10.47
distinction, clear, need for, 10.43
liabilities defined, 10.46–10.47
proposal, effects of, 10.45–10.46

goodwill, 10.33

guarantees, expansion of disclosure requirements (Exposure Draft), 10.24

Improving Business Reporting Insights into Enhancing Voluntary Disclosures, 10.47–10.48

International Joint Working Group (JWG), 10.19

redundancies, report on, 10.50

research and technical activities, reorganization of, 10.07

retrievability, 10.21–10.22

revenue recognition project, 10.25

sale, assets accounted for as, 10.28–10.29

special-purpose entities (SPEs)
consolidation of, proposed standard on, 10.02–10.03
earlier FASB action related to, 10.03–10.04
synthetic leases, 10.04–10.05

standards overload, project to consider, 10.19–10.21
cost benefit analysis, 10.21
simplification, 10.20–10.21

Statement 133, *Accounting for Certain Derivative Instruments and Hedging Activities,* 10.17
amendment of, 10.22–10.23

Statement 139, *Rescission of FASB Statement 53 and Amendments to FASB Statements 63, 89, and 121,* 10.26–10.28

Statement 140, *Accounting for Transfers and Servicing of Financial Assets and Extinguishments of Liabilities,* 10.28

Financial Accounting Standards Board (FASB)
(*cont.*)
additional disclosures, 10.30
assets and liabilities, measurement of, 10.28–
10.29
earlier standards, effect upon, 10.30
effective dates, 10.31–10.32
implementation guidelines, 10.29
sale, assets accounted for as, 10.28
special report on, 10.31
Statements 141 and 142, 10.34–10.35
Statement 143, *Accounting for Asset Retirement
Obligations,* 10.35–10.39
ARO liability, subsequent measurement, 10.38
capitalization, 10.36
disclosures, 10.38–10.39
fair value methodology, 10.36–10.37
objective of project, 10.36–10.37
obligating events, 10.38–10.39
recognition, 10.37–10.38
requirements, 10.36–10.37
transition, 10.39
streamlining of process, changes considered by
FAF, 10.05–10.07
voluntary disclosures, report on, 10.47–10.49
voting, changes to increase efficiency, 10.06–10.07
Financial budgets, 14.02–14.03. *See also* Budgeting
for profit planning and budgetary control
Financial control
independent contractor or employee, 34.09–34.11
Financial Executives Institute (FEI), 8.02
Financial expenses
internal control system, 16.25
Financial instruments with characteristics of liabilities, equity, or both, accounting for, 10.42–
10.48. *See also* Financial Accounting Standards Board
Financial planner
CPA as, 17.01–17.32
accelerating client planning process, 17.05
accreditation requirements for PFS designation,
17.32
active versus passive investments, 17.07
asset allocation and, 17.20–17.29
checklist, 17.13
college planning, 17.08–17.09
dialogue with client, planning, 17.03–17.04
employee benefits, 17.10–17.11
estate planning, 17.10
fees, setting, 17.02
inflation, 17.02–17.03
insurance, 17.10–17.11
investments, advising clients on, 17.14–17.32.
See also Investments, advising clients on
investment versus personal assets, 17.07
key areas of financial planning, 17.05–17.12
liquid versus illiquid assets, 17.07
need-based planning, 17.04

need for financial plan, 17.03
net worth of client, 17.05–17.07
retirement planning, 17.07–17.08
sample questions, 17.12
Social Security of client, 17.07
Personal Financial Specialist (PSF), 17.02. *See also
lines throughout this topic*
Financial reporting
fraudulent, 16.46–16.47
Financial Reporting Council (FRC) of Australia,
5.07–5.08
Financial Reporting Release
FRR 36, 2.21–2.22
Financial statements
analysis and interpretation, 1.21–1.22
bankers' use of, 4.11–4.14
direct costing, effect of, 15.16
interim. *See* Interim financial statements
presentation, twelve principles of, 1.02–1.05
Finished goods inventories, 16.17–16.18
*First-time Application of IASs on the Primary Basis
of Accounting* (SIC-8), 5.13–5.14
Fiscal year for taxpayer, 36.17–36.18
Fixed expenses, 14.11
vs. variable, 14.12
Footnote information, 1.11
Forecasting sales, 14.03–14.04
Foreclosures, 19.18–19.19
Foreign Corrupt Practices Act (FCPA), 16.05–16.12
accounting provisions, 16.07
financial policies and internal controls, 16.08–
16.09
anti-bribery provisions, 16.07–16.08
definitions, 16.09–16.10
discussion, 16.09–16.12
foreign official, defined, 16.10
1988 amendment, 16.11
non-compliance, prevention, 16.11–16.12
OECD Anti-Bribery Convention, 16.12
red flags, 16.10–16.11
U.S. person, defined, 16.07, 16.09–16.10
violations, sanctions, 16.10
compliance problems, 16.06–16.07
financial policies and internal controls, 16.08–16.09
importance of, 16.05
internal control, 16.08–16.09
1988 amendment, 16.07, 16.11
Opinion Procedure, 16.09
responsibility of accountant, 16.05–16.06
Foreign currency exposure hedge, 7.14
Foreign currency translations and derivative disclosure
definitions, 7.02–7.04
FASB Statement 52, *Foreign Currency Translation,*
7.01–7.10
background, 7.05–7.06
functional currency approach, 7.06–7.09
measurement, 7.17
requirements of, 7.04–7.05

transactions, 7.10

translation, 7.09–7.10

FASB Statement 107, *Disclosure about Fair Value of Financial Instruments,* 7.10–7.12

exceptions, 7.12

FASB Statement 133, *Accounting for Derivative Instruments and Hedging Activities,* 7.12–7.18

accounting literature, effect on other, 7.16–7.17

amendments, 7.17–7.18

derivatives, 7.15–7.16

not-for-profit organizations, application to, 7.17

underlyings, 7.15

FASB Statement 137, *Accounting for Derivative Instruments and Hedging Activities—Deferral of Effective Date of FASB Statement,* 7.13

hedge accounting, 7.14–7.15. *See also* Hedging

modification, 7.13

not-for-profit organizations, application to, 7.17

notional amount, 7.16

timing of effective date, 7.13

underlying, 7.15

Foreign-earned income exclusion, 40.33

Foreign private investors in U.S. securities markets, 5.33

Foreign tax deduction or credit on mutual funds, 29.03

Form 56, *Notice Concerning Fiduciary Relationship,* 37.10

Form 1045, *Application for Tentative Refund,* 41.02, 41.03

Forum of Firms, 6.07–6.09. *See also* International Federation of Accountants

constitution, approval of, 6.08–6.09

establishment of, 6.07

requirements, 6.07–6.08

structure of, 6.07–6.08, 6.09

Transnational Audit Committee (TAC), 6.09

Foster care, 41.13

401(k) plans

catch-up contributions, 39.12

contribution limits, increase in, 39.12

elective deferrals, 40.22

403(b) plans, 40.24–40.25

Job Creation and Worker Assistance Act of 2002, 41.07–41.08

457 deferred compensation plans. *See* Section 457 deferred compensation plans

Fraud

Corporate and Criminal Fraud Accountability Act of 2002, 9.13

financial reporting, 16.46–16.47

International Auditing Practices Committee, guidance, 6.20

Fraudulent Financial Reporting 1987-1997: An Analysis of U.S. Public Companies, 2.15

Front-ended load, defined

mutual funds, 30.06

Fuel economy tax, 35.10–35.11

Full-cost accounting by mining enterprises, 5.29

Functional currency approach, 7.06–7.09

Fund-raising foundations and similar organizations, financial reporting guidance, 11.05

Funds, governmental

Capital Project, 12.09, 12.12–12.13

Debt Service, 12.09, 12.12

definition, 12.09

Enterprise, 12.09, 12.13

Fiduciary, 12.09

General, 12.09, 12.10–12.11

General Fixed Assets Account Group, 12.16

Intergovernmental Service Funds, 12.14–12.15

Internal Service, 12.09, 12.14–12.15

Long-Term Debt Group, 12.16–12.17

Special Revenue, 2.11–2.12, 12.09

Trust and Agency Fund (TAF), 12.13–12.14

Working Capital funds, 12.14–12.15

Futures contracts, 40.05

Future value, 2.10

of annuity, 2.11–2.12

G

GAAP, precedence over industry practice

SEC materiality, 24.13–24.14

GAAP 2000: A Survey of National Accounting Rules in 53 Countries, 6.11

GAAP 2001 report, 6.10

GASB Statement 33, *Accounting and Financial Reporting for Nonexchange Transactions,* 11.26, 11.29–11.30

GASB Statement 34, *Basic Financial Statements—and Management's Discussion and Analysis—for State and Local Governments,* 12.02

amendment, 11.28

GASB Statement 35, 11.27–11.28

GASB Statement 36, on symmetry between recipients and providers in accounting for certain shared revenue, 11.30

GASB Statement 37, *Basic Financial Statements—and Management's Discussion and Analysis—for State and Local Governments; Omnibus—An Amendment of GASB Statements 21 and 24,* 11.02–11.03

GASB Statement 38, *Certain Financial Statement Note Disclosures,* 11.04

GASB Statement 39, *Determining Whether Certain Organizations Are Component Units, an Amendment of GASB Statement 14,* 11.05

Gas-guzzler tax, 35.10–35.11

General asset accounts, 33.11–33.12. *See also* Depreciation

General Depreciation System (GDS), 33.08

General Fixed Assets Account Group, 12.16

General Fund, 12.09, 12.10–12.11

Generation-skipping transfer tax (GST) exemption, 40.30

Geographic areas
  segment reporting
    Codification of Financial Reporting Policies
      (CFRP), 26.15–26.16
    required reporting, 26.12–26.13
Gift tax, 39.06
  exclusion for gifts, increased, 40.29
  maximum tax rate, reduction, 40.29
Global accounting standards, importance of, 5.42–
  5.44. *See also* International Accounting
  Standards
Global bond funds, 30.12–30.13
Global Corporate Governance Forum (GCGF), 6.30
Global peer reviews, ED on guidelines for, 6.09
Goodwill, 3.07, 10.33
  not depreciable, 33.03
Governmental accounting, 11.01–11.30
  asset impairment/preservation method, 11.13–
    11.14
  budget, governmental, 11.19
    RSI (required supplemental information),
      11.19, 11.21
  "Cliffies" for government financial statements,
    11.11–11.12
  communication methods, 11.14
  deposit and investment risk disclosures (Exposure
    Draft), 11.06–11.07
  economic condition, 11.14–11.15
  effective date and transition, 11.26
    GASB Statement 33, *Accounting and Financial
      Reporting for Nonexchange Transactions,*
      11.26
  environmental liabilities, 11.15
  existing standards, review of, 11.13–11.14
  financial analysts, guide for, 11.10–11.11
    *An Analyst's Guide to Government Financial
      Statements,* 11.10–11.11
  fund accounting, retention of, 11.18
  fund financial statements, 11.21, 11.24–11.25
    fiduciary funds report, 11.24
    governmental funds report, 11.24
    major funds, 11.24–11.25
    nonmajor funds, 11.25
    proprietary funds report, 11.24
  fund-raising foundations and similar organizations,
    financial reporting guidance, 11.05
  GASB Statement 33, *Accounting and Financial
    Reporting for Nonexchange Transactions,*
    11.26, 11.29–11.30
  GASB Statement 34, *Basic Financial Statements—
    and Management's Discussion and Analysis—
    for State and Local Governments,* 11.12
    accountability, 11.17–11.18
    amendment, 11.28
    background information, 11.17
    concepts Statement, *Objectives of Financial Re-
      porting,* 11.16
    consulting opportunities, 11.18
    as dual-perspective report, 11.17
    infrastructures, accountability for cost of, 11.17
    provisions of, 11.16
  GASB Statement 35, 11.27–11.28
  GASB Statement 36, on symmetry between recipi-
    ents and providers in accounting for certain
    shared revenue, 11.30
  GASB Statement 37, *Basic Financial Statements—
    and Management's Discussion and Analysis—
    for State and Local Governments; Om-
    nibus—An Amendment of GASB Statements
    21 and 24,* 11.02–11.03
  GASB Statement 38, *Certain Financial Statement
    Note Disclosures,* 11.04
  GASB Statement 39, *Determining Whether Cer-
    tain Organizations Are Component Units, an
    Amendment of GASB Statement 14,* 11.05
  Governmental Accounting Standards Board, in-
    creased stature of, 11.16
  government-wide financial statements, 11.21,
    11.22–11.24
    special items, 11.24
  guide for implementing new financial statements,
    11.07
  compliance, in-depth instructions for, 11.07
  interpretation relating to modified accrual stan-
    dards, 11.12–11.13
  local government financial statements, guide to,
    11.08
    *What You Should Know about Your Local Gov-
      ernment's Finances: A Guide to Financial
      Statements,* 11.08
  management's discussion and analysis (MD&A),
    content of, 11.19, 11.20–11.21, 11.22
  modified accrual, proposed interpretation on,
    11.27
    *Recognition and Measurement of Certain Liabil-
      ities and Expenditures in Governmental Fund
      Financial Statements,* 11.27
  modified accrual standards, 11.12–11.13
  new information required, 11.19–11.20
    basic financial statements, 11.21
    fiduciary fund financial statements, 11.21
    fund financial statements, 11.21, 11.24–11.25
    government fund financial statements, 11.21
    government-wide financial statements, 11.21,
      11.22–11.24
    management's discussion and analysis
      (MD&A), 11.19, 11.20–11.21, 11.22
    notes to financial statements, 11.21
    proprietary fund financial statements, 11.21
    RSI (required supplementary information),
      11.25–11.26
    users, benefits to, 11.20
  other postemployment benefits (OPEB), 11.15
  prospective reporting, requirements for, 11.26–
    11.27
  public colleges and universities, 11.27–11.28

RSI (required supplementary information), 11.19, 11.21, 11.25–11.26
  budgetary comparison schedules, 11.26
  school district's financial statements, guide to, 11.09–11.10
  What You Should Know about Your School District's Finances: A Guide to Financial Statements, 11.09
  state and local government, 11.15
Governmental Accounting Standards Board (GASB), 12.08–12.09. *See also* Governmental accounting
  increased stature of, 11.16
Governmental fund accounting, 12.01–12.17
  and commercial accounting, differences between, 12.01–12.02
  complexity of, 12.03
  legal provisions, 12.02–12.03
  nonbusiness organizations, objectives of financial reporting by, 12.17
  retention of, 11.18. *See also* Governmental accounting, new
  systems, 12.08–12.17
    funds, types of, 12.09–12.10
    Governmental Accounting Standards Board (GASB), 12.08–12.09
  terminology, 12.03–12.07
Government-wide financial statements, requirement of by GASB 34, 11.21, 11.22–11.24. *See also* Governmental accounting, new
Gross profit ratio, 1.34–1.35
GST. *See* Generation-skipping transfer tax (GST)
Guarantees, expansion of disclosure requirements (Exposure Draft), 10.24

H

Hardship
  distributions, rollovers, 40.27
  significant, recognition of by IRS, 38.10–38.11
Health insurance
  self-employed health insurance deduction, 40.33
Hedge accounting, IAS 39 and, 5.66–5.67
  cash flow hedge, 5.67
  fair value hedge, 5.67
Hedging
  accounting, 7.14–7.15
    cash flow hedge, 7.14
    fair value hedge, 7.14
    foreign currency exposure hedge, 7.14–7.15
  definition, 7.03
Higher education expense, new deduction for
  coordination with credits and other deductions, 40.10
  coordination with exclusions, 40.11
  income limits, 40.10
  limits on eligibility, 40.11
  maximum deduction, 40.10

qualified tuition and related expenses, 40.09–40.10
  student name and ID number, 40.1
  termination, 40.1
  year of deduction, 40.11
Holocaust victims, restitution, 40.03
Home
  office. *See* Business use of home
  sale of. *See* Real estate as asset
HOPE credits, 39.09
  Coverdell ESAs, coordination with, 40.08–40.09
Horizontal analysis, 1.23
Human resources, 22.06

I

IAASB. *See* International Auditing and Assurance Standards Board (IAASB)
IAS 2, *Inventories,* 5.26
IAS 10, *Contingencies and Events Occurring After Balance Sheet Date,* 5.61
IAS 12, *Income Taxes,* 5.28
IAS 14, *Segment Reporting,* 5.54, 26.01
IAS 19, *Employee Benefits,* 5.18, 5.28
IAS 21, *The Effects of Changes in Foreign Exchange Rates,* 5.67
IAS 22, *Business Combinations,* 5.63
IAS 28, *Accounting for Investments in Associates,* 5.28
IAS 31, *Financial Reporting of Interests in Joint Ventures,* 5.28
IAS 32, *Financial Instruments Disclosure and Presentation,* 5.11, 5.65, 43.06
IAS 33, *Earnings per Share,* 5.50
IAS 34, *Interim Financial Reporting,* 5.50–5.53
  comparability, 5.53
  costs, 5.53
  dependent approach, 5.52
  dependent/independent approach, 5.52
  independent theory, 5.51–5.52
  mandated/suggested approach, 5.52–5.53
IAS 35, *Discontinuing Operations,* 5.53–5.56
  considerations, other, 5.55
  definition, 5.54
  disclosure requirements, 5.54–5.55
  uniform approach, 5.56
  U.S. GAAP, comparison to, 5.55–5.56
IAS 36, *Impairment of Assets,* 5.56–5.60, 5.63
  book value, 5.57
  cash-generating unit, 5.58
  GAAP, differences from, 5.59–5.60
  IASC-UK cooperation, 5.58–5.59
  requirements, 5.57–5.58
IAS 37, *Provisions, Contingent Liabilities and Contingent Assets,* 5.60–5.62, 43.06
  applications, three, of requirements, 5.61
  "big bath," 5.60, 5.61
  global aspects, 5.62
  UK-IASC cooperation, 5.61

IAS 38, *Intangible Assets,* 5.62–5.64
  GAAP, comparison to, 5.64
  requirements, 5.62–5.64
  Web site costs, 5.16–5.18
IAS 39, *Financial Instruments Recognition and Measurement,* 5.30–5.31, 5.64–5.69, 8.03, 43.05, 43.06
  background, 5.65
  derecognition, 5.67–5.68
  disclosure requirements, additional, 5.68
  hedge accounting, 5.66–5.67
  IAS 32, *Financial Instruments Disclosure and Presentation,* 5.65
  requirements, principal, 5.65–5.66
  stop-gap solution, 5.68–5.69
  uniformity, need for greater, 5.65
IAS 40, *Investment Property,* 5.48–5.49
IASC. *See* International Accounting Standards; International Accounting Standards Commission (IASC)
  insurance accounting, paper on, 43.01–43.06. *See also* Insurance
IC-DISC, 36.25, 36.26
Illiquid assets
  financial planning, 17.07
Improper tax year, 36.18
Improvements
  rental property, 19.04
Improving Business Reporting Insights into Enhancing Voluntary Disclosures, 10.47–10.49
Imputed interest, 2.05–2.07. *See also* Revenue and expenses
"Incidents of ownership," depreciation and, 33.03
Income Statement, 1.03
  analysis, 1.28–1.30
  income taxes, presentation of, 1.20–1.21
Income tax
  independent contractor or employee, 34.04
Independent contractor or employee, 34.01–34.21
  accountant's concerns, 34.05–34.06
  behavioral control, 34.08–34.09
  categories, emphasis on, 34.16
  checklist, 33.14–33.16
  common law employees, 34.02–34.03
  decision, 34.07
  defined, 34.02
  determination, 34.02–34.05
  direct sellers, 34.04–34.05
  employment tax, 34.16–34.21
    appeals jurisdiction, 34.20
    assessment, restrictions, 34.20
    eligibility to seek review, 34.18
    notice of determination, 34.18–34.19
    prerequisite for seeking review, 34.19
    Section 7436, 34.17–34.18
    settlements, agreed, 34.20–34.21
    statute of limitations, suspension of, 34.20
    timing of filing, 34.19

Federal Unemployment Tax Act (FUTA), 34.04
  financial control, 34.09–34.11
  income tax, 34.04
  leased employees, 34.03
  Medicare taxes, 34.04
  permanent/indefinite relationships, 34.13–34.14
  primary categories, 34.07–34.14
  reasonable basis, 34.06
  relationship of the parties, 34.11–34.14
  reporting consistency, 34.06–34.07
  Section 530 relief requirements, 34.06–34.07
  Small Business Jobs protection Act of 1996, 34.01
  Social Security taxes, 34.04
  statutory employees, 34.03–34.04
  statutory nonemployees, 34.04–34.05
  substantive consistency, 34.06
  termination rights, 33.12–33.13
  worker classification, 34.05, 34.07–34.14
Independent fund advisors, SEC final rules and amendments, 29.08–29.21
Independent fund directors, mutual funds. *See* Mutual funds
Indirect labor expense, 14.07–14.08, 14.12
Indirect method, 4.09–4.10
Indirect reconciliation method, 4.04
Individual retirement arrangements (IRAs), 40.19–40.21
  catch-up contribution, 39.12
  contributions, 39.11, 39.12
    catch-up contribution, 39.12
    saver's credit, 40.17–40.19
  deemed IRAs, 40.27
    Job Creation and Worker Assistance Act of 2002, 41.08
  Job Creation and Worker Assistance Act of 2002, 41.06–41.07
  rollovers, 40.20–40.21
  Roth IRAs. *See* Roth IRAs
Individuals, tax filing period for, 36.17
Individual sales performance, measuring, 14.04–14.05
Inflation
  financial planning and, 17.02–17.03
  risk, 17.19
Infrastructure, governmental accountability for cost of, 11.17
Inheritance
  basis in property other than cost, 35.14–35.15
  mutual funds, 29.04
Innocent spouse relief, 38.05
Insider trading
  Sarbanes-Oxley Act of 2002, 9.11
  Securities and Exchange Commission (SEC), 23.23
Installment agreement to pay taxes, 38.08–38.10
  estate tax, 40.30
Installment method of accounting
  election out of, 40.05
  income determination, 2.02

Installment sales of home, 19.24
Insurance
 financial planning, 17.10–17.11
 internal control system, checklist, 16.42
Insurance accounting, 43.01–43.14
 FASB 60, *Accounting and Reporting by Insurance Enterprises,* 43.06, 43.10, 43.14
 FASB 97, *Accounting and Reporting by Insurance Enterprises for Certain Long-Duration Contracts and for Realized Gains and Losses from Sale of Investments,* 43.07–43.08, 43.12, 43.14
 FASB 105, *Disclosures of Information about Financial Instruments with Off-Balance-Sheet Risk and Financial Instruments with Concentrations of Credit Risk,* 43.11
 FASB 113, *Accounting and Reporting for Reinsurance of Short-Duration and Long-Duration Contracts,* 43.08–43.13, 43.14
 FASB 120, *Accounting and Reporting by Mutual Life Insurance Enterprises and by Insurance Enterprises for Certain Long-Duration Participating Contracts,* 43.13–43.14
 FASB Statements for accounting and reporting, 43.06–43.14
 IASC paper on, 43.01–43.06
  contracts, 43.02–43.03
  full fair value accounting, anticipated requirement of, 43.05
  IAS 39, *Financial Instruments Recognition and Measurement,* 43.05
  insurance risks, types of, 43.03–43.04
  measurement issues, discussion of, 43.05–43.06
  presentation and disclosure, 43.06
  recognition and measurement, 43.04–43.05
  topics, 43.01–43.02
 mortality or morbidity risk, policies not covering, 43.08
Insurance expense, 14.12
Intangible assets
 not-for-profit organizations (NPOs)
  business combinations, methods of accounting for, 13.21
  FASB Project on NPO combinations, 13.17
Intangible Assets—Web Site Costs (SIC-32), 5.16–5.17
Intangible business assets, 35.06
Intangible property
 ineligible for depreciation, 33.03
Intellectual capital management, accountant's role in, 6.33
Interest-conversion period, 2.11
Interest rate risk, 17.19
 bond mutual funds, 30.15
Intergovernmental Service Funds, 12.14–12.15
Interim financial statements
 appropriateness of rules, gauging, 22.14
 Blue Ribbon Panel, 22.13–22.14
 SEC's new rules, 22.12–22.13

Interim reporting
 segment information added to interim reports, 26.13–26.14
Internal auditor
 internal control system, 16.14
Internal audit services, 22.06
Internal charges, defined
 mutual funds, 30.06
Internal control. *See also* Internal control system (ICS)
 COSO framework for, 16.03–16.05
 FCPA, accounting provisions, 16.08–16.09
Internal control system, 16.12–16.43
 accounting control, 16.13
 accounts payable, checklist, 16.39–16.40
 accounts receivable
  cash, 16.28–16.29
  checklist, 16.36
 administrative control, 16.13–16.14
 basic elements of, 16.14–16.15
 cash, for, 16.27–16.31
  accounts receivable, 16.28–16.29
  bank reconciliations and cash, 16.29–16.31
  block-proofs of cash, 16.30
  cash disbursements, 16.28
  cash receipts, 16.27–16.28
  notes receivable, 16.29
  petty cash, 16.28
 cash receipts, 16.27–16.28
  checklist, 16.38
 computer files, 16.32
 credit manager, 16.25
 defined, 16.12–16.13
 division of duties, 16.14
 expenses, for, 16.23–16.27
  administrative expenses, 16.25
  financial expenses, 16.25
  manufacturing expenses, 16.23–16.24
  office payroll, 16.26–16.27
  salaries and wages, 16.25–16.26
  selling expenses, 16.24
 file maintenance, 16.31–16.32
 forms and documents, use of, 16.14
 fundamentals of system, 16.14
 insurance checklist, 16.42
 internal auditor, 16.14
 inventories, 16.15–16.23
  finished goods, 16.17–16.18
  merchandise purchased for resale and supplies, 16.16–16.17
  physical inventory, 16.20–16.23
  raw materials and supplies, 16.18–16.19
  work-in-process, 16.19–16.20
 outside accountants, relationship to, 16.15
 responsibility, 16.14
 small business enterprise, 16.32–16.43
  accounts payable checklist, 16.39–16.40
  accounts receivable checklist, 16.36
  cash receipts checklist, 16.37

Internal control system (*cont.*)
  checklists, 16.32–16.43
  disbursements, checklist, 16.39–16.40
  insurance checklist, 16.42
  investments checklist, 16.41
  property, plant, and equipment checklist, 16.42
  purchases, checklist, 16.39–16.40
  sales checklist, 16.36
Internal Revenue Code, Section 179, 33.04–33.07.
  See also Depreciation
Internal Revenue Service. *See* IRS
Internal Service, 12.14–12.15
Internal Service Funds, 12.09
International accounting, 5.01–5.67
  advertising services, 5.19
  agreement on IASs to help investors and business
    in EU, 5.07
  Agriculture, Standard on, 5.26–5.27
    biological asset, 5.27
    fair value measurement, 5.27–5.28
    unique aspects of agriculture, 5.27
  AICPA, SEC practice section, 5.34–5.35
  Australia, 5.07–5.08
  biological asset, measurement of fair value for, 5.27
  business combinations, 5.10–5.11, 5.19
  Canada, foreign issuers, 5.05
  consolidation method, 5.20
  cooperative standard setting, examples of, 5.31–5.32
  currency, reporting, 5.19
  disclosure requirements, amendments to, 5.35
  e-commerce, tax treatment of, 5.37–5.41
  EFRAG recommends endorsement of IASB stan-
    dards, 5.05–5.06
  employee benefits, 5.18
  European Parliament's changes to accounting di-
    rectives, 5.36
  European Union
    agreement on IASs to help investors and busi-
      nesses, 5.07
    new regulatory body created by, 5.07
    plans to adopt IASs and IFRSs, 5.05
  existing standards, need to improve, 5.15–5.16
  financial instruments, 5.30
  foreign integrated disclosure system, 5.35–5.36
  global standard setting, 5.04
  history of international body, 5.41
  implementation guides, 5.30–5.31
  improvements, stepped-up efforts, 5.15
  leases, 5.19
  new regulatory body created by EU, 5.07
  revenue-barter transactions, 5.19–5.20
  service concession arrangements, 5.19
  standards currently in force or issued recently
    core standards, 5.69–5.71
  United Kingdom, 5.08–5.09
  Web site costs, interpretation on, 5.16–5.18
International Accounting Standards Board (IASB)
  agenda for improving standards, 5.03
  business combinations, 5.10–5.11

EFRAG recommends endorsement of standards,
    5.05–5.06
  employee stock options, 2.14–2.15
  improvements proposed by, 5.14–5.15
    financial instrument standards, 5.11–5.12
  IPSAS based on standards of, 6.05
  long-range plans, 5.10
  Preface to International Financial Reporting, 5.13
  Proposals to Ease Transition to IAS, 5.13–5.14
International Accounting Standards Commission
    (IASC), 5.41–5.70, 26.01–26.02. *See also* In-
    ternational accounting
  acceptance of international standards, growing
    FASB's attitude, 5.46–5.47
    NYSE and securities dealers, attitude of, 5.46
    structure, new, support for, 5.47
  Accounting for Investments and *Financial Instru-
    ments: Recognition and Measurement,* 5.41
  accounting standards, global, importance of, 5.42–
    5.44
    comparability, 5.43
    core standards, 5.43–5.44
    European Union (EU), 5.43
    transparency, 5.43
  constitution, revised, 5.22–5.26
    board, 5.23–5.24
    International Financial Reporting Interpreta-
      tions Committee, 5.24
    relationship with other international groups,
      5.24–5.25
    trustees, distribution, 5.23
  exposure drafts, revised, 5.28
  Foundation
    Assessment and Certification Program, 5.12–
      5.13
    Standards Advisory Council (SAC), 5.21
  International Financial Reporting Interpretations
    Committee, 5.44
    SIC, new interpretations, 5.19–5.22
    SIC-8, *First-time Application of IASs as the Pri-
      mary Basis of Accounting,* 5.14
    SIC-27, *Evaluating the Substance of Transac-
      tions in the Legal Form of a Lease,* 5.19
    SIC-28, *Business Combinations—"Date of Ex-
      change" and Fair Value of Equity Instru-
      ments,* 5.19
    SIC-29, *Disclosure—Service Concession
      Arrangements,* 5.19
    SIC-30, *Reporting Currency—Translation from
      Measurement Currency to Presentation Cur-
      rency,* 5.19
    SIC-31, *Revenue—Barter Transactions Involving
      Advertising Services,* 5.20
    SIC-33, *Consolidation and Equity Method—Po-
      tential Voting Rights and Allocation of Own-
      ership Interests,* 5.20
  International Organization of Securities Commis-
    sions (IOSCO), 5.41
    role of, 5.44–5.45

mining/oil and gas companies accounting by, 5.28–5.30

relationship with IFAC, 6.31

relationship with other groups, 5.24

revised organization, 5.21

SEC, cautious appraisal of, 5.48

   IAS 40, *Investment Property,* 5.48–5.49

selected IASC standards with comparison to U.S. GAAP, 5.49–5.70

   IAS 33, *Earnings per Share,* 5.50

   IAS 34, *Interim Financial Reporting,* 5.50–5.53

   IAS 35, *Discontinuing Operations,* 5.53–5.56

   IAS 36, *Impairment of Assets,* 5.56–5.60, 5.63

   IAS 37, *Provisions, Contingent Liabilities and Contingent Assets,* 5.60–5.62

   IAS 38, *Intangible Assets,* 5.62–5.64

   IAS 39, *Financial Instruments: Recognition and Measurement,* 5.64–5.69

Standard on Agriculture (AIS 41), 5.26–5.27

standards (IASs)

   core standards, launching of, 5.32–5.33

   future development of, 5.33

   three revised, 5.28

Standing Interpretations Committee (SIC), 5.44. *See also* International Financial Reporting Interpretations Committee

2000 standards, 5.32

U.S. securities markets, internationalization of, 5.33–5.34

   foreign issuers in U.S. market, 5.34

world economy, changing, 5.41–5.42

   Securities and Exchange Commission, 5.42

International Anti-Bribery and Fair Competition Act of 1998, 16.11

International Auditing and Assurance Standards Board (IAASB), 6.19

International Federation of Accountants (IFAC), 6.01–6.45

accountability of accountants, actions to improve, 6.05–6.06

The Accountancy Profession and the Fight against Corruption, 6.40

accountant competencies, addressing, 6.26–6.27

The Accountant's Role in Intellectual Capital Management, 6.33

Acquiring Information Technology, Implementation of Information Technology Solutions, and IT Delivery and Support, 6.37

anti-corruption, 6.40–6.43

   The Accountancy Profession and the Fight against Corruption, 6.40

   proposals of IFAC, 6.42–6.43

Articles of Merit, 6.33

Assuring the Quality of Professional Services, 6.32

coalition to advance accountancy development, 6.37–6.40

   International Forum on Accountancy Development (IFAD), 6.38

Code of Ethics for Professional Accountants, 6.23–6.24

continuing education, 6.25–6.26

corruption, fight against, 6.40–6.43

credibility of financial statements, 6.06–6.07

e-business, paper issued on, 6.28

E-Business and the Accountant: Risk Management for Accounting Systems in an E-Business Environment, 6.28–6.29, 27.14

E-commerce and e-communication, 27.12–27.14

Education Committee, 6.24–6.26

   accountant competencies, 6.27

Financial and Management Accounting Committee (FMAC), 6.33

   intellectual capital, 6.33

Forum of Firms, 6.07–6.09

   constitution, approval of, 6.08–6.09

   establishment of, 6.07

   requirements, 6.07–6.08

   structure of, 6.07–6.08, 6.09

   Transnational Audit Committee (TAC), 6.09

GAAP 2000: A Survey of National Accounting Rules in 53 Countries, 6.11

GAAP 2001 report, 6.10

global peer reviews, ED on guidelines for, 6.09

Glossary of Defined Terms, 6.04

Going Concern (ISA 570), 6.33–6.35

history of, 6.31

IASC, relationship with, 5.24

IFAC and IASC relationship, 6.31

   as two separate international organizations, 6.31–6.32

independence rules and *Code of Ethics,* 6.23–6.24

Information Technology Committee (ITC), 6.37

International Auditing Practices Committee (IAPC), 6.15–6.22, 6.33–6.37

   Assurance Engagements, 6.35

   assurance of credibility, 6.35–6.36

   audit matters, communications of, 6.36–6.37

   auditors and bank supervisors, role of, 6.16–6.17

   The Auditor's Report on Financial Statements, 6.15

   banks and banking, 6.16–6.19

   Basel Committee on Banking Supervision, 6.17–6.19

   derivatives, guidance on, 6.20–6.21

   fair value measurements, auditing, 6.19–6.20

   fraud, guidance on, 6.20

   Going Concern (ISA 570), 6.33–6.35

   IAPS 1004, *The Relationship Between Banking Supervisors and Banks' External Auditors,* 6.18–6.19

   IAPS 1006, *Audits of Bank Financial Statements,* 6.18

   International Auditing Practice Statement (IAPS), 6.17

   publications, 6.15–6.16

   The Relationship between Banking Supervisors and Banks' External Auditors, 6.16–6.17

   standard, international, 6.16

International Federation of Accountants (IFAC)
(*cont.*)

International Forum on Accountancy Development (IFAD), 6.13

creation of, 6.11

IPSAS

IASB's standards, based on, 6.05

IPSAS 1, *Presentation of Financial Statements,* 6.43

IPSAS 2, *Cash Flow Statements,* 6.43

IPSAS 3, *Net Surplus or Deficit for the Period, Fundamental Errors and Changes in Accounting Policies,* 6.43–6.44

IPSAS 4, *The Effect of Changes in Foreign Exchange Rates,* 6.44

IPSAS 5, *Borrowing Costs,* 6.44

IPSAS 6, *Consolidating Financial Statements and Accounting for Controlled Entities,* 6.44

IPSAS 7, *Accounting for Investments in Associates,* 6.44

IPSAS 8, *Financial Reporting of Interests in Joint Ventures,* 6.44

IPSAS 9, *Revenue from Exchange Transactions,* 6.44

IPSAS 10, *Financial Reporting in Hyperinflationary Economies,* 6.44

IPSAS 11, *Construction Contracts,* 6.45

IPSAS 12, *Inventories,* 6.45

IPSAS 13, *Leases,* 6.03

IPSAS 14, *Events After the Reporting Date,* 6.03

IPSAS 15, *Financial Instruments: Disclosure and Presentation,* 6.03

IPSAS 16, *Investment Property,* 6.03

IPSAS 17, *Property, Plant and Equipment,* 6.03–6.04

IPSAS 18, *Segment Reporting,* 6.04

public sector, standards for, 6.01–6.03

standards set for government and public sector bodies, 6.01–6.03

management accountants

changing environment of management accountancy, 6.22–6.23

Competency: Profiles for Management Accounting Practice and Practitioners, 6.21

value to organizations, 6.21–6.22

Managing Information Technology Monitoring, 6.27–6.28

Managing Information Technology Planning for Business Impact, 6.37

Managing Security in Information and Communications, 6.37

money laundering, 6.29–6.30

projects, implementing, 6.12

public sector, standards for, 6.01–6.03

Public Sector Committee (PSC)

accrual accounting, 6.43–645

governments not ready for accrual basis, 6.05

Study 11, *Governmental Financial Reporting: Accounting Issues and Practices,* 6.05

Study to Assist Public Sector Entities' Transition from Cash to Accrual Basis, 6.04–6.05

quality assurance, 6.32

risk, IT monitoring guidelines, 6.27–6.28

small and medium practices (SMPs), 6.30

Transnational Audit Committee (TAC), 6.09

U.S. organizations, comparison to, 6.32

XBRL (eXtensible Business Reporting Language) Consortium, 6.13–6.15

accomplishments, 6.14

dissemination of information, 6.14–6.15

value of, 6.14

International Financial Reporting Interpretations Committee (IFRIC)

Web site costs, interpretation on, 5.16–5.18

International Forum on Accountancy Development (IFAD), 6.11, 6.13, 6.38

International Joint Working Group (JWG), 10.19. *See also* International accounting

International Organization of Securities Commissions (IOSCO)

IASC, relationship with, 5.24

matters raised by IOSCO, 5.26

International Disclosure Standards, 5.36

Internet. *See also* E-commerce and E-communication accounting. *See* Internet accounting

mutual funds, services, 30.18

Internet accounting, 28.01–28.38

advertising arrangements

prepaid/intangible assets versus period costs, 28.31–28.32

revenue recognition, 28.08–28.09, 28.27–28.28

auction sites on Internet, 28.19–28.20

classification issues, 28.34–28.35

coupons, 28.35–28.36

customer or membership base, 28.32–28.33

EITF 00-8, *Accounting by a Grantee for an Equity Instrument to Be Received in Conjunction with Providing Goods or Services,* 28.33–28.34

EITF 00-22, 28.30

EITF 00-25, *Vendor Income Statement Characterization of Consideration from a Vendor to a Retailer,* 28.36

EITF 01-9, *Accounting for Consideration Given by a Vendor to a Customer or a Reseller of the Vendor's Products,* 28.04–28.07

EITF 099-19, *Reporting Revenue Gross as a Principal versus Net as an Agent,* 28.07

Emerging Issues Task Force of FASB, 28.03–28.07

equity instruments, 28.33–28.34

FASB 131, *Disclosures about Segments of an Enterprise and Related Information,* 28.34

gross versus net issue, 28.07–28.16

advertising barter transactions, 28.08–28.09

discounts, 28.13–28.15

personal computer retailers, 28.10–28.12

service outages, 28.15–28.16

shipping and handling costs, 28.12–28.13

third-party products, resale of, 28.07–28.08
incentives, 28.30
"point" and loyalty programs, 28.28–28.30
prepaid/intangible assets versus period costs,
    28.31–28.33
  advertising arrangements, 28.31–28.32
  customer or membership base, 28.32–28.33
  long-term contractual rights, 28.31
quality accounting, need for, 28.03
revenue recognition, 28.19–28.30
  advertising arrangements, 28.08–28.09, 28.27–
    28.28
  IASB, request by SEC to consider project,
    28.26–28.30
  listing fees, auctions, 28.19–28.20
  multiple element arrangements, 28.25
  "point" and loyalty programs, 28.28–28.30
  Web site access or maintenance, 28.21–28.25
and Securities and Exchange Commission (SEC),
    28.02–28.03
  issues, related, 28.02
  quality accounting, need for, 28.03
  targeted areas, 28.02–28.03
segment reporting, 28.34
software
  definition, 28.16–28.19
  revenue recognition, 28.20–28.21
top 10 technologies and issues, 28.38–28.39
Web site, costs of developing, 28.18–28.19
Internet Tax Freedom Act of 1998, 27.10
Intrinsic value method
employee stock options, 2.23
Inventories
control, 1.27, 14.10
  small business enterprise, payroll checklist,
    16.43
internal control system, 16.15–16.23
  finished goods, 16.17–16.18
  merchandise purchased for resale and supplies,
    16.16–16.17
  raw materials and supplies, 16.18–16.19
  work-in-process, 16.19–16.20
physical inventory, 16.20–16.23
  perpetual system, 16.20–16.21
  physical count, 16.21–16.23
Investment Advisers Act of 1940, 17.14, 23.39
Investment expenses for mutual funds, 29.07–29.08
Investments
advising clients on. *See* Investments, advising
    clients on
real estate, 19.15–19.16
vocabulary, 18.01–18.25
Investments, advising clients on, 17.14–17.32
asset allocation and, 17.20–17.29
client investment profile, 17.16–17.18
good advice, listing, 17.31–17.32
knowledge, 17.14–17.15
market risk, 17.19–17.20
mistakes, common, 17.30–17.31

ramifications, 17.14
risk
  credit risk, 17.19–17.20
  event risk, 17.20
  exchange risk, 17.19
  inflation risk, 17.19
  interest rate risk, 17.19
  liquidity risk, 17.19
  market risk, 17.19–17.20
  minimizing, 17.32
  principal risk, 17.20
  regulatory risk, 17.20
  tolerance, 17.15–17.16
IRAs. *See* Individual retirement arrangements (IRAs)
IRS
change in accounting methods, 36.01–36.27. *See
    also* Change in accounting methods and con-
    sideration of accounting periods
collection process, 38.06–38.11
filing, 36.06
Form 3115, *Application for Change in Accounting
    Method,* 33.18, 36.01–36.27. *See also* Change
    in accounting methods and consideration of
    accounting periods
IRS-initiated method changes, 36.14–36.15. *See
    also* Change in accounting methods and con-
    sideration of accounting periods
  material item, 36.05
  tax year, 36.16–36.17
Rulings for not-for-profit organizations, 13.06–
    13.08. *See also* Not-for-profit organizations
  fraudulent information, penalties for, 13.08
  noncompliance, penalties for, 13.08
IRS, practice before, and power of attorney, 37.01–
    37.11
confidentiality privilege between taxpayer and
    federally authorized tax practitioner, 37.01–
    37.02
explained, 37.02
power of attorney, 37.07–37.08
  Centralized Authorized File (CAF), 37.09, 37.10
  Declaration of Representative, 37.09
  described, 37.07–37.08
  documents, completed, 37.10–37.11
  fiduciary, 37.10. *See also* Fiduciary
  filing, 37.09
  income tax return, 37.08
  non-IRS power of attorney, when allowed, 37.09
  revoking, 37.11
  Tax Matters Partner/Person (TMP), 37.10
  when not required, 37.10
  when required, 37.08–37.09
practicing before IRS
  Centralized Authorization File number, mean-
    ing of, 37.04, 37.10
  denial of right to limited practice, 37.04
  disreputable conduct, 37.07
  due diligence, required, 37.06
  enrollment, methods of, 37.05

IRS, practice before, and power of attorney (*cont.*)
  government employees, former, restrictions on,
    37.06
  recognized representative, who can become,
    37.03–37.05
  restrictions, 37.06
  rules of practice, 37.05–37.07
  special appearance, authorization for, 37.04
  who cannot practice, 37.04–37.05
IRS Restructuring and Reform Act of 1998, 38.01,
  38.02

J

Jobbing plants, cost accounting, 15.05
Job Creation and Worker Assistance Act of 2002,
    33.01, 33.14, 41.01–41.15
  Archer MSAs, 41.13
  business incentives, 41.04–41.06
    empowerment zone tax incentives, 41.05–41.06
    expiring business tax credits, 41.06
    non-accrual experience method of accounting,
      41.05
    pension plan start-up costs, credit for, 41.05
    tax incentives for New York City Liberty Zone,
      41.04–41.05
  carryback period, election to forgo, 41.03
  child and dependent care credit, 41.13
  deemed IRAs, 41.08
  defined benefit plans, contributions to, 41.08
  educator expenses, deduction for, 41.12–41.13
  electronic filing of 1099s, 41.09
  five-year carryback for NOLs, 41.02–41.03
  foster care, 41.13
  403(b) plans, 41.07–41.08
  highlights of, 41.02
  individual incentives, 41.10–41.13
    Archer MSAs, 41.13
    child and dependent care credit, 41.13
    educator expenses, deduction for, 41.12–41.13
    foster care, 41.13
    personal credits against AMT, 41.10–41.12
  individual retirement arrangements (IRAs),
    41.06–41.07
  New York City Liberty Zone, 41.09–41.10
    business incentives, 41.04–41.05
  personal credits against AMT, 41.10–41.12
  retirement plans, 41.06–41.07
  Salary reduction SEP (SARSEP), 41.07
  S corporation indebtedness, discharge of, 41.08–
    41.09
  simplified employee pensions (SEPs), 41.06–
    41.07
  technical corrections, 41.13–41.15
Joint Board for Enrollment of Actuaries, 37.03
Joint Working Group (JWG), International, 10.19
Junk bond funds, 30.12

K

Kidnapped children, tax benefits for parents of,
  40.02–40.03

L

Labor budget, 14.07–14.09. *See also* Budgeting for
    profit planning and budgetary control
Land and buildings, allocating cost basis of, 35.07–
    35.08
Lapping, 16.44–16.45
Leased employees
  independent contractor or employee, 34.03
Leased property, depreciation of
  Section 179 deduction, 33.05
Leases
  international accounting, 5.19
  synthetic, 10.04–10.05
Legalese in prospectus, eliminating, 32.19. *See also*
    Plain English Disclosure Rule
Level-load, defined
  mutual funds, 30.06
Liability defined, 10.45–10.46
  changes, resulting, 10.46–10.47
Lifetime learning credits, 39.09
  Coverdell ESAs, coordination with, 40.08–40.09
Like-kind exchanges, basis of, 35.12–35.14
  partial business use of property, 35.13–35.14
  partially nontaxable exchange, 35.13
Limited-payment policies, 43.07–43.08
Liquid assets
  financial planning, 17.07
Liquidity ratios, 1.22
Listed property
  business use of home, 20.08–20.09
Load, defined
  mutual funds, 30.06
Load charge in mutual funds, 29.03
Loans, student, 39.10–39.11
  interest deduction, 40.11–40.12
Long-lived assets
  FASB statement 144
    conceptual framework of FASB, relation to,
      10.14
    discontinued operations, 10.13
    effective date, 10.15
    held or used, 10.10
    later standards, coverage by, 10.14
    other than sale, disposal of assets by, 10.12–
      10.13
    reason for issuing statement, 10.09
    sale, disposal of assets by, 10.11–10.12
    SEC, cautions from, 10.08–10.09
Long-Term Debt Group, 12.16–12.17
Long-term growth
  diversification, 17.27

Losses. *See specific topic*
Luxury taxes, 40.31

M

MACRS. *See* Modified accelerated cost recovery system (MACRS)
MAGI. *See* Modified adjusted gross income (MAGI)
Maintenance expenses, 14.12
Management accountancy, 6.21–6.23
Management evaluation by bankers, 4.13
Management fees
    mutual funds, 30.06
Management's Discussion and Analysis (MD&A)
    content of, 11.22
    segment reporting, 26.10–26.12
Managing Information Technology Monitoring, 6.27–6.28
Manufacturing expense budget, 14.07–14.08, 14.11–14.13. *See also* Budgeting for profit planning and budgetary control
Manufacturing expenses
    internal control system, 16.23–16.24
Margin trading
    Securities and Exchange Commission (SEC), 23.23
Market analysis, 14.04
Market risk, 17.19–17.20
Markup, 1.34
Marriage penalty relief, 39.06–39.07
"Matching," 2.04
Materiality
    e-commerce, related to, 27.07
    financial statement, 1.05–1.07
        as abstract concept, 1.06
        disclosure, distinction between, 1.06
        "landmark" *Bar Chris* case, 1.05
        material required to be recognized, 1.07–1.08
        Securities and Exchange Commission, 1.06, 24.03. *See also* SEC materiality
        Supreme Court, definition of, 1.05–1.06
        who decides, 1.07
    material item, 36.05
Materials budget, 14.09–14.11. *See also* Budgeting for profit planning and budgetary control
Meal expense and "hours of service" limits, 40.32–40.33
Medical savings accounts program, 40.06. *See also* Archer MSAs
Medicare taxes, 40.16
    independent contractor or employee, 34.04
Merchandise purchased for resale and supplies, inventories, 16.16–16.17
Mergers and acquisitions in e-commerce, 27.04
Mileage rate, standard, use of, 33.11, 40.33
Mining companies, IASC consideration of accounting for, 5.28–5.30

Modified accelerated cost recovery system (MACRS), 33.07–33.11. *See also* Depreciation
Modified accrual, proposed interpretation on, 11.27
Modified accrual accounting in governmental accounting, 11.12–11.13
Modified adjusted gross income (MAGI)
    Coverdell ESAs, 40.07
    earned income credit, 40.13
    higher-education expense deduction, 40.10
    student loan interest deduction, 40.12
Money laundering
    IFAC and, 6.29–6.30
Mortgages
    in cost basis of property, 35.04–35.05
    end of, "points" and, 19.06
Municipal bond funds, 30.14–30.15
Mutual funds, 29.01–29.21
    back-ended (trailing) load, 30.06
    basis, 29.03–29.04
        adjusted basis, 29.04
        average basis, 29.06–29.07
        commissions, 29.03
        double-category method, 29.06–29.07
        inheritance, shares adjusted by, 29.04
        keeping track of, 29.03–29.04
        load charge, 29.03
        reduction, 29.04
        single-category method, 29.06
    bond mutual funds
        costs, 30.11–30.12
        emerging markets bond funds, 30.13–30.14
        global bond funds, 30.12–30.13
        insured municipal bond funds, 30.14–30.15
        junk bond funds, 30.12
        municipal bond funds, 30.14–30.15
        risk and, 30.15–30.16
    closed-ended funds, 30.05
    computer software, 30.17–30.18
    defined, 30.03–30.05
    demystifying, 30.01–30.20
        advice, generally, 30.19
        bond mutual funds, 30.11–30.16
        closed-ended funds, 30.05
        computer software, 30.17–30.18
        definition, 30.03–30.05
        industry, overview, 30.02–30.03
        Internet services, 30.18
        open-ended funds, 30.05
        periodicals, 30.17
        professional rating services, 30.16–30.17
        returns, generally, 30.03
        sales costs, 30.06–30.10
        selection of mutual funds, 30.16–30.17, 30.19
        steps to avoid, 30.19–30.20
        stock mutual funds, 30.10–30.11
    distributions, kinds of, 29.02–29.03
        capital, return of, 29.02
        reinvestment of distributions, 29.03

Mutual funds (*cont.*)
  equity funds, 30.11
  foreign tax deduction or credit, 29.03
  front-ended load, defined, 30.06
  holding period, 29.07
  independent fund advisors, SEC final rules and
      amendments, 29.08–29.21
    adoption of final rules, 29.10–29.13
    basic information about fund directors, 29.17
    beneficial ownership, disclosure, 29.18
    conflicts of interest, disclosure, 29.19–29.21
    disclosure requirements, 29.16–29.21
    equity securities, disclosure of ownership,
        29.17–29.21
    exemptive rules to enhance director indepen-
        dence and effectiveness, 29.14
    independent audit committee, 29.15
    joint insurance policies, 29.15
    legal counsel for independent directors, 29.12–
        29.13
    nomination and selection of independent direc-
        tors, 29.11–29.12
    ownership of funds within same family of in-
        vestments, disclosure, 29.18–29.19
    qualifications of independent director, 29.16
    recordkeeping requirements, 29.16
    role of independent directors, SEC study,
        29.09–29.10
  industry, overview, 30.02–30.03
  internal charges, defined, 30.06
  Internet services, 30.18
  investment expenses, 29.07–29.08
  level-load, defined, 30.06
  load, defined, 30.06
  management fees, 30.06
  no-load, defined, 30.06
  open-ended funds, 30.05
  periodicals, 30.17
  professional rating services, 30.16–30.17
  "profile" disclosure option, 31.01–31.10
    application to purchase shares, 31.10
    cover page, 31.04–31.05
    for defined contribution plans, 31.10
    fees and expenses of fund, 31.07–31.08
    filing requirements, 31.10
    fund distribution and tax information, 31.09
    fund shares, purchase of, 31.09
    fund shares, sale of, 31.09
    insurance contracts, variable, funds offered
        through, 31.10
    investment adviser(s), identification of, 31.08
    investment companies, other, excluded, 31.04
    investment strategy, 31.06
    modified for certain funds, 31.10
    multiple funds described in, 31.04
    need for simplified disclosure, 31.02
    objectives and goals of fund investment, 31.05–
        31.06

    pilot program, 31.03–31.04
    Plain English rule, 31.03
    portfolio manager(s), identification of, 31.08
    profiles, modified, for certain funds, 31.10
    risk/return bar chart and table, 31.06–31.07
    risk/return summary, 31.05–31.08, 31.06–31.07
    risks of investing, principal, 31.06–31.07
  reinvestment of distributions, 29.03
  returns, generally, 30.03
  Rule 498, requirements under
    described, 31.03
    services provided by fund, other, 31.09
    special risk disclosure requirements, 31.06
    as summary disclosure document, 31.06
    tax information, 31.09
    "uninitiated" investors, goal of protecting, 31.02
  sales, exchanges and redemptions, 29.04–29.07
    average basis, 29.06–29.07
    cost basis, 29.05
    exchange of one fund for another as taxable,
        29.05
    gain or loss, 29.04–29.05
    holding period, 29.07
    identifying shares sold, 29.05
    trade date, 29.07
  sales costs, 30.06–30.10
    back-ended (trailing) load, 30.06
    fees, definitions, 30.06–30.07
    front-ended load, defined, 30.06
    internal charges, defined, 30.06
    level-load, defined, 30.06
    load, defined, 30.06
    management fees, 30.06
    no-load, defined, 30.06
    performance, effect on, 30.07–30.08
    significance of, 30.07
    12b-1 fees, 30.06
  selection of mutual funds, 30.16–30.17, 30.19
  software, 30.17–30.18
  steps to avoid, 30.19–30.20
  stock mutual funds, 30.10–30.11
    equity funds, 30.11
    special and sector equity funds, 30.11
  tax-exempt distributions, 29.02
  12b-1 fees, 30.06
  typical investor, 30.01
Mutual fund shares, cost basis of, 35.03

N

National Arbitration Forum, 27.20
National Association of Securities Dealers (NASD or
    NASDAQ), 22.11–22.12
National Commission on Fraudulent Financial Re-
    porting, 16.02
National Taxpayer Advocate's Problem Resolution
    Program, 38.03

Natural business year for taxpayer, 36.19–36.20

Net operating loss (NOL), 36.20
  Job Creation and Worker Assistance Act of 2002, 41.02–41.03

Net worth. *See also* Stockholders' equity
  financial planning and, 17.05–17.07

New basis accounting
  business combinations, 10.18–10.19

New York City
  Job Creation and Worker Assistance Act of 2002. *See* Job Creation and Worker Assistance Act of 2002

New York City Liberty Zone, 41.09–41.10
  depreciation. *See* New York City Liberty Zone depreciation
  tax expenses, 41.04–41.05
  work opportunity credit, expansion, 41.04–41.05

New York City Liberty Zone depreciation, 33.14, 33.17, 33.19–33.23, 41.10
  election not to claim, 33.22
  qualified liberty zone property, 33.20–33.22
  qualifying tests, 33.21
  Section 179 deduction, increased, 33.22–33.23
  special Liberty Zone Depreciation Allowance, 33.20

New York Society of Security Analysts (NYSSA), 5.03

New York Stock Exchange (NYSE), 22.11
  and securities dealers, attitude of to international standards, 5.46

No-load, defined
  mutual funds, 30.06

Nonbusiness organizations, objectives of financial reporting by, 12.17

Noncumulative preferred stock, 3.04

No-par stock, 3.03

Notes receivable
  internal control system, 16.29

Not-for-profit organizations (NPOs), 3.01–3.21
  application of FASB 133 to, 7.17
  business combinations, methods of accounting for, 13.17–13.21
    acquiring organization, identifying, 13.19–13.21
    collection acquired, 13.21
    exchange of cash or other assets as consideration, 13.18–13.19
    intangible assets, identification of, 13.21
  business entities, differences between, 13.02
  characteristics, distinguishing, 13.02
  FASB 93, *Recognition of Depreciation by Not-for-Profit Organizations,* 13.08–13.09
  FASB 116, *Accounting for Contributions Received and Contributions Made,* 13.09
    accounting standards, 13.09
    collections, disclosure requirements for, 13.10
    contributions, three classes of, 13.10
    volunteer services, provisions for, 13.09

FASB 117, *Financial Statements of Not-for-Profit Organizations,* 13.09–13.13
  contributions, three classes of, 13.10
  expenses, three classes of, 13.12
  FASB 95, *Statement of Cash Flows,* 13.11
  financial statements required, three, 13.11
  service aspect of NPOs, emphasis on, 13.12
  Statement of Activities, 13.11, 13.12–13.13, 13.14–13.15
  Statement of Cash Flows, 13.11, 13.13
  Statement of Financial Position, 13.11, 13.12, 13.15
  uniformity of financial statements as purpose, 13.11
  Voluntary Health and Welfare organizations, requirement for, 13.11

FASB 124, *Accounting for Certain Investments Held by Not-for-Profit Organizations,* 13.13–13.15
  accounting procedures, 13.14
  disclosure and reporting, 13.14–13.15
  fair value requirements, 13.13–13.14
  FASB 107, *Disclosure about Fair Value of Financial Instruments,* 13.14
  FASB 115, *Accounting for Certain Investments in Debt and Equity Securities,* 13.13
  FASB 133, *Accounting for Derivative Instruments and Hedging Activities,* 13.14

FASB 136, *Transfers of Assets to a Not-for-Profit Organization or Charitable Trust That Raises or Holds Contributions for Others,* 13.02–13.05
  beneficiary's rights, 13.03–13.04
  FASB 42, *Accounting for Transfers of Assets in Which a Not-for-Profit Organization Is Granted Variance Power,* 13.05
  financial statements, requirements for, 3.02–3.03
  interrelatedness, financial, 13.03
  requirements for NPOs, 3.02–3.03
  time framework, 13.05
  variance power, 13.04
  when transfer of assets is liability for recipient, four circumstances, 13.04–13.05

FASB Project on NPO combinations, 13.15–13.17
  board deliberations, 13.16–13.17
  current practice, diversity in, 13.15–13.16
  intangibles, decisions relating to, 13.17
  mergers, 13.16
  pooling-of-interests, effect of elimination, 13.16

IRS Rulings and legislation relating to disclosure, 13.06–13.08
  documents to be accessible for inspection, 13.06–13.07
  exempt organizations included, 13.05
  fraudulent information, penalty for, 13.08
  Internet, placing required documents on, 13.07
  noncompliance, penalties for, 13.08

Not-for-profit organizations (NPOs) (*cont.*)
Omnibus Budget Reconciliation Act of 1987, 13.06
procedures for document availability, 13.07–13.08
Taxpayer Bill of Rights 2, 13.06
Notional amount, 7.16
NYSSA. *See* New York Society of Security Analysts (NYSSA)

O

Office of Internet Enforcement (OIE), 28.37–28.38
Office of Management and Budget (OMB)
Circular A-123, "Management Accountability and Control," 16.03
Office payroll
internal control system, 16.26–16.27
Officer and director penalties
Sarbanes-Oxley Act of 2002, 9.09, 9.10
OIE. *See* Office of Internet Enforcement (OIE)
Oil and gas companies, IASC consideration of accounting for, 5.28–5.30
Oklahoma City bombing
tax relief for victims of, 40.03–40.04
Omnibus Budget Reconciliation Act of 1987, 13.06
150% declining balance method of depreciation, 33.08
Operating budget, 14.02–14.03. *See also* Budgeting for profit planning and budgetary control
Operating profit, 1.33–1.35
Organization for Economic Cooperation and Development (OECD), 6.30. *See also* International accounting
Anti-Bribery Convention, 16.12
e-commerce, tax treatment of, 5.37–5.41
consumption tax issues, 5.39
direct tax issues, 5.38–5.39
future process, 5.39–5.40
Model Tax Convention, 5.38
Ottawa Taxation Framework Conditions, 5.38
tax administration issues, 5.39
Technical Advisory Group (TAG) on Treaty Characterization, 5.38, 5.40–5.41
of e-commerce payments, 5.38, 5.40–5.41
Original use test
depreciation, 33.17, 33.21
Other postemployment benefits (OPEB)
governmental accounting, 11.15
Ottawa Taxation Framework Conditions, 5.38
Oversight Board. *See* Sarbanes-Oxley Act of 2002
Ownership tax year test, 36.19–36.20

P

Par stock, 3.03, 3.04–3.05
Partnerships
tax filing period for, 36.17, 36.21–36.22

Passive activity rules
rental property, 19.14
Passive investments
financial planning, 17.07
Patent, cost basis of, 35.06
Payment period of annuity, 2.11
Payroll
fraud, 16.46
inventory control system, checklist, 16.43
Pension plan start-up costs, credit for, 40.16–40.17, 41.05
Pension provisions, 39.11–39.13
Percentage of completion method to determine income, 2.02
Period expenses, 2.04–2.05
Permitted tax year, 36.22
Personal assets, financial planning, 17.07
Personal Financial Specialist (PSF). *See* Financial planner
Personal service corporation as taxpayer, 36.22–36.23
Petroleum companies, IASC consideration of accounting for, 5.28–5.30
Petty cash, internal control system, 16.28
Placed in service date test
depreciation, 33.16–33.17, 33.21
Plain English Disclosure rule, 32.01–32.19
comments on requirements, 32.10–32.11
cost factors, 32.11
investor protection, 32.01
pilot program, 32.03
Plain English Handbook: How to Create Clear SEC Disclosure Documents, 32.03
profile requirement, 31.03
prospectus simplification, 32.02–32.03
Regulations S-K and S-B, revisions to, 32.06
cover page format, 3.07–3.08
Forms S-2, S-3, S-4, F-2, F-3, F-4, 32.09
Item 501, 32.06–32.07
Item 502, 32.08–32.09
Item 503, 32.09–32.10
limited partnership offerings risk, 32.08
ratio of earnings to fixed charges, 32.10
"red herring" legend, 32.07
risk factors, 32.10
summary information, 32.09–32.10
Rule 421(B), 32.04–32.06, 32.13–32.14
complying, 32.05
concerning prospectus, 32.04–32.05
legal documents, 32.06
risk factor guidance, 32.11–32.12
tactics to avoid, 32.05
technical terminology, 32.05–32.06
writing techniques, 32.05
Rule 421(D), 32.03–32.04
Securities and Exchange Commission, adoption by in 1998, 31.01–31.02
Staff Legal Bulletin 7, 32.11
acceleration requests, 32.17

"bundling" of risk factors, avoiding, 32.12

cautions and suggestions re risk disclosure, 32.12–32.13

cautions for entire prospectus, 32.18–32.19

clarity as goal, 32.16

cover page reminders, 32.17

documents incorporated by reference, 32.14

EDGAR, 32.16

electronic filers selected for review, 32.16–32.17

footnotes, 32.18

glossaries and defined terms, 32.13–32.14

legal documents, use of in prospectus, 32.15

post-effective amendments to registration statements, 32.14–32.15

risk factor guidance, 32.11–32.12

risks, types of, 32.12

summary, 32.17–32.18

technical business description, 32.15–32.16

"Point" and loyalty programs

Internet accounting, 28.28–28.30

Points and cost basis of property, 35.04–35.05

"Points," real estate, 19.05–19.06

constant yield method, 19.05–19.06

mortgage, end of, 19.06

Pooling-of-interests method of accounting, eliminating, 13.16

Portfolio management, 17.22–17.23

Power of attorney. *See* IRS, practice before, and power of attorney

Preface to International Financial Reporting (IASB), 5.13

Preferred stock, 3.03–3.04

convertible, 3.03–3.04

cumulative/noncumulative, 3.04

participating/nonparticipating, 3.03

Premium Account, 2.13

Prepaid/intangible assets vs. priced costs of Internet businesses. *See* Internet accounting

Present value, 2.05, 2.10–2.11. *See also* Revenue and expenses

Present worth of annuity, 2.12

Presidentially declared disaster areas, postponed tax deadlines, 40.03

Pricing policy, deciding on, 14.04

Principles of financial statements, disclosure, analysis and interpretation, 1.01–1.42

comprehensive income, 1.37–1.41

components, 1.39–1.40

definition, 1.38

Disclosure of Accounting Policies, 1.41–1.42

format for presentation of, 1.38–1.39

terminology, 1.40

disclosures required in, 1.07–1.16. *See also* Disclosure

content and format of, 1.41–1.42

FASB 130, *Reporting Comprehensive Income,* 1.37–1.41

in financial reporting, 1.09–1.16

full disclosure, 1.09

financial statement

analysis and interpretation, 1.21–1.22

GAAP, fair presentation conforming to, 1.02

income statement analysis, 1.28–1.30

presentation, twelve principles of, 1.02–1.05

income taxes

balance sheet presentation, 1.20

considerations, other, 1.20

timing and permanent differences, 1.18

timing differences, 1.18–1.20

inventory control, 1.27

materiality, 1.05–1.07

what must be recognized, 1.07–1.08

operating profit, 1.33–1.35

ratios, 1.22–1.28

asset turnover, 1.28

book value of securities, 1.28–1.29

of cost of goods sold to inventory, 1.27

of current assets to current liabilities, 1.24–1.25

of current liabilities to stockholders' equity, 1.25–1.26

dividend payout, 1.37

dividend yield, 1.36

earnings per share, 1.30–1.33

of fixed assets to long-term liabilities, 1.26–1.27

of fixed assets to stockholders' equity, 1.26

gross profit, 1.34–1.35

of inventory to working capital, 1.27–1.28

of long-term debt to equity, 1.30

of net sales to stockholders' equity, 1.35

of net sales to working capital, 1.35

profit margins on sales, 1.35–1.36

rate of return on common stock equity, 1.36

receivables turnover, 1.28

return on equity, 1.36

return to investors, 1.37

times interest earned, 1.36

of total liabilities to stockholders' equity, 1.26

Reporting Comprehensive Income, FASB 130, 1.37–1.41

cash flow not affected, 1.40–1.41

components, 1.39–1.40

definition, 1.38

equity valuation not affected, 1.38, 1.40–1.41

FASB 102, 1.39

FASB 117, 1.39

format for presentation, 1.38–1.39

requirements, application of, 1.39

restatements, 1.16–1.18

sales growth, 1.33

securities, book value of, 1.28–1.29

statement of changes in stockholders' equity, 1.36–1.37

timing differences, 1.18–1.20

timing and permanent differences-income taxes, 1.18

Prior period adjustments, 3.07–3.08

Private Securities Litigation Reform Act of 1995
  abusive litigation
    presumption in favor of attorneys' fees and costs, 25.10
    rebuttal evidence for sanctions against, 25.10
  aiding and abetting, 25.13
  attorney privilege, nonwaiver of, 25.05
  attorneys' fees and expenses, restrictions on payment of, 25.07
  authority, other, of Commission, 25.11
  causation of loss, 25.09
  certification filed with complaint, 25.05
  class actions
    private, 25.10
    reforms, 25.13
    security for payment of costs in, 25.08
  damages, limitation on, 25.09
  discovery, 25.06
    stay of, 25.14
  documents, availability of, 25.10
  e-commerce, related to, 27.11
  evidence, preservation of, 25.14
  exception provision, 25.16
  exemption authority, 25.11
  forward-looking statement, definition of, 25.11
    safe harbor for, 25.12–25.13
  frivolous lawsuits, deterrent of, 25.02–25.03
  indemnification agreements, 25.15
  investment retirement plans, qualified, protections for, 25.14
  lead counsel, selection of, 25.06
  lead plaintiff, appointment of, 25.05
  misleading statements and omissions, 25.08–25.09
  multiple actions, 25.10
  notice, 25.05–25.06
  plaintiffs
    conflict of interest by attorney, 25.08
    disclosure of settlement terms to class members, 25.07–25.08
    professional plaintiffs, restrictions on, 25.06
    recovery by, 25.06–25.07
    settlements under seal, restrictions on, 25.07
  preservation of evidence, 25.14
  proportionate liability, 25.03, 25.14–25.15
    and contributions, 25.13
  provisions of act, 25.03–25.05
  qualified investment retirement plans, protections for, 25.14
  Racketeer Influenced and Corrupt Organization Act (RICO), 25.14
  reason for passage of, 25.02–25.03
  rebuttable presumption, 25.06
  required state of mind, 25.09
  rescission, right of, 25.13
  rule of construction, 25.15
  sanctions against abusive litigation, rebuttal evidence for, 25.10
  security for payment of costs in class actions, 25.08
  senior citizens, protections for, 25.14
  stay pending decision on motion exemption authority, 25.10–25.11
  willful violation, sanction for, 25.09
Production budget, 14.05–14.07. *See also* Budgeting for profit planning and budgetary control
Professional rating services
  mutual fund selection, 30.16–30.17
Profitability ratios, 1.22
Property, plant, and equipment
  small business enterprise, internal control system, 16.42
Proposals to Ease Transition to IAS (IASB), 5.13–5.14
Prospectus preparation and Plain English Disclosure rule, 32.01–32.19. *See also* Plain English Disclosure Rule
Proxy disclosure requirement, 22.08
Prudent man concept
  SEC materiality, 24.10
Public accountability for governmental spending, 11.17–11.18
Public colleges and universities, GASB Statement 35, 11.27–11.28
Public Company Audit Committees. *See* Sarbanes-Oxley Act of 2002
Public education
  qualified public educational facilities, tax-exempt bond funding, 40.12
Public Oversight Board (POB), 22.02
  Panel on Audit Effectiveness ("O'Malley Panel"), 22.15
Public Sector Committee (PSC). *See* International Federation of Accountants (IFAC)
Public Utility Holding Company Act of 1935, 23.37–23.38
  acquisitions, 23.37–23.38
  integrated utility system, 23.37
  issuance and sale of securities, 23.38
Purchase method procedures
  business combinations, 10.15–10.17
    assets and liabilities, recognition and measurement, 10.17
    contingent consideration, 10.16
    measurement issues, acquired businesses, 10.17
    tentative decisions, 10.15–10.16

Q

QFOBI. *See* Qualified family-owned business interest (QFOBI)
QTPs. *See* Qualified tuition programs (QTPs)
Qualified family-owned business interest (QFOBI), 40.30
Qualified plans, tax matters, 40.21–40.23
  contributions and benefits, limits on, 40.22
  deduction limits, 40.21
  EGTRRA, conformity, 40.23

elective deferrals, 40.22
involuntary payment of benefits, 40.22–40.23
retirement planning, 40.21
Qualified public educational facilities, tax-exempt
    bond funding, 40.12
Qualified tuition programs (QTPs), 40.06–40.07
    Coverdell ESAs, coordination with, 40.09
    expansion of, 39.11
Qualified zone academy bonds, 41.05
Quality control, 22.07–22.08
Quasi-reorganizations, 3.11–3.12
Questionnaire for market analysis, 14.04
Quick ratio, 1.25

R

Racketeer Influenced and Corrupt Organization Act
    (RICO), 25.14
Ratios, 1.22–1.28
    accountant's responsibility, 1.22–1.23
    acid test, 1.25
    asset turnover, 1.28
    balance sheet analysis, 1.23–1.24
    book value of securities, 1.28–1.29
    of cost of goods sold to inventory, 1.27
    current, 4.13
    of current assets to current liabilities, 1.24–1.25
    of current liabilities to stockholders' equity, 1.25–
        1.26
    debt-to-net-worth, 4.13
    defensive-interval, 1.25
    dividend payout, 1.37
    dividend yield, 1.36
    earnings per share, 1.30–1.33
    financial, bankers' evaluation of, 4.12–4.13
    fixed assets
        to long-term liabilities, 1.26–1.27
        to stockholders' equity, 1.26
    gross profit, 1.34–1.35
    horizontal analysis, 1.23
    income statement analysis, 1.28–1.30
    inventory to working capital, 1.27–1.28
    long-term debt to equity, 1.30
    net sales
        to stockholders' equity, 1.35
        to working capital, 1.35
    profit margins on sales, 1.35–1.36
    quick, 1.25
    rate of return on common stock equity, 1.36
    receivables turnover, 1.28
    return on equity, 1.36
    return to investors, 1.37
    times interest earned, 1.36
    of total liabilities to stockholders' equity, 1.26
    vertical analysis, 1.23
Raw materials and supplies inventories, 16.18–16.19
Readjustment, 3.11

Real estate as asset, 19.01–19.25
    importance to client, 19.16
    income-producing rental property, 19.02–19.15
        advance rent, 19.02
        casualties, 19.13
        change of property to rental use, 19.08
        condominiums, 19.07–19.08
        cooperatives, 19.08
        deductibility of expenses, 19.04–19.05
        deductions, limit on, 19.12
        depreciation, 19.13
        dividing property, 19.12
        donation of use of property, 19.11
        dwelling unit, defined, 19.09–19.10
        dwelling unit used as home, 19.10–19.11
        fair rental price, 19.10
        figuring rental income and deductions, 19.12
        losses, limits on, 19.13–19.15
        part of property, rental of, 19.09
        personal use of dwelling, 19.09
        "points," 19.05–19.06
        rental expenses, 19.03
        rental income, 19.02–19.03
        repairs and improvements, differentiating be-
            tween, 19.04
        repairs and maintenance, days used for, 19.11
        sale of home used for business or rent, 19.22–
            19.23
        security deposit, 19.02
        shared equity financing agreements, 19.11
        tax return preparation, 19.06–19.07
        thefts, 19.13
        travel expenses, 19.06
        use as main home before or after renting,
            19.10–19.11
        vacation homes, 19.09
    investing in real estate, 19.15–19.16
        appreciation, 19.15–19.16
        cash flow, 19.15
        equity, increase, 19.15
        tax savings, 19.16
    market, real estate, 19.24–19.25
    "points," 19.05–19.06
    sale of home, 19.16–19.25
        abandonment, 19.18–19.19
        business or rental of home, 19.22–19.23
        exclusion of gain, 19.16–19.17, 19.19–19.20
        expatriate tax, 19.23
        foreclosures, 19.18–19.19
        gain or loss, figuring, 19.17–19.19
        installment sales, 19.24
        main home, 19.16–19.17
        market, real estate, 19.24–19.25
        married persons, ownership and use tests, 19.22
        more than one home, sale of, 19.20
        option to buy, 19.17–19.18
        ownership and use tests, 19.20–19.23
        real estate taxes, 19.24

Real estate as asset (*cont.*)
  remainder interests, 19.23
  reporting gain, 19.23
  repossession, 19.18–19.19
  rules for sales, 19.17–19.24
  seller-financed mortgages, 19.24
  transfers, effect of, 19.19
  transfer taxes, 19.24
Real property, cost basis of, 35.03–35.05
  points and mortgages, 35.04–35.05
  settlement costs, 35.03
Reasonableness
  SEC materiality, 24.10–24.12
Recapitalizations, 3.09–3.12. *See also* Stockholders'
      equity
Receivables turnover, 1.28
Reconciliation method, 4.04, 4.09–4.10
Redemptions of mutual funds, 29.04–29.07
"Red herring" legend, 32.07
Redundancies, FASB report on, 10.50
Regulation S-B, 8.09, 32.06
Regulation S-K, 8.05–8.09, 23.25
Regulation S-X, 8.11–8.12, 23.25
Regulatory risk, 17.20
Reinsurance, 43.08–43.13
  concern, cause for, 43.11–43.13
  definitions, 43.08–43.10
  disclosure requirements, 43.13
  FASB 97, *Accounting and Reporting by Insurance
      Enterprises for Certain Long-Duration Con-
      tracts and for Realized Gains and Losses
      from Sale of Investments,* 43.12
  FASB 113, *Accounting and Reporting for Reinsur-
      ance of Short-Duration and Long-Duration
      Contracts,* 43.08–43.13
  provisions of Statement, 43.10–43.11
Related persons
  depreciation, 33.16
  like-kind exchanges between, 35.13
Relationship of the parties
  independent contractor or employee, 34.11–34.14
Renewal communities, 40.28
Rental property, 19.02–19.15
  advance rent, 19.02
  casualties, 19.13
  change of property to rental use, 19.08
  condominiums, 19.07–19.08
  cooperatives, 19.08
  deductions
    expenses, deductibility, 19.04–19.05
    limit on, 19.12
  depreciation, 19.13
  dividing property, 19.12
  donation of use of property, 19.11
  dwelling unit
    defined, 19.09–19.10
    used as home, 19.10–19.11
  fair rental price, 19.10

  figuring rental income and deductions, 19.12
  losses, limits on, 19.13–19.15
    at-risk rules, 19.14
    passive activity limits, 19.14
    rental real estate activities, 19.14–19.15
  part of property, rental of, 19.09
  personal use of dwelling, 19.09
  "points," 19.05–19.06
  rental expenses, 19.03
  rental income, 19.02–19.03
  repairs and improvements, differentiating be-
      tween, 19.04
  repairs and maintenance, days used for, 19.11
  sale of home used for business or rent, 19.22–
      19.23
  security deposit, 19.02
  shared equity financing agreements, 19.11
  tax return preparation, 19.06–19.07
  thefts, 19.13
  travel expenses, 19.06
  use as main home before or after renting, 19.10–
      19.11
  vacation homes, 19.09
Reorganization proceedings, 23.40–23.41
Repairs and maintenance
  expense, 14.12
    manufacturing expense budget, 14.12
  rental property
    days used for, 19.11
    expense, 19.04
Reporting Comprehensive Income, FASB 130, 1.37–
      1.41. *See also* Principles of financial state-
      ments, disclosure, analysis and interpretation
Repossession, real estate, 19.18–19.19
Required supplemental information (RSI) in new
      governmental accounting, 11.19, 11.21,
      11.25–11.26
Residential property, sale of. *See* Real estate as asset
Restatements, 1.16–1.18
Retained earnings, 3.06–3.07
Retirement and benefit plans, tax matters, 40.16–
      40.27. *See also specific type of plan*
  contributions to, saver's credit, 40.17–40.19
Retirement planning
  financial planning and, 17.07–17.08
  qualified plans, tax matters, 40.21
Retirement savings programs, 39.11–39.13
Revenue and expenses, 2.01–2.24
  annuities, 2.11–2.13
    Bond Discount account, 2.13
    definition, 2.11
    future worth, 2.11–2.12
    interest-conversion period, 2.11
    payment period, 2.11
    Premium Account, 2.13
    present worth, 2.12
  disclosures for revenue recognition, 2.20–2.22
    fair value method, 2.22–2.23

Management's Discussion and Analysis (MD&A), 2.21
  Regulation S-X, 2.21
employee stock options, 2.13–2.15
  additional requirements, 2.24
  controversy, 2.24
  exceptions, 2.24
  fair value, 2.14–2.15, 2.22–2.23
  forced compromise, 2.13–2.14
  intrinsic value method, 2.23
  transition questions, 2.14
expenses, 2.03–2.05
  definition, 2.04
  extraordinary items, 2.05
  gains and losses, 2.05
  "matching," 2.04
  as part of "cost," 2.03
  period expenses, 2.04–2.05
  recognizing, three principles as basis of, 2.04–2.05
  systematic and rational allocation, 2.04
  unusual items, 2.05
extraordinary items, classifying and reporting, 2.08–2.09
  criteria for, 2.09
  definition, 2.09
  discontinued operations, 2.08
FASB revenue recognition project, 10.25–10.26
imputed interest on notes receivable or payable, 2.05–2.07
  accounting considerations, 2.05–2.07
  discounting, 2.06
  imputed rate, 2.06
  present value, 2.05
present value computation and application, 2.10–2.11
  caution, 2.11
  compounding, 2.10–2.11
  time as continuous, not discrete, function, 2.10
revenue (income), 2.01–2.03
  determining, methods of, 2.02–2.03
  right of return to seller, 2.03
  of shareholder, 2.03
revenue recognition accounting literature, 2.19–2.20
SAB 101, *Revenue Recognition in Financial Statements,* 2.15–2.19, 28.22
  conditions for recognition, 2.16
  corrections required, 2.16
  effect of, 2.16–2.19
Revenue-barter transactions
international accounting, 5.19–5.20
Revenue Procedure 2002-37, 36.02–36.03
Revenue Procedure 2002-38, 36.03–36.04
Revenue recognition
  Internet accounting, 28.19–28.30
    advertising arrangements, 28.08–28.09, 28.27–28.28

IASB, request by SEC to consider project, 28.26–28.30
  listing fees, auctions, 28.19–28.20
  multiple element arrangements, 28.25
  "point" and loyalty programs, 28.28–28.30
  software applications, 28.20–28.21
  Web site access or maintenance, 28.21–28.25
Reverse stock split-up, 3.10
Risk
  bond mutual funds, 30.15–30.16
    credit risk, 30.15
    interest rate risk, 30.15
    sector risk, 30.15–30.16
  e-commerce and e-communication
    international guidance on, 27.12–27.14
  investments, advising clients on
    asset allocation and, 17.20–17.29
    credit risk, 17.19–17.20
    event risk, 17.20
    inflation risk, 17.19
    interest rate risk, 17.19
    liquidity risk, 17.19
    market risk, 17.19–17.20
    minimizing risk, 17.32
    principal risk, 17.20
    regulatory risk, 17.20
    risk tolerance, 17.15–17.16
  IT monitoring guidelines, 6.27–6.28
Rollovers, 40.27
  empowerment zone assets, rollover of gain, 40.28
  IRAs, 40.20–40.21
Roth IRAs, 39.11
  contribution limit, 40.19–40.20
  saver's credit, 40.17–40.18
Rule 421(B) of Securities Act, 32.04–32.06. *See also* Plain English Disclosure Rule
Rule 421(D) of Securities Act, the Plain English Rule, 32.03–32.04

S

SAB 99, *Materiality,* 24.01–24.02, 24.04, 24.13. *See also* SEC Materiality
SAB 101, *Revenue Recognition in Financial Statements,* 2.15–2.19, 28.22. *See also* Revenue and expenses
Safe harbor
  excise taxes, 40.31
  Private Securities Litigation Reform Act of 1995, 25.12–25.13
Salaries and wages
  internal control system, 16.25–16.26
Salary reduction SEP (SARSEP)
  elective deferrals, 40.23
  Job Creation and Worker Assistance Act of 2002, 41.07
  saver's credit, 40.17

Sale of home. *See* Real estate as asset
Sales budget, 14.03–14.05. *See also* Budgeting for profit planning and budgetary control
Sales growth, 1.33
Sales method to determine income, 2.02
Sales of mutual funds, 29.04–29.07
Sarbanes-Oxley Act of 2002, 9.01–9.14
 amendments to Senate bill, 9.13
 audit partner rotation, 9.12
 awareness of provisions, importance of, 9.14
 conflicts of interest, 9.12
 conviction of crime, penalties, 9.03
 Corporate and Criminal Fraud Accountability Act of 2002, 9.13
 corporate responsibility for financial reports, 9.09
 financial report requirements, 9.08–9.09
 forecasting, 9.02
 GAO studies, 9.12
 improper influence on conduct of audits, 9.09
 insider trading, prohibition of, 9.11
 management assessment of internal controls, 9.08
 officers and directors
  measures relating to, 9.11–9.12
  penalties, 9.09, 9.10
 Oversight Board
  auditing standards, responsibilities related to, 9.04–9.05
  functions of, 9.05–9.06
  generally, 9.03–9.04
  mandatory registration, 9.05–9.06
  SEC oversight of, 9.02, 9.06–9.07
 personal loans to executives, prohibition of, 9.11–9.12
 Public Company Audit Committees
  auditor reports to, 9.08
  qualifications, 9.07
  responsibilities, 9.07
 SEC involvement, 9.09–9.11
  appearance and practice before, 9.10–9.11
  oversight board, 9.02, 9.06–9.07
  temporary freeze authority, 9.11
 securities analysts, treatment by registered securities associations, 9.12
 special-purpose entities, SEC study and report, 9.10
 tampering with official proceeding, 9.12
 timely disclosures, 9.12
 types of services considered unlawful, 9.02–9.03
 White-Collar Crime Penalty Enhancement Act of 2002, 9.13–9.14
SARSEP. *See* Salary reduction SEP (SARSEP)
Saver's credit, 40.17–40.19
 eligible contributions and reduction, 40.17–40.18
 ineligibility for, 40.18–40.19
S corporations
 indebtedness, discharge of, 41.08–41.09
 shareholders, tax filing year for, 36.17, 36.20, 36.22
SEC materiality, 24.01–24.14

 defined, 1.06, 24.03
 determining appropriate accounting treatment, 24.13–24.14
 FASB and, 24.03–24.04
 GAAP, precedence over industry practice, 24.13–24.14
 investor, considerations, 24.06–24.07
 managed earnings, 24.06–24.07
 misstatements, 24.05–24.06
  aggregating and netting, 24.07–24.09
  cost of correcting, 24.11
  how arose, 24.11
  intentional immaterial misstatements, 24.09–24.10
  response to intentional misstatements, 24.12–24.13
 prudent man concept, 24.10
 qualitative and quantitative factors, 24.03–24.04
 qualitatively material, 24.07
 quantitatively immaterial, 24.07
 reasonableness, 24.10–24.12
 "rule of thumb," misuse of, 24.02
 size of figures, 24.04–24.05
Section 179 deduction
 business use of home, 20.10
 generally, 40.32
 use of, 33.04–33.07. *See also* Depreciation
Section 444 election of IRS Code, 36.22, 36.23–36.25
 deferral period, 36.24
Section 457 deferred compensation plans, 40.25–40.26
Section 530 relief
 independent contractor or employee, 34.06–34.07
Section 7436, 34.17–34.18. *See also* Independent contractor
Securities, book value of, 1.28–1.29
Securities Act of 1933
 disclosure, development of, 23.24–23.26
 overview, 23.16–23.17
 synopsis, 23.26–23.30
Securities and Exchange Commission (SEC), 5.42
 Accounting Oversight Board, 9.02, 9.06–9.07
 derivatives, 8.01–8.15
 disclosure
  development of, 23.24–23.26
  overload, combined efforts of SEC and FASB, 10.22
 Division of Corporation Finance, 23.23
 on e-communication and e-trading, 27.17–27.18. *See also* E-commerce and E-communication
 FASB 131, response to, 26.07–26.13
 Form S-15, 23.26
 IASC, appraisal, 5.48
 IASC, interaction with, 5.35
 independent fund advisors, SEC final rules and amendments, 29.08–29.21
 insider trading, 23.23
 and internationalization of securities markets, 5.33–5.34

and Internet accounting, 28.02–28.03. *See also* Internet accounting
long-lived assets, caution, 10.08–10.09
margin trading, 23.23
materiality. *See* SEC-Materiality
mutual funds
  independent fund advisors, SEC final rules and amendments, 29.08–29.21
online trading, 27.17–27.18
organization and Acts, 23.01–23.41
  composition of SEC, 23.04
  history, 23.02
  Investment Advisers Act of 1940, 23.39
  members of, 23.04
  offices, regional and district, 23.02–23.04
  overview of SEC, 23.04–23.05
  Public Utility Holding Company Act of 1935, 23.37–23.38
  registration, 23.17–23.22
  reorganization proceedings, 23.40–23.41
  Securities Act of 1933, 23.16–23.17, 23.24–23.30
  Securities Exchange Act of 1934, 23.22, 23.24–23.26, 23.31–23.36
  terminology, glossary, 23.05–23.16
  Trust Indenture Act of 1939, 23.23, 23.38–23.39
  Trust Investment Company Act of 1940, 23.39–23.40
Private Securities Litigation Reform Act of 1995, 25.01–25.06. *See also* Private Securities Litigation Reform Act of 1995 *for detailed treatment*
Public Oversight Board (POB), 22.02
recent accomplishments, 22.15–22.16
registration, 23.17–23.22
  process, 23.18–23.22
  small business exemption, 23.19
Regulation S-K, 8.05–8.06, 23.25
Regulation S-X, disclosure rule in, 8.11–8.12, 23.25
reorganization proceedings, 23.40–23.41
Sarbanes-Oxley Act of 2002
  appearance and practice before, 9.10–9.11
  involvement in, 9.09–9.11
  oversight board and, 9.02, 9.06–9.07
  temporary freeze authority, 9.11
SEC Accounting Bulletin, SAB 101, 28.03
Transition Oversight Staff (TOS), 22.02
Trust Indenture Act of 1939, 23.23
truth in securities laws, 23.24
Securities Exchange Act of 1934
  disclosure, development of, 23.24–23.26
  overview, 23.22
  Regulation S-X
    extension of disclosure doctrine, 8.11–8.12
    Form 20-F, 26.12
  synopsis, 23.31–23.36
Securities futures contracts, 40.05
Securities markets of U.S., internationalization of, 5.33–5.34

foreign issuers in, 5.34
Segment reporting, 26.01–26.16
  FASB Statement 131, *Disclosures about Segments of an Enterprise and Related Information,* 26.01–26.16
  geographic areas
    Codification of Financial Reporting Policies (CFRP), 26.15–26.16
    required reporting, 26.12–26.13
  IASC's revised segment reporting standard, 26.04
  information from within, 26.03
  interim reports, segment information, 26.13–26.14
  management approach, 26.03–26.04
  management's discussion and analysis (MD&A), 26.10–26.12
  objectives of standard, 26.03
  operating segments defined, 26.04–26.05
  protests, 26.05
  secrecy and, 26.05
  Security and Exchange Commission's response to FASB 131, 26.07–26.13
    business, description of—Item 101, 26.09–26.10
    Codification of Financial Reporting Policies (CFRP), 26.14–26.16
    differences from FASB 131 standards, 26.09–26.10
    FASB 14, contrast with, 26.07
    Form 20-F, 26.12
    geographic areas, required reporting about, 26.12–26.13
    major customers, required reporting about, 26.13
    management's discussion and analysis (MD&A), 26.10–26.12
    operating segment disclosure rules, change in, 26.07–26.09
    property-Item 102, 26.10
    Regulation S-K, amendment to, 26.07
    Regulation S-X, amendment to, 26.07
    retroactive restatement of information, SEC requirement for, 26.10
    rules, change of, 26.07–26.09
    Schedule 14A, amendment to, 26.07
  segment quantitative thresholds, 26.05–26.06
    asset test, 26.05
    profitability test, 26.05
    revenue test, 26.05
    single segment entities, 26.06–26.07
Self-employed health insurance deduction, 40.33
Self-employment tax, 40.33
Selling expenses
  internal control system, 16.24
Separate trades or businesses, change in accounting for, 36.12
SEPs. *See* Simplified employee pensions (SEPs)
September 11 terrorist attacks
  tax relief for victims of, 40.03–40.04
  Victims of Terrorism Tax Relief Act of 2001, 41.10

Service concession arrangements
  international accounting, 5.19
Service establishments, cost accounting, 15.05
Service outages
  Internet accounting, 28.15–28.16
Settlement costs as cost basis of assets, 35.03
Shareholder
  income, 2.03
  S corporations. *See* S corporations
Shipping and handling costs
  Internet accounting, 28.12–28.13
SIMPLE 401(K) plans
  Saver's credit, 40.17
SIMPLE IRAs
  Saver's credit, 40.17
SIMPLE plans, 40.24
  increase in deferrals to, 39.13
Simplified employee pensions (SEPs), 40.23
  Job Creation and Worker Assistance Act of 2002,
    41.06–41.07
Small business enterprise
  internal control system, 16.32–16.43
    accounts payable checklist, 16.39–16.40
    accounts receivable checklist, 16.36
    cash receipts checklist, 16.37
    checklists, 16.32–16.43
    disbursements, checklist, 16.39–16.40
    insurance checklist, 16.42
    investments checklist, 16.41
    property, plant, and equipment checklist, 16.42
    purchases, checklist, 16.39–16.40
    sales checklist, 16.36
  inventory control system, payroll checklist, 16.43
  WebTrust, 27.18–27.20
Small business exemption
  SEC registration, 23.19
Small Business Jobs Protection Act of 1996, 34.01
Social Security
  financial planning and, 17.07
Social Security and Medicare taxes, 40.16
  independent contractor or employee, 34.04
Software
  accounting rules, internally developed software,
    27.03–27.04
  definition of and accounting for, 28.16–28.19
  mutual funds and, 30.17–30.18
Sole proprietorships, tax filing period for, 36.17
SOP 81-1, *Accounting for Performance of Construc-
  tion-Type and Certain Production-Type Con-
  tracts,* 28.26
SOP 97-2, *Software Revenue Recognition,* 28.26
Special-purpose entity (SPE)
  consolidation of, proposed standard, 10.02–10.03
  earlier FASB action related to, 10.03–10.04
  synthetic leases, 10.04–10.05
Special Revenue Fund, 2.11–2.12, 12.09
Spouse, basis of property transferred from, 35.14
Standards Advisory Council (SAC), IASC, 5.21

Standards overload, FASB project to consider,
  10.19–10.21
Standing Interpretations Committee (SIC). *See* In-
  ternational Financial Reporting Interpreta-
  tions Committee
Start-up costs
  pension plans, credit for, 40.16–40.17, 41.05
Stated capital, 3.04–3.05
State death taxes, reduction of credit for, 40.29
Statement of cash flows, 4.01–4.16. *See also* Cash flows
Statute of limitations
  independent contractor or employee
    employment tax cases, 34.20
Statutory employees
  independent contractor or employee, 34.03–34.04
Statutory nonemployees
  independent contractor or employee, 34.04–34.05
Stock dividends, 3.10
Stockholders' equity, 3.01–3.14
  capital in excess of par or stated value, 3.06
  capital stock, 3.02–3.06
    common stock, 3.02–3.03. *See also* Common
      stock
    issued for property, 3.05–3.06
    par/no-par stock, 3.03, 3.04–3.05
    preferred stock, 3.03–3.04. *See also* Preferred
      stock
  capital stock issued for property, 3.05–3.06
  capital surplus, 3.06
  changes in, causes of, 3.02
  contingency reserves, 3.08–3.09
    definition, 3.08
  par value, stated capital, and capital stock ac-
    counts, 3.04–3.05
  prior period adjustments, 3.07–3.08
  ratios of current liabilities to, 1.25–1.26
  recapitalizations, 3.09–3.12
    changing par or stated value of stock, 3.11
    quasi-reorganizations, 3.11–3.12
    readjustment, 3.11
    reverse stock split-up, 3.10
    stock dividends, 3.10
    stock reclassifications, 3.12
    stock split-ups effected in form of dividend,
      3.10–3.11
    substituting debt for stock, 3.12
  retained earnings, 3.06–3.07
    definition, 3.06
  retroactive adjustments, 3.07
  source classifications, 3.01–3.02
  Statement of Changes in Retained Earnings re-
    quired, 3.06
  treasury stock, 3.13–3.14
    as asset, 3.13–3.14
    shown at cost, 3.13
    shown at par or stated value, 3.13
Stock mutual funds, 30.10–30.11
Stock reclassifications, 3.12

Stocks
  asset allocation, 17.24–17.25
  cost basis of, 35.02–35.03
  split-ups, 3.10
    effected in form of dividend, 3.10–3.11
    reverse, 3.10
Straight line method of depreciation, 33.08
Student loans
  deductions, enhanced, 39.10–39.11
  interest deduction, 40.11–40.12
Subdivided lots, allocating cost basis of, 35.08
Subpart F, electronic filing of 1099s, 41.09
Substantial-use test
  depreciation, 33.21
Substituting debt for stock, 3.12
Successful efforts accounting by mining and petro-
    leum companies, 5.29
Synthetic leases, 10.04–10.05
SysTrust, 27.20–27.22
  defined, 27.20–27.21
  WebTrust, plans to combine, 27.21–27.22

T

Tangible property
  ineligible for depreciation, 33.02–33.03
Tax advice communication, confidentiality protection
    of, 37.01–37.02
Tax Court proceedings, change in
  burden of proof, 38.14
  overpayments, refund/credit of before final deci-
      sion, 38.14–38.15
  penalties, 38.14
  small case procedures, 38.15
  statistical information, use of, 38.14
Tax-exempt mutual fund, 29.02
Tax matters, 40.01–40.33
  Afghanistan, designation as combat zone, 40.04
  air transportation taxes, 40.31
  anthrax attacks, tax relief for victims of, 40.03
  Archer MSAs, 40.06, 41.13
  business incentives, 41.04–41.06
  capital gain, lower tax rates, 40.06
  cash method of accounting, 40.05
  child-oriented tax benefits and considerations,
      40.13–40.15
  community renewal and environmental credits and
      deductions, 40.27–40.29
  deemed IRAs, 40.27
  disaster areas, postponed tax deadlines, 40.03
  earned income credit, 40.12–40.13
  e-commerce, 27.10–27.11
  education, tax benefits for, 40.06–40.12
    Coverdell ESAs, 40.07–40.09
    employer-provided educational assistance, 40.06
    higher education expense, new deduction for,
        40.09–40.11

  HOPE and Lifetime Learning credits, 39.09,
      40.08–40.09
  qualified public educational facilities, tax-ex-
      empt bond funding, 40.12
  qualified tuition programs (QTPs), 40.06–
      40.07
  student loan interest deduction, 40.11–40.12
  tax cuts, 39.09
  educator expenses, deduction for, 41.12–41.13
  empowerment zones, 40.28, 41.05–41.06
  estate and gift tax. See Estate tax; Gift tax
  estimated tax payments for 2002, need to adjust,
      40.02, 40.04
  excise taxes. See Excise taxes
  expiring business tax credits, 41.06
  financial planning and, 17.10, 17.12
  foreign-earned income exclusion, 40.33
  403(b) plans, 40.24–40.25
  generation-skipping transfer tax (GST), 40.30
  higher education expense, new deduction for,
      40.09–40.11
  higher-income taxpayers, estimated tax for, 40.31–
      40.32
  Holocaust victims, restitution, 40.03
  individual retirement arrangements (IRAs),
      40.19–40.21
    deemed IRAs, 40.27
  installment method, election out of, 40.05
  kidnapped children, tax benefits for parents of,
      40.02–40.03
  later years, changes for, 40.16
  luxury taxes, 40.31
  meal expense and "hours of service" limits, 40.32–
      40.33
  medical savings accounts program, 40.06
  mileage rate, standard, use of, 33.11, 40.33
  pension plan start-up costs, credit for, 40.16–
      40.17, 41.05
  presidentially declared disaster areas, postponed
      tax deadlines, 40.03
  qualified family-owned business interest (QFOBI),
      40.30
  qualified plans, 40.21–40.23
  qualified tuition programs (QTPs)
    Coverdell ESAs, coordination with, 40.09
    expansion of, 39.11
  real estate investments, tax savings, 19.16
  retirement and benefit plans, 40.16–40.27. See also
      specific type of plan
  rollovers, 40.27
  salary reduction SEP (SARSEP), 40.23
  Section 457 deferred compensation plans, 40.25–
      40.26
  securities futures contracts, 40.05
  self-employed health insurance deduction, 40.33
  self-employment tax, 40.33
  SIMPLE plans, 40.24
  Social Security and Medicare taxes, 40.16

Tax matters (*cont.*)
  terrorist attacks, tax relief for victims of, 40.03–40.04
  2001 changes affecting later years, 40.02–40.06
  welfare-to-work credit, 40.32
  withholding
    decrease of rates, 40.32
    2002, need to adjust, 40.02
  work opportunity credit, 40.32, 41.04–41.05, 41.10
Tax Matters Partner/Person (TMP), 37.10
Taxpayer Bill of Rights 2, 13.06, 38.01
Taxpayer Bill of Rights 3, 38.01, 38.02. *See also* Taxpayer rights
Taxpayer Bill of Rights 4, 38.02
Taxpayer Relief Act of 1997 (TRA '97)
  independent contractor or employee, 34.16
  technical corrections, 41.14
Taxpayer rights, 38.01–38.17
  administrative costs, award of, 38.12–38.13
    attorney fees, 38.13
    qualified offer, 38.12–38.13, 38.15–38.16
    qualified offer rule, 38.12
  appeals, 38.05
  attorney fees, 38.13, 38.16
  audits, 38.04
    by interview, 38.04
    by mail, 38.04
    repeat, 38.04–38.05
  collection process of IRS, 38.06–38.11
    Application for Taxpayer Assistance Order, 38.11
    bankruptcy proceeding of taxpayer, 38.07
    child support owed by taxpayer, 38.07
    Collection Information Statement, 38.08, 38.09
    compromise offer, 38.10
    delay, temporary, 38.10
    disagreement with IRS decision, 38.06
    error, taxpayer's belief of, 38.08
    hardship, significant, 38.10–38.11
    installment agreement, 38.08–38.10
    Notice of Federal Tax Lien, 38.09, 38.10
    Notice of Tax Due and Demand for Payment, 38.07
    Offer in Compromise, 38.10
    problem resolution program, 38.06–38.07
    representation of taxpayer, 38.06
    sharing information, 38.07
    third parties, contacting, 38.07, 38.16
    when taxpayer cannot pay, 38.07–38.08
  declaration of, 38.02–38.03
  employment taxes for employers, 38.11–38.12
    responsible person, 38.11
    trust fund recovery penalty, assessing, 38.11–38.12
  equitable relief, 38.05
  examinations, 38.04
  explanation of disallowance of claim for refund, 38.13–38.14, 38.17

  innocent spouse relief, 38.05
  IRS Restructuring and Reform Act of 1998, 38.01
  National Taxpayer Advocate's Problem Resolution Program, 38.03
  new image for IRS, 38.01–38.02
  provisions, additional, 38.15–38.16
  qualified offer, 38.12–38.13, 38.15–38.16
  reasonable costs, awarding, 38.15
  refunds, 38.05–38.06
    disallowance, explanation of, 38.13–38.14, 38.17
  separation of liability, 38.05
  Tax Court proceedings, 38.14–38.15
    petition, last date for filing, 38.16
  Taxpayer Bill of Rights 3, 38.01
  trust fund taxes, 38.11–38.12
Tax return preparation
  rental income and, 19.06–19.07
Tax year, 36.16–36.17
  business purpose, 36.18–36.19
  change in, 36.20–36.21
  improper, 36.18
  permitted, 36.22
  short, 36.20
  year of change, 36.21
Technical Advisory Group (TAG) on Treaty Characterization, 5.38, 5.40–5.41
Technical and Miscellaneous Revenue Act of 1988
  corrections, 41.15
Termination rights
  independent contractor or employee, 33.12–33.13
Terrorist attacks, tax relief for victims of, 40.03–40.04
Thefts, rental property, 19.13
Third parties, contact of by IRS, 38.07, 38.16
Times interest earned, 1.36
Time-value-of-money approach, 36.13
Tip income, 42.01–42.13
  aggregation method, 42.12–42.13
  allocation of tips, 42.07, 42.10–42.11
    formula, 42.10–42.11
  annual review, 42.09
  District Director review, 42.09
  employer submission, 42.09
  rules relating to reporting, 42.04–42.05
    daily tip record, 42.05–42.06
    employer, reporting tip income to, 42.06
    employer records for tip allocation, 42.07
    penalties for nonreporting, 42.07–42.08
    what to report, 42.07
  tip rates, 42.08–42.09
    methods for determining, 42.08–42.09
Tipped Employee Participation Agreement (TEPA), 42.02
Tip Rate Determination Agreement (TRDA), 42.02–42.03
Tip Rate Determination/Education Program (TRD/EP), 42.01–42.04
Tip Reporting Alternative Commitment (TRAC). *See also* TRAC

TMP. *See* Tax Matters Partner/Person (TMP)
TRAC agreement, 42.03–42.04
Trade, cost basis of
  allocating, 35.06–35.07
Trademarks and trade names
  cost basis of, 35.06
  not depreciable, 33.03
Trade or business use test
  business use of home, 20.06
Transition Oversight Staff (TOS), 22.02
Travel expenses
  rental income and, 19.06
Treadway Commission. *See* National Commission on
  Fraudulent Financial Reporting
Treasury stock, 3.13–3.14. *See also* Stockholders'
  equity
Trust and Agency Fund (TAF), 12.13–12.14
Trust Indenture Act of 1939, 23.23, 23.38–23.39
Trust Investment Company Act of 1940, 23.39–23.40
Truth in securities laws, 23.24
12b-1 fees, mutual funds, 30.06
200% declining balance method of depreciation, 33.08

U

Uncertainty
  e-commerce and e-communication, 27.07
Under examination by IRS, 36.10
Underlying, 7.15
Uniform capitalization rules for business assets,
  35.05–35.06
United Kingdom
  accounting standards, amendment, 5.08–5.09
  Accounting Standards Board (ASB), 5.08–5.09,
  5.58–5.59, 5.61
Universal life-type policies, 43.07
U.S. Patriot's Act, 6.30

V

Vacation homes, 19.09
Valuation of assets for tax purposes, 35.01–35.16. *See
  also* Asset valuation for tax purposes
Valuation services, 22.05
Vertical analysis, 1.23

Victims of Terrorism Tax Relief Act of 2001, 41.10
Voluntary disclosures, report on, 10.47–10.48
Volunteer services, valuation and reporting of, 13.09
Voting rights
  international accounting, 5.20

W

Web-based business reporting, code of conduct for,
  27.15
Web site access or maintenance
  international accounting, costs, 5.16–5.18
  Internet accounting, 28.21–28.25
WebTrust, 27.18–27.20. *See also* E-commerce and
  E-communication
  SysTrust, plans to combine, 27.21–27.22
Welfare-to-work credit, 40.32
Whistleblowers, 16.46
White-Collar Crime Penalty Enhancement Act of
  2002, 9.13–9.14
Windows period for IRS filing, 36.09. *See also*
  Change
Withholding
  decrease of rates, 40.32
  2002, need to adjust, 40.02
Working capital, 1.24
  funds, 12.14–12.15
Work-in-process inventory, 16.19–16.20
Work opportunity credit, 40.32, 41.04–41.05, 41.10
World Bank, 5.26, 6.30
World economy, changing, 5.41–5.42x

X

XBRL (eXtensible Business Reporting Language)
  Consortium, 6.13–6.15. *See also* International Federation of Accountants

Z

Zero-base budgeting (ZBB), 14.02, 14.17–14.20. *See
  also* Budgeting for profit planning and budgetary control
  decision package concept, 14.18–14.20